3D Imaging, Analysis and Applications

Yonghuai Liu · Nick Pears · Paul L. Rosin · Patrik Huber

Editors

3D Imaging, Analysis and Applications

Second Edition

 Springer

Editors
Yonghuai Liu
Department of Computer Science
Edge Hill University
Ormskirk, Lancashire, UK

Nick Pears
Department of Computer Science
University of York
York, UK

Paul L. Rosin
School of Computer Science and Informatics
Cardiff University
Cardiff, UK

Patrik Huber
Department of Computer Science
University of York
York, UK

ISBN 978-3-030-44072-5   ISBN 978-3-030-44070-1   (eBook)
https://doi.org/10.1007/978-3-030-44070-1

This Springer imprint is published by the registered company Springer Nature Switzerland AG
The registered company address is: Gewerbestrasse 11, 6330 Cham, Switzerland

Preface

This book is primarily a graduate text on 3D imaging, shape analysis, and associated applications. In addition to serving masters-level and doctoral-level research students, much of the text is accessible enough to be useful to final-year undergraduate project students. Also, we hope that it will serve wider audiences, for example, as a reference text for professional academics, people working in commercial research and development labs, and industrial practitioners.

We believe that this text is unique in the literature on 3D imaging in several respects: (1) it provides a wide coverage of topics in 3D imaging; (2) it pays special attention to the clear presentation of well-established core techniques; (3) it covers a wide range of the most promising recent techniques that are considered to be state-of-the-art.

This second edition (2020) upgrades existing topics presented in the first edition (2012) with the most significant novel findings in the intervening period. Additionally, it has new material covering consumer-grade RGB-D cameras, 3D morphable models, deep learning on 3D datasets, as well as new applications in the 3D digitization of cultural heritage and the 3D phenotyping of plants.

3D Imaging, Analysis and Applications

Three-dimensional (3D) imaging techniques have been developed within the field of computer vision that *automatically* reconstruct the 3D shape of the imaged objects and scene. This is referred to as a 3D scan or 3D image and it often comes with a registered color-texture image that can be pasted over the captured shape and rendered from many viewpoints (if desired) on a computer display.

The techniques developed include both active systems, where some form of illumination is projected onto the scene, and passive systems, where the natural illumination of the scene is used. Perhaps the most intensively researched area of 3D shape acquisition has been focused on stereo vision systems, which, like the human visual system, uses a pair of views (images) in order to compute 3D structure. Here, researchers have met challenging problems such as the establishment of correspondences between overlapping images for the dense reconstruction of the imaged scene. Many applications require further processing and data analysis once 3D shape data has been acquired. For example, identification of salient points within the 3D data, segmentation into semantic parts, registration of multiple partial 3D data scans, computation of 3D symmetry planes, and matching of whole 3D objects.

It is one of today's challenges to design a technology that can cover the whole pipeline of 3D shape capture, processing, and visualization. The different steps of this pipeline have raised important topics in the research community for decades, owing to the numerous theoretical and technical problems that they induce. Capturing the 3D shape, instead of just a 2D projection as a standard camera does, makes an extremely wide array of new kinds of application possible. For instance, computer aided geometric design, 3D and free-viewpoint TV, virtual and augmented reality, natural user interaction based on monitoring gestures, 3D object recognition and 3D recognition for biometrics, 3D medical imaging, 3D remote sensing, industrial inspection, and robot navigation, to name just a few. These applications, of course, involve much more technological advances than just 3D shape capture; storage, analysis, transmission, and visualization of the 3D shape are also part of the whole pipeline.

While 3D imaging provides opportunities for numerous applications in the real world, these applications also provide a platform to test the techniques developed. 3D phenotyping of plants is one of the representative applications that spans the whole spectrum and different stages of 3D imaging: data capture, plant modeling, segmentation, skeletonization, feature extraction and measurements, and tracking. As discussed later in the book, despite the rapid progress of research and development in the past four decades, the problem is far from being solved, especially in the sense of real-time and high throughput, and thus will continue to attract intensive attention from the community.

3D imaging and analysis is closely associated with computer vision, but it also intersects with a number of other fields, for example, image processing, pattern recognition, machine learning, computer graphics, information theory, statistics, computational geometry, and physics. It involves building sensors, modeling them, and then processing the output images. In particular, 3D image analysis bridges the gap between low-level and high-level vision in order to deduce high-level (semantic) information from basic 3D data.

Book Objective and Content

The objective of this book is to bring together a set of core topics in 3D imaging, analysis, and applications, both in terms of well-established fundamental techniques and the most promising recent techniques. Indeed, we see that many similar techniques are being used in a variety of subject areas and applications and we feel that we can unify a range of related ideas, providing clarity to both academic and industrial practitioners, who are acquiring and processing 3D datasets. To ensure the quality of the book, all the contributors we have chosen have attained a world-class standing by publishing in the top conferences and journals in this area. Thus, the material presented in this book is informative and authoritative and represents mainstream work and opinions within the community.

After an introductory chapter, the book covers 3D image capture methods, particularly those that use two cameras, as in passive stereo vision, or one or more cameras and light projector, as in active 3D imaging. It also covers how 3D data is represented, stored, and visualized. Later parts of the book cover 3D shape analysis and inference, firstly in a general sense, which includes feature extraction, shape registration, shape matching, 3D morphable models, and deep learning on 3D datasets. The final part of the book focuses on applications including 3D face recognition, 3D cultural heritage, and 3D phenotyping of plants.

Ormskirk, UK   Yonghuai Liu
York, UK   Nick Pears
Cardiff, UK   Paul L. Rosin
York, UK   Patrik Huber

Acknowledgements We would like to express our sincere gratitude to all chapter authors for their contributions, their discussions, and their support during the book preparation. It has been our honor to work with so many truly world leading academics and, without them, the production of this book would not have been possible.

We would also like to thank all of the chapter reviewers for their insightful comments, which have enabled us to produce a high quality book. In particular, we thank Song Bai, Francesco Banterle, Stefano Berretti, Stefano Brusaporci, Benjamin Bustos, Umberto Castellani, Chi Chen, Andrew French, Ryo Furukawa, Yulan Guo, Lasse Klingbeil, Huibin Li, Feng Liu, Andreas Morel-Forster, Michael Pound, Tomislav Pribanić, Stephen Se, Boxin Shi, Ferdous Sohel, Hedi Tabia, Damon L. Woodard, Jin Xie, and Ruigang Yang.

We are grateful for the support of our publisher, Springer; in particular, we would like to thank Helen Desmond who worked with us in a friendly and effective way throughout all stages of the book production process.

Contents

Contributors

John L. Barron Department of Computer Science, University of Western Ontario, London, Canada

Adrien Bartoli Université d'Auvergne, Clermont-Ferrand, France

Jean-Angelo Beraldin National Research Council Canada (formerly), Ottawa, Canada

Johannes Brünger Institute of Computer Science, Christian-Albrechts-University of Kiel, Kiel, Germany

Benjamin Bustos Department of Computer Science, University of Chile, Santiago, Chile

Umberto Castellani University of Verona, Verona, Italy

Ayan Chaudhury School of EECS, KTH Royal Institute of Technology, Stockholm, Sweden;
Department of Computer Science, University of Western Ontario, London, Canada

Hang Dai Department of Computer Science, University of York, York, UK

Marc-Antoine Drouin National Research Council Canada, Ottawa, Canada

Bernard D. Frischer Indiana University, Bloomington, IN, USA

Gabriele Guidi Politecnico di Milano, Milan, Italy

Ismail Hamieh National Research Council Canada (formerly), Ottawa, Canada

Patrik Huber Department of Computer Science, University of York, York, UK

Reinhard Koch Institute of Computer Science, Christian-Albrechts-University of Kiel, Kiel, Germany

Yonghuai Liu Department of Computer Science, Edge Hill University, Ormskirk, Lancashire, UK

Ajmal Mian School of Computer Science and Software Engineering, University of Western Australia, Crawley, WA, Australia

Nick Pears Department of Computer Science, University of York, York, UK

Paul L. Rosin School of Computer Science & Informatics, Cardiff University, Cardiff, UK

Charles Ruizhongtai Qi Stanford University, Stanford, CA, USA

Samuele Salti University of Bologna, Bologna, Italy

Stephen Se FLIR Systems Inc., Richmond, BC, Canada

Lama Seoud Polytechnique Montreal, Montreal, Canada

Ivan Sipiran Department of Engineering, Pontifical Catholic University of Peru, Lima, Peru

William A. P. Smith Department of Computer Science, University of York, York, UK

Riccardo Spezialetti University of Bologna, Bologna, Italy

Luigi Di Stefano University of Bologna, Bologna, Italy

Federico Tombari TU Munich and Google, Munich, Germany

Chapter 1
Introduction

Johannes Brünger, Reinhard Koch, Nick Pears, Yonghuai Liu,
and Paul L. Rosin

Abstract *3D Imaging, Analysis, and Applications* is the second edition of a comprehensive textbook on 3D shape capture, 3D shape analysis, and how such capture and analysis can be employed in applications. Fourteen chapters cover a broad range of concepts, algorithms, and applications. After this introduction, the chapters are split into three parts, as follows: Part I, *3D Image Acquisition, Representation, and Visualization*, presents techniques for capture, representation, and visualization of 3D data; Part II, *3D Shape Analysis and Inference*, presents hand-crafted and learned 3D local shape descriptors, shape registration and matching, statistical shape modeling and deep learning on 3D datasets. Finally, Part III, *3D Imaging Applications*, presents application areas in 3D face recognition, 3D heritage modeling, and 3D phenotyping of plants. This introduction provides the reader with historical and background information, such as that relating to the development of computer vision; in particular, the development of automated 3D imaging. It briefly discusses general depth estimation principles for 3D imaging, details a selection of seminal papers, sketches applications of 3D imaging, and concludes with an outline of the book's remaining chapters.

J. Brünger · R. Koch (✉)
Institute of Computer Science, Christian-Albrechts-University of Kiel, Kiel, Germany
e-mail: rk@informatik.uni-kiel.de

J. Brünger
e-mail: jobr@informatik.uni-kiel.de

N. Pears
Department of Computer Science, University of York,
Deramore Lane, York YO10 5GH, UK
e-mail: nick.pears@york.ac.uk

Y. Liu
Department of Computer Science, Edge Hill University,
Ormskirk, Lancashire L39 4QP, UK
e-mail: Liuyo@edgehill.ac.uk

P. L. Rosin
School of Computer Science & Informatics, Cardiff University,
Cardiff CF24 3AA, UK
e-mail: Paul.Rosin@cs.cf.ac.uk

© Springer Nature Switzerland AG 2020
Y. Liu et al. (eds.), *3D Imaging, Analysis and Applications*,
https://doi.org/10.1007/978-3-030-44070-1_1

1

1.1 Introduction

Three-dimensional (3D) imaging seeks to capture the 3D structure of scenes and objects within our environment. The computed set of data points in 3D space is often accompanied by color-texture information in the form of a registered 2D image, typically obtained from standard digital image capture. Such 3D data, with or without accompanying color/texture, is referred to by various names, such as a *3D model,*[1] a *3D scan*[2], or a *3D image.*[3]

The output of a 3D imaging process can be analyzed and processed to extract information that supports a wide range of applications, such as object recognition, shape search on the web, face recognition for security and surveillance, robot navigation, mapping of the Earth's surface, forests or urban regions, and clinical procedures in medicine.

Chapter Outline
The main sections in this chapter cover the following:

- A historical perspective on 3D imaging;
- The development of the broader field of Computer Vision for context;
- Acquisition techniques for 3D imaging;
- Milestones in 3D imaging and shape analysis from recent decades (post 1970).

We conclude by giving a 'road map' for the remaining chapters in this book.

1.2 A Historical Perspective on 3D Imaging

To understand the roots of 3D imaging, we first need to consider the history of the more general concepts of image formation and image capture. After this, the remainder of this section discusses the binocular depth perception and stereoscopic displays.

1.2.1 Image Formation and Image Capture

Since ancient times, humans have tried to capture their surrounding 3D environment and important aspects of social life on wall paintings. Early drawings, mostly animal paintings, are thought to date back 32,000 years, such as the early works in the

---

[1]Typically, this term is used when the 3D data is acquired from multiple-viewpoint 2D images. We prefer to avoid the use of this term for what we see as raw 3D data, as this is easily confused with 3D statistical shape models.

[2]Typically, this term is used when a scanner acquires the 3D data, such as a laser stripe scanner.

[3]Typically, this term is used when the data is ordered in a regular grid, such as the 2D array of depth values in a range image, or a 3D array of data in volumetric medical imaging.

Chauvet Cave, France. Drawings in the famous Lascaux Caves near Montignac, France are also very old and date back to around 17,000 years [16]. These drawings were not correct in terms of perspective, but did capture the essence of the objects in an artistic way.

A rigorous mathematical treatment of vision was postulated by Euclid[4] in his book *Optics* [13]. Thus, already early on in history, some aspects of perspective were known. Another very influential mathematical text was the *Kitab al-Manazir* (Book of Optics) by Alhazen[5] [72].

In parallel with the mathematical concepts of vision and optics, physical optics developed by the use of lenses and mirrors form the basis of modern optical instruments. Very early lenses were found as polished crystals, like the famous *Nimrud lens* that was discovered by Austen Henry Layard.[6] The lens quality is far from perfect but allows light focusing at a focal point distance of 110 mm. Lenses were used as *burning lenses* to focus sunlight and as magnification lenses. An early written record of such use is found with Seneca the Younger[7] who noted

> Letters, however small and indistinct, are seen enlarged and more clearly through a globe or glass filled with water [42].

Thus, he describes the effect of a spherical convex lens. Early on, the use of such magnification for observing distant objects was recognized and optical instruments were devised, such as corrective lenses for bad eye-sight in the thirteenth–fifteenth century CE and the telescope at the beginning of the seventeenth century. It is unclear who invented the telescope, as several lens makers observed the magnification effects independently. The German-born Dutch lens maker Hans Lippershey (1570–1619) from Middelburg, province Zeeland, is often credited as the inventor of the telescope, since he applied for a patent, which was denied. Other lens makers like his fellow Middelburg lens maker Zacharias Janssen were also claiming the invention [38]. Combined with the camera obscura, optically a pinhole camera, they form the basic concept of modern cameras. The *camera obscura*, Latin for *dark room,* has been used for a long time to capture images of scenes. Light reflected from a scene enters a dark room through a very small hole and is projected as an image onto the back wall of the room. Already Alhazen had experimented with a camera obscura and it was used as a drawing aid by artists and as a visual attraction later on. The name *camera* is derived from the camera obscura. The pinhole camera generates an inverse image of the scene with a scale factor $f = i/o$, where i is the image distance between pinhole and image and o is the object distance between object and pinhole. However,

---

[4]Euclid of Alexandria, Greek mathematician, also referred to as the *Father of Geometry*, lived in Alexandria during the reign of Ptolemy I (323–283 BC).

[5]Alhazen (Ibn al-Haytham), born 965 CE in Basra, Iraq, died in 1040. Introduced the concept of *physical optics* and experimented with lenses, mirrors, camera obscura, refraction, and reflection.

[6]Sir Austen Henry Layard (1817–1894), British archeologist, found a polished rock crystal during the excavation of ancient Nimrud, Iraq. The lens has a diameter of 38 mm, presumed creation date 750–710 BC and now on display at the British Museum, London.

[7]Lucius Annaeus Seneca, around 4 BC–65 CE, was a Roman philosopher, statesman, dramatist, tutor, and adviser of Nero.

the opening aperture of the pinhole itself has to be very small to avoid blurring. A light-collecting and focusing lens is then used to enlarge the opening aperture and brighter, yet still sharp images can be obtained for thin convex lenses.[8] Such lenses follow the Gaussian thin lens equation: $1/f = 1/i + 1/o$, where f is the focal length of the lens. The drawback, as with all modern cameras, is the limited depth of field, in which the image of the scene is in focus.

Until the mid-nineteenth century, the only way to capture an image was to manually paint it onto canvas or other suitable backgrounds. With the advent of photography,[9] images of the real world could be taken and stored for future use. This invention was soon expanded from monochromatic to color images, from monoscopic to stereoscopic[10] and from still images to film sequences. In our digital age, electronic sensor devices have taken the role of chemical film and a variety of electronic display technologies have taken over the role of painted pictures.

It is interesting to note, though, that some of the most recent developments in digital photography and image displays have their inspiration in technologies developed over 100 years ago. In 1908, Gabriel Lippmann[11] developed the concept of *integral photography*, a camera composed of very many tiny lenses side by side, in front of a photographic film [45]. These lenses collect view-dependent light rays from all directions onto the film, effectively capturing a three-dimensional field of light rays, the *light field* [1]. The newly established research field of *computational photography* has taken on his ideas and is actively developing novel multilens-camera systems for capturing 3D scenes, enhancing the depth of field, or computing novel image transfer functions. In addition, the reverse process of projecting an integral image into space has led to the development of lenticular sheet 3D printing and to auto-stereoscopic (glasses-free) multi-view displays that let the observer see the captured 3D scene with full depth parallax without wearing special purpose spectacles (glasses). These 3D projection techniques have spawned a huge interest in the display community, both for high-quality auto-stereoscopic displays with full 3D parallax as used in the advertisement (3D signage) and for novel 3D-TV display systems that might eventually conquer the 3D-TV home market. This technique is discussed further in Sect. 1.2.3. However, the market today is still dominated by traditional stereoscopic displays, either based on actively switched shutter glasses for gamers or based on passive polarization techniques for 3D cinema production.

---

[8] Small and thin bi-convex lenses look like lentils, hence the name *lens*, which is Latin for *lentil*.

[9] Nicéphore Niépce, 1765–1833, is credited as one of the inventors of photography by solar light etching (Heliograph) in 1826. He later worked with Louis-Jacques-Mandé Daguerre, 1787–1851, who acquired a patent for his Daguerreotype, the first practical photography process based on silver iodide, in 1839. In parallel, William Henry Fox Talbot, 1800–1877, developed the calotype process, which uses paper coated with silver iodide. The calotype produced a negative image from which a positive could be printed using silver chloride coated paper [28].

[10] The Greek word *stereos* for solid is used to indicate a spatial 3D extension of vision, hence stereoscopic stands for a 3D form of visual information.

[11] Gabriel Lippmann, 1845–1921, French scientist, received the 1908 Nobel prize in Physics for his method to reproduce color pictures by interferometry.

Fig. 1.1 Left: Human binocular perception of 3D scene. Right: the perceived images of the left and right eye, showing how the depth-dependent disparity results in a parallax shift between foreground and background objects. Both observed images are fused into a 3D sensation by the human eye–brain visual system

1.2.2   Binocular Perception of Depth

It is important to note that many visual cues give the perception of depth, some of which are monocular cues (e.g., occlusion, shading, and texture gradients) and some of which are binocular cues (e.g., retinal disparity, parallax, and eye convergence). Of course, humans, and most predator animals, are equipped with a very sophisticated binocular vision system and it is the binocular cues that provide us with accurate short range depth perception. Clearly, it is advantageous for us to have good depth perception to a distance at least as large as the length of our arms. The principles of binocular vision were already recognized in 1838 by Sir Charles Wheatstone,[12] who described the process of binocular perception:

> ... the mind perceives an object of three dimensions by means of the two dissimilar pictures projected by it on the two retinae... [82]

The important observation was that the binocular perception of two correctly displaced 2D-images of a scene is equivalent to the perception of the 3D scene itself.

Figure 1.1 illustrates the human binocular perception of a 3D scene, comprised of a cone in front of a torus. At the right of this figure are the images perceived by the left and the right eye. If we take a scene point, for example, the tip of the cone, this projects to different positions on the left and right retina. The difference between these two positions (retinal correspondences) is known as *disparity* and the disparity associated with nearby surface points (on the cone) is larger than the disparity associated with more distant points (on the torus). As a result of this difference between foreground

---

[12]Sir Charles Wheatstone, 1802–1875, English physicist and inventor.

and background disparity, the position (or alignment) of the foreground relative to the background changes as we shift the viewpoint from the left eye to the right eye. This effect is known as parallax.[13]

Imagine now that the 3D scene of the cone in front of the torus is observed by a binocular camera with two lenses that are separated horizontally by the inter-eye distance of a human observer. If these images are presented to the left and right eyes of the human observer later on, she or he cannot distinguish the observed real scene from the binocular images of the scene. The images are fused inside the binocular perception of the human observer to form the 3D impression. This observation led to the invention of the stereoscope by Sir David Brewster[14] [11], where two displaced images could convey 3D information to the human observer.

1.2.3   Stereoscopic Displays

Since Brewster's stereoscope, a wealth of technical devices for presenting stereo-scopic images to the human observer has been designed. Virtually all of the modern stereoscopic display technologies are based on the same principle, namely that of presenting two different views to the two eyes on a single display. To do this, techniques have been employed that

- Separate them by color-coding (the anaglyph technique with red-green glasses or spectral comb filters),
- Use polarization properties of light (circularly or linearly polarized eye glasses),
- Perform time-coding with left–right time-interleaving and actively synchronized shutter glasses, or
- Exploit lens systems to project different images directly into the eyes of the observer.

While the first three techniques all use separating glasses to be worn by the user, the latter lens projection systems allow glasses-free, auto-stereoscopic perception, even for more than two different views. Figure 1.2 sketches the stereoscopic perception with either two-view stereoscopic or glasses-free auto-stereoscopic multi-view displays. In the binocular display, polarization serves to decouple left and right eye information. The auto-stereoscopic display exploits optical lenticular sheet lenses or

---

[13]The terms disparity and parallax are sometimes used interchangeably in the literature and this misuse of terminology is a source of confusion. One way to think about parallax is that it is induced by the difference in disparity between foreground and background objects over a pair of views displaced by a translation. The end result is that the foreground is in alignment with different parts of the background. The disparity of foreground objects and parallax then only become equivalent when the distance of background objects can be treated as infinity (e.g., distant stars); in this case, the background objects are stationary in the image.

[14]Sir David Brewster, 1781–1868, Scottish physicist and inventor.

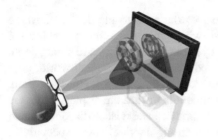

Fig. 1.2 Left: Stereoscopic displays use glasses-based polarization light separators to produce the two images required for stereoscopic reception. Right: Lens-based auto-stereoscopic displays project multiple, slightly displaced images by the use of lenses or parallax barrier systems, allowing glasses-free stereoscopic reception. Such systems allow for slight head motion

light barrier systems to selectively project the displaced images into different angular sections in front of the display. If the observer moves in front of the display, each eye receives a differently displaced image, resulting in a look-around capability.

Binocular stereoscopic movies and selected stereoscopic television programs have now entered the market quite successfully. These display techniques are commonly given the branding *3D*, but actually, they do not contain or need true 3D information. In a stereo movie recording, two displaced movie cameras are synchronously used to capture left and right eye views, and stereoscopic digital movie projectors utilize polarization filters to separate both views. The spectator needs to wear a similar set of polarized glasses for binocular perception. The perceived depth impression is fixed by the inter-camera eye distance of the recording stereo camera and can only be adjusted during recording. This is a drawback of binocular stereo camera recordings because it is difficult to scale depth perception later on. Hence, different recordings must be undertaken for large screen movie theaters and for home TV settings. Even more severe is the stereoscopic image capture for auto-stereoscopic displays. In this case, not two but many slightly displaced views need to be recorded simultaneously. Typical displays require 8–28 simultaneous views and it is not feasible to record all views directly, because the amount of data would grow enormously. Also, the design of such multi-ocular cameras is difficult and expensive. Instead, a true 3D movie format is needed that allows us to synthesize the required views from a generic 3D image format. Currently, MPEG allows for stereoscopic Multi-View Coding (H.264 MVC 3D) formats, and dedicated 3D data formats like Multi-View Depth (MVD) or Layered Depth Video (LDV) are under discussion [4]. MVD and LDV record both depth and color from a few camera positions that capture the desired angular sections in front of the display. The many views needed to drive the display are then rendered by depth-compensated interpolation from the recorded data. Thus, a true 3D format will greatly facilitate data capture for future 3D-TV systems.

There is another obstacle to the binocular perception that was not discussed in early binocular display systems. The observed disparity is produced on the image plane and both eyes of the human observer are accommodating their focus on the display plane. However, the binocular depth cue causes the eyes to physically converge toward the virtual 3D position of the object, which may be before or behind the display plane. Both eye accommodation and eye convergence angle are strong depth cues to our visual system, and depth is inferred from both. In the real world, both cues coincide since the eyes focus and converge toward the same real object position. On a binocular display, the eyes always accommodate toward the display, while the convergence angle varies with depth. This conflict causes visual discomfort and is a major source of headaches when watching strong depth effects, especially in front of the screen. Stereographers nowadays take great care to balance these effects during recording. The only remedy to this disturbing effect is to build volumetric displays where the image is truly formed in 3D space rather than on the 2D display. In this case, the convergence and accommodation cues coincide and yield stress-free stereoscopic viewing. There is an active research community underway developing volumetric or holographic displays, that rely either on spatial pattern interference, on volume-sweeping surfaces, or on 3D light fields. Blundell and Schwarz give a good classification of volumetric displays and sketch current trends [8]. All these 3D displays need some kind of 3D scene representation, and binocular imaging is not sufficient. Hence, these displays also are in need of true 3D data formats.

1.3   The Development of Computer Vision

Although the content of this book derives from a number of research fields, the field of computer vision is the most relevant large-scale research area. It is a diverse field that integrates ideas and methods from a variety of pre-existing and co-existing areas, such as image processing, statistics, pattern recognition, geometry, photogrammetry, optimization, scientific computing, computer graphics, and many others. In 1960–1980s, Artificial Intelligence was the driving field that tried to exploit computers for understanding the world that, in various ways, corresponded to how humans understand it. This included the interpretation of 3D scenes from images and videos.

The process of scene understanding was thought of as a hierarchy of vision levels, similar to visual perception, with three main levels [52], as follows:

- **Low-level vision:** early 2D vision processes, such as filtering and extraction of local image structures.
- **Mid-level vision:** processes such as segmentation, generation of 2.5D depth, optical flow computation, and extraction of regional structures.
- **High-level vision:** semantic interpretation of segments, object recognition, and global 3D scene reasoning.

This general approach is still valid, but it was not successful at the first attempt, because researchers underestimated the difficulties of the first two steps and tried to directly handle high-level vision reasoning. In his textbook *Computer Vision: Algorithms and Applications* [76], Rick Szeliski reports an assignment of Marvin

Minsky, MIT, to a group of students to develop a computer vision program that could reason about image content:

> According to one well-known story, in 1966, Marvin Minsky at MIT asked his undergraduate student Gerald Jay Sussman to "spend the summer linking a camera to a computer and getting the computer to describe what it saw".[15]

Soon, it became clear that Minsky underestimated this challenge. However, the attempts to resolve the various problems of the three levels proved fruitful to the field of computer vision, and very many approaches to solve partial problems on all levels have appeared. Although some vision researchers follow the path of cognitive vision that builds on the working of the human brain, most techniques today are driven by engineering demands to extract relevant information from the images.

Computer vision is developed roughly along with the above-mentioned three levels of vision. Research in low-level vision has deepened the understanding of local image structures. Digital images can be described without regard to scanning resolution by the image scale space [83] and image pyramids [77]. Image content can be described in the image domain or equivalently in the frequency (Fourier) domain, leading to a theory of filter design to improve the image quality and to reduce noise. Local structures are defined by their intrinsic dimension[16] [5], which leads to interest operators [30] and to feature descriptors [7].

Regional relations between local features in an image or between images are powerful descriptions for mid-level vision processes, such as segmentation, depth estimation, and optical flow estimation. Marr [52] coined the term *2.5D model*, meaning that information about scene depth for a certain region in an image exists, but only viewed from a single viewpoint. Such is the case for range estimation techniques, which include stereo, active triangulation or time-of-flight depth measurement devices, where not a full 3D description is measured but a range image $d(u, v)$ with one distance value per image pixel. This range value, along with some intrinsic parameters of the range sensing device, allows us to invert the image projection and to reconstruct scene surfaces. Full 3D depth can be reconstructed from multi-view range images if suitably fused from different viewpoints.

The special branch of computer vision that deals with viewing a scene from two or more viewpoints and extracting a 3D representation of the geometry of the imaged scene is termed *geometric computer vision*. Here, the camera can be thought of as a measurement device. Geometric computer vision developed rapidly in the 1990s and 2000s and was influenced strongly by geodesy and photogrammetry. In fact, those disciplines are converging. Many of the techniques well known in photogrammetry have found their way into computer vision algorithms. Most notably is the method of bundle adjustment for optimally and simultaneously estimating camera parameters and 3D point estimates from uncertain image features [78].

Combining the geometric properties of scene objects with image-based reflectance measurements allows us to model the visual-geometric appearance of scenes. There is

---

[15]Szeliski, Computer Vision: Algorithms and Applications, page. 10 [76].

[16]Intrinsic Image Dimension (IID) describes the local change in the image. Constant image: 0D, linear structures: 1D, point structures: 2D.

now a strong relationship between computer vision and computer graphics that developed during the last decade. While computer graphics displays computer-defined objects with given surface properties by projecting them into a synthetic camera, vision estimates the surface properties of real objects as seen by a real camera. Hence, vision can be viewed as the inverse problem of graphics. One of the key challenges in computer vision is that, due to the projection of the objects into the camera, the range information is lost and needs to be recovered. This makes the inverse problem of recovering depth from images especially hard and often ill-posed. Today, both disciplines are still converging, for example, in the area of image-based rendering in computer graphics and by exploiting the computing capabilities of Graphics Processing Units for computer vision tasks.

High-level vision attempts to interpret the observed scene and to assign semantic meaning to scene regions. Much progress has been made recently in this field, starting with simple object detection to object recognition, ranging from individual objects to object categories. Machine learning is vital for these approaches to work reliably and has been exploited extensively in computer vision over the last decade [67]. The availability of huge amounts of labeled training data from databases and the Web and advances in high-dimensional learning techniques are keys to the success of machine learning techniques. Successful applications range from face detection, face recognition, and biometrics to visual image retrieval and scene object categorization, to human action and event analysis. The merging of machine learning with computer vision algorithms is a very promising ongoing development and will continue to solve vision problems in the future, converging toward the ultimate goal of visual scene understanding. From a practical point of view, this will broaden the range of applications from highly controlled scenes, which is often the necessary context for the required performance in terms of accuracy and reliability, to natural, uncontrolled, real-world scenes with all of their inherent variability.

Particularly successful in the processing of image data from real-world scenes in recent years have been the Deep Convolutional Neural Networks (DCNN). Although the concept of neural networks, like other methods of machine learning, has existed since the 1960s, some hurdles had to be overcome before they became such a powerful tool [66]. With the application of convolutions and the adjustment of weights by means of backpropagation even with many intermediate layers, the first successes on realistic practical applications could be achieved in the 80s and 90s. The big breakthrough for deep neural networks took place in the 2010s after large datasets were available and computers (or GPUs) had become faster. Thanks to new activation functions and regularization, the networks have now achieved considerable success in computer vision competitions [43]. With new architectures, this trend has continued in recent years, so that the winners of big computer vision competitions are now almost exclusively solutions based on neural networks. Meanwhile, they are universally applicable as single building blocks (depth estimation, camera pose estimation, etc.) and thus are also integrated with classical approaches to achieve high-performance results.

Closely following the classical processing of image data, DCNNs are optimized for the processing of 2D data in Euclidean space. But by combining the information from multiple 2D input images, networks can reconstruct the 3D structure of objects, similar to the reconstruction with classical triangulation [74]. With some tricks, they can also be applied to sphere-like surface meshes [51] or 3D objects represented by a voxel grid of binary variables [84]. But even on intrinsic non-Euclidean data, such as graphs or surfaces, they can show their potential by finding keypoint-correspondences in 2D and 3D [14, 87].

Despite the continuing trend to solve problems or parts of problems with the help of learned methods, one should not ignore what these methods are based on. For example, most problems require a large amount of data to train on, and in the case of a supervised learning method, this training data must be annotated manually. Furthermore, there is always the danger that the existing training data does not cover all theoretically possible scenarios and that the networks may react unexpectedly in these cases. So the disadvantages of learned methods are their dependence on training data and the difficulty of clearly explaining their performance. Hand-crafted features, on the other hand, have the advantage that they are based on geometric formulas and always deliver correct, clear, and explainable results if the input data is correct. In summary, it can be said that manually generated features produce good results under good conditions (lighting, textures) without the need for training data. Neural networks, on the other hand, can build on what has been learned, even under difficult conditions, and usually deliver realistic (albeit often inexplicable) results. However, at the time of writing (2020), a new push for explainable AI is emerging, which includes often opaque approaches, such as deep learning.

1.3.1 Further Reading in Computer Vision

Computer vision has matured over the last 50 years into a very broad and diverse field and this book does not attempt to cover that field comprehensively. However, there are some very good textbooks available that span both individual areas as well as the complete range of computer vision. An early book on this topic is the above-mentioned text by David Marr: *Vision. A Computational Investigation into the Human Representation and Processing of Visual Information* [52]; this is one of the forerunners of computer vision concepts and could be used as a historical reference. A recent and very comprehensive textbook is the work by Rick Szeliski: *Computer Vision: Algorithms and Applications* [76]. This work is exceptional as it covers not only the broad field of computer vision in detail, but also gives a wealth of algorithms, mathematical methods, practical examples, an extensive bibliography, and references to many vision benchmarks and datasets. The introduction gives an in-depth overview of the field and of recent trends.[17] If the reader is interested in a detailed analysis of geometric computer vision and projective multi-view geometry, we refer to the standard book *Multiple View Geometry in Computer Vision* by Richard Hartley and Andrew Zisserman [31]. Here, most of the relevant geometrical algorithms as well as

---

[17] A PDF version is also available for personal use on the website http://szeliski.org/Book/.

the necessary mathematical foundations are discussed in detail. Other textbooks that cover the computer vision theme at large are *Computer Vision: a modern approach* [21], *Introductory Techniques for 3-D Computer Vision* [79], or *An Invitation to 3D Vision: From Images to Models* [49].

1.4 Acquisition Techniques for 3D Imaging

The challenge of 3D imaging is to recover the distance information that is lost during projection into a camera, with the highest possible accuracy and reliability, for every pixel of the image. We define a *range image*[18] as an image where each pixel stores the distance between the imaging sensor (for example, a 3D range camera) and the observed surface point. Here, we can differentiate between passive and active methods for 3D imaging, which will be discussed briefly in the following section. In-depth presentations are given in Chap. 2 for passive methods and Chaps. 3–5 for active methods.

1.4.1 Passive 3D Imaging

Passive 3D imaging relies on images of the ambient-lit scene alone, without the help of further information, such as projection of light patterns onto the scene. Hence, all information must be taken from standard 2D images. More generally, a set of techniques called *Shape from X* exists, where *X* represents some visual cue. These include

- Shape from focus, which varies the camera focus and estimates depth pointwise from image sharpness [54].
- Shape from shading, which uses the shades in a grayscale image to infer the shape of the surfaces, based on the reflectance map. This map links image intensity with surface orientation [34]. There is a related technique, called *photometric stereo*, that uses several images, each with a different illumination direction.
- Shape from texture, which assumes the object is covered by a regular surface pattern. Surface normal and distance are then estimated from the perspective effects in the images.
- Shape from stereo disparity, where the same scene is imaged from two distinct (displaced) viewpoints and the difference (disparity) between pixel positions (one from each image) corresponding to the same scene point is exploited.

The most prominent, and the most detailed in this book, is the last mentioned of these. Here, depth is estimated by the geometric principle of triangulation, when the

---

[18]Range images are often combined with standard RGB color images, and referred to as *RGB-D images*.

Fig. 1.3 A rectilinear stereo
rig. Note the increased image
disparity for the near scene
point (blue) compared to the
far scene point (black). The
scene area marked in red
cannot be imaged by the
right camera and is a
'missing part' in the
reconstructed scene

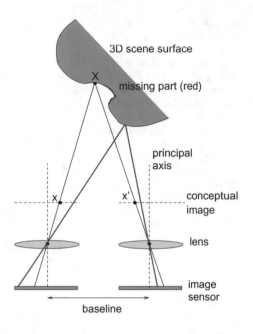

same scene point can be observed in two or more images. Figure 1.3 illustrates this
principle in detail. Here, a rectilinear stereo rig is shown where the two cameras are
side by side with the principal axes of their lenses parallel to each other. Note that
the origin (or center) of each camera is the optical center of its lens and the *baseline*
is defined as the distance between these two camera centers. Although the real image
sensor is behind the lens, it is a common practice to envisage and use a conceptual
image position in front of the lens so that the image is in the same orientation as
the scene (i.e., not inverted top to bottom and left to right) and this is shown by the
dashed horizontal line in Fig. 1.3. The term *triangulation* comes from the fact that the
scene point, $\mathbf{X}$, can be reconstructed from the triangle[19] formed by the baseline and
the two coplanar vector directions defined by the left camera center to image point $\mathbf{x}$
and the right camera center to image point $\mathbf{x}'$. In fact, the depth of the scene is related
to the disparity between the left and right image correspondences. For closer objects,
the disparity is greater, as illustrated by the blue lines in Fig. 1.3. It is clear from this
figure that the scene surface colored red cannot be observed by the right camera, in
which case no 3D shape measurement can be made. This scene portion is sometimes
referred to as a *missing part* and is the result of self-occlusion or occlusion by a
different foreground object. Image correspondences are found by evaluating image
similarities through image feature matching, either locally or globally over the entire
image. Problems might occur if the image content does not hold sufficient information
for unique correspondences, for example in smooth, textureless regions. Hence, a
dense range estimation cannot be guaranteed and, particularly in man-made indoor

---

[19]This triangle defines an *epipolar plane*, which is discussed in Chap. 2.

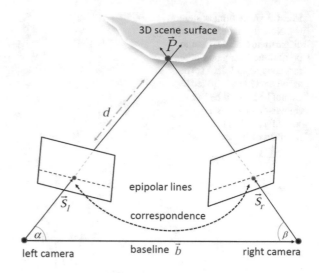

Fig. 1.4 A verged stereo system. Note that this diagram uses a simplified diagrammatic structure seen in much of the literature where only camera centers and conceptual image planes are shown. The intersection of the epipolar plane with the (image) planes defines a pair of epipolar lines. This is discussed in detail in Chap. 2. Figure with permission from [39]

scenarios, the resulting range images are often sparse. Algorithms, test scenarios, and benchmarks for such systems may be found in the Middlebury database [65], and Chap. 2 in this book will discuss these approaches in detail. Note that many stereo rigs turn the cameras toward each other so that they are *verged*, which increases the overlap between the fields of view of the camera and increases the scene volume over which 3D reconstructions can be made. Such a system is shown in Fig. 1.4.[20]

1.4.2 Active 3D Imaging

Active 3D imaging avoids some of the difficulties of passive techniques by introducing controlled additional information, usually controlled lighting or other electromagnetic radiation, such as infrared. Active stereo systems, for example, have the same underlying triangulation geometry as the above-mentioned passive stereo systems, but they exchange one camera by a projector, which projects a spot or a stripe, or a patterned area that does not repeat itself within some local neighborhood. This latter type of non-scanned system is called a *structured light* projection. Advances in optoelectronics for the generation of structured light patterns and other illumination, accurate mechanical laser scanning control, and high-resolution, high sensitivity image sensors have all had their impact on advancing the performance of active 3D imaging.

Note that, in structured light systems, all of the image feature shift that occurs due to depth variations, which causes a change in disparity, appears in the sensor's one camera, because the projected image pattern is fixed. (Contrast this with a passive

---

[20]Figures 1.4 and 1.5 are a preprint from the forthcoming Encyclopedia of Computer Vision, 2nd Ed. [39].

binocular stereo system, where the disparity change, in general, is manifested as feature movement across two images.) The projection of a pattern means that smooth, textureless areas of the scene are no longer problematic, allowing dense, uniform reconstructions, and the correspondence problem is reduced to finding the known projected pattern. (In the case of a projected spot, the correspondence problem is removed altogether.) In general, the computational burden for generating active range triangulations is relatively light, the resulting range images are mostly dense and reliable, and they can be acquired quickly.

An example of such systems are coded light projectors that use either a time-series of codes or color codes [10]. A recent example of a successful projection system is the Kinect-camera[21] that projects a random infrared pattern and is able to recover dense range images up to several meters distance at 30 frames per second (fps). One problem with all triangulation-based systems, passive and active, is that depth accuracy depends on the triangulation angle, which means that a large baseline is desirable. On the other hand, with a large baseline, the 'missing parts' problem described above is exacerbated, yielding unseen, occluded regions at object boundaries. This is unfortunate, since precise object boundary estimation is important for geometric reconstruction.

An alternative class of active range sensors that avoids the occlusion problem are coaxial sensors, which exploit the time-of-flight principle. Here, light is emitted from a light source that is positioned in line with the optical axis of the receiving sensor (for example, a camera or photo-diode) and is reflected from the object surface back into the sensor. Figure 1.5 gives a schematic view of an active coaxial range sensor [39]. The traveling time delay between outgoing and reflected wave is then measured by phase correlation or direct run-time shuttering, as a direct measure of object distance. Classical examples of such devices are laser-based systems, such as the *LIght Detection And Ranging* (LIDAR) scanner for long-distance depth estimation. The environment is scanned by deflecting a laser with a rotating mirror and distances are measured pointwise, delivering 3D point clouds. Recently, camera-based receivers are utilized that avoid the need for coherent laser light but use inexpensive LED light sources instead. (Such light sources are also easier to make eye-safe.) Again, the time shift of the reflected light is measured, either by gating very short light pulses directly or by phase correlation of the time shift between the emitted and reflected light of a modulated continuous LED light source. Such range cameras [68] are depth estimation devices that, in principle, may deliver dense and accurate depth maps in real time and can be used for depth estimation of dynamic time-varying scenes [40, 41]. Active sensing devices will be discussed in more detail in Chaps. 3–5.

---

[21] Kinect is trademark of Microsoft.

Fig. 1.5 Active coaxial time-of-flight range estimation by phase shift correlation. Figure with permission from [39]

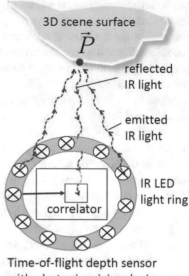

1.4.3 Passive Stereo Versus Active Stereo Imaging

What are the relative merits of passive and active stereo imaging systems? In summary, since the computational burden of passive correspondences is alleviated, it is generally easier to build active systems that can generate dense range images at high frames rates (e.g., 30 fps for the Kinect). Lack of surface features or sufficiently large-scale texture on the scene object can result in passive stereo giving low density 3D reconstructions, at least in the local regions where the surface texture or features (e.g., corners) are missing. This has a number of effects. Firstly, it makes it difficult to comprehensively determine the size and shape of the imaged object. Secondly, it is difficult to get good shape visualizations, when the imaged object is rendered from many different viewpoints. In contrast, as long as the surface is not too dark (low reflectivity) or specular, and does not have too many deep concavities ('missing parts'), active stereo systems allow comprehensive shape measurements and give good renderings for multi-viewpoint visualizations. Thus, when the density of features is low, or the resolution of image sensing is low compared to the scale of the imaged texture, an active stereo system is a preferred solution. However, the need to scan a laser spot or stripe or to project a structured light pattern brings with it extra complexity and expense, and potential eye-safety issues. The use of spot or stripe scanning also brings with it additional reliability issues associated with moving parts.

There is another side to this discussion, which takes into account the availability of increasingly high-resolution CCD/CMOS image sensors. For passive stereo systems, these now allow previously smooth surfaces to appear textured, at the higher resolution scale. A good example is the human face where the random pattern of facial pores can be extracted and hence used to solve the correspondence problem in a passive system. Of course, higher resolution sensors bring with them higher data rates and hence a higher computational burden. Thus, to achieve reasonable real-time performance, improved resolution is developing in tandem with faster processing architectures, such as GPUs, which are starting to have a big impact on dense, real-time passive stereo [86].

1.4.4 Learned Depth Estimation

Besides the two mentioned techniques for range image acquisition, there is nowadays also a third approach, based on machine learning techniques. Similar to the task of semantic segmentation, where each pixel is assigned a class label, the task of depth estimation is defined as estimating the depth value of each pixel of an monocular input image. Using a vast amount of monocular images and the corresponding range images [26], supervised approaches can use these training examples to infer the underlying structure and pattern of the processed data as a mathematical function. Solutions have been proposed with Markov Random Fields [64], neural networks [17, 44] or a combination of both [46].

Since the projection into the camera has irretrievably discarded the depth information, theoretically an infinite number of 3D scenes can be considered as the origin of the processed image. To resolve this ambiguity, the employed techniques need to evaluate the global context of the entire image in addition to local image information to determine the depth values. For example, instead of the absolute distance, the relation between different points in the image can be evaluated [17]. Alternatively, the error function is based on a spacing-increasing discretization and the optimizer executes an ordinal regression [22]. Neural networks also can learn the principles of triangulation. With unsupervised approaches, the disparity estimation of individual image positions can be learned from existing stereo image pairs. This exploits the advantages of the existing (even larger) datasets of stereo images without depth maps. By warping the second stereo image from the disparities into the first image, visualization errors can be measured and used as a loss function [24, 29].

In summary, this new field of learned depth estimation shows very promising results and huge potential for monocular depth conversion.

1.5 Milestones in 3D Imaging and Shape Analysis

In the development toward the current state-of-the-art in 3D imaging and analysis systems, we now outline a small selection of scientific and technological milestones. As we have pointed out, there are many historical precursors to this modern subject area, from the ancient Greeks referring to the optical projection of images (Aristotle, circa 350 BC) to Albrecht Dürer's first mechanical perspective drawing (1525 CE)

to Hauck's establishment of the relationship between projective geometry and photogrammetry (1883 CE). Here, however, we will present a very small selection of
relatively modern milestones[22] from half a century of research (1970–2020) that are
generally thought to fall within the fields of computer vision or computer graphics.

1.5.1 Active 3D Imaging: An Early Optical Triangulation System

The development of active rangefinders based on optical triangulation appears regularly in the literature from the early 1970s. In 1972, Shirai [69] presented a system
that used a stripe projection system and a TV camera to recognize polyhedral objects.
The stripe projector is rotated in steps so that a vertical plane of light passes over a
polyhedral object of interest. A TV camera captures and stores the deformation of the
projected stripe at a set of projection angles. A set of processing steps enabled shapes
to be recognized based on the interrelation of their scene planes. The assumption of
polyhedral scene objects reduced the complexity of their processing which suited
the limitations of the available computational power at that time.

1.5.2 Passive 3D Imaging: An Early Stereo System

One of the first computer-based passive stereo systems employed in a clearly defined
application was that of Gennery who, in 1977, presented a stereo vision system for
an autonomous vehicle [27]. In this work, interest points are extracted and area-
based correlation is used to find correspondences across the stereo image pair. The
relative pose of the two cameras is computed from these matches, camera distortion
is corrected, and, finally, 3D points are triangulated from the correspondences. The
extracted point cloud is then used in the autonomous vehicle application to distinguish
between the ground and objects above the ground surface.

1.5.3 Passive 3D Imaging: The Essential Matrix

When eight or more image correspondences are given for a stereo pair, captured
by cameras with known intrinsic parameters, it is possible to linearly estimate the
relative position and orientation (pose) of the two viewpoints from which the two
projective images were captured. Once these relative viewpoints are known, then
the 3D structural information of the scene can be easily recovered from the image

---

[22]The selection is subjective and open to debate. We are merely attempting to give a glimpse of the
subject's development and diversity, not a definitive and comprehensive history.

correspondences. The origin of this approach, where the relative viewpoint pose is captured in a 3×3 *Essential Matrix*, is due to Longuet-Higgins in his 1981 *Nature* paper entitled: *A computer algorithm for reconstructing a scene from two projections* [47]. It was previously known that relative camera viewpoints could be determined iteratively with just five correspondences, but the extra correspondences allowed Longuet-Higgins to present a much more direct linear solution. Note that only the direction of the displacement between the two viewpoints can be recovered, which means that the absolute scale of the 3D scene reconstruction is unknown. (Put simply, shape but not size is recovered, but the correct scale can be determined with a known dimension in the scene.)

1.5.4 Model Fitting: The RANSAC Approach to Feature Correspondence Analysis

Matching corresponding features between images or surfaces is essential for both 3D shape reconstruction methods and 3D shape matching techniques. Selecting, for example, a set of eight correct correspondences is vital to the estimation of the Essential Matrix. Unfortunately, this is a very difficult problem and often mismatches occur. Hence, a robust selection of feature correspondences is of utmost importance. The 1981 seminal paper by Fishler and Bolles: *Random Sample Consensus: A Paradigm for Model Fitting with Applications to Image Analysis and Automated Cartography* [50] opened the way to handle correspondence errors with a large percentage of outliers. From the available set of n candidate correspondences, which are matched on the basis of local properties, random subsets of $p = 8$ correspondences are drawn and a candidate Essential Matrix is computed for each. The other $n - p$ candidate correspondences are then tested against the random set solutions and the solution with the largest 'consensus' (i.e., the most support in terms of the number of inliers) is selected as the best solution. Although computationally expensive, it yields excellent results. From the 1990s, many variants of this basic algorithm, with improved performance, have been employed in computer vision and 3D shape analysis.

1.5.5 Active 3D Imaging: Advances in Scanning Geometries

The practical development of 3D laser range sensors closely follows the availability of new electronic components and electro-optical technologies. A novel active triangulation method was proposed by Rioux in 1984 [60]. To obtain a large field of view using small triangulation angles, without sacrificing precision, the concept of synchronized scanners was proposed. Such a system has the advantage that the number of 'missing parts' (i.e., the 'shadow effect') can be reduced. These occur where parts of the scene are not simultaneously accessible to both the laser and the image sensor. Using a special scanning mirror arrangement, both the emitted laser beam and receiver optics are rotated simultaneously, in a synchronized fashion, so that the laser spot in the sensor plane can be maintained closer to the image center, while the projected beam remains inherently in focus over a large depth of field and high resolution can be maintained despite a short physical baseline.

1.5.6 3D Registration: Rigid Transformation Estimation from 3D Correspondences

Given a set of surface correspondences between two 3D datasets of the same or similar objects in different poses, how do we compute the six degrees of freedom rigid transformation between them? If we have this rotation and translation information, we can bring the two scans into alignment; a process called *registration*. In the second half of the 1980s, several researchers presented solutions to this problem; for example, both Faugeras and Hebert [20] and Horn [35] derived formulations where the rigid body rotation is represented using quaternions. In Horn's work, an optimal unit quaternion (4-vector) is estimated as the eigenvector corresponding to the maximum eigenvalue of a matrix. Once the rotation has been estimated, it is trivial to compute the estimated translation using this rotation and the centroids of the two point clouds.

The Singular Value Decomposition (SVD) approach of Arun et al. [3] is also very widely used. Here, a 3×3 cross-covariance matrix H is formed using the correspondences and an SVD of this matrix, $H = USV^T$, yields the estimated rotation matrix as $\hat{R} = VU^T$. This is further refined by Kanatani [37] as

$$\hat{R} = V \begin{pmatrix} 1 & & \\ & 1 & \\ & & det(VU^T) \end{pmatrix} U^T \tag{1.1}$$

to avoid the case that $\hat{R}$ is a reflection, instead of a rotation, matrix.

Rigid body transformation estimation forms the core of 3D registration algorithms, such as Iterative Closest Points, which is described next.

1.5.7 3D Registration: Iterative Closest Points

As long as three or more correspondences in a general position (non-colinear) are given between two overlapping 3D point clouds, then the resulting rigid body transformation can be estimated, using one of several methods, as previously mentioned. In 1992, Besl and McKay proposed the seminal Iterative Closest Point (ICP) algorithm [6]. Algorithms based on the ICP algorithm are currently the *de facto* standard

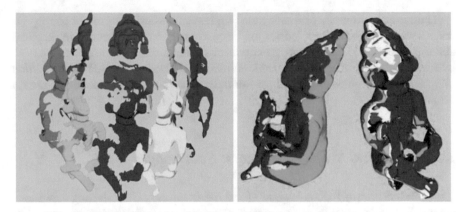

Fig. 1.6 Example of model reconstruction. Partial 3D views of the object of interest are acquired (left). After registration, all the 3D views are transformed to the common reference system and merged (right). Figure generated by Alessandro Negrente, reproduced from [23]

for rigid 3D shape registration tasks. The basis of the algorithm is that it iterates two steps until convergence: tentative correspondences establishment via 'closest points' across the two shapes and rigid transformation parameters update. As long as the initial rotational and translational displacement between a pair of 3D shapes is sufficiently small, then convergence to a global minimum is always possible and high-quality correspondences can be established. Over the last two decades, many variants of ICP have been proposed to improve the speed and accuracy of the registration process [56, 62]. An example of the registration required for model construction from partial 3D views is given in Fig. 1.6.

1.5.8 Passive 3D Imaging: The Fundamental Matrix and Camera Self-calibration

In 1992 Luong, Faugeras, and Maybank extended the Essential Matrix to uncalibrated cameras through the Fundamental Matrix. While for the Essential Matrix estimation, the camera intrinsic parameters had to be known in advance, now arbitrary cameras could be used and calibrated from the image data alone. The papers by Faugeras: *What can be seen in three dimensions with an uncalibrated stereo rig?* [18] and by Faugeras, Luong, and Maybank: *Camera self-calibration: Theory and experiments* [19] started a new research area within computer vision that today allows us to reconstruct large 3D environments from arbitrary image collections; for example, those taken by tourists and uploaded to the web. There are even web services available that enable us to simply upload our pictures of a scene and obtain 3D representations from them.

The basic algorithm for estimating the Fundamental Matrix from eight correspondences was rather sensitive to correspondence errors and researchers were skeptical about its usability in noisy imaging conditions. This problem was tackled in 1995 by Richard Hartley in his famous work entitled *In Defense of the 8-Point Algorithm* [32, 33]. Hartley showed that image normalization is vital for practical F-matrix estimation.

1.5.9   3D Local Shape Descriptors: Spin Images

The ICP algorithm might converge to a local minimum only if the starting conditions are non favorable. A common approach to prevent this is to determine a sparse set of three or more strong local descriptor (feature) matches across the pair of 3D shapes, which allows coarse 3D registration within the convergence basin of ICP. Probably the most well-known 3D local shape descriptor is the spin images [36], presented by Johnson and Hebert in 1997. Here, the local normal of a 3D point is used to encode neighboring points by measuring their height in the direction of the normal and their radius in the tangential plane described by the normal. Thus, a spin image encodes the relative positions of neighboring points in a cylindrical-polar coordinate system. The neighbor's angles in the tangential plane are discarded in order to give pose-invariance to the descriptor and the heights and radius values of the neighbors are built into a two-dimensional histogram, which forms the spin image descriptor. A large number of experiments in the literature have shown that the spin images are powerful for several tasks that include the registration of overlapping shapes, 3D object recognition, and 3D shape retrieval (shape search).

Figure 1.7 shows some examples of spin images computed on 3D captures of human faces [15]. In this case, the spin images are taken over a limited local range, as the 3D face surfaces are partial scans taken from a single viewpoint (there is no scanned surface for the back of the head). In the figure, the spin images for a given landmark appear quite similar across two different faces. For complete 3D scans, it is possible for spin images to encode the full extent of the object.

1.5.10   Passive 3D Imaging: Flexible Camera Calibration

Camera calibration is the process whereby *intrinsic* camera parameters are established, such as the focal length of the lens and the size and aspect ratio of the image sensor pixels. The position and orientation of the camera relative to the scene is also established and the parameters describing this are referred to as *extrinsic* parameters. Many current approaches to camera calibration are based on the easy-to-use, yet accu-

Fig. 1.7 Example spin images computed for 14 landmarks on two different faces from the FRGC dataset. Here, a bin size of 5 mm is used. The size of the spin image is 18×9 pixels. The middle top part of the spin image is the 3D surface point whose local shape we are encoding; the left part of the spin image corresponds to points above this 3D point in the direction of the normal; the right part corresponds to points below, using this same direction. Figure adapted from [15], courtesy of Clement Creusot

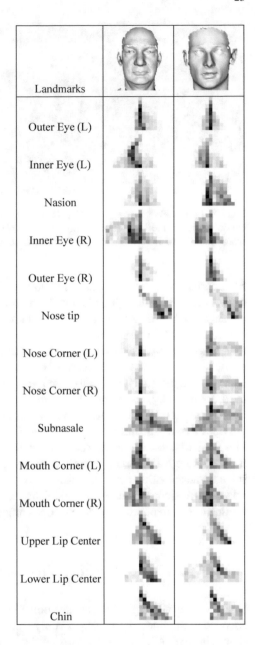

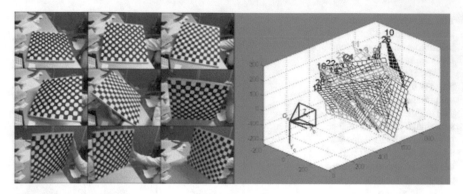

Fig. 1.8 Left: calibration targets used in a camera calibration process. Right: after calibration, it is possible to determine the positions of the calibration planes using the estimated extrinsic parameters. Image courtesy of Jean-Yves Bouguet from the *Camera Calibration Toolbox for Matlab* webpage

rate approach presented by Zhang in 2000,[23] where calibration can be achieved from n-views of a calibration grid of known grid dimensions [88]. This calibration grid is a planar 'chessboard' pattern of alternate black and white squares which can be freely moved as the calibration images are captured, the motion between the captures is not required, hence the system is easy to use. Although the minimum number of images captured is 2, around 20 are commonly used for improved accuracy. The estimation is in two stages: firstly, a closed-form linear solution for the camera's parameters is used, followed by a non-linear refinement based on the maximum-likelihood criterion. In the first stage, lens distortion is assumed to be zero, whereas the second stage provides a mechanism for radial distortion parameters to be estimated, if required. Figure 1.8 illustrates a typical set of calibration plane positions to calibrate a camera, with the automatic corner detections on the grid shown as a colored overlay. The same corner position input data can be used to calibrate a stereo rig, whereby two sets of intrinsic parameters are established and the extrinsic parameters define the six degrees of freedom rigid pose of one camera relative to another.

1.5.11   3D Shape Matching: Heat Kernel Signatures

One problem with spin images and other local shape descriptors is that they are encoded in Euclidean space and are only valid for rigid local shapes. Understanding shapes in terms of their geodesic distances[24] can yield more generic approaches that are not degraded by the bending of the shape (i.e., they are isometric invariant). In

---

[23]Zhang's seminal work is pre-dated by a large body of pioneering work on calibration, such as D. C. Brown's work in the context of photogrammetry, which dates back to the 1950s and many other works in computer vision, such as the seminal two-stage method of Tsai [80].

[24]A geodesic distance between two points on a surface is the minimal across surface distance.

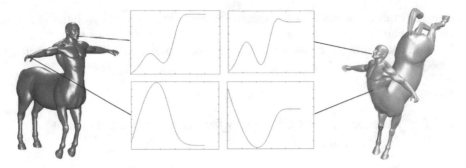

Fig. 1.9 Heat kernel signatures calculated on two isometric shapes. The top row shows that signatures at corresponding points look very similar. The bottom row shows that signatures at different points on the mesh differ. Figure courtesy of Benjamin Bustos

2009, Sun et al. [75] presented a multi-scale shape signature that is isometric invariant. It is based on the properties of the heat diffusion process over a meshed surface and belongs to a class of methods known as diffusion geometry approaches. The concise signature is obtained by restricting the heat kernel to the temporal domain. This technique and other approaches involving diffusion geometry enable high-performance 3D shape matching under isometric deformation and are thus finding their way into 3D object recognition and 3D shape retrieval (search) applications. Figure 1.9 shows heat kernel signatures extracted on two instances of an isometrically deformed shape.

1.5.12 Active 3D Imaging: Kinect

The Kinect was primarily developed by Microsoft for gaming applications. Brought to market amid great publicity in 2010, it was literally a game changer, and a huge success with tens of millions of units sold. However, the impact of the Kinect reached beyond the Xbox. Initially with a reverse engineered open source driver, and subsequently with the Microsoft official SDK for Windows, the Kinect has been redeployed by researchers, practitioners and enthusiasts for other applications benefiting from 3D capture and analysis. The combination of a low cost ($149.99) system with access to not only the raw sensor streams from the depth sensor, color camera sensor, and microphone array, but also multi-person skeletal tracking, gesture recognition, facial recognition, and voice recognition, meant that for the first time, such applications became much more affordable and easy to develop compared to traditional 3D-cameras. Many examples of applications of the Kinect can be found in healthcare [55], education [25], cultural heritage [9], agricultural [61], etc.

The Kinect has undergone several technical developments during its lifetime [63]. The initial Kinect for Xbox used structured light for 3D reconstruction; an infrared speckle dot pattern was projected and captured by an infrared sensor. Color information was acquired using a separate RGB camera. The second-generation Kinect changed to use time-of-flight, with three infrared projectors and an infrared sensor, and achieved greater accuracy as well as a larger capture volume. More recently Microsoft has shifted focus, and subsequent iterations of Kinect technology are being incorporated into the Microsoft HoloLens.

1.5.13 Random-Forest Classifiers for Real-Time 3D Human Pose Recognition

In 2011, Shotton et al. [70, 71] presented a system that was able to segment the whole body into a set of parts based on a single range image (i.e., no temporal information is used) and thereby determine, in real time, the position of human body joints. This process is illustrated in Fig. 1.10. A design aim was high frame rates and they achieved 200 frames per second on consumer hardware, thus the system can run comfortably on an inexpensive 3D camera and the algorithm forms a core component of the Kinect-Xbox gaming platform. To achieve high frame rates, extremely simple and computationally cheap 3D features were employed based on depth comparisons, and randomized decision forest classifiers were trained and implemented to run on a GPU. The training data uses 100 000 captured poses, each of which generates a synthetic set of 15 base meshes, spanning a range of different body sizes, shapes, viewpoints, clothing, and hairstyles. This system is an archetypal modern, successful

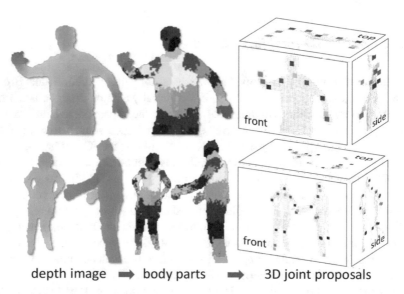

depth image ➡ body parts ➡ 3D joint proposals

Fig. 1.10 From a single depth image, range pixels can be labeled as belonging to certain body parts, which are colored differently in the figure. From this labeling, 3D joint positions can be inferred. Figure courtesy of [71]

3D recognition system that shows what can be achieved when machine learning techniques, a large corpus of training data, and fast computational architectures are brought together.

1.5.14 Convolutional–Recursive Deep Learning for 3D Object Classification

The deep learning revolution in AI has had a massive impact across many areas. Its benefits were clear to the computer vision community from as early as 2012, with deep learning's breakthrough result in the ImageNet *large-scale visual recognition challenge* [43] significantly outperforming traditional methods. In the same year, Socher et al. [73] presented a deep learning approach to the problem of classifying 3D objects in an RGB-D dataset. They employed a combination of Convolutional Neural Networks (CNNs) and Recursive Neural Networks (RNNs). The CNNs learn low-level features on the RGB and depth modalities separately and then pass them to multiple, fixed-tree RNNs, which learn hierarchical feature representations by applying the same neural network recursively in a tree structure. Such RNNs are able to learn compositional features and part interactions. Finally, the concatenation of all the feature vectors is passed to a softmax classifier. The authors were able to demonstrate that RNNs can extract powerful features, even with random weights. They used an RGB-D dataset of 41.6 K images of 51 object classes with a ten-fold random train/test split and were able to demonstrate an 88% classification accuracy which, at the time, was state-of-the-art.

1.5.15 VoxNet: A 3D Convolutional Neural Network for Real-Time Object Recognition

Given the success of CNNs on 2D images, it is natural to extend the same ideas to 3D data, and this is relatively straightforward if that data is represented in a Euclidean domain, such as the flat, grid-like structure of voxels. In 2015, Maturana and Scherer [53] presented VoxNet, a deep learning approach, and they demonstrated its application to the object recognition task for LiDAR point clouds, RGB-D data, and CAD models. The authors use a volumetric occupancy grid representation of size $32 \times 32 \times 32$ that captures a probability of occupancy for each voxel. The network is relatively small with around 922 K parameters in five layers, two convolutional layers, a pooling layer, and two fully connected layers. The authors found that their best system gave state-of-the-art performance on several benchmark datasets including ModelNet10, ModelNet40, Sydney Objects, and NYUv2, with various accuracies reported between 71% and 92%. A limitation of a straightforward voxelization approach is that, due to memory limitations, it is unable to scale up from the very coarse resolution without reducing the depth of the network. Subsequent methods, such as Octnet [59], represent space in a more dynamic manner, e.g., using a set of unbalanced octrees.

1.5.16 PointNet: Deep Learning on Point Sets for 3D Classification and Segmentation

At the 2017 CVPR conference, the PointNet architecture was presented by Qi et al. [57]. Significantly, this broke away from the requirement of processing 3D on Euclidean domains and allowed the direct consumption of unordered 3D point cloud data. The application of deep learning to such non-Euclidean domains has been termed *Geometric Deep Learning* by Bronstein et al. [12]. The idea of PointNet is to construct a network whose response is invariant to the $n!$ permutations of its n-point input data. Such permutation invariance is achieved by processing all n input points identically. The architecture is presented in detail in Chap. 11, here we give a brief overview. Initially, a transformer net is applied at the input to map the 3D data to a canonical frame (normalization of pose, aspect ratio, and size). This is achieved by predicting an affine transform using a mini-network with a similar structure to the overall network. After that, Multi Layer Perceptrons (MLPs) with shared weights across all points are used to map the points to a higher dimensional feature space. This is then followed by max pooling (a symmetric operation) to aggregate features. Finally, fully connected layers generate a set of m output scores for the m object classes in the training data. A segmentation network concatenates global and local features from the classification network and outputs per-point scores.

PointNet is evaluated on the ModelNet40 shape classification benchmark, which contains 12311 CAD models from 40 man-made object categories, split into 9843 for training and 2468 for testing. At the time, the classifier achieved a state-of-the-art accuracy of 89.2% averaged over all classes. Segmentation was evaluated on the ShapeNet part dataset. This contains 16881 shapes from 16 categories, annotated with 50 parts in total and with most object categories labeled with two to five parts. The *mean Intersection over Union* (mIoU) metric was used to evaluate parts segmentation and PointNet achieved a value of 83.7%. Further work has extended PointNet to form PointNet++ [58], which recursively applies PointNet to the input point cloud, enabling it to combine features from multiple scales from varying densities.

1.5.17 Dynamic Graph CNN for Learning on Point Clouds

In 2019, Wang et al. [81] presented the Dynamic Graph CNN (DGCNN) for learning on 3D point clouds, an approach inspired by PointNet. The method constructs a local-neighborhood graph and applies convolution-like operations on the graph's edges and thus a key contribution is the *EdgeConv* block, which can be integrated into existing point cloud networks. Specifically, the EdgeConv block is placed after the initial spatial transform layer and after each subsequent feature embedding layer, in order to improve the overall network performance. The core idea is to better capture local geometric features of point clouds, while still maintaining the permutation invariance of PointNet-style architectures. The term *dynamic* graph in DGCNNs comes from the fact that the k-nearest neighbors change from layer to layer, i.e., through the sequence of high-dimensional embeddings. For the edge convolution itself, edge features between each pair of local graph vertices are extracted with a non-linear function with learnable parameters, in this case implemented with a Multi Layer Perceptron (MLP). These features are then aggregated over all edges of the local graph in a symmetric manner by taking the maximum. The DGCNN architecture was evaluated on ModelNet40 and achieved a state-of-the-art accuracy of 93.5%.

1.5.18 PointNetLK: Robust and Efficient Point Cloud Registration Using PointNet

The work of Aoki et al. [2] is the first to apply PointNet to the 3D point cloud registration problem. They envisage PointNet as a kind of imaging function in the sense that the network consumes an unordered, unstructured set of points and generates an output of fixed structure and size. The idea is that the PointNet architecture encodes a pair of 3D point clouds via its usual shared MLP structure to yield a pair of symmetric function encodings. Viewing these encodings as 'images' motivates their alignment by a classical registration approach, in particular, the Lucas–Kanade (LK) algorithm [48].[25]

A core contribution was to show how to circumvent the grid-like convolutions employed in the standard LK algorithm (used to establish the spatial gradients), as such convolutions cannot be applied to PointNet representations. The suitably modified LK form is implemented as a recurrent network and integrated with PointNet to yield PointNetLK. Crucially, correspondences are not explicitly computed, which results in computationally efficiency ($O(n)$) as compared to ICP-style approaches ($O(n^2)$). A further advantage over ICP is robustness to initial point cloud pose, since ICP is vulnerable to local minima. The PointNetLK approach is fully differentiable, making it a general computation block for incorporation into deep learning systems, imbuing them with an explicit encoding of the alignment process. The authors demonstrate that PointNetLK evaluates favorably against ICP on ModelNet40 [84, 85].

---

[25]Originally conceived for 2D image optical flow estimation, by relating spatial and temporal image gradients.

1.6 Book Roadmap

We conclude this chapter with a roadmap of the remaining chapters of this book. Although there is a natural order to the chapters, they are relatively self-contained, so that they can also be read as stand-alone chapters. The book is split into three parts: Part I is comprised of Chaps. 2–6 and it presents the fundamental techniques for the capture, representation, and visualization of 3D data; Part II is comprised of Chaps. 7–11 and is concerned with 3D shape analysis and inference; finally, Part III is comprised of Chaps. 12–14 and focusses on three specific application areas, namely, 3D face recognition, 3D heritage modeling, and the 3D phenotyping of plants.

1.6.1 Part I: 3D Image Acquisition, Representation, and Visualization

Chapter 2 describes passive 3D imaging, which recovers 3D information from camera systems that do not project light or other electromagnetic radiation onto the imaged scene. An overview of the common techniques used to recover 3D information from camera images is presented first. The chapter then focuses on 3D recovery from multiple views, which can be obtained using two or more cameras at the same time (stereo), or a single moving camera at different times (structure from motion). The aim is to give a comprehensive presentation that covers camera modeling, camera calibration, image rectification, correspondence search, and the triangulation to compute 3D scene structure. Several 3D passive imaging systems and their real-world applications are highlighted later in this chapter.

Chapters 3–5 are all related to active 3D image capture. We have designed these chapters so that they can be read independently of each other and this inevitably generates some content overlap. To deal with this, we have added signposting that directs readers to skip various sections if they have already been covered in an earlier chapter. In the first of these, Chap. 3, active 3D imaging based on artificial illumination and triangulation is discussed, particularly in the context of industrial inspection. These systems have the same underlying geometry as the passive vision systems presented in Chap. 2, but the use of artificial illumination allows the acquisition of dense and accurate range images of texture-free objects that are difficult to acquire using passive vision systems. The characterization of such triangulation-based systems is discussed using both an error propagation framework and experimental protocols.

Chapter 4 covers Time-of-Flight (ToF) technologies, which are suitable for medium-range applications. Such technologies allow the development of a plethora of systems that can operate from a range of a few meters to many kilometers while systems based on triangulation typically operate at a range of a few millimeters to a few meters. The characterization of those systems is discussed and experimental results using systems related to the construction and engineering industry and the automobile industry are shown.

Chapter 5 discusses a relatively new family of affordable active 3D imaging systems referred to as range cameras or RGB-D cameras. These systems operate in the range of 0.4–10 m and are targeted directly at cost-sensitive consumers. They are typically specialized for capturing dynamic human activities and are designed to minimally interfere with such activities. They use infrared-light sources and produce a continuous stream of 3D data at video frame rate using either active stereo vision, structured light, or time-of-flight.

Chapter 6 focusses on 3D data representation, storage, and visualization. It begins by providing a taxonomy of 3D data representations and then presents more detail on a selection of the most important 3D data representations and their processing, such as triangular meshes and subdivision surfaces. This chapter also discusses the local differential properties of surfaces, mesh simplification and compression.

1.6.2 Part II: 3D Shape Analysis and Inference

Chapter 7 presents a comprehensive review of local 3D shape descriptors, including both classical hand-crafted features and those that are learned. Description of local features lays the foundations for a variety of applications that process 3D data, such as 3D object recognition, 3D registration and reconstruction, and mobile robot mapping and navigation.

Chapter 8 details 3D shape registration, which is the process of bringing together two or more 3D shapes, either of the same object or of two different but similar objects. This chapter first introduces the classical Iterative Closest Point (ICP) algorithm [6], which represents the gold standard registration method. Current limitations of ICP are addressed and the most popular variants of ICP are described to improve the basic implementation in several ways. Challenging registration scenarios are analyzed and a taxonomy of promising alternative registration techniques is introduced. Four case studies are described with an increasing level of difficulty, including an algorithm capable of dealing with deformable objects.

Chapter 9 presents 3D shape matching with a view to applications in shape retrieval (e.g., web search) and object recognition. In order to present the subject, four approaches are described in detail with good balance among maturity and novelty, namely, the PANORAMA descriptor, spin images, functional maps, and heat kernel signatures.

In Chap. 10, the idea of a 3D Morphable Model (3DMM) is introduced. A 3DMM is a compact description of an object class that captures the model's training set shape variance, and thus can act as a useful prior in many Computer Vision applications. 3DMMs are also able to model the associated texture, where that texture is registered (i.e., aligned) with shape data. In this chapter, the historical context and recent literature are introduced, and both classical and modern 3DMM construction pipelines are described. Finally, the power of 3DMMs is illustrated via case studies and examples.

The final chapter in Part II, Chap. 11, shows how to apply deep learning to 3D data. 3D data has many popular representations, such as point clouds (from raw sensor input) or meshes (widely used in shape modeling) but both these representations are not defined on a regular grid. Due to their irregular format, current convolutional deep learning methods cannot be directly used. So, in this chapter, two major branches of methods to work with 3D data are introduced. One family of methods firstly converts such irregular data to regular structures, the other (rather new) family of methods studies how to design deep neural networks that directly consume irregular data and respect the special properties of the input 3D representations, such as the permutation invariance of the points in a point cloud, or the intrinsic surface structure in a mesh. The chapter closes with a showcase of successful applications that use deep learning on 3D images.

1.6.3 Part III: 3D Imaging Applications

Chapter 12 gives an overview of 3D face recognition and discusses both well-established and more recent state-of-the-art 3D face recognition techniques in terms of their implementation and expected performance on benchmark datasets. In contrast to 2D face recognition methods that have difficulties when handling changes in illumination and pose, 3D face recognition algorithms have often been more successful in dealing with these challenges. 3D face shape data is used as an independent cue for face recognition and has also been combined with texture to facilitate multimodal face recognition. Furthermore, 3D face recognition can achieve some invariance to expression by modeling the non-rigid surface deformations of the face. The chapter presents both classical approaches and recent approaches that exploit deep learning.

Chapter 13 covers the use of 3D technologies for digitizing Cultural Heritage (CH). After the analysis of the motivations and an overview of the history of the application of 3D technologies, a review of the current state-of-the-art in the field is given. A methodological section points out which 3D technologies are used in the field and how they can be best applied, taking into account digitization approaches appropriate to the different classes of CH objects as well as the relative strengths and weaknesses of the various technologies. The chapter continues with a discussion of how CH can be modeled from raw data and a section about the different 3D processing pipelines. The last section treats the creation of a 3D content repository for CH, taking into account both the relevant articulated metadata as well as the ways 3D data are stored and visualized for online access.

In Chap. 14, a broad overview of computer vision based 3D plant phenotyping techniques is given. Due to their non-invasive and non-contact properties, imaging techniques have become state-of-the-art in automated plant phenotyping analysis. There are several aspects of phenotyping, including plant growth, plant organ classification and tracking, and disease detection. This chapter presents a broad overview of computer vision based 3D plant phenotyping techniques. The chapter covers multiple case studies with automated robotic systems for 3D plant phenotyping, general registration techniques for 3D point clouds, and alignment of challenging multiple-view 3D point clouds of plants.

References

1. Adelson, E.H., Bergen, J.R.: The Plenoptic Function and the Elements of Early Vision. In: Landy, M., Movshon, J.A. (eds.) Computational Models of Visual Processing (1991)
2. Aoki, Y., Goforth, H., Srivatsan, R.A., Lucey, S.: PointNetLK: robust and efficient point cloud registration using pointnet. In: The IEEE Conference on Computer Vision and Pattern Recognition (CVPR) (2019)
3. Arun, K.S., Huang, T.S., Blostein, S.D.: Least-squares fitting of two 3D point sets. IEEE Trans. Pattern Anal. Mach. Intell. **9**(5), 698–700 (1987)
4. Bartczak, B., Vandewalle, P., Grau, O., Briand, G., Fournier, J., Kerbiriou, P., Murdoch, M., Müller, M., Goris, R., Koch, R., van der Vleuten, R.: Display-independent 3D-TV production and delivery using the layered depth video format. IEEE Trans. Broadcast. **57**(2), 477–490 (2011)
5. Bennet, R.: Representation and analysis of signals – part XXI: the intrinsic dimensionality of signal collections. Report No. 163, The Johns Hopkins University, Baltimore, MD (1965)
6. Besl, P., McKay, N.D.: A method for registration of 3D shapes. IEEE Trans. Pattern Anal. Mach. Intell. **14**(2), 239–256 (1992)
7. Bigun, J., Granlund, G.: Optimal orientation detection of linear symmetry. In: 1st International Conference on Computer Vision, pp. 433–438. IEEE Computer Society (1987)
8. Blundell, B., Schwarz, A.: The classification of volumetric display systems: characteristics and predictability of the image space. IEEE Trans. Vis. Comput. Graph. **8**, 66–75 (2002)
9. Bostanci, E., Kanwal, N., Clark, A.F.: Augmented reality applications for cultural heritage using Kinect. Hum.-Centric Comput. Inf. Sci. **5**(1), 20 (2015)
10. Boyer, K., Kak, A.: Color-encoded structured light for rapid active ranging. IEEE Trans. Pattern Anal. Mach. Intell. **9**(1) (1987)
11. Brewster, S.D.: The Stereoscope: Its History, Theory, and Construction with Applications to the Fine and Usefull Arts and to Education. John Murray, London (1856)
12. Bronstein, M.M., Bruna, J., LeCun, Y., Szlam, A., Vandergheynst, P.: Geometric deep learning: going beyond euclidean data. IEEE Signal Process. Mag. **34**(4), 18–42 (2017)
13. Brownson, C.D.: Euclid's optics and its compatibility with linear perspective. Arch. Hist. Exact Sci. **24**, 165–194 (1981). https://doi.org/10.1007/BF00357417
14. Cosmo, L., Rodola, E., Masci, J., Torsello, A., Bronstein, M.M.: Matching deformable objects in clutter. In: 2016 4th International Conference on 3D Vision (3DV), pp. 1–10. IEEE (2016)
15. Creusot, C.: Automatic landmarking for non-cooperative 3D face recognition. Ph.D. thesis, Department of Computer Science, University of York, UK (2011)
16. Curtis, G.: The Cave Painters. Knopf, New York (2006)
17. Eigen, D., Puhrsch, C., Fergus, R.: Depth map prediction from a single image using a multi-scale deep network. In: Advances in Neural Information Processing Systems, pp. 2366–2374 (2014)
18. Faugeras, O.: What can be seen in three dimensions with an uncalibrated stereo rig? In: Sandini, G. (ed.) Computer Vision: ECCV'92. Lecture Notes in Computer Science, vol. 588, pp. 563–578. Springer, Berlin/Heidelberg (1992)
19. Faugeras, O., Luong, Q., Maybank, S.: Camera self-calibration: Theory and experiments. In: Sandini, G. (ed.) Compure Vision: ECCV'92. Lecture Notes in Computer Science, vol. 588, pp. 321–334. Springer, Berlin/Heidelberg (1992)
20. Faugeras, O.D., Hebert, M.: The representation, recognition and locating of 3-d objects. Int. J. Robot. Res. **5**(3), 27–52 (1986)
21. Forsyth, D., Ponce, J.: Computer Vision: A Modern Approach. Prentice Hall, Upper Saddle River (2003)
22. Fu, H., Gong, M., Wang, C., Batmanghelich, K., Tao, D.: Deep ordinal regression network for monocular depth estimation. In: Proceedings of the IEEE Conference on Computer Vision and Pattern Recognition, pp. 2002–2011 (2018)
23. Fusiello, A.: Visione computazionale. Appunti delle lezioni. Technical Report, Informatic Department, University of Verona (2008)

24. Garg, R., BG, V.K., Carneiro, G., Reid, I.: Unsupervised CNN for single view depth estimation: geometry to the rescue. In: European Conference on Computer Vision, pp. 740–756. Springer (2016)
25. Ge, Z., Fan, L.: Social development for children with autism using Kinect gesture games: a case study in Suzhou industrial park Renai school. In: Simulation and Serious Games for Education, pp. 113–123. Springer, Berlin (2017)
26. Geiger, A., Lenz, P., Stiller, C., Urtasun, R.: Vision meets robotics: the KITTI dataset. Int. J. Robot. Res. **32**(11), 1231–1237 (2013)
27. Gennery, D.B.: A stereo vision system for an autonomous vehicle. In: Proceedings of the 5th International Joint Conference on Artificial Intelligence (IJCAI), pp. 576–582 (1977)
28. Gernsheim, H., Gernsheim, A.: The History of Photography. McGraw-Hill, New York (1969)
29. Godard, C., Mac Aodha, O., Brostow, G.J.: Unsupervised monocular depth estimation with left-right consistency. In: Proceedings of the IEEE Conference on Computer Vision and Pattern Recognition, pp. 270–279 (2017)
30. Harris, C., Stephens, M.J.: A combined corner and edge detector. In: Alvey Vision Conference (1988)
31. Hartley, R., Zisserman, A.: Multiple View Geometry in Computer Vision. Cambridge University Press, Cambridge (2003). ISBN 0-521-54051-8
32. Hartley, R.I.: In defence of the 8-point algorithm. In: Proceedings of the IEEE International Conference on Computer Vision (ICCV), pp. 1064–1070 (1995)
33. Hartley, R.I.: In defence of the 8-point algorithm. IEEE Trans. Pattern Anal. Mach. Intell. **19**(6), 580–593 (1997)
34. Horn, B.K.P.: Shape from shading: a method for obtaining the shape of a smooth opaque object from one view. PhD thesis, MIT, Cambridge, MA, USA (1970)
35. Horn, B.K.P.: Closed-form solution of absolute orientation using unit quaternions. J. Opt. Soc. Am. A **4**(4), 629–642 (1987)
36. Johnson, A.E., Hebert, M.: Using spin images for efficient object recognition in cluttered 3D scenes. IEEE Trans. Pattern Anal. Mach. Intell. **21**(5), 433–449 (1997)
37. Kanatani, K.I.: Analysis of 3-D rotation fitting. IEEE Trans. Pattern Anal. Mach. Intell. **16**(5), 543–549 (1994)
38. King, H.: The History of Telescope. Griffin, London (1955)
39. Koch, R.: Depth estimation. In: Ikeuchi, K. (ed.) Encyclopedia of Computer Vision, 2nd edn. Springer, New York (2020)
40. Kolb, A., Barth, E., Koch, R., Larsen, R.: Time-of-flight cameras in computer graphics. Comput. Graph. Forum **29**(1), 141–159 (2010)
41. Kolb, A., Koch, R. (eds.): Dynamic 3D Imaging. Lecture Notes in Computer Science, vol. 5742. Springer, Berlin (2009)
42. Kriss, T.C., Kriss, V.M.: History of the operating microscope: from magnifying glass to microneurosurgery. Neurosurgery **42**(4), 899–907 (1998)
43. Krizhevsky, A., Sutskever, I., Hinton, G.E.: ImageNet classification with deep convolutional neural networks. In: Advances in Neural Information Processing Systems, pp. 1097–1105 (2012)
44. Laina, I., Rupprecht, C., Belagiannis, V., Tombari, F., Navab, N.: Deeper depth prediction with fully convolutional residual networks. In: 2016 4th International Conference on 3D Vision (3DV), pp. 239–248. IEEE (2016)
45. Lippmann, G.: La photographie integrale (English Translation Fredo Durant, MIT-CSAIL). In: Academy Francaise: Photography-Reversible Prints. Integral Photographs (1908)
46. Liu, F., Shen, C., Lin, G., Reid, I.: Learning depth from single monocular images using deep convolutional neural fields. IEEE Trans. Pattern Anal. Mach. Intell. **38**(10), 2024–2039 (2016)
47. Longuet-Higgins, H.C.: A computer algorithm for re-constructing a scene from two projections. Nature **293**, 133–135 (1981)
48. Lucas, B., Kanade, T.: An iterative image registration technique with an application to stereo vision. In: IJCAI'81 (1981)

49. Ma, Y., Soatto, S., Kosecka, J., Sastry, S.: An Invitation to 3D Vision: From Images to Geometric Models. Springer, Berlin (2003)
50. Fischler, M.A., Bolles, R.: Random sample consensus: a paradigm for model fitting with applications to image analysis and automated cartography. Commun. ACM **24**, 381–395 (1981)
51. Maron, H., Galun, M., Aigerman, N., Trope, M., Dym, N., Yumer, E., Kim, V.G., Lipman, Y.: Convolutional neural networks on surfaces via seamless toric covers. ACM Trans. Graph. **36**(4), 71–1 (2017)
52. Marr, D.: Vision. A Computational Investigation into the Human Representation and Processing of Visual Information. W.H. Freeman and Company, New York (1982)
53. Maturana, D., Scherer, S.: Voxnet: A 3D convolutional neural network for real-time object recognition. In: 2015 IEEE/RSJ International Conference on Intelligent Robots and Systems (IROS), pp. 922–928 (2015)
54. Nayar, S.K., Watanabe, M., Noguchi, M.: Real-time focus range sensor. IEEE Trans. Pattern Anal. Mach. Intell. **18**(12), 1186–1198 (1996)
55. Pöhlmann, S.T., Harkness, E.F., Taylor, C.J., Astley, S.M.: Evaluation of Kinect 3D sensor for healthcare imaging. J. Med. Biol. Eng. **36**(6), 857–870 (2016)
56. Pomerleau, F., Colas, F., Siegwart, R., Magnenat, S.: Comparing ICP variants on real-world data sets. Auton. Robot. **34**(3), 133–148 (2013)
57. Qi, C.R., Su, H., Mo, K., Guibas, L.J.: PointNet: deep learning on point sets for 3D classification and segmentation. In: Proceedings of the IEEE Conference on Computer Vision and Pattern Recognition, pp. 652–660 (2017)
58. Qi, C.R., Yi, L., Su, H., Guibas, L.J.: PointNet++: deep hierarchical feature learning on point sets in a metric space. In: Advances in Neural Information Processing Systems (NIPS), pp. 5099–5108 (2017)
59. Riegler, G., Osman Ulusoy, A., Geiger, A.: OctNet: learning deep 3D representations at high resolutions. In: Proceedings of the IEEE Conference on Computer Vision and Pattern Recognition, pp. 3577–3586 (2017)
60. Rioux, M.: Laser range finder based on synchronized scanners. Appl. Opt. **23**(21), 3837–3844 (1984)
61. Rosell-Polo, J.R., Gregorio, E., Gené, J., Llorens, J., Torrent, X., Arnó, J., Escolà, A.: Kinect v2 sensor-based mobile terrestrial laser scanner for agricultural outdoor applications. IEEE/ASME Trans. Mechatron. **22**(6), 2420–2427 (2017)
62. Rusinkiewicz, S., Levoy, M.: Efficient variants of the ICP algorithm. In: International Conference on 3D Digital Imaging and Modeling, p. 145 (2001)
63. Sarbolandi, H., Lefloch, D., Kolb, A.: Kinect range sensing: structured-light versus time-of-flight Kinect. Comput. Vis. Image Underst. **139**, 1–20 (2015)
64. Saxena, A., Chung, S.H., Ng, A.Y.: Learning depth from single monocular images. In: Advances in Neural Information Processing Systems, pp. 1161–1168 (2006)
65. Scharstein, D., Szeliski, R.: A taxonomy and evaluation of dense two-frame stereo correspondence algorithms. Int. J. Comput. Vis. **47**, 7–42 (2002)
66. Schmidhuber, J.: Deep learning in neural networks: an overview. Neural Netw. **61**, 85–117 (2015)
67. Schölkopf, B., Smola, A.: Learning with Kernels: Support Vector Machines, Regularization, Optimization and Beyond. MIT Press, Cambridge (2002)
68. Schwarte, R., Xu, Z., Heinol, H.G., Olk, J., Klein, R., Buxbaum, B., Fischer, H., Schulte, J.: New electro-optical mixing and correlating sensor: facilities and applications of the photonic mixer device (PMD). In: Proceedings of SPIE, vol. 3100 (1997)
69. Shirai, Y.: Recognition of polyhedons with a range finder. Pattern Recognit. **4**, 243–250 (1972)
70. Shotton, J., Fitzgibbon, A., Cook, M., Sharp, T., Finocchio, M., Moore, R., Kipman, A., Blake, A.: Real-time human pose recognition in parts from single depth images. In: CVPR (2011)
71. Shotton, J., Fitzgibbon, A., Cook, M., Sharp, T., Finocchio, M., Moore, R., Kipman, A., Blake, A.: Real-time human pose recognition in parts from single depth images, pp. 119–135. Springer, Berlin (2013)

72. Smith, A.M.: Alhacen's Theory of Visual Perception: A Critical Edition, with English Translation and Commentary, of the First Three Books of Alhacen's De Aspectibus, the Medieval Latin Version of Ibn Al-Haytham's Kitab Al-Manazir. In: Transactions of the American Philosophical Society, vol. 91 (2001)
73. Socher, R., Huval, B., Bhat, B., Manning, C.D., Ng, A.Y.: Convolutional-recursive deep learning for 3D object classification. In: Proceedings of the 25th International Conference on Neural Information Processing Systems (NIPS), vol. 1, p. 656–664 (2012)
74. Su, H., Maji, S., Kalogerakis, E., Learned-Miller, E.: Multi-view convolutional neural networks for 3D shape recognition. In: Proceedings of the IEEE International Conference on Computer Vision, pp. 945–953 (2015)
75. Sun, J., Ovsjanikov, M., Guibas, L.: A concise and provably informative multi-scale signature based on heat diffusion. Comput. Graph. Forum **28**(5), 1383–1392 (2009)
76. Szeliski, R.: Computer Vision, Algorithms and Applications. Springer, Berlin (2010)
77. Tanimoto, S., Pavlidis, T.: A hierarchical data structure for picture processing. Comput. Graph. Image Process. **4**, 104–113 (1975)
78. Triggs, B., McLauchlan, P.F., Hartley, R.I., Fitzgibbon, A.W.: Bundle adjustment – a modern synthesis. In: Proceedings of the International Workshop on Vision Algorithms: Theory and Practice (ICCV'99), pp. 298–372 (2000)
79. Trucco, E., Verri, A.: Introductory Techniques for 3-D Computer Vision. Prentice Hall, Upper Saddle River (1998)
80. Tsai, R.Y.: A versatile camera calibration technique for high accuracy 3D machine vision metrology using off-the-shelf TV cameras and lenses. IEEE J. Robot. Autom. **3**(4), 323–344 (1987)
81. Wang, Y., Sun, Y., Liu, Z., Sarma, S.E., Bronstein, M.M., Solomon, J.M.: Dynamic graph CNN for learning on point clouds. ACM Trans. Graph. **38**(5) (2019)
82. Wheatstone, C.: Contributions to the physiology of vision. Part the first. On some remarkable, and hitherto unobserved, phenomena of binocular vision. Philos. Trans. R. Soc. Lond. 371–394 (1838)
83. Witkin, A.P.: Scale-space filtering. In: Proceedings of the 8th International Joint Conference on Artificial Intelligence, vol. 2, pp. 1019–1022 (1983)
84. Wu, Z., Song, S., Khosla, A., Yu, F., Zhang, L., Tang, X., Xiao, J.: 3D ShapeNets: a deep representation for volumetric shapes. In: Proceedings of the IEEE Conference on Computer Vision and Pattern Recognition, pp. 1912–1920 (2015)
85. Wu, Z., Song, S., Khosla, A., Yu, F., Zhang, L., Tang, X., Xiao, J.: Princeton ModelNet - a 3D CAD model dataset. https://modelnet.cs.princeton.edu/ (2015). Accessed 1 Mar 2020
86. Yang, R., Pollefeys, M.: A versatile stereo implementation on commodity graphics hardware. Real-Time Imaging **11**, 7–18 (2005)
87. Yi, K.M., Trulls, F.E., Ono, Y., Lepetit, V., Salzmann, M., Fua, P.: Learning to find good correspondences. In: Proceedings of the IEEE/CVF Conference on Computer Vision and Pattern Recognition (CVPR) (2018)
88. Zhang, Z.: A flexible new technique for camera calibration. IEEE Trans. Pattern Anal. Mach. Intell. **22**(11), 1330–1334 (2000)

Part I
3D Shape Acquisition, Representation and Visualisation

In this part, we discuss 3D imaging using both passive techniques (Chap. 2) and active techniques (Chaps. 3–5). The former uses ambient illumination (i.e. sunlight or standard room lighting), whilst the latter projects its own illumination (usually visible or infra-red) onto the scene. Chapter 3 discusses triangulationbased sensing, whilst Chap. 4 covers sensors based on time of flight. Chapter 5 covers consumer-grade RGB-D cameras. Finally, Chap. 6 discusses how to represent the captured data, both for efficient algorithmic 3D data processing and efficient data storage. This provides a bridge to the following part of the book, which deals with 3D shape analysis and inference.

Chapter 2
Passive 3D Imaging

Stephen Se and Nick Pears

Abstract We describe passive 3D imaging systems that recover 3D information from scenes that are illuminated only with ambient lighting. Although we briefly overview monocular reconstruction, much of the material is concerned with using the geometry of stereo 3D imaging to formulate estimation problems. Firstly, we present an overview of the common techniques used to recover 3D information from camera images. Secondly, we discuss camera modeling and camera calibration as an essential introduction to the geometry of the imaging process and the estimation of geometric parameters. Thirdly, we focus on 3D recovery from multiple views, which can be obtained using multiple cameras at the same time (stereo), or a single moving camera at different times (structure from motion). Epipolar geometry and finding image correspondences associated with the same 3D scene point are two key aspects for such systems, since epipolar geometry establishes the relationship between two camera views, and depth information can be inferred from the correspondences. The details of both stereo and structure from motion, the two essential forms of multiple-view 3D reconstruction technique, are presented. We include a brief overview of the recent trend of applying deep learning to passive 3D imaging. Finally, we present several real-world applications.

2.1 Introduction

Passive 3D imaging has been studied extensively for several decades, and it is a core topic in many of the major computer vision conferences and journals. Essentially, a *passive* 3D imaging system, also known as a passive 3D vision system, is one in which we can recover 3D scene information, without that system having to project

S. Se (✉)
FLIR Systems Inc., 12051 Riverside Way, Richmond, BC V6W 1K7, Canada
e-mail: stephen.se@flir.com

N. Pears
Department of Computer Science, University of York,
Deramore Lane, York YO10 5GH, UK
e-mail: nick.pears@york.ac.uk

© Springer Nature Switzerland AG 2020   39
Y. Liu et al. (eds.), *3D Imaging, Analysis and Applications*,
https://doi.org/10.1007/978-3-030-44070-1_2

its own source of light or other source of electromagnetic radiation (EMR) onto that scene. By contrast, an *active* 3D imaging system has an EMR projection subsystem, which is commonly in the infrared or visible wavelength region.

Several passive 3D information sources (cues) relate closely to human vision and other animal vision. For example, in stereo vision, fusing the images recorded by our two eyes and exploiting the difference between them gives us a sense of depth. The aim of this chapter is to present the fundamental principles of passive 3D imaging systems so that readers can understand their strengths and limitations, as well as how to implement a subset of such systems, namely, those that exploit multiple views of the scene.

Passive, multiple-view 3D imaging originates from the mature field of photogrammetry and, more recently, from the younger field of computer vision. In contrast to photogrammetry, computer vision applications rely on fast, automatic techniques, sometimes at the expense of precision. Our focus is on the computer vision perspective.

A recurring theme of this chapter is that we consider some aspect of the geometry of 3D imaging and formulate a linear least squares estimation problem to estimate the associated geometric parameters. These estimates can then optionally be improved, depending on the speed and accuracy requirements of the application, using the linear estimate as an initialization for a non-linear least squares refinement. In contrast to the linear stage, this non-linear stage usually optimizes a cost function that has a well-defined geometric meaning.[1] Multi-view 3D reconstruction is now a mature technology. Figure 2.1 shows a 3D reconstruction of a building from a 2D image sequence.

2.1.1 Chapter Outline

We will start with an overview of various techniques for passive 3D imaging systems, including single-view and multiple-view approaches. However, the main body of this chapter is focused on 3D recovery from multiple views, which can be obtained using multiple cameras simultaneously (stereo) or a single moving camera (structure from motion). A good starting point to understand this subject matter is knowledge of the image formation process in a single camera and how to capture this process in a camera model. This modeling is presented in Sect. 2.3, and the following section describes camera calibration: the estimation of the parameters in the developed camera model. In order to understand how to search efficiently for left–right feature pairs that correspond to the same scene point in a stereo image pair (the *correspondence* problem), a good understanding of two-view geometry is required, which establishes the relationship between two camera views. Hence, Sect. 2.5 details this geometry, known as *epipolar geometry*, and shows how it can be captured and used in linear (vector–matrix) form. Following this, we can begin to consider the correspondence

---

[1] Parameters obtained from a linear estimate are often a complex function of geometric parameters.

Fig. 2.1 Top: partial image sequence of the library building at the Chinese University of Hong Kong. Bottom: 3D reconstruction of the library building, obtained automatically from the uncalibrated image sequence (left: Delaunay triangulation; right: with texture). Figure courtesy of [16]

problem and the first step is to simplify the search to be across the same horizontal scan lines in each image, by warping the stereo image pair in a process known as *rectification*. This is described in Sect. 2.6. The following section then focuses on the correspondence search itself, and then Sect. 2.8 details the process of generating a 3D point cloud from a set of image correspondences. A brief overview is included on how deep learning techniques, such as convolutional neural networks and recurrent neural networks, have been applied to passive 3D imaging recently and had had a big impact. Despite this, we believe that it is important that this chapter covers the underlying mathematical modeling explicitly for a good understanding of the subject area.

With increasing computer processing power and decreasing camera prices, many real-world applications of passive 3D imaging systems have been emerging in recent years. Thus, later in the chapter (Sect. 2.10), some recent applications involving such systems are discussed. Several commercially available stereo vision systems will first be presented, as well as stereo cameras for people counting in retail analytics. We then describe 3D modeling systems that generate photo-realistic 3D models from image sequences, which have a wide range of applications. Later in this section, passive 3D imaging systems for mobile robot pose estimation and visual SLAM are described. In the following section, multiple-view passive 3D imaging systems are compared to their counterpart within active 3D imaging systems.

The final sections in the chapter cover concluding remarks, further reading, software resources, questions, and exercises for the reader.

2.2   An Overview of Passive 3D Imaging Systems

Most cameras today use either a *Charge Coupled Device* (CCD) image sensor or a *Complementary Metal Oxide Semiconductor* (CMOS) sensor, both of which capture light and convert it into electrical signals. Historically, CCD sensors have provided higher quality, lower noise images, whereas CMOS sensors have been cheaper, more compact, and consume less power. Presently, CMOS sensors are more prevalent perhaps due to their now highly favorable performance-to-cost ratio. The cameras employing such image sensors can be hand-held or mounted on different platforms such as *Unmanned Ground Vehicles* (UGVs), *Unmanned Aerial Vehicles* (UAVs), *Unmanned Underwater Vehicles* (UUVs), and optical satellites.

Passive 3D vision techniques can be categorized as follows: (i) Multiple-view approaches and (ii) single-view approaches. We outline each of these in the following two subsections.

2.2.1   Multiple-View Approaches

In multiple-view approaches, the scene is observed from two or more viewpoints, by either multiple cameras at the same time (stereo) or a single moving camera at different times (structure from motion). From the gathered images, the system is to infer information on the 3D structure of the scene.

Stereo refers to multiple images taken simultaneously using two or more cameras, which are collectively called a stereo camera. For example, binocular stereo uses two viewpoints, trinocular stereo uses three viewpoints, or alternatively there may be many cameras distributed around the viewing sphere of an object. *Stereo* derives from the Greek word *stereos* meaning *solid*, thus implying a 3D form of visual information. In this chapter, we will use the term *stereo vision* to imply a binocular stereo system. At the top of Fig. 2.2, we show an outline of such a system.

If we can determine that imaged points in the left and right cameras correspond to the same scene point, then we can determine two directions (3D rays) along which the 3D point must lie. (The camera parameters required to convert the 2D image positions to 3D rays come from a camera calibration procedure.) Then, we can intersect the 3D rays to determine the 3D position of the scene point, in a process known as *triangulation*. A scene point, $\mathbf{X}$, is shown in Fig. 2.2 as the intersection of two rays (colored black) and a nearer point is shown by the intersection of two different rays (colored blue). Note that the difference between left and right image positions, the *disparity*, is greater for the nearer scene point and inversely proportional to the range. In fact, at some maximum range, the disparity becomes so small and corruptable by noise, which usefully accurate range measurements can no longer be made. Compared to some other 3D imaging modalities, stereo is relatively short range. Also, regions close to the stereo camera rig are outside of the field of view of either one or both cameras, and so stereo cameras have some defined minimum

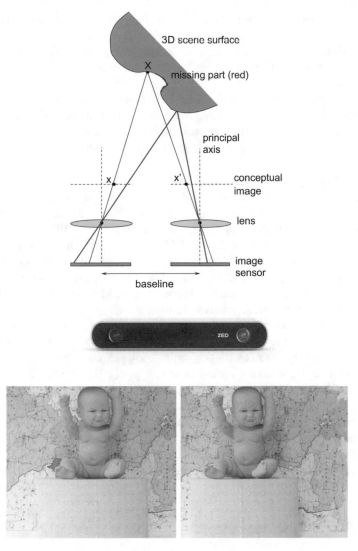

Fig. 2.2 Top: Plan view of the operation of a simple stereo rig. Here the optical axes of the two cameras are parallel to form a rectilinear rig. However, often the cameras are rotated toward each other (verged) to increase the overlap in their fields of view. Center: The commercial ZED stereo camera, supplied by Stereolabs [82]. Bottom: Left and right views of a stereo pair (images courtesy of [74])

range of operation. Note also that the scene surface colored red cannot be observed by the right camera, in which case no 3D shape measurement can be made. This scene portion is sometimes referred to as a *missing part* and is the result of self-occlusion. The baseline length of a stereo camera is a trade-off between accuracy and missing parts.

A modeling point to note is that, although the real image sensor is behind the lens, it is common practice to envisage and use a conceptual image position in front of the lens so that the image is the same orientation as the scene (i.e., not inverted top to bottom and left to right), and this is shown by the dashed horizontal line in the figure.

Despite the apparent simplicity of Fig. 2.2(top), a large part of this chapter is required to present the various aspects of stereo 3D imaging in detail, such as calibration, determining left-to-right image correspondences and dense 3D shape reconstruction. A typical commercial stereo camera, called the ZED and supplied by Stereolabs [82], is shown in the center of Fig. 2.2, although many computer vision researchers build their own stereo rigs, using off-the-shelf digital cameras and a slotted steel bar mounted on a tripod. Finally, at the bottom of Fig. 2.2, we show the left and right views of a typical stereo pair taken from the Middlebury webpage [74].

In contrast to stereo vision, *structure from motion* (SfM) refers to a single moving camera scenario, where image sequences are captured over a period of time. While stereo refers to fixed relative viewpoints with synchronized image capture, SfM refers to variable viewpoints with sequential image capture. For image sequences captured at a high frame rate, optical flow can be computed, which estimates the motion field from the image sequences, based on the spatial and temporal variations of the image brightness. Using the local brightness constancy alone, the problem is under-constrained as the number of variables is twice the number of measurements. Therefore, it is augmented with additional global smoothness constraints, so that the motion field can be estimated by minimizing an energy function [41, 49]. 3D motion of the camera and the scene structure can then be recovered from the motion field.

2.2.2   Single-View Approaches

In contrast to these two multiple-view approaches, 3D shape can be inferred from a single viewpoint using information sources (cues) such as shading, texture, and focus. The collection of such approaches is sometimes termed *Shape from X*. Not surprisingly, the mentioned techniques are called *Shape from Shading*, *Shape from Texture*, and *Shape from Focus*, respectively.

Shading on a surface can provide information about local surface orientations and overall surface shape, as illustrated in Fig. 2.3, where the technique in [42] has been used. Shape from shading [40] uses the shades in a grayscale image to infer the shape of the surfaces, based on the reflectance map which links image intensity with surface orientation. After the surface normals have been recovered at each pixel, they can be integrated into a depth map using regularized surface fitting. The

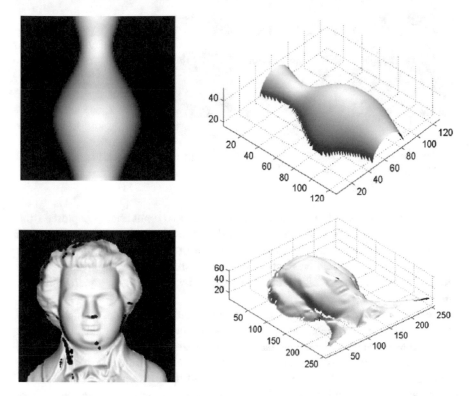

Fig. 2.3 Examples of synthetic shape from shading images (left column) and corresponding shape from shading reconstruction (right column)

computations involved are considerably more complicated than for multiple-view approaches. Moreover, various assumptions, such as uniform albedo, reflectance, and known light source directions, need to be made and there are open issues with convergence to a solution. The survey in [97] reviews various techniques and provides some comparative results. The approach can be enhanced when lights shining from different directions can be turned on and off separately. This technique is known as *photometric stereo* [91], and it takes two or more images of the scene from the same viewpoint but under different illuminations in order to estimate the surface normals.

The foreshortening of regular patterns depends on how the surface slants away from the camera viewing direction and provides another cue on the local surface orientation. Shape from texture [34] estimates the shape of the observed surface from the distortion of the texture created by the imaging process, as illustrated in Fig. 2.4. Therefore, this approach works only for images with texture surfaces and assumes the presence of a regular pattern. Shape from shading is combined with shape from texture in [90] where the two techniques can complement each other. While the texture components provide information in textured region, shading helps in the uniform region to provide detailed information on the surface shape.

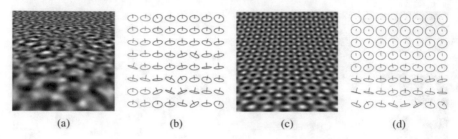

Fig. 2.4 Examples of synthetic shape from texture images (**a, c**) and corresponding surface normal estimates (**b, d**). Figure courtesy of [34]

Shape from focus [58, 65] estimates depth using two input images captured from the same viewpoint but at different camera depths of field. The degree of blur is a strong cue for object depth as it increases as the object moves away from the camera's focusing distance. The relative depth of the scene can be constructed from the image blur where the amount of defocus can be estimated by averaging the squared gradient values in a region.

Another approach that is specialized for a particular object class is the *Analysis by Synthesis* approach. Here, the assumption is that we have a 3D model of the object class of interest, such as the human face [10] or human head [22]. If we also model all the physical components that generate an image, such as surface reflectance, scene lighting, and the projective imaging processes, and if we parameterize these model components accurately by model fitting, we can synthesize an image that is very similar to the actual image. The 3D structure obtained from the parametrization of the 3D model is then the 3D reconstruction of the single-viewpoint image [9].

Single-view metrology [21] allows shape recovery from a single perspective view of a scene given some geometric information determined from the image. By exploiting scene constraints such as orthogonality and parallelism, a vanishing line and a vanishing point in a single image can be determined. Relative measurements of shape can then be computed, which can be upgraded to absolute metric measurements if the dimensions of a reference object in the scene are known.

While 3D recovery from a single view is possible, such methods are often not practical in terms of either robustness or speed or both. Therefore, the most commonly used approaches are based on multiple views, which is the focus of this chapter. The first step to understanding such approaches is to understand how to model the image formation process in the cameras of a stereo rig. Then we need to know how to estimate the parameters of this model. Thus camera modeling and camera calibration are discussed in the following two main sections.

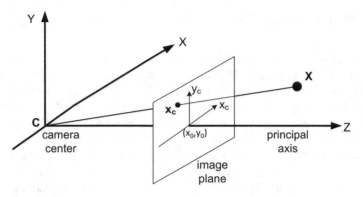

Fig. 2.5 Projection based on a pinhole camera model where a 3D object is projected onto the image plane. Note that, although the real image plane is behind the camera center, it is common practice to employ a virtual image plane in front of the camera, so that the image is conveniently at the same orientation as the scene

2.3   Camera Modeling

A camera is a device in which the 3D scene is projected down onto a 2D image. The most commonly used projection in computer vision is 3D perspective projection. Figure 2.5 illustrates perspective projection based on the pinhole camera model, where **C** is the position of the pinhole, termed the camera center or the *center of projection*. Note that, although the real image plane is behind the camera center, it is common practice to employ a virtual image plane in front of the camera, so that the image is conveniently at the same orientation as the scene.

Clearly, from this figure, the path of imaged light is modeled by a ray that passes from a 3D world point **X** through the camera center. The intersection of this ray with the image plane defines where the image, $\mathbf{x_c}$, of the 3D scene point, **X**, lies. We can reverse this process and say that, for some point on the image plane, its corresponding scene point must lie somewhere along the ray connecting the center of projection, **C**, and that imaged point, $\mathbf{x_c}$. We refer to this as *back-projecting* an image point to an infinite ray that extends out into the scene. Since we do not know how far along the ray the 3D scene point lies, explicit depth information is lost in the imaging process. This is the main source of geometric ambiguity in a single image and is the reason why we refer to the recovery of the depth information from stereo and other cues as *3D reconstruction*.

Before we embark on our development of a mathematical camera model, we need to digress briefly and introduce the concept of homogeneous coordinates (also called projective coordinates), which is the natural coordinate system of analytic projective geometry and hence has wide utility in geometric computer vision.

2.3.1 Homogeneous Coordinates

We are all familiar with expressing the position of some point in a plane using a pair of coordinates as $[x, y]^T$. In general for such systems, n coordinates are used to describe points in an n-dimensional space, $\mathbb{R}^n$. In analytic projective geometry, which deals with algebraic theories of points and lines, such points and lines are typically described by *homogeneous coordinates*, where $n + 1$ coordinates are used to describe points in an n-dimensional space. For example, a general point in a plane is described as $\mathbf{x} = [x_1, x_2, x_3]^T$, and the general equation of a line is given by $\mathbf{l}^T \mathbf{x} = 0$ where $\mathbf{l} = [l_1, l_2, l_3]^T$ are the homogeneous coordinates of the line.[2] Since the right-hand side of this equation for a line is zero, it is a homogeneous equation, and any non-zero multiple of the point $\lambda[x_1, x_2, x_3]^T$ is the same point; similarly, any non-zero multiple of the line's coordinates is the same line. The symmetry in this equation is indicative of the fact that points and lines can be exchanged in many theories of projective geometry; such theories are termed *dual* theories. For example, the cross-product of two lines, expressed in homogeneous coordinates, yields their intersecting point, and the cross-product of a pair of points gives the line between them. This is very useful for manipulating points and lines in the image plane. For example, if we had four image points, then to determine the point of intersection, $\mathbf{x}$, of any two lines defined by any two points we simply compute:

$$\mathbf{x} = (\mathbf{x}_i \times \mathbf{x}_j) \times (\mathbf{x}_k \times \mathbf{x}_l).$$

Note that we can easily convert from homogeneous to inhomogeneous coordinates, simply by dividing through by the third element, thus $[x_1, x_2, x_3]^T$ maps to $[\frac{x_1}{x_3}, \frac{x_2}{x_3}]^T$. A key point about homogeneous coordinates is that they allow the relevant transformations in the imaging process to be represented as linear mappings, which of course are expressed as matrix–vector equations. However, although the mapping between homogeneous world coordinates of a point and homogeneous image coordinates is linear, the mapping from homogeneous to inhomogeneous coordinates is non-linear, due to the required division.

The use of homogeneous coordinates fits well with the relationship between image points and their associated back-projected rays into the scene space. Imagine a mathematical (virtual) image plane at a distance of one metric unit in front of the center of projection, as shown in Fig. 2.5. With the camera center, $\mathbf{C}$, the homogeneous coordinates $[x, y, 1]^T$ define a 3D scene ray as $[\lambda x, \lambda y, \lambda]^T$, where λ is the unknown distance ($\lambda > 0$) along the ray. Thus there is an intuitive link between the depth ambiguity associated with the 3D scene point and the equivalence of homogeneous coordinates up to an arbitrary non-zero scale factor.

Extending the idea of thinking of homogeneous image points as 3D rays, consider the cross-product of two homogeneous points. This gives a direction that is the normal

---

[2] You may wish to compare $\mathbf{l}^T \mathbf{x} = 0$ to two well-known parameterizations of a line in the (x,y) plane, namely, $ax + by + c = 0$ and $y = mx + c$ and, in each case, write down homogeneous coordinates for the point $\mathbf{x}$ and the line $\mathbf{l}$.

of the plane that contains the two rays. The line between the two image points is the intersection of this plane with the image plane. The dual of this is that the cross product of two lines in the image plane gives a point on the image plane whose associated 3D ray represents the intersection of their associated planes. The 3D ray has a direction orthogonal to the normals of both of these planes and is the direction of the ray that defines the point of intersection of the two lines in the image plane. Note that any point with its third homogeneous element zero defines a ray parallel to the image plane and hence meets it at infinity. Such a point is termed a *point at infinity*, and there is an infinite set of these points $[x_1, x_2, 0]^T$ that lie on the *line at infinity* $[0, 0, 1]^T$; Finally, note that the 3-tuple $[0, 0, 0]^T$ has no meaning and is undefined. For further reading on homogeneous coordinates and projective geometry, please see [20, 38].

2.3.2 Perspective Projection Camera Model

We now return to the perspective projection (central projection) camera model, and we note that it maps 3D world points in standard metric units into the pixel coordinates of an image sensor. It is convenient to think of this mapping as the concatenation of three successive stages:

1. A six degree-of-freedom (DOF) rigid transformation consisting of a rotation, R (3 DOF), and translation, $\mathbf{t}$ (3 DOF), that maps points expressed in world coordinates to the same points expressed in camera-centered coordinates.
2. A perspective projection from the 3D world to the 2D image plane.
3. A mapping from metric image coordinates to pixel coordinates.

We now discuss each of these projective mappings in turn.

2.3.2.1 Camera Modeling: The Coordinate Transformation

As shown in Fig. 2.5, the camera frame has its (X,Y) plane parallel to the image plane and Z is in the direction of the principal axis of the lens and encodes depth from the camera. Suppose that the camera center has *inhomogeneous* position $\tilde{\mathbf{C}}$ in the world frame[3] and the rotation of the camera frame is R_c relative to the world frame orientation. This means that we can express any *inhomogeneous* camera frame points as:

$$\tilde{\mathbf{X}}_c = \mathsf{R}_c^T (\tilde{\mathbf{X}} - \tilde{\mathbf{C}}) = \mathsf{R}\tilde{\mathbf{X}} + \mathbf{t}. \tag{2.1}$$

Here $\mathsf{R} = \mathsf{R}_c^T$ represents the rigid rotation and $\mathbf{t} = -\mathsf{R}_c^T \tilde{\mathbf{C}}$ represents the rigid translation that maps a scene point expressed in the world coordinate frame into a camera-

---

[3] We use a tilde to differentiate n-tuple inhomogeneous coordinates from (n+1)-tuple homogeneous coordinates.

centered coordinate frame. Equation 2.1 can be expressed as a projective mapping, namely, one that is linear in homogeneous coordinates, to give

$$
\begin{bmatrix} X_c \\ Y_c \\ Z_c \\ 1 \end{bmatrix} = \begin{bmatrix} \mathbf{R} & \mathbf{t} \\ \mathbf{0}^T & 1 \end{bmatrix} \begin{bmatrix} X \\ Y \\ Z \\ 1 \end{bmatrix}.
$$

We denote $\mathbf{P}_r$ as the 4×4 homogeneous matrix representing the rigid coordinate transformation in the above equation.

2.3.2.2   Camera Modeling: Perspective Projection

Observing the similar triangles in the geometry of perspective imaging, we have

$$
\frac{x_c}{f} = \frac{X_c}{Z_c}, \quad \frac{y_c}{f} = \frac{Y_c}{Z_c}, \tag{2.2}
$$

where (x_c, y_c) is the position (metric units) of a point in the camera's image plane and f is the distance (metric units) of the image plane to the camera center. (This is usually set to the focal length of the camera lens.) The two equations above can be written in linear form as

$$
Z_c \begin{bmatrix} x_c \\ y_c \\ 1 \end{bmatrix} = \begin{bmatrix} f & 0 & 0 & 0 \\ 0 & f & 0 & 0 \\ 0 & 0 & 1 & 0 \end{bmatrix} \begin{bmatrix} X_c \\ Y_c \\ Z_c \\ 1 \end{bmatrix}.
$$

We denote $\mathbf{P}_p$ as the 3×4 perspective projection matrix, defined by the value of f, in the above equation. If we consider an abstract image plane at $f = 1$, then points on this plane are termed *normalized image coordinates*[4] and from Eq. 2.2, these are given by

$$
x_n = \frac{X_c}{Z_c}, \quad y_n = \frac{Y_c}{Z_c}.
$$

2.3.2.3   Camera Modeling: Image Sampling

Typically, the image on the image plane is sampled by an image sensor, such as a CCD or CMOS device, at the locations defined by an array of pixels. The final part of camera modeling defines how that array is positioned on the $[x_c, y_c]^T$ image plane,

---

[4]We need to use a variety of image coordinate normalizations in this chapter. For simplicity, we will use the same subscript n, but it will be clear about how the normalization is achieved.

so that pixel coordinates can be generated. In general, pixels in an image sensor are not square and the number of pixels per unit distance varies between the x_c and y_c directions; we will call these scalings m_x and m_y. Note that pixel positions have their origin at the corner of the sensor and so the position of the principal point (where the principal axis intersects the image plane) is modeled with pixel coordinates $[x_0, y_0]^T$. Finally, many camera models also cater for any skew,[5] s, so that the mapping into pixels is given by

$$
\begin{bmatrix} x \\ y \\ 1 \end{bmatrix} = \begin{bmatrix} m_x & s & x_0 \\ 0 & m_y & y_0 \\ 0 & 0 & 1 \end{bmatrix} \begin{bmatrix} x_c \\ y_c \\ 1 \end{bmatrix}.
$$

We denote P_c as the 3×3 projective matrix defined by the five parameters m_x, m_y, s and x_0, y_0 in the above equation.

2.3.2.4 Camera Modeling: Concatenating the Projective Mappings

We can concatenate the three stages described in the three previous subsections to give

$$
\lambda \mathbf{x} = P_c P_p P_r \mathbf{X}
$$

or simply

$$
\lambda \mathbf{x} = P \mathbf{X}, \tag{2.3}
$$

where λ is non-zero and positive. We note the following points concerning the above equation:

1. For any homogeneous image point scaled to $\lambda[x, \; y, \; 1]^T$, the scale λ is equal to the imaged point's depth in the camera-centered frame ($\lambda = Z_c$).
2. Any non-zero scaling of the projection matrix $\lambda_P P$ performs the same projection since, in Eq. 2.3, any non-zero scaling of homogeneous image coordinates is equivalent.
3. A camera with projection matrix P, or some non-zero scalar multiple of that, is informally referred to as *camera P* in the computer vision literature and, because of point 2 above, it is referred to as being defined *up to scale*.

The matrix P is a 3×4 projective camera matrix with the following structure:

$$
P = K[R|t]. \tag{2.4}
$$

The parameters within K are the camera's *intrinsic parameters*. These parameters are those combined from Sects. 2.3.2.2 and 2.3.2.3 above, so that

---

[5] Skew models a lack of orthogonality between the two image sensor sampling directions. For most imaging situations, it is zero.

$$\mathsf{K} = \begin{bmatrix} \alpha_x & s & x_0 \\ 0 & \alpha_y & y_0 \\ 0 & 0 & 1 \end{bmatrix},$$

where $\alpha_x = f m_x$ and $\alpha_y = f m_y$ represent the focal length in pixels in the x and y directions, respectively. Together, the rotation and translation in Eq. 2.4 are termed the camera's *extrinsic parameters*. Since there are 5 DOF from intrinsic parameters and 6 DOF from extrinsic parameters, a camera projection matrix has only 11 DOF, not the full 12 of a general 3×4 matrix. This is also evident from the fact that we are dealing with homogeneous coordinates and so the overall scale of P does not matter.

By expanding Eq. 2.3, we have

$$\lambda \overbrace{\begin{bmatrix} x \\ y \\ 1 \end{bmatrix}}^{\substack{homogeneous \\ image \\ coordinates}} = \overbrace{\begin{bmatrix} \alpha_x & s & x_0 \\ 0 & \alpha_y & y_0 \\ 0 & 0 & 1 \end{bmatrix}}^{\substack{intrinsic \\ camera \\ parameters}} \overbrace{\begin{bmatrix} r_{11} & r_{12} & r_{13} & t_x \\ r_{21} & r_{22} & r_{23} & t_y \\ r_{31} & r_{32} & r_{33} & t_z \end{bmatrix}}^{\substack{extrinsic \\ camera \\ parameters}} \overbrace{\begin{bmatrix} X \\ Y \\ Z \\ 1 \end{bmatrix}}^{\substack{homogeneous \\ world \\ coordinates}}, \quad (2.5)$$

which indicates that both the intrinsic and extrinsic camera parameters are necessary to fully define a ray (metrically, not just in pixel units) in 3D space and hence make absolute measurements in multiple-view 3D reconstruction. Finally, we note that any non-zero scaling of scene homogeneous coordinates $[X, Y, Z, 1]^T$ in Eq. 2.5 gives the same image coordinates[6] which, for a single image, can be interpreted as ambiguity between the scene scale and the translation vector $\mathbf{t}$.

2.3.3 Radial Distortion

Typical cameras have a lens distortion which disrupts the assumed linear projective model. Thus a camera may not be accurately represented by the pinhole camera model that we have described, particularly if a low-cost lens or a wide field-of-view (short focal length) lens such as a fish-eye lens is employed. Some examples of lens distortion effects are shown in Fig. 2.6. Note that the effect is non-linear and, if significant, it must be corrected so that the camera can again be modeled as a linear device. The estimation of the required distortion parameters to do this is often encompassed within a camera calibration procedure, which is described in Sect. 2.4. With reference to our previous three-stage development of a projective camera in Sect. 2.3.2, lens distortion occurs at the second stage which is the 3D to 2D projection, and this distortion is sampled by the image sensor.

---

[6]The same homogeneous image coordinates *up to scale* or the same inhomogeneous image coordinates.

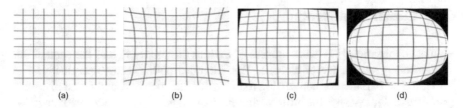

Fig. 2.6 Examples of radial distortion effects in lenses: (**a**) No distortion, (**b**) Pincushion distortion, (**c**) Barrel distortion, (**d**) Fish-eye distortion

Detailed distortion models contain a large number of parameters that model both radial and tangential distortions [13]. However, radial distortion is the dominant factor and usually it is considered sufficiently accurate to model this distortion only, using a low-order polynomial such as

$$\begin{bmatrix} x_{nd} \\ y_{nd} \end{bmatrix} = \begin{bmatrix} x_n \\ y_n \end{bmatrix} + \begin{bmatrix} x_n \\ y_n \end{bmatrix} (k_1 r^2 + k_2 r^4),$$

where $[x_n, y_n]^T$ is the undistorted image position (i.e., that obeys our linear projection model) in normalized coordinates, $[x_{nd}, y_{nd}]^T$ is the distorted image position in normalized coordinates, k_1 and k_2 are the unknown radial distortion parameters, and $r = \sqrt{x_n^2 + y_n^2}$. Assuming zero skew, we also have

$$\begin{bmatrix} x_d \\ y_d \end{bmatrix} = \begin{bmatrix} x \\ y \end{bmatrix} + \begin{bmatrix} (x - x_0) \\ (y - y_0) \end{bmatrix} (k_1 r^2 + k_2 r^4), \tag{2.6}$$

where the distorted position $[x_d, y_d]^T$ is now expressed in pixel coordinates and $[x, y]^T$ are the usual pixel coordinates predicted by the linear pinhole model. Note that r is still defined in normalized image coordinates and so a non-unity aspect ratio ($m_x \neq m_y$) in the image sensor does not invalidate this equation. Also note that both Eq. 2.6 and Fig. 2.6 indicate that distortion increases away from the center of the image. In the barrel distortion, shown in Fig. 2.6c, distortion correction requires that image points are moved slightly toward the center of the image, more so if they are near the edges of the image. Correction could be applied to the whole image, as in dense stereo, or just a set of relevant features, such as extracted corner points. Clearly, the latter process is computationally cheaper.

Now that we have discussed the modeling of a camera's image formation process in detail; we now need to understand how to estimate the parameters within this model. This is the focus of the next section, which details camera calibration.

2.4   Camera Calibration

Camera calibration [14] is the process of finding the parameters of the camera that produced a given image of a scene. This includes both extrinsic parameters R, t and intrinsic parameters, comprising those within the matrix K and radial distortion parameters, k_1, k_2. Once the intrinsic and extrinsic camera parameters are known, we know the camera projection matrix P and, taking into account any radial distortion present, we can back-project any image pixel to a 3D ray in space. Clearly, as the intrinsic camera calibration parameters are tied to the focal length, changing the zoom on the lens would make the calibration invalid. It is also worth noting that calibration is not always required. For example, we may be more interested in approximate shape, where we need to know what objects in a scene are co-planar, rather than their absolute 3D position measurements. However, for stereo systems at least, camera calibration is commonplace.

Generally, it is not possible for an end user to get the required calibration information to the required accuracy from camera manufacturer's specifications and external measurement of the position of cameras in some frames. Hence, some sort of camera calibration procedure is required, of which there are several different categories. The longest established of these is *photogrammetric calibration*, where calibration is performed using a scene object of precisely known physical dimensions. Typically, several images of a special 3D target, such as three orthogonal planes with calibration grids (chessboard patterns of black and white squares), are captured and precise known translations may be used [89]. Although this gives accurate calibration results, it lacks flexibility due to the need for precise scene knowledge.

At the other end of the spectrum is *self-calibration* (auto-calibration) [38, 55], where no calibration target is used. The correspondences across three images of the same rigid scene provide enough constraints to recover a set of camera parameters which allow 3D reconstruction up to a similarity transform. Although this approach is flexible, there are many parameters to estimate and reliable calibrations cannot always be obtained.

Between these two extremes are "desktop" camera calibration approaches that use images of planar calibration grids, captured at several unknown positions and orientations (i.e., a single planar chessboard pattern is manually held at several random poses, and calibration images are captured and stored). This gives a good compromise between the accuracy of photogrammetric calibration and the ease of use of self-calibration. A seminal example is given by Zhang [98].

Although there are a number of publicly available camera calibration packages on the web, such as the Caltech camera calibration toolbox for MATLAB [11] and in the OpenCV computer vision library [62], a detailed study of at least one approach is essential to understand calibration in detail. We will use Zhang's work [98] as a seminal example, and this approach consists of two main parts:

1. A *basic* calibration that is based on linear least squares and hence has a closed-form solution. In the formulation of the linear problem, a set of nine parameters need to be estimated. These are rather complicated combinations of the camera's intrinsic

parameters, and the algebraic least squares minimization to determine them has no obvious geometric meaning. Once intrinsic parameters have been extracted from these estimated parameters, extrinsic parameters can be determined using the homography associated with each calibration grid image.

2. A *refined* calibration is based on non-linear least squares and hence has an iterative solution. Here, it is possible to formulate a least squares error between the observed (inhomogeneous) image positions of the calibration grid corners and the positions predicted by the current estimate of intrinsic and extrinsic camera parameters. This has a clear geometric interpretation, but the sum of squares function that we wish to minimize is non-linear in terms of the camera parameters. A standard approach to solving this kind of problem is the *Levenberg–Marquardt* (LM) algorithm, which employs gradient descent when it is far from a minimum and Gauss–Newton minimization when it gets close to a minimum. Since the LM algorithm is a very general procedure, it is straightforward to employ more complex camera models, such as those that include parameters for the radial distortion associated with the camera lens.

The iterative optimization in (2) above needs to be within the basin of convergence of the global minimum and so the linear method in (1) is used to determine an initial estimation of camera parameters. The raw data used as inputs to the process consists of the image corner positions, as detected by an automatic corner detector [37] [81], of all corners in all calibration images and the corresponding 2D world positions, $[X, Y]^T$, of the corners on the calibration grid. Typically, correspondences are established by manually clicking one or more detected image corners, and making a quick visual check that the imaged corners are matched correctly using overlaying graphics or text. A typical set of targets is shown in Fig. 2.7.

In the following four subsections, we outline the theory and practice of camera calibration. The first subsection details the estimation of the planar projective map-

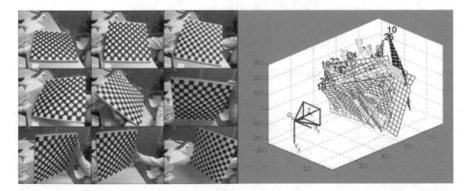

Fig. 2.7 Left: calibration targets used in a camera calibration process. Right: after calibration, it is possible to determine the positions of the calibration planes using the estimated extrinsic parameters (Figure courtesy of the *Camera Calibration Toolbox for MATLAB* webpage at Caltech by Jean-Yves Bouguet [11])

ping between a scene plane (calibration grid) and its image. The next two subsections closely follow Zhang [98] and detail the basic calibration and then the refined calibration, as outlined above. These subsections refer to the case of a single camera, and so a final fourth subsection is used to describe the additional issues associated with the calibration of a stereo rig.

2.4.1 Estimation of a Scene-to-Image Planar Homography

A homography is a projective transformation (*projectivity*) that maps points to points and lines to lines. It is a highly useful imaging model when we view planar scenes, which is common in many computer vision processes, including the process of camera calibration.

Suppose that we view a planar scene, then we can define the (X, Y) axes of the world coordinate system to be within the plane of the scene, and hence $Z = 0$ everywhere. Equation 2.5 indicates that, as far as a planar scene is concerned, the imaging process can be reduced to

$$\lambda \mathbf{x} = \mathsf{K}[\mathbf{r}_1 \ \mathbf{r}_2 \ \mathbf{t}][X, Y, 1]^T,$$

where $\mathbf{r}_1$ and $\mathbf{r}_2$ are the first and second columns of the rotation matrix R; hence,

$$\lambda \mathbf{x} = \mathsf{H}[X, Y, 1]^T, \quad \mathsf{H} = \mathsf{K}[\mathbf{r}_1 \ \mathbf{r}_2 \ \mathbf{t}]. \tag{2.7}$$

The 3×3 matrix H is termed a planar homography, which is defined up to a scale factor,[7] and hence has eight degrees of freedom instead of nine.

By expanding the above equation, we have

$$\lambda \begin{bmatrix} x \\ y \\ 1 \end{bmatrix} = \begin{bmatrix} h_{11} & h_{12} & h_{13} \\ h_{21} & h_{22} & h_{23} \\ h_{31} & h_{32} & h_{33} \end{bmatrix} \begin{bmatrix} X \\ Y \\ 1 \end{bmatrix}. \tag{2.8}$$

If we map homogeneous coordinates to inhomogeneous coordinates, by dividing through by λ, this gives

$$x = \frac{h_{11}X + h_{12}Y + h_{13}}{h_{31}X + h_{32}Y + h_{33}} \tag{2.9}$$

$$y = \frac{h_{21}X + h_{22}Y + h_{23}}{h_{31}X + h_{32}Y + h_{33}}. \tag{2.10}$$

---

[7]Due to the scale equivalence of homogeneous coordinates.

From a set of four correspondences in a general position,[8] we can formulate a set of eight linear equations in the eight unknowns of a homography matrix. This is because each correspondence provides a pair of constraints of the form given in Eqs. 2.9 and 2.10.

Rearranging terms in four pairs of those equations allows us to formulate the homography estimation problem in the form:

$$\mathbf{Ah} = \mathbf{0}, \tag{2.11}$$

where $\mathbf{A}$ is an 8×9 data matrix derived from image and world coordinates of corresponding points and $\mathbf{h}$ is the 9-vector containing the elements of the homography matrix. Since $\mathbf{A}$ has rank 8, it has a one-dimensional null space, which provides a non-trivial (non-zero vector) solution for Eq. 2.11. This can be determined from a Singular Value Decomposition (SVD) of the data matrix, which generates three matrices $(\mathbf{U}, \mathbf{D}, \mathbf{V})$ such that $\mathbf{A} = \mathbf{UDV}^T$. Here, $\mathbf{D}$ is a diagonal matrix of singular values and $\mathbf{U}$, $\mathbf{V}$ are orthonormal matrices. Typically, SVD algorithms order the singular values in descending order down the diagonal of $\mathbf{D}$ and so the required solution, corresponding to a singular value of zero, is extracted as the last column of $\mathbf{V}$. Due to the homogeneous form of Eq. 2.11, the solution is determined up to a non-zero scale factor, which is acceptable because $\mathbf{H}$ is only defined up to scale. Often a unit scale is chosen (i.e., $||\mathbf{h}|| = 1$), and this scaling is returned automatically in the columns of $\mathbf{V}$.

In general, a larger number of correspondences than the minimum will not exactly satisfy the same homography because of image noise. In this case, a least squares solution to $\mathbf{h}$ can be determined in an over-determined system of linear equations. We follow the same procedure as above but this time the data matrix is of size $2n \times 9$ where $n > 4$ is the number of correspondences. When we apply SVD, we still select the last column of V corresponding to the smallest singular value in D. (Note that, in this case, the smallest singular value will be non-zero.)

Data normalization prior to the application of SVD is *essential* to give stable estimates [38]. The basic idea is to translate and scale both image and world coordinates to avoid orders of magnitude difference between the columns of the data matrix. Image points are translated so that their centroid is at the origin and scaled to give a root-mean-squared (RMS) distance of $\sqrt{2}$ from that origin, so that the "average" image point has coordinates of unity magnitude. Scene points should be normalized in a similar way except that they should be scaled to give an RMS distance of $\sqrt{3}$.

When using homogeneous coordinates, the normalizations can be applied using matrix operators $\mathbf{N}_i$, $\mathbf{N}_s$, such that new *normalized* coordinates are given as

$$\mathbf{x}_n = \mathbf{N}_i \mathbf{x}, \quad \mathbf{X}_n = \mathbf{N}_s \mathbf{X}$$

---

[8]No three points collinear.

for the image points and scene points, respectively. Suppose that the homography computed from normalized coordinates is $\tilde{H}$, then the homography relating the original coordinates of the correspondences is given as

$$H = N_i^{-1}\tilde{H}N_s.$$

2.4.2 Basic Calibration

From the known planar scene target and the resulting image, a scene-to-image planar homography can be estimated as described in the previous subsection. Suppose that we describe such a homography as a set of 3×1 column vectors, i.e., $H = [h_1\ h_2\ h_3]$, then comparing this to Eq. 2.7 we have

$$\lambda_H h_1 = Kr_1, \quad \lambda_H h_2 = Kr_2, \tag{2.12}$$

where λ_H is a scale factor, accounting for the particular scale of an estimated homography. Noting that the columns of the rotation matrix, r_1, r_2 are orthonormal,

$$r_1^T r_2 = h_1^T K^{-T} K^{-1} h_2 = 0, \tag{2.13}$$

$$r_1^T r_1 = r_2^T r_2 \Rightarrow h_1^T K^{-T} K^{-1} h_1 = h_2^T K^{-T} K^{-1} h_2. \tag{2.14}$$

These equations provide one constraint each on the intrinsic parameters.

We construct a symmetric matrix B such that

$$B = K^{-T}K^{-1} = \begin{bmatrix} B_{11} & B_{12} & B_{13} \\ B_{12} & B_{22} & B_{23} \\ B_{13} & B_{23} & B_{33} \end{bmatrix}.$$

Let the ith column vector of H be $h_i = [h_{1i}, h_{2i}, h_{3i}]^T$, we have

$$h_i^T B h_j = v_{ij}^T b,$$

where

$$v_{ij} = [h_{1i}h_{1j}, h_{1i}h_{2j} + h_{2i}h_{1j}, h_{2i}h_{2j}, h_{3i}h_{1j} + h_{1i}h_{3j}, h_{3i}h_{2j} + h_{2i}h_{3j}, h_{3i}h_{3j}]^T$$

and b is the vector containing six independent entries of the symmetric matrix B:

$$b = [B_{11}, B_{12}, B_{22}, B_{13}, B_{23}, B_{33}]^T.$$

Therefore, the two constraints in Eqs. 2.13 and 2.14 can be rewritten as

$$\begin{bmatrix} \mathbf{v}_{12}^T \\ (\mathbf{v}_{11} - \mathbf{v}_{22})^T \end{bmatrix} \mathbf{b} = \mathbf{0}.$$

If n images of the planar calibration grid are observed, n sets of these equations can be stacked into a matrix–vector equation as

$$\mathbf{V}\mathbf{b} = \mathbf{0},$$

where $\mathbf{V}$ is a $2n \times 6$ matrix. Although a minimum of three planar views allows us to solve for $\mathbf{b}$, it is recommended to take more and form a least squares solution. In this case, the solution for $\mathbf{b}$ is the eigenvector of $\mathbf{V}^T\mathbf{V}$ associated with the smallest eigenvalue. Once $\mathbf{b}$ is estimated, we know the matrix $\mathbf{B}$ up to some unknown scale factor, λ_B, and all of the intrinsic camera parameters can be computed by expanding the right-hand side of $\mathbf{B} = \lambda_B \mathbf{K}^{-T}\mathbf{K}^{-1}$ in terms of its individual elements. Although this is somewhat laborious, it is straightforward algebra of simultaneous equations, where five intrinsic camera parameters plus one unknown scale factor can be derived from the six parameters of the symmetric matrix $\mathbf{B}$. Zhang [98] presents the solution:

$$y_0 = \frac{(B_{12}B_{13} - B_{11}B_{23})}{(B_{11}B_{22} - B_{12}^2)}$$

$$\lambda_B = B_{33} - \frac{[B_{13}^2 + y_0(B_{12}B_{13} - B_{11}B_{23})]}{B_{11}}$$

$$\alpha_x = \sqrt{\frac{\lambda_B}{B_{11}}}$$

$$\alpha_y = \sqrt{\frac{\lambda_B B_{11}}{(B_{11}B_{22} - B_{12}^2)}}$$

$$s = \frac{-B_{12}\alpha_x^2\alpha_y}{\lambda_B}$$

$$x_0 = \frac{s y_0}{\alpha_y} - \frac{B_{13}\alpha_x^2}{\lambda_B}.$$

Once $\mathbf{K}$ is known, the extrinsic camera parameters for each image can be computed using Eq. 2.12:

$$\mathbf{r}_1 = \lambda_H \mathbf{K}^{-1}\mathbf{h}_1$$
$$\mathbf{r}_2 = \lambda_H \mathbf{K}^{-1}\mathbf{h}_2$$
$$\mathbf{r}_3 = \mathbf{r}_1 \times \mathbf{r}_2$$
$$\mathbf{t} = \lambda_H \mathbf{K}^{-1}\mathbf{h}_3,$$

where here

$$\lambda_H = \frac{1}{||\mathsf{K}^{-1}\mathbf{h}_1||} = \frac{1}{||\mathsf{K}^{-1}\mathbf{h}_2||}.$$

The vectors $\mathbf{r}_1$, $\mathbf{r}_2$ will not be exactly orthogonal and so the estimated rotation matrix does not exactly represent a rotation. Zhang [98] suggests performing SVD on the estimated rotation matrix so that $\mathsf{USV}^T = \mathsf{R}$. Then the closest pure rotation matrix in terms of Frobenius norm to that estimated is given as $\mathsf{R}' = \mathsf{UV}^T$.

2.4.3 Refined Calibration

After computation of the linear solution described above, it can be iteratively refined via a non-linear least squares minimization using the *Levenberg–Marquardt* (LM) algorithm. As previously mentioned, the camera parameters can be extended at this stage to include an estimation for the lens distortion parameters, to give us the following minimization:

$$\hat{\mathbf{p}} = \min_{\mathbf{p}} \left\{ \sum_{i=1}^{n} \sum_{j=1}^{m} ||\mathbf{x}_{i,j} - \hat{\mathbf{x}}_{i,j}(\mathsf{K}, k_1, k_2, \mathsf{R}_i, \mathbf{t}_i, \mathbf{X}_j)||^2 \right\},$$

where $\mathbf{x}_{i,j}$ is the image of world point $\mathbf{X}_j$ in image i and $\hat{\mathbf{x}}_{i,j}$ is the predicted projection of the same world point according to Eq. 2.7 (using estimated intrinsic and extrinsic camera parameters) followed by radial distortion according to Eq. 2.6.

The vector $\mathbf{p}$ contains all of the free parameters within the planar projection (homography) function plus two radial distortion parameters k_1 and k_2 as described in Sect. 2.3.3. Initial estimates of these radial distortion parameters can be set to zero. LM iteratively updates all parameters according to the equation:

$$\mathbf{p}_{k+1} = \mathbf{p}_k + \delta\mathbf{p}_k$$
$$\delta\mathbf{p}_k = -(\mathsf{J}^T\mathsf{J} + \lambda_J diag(\mathsf{J}^T\mathsf{J}))^{-1}\mathsf{J}^T\mathbf{e},$$

where J is the Jacobian matrix containing the first derivatives of the residual $\mathbf{e}$ with respect to each of the camera parameters.

Thus computation of the Jacobian is central to LM minimization. This can be done either numerically or with a custom routine, if analytical expressions for the Jacobian entries are known. In the numerical approach, each parameter is incremented and the function to be minimized (the least squares error function in this case) is computed and divided by the increment, which should be the maximum of 10^{-6} and $10^{-4} \times |p_i|$, where p_i is some current parameter value [38]. In the case of providing a custom Jacobian function, the expressions are long and complicated in the case of camera calibration, and so the use of a symbolic mathematics package can help reduce human error in constructing the partial differentials.

Note that there are LM implementations available on many platforms, for example, in MATLAB's optimization toolbox, or the C/C++ *levmar* package. A detailed discussion of iterative estimation methods including LM is given in Appendix 6 of Hartley and Zisserman's book [38].

2.4.4   Calibration of a Stereo Rig

As a mathematical convenience, it is common practice to choose the optical center of one camera to be the origin of a stereo camera's 3D coordinate system. Then, the relative rigid location of the other camera, [R, t], within this frame, along with both sets of intrinsic parameters, is required to generate a pair of projection matrices and hence a pair of 3D rays from corresponding image points that intersect at their common scene point.

The previous two subsections showed how we can calculate the intrinsic parameters for any single camera. If we have a stereo pair, which is our primary interest, then we would compute a pair of intrinsic parameter matrices, one for the left camera and one for the right. In most cases, the two cameras are the same model, and hence we would expect the two intrinsic parameter matrices to be very similar.

Also, we note that, for each chessboard position, two sets of extrinsic parameters, [R, t], are generated, one for the left camera's position relative to the calibration plane and one for the right. Clearly, each left–right pair of extrinsic parameters should have approximately[9] the same relationship, which is due to the fixed rigid rotation and translation of one camera relative to another in the stereo rig.

Once two sets of intrinsic parameters and *one* set of extrinsic parameters encoding the *relative* rigid pose of one camera relative to another has been computed, the results are often refined in a global stereo optimization procedure, again using the Levenberg–Marquardt approach. To reduce n sets of relative extrinsic parameters to one set, we could choose the set associated with the closest calibration plane or compute some form of average.

All parameter estimates, both intrinsic and extrinsic, can be improved if the optimization is now performed over a minimal set of parameters, since the extrinsic parameters are reduced from 12 (two rotations and two translations) to 6 (one relative rotation and one relative translation) per calibration grid location. This approach ensures global rigidity of the stereo rig going from left-to-right camera. An implementation of global stereo optimization to refine stereo camera parameters is given in the Caltech camera calibration toolbox for MATLAB [11].

---

[9]"Approximately", because of noise in the imaged corner positions supplied to the calibration process.

2.5 Two-View Geometry

3D reconstruction from an image pair must solve two problems: the correspondence problem and the reconstruction problem.

- *Correspondence problem.* For a point $\mathbf{x}$ in the left image, which is the corresponding point $\mathbf{x}'$ in the right image, where $\mathbf{x}$ and $\mathbf{x}'$ are images of the same physical scene point $\mathbf{X}$?
- *Reconstruction problem.* Given two corresponding points $\mathbf{x}$ and $\mathbf{x}'$, how do we compute the 3D coordinates of scene point $\mathbf{X}$?

Of these problems, the correspondence problem is significantly more difficult as it is a search problem whereas, for a stereo camera of known calibration, reconstruction to recover the 3D measurements is a simple geometric mechanism. Since we have sets of three unique points, $(\mathbf{x}, \mathbf{x}', \mathbf{X})$, this mechanism is called triangulation (not to be confused with surface mesh triangulation, described in Chap. 6).

This section is designed to give the reader a good general grounding in two-view geometry and estimation of the key two-view geometric relations that can be useful even when extrinsic or intrinsic camera calibration information is not available.[10] As long as the concept of epipolar geometry is well understood, the remaining main sections of this chapter can be easily followed.

2.5.1 Epipolar Geometry

Epipolar geometry establishes the relationship between two camera views. When we have calibrated cameras and we are dealing with metric image coordinates, it is dependent only on the relative pose between the cameras. When we have uncalibrated cameras and we are dealing with pixel-based image coordinates, it is additionally dependent on the cameras' intrinsic parameters; however, it is independent of the scene.

Once the epipolar geometry is known, for any image point in one image, we know that its corresponding point (its match) in the other image must lie on a line, which is known as the *epipolar line* associated with the original point. This epipolar constraint greatly reduces the correspondence problem from a 2D search over the whole image to a 1D search along the epipolar line only, and hence reduces computational cost and ambiguities.

The discussion here is limited to two-view geometry only. A similar constraint called the *trifocal tensor* is applicable for three views but is outside the scope of this chapter. For further information on the trifocal tensor and n-view geometries, please refer to [38].

---

[10]Extrinsic parameters are always not known in a structure from motion problem; they are part of what we are trying to solve for. Intrinsic parameters may or may not be known, depending on the application.

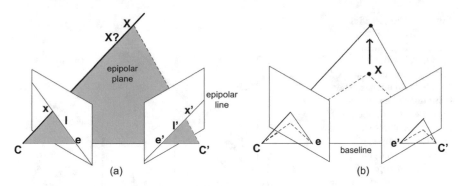

Fig. 2.8 a The epipolar geometry establishes the relationship between the two camera views. **b** The epipolar planes rotate around the baseline, and all epipolar lines intersect at the epipole

As shown in Fig. 2.8a, the image points **x** and **x′**, world point **X**, and the camera centers are co-planar, and this plane is called the epipolar plane, which is shaded in the figure. If we only know **x**, how is the corresponding point **x′** constrained? The line **l′** is the intersection of the epipolar plane with the second image plane. **l′** is called the epipolar line, which is the image in the second view of the ray back-projected from **x**. As the point **x′** lies on **l′**, the correspondences search does not need to cover the entire image but can be restricted only to the line **l′**. In fact, if any point on epipolar line **l** has a corresponding point in the second image, it must lie on epipolar line **l′** and vice versa. Thus **l** and **l′** are called *conjugate* epipolar lines.

The epipole is the point of intersection of the line joining the camera centers with the image plane. The epipole **e** is the projection of the second camera center on the first image, while the epipole **e′** is the projection of the first camera center on the second image.

In essence, two-view epipolar geometry describes the intersection of the image planes with the pencil of planes having the baseline as the pencil axis, as illustrated in Fig. 2.8b. Note that the baseline is the line joining the two camera centers.[11] All epipolar lines intersect at the epipole of the respective image to give a pencil of epipolar lines in each image. Note that the epipoles are not necessarily within the boundaries of the image. A special case is when the cameras are oriented in the same direction, and they are separated by a translation parallel to both image planes. In this case, the epipoles are at infinity and the epipolar lines are parallel. Furthermore, if the translation is in the X direction only and the cameras have the same intrinsic parameters, the conjugate epipolar lines lie on the same image rows. This is an ideal set up when we search for correspondences between the two images. However, we may prefer some camera vergence to improve the field-of-view overlap between the two cameras for certain distance and, in this case, the images need to be warped so that the epipolar lines become horizontal again. This *rectification* process is discussed later in the chapter.

---

[11] The length of the baseline is the magnitude of the extrinsic translation vector, **t**.

Fig. 2.9 The essential
matrix $\mathsf{E} = [\mathbf{t}]_x \mathsf{R}$ encodes
the epipolar geometry. It is
used to relate the
correspondences $\mathbf{x}_c$ and $\mathbf{x}_c'$
between two images, when
these image locations are
expressed in metric units. If
pixel-based coordinates are
used (for example, if
intrinsic camera parameters
are unknown) epipolar
geometry is encoded by the
fundamental matrix F

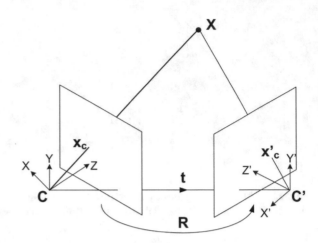

The epipolar constraint can be represented algebraically by a 3×3 matrix called the *fundamental matrix* (F), when we are dealing with raw pixel coordinates, and by the *essential matrix* (E) when the intrinsic parameters of the cameras are known and we are dealing with metrically expressed coordinates (e.g., millimeters) in the image plane.

2.5.2 Essential and Fundamental Matrices

Both the essential and fundamental matrices derive from a simple co-planarity constraint. For simplicity it is best to look at the epipolar relation using the essential matrix first and then adapt it using the camera intrinsic parameters to obtain a relation for pixel-based image coordinates, which involves the fundamental matrix.

Referring to Fig. 2.9, we have a world point $\mathbf{X}$ that projects to points $\mathbf{x}_c$ and $\mathbf{x}_c'$ in the image planes. These image plane points are expressed as 3-vectors, so that they are effectively the 3D positions of the imaged points expressed metrically in their own camera frame, hence the subscript c. (Note also that they can be regarded as normalized homogeneous image coordinates, with the scale set to the focal length, f, although any non-zero scale would suffice.) We know that the three vectors $\mathbf{Cx}_c$, $\mathbf{C}'\mathbf{x}_c'$ and $\mathbf{t}$ are co-planar, so we can choose one of the two camera frames to express this co-planarity, using the scalar triple product. If we choose the right frame (primed), then we must rotate vector $\mathbf{Cx}_c$ using rotation matrix R, to give

$$\mathbf{x}_c'^T (\mathbf{t} \times \mathsf{R}\mathbf{x}_c) = 0.$$

Expressing the cross-product with $\mathbf{t}$ by the multiplication with the skew-symmetric matrix $[\mathbf{t}]_x$, we have

$$\mathbf{x}_c'[\mathbf{t}]_x \mathsf{R}\mathbf{x}_c = 0,$$

where

$$[\mathbf{t}]_x = \begin{bmatrix} 0 & -t_z & t_y \\ t_z & 0 & -t_x \\ -t_y & t_x & 0 \end{bmatrix}$$

and thus we have

$$\mathsf{E} = [\mathbf{t}]_x \mathsf{R} \tag{2.15}$$

and

$$\mathbf{x}_c'^T \mathsf{E} \mathbf{x}_c = 0. \tag{2.16}$$

Thus the essential matrix encapsulates only extrinsic parameters, namely, the rotation and translation associated with the *relative* pose of the two cameras. The implication of this is that, in applications where R and $\mathbf{t}$ have not been computed in a calibration procedure, they may be recoverable from E, which will be discussed further in Sect. 2.8.2 in the context of structure from motion.

In many practical situations, we also need to deal with uncalibrated cameras where the intrinsic parameters are unknown (i.e., the mapping between metric image coordinates and raw pixel values is unknown). The shifting and scaling operations required for this conversion can be encapsulated in matrices K and K', as follows:

$$\mathbf{x} = \mathsf{K}\mathbf{x}_c, \quad \mathbf{x}' = \mathsf{K}'\mathbf{x}_c',$$

where K and K' are the 3×3 matrices containing the intrinsic camera parameters for the two cameras. Inserting these relations into Eq. 2.16 gives

$$\mathbf{x}'^T \mathsf{K}'^{-T} \mathsf{E} \mathsf{K}^{-1} \mathbf{x} = 0$$

$$\mathbf{x}'^T \mathsf{F} \mathbf{x} = 0$$

thus

$$\mathsf{F} = \mathsf{K}'^{-T} \mathsf{E} \mathsf{K}^{-1} = \mathsf{K}'^{-T} [\mathbf{t}]_x \mathsf{R} \mathsf{K}^{-1}$$

and we can see that the fundamental matrix encapsulates both intrinsic and extrinsic parameters. The interpretation of the epipolar constraint given by the fundamental matrix is that, if points $\mathbf{x}$ and $\mathbf{x}'$ correspond, then $\mathbf{x}'$ must lie on the epipolar line given by $\mathbf{l}' = \mathsf{F}\mathbf{x}$ and therefore the dot product between $\mathbf{x}'$ and $\mathsf{F}\mathbf{x}$ is zero.

Some key properties of the fundamental matrix are summarized below:

- If F is the fundamental matrix between camera P and camera P', then F^T is the fundamental matrix between camera P' and camera P.
- F is a projective mapping taking a point to a line. If $\mathbf{l}$ and $\mathbf{l}'$ are corresponding (i.e., conjugate) epipolar lines, then any point $\mathbf{x}$ on $\mathbf{l}$ maps to the same line $\mathbf{l}'$. Hence, there is no inverse mapping (zero determinant, rank 2).

- F has seven degrees of freedom. While a 3×3 homogeneous matrix has eight independent ratios, there is also an additional constraint that the determinant of F is zero (F is rank 2), which further removes one degree of freedom.
- For any point $\mathbf{x}$ in the first image, the corresponding epipolar line in the second image is $\mathbf{l}' = F\mathbf{x}$. Similarly, $\mathbf{l} = F^T\mathbf{x}'$ represents the epipolar line in the first image corresponding to $\mathbf{x}'$ in the second image.
- The epipoles are determined as the left and right nullspaces of the fundamental matrix. This is evident, since each epipole is on every epipolar line in their respective image. This is written as $\mathbf{e}'^T\mathbf{l}' = \mathbf{e}'^T F\mathbf{x} = 0 \ \forall \mathbf{x}$, hence $\mathbf{e}'^T F = 0$. Similarly $\mathbf{l}^T\mathbf{e} = \mathbf{x}'^T F\mathbf{e} = 0 \ \forall \mathbf{x}'$, hence $F\mathbf{e} = 0$.
- The SVD (*Singular Value Decomposition*) of F is given as

$$F = U \ diag(\sigma_1, \sigma_2, 0) \ V^T,$$

where $U = [\mathbf{u}_1, \mathbf{u}_2, \mathbf{e}']$, $V = [\mathbf{v}_1, \mathbf{v}_2, \mathbf{e}]$. Thus finding the column in V that corresponds to the zero singular value gives a simple method of computation of the epipoles from the fundamental matrix.
- For cameras with some vergence (epipoles not at infinity) to give camera projection matrices: $P = K[I|0]$ and $P' = K'[R|t]$, then we have $F = K'^{-T}[t]_\times RK^{-1} = [K't]_\times K'RK^{-1} = K'^{-T}RK^T[KR^Tt]_\times$ [38].

2.5.3 The Fundamental Matrix for Pure Translation

If the two identical cameras ($K = K'$) are separated by a pure translation ($R = I$), the fundamental matrix has a simple form, which can be shown to be [38]

$$F = [Kt]_x = [\mathbf{e}']_x = \begin{bmatrix} 0 & -e'_z & e'_y \\ e'_z & 0 & -e'_x \\ -e'_y & e'_x & 0 \end{bmatrix}.$$

In this case, the epipoles are at the same location in both images. If the translation is parallel to the image plane, the epipoles are at infinity with $e_z = e'_z = 0$ and the epipolar lines are parallel in both images. When discussing rectilinear stereo rigs and rectification later, we will be particularly interested in the case when the translation is parallel to the camera's x-axis, in which case the epipolar lines are parallel and horizontal and thus correspond to image scan (raster) lines. In this case $\mathbf{e}' = [1, 0, 0]^T$ and the fundamental matrix is

$$F = \begin{bmatrix} 0 & 0 & 0 \\ 0 & 0 & -1 \\ 0 & 1 & 0 \end{bmatrix}$$

and hence the relationship between corresponding points $\mathbf{x}$ and $\mathbf{x}'$ is given by $\mathbf{x}'^T \mathbf{F} \mathbf{x} = 0$ which reduces to $y = y'$.

2.5.4   Computation of the Fundamental Matrix

As the fundamental matrix is expressed in terms of corresponding image points, $\mathbf{F}$ can be computed from image correspondences alone. No camera calibration information is needed, and pixel coordinates are used directly. Note that there are degenerate cases in the estimation of $\mathbf{F}$. These occur in two common and well-known instances: (i) when the relative pose between the two views can be described by a pure rotation and (ii) when the scene is planar. For now we consider scenarios where such degeneracies do not occur and we return to them later.

By expanding $\mathbf{x}'^T \mathbf{F} \mathbf{x} = 0$ where $\mathbf{x} = [x, y, 1]^T$ and $\mathbf{x}' = [x', y', 1]^T$ and

$$
\mathbf{F} = \begin{bmatrix} f_{11} & f_{12} & f_{13} \\ f_{21} & f_{22} & f_{23} \\ f_{31} & f_{32} & f_{33} \end{bmatrix}
$$

we obtain

$$
x'x f_{11} + x'y f_{12} + x' f_{13} + y'x f_{21} + y'y f_{22} + y' f_{23} + x f_{31} + y f_{32} + f_{33} = 0.
$$

As each feature correspondence provides one equation, for n correspondences, we get the following set of linear equations:

$$
\begin{bmatrix} x'_1 x_1, & x'_1 y_1, & x'_1, & y'_1 x_1, & y'_1 y_1, & y'_1, & x_1, & y_1, & 1 \\ \vdots & \vdots & \vdots & \vdots & \vdots & \vdots & \vdots & \vdots & \vdots \\ x'_n x_n, & x'_n y_n, & x'_n, & y'_n x_n, & y'_n y_n, & y'_n, & x_n, & y_n, & 1 \end{bmatrix} \begin{bmatrix} f_{11} \\ f_{12} \\ f_{13} \\ f_{21} \\ f_{22} \\ f_{23} \\ f_{31} \\ f_{32} \\ f_{33} \end{bmatrix} = \mathbf{0} \qquad (2.17)
$$

or more compactly,

$$
\mathbf{Af} = \mathbf{0},
$$

where $\mathbf{A}$ is termed the data matrix and $\mathbf{f}$ is the vector of unknown elements of $\mathbf{F}$.

The eight-point algorithm[12] [47] can be used as a very simple method to solve for
F linearly using eight correspondences. As this is a homogeneous set of equations,
f can only be determined up to a scale factor. With eight correspondences, Eq. 2.17
can be solved by linear methods, where the solution is the nullspace of A. (This can
be found from the column in V that corresponds to the *zero* singular value in D in the
singular value decomposition $A = UDV^T$.) However, a solution with a minimal set
of correspondences is often inaccurate, particularly if the correspondences are not
well spread over the images, or they may not provide enough strong constraints if
some of them are near-collinear or co-planar. It is preferable to use more than eight
correspondences, then the least squares solution for f is given by the singular vector
corresponding to the *smallest* singular value of A.

Note that this approach is similar to that for determining the homography matrix,
discussed earlier in Sect. 2.4.1. As with that approach, it is essential to normalize
the pixel coordinates of each image before applying SVD [38, 39], using a mean-
centering translation and a scaling so that the RMS distance of the points to the origin
is $\sqrt{2}$. When using homogeneous coordinates, this normalization can be applied using
matrix operators N, N', such that new *normalized* image coordinates are given as
$x_n = Nx$, $x'_n = N'x'$.

In general, the solution for F_n (the subscript n now denotes that we have based
the estimate on normalized image coordinates) will not have zero determinant (its
rank will be 3 and not 2), which means that the epipolar lines will not intersect at
a single point. In order to enforce this, we can apply SVD a second time, this time
to the initially estimated fundamental matrix so that $F_n = UDV^T$. We then set the
smallest singular value (in the third row and third column of D) to zero to produce
matrix D' and update the estimate of the fundamental matrix as $F_n = UD'V^T$.

Of course, the estimate of F_n maps points to epipolar lines in the normalized
image space. If we wish to search for correspondences within the original image
space, we need to de-normalize the fundamental matrix estimate as $F = N'^T F_n N$.

Typically, there are many correspondences between a pair of images, including
mostly inliers but also some outliers. This is inevitable, since matching is a local
search and ambiguous matches exist, which will be discussed further in Sect. 2.7.
Various robust methods for estimating the fundamental matrix, which address the
highly corrupting effect of outliers, are compared in [86]. In order to compute F
from these correspondences automatically, a common method is to use a robust
statistics technique called Random Sample Consensus (RANSAC) [32], which we
now outline:

1. Extract features in both images, for example, from a corner detector [37].
2. Perform feature matching between images (usually over a local area neighborhood) to obtain a set of potential matches or *putative correspondences*.
3. Repeat the following steps N times:

   - Select eight putative correspondences randomly.
   - Compute F using these eight points, as described above.

---

[12]There are several other approaches, such as the seven-point algorithm.

Table 2.1 Number of samples required to get at least one good sample with 99% probability for various sample sizes s and outlier fraction ϵ.

Sample size s	$\epsilon = 10\%$	$\epsilon = 20\%$	$\epsilon = 30\%$	$\epsilon = 40\%$	$\epsilon = 50\%$
4	5	9	17	34	72
5	6	12	26	57	146
6	7	16	37	97	293
7	8	20	54	163	588
8	9	26	78	272	1177

- Find the number of inliers[13] that support F.

4. Find the F with the highest number of inliers (largest support) among the N trials.
5. Use this F to look for additional matches outside the search range used for the original set of putative correspondences.
6. Re-compute a least squares estimate of F using all inliers.

Note that re-computing F in the final step may change the set of inliers, as the epipolar lines are adjusted. Thus, a possible refinement is to iterate computation of a linear least squares estimate of F and its inliers, until a stable set of inliers is achieved or some maximum number of iterations is reached. The refinement achieved is often considered to be not worth the additional computational expense if processing time is considered important or if the estimate of F is to be used as the starting point for more advanced iterative non-linear refinement techniques, described later.

In the RANSAC approach, N is the number of trials (putative F computations) needed to get at least one good sample with a high probability (e.g., 99%). How large should N be? The probability p of getting a good sample is given by

$$p = 1 - (1 - (1 - \epsilon)^s)^N,$$

where ϵ is the fraction of outliers (incorrect feature correspondences) and s is the number of correspondences selected for each trial. The above equation can be re-arranged as

$$N = \frac{log(1 - p)}{log(1 - (1 - \epsilon)^s)}. \tag{2.18}$$

The number of samples required for various sample sizes and outlier fractions based on Eq. 2.18 are shown in Table 2.1. It can be seen that the number of samples gets higher as the outlier fraction increases.

By repeatedly selecting a group of correspondences, the inlier support would be high for a correct hypothesis in which all the correspondences within the sample

---

[13] An inlier is a putative correspondence that lies within some threshold of its expected position predicted by F. In other words, image points must lie within a threshold from their epipolar lines generated by F.

size, s, are correct. This allows the robust removal of outliers and the computation of F using inliers only. As the fraction of outliers may not be known in advance, an adaptive RANSAC method can be used where the number of outliers at each iteration is used to re-compute the total number of iterations required.

As the fundamental matrix has only seven degrees of freedom, a minimum of seven correspondences are required to compute F. When there are only seven correspondences, $det(\mathsf{F}) = 0$ constraint also needs to be imposed, resulting in a cubic equation to solve, and hence may produce up to three solutions and all three must be tested for support. The advantage of using seven correspondences is that fewer trials are required to achieve the same probability of getting a good sample, as illustrated in Table 2.1.

Fundamental matrix refinement techniques are often based on the Levenberg–Marquardt algorithm, such that some non-linear cost function is minimized. For example, a geometric cost function can be formulated as the sum of the squared distances between image points and the epipolar lines generated from their associated corresponding points and the estimate of F. This is averaged over both points in a correspondence and over all corresponding points (i.e., all those that agree with the estimate of F). The minimization can be expressed as

$$\mathsf{F} = \min_{\mathsf{F}} \left(\frac{1}{N} \Sigma_{i=1}^{N} \left(d(\mathbf{x}'_i, \, \mathsf{F}\mathbf{x}_i)^2 + d(\mathbf{x}_i, \, \mathsf{F}^T\mathbf{x}'_i)^2 \right) \right),$$

where $d(\mathbf{x}, \mathbf{l})$ is the distance of a point $\mathbf{x}$ to a line $\mathbf{l}$, expressed in pixels. For more details of this and other non-linear refinement schemes, the reader is referred to [38].

2.5.5   Two Views Separated by a Pure Rotation

If two views are separated by a pure rotation around the camera center, the baseline is zero, the epipolar plane is not defined, and a useful fundamental matrix cannot be computed. In this case, the back-projected rays from each camera cannot form a triangulation to compute depth. This lack of depth information is intuitive because, under rotation, all points in the same direction move across the image in the same way, regardless of their depth. Furthermore, if the translation magnitude is small, the epipolar geometry is close to this degeneracy and computation of the fundamental matrix will be highly unstable.

In order to model the geometry of correspondences between two rotated views, a *homography*, described by a 3×3 matrix H, should be estimated instead. As described earlier, a homography is a projective transformation (*projectivity*) that maps points to points and lines to lines. For two identical cameras ($\mathsf{K} = \mathsf{K}'$), the scene-to-image projections are

$$\mathbf{x} = \mathsf{K}[\mathsf{I}|\mathbf{0}]\mathbf{X}, \quad \mathbf{x}' = \mathsf{K}[\mathsf{R}|\mathbf{0}]\mathbf{X}$$

Fig. 2.10 The homography induced by a plane π, where a point $\mathbf{x}$ in the first image can be transferred to the point $\mathbf{x}'$ in the second image

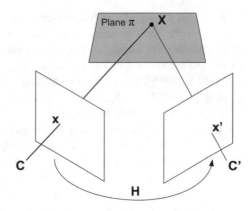

hence

$$\mathbf{x}' = \mathsf{KRK}^{-1}\mathbf{x} = \mathsf{H}\mathbf{x}. \tag{2.19}$$

We can think of this homography as a mapping of image coordinates onto normalized coordinates (centered on the principal point at a unit metric distance from the camera). These points are rotated and then multiplying by K generates the image coordinates on the focal plane of the second, rotated camera.

2.5.6 Two Views of a Planar Scene

A homography should also be estimated for planar scenes where correspondences cannot uniquely define the epipolar geometry and hence the fundamental matrix. Similar to Eq. 2.7, the *2D-to-2D* projection of the world plane π in Fig. 2.10 to the left and right images is given by

$$\lambda_x \mathbf{x} = \mathsf{H}_x \mathbf{X}, \qquad \lambda_{x'}\mathbf{x}' = \mathsf{H}_{x'}\mathbf{X},$$

where H_x, $\mathsf{H}_{x'}$ are 3×3 homography matrices (homographies) and $\mathbf{x}, \mathbf{x}'$ are homogeneous image coordinates. The planar homographies form a group, and hence we can form a composite homography as $\mathsf{H} = \mathsf{H}_{x'}\mathsf{H}_x^{-1}$ and it is straightforward to show that

$$\lambda\mathbf{x}' = \mathsf{H}\mathbf{x}.$$

Figure 2.10 illustrates this mapping from $\mathbf{x}$ to $\mathbf{x}'$ and we say that a homography is induced by the plane π. Homography estimation follows the same approach as was described in Sect. 2.4.1 for a scene-to-image planar homography (replacing $\mathbf{X}$ with $\mathbf{x}$ and $\mathbf{x}$ with $\mathbf{x}'$ in Eqs. 2.8 to 2.10).

Note that a minimum of four correspondences (no three points collinear in either image) are required because, for the homography, each correspondence generates a pair of constraints. Larger numbers of correspondences allow a least squares solution to an over-determined system of linear equations. Again suitable normalizations are required before SVD is applied to determine the homography.

A RANSAC-based technique can also be used to handle outliers, similar to the fundamental matrix estimation method described in Sect. 2.5.4. By repeatedly selecting the minimal set of four correspondences randomly to compute H and counting the number of inliers, the H with the largest number of inliers can be chosen. Additional matches that are not in the original set of putative correspondences can be obtained using the best H. Then, H can be re-computed using all supporting matches in a linear least squares minimization using SVD.

Finally, we note that, as in the case of the fundamental matrix, a non-linear optimization can be applied to refine the homography solution, if required by the application. The interested reader is referred to [38] for the details of the geometric cost function to be minimized.

2.6 Rectification

Typically, in a stereo rig, the cameras are horizontally displaced and rotated toward each other by an equal amount (verged), in order to overlap their fields of view. In this case, epipolar lines lie at a variety of angles across the two images, complicating the search for correspondences. In contrast, if these cameras had their principal axes parallel to each other (no vergence) and the two cameras had identical intrinsic parameters, conjugate (corresponding) epipolar lines would lie along the same horizontal scanline in each image, as observed in Sect. 2.5.3. This configuration is known as a standard rectilinear stereo rig. Clearly, it is desirable to retain the improved stereo viewing volume associated with verged cameras and yet have the simplicity of correspondence search associated with a rectilinear rig.

To achieve this, we can warp or *rectify* the raw images associated with the verged system such that corresponding epipolar lines become collinear and lie on the same scanline. A second advantage is that the equations for 3D reconstruction are very simply related to image disparity after image rectification, since they correspond to those of a simple rectilinear stereo rig. This triangulation computation is described later in the chapter.

Rectification can be achieved either with camera calibration information, for example, in a typical stereo application, or without calibration information, for example, in a typical structure from motion application. We discuss the calibrated case in the following subsection and give a brief mention of uncalibrated approaches in Sect. 2.6.2.

2.6.1   Rectification with Calibration Information

Here, we assume a calibrated stereo rig, where we know both the intrinsic and the extrinsic parameters. Knowing this calibration information gives a simple rectification approach, where we find an image mapping that generates, from the original images, a pair of images that would have been obtained from a rectilinear rig. Of course, the field of view of each image is still bound by the real original cameras, and so the rectified images tend to be a different shape than the originals (e.g., slightly trapezoidal in a verged stereo rig).

Depending on the lenses used and the required accuracy of the application, it may be considered necessary to correct for radial distortion, using estimated parameters k_1 and k_2 from the calibration. To do the correction, we employ Eq. 2.6 in order to compute the unknown, undistorted pixel coordinates, $[x, y]^T$, from the known distorted coordinates, $[x_d, y_d]^T$. There are various ways to solve this non-linear equation, such as approximation of the Taylor series with the first-order derivatives, a look-up table, or an iterative solution where the distorted pixel coordinates can be used as the initial estimate.

Assuming some vergence, we wish to map the image points onto a pair of (virtual) image planes that are parallel to the baseline and in the same plane. Thus we can use the homography structure in Eq. 2.19 that warps images between a pair of rotated views. Given that we already know the intrinsic camera parameters, we need to determine the rotation matrices associated with the rectification of the left and right views. We will assume that the origin of the stereo system is at the optical center of the left camera and calibration information gives [R, t] to define the rigid position of the right camera relative to this. To get the rotation matrix that we need to apply to image points of the left camera, we define the rectifying rotation matrix as

$$\mathsf{R}_{rect} = \begin{bmatrix} \mathbf{r}_1^T \\ \mathbf{r}_2^T \\ \mathbf{r}_3^T \end{bmatrix},$$

where $\mathbf{r}_i$, $i = 1 \ldots 3$ are a set of mutually orthogonal unit vectors. The first of these is in the direction of the epipole or, equivalently, the direction of the translation to the right camera, $\mathbf{t}$. (This ensures that epipolar lines will be horizontal in the rectified image.) Hence, the unit vector that we require is

$$\mathbf{r}_1 = \frac{\mathbf{t}}{||\mathbf{t}||}.$$

The second vector $\mathbf{r}_2$ is orthogonal to the first and obtained as the cross-product of $\mathbf{t}$ and the original left optical axis $[0, 0, 1]^T$ followed by a normalization to unit length to give

$$\mathbf{r}_2 = \frac{1}{\sqrt{t_x^2 + t_y^2}}[-t_y, t_x, 0]^T.$$

The third vector is mutually orthogonal to the first two and so is computed using the cross-product as $\mathbf{r}_3 = \mathbf{r}_1 \times \mathbf{r}_2$.

Given that the real right camera is rotated relative to the real left camera, we need to apply a rotation $\mathsf{R}\mathsf{R}_{rect}$ to the image points of the right camera. Hence, applying homographies to left and right image points, using the form of Eq. 2.19, we have

$$\mathbf{x}_{rect} = \mathsf{K}\mathsf{R}_{rect}\mathsf{K}^{-1}\mathbf{x}$$

$$\mathbf{x}'_{rect} = \mathsf{K}'\mathsf{R}\mathsf{R}_{rect}\mathsf{K}'^{-1}\mathbf{x}',$$

where K and K' are the 3×3 matrices containing the intrinsic camera parameters for the left and right cameras, respectively. Note that, even with the same make and model of camera, we may find that the focal lengths associated with K and K' are slightly different. Thus we need to scale one rectified image by the ratio of focal lengths in order to place them on the same focal plane.

As the rectified coordinates are, in general, not integer, *resampling* using some form of interpolation is required. The rectification is often implemented in reverse, so that the pixel values in the new image plane can be computed as a bilinear interpolation of the four closest pixels values in the old image plane. Rectified images give a very simple triangulation reconstruction procedure, which is described later in Sect. 2.8.1.2.

2.6.2 Rectification Without Calibration Information

When calibration information is not available, rectification can be achieved using an estimate of the fundamental matrix, which is computed from correspondences within the raw image data. A common approach is to compute a pair of rectifying homographies for the left and right images [38, 54] so that the fundamental matrix associated with the rectified images is the same form as that for a standard rectilinear rig and the "new cameras" have the same intrinsic camera parameters. Since such rectifying homographies map the epipoles to infinity ($[1, 0, 0]^T$), this approach fails when the epipole lies within the image. This situation is common in structure from motion problems, when the camera translates in the direction of its Z-axis. Several authors have tackled this problem by directly resampling the original images along their epipolar lines, which are specified by an estimated fundamental matrix. For example, the image is reparameterized using polar coordinates around the epipoles to reduce the search ambiguity to half epipolar lines [67, 68]. Figure 2.11 shows an example of an image pair before and after rectification for this scheme, where the corresponding left and right features lie on the same image row afterward. Specialized rectifications exist, for example, [17] that allow image matching over large forward translations of the camera although, in this scheme, rotations are not catered for.

(a)   (b)

Fig. 2.11 An image pair before rectification (**a**) and after rectification (**b**). The overlay shows that the corresponding left and right features lie on the same image row after rectification. Figure courtesy of [68]

2.7   Finding Correspondences

Finding correspondences is an essential step for 3D reconstruction from multiple views. The correspondence problem can be viewed as a search problem, which asks, given a pixel in the left image, which is the corresponding pixel in the right image? Of course there is something of a circular dependency here. We need to find correspondences to determine the epipolar geometry, yet we need the epipolar geometry to find (denser) correspondences in an efficient manner. The RANSAC sampling approach described earlier showed us how to break into this loop. Once we have the epipolar geometry constraint, the search space is reduced from a 2D search to the epipolar line only.

The following assumptions underpin most methods for finding correspondences in image pairs. These assumptions hold when the distance of the world point from the cameras is much larger than the baseline.

- Most scene points are visible from both viewpoints.
- Corresponding image regions are similar.

Two questions are involved: what is a suitable image element to match and what is a good similarity measure to adopt? There are two main classes of correspondence algorithms: correlation-based and feature-based methods. Correlation-based methods recover dense correspondences where the element to match is an image window centered on some pixel and the similarity measure is the correlation between the windows. Feature-based methods typically establish sparse correspondences where the element to match is an image feature and the similarity measure is the distance between descriptors of the image features.

2.7.1   Correlation-Based Methods

If the element to match is only a single image pixel, ambiguous matches exist. Therefore, windows are used for matching in correlation-based methods, and the similarity criterion is a measure of the correlation between the two windows. A larger

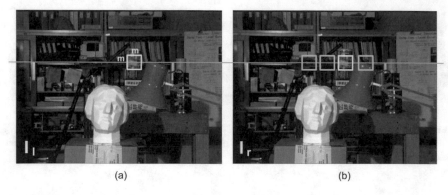

Fig. 2.12 Correlation-based methods look for the matching image window between the left and right rectified images. An m by m window centering at the pixel is used for correlation. (Raw image pair courtesy of the Middlebury Stereo Vision Page [74], originally sourced from Tsukuba University.)

window gives larger image context which can reduce the probability of ambiguities, but this has its own problems which will be discussed in Sect. 2.8.1.1. The selected correspondence is given by the window that maximizes a similarity criterion or minimizes a dissimilarity criterion within a search range. Once a match is found, the offset between the two windows can be computed, which is called the *disparity* from which the depth can be recovered. Some commonly used criteria for correlation-based methods are described next.

Based on the rectified images in Fig. 2.12, we define the window function, where m, an odd integer, is the image window size so that

$$W_m(x, y) = \{(u, v) | x - \frac{(m-1)}{2} \le u \le x + \frac{(m-1)}{2}, y - \frac{(m-1)}{2} \le v \le y + \frac{(m-1)}{2}\}.$$
$$(2.20)$$

The dissimilarity can be measured by the *Sum of Squared Differences* (SSD) cost, for instance, which is the intensity difference as a function of disparity d:

$$SSD(x, y, d) = \sum_{(u,v) \in W_m(x,y)} [I_l(u, v) - I_r(u - d, v)]^2,$$

where I_l and I_r refer to the intensities of the left and right images, respectively.

If two image windows correspond to the same world object, the pixel values of the windows should be similar, and hence the SSD value would be relatively small. As shown in Fig. 2.12, for each pixel in the left image, correlation-based methods would compare the SSD measure for pixels within a search range along the corresponding epipolar line in the right image. The disparity value that gives the lowest SSD value indicates the best match.

A slight variation of SSD is the *Sum of Absolute Differences* (SAD) where the absolute values of the differences are added instead of the squared values:

$$SAD(x, y, d) = \sum_{(u,v)\in W_m(x,y)} |I_l(u, v) - I_r(u - d, v)|.$$

This cost measure is less computationally expensive as it avoids the multiplication operation required for SSD. On the other hand, the SSD cost function penalizes the large intensity difference more due to the squaring operation.

The intensities between the two image windows may vary due to illumination changes and non-Lambertian reflection. Even if the two images are captured at the same time by two cameras with identical models, non-Lambertian reflection and differences in the gain and sensitivity can cause variation in the intensity. In these cases, SSD or SAD may not give a low value even for the correct matches. For these reasons, it is a good idea to normalize the pixels in each window. A first level of normalization would be to ensure that the intensities in each window are zero-mean. A second level of normalization would be to scale the zero-mean intensities so that they either have the same range or, preferably, unit variance. This can be achieved by dividing each pixel intensity by the standard deviation of window pixel intensities, after the zero-mean operation, i.e., normalized pixel intensities are given as

$$I_n = \frac{I - \bar{I}}{\sigma_I},$$

where $\bar{I}$ is the mean intensity and σ_I is the standard deviation of window intensities. While SSD measures the dissimilarity and hence the smaller the better, *Normalized Cross-Correlation* (NCC) measures the similarity and hence, the larger the better. Again, the pixel values in the image window are normalized first by subtracting the average intensity of the window so that only the relative variation would be correlated. The NCC measure is computed as follows:

$$NCC(x, y, d) = \frac{\sum_{(u,v)\in W_m(x,y)}(I_l(u, v) - \overline{I_l})(I_r(u - d, v) - \overline{I_r})}{\sqrt{\sum_{(u,v)\in W_m(x,y)}(I_l(u, v) - \overline{I_l})^2(I_r(u - d, v) - \overline{I_r})^2}},$$

where

$$\overline{I_l} = \frac{1}{m^2} \sum_{(u,v)\in W_m(x,y)} I_l(u, v), \quad \overline{I_r} = \frac{1}{m^2} \sum_{(u,v)\in W_m(x,y)} I_r(u, v).$$

2.7.2 Feature-Based Methods

Rather than matching each pixel, feature-based methods only search for correspondences to a sparse set of features, such as those located by a repeatable, well-localized interest point detector (e.g., a corner detector). Apart from locating the features, feature extraction algorithms also compute some sort of feature descriptors for their representation, which can be used for the similarity criterion. The correct correspondence is given by the most similar feature pair, the one with the minimum distance between the feature descriptors.

Stable features are preferred in feature-based methods to facilitate matching between images. Typical examples of image features are edge points, lines, and corners. For example, a feature descriptor for a line could contain the length, the orientation, coordinates of the mid-point, or the average contrast along the edge line. A problem with linear features is that the matching can be poorly localized along the length of a line particularly if a linear feature is fragmented (imagine a smaller fragment from the left image sliding along a larger fragment from the right image). This is known as the aperture problem, referring to the fact that a *local* match "looks through" a small aperture.

As a consequence, point-based features that are well localized in two mutually orthogonal directions have been preferred by researchers and practitioners in the field of computer vision. For example, the Harris corner detector [37] extracts points that differ as much as possible from neighboring points. This is achieved by looking for high curvatures in two mutually orthogonal directions, as the gradient is ill-defined in the neighborhood of corners. The corner strength or the grayscale values in a window region around each corner could be used as the descriptor. Another corner detector SUSAN [81] detects features based on the size, centroid, and second moments of the local areas. As it does not compute image derivatives, it is robust to noise and does not require image smoothing.

Wide baseline matching refers to the situation where the two camera views differ considerably. Here, matching has to operate successfully over more difficult conditions, since there are larger geometric and photometric variations between the images.

In recent years, many interest point detection algorithms have been proposed that are scale-invariant and viewpoint invariant to a certain extent which facilitates wide baseline matching. An interest point refers to an image feature that is stable under local and global perturbations, and the local image structure is rich in terms of local image contents. These features are often described by a distinctive feature descriptor which is used as the similarity criterion. They can be used even when epipolar geometry is not yet known, as such distinctive descriptors allow correspondences to be searched over the whole image relatively efficiently.

For example, the *Scale-Invariant Feature Transform* (SIFT) [48] and the *Speeded-Up Robust Feature* (SURF) [5] are two traditional features which were developed for image feature generation in object recognition applications. The SIFT feature is described by a local image vector with 128 elements, which is invariant to image translation, scaling, rotation, and partially invariant to illumination changes and affine or 3D projections. Fig. 2.13 shows an example of matching SIFT features across large baseline and viewpoint variation. It can be seen that most matches are correct, thanks to the invariance and discriminative nature of SIFT features. Extraction of such traditional features has been shown to be accurate and stable across views, but they are rather slow to compute compared to more recent binary descriptors.

Fig. 2.13 Wide baseline matching between two images with SIFT. The size and orientation of the squares correspond to the scale and orientation of the matching SIFT features. The color lines highlight some of the matches between the two images

These include BRIEF [15], BRISK [45], ORB [73], and FREAK [2], which are more suitable for real-time performance on portable hardware of relatively limited computational power.

2.8   3D Reconstruction

Different types of 3D reconstruction can be obtained based on the amount of *a priori* knowledge available, as illustrated in Table 2.2. The simplest method to recover 3D information is stereo where the intrinsic and extrinsic parameters are known, and the *absolute metric* 3D reconstruction can be obtained. This means we can determine the actual dimensions of structures, such as *height of door*=1.93 m.

For structure from motion, if no such prior information is available, only a projective 3D reconstruction can be obtained. This means that 3D structure is known only up to an arbitrary projective transformation so we know, for example, how many planar faces the object has and what point features are collinear, but we do not know anything about the scene dimensions and angular measurements within the scene. If intrinsic parameters are available, the projective 3D reconstruction can be upgraded to a metric reconstruction, where the 3D reconstruction is known up to a scale factor (i.e., a scaled version of the original scene). There is more detail to this hierarchy of

Table 2.2 Different Types of 3D Reconstruction

A Priori Knowledge	3D Reconstruction
Intrinsic and extrinsic parameters	Absolute 3D reconstruction
Intrinsic parameters only	Metric 3D reconstruction (up to a scale factor)
No information	Projective 3D reconstruction

reconstruction than we can present here (for example, *affine* 3D reconstruction lies between the metric and projective reconstructions) and we refer the interested reader to [38].

2.8.1 Stereo

Stereo vision refers to the ability to infer information on the 3D structure and distance of a scene from two or more images taken from different viewpoints. The disparities of all the image points form the *disparity map*, which can be displayed as an image. If the stereo system is calibrated, the disparity map can be converted to a 3D point cloud representing the scene.

The discussion here focuses on binocular stereo for two image views only. Please refer to [80] for a survey of multiple-view stereo methods that reconstruct a complete 3D model instead of just a single disparity map, which generates *range image* information only. In such a 3D imaging scenario, there is at most one depth per image plane point, rear-facing surfaces, and other self-occlusions are not imaged and the data is sometimes referred to as 2.5D.

2.8.1.1 Dense Stereo Matching

The aim of dense stereo matching is to compute disparity values for all the image points from which a dense 3D point cloud can be obtained. Correlation-based methods provide dense correspondences, while feature-based methods only provide sparse correspondences. Dense stereo matching is challenging as textureless regions do not provide information to distinguish the correct matches from the incorrect ones. The quality of correlation-based matching results depends highly on the amount of texture available in the images and the illumination conditions. Repetitive texture does not help though as the matching would be ambiguous.

Figure 2.14 shows a sample disparity map after dense stereo matching. The disparity map is shown in the middle with disparity values encoded in grayscale level. The brighter pixels refer to larger disparities which means the object is closer. For example, the ground pixels are brighter than the building pixels. An example of correspondences is highlighted in red in the figure. The pixel itself and the matching pixel are marked and linked to the right image. The length of the line corresponds to the disparity value highlighted in the disparity map.

Comparing image windows between two images could be ambiguous. Various matching constraints can be applied to help reduce the ambiguity, such as

- Epipolar constraint,
- Ordering constraint,
- Uniqueness constraint, and
- Disparity range constraint.

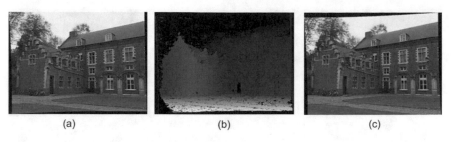

(a)   (b)   (c)

Fig. 2.14 A sample disparity map (**b**) obtained from the left image (**a**) and the right image (**c**). The disparity value for the pixel highlighted in red in the disparity map corresponds to the length of the line linking the matching features in the right image. Figure courtesy of [68]

The epipolar constraint reduces the search from 2D to the epipolar line only, as has been described in Sect. 2.5. The ordering constraint means that if pixel b is to the right of a in the left image, then the correct correspondences a' and b' must also follow the same order (i.e., b' is to the right of a' in the right image). This constraint fails if there is occlusion.

The uniqueness constraint means that each pixel has at most one corresponding pixel. In general, there is a one-to-one correspondence for each pixel, but there is none in the case of occlusion or noisy pixels. The left-right consistency check can be applied to ensure that the same match is obtained via both left-to-right and right-to-left matching.

The disparity range constraint limits the disparity search range according to the prior information of the expected scene. Maximum disparity sets how close the object can be, while the minimum disparity sets how far the object can be. Zero disparity refers to objects at infinity.

One important parameter for these correlation-based methods is the window size m in Eq. 2.20. While using a larger window size provides more intensity variation and hence more context for matching, this may cause problems around the occlusion area and at object boundaries, particularly for wide baseline matching.

Figure 2.15 shows the effect of window size on the resulting disparity map. The disparity map in the middle is for a window size of 3×3. It can be seen that, while it captures details well, it is very noisy, as the smaller window provides less information for matching. The disparity map on the right is for a window size of 15×15. It can be seen that while it looks very clean, the boundaries are not well defined. Moreover, the use of a larger window size typically increases the processing time as more pixels need to be correlated. The best window size is a trade-off between these two effects and is dependent on the level of fine detail in the scene.

For local methods, disparity computation at a given point depends on the intensity value within a local window only. The best matching window is indicated by the lowest dissimilarity measure or the highest similarity measure which uses information in the local region only. As pixels in an image are correlated (they may belong to the same object, for instance), global methods could improve the stereo matching quality by making use of information outside the local window region.

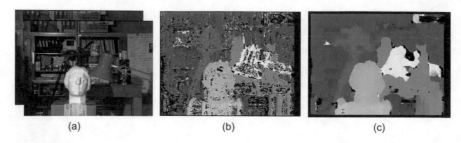

(a)   (b)   (c)

Fig. 2.15 The effect of window size on correlation-based methods: (**a**) input images (**b**) disparity map for a small correlation window (**c**) disparity map for a large correlation window. (Raw image pair courtesy of the Middlebury Stereo Vision Page [74], originally sourced from Tsukuba University.)

Global methods perform optimization across the image and are often formulated as an energy minimization problem. Dynamic programming approaches [6, 8, 19] compute the minimum-cost path through the matrix of all pairwise matching costs between two corresponding scanlines so that the best set of matches that satisfy the ordering constraint can be obtained. Dynamic programming utilizes information along each scanline independently; therefore, it may generate results that are not consistent across scanlines.

The *Graph Cuts* [12, 44] optimization technique makes use of information across the whole image and produces high-quality disparity maps. There is a trade-off between stereo matching quality and the processing time. Global methods such as this, max flow [72], and belief propagation [83, 84] produce better disparity maps than local methods, but they are computationally intensive.

Apart from the algorithm itself, the processing time also depends on the image resolution, the window size, and the disparity search range. The higher the image resolution, the more pixels need to be processed to produce the disparity map. The similarity measure needs to correlate more pixels for a larger window size. The disparity search range affects how many such measures need to be computed in order to find the correct match.

Hierarchical stereo matching methods have been proposed by down-sampling the original image into a pyramid [7, 70]. Dense stereo matching is first performed on the lowest resolution image, and disparity ranges can be propagated back to the finer resolution image afterward. This coarse-to-fine hierarchical approach allows fast computation to deal with a large disparity range, as a narrower disparity range can be used for the original image. Moreover, the more precise disparity search range helps to obtain better matches in the low texture areas.

The Middlebury webpage [74] provides standard datasets with ground truth information for researchers to benchmark their algorithms so that the performance of various algorithms can be evaluated and compared. A wide spectrum of dense stereo matching algorithms has been benchmarked, as illustrated in Fig. 2.16 [75]. Researchers can submit results of new algorithms which are ranked based on various metrics, such as RMS error between computed disparity map and ground truth map, percentage of bad matching pixels, and so on. It can be observed from Fig. 2.16 that

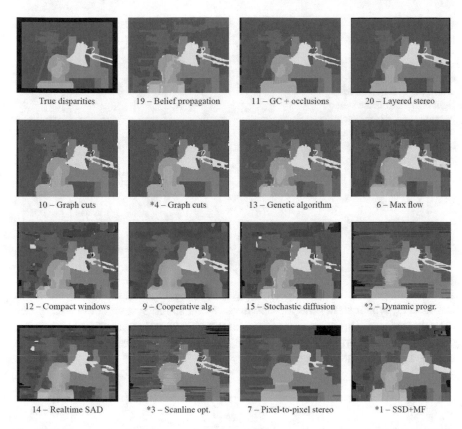

True disparities   19 – Belief propagation   11 – GC + occlusions   20 – Layered stereo

10 – Graph cuts   *4 – Graph cuts   13 – Genetic algorithm   6 – Max flow

12 – Compact windows   9 – Cooperative alg.   15 – Stochastic diffusion   *2 – Dynamic progr.

14 – Realtime SAD   *3 – Scanline opt.   7 – Pixel-to-pixel stereo   *1 – SSD+MF

Fig. 2.16 Comparative disparity maps for the top 15 dense stereo matching algorithms in [75] in decreasing order of performance. The top left disparity map is the ground truth. Performance here is measured as the percentage of bad matching pixels in regions where there are no occlusions. This varies from 1.15% in algorithm 19 to 5.23% in algorithm 1. Algorithms marked with a ∗ were implemented by the authors of [75], who present a wider range of algorithms in their publication. Figure courtesy of [75]

it is very difficult to understand algorithmic performance by qualitative inspection of disparity maps and the quantitative measures presented in [75] are required.

2.8.1.2   Triangulation

When the corresponding left and right image points are known, two rays from the camera centers through the left and right image points can be back-projected. The two rays and the stereo baseline lie on a plane (the epipolar plane) and form a triangle; hence, the reconstruction is termed "triangulation". Here, we describe triangulation for a rectilinear arrangement of two views or, equivalently, two rectified views.

Fig. 2.17 The stereo geometry becomes quite simple after image rectification. The world coordinate frame is arbitrarily centered on the right camera. B is the stereo baseline, and f is the focal length. Disparity is given by $d = x_c - x_c'$

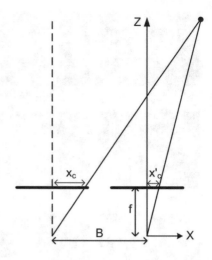

After image rectification, the stereo geometry becomes quite simple as shown in Fig. 2.17, which shows the top-down view of a stereo system composed of two pinhole cameras. The necessary parameters, such as baseline and focal length, are obtained from the original stereo calibration. The following two equations can be obtained based on the geometry:

$$x_c' = f\frac{X}{Z}$$

$$x_c = f\frac{X + B}{Z},$$

where x_c' and x_c are the corresponding horizontal image coordinates (in metric units) in the right and left images, respectively, f is the focal length, and B is the baseline distance.

Disparity d is defined as the difference in horizontal image coordinates between the corresponding left and right image points, given by

$$d = x_c - x_c' = \frac{fB}{Z}.$$

Therefore,

$$Z = \frac{fB}{d} \tag{2.21}$$

$$X = \frac{Zx_c'}{f}, \quad Y = \frac{Zy_c'}{f},$$

where y_c' is the vertical image coordinates in the right image.

This shows that the 3D world point can be computed once disparity is available: $(x'_c, y'_c, d) \mapsto (X, Y, Z)$. Disparity maps can be converted into depth maps using these equations to generate a 3D point cloud. It can be seen that triangulation is straightforward compared to the earlier stages of computing the two-view relations and finding correspondences.

Stereo matches are found by seeking the minimum of some cost functions across the disparity search range. This computes a set of disparity estimates in some discretized space, typically integer disparities, which may not be accurate enough for 3D recovery. 3D reconstruction using such quantized disparity maps leads to many thin layers of the scene. Interpolation can be applied to obtain sub-pixel disparity accuracy, such as fitting a curve to the SSD values for the neighboring pixels to find the peak of the curve, which provides more accurate 3D world coordinates.

By taking the derivatives of Eq. 2.21, the standard deviation of depth, which represents uncertainty of depth estimation, is given by

$$\Delta Z = \frac{Z^2}{Bf} \Delta d,$$

where Δd is the standard deviation of the disparity. This equation shows that the depth uncertainty increases quadratically with depth. Therefore, stereo systems typically are operated within a limited range. If the object is far away, the depth estimation becomes more uncertain. The depth error can be reduced by increasing the baseline, focal length, or image resolution. However, each of these has detrimental effects. For example, increasing the baseline makes matching harder as features appear less similar and causes viewed objects to self-occlude, increasing the focal length reduces the depth of field, and increasing image resolution increases processing time and data bandwidth requirements. Thus, we can see that design of stereo cameras typically involves a range of performance trade-offs, where trade-offs are selected according to the application requirements.

Figure 2.18 compares the depth uncertainty for three stereo configurations assuming a disparity standard deviation of 0.1 pixel. A stereo camera with higher resolution (dashed line) provides better accuracy than the one with lower resolution (dotted line). A stereo camera with a wider baseline (solid line) provides better accuracy than the one with a shorter baseline (dashed line).

A quick and simple method to evaluate the accuracy of 3D reconstruction is to place a highly textured planar target at various depths from the sensor, fit a least squares plane to the measurements, and measure the residual RMS error. In many cases, this gives us a good measure of depth repeatability, unless there are significant systematic errors, for example, from inaccurate calibration of stereo camera parameters. In this case, more sophisticated processes and ground truth measurement equipment are required. Capturing images of a target of known size and shape at various depths, such as a textured cube, can indicate how reconstruction performs when measuring in all three spatial dimensions.

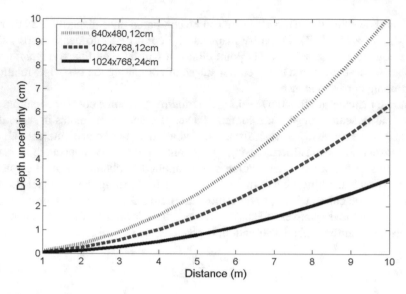

Fig. 2.18 A plot illustrating the stereo uncertainty with regard to image resolution and baseline distance. A larger baseline and higher resolution provide better accuracy, but each of these has other costs

2.8.2 Structure from Motion

Structure from motion (SfM) is the simultaneous recovery of 3D structure and camera relative pose (position and orientation) from image correspondences, and it refers to the situation where images are captured by a moving camera. There are three sub-problems in structure from motion.

- Correspondence: which elements of an image frame correspond to which elements of the next frame.
- Ego-motion and reconstruction: determination of camera motion (sometimes called ego-motion) and structure of the observed world.
- Segmentation: extraction of regions corresponding to one or more moving objects.

The third sub-problem is a relatively recent problem in structure from motion, where some objects in the scene may have moved between frames. For dynamic scenes, features belonging to moving objects could be identified and removed as outliers. Alternatively one could consider an environment to contain an unknown number (n) of independently moving objects and a static environment as $n + 1$ SfM sub-problems, each having their own F matrix. However, for the following discussion, we assume that the scene is static, without any moving objects.

By matching features between frames, we obtain at least eight correspondences from which the fundamental matrix can be recovered as described in Sect. 2.5.4. Without camera calibration parameters, only the projective reconstruction can be obtained where orthogonal lines in the world may not be reconstructed as orthogonal.

While this may be useful by itself, most practical applications require at least metric reconstruction where the reconstructed 3D model is a scaled version of the real scene.

Metric reconstruction requires camera intrinsic parameters which can be estimated from the images themselves using self-calibration (auto-calibration) techniques [38, 55] developed in recent years. Such methods exploit some prior information of the scene itself such as parallel lines, vanishing points, and so on. For better accuracy and more robustness, the camera intrinsic parameters can be obtained with a calibration procedure using a known calibration grid, as discussed in Sect. 2.4.

Once the camera intrinsic parameters are known, the essential matrix E can be computed from the fundamental matrix. According to Eq. 2.15, the motion can be recovered from E, where t is determined up to a scale factor only (since we can multiply Eq. 2.16 by an arbitrary non-zero scale factor). The physical insight into this is that the same image disparity between a pair of views can occur for a point close to the camera positions and a point n-times the distance away with n-times the translation. Effectively, we have scaled similar triangles in the triangulation-based reconstruction process.

SVD can be applied to extract t and R from E as follows [38]. Application of SVD gives the factorization $E = UDV^T$. By defining

$$W = \begin{bmatrix} 0 & -1 & 0 \\ 1 & 0 & 0 \\ 0 & 0 & 1 \end{bmatrix}, \quad Z = \begin{bmatrix} 0 & 1 & 0 \\ -1 & 0 & 0 \\ 0 & 0 & 0 \end{bmatrix},$$

the solution is given by

$$R = UWV^T \;\; or \;\; UW^TV^T$$

$$t = \pm u_3,$$

where u_3 is the third column of matrix U. With two possible choices of R and t, there are four possible solutions. Testing with a single point to determine if it is in front of both cameras is sufficient to decide among the four different solutions. For further details, please refer to [38].

Once t (up to scale) and R have been extracted from E, the sparse scene structure can be recovered by computing the intersection between the back-projected rays. In general, due to measurement noise, these will not intersect in 3D space. The simplest solution is to compute the mid-point of the shortest perpendicular line between the two rays. However, a refined solution is to choose a reconstructed scene point X, such that it minimizes the sum of square errors between the actual image positions and their positions predicted by their respective camera projection matrices. The scene structure is only determined up to a scale factor but in some applications this could be constrained, for example, if some measurement is known in the scene, or the translation can be estimated from the wheel odometry of a mobile robot. In summary, this method first estimates the intrinsic camera parameters (or uses an existing calibration) after which the extrinsic camera parameters are recovered. Both the intrinsic and extrinsic camera parameters are then used to compute the scene structure.

Alternatively, *bundle adjustment*[14] offers a more accurate method that simultaneously optimizes the 3D structure and the 6-DOF camera pose (extrinsic camera parameters) for each view in an image sequence [88]. Sometimes the intrinsic camera parameters are also refined in the procedure. This is a batch process that iteratively refines the camera parameters and the 3D structure in order to minimize the sum of the reprojection errors. (A reprojection error is the Euclidean distance between an image feature and its reprojection into the image plane after computing the 3D world coordinate and the camera pose associated with that image point.) Since a specific reprojection error is only dependent on its own scene point and own viewpoint, the structure of the equations is sparse. Thus, even though bundle adjustments are thought to be fairly computationally expensive, exploitation of sparse linear algebra algorithms can significantly mitigate this. Such procedures are referred to as *sparse bundle adjustment*.

Using consecutive video frames gives poor 3D accuracy due to the very short baseline. An image pair formed by a larger time increment would provide better 3D information. However, if the time increment is too large, the camera could have moved significantly and it would be harder to establish correct correspondences. One possible solution to this is to track features over several short baseline frames using a small, local area-based search, before computing 3D from a pair of frames tracked over a significantly longer baseline.

2.9 Deep Learning for Passive 3D Imaging

Recently, deep learning has proved to provide the best solutions to many problems in image classification, speech recognition, and natural language processing. Essentially, application of this powerful technology involves formulation of optimization problems that have well-behaved differentials, thus enabling gradient descent to function well. Deep learning has also been applied successfully to passive 3D imaging in two modalities: improving stereo matching and inferring depth from monocular imagery.

2.9.1 Deep Learning for Stereo Matching

A Convolutional Neural Network (CNN) was trained to predict how well two image patches match and it was used to compute the stereo matching cost [96]. The proposed network consisted of eight layers and achieved the best performance in the KITTI

---

[14]Bundle adjustment methods appeared several decades ago in the photogrammetry literature and are now used widely in the computer vision community.

dataset [35]. While [96] focused on comparing patches in narrow baseline stereo, a general similarity function was learned from image data in [95] to handle a broader set of appearance changes so that it can be used in more challenging set of applications including wide baseline stereo. Various neural network architectures such as Siamese and 2-channel models were explored, showing that they exhibited good performance and outperformed the state-of-the-art on wide baseline stereo matching. A dot product layer was exploited to compute the inner product between the two representations of a Siamese architecture, which achieved an order of magnitude faster computation [50]. The network was trained by treating the problem as multi-class classification where the classes are all possible disparities. As a result, correlations between different disparities can be captured implicitly, whereas the previous approaches performed independent binary predictions on image patches.

2.9.2   Deep Learning for Monocular Reconstruction

Depth was estimated from a single image by integrating both global and local information from various cues [27]. A multi-scale CNN approach was proposed by employing two deep network stacks: one for a coarse global prediction based on the entire image and another to refine the prediction locally. A scale-invariant error was applied to help measure depth relations rather than scale. The proposed method achieved state-of-the-art results on both NYU Depth and KITTI datasets. A deep structured learning scheme was proposed to learn the unary and pairwise potentials of continuous Conditional Random Field (CRF) in a unified deep CNN framework [46]. Using a faster model based on fully convolutional networks and a novel superpixel pooling method resulted in 10 times speedup while producing similar prediction accuracy. The proposed method outperformed state-of-the-art results on various indoor and outdoor scenes. While both [27] and [46] require vast quantities of ground truth depth data for training, an unsupervised approach was proposed in [36] to perform single image depth estimation without the use of ground truth depth data for training. Disparity images were generated by training the CNN with an image reconstruction loss using binocular stereo data. A novel training loss that enforced left–right consistency was employed to improve performance and robustness. The proposed method produced state-of-the-art results for monocular depth estimation on KITTI dataset, even outperforming supervised methods that have been trained with ground truth depth data. Recently, Wu et al. [92] described how to learn shape priors for monocular 3D completion. Their approach integrates deep generative models with adversarially learned shape priors, where the learned priors act as a regularizer, penalizing the model if its output is unrealistic.

2.10 Passive Multiple-View 3D Imaging Systems

Examples of passive multiple-view 3D imaging systems and their applications will now be presented, including stereo cameras, people counting, 3D modeling, and visual SLAM. 3D modeling systems generate photo-realistic 3D models from sequences of images and have a wide range of applications. For mobile robot applications, passive multiple-view 3D imaging systems are used for localization, building maps, and obstacle avoidance.

2.10.1 Stereo Cameras

Stereo cameras can be custom-built by mounting two individual cameras on a rigid platform separated by a fixed baseline. However, it is important that, for non-static scenes or for mobile platforms, the two cameras are synchronized so that they capture images at the same time. In order to obtain absolute 3D information, as discussed earlier in Table 2.2, the stereo camera needs to be calibrated to recover the intrinsic and extrinsic parameters. It is also critical that the relative camera pose does not change over time; otherwise, re-calibration would be required.

Commercial off-the-shelf (COTS) stereo vision systems have been emerging in recent years. These cameras often have a fixed baseline and are pre-calibrated by the vendor. Typically, they are nicely packaged and convenient to use. There are a number of pre-calibrated COTS stereo camera available such as Tara from E-con Systems with 6 cm baseline [26] and DUO MC from Code Laboratories with 3 cm baseline [25]. The FLIR Bumblebee camera [33] is another example with 12 cm baseline, which comes pre-calibrated, and an application programming interface (API) is provided to configure the camera and grab images, as well as rectify the images and perform dense stereo matching. FLIR also offers Bumblebee XB3 which is a three-sensor multi-baseline stereo camera which has both 12 cm and 24 cm baselines available for stereo processing. The wide baseline provides more precision at longer range, while the narrow baseline improves close range matching and minimum-range limitation.

It is desirable to obtain disparity maps in real time in many applications, for example, obstacle detection for mobile robots. Dense stereo matching can be highly parallelized; therefore, such algorithms are highly suitable to run on graphics processing units (GPUs) to free up the CPU for other tasks. GPUs have a parallel throughput architecture that supports executing many concurrent threads, providing immense speedup for highly parallelized algorithms. A dense stereo matching algorithm has been implemented on a commodity graphics card [94] to perform several hundred millions of disparity evaluations per second. This corresponds to 20 Hz for 512×512 image resolution with 32 disparity search range.

Stereolabs ZED stereo camera [82] is a stereo camera with 12 cm baseline for depth sensing and motion tracking. It relies on the use of NVIDIA GPU for processing and provides real-time depth data as well as camera pose. Stereolabs also offers a mini

Fig. 2.19 FLIR Bumblebee XB3 stereo camera with three cameras provides both narrow and wide baseline configurations (left) and Stereolabs ZED stereo camera (right)

Fig. 2.20 Examples of hazard detection using stereo images: a truck (left) and a person (right). Hazards are shown in red on the hazard map

version with 6 cm baseline for augmented reality application. Two of the COTS stereo cameras mentioned are shown in Fig. 2.19.

Stereo cameras are often used for obstacle/hazard detection in mobile robots as they can capture the 3D scene instantaneously. Figure 2.20 shows the stereo images from Bumblebee XB3 and the resulting hazard maps for a truck and a person, respectively. Correlation-based matching is performed to generate a dense 3D point cloud. Clusters of point cloud that are above the ground plane are considered as hazards.

2.10.2   People Counting

People counting for retail analytics is a key market for passive stereo cameras. The stereo cameras are mounted on the ceiling of retail store entrances, pointing down to count the number of people walking in and out of the store. Based on the disparity or 3D point cloud, people are detected and tracked as they walk across the camera field-of-view. Enter/exit counts are incremented when the tracks cross a pre-defined count line. Such information can be used to generate retail analytics such as conversion rates (proportion of customers who make a purchase), to optimize staff scheduling, and so on.

Stereo cameras provide better counting accuracy than monocular cameras, as they are more tolerant of lighting changes and can avoid counting shadows. Moreover, the 3D data can be used to distinguish between people and shopping carts as well as between adults and children. Currently, there are a number of successful stereo-based

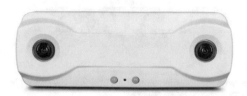 

Fig. 2.21 Examples of stereo-based people counters for retail analytics: FLIR Brickstream camera (left) and Xovis PC2 camera (right)

people counters offered by various vendors including FLIR, Xovis, Axper, and Hella. Two of these are shown in Fig. 2.21.

2.10.3 3D Modeling

The creation of photo-realistic 3D models of observed scenes has been an active research topic for many years. Such 3D models are very useful for both visualization and measurements in various applications such as planetary rovers, defense, mining, forensics, archaeology, and virtual reality.

Pollefeys et al. [68] and Nister [60] presented systems which create surface models from a sequence of images taken with a hand-held video camera. The camera motion is recovered by matching corner features in the image sequence. Dense stereo matching is carried out between the frames. The input images are used as surface texture to produce photo-realistic 3D models. These monocular approaches only output a scaled version of the original scene but can be scaled with some prior information. Moreover, it requires a long processing time.

The objective of the DARPA Urbanscape project [56] is to develop a real-time data collection and processing system for the automatic geo-registered 3D reconstruction of urban scenes from video data. Multiple video streams as well as *Global Positioning System* (GPS) and *Inertial Navigation System* (INS) measurements are collected to reconstruct photo-realistic 3D models and place them in geo-registered coordinates. An example of a large-scale 3D reconstruction is shown in Fig. 2.22.

A stereo camera-based 3D vision system is capable of quickly generating calibrated photo-realistic 3D models of unknown environments. *Instant Scene Modeler* (iSM) can process stereo image sequences captured by an unconstrained hand-held stereo camera [77]. Dense stereo matching is performed to obtain 3D point clouds from each stereo pair. 3D point clouds from each stereo pair are merged together to obtain a color 3D point cloud. Furthermore, a surface triangular mesh is generated from the point cloud. This is followed by texture mapping, which involves mapping image textures to the mesh triangles. As adjacent triangles in the mesh may use different texture images, seamlines may appear unless texture blending is performed.

Fig. 2.22 An example of 3D modeling of urban scene from the Urbanscape project. Figure courtesy of [56]

Fig. 2.23 The user points the stereo camera freely at the scene of interest (left), and the photo-realistic 3D model of the scene is generated (right). Figure adapted from [77]

The resulting photo-realistic 3D models can be visualized from different views, and absolute measurements can be performed on the models. Figure 2.23 shows the user pointing the hand-held COTS stereo camera to freely scan the scene and the resulting photo-realistic 3D model, which is a textured triangular mesh.

For autonomous vehicles and planetary rovers, the creation of 3D terrain models of the environment is useful for visualization and path planning [4]. Moreover, the 3D modeling process achieves significant data compression, allowing the transfer of data as compact surface models instead of raw images. This is beneficial for planetary rover exploration due to the limited bandwidth available. Figure 2.24 shows a photo-realistic 3D model created from a moving autonomous vehicle that traveled in a desert in Nevada.

One of the key technologies required for planetary rover navigation is the ability to sense the nearby 3D terrain. Stereo cameras are suitable for planetary exploration, thanks to their low power, low mass requirements, and the lack of moving parts. The NASA *Mars Exploration Rovers* (MERs), named *Opportunity* and *Spirit*, use passive stereo image processing to measure geometric information about the environment [52]. This is done by matching and triangulating pixels from a pair of rectified stereo images to generate a 3D point cloud. Figure 2.25 shows an example of the

Fig. 2.24 First image of a sequence captured by an autonomous rover in a desert in Nevada (left). Terrain model generated with virtual rover model inserted (right). Resulting terrain model and rover trajectory (bottom). Figure courtesy of [4]

Fig. 2.25 Mars Exploration Rover stereo image processing (left) and the reconstructed color 3D point cloud (right), with a virtual rover model inserted. Figure courtesy of [52]

stereo images captured and the color 3D point cloud generated which represents the imaged terrain.

Documenting crime scenes is a tedious process that requires the investigators to record vast amounts of data by using video, still cameras, and measuring devices, and by taking samples and recording observations. With passive 3D imaging systems, 3D models of the crime scene can be created quickly without much disturbance to the crime scene. The police can also perform additional measurements using the 3D model after the crime scene is released. The 3D model can potentially be shown in court so that the judge and the jury can understand the crime scene better. Figure 2.26

Fig. 2.26 3D model of a mock crime scene obtained with a hand-held stereo camera. Figure courtesy of [78]

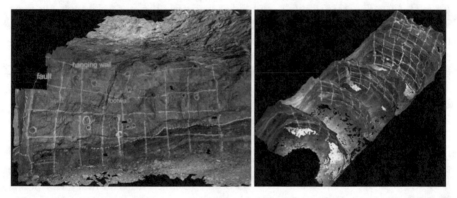

Fig. 2.27 Underground mine 3D model (left) and consecutive 3D models as the mine advances (right). The red and blue lines on the left are geological features annotated by geologists to help with the ore body modeling. Figure courtesy of [78]

shows a 3D reconstruction of a mock crime scene generated from a hand-held stereo sequence within minutes after acquisition [78].

Photo-realistic 3D models are useful for survey and geology in underground mining. The mine map can be updated after each daily drill/blast/ore removal cycle to minimize any deviation from the plan. In addition, the 3D models can also allow the mining companies to monitor how much ore is taken at each blast. Figure 2.27 shows a photo-realistic 3D model of an underground mine face annotated with geological features and consecutive 3D models of a mine tunnel created as the mine advances [78].

Airborne surveillance and reconnaissance are essential for successful military missions. *Unmanned Aerial Vehicles* (UAVs) are becoming the platform of choice

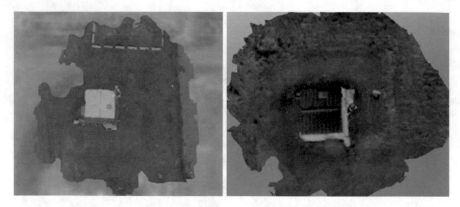

Fig. 2.28 3D reconstruction of a building on the ground using video (left) and using infrared video (right) captured by an UAV (Unmanned Aerial Vehicle). Figure courtesy of [76]

for such surveillance operations, and video cameras are among the most common sensors onboard UAVs. Photo-realistic 3D models can be generated from UAV video data to provide situational awareness as it is easier to understand the scene by visualizing it in 3D. The 3D model can be viewed from different perspectives and allow distance measurements and line-of-sight analysis. Figure 2.28 shows a 3D reconstruction of a building on the ground using video and infrared video captured by an UAV [76]. The photo-realistic 3D models are geo-referenced and can be visualized in 3D *Geographical Information System* (GIS) viewers such as Google Earth.

Deep learning has also been applied to 3D reconstruction. A novel recurrent neural network architecture was proposed for single- and multi-view 3D object reconstruction by learning a mapping from observations to their underlying 3D shape [18]. The network took one or more images of an object instance from arbitrary viewpoints to output a reconstruction of the object in the form of a 3D occupancy grid. Experimental results showed that the proposed framework outperformed the state-of-the-art method for single-view reconstruction. It worked well in situations where traditional SfM methods failed due to the lack of texture or wide baselines. An encoder–decoder network was proposed for single-view 3D object reconstruction with a novel projection loss defined by the perspective transformation [93]. The projection loss enabled unsupervised learning using 2D observation without ground truth 3D training data. A single network for multi-class 3D object reconstruction was trained, with generalization potential to unseen categories.

2.10.4 Visual SLAM

Mobile robot localization and mapping is the process of simultaneously tracking the position of a mobile robot relative to its environment and building a map of the

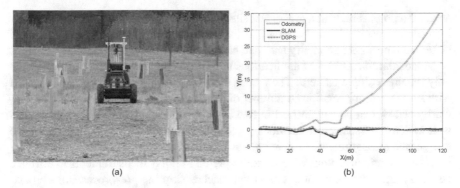

(a)   (b)

Fig. 2.29 (**a**) Autonomous rover on a gravel test site with obstacles (**b**) Comparison of the estimated path by SLAM, wheel odometry, and DGPS (Differential GPS). Figure courtesy of [4]

environment. Accurate localization is a prerequisite for building a good map and having an accurate map is essential for good localization. Therefore, *Simultaneous Localization and Mapping* (SLAM) is a critical underlying capability for successful mobile robot applications. To achieve a SLAM capability, high-resolution passive vision systems can capture images in milliseconds, and hence they are suitable for moving platforms such as mobile robots.

Stereo vision systems are commonly used on mobile robots, as they can measure the full six degrees of freedom (DOF) of the change in robot pose. This is known as visual odometry. By matching visual landmarks between frames to recover the robot motion, visual odometry is not affected by wheel slip and hence is more accurate than the wheel-based odometry. For outdoor robots with GPS receivers, visual odometry can also augment the GPS to provide better accuracy, and it is also valuable in environments where GPS signals are not available.

Unlike in 3D modeling where correlation-based dense stereo matching is typically performed, feature-based matching is sufficient for visual odometry and SLAM; indeed, it is preferable for real-time robotics applications, as it is computationally less expensive. Such features are used for localization, and a feature map is built at the same time.

The MERs *Opportunity* and *Spirit* are equipped with visual odometry capability [53]. An update to the rover's pose is computed by tracking the motion of autonomously selected terrain features between two pairs of stereo images. It has demonstrated good performance and successfully detected slip ratios as high as 125% even while driving on slopes as high as 31 degrees.

As SIFT features [48] are invariant to image translation, scaling, rotation, and fairly robust to illumination changes and affine or even mild projective deformation, they are suitable landmarks for robust SLAM. When the mobile robot moves around in an environment, landmarks are observed over time but from different angles, distances, or under different illuminations. SIFT features are extracted and matched between the stereo images to obtain 3D SIFT landmarks which are used for indoor SLAM [79] and for outdoor SLAM [4]. Figure 2.29 shows a field trial of an autonomous vehicle at a gravel test site with obstacles and a comparison of rover localization results. It can be seen that the vision-based SLAM trajectory is much better than the wheel odometry and matches well with the *Differential GPS* (DGPS).

Monocular visual SLAM applications have been emerging in recent years which only require a single camera. The results are up to a scale factor but can be scaled with some prior information. A number of different approaches have gained in popularity, which can be categorized in two axes: direct versus indirect approaches as well as dense versus sparse methods [29]. Indirect approaches first pre-process the raw sensor measurements to generate an intermediate representation such as feature correspondences, which are then interpreted as noisy measurements to estimate geometry and camera motion. Direct approaches skip the pre-processing step and use the actual sensor values directly as measurement. In the case of passive vision, direct approaches optimize a photometric error, while indirect approaches optimize a geometric error.

Dense methods use and reconstruct all pixels in the 2D image, while sparse methods use and reconstruct only a selected set of feature points such as corners. In sparse formulation, there is no notion of neighborhood, as feature positions are conditionally independent given the camera poses and intrinsics. Dense methods exploit the connectedness of the image region to formulate a geometry prior, favoring smoothness, which is often necessary to make a dense world model. Such a geometric prior may introduce bias which could reduce long-term large-scale accuracy and may make it infeasible to have a consistent joint optimization in real time. The various visual SLAM approaches can be categorized into the following four categories:

- Sparse + indirect approach is the most widely used formulation where keypoint correspondences are used to estimate 3D geometry, such as MonoSLAM [23], PTAM [43], and ORB-SLAM [57].
- Dense + indirect approach estimates 3D geometry from a dense, regularized optical flow field, such as [71].
- Dense + direct approach employs a photometric error as well as a geometric prior to estimate dense geometry, such as DTAM [59] and LSD-SLAM [28].
- Sparse + direct approach optimizes a photometric error without incorporating a geometric prior, such as [29].

Given the recent advances in depth prediction from monocular imagery using CNNs, researchers have investigated how to improve visual SLAM with deep learning. CNN-predicted dense depth maps were fused together with depth measurements obtained from direct monocular SLAM [85]. The fusion scheme prioritized CNN depth prediction in image locations where monocular SLAM approaches tend to fail. CNN depth prediction also estimated the absolute scale of the reconstruction, hence overcoming one of the major limitations of monocular SLAM.

2.11   Passive Versus Active 3D Imaging Systems

Before concluding, we briefly compare passive multiple-view 3D imaging systems and their active imaging counterpart, as a bridge between this and the following chapter. Passive systems do not emit any illumination and only perceive the ambient light reflected from the scene. Typically, this is reflected sunlight when outdoors, or the light, reflected from standard room lighting when indoors. On the other hand, active systems include their own source of illumination, which has two main benefits:

- 3D structure can be determined in smooth, textureless regions. For passive stereo, it is impossible to extract features and correspondences in such circumstances.
- The correspondence problem either disappears, for example, a single spot of light may be projected at any one time, or is greatly simplified by controlling the structure of the projected light.

The geometric principle of determining depth from a light (or other EMR) projector (e.g., laser) and a camera is identical to the passive binocular stereo situation. The physical difference is that, instead of using triangulation applied to a pair of back-projected rays, we apply triangulation to the axis of the projected light and a single back-projected ray.

Compared with active approaches, passive systems are computationally intensive as the 3D data is computed from processing the images and matching image features. Moreover, the depth data could be noisier as it relies on the natural texture in the scene and ambient lighting condition. Unlike active scanning systems such as laser scanners, cameras could capture complete images in milliseconds; hence, they can be used as mobile sensors or operate in dynamic environments. The cost, size, mass, and power requirements of cameras are generally lower than those of active sensors.

2.12   Concluding Remarks

One of the key challenges for 3D vision researchers is to develop algorithms to recover accurate 3D information robustly under a wide range of illumination conditions, a task that can be done by humans so effortlessly. While 3D passive vision algorithms have been maturing over the years, this is still an active topic in the research community and at major computer vision conferences. Many algorithms perform reasonably well with test data but there are still challenges to handle scenes with uncontrolled illumination. Deep learning, in the form of many-layered neural networks, continues to have a big impact on this area. Passive 3D imaging systems are becoming more prevalent as cameras are getting cheaper and computers are fast enough to handle the intensive processing requirements. Thanks to hardware acceleration and GPUs, embedded real-time applications are becoming more robust, leading to a growing number of real-world applications.

After working through this chapter, you should be able to

- Explain the fundamental concepts and challenges of passive 3D imaging systems.
- Explain the principles of epipolar geometry.
- Solve the correspondence problem by correlation-based and feature-based techniques (using off-the-shelf feature extractors).
- Estimate the fundamental matrix from correspondences.
- Perform dense stereo matching and compute a 3D point cloud.
- Explain the principles of structure from motion.
- Explain how deep learning can be applied to 3D imaging.
- Provide example applications of passive 3D imaging systems.

2.13 Further Reading

Two-view geometry is studied extensively in [38], which also covers the equivalent of epipolar geometry for three or more images. The eight-point algorithm was proposed in [39] to compute the fundamental matrix, while the five-point algorithm was proposed in [61] for calibrated cameras. Reference [88] provides a good tutorial and survey on bundle adjustment, which is also covered in textbooks [30, 38] and a recent survey article [55].

Surveys such as [75] serve as a guide to the extensive literature on stereo imaging. Structure from motion is extensively covered in review articles such as [55]. A step-by-step guide to 3D modeling from images is described in detail in [51]. Non-rigid structure from motion for dynamic scenes is discussed in [87].

Multiple-view 3D vision, particularly in the context of deep learning, continues to be highly active research topics, and some of the major computer vision conferences include the International Conference on Computer Vision (ICCV), IEEE Conference on Computer Vision and Pattern Recognition (CVPR), and the European Conference on Computer Vision (ECCV). Some of the relevant major journals include International Journal of Computer Vision (IJCV), IEEE Transactions on Pattern Analysis and Machine Intelligence (PAMI), and Image and Vision Computing (IVC).

The following websites provide comprehensive online resources for computer vision including 3D passive vision topics and are being updated regularly.

- CVonline [31] provides an online compendium of computer vision.
- VisionBib.Com [69] contains annotated bibliography on a wide range of computer vision topics, as well as references to available datasets.

Due to limited space, there are areas of passive 3D imaging that we were unable to cover. For example, we have assumed that we are using imaging in the medium of air, yet many applications require underwater imaging, such as Unmanned Underwater Vehicles (UUVs). A useful function of such UUVs is to perform a reconstruction of the seabed or some artefact on the seabed, such as a shipwreck. This poses several problems that we have not considered, such as the refractive properties of the air–glass–water interface affecting the camera's intrinsic parameters. Furthermore, images are blurred due to light scattering, and visibility is often poor due to suspended particles. An interesting case study of the Xlendi Wreck in Malta is provided by Drap et al. [24], which employs underwater photogrammetry and object modeling.

Also, we did not extensively detail methods that can deal with missing parts due to insufficient texture for multiple-view matching, or due to self-occlusion. In applications when the class of object to be reconstructed is known, it is possible to learn a shape prior, for example, as a 3D Morphable Model (3DMM). Given a 3DMM, missing parts can then be inferred from the reconstructed parts. Such models are discussed extensively in a later chapter of this book. Furthermore, recent work has applied deep learning to the combined problem of monocular reconstruction and shape completion [92].

2.14   Software Resources

As 3D reconstruction is now a mature technology, there are a variety of software packages that can perform 3D reconstruction from a series of 2D images. Open-source 3D modeling packages include OpenMVG [63] and OpenMVS [64]. Open Multiple-View Geometry (OpenMVG) is a library for computer vision scientists targeted the multiple-view geometry community. It provides an easy access to classical problem solvers in multiple-view geometry, such as *structure from motion*, which recovers camera poses and a sparse 3D point cloud from a set of input images. Open Multi-View Stereo (OpenMVS) focuses on the last part of the reconstruction pipeline by providing a set of algorithms to recover the full surface of the scene. The input is a set of camera poses plus the sparse point cloud, and the output is a photo-realistic 3D model in the form of a textured mesh. There are other free open-source 3D reconstruction software packages, such as AliceVision's *Meshroom* [3]. Furthermore, *OpenCV* [62] is a free general open-source computer vision library that is useful in a wide range of passive 3D applications. There are several commercial 3D reconstruction packages available, sometimes called *photogrammetry* packages and sometimes with educational licenses. For example, the Agisoft company has the *Metashape* package [1], which is a development of their earlier *Photoscan* product. Another is *Pix4D* [66], which is targeted at drone-based aerial mapping.

2.15   Questions

1. What are the differences between passive and active 3D vision systems?
2. Name two approaches to recover 3D from single images and two approaches to recover 3D from multiple images.
3. What is the epipolar constraint and how can you use it to speed up the search for correspondences?
4. What are the differences between essential and fundamental matrices?
5. What is the purpose of rectification?

6. What are the differences between correlation-based and feature-based methods for finding correspondences?
7. What are the differences between local and global methods for dense stereo matching?
8. What are the differences between stereo and structure from motion?
9. What are the factors that affect the accuracy of stereo vision systems?
10. What are two use cases of applying deep learning to 3D imaging?

2.16 Exercises

Experimenting with stereo imaging requires that you have two images of a scene from slightly different viewpoints, with a good overlap between the views, and a significant number of well-distributed corner features that can be matched. You will also need a corner detector. There are many stereo image pairs and corner detector implementations available on the web [62]. Of course, you can collect your own images either with a pre-packaged stereo camera or with a pair of standard digital cameras. The following programming exercises should be implemented in a language of your choice.

1. *Fundamental matrix with manual correspondences.* Run a corner detector on the image pair. Use a point-and-click GUI to manually label around 20 well-distributed correspondences. Compute the fundamental matrix and plot the conjugate pair of epipolar lines on the images for each correspondence. Experiment with different numbers and combinations of correspondences, using a minimum of eight in the eight-point algorithm. Observe and comment on the sensitivity of the epipolar lines with respect to the set of correspondences chosen.
2. *Fundamental matrix estimation with outlier removal.* Add 4 incorrect corner correspondences to your list of 20 correct ones. Observe the effect on the computed fundamental matrix and the associated (corrupted) epipolar lines. Augment your implementation of fundamental matrix estimation with the RANSAC algorithm. Use a graphical overlay on your images to show that RANSAC has correctly identified the outliers, and verify that the fundamental matrix and its associated epipolar lines can now be computed without the corrupting effect of the outliers.
3. *Automatic feature correspondences.* Implement a function to *automatically* match corners between two images according to the *Sum of Squared Differences* (SSD) measure. Also, implement a function for the *Normalized Cross-Correlation* (NCC) measure. Compare the matching results with test images of similar brightness and also of different brightnesses.
4. *Fundamental matrix from automatic correspondences.* Use your fundamental matrix computation (with RANSAC) with the automatic feature correspondences. Determine the positions of the epipoles and, again, plot the epipolar lines.

The following additional exercises require the use of a stereo rig, which could be a pre-packaged stereo pair or a homemade rig with a pair of standard digital cameras. The cameras should have a small amount of vergence to overlap their fields of view.

5. *Calibration.* Create your own calibration target by printing off a chessboard pattern and pasting it to a flat piece of wood. Use a point-and-click GUI to semi-automate the corner correspondences between the calibration target and a set of captured calibration images. Implement a camera calibration procedure for a stereo pair to determine the intrinsic and extrinsic parameters of the stereo rig. If you have less time available, you may choose to use some of the calibration libraries available on the web [11, 62].

6. *Rectification.* Compute an image warping (homography) to apply to each image in the stereo image pair, such that conjugate epipolar lines are horizontal (parallel to the x-axis) and have the same y-coordinate. Plot a set of epipolar lines to check that this rectification is correct.

7. *Dense stereo matching.* Implement a function to perform local dense stereo matching between left and right rectified images, using NCC as the similarity measure, and hence generate a disparity map for the stereo pair. Capture stereo images for a selection of scenes with varying amounts of texture within them and at varying distances from the cameras, and compare their disparity maps.

8. *3D reconstruction.* Implement a function to perform a 3D reconstruction from your disparity maps and camera calibration information. Use a graphics tool to visualize the reconstructions. Comment on the performance of the reconstructions for different scenes and for different distances from the stereo rig.

References

1. Agisoft: Agisoft's Metashape. Photogrammetric processing of digital images and 3D spatial data generation. https://www.agisoft.com (2020). Accessed 3 Jan 2020
2. Alahi, A., Ortiz, R., Vandergheynst, P.: FREAK: Fast retina keypoint. In: 2012 IEEE Conference on Computer Vision and Pattern Recognition, pp. 510–517 (2012)
3. AliceVision: AliceVision: Photogrammetric Computer Vision Framework. https://alicevision. org/#meshroom (2020). Accessed 3 Jan 2020
4. Barfoot, T., Se, S., Jasiobedzki, P.: Vision-based localization and terrain modelling for planetary rovers. In: A. Howard, E. Tunstel (eds.) Intelligence for Space Robotics, pp. 71–92. TSI Press, Beijing (2006)
5. Bay, H., Ess, A., Tuytelaars, T., Gool, L.V.: Speeded-up robust features (SURF). Comput. Vis. Image Underst. **110**(3), 346–359 (2008)
6. Belhumeur, P.N.: A bayesian approach to binocular steropsis. Int. J. Comput. Vis. **19**(3), 237–260 (1996)
7. Bergen, J.R., Anandan, P., Hanna, K.J., Hingorani, R.: Hierarchical model-based motion estimation. In: G. Sandini (ed.) Computer Vision— ECCV'92, pp. 237–252 (1992)
8. Birchfield, S., Tomasi, C.: Depth discontinuities by pixel-to-pixel stereo. Int. J. Comput. Vis. **35**(3), 269–293 (1999)
9. Blanz, V., Vetter, T.: Face recognition based on fitting a 3D morphable model. IEEE Trans. Pattern Anal. Mach. Intell. **25**(9), 1063–1074 (2003)

10. Booth, J., Roussos, A., Ponniah, A., Dunaway, D., Zafeiriou, S.: Large scale 3D morphable models. Int. J. Comput. Vis. **126**(2), 233–254 (2018)
11. Bouguet, J.Y.: Camera calibration toolbox for MATLAB. http://www.vision.caltech.edu/bouguetj/calib_doc/ (2015). Accessed 3 Jan 2020
12. Boykov, Y., Veksler, O., Zabih, R.: Fast approximate energy minimization via graph cuts. IEEE Trans. Pattern Anal. Mach. Intell. **23**(11), 1222–1239 (1999)
13. Brown, D.H.: Decentering distortion of lenses. Photom. Eng. **32**(3), 444–462 (1966)
14. Brown, D.H.: Close-range camera calibration. Photom. Eng. **37**(8), 855–866 (1971)
15. Calonder, M., Lepetit, V., Strecha, C., Fua, P.: BRIEF: Binary robust independent elementary features. In: Computer Vision—ECCV 2010, pp. 778–792. Springer, Berlin, Heidelberg (2010)
16. Chen, Z., Wu, C., Liu, Y., Pears, N.E.: 3D Euclidean reconstruction of buildings from uncalibrated image sequences. Int. J. Shape Modell. **10**(1), 115–131 (2004)
17. Chen, Z., Pears, N.E., Liang, B.: Monocular obstacle detection using reciprocal-polar rectification. Image Vis. Comput. **24**(12), 1301–1312 (2006)
18. Choy, C., Xu, D., Gwak, J., Chen, K., Savarese, S.: 3D-R2N2: A unified approach for single and multi-view 3D object reconstruction. In: European Conference on Computer Vision (ECCV), pp. 628–644 (2016)
19. Cox, I.J., Hingorani, S.L., Rao, S.B., Maggs, B.M.: A maximum likelihood stereo algorithm. Comput. Vis. Image Underst. **63**(3), 542–567 (1996)
20. Coxeter, H.: Projective Geometry, 2nd edn. Springer, Berlin (2003)
21. Criminisi, A., Reid, I., Zisserman, A.: Single view metrology. Int. J. Comput. Vis. **40**(2), 123–148 (2000)
22. Dai, H., Pears, N., Smith, W.A.P., Duncan, C.: A 3D morphable model of craniofacial shape and texture variation. In: IEEE International Conference on Computer Vision (ICCV), pp. 3104–3112 (2017)
23. Davison, A.J., Reid, I.D., Molton, N.D., Stasse, O.: MonoSLAM: Real-time single camera SLAM. IEEE Trans. Pattern Anal. Mach. Intell. **29**(6), 1052–1067 (2007)
24. Drap, P., Merad, D., Hijazi, B., Gaoua, L., Nawaf, M., Saccone, M., Chemisky, B., Seinturier, J., Sourisseau, J.C., Gambin, T., Castro, F.: Underwater photogrammetry and object modeling: A case study of xlendi wreck in malta. Sensors **15**, 30351–30384 (2015)
25. duo3d: The DUO MC ultra-compact, configurable stereo camera. https://duo3d.com/product/duo-mc-lv1 (2020). Accessed 3 Jan 2020
26. e-con systems: Tara—USB 3.0 Stereo Vision Camera. https://www.e-consystems.com/3D-USB-stereo-camera.asp (2020). Accessed 3 Jan 2020
27. Eigen, D., Puhrsch, C., Fergus, R.: Depth map prediction from a single image using a multi-scale deep network. In: Advances in Neural Information Processing Systems 27 (NIPS), pp. 2366–2374 (2014)
28. Engel, J., Schöps, T., Cremers, D.: LSD-SLAM: Large-scale direct monocular SLAM. In: Computer Vision – ECCV 2014, pp. 834–849. Springer International Publishing, Berlin (2014)
29. Engel, J., Koltun, V., Cremers, D.: Direct sparse odometry. IEEE Trans. Pattern Anal. Mach. Intell. **40**(3), 611–625 (2018)
30. Faugeras, O., Luong, Q.: The Geometry of Multiple Images. MIT Press, Cambridge, MA (2001)
31. Fischer, R.: CVonline: The Evolving, Distributed, Non-Proprietary, On-Line Compendium of Computer Vision. http://homepages.inf.ed.ac.uk/rbf/CVonline/ (1999–2020). Accessed 10 Mar 2020
32. Fischler, M., Bolles, R.: Random sample consensus: A paradigm for model fitting with applications to image analysis and automated cartography. Commun. ACM **24**(6), 381–395 (1981)
33. FLIR systems: Bumblebee 3D cameras. https://www.flir.com/iis/machine-vision/stereo-vision (2020). Accessed 10 Mar 2020
34. Garding, J.: Shape from texture for smooth curved surfaces in perspective projection. J. Math. Imaging Vis. **2**, 630–638 (1992)
35. Geiger, A., Lenz, P., Stiller, C., Urtasun, R.: Vision meets robotics: The kitti dataset. Int. J. Robot. Res. **32**, 1231–1237 (2013)

36. Godard, C., Mac Aodha, O., Brostow, G.J.: Unsupervised monocular depth estimation with left-right consistency. In: IEEE Conference on Computer Vision and Pattern Recognition (CVPR) (2017)
37. Harris, C., Stephens, M.: A combined corner and edge detector. In: Proceedings of the 4th Alvey Vision Conference, pp. 147–151 (1988)
38. Hartley, R.I., Zisserman, A.: Multiple View Geometry in Computer Vision, 2nd edn. Cambridge University Press, Cambridge. ISBN: 0521540518 (2004)
39. Hartley, R.I.: In defense of the eight-point algorithm. IEEE Trans. Pattern Anal. Mach. Intell. **19**(6), 580–593 (1997)
40. Horn, B.K.P., Brooks, M.J. (eds.): Shape from Shading. MIT Press, Cambridge, MA, USA (1989)
41. Horn, B.K., Schunck, B.G.: Determining optical flow. Artif. Intell. **17**(1), 185–203 (1981)
42. Huang, R., Smith, W.: A shape-from-shading framework for satisfying data-closeness and structure-preserving smoothness constraints. In: Proceedings of the British Machine Vision Conference (BMVC) (2009)
43. Klein, G., Murray, D.: Parallel tracking and mapping for small ar workspaces. In: 6th IEEE and ACM International Symposium on Mixed and Augmented Reality, pp. 225–234 (2007)
44. Kolmogorov, V., Zabih, R.: Computing visual correspondence with occlusions using graph cuts. In: Proceedings Eighth IEEE International Conference on Computer Vision. ICCV 2001, vol. 2, pp. 508–515 (2001)
45. Leutenegger, S., Chli, M., Siegwart, R.Y.: BRISK: Binary robust invariant scalable keypoints. In: 2011 International Conference on Computer Vision, pp. 2548–2555 (2011)
46. Liu, F., Shen, C., Lin, G., Reid, I.: Learning depth from single monocular images using deep convolutional neural fields. IEEE Trans. Pattern Anal. Mach. Intell. **38**(10), 2024–2039 (2016)
47. Longuet-Higgins, H.: A computer algorithm for reconstructing a scene from two projections. In: Fischler, M.A., Firschein, O. (eds.) Readings in Computer Vision, pp. 61–62. Morgan Kaufmann, San Francisco (CA) (1987)
48. Lowe, D.G.: Distinctive image features from scale-invariant keypoints. Int. J. Comput. Vis. **60**, 91–110 (2004)
49. Lucas, B.D., Kanade, T.: An iterative image registration technique with an application to stereo vision (ijcai). In: Proceedings of the 7th International Joint Conference on Artificial Intelligence (IJCAI '81), pp. 674–679 (1981)
50. Luo, W., Schwing, A.G., Urtasun, R.: Efficient deep learning for stereo matching. In: 2016 IEEE Conference on Computer Vision and Pattern Recognition (CVPR), pp. 5695–5703 (2016)
51. Ma, Y., Soatto, S., Kosecka, J., Sastry, S.S.: An Invitation to 3-D Vision: From Images to Geometric Models. Springer, Berlin (2003)
52. Maimone, M., Biesiadecki, J., Tunstel, E., Cheng, Y., Leger, C.: Surface navigation and mobility intelligence on the mars exploration rovers. In: A. Howard, E. Tunstel (eds.) Intelligence for Space Robotics, pp. 45–69. TSI Press, San Antonio (2006)
53. Maimone, M., Cheng, Y., Matthies, L.: Two years of visual odometry on the mars exploration rovers. J. Field Robot. **24**(3), 169–186 (2007)
54. Mallon, J., Whelan, P.F.: Projective rectification from the fundamental matrix. Image Vis. Comput. **23**(7), 643–650 (2005)
55. Moons, T., Gool, L.V., Vergauwen, M.: 3d reconstruction from multiple images part 1: Principles. Found. Trends Comput. Graph. Vis. **4**(4), 287–404 (2010)
56. Mordohai, P., Frahm, J.M., Akbarzadeh, A., Engels, C., Gallup, D., Merrell, P., Salmi, C., Sinha, S., Talton, B., Wang, L., Yang, Q., Stewenius, H., Towles, H., Welch, G., Yang, R., Pollefeys, M., Nistér, D.: Real-time video-based reconstruction of urban environments. In: Proceedings of 3DARCH: 3D Virtual Reconstruction and Visualization of Complex Architectures (2007)
57. Mur-Artal, R., Montiel, J.M.M., Tardós, J.D.: ORB-SLAM: A versatile and accurate monocular SLAM system. IEEE Trans. Robot. **31**(5), 1147–1163 (2015)
58. Nayar, S.K., Nakagawa, Y.: Shape from focus. IEEE Trans. Pattern Anal. Mach. Intell. **16**(8), 824–831 (1994)

59. Newcombe, R.A., Lovegrove, S.J., Davison, A.J.: Dtam: Dense tracking and mapping in real-time. In: 2011 International Conference on Computer Vision, pp. 2320–2327 (2011)
60. Nister, D.: Automatic passive recovery of 3D from images and video. In: Proceedings 2nd International Symposium on 3D Data Processing, Visualization and Transmission, 2004. 3DPVT 2004, pp. 438–445 (2004)
61. Nister, D.: An efficient solution to the five-point relative pose problem. IEEE Trans. Pattern Anal. Mach. Intell. **26**(6), 756–770 (2004)
62. OpenCV: Open source Computer Vision library. https://opencv.org/ (2020). Accessed 4 Jan 2020
63. OpenMVG: Open Multiple View Geometry library. https://github.com/openMVG/openMVG/ (2020). Accessed 10 Mar 2020
64. OpenMVS: Open Multi-View Stereo reconstruction library (Accessed Jan 4th, 2020). https://github.com/cdcseacave/openMVS/ (2020). Accessed 4 Mar 2020
65. Pentland, A.P.: A new sense for depth of field. IEEE Trans. Pattern Anal. Mach. Intell. **9**(4), 523–531 (1987)
66. Pix4D: Pix4D Photogrammetry software suite for drone mapping. https://www.pix4d.com/ (2020). Accessed 4 Jan 2020
67. Pollefeys, M., Koch, R., Van Gool, L.: A simple and efficient rectification method for general motion. Proc. Seventh IEEE Int. Conf. Comput. Vis. **1**, 496–501 (1999)
68. Pollefeys, M., Van Gool, L., Vergauwen, M., Verbiest, F., Cornelis, K., Tops, J., Koch, R.: Visual modeling with a hand-held camera. Int. J. Comput. Vis. **59**(3), 207–232 (2004)
69. Price, K.: VisionBib.com: Computer Vision Information Pages. http://www.visionbib.com/index.php (2020). Accessed 10 Mar 2020
70. Quam, L.H.: Hierarchical warp stereo. In: Fischler, M.A., Firschein, O. (eds.) Readings in Computer Vision, pp. 80–86. Morgan Kaufmann, San Francisco (CA) (1987)
71. Ranftl, R., Vineet, V., Chen, Q., Koltun, V.: Dense monocular depth estimation in complex dynamic scenes. In: IEEE Conference on Computer Vision and Pattern Recognition (CVPR), pp. 4058–4066 (2016)
72. Roy, S., Cox, I.J.: A maximum-flow formulation of the n-camera stereo correspondence problem. In: International Conference on Computer Vision, pp. 492–499 (1998)
73. Rublee, E., Rabaud, V., Konolige, K., Bradski, G.: Orb: An efficient alternative to SIFT or SURF. In: International Conference on Computer Vision, pp. 2564–2571 (2011)
74. Scharstein, D., Szeliski, R., Hirschmüller, H.: The Middlebury stereo vision page. http://vision.middlebury.edu/stereo (2020). Accessed 3 Jan 2020
75. Scharstein, D., Szeliski, R.: A taxonomy and evaluation of dense two-frame stereo correspondence algorithms. Int. J. Comput. Vis. **47**(1), 7–42 (2002)
76. Se, S., Firoozfam, P., Goldstein, N., Dutkiewicz, M., Pace, P.: Automated uav-based video exploitation for mapping and surveillance. In: International Society for Photogrammetry and Remote Sensing (ISPRS) Commission I Symposium, vol. 38 (2010)
77. Se, S., Jasiobedzki, P.: Photo-realistic 3D model reconstruction. In: Proceedings IEEE International Conference on Robotics and Automation (ICRA), pp. 3076–3082 (2006)
78. Se, S., Jasiobedzki, P.: Stereo-vision based 3D modeling and localization for unmanned vehicles. Int. J. Intell. Control Syst. **13**(1), 47–58 (2008)
79. Se, S., Lowe, D., Little, J.: Mobile robot localization and mapping with uncertainty using scale-invariant visual landmarks. Int. J. Robot. Res. **21**(8), 735–758 (2002)
80. Seitz, S.M., Curless, B., Diebel, J., Scharstein, D., Szeliski, R.: A comparison and evaluation of multi-view stereo reconstruction algorithms. In: Proceedings of the IEEE Computer Society Conference on Computer Vision and Pattern Recognition, pp. 519–528 (2006)
81. Smith, S.M., Brady, J.M.: Susan—A new approach to low level image processing. Int. J. Comput. Vis. **23**(1), 45–78 (1997)
82. Stereolabs: The Stereolab ZED camera. https://www.stereolabs.com/zed/ (2020). Accessed 4 Jan 2020
83. Sun, Jian, Zheng, Nan-Ning, Shum, Heung-Yeung: Stereo matching using belief propagation. IEEE Trans. Pattern Anal. Mach. Intell. **25**(7), 787–800 (2003)

84. Tappen, Freeman: Comparison of graph cuts with belief propagation for stereo, using identical mrf parameters. Proc. Ninth IEEE Int. Conf. Comput. Vis. **2**, 900–906 (2003)
85. Tateno, K., Tombari, F., Laina, I., Navab, N.: CNN-SLAM: Real-time dense monocular SLAM with learned depth prediction. In: 2017 IEEE Conference on Computer Vision and Pattern Recognition (CVPR) (2017)
86. Torr, P., Murray, D.: The development and comparison of robust methods for estimating the fundamental matrix. Int. J. Comput. Vis. **24**(3), 271–300 (1997)
87. Torresani, L., Hertzmann, A., Bregler, C.: Nonrigid structure-from-motion: Estimating shape and motion with hierarchical priors. IEEE Trans. Pattern Anal. Mach. Intell. **30**(5), 878–892 (2008)
88. Triggs, B., McLauchlan, P., Hartley, R., Fitzgibbon, A.: Bundle adjustment—A modern synthesis. In: Vision Algorithms: Theory and Practice, LNCS, pp. 298–375 (2000)
89. Tsai, R.: A versatile camera calibration technique for high-accuracy 3D machine vision metrology using off-the-shelf tv cameras and lenses. IEEE J. Robot. Autom. **3**(4), 323–344 (1987)
90. White, R., Forsyth, D.A.: Combining cues: Shape from shading and texture. In: 2006 IEEE Computer Society Conference on Computer Vision and Pattern Recognition (CVPR'06), vol. 2, pp. 1809–1816 (2006)
91. Woodham, R.J.: Analysing images of curved surfaces. Artif. Intell. **17**(1), 117–140 (1981)
92. Wu, J., Zhang, C., Zhang, X., Zhang, Z., Freeman, W., Tenenbaum, J.: Learning shape priors for single-view 3D completion and reconstruction. ECCV **2018**, 673–691 (2018)
93. Yan, X., Yang, J., Yumer, E., Guo, Y., Lee, H.: Perspective transformer nets: Learning single-view 3D object reconstruction without 3D supervision. In: Advances in Neural Information Processing Systems (NIPS), vol. 29, pp. 1696–1704 (2016)
94. Yang, R., Pollefeys, M.: A versatile stereo implementation on commodity graphics hardware. Real-Time Imaging **11**(1), 7–18 (2005)
95. Zagoruyko, S., Komodakis, N.: Learning to compare image patches via convolutional neural networks. In: IEEE Conference on Computer Vision and Pattern Recognition, CVPR, pp. 4353–4361 (2015)
96. Zbontar, J., LeCun, Y.: Computing the stereo matching cost with a convolutional neural network. In: IEEE Conference on Computer Vision and Pattern Recognition. CVPR, pp. 1592–1599 (2015)
97. Zhang R., Tsai P.-S., Cryer, J.E., Shah, M.: Shape-from-shading: A survey. IEEE Trans. Pattern Anal. Mach. Intell. **21**(8), 690–706 (1999)
98. Zhang, Z.: A flexible new technique for camera calibration. IEEE Trans. Pattern Anal. Mach. Intell. **22**(11), 1330–1334 (2000)

Chapter 3
Active Triangulation 3D Imaging Systems for Industrial Inspection

Marc-Antoine Drouin and Jean-Angelo Beraldin

Abstract Active 3D imaging systems use artificial illumination in order to capture and record digital representations of objects. The use of artificial illumination allows the acquisition of dense and accurate range images of textureless objects that are difficult to acquire using passive vision systems. An active 3D imaging system can be based on different measurement principles that include time-of-flight, triangulation, and interferometry. Here, an in-depth presentation of triangulation-based 3D imaging is provided, including both scanning laser and structured light projection systems, with a focus on industrial applications. The characterization of triangulation is discussed using both an error-propagation framework and experimental protocols.

3.1 Introduction

Three-dimensional (3D) imaging systems, also known as 3D vision systems, capture and record a digital representation of the geometry and appearance (e.g., color-texture) information of visible 3D surfaces of people, animals, plants, objects, and sites. This digital surrogate of the physical world is then processed in order to extract useful information from the raw data and finally, communicate the results. *Active* 3D imaging systems use an artificial illumination, usually either a spatially coherent light source (e.g., laser) or an incoherent one (e.g., halogen lamp), to acquire dense range maps with a minimum of ambiguity. The term is also used for systems that project non-visible electromagnetic radiation, such as near infrared onto the scene. The use of an artificial light source makes it possible for active 3D imaging systems

M.-A. Drouin (✉)
National Research Council Canada, Ottawa, Canada
e-mail: Marc-Antoine.Drouin@nrc-cnrc.gc.ca

J.-A. Beraldin
National Research Council Canada (formerly), Ottawa, Canada

Y. Liu et al. (eds.), *3D Imaging, Analysis and Applications*,
https://doi.org/10.1007/978-3-030-44070-1_3

to generate a model of a surface geometry, even when the surface appears featureless to the naked eye or to a photographic/video camera and, hence, require minimal
operator assistance. Furthermore, the 3D information can be made relatively insensitive to ambient illumination and surface color. They are, by their nature, noncontact
measurement instruments and produce a quantifiable 3D digital representation (e.g.,
point cloud or range image) of a surface in a specified finite volume of interest and
with a particular measurement uncertainty.

3.1.1 Historical Context

The desire to capture and record shape using optical instruments can be traced back
to the invention of rudimentary surveying instruments and the camera obscura [84].
The invention of photography, in which images are recorded on semi-permanent
recording media, is certainly the catalyst of modern methods. In the 1860s, François
Willème invented a process known as photo-sculpture that used many cameras [72,
94]. Profiles of the subject to be reproduced were taken on photographic plates, projected onto a screen, and transferred to a piece of clay using a pantograph. The process
supplied many profiles, which were used to rough down the piece of clay, leaving
a large amount of manual work. Commercial applications developed rapidly and
studios stayed in operation from 1863 to 1867, when it was realized that the photo-
sculpture process was not more economical than the traditional sculpture technique.
A professional sculptor was needed and the photo-sculpture process required a significant investment in cameras, projection and reproduction systems, and skilled labor
to operate them.

It is only with the advances made during the last half of the twentieth century in the
field of solid-state electronics, photonics, computer vision, and computer graphics
that the process of capturing and recording detailed shapes by optical means regained
substantial interest. Indeed, obvious changes have been instrumental in the growth
of active 3D imaging systems technology, i.e., the availability of affordable and
fast digital computers and reliable light sources (lasers, halogen lamps, LEDs). It
is now possible to build reliable, accurate, high-resolution 3D active vision systems
that can capture large amounts of 3D data. In addition, the ability to process these
dense point clouds in an efficient and cost-effective way has opened up a myriad
of applications in many diverse areas, such as defense, medicine, entertainment,
industry, and commerce.

3.1.2 Basic Measurement Principles

Active 3D imaging systems can be based on different measurement principles. The
three most used principles in commercially available systems are time-of-flight (ToF),
interferometry, and triangulation. Seitz describes ToF as based on an accurate clock,

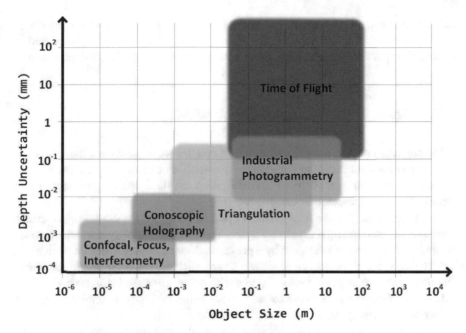

Fig. 3.1 Diagram showing typical accuracy at different operating distances for the most common active 3D imaging technologies. Figure courtesy of NRC

interferometry as one that uses accurate wavelengths and triangulation as a method based on geometry [83]. Figure 3.1 summarizes the typical accuracy of each type of active 3D imaging system technology, found on the market, as a function of the operating distance. It can be observed that each optical technique covers a particular range of operation. Furthermore, many in-depth classifications of optical distance measurement principles have been published [11, 13, 59, 73].

The fundamental work on ToF systems can be traced back to the era of RADAR, which is based on radio waves. With the advent of lasers in the late 1950s, it became possible to image a surface with angular and range resolutions much higher than possible with radio waves. Different strategies have been devised to exploit this basic measurement principle [1, 6, 59].

Interferometry is based on the superposition of two beams of light [59]. Typically, a laser beam is split into two paths. One path is of known length, while the other is of unknown length. The difference in path lengths creates a phase difference between the light beams. The two beams are then combined together before reaching a photodetector. The interference pattern seen by the detector resulting from the superposition of these two light beams depends on the path difference (a distance). Note that commercially available systems based on other principles such as conoscopic holography are available for small operating distances (see Fig. 3.1). Technologies for small operating distances are covered in [59, 61] and ToF methods are described in the next chapter. The remainder of this chapter will focus on triangulation-based methods that use the same principle as the passive triangulation systems presented in Chap. 2 of this book. Active triangulation systems are frequently encountered in industrial inspection applications and so we cover that aspect of their deployment.

3.1.3 Active Triangulation-Based Methods

In the previous chapter, passive triangulation systems were presented, namely, standard stereo configurations and structure-from-motion. In this chapter, we assume that the reader is familiar with camera calibration and the epipolar geometry of two camera views, as presented in Chap. 2.

Both active and passive triangulation systems are based on the same geometric principle: intersecting light rays in 3D space. Typically, an active system replaces one camera of a passive stereo system by a projection device. This projection device can be a digital video projector, an analogue slide projector or a laser. (Note, however, that many active systems use two cameras with a projection device. Although this is at first sight redundant, there are sound reasons behind this design choice, such as a reduction in 'missing parts' due to self-occlusion.)

There are many ways to classify active triangulation sensors, according to their opto-mechanical components, opto-mechanical construction, and performance. One of the key dimensions within this taxonomy is the way in which the active 3D imaging system illuminates the scene. Here we will consider four distinct categories: spot scanners, stripe scanners, systems that use structured light patterns, and handheld scanners.

The simplest of these is the spot scanner (also known as a point-based scanner) where, typically, a collimated or focused laser beam illuminates a very small circular or elliptical part of the scene for each image capture. One advantage of this approach is that the spatial correspondence problem is non-existent, because the illumination of the object's surface is spread temporally (i.e., in the time dimension). Moreover, a spot scanner allows us to control the spatial sampling on the scene surfaces. The laser power can also be controlled on a per-3D-sample basis. However, this is at the expense of additional opto-mechanical complexity because the spot must be scanned either by mounting the sensor on a 2D translation stage, or by orienting the laser around two axes of rotation using two galvanometer-mounted mirrors (see Fig. 3.2-left). In addition, the significant time taken to capture a range image precludes the use of this type of scanner in dynamic scenes.

Typically, in the second type of scanner, a collimated laser beam is passed through a cylindrical lens in order to generate a 'sheet-of-light' that illuminates the scene with a thin stripe (see Fig. 3.2-middle). Other implementations are possible, for example, the cylindrical lens could be replaced by a diffractive optical element (DOE) or a diffraction grating. This stripe now only needs to be scanned in one dimension relative to the scene in order to assemble a range image and, again, this may be done by translation of the sensor (or, alternatively, the object) or the rotation of a single mirror. These 3D imaging devices are called stripe scanners or profile scanners. Note

Fig. 3.2 Left: a spot-based system where the orientation along one axis of the laser is controlled by a galvanometer-mounted mirror. The complete scanner head is translated. This design is described in Sect. 3.9.2. Center: a commercial stripe-based system where the scanner head is translated. Right: a commercial area-based system. Figure courtesy of the NRC

that although the complexity of scanning has reduced from two-dimensional to one-dimensional, some ambiguity in the direction of illumination is introduced, which needs to be resolved using the epipolar constraint.

The third type of scanner that we discuss is the type that projects a structured light pattern onto the scene [59] (see Fig. 3.2-right). These 3D imaging devices are also known as area scanners [91]. Typically these systems do not scan the projected light over the scene object at all, since the object is usually completely illuminated by the pattern, although the term 'scanner' is often still applied in an informal sense. These systems provide the advantage of the shortest capture times, thus minimizing distortion due to motion in dynamic scenes. The correspondence problem, however, is more challenging (although not as difficult as for passive stereo) and the projected light is structured either spatially, temporally, or both in order to determine which part of the projected pattern corresponds to which part of the imaged pattern.

The last type of scanner is a handheld device and this is very popular because of its ease of use. As the name implies, a scanner of this type is held by the operator, who moves it in front of the object to be digitized. These scanners perform range image alignment and fusion in real time, thus providing the user with instantaneous feedback. A handheld scanner is composed of a measurement system, a positioning system, and a sophisticated software pipeline. The measurement system is typically a stripe-based scanner or a structured light system. The positioning system is typically a passive triangulation system (labeled as industrial photogrammetry in Fig. 3.1) that relies on cooperative 2D targets (usually stickers). This type of positioning system can be part of the handheld device. In this case, the 2D targets are installed on the object to be digitalized. An alternative is to use an external passive system that tracks the movement of the scanner. In that case, the 2D targets are installed on the scanner. Another variant mounts the 3D scanner on a portable arm and, in that case, the positioning of the scanner is computed using the information provided by the arm encoders. In Sects. 3.3 and 3.4, we discuss both stripe-based and structured light subsystems of handheld scanners. More information about positioning systems and software pipelines can be found in [54, 88, 89].

When working with coherent light sources (lasers) eye safety is of paramount importance and one should never operate laser-based 3D imaging sensors without appropriate eye-safety training. Many 3D imaging systems use a laser in the visible spectrum where fractions of a milliwatt are sufficient to cause eye damage, since the laser light density entering the pupil is magnified, at the retina, through the lens. For an operator using any laser, an important safety parameter is the maximum permissible exposure (MPE), which is defined as the level of laser radiation to which a person may be exposed without hazardous effect or adverse biological changes in the eye or skin [2]. The MPE varies with wavelength and operating conditions of a system. We do not have space to discuss eye safety extensively here and refer the reader to the *American National Standard for Safe use of Lasers* [2]. Note that high power low coherence (and non-coherent) light sources can also pose eye-safety issues [21].

3.1.4 Chapter Outline

The core sections in this chapter cover the following materials:

- Spot scanners.
- Stripe scanners.
- Area-based structured light systems.
- System calibration.
- Measurement uncertainty.[1]
- Experimental characterization.

In Sects. 3.8 and 3.9, further advanced topics are included on modeling sensors, understanding their uncertainty, and designing synchronized scanning systems.[2] Toward the end of the chapter, we present the main challenges for future research, concluding remarks, and suggestions for further reading. Finally a set of questions and exercises are presented for the reader to develop and consolidate their understanding of active 3D imaging systems.

3.2 Spot Scanners

Usually, spot scanners use a laser. We limit the discussion to this type of technology and in order to study the basic principle of triangulation, we assume an infinitely thin laser beam diameter and constrain the problem to the plane (X, Z), i.e., $Y = 0$. The basic geometrical principle of optical triangulation for a spot scanner is shown in Fig. 3.3 and is identical to the one of passive stereo discussed in Chap. 2.

---

[1] Optional advanced material that may be omitted on the first reading.

[2] May also be omitted on the first reading.

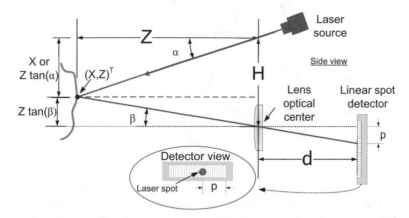

Fig. 3.3 Schematic diagram of a single point optical triangulation sensor based on a laser beam and a linear spot detector. The baseline is H and d is the distance between the lens and the linear spot detector. The projection angle is α. The collection angle is β, which is computed using the distance d and the position p on the linear spot detector. The point $[X, Z]^T$ is determined by the baseline H, the projection angle α, and the collection angle β. Figure courtesy of [7]

In Fig. 3.3, a laser source projects a beam of light on a surface of interest. The light scattered by that surface is collected from a vantage point spatially distinct from the projected light beam. This light is focused (imaged) onto a linear spot detector.[3] Knowledge of both projection and collection angles (α and β) relative to a baseline (H) determines the $[X, Z]^T$ coordinate of a point on a surface. Note that it is assumed that the only light that traverses the lens goes through the optical center, which is the well-known *pinhole* model of the imaging process. Furthermore, we refer to *projection* of the laser light onto the scene and we can think of the imaged spot position on the detector and the lens optical center as a *back-projected* ray, traveling in the opposite direction to the light, back into the scene. This intersects with the projected laser ray to determine the 3D scene point.

The linear spot detector acts as an angle sensor and provides signals that are interpreted as a position p. Explicitly, given the value of p, the value of β in radians is computed as

$$\beta = \arctan\left(\frac{p}{d}\right) \tag{3.1}$$

where d is the distance between the laser spot detector and the collection lens. Typically this distance will be slightly larger than the focal length of the lens, such that the imaged spot is well focused at the depth at which most parts of the object surface are imaged. The relevant thin lens equation is discussed in Sect. 3.8.1.

The position of p on the linear spot detector is computed using a peak detector, which will be described later. Using simple trigonometry, one can verify that

---

[3] A linear spot detector can be conceptually viewed as a camera that has a singe row of pixels. Many linear spot detectors have been proposed in the past for 3D imaging [7].

$$Z = \frac{H}{\tan \alpha + \tan \beta} \qquad (3.2)$$

and

$$X = Z \tan \alpha. \qquad (3.3)$$

Substituting Eq. 3.1 into Eq. 3.2 gives

$$Z = \frac{Hd}{p + d \tan \alpha}. \qquad (3.4)$$

In order to acquire a complete profile without using a translation stage, the laser beam can be scanned around some $[X, Z]^T$ coordinate using a mirror mounted on a mechanical scanner (typically a galvanometer drive). In this case, the angle α is varied according to a predefined field of view. For practical reasons, the total scanned angle for a configuration like the one in Fig. 3.3 is about $30°$. Larger angles may be scanned by more sophisticated optical arrangements called synchronized scanners, where the field of view of the camera is scanned using the same mirror that scans the laser. Sometimes the reverse side of a double-sided mirror is used [19, 77].

3.2.1 Spot Position Detection

It is crucial to obtain the position of the laser spot on the linear spot detector to sub-pixel accuracy. In order to accomplish this, the image of the laser spot must be a few pixels wide on the detector, which is easy to achieve in a real system. Many peak detectors have been proposed to compute the position of the laser spot and two studies compare different peak detectors [38, 69]. We examine two peak detectors [16, 38, 69]. The first one localizes the 'center of mass' of the imaged spot intensity. In this method, the pixel i_M with the maximum intensity is found in the 1D image I. Then a window of size $2N + 1$ centered on i_M is used to compute the centroid position. Explicitly, the peak position p is defined as

$$p = i_M + \frac{\sum_{i=-N}^{N} I(i_M + i)i}{\sum_{i=-N}^{N} I(i_M + i)}. \qquad (3.5)$$

The second peak detector uses convolution with a derivative filter, followed by a linear interpolation. Explicitly, for each pixel, i, let

$$g(i) = \sum_{j=-N}^{N} I(i - j)F(j + N) \qquad (3.6)$$

where $F = [1, 1, 1, 1, 0, -1, -1, -1, -1]$ and $N = 4$. Finally, the linear interpolation process is implemented as

$$p = i_0 + \frac{g(i_0)}{g(i_0) - g(i_0 + 1)} \tag{3.7}$$

where i_0 is a pixel such that $g(i_0) \geq 0$ and $g(i_0 + 1) < 0$. Moreover, F has the property of filtering out some of the frequency content of the image [16]. This makes it possible to filter out the ambient illumination and some of the noise and interference introduced by the linear detector electronics. Note that other filters could be used. It has been shown that the second peak detector outperforms the first in an actual implementation of laser triangulation [16].

3.3 Stripe Scanners

As shown previously, spot scanners intersect a detection direction (a line in a plane, which is a back-projected ray) with a projection direction (another line in the same plane) to compute a point in a 2D scene space. Stripe scanners and structured light systems intersect a back-projected 3D ray, generated from a pixel in a camera, and a projected 3D plane of light, in order to compute a point in the 3D scene. Clearly, the scanner baseline should not be contained within the projected plane, otherwise we would not be able to detect the deformation of the stripe. (In this case, the imaged stripe lies along an epipolar line in the scanner camera.)

A stripe scanner is composed of a camera and a laser 'sheet-of-light' or plane, which is rotated or translated in order to scan the scene. (Of course, the object may be rotated on a turntable instead, or translated, and this is a common set up for industrial 3D scanning of objects on conveyer belts.) Figure 3.4 illustrates three types of stripe scanners. Note that other configurations exist, but are not described here [13]. In the

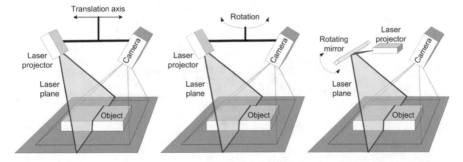

Fig. 3.4 Left: a stripe scanner where the scanner head is translated. Center: a stripe scanner where the scanner head is rotated. Right: a stripe scanner where a mirror rotates the laser beam. Figure courtesy of NRC

remainder of this chapter, we will discuss systems in which only the plane of projected light is rotated and an image is acquired for each laser plane orientation. The camera pixels that view the intersection of the laser plane with the scene can be transformed into observation directions (see Fig. 3.4). Depending on the roll orientation of the camera with respect to the laser plane, the observation directions in the camera are obtained by applying a peak detector on each row or column of the camera image. We assume a configuration where a measurement is performed on each row of the camera image using a peak detector.

Next, the pinhole camera model presented in the previous chapter is revisited. Then, a laser-plane-projector model is presented. Finally, triangulation for a stripe scanner is presented.

3.3.1 Camera Model

The simplest mathematical model that can be used to represent a camera is the pinhole model. Readers familiar with the camera model presented in the previous chapter can go directly to the last paragraph of this section. A pinhole camera can be assembled using a box in which a small hole (i.e., the aperture) is made on one side and a sheet of photosensitive paper is placed on the opposite side. Figure 3.5 is an illustration of a pinhole camera. The pinhole camera has a very small aperture so it requires long integration times; thus, machine vision applications use cameras with lenses which collect more light and hence require shorter integration times. Nevertheless, for many applications, the pinhole model is a valid approximation of a camera. In this mathematical model, the aperture and the photosensitive surface of the pinhole are represented, respectively, by the center of projection and the image plane. The center of projection is the origin of the camera coordinate system and the optical axis coincides with the Z-axis of the camera. Moreover, the optical axis

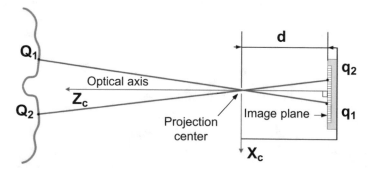

Fig. 3.5 Cross section of a pinhole camera. The 3D points Q_1 and Q_2 are projected into the image plane as points q_1 and q_2, respectively, and d is the distance between the image plane and the projection center. Figure courtesy of NRC

is perpendicular to the image plane and the intersection of the optical axis and the image plane is the principal point (image center). Note that when approximating a camera with the pinhole model, the geometric distortions of the image introduced by the optical components of an actual camera are not taken into account. Geometric distortions will be discussed in Sect. 3.5. Other limitations of this model are described in Sect. 3.8.

A 3D point $[X_c, Y_c, Z_c]^T$ in the camera reference frame can be transformed into pixel coordinates $[x, y]^T$ by first projecting $[X_c, Y_c, Z_c]^T$ onto the normalized camera frame using $[x', y']^T = [X_c/Z_c, Y_c/Z_c]^T$. This normalized frame corresponds to the 3D point being projected onto a conceptual imaging plane at a distance of one unit from the camera center. The pixel coordinates can be obtained from the normalized coordinates as

$$\begin{bmatrix} x \\ y \end{bmatrix} = d \begin{bmatrix} \frac{x'}{s_x} \\ \frac{y'}{s_y} \end{bmatrix} + \begin{bmatrix} o_x \\ o_y \end{bmatrix} \tag{3.8}$$

where s_x and s_y are the dimensions of the sensor in millimeters divided by the number of pixels along the X and Y-axis, respectively. Moreover, d is the distance in millimeters between the aperture and the sensor chip and $[o_x, o_y]^T$ is the position in pixels of the principal point (image center) in the image. The parameters s_x, s_y, d, o_x, and o_y are the intrinsic parameters of the camera.

The extrinsic parameters of the camera must be defined in order to locate the position and orientation of the camera in the world coordinate system. This requires three parameters for the rotation and three parameters for the translation. (Note that in many design situations, we can define the world coordinate system such that it coincides with the camera coordinate system. However, we still would need to estimate the pose of the light projection system, which can be viewed as an *inverse camera*, within this frame. Also, many active 3D imaging systems use multiple cameras, which can reduce the area of the 'missing parts' caused by self-occlusion.)

The rotation is represented using a 3×3 rotation matrix

$$\mathsf{R}_c = \begin{bmatrix} 1 & 0 & 0 \\ 0 & \cos\theta_x & -\sin\theta_x \\ 0 & \sin\theta_x & \cos\theta_x \end{bmatrix} \begin{bmatrix} \cos\theta_y & 0 & \sin\theta_y \\ 0 & 1 & 0 \\ -\sin\theta_y & 0 & \cos\theta_y \end{bmatrix} \begin{bmatrix} \cos\theta_z & -\sin\theta_z & 0 \\ \sin\theta_z & \cos\theta_z & 0 \\ 0 & 0 & 1 \end{bmatrix} \tag{3.9}$$

where θ_x, θ_y and θ_z are the rotation angles around the X, Y, and Z axis and translation is represented by a vector $\mathbf{T}_c = [T_x, T_y, T_z]^T$. Note that the rotation matrix R_c is orthogonal (i.e., $\mathsf{R}_c^T = \mathsf{R}_c^{-1}$) and $\det(\mathsf{R}_c) = 1$.

A 3D point $\mathbf{Q}_w = [X_w, Y_w, Z_w]^T$ in the world reference frame can be transformed into a point $\mathbf{Q}_c = [X_c, Y_c, Z_c]^T$ of the camera reference frame by using

$$\mathbf{Q}_c = \mathsf{R}_c \mathbf{Q}_w + \mathbf{T}_c \tag{3.10}$$

Then, the point $\mathbf{Q}_c$ is projected onto the normalized camera frame $[x', y']^T = [X_c/Z_c, Y_c/Z_c]^T$. Finally, the point in the normalized camera frame $[x', y']^T$ can be transformed into the pixel coordinate $[x, y]^T$ using Eq. 3.8. Explicitly, the transformation from $\mathbf{Q}_w$ to pixel $[x, y]^T$ is

$$\begin{bmatrix} x \\ y \end{bmatrix} = \begin{bmatrix} \frac{d}{s_x} \frac{(r_{11}, r_{12}, r_{13}) \mathbf{Q}_w + T_x}{(r_{31}, r_{32}, r_{33}) \mathbf{Q}_w + T_z} \\ \frac{d}{s_y} \frac{(r_{21}, r_{22}, r_{23}) \mathbf{Q}_w + T_y}{(r_{31}, r_{32}, r_{33}) \mathbf{Q}_w + T_z} \end{bmatrix} + \begin{bmatrix} o_x \\ o_y \end{bmatrix} \tag{3.11}$$

where the r_{ij} are the elements of matrix $\mathbf{R}_c$. Note that a pixel $[x, y]^T$ can be transformed into the normalized camera frame using

$$\begin{bmatrix} x' \\ y' \end{bmatrix} = \frac{1}{d} \begin{bmatrix} s_x (x - o_x) \\ s_y (y - o_y) \end{bmatrix}. \tag{3.12}$$

Moreover, one may verify using Eq. 3.10 that a point in the camera reference frame can be transformed to a point in the world reference frame by using

$$\mathbf{Q}_w = \mathbf{R}_c^T [\mathbf{Q}_c - \mathbf{T}_c] \tag{3.13}$$

Note that the camera model used in this chapter is similar to the one used in the previous chapter, with one minor difference: $f k_x$ and $f k_y$ are replaced by d/s_x and d/s_y, respectively. This change is partly notational ($k_x = \frac{1}{s_x}$, $k_y = \frac{1}{s_y}$) and partly to do with where the image is in focus relative to the camera center (in general, d and f are not equal, with d often being slightly larger). This will be discussed further in Sect. 3.8. Note that intrinsic camera parameters can be determined using the method described in Chap. 2.

3.3.2 Sheet-of-light Projector Model

In the projective-geometry framework of the pinhole camera, a digital projector can be viewed as an inverse camera and both share the same parameterization. Similarly, a sheet-of-light projection system can be geometrically modeled as a pinhole camera with a single infinitely thin column of pixels. Although this parameterization is a major simplification of the physical system, it allows the presentation of the basic concepts of a sheet-of-light scanner using the same two-view geometry that was presented in Chap. 2. This column of pixels can be back-projected as a plane in 3D and the projection center of this simplified model acts as the laser source (see Sect. 3.8.5).

In order to acquire a complete range image, the laser source is rotated around a rotation axis by an angle α. The rotation center is located at $\mathbf{T}_\alpha$ and $\mathbf{R}_\alpha$ is the corresponding rotation matrix.[4] For a given α, a point $\mathbf{Q}_\alpha$ in the laser coordinate frame can be transformed into a point $\mathbf{Q}_w$ in the world coordinate frame using

---

[4]The rotation matrix representing a rotation of θ around an axis $[a, b, c]^T$ of unit magnitude is

$$\mathbf{Q}_w = \mathbf{T}_\alpha + \mathbf{R}_\alpha [\mathbf{Q}_\alpha - \mathbf{T}_\alpha]. \tag{3.14}$$

In a practical implementation, a cylindrical lens can be used to generate a laser plane and optical components such as a mirror are used to change the laser plane orientation.

3.3.3 Triangulation for Stripe Scanners

Triangulation for stripe scanners essentially involves intersecting the back-projected ray associated with a camera pixel with the sheet-of-light, projected at some angle α. Consider a stripe scanner, where projector coordinates are subscripted with 1 and camera coordinates are subscripted with 2. Suppose that an unknown 3D scene point, $\mathbf{Q}_w$, is illuminated by the laser for a given value of α and this point is imaged in the scanner camera at *known* pixel coordinates $[x_2, y_2]^T$. The normalized camera point $[x_2', y_2']^T$ can be computed from $[x_2, y_2]^T$ and the intrinsic camera parameters (known from a camera calibration) using Eq. 3.12. Considering the sheet-of-light projector model, described above, the 3D scene point $\mathbf{Q}_w$ is back-projected to an *unknown* normalized coordinate $[0, y_1']^T$ for the given value of α.

Clearly there are three unknowns here, which includes the depth associated with the back-projected camera ray to the 3D scene point, and a pair of parameters that describe the planar position in the projected sheet-of-light of the 3D scene point. If we can form an independent equation for each of the coordinates X_w, Y_w, Z_w of $\mathbf{Q}_w$, then we can solve for that point's unknown 3D scene position.

By rearranging Eqs. 3.13 and 3.14, one may obtain

$$\mathbf{Q}_w = \mathbf{R}_\alpha [0, \lambda_1 y_1', \lambda_1]^T + \mathbf{T}_\alpha - \mathbf{R}_\alpha \mathbf{T}_\alpha = \mathbf{R}_c^T [[\lambda_2 x_2', \lambda_2 y_2', \lambda_2]^T - \mathbf{T}_c] \tag{3.15}$$

where λ_1 and λ_2 are the range (i.e., the distance along the Z-axis) between the 3D point $\mathbf{Q}_w$ and the laser source and the camera, respectively. Moreover, $\mathbf{R}_\alpha$ and $\mathbf{T}_\alpha$ are the parameters related to the laser plane orientation and position and $\mathbf{R}_c$ and $\mathbf{T}_c$ are the extrinsic parameters of the camera. (Note that these can be simplified to the 3 x 3 identity matrix and the zero 3-vector, if the world coordinate system is chosen to coincide with the camera coordinate system.) When $\mathbf{R}_\alpha$ and $\mathbf{T}_\alpha$ are known, the vector equality on the right of Eq. 3.15 is a system of three equations with three unknowns λ_1, λ_2, and y_1'. These can easily be determined and then the values substituted in the vector equality on the left of Eq. 3.15 to solve for the unknown $\mathbf{Q}_w$. (A question about the independence of these equations is given in Sect. 3.13).

$$\mathbf{R}_\theta = \begin{bmatrix} a^2(1-\cos\theta) + \cos\theta & ab(1-\cos\theta) - c\sin\theta & ac(1-\cos\theta) + b\sin\theta \\ ab(1-\cos\theta) + c\sin\theta & b^2(1-\cos\theta) + \cos\theta & bc(1-\cos\theta) - a\sin\theta \\ ac(1-\cos\theta) - b\sin\theta & bc(1-\cos\theta) + a\sin\theta & c^2(1-\cos\theta) + \cos\theta \end{bmatrix}.$$

For a given α, a 3D point can be computed for each row of the camera. Thus, in Eq. 3.15 the known y_2 and α and the measured value of x_2 which is obtained using a peak detector can be used to compute a 3D point. A range image is obtained by taking an image of the scene for each value of α. In the next section, we examine scanners that project structured light patterns over an area of the scene.

3.4 Area-Based Structured Light Systems

The stripe scanner presented earlier requires the head of the scanner to be rotated or translated in order to produce a range image (see Fig. 3.4). Other methods project many planes of light simultaneously and use a coding strategy to recover which camera pixel views the light from a given plane. There are many coding strategies that can be used to establish the correspondence [80] and it is this coding that gives the name *structured* light. The two main categories of coding are spatial coding and temporal coding, although the two can be mixed [32]. In temporal coding, patterns are projected one after the other and an image is captured for each pattern. Matching to a particular projected stripe is done based only on the time sequence of imaged intensity at a particular location in the scanner's camera. In contrast, spatial coding techniques project just a single pattern, and the greyscale or color pattern within a local neighborhood is used to perform the necessary correspondence matching. Clearly this has a shorter capture time and is generally better suited to dynamic scene capture. (One example could be the sequence of 3D face shapes that constitute changes in facial expression.) However, due to self occlusion, the required local area around a pixel is not always imaged, which can pose more difficulty when the object surface is complex, for example, with many surface concavities. Moreover, systems based on spatial coding usually produce a sparse set of correspondences, while systems based on temporal coding produce a dense set of correspondences.

Usually, structured light systems use a non-coherent projector source (e.g., video projector) [5, 93]. We limit the discussion to this type of technology and we assume a digital projection system. Moreover, the projector images are assumed to contain vertical lines referred to as *fringes*.[5] Thus the imaged fringes cut across the camera's epipolar lines, as required. With L intensity levels and F different projection fringes to distinguish, $N = \lceil \log_L F \rceil$ patterns are needed to remove the ambiguity. When these patterns are projected temporally, this strategy is known as a *time-multiplexing codification* [80]. Codes that use two (binary) intensity levels are very popular because the processing of the captured images is relatively simple. The *Gray code* is probably the best known time-multiplexing code. These codes are based on intensity measurements. Another coding strategy is based on phase measurement and both approaches are described in the remainder of this section. For spatial neighborhood methods, the reader is referred to the next chapter.

---

[5]Fringe projection systems are a subset of structured light systems, but we use the two terms somewhat interchangeably in this chapter.

3.4.1 Gray Code Methods

Gray codes were first used for telecommunication applications. Frank Gray from Bell Labs patented a telecommunication method that used this code [47]. A structured light system that used Gray codes was presented in 1984 by Inokuchi et al. [56]. A Gray code is an ordering of 2^N binary numbers in which only one bit changes between two consecutive elements of the ordering. For $N > 3$ the ordering is not unique. Table 3.1 contains two ordering for $N = 4$ that obey the definition of a Gray code. The table also contains the natural binary code. Figure 3.6 contains the pseudocode used to generate the first ordering of Table 3.1.

Let us assume that the number of columns of the projector is 2^N, then each column can be assigned to an N bit binary number in a Gray code sequence of 2^N elements. This is done by transforming the index of the projector column into an element (i.e., N-bit binary number) of a Gray code ordering, using the pseudocode of Fig. 3.6. The projection of darker fringes is associated with the binary value of 0 and the projection of lighter fringes is associated with the binary value of 1. The projector needs to project N images, indexed $i = 0...N - 1$, where each fringe (dark/light) in the ith image is determined by the binary value of the ith bit (0/1) within that column's N-bit Gray code element. This allows us to establish the correspondence between the projector fringes and the camera pixels. Figure 3.7 contains an example of a Gray code pattern. Usually, the image in the camera of the narrowest projector fringe is many camera pixels wide and all of these pixels have the same code. It is possible to compute either the centers of the fringes or the edges between adjacent fringes in order to define the projector plane with which triangulation is performed. Generally edge-based schemes give better performance [80].

3.4.1.1 Decoding of Binary Fringe-Based Codes

Two algorithms for transforming the camera images into correspondences between projector fringes and camera pixels are presented. In the first algorithm, the camera pixels are at known positions and the projector fringe for these positions is measured. In the second algorithm, the fringe indices are known in the projector and for each row of the camera the fringe transitions are measured.

The first algorithm uses a simple thresholding approach where a threshold is computed individually for each pixel of the camera [80]. The threshold values are computed using the images of the projection of a white and a black frame. For every camera pixel, the mean value of the white and black frames is used as the threshold value. This method does not allow a sub-pixel localization of the boundary between fringes, which is important in order to increase the precision of the system (see Sect. 3.6). This method simply classifies the camera pixel as being lit by which projector pixel and supports other coding strategies such as phase measurement methods covered in Sect. 3.4.2.

Table 3.1 Two different orderings with $N = 4$ that respect the definition of a Gray code. Also, the natural binary code is also represented. Table courtesy of NRC

Ordering 1	Binary	0000	0001	0011	0010	0110	0111	0101	0100	1100	1101	1111	1110	1010	1011	1001	1000
	Decimal	0	1	3	2	6	7	5	4	12	13	15	14	10	11	9	8
Ordering 2	Binary	0110	0100	0101	0111	0011	0010	0000	0001	1001	1000	1010	1011	1111	1101	1100	1110
	Decimal	6	4	5	7	3	2	0	1	9	8	10	11	15	13	12	14
Natural binary	Binary	0000	0001	0010	0011	0100	0101	0110	0111	1000	1001	1010	1011	1100	1101	1110	1111
	Decimal	0	1	2	3	4	5	6	7	8	9	10	11	12	13	14	15

CONVENTION FROM GRAY TO BINARY$(gray[0...n-1])$
$bin[0] = gray[0]$
for $i = 1$ **to** $n-1$ **do**
    $bin[i] = bin[i-1]$ **xor** $gray[i]$
end for
return bin

CONVENTION FROM BINARY TO GRAY$(bin[0...n-1])$
$gray[0] = bin[0]$
for $i = 1$ **to** $n-1$ **do**
    $gray[i] = bin[i-1]$ **xor** $bin[i]$
end for
return gray

Fig. 3.6 Pseudocode allowing to convert the natural binary code into a Gray code and *vice versa*. Figure courtesy of [36]

Fig. 3.7 From left to right: an image of the object with surface defects; an image of the object when a Gray code pattern is projected; the camera image of a phase-shift pattern; the recovered phase for each camera pixel coded in greyscale level. Figure courtesy of NRC

The second algorithm provides a robust way for achieving sub-pixel accuracy [87]. The method requires the projection of both a Gray code and the associated reverse Gray code (white fringes are replaced by black ones and *vice versa*). Figure 3.8 illustrates the process of computing the position of a stripe's transition into the camera image. An intensity profile is constructed using linear interpolation for both the images of a Gray code and those of the associated reverse Gray code (Fig. 3.8, left and center). The intersection of both profiles is the sub-pixel location of the fringe transition (Fig. 3.8, right).

3.4.1.2 Advantage of the Gray Code

The Gray code offers a significant advantage over the natural binary code when using the previously described thresholding algorithm with noisy images. The reason for this is that more decoding errors occur on fringe transitions, namely, pixels where

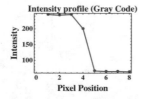 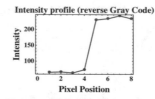 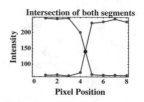

Fig. 3.8 Left: intensity profile of a white-to-black transition in the image of a Gray code. The values between pixels are obtained using linear interpolation. The transition is located between the 4th and 5th pixel. Center: the same intensity profile for the associated reverse Gray code. Right: the two previous graphs are superimposed and the intersection is marked with a dot. The transition is localized at pixel position 4.45. Figure courtesy of NRC

the pattern changes from dark to light or light to dark. For the Gray code, there are significantly fewer fringe transitions over the N patterns when compared to the natural binary code. In fact the natural binary code has the highest possible frequency of transitions in the Nth projected pattern, which corresponds to the least significant bit of the code.

Let us assume that the probability of getting an error when thresholding a camera image at a pixel located at a fringe transition is p, and that the probability of getting an error when no transition occurs is q, the probability of getting an error using a Gray code is $p \times q^{N-1}$ for all camera pixels located at a transition independent of the transition location. In this case, the Gray code results in a uniform distribution of error at the transition which is not the case with the natural binary code. The natural binary code has a probability of getting an error at a transition that ranges from p^N to $p \times q^{N-1}$. As an example, the probability of getting an error at the transition between 7 and 8 and between 0 and 1 in the natural binary code shown in Table 3.1 are p^4 (all bits change) and $p \times q^3$, respectively, (only one bit changes). As we have already mentioned, in a fringe projection system, it is expected that p is larger than q. Thus, the mean error rate at fringe transitions when using a Gray code is expected to be smaller than the one obtained using a natural binary code.

The narrowest fringes of a Gray code may be difficult to decode and are error-prone when the images are out-of-focus (see Sect. 3.8). For this reason, some systems use an ordering of the Gray code named large-gap Gray code which significantly reduces the measurement uncertainty [52]. The narrowest fringes of this ordering are larger than the narrowest fringes of the ordering generated by the pseudocode in Fig. 3.6. Another solution is to use the Gray code for establishing a coarse correspondence using the widest patterns and another code based on *phase measurement* replaces the narrowest patterns. Phase measurement methods (also known as phase shift) are presented next.

3.4.2 Phase-Shift Methods

While a Gray code is binary in nature (through a suitable thresholding of intensity images), phase-shift approaches use patterns containing periodic and smooth variations in greyscale level. The phase-shift patterns contain vertical fringes and each projector column, x_2, is associated with a phase value $\phi(x_2)$ using

$$\phi(x_2) = \frac{2\pi}{\omega} \text{mod}\,(x_2, \omega) \tag{3.16}$$

where ω is the spatial period of the pattern and mod is the modulo operator.

The intensity profile for each row is defined by $I(x_2) = A + B\cos(\phi(x_2) - \theta)$ where A and B are constants and θ is a phase offset. Many patterns with different phase offsets, θ, are required to establish the correspondence between the phase measured at a camera pixel and the phase associated with a projector fringe. Note that, because the modulo operator is used, this mapping is not unique and an extra unwrapping step is necessary to establish an unambiguous correspondence. Figure 3.7 shows a phase-shift pattern and the recovered phase.

The intensity of each pixel of the camera viewing the projected phase-shift patterns can be modeled using the following system of equations:

$$I_0(x_1, y_1) = A(x_1, y_1) + B(x_1, y_1)\cos(\phi(x_1, y_1) - \theta_0) \tag{3.17}$$
$$I_1(x_1, y_1) = A(x_1, y_1) + B(x_1, y_1)\cos(\phi(x_1, y_1) - \theta_1) \tag{3.18}$$
$$...$$
$$I_{N-1}(x_1, y_1) = A(x_1, y_1) + B(x_1, y_1)\cos(\phi(x_1, y_1) - \theta_{N-1}) \tag{3.19}$$

where $A(x_1, y_1)$, $B(x_1, y_1)$ and $\phi(x_1, y_1)$ are unknowns and θ_i are the known phase offsets in the projector. The number of patterns is N. $I_i(x_1, y_1)$ is the measured image intensity for camera pixel $[x_1, y_1]^T$ when the pattern with the phase offset θ_i is projected. Using the trigonometric identity $\cos(\alpha - \beta) = \cos\alpha\cos\beta + \sin\alpha\sin\beta$, the previous system of equations is equivalent to

$$I_0(x_1, y_1) = A(x_1, y_1) + B_1(x_1, y_1)\cos(\theta_0) + B_2(x_1, y_1)\sin(\theta_0) \tag{3.20}$$
$$I_1(x_1, y_1) = A(x_1, y_1) + B_1(x_1, y_1)\cos(\theta_1) + B_2(x_1, y_1)\sin(\theta_1) \tag{3.21}$$
$$...$$
$$I_{N-1}(x_1, y_1) = A(x_1, y_1) + B_1(x_1, y_1)\cos(\theta_{N-1}) + B_2(x_1, y_1)\sin(\theta_{N-1}) \tag{3.22}$$

where

$$B_1(x_1, y_1) = B(x_1, y_1)\cos(\phi(x_1, y_1)) \tag{3.23}$$

and

$$B_2(x_1, y_1) = B(x_1, y_1)\sin(\phi(x_1, y_1)). \tag{3.24}$$

Since the θ_i are known, $\cos\theta_i$ and $\sin\theta_i$ are scalar coefficients. The following more compact matrix notation can be used

$$\mathbf{M}\mathbf{X}(x_1, y_1) = \mathbf{I}(x_1, y_1) \tag{3.25}$$

where $\mathbf{I}(x_1, y_1) = [I_0(x_1, y_1), I_1(x_1, y_1), ..., I_{N-1}(x_1, y_1)]^T$,

$$M = \begin{bmatrix} 1 & \cos(\theta_0) & \sin(\theta_0) \\ 1 & \cos(\theta_1) & \sin(\theta_1) \\ & \cdots & \\ 1 & \cos(\theta_{N-1}) & \sin(\theta_{N-1}) \end{bmatrix} \tag{3.26}$$

and $\mathbf{X}(x_1, y_1) = [A(x_1, y_1), B_1(x_1, y_1), B_2(x_1, y_1)]^T$. In the presence of noise and when using more than three patterns, the system of equations may be over determined. In this case, the vector $\mathbf{X}(x_1, y_1)$ is obtained using the pseudoinverse and explicitly,

$$\mathbf{X}(x_1, y_1) = (M^T M)^{-1} M^T \mathbf{I}(x_1, y_1). \tag{3.27}$$

Note that $M^T M$ is invertible when M has rank 3. Alternative presentations can be found in [46, 74]. Once $\mathbf{X}(x_1, y_1)$ is computed,

$$B(x_1, y_1) = \sqrt{B_1(x_1, y_1)^2 + B_2(x_1, y_1)^2} \tag{3.28}$$

and

$$\phi(x_1, y_1) = \arctan(B_2(x_1, y_1), B_1(x_1, y_1)) \tag{3.29}$$

where $\arctan(n, d)$ represents the usual $\arctan(n/d)$ where the sign of n and d are used to determinate the quadrant.

We provide the details for the case $\theta_i = \frac{2\pi i}{N}$ for which

$$M^T M = \begin{bmatrix} N & 0 & 0 \\ 0 & \frac{N}{2} & 0 \\ 0 & 0 & \frac{N}{2} \end{bmatrix} \text{ and } M^T \mathbf{I}(x_1, y_1) = \begin{bmatrix} \sum_{i=0}^{N-1} I_i(x_1, y_1) \\ \sum_{i=0}^{N-1} I_i(x_1, y_1) \cos\left(\frac{2i\pi}{N}\right) \\ \sum_{i=0}^{N-1} I_i(x_1, y_1) \sin\left(\frac{2i\pi}{N}\right) \end{bmatrix}.$$

Explicitly, $A(x_1, y_1)$, $B_1(x_1, y_1)$ and $B_2(x_1, y_1)$ are computed using

$$A(x_1, y_1) = \frac{1}{N} \sum_{i=0}^{N-1} I_i(x_1, y_1) \tag{3.30}$$

$$B_1(x_1, y_1) = \frac{2}{N} \sum_{i=0}^{N-1} I_i(x_1, y_1) \cos\left(\frac{2i\pi}{N}\right) \tag{3.31}$$

$$B_2(x_1, y_1) = \frac{2}{N} \sum_{i=0}^{N-1} I_i(x_1, y_1) \sin\left(\frac{2i\pi}{N}\right) \tag{3.32}$$

and $B(x_1, y_1)$ and $\phi(x_1, y_1)$ are computed using Eqs. 3.28 and 3.29, respectively.

3.4.2.1   Removing the Phase Ambiguity

Once the phases have been computed, projector position x_2 corresponding to the camera pixel (x_1, y_1) is given as

$$x_2 = \frac{\omega}{2\pi}\phi(x_1, y_1) + k(x_1, y_1) \tag{3.33}$$

where $k(x_1, y_1)$ are unknown integers that represents the phase ambiguity. The value of $k(x_1, y_1)$ must be recovered in order to compute the location of the 3D points. We will briefly describe two different approaches that allow the removal of this phase ambiguity.

Fiducial markers can be embedded into the phase-shift patterns. These markers can simply be a white or black point. When there is only one marker, the 3D position of the surface on which the fiducial maker is projected can be computed by triangulation. This allows one to know the value of k for the camera pixel around a fiducial marker. It is then possible to propagate this information to neighboring pixels using a phase unwrapping algorithm. Phase unwrapping is frequently encountered in other fields such as synthetic aperture radar and interferometry. This is a complex subject and an entire book is devoted to it [42]. For these reasons, phase unwrapping will not be discussed further. When the projection patterns contain many fiducial markers, the epipolar constraint and the ordering constraint which are described in the previous chapter can be used to establish unambiguous matches between fiducial markers. Note that a similar fiducial approach is implemented in [57].

The second approach combines phase shift and Gray codes [82]. Binary codes, such as the Gray code, are often used to establish a coarse correspondence between projector and camera pixels using the thresholding algorithm presented previously. The patterns with the smallest stripes are not projected and are replaced by phase-shift patterns whose spatial periods are selected to match the smallest stripes projected. Combining binary and phase-shift code is a solution used in many experimental [79, 80] and commercial scanners. Note that phase shift with multiple spatial periods could also be used to remove the phase ambiguity.

3.4.3   Triangulation for a Structured Light System

In the projective-geometry framework of the pinhole camera, a digital projector can be viewed as an inverse camera and both share the same parametrization. Each implementation of an analogue slide projector can have its own parametrization. Nevertheless, they remain similar to a pinhole camera. Two commercial implementations are presented in [57] and [20]. Again, we consider an area-based scanner composed of a digital projector and a digital camera where phase-shift patterns are used. It is assumed that the projected fringes are vertical.

Suppose that the world coordinate system of the camera coincides with the world coordinate system and the extrinsic parameters of the projector are R_p and $\mathbf{T}_p$. A point in the camera is at a known position $[x_1, y_1]^T$ and one coordinate in the projector (i.e., x_2) is measured using phase shift. Again, x_1', y_1' and x_2' can be computed from x_1, y_1 and x_2 using Eq. 3.12. Moreover, the x_1', y_1', and x_2' provide the three following constraints on the 3D point $[X_w, Y_w, Z_w]^T$:

$$
\begin{bmatrix} x_1' \\ y_1' \\ x_2' \end{bmatrix} = \begin{bmatrix} \frac{X_w}{Z_w} \\ \frac{Y_w}{Z_w} \\ \frac{(r_{11}, r_{12}, r_{13})[X_w, Y_w, Z_w]^T + T_x}{(r_{31}, r_{32}, r_{33})[X_w, Y_w, Z_w]^T + T_z} \end{bmatrix}
\tag{3.34}
$$

where the r_{ij} are the elements of matrix R_p and $[T_x, T_y, T_z]^T = \mathbf{T}_p$. Assuming that, x_1' and y_1' define a known position in the camera, that x_2' is measured in the projector and that the three previous equations are linearly independent, we denote the 3D point $[X_w, Y_w, Z_w]^T$ corresponding to $[x_1', y_1']^T$ as $\mathbf{Q}_{(x_1', y_1')}(x_2')$. Explicitly, using Eq. 3.34 we obtain

$$
\mathbf{Q}_{(x_1', y_1')}(x_2') = \frac{(T_x - x_2' T_z)}{-x_1' r_{11} - y_1' r_{12} - r_{13} + x_2' x_1' r_{31} + x_2' y_1' r_{32} + x_2' r_{33}} \begin{bmatrix} x_1' \\ y_1' \\ 1 \end{bmatrix}.
\tag{3.35}
$$

3.5 System Calibration

There are three types of method that can be used to calibrate a triangulation-based scanner. Some methods are purely parametric, others are non-parametric, and, finally, some methods combine parametric and non-parametric elements. Non-parametric methods are well adapted to small reconstruction volumes and to the modeling of local distortions that can include mirror surface defects, or other nonlinearities that may be difficult to identify or model. Parametric methods make it possible to modify some parameters of the system without requiring a full recalibration. For example, the baseline of the system could be changed. The recalibration procedure would only need to recompute the pose between the camera and projection system; clearly, the intrinsic parameters would remain the same. This is not possible with non-parametric methods. While different cameras may use the same parametric model, an area-based digital projection system has a parameterization that is significantly different from a sheet-of-light laser projection system. We present a hybrid parametric and non-parametric method that could be adapted for the calibration of a large class of stripe and area-based triangulation scanners. Here, we will assume a fringe projection scanner that uses phase shift. The calibration of other scanners will be discussed briefly at the end of this section.

A parametric model is used to represent the camera while the projection system is viewed as a black box and a look-up table is built in order to calibrate the system.

This method requires a calibration bench consisting of an auxiliary camera and a planar surface mounted on a translation stage. Firstly, the scanner camera and the auxiliary camera, which together form a passive stereo rig, are calibrated using the methods described in Chap. 2. Given a pixel from the scanner camera and using the epipolar geometry presented in the previous chapter, it is possible to identify the corresponding epipolar line in the auxiliary camera. Moreover, the scanner-camera pixel and the corresponding point on this line must be lit by the same point of the projection system. The projection system is used to remove the ambiguity in the matching between the two cameras and the 3D points can be easily and accurately computed using this setup [32]. This two-camera-and-one-projector system is another type of triangulation scanner and products based on this principle are commercially available. Here, we use this two-camera setup only during the calibration stage. The planar surface is moved to different positions in the reconstruction volume. At each position i, a range image is produced using the method described above and the coordinate system of the scanner camera is used as the world coordinate system. Each 3D point is associated with a scanner-camera pixel $[x_1, y_1]^T$ and a measured position x_2 in the projection system. Two tables of the form $t_i(x_1, y_1) = x_2$ and $t_i'(x_1, y_1) = Z$ can be filled for each plane position i. Once the tables are filled, the auxiliary camera is no longer needed and the scanner can be used to acquire range images of unknown objects. For a given pixel $[x_1, y_1]^T$ in the camera and a measured position x_2 in the projector, one can find the entries $t_j(x_1, y_1)$ and $t_{j+1}(x_1, y_1)$ such that $t_j(x_1, y_1) < x_2 \leq t_{j+1}(x_1, y_1)$. Once these entries are found, the value of Z can be interpolated using $t_j'(x_1, y_1)$ and $t_{j+1}'(x_1, y_1)$ and the values of X and Y can be computed using Eq. 3.34. Note that the computation of the pixel coordinates $[x, y]^T$ from the normalized coordinates $[x', y']^T$ of Eq. 3.8 does not take into account the lens distortion. The following transformation takes into account lens distortion:

$$
\begin{bmatrix} x \\ y \end{bmatrix} = \begin{bmatrix} \frac{d}{s_x} & 0 \\ 0 & \frac{d}{s_y} \end{bmatrix} \left[k' \begin{bmatrix} x' \\ y' \end{bmatrix} + \begin{bmatrix} 2k_3 x'y' + k_4(r^2 + 2x'^2) \\ k_3(r^2 + 2y'^2) + 2k_4 x'y' \end{bmatrix} \right] + \begin{bmatrix} o_x \\ o_y \end{bmatrix} \tag{3.36}
$$

where $r^2 = x_2'^2 + y_2'^2$, $k' = 1 + k_1 r^2 + k_2 r^4 + k_5 r^6$ and the k_i are the radial and tangential distortion coefficients. This model is known as the Brown–Conrady model [22] and is widely used. Camera calibration packages often use similar distortion models. The computation of pixel coordinates from normalized coordinates is straightforward. However, the reverse computation, which is what we need, requires the use of iterative algorithms such as Levenberg–Marquardt and can be time-consuming. At calibration time, another table can be computed. This table, given a camera pixel $[x_1, y_1]^T$, provides the distortion-free normalized coordinates $[x_1', y_1']^T$ that are used to compute X and Y using Eq. 3.35.

A sheet-of-light system such as the one illustrated at Fig. 3.4-right can be calibrated similarly by replacing the tables $t_i(x_1, y_1) = x_2$ and $t_i'(x_1, y_1) - Z$ by $t_i(\alpha, y_2) = x_2$ and $t_i'(\alpha, y_2) = Z$, where α is the angle controlling the orientation of the laser plane, y_2 is a row of the camera, and x_2 is the measured laser peak position for the camera row y_2. Systems that use a Gray code with sub-pixel localization of the fringe transitions could be calibrated similarly. Note that tables t_i and t_i' can be large and the values inside these tables vary smoothly. It is, therefore, possible to fit a *nonuniform rational B-spline* (NURBS) surface or polynomial surface over these tables in order to reduce the memory requirement. Moreover, different steps are described in [24] that make it possible to reduce the sensitivity to noise of a non-parametric calibration procedure.

3.6 Measurement Uncertainty

In this section,[6] we examine the uncertainty associated with 3D points measured by an active triangulation scanner. Some errors are systematic in nature while others are random. Systematic errors may be implementation dependent and an experimental protocol is proposed to detect them in Sect. 3.7, while, in this section, random errors are discussed. This study is performed for area-based scanners that use phase shift. An experimental approach for modeling random errors for the Gray code method will be presented in Sect. 3.7. Moreover, because the description requires advanced knowledge of the image formation process, the discussion of random errors for laser-based scanners is postponed until Sect. 3.8.

In this section, we examine how the noise in the images of the camera influences the position of 3D points. First, the error propagation from image intensity to pixel coordinate is presented for the phase-shift approach described in Sect. 3.4.2. Then, this error on the pixel coordinate is propagated through the intrinsic and extrinsic parameters. Finally, the error-propagation chain is used as a design tool.

3.6.1 Uncertainty Related to the Phase-Shift Algorithm

In order to perform the error propagation from the noisy images to the phase value associated with a pixel $[x_1, y_1]^T$, we only consider the $B_1(x_1, y_1)$ and $B_2(x_1, y_1)$ elements of vector $\mathbf{X}(x_1, y_1)$ in Eq. 3.27. Thus, Eq. 3.27 becomes

$$[B_1(x_1, y_1), B_2(x_1, y_1)]^T = \mathbf{M'I}(x_1, y_1) \tag{3.37}$$

where $\mathbf{M'}$ is the last two rows of the matrix $(\mathbf{M}^T\mathbf{M})^{-1}\mathbf{M}^T$ used in Eq. 3.27. First, assuming that the noise is spatially independent, the joint probability density function $p(B_1(x_1, y_1), B_2(x_1, y_1))$ must be computed. Finally, the probability density function for the phase error $p(\Delta\phi)$ is obtained by changing the coordinate system from Cartesian to polar coordinates and integrating over the magnitude. Assuming that the noise contaminating the intensity measurement in the images is a zero-mean Gaussian noise, $p(B_1(x_1, y_1), B_2(x_1, y_1))$ is a zero-mean multivariate Gaussian distribution [30, 31]. Using Eq. 3.37, the covariance matrix Σ_B associated with this

---

[6]Contains advanced material and may be omitted on first reading.

distribution can be computed as

$$\Sigma_B = \mathbf{M}' \Sigma_I \mathbf{M}'^T \tag{3.38}$$

where Σ_I is the covariance matrix of the zero-mean Gaussian noise contaminating the intensity measured in the camera images [30, 31].

We give the details for the case $\theta_i = 2\pi i / N$ when the noise on each intensity measurement is independent with a zero mean and a uniform variance σ^2. One may verify that

$$\Sigma_B = \sigma^2 \begin{bmatrix} 2/N & 0 \\ 0 & 2/N \end{bmatrix}. \tag{3.39}$$

This is the special case of the work presented in [76] (see also [75]).

Henceforth, the following notation will be used: quantities obtained from measurement will use a hat symbol to differentiate them from the unknown real quantities. As an example $B(x_1, y_1)$ is the real unknown value while $\hat{B}(x_1, y_1)$ is the value computed from the noisy images. The probability density function is

$$p(\hat{B}_1(x_1, y_1), \hat{B}_2(x_1, y_1)) = \frac{N}{4\pi\sigma^2} e^{-\gamma(x_1, y_1)} \tag{3.40}$$

where

$$\gamma(x_1, y_1) = \frac{N((B_1(x_1, y_1) - \hat{B}_1(x_1, y_1))^2 + (B_2(x_1, y_1) - \hat{B}_2(x_1, y_1))^2)}{4\sigma^2} \tag{3.41}$$

Now changing to a polar coordinate system using $\hat{B}_1 = r\cos(\phi + \Delta\phi)$ and $\hat{B}_2 = r\sin(\phi + \Delta\phi)$ and $B_1 = B\cos\phi$ and $B_2 = B\sin\phi$ and integrating over r in the domain $[0, \infty]$ we obtain the probability density function

$$p(\Delta\phi) = \frac{e^{-\frac{B^2 N \sin^2 \Delta\phi}{4\sigma^2}} \left(2\sigma e^{-\frac{B^2 N \cos^2 \Delta\phi}{4\sigma^2}} + B\sqrt{N\pi} \cos\Delta\phi \left(1 + \mathrm{erf}(\frac{B\sqrt{N}\cos\Delta\phi}{2\sigma})\right)\right)}{4\pi\sigma} \tag{3.42}$$

which is independent of ϕ and where

$$\mathrm{erf}(z) = \frac{2}{\sqrt{\pi}} \int_0^z e^{-t^2} dt. \tag{3.43}$$

When σ is small and B is large, $p(\Delta\phi)$ can be approximated by the probability density function of a zero-mean Gaussian distribution of variance $\frac{2\sigma^2}{B^2 N}$ (see [76] for details). Assuming that the spatial period of the pattern is ω, the positional error on x_2 is a zero-mean Gaussian noise with

$$\sigma_{x_2}^2 = \frac{\omega^2 \sigma^2}{2\pi^2 B^2 N}. \tag{3.44}$$

The uncertainty interval can be reduced by reducing either the spatial period of the pattern, or the variance σ^2, or by increasing either the number of patterns used or the intensity ratio (i.e., B) of the projection system. Note that even if B is unknown, it can be estimated by projecting a white and a black image; however, this is only valid when the projector and camera are in focus (see Sect. 3.8).

3.6.2 Uncertainty Related to Intrinsic Parameters

When performing triangulation using Eq. 3.35, the pixel coordinates of the camera are known and noise is only present on the measured pixel coordinates of the projector. Thus, the intrinsic parameters of the camera do not directly influence the uncertainty on the position of the 3D point. The error propagation from the pixel coordinates to the normalized view coordinates for the projector can easily be computed. The transformation in Eq. 3.12 is linear and the variance associated with x_2' is

$$\sigma_{x_2'}^2 = \frac{\sigma_{x_2}^2 s_{x_2}^2}{d^2} \tag{3.45}$$

where s_{x_2} and d are intrinsic parameters of the projector and $\sigma_{x_2}^2$ is computed using Eq. 3.44. According to Eq. 3.45, as the distance d increases, or s_{x_2} is reduced, the variance will be reduced. However, in a real system, the resolution may not be limited by the pixel size but by the optical resolution (see Sect. 3.8). and increasing d may be the only effective way of reducing the uncertainty. As will be explained in Sect. 3.8, when d is increased while keeping the standoff distance constant the focal length must be increased; otherwise, the image will be blurred. Note that when d is increased the field of view is also reduced. The intersection of the field of view of the camera and projector defines the reconstruction volume of a system. Figure 3.9 illustrates the reconstruction volume of two systems that differs only by the focal length of the projector (i.e., the value of d also varies). Thus, there is a trade-off between the size of the reconstruction volume and the magnitude of the uncertainty.

3.6.3 Uncertainty Related to Extrinsic Parameters

The transformation of Eq. 3.35 from a normalized image coordinates to 3D points is nonlinear, hence we introduce a first-order approximation using Taylor's expansion. The solution close to $\hat{x}_2'$ can be approximated by

$$\mathbf{Q}_{(x_1',y_1')}(\hat{x}_2' + \Delta x_2') \approx \mathbf{Q}_{(x_1',y_1')}(\hat{x}_2') + \frac{d}{d\hat{x}_2'}\mathbf{Q}_{(x_1',y_1')}(\hat{x}_2')\Delta x_2' \tag{3.46}$$

where

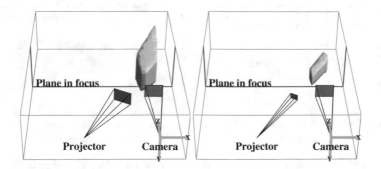

Fig. 3.9 The reconstruction volume of two systems where only the focal length of the projector is different (50 mm at left and 100 mm at right). The red lines define the planes in focus in the cameras. Figure courtesy of NRC

$$\frac{d}{d\hat{x}_2'}\mathbf{Q}_{(x_1',y_1')}(\hat{x}_2') = \frac{(-r_{33}T_x + r_{13}T_z - r_{31}T_x x_1' + r_{11}T_z x_1' - r_{32}T_x y_1' + r_{12}T_z y_1')}{(r_{13} + r_{11}x_1' - r_{33}\hat{x}_2' - r_{31}x_1'\hat{x}_2' + r_{12}y_1' - r_{32}\hat{x}_2'y_1')^2}\begin{bmatrix}x_1'\\y_1'\\1\end{bmatrix}.$$

(3.47)

Since a first-order approximation is used, the covariance matrix associated to a 3D point can be computed similarly as Σ_B in Eq. 3.39 [30, 31]. Explicitly, the covariance matrix associated with a 3D point is

$$\Sigma = \begin{bmatrix}x_1'^2 & x_1'y_1' & x_1'\\x_1'y_1' & y_1'^2 & y_1'\\x_1' & y_1' & 1\end{bmatrix}\frac{(-r_{33}T_x + r_{13}T_z - r_{31}T_x x_1' + r_{11}T_z x_1' - r_{32}T_x y_1' + r_{12}T_z y_1')^2}{(r_{13} + r_{11}x_1' - r_{33}\hat{x}_2' - r_{31}x_1'\hat{x}_2' + r_{12}y_1' - r_{32}\hat{x}_2'y_1')^4}\sigma_{x_2'}^2$$

(3.48)

where $\sigma_{x_2'}^2$ is computed using Eqs. 3.44 and 3.45.

The covariance matrix can be used to compute a confidence region which is the multi-variable equivalent to the confidence interval.[7] The uncertainty over the range (i.e., Z-axis) is an important design characteristic. Figure 3.10-left illustrates the confidence interval for different range values for the geometric configuration at the left of Fig. 3.9. As the range increases, the size of the confidence interval also increases. This is a characteristic of triangulation systems and this explains why triangulation systems are often used for short-range measurements [6]. Note that the results presented in Fig. 3.10 ignore many things such as the effect of optical components (see Sect. 3.8).

The usable measurement volume is the portion of the reconstruction volume for which the error on the position of a 3D point is expected to be smaller than a maximum permissible error. The depth of field of a scanner is the size of the interval of Z values inside this usable measurement volume. Note that because of optical limitations, such

---

[7]A confidence interval is an interval within which we are $(1 - \alpha)100\%$ confident that a point measured under the presence of Gaussian noise (of known mean and variance) will be within this interval (a typical value for α is 0.05).

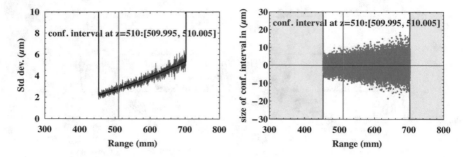

Fig. 3.10 Left: the standard deviation obtained from the first-order approximation and the Monte Carlo simulation points displayed in black and blue, respectively. Right: confidence interval size computed for many range values using a first-order approximation. The Monte Carlo simulation points are displayed at the top of the confidence interval. The reconstruction volume covers a range from 450 to 700 mm and is shown in Fig. 3.9-left. The confidence interval for $Z = 510$ mm is given. Figure courtesy of NRC

as blurring effects, the usable measurement volume can be significantly smaller than the reconstruction volume (see Sect. 3.8).

Since a first-order approximation is used when computing the uncertainty with Eq. 3.48, it is important to validate the results using Monte Carlo simulations. Figure 3.10 right shows the results of one such simulation. The simulation process consisted of the following steps:

- 50000 values of x_2' were generated using a uniform distribution.
- Zero-mean Gaussian noise was added to each point.
- The points were triangulated using Eq. 3.35 at $[x_1', y_1']^T = [0, 0]^T$.
- The variance of the range values obtained previously was compared with the one computed using the first-order approximation.

3.6.4 Uncertainty as a Design Tool

For design purposes, it is useful to fix the position of a 3D point and examine how the uncertainty varies when modifying the parameters of the system. In order to do so, it is possible to modify Eq. 3.48 such that x_2' is replaced by Z_w. As the distance between the views is increased, the size of the uncertainty interval for the range value is reduced. Moreover, configurations with vergence produce lower uncertainty than those without, due to the preferable large angle that a back-projected ray intersects a projected plane of light. Note that the baseline and the vergence angle are usually varied together to minimize the variation of the shape and the position of the reconstruction volume. Figure 3.11 illustrates the impact of varying these extrinsic parameters of the system on the confidence interval for a fixed 3D point. As the distance between the views is increased, the amount of occlusion that occurs is also

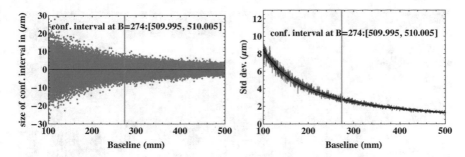

Fig. 3.11 Left: the size of the confidence interval when varying both the vergence (i.e., the angle around the Y axis) and the baseline for the the geometric configuration shown in Fig. 3.9 left. Right: the standard deviation for this geometric configuration. The confidence interval for a baseline value of 274 mm is given. This is the baseline value used by the geometric configuration shown in Fig. 3.9 left. Figure courtesy of NRC

increased. An occlusion occurs when a 3D point is visible in one view but not in the other one. This can occur when a 3D point is outside the reconstruction volume of a scanner or when one part of the surface occludes another. Thus, there is a trade-off between the size of the confidence interval and the amount of occlusion that may occur. The use of a Monte Carlo method for evaluating uncertainty is discussed further in [30].

3.7 Experimental Characterization

Manufacturers of 3D scanners and end users are interested in verifying that their scanner performs within predetermined specifications. In this section, we will show scans of known objects that can be used to characterize a scanner. Objects composed of simple surfaces such as a plane or a sphere can be manufactured with great accuracy. These objects can then be scanned by the 3D imaging system and the measurements taken can be compared with nominal values. Alternatively, a *coordinate measuring machine* (CMM) can be used to characterize the manufactured object. This object can then be scanned by the 3D imaging system and the measurements taken can be compared with those obtained by the CMM. As a rule of thumb, the measurements acquired by the reference instrument need to be a minimum of four times and preferably an order of magnitude more accurate than the measurements acquired by the 3D scanner.

We propose to examine three types of test for characterizing 3D imaging systems. Note that, the range images generated by a 3D imaging system are composed of 3D points usually arranged in a grid format. The first type of test looks at the error between 3D points that are contained in a small area of this grid. This type of test is not affected by miscalibration and makes it possible to perform a low-level characterization of a scanner. The second type of test looks at the error introduced

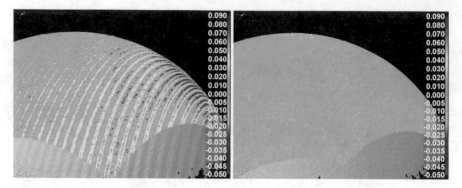

Fig. 3.12 An object scanned twice under the same conditions. A sphere was fitted to each set of 3D points. The residual error in millimeters is shown using a color coding. The artifacts visible in the left image are suspected to be the result of a human error. Figure courtesy of NRC

when examining the interactions between many small areas of the grid. This type of test makes it possible to perform a system-level characterization and is significantly affected by miscalibration. The last family of test is based on an industrial application and evaluates the fitness of a scanner to perform a given task.

In this section, we present the scans of objects obtained using different short-range technologies. Most of the scanners used are triangulation-based and there is currently a plethora of triangulation-based scanners available on the market. Different scanners that use the same technology may have been designed for applications with different requirements; thus, a scanner that uses a given implementation may not be representative of all the scanners that use that technology. Establishing a fair comparison between systems is a challenging task that falls outside of the scope of this chapter. The results shown in this section are provided for illustration purposes.

The human operator can represent a significant source of error in the measurement chain. The user may select a 3D imaging system whose operating range or operating conditions (i.e., direct sunlight, vibration, *etc.*) are inadequate for a given task. Alternatively, a user can misuse a system that is well adapted to a given task. Usually, this is a result of lack of experience, training, and understanding of the performance limitations of the instrument. As an example, in Fig. 3.12, a sphere was scanned twice by the same fringe projection system under the same environmental conditions. The scan shown on the left of the figure contains significant artifacts, while the other does not. One plausible explanation for these artifacts is that the selected projector intensity used while imaging the phase-shift patterns induces saturation for some camera pixels. Another plausible explanation is that the scanned object was inside the reconstruction volume of the scanner, but outside the usable measurement volume. Moreover, user fatigue and visual acuity for spotting details to be measured also influence the measurement chain.

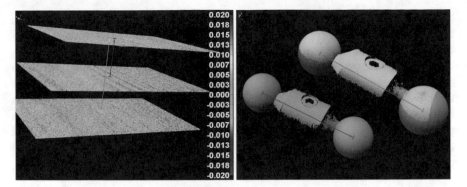

Fig. 3.13 Left: a point-based laser scanner was used to scan the same plane at three different positions. The residual error in millimeters is shown using a color coding. Right: a profile-based laser scanner was used to perform a center-to-center distance measurement between the centers of two spheres. The experiment was repeated at two different positions. Figure courtesy of NRC

3.7.1 Low-Level Characterization

Figure 3.13 shows multiple scans of a planar surface at different positions in the reconstruction volume. This type of experiment is part of a standard that addresses the characterization of the flatness measurement error of optical measurement devices [91]. When the area used to fit a plane is small with respect to the reconstruction volume, miscalibration has a very limited impact. A point-based laser triangulation scanner was used to illustrate this type of experiment. As expected from the results of the previous section, the root mean square (RMS) for each plane fit increases as the distance from the scanner increases (see Fig. 3.10). The RMS values are 6.0, 7.0, and 7.5 μm. However, it is not the error value which is important but the distribution of the error which can be seen in Fig. 3.13 using a color coding. This type of experiment makes it possible to identify systematic errors that are independent of the calibration. As a result, lens, geometric configuration, and other components of the system can be changed and the system can be retested quickly. Usually, the error analysis is performed using the raw output of the scanner and not the 3D points. This makes it possible to decorrelate the different error sources and thereby simplify the identification of the error sources. As an example, for a phase-shift triangulation system, the fitting of a primitive is not performed using the $[X_w, Y_w, Z_w]^T$ points obtained from the point triangulation procedure described in Sect. 3.4.3, but using the $[x_1, y_1, x_2]^T$ directly. Moreover, in order to take into account the distortion of the lens, the rotation of the mirrors and other nonlinear distortions, the raw data from the scanner is fitted to a NURBS surface rather than a plane.

We now examine an experimental protocol for measuring the error of the sub-pixel fringe localization of a Gray code fringe projection system[76]. It is assumed that no error in the decoding of Gray code occurs and the only error is in the sub-pixel localization of the fringe frontiers. Under projective geometry, the image in the camera of a projector fringe that is projected on a planar surface should remain a line. In a noise-free environment, and assuming that the line in the projector image is vertical with respect to the camera, each row y_1 of the camera should provide an equation of the form $[x_1, y_1, 1][1, a, b]^T = 0$, where x_1 is the measured frontier and a and b are the unknown parameters defining the line. Our camera contains more than two rows and the images are noisy, thus it is possible to use linear regression to estimate a and b. Once the parameters a, b of the line have been estimated, it is possible to compute the variance of the error on x_1. Since the optical components introduce distortion, a projected line may no longer be a line in the camera and polynomials can be fitted rather than straight lines.

3.7.2 System-Level Characterization

The results of fitting a model on a small patch of 3D points is not significantly affected by miscalibration. However, other measurements such as angles and sphere-to-sphere measurement are very sensitive to miscalibration. Sphere-to-sphere measurement is part of a guideline that addresses the characterization of optical measurement devices [91]. Two spheres are mounted on a bar with a known center-to-center distance. This object is known as a *ball bar*. This ball bar is placed at different predetermined positions in the reconstruction volume and the errors of center-to-center distance are used to characterize the scanner. Two scans of this object at two different positions are shown in Fig. 3.13.

MacKinnon et al. have presented a Portable Characterization Target (PCT) kit which consists of metrics, a reference object, software, and best practices for characterizing and verifying the operating limits of short-range 3D imaging systems [25, 65]. The metrics have been designed to correspond to some of the Geometric Dimensioning and Tolerancing (GD&T) metrics. GD&T is a universal language developed by mechanical engineers and used to define parts with their admissible errors. The PCT is shown in Fig. 3.14. The procedure and associated reference objects consists of 16 tests in 6 categories that are listed in Table 3.2. All computations are integrated within the Polyworks ImInspect®software from InnovMetric.[8] An example of form error on a plane and plane fit residual is shown in Fig. 3.14-right . The system-level characterization of active 3D imaging systems is further discussed in [9, 17, 23, 39, 62, 63].

3.7.3 Application-Based Characterization

We illustrate the principle behind this family of tests using a surface defect detection application. The objective of this application is to localize defects that create a vari-

---

[8]www.innovmetric.com.

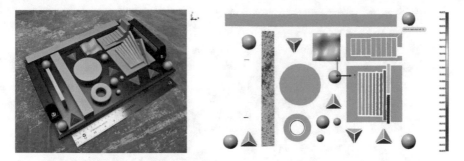

Fig. 3.14 Second generation of the Portable Characterization Target (PCT). Left: picture of the PCT. Right: illustration of the analysis results for one of the planes. The RMS plane fit residual (Gaussian deviation) is $8\,\mu m$ and the flatness (form error) is $50\,\mu m$. Figure courtesy of NRC

Table 3.2 List of the tests that can be performed using the PCT. The references values were obtained using a coordinate measuring machine. Figure courtesy of NRC

Category	Type	Test	Reference Values
Geometry	Form	Flatness	2
		Circularity	8
	Size	Sphere diameter error	8
		Sphere-spacing error	28
		Angle error	10
		Unidirectional plane-spacing error	9
		Bidirectional plane-spacing error	1
	Orientation	Angularity	10
	Location	Sphere position error	8
		Corner position error	5
		Hole position error	1
	Profile	Surface profile	1
Gaussian Dispersion		RMS plane-fit residuals	2
		RMS sphere-fit residuals	8
		RMS plane-fit residuals versus orientation	10
		RMS surface-fit residuals	1

ation on the surface of a product. In this type of application, the calibration of the system is not very important; however, the capability of the system to image small structural details is very important. In this test, an object which is known to contain defects is scanned and it is possible to verify the presence of these defects in the 3D data. Figure 3.15 illustrates surface defects as detected by four different systems. It is important to note that surface properties can significantly influence the performance of a scanner (see Sect. 3.8.6).

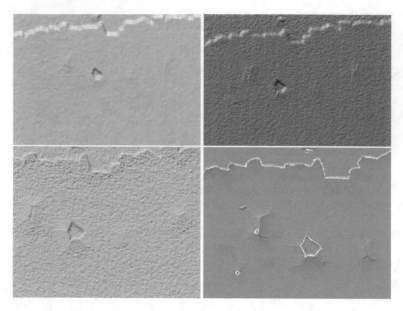

Fig. 3.15 The same surface containing defects scanned by four different scanners. Top left: point-based laser triangulation system. Top right: profile-based laser triangulation system. Bottom left: fringe projection system. Bottom right: scanner based on conoscopic holography. Figure courtesy of NRC

3.8 Selected Advanced Topics

This section[9] contains material that requires in-depth knowledge of the image formation process. Section 3.8.1 will present the thin lens equation. Sections 3.8.2 and 3.8.3 examine the depth of field of a triangulation-based 3D camera. Sections 3.8.4 and 3.8.5 give some important results whose derivations would require in-depth knowledge of diffraction and Gaussian beam optics. Section 3.8.6 discusses issues related to the laser beam thickness induced by Gaussian beam optics. Section 3.8.7 uses the results of Sect. 3.8.5 to discuss the lateral resolution of phase shift and spot scanners. Finally, Sect. 3.8.8 examines the impact of interreflection and the strategies that can be used to minimize interreflection artifacts. Further information concerning optical issues can be found in [12, 59, 85].

3.8.1 Thin Lens Equation

Optical systems are complex and difficult to model. A very useful approximation is the thin lens equation which provides a first-order approximation of a lens with

---

[9]May be omitted at the first reading.

negligible thickness. Given the distance Z between an object and the optical center of the lens and the focal length f of this lens, one may compute, using the thin lens equation the distance between the optical center and the image plane needed in order to obtain a sharp image of the object. Since optical engineering falls outside the scope of this chapter, we provide the thin lens equation without derivation (see for details [85]). The thin lens equation is

$$\frac{1}{Z} + \frac{1}{d} = \frac{1}{f} \tag{3.49}$$

where f is the lens focal length, Z is the distance between the optical center and the object plane, and d is the distance between the optical center and the image plane (i.e., the CCD or CMOS sensor).

Since $d \approx f$ when the distance between the camera and the object is sufficiently large, Chap. 2 and other textbooks use f (for focal length) rather than using d in their camera models (see Sect. 3.3.1).

Usually, 3D imaging systems are used for applications that require the scan of non-planar objects. Thus, Eq. 3.49 is not fulfilled for all the points on the surface of the object. As will be explained next, this induces out-of-focus blurring in some parts of the image.

3.8.2   Depth of Field

The point located at Z' in Fig. 3.16, will be imaged as a circle of diameter c on the image plane. This circle is named a *circle of confusion*. Using simple trigonometry and the thin lens equation, the diameter of this circle can be computed as

$$c = \Phi \frac{|Z' - Z|}{Z'} \frac{f}{Z - f} \tag{3.50}$$

where Φ is the size of the lens aperture. The proof is left as an exercise to the reader. Given a maximum diameter c_{max} for the circle of confusion and assuming that $Z' > Z > f$, the depth of field can be computed, using Eq. 3.50, as

$$D_f = 2(Z' - Z) \tag{3.51}$$

where

$$Z' = \frac{\Phi f Z}{\Phi f + (f - Z)c_{max}}. \tag{3.52}$$

Thus, a large lens diameter will induce a small focusing range, even though more light is captured by the imaging system.

Figure 3.17 right illustrates the impact of out-of-focus blurring on the magnitude of sinusoidal patterns used by a phase shift scanner. As the ratio between the circle-

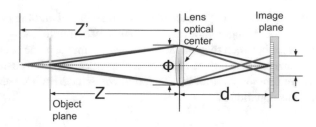

Fig. 3.16 The image of the point at distance Z from the optical center is in focus on the image plane, while the point at distance Z' from the optical center is imaged as a circle of diameter c on the image plane. The lens aperture is Φ and the distance between the image plane and the optical center is d. Figure courtesy of NRC

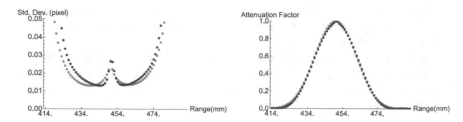

Fig. 3.17 Impact of the out-of-focus blurring of the camera on the performance of the scanner for both the model proposed by [37] in orange and the real data in blue. On the left is the standard deviation of the residual error of the surface fit of an optical flat in the unwrapped-phase image for different out-of-focus distances. On the right is the sine wave attenuation factor for different ranges (both the orange and blue curves are overlapping). Note that the in-focus distance is 450 mm; it corresponds to the position at which the attenuation factor is one (no attenuation) and to a local maximum for the range uncertainty. The point spacing of the system is $16\,\mu$m, the focal length of the camera is 100 mm and the magnification is $\frac{1}{2}$ (see [37] for more details). Figure courtesy of NRC

of-confusion diameter and spatial period of the pattern increases, the magnitude of the signal is reduced. In Eq. 3.44, it can be seen that reducing the spatial period reduces the uncertainty. However, once the optical components of the system are taken into account, one can see that reducing the spatial period, may also reduce the magnitude of the sinusoidal pattern, possibly increasing the uncertainty rather than reducing it. Both the projection lenses and the camera lenses induce this range-dependent attenuation of the sine wave. Moreover, the camera blurring induces a noise reduction by acting as a spatial filter. Drouin et al. presented a range-dependent correction coefficient for Eq. 3.44 that takes these effects into account [37]. For a high-resolution system, this coefficient varies with the range and exhibits a W-shape (see Fig. 3.17-left). Note than even when a system is perfectly in-focus, sensor resolution, diffraction, and aberrations induce a degradation of the image [85]. This can affect the W-shape by reducing the magnitude of the central peak. All of this demonstrates the important of factoring in the optically induced blurring and other optical related degradation when designing a system.

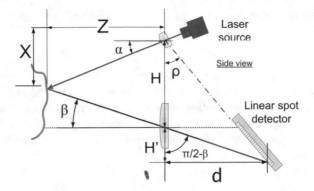

Fig. 3.18 Scheimpflug geometry for a point-based triangulation sensor. The baseline is H. The projection and collection angles are α and β, respectively. The angle between the photodetector and the collecting lens is ρ. The distance between the lens optical center and the position of the laser spot on the detector along the Z-axis is d, and H' is that separation along the X-axis. Figure courtesy of NRC

3.8.3   Scheimpflug Condition

As explained earlier, a large lens diameter will induce a small focusing range. This affects all triangulation-based 3D cameras and many of them use the *Scheimpflug condition* in order to mitigate the impact of this reduced focusing range [13]. In order to simplify the discussion, the Scheimpflug condition will be presented for a point-based scanner. Nevertheless, it could be used with profile-based and area-based scanners. Figure 3.18 shows an optical geometry based on the Scheimpflug condition for the point-based scanner presented in Sect. 3.2. Note that the optical axis is no longer perpendicular to the photodetector. The angle between the photodetector and the collecting lens is set to ρ and, as will be shown, this ensures that for a given illumination direction (i.e., angle α) all the points along the laser beam path will be in-focus on the position detector. Using simple trigonometry, one can verify that

$$\tan \rho = \frac{d}{H + H'} \tag{3.53}$$

and

$$H' = \frac{d}{\tan(\pi/2 - \beta)}. \tag{3.54}$$

where H' is a line segment in Fig. 3.18. We obtain

$$d = \frac{H \tan \rho}{1 - \tan \beta \tan \rho} \tag{3.55}$$

by substituting Eq. 3.54 in Eq. 3.53. Finally, substituting Eqs. 3.55 and 3.2 in Eq. 3.49, we obtain

$$\cot \rho = \frac{H - f \tan \alpha}{f}.$$ (3.56)

Thus, for a given α, the angle ρ can be computed such that any point along the laser beam path is in-focus on the position detector. This condition allows one to design a system with a large aperture to increase light collection power. As will be explained next, for a laser-based scanner, this allows the reduction of noise without affecting the focusing range.

3.8.4 Speckle and Uncertainty

In Sect. 3.6.1, the error propagation from image intensity to pixel coordinate was examined for area-based scanners that use phase shift and an expression for the variance $\sigma_{x_2}^2$ was provided. As shown, the variance $\sigma_{x_2}^2$ can then be used to compute the uncertainty on the 3D points computed by a triangulation scanner. Here, we give the result of a similar analysis performed for point-based systems that use a laser.

For laser-based system, the value of $\sigma_{x_2}^2$ depends on the type of laser spot detector used (e.g., CMOS, CCD, lateral-effect photodiode, split diodes), the laser peak detector algorithm, the signal-to-noise ratio (SNR) and the imaged laser spot shape [7]. The laser spot shape is influenced by lens aberrations, vignetting, surface artifacts, etc. In the case of discrete response laser spot sensors, assuming both a high SNR and a centroid-based method for peak detection, the dominant error source will be speckle noise.

Speckle noise is the result of the interference of many light waves having the same wavelength but having different phases. Different waves emitted by the projection system are reflected on the object at slightly different positions and thus reach the detector with slightly different phases. The light waves are added together at the detector which measures an intensity that varies. The speckle depends on the surface microstructure or roughness (of the order of the source wavelength) of the object which is scanned. Note that with a high-quality imaging system, speckle noise is more a multiplicative noise source than an additive source [90]. Explicitly, the variance $\sigma_{x_2}^2$ can be approximated as

$$\sigma_{x_2}^2 \approx \frac{\lambda^2 d^2}{2\pi \Phi^2}$$ (3.57)

where Φ is the lens aperture diameter, λ is the laser wavelength, and d is the distance between the laser spot detector and the collection lens [13]. The effects of speckle on the peak detection have also been studied by [4, 34, 61]. Note that when substituting Eq. 3.57 back into Eq. 3.45, one can verify that the presence of speckle noise caused by a laser does not depend on d. When λ is reduced or when Φ is increased, the uncertainty is reduced. While a large lens diameter reduces the uncertainty, it also limits the focusing range when a Scheimpflug condition is not used.

Note that speckle can be an important error source even for a fringe projection system that uses a spatially incoherent light source with a relatively long coherence length such as LED. The coherence length is proportional to the square of the nominal wavelength of the source and inversely proportional to the wavelength range [61].

The object surface microstructure combined with the light source spectral distribution can greatly influence the performance of a system. As an example, an optical flat surface was scanned with the same fringe projection system using two different light sources. The first one is a tungsten-halogen source with a large wavelength range, while the second one is a red LED having a narrow wavelength range. The experimentation was conducted in a controlled environment. The RMS values obtained using the two sources are 21 and 32 μm, respectively.

3.8.5   Laser Beam Thickness

Until now, the laser beam and collected ray were assumed to be infinitely thin. Though convenient to explain the basic principles, this is an over-simplification. Taking into account the properties of Gaussian beams associated with lasers is fundamental to understanding the limitations of some 3D laser-based vision systems [14, 18, 78]. As a result of diffraction, even in the best laser emitting conditions, a laser beam does not maintain focus with distance (see Fig. 3.19). Note that in many close-range 3D laser scanners, a focused laser beam is the preferred operating mode. This is a complex topic whose details fall outside the scope of this chapter. Nevertheless, because it is fundamental to understanding the resolution limitations of some 3D imaging systems, we give two important results concerning Gaussian beam propagation. Using the Gaussian beam propagation formula, the beam radius measured

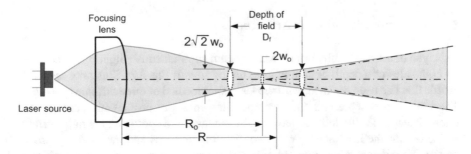

Fig. 3.19 The focus of an actual laser beam is governed by diffraction. We show the case of a focused laser beam with a Gaussian shape transversal profile. The minimum beam diameter is $2w_0$ and R_0 is the distance from the lens to the point at which the beam diameter is minimal. A maximum beam diameter of $2\sqrt{2}w_0$ is used to compute the depth of field, D_f, of the laser. Figure courtesy of NRC

orthogonally to the beam axis, denoted by $w(R)$ at the e^{-2} irradiance contour in the direction of propagation R is

$$w(R) = w_0\sqrt{1 + \left(\frac{\lambda(R - R_0)}{\pi w_0^2}\right)^2} \qquad (3.58)$$

where the distance R_0 is the distance from the lens to the point at which the beam radius is minimal. The minimum radius is denoted by w_0 and λ is the wavelength of the laser source. More details information concerning Eq. 3.58 can be found in [12, 59, 85]. In accordance with the Rayleigh criterion, the depth of field D_f for a focused Gaussian beam is $R_{max} - R_{min}$ where $w(R_{max}) = w(R_{min}) = \sqrt{2}w_0$ and $R_{min} < R_{max}$ and explicitly,

$$D_f = \frac{2\pi w_0^2}{\lambda}. \qquad (3.59)$$

For a point-based scanner, the depth of field D_f, the distance R_0, and the angular interval for the scanning angle α can be used to compute the usable measurement volume of the scanner. Moreover, the usable measurement volume of a sheet-of-light scanner could be computed similarly.

3.8.6 Artifacts Induced by the Laser Beam Thickness

In this section, we examine two types of artifact induced by the laser beam thickness. The first one is related to depth discontinuities and the second one is related to texture variations of the object being scanned. The presentation focuses on spot-based scanners, but all types of triangulation-based systems are affected by these artifacts.

3.8.6.1 Depth-Discontinuity Artifacts

This type of artifact results from the laser beam simultaneously lighting the surfaces on both sides of a depth discontinuity. The top row of Fig. 3.20 illustrates an actual profile that has been scanned, with the laser spot located at three different positions. The bottom part represents the corresponding intensity profiles measured on the linear detector. At the left, we have the case where the spot is on a single surface. In the center, the laser spot covers two different surfaces and the intensity profile on the linear detector is composed of two overlapping peaks. This creates a bias in the detected position of the peak. On the right side of the figure, the two peaks are no longer overlapping. The transition from one peak toward two distinct peaks is progressive which leads to artifacts that are spatially smooth near spatial discontinuities. On the top right side of Fig. 3.25 such artifacts are visible. Note that this type

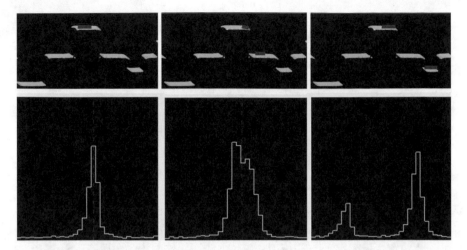

Fig. 3.20 Depth-discontinuity artifacts Top: example of the laser footprint (in red) at three positions on a surface. Bottom: actual intensity profiles on the linear detector corresponding to the laser spots shown on the top row. The linear detector intensity profile are generated by the scanner presented in Sect. 3.9.2 that uses the spot position detector presented in Sect. 3.2.1. When a peak is found its position is mark by a dashed red line. Figure courtesy of NRC

of artifact is dependent on the orientation of the imaging system with respect to the object being digitized.

3.8.6.2 Reflectance-Discontinuity Artifacts

The amount of light emitted by the projection system which is returned to the linear detector depends on the variations of reflectance of the object been scanned. When the laser spot covers a region with a varying reflectance, the values of some pixels on the linear detector can be significantly attenuated leading to a bias on the position of the measured peak. When successive 3D measurements have overlapping laser spots, very characteristic artifacts are created near sharp reflectance discontinuities (see Fig. 3.21). The artifacts depend on the relative orientation of the reflectance transition with respect to the scanner (see the right column of Fig. 3.21).

3.8.7 Lateral Resolution

Intuitively, the lateral resolution is the capability of a scanner to discriminate two adjacent structures on the surface of a sample. A formal definition can be found in [92]. For some applications such as the one presented in Sect. 3.7.3, it is critical to

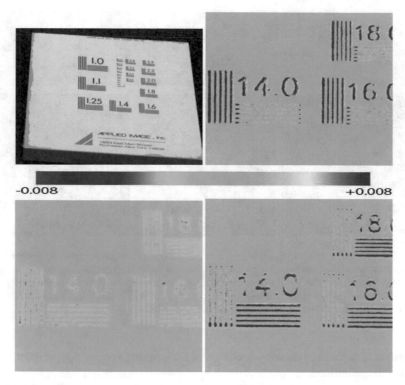

Fig. 3.21 A USAF resolution target used to evaluate the resolution of 2D imaging. An image of the target (top left). Multiple scans of the highest frequency region of the target are shown. For each scan, the deviation of the measured 3D points with respect to a plane is displayed using a color map (the unit is the millimeter). The top right and bottom right results were obtained using two different orientations of the target with respect to the baseline of the scanner. For the top scan the baseline is aligned with the horizontal line of the target, while the baseline is aligned with the vertical line for the bottom scan. The bottom-left image shows the result of an artifact-mitigation strategy that is presented in Sect. 3.9.3. The scanner presented in Sect. 3.9.3 was used to generate all of these results. Figure courtesy of NRC

use a 3D scanner with sufficient lateral resolution. The lateral resolution is limited by two factors which are the structural and the spatial resolution [92].

For a phase-shift system, when working out-of-focus, the lateral resolution of a system is not limited by the camera resolution (spatial resolution), but by the optical resolution (structural resolution) of the camera lens. Thus, to increase the lateral resolution, one may have to reduce the depth of field of the scanner or the lens aperture size. When a digital projector is used, artifacts induced by inter-pixel gaps and discretization may limit the lateral resolution of the system (see Sect. 3.9.4).

For a laser spot scanner, the knowledge of the beam radius on the scene allows one to determine the structural component of the lateral resolution of the system. The spatial resolution is the smallest possible variation of the scan angle α. Increasing the angular resolution of α can improve the lateral resolution as long as the spatial resolution does not exceed the structural one. Thus, reducing the beam radius may be the only way to increase the lateral resolution unless an auto-focusing method is used while measuring (see Sect. 3.9.2). When the beam radius is reduced, the depth of field is also reduced. Thus, there is a trade-off between lateral resolution and the depth of field. The evaluation of the lateral resolution of 3D imaging systems is further discussed in [45, 64].

3.8.8   Interreflection

Shiny objects with concavities are frequently encountered in industrial applications and they can represent a significant challenge for 3D imaging systems. In Sect. 3.2, it is assumed that the light emitted by the laser is directly reflected by the scene back to the detector. In the presence of shiny surfaces with concavities, a part of the laser beam can reach the surface and can be reflected onto a second surface before being indirectly reflected back to the sensor. The detector can thus register multiple peaks. One peak is created by the direct illumination, while other peaks are generated by indirect illumination (i.e., generated by interreflection). Sections 3.9.1 and 3.9.3 present two designs that are robust to indirect illumination. Another approach to mitigate interreflection is to positioned next to the diaphragm of the collection lens a dual-aperture mask. Using this modified collection lens, a laser spot will register as two peaks on the detector. The position of each peak can be independently used to compute the range. Moreover, the distance between the two peaks also depends on the range of the 3D point and this information can be used to filter out 3D points generated by indirect illumination [13].

Since area-based systems illuminate the entire scene simultaneously they are usually more affected by indirect illumination than point-based and stripe-based systems. They are three main approaches to reduce the impact of interreflection in area-based systems. One approach for 3D shape reconstruction in the presence of interreflections is based on explicit separation of direct and global illuminations. The global illumination excludes the direct illumination and includes the indirect illumination and all other illuminations that reach the detector. Nayar et al. [71] demonstrated that high-frequency patterns can be used to achieve a separation between the two types of illumination. Chen et al. [26] proposed the modulated phase-shift method where high-frequency patterns modulate low frequency patterns to separate the illumination components. Gu et al. [48] proposed a multiplexed illumination method for separating direct and global illumination. A codification method that associates a frequency to every projector column rather than a phase to every column is presented in [33]. In this frequency shift method, many patterns composed of sine wave with different frequencies are projected. The method allows the separation of direct and indirect illuminations. Figure 3.22 shows a comparison between phase shift (see Sect. 3.4.2) and frequency shift. Some approaches are designed to increase the resilience to global illumination. Gupta et al. [51] proposed the microphase shifting method that used groups of sine pattern frequencies selected in a high-frequency narrow band.

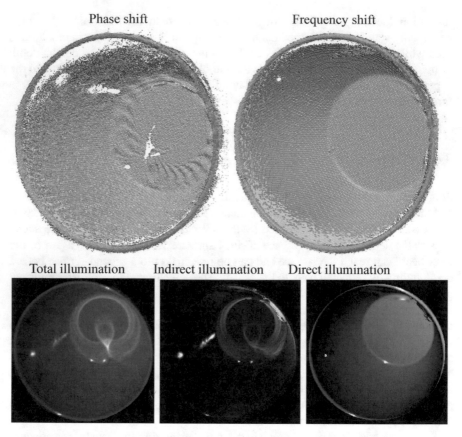

Fig. 3.22 3D reconstruction of a glazed ceramic bowl using an area-based system that employs phase shift and frequency shift. This object presents strong interreflections in its concavity. The bottom row shows the separation of direct and indirect illuminations obtained using the frequency shift method. To increase contrast, images have been scaled independently of each other. Figure courtesy of NRC

Gupta el al. [49] proposed the code ensemble method constituted by four groups of binary patterns among which we have high-frequency patterns, band-pass patterns, and standard Gray code. In Embedded Phase Shifting, high frequencies are chosen so that they can be combined to give low frequencies [68]. Two methods based on Hamiltonian coding robust to interreflection are presented in [50]. An unstructured light scanning method which use band-pass white noise patterns to mitigate inter-reflections is presented in [29, 66]. Other approaches are adaptive and the patterns they use are modified based on the projected images of patterns already acquired [27, 28, 95, 96].

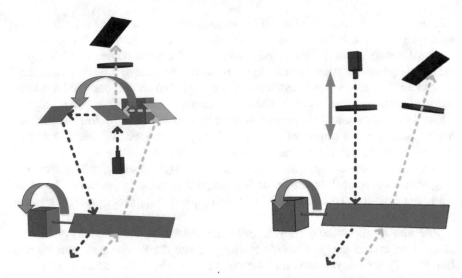

Fig. 3.23 Left: illustration of an auto-synchronized scanner with Scheimpflug geometry (see Sect. 3.9.1). Right: illustration of a lateral-synchronized scanner with Scheimpflug geometry (see Sect. 3.9.2). The static mirrors are shown in green, the galvanometers are in orange, and the lenses are blue. The laser sources are in red and the linear detectors are shown in black. The directions of movement of components are illustrated using gray arrows. The light beam that is emitted by the laser toward the scene is illustrated using a dashed red line. The light beam that is reflected from the scene toward the linear detectors is drawn using a dashed orange line. Figure courtesy of NRC

3.9 Advanced Designs

In this section,[10] four advanced designs are presented. The first two designs are point-based scanners, while the third one is a hybrid point-based and stripe-based scanner. The last design is for a high-resolution fringe projection.

3.9.1 Auto-Synchronized Design

The geometry of the point-based scanner presented in Sect. 3.2 can be modified using mirrors that fold the baseline such that the baseline of a system is larger than the physical scanner. The orientation of mirrors can be dynamically modified to limit the field of view of the camera such that the sensor only sees a small area around the laser spot [77]. This makes this design robust to indirect illumination. This type of point-based scanner is known as an auto-synchronized scanner and such a system is shown in the left side of Fig. 3.23. The basic system is composed of a double-side mirror mounted on a galvanometer and two fixed mirrors. One side of the double-

---

[10]May be omitted at the first reading and it is based on the material presented in Sect. 3.8.

side mirror is used for collection while the other one is used for the projection. By modifying the orientation of the double-side mirror, it is possible to acquire a profile. Notice the angle between the collection lenses and the linear detector which allows the Scheimpflug condition. In order to obtain a complete range image, another mirror can be mounted on a galvanometer. A scanner based on that designed has been used for space applications [81]. The simultaneous control of both galvanometers allowed complex scanning patterns that have been exploited to perform simultaneously tracking and scanning of moving objects [15]. A modified design replaces the second galvanometer by a translation stage and uses simultaneously three lasers having different wavelengths (red,green, and blue). By measuring the position and magnitude of each peak on the linear detector, it is possible to generate a 3D point with color attributes. This design has been used in many cultural heritage applications [44].

The auto-synchronized design has two main drawbacks: the assembly and alignment of the optical components are challenging and the Scheimpflug condition is fulfilled only for one orientation of the double-side mirror. The next design eliminates the folding of the baseline in order to simplify the assembly and allows the Scheimpflug condition to be valid for all measurements.

3.9.2 Lateral-Synchronized Design

A schematic of lateral-synchronized scanner is shown on the right side of Fig. 3.23. This type of scanner is composed of a single mirror for which the orientation is controlled by a galvanometer. One part of the mirror is used for collection, while the other part is used for projection. This configuration is discussed in [13]. Using this configuration, the Scheimpflug condition is valid for every orientation of the mirror. The spot diameter on the detector depends only on the projection optics and the depth of the surface of interest. It is thus possible to use an auto-focus optical component in the projection optics in order to have a small spot diameter over a large depth of field. A possible implementation uses lenses mounted on a piezo. The position of the piezo determines the focusing distance and it can be dynamically modified by predicting the depth of the point to be measured based on the points already measured. Systems using this configuration can simultaneously achieve a large depth of field and a high-lateral resolution. Figure 3.2 left contains a picture of lateral-synchronized scanner. This design is well adapted to the challenging application of turbine blades inspection. Figure 3.24 shows result from scanning a kitchen knife.[11] The system that produced this model had a point spacing of 7.5 μm, a laser spot diameter of 20 μm, and a dynamic depth-of-field of 1.5 mm. The wavelength of the laser is 405 nm and the standoff distance is 75 mm.

---

[11] The inspection results of turbine blades are usually confidential.

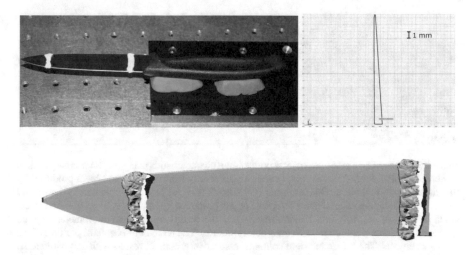

Fig. 3.24 Top left: picture of a knife. The white stripes on the blades are used to align multiple scans together using software from InnovMetric. Bottom: a shaded view of a complete model of the blade. Right: a cross-sectional view of the blade. The scans were obtained using the scanner presented in Sect. 3.9.2. Figure courtesy of NRC

3.9.3 Modified Lateral-Synchronized Design

The scanner design presented in this section is optimized to reduce the impact of the orientation dependent artifacts presented in Sect. 3.8.6. It is based on the lateral-synchronized design. One modification is that the linear detector is replaced by a 2D detector making the system similar to a stripe-based scanner. The projection subsystem remains point-based and it uses per point control of the focus and power output of the laser. This design preserves most of the advantage of the point-based scanners while having the acquisition rate of stripe-based scanners. The second modification is that the baseline was increased and the standoff distance was reduced thereby reducing the measurement uncertainty. The third modification is related to the peak detector software. The software preserves the peak position and other attributes of the peak that can be used during post-processing. The scanner is installed on top of a rotation table on which the object to digitize is fixed. The position and orientation of the scanner with respect to each orientation of the rotation stage need to be known. This mechanical calibration is critical, but the details fall outside the scope of this chapter. The object is digitized using many orientations and the different scans are merged together using the low-level attributes (which can include height, width, and number of peaks) and the prior knowledge of the variation of these attributes near depth and intensity discontinuities (see Fig. 3.20). Figure 3.21 demonstrates the reduction of intensity artifacts and preservation of the lateral resolution (the point spacing is 7.5 μm). Figure 3.25 top illustrates the robustness to interreflection and depth discon-

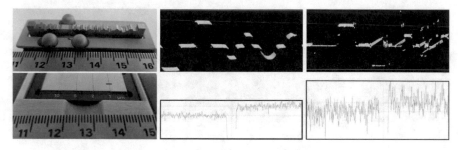

Fig. 3.25 Scans of two reference objects with known characteristics using the 3D imaging system presented in Sect. 3.9.3. The first row contains scan results from a reference object produced by the Physikalisch-Technische Bundesanstalt (Germany's national metrology institute). The second row contains scanning results from a reference object produced by Mututoyo. The reference object contains steps of 10, 5, 2, and 1 micrometer. Only the results for the one micrometer step are displayed (see the red line on the reference object picture). The left column contains pictures of the reference objects. The center and right columns, respectively, contain results with and without the artifact reduction strategy presented in Sect. 3.9.3. Figure courtesy of NRC

tinuities. Since speckle is also an orientation dependent noise, the proposed method can be used to significantly reduce the impact of the speckle noise. Figure 3.25 bottom illustrates the capability of the system to measure a one micrometer height step. A simpler mitigation strategy which is regularly encountered in commercial systems is to use two detectors, one on each side of the projection system.

3.9.4 High-Resolution Fringe Projection Design

In Sect. 3.4, fringe projection technologies are presented assuming digital projection systems. Digital systems have the advantage of being based on mass-produced devices. They have no moving mechanical component which provides greater stability and repeatability. They are programmable and can achieve high projection rates. However, digital projectors have limited resolution and each pixel is composed of an active region where the emissivity can be controlled and a passive one where emissivity cannot be controlled. We assume that the emissivity of a pixel is constant over its active region. The passive region, which surrounds its active region, is referred to as the inter-pixel gaps (see Fig. 3.26-left).

Drouin et al. presents a simple method to assemble a high-resolution 3D imaging system using a low-resolution projection device such as multimedia projector [35]. An optical element, such as a cylindrical lens, is installed on top of the projection optic. This element acts as a one-dimensional uniform blurring kernel tilted by an angle of 8° with respect to the pixel grid. The concept is illustrated in the right side of Fig. 3.26 using a digital device having two rows of pixels. Each row of the projector image contains the same discrete approximation of a sine wave. Figure 3.26 contains a sine wave approximated by a digital device. One can see that there is a large

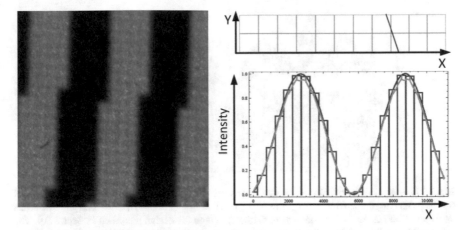

Fig. 3.26 Left: camera image of a binary pattern projected by a digital micromirror device chip. The inter-pixel gaps are clearly visible. Top right: a digital projector having two rows. The one-dimensional blurring kernel induced by the cylindrical lens is illustrated as a red and blue line. The color is used to illustrate the relative contribution to the final intensity of each row of pixels. Bottom right: the intensity profile generated by the configuration shown on the top. The ideal signal is shown in blue, in red is the discrete approximation, and in gold is the approximation obtained using the proposed method on the two-row digital device. Figure courtesy of NRC

difference between the sine wave and the digital approximation. The periodic drop of intensity to zero when inter-pixel gaps are encountered is particularly important. The method proposed in [35] improves significantly the sine wave approximation as shown on the bottom right of Fig. 3.26. The bottom left of Fig. 3.15 shows a scan that was acquired using a fringe projection system based on the presented method. The system uses a region of 1024 by 400 pixels from a digital micromirror device and a mosaic of two 16-million-pixel cameras.

3.10   Research Challenges

In Sect. 3.6, we presented the error propagation from the image formation to the 3D points for some area scanners. To the best of our knowledge, no commercial scanner associates a covariance matrix to each 3D point that can be used for performing a first-order error propagation. An important research issue is the understanding and modeling of error propagation from the calibration step to the visualization step of the modeling pipeline. This is challenging because the modeling pipeline can contain a significant amount of geometric processing such as the fusion of multiple scans, the transformation of point clouds into meshes, the decimation of triangles, and the fitting of geometric primitives. This understanding is now becoming critical as the use of handheld scanners for industrial applications has significantly increased in the last few year. These scanners perform many modeling tasks within the device [88,

Fig. 3.27 Shaded views of 3D models obtained by merging multiple scans of a new machining tool tip (left) and a used one (right). A picture of the machining tool is shown at the bottom. The scans were performed using a fringe projection system based on the design presented in Sect. 3.9.4. The point spacing is 7.5 μm. Note the presence of damage clearly visible on the tip of the tool. Figure courtesy of NRC

89]. In Givi et al., some of the error sources of a handheld scanner were quantified [43].

As the individual components of 3D imaging systems continue to improve, it is expected that the spatial resolution of 3D imaging systems will increase up to the limits imposed by physics. As an example, in recent years the resolution of cameras has significantly increased. This had a significant impact on the performance of fringe projection systems; however, there are physical limitations that make further improvement of a 3D scanner impossible. As an example, a laser point scanner can be designed to reduce the speckle noise, but the presence of coherence in the optical system induces a limit to this noise reduction [53]. Another example of physical limitations is the diffraction introduced by the finite size of a lens aperture. Thus, one of the main challenges in the development of 3D imaging systems is to combine the improvements in commercially available components with innovative new designs and algorithms in order to bring the performance of the system as close as possible to the physical limits. Adapting 3D imaging systems for the newest materials used in advanced manufacturing is an ongoing challenge.

Finally, as the cost of components for 3D imaging systems drops, high performance 3D systems are expected to become affordable. This creates opportunities to revisit manufacturing processes and incorporate vision systems in ways that were not considered financially viable a few years ago (see Fig. 3.27 for a machining application).

3.11 Concluding Remarks

Many of the traditional measurement instruments like theodolites and coordinate measuring machines are being replaced by noncontact optical scanners based on triangulation, time-of-flight, or interferometry technology. This sudden change in process design and quality assurance practices needs to be addressed by research organizations and companies. When the goal of a business is to make a quality product for a profit, then metrology will have a direct impact on that business. The quality of measurements planned in the design stage, applied during manufacturing, and performed during inspection directly affect the quality of a product. Poor measurements (those without an accuracy statement) may even lead to creating waste with scrapped products. Conversely, precise measurements (those with an accuracy statement) lead to superior products. The dimensional deviations between as-designed, as-built, and as-measured devices can only be understood and controlled if traceable measurements can be made in compliance with clear standards. While 3D imaging systems are more widely available, standards, best practices, and comparative data are limited. In the near future, we hope to see more comparative data in scientific publications and industrial standards aimed at active triangulation systems [9].

3.12 Further Reading

One of the earliest papers on triangulation-based spot scanning for the capture and recording of 3D data was published by Forsen in 1968 [40]. Kanade presents a collection of chapters from different authors that describe a number of close-range active 3D imaging systems [60]. Many survey papers that review range sensors have been published [1, 13]. The calibration of point-based triangulation scanners is discussed in [8, 10, 24].

Two articles published by Salvi et al. [79, 80] present an in-depth classification of different types of structured light patterns. Davis et al. [32] present a unifying framework within which one can categorize 3D triangulation sensors, for example, on the basis of their coding within the spatial and temporal domains. Moreover, an analysis of the uncertainty of a white light fringe projection based on Gray codes is presented in [87]. Many analyses of the impact of random noise on phase-shift methods have been conducted [46, 55, 76, 86]. In Sect. 3.6, the effect on the measurement uncertainty of changes on the geometric configuration of a structured light system was presented. A related topics explored by Mirdehghan et al. is the selection of the best structured light patterns given a geometric configuration [67].

An active area of research is the design of structured light systems that must scan very challenging objects, such as translucent objects [70]. More details about the measurement system and the positioning systems of handheld devices can be found in[54]. Some components of the sophisticated software pipeline used by handheld devices are described in [88, 89].

The two authoritative texts on the matter of uncertainty and vocabulary related to metrology are the *Guide to the Expression of Uncertainty in Measurement* (GUM) and the *International Vocabulary of Metrology* (VIM) [41, 58]. The document designated E 2544 from the American Society for Testing and Materials (ASTM) provides the definition and description of terms for 3D imaging systems [3]. Moreover, VDI 2634 is a document from a standardization body that addresses the characterization of optical distance sensors [91]. Error propagation in the context of multiple-view geometry is discussed in [31] .

3.13 Questions

1. Name and explain four categories of triangulation scanner, based on different methods of scene illumination.
2. In recent years, the resolution of cameras has significantly increased. What are the impacts of this on each type of triangulation scanner?
3. What are the impacts on the 3D data of varying the distance between the camera and the laser source of a laser stripe scanner without recalibrating the system?
4. What are the impacts on the 3D data of varying the distance, d, (the distance between the camera center and image plane) of a laser stripe scanner without recalibrating the system?
5. What are the values of R_p, $\mathbf{T}_p$, x_1', y_1' and x_2' for which the three constraints in Eq. 3.34 are not linearly independent?
6. What is the static depth of field of the scanner described in Sect. 3.9.2?
7. What are the elements that can limit the lateral resolution of a stripe scanner? Classify those elements as belonging to the spatial or structural resolution.

3.14 Exercises

1. Using a programming environment of your choice, develop a 2D simulator of a phase-shift fringe projection scanner that can reproduce the intensity artifact described into Sect. 3.8.6.2. Assume that optical-induced blurring is only present in the camera images and that the camera has an infinite spatial resolution. Repeat the experiment for a fringe projection system that uses a Gray code.
2. Modify the previously developed prototype in order to apply it to a stripe scanner. Plot a graph that shows the variation of error due to the width of the stripe.
3. Perform the error propagation computation for a stripe scanner that includes uncertainty on the angles α.
4. Using Fig. 3.16, trigonometry and the thin lens equation, give the derivation of Eq. 3.50.
5. Modify the camera model presented in Sect. 3.3.1 to incorporate a Scheimpflug condition.

6. Some projectors have a digital micromirror device (DMD) chip having diamond-shaped pixels rather than square shaped ones. Generate a version of Fig. 3.26 for a diamond-shaped DMD.
7. Implement the projection system presented in Sect. 3.9.4 using a multimedia projector.
8. Using the projection system previously implemented, developed a phase-shift method that uses multiple spatial periods to remove the phase ambiguity.

Acknowledgements The authors would like to acknowledge the numerous contributions of their colleagues at the National Research Council, Canada. In particular, Sect. 3.9 presents innovations based on contributions from many colleagues.

References

1. Amann, M.C., Bosch, T., Lescure, M., Myllylä, R., Rioux, M.: Laser ranging: a critical review of usual techniques for distance measurement. Opt. Eng. **40**(1), 10–19 (2001)
2. American National Standards Institute (ANSI): ANSI Z136 Part 1-6, American National Standard for Safe use of Lasers (2007)
3. American Society for Testing and Materials: ASTM E2544 - 10 Standard Terminology for Three-Dimensional (3D) Imaging Systems (2010)
4. Baribeau, R., Rioux, M.: Influence of speckle on laser range finders. App. Opt. **30**(20), 2873–2878 (1991)
5. Benoit, P., Mathieu, E., Hormière, J., Thomas, A.: Characterization and control of three-dimensional objects using fringe projection techniques. Nouvelle Revue d'Optique **6**(2), 67–86 (1975)
6. Beraldin, J.A., Blais, F., Lohr, U.: Laser scanning technology. In: Vosselman, G., Mass, H-G. (eds) Airborne and Terrestrial Laser Scanning. Whittles Publishers, Dunbeath (2010)
7. Beraldin, J.A., Blais, F., Rioux, M., Domey, J., Gonzo, L., Nisi, F.D., Comper, F., Stoppa, D., Gottardi, M., Simoni, A.: Optimized position sensors for flying-spot active triangulation systems. In: Proceedings of International Conference on 3D Digital Imaging and Modeling, pp. 29–36 (2003)
8. Beraldin, J.A., El-Hakim, S.F., Cournoyer, L.: Practical range camera calibration. SPIE Proc., Videometrics **II**, 21–31 (1993)
9. Beraldin, J.A., Mackinnon, D., Cournoyer, L.: Metrological characterization of 3D imaging systems: progress report on standards developments. In: 17th International Congress of Metrology, p. 13003. EDP Sciences (2015)
10. Beraldin, J.A., Rioux, M., Blais, F., Godin, G., Baribeau, R.: Model-based calibration of a range camera (1992)
11. Besl, P.J.: Active, optical range imaging sensors. Mach. Vis. Appl. **1**(2), 127–152 (1988)
12. Blahut, R.E.: Theory of Remote Image Formation. Cambridge University Press, Cambridge (2004)
13. Blais, F.: Review of 20 years of range sensor development. J. Electron. Imaging **13**(1), 231–243 (2004)
14. Blais, F., Beraldin, J.A.: Recent developments in 3D multi-modal laser imaging applied to cultural heritage. Mach. Vis. Appl. **17**(3), 395–409 (2006)
15. Blais, F., Beraldin, J.A., Cournoyer, L.., El-Hakim, S., Picard, M., Domey, J., Rioux, M.: The nrc 3-D laser tracking system: Iit's contribution to the international space station project. In: Proceedings of the 2001 Workshop of Italy-Canada on 3D Digital Imaging and Modeling Application of : Heritabe, Industry, Medicine, and Land (2001)

16. Blais, F., Rioux, M.: Real-time numerical peak detector. Sig. Process. **11**(2), 145–155 (1986)
17. Boehler, W., Marbs, A.: Investigating scanner accuracy. Technical report, German University FH Mainz (2003)
18. Born, M., Wolf, E.: Principles of Optics: Electromagnetic Theory of Propagation, Interference and Diffraction of Light, 7 edn. Cambridge University Press, Cambridge (1999)
19. Bosch, T., Lescure, M. (eds.): Selected Papers on Laser Distance Measurements, vol. MS 115, B. J. Thompson General editor SPIE Milestone Series (1995)
20. Breuckmann, GmbH: Projector for an arrangement for three-dimensional optical measurement of object. United State Patent Office 7532332 (2009)
21. British Standards Institution: BS EN 62471:2008, British Standards photobiological safety of lamps and lamp systems (2008)
22. Brown, D.: Decentering distortion of lenses. Photom. Eng. **32**(3), 444–462 (1966)
23. Brownhill, A., Brade, R., Robson, S.: Performance study of non-contact surface measurement technology for use in an experimental fusion device. In: 21st Annual IS&T/SPIE Symposium on Electronic Imaging (2009)
24. Bumbaca, F., Blais, F.: Real-time correction of three-dimensional non-linearities for a laser range finder. Opt. Eng. (1986)
25. Carrier, B., Mackinnon, D., Cournoyer, L., Beraldin, J.A.: Proposed nrc portable target case for short-range triangulation-based 3-D imaging systems characterization. In: 23st Annual IS&T/SPIE Symposium on Electronic Imaging (2011)
26. Chen, T., Seidel, H.P., Lensch, H.P.A.: Modulated phase-shifting for 3D scanning. In: Proceedings of the IEEE Conference on Computer Vision and Pattern Recognition (CVPR), pp. 1–8 (2008)
27. Chen, X., Yang, Y.H.: Scene adaptive structured light using error detection and correction. Pattern Recogn. **48**(1), 220–230 (2015)
28. Chiba, N., Arai, S., Hashimoto, K.: Feedback projection for 3D measurements under complex lighting conditions. In: 2017 American Control Conference (ACC), pp. 4649–4656 (2017)
29. Couture, V., Martin, N., Roy, S.: Unstructured light scanning robust to indirect illumination and depth discontinuities. Int. J. Comput. Vis. **108**(3), 204–221 (2014)
30. Cox, M.G., Siebert, B.R.L.: The use of a monte carlo method for evaluating uncertainty and expanded uncertainty. Metrologia **43**(4), S178 (2006)
31. Criminisi, A.: Accurate Visual Metrology from Single and Multiple Uncalibrated Images. Springer, New York (2001)
32. Davis, J., Nehab, D., Ramamoorthi, R., Rusinkiewicz, S.: Spacetime stereo: a unifying framework for depth from triangulation. IEEE Trans. Pattern Anal. Mach. Intell. **27**(2), 296–302 (2005)
33. Dizeu, F.B.D., Boisvert, J., Drouin, M.A., Godin, G., Rivard, M., Lamouche, G.: Frequency shift method: a robust fringe projection technique for 3d shape acquisition in the presence of strong interreflections. In: International Conference on 3D Vision (2019)
34. Dorsch, R.G., Häusler, G., Herrmann, J.M.: Laser triangulation: fundamental uncertainty in distance measurement. Appl. Opt. **33**(7), 1306–1314 (1994)
35. Drouin, M., Blais, F., Godin, G.: High resolution projector for 3D imaging. In: 2014 2nd International Conference on 3D Vision, pp. 337–344 (2014)
36. Drouin, M.A.: Mise en correspondance active et passive pour la vision par ordinateur multivue. Université de Montréal (2007)
37. Drouin, M.A., Blais, F., Picard, M., Boisvert, J., Beraldin, J.A.: Characterizing the impact of optically induced blurring of a high-resolution phase-shift 3D scanner. Mach. Vis. Appl. **28**(8), 903–915 (2017)
38. Fisher, R.B., Naidu, D.K.: A comparison of algorithms for subpixel peak detection. In: Image Technology, Advances in Image Processing, Multimedia and Machine Vision, pp. 385–404. Springer, Berlin (1996)
39. Forbes, A.B., Hughes, B., Sun, W.: Comparison of measurements in co-ordinate metrology. Measurement **42**(10), 1473–1477 (2009)

40. Forsen, G.: Processing visual data with an automaton eye. In: Pictorial Pattern Recognition, pp. 471–502 (1968)
41. French College of Metrology: CGM 200:2008, International Vocabulary of metrology – Basic and general concepts and associated terms (VIM) (2008)
42. Ghiglia, D.C., Pritt, M.D.: Two-dimensional Phase Unwrapping Theory, Algorithms and Software. Wiley, Hoboken (1998)
43. Givi, M., Cournoyer, L., Reain, G., Eves, B.: Performance evaluation of a portable 3D imaging system. Precis. Eng. (2019)
44. Godin, G., Beraldin, J.A., Taylor, J., Cournoyer, L., Rioux, M., El-Hakim, S., Baribeau, R., Blais, F., Boulanger, P., Domey, J., Picard, M.: Active optical 3D imaging for heritage applications. IEEE Comput. Graph. Appl. **22**(5), 24–35 (2002)
45. Goesele, M., Fuchs, C., Seidel, H.P.: Accuracy of 3D range scanners by measurement of the slanted edge modulation transfer function. In: International Conference on 3D Digital Imaging and Modeling, p. 37 (2003)
46. Goldberg, K.A., Bokor, J.: Fourier-transform method of phase-shift determination. Appl. Opt. **40**(17), 2886–2894 (2001)
47. Gray, F.: Pulse code communication. United States Patent Office 2632058 (1953)
48. Gu, J., Kobayashi, T., Gupta, M., Nayar, S.K.: Multiplexed illumination for scene recovery in the presence of global illumination. In: Proceedings of the IEEE International Conference on Computer Vision (ICCV), pp. 691–698 (2011)
49. Gupta, M., Agrawal, A., Veeraraghavan, A., Narasimhan, S.G.: A practical approach to 3D scanning in the presence of interreflections, subsurface scattering and defocus. Int. J. Comput. Vis. **102**(1), 33–55 (2013)
50. Gupta, M., Nakhate, N.: A geometric perspective on structured light coding. In: Ferrari, V., Hebert, M., Sminchisescu, C., Weiss, Y. (eds.) Computer Vision - ECCV 2018, pp. 90–107 (2018)
51. Gupta, M., Nayar, S.K.: Micro phase shifting. In: Proceedings of the 2012 IEEE Conference on Computer Vision and Pattern Recognition (CVPR), CVPR '12, pp. 813–820 (2012)
52. Hansen, K., Pedersen, J., Sølund, T., Aanæs, H., Kraft, D.: A structured light scanner for hyper flexible industrial automation. In: 2nd International Conference on 3D Vision, vol. 1, pp. 401–408 (2014)
53. Häusler, G., Kreipl, S., Lampalzer, R., Schielzeth, A., Spellenberg, B.: New range sensors at the physical limit of measuring uncertainty of measuring uncertainty. In: Proceedings of the EOS Topical Meeting on Optoelectronics Distance Measurements and Applications (1997)
54. Hebert, P.: A self-referenced hand-held range sensor. In: Proceedings Third International Conference on 3-D Digital Imaging and Modeling, pp. 5–12 (2001)
55. Hibino, K.: Susceptibility of systematic error-compensating algorithms to random noise in phase-shifting interferometry. Appl. Opt. **36**(10), 2084–2093 (1997)
56. Inokuchi, S., Sato, K., Matsuda, F.: Range imaging system for 3-D object recognition. In: Proceedings of International Conference on Pattern Recognition, pp. 806–808 (1984)
57. Inc, Inspect: Optional 3D digitizer, system and method for digitizing an object. United States Patent Office 6493095 (2002)
58. International Standards Organization (ISO): ISO Guide 98-3, Uncertainty of Measurement – Part 3: Guide to the Expression of Uncertainty in Measurement, GUM (1995)
59. Jahne, B., Haussecker, H.W., Geissler, P.: Handbook of Computer Vision and Applications. 1. Sensors and Imaging. Academic, Cambridge (1999)
60. Kanade, T. (ed.): Three-dimensional Machine Vision. Kluwer Academic Publishers, Norwell (1987)
61. Leach, R. (ed.): Optical Measurement of Surface Topography. Springer, Berlin (2011)
62. Luhmann, T., Bethmann, F., Herd, B., Ohm, J.: Comparison and verification of optical 3-D surface measurment systems. In: The International Archives of the Photogrammetry, Remote Sensing and Spatial Information Sciences, vol. XXXVII. Part B5. Beijing (2008)
63. MacKinnon, D., Aitken, V., Blais, F.: Review of measurement quality metrics for range imaging. J. Electron. Imaging **17** (2008)

64. MacKinnon, D.K., Beraldin, J.A., Cournoyer, L., Picard, M., Blais, F.: Lateral resolution challenges for triangulation-based three-dimensional imaging systems. Optical Engineering **51**(2), 1–16 (2012)
65. MacKinnon, D.K., Carrier, B., Beraldin, J., Cournoyer, L.: GD&T-based characterization of short-range non-contact 3D imaging systems. Int. J. Comput. Vis. **102**(1–3), 56–72 (2013)
66. Martin, N., Couture, V., Roy, S.: Subpixel scanning invariant to indirect lighting using quadratic code length. In: The IEEE International Conference on Computer Vision (ICCV) (2013)
67. Mirdehghan, P., Chen, W., Kutulakos, K.N.: Optimal structured light à la carte. In: The IEEE Conference on Computer Vision and Pattern Recognition (CVPR) (2018)
68. Moreno, D., Son, K., Taubin, G.: Embedded phase shifting: robust phase shifting with embedded signals. In: The IEEE Conference on Computer Vision and Pattern Recognition (CVPR) (2015)
69. Naidu, K., Fisher, R.B.: A comparative analysis of algorithms for determining the peak position of a stripe to sub-pixel accuracy. In: Proceedings of British Machine Vision Conference (1991)
70. Narasimhan, S.G., Nayar, S.K., Sun, B., Koppal, S.J.: Structured light in scattering media. In: Proceedings of the 10th IEEE International Conference on Computer Vision (ICCV), pp. 420–427 (2005)
71. Nayar, S.K., Krishnan, G., Grossberg, M.D., Raskar, R.: Fast separation of direct and global components of a scene using high frequency illumination. In: ACM SIGGRAPH 2006 Papers, SIGGRAPH '06, pp. 935–944 (2006)
72. Newhall, B.: Photosculture. Image: J. Photogr. Motion Pict. Georg. Eastman House **7**(5), 100–105 (1958)
73. Nitzan, D.: Three-dimensional vision structure for robot applications. IEEE Trans. Pattern Anal. Mach. Intell. **10**(3), 291–309 (1988)
74. Ohyama, N., Kinoshita, S., Cornejo-Rodriguez, A., Tsujiuchi, J.: Accuracy of phase determination with unequal reference phase shift. J. Opt. Soc. Am. A **12**(9), 1997–2008 (1995)
75. Rathjen, C.: Optical Shop Testing. Malacara (ed.). Wiley, Hoboken (1978)
76. Rathjen, C.: Statistical properties of phase-shift algorithms. J. Opt. Soc. Am. A **12**(9), 1997–2008 (1995)
77. Rioux, M.: Laser range finder based on synchronized scanners. App. Opt. **23**(21), 3837–3855 (1984)
78. Rioux, M., Taylor, D., Duggan, M.: Design of a large depth of view three-dimensional camera for robot vision. Opt. Eng. **26**(12), 1245–1250 (1987)
79. Salvi, J., Fernandez, S., Pribanic, T., Llado, X.: A state of the art in structured light patterns for surface profilometry. Pattern Recogn. **43**(8), 2666–2680 (2010)
80. Salvi, J., Pages, J., Batlle, J.: Pattern codification strategies in structured light systems. Pattern Recogn. **37**(4), 827–849 (2004)
81. Samson, C., English, C.E., DesLauriers, A.M., Christie, I., Blais, F.: Imaging and tracking elements of the international space station using a 3D autosynchronized scanner. In: Proceedings of SPIE, vol. 4714, pp. 4714–4714–10 (2002)
82. Sansoni, G., Patrioli, A.: Noncontact 3D sensing of free-form complex surfaces. In: Proceedings of SPIE, vol. 4309 (2001)
83. Seitz, P.: Photon-noise limited distance resolution of optical metrology methods. In: Proceedings of SPIE, vol. 6616. Optical Measurement Systems for Industrial Inspection V (2007)
84. Singer, C.J., Williams, T.I., Raper, R.: A History of Technology. Clarendon Press, Oxford (1954)
85. Smith, W.J.: Modern Optical Engineering, 3rd edn. McGraw-Hill, New York (2000)
86. Surrel, Y.: Additive noise effect in digital phase detection. Appl. Opt. **36**(1), 271–276 (1994)
87. Trobina, M.: Error model of a coded-light range sensor. Technical report, BIWI-TR-164, ETH-Zentrum (1995)
88. Tubic, D., Hébert, P., Laurendeau, D.: A volumetric approach for interactive 3D modeling. Comput. Vis. Image Underst. **92**, 56–77 (2003)
89. Tubic, D., Hébert, P., Laurendeau, D.: 3D surface modeling from curves. Image Vis. Comput. **22**, 719–734 (2004)

90. Tur, M., Chin, K.C., Goodman, J.W.: When is speckle noise multiplicative? Appl. Opt. **21**(7), 1157–1159 (1982)
91. Verein Deutscher Ingenieure (VDI, Association of German Engineers): VDI 2634 Part 2 Optical 3-D measuring systems Optical system based on area scanning (2002)
92. Verein Deutscher Ingenieure (VDI, Association of German Engineers): VDI 2617 Part 6.2, Accuracy of coordinate measuring machines – Characteristics and their testing – Guideline for the application of DIN EN ISO 10360 to coordinate measuring machines with optical distance sensors, Beuth Verlag GmbH. (2005)
93. Will, P.M., Pennington, K.S.: Grid coding: a novel technique for image processing. Proc. IEEE **60**(6), 669–680 (1972)
94. Willéme, F.: Photo-Sculpture, United States Patent Office 43822 (1864)
95. Xu, Y., Aliaga, D.G.: An adaptive correspondence algorithm for modeling scenes with strong interreflections. IEEE Trans. Vis. Comput. Graph. **15**(3), 465–480 (2009)
96. Zhao, H., Xu, Y., Jiang, H., Li, X.: 3D shape measurement in the presence of strong inter-reflections by epipolar imaging and regional fringe projection. Opt. Express **26**(6), 7117–7131 (2018)

Chapter 4
Active Time-of-Flight 3D Imaging Systems for Medium-Range Applications

Marc-Antoine Drouin and Ismail Hamieh

Abstract Active 3D imaging systems use artificial illumination in order to capture and record digital representations of objects. The use of artificial illumination allows the acquisition of dense and accurate range images of textureless objects. An active 3D imaging system can be based on different measurement principles that include time-of-flight, triangulation, and interferometry. The different time-of-flight technologies allow the development of a plethora of systems that can operate at a range of a few meters to many kilometers. In this chapter, we focus on time-of-flight technologies that operate from a few meters to a few hundred meters. The characterization of these systems is discussed and experimental results are presented using systems related to construction, engineering, and the automobile industry.

4.1 Introduction

Three-dimensional (3D) vision systems capture and record a digital representation of the geometry and appearance information of visible 3D surfaces of people, animals, plants, objects, and sites. Active 3D imaging systems use an artificial illumination (visible or infrared) to acquire dense range maps with a minimum of ambiguity. In the previous chapter, active 3D imaging systems based on triangulation that operate at a range of a few centimeters to a few meters were presented. In contrast, Time-of-Flight (ToF) technologies allow the development of a plethora of systems that can operate from a range of a few meters to many kilometers. Systems that operate up to a few meters (approx. 5 m) are typically called range cameras or RGB-D cameras and are typically dedicated to indoor applications. Systems that operate at greater ranges are termed LiDAR (Light Detection and Ranging). LiDAR started as a method to directly and accurately capture digital elevation data for Terrestrial

M.-A. Drouin (✉)
National Research Council Canada, Ottawa, Canada
e-mail: Marc-Antoine.Drouin@nrc-cnrc.gc.ca

I. Hamieh
National Research Council Canada (formerly), Ottawa, Canada
e-mail: ismail.hamieh@gmail.com

©2020 Her Majesty the Queen in Right of Canada,
as represented by the National Research Council of Canada
Y. Liu et al. (eds.), *3D Imaging, Analysis and Applications*,
https://doi.org/10.1007/978-3-030-44070-1_4

Laser Scanning (TLS) and Airborne Laser Scanning (ALS) applications. In the last few years, the appealing features of LiDAR have attracted the automotive industry and LiDAR became one of the most important sensors in autonomous vehicle applications where it is called Mobile Laser Scanning (MLS). Terrestrial, airborne, and mobile laser scanning differ in terms of data capture mode, typical project size, scanning mechanism, and obtainable accuracy and resolution; however, they share many features. In this chapter, we focus on time-of-flight technologies that operate from a few meters to a few hundred meters. They are, by their nature, non-contact measurement instruments and produce a quantifiable 3D digital representation of a surface in a specified finite volume of interest and with a particular measurement uncertainty.

4.1.1 Historical Context

The fundamental work on Time-of-Flight systems can be traced back to the era of RADAR (Radio Detection And Ranging), which is based on radio waves. With the advent of lasers in the late 1950s, it became possible to image a surface with angular and range resolutions much higher than possible with radio waves. This new technology was termed LiDAR and one of its initial uses was for mapping particles in the atmosphere [38]. During the 1980s, the development of the Global Positioning System (GPS) opened up the possibility of moving sensor systems such as airborne LiDAR and Bathymetric LiDAR were actually one of the first uses [98]. The early 1990s saw the improvement of the Inertial Measurement Unit (IMU) and the ability to begin achieving decimeter accuracies. Some of the earlier non-bathymetric airborne applications were in the measurement of glaciers and how they were changing [113]. TLS systems are also beginning to be used as a way to densely map the three-dimensional nature of features and ground surfaces to a high level of accuracy [79]. TLS is now an important tool in the construction and engineering industry. Many modern ToF systems work in the near and short-wave infrared regions of the electromagnetic spectrum. Some sensors also operate in the green band to penetrate water and detect features at the bottom of it. In recent years, the automotive industry has adopted ToF systems and this is now an essential technology for automated and advanced driver-assistance systems. The entertainment industry has also adopted ToF systems. The progressive addition of motion-sensitive interfaces to gaming platforms and the desire to personalize the gaming experience led to the development of short-range time-of-flight cameras targeted at a wide range of cost-sensitive consumers.

4.1.2   Basic Measurement Principles

Active three-dimensional (3D) imaging systems can be based on different measurement principles. The three most used principles of commercially available systems are triangulation, interferometry, and time-of-flight. Seitz describes triangulation as a method based on geometry, interferometry as one that uses accurate wavelengths and time-of-flight as based on an accurate clock [92]. Figure 4.1 summarizes the typical accuracy of each type of active 3D imaging system technology found on the market as a function of the operating distance. It can be observed from that figure that each optical technique covers a particular range of operations. Many in-depth classifications of optical distance measurement principles have been published in important references in the field of 3D vision, e.g., [17, 19, 52, 78]. Both active and passive triangulation systems are based on the same geometric principle: intersecting light rays in 3D space. Typically, an active system replaces one camera of a passive stereo system by a projection device. This projection device can be a digital video projector, an analog slide projector, or a laser. Interferometry is based on the superposition of two beams of light [52]. Typically, a laser beam is split into two paths. One path is of known length, while the other is of unknown length. The difference in path lengths creates a phase difference between the light beams. The two beams are then combined together before reaching a photodetector. The interference pattern seen by the detector resulting from the superposition of these two light beams depends on

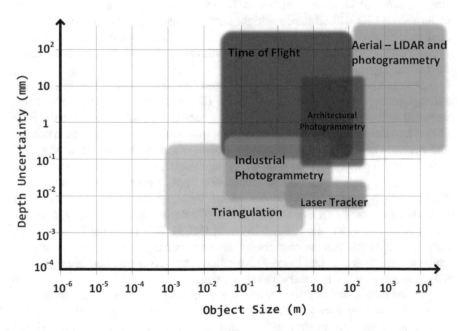

Fig. 4.1 Typical accuracy at different operating distances for the most common active 3D imaging technologies. Figure courtesy of NRC

the path difference (i.e., the distance). The remainder of this chapter will focus on the time-of-flight.

4.1.3 Time-of-Flight Methods

Most Time-of-Flight (ToF) technologies presented in this chapter are classified as active optical non-contact 3D imaging systems because they emit light into the environment and use the reflected optical energy to estimate the distance to a surface in the environment. The distance is computed from the round-trip time which may be estimated directly using a high-resolution clock to measure the time between outgoing and incoming pulses (Pulse-based ToF), or indirectly by measuring the phase shift of an amplitude-modulated optical signal (Phase-based ToF) [105].

There are many ways to classify ToF sensors, according to their components, application fields, and performance. One of the key dimensions within this taxonomy is the way in which the active 3D imaging system illuminates the scene. Some measurement systems are points based and need to scan the laser spot along two axes in order to acquire a range image, other systems used multiple laser spots and require the scanning along a single axis to obtain a range image. Finally, some systems illuminate the entire scene simultaneously.

The first family of systems that we present are point-based scanners. A large subset within this family are known as Terrestrial Laser Scanning (TLS) systems or Terrestrial LiDAR and have multiple applications within the construction and engineering industry (see top left of Fig. 4.2). Many TLS systems contain a biaxial leveling compensator used to align the coordinate system of the generated range image with respect to gravity.

A second type of point-based system, frequently encountered in the construction and engineering industry, is the Laser Tracker (LT) which is the only type of systems presented in this chapter that is classified as a contact technology because the light emitted into the environment is reflected by a retroreflector, which is placed in contact with a surface at the time of measurement (see top right and bottom left of Fig. 4.2).

Systems using multiple laser spots are typically referred as multi-channel LiDAR. These systems are encountered in automotive applications (see bottom right of Fig. 4.2). Multi-channel LiDAR is considered by many automobile manufacturers to be a key technology for autonomous driving. In the automotive industry, the technology is known as Mobile LiDAR Systems (MLS). Multi-channel LiDAR emits multiple laser beams that are contained within a plane. Each acquisition generates a profile contained within that plane and by modifying the orientation or position of this plane it is possible to generate a range image.

Systems that illuminate the entire scene simultaneously are now frequently encountered in consumer-grade applications. These systems are referred as area-based systems and the detection of the incoming light is done by a two-dimensional (2D) array of detectors. The second generation Microsoft Kinect is a popular area-based system. Typically, because of constraints imposed by eye-safety requirements

Fig. 4.2 Various ToF systems. (These are used to generate the experimental results shown in Sect. 4.7.) Top left: a terrestrial LiDAR system. Top right: a laser tracker. Bottom left: a retroreflector used by the laser tracker. Bottom right: a multi-channel LiDAR mounted on the top of a car. Note the GPS receiver on the left and the inertial measurement unit on the right of the LiDAR system. Figure courtesy of NRC

for consumer-grade products, their operational range is smaller than other types of ToF system.

ToF systems measure the distance to a point by calculating the round-trip time of light reflected from the surface [24, 105], based on an assumption of the speed at which the light is able to travel through the medium (typically air). Factors such as air temperature and pressure [20, 70], relative humidity, CO_2 concentration [24], atmospheric turbulence [109], and the presence of particulate matter [11, 24] or fog [89] can all affect the speed at which light can travel through the medium. This is further complicated by gradients in these factors along the beam path [42].

Moreover, the measurement quality is strongly dependent on the surface being measured due to factors such as reflectance [46], surface orientation [42], optical penetration [34, 40, 44], and substances, such as water, on the surface [61, 67].

The output of a ToF system is typically a point cloud or range image. A point cloud is an unorganized set of 3D points, while a range image is an organized array of 3D points that implicitly encode the neighborhood relation between points. This neighborhood structure is related to the physical acquisition process. As an example, for a range image produced by a multi-channel LiDAR, one axis represents the laser beam index while the other represents the angular position of the laser beam along the scanning axis. For historical reasons, unstructured point clouds saved into ASCII file format are still encountered today. Wherever possible, we advocate the preservation of the neighborhood structure associated with the physical acquisition process of the ToF system employed.

As discussed in Chap. 3, when working with coherent light sources (lasers) eye safety is of paramount importance and one should never operate laser-based 3D imaging sensors without appropriate eye-safety training. Many 3D imaging systems use a laser in the visible spectrum where fractions of a milliwatt are sufficient to cause eye damage, since the laser light density entering the pupil is magnified, at the retina, through the lens. For an operator using any laser, an important safety parameter is the Maximum Permissible Exposure (MPE) which is defined as the level of laser radiation to which a person may be exposed without hazardous effect or adverse biological changes in the eye or skin [4]. The MPE varies with wavelength and operating conditions of a system. One possible mitigation strategy used by scanner manufacturers is to use a laser at $1.55\,\mu m$. At this wavelength, the light is absorbed by the eye fluids before being focused on the retina. This tends to increase the MPE to the laser source. We do not have space to discuss eye safety extensively here and refer the reader to the *American National Standard for Safe Use of Lasers* [4].

4.1.4 Chapter Outline

The core sections in this chapter cover the following materials:

- Point-based systems.
- Laser trackers—a special type of point-based system using retroreflectors.
- Multi-channel systems.
- Area-based systems (these are used in consumer-grade products).
- Characterization of ToF system performance.
- Experimental results for random and systematic ranging errors.
- Sensor fusion and navigation.
- ToF versus photogrammetry for some specific applications.

Toward the end of the chapter, we will present the main challenges for future research followed by concluding remarks and suggestions for further reading. A set of questions and exercises are provided at the end for the reader to develop a good understanding and knowledge of ToF technologies.

4.2 Point-Based Systems

Point-based systems measure distance one point at a time and need to be scanned along two axes in order to acquire a range image. TLS systems are a large subset within this family and this section will mostly focus on this type of system, which is now commonly used as a survey method for monitoring large structures such as bridges and for as-built building information modeling. TLS can be used for forensic applications in large environments and they are regularly used to document cultural heritage sites. In TLS, the scanning is performed by two rotating components. One controls the elevation, while the other determines the azimuth. Many TLS systems contain a biaxial leveling compensator used to align the coordinate system of the generated range image with respect to gravity. Point-based systems that do not include scanning mechanisms are commercially available and are refereed as laser range finders.[1]

One configuration that can be encountered in a TLS system uses a galvanometer with a mirror to control the elevation and azimuth is controlled by rotating the complete scanner head. Using this configuration, the elevation can be scanned at a higher frequency than the azimuth. A typical configuration could have a 360° field of view in the azimuth and 30–120° of field of view in elevation. Note that galvanometer scan angles are limited to about ±45°. For larger scan angle, a motor with encoders must be used. In the idealized case, each time a distance measurement is made, the value of the optical encoder of the rotating head and the readout value for the galvanometer are recorded. When the system is calibrated, these values can be converted into angles. Using the distance measurement and the angles it is possible to compute the position of the 3D points. In the non-idealized case, the rotation axis of the scanner head and that of the galvanometer may not be perpendicular and some small translation offsets can result from the misalignment of the laser and galvanometer with respect to the rotation center of the scanner head. Moreover, the rotation axis may wobble. For high-end systems, all these issues and others have to be taken into account. Since access to a facility capable of calibrating a TLS system is rare, this topic is not discussed in this chapter. However, the characterization of systems will be discussed in Sect. 4.6. For the remainder of this section, two technologies for the distance measurement known as pulse-based and phase-based are presented. Pulse-based systems perform a direct measurement of the time required by the light to do a round trip between the scanner and the scene. Phase-based systems perform an indirect measurement of the time by measuring a phase offset. Some authors reserved the name *time-of-flight* for systems performing direct measurement. In this chapter, a less restricting definition of time-of-flight is used.

4.2.1   Pulse-Based Systems

Pulse-based systems continually pulse a laser, and measure how long it takes for each light pulse to reach a surface within the scene and return to the sensor. Typically, the pulse has a Gaussian shape with a half-beam width of 4–10 ns. Since the speed of light is known, the range $r(\Delta t)$ of the scene surface is defined as

---

[1]Note that some range finders are based on triangulation.

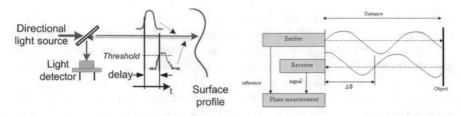

Fig. 4.3 Range measurement techniques employed by common ToF systems. Left: pulse-based. Right: phase-based (more specifically amplitude modulation). Figure courtesy of NRC

$$r(\Delta t) = \frac{c\Delta t}{2} \tag{4.1}$$

where c is the speed of light, and Δt is the time between the light being emitted and it being detected. Typically, the detector performs a sampling of the signal for every 1 or 2 ns. Different algorithms that perform the detection of pulses in the incoming signal are discussed in Sect. 4.2.1.2. In many applications, the detection of the peak of a pulse with a sub-nanosecond accuracy is critical as the pulse travels approximately 30 cm in one nanosecond. Figure 4.3-left illustrates the principle.

The simplest implementation assumes that a detected pulse corresponds to the last pulse emitted. In some situations, the ordering of the outgoing pulses may be different from the order of the returning pulses. This can occur in scenes with large depth variations. A pulse can reach a distant surface and by the time the pulse returns to the sensor, a second pulse is emitted to a close surface and back to the sensor. In order to avoid this situation, the maximum pulsing rate f_p of a pulse-based system is limited by the maximum range R_{max} of the system using

$$f_p \leq \frac{c}{2R_{max}}. \tag{4.2}$$

As an example, a system having a maximum range of 1.5 km is expected to generate at most 100,000 range measurements per second.

4.2.1.1 Multiple Returning Pulses

A property of pulse-based system is that it may register multiple return signals per emitted pulse. An emitted laser pulse may encounter multiple reflecting surfaces and the sensor may register as many returns as there are reflective surfaces (i.e., the laser beam diameter is not infinitely thin [94]). This situation is frequently encountered in airborne applications related to forestry and archaeology where it may simultaneously register the top of the vegetation and the ground [25, 59, 84]. Note that a pulse can hit a thick branch on its way to the ground and it may not actually reach the ground. For terrestrial applications, the analysis of multiple return signals can sometimes allow detection of a building behind vegetation or can detect both the position of a

Fig. 4.4 Some spurious data points are induced by inter-reflection. Figure courtesy of NRC

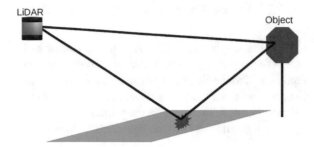

building's window and a surface within the building. Finally, some systems record the complete return signal, which forms a vector of intensity values where each value is associated with a time stamp. These systems are known as waveform LiDAR [68]. Waveform LiDAR is capable of measuring the distance of several objects within the laser footprint and this allows characterization of the vegetation structure [1, 59, 106]. Finally, some detected pulses can be the result of an inter-reflection within the scene. This situation is illustrated in Fig. 4.4. In this figure, a part of the laser light emitted by the system is first reflected on the ground and then reflected on the road sign before reaching the sensor. Typically, multi-channel and area-based systems are more sensitive to inter-reflection artifacts than point-based systems.

4.2.1.2   Detecting a Returning Pulse

The detection of the peak of the returning signal with a sub-nanosecond accuracy is critical for many commercially available systems and scanner manufacturers provide few implementation details. An electronic circuit that can be used to locate the peak is the constant fraction discriminator circuit. This approximates the mathematical operation of finding the maximum of the returning pulse by locating the zero of the first derivative [60]. Implementation details about the peak detector of experimental systems developed for the landing of spacecraft are discussed in [22, 39]. In [39], the returning signal is convolved with a Gaussian and the peaks are located by examining the derivative. The standard deviation of the Gaussian is derived from the physical characteristics of the system. In [22], a 6° polynomial is fitted on the returning signal. Waveform LiDAR records the complete return signal and makes it available to the end user. The end user can implement specialized peak detectors adapted to specific applications. A significant body of knowledge about peak detection for waveform LiDAR is available [68]. One approach is to model the waveform as a series of Gaussian pulses. The theoretical basis for this modeling is discussed in [104].

4.2.2 Phase-Based Systems

Phase-based systems emit an Amplitude-Modulated (AM) laser beam [3]. The systems presented in this section are also known as continuous-wave ToF system. Frequency Modulation (FM) is rarely used so it is not considered here.[2] The range is deduced from the phase difference between the detected signal and the emitted signal. Figure 4.3b illustrates the principle of the phase-based system. The temporal intensity profile $I_s(t)$ for the illumination source is

$$I_s(t) = A_s + B_s \cos(\phi(t) + \theta_s) \tag{4.3}$$

where A_s, B_s, and θ_s are constants and $\phi(t) = 2\pi t f_{cw}$ where f_{cw} is the modulation frequency. The temporal intensity profile $I_d(t)$ for the detected signal is

$$I_d(t) = A_d + B_d \cos(\phi(t) + \theta_d + \delta\phi) \tag{4.4}$$

where $\delta\phi$ is the phase offset related to the range. Note that A_d, B_d depend on A_s, B_s the scene surface properties and the sensor characteristics. In general, the value of θ_s and θ_d are assumed to be constant but their values are unknown. The conversion from phase offset to range can be achieved using

$$r(\delta\phi) = \frac{c\delta\phi}{4\pi f_{cw}} \tag{4.5}$$

where c is the speed of light in the medium. The range over which the system can perform unambiguous measurement can be computed from the modulation frequency. This unambiguous range r_{max} is defined as

$$r_{max} = r(2\pi) = \frac{c}{2f_{cw}}. \tag{4.6}$$

Increasing the modulation frequency f_{cw} will simultaneously reduce the value of r_{max} and the measurement uncertainty.

4.2.2.1   Measuring Phase Offset

Phase-based systems combine the detected signal with the emitted signal in order to perform the phase offset measurement. At this point, one should realize a similarity with interferometry. A unified presentation of phase-based ToF and interferometry can be found in [29]. Combining the detected signal with the emitted signal is mathematically equivalent to the cross-correlation between Eqs. 4.3 and 4.4 which results in another sinusoidal function $I_c(t)$ defined as

---

[2]FM systems for small measurement volumes exist.

$$I_c(t) = A_c + B_c \cos(\phi(t) + \theta_c + \delta\phi) \tag{4.7}$$

where A_c, B_c and $\delta\phi$ are unknown and $\phi(t)$ and θ_c are known. Typically, θ_c is assumed to be zero during the processing of the signal as a nonzero value simply creates a bias in the range measurement that can be compensated by the calibration. By sampling Eq. 4.7 three or more times with different values of t_i, it is possible to construct a system of equations that allows us to solve for A_c, B_c, and $\delta\phi$. This is done in the same way as is described in the previous chapter and the details are not repeated here. After selecting different sampling times t_i such that $\phi(t_i) = \frac{2\pi i}{N}$, where N is the number of samples, we can compute the following:

$$A_c = \frac{1}{N} \sum_{i=0}^{N-1} I(t_i), \tag{4.8}$$

$$B_c = \frac{\sqrt{\left(\sum_{i=0}^{N-1} I(t_i) \sin\left(\frac{2i\pi}{N}\right)\right)^2 + \left(\sum_{i=0}^{N-1} I(t_i) \cos\left(\frac{2i\pi}{N}\right)\right)^2}}{N} \tag{4.9}$$

and

$$\delta\phi = \arctan\left(\sum_{i=0}^{N-1} I(t_i) \sin\left(\frac{2i\pi}{N}\right), \sum_{i=0}^{N-1} I(t_i) \cos\left(\frac{2i\pi}{N}\right)\right) \tag{4.10}$$

where $\arctan(n, d)$ represents the usual $\tan^{-1}(n/d)$ where the sign of n and d are used to determinate the quadrant.

4.2.2.2 Removing the Phase Offset Ambiguity

Once the phase difference $\Delta\Phi$ is computed, the range is defined as

$$r(\Delta\Phi) = \frac{c(\Delta\Phi + 2k\pi)}{4\pi f_{cw}} \tag{4.11}$$

where k is an unknown integer that represents the phase ambiguity. The value of k must be recovered in order to compute the location of the 3D points. A simple method uses multiple modulation frequencies denoted as f_{cw}^i with $i > 0$. When using this scheme, a value of k^i must be recovered for each f_{cw}^i. The lower modulation frequencies are used to remove the range ambiguity while the higher ones are used to improve the accuracy of the measurement. In that scheme, the value of f_{cw}^1 and r_{max} are selected such that k^1 is always zero and the value of $\Delta\Phi^i$ for $i \geq 1$ can be used to determinate the value of k^{i+1} (assuming that $f_{cw}^i < f_{cw}^{i+1}$).

4.3 Laser Trackers

In this section, we are specifically interested in a type of measurement system known as a laser trackers, also known as portable coordinate measurement machines. Laser trackers are classified as contact systems because the light emitted into the environment is reflected by a retroreflector, often referred to as Spherically Mounted Reflector or SMR, which is placed in contact with a surface at the time of measurement (see Fig. 4.5). Measurement results obtained by laser tracker systems are also relatively independent of the type of surface being measured because the point of reflection is the retroreflector. Every point obtained by a laser tracker system requires human intervention. For this reason, these systems are used where only a few points need to be measured, but must be measured at high accuracy. The laser tracker instrument is relatively easy to use and it can be employed to evaluate the performance of a time-of-flight 3D imaging system. The laser tracker is used as a reference instrument for medium-range 3D imaging systems in the American Society for Testing and Materials (ASTM) standard ASTM E2641-09 (2017). As seen in Fig. 4.1, laser tracker systems operate in the same range as ToF systems, from the tenth-of-a-meter to the hundreds-of-meters range. They have a measurement uncertainties one order of magnitude or more better than ToF. The performance of the laser tracker is covered by the American Society of Mechanical Engineers (ASME) ASME B89.4.19-2006 standard which uses the interferometer as a reference instrument [77]. Laser tracker systems use interferometry, ToF or a combination of both to calculate the distance. Distance measurement using interferometry is known as Interferometry Mode (IFM), while distance calculated using ToF is known as Absolute Distance Mode (ADM).

Typically, specifications for laser trackers are given as a Maximum Permissible Error (MPE) [55]. Specifically,

$$E_{L,MPE} = \pm (A + L/K) \tag{4.12}$$

where A and K are constants that depend on the laser tracker and L is the range of the SMR. Incidentally, MPE estimates are Type B uncertainties, which are described in GUM JCGM 104:2008 [53]. There are two types of uncertainty defined in [53]. Type A uncertainties are obtained using statistical methods, while Type B is obtained by means other than statistical analysis. FARO X Laser Tracker[3] specifications are given in Table 4.1.

Measurement accuracy is affected not only by tracker performance but also by the variation in air temperature and procedures used to perform the measurement which is not discussed. In the remainder of this section, we described best practices that should be adopted when using laser trackers.

---

[3]See user manual available at https://knowledge.faro.com/Hardware/Laser_Tracker/Tracker.

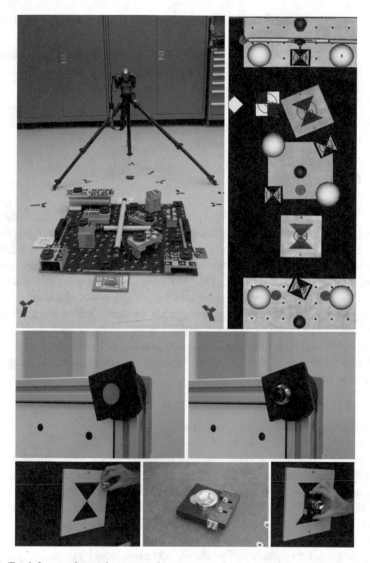

Fig. 4.5 Top left: experimental setup used to compare close-range photogrammetry and LT. Top right: a range image with different targets extracted, shown in red. Center left: a half-sphere mounted on a kinetic mount. Center right: the same setup with the half sphere substituted with an SMR. Bottom left: a specialized target containing a recessed black bow tie. An operator is currently probing the planar surface using LT. Bottom center: the specialized probing tool with the SMR's nest but without the SMR. Bottom right: the specialized probing tool with the SMR, as used to probe the center of the bow tie. Figure courtesy of NRC

Table 4.1 MPE quantities related to tracker performance where L is the range in meters (Transverse: perpendicular to the laser beam and Radial: along the laser beam). The R0 (range zero) error is described in Sect. 4.3.1

Tracker subsystem	Symbol	MPE
ADM-radial	E_{ADM}	$20\,\mu m + L\,0.8\,\mu m/m$
Transverse	E_T	$36\,\mu m + L\,6\,\mu m/m$
Range zero (R0)	E_{R0}	$20\,\mu m$

4.3.1 Good Practices

Before a laser tracker can be used to obtain measurement results, the quality of data produced must be verified by a set of basic tests using SMR nests in fixed positions. These tests are often divided into two categories: ranging tests that assess the radial measurement performance, and system tests that evaluate volumetric measurement performance. The ASME B89.4.19 [70, 76] standard is the most applicable to the average laser tracker user because it provides a clear and well-recognized method for evaluating whether the performance of the laser tracker is within the manufacturer provided Maximum Permissible Error (MPE). More recently, other research institutes including NIST and NPL have published additional in-field test procedures that can be used to establish the measurement uncertainty associated with any laser tracker measurement result.

4.3.1.1 Range Measurement Evaluation

A laser tracker performance assessment typically starts by assessing the range (radial) measurement performance of a laser tracker. These systems can use either one of the two operating modes to measure the radial distance to a Spherically Mounted Retroreflector (SMR). The two operating modes are Interferometric distance Measurement (IFM) or Absolute Distance Meter (ADM) [72, 75]. In IFM mode the SMR must initially be placed in the home position, then moved without breaking the beam to the position of interest. The distance is calculated by counting the number of fringes from the measurement beam relative to an internal reference beam, which corresponds to the distance traveled [35]. The distance between each fringe is one wavelength, and the result is a highly accurate measurement result. ADM mode, by contrast, uses a form of time-of-flight measurement so it is less accurate; however, it does not require SMRs to start the measurement process in the home position.

The range measurement results of laser trackers that operate in IFM mode are typically compared with displacement measurement results obtained from a calibrated reference interferometer with measurement uncertainty traceable to the meter [35]. These results are used to verify that the laser tracker range measurement performance is within the specifications provided by the manufacturer. This is normally performed in-factory of the manufacturer and periodically as required by the manufacturer to ensure that the laser scanner continues to operate within specification. The performance of laser trackers that operate in both IFM and ADM mode can be validated on site by calculating the deviation between range measurements obtained in IFM mode (reference) and ADM mode (test).

4.3.1.2   Angular Encoder Evaluation

Once the radial axis measurement performance has been verified, the performance of the horizontal and vertical angle encoders can be assessed using system tests. The following encoder errors can be identified [76]: beam offset, transit offset, vertex index offset, beam tilt, transit tilt, encoder eccentricity, bird-bath error, and encoder scale errors. A complete calibration requires quantification of each error source using a more comprehensive test regime. For in-field evaluation, however, most error sources can be bundled to reduce the number of encoder performance tests required to complete an in-field calibration.

4.3.1.3   In-Field Evaluation

The first in-field system test to perform is referred to as the two-faced test because it compares the performance of the system between front-face and back-face mode [70, 74, 76]. An SMR is placed in a fixed position relative to the laser tracker and its position is determined in both front-face and in back-face mode. Any deviations between the measurement result obtained in each mode indicate that compensation will need to be applied to minimize the deviation. The compensation procedure to correct for what is referred to as R0 (range zero) error is normally available in most software packages provided with the laser tracker. For most applications a deviation less than $50\,\mu$m is considered negligible. The two-face test must be repeated after compensation has been applied to verify that the deviation between front-face and back-face mode measurement results has been minimized; however, it may also need to be repeated often during the day if the test situation changes, such as a change in temperature, or if the equipment needs to be turned off and moved to another location.

The second in-field test compares the distance between two SMR positions where the distance has been previously established using a more accurate method. A common reference is a fixed-length bar with SMR nests at each end in which the SMR-to-SMR distance has been previously established using a distance measurement device more accurate than the laser tracker encoders, such as a Coordinate Measuring Machine (CMM) [70]. The SMR-to-SMR distance can also be established using the range axis of the laser tracker in IFM mode because the IFM radial uncertainty is typically much smaller than the encoder uncertainty. The second option is feasible only for bars in which the SMR nests are mounted on one side, which permits the SMR nests to be aligned along the radial axis in what is referred to as the "bucked-in" position. An example of one such bar available commercially is the Kinary, recently developed as part of a collaboration between NIST and Brunson Instruments [58].

Having established a fixed-length reference artifact, the encoder performances are evaluated by placing the artifacts in different positions and orientations. The ASME B89.4.19 [70] describes a series of test positions to evaluate whether the performance of the laser tracker is within the stated Maximum Permissible Error (MPE) of the laser tracker, as stated by the manufacturer.

4.3.2 Combining Laser Trackers with Other 3D Imaging Systems

Some applications may require the combined use of a laser tracker and a TLS system. A Laser Tracker (LT) can be used to measure some features with high accuracy and a TLS system can be used to obtain lower accuracy dense point clouds of the surroundings. Aligning the coordinate system of the LT and the TLS system requires pairs of corresponding 3D points. We present the following three methods to compute a correspondence:

- The first method uses three planes which intersect into a 3D point. The LT can be used to probe 3D points on the surfaces of each plane. It is possible to compute the equation of each plane and compute the intersection of the three planes [66]. Using the 3D points scanned by the TLS system, it is possible to compute the equation of the three planes and compute their intersection. Note that the intersection of the planes does not necessarily correspond to an actual physical structure in the scene.
- The second method uses a sphere. The LT can be used to probe points on the surface of a sphere. From these 3D points, it is possible to compute the position of the center of the sphere. Using the 3D points scanned by the TLS, it is also possible to compute the center of the sphere. A specific algorithm has been developed to compute the position of the center of a sphere using the 3D points of the surface of the sphere generated by the TLS system [86].
- The third method uses a specifically designed target and designed probing tool [30]. This target can be used simultaneously for photogrammetry (shape from motion), LT and TLS. The last row of Fig. 4.5 shows the target and probing tool.

The top right image of Fig. 4.5 shows a range image where inferred 3D points are computed based on the last two presented methods. The combined use of LT and TLS is further discussed in Sects. 4.6.2 and 4.7.1.3.

The measurements of an LT and photogrammetry can also be combined using a kinetic mount, half spheres, and SMRs [80]. The middle row of Fig. 4.5 shows a half-sphere installed on a kinetic mount (left) and a SMR is installed on the same kinetic mount (right). The center of the circle formed by the planar surface of the half-sphere is located at the same position as the center of the SMR. The top left part of Fig. 4.5 contains a picture of the experimental setup used to compare close-range photogrammetry and a LT [80]. Note the two yellow scale bars used to compute the scale of the sparse point cloud obtained by a shape-from-motion algorithm.

4.4   Multi-channel Systems

Typically, a multi-channel LiDAR emits multiple laser beams that are contained within a plane. Each acquisition generates a profile contained within that plane and, by modifying the orientation or position of this plane, it is possible to generate a range image. Multi-channel LiDAR is now considered by many automobile manufacturers as a key technology required for autonomous driving and for the remainder of this section we will focus on imaging systems typically encountered in autonomous driving vehicles. Two variants of this concept are presented in the following two subsections. The first one uses physical scanning, while the second one uses a time-multiplexing strategy to perform digital scanning. In both cases, the distance measurement is performed using a pulse-based method.

4.4.1   Physical Scanning

A simple modification to the point-based approach is the integration into a single scanning head of multiple point-based systems having their laser beams contained within a plane. By scanning the head perpendicularly to this plane, it is possible to generate a range image. This configuration limits the lateral resolution and/or field of view along one axis, but allows a higher sampling rate than point-based systems. This type of system is well adapted to navigation applications where the horizontal orientation requires a larger field of view and higher resolution than the vertical one. A typical system for navigation could generate a range image of 20000×16 3D points by rotating a 16-channel scanner head over $360°$. Section 4.7.2 presents results from a 16-channel scanner. Typically, the 3D information along the vertical axis is used to verify that the proper clearance is available for the vehicle, while the horizontal axis is used for obstacles avoidance. For some autonomous driving applications, the desired vertical field of view is about $30°$. As shown in Fig. 4.6, a $30°$ vertical field of view allows the detection of objects on the road just in front of

Fig. 4.6 Left: a $30°$ field-of-view collision avoidance system on the top of a vehicle. Center: vehicle just before driving uphill. Right: vehicle just before driving downhill. Figure courtesy of NRC

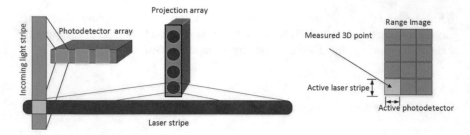

Fig. 4.7 An example of forward-looking LiDAR with digital scanning. The system is composed of arrays of three photodetectors and four lasers. This system generates a range image of four by three, which is shown on the right. The pixel in yellow represents the 3D point that is being measured, as illustrated on the left. For illustrative purposes, a single photodetector is active. Figure courtesy of NRC

the autonomous vehicle and approaching hills, and it allows the monitoring of the vertical clearance of garage entrances and other structures. For moving vehicles, the limitation of vertical lateral resolution can be compensated by integrating multiple range images into a single point cloud.

4.4.2 Digital Scanning

While physical scanning systems can generate 360° range images, the design discussed in this section is adapted for the forward-looking configuration. This simplified solid-state design is inspired by the commercial documentation by LeddarTech.[4] The system is composed of a linear array of M photodetectors and a linear array of N laser sources. The projection and collection linear arrays are mounted side by side such that the arrays are perpendicular (see Fig. 4.7). Without loss of generality, it will be assumed that the projection array is oriented vertically, while the detector array is oriented horizontally. There is an optical element installed in front of the projection array that spreads the laser spots into stripes. The optical element is mounted such that the laser stripes are perpendicular to the linear array of projectors. Each individual laser will generate a horizontal stripe on the scene at a given elevation. By successively firing each laser, it is possible to scan (with a discrete number of samples) a horizontal laser line on the scene. Each laser pulse can be detected by the M photodetectors and the range of M 3D points can be computed. This is made possible by the installation, in front of the photodetector array, an optical element that collects a stripe of laser light reflected from the scene. For a system that generates horizontal laser stripes, the orientation of the collection optical element is arranged such that the stripes of incoming light are vertical. A range image of N by M 3D

---

[4]https://leddartech.com.

points can be generated by projecting N laser stripes. Note that the array of N laser stripes could be replaced by a single laser stripe whose orientation is controlled using a Microelectromechanical Systems (MEMS).

4.5 Area-Based Systems

Area-based ToF systems typically use a single illumination source and a 2D array of detectors that share the same collection optics. They are, to some extent, similar to a regular camera equipped with a flash. This type of system can be based on pulse or phase technologies. Pulse-based systems are also referred to as flash LiDAR. The camera model for the area-based system is presented in Sect. 4.5.1. Phase-based products are now mass produced and distributed as accessories for popular computing platforms. Due to the popularity of these platforms, an overview of the sensors is presented in Sect. 4.5.2. The last type of system presented in Sect. 4.5.3 is *range-gated imaging*, which is an active vision system for challenging environments that scatter light.

4.5.1 Camera Model

The simplest mathematical model that can be used to represent a camera is the pinhole model. A pinhole camera can be assembled using a box in which a small hole (i.e., the aperture) is made on one side and a sheet of photosensitive paper is placed on the opposite side. Figure 4.8 is an illustration of a pinhole camera. The pinhole camera has a very small aperture so it requires long integration times; thus, machine vision

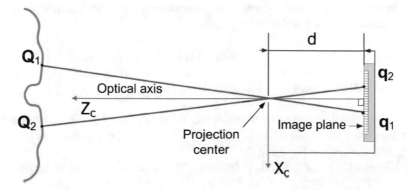

Fig. 4.8 Cross-section of a pinhole camera. The 3D points $\mathbf{Q}_1$ and $\mathbf{Q}_2$ are projected into the image plane as points $\mathbf{q}_1$ and $\mathbf{q}_2$, respectively, and d is the distance between the image plane and the projection center. Figure courtesy of NRC

applications use cameras with lenses which collect more light and hence require shorter integration times. Nevertheless, for many applications, the pinhole model is a valid approximation of a camera. The readers familiar with the camera modeling material presented in Chaps. 2 and 3 can omit the following section.

4.5.1.1 Pinhole Camera Model

In this mathematical model, the aperture and the photosensitive surface of the pinhole are represented by the center of projection and the image plane, respectively. The center of projection is the origin of the camera coordinate system and the optical axis coincides with the Z-axis of the camera. Moreover, the optical axis is perpendicular to the image plane and the intersection of the optical axis and the image plane is the principal point (image center). Note that when approximating a camera with the pinhole model, the geometric distortions of the image introduced by the optical components of an actual camera are not taken into account (see Chap. 2 and [94] for more details). A 3D point $[X_c, Y_c, Z_c]^T$ in the camera reference frame can be transformed into pixel coordinates $[x, y]^T$ using

$$\begin{bmatrix} x \\ y \end{bmatrix} = \frac{d}{Z_c} \begin{bmatrix} \frac{X_c}{s_x} \\ \frac{Y_c}{s_y} \end{bmatrix} + \begin{bmatrix} o_x \\ o_y \end{bmatrix} \tag{4.13}$$

where s_x and s_y are the dimensions of the sensor in millimeters divided by the number of pixels along the X and Y-axis, respectively. Moreover, d is the distance in millimeters between the aperture and the sensor chip and $[o_x, o_y]^T$ is the position in pixels of the principal point (image center) in the image. The parameters s_x, s_y, d, o_x, and o_y are the intrinsic parameters of the camera.

The extrinsic parameters of the camera must be defined in order to locate the position and orientation of the camera in the world coordinate system. This requires three parameters for the rotation and three parameters for the translation. The rotation is represented using a 3×3 rotation matrix

$$\mathsf{R}_c = \begin{bmatrix} 1 & 0 & 0 \\ 0 & \cos\theta_x & -\sin\theta_x \\ 0 & \sin\theta_x & \cos\theta_x \end{bmatrix} \begin{bmatrix} \cos\theta_y & 0 & \sin\theta_y \\ 0 & 1 & 0 \\ -\sin\theta_y & 0 & \cos\theta_y \end{bmatrix} \begin{bmatrix} \cos\theta_z & -\sin\theta_z & 0 \\ \sin\theta_z & \cos\theta_z & 0 \\ 0 & 0 & 1 \end{bmatrix} \tag{4.14}$$

where θ_x, θ_y, and θ_z are the rotation angles around the X, Y, and Z axis and translation is represented by a vector $\mathbf{T}_c = [T_x, T_y, T_z]^T$. Note that the rotation matrix R_c is orthogonal (i.e., $\mathsf{R}_c^T = \mathsf{R}_c^{-1}$) and $\det(\mathsf{R}_c) = 1$.

A 3D point $\mathbf{Q}_w = [X_w, Y_w, Z_w]^T$ in the world reference frame can be transformed into a point $\mathbf{Q}_c = [X_c, Y_c, Z_c]^T$ of the camera reference frame by using

$$\mathbf{Q}_c = \mathsf{R}_c \mathbf{Q}_w + \mathbf{T}_c. \tag{4.15}$$

A point in the camera reference frame can be transformed to a point in the world reference frame by using

$$\mathbf{Q}_w = \mathbf{R}_c^T [\mathbf{Q}_c - \mathbf{T}_c].$$ (4.16)

4.5.1.2 Camera Models for Area-Based Systems

For a pulse-based system, a pixel $[x, y]^T$ with a time delay of $\Delta t (x, y)$ can be transformed into a 3D point using Eqs. 4.13, 4.16, and 4.1

$$\begin{bmatrix} X_w \\ Y_w \\ Z_w \end{bmatrix} = \mathbf{R}_c^T \left[\frac{c \Delta t (x, y) + o_r (x, y)}{2} \begin{bmatrix} \frac{s_x}{d} (x - o_x) \\ \frac{s_y}{d} (y - o_y) \\ 1 \end{bmatrix} - \mathbf{T}_c \right].$$ (4.17)

where $o_r (x, y)$ are an offset recovered at calibration time that compensate for a systematic error in range. The intensity of the peaks can be used to create an intensity image associated with the range image.

For a phase-based system, a pixel $[x, y]^T$ with a phase offset of $\Delta \Phi (x, y)$ can be transformed into a 3D point using Eqs. 4.13, 4.16, and 4.11

$$\begin{bmatrix} X_w \\ Y_w \\ Z_w \end{bmatrix} = \mathbf{R}_c^T \left[\frac{c (\Delta \Phi (x, y) + 2k\pi + o_r (x, y))}{4\pi f_{cw}} \begin{bmatrix} \frac{s_x}{d} (x - o_x) \\ \frac{s_y}{d} (y - o_y) \\ 1 \end{bmatrix} - \mathbf{T}_c \right].$$ (4.18)

where $o_r (x, y)$ is an offset recovered at calibration time and k is the unknown integer that represents the phase ambiguity (see Sect. 4.2.2.2). The sine-wave magnitude, B_c, allows the creation of the intensity image.

The intensity images associated with the range image can be use to calibrate the camera [101, 110] (see Chap. 2). This allows recovery of the intrinsic and extrinsic parameters of the camera. Once the parameters are recovered and using the pairs of known 3D points and their image coordinates, it is possible to use Eq. 4.17 or Eq. 4.18 to compute the value of the offset o_r. Note that the offset o_r could also vary with the distance of the 3D points.

4.5.2 Phase-Based ToF for the Consumer Market

Consumer-grade products that use phase-based technology typically use a modulation frequency in the range of 10–300 MHz. Some major industrial players are designing dedicated imaging sensors for ToF [12, 83]. Table 4.2 contains some characteristics of these sensors. These dedicated designs are made viable by the expected large volume of production associated with consumer-grade products. Rather than examining the actual physical implementation, we will present the guiding principles

Table 4.2 Table of specifications for two phase-based systems. The table is adapted from [12]. The operating distance of the Kinect v2 is different depending on the drive used (i.e., the official drive or the open source drive)

	ToF systems	
	Kinect v3, rumored data	Kinect v2
Number of lines	1024	512
Number of columns	1024	424
Frame rate	30 fps	30 fps
Horizontal field of view	120°	70°
Vertical field of view	120°	60°
Minimum operating distance	0.4 m	0.8 m
Maximum operating distance	4.2 m	4.2 m
Minimum modulation frequency	10 MHz	10 MHz
Maximum modulation frequency	320 MHz	130 MHz
Average modulation frequency	200 MHz	80 MHz
Wavelength	860 μm	860 μm

of these specialized designs. While they are multiple reasons to design a specialized ToF sensor chip, we identify three main reasons as follows:

1. Increasing the dynamic range of the system. For most 3D active imaging systems, increasing the dynamic range usually results in a reduction of the measurement uncertainty. Some specialized ToF sensors achieved this by using a per-pixel gain.
2. Reducing the power consumption of the system. This can be achieved by reducing the power requirement of the sensor chip itself or by increasing the fill factor and quantum efficiency of the sensor, which allows a reduction of the power output of the illumination source. This reduction is key to the integration of ToF cameras into augmented-reality and mixed-reality helmets, which require a 3D map of the user environment.
3. Immunizing the system from ambient lighting variation. To achieve this, some chips acquire two images quasi-simultaneously and output the difference of both images. The difference of two sine waves with the same frequency, but with a phase offset π, is a sine wave with twice the amplitude, centered on zero (i.e., without ambient illumination).

4.5.3 Range-Gated Imaging

Range-gated imaging is a technology typically used for night vision and challenging environments that scatter light. Typically, it is composed of an infrared camera coupled with an infrared light source. When the light source is pulsed and the exposure delay and integration time of the camera are controlled, it is possible to perform some rudimentary range measurements. The integration time (typically referred to as the gate) and exposure delay (referred to as the gate delay) can be specified such that light emitted by the source and captured by the sensor had to be reflected by an object located within a given range interval. One interesting aspect of range-gated imaging is that it can be used during a snowstorm, rain, fog, or underwater to image objects that would be difficult to image using passive 2D imaging technology. However, the resulting images become noisier and, in these weather conditions, the power output of the light source may need to be increased to levels that pose eye-safety issues. One possible mitigation strategy is to use a laser at $1.55\,\mu m$. At this wavelength (known as shortwave infrared or SWIR), the light is absorbed by the eye fluids before being focused on the retina. This tends to increase the maximum permissible exposure to the laser source. Due to possible military applications, some SWIR imagers are regulated by stringent exportation laws. Moreover, they are expensive as they require Indium Gallium Arsenide semiconductors (InGaAs) rather than the more usual Complementary Metal Oxide Semiconductors (CMOS). While range-gated imaging technology is typically used for enhancing 2D vision, it can be used to construct a range image by acquiring multiple images with different acquisition parameters [23, 108]. Moreover, codification techniques, similar to the one used for structured light (see Chap. 3), can also be used [57].

4.6   Characterization of ToF System Performance

A prerequisite for the characterization of ToF systems is the definition of uncertainty, accuracy, precision, repeatability, reproducibility, and lateral resolution. None of these terms are interchangeable. Two authoritative texts on the matter of uncertainty and the vocabulary related to metrology are the *Guide to the Expression of Uncertainty in Measurement* (GUM) and the *International Vocabulary of Metrology* (VIM) [51, 54]. The document designated E2544 from the ASTM provides the definition and description of terms for 3D imaging systems [6]. Due to space constraints, we provide concise intuitive definitions. For formal definitions, we refer the reader to the abovementioned authoritative texts.

Uncertainty is the expression of the statistical dispersion of the values associated with a measured quantity. There are two types of uncertainty defined in [53]. Type A uncertainties are obtained using statistical methods (standard deviation), while Type B is obtained by other means than statistical analysis (a frequently encountered example is the maximum permissible error). In metrology, a measured quantity must be reported with an uncertainty.

For a metrologist, an accuracy is a qualitative description of the measured quantity (see the definition of exactitude in the VIM [54]). However, many manufacturers are referring to quantitative values that they describe as the accuracy of their systems. Note that often accuracy specifications provided by the manufacturer do not include information about the test procedures used to obtain these values. For many applica-

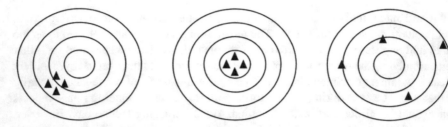

Fig. 4.9 The throwing of darts represents the measurement process. The position of the darts on the far left board is precise but not accurate, on the centerboard it is both precise and the accurate, and on the right board it is both imprecise and inaccurate. Figure courtesy of NRC

tions, the measured quantities need to be georeferenced and one may encounter the terms *relative* and *absolute* accuracy, the latter being critical for autonomous vehicle applications, for example. Relative accuracy relates to the position of something relative to another landmark. It is how close a measured value is to a standard value in relative terms. For example, you can give your location by referencing a known location, such as 100 km West of the CN Tower located in downtown Toronto. Absolute accuracy relates to a fixed position that never changes, regardless of your current location. It is identified by specific coordinates, such as latitude and longitude. Manufacturers are usually referring to accuracy specifications of their system as relative and not absolute. Relative measurement is generally better than absolute for a given acquisition.

Intuitively, precision is how close multiple measurements are to each other. Precise measurements are both repeatable and reproducible. You can call it repeatable if you can get the same measurement using the same operator and instrument. It is reproducible if you can get the same measurement using multiple operators and instruments. Figure 4.9 shows the difference between precision and accuracy with a dartboard example. Precision is the grouping of the shots (how close they are to each other on average), whereas accuracy is how close the darts are, on average, to the bullseye.

Intuitively, the lateral resolution is the capability of a scanner to discriminate two adjacent structures on the surface of a sample. The lateral resolution is limited by two factors: structural resolution and spatial resolution. The knowledge of beam footprint (see discussion on laser spot size in Chap. 3) on the scene allows one to determine the structural component of the lateral resolution of the system. The spatial resolution is the smallest possible variation of the scan angle. Increasing the resolution of the scan angle can improve the lateral resolution, as long as the spatial resolution does not exceed structural resolution.

For the remainder of this section, we will first review the use of reference instruments to compare ToF systems. This is used to introduce current standards and guidelines. Then other related studies on the characterization of 3D imaging system are presented. We then present methods to find inconsistencies in instrument measurement results.

4.6.1   Comparison to a Reference System

The performance of a 3D imaging system (instrument under test or IUT) is usually evaluated by comparing it to the performance of a reference system to determine if the IUT can be used to accomplish the same task as the reference system. This requires the reference system to be considered the "gold standard" for system performance. The objective is to validate whether, for a given task, both instruments can provide similar measurement results. Many governments have been active in developing standards to test the performance of TLS systems using an LT system as the reference instrument [14, 63–65]. For small objects, obtaining 3D reference models can be relatively simple because they can be manufactured with great accuracy or they can easily be characterized using a Coordinate Measuring Machine (CMM) [62]. When quantitatively evaluating the performance of a large-volume TLS system, a significant problem is how to acquire reliable 3D reference models. For example, manufacturing a reference object the size of a building would be cost-prohibitive. Moreover, creating a digital reference model of such an object would require the use of a complex software pipeline to merge many 3D scans. It may be difficult to properly characterize the impact of the software pipeline on the uncertainty of the data points comprising the 3D model. For example, consider the study presented in [99, 100] that compared the task-specific performance of a TLS system and a photogrammetry system being used to create a digital model of the entrance of a patrimonial building ($10\,\mathrm{m} \times 10\,\mathrm{m}$). For the large-volume digital reference model, the authors used a combination of measurements results obtained by both a total station and a TLS system. For a smaller volume digital reference model they combined measurement results obtained using both an LT system and a TLS system. In another study, the authors compared the performance of a photogrammetry system with that of a laser scanning system [18, 41]. Yet another study compared the performance of a photogrammetry system to a manual survey for the task of generating the as-built model of a building [31, 56]. A best practice methodology for acquiring reference models of building-sized object is presented in [33]. The method uses a TLS system and an LT. A study that uses a LT to evaluate close-range photogrammetry with tilt-shift lenses is presented in [80]. The comparison of TLS and LT with photogrammetry is further discussed in Sect. 4.9.

4.6.2   Standards and Guidelines

There are relatively few guidelines and standards available for optical non-contact 3D imaging systems, most of which have emerged from the world of CMMs. The primary organizations that develop standards for optical non-contact 3D imaging systems are the International Organization for Standardization (ISO), American Society for Testing and Materials (ASTM), and American Society of Mechanical Engineers

(ASME). There is also a set of guidelines published by the Association of German Engineers (the VDI).

ISO 10360 encompasses a group of international standards that provides methods for the acceptance and reverification of 3D imaging systems [49]. Parts 1 through 6 apply specifically to CMMs, but a part 7 was added to include CMMs with imaging probing systems. Parts 8, 9, and 10 apply to the broader class of Coordinate Measuring System (CMS), which includes both CMMs and LT systems. A part 12 is under development to include articulated arm systems under the CMS umbrella. All four of these standards, however, apply only to contact 3D imaging systems. ISO 17123-9 was developed to provide a standard for in-field test procedures for TLS systems [36, 50].

VDI 2634, a set of German guidelines, is devoted to acceptance and reverification testing of optical non-contact 3D imaging systems, but is limited to optical non-contact 3D imaging systems that perform area scanning from a single viewpoint [103]. Part 3 extends the test procedures to multi-view non-contact 3D imaging systems. VDI 2634 was written as an extension to ISO 10360, so it drew heavily from CMM standards; however, 3D imaging systems utilize measurement principles that differ substantially from those of CMMs. VDI 2617 part 6.2 makes some attempt to bridge the gap between contact and non-contact 3D imaging systems, but still approaches acceptance and reverification from the CMM perspective.

The ASTM E57 committee for 3D imaging systems has developed standards specifically for TLS systems. ASTM E2611-09 is a guideline to the best practices for safe use of 3D imaging system technology. This standard was followed by ASTM E2544-11, which provides a set of terminology to facilitate discussion regarding 3D imaging systems. Parallel with this effort was the development of ASTM E2807 to provide a common and vendor-neutral way to encode and exchange LiDAR data, although this was focused mostly on airborne LiDAR systems rather than TLS systems. The most recent standard developed by the committee is ASTM E2938-15, which evaluates the range measurement performance of a TLS system using an LT as the reference instrument. A proposed standard WK43218 is under development to evaluate the volumetric measurement performance of a TLS system, building on the method developed for the E2939-15. More details on the development of standards can be found in [15].

4.6.3 Other Research

Outside the realm of official standards and guidelines, there have been many attempts to quantify the performance of LiDAR systems. Hebert and Krotkov [2] identified a variety of issues that can affect LiDAR data quality, including mixed pixels, range/intensity cross-talk, synchronization problems among the mirrors and range measuring system, motion distortion, incorrect sensor geometry model, and range drift. Mixed pixels refer to multiple return signals associated with a single outgoing signal, each resulting from a different surface along the beam path, and occurs when the beam footprint is only partially intersected by a surface. They assessed the accuracy of a LiDAR system from 5 trials of measuring the positions of 6 targets of different materials (untreated cardboard, black-painted cardboard, wood) at known distances from 6 to 16 m under different lighting conditions (sunny and cloudy, with and without lights). Range accuracy was evaluated by averaging 100 scans of each of 6 black-painted cardboard targets at different distances from 6 to 16 m. Angular accuracy was evaluated by measuring the lateral drift of 1000 scans of white circles with radius 12 cm, which were extracted from each image using thresholding.

Tang et al. [96] focused their efforts on quantifying the effect of spatial discontinuities, or edges, on LiDAR data. This is related to the mixed pixel problem discussed by Hebert and Krotkov, but focused on the spatial measurement error that occurs as progressively less of the surface intersects the beam footprint. Indeed, Tang et al. referred specifically to the mixed pixel effect as a significant issue in which both foreground and background surfaces are simultaneously imaged. Different LiDAR systems handle multiple return signals in different ways such as reporting only the first or the last returns, or averaging the returns. In all cases, measurements at discontinuities are extremely noisy, so a challenge is to detect and remove them; however, zero-tolerance removal can significantly degrade the quality of the resulting depth map, especially when surfaces narrower than the beam footprint are removed as noise. In some cases, strips of up to several centimeters wide may be removed at spatial discontinuities.

Cheok and Stone [27], as part of the NIST's Construction and Metrology Automation Group, have conducted significant research into the problem of characterizing the performance of LiDAR systems. In addition to their participation in the ASTM E57 standard development, they built a facility devoted to the performance assessment and calibration of LiDAR systems. Some of this work was discussed in Sect. 4.6.2. They noted that LiDAR performance is not simply a function of range measurement. Rather, it is complicated by having to function in a multi-system environment that may include equipment to determine the pose of the LiDAR system and other imaging systems such as triangulation or photogrammetry that may be included in the final model. For individual LiDAR systems, range measurement accuracy, surface color, surface reflectivity (shiny to matt), surface finish (rough to smooth), and angle of incidence with the systems are significant factors in assessing LiDAR system performance. As impediments to assessing LiDAR performance, they identified a lack of standard procedures for in-site test setup and equipment alignment, how to obtain reference measurements, lack of standards related to target size or reflectivity, and no guidelines regarding the required number of data points.

Zhu and Brilakis [111] examined different approaches to collecting spatial data from civil infrastructure and how they are converted into digital representations. They noted that while there were many types of optical-spatial data collection systems, no system was ideally suited for civil infrastructure. In their study they compared system accuracy, methods of automating spatial-data acquisition, instrument cost, and portability. According to Teizer and Kahlmann [97], the ideal system for generating digital models of civil infrastructure would be highly accurate, capable of updating information in real time, be affordable, and be portable. Zhu and Brilakis tabulated the benefits and limitations of four classes of optical spatial imaging systems: terrestrial photogrammetry, videogrammetry, terrestrial laser scanning, and video camera ranging. They classified each according to measurement accuracy, measurement spatial resolution, equipment cost, portability, spatial range, and whether or not data about the infrastructure could be obtained in real time (fast and automated data collection).

4.6.4   Finding Inconsistencies in Final 3D Models

As noted in the previous section, partial or complete automation of a spatial data collection system is the ideal; however, measurement errors often require manual intervention to locate and remove data prior to merging the data into the final model. Moreover, inaccuracies in the final model due to problems in the registration process must also be located and addressed.

Salvi et al. [90] completed a review of image registration techniques in which model accuracy was assessed as part of the process. Image registration is used to address the physical limitation to accurately modeling a surface by most spatial imaging systems. These limitations include occluded surfaces and the limited field of view of typical sensor system. The registration process determines the motion and orientation change required of one range image to fit a second range image. They divided registration techniques into coarse and fine methods. Coarse methods can handle noisy data and are fast. Fine methods are designed to produce the most accurate final model possible given the quality of the data; however, they are typically slow because they are minimizing the point-to-point or point-to-surface distance. Salvi et al. experimentally compared a comprehensive set of registration techniques to determine the rotation error, translation error, and Root-Mean-Square (RMS) error, as well as computing time of both synthetic and real datasets.

Bosche [21] focused on automated CAD generation from laser scans to update as-built dimensions. These dimensions would be used to determine whether as-built features were in compliance with as-designed building tolerances. Even this system, though, was only quasi-automated in that the image registration step required manual intervention. The automated part of the system used the registered laser scans to find a best-fit match to the as-designed CAD with an 80% recognition rate. They noted that fit accuracy could not be properly assessed because it depended on the partially manual registration process in which a human operator was required to provide the match points for the registration system. The system, though, assumed each CAD object corresponded to a pre-cast structure that was already in compliance, so only assessed whether the resulting combination of those structures was in compliance.

Anil et al. [7, 8] tackled the problem of assessing the quality of as-built Building Information Modeling (BIM) models generated from point-cloud data. Significant deviations between as-built and as-designed BIM models should be able to provide information about as-built compliance to as-designed tolerance specifications, but only if the digital model is a reasonably accurate representation of the physical structure. In their case study, they determined that the automated compliance testing identified six times as many compliance deviations as physical test measurement methods alone. Moreover, the errors were discovered more quickly, resulting in a 40% time savings compared to physical measurement methods. The authors did, however, note that automated methods were not as well suited to detecting scale errors. This issue is balanced by limitations to physical measurements that include limited accuracy of tape- and contact-based methods, limited number of measurements, and the physical measurement process is time and labor intensive. They identified the primary sources of measurement errors in scanned data as data collection errors (mixed pixels, incidence angle, etc.), calibration errors in scanning systems, data artifacts, registration errors, and modeling errors (missing sections, incorrect geometry, location, or orientation). They observed that these errors were, in practice, typically within the building-design tolerance so were well suited to identifying actual deviations in the as-built structure.

4.7   Experimental Results

In this section, we present some experimental results that illustrate some of the applications of terrestrial and mobile LiDAR systems. The discussions about range uncertainty and systematic error of the measurements produced by TLS is also applicable to MLS.

4.7.1   Terrestrial LiDAR Systems (TLS)

First, the range uncertainty of a pulse-based TLS on different diffuse reflectance surfaces is presented. Then, the impact of sub-surface scattering on pulse-based and phase-based TLS is discussed. Finally, a case study of the use of pulse-based TLS and LT is showcased.

4.7.1.1   Range Uncertainty

The performance of a Leica ScanStation 2 was verified under laboratory conditions (ISO 1) for distances below 10 m and in a monitored corridor for distances up to 40 m. Figure 4.10 shows two sets of curves for evaluating the noise level on a flat surface (RMS value of the residuals after plane fitting to the data) as a function of distance, and the diffuse reflectance of different materials [5]. Using a Munsell cardboard reference with a diffuse reflectance of 3.5%, we get a maximum range of 20 m; therefore, the measurement of dark areas is limited by distance. At a range that varies between 1 and 90 m, on a surface with diffuse reflectance that varies between 18 and 90%, the RMS noise levels vary between 1.25 and 2.25 mm.

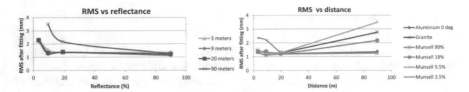

Fig. 4.10 Left: graphical representation of the RMS values obtained after fitting a plane to the 3D point cloud at different distances and as a function of material diffuse reflectance. Right: graphical representation of the RMS values obtained after fitting a plane to the 3D point clouds for different material diffuse reflectance as a function of distance. Figure courtesy of NRC

Fig. 4.11 Left: example of light penetration in marble. The paper sheet appears to be 5 mm thick. Note that green is no offset, red is 7 mm positive offset, and purple is 7 mm negative offset. Right: a 15 mm thick metallic plate (with four holes) in front of a marble plate. Figure courtesy of NRC

4.7.1.2   Systematic Range Error

Figure 4.11 left shows the range measurement systematic error resulting from optical penetration of a marble surface. This image was acquired in-situ, while performing the 3D data acquisition of the Erechtheion at the Acropolis in Athens [34]. An approximately 0.1 mm thick piece of paper represents an opaque surface held flat onto the semi-opaque marble surface. The penetration makes the marble surface appear offset by almost 5 mm from the paper. This systematic range error may be attributed to a combination of laser penetration and unusual backscattering properties of the laser light on this type of marble. This systematic error was observed in the field using a pulse-based TLS and a phase-based TLS. While both scanners register a systematic error, the magnitude varies depending on the technology used and the type of marble.

Figure 4.11 right shows an experiment conducted under laboratory conditions (ISO 1) that validates this in-situ observation. A 15 mm thick well-characterized metallic plate is installed in front of a polished marble plate. When analyzing scans from a TLS, the metallic plate appears 8.4 mm thicker. Again, this systematic error was observed using a pulse-based TLS and a phase-based TLS and the magnitude of the error varies depending on the technology used.

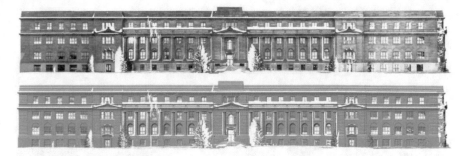

Fig. 4.12 Facade of a building facing south, Top: color from the onboard laser scanner 2D camera mapped onto the final 3D point cloud. Bottom: shaded view of the 3D point cloud. The polygonal mesh was created without using a hole-filling algorithm, using Polyworks IMMerge (no scale provided on this drawing). Figure courtesy of NRC

4.7.1.3   A Case Study in Combining TLS and LT

This section presents a dataset containing a reference model composed of a 3D point cloud of the exterior walls and courtyards of a 130 m × 55 m × 20 m building that was acquired using the methodology proposed in [33]. This building is located at 100 Sussex Drive in Ottawa and was built from 1930 to 1932 to host the National Research Council Canada. The building is made of large sandstone and granite and it is designated as a classified federal heritage building under the Treasury Board heritage buildings policy of the Government of Canada (see Fig. 4.12). The two courtyards require special attention because they had to be attached to the 3D images of the exterior walls. Multiple scan positions were required and Fig. 4.14 illustrates the different range images that were acquired. The range images, once acquired, were aligned in a reference system linked to the measurement results from the laser tracker. This was possible by the combined use of TLS, LT, and spherical reference objects. The spherical object was used to combine the TLS and LT coordinate systems (see Sect. 4.3.2). Some contrast targets were used for quality control purposes (see Fig. 4.13). Polyworks IMAlign, IMInspect, and IMMerge[5] were used together to perform most of the work.

Due to the combined use of both measurement instruments, it was possible to quantitatively evaluate the quality of the alignment of the different range images produces at different scanning positions. The final model has 47 million polygons and can be characterized by an expanded uncertainty (Type B) U(k=3) of 33.63 mm [33]. Locally, the RMS on the surface is about 2.36 mm (1σ) and the average spatial resolution is about 20 mm (between 10 and 30 mm).

---

[5]www.innovmetric.com.

Fig. 4.13 View of the south facade. The contrast target positions are extracted with the laser scanner interface software Cyclone 2.0. The results are embedded in IMInspect and mapped onto the final 3D point cloud (top). Bottom: close-up of the coordinates of some contrast targets on the west side of the south facade (no scale provided on this drawing). Figure courtesy of NRC

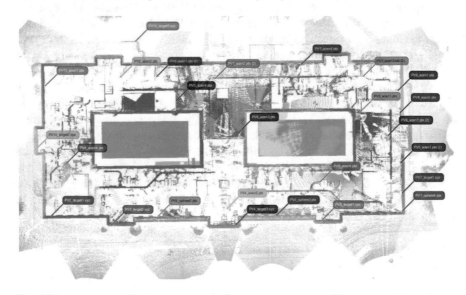

Fig. 4.14 Top view of the 3D point cloud after alignment of the different acquisitions for the courtyards and exterior of the building, one color per range image (Polyworks IMAlign, no scale provided on this drawing). Figure courtesy of NRC

Fig. 4.15 Snapshot of an area using a camera (left) and a view of the same area using VLP-16 LiDAR (right). Note the stop sign, the street sign and the street light pole contained in the red, purple, and yellow rectangles, respectively. Figure courtesy of NRC

4.7.2   Mobile LiDAR Systems (MLS)

Some LiDARs installed on mobile platforms are used for acquiring high-resolution mappings of urban environments, while others are used for the vehicular navigational purposes. In the remainder of this section, 3D scans obtained using a 16-channel LiDAR system installed on top of an automobile are presented. The results shown in this section target navigation applications.

4.7.2.1   Static Scan

In Fig. 4.15, a 360° range image and an image from a front-facing camera are presented. These were obtained while the automobile was parked. Generally, standard 2D cameras must deal with lighting variation and shadows. This is a significant disadvantage. However, LiDAR can provide a 3D representation of the surrounding environment largely independently of ambient light. Another example of a 360° scan is presented in Fig. 4.16. The accompanying image was generated using the panoramic feature on a smart phone.

4.7.2.2   Simultaneous Localization and Mapping (SLAM)

A typical robot integrated with a SLAM system will build a model of the surrounding environment and estimate its trajectory simultaneously. SLAM systems rely on several key algorithms, like feature extraction, registration, and loop closure detection. SLAM is a central challenge in mobile robotics and SLAM solutions enable autonomous navigation through large, unknown, and unstructured environments. In recent years, SLAM became an important research topic that has been investigated heavily [9]. In autonomous vehicle and mobile robotics applications, both cameras and the LiDAR can be used for localization [95]. As stated above, LiDAR has the advantage of being largely independent of external lighting and making use of the full 3D representation. Figure 4.17 shows the result of a map of the environment made

Fig. 4.16 Top: a panoramic picture taken by a smartphone. Bottom: 3D data collected by a Velodyne VLP-16 LiDAR from the same location. Figure courtesy of NRC

Fig. 4.17 3D Map of the Collip Circle road located in London (Canada) generated using a SLAM algorithm. The trajectory of the vehicle is shown using a dotted line. This result was obtained using the system presented in [45]. Figure courtesy of NRC

using the Velodyne VLP-16 LiDAR previously used. Note that the SLAM method that produced this result exploited the 360° field of view of the VLP-16 LiDAR and the availability of odometry data.

4.8   Sensor Fusion and Navigation

Sensor fusion is the process of integrating data from different sensors in order to construct a more accurate representation of the environment than otherwise would be obtained using any of the independent sensors alone. In recent years, significant progress has been made in the development of autonomous vehicles and Advanced Driver-Assistance Systems (ADAS). LiDAR is an important sensor that made possible such progress. Nevertheless, LiDAR data must be fused with other sensor's data in order to improve the situational awareness and the overall reliability and security of autonomous vehicles.

4.8.1   Sensors for Mobile Applications

For autonomous driving, ADAS and navigation applications, the sensors may include stereo cameras, cameras, radar, sonar, LiDAR, GPS, Inertia Navigation System (INS), and so on. Radar is one of the most reliable sensors. It can operate through various conditions such as fog, snow, rain, and dust when most optical sensors fail. However, radar has a limited lateral resolution. Cameras are cheap and have high resolution, but are affected by ambient illumination. Stereo cameras are cheap, but can be computationally expensive and do not cope well with low-texture areas. Sonar is useful for parking assistance, but has a limited range. The main disadvantage of sensor fusion is that different sensors can have incompatible perceptions of the environment; for example, some may detect an obstacle, while others may not.

In autonomous systems and ADAS, all sensor data is fed into the Data Acquisition System (DAQ). The gathering of the data by the DAQ can also be used for testing, developing, improving efficiency, ensuring reliability, and safety. Figure 4.18 explains the collaboration of the main sensors in an autonomous or ADAS application. The sensor fusion process starts by using information provided by GPS, INS, and odometery in order to determine the absolute position and orientation of the vehicle. Then sensor information from cameras and LiDARs is compared to known maps that are downloaded from the cloud (Web Security Services).

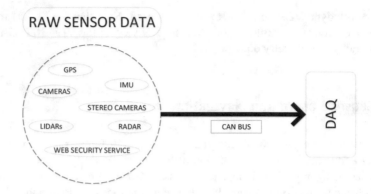

Fig. 4.18 Data acquisition is a sampling process that measures real-world physical conditions and converts the resulting samples into a digital representation recorded on the Data Acquisition System (DAQ). In automotive applications, the data from the different sensors are typically transferred on a data bus known as a Controller Area Network (CAN) or CAN bus. Figure courtesy of NRC

4.8.2 Cloud-Based, High-Definition Map

The cloud-based information is typically referred to as a High-Definition (HD) map and it allows adaptation of the driving to potential obstacles, including traffic, in order to avoid potential accidents. An HD map consists of geo-spatial coordinates of the static elements that describe roadway features such as lane markings, traffic signs, landmarks, road-edges, and so on. In order to construct these maps, special mapping vehicles are augmented with a number of high-accuracy sensors [91]. This allows the determination of a geo-spatial representation of the roadways that can be used by autonomous vehicles or ADAS that uses cheaper sensors. However, this HD-map approach creates significant data storage, computation, data delivery, and cyber-security issues that fall outside the scope of this chapter.

4.8.3 Absolute Positioning Systems

The Global Positioning System is not as accurate as a Global Navigation Satellite System/Inertia Navigation System (GNSS/INS), which is heavily used in various autonomous applications. A GNSS receiver provides accurate position and time to the navigation system. When the GNSS signal deteriorates, the INS sensor provides the position and navigation until the GNSS conditions improve. A GNSS/INS is expensive and, for some applications, GPS is the only economically viable geo-location solution. To reach a high-accuracy potential, LiDAR systems must be well calibrated and equipped with a high-end GNSS/INS navigation unit. A typical LiDAR sensor range accuracy is 1–5 cm, the GPS accuracy is 2–5 cm, INS accuracy for pitch/roll is 0.005°, and for heading is 0.008° with the laser beam divergence being

0.25–5 mrad. Note that some systematic errors may be due to misalignment of the laser with respect to the vehicle roll, pitch and yaw axes, or a measurement error of the relative position of the GPS antenna with respect to the INS reference system.

4.9   ToF Versus Photogrammetry

As seen in the Fig. 4.1, active triangulation systems and ToF systems operate over different ranges. The limitation of the range for triangulation systems is induced by the practical limitation on the physical size of the system. There are many passive triangulation methods that simultaneously compute 3D structure and camera position (see Chap. 2). These methods are known as stereo or structure-from-motion in the computer vision community or simply as photogrammetry in the photogrammetry community. Typically, photogrammetry requires smaller power consumption during the acquisition. The equipment is generally less expensive and smaller. However, the processing of the images is significantly more computationally intensive than ToF. In recent years, the increase in performance of computing platforms combined with algorithm development has made passive triangulation methods an attractive alternative to active ToF for some application fields. For the remainder of this section, we present three application fields where both technologies coexist (see Fig. 4.1).

4.9.1   TLS Versus Architectural Photogrammetry

Architectural Photogrammetry is typically aimed at the 3D reconstruction of patrimonial buildings or parts of buildings. Many studies have compared the performance of a photogrammetry system with that of ToF systems [18, 41, 99, 100]. Figure 4.19 shows results of a comparison between photogrammetry and a reference model produced by combining the measurements obtained using both TLS system and LT. The left image shows a result obtained in 2008, while the right one contains a result obtained in 2014. The same TLS and LT were used in both experiences, the reconstruction software, the cameras, and acquisition methodologies were different, reflecting the advances in the field. Both experiments were conducted in controlled laboratory conditions (ISO 1) at NRC Canada. The 2014 result was published in a study [99, 100].

4.9.2   LiDAR Versus Aerial Photogrammetry

Aerial photogrammetry and aerial LiDAR are two technologies used to produce Digital Elevation Models (DEMs). Low-cost Unmanned Aerial Vehicles (UAV) equipped with high-resolution cameras are now available. These systems allow low-altitude

Fig. 4.19 Comparison between photogrammetry and a reference model produced by combining the measurements obtained using both a TLS system and a LT. The left image shown a result obtained in 2008, while the right one contains a result obtained in 2014. Figure courtesy of NRC

photogrammetric survey. Using structure-from-motion at low altitude reduces the uncertainty associated with triangulation. For some applications, the use of UAVs can replace aerial photogrammetry, aerial LiDAR and, in some cases, TLS. UAV photogrammetry is a relatively recent and it faces technological, regulation, and methodology challenges [87].

4.9.3 LT Versus Industrial Photogrammetry

Industrial photogrammetric systems are composed of two or more cameras. The relative position and orientation between the cameras are known and the software extracts the position in the images of photogrammetric markers. The marker positions are used to triangulate 3D points. Photogrammetric markers are typically dots made of retroreflector material. They are either installed at known positions or they are printed on stickers that are put on the scene at unknown positions. Industrial photogrammetric systems are also known as optically tracked CMMs [16]. Industrial photogrammetry and conventional photogrammetry can replace a laser tracker up to a few meters for some applications [37, 69, 73, 81]. Industrial photogrammetry can compute the position of multiple markers at the same time and can be significantly cheaper than a laser tracker. The laser trackers can operate at greater ranges, they have a larger field of view and the measurements they provide are traceable [77]. A study that uses an LT to evaluate close-range photogrammetry with tilt-shift lenses is presented in [80]. The experimental setup for this study is shown in Fig. 4.5.

4.10 Research Challenges

The combination of modern imagery technologies, including 3D imaging, and machine learning is a very active topic for both academic and applied industrial researchers. In recent years, researchers have contributed to progress in application fields as diverse as agriculture, aerospace, archaeology, construction, manufacturing, aeronautic, automotive, medical technology, and security.

Currently, researchers, engineers, and entrepreneurs are researching new methods and technologies to improve packaging and performance, and to reduce production costs of ToF systems intended for automotive applications. The MEMS LiDAR is in an early stage of development as a low-cost LiDAR solution for automotive applications. The Solid-state Hybrid LiDAR (SH LiDAR) was introduced in 2005 as a result of the DARPA Robotic Car Races and simplified the design of 16-and-more-channel systems. The technology has been tested for autonomous safety over the years and the cost of multi-channel LiDAR dropped dramatically in 2015. With planned mass production to meet the growing demand for autonomous navigation and advanced safety, further dramatic cost reduction is expected. This should further increase industrial adoption and create new research opportunities in the development of low-cost autonomous vehicles.

Conventional LiDAR, can only provide indirect velocity data; it rapidly beams individual pulses of coherent light, producing frames milliseconds apart that can be used to estimate speed. The development of LiDAR systems that can simultaneously compute range and velocity is a challenging and active industrial research topic that could have a profound impact in the automotive industry.

As seen in Sect. 4.9, with the increase in computation power and improvement of machine learning algorithms, some problems that were mainly addressed using active 3D imaging systems can now be tackled with passive imaging systems or hybrid (active and passive). The development of reliable hybrid and passive systems are challenging research topics that could also lead to significant cost reduction for autonomous vehicles. The evaluation of the performance and safety of autonomous vehicles remains a major research challenge.

Finally, the field of robot vision guidance is developing rapidly. The benefits of sophisticated vision technology include savings, improved quality, reliability, safety, and productivity. The use of cheap, safe, and reliable mobile robots with vision systems could lead to major changes in the organization of warehouses and factories. The impact of such changes needs to be investigated.

4.11 Concluding Remarks

Time-of-flight technology is relatively new compared to more established measurement systems but the advantages that this technology offers cannot be ignored. Already, ToF systems have entered our living room through gaming consoles and are

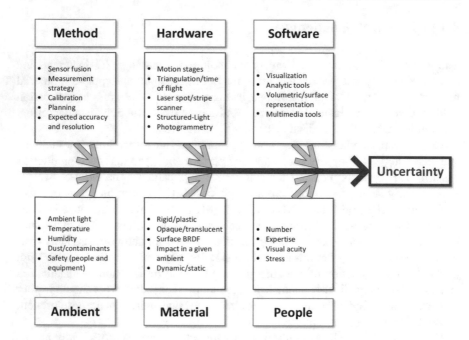

Fig. 4.20 The different sources of uncertainty affecting the measurements made by a 3D imaging system. Figure courtesy of NRC

now being integrated into high-end cellphones. LiDAR is viewed as an important technology that paves the way for self-driving cars. TLS and LT are regularly used in medium and large-scale civil engineering projects. Recognized standards for TLS and LT are now available and traceable measurements can be made in compliance with these standards.

Publicly available literature on active 3D imaging systems sometimes heavily focuses on the measurement instruments (i.e., the hardware means). The instrument is an important element that contributes to the uncertainty of a measurement. Nevertheless, they are many other uncertainty sources that an operator needs to be familiar with. Figure 4.20 shows other sources that affect the uncertainty associated with a measurement. The impact of ambient conditions was briefly discussed toward the end of Sect. 4.1.3. Some of the issues related to materiel properties of the object being measured were presented in Sect. 4.7. The software used to process the data also has an influence on the uncertainty of the measurements. Finally, two important sources of uncertainty that are often neglected are related to the people and the methodology that they used to operate the instrument and manipulate the data.

4.12 Further Reading

Due to space limitations, many topics related to time-of-flight technologies could not be covered in this chapter. In this section, we provide the reader with references to resources for exploring some of these topics.

Two aspects that were not discussed are the photonics and semiconductor challenges that include high-frequency laser pulsing, high-accuracy time measurement, and numerous other important implementation details. A good starting point for someone interested in the implementation of time-of-flight technologies is [88].

The exploitation of point clouds acquired from airborne and space-based platforms is an important topic for the remote sensing community [13]. The specificity of airborne and space-based LiDAR was not discussed in this chapter and we refer the reader to [10, 26, 32] for more information about remote sensing application of LiDAR. The use of space-based LiDAR for space operations is investigated in [28, 82, 102].

The development of autonomous vehicles is currently a popular academic and industrial research field. The current trend is to use multiple sensors some of which are 2D in nature while others are 3D. A survey of advanced driver-assistance system technologies that focuses on sensor fusion can be found in [112]. A survey of sensing technologies for autonomous vehicles is presented in [48]. The detection of traffic signs is discussed in [47, 71]. More details about the HD-map for autonomous vehicles can be found in [91] and a survey of vision-based vehicle detection is presented in [93]. More details about the use of Global Navigation Satellite System and Inertia Navigation System (GNSS/INS) can be found in [43, 85].

Acknowledgements The authors would like to acknowledge the numerous contributions of their colleagues at the National Research Council Canada.

4.13 Questions

1. Explain the difference between a pulse-based and a phase-based ToF?
2. What is the impact of multiple return signals for phase-based systems?
3. What type of applications would be better adapted to the use of a pulse-based system rather than a phase-based system?
4. How would you design an outfit for a human that would make a human invisible to a multi-channel scanner or that would induce a significant systematic range error?
5. A point-based scanner is acquiring a range image of a moving sphere. For different possible trajectories of the sphere with respect to the scanner, what type of artifacts are expected to be part of the point cloud?
6. Select an application that requires the use of a 3D imaging system. For that application what would be the advantages and disadvantages of using a passive triangulation system, an active triangulation system, and a ToF system?

7. You are given the mandate to scan in 3D the facade of a historic building. The resulting 3D model will be used to warp videos that will be projected on the building facade during a multimedia show. Explain your acquisition plan for this mandate and give a list of equipment and software that you would use.

4.14 Exercises

1. Transform a commercially available laser range finder into a TLS by developing your own scanning mechanisms (see [107] for a possible implementation).
2. For some applications that use a pulse-based system, the closest object in the scene can be far from the sensor. For these applications, a minimum range R_{min} can be defined. What is the fastest pulsing frequency f_p given R_{min} and R_{max}? In this case, does a detected pulse correspond to the last pulse emitted?
3. A pedestrian is located at 20 m in front of a pulse-based multi-channel LiDAR that acquires 55 3D points per degree and has a laser with beam divergence of 0.25 mrad. How many 3D points in the range image profile will belong to the pedestrian?
4. Given a point cloud generated by a multi-channel LiDAR, where each 3D point has a unique time stamp and assuming a single 3D measurement per laser pulse, develop an algorithm to reconstruct the range image from the point cloud.
5. Modify the previous algorithm for the case where the resolution of the time stamp is not sufficient for differentiating every 3D point and assume that some pulses may not have a return signal.
6. Compute the maximum operating distance of the systems listed in Table 4.2 using their minimum modulation frequencies and compare the value with the maximum operating distance given in the table.
7. Using the maximum and minimum modulation frequencies in Table 4.2, develop a multi-frequency phase disambiguation method for phase-based ToF, similar to the one presented in Sect. 4.2.2.2, that would be compatible with the average modulation frequency given in Table 4.2.
8. Assuming an area-based system with a light source located at distance D to the left of the detector and having a range uncertainty of σ, what is the range R of an object in front of the system for which the difference of the length of the light path from the source to the object and the object to the sensor is non-negligible? Compute a correction coefficient to be added to Eq. 4.17 that would compensate for this effect.
9. Replace the linear array of photodetectors of the system described in Sect. 4.4.2 by a bidirectional array of photodetectors such that the resulting system is able to compute range by using ToF and triangulation. Increase the pulse rate of the system such that Eq. 4.2 is no longer fulfilled and develop a method that uses the triangulation to pair the outgoing and incoming pulses.
10. At the time of publication, RoboSense and LeddarTech are advertising solid-state LiDAR technologies targeted at the automobile market. Using the marketing

material available from each company, compare both technologies and highlight the similarities and differences.

11. Make a list of the different error sources for a modeling project similar to the one presented in Sect. 4.7.1.3 and classify them according to the categories listed in Fig. 4.20. Provide mitigation strategies for the error sources identified.

References

1. Adams, T., Beets, P., Parrish, C.: Extracting more data from lidar in forested areas by analyzing waveform shape. Remote Sens. **4**(3), 682–702 (2012)
2. Aggarwal, J., Vemuri, B., Hebert, M., Krotkov, E.: Range image understanding 3D measurements from imaging laser radars: how good are they? Image Vis. Comput. **10**(3), 170–178 (1992)
3. Amann, M.C., Bosch, T., Lescure, M., Myllyla, R., Rioux, M.: Laser ranging: a critical review of usual techniques for distance measurement. Opt. Eng. **40**(1) (2001)
4. American National Standards Institute (ANSI): ANSI Z136 Part 1–6, American National Standard for Safe Use of Lasers (2007)
5. American Society of Tool and Manufacturing Engineers: ASTM E284-13b Standard Terminology of Appearance (2002)
6. American Society of Tool and Manufacturing Engineers: ASTM E2544 - 10 Standard Terminology for Three-Dimensional (3D) Imaging Systems (2010)
7. Anil, E., Tang, P., Akinci, B., Huber, D.: Assessment of quality of as-is building information models generated from point clouds using deviation analysis. In: Proceedings of SPIE, vol. 7864a (2011)
8. Anil, E.B., Tang, P., Akinci, B., Huber, D.: Deviation analysis method for the assessment of the quality of the as-is building information models generated from point cloud data. Autom. Constr. **35**, 507–516 (2013)
9. Aulinas, J., Petillot, Y.R., Salvi, J., Lladó, X.: The SLAM problem: a survey. CCIA **184**(1), 363–371 (2008)
10. Baghdadi, N., Zribi, M. (eds.): Land Surface Remote Sensing in Urban and Coastal Areas. Elsevier, Amsterdam (2016)
11. Baltsavias, E.P.: Airborne laser scanning: basic relations and formulas. ISPRS J. Photogramm. Remote Sens. **54**(2), 199–214 (1999)
12. Bamji, C.S., Mehta, S., Thompson, B., Elkhatib, T., Wurster, S., Akkaya, O., Payne, A., Godbaz, J., Fenton, M., Rajasekaran, V., Prather, L., Nagaraja, S., Mogallapu, V., Snow, D., McCauley, R., Mukadam, M., Agi, I., McCarthy, S., Xu, Z., Perry, T., Qian, W., Chan, V., Adepu, P., Ali, G., Ahmed, M., Mukherjee, A., Nayak, S., Gampell, D., Acharya, S., Kordus, L., O'Connor, P.: Impixel 65 nm bsi 320 mhz demodulated tof image sensor with 3μm global shutter pixels and analog binning. In: 2018 IEEE International Solid - State Circuits Conference - (ISSCC), pp. 94–96 (2018)
13. Beraldin, J.A., Blais, F., Lohr, U.: Laser scanning technology. In: Vosselman, G., Mass, H.-G. (eds.) Airborne and Terrestrial Laser Scanning. Whittles Publishers, Dunbeath (2010)
14. Beraldin, J.A., Cournoyer, L., Picard, M., Blais, F.: Proposed procedure for a distance protocol in support of ASTM-E57 standards activities on 3D imaging. In: Three-Dimensional Imaging Metrology - Proceedings of the SPIE-IS&T Electronic Imaging (2009)
15. Beraldin, J.A., Mackinnon, D., Cournoyer, L.: Metrological characterization of 3D imaging systems: progress report on standards developments. In: 17th International Congress of Metrology, p. 13003. EDP Sciences (2015)
16. Beraldin, J.A., MacKinnon, D.K., Cournoyer, L.: Testing proposal for an optically tracked CMM (OTCMM) in a pre-normative context. In: The Coordinate Metrology Society Conference (CMSC) (2016)

17. Besl, P.J.: Active, optical range imaging sensors. Mach. Vis. Appl. **1**(2), 127–152 (1988)
18. Bhatla, A., Choe, S.Y., Fierro, O., Leite, F.: Evaluation of accuracy of as-built 3D modeling from photos taken by handheld digital cameras. Autom. Constr. **28**, 116–127 (2012)
19. Blais, F.: Review of 20 years of range sensor development. J. Electron. Imaging **13**(1), 231–243 (2004)
20. Boehler, W., Marbs, A.: Investigating scanner accuracy. Technical Report, German University FH Mainz (2003)
21. Bosche, F.: Automated recognition of 3D CAD model objects in laser scans and calculation of as-built dimensions for dimensional compliance control in construction. Adv. Eng. Inform. **24**(1), 107 – 118 (2010). Informatics for cognitive robots
22. Bulyshev, A., Amzajerdian, D.P.F., Busch, G., Vanek, M., Reisse, R.: Processing of three-dimensional flash lidar terrain images generating from an airborne platform. In: Proceedings of SPIE, vol. 7329, pp. 7329–9 (2009)
23. Busck, J., Heiselberg, H.: Gated viewing and high-accuracy three-dimensional laser radar. Appl. Opt. **43**(24), 4705–4710 (2004)
24. Carmer, D.C., Peterson, L.M.: Laser radar in robotics. Proc. IEEE **84**(2), 299–320 (1996)
25. Chase, A.F., Chase, D.Z., Weishampel, J.F., Drake, J.B., Shrestha, R.L., Slatton, K.C., Awe, J.J., Carter, W.E.: Airborne lidar, archaeology, and the ancient maya landscape at Caracol, Belize. J. Archaeol. Sci. **38**(2), 387–398 (2011)
26. Chen, H.S.: Space Remote Sensing Systems: An Introduction. Academic, Cambridge (2014)
27. Cheok, G.S., Stone, W.: Performance evaluation facility for LADARs. In: Proceedings of SPIE, vol. 5412, pp. 54–65 (2004)
28. Christian, J.A., Cryan, S.: A survey of lidar technology and its use in spacecraft relative navigation. In: AIAA Guidance, Navigation, and Control (GNC) Conference (2013)
29. Conde, M.H.: Compressive Sensing for the Photonic Mixer Device - Fundamentals Methods and Results. Springer Vieweg, Berlin (2017)
30. Cournoyer, L., Picard, M.: Method, kit and target for multimode 3D imaging systems. US Patent Application US20180238677A1 (2016)
31. Dai, F., Lu, M.: Assessing the accuracy of applying photogrammetry to take geometric measurements on building products. J. Constr. Eng. Manag. **136**(2), 242–250 (2010)
32. Dong, P., Chen, Q.: LiDAR Remote Sensing and Applications. CRC Press, Boca Raton (2017)
33. Drouin, M., Beraldin, J., Cournoyer, L., Borgeat, L., Mackinnon, D., Godin, G., Fournier, J.: A methodology for creating large scale reference models with known uncertainty for evaluating imaging solution. In: 2014 2nd International Conference on 3D Vision, vol. 2, pp. 137–144 (2014)
34. El-Hakim, S., Beraldin, J.A., Picard, M., Cournoyer, L.: Surface reconstruction of large complex structures from mixed range data-the Erechtheion experience. In: Proceedings of the XXI Congress of the International Society for Photogrammetry and Remote Sensing (2008)
35. Estler, W.T., Edmundson, K.L., Peggs, G.N., Parker, D.H.: Large-scale metrology - an update. CIRP Ann. - Manuf. Technol. **51**, 587–609 (2002)
36. Federation Internationale des Geometres Standards Network: FIG Standards Network Report to 2013. FIG General Assembly (2013)
37. Filion, A., Joubair, A., Tahan, A.S., Bonev, I.A.: Robot calibration using a portable photogrammetry system. Robot. Comput.-Integr. Manuf. **49**, 77–87 (2018)
38. Fiocco, G., Smullin, L.: Detection of scattering layers in the upper atmosphere (60–140 km) by optical radar. Nature **199**(4900), 1275 (1963)
39. Gelbart, A., Bybee-Driscoll, S., Freeman, J., Fetzer, G.J., Wasson, D., Hanna, K., Zhao, W.Y.: Signal processing, image registration, and visualization of flash lidar data. In: Proceedings of SPIE, vol. 5086, p. 5086 (2003)
40. Godin, G., Rioux, M., Beraldin, J.A., Levoy, M., Cournoyer, L., Blais, F.: An assessment of laser range measurement on marble surfaces. In: Proceedings of the 5th Conference on Optical 3D Measurement Techniques Vienna Austria (2001)
41. Golparvar-Fard, M., Bohn, J., Teizer, J., Savarese, S., Peña-Mora, F.: Evaluation of image-based modeling and laser scanning accuracy for emerging automated performance monitoring techniques. Autom. Constr. **20**(8), 1143–1155 (2011)

42. Grönwall, C., Steinvall, O., Gustafsson, F., Chevalier, T.: Influence of laser radar sensor parameters on range-measurement and shape-fitting uncertainties. Opt. Eng. **46**(10), 106201 (2007)
43. Groves, P.D.: Principles of GNSS, Inertial, and Multisensor Integrated Navigation Systems, 2nd edn. Artech House, Norwood (2013)
44. Guidi, G., Remondino, F., Russo, M., Spinetti, A.: Range sensors on marble surfaces: quantitative evaluation of artifacts. In: SPIE Optical Engineering + Applications, p. 744703. International Society for Optics and Photonics (2009)
45. Hamieh, I., Myers, R., Rahman, T.: Construction of autonomous driving maps employing LiDAR odometry using real-time simulator. In: Canadian Conference on Electrical and Computer Engineering (2019)
46. Hancock, J., Langer, D., Hebert, M., Sullivan, R., Ingimarson, D., Hoffman, E., Mettenleiter, M., Froehlich, C.: Active laser radar for high-performance measurements. In: Proceedings. 1998 IEEE International Conference on Robotics and Automation, vol. 2, pp. 1465–1470 (1998)
47. Hussain, S., Abualkibash, M., Tout, S.: A survey of traffic sign recognition systems based on convolutional neural networks. In: 2018 IEEE International Conference on Electro/Information Technology (EIT), pp. 0570–0573 (2018)
48. Ilas, C.: Electronic sensing technologies for autonomous ground vehicles: a review. In: International Symposium on Advanced Topics in Electrical Engineering (ATEE), pp. 1–6 (2013)
49. International Organization for Standardization: ISO 10360, Geometrical Product Specifications (GPS) -Acceptance and Re-verification Tests for Coordinate Measuring Machines (2011)
50. International Organization for Standardization: ISO 17123, Optics and Optical Instruments – Field Procedures for Testing Geodetic and Surveying Instruments (2014)
51. International Standards Organization (ISO): ISO Guide 98-3, Uncertainty of Measurement – Part 3: Guide to the Expression of Uncertainty in Measurement: GUM:1995 (1995)
52. Jahne, B., Haussecker, H.W., Geissler, P.: Handbook of Computer Vision and Applications. Volume 1. Sensors and Imaging. Academic, Cambridge (1999)
53. Joint Committee for Guides in Metrology: Guide to the Expression of Uncertainty in Measurement (2008)
54. Joint Committee for Guides in Metrology: International Vocabulary of Metrology – Basic and General Concepts and Associated Terms: VIM (2008)
55. Joint Committee for Guides in Metrology: International Vocabulary of Metrology – Basic and General Concepts and Associated Terms (2012)
56. Laura, K., Nan, L., Burcin, B.G.: Comparison of image-based and manual field survey methods for indoor as-built documentation assessment. In: Computing in Civil Engineering (2011), pp. 59–66. ASCE Publications, Reston (2011)
57. Laurenzis, M., Bacher, E.: Image coding for three-dimensional range-gated imaging. Appl. Opt. **50**(21), 3824–3828 (2011)
58. Lee, V.D., Blackburn, C.J., Muralikrishnan, B., Sawyer, D.S., Meuret, M., Hudlemeyer, A.: A Proposed Interim Check for Field Testing a Laser Trackers 3-D Length Measurement Capability Using a Calibrated Scale Bar as a Reference Artifact. NIST Interagency/Internal Report (NISTIR) - 8016 (2014)
59. Lefsky, M.A., Cohen, W.B., Parker, G.G., Harding, D.J.: Lidar remote sensing for ecosystem studies: Lidar, an emerging remote sensing technology that directly measures the three-dimensional distribution of plant canopies, can accurately estimate vegetation structural attributes and should be of particular interest to forest, landscape, and global ecologists. AIBS Bull. **52**(1), 19–30 (2002)
60. Li, X., Wang, H., Yang, B., Huyan, J., Xu, L.: Influence of time-pickoff circuit parameters on lidar range precision. Sensors **17**(10), (2017)
61. Lichti, D.D., Harvey, B.: The effects of reflecting surface material properties on time-of-flight laser scanner measurements. In: Proceedings of the Symposium on Geospatial Theory, Processing and Applications. ISPRS Commission IV (2002)

62. MacKinnon, D., Carrier, B., Beraldin, J.A., Cournoyer, L.: GD&T-based characterization of short-range non-contact 3D imaging systems. Int. J. Comput. Vis. **102**(1–3), 56–72 (2013)
63. MacKinnon, D., Cournoyer, L.: NRCC experiments for ASTM E57 medium-range measurement error standards development. J. CMSC (2014)
64. MacKinnon, D., Cournoyer, L., Beraldin, J.A.: Single-plane versus three-plane methods for relative range error evaluation of medium-range 3D imaging systems. In: SPIE Optical Metrology (2015)
65. MacKinnon, D., Cournoyer, L., Saidi, K.S., Cheok, G.S., Bridges, R., Ingimarson, D.: Proposed E57.02 range measurement performance standard for medium range 3D imaging systems. J. CMSC 4–9 (2013)
66. MacKinnon, D.K., Cournoyer, L.: Single-plane versus three-plane methods for relative range error evaluation of medium-range 3D imaging systems. In: Proceedings of SPIE, vol. 9528 (2015)
67. Mak, N., Beraldin, J.A., Cournoyer, L., Picard, M., et al.: A distance protocol for mid-range TLS in support of ASTM-E57 standards activities. In: Proceedings of the ISPRS Commission V Mid-Term Symposium on Close Range Image Measurement Techniques, vol. 38, Part 5, pp. 428–433. Citeseer (2010)
68. Mallet, C., Bretar, F.: Full-waveform topographic lidar: state-of-the-art. ISPRS J. Photogramm. Remote Sens. **64**(1), 1–16 (2009)
69. Gaudreault, M., Joubair, A., Bonev, I.: Self-calibration of an industrial robot using a novel affordable 3D measuring device. Sensors **18**(10), 3380 (2018)
70. For Mechanical Engineers, A.S.: ASME B89.4.19 Performance Evaluation Tests and Geometric Misalignments in Laser Trackers (2009)
71. Mogelmose, A., Trivedi, M.M., Moeslund, T.B.: Vision-based traffic sign detection and analysis for intelligent driver assistance systems: perspectives and survey. IEEE Trans. Intell. Transp. Syst. **13**(4), 1484–1497 (2012)
72. Morse, E., Welty, V.: Dynamic testing of laser trackers. CIRP Ann. - Manuf. Technol. **64** (2015)
73. Muelaner, J., Maropoulos, P.: Large scale metrology in aerospace assembly. In: 5th International Conference on Digital Enterprise Technology; Conference Date: 22-10-2008 Through 24-10-2008 (2008)
74. Muralikrishnan, B., Blackburn, C., Sawyer, D., Phillips, S.: Measuring scale errors in a laser tracker's horizontal angle encoder through simple length measurement and two-face system tests. J. Res. Natl. Inst. Stand. Technol. **115**(5), (2010)
75. Muralikrishnan, B., Phillips, S., Sawyer, D.: Laser trackers for large-scale dimensional metrology: A review. Precis. Eng. **44** (2016)
76. Muralikrishnan, B., Sawyer, D.S., Blackburn, C.J., Phillips, S.D., Borchardt, B.R., Estler, W.T.: ASME B89.4.19 performance evaluation tests and geometric misalignments in laser trackers. J. Res. Natl. Inst. Stand. Technol. (2009)
77. Nasr, K.M., Forbes, A.B., Hughes, B., Lewis, A.: ASME B89.4.19 standard for laser tracker verification – experiences and optimisations. Int. J. Metrol. Qual. Eng. **3**, 89–95 (2012)
78. Nitzan, D.: Three-dimensional vision structure for robot applications. IEEE Trans. Pattern Anal. Mach. Intell. **10**(3), 291–309 (1988)
79. NOAA: Lidar 101: And Introduction to Lidar Technology, Data, and Applications. Revised (2012)
80. Nocerino, E., Menna, F., Remondino, F., Beraldin, J.A., Cournoyer, L., Rein, G.: Experiments on calibrating tilt-shift lenses for close-range photogrammetry. ISPRS-Int. Arch. Photogramm. Remote. Sens. Spat. Inf. Sci. **XLI-B5**, 99–105 (2016)
81. Nubiola, A., Slamani, M., Joubair, A., Bonev, I.A.: Comparison of two calibration methods for a small industrial robot based on an optical cmm and a laser tracker. Robotica **32**(3), 447–466 (2014)
82. Opromolla, R., Fasano, G., Rufino, G., Grassi, M.: Uncooperative pose estimation with a lidar-based system. Acta Astronaut. **110**, 287–297 (2015)

83. Payne, A., Daniel, A., Mehta, A., Thompson, B., Bamji, C.S., Snow, D., Oshima, H., Prather, L., Fenton, M., Kordus, L., et al.: A 512× 424 CMOS 3D time-of-flight image sensor with multi-frequency photo-demodulation up to 130 mhz and 2 gs/s adc. In: 2014 IEEE International Solid-State Circuits Conference Digest of Technical Papers (ISSCC), pp. 134–135. IEEE (2014)
84. Petrie, G., Toth, C.K.: Topographic Laser Ranging and Scanning. CRC Press, Boca Raton (2009)
85. Quan, W., Li, J., Gong, X., Fang, J.: INS/CNS/GNSS Integrated Navigation Technology. Springer, Berlin (2015)
86. Rachakonda, P., Muralikrishnan, B., Cournoyer, L., Cheok, G., Lee, V., Shilling, M., Sawyer, D.: Methods and considerations to determine sphere center from terrestrial laser scanner point cloud data. Meas. Sci. Technol. 28(10), 105001 (2017)
87. Remondino, F., Barazzetti, L., Nex, F., Scaioni, M., Sarazzi, D.: Uav photogrammetry for mapping and 3D modeling - current status and future perspectives. ISPRS-Int. Arch. Photogramm. Remote. Sens. Spat. Inf. Sci. 3822, 25–31 (2011)
88. Remondino, F., Stoppa, D. (eds.): TOF Range-Imaging Cameras. Springer, Berlin (2013)
89. Ryan, J., Carswell, A.: Laser beam broadening and depolarization in dense fogs. J. Opt. Soc. Am. A 68(7), 900–908 (1978)
90. Salvi, J., Matabosch, C., Fofi, D., Forest, J.: A review of recent range image registration methods with accuracy evaluation. Image Vis. Comput. 25(5), 578–596 (2007)
91. Seif, H.G., Hu, X.: Autonomous driving in the iCity—HD maps as a key challenge of the automotive industry. Engineering 2(2), 159–162 (2016)
92. Seitz, P.: Photon-noise limited distance resolution of optical metrology methods. In: Proceedings of SPIE, vol. 6616 (2007)
93. Sivaraman, S., Trivedi, M.M.: Looking at vehicles on the road: a survey of vision-based vehicle detection, tracking, and behavior analysis. IEEE Trans. Intell. Transp. Syst. 14(4), 1773–1795 (2013)
94. Smith, W.J.: Modern Optical Engineering, 3rd edn. McGraw-Hill, New York (2000)
95. Taketomi, T., Uchiyama, H., Ikeda, S.: Visual SLAM algorithms: a survey from 2010 to 2016. IPSJ Trans. Comput. Vis. Appl. 9(1), 16 (2017)
96. Tang, P., Akinci, B., Huber, D.: Quantification of edge loss of laser scanned data at spatial discontinuities. Autom. Constr. 18(8), 1070–1083 (2009)
97. Teizer, J., Kahlmann, T.: Range imaging as emerging optical three-dimension measurement technology. Transp. Res. Rec. 2040(1), 19–29 (2007)
98. Thomas, R., Guenther, G.: Theoretical characterization of bottom returns for bathymetric lidar. In: International Conference on Lasers, pp. 48–59 (1979)
99. Toschi, I., Beraldin, J.A., Cournoyer, L., Luca, L.D., Capra, A.: Evaluating dense 3D surface reconstruction techniques using a metrological approach. NCSLI Meas. 10(1), 38–48 (2015)
100. Toschi, I., Capra, A., De Luca, L., Beraldin, J.A., Cournoyer, L.: On the evaluation of photogrammetric methods for dense 3D surface reconstruction in a metrological context. ISPRS Ann. Photogramm. Remote Sens. Spat. Inf. Sci. 371–378 (2014)
101. Tsai, R.: A versatile camera calibration technique for high-accuracy 3D machine vision metrology using off-the-shelf TV cameras and lenses. IEEE J. Robot. Autom. 3(4), 323–344 (1987)
102. Tzschichholz, T., Boge, T., Schilling, K.: Relative pose estimation of satellites using pmd-/ccd-sensor data fusion. Acta Astronaut. 109, 25–33 (2015)
103. Verein Deutscher Ingenieure (VDI, Association of German Engineers): VDI 2634 Part 3 Optical 3-D Measuring Systems Optical System Based on Area Scanning (2008)
104. Wagner, W., Ullrich, A., Ducic, V., Melzer, T., Studnicka, N.: Gaussian decomposition and calibration of a novel small-footprint full-waveform digitising airborne laser scanner. ISPRS J. Photogramm. Remote Sens. 60(2), 100–112 (2006)
105. Wehr, A., Lohr, U.: Airborne laser scanning–an introduction and overview. ISPRS J. Photogramm. Remote Sens. 54(2), 68–82 (1999)
106. Whitehurst, A.S., Swatantran, A., Blair, J.B., Hofton, M.A., Dubayah, R.: Characterization of canopy layering in forested ecosystems using full waveform lidar. Remote Sens. 5(4), 2014–2036 (2013)

107. Willis, A., Sui, Y., Ringle, W., Galor, K.: Design and implementation of an inexpensive lidar scanning system with applications in archaeology. In: Proceedings of SPIE, vol. 7239 (2009)
108. Wu, L., Zhao, Y., Zhang, Y., Jin, C., Wu, J.: Multipulse gate-delayed range gating imaging lidar. Opt. Lett. **36**(8), 1365–1367 (2011)
109. Yura, H.T.: Atmospheric turbulence induced laser beam spread. Appl. Opt. **10**(12), 2771–2773 (1971)
110. Zhang, Z.: A flexible new technique for camera calibration. IEEE Trans. Pattern Anal. Mach. Intell. **22** (2000)
111. Zhu, Z., Brilakis, I.: Comparison of optical sensor-based spatial data collection techniques for civil infrastructure modeling. J. Comput. Civ. Eng. **23**(3), 170–177 (2009)
112. Ziebinski, A., Cupek, R., Erdogan, H., Waechter, S.: A survey of ADAS technologies for the future perspective of sensor fusion. In: Nguyen, N.T., Iliadis, L., Manolopoulos, Y., Trawiński, B. (eds.) Computational Collective Intelligence, pp. 135–146. Springer International Publishing, Cham (2016)
113. Zwally, H.J., Bindschadler, R., Thomas, R.: Ice-sheet dynamics by satellite laser altimetry. In: International Geoscience and Remote Sensing Symposium, pp. 1012–1022 (1981)

Chapter 5
Consumer-Grade RGB-D Cameras

Marc-Antoine Drouin and Lama Seoud

Abstract A new family of affordable active 3D imaging systems referred to as range cameras or RGB-D cameras has emerged in the last decade. These systems operate in the range of 0.4–10 m and are targeted directly at cost-sensitive consumers. They are typically specialized for capturing dynamic human activities and are designed to interfere only minimally with such activities. They use infrared-light sources and produce a continuous stream of 3D data at video frame rate. This chapter provides an overview of the three measurement principles that are behind most of today's commercial RGB-D cameras, namely, active stereo vision, structured-light, and time-of-flight. Examples of range images acquired using different RGB-D cameras are provided to support the comparison. Advanced material regarding range uncertainty and lateral resolution is also provided to identify the limitations of various RGB-D cameras currently available on the market.

5.1 Introduction

In recent years, affordable 3D active imaging systems have been introduced into the market. These vision systems capture and record a digital representation of geometry and appearance (e.g., color texture) information of visible 3D surfaces. Usually, they are not marketed to service providers or manufacturers of goods; they are marketed directly to consumers or embedded in products that are targeting the consumer market. These active 3D imaging systems are usually referred to as a range camera or RGB-D camera. RGB-D cameras are typically specialized for capturing human activities and have many characteristics that are not encountered in industrial 3D imaging systems. Usually, they are operated by untrained personnel who will use the device only if it brings instant gratification. This makes the user's experience

M.-A. Drouin (✉)
National Research Council, Ottawa, Canada
e-mail: Marc-Antoine.Drouin@nrc-cnrc.gc.ca

L. Seoud
Polytechnique Montreal, Montreal, Canada
e-mail: lama.seoud@polymtl.ca

©2020 Her Majesty the Queen in Right of Canada,
as represented by the National Research Council of Canada
Y. Liu et al. (eds.), *3D Imaging, Analysis and Applications*,
https://doi.org/10.1007/978-3-030-44070-1_5

dominate all other technical requirements and has a profound impact on the design of these systems (latency, calibration, performance, and data processing). RGB-D cameras are mainly focused toward dynamic human activities and are designed to minimally interfere with such activities. They use infrared-light sources and produce a continuous stream of 3D data at video frame rate. The intended application, eye safety, the price of components, and production cost are the limiting factors for the performances of these systems. Some systems are based on triangulation, while others are based on Time-of-Flight (ToF). Note that two products from the same company having a similar designation can be based on different measurement principles.

The power output of the laser used in RGB-D cameras is typically selected such that the device is class 1 in terms of eye safety. Such devices are safe under all conditions during the normal use (including when using typical magnifying optics). More details about the classification of lasers can be found in [1]. However, many exercises in this chapter propose to build systems similar to commercially available RGB-D cameras that will probably not meet the safety requirements for class 1 devices. When working with coherent light sources (lasers), eye safety is of paramount importance and one should never operate laser-based 3D imaging sensors without appropriate eye-safety training. For an operator using any laser, an important safety parameter is the Maximum Permissible Exposure (MPE) which is defined as the level of laser radiation to which a person may be exposed without hazardous effect or adverse biological changes in the eye or skin [1]. The MPE varies with wavelength and operating conditions of a system. We do not have space to discuss eye safety extensively here and refer the reader to the *American National Standard for Safe use of Lasers* [1]. Note that high power low coherence (and non-coherent) light sources can also pose eye safety issues [9].

5.1.1 Learning Objectives

After reading this chapter, the reader should have acquired knowledge of the operation of the different types of RGB-D cameras and should be able to assemble 3D imaging systems that are similar to some consumer-grade RGB-D cameras using commercially available components. This knowledge should also help in selecting which type of RGB-D camera best fits an application's needs. In this chapter, we present the scans of an object obtained using commercially available or legacy RGB-D cameras. The resulting images are provided for illustrating the working principles of the different types of RGB-D cameras. These results should not be used to assert the performance of the devices. Toward the end of this chapter, different studies that evaluate the performance of RGB-D cameras are discussed. We discourage the reader from comparing numerical values taken from different studies, as experimental protocol may vary between studies.

5.1.2 Historical Context

The entertainment industry has used active 3D imaging systems for years. The use was first limited to acquire digital representations of sites, professional actors, and athletes in order to add realistic synthetic imagery into movies and video games. The progressive addition of motion sensitive interface to gaming platforms and the desire to personalize the gaming experience led to the development of consumer-grade RGB-D cameras, targeted at a large demography of cost-sensitive consumers. Shortly after the release of a consumer-grade structured-light scanner, known as Microsoft's Kinect, a community of hobbyists, electrical and software engineers started reverse-engineering the device [36]. The scientific community began exploring the capability of the device in various applications and a significant body of scientific literature has been produced yearly since then. Figure 5.1 illustrates the number of publications with reference to Microsoft Kinect and RGB-D cameras for the year 2010–2018. Since the introduction of the first Kinect, other systems from Intel, Asus, Orbbec, and Occipital were introduced to the market. Moreover, the second and the third generation of Kinect sensor based on ToF were developed.

The information technology industry has members whose business models are built around the consumption of multimedia contents by large communities of users. These software and hardware giants have invested considerable resources in the development of headsets, or other devices, that allow augmented, virtual, and mixed reality. Some of these devices need to acquire a 3D representation of their environment in order to operate properly. While the development of these devices at an affordable retail price is challenging, the production of appealing content to a large community is also problematic. Part of this content is expected to be produced by the entertainment industry, while another part is produced by the community itself using consumer-grade RGB-D cameras. At the time of writing, RGB-D cameras that use ToF are viewed as an important new feature for smartphones, and manufacturers such as LG, Samsung, Huawei, Honor, and Oppo offer products with RGB-D cameras. While Apple had initially included a structured-light sensor in its flagship

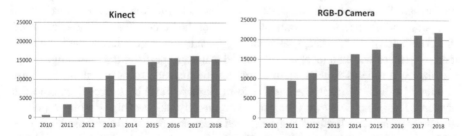

Fig. 5.1 Number of publications that mention Microsoft's Kinect (left) and RGB-D cameras in general (right) for the years 2010–2018. The results were generated using Google Scholar. A similar figure produced using the number of publications calculated from Scopus is presented in [111]. Figure courtesy of NRC

smartphone, its newest products now include a ToF sensor. These integrated RGB-D cameras are mostly targeting selfie types of application and face-unlock technology.

5.1.3 Basic Measurement Principles

One classification of optical distance measurement uses the illumination method to divide the imaging systems into three categories. Some measurement systems are point-based and scan the illumination source along two axes in order to acquire a range image. Other systems are profile-based and scan the illumination source along a single axis. Finally, some systems are area-based and they simultaneously illuminate the entire scene. Most, if not all, RGB-D cameras can be classified as area-based 3D imaging systems.

RGB-D cameras use either triangulation or Time-of-Flight (ToF) approaches. Triangulation approaches consist of finding light rays intersections in the 3D space. Two categories of triangulation-based sensing approaches exist: passive triangulation and active triangulation. Consumer-grade passive systems generally require two calibrated cameras and are thus referred to as stereo vision systems.

In stereo vision systems, the first step consists of finding point correspondences between the two camera views. Then, to retrieve the 3D position of the point that gave rise to a pair of matching points, the intersection of the two light rays passing through the point correspondences is computed. However, finding stereo matching points usually fails in low texture areas of the scene, resulting in dropouts [60]. One method for removing these dropouts is to artificially add texture to the scene using a light projector. This method is thus called *active stereo vision* or *projected texture stereo vision*.

In active triangulation systems, the second camera is replaced by a calibrated light projector. The term *active* refers to the fact that the scene is altered by projecting a specific light pattern onto it. Active systems are referred to as structured-light systems. In structured-light systems, the correspondences between the camera and the projector are implicitly encoded in the light pattern, either temporally or spatially, which simplifies the depth computation compared to the stereo vision approach. In temporal coding, patterns are projected one after the other and an image is captured for each pattern. In contrast, spatial coding techniques project just a single pattern, and the pattern within a local neighborhood is used to perform the matching.

Finally, a time-of-flight system computes the distance from the round-trip time required by light to reach the surface to be digitized and be reflected back to the system. This time delay may be estimated directly using a high-resolution clock to measure the time between outgoing and incoming pulses (pulse-based ToF), or indirectly by measuring the phase shift of an amplitude-modulated optical signal (phase-based ToF). For the remainder of this chapter, the discussions on ToF systems will focus on the phase-based system as the Kinect II and Azure devices are phase-based. The reader is referred to Chap. 4 for more details on pulse-based systems.

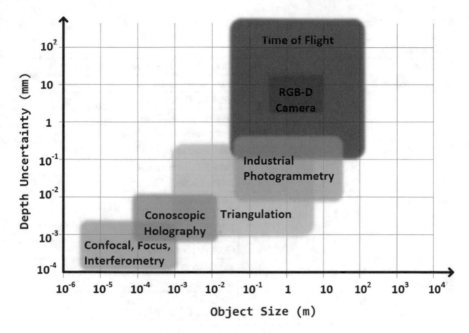

Fig. 5.2 Typical accuracy at different operating distances for the most common active 3D imaging technologies. Figure courtesy of NRC

Figure 5.2 summarizes the typical accuracy of each type of industrial active 3D imaging system technology found on the market as a function of the operating distance. Note that the operational range of RGB-D cameras falls within the end of the object-size range of triangulation system, but with a significant higher range uncertainty. This allows the design of RGB-D cameras based on triangulation using significantly cheaper components than industrial inspection systems based on triangulation. Table 5.1 presents a classification of the different commercially available or legacy RGB-D cameras.

5.1.4   Basic Design Considerations

In this section, we present the basic geometric constraints that influence the physical layout of components within RGB-D cameras. Other criteria such as the mechanical considerations, heat dissipation, and application constraints are not covered in this section. Figure 5.4 shows three popular designs of RGB-D cameras that can be found on the market. In all cases, RGB-D cameras are composed of a range subsystem working in the Near-Infrared (NIR) and a color camera used to add texture information to the 3D data. Typically, RGB-D cameras are designed such that the distance between the texture or RGB camera and the NIR camera used by the range

Table 5.1 Classification of some RGB-D cameras available on the market in four categories based on their measurement principle. Some of these RGB-D cameras are shown in Fig. 5.3. Figure courtesy of NRC

Measurement principle	Examples of commercial RGB-D sensors
Active stereo vision	Intel RealSense R200
	Intel RealSense D400 series
	Orbbec Astra Stereo
	Occipital Structure Core
Structured-light (temporal encoding)	Intel RealSense F200
	Intel RealSense SR300
	Intel RealSense SR305
Structured-light (spatial encoding)	Microsoft Kinect I
	Asus XTion 2
	Orbbec Astra
	Occipital Structure
	3D systems iSense
Time-of-flight	Microsoft Kinect II
	Microsoft Kinect Azure
	Intel RealSense L515

subsystem is as small as possible. This helps in reducing the amount of occlusion. Occlusion occurs when part of the scene is viewed by one camera but not by the other one. The problematic case is when the measurement camera views part of the scene that is not viewed by the color camera. In this situation, part of the recovered geometry cannot be textured. Some designs may also include microphone, accelerometers, gyroscopes, motor that controls the pan/tilt of the unit and other accessories not directly related to the generation of the textured range image. Figure 5.3 shows the RGB-D cameras discussed in this chapter.

Figure 5.4 shows on the left a schematized active stereo vision system. Typically, the projector is centered between the two NIR cameras used for stereo matching. The measurement uncertainty is directly related to the size of the baseline which is the distance between the two NIR cameras. For this reason, engineers have a strong incentive to position the measuring cameras at the extremity of the device in order to maximize the baseline.

On the right side of Fig. 5.4, a structured-light based RGB-D camera is schematized. Structured-light systems can use many coding strategies to establish the correspondence between the camera's pixels and the projector's pixels. The two main categories of coding are spatial coding and temporal coding. Both codification approaches are encountered in commercially available RGB-D cameras. The measurement uncertainty is directly related to the size of the baseline which is the distance between the measurement camera and the light projector. Again, there is a strong incentive to

Fig. 5.3 Some of the RGB-D cameras discussed in this chapter. Top-left: Intel RealSense D430 which is based on active stereo. Top-right: Intel RealSense SR300 which is based on time-multiplexed structured-light Bottom-left: Microsoft Kinect I which is based on spatially encoded structured-light. Bottom-right: Microsoft Kinect Azure based on ToF. Figure courtesy of NRC

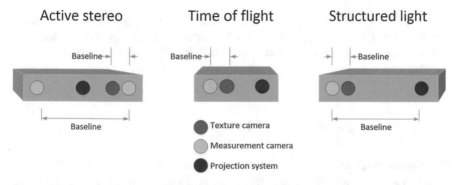

Fig. 5.4 Generic designs of RGB-D cameras. Left: an active stereo RGB-D camera composed of two measurement cameras, an RGB texture camera, and a light projector. Center: a time-of-flight RGB-D camera composed of an illumination projector, a specialized measurement camera, and an RGB texture camera. Right: a structured-light RGB-D camera composed of a measurement camera, a projector, and an RGB texture camera. The same design could be used for temporal and spatial encoding. Figure courtesy of NRC

position the measuring camera and the projector at the extremity of the device in order to maximize the baseline.

In the center of Fig. 5.4, a time-of-flight design is shown. ToF-based RGB-D cameras are composed of an illumination projector (or illumination source) and a measurement camera. While triangulation-based measurement cameras are monochromatic cameras optimized for NIR vision, ToF-based systems use specialized sensors (see [5] for some examples). Contrary to triangulation-based RGB-D systems, the performance of ToF-based systems is not affected by their physical dimensions [39].

In order to minimize the occlusions and parallax effect between the illumination projector and the measurement camera, it is useful to minimize the physical distance between both components. This allows the development of small footprint range sensors that can be integrated into consumer-grade products, such as augmented reality headsets or smartphones.

5.1.5 Chapter Outline

The core sections in this chapter cover the following material:

- Camera and projector models.
- Active stereo vision RGB-D cameras.
- Structured-light RGB-D cameras.
- Phase-based time-of-flight RGB-D cameras.
- Texture mapping.
- Range uncertainty and lateral resolution.
- System characterization and calibration.

Toward the end of the chapter, we present the main challenges for future research, concluding remarks, and suggestions for further reading. Finally, a set of questions and exercises are presented in order to consolidate the understanding of RGB-D cameras.

5.2   Camera and Projector Models

The simplest mathematical model that can be used to represent a camera is the pinhole model. A pinhole camera can be assembled using a box in which a small hole (i.e., the aperture) is made on one side and a sheet of photosensitive paper is placed on the opposite side. Figure 5.5 is an illustration of a pinhole camera. The pinhole camera has a very small aperture so it requires long integration times; thus, machine vision applications use cameras with lenses that collect more light and hence require shorter integration times. Nevertheless, for many applications, the pinhole model is a valid approximation of a camera. The readers that are familiar with the pinhole model material presented in Chap. 2–4 can omit Sect. 5.2.1.

5.2.1   Pinhole Model

In this mathematical model, the aperture and the photosensitive surface of the pinhole are represented, respectively, by the center of projection and the image plane. The center of projection is the origin of the camera coordinate system and the optical axis

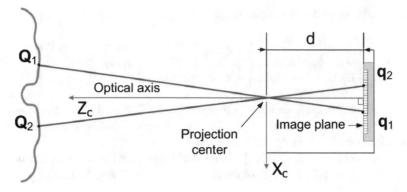

Fig. 5.5 Cross section of a pinhole camera. The 3D points $\mathbf{Q}_1$ and $\mathbf{Q}_2$ are projected into the image plane as points $\mathbf{q}_1$ and $\mathbf{q}_2$, respectively, and d is the distance between the image plane and the projection center. Figure courtesy of NRC

coincides with the Z-axis of the camera. Moreover, the optical axis is perpendicular to the image plane and the intersection of the optical axis and the image plane is the principal point (image center). Note that when approximating a camera with the pinhole model, the geometric distortions of the image introduced by the optical components of an actual camera are not taken into account (see Chap. 2 and [101] for more details). A 3D point $[X_c, Y_c, Z_c]^T$ in the camera reference frame can be transformed into pixel coordinates $[x, y]^T$ using

$$\begin{bmatrix} x \\ y \end{bmatrix} = \frac{d}{Z_c} \begin{bmatrix} \frac{X_c}{s_x} \\ \frac{Y_c}{s_y} \end{bmatrix} + \begin{bmatrix} o_x \\ o_y \end{bmatrix} \tag{5.1}$$

where s_x and s_y are the dimensions of the sensor in millimeters divided by the number of pixels along the X and Y-axis, respectively. Moreover, d is the distance in millimeters between the aperture and the sensor chip and $[o_x, o_y]^T$ is the position in pixels of the principal point (image center) in the image. The parameters s_x, s_y, d, o_x, and o_y are the intrinsic parameters of the camera. Note that when illustrating cameras in a 3D drawing, it is possible to improve the legibility of the illustration by positioning the image plane in front of the projection center. This representation is used for the remainder of this chapter. Note that the projector center is sometimes referred to as center point.

5.2.2 Extrinsic Parameters

The extrinsic parameters of the camera must be defined in order to locate the position and orientation of the camera in the world coordinate system. This requires three parameters for the rotation and three parameters for the translation. The rotation is represented using a 3×3 rotation matrix

$$R_c = \begin{bmatrix} 1 & 0 & 0 \\ 0 & \cos\theta_x & -\sin\theta_x \\ 0 & \sin\theta_x & \cos\theta_x \end{bmatrix} \begin{bmatrix} \cos\theta_y & 0 & \sin\theta_y \\ 0 & 1 & 0 \\ -\sin\theta_y & 0 & \cos\theta_y \end{bmatrix} \begin{bmatrix} \cos\theta_z & -\sin\theta_z & 0 \\ \sin\theta_z & \cos\theta_z & 0 \\ 0 & 0 & 1 \end{bmatrix} \quad (5.2)$$

where θ_x, θ_y, and θ_z are the rotation angles around the X, Y, and Z axis and translation is represented by a vector $\mathbf{T}_c = [T_x, T_y, T_z]^T$. Note that the rotation matrix R_c is orthogonal (i.e., $R_c^T = R_c^{-1}$) and $\det(R_c) = 1$.

A 3D point $\mathbf{Q}_w = [X_w, Y_w, Z_w]^T$ in the world reference frame can be transformed into a point $\mathbf{Q}_c = [X_c, Y_c, Z_c]^T$ of the camera reference frame by using

$$\mathbf{Q}_c = R_c \mathbf{Q}_w + \mathbf{T}_c. \quad (5.3)$$

A point in the camera reference frame can be transposed into the world reference frame by using

$$\mathbf{Q}_w = R_c^T [\mathbf{Q}_c - \mathbf{T}_c]. \quad (5.4)$$

A projector system can be viewed as an *inverse camera*. This model is also suitable for a Diffraction Optical Element (DOE) projector [18]. Using a DOE projector is a compact and cost-efficient method that is used by some RGB-D cameras to project a static pattern. Some 3D systems used in the context of an endoscope also used this type of projector. The extrinsic parameters of the projector must also be defined in order to locate the position and orientation of the projector in the world coordinate system. The matrix R_p and the vector $\mathbf{T}_p$ can be defined similarly as R_c and $\mathbf{T}_c$.

A 3D point $\mathbf{Q}_p = [X_p, Y_p, Z_p]^T$ in the projector reference frame can be transformed into a point $\mathbf{Q}_c = [X_c, Y_c, Z_c]^T$ in the camera reference frame by using

$$\mathbf{Q}_c = R_c R_p^T [\mathbf{Q}_p - \mathbf{T}_p] + \mathbf{T}_c. \quad (5.5)$$

All components of an RGB-D camera are usually mounted on the same Printed Circuit Board (PCB), they have the very similar orientations ($R_c \approx R_p$) and are physically aligned on the board. In this case, Eq. 5.5 can be approximated by

$$\mathbf{Q}_c \approx \mathbf{Q}_p - (b, 0, 0)^T. \quad (5.6)$$

where $\mathbf{T}_p + \mathbf{T}_c = (b, 0, 0)^T$ with b being the baseline between the projector and camera. Using image rectification (see Chap. 2), the approximation in Eq. 5.6 can be replaced by an equality. RGB-D cameras based on active stereo vision use two measurement cameras. The transformation from the reference frame of one camera to the second one is performed similarly. This type of RGB-D camera is presented in the next section.

5.3 Active Stereo Vision RGB-D Cameras

This section covers active stereo vision, which is becoming increasingly prevalent
in the RGB-D market. As its name suggests, the method is based on two-camera
triangulation, aiming at identifying corresponding points between two images to
retrieve the depth of the scene. The word *active* refers to the fact that a highly textured
unstructured light pattern is projected onto the scene to facilitate the matching in scene
regions that are devoid of rich texture. This section broadly presents the steps for
classic, passive stereo vision, followed by the specific requirements of active stereo
vision and an example of a commercial RGB-D sensor that is based on this range
sensing technique.

5.3.1 Stereo Vision

Stereo vision based RGB-D cameras usually consist of two cameras mounted on a rig
and separated by a distance referred to as the baseline b. Cameras are calibrated so that
all implicit and explicit parameters are known. Similar to the human vision system,
each camera acquires a slightly different view of the scene. The two resulting images
are then processed such that pixels with similar features are matched between the two
views to create stereo-corresponding pairs of points. Matching points are actually
2D projections of the same unique point in 3D. From a pair of stereo-corresponding
points, the 3D reconstruction consists of computing the intersection between the rays
passing through each of the corresponding camera center points and some pixel in
the image plane (see Fig. 5.6).

Fig. 5.6 Stereo vision
consists of finding
corresponding points p_l and
p_r in a pair of images
acquired with left and right
cameras, the center points of
which are denoted by C_l and
C_r, respectively. The 3D
point P corresponds to the
intersection of the light rays.
Figure courtesy of NRC

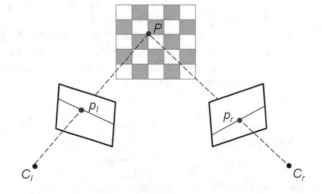

5.3.1.1 Image Rectification

In stereo vision, the matching process is usually the most challenging step in terms of computation. One step to simplify the problem is to convert the 2D search to a 1D search, along a line. This can be done by exploiting the epipolar geometry of the whole system and by rectifying the images so that both camera optical axes are parallel and each horizontal line in the first image matches the similar line in the second rectified image. Please refer to Chap. 2 for more details on image rectification and epipolar geometry (see Fig. 5.6).

One of the main differences between triangulation-based consumer-grade RGB-D cameras and industrial range systems is the geometric configuration. Consumer RGB-D cameras have a limited physical size which constrains the baseline to relatively small values (usually below 10 cm). All components of a RGB-D camera are usually mounted on the same printed circuit board, thus image pairs can be hardware-rectified ($\theta_x \approx 0$, $\theta_y \approx 0$, $\theta_z \approx 0$), and $T_y \approx 0$, and $T_z \approx 0$ and $T_x = b$ is a few centimeters. Moreover, since these cameras are usually targeted for human-centered applications, they generally require a standoff distance of a few meters. Whereas in range systems designed for industrial applications, larger baselines and shorter standoff distances are used.

5.3.1.2 Block Matching

In rectified images, the search for corresponding points along a line is based on a measure of similarity or dissimilarity of the local intensity information, a task commonly referred to as block matching. The distance between a point p and its corresponding point along the epipolar line is called disparity and noted D_p. The disparities of all the points in the image form a disparity map D, which can be displayed as an image. Different algorithms exist for block matching, they are generally divided into three categories: local, global, and semi-global.

Local block matching consists of finding corresponding pixels by matching $n \times n$ blocks in one image to N blocks of $n \times n$ along the search line in the other image. To score the matching, the most commonly used dissimilarity measure is the Sum of Absolute Distances (SAD) due to its computational simplicity. Explicitly, it is defined as

$$SAD(p(x, y), D_p) = \sum_{i=-n/2}^{n/2} \sum_{j=-n/2}^{n/2} |I_l(x + i, y + j) - I_r(x + i + D_p, y + j)|$$

$$(5.7)$$

with $0 < D_p < N$, N being generally referred to as the search range, I_l and I_r are respectively the left and right images. Other metrics can be used as well such as the Normalized Cross-Correlation (NCC) or the Sum of Squared Differences (SSD) among others (see Chap. 2). The main drawback of local block matching is that it can lead to discontinuities in the estimated disparity map.

Global block matching methods consist of determining the best transformation of one image to the other by optimizing a global energy function. The latter is generally composed of a pixel-wise matching cost similar to the local method over the whole image and a regularization term to deal with local discontinuities. Due to the regulation terms that are typically used, the optimization problem is often NP-complete. The most common approximate solutions to this NP-complete problem are graph cuts and belief propagation. However, the limitations of global methods are the computational cost and memory consumption associated with it [105].

Semi-Global block Matching (SGM) allows a good tradeoff between accuracy and run time by combining concepts from both local and global matching [48]. Like global matching, SGM is formulated as finding the disparity map D that minimizes the cost function $E(D)$ defined as

$$E(D) = \sum_p (SAD(p, D_p)) + \sum_p \sum_{q \in N_p} P_1 T[|D_p - D_q| = 1] +$$
$$\sum_p \sum_{q \in N_p} P_2 T[|D_p - D_q| > 1]. \tag{5.8}$$

The operator $T[.]$ returns 1 when its argument is true, and 0 otherwise. N_p refers to the neighborhood of the pixel p. The first term of the cost function is the dissimilarity measure computed for all pixels p along one dimension. The second term penalizes small disparity variations in the neighborhood of a pixel p by a factor of P_1. The third term penalizes large disparity variations by a factor of P_2 to preserve discontinuities. However, this optimization is not performed globally on the whole image as in global methods, but rather along several one-dimensional paths around a pixel p. The energy of all the paths is then summed for each pixel and the disparity is determined by *winner takes all*.

5.3.1.3 Triangulation

Considering an identical pair of calibrated cameras separated by a baseline b and the disparity map D, a 3D point $\mathbf{Q}^{\Delta}_{(x,y)}(D(x, y))$ can be computed when $s_x = s_y$ using

$$\mathbf{Q}^{\Delta}_{(x,y)}(D(x, y)) = \begin{bmatrix} X_W \\ Y_W \\ Z_W \end{bmatrix} = \frac{b}{D(x, y)} \begin{bmatrix} x - o_x \\ y - o_y \\ \frac{d}{s_x} \end{bmatrix} \tag{5.9}$$

where (X_W, Y_W, Z_W) are the coordinates of the scene's points in the world coordinate system.

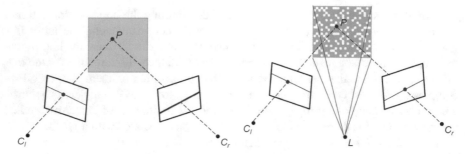

Fig. 5.7 Left: finding corresponding points in texture-poor areas is difficult, resulting in dropouts in the computed depth map. Right: active stereo vision enhances the scene by projecting a highly textured light pattern. This facilitates the matching between the left and right images. Figure courtesy of NRC

5.3.2 Active Stereo Vision

Finding correspondences between two images works well in highly textured scenes. However, in areas with poor texture, such as uniform surfaces (Fig. 5.7-left), matching methods fail, resulting in missing 3D points. To address this limitation, active stereo vision or projectedtexture stereo vision consists in artificially enhancing the texture of the scene by projecting a highly textured light pattern onto it [60, 66, 73] (Fig. 5.7-right). This simplifies the search for matching points and allows for a much denser 3D reconstruction of the scene.

Active stereo vision should not be confused with one-shot, spatially encoded, structured-light approaches. In active stereo vision systems, the light pattern can even be unstructured. Moreover, such systems make use of two calibrated cameras and a light projector that does not need to be calibrated.

5.3.2.1 Projector

In active stereo vision, the projector is only required to add enough texture to featureless surfaces to enable block matching to work, regardless of ambient light or poorly reflective materials. Grunnet-Jepsen et al. provide guidelines on projector design [40] and these include the following.

1. Projection in the infrared spectrum in order not to interfere with human vision and enable simultaneous RGB image capture.
2. Projection of a dense semi-random dot pattern. The spatial density of the dots determines the resolution of the texture and it was found that a pattern density beyond 10% of image resolution does not result in significantly improved performance.
3. High contrast, so that the pattern can be visible even in bright daylight. The intrinsic contrast provided by a projector is usually reduced due to ambient light

or poorly reflective materials. Thus maximizing the intrinsic contrast makes the imaging system more robust to real-world conditions. In practice, maximizing the contrast consists in concentrating as much of the available projector power into the pattern and minimizing any background projector power that appears as uniform light between the projected features and effectively augments the ambient lighting.

4. Minimum laser speckle, which leads to different views from both cameras and thus can deteriorate the depth performance.
5. Dynamic projection with a programmable dot density to adapt to imaging resolution.
6. A large depth-of-field, so that the pattern is not blurred across the operating depth range.

5.3.2.2 Projected Light Pattern

The basic idea behind active stereo vision is to have a projected light pattern P made of $n \times n$ blocks as dissimilar as possible across the search range of size $n \times N$. So is there an ideal light pattern P to augment the texture of a scene? This question has been largely addressed in the literature. Some have proposed to incrementally fill a pattern with randomly generated binary pixels while testing that each $n \times n$ blocks is unique [73]. Others have used the DeBruijn sequences [66] or Hamming codes [60]. To assess how good a pattern P is for stereo matching, one can measure the minimum difference $S(P)$ between all its blocks. Using the Sum of Absolute Differences (SAD) as correlation measure, the score of a pattern is given by

$$S(P) = \min_{0 < D_p < N} SAD(p, D_p). \tag{5.10}$$

However, finding the best object onto a scene is not only influenced by the pattern itself but also by characteristics of the projector and the pair of cameras. Figure 5.8 shows how a projected pattern P is blurred by the projector and the camera and then sampled to adjust to the sensor's resolution. Konolige [60] compared random patterns, De Bruijn patterns, and patterns created with Hamming codes, while taking into consideration the imperfections of both cameras and projector in terms of resolution and blur.

In active stereo vision, no prior knowledge of the projected light pattern is necessary, thus the term "unstructured" light. Consequently, strict stability over time of the light pattern is not a critical requirement. Moreover, using multiple projectors or a combination of active stereo vision systems simultaneously is possible and can further improve the performance, since more texture is added to the scene.

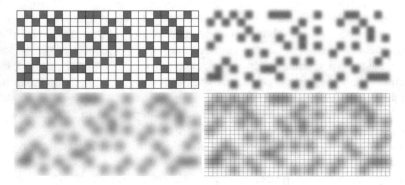

Fig. 5.8 Effect of resolution and blur on the projected light pattern. The light pattern (top-left) is blurred by the lenses of both projector (top-right) and camera (bottom-left) and resampled by the camera's sensor grid. Figure adapted from [60], courtesy of NRC

5.3.2.3 Intel RealSense D400 Series

Intel develops and offers consumer-grade RGB-D sensors based on a variety of range sensing technologies, each of which has its own technological tradeoffs. The RealSense D400 series is based on active stereo vision. The D400 series takes full advantage of the Intel RealSense Vision Processor D4, an Application-Specific Integrated Circuit (ASIC), onto which a customized variant of the semi-global block matching algorithm is embedded, allowing a depth throughput of up to 36 million depth points per second (848×480, 90 fps), with a search range of $N = 128$. Since stereoscopic systems are highly flexible in their design, the D400 series offers a large variety of depth modules, all incorporating the same processor. This flexibility allows for a tradeoff between price, size, range, and performance, depending on the targeted application. Only the D410, D415, D430, and D435 use active stereo vision, the rest of the modules being based solely on the passive stereo. Among the active stereo modules, D415 and D435 are the only ready-to-use RGB-D cameras, whereas the other modules are customizable. The main differences between D415 and D435 are as follows.

1. Baseline: 5.5 cm for D415 or 5 cm for D435
2. Shutter type: rolling for D415 versus global for D435. Global shutter provides better performance in case of low-lighting or high-speed motion.
3. Cameras Field of View (FOV): standard 70° FOV for D415 or wide angle 90° FOV for D435.
4. RGB-D calibration: in the D415 depth module, all the components (projector, depth cameras, and RGB camera) are mounted on the same computer board which facilitates calibration and rectification. Whereas the D435 camera is based on the D430 depth module which comes with a separated RGB camera making the calibration between the RGB and depth more difficult.

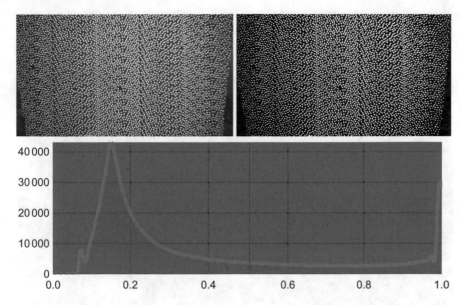

Fig. 5.9 Intel RealSense D435 infrared dot pattern. The light pattern is projected onto a planar surface in an environment without ambient lighting and seen by the left infrared camera (top-left). The corresponding intensity histogram reveals two clear peaks (bottom) easing image binarization (top-right). This illustrates the good contrast provided by the infrared projector. Figure courtesy of NRC

Considering these characteristics, the D415 is usually favored for applications requiring high accuracy, whereas the D435 is best for applications that require a wider FOV such as drone navigation.

The D415 and D435 cameras use different types of projector. The D415 uses two AMS Heptagon projectors placed side by side, while the D435 uses an AMS Princeton Optronics projector with a wider emission angle but fewer dots ($\approx$5000 dots). However, in both cases, the wavelength of the class 1 laser is 850 nm and the reported range varies between 11 cm up to 10 m. Figure 5.9 illustrates the infrared dot pattern of the Intel RealSense D435 projected onto a planar surface in an environment with minimal ambient light (top-left). The intensity histogram at the bottom of Fig. 5.9 reveals two clearly distinguishable peaks (around 0.18 and 1.0, respectively), demonstrating the good contrast provided by the projector.

To demonstrate the benefit of active stereo vision over passive stereo vision, we conducted a simple experiment using the Intel RealSense D435 RGB-D sensor. The same scene is acquired with the IR projector turned off (passive stereo) and then on (active stereo). The resulting depth maps are illustrated on the bottom row of Fig. 5.10. It clearly shows that texture augmentation provides a much denser depth map, with significantly less dropouts on uniform surfaces such as the wall and the table.

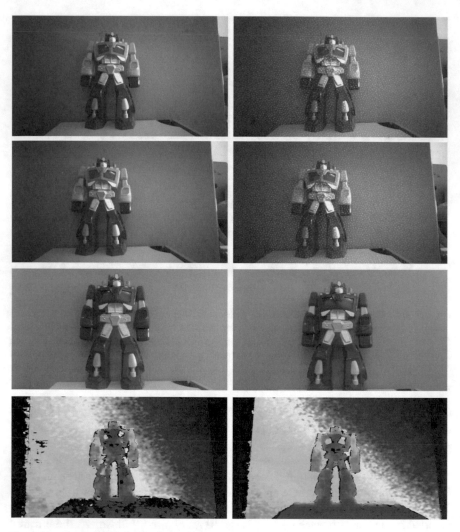

Fig. 5.10 Results from the Intel RealSense D435 RGB-D Camera. Results are shown with the infrared projector off (left) and on (right). First row: images of the left infrared camera used for the range measurement. Note, on the right, the pattern "painted" on the scene by the infrared projector. Second row: images of the right infrared camera used for the range measurement. Third row: image of the RGB camera used for the texturing. Fourth row: the computed depth image. The range is displayed using a color code. Figure courtesy of NRC

5.4 Structured-Light RGB-D Cameras

An RGB-D camera based on structured-light is conceptually a passive stereo system where one of the measurement cameras is replaced by a calibrated projector. The projector can either display a single pattern (spatial codification) or series of patterns (temporal codification). In temporal codification (also known as time-multiplexing), patterns are projected one after the other and an image is captured for each pattern. The camera–projector matching is done based only on the time sequence of image intensity at a particular location in the camera. In contrast, spatial codification techniques project just a single pattern, and the grayscale pattern within a local neighborhood is used to perform the necessary correspondence matching. A detailed presentation of the different codification methods can be found in [90, 91].

The affordable price of RGB-D cameras significantly limits the cost of the projection subsystem. In the remainder of this chapter, temporal encoding will be presented assuming a 1-D scanning device and a modulated laser source. For spatial encoding, the same type of projector as the one used for active stereo is assumed (see Sect. 5.3.2.1). Note that producing projection subsystems that are stable in time and robust to variations in temperature, while remaining affordable, is challenging. In some cases, it can be more affordable to add an extra camera with an unstable projector (active stereo) rather than increasing the stability of the projection subsystem. Microsoft's Kinect I, which was based on spatial codification, was a revolutionary 3D sensor that had a profound impact on the democratization of 3D imaging systems. A picture of the Kinect I is shown in Fig. 5.3. Figure 5.11 contains a range image produced by a Kinect I. Figure 5.12 illustrates the infrared dot pattern in the Microsoft Kinect I projected onto a planar surface in an environment with minimal ambient light (top-left). The intensity histogram at the bottom of Fig. 5.12 does not show two clearly distinguishable peaks as contained in the histogram shown in Fig. 5.9. When examining the commercial offering of RGB-D cameras in the past 5 years, we can clearly notice a trend where companies are moving away from spatial encoding, toward active stereo vision systems. For these reasons, the remainder of this section focuses on structured-light sensors based solely on temporal encoding.

5.4.1 Temporal Encoding

Temporal encoding methods project many planes of light simultaneously and use a coding strategy to recover which camera pixel views the light from a given plane. The camera and projector are side by side, as shown in Fig. 5.4. The projector images are assumed to contain vertical lines referred to as fringes. The Gray code is probably the best-known time-multiplexing code and was presented in Chap. 3 in the context of digital projection. Figure 5.16-bottom contains the images of two Gray code patterns. In the digital context, and assuming that the number of columns of the projector is 2^N, then each column can be assigned to an N-bit binary number in a Gray code sequence

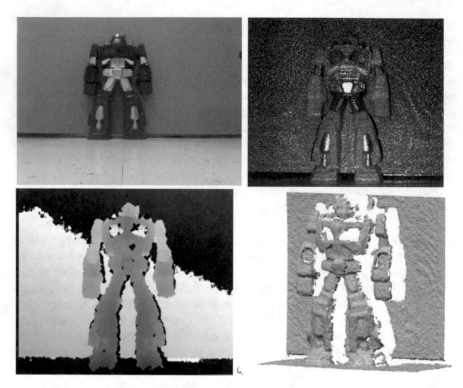

Fig. 5.11 Results from the Microsoft Kinect I RGB-D Camera. Top-left: image from the RGB camera used for texture mapping. Top-right: an image of the infrared camera used for the range measurement. Note the pattern of the infrared projector. Bottom-left: the range image from the infrared camera used for the range measurement. The range is displayed using a Gray level coding. Bottom-right: a shaded view of a polygonal model created using the range image display on the left. Figure courtesy of NRC

of 2^N elements. This is done by transforming the index of the projector column into an element (i.e., N-bit binary number) of a Gray code ordering, using the pseudo-code of Fig. 5.13. Table 5.2 contains results of the pseudo-code. The projection of darker fringes is associated with the binary value of 0 and the projection of lighter fringes is associated with the binary value of 1. In the remainder of this chapter, we focus on cheaper projection systems that have an analog nature.

5.4.1.1   Generating the Gray Code

Figure 5.14 shows the Gray code patterns generated by scanning a pulsing laser. These patterns are used by the Intel RealSense F200, SR300, and R305, and the corresponding Gray code ordering is shown in Table 5.2. By examining Fig. 5.14, one should realize that each pattern (bit i) of the Gray code can be generated using a

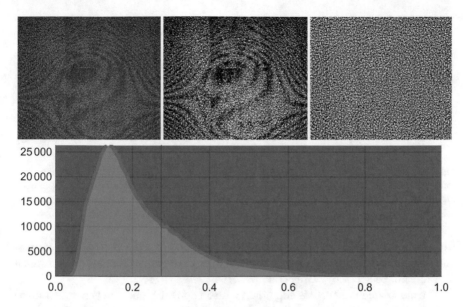

Fig. 5.12 Microsoft Kinect I infrared dot pattern. The light pattern is projected onto a planar surface in an environment without ambient lighting and seen by the infrared camera (top-left). The corresponding intensity histogram reveals two overlapping peaks (bottom) that make image binarization using a single threshold very difficult. The threshold value used for the binarization (top-center) is shown using a red line on the histogram. The binarization is still possible using an adaptive thresholding method (top-right). Figure courtesy of NRC

Fig. 5.13 Pseudo-code allowing the conversion of a natural binary code into a Gray code and *vice versa.* Figure courtesy of [29]

CONVENTION FROM GRAY TO BINARY(*gray*[0...*n* − 1])
bin[0] = *gray*[0]
for *i* = 1 **to** *n* − 1 **do**
    bin[*i*] = *bin*[*i* − 1]   **xor**   *gray*[*i*]
end for
return bin

CONVENTION FROM BINARY TO GRAY(*bin*[0...*n* − 1])
gray[0] = *bin*[0]
for *i* = 1 **to** *n* − 1 **do**
    gray[*i*] = *bin*[*i* − 1]   **xor**   *bin*[*i*]
end for
return gray

square wave. A Gray code pattern G_i for bit i at time t can be generated by pulsing a laser using

$$G_i(t) = \frac{sign\left(\sin\left(\frac{2\pi t 2^{i-1}}{f_p} + 3\pi/2 + \theta\right)\right) + 1}{2} V_p \qquad (5.11)$$

where $sign(x)$ is a function that gives, respectively, -1, 0, or 1 when x is negative, zero, or positive. Moreover, f_p is the frequency of the acquisition camera, and V_p is the voltage input of the modulating signal of the laser. When the laser is scanned

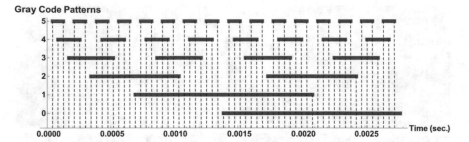

Fig. 5.14 Illustration of the six patterns of a 6-bit Gray code. Note that the X-axis is time in seconds (rather than the projector pixel). The transition timing is adjusted for a 600 fps measurement camera. Figure courtesy of NRC

from right to left and for the pattern representing the bit zero (i.e., $i = 0$), $\theta = \pi$; otherwise, θ is always zero. The first row of Fig. 5.15 illustrates the modulation signal for projecting a set of five Gray code patterns.

The modulated laser spot is combined with an optical element to generate a stripe and this stripe needs to be mechanically scanned in order to generate a Gray code pattern. A cost-efficient implementation could use a one-dimensional Micro Electro-Mechanical System (MEMS) to scan the laser stripe on the scene. It is possible to use a galvanometer that moves a mirror rather than a MEMS and the remaining description assumes a galvanometer-based implementation. The orientation of the mirror can be changed by varying the input voltage of the galvanometer. A typical voltage range that can be encountered is -10 V to 10 V. We assume that a voltage of -10 V corresponds to the left most orientation and a voltage of 10 V corresponds to the right most orientation. To generate an image, the driving voltage waveform is triangular with a frequency of $f_p/2$. At each cycle, two images are generated, one from left to right (-10 V to 10 V) and one from right to left (10 V to -10 V). In order to avoid damaging the galvanometer, the input triangular wave is filtered so that the resulting signal is differentiable. This is shown in the second row of Fig. 5.15. Both the control signals of the galvanometer and laser allow one to define the actual field of view of the projector. The effective field of view also takes into account the camera integration timing. The third row of Fig. 5.15 illustrates the camera timing. Note that the camera is not sensitive to projector light at the extremity of the field of view of the scanner. This corresponds to regions near the maximum and minimum of the filtered triangular wave (see the second row of Fig. 5.15). The last row of Fig. 5.15 contains effective patterns generated by the projection system after taking into account the modulation of the laser, the mirror orientation, and the camera integration timing. Generally, the actual orientation of the mirror may differ from the expected one. It is possible to read an output signal that gives the actual orientation of the mirror. The difference between both signals can be used to distort the triangular waveform so that the actual orientation fits the expected one. This allows one to dynamically modify the projected patterns, in order to compensate for some of the non-linearity present in the projection patterns.

Table 5.2 The Gray code ordering for four patterns as generated by both the pseudo-code presented in Fig. 5.13 and the method presented in Sect. 5.4.1.1. Also, the natural binary code is represented. Table courtesy of NRC

Gray code	Bir.	0000	0001	0011	0010	0110	0111	0101	0100	1100	1101	1111	1110	1010	1011	1001	1000
	Dec.	0	1	3	2	6	7	5	4	12	13	15	14	10	11	9	8
Binary	Bin.	0000	0001	0010	0011	0100	0101	0110	0111	1000	1001	1010	1011	1100	1101	1110	1111
	Dec.	0	1	2	3	4	5	6	7	8	9	10	11	12	13	14	15

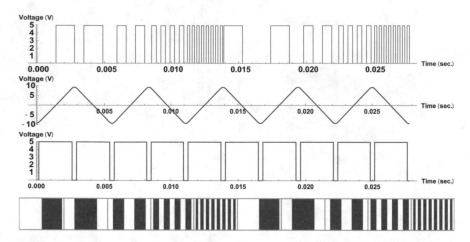

Fig. 5.15 Description of the timing of the different components of an analog projection system described in Sect. 5.4.1.1. The graph on the first row contains the signal controlling the pulsing of the laser. The graph on the second row contains the signal that controls the position of the galvanometer. The third row displays the integration timing of the camera. The last row contains the images generated by the signals in the previous rows. Figure courtesy of NRC

5.4.1.2   Decoding the Gray Code

For each Gray code pattern and for each row of the camera, the position of the fringe transitions is measured. Thus, the number of 3D points generated during one acquisition is equal to the number of fringe transitions multiplied by the number of camera rows. In Chap. 3, a method was presented that requires the projection of both a Gray code and the associated reverse Gray code [107]. This algorithm provides a robust way for achieving subpixel accuracy [107]; however, it requires the projection of twice the number of patterns. For industrial applications, this could be acceptable but in the context of consumer-grade RGB-D cameras, where the scene is expected to be dynamic, this is not acceptable. The algorithm used in the Intel RealSense F200, R300, and R305 is presented in [119]. More details about such RGB-D cameras are given in the next section.

5.4.1.3   Intel RealSense F200, SR300, and SR305

The Intel RealSense F200, SR300, and SR305 are RGB-D cameras that use the Gray code. A picture of the RealSense SR300 is shown in Fig. 5.3. The SR300 provides a VGA-resolution range image at a frequency of 60 fps. The sensor also provides an infrared VGA video stream and an HD-RGB video stream. Both video streams operate at 30 fps and all video streams are synchronized. The measuring camera has a VGA resolution and uses a global shutter and acquires image at 600 fps. The SR300

Fig. 5.16 Results from the Intel RealSense SR300 RGB-D Camera. Top-left: image from the RGB camera used for texture mapping. Top-center: the range image from the infrared camera used for the range measurement. The range is displayed using a color coding. Top-right: a shaded view of a polygonal model created using the range image display in the center. Bottom: two images of a scene taken by an industrial camera with a filter that blocks all light with wavelength smaller than 705 nm while the SR300 is acquiring images of the scene. On the right, a high-frequency pattern of the Gray code and on the left, a lower frequency pattern. Figure courtesy of NRC

uses a 9-bit Gray code. A dark frame and a fully illuminating frame are also used in order to simplify the decoding of the Gray code.

The projection system uses a class-1 laser with a wavelength of 860 nm. The laser point source is combined with an optical element to generate a stripe. A Micro Electro-Mechanical System (MEMS) is used to scan the laser stripe on the scene. Figure 5.16-bottom contains the images of two Gray code patterns. The properties of the MEMS change over time and vary with temperature and such changes need to be compensated for in order to obtain a repeatable measurement system. In this RGB-D camera, the position of the mirror is measured at different orientations. These measurements are used in real time to modify the electric load. More information about the projection subsystem can be found in [10, 104, 119]. An in-depth presentation of the implementation of the SR300 can be found in [119]. Figure 5.16-top illustrates a color-coded range image and a shaded view of the reconstructed surface mesh, obtained using the Intel RealSense SR300.

5.5 Phase-Based Time-of-Flight RGB-D Cameras

The reader familiar with the phase-based Time-of-Flight (ToF) material, presented in Chap. 4, may omit this section. A phase-based ToF system computes the distance between the sensor and a surface to be digitized using the round-trip time required by light to reach the surface and be reflected back to the sensor, which may be estimated indirectly. The range is deduced from the phase difference between the detected signal and the emitted signal. Figure 5.17 illustrates the principle of the phase-based system. Note that such systems are also known as continuous-wave ToF. The Kinect II and Kinect Azure are phase-based ToF RGB-D cameras [5, 81]. The temporal intensity profile $I_s(t)$ for the illumination source is

$$I_s(t) = A_s + B_s \cos(\phi(t) + \theta_s) \tag{5.12}$$

where A_s, B_s, and θ_s are constant and $\phi(t) = 2\pi t f_{cw}$ where f_{cw} is the modulation frequency of the continuous wave. The temporal intensity profile $I_d(t)$ for the detected signal is

$$I_d(t) = A_d + B_d \cos(\phi(t) + \theta_d + \delta\phi) \tag{5.13}$$

where $\delta\phi$ is the phase offset related to the range. Note that A_d, B_d depend on A_s, B_s, the scene surface properties, and the sensor's characteristics. In general, the value of θ_s and θ_d are assumed to be constant but their values are unknown. We refer the reader to the previous chapter for details related to the phase offset measurement.

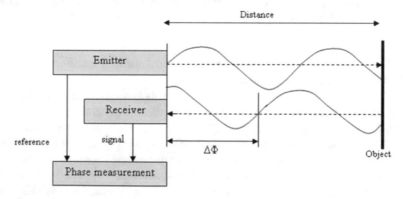

Fig. 5.17 Continuous-wave measurement techniques employed by Time-of-Flight RGB-D cameras. Figure courtesy of NRC

The conversion from phase offset to range is achieved using

$$r(\delta\phi) = \frac{c\delta\phi}{4\pi f_{cw}}$$
(5.14)

where c is the speed of light in the medium. The range over which the system can perform unambiguous measurement can be computed from the modulation frequency. This unambiguous range r_{max} is defined as

$$r_{max} = r(2\pi) = \frac{c}{2f_{cw}}.$$
(5.15)

Increasing the modulation frequency f_{cw} will simultaneously reduce the value of r_{max} and the measurement uncertainty. A simple method to achieve a large value for r_{max} and a small uncertainty uses multiple acquisitions with different modulation frequencies. The lower modulation frequencies are used to obtain a large range interval, while the higher ones are used to improve the accuracy of the measurement.

For a phase-based system, a pixel $[x, y]^T$ with a phase offset of $\delta\Phi(x, y)$ can be transformed into a 3D point using

$$\mathbf{Q}^{ToF}_{(x,y)}(\delta\Phi(x, y)) = \begin{bmatrix} X_w \\ Y_w \\ Z_w \end{bmatrix} = \frac{c\,(\delta\Phi(x, y) + 2k\pi + o_r(x, y))}{4\pi f_{cw}} \begin{bmatrix} \frac{s_x}{d}(x - o_x) \\ \frac{s_y}{d}(y - o_y) \\ 1 \end{bmatrix}$$
(5.16)

where $o_r(x, y)$ is an offset recovered at calibration time and k is the unknown integer that is resolved using multiple modulation frequencies.

5.5.1 Microsoft's Kinect II and Kinect Azure

Table 5.3 presents some characteristics of Kinect II and Azure. Among the improvements of both systems is a significant reduction of power requirements of the sensor chip. The maximum modulation frequency and the modulation contrast are significantly larger for the Kinect Azure. Typically, an increase of these values induces a reduction of the range uncertainty as discussed in Sect. 5.7.2. In order to provide robustness to ambient lighting variation, some chips acquire two images quasi-simultaneously and output the difference of both images. The difference of two sine waves with the same frequency, but with a phase offset π, is a sine wave with twice the amplitude centered on zero (i.e., without ambient illumination). This type of feature is implemented within the Kinect Azure using a design that allows a very high fill factor [5]. Figure 5.18 illustrates a range image obtained using the Kinect Azure. More details about Kinect II and the Kinect Azure, which is shown in Fig. 5.3, can be found in [5, 81].

Table 5.3 Table of specifications for two phase-based ToF systems. The table is adapted from [5]. The operating distance of the Kinect II is different depending on the software driver used (i.e., the official software driver or the open source one)

	Gaming Platforms	
	Kinect Azure	Kinect II
Technology	TSMC 65 nm BSI 1P8M	TSMC 0.13 µm 1P5M
Pixel pitch	3.5 µm × 3.5 µm	10 µm × 10 µm
Number of lines	1024	512
Number of columns	1024	424
Frame rate	30 fps	30 fps
Horizontal field of view	120°	70°
Vertical field of view	120°	60°
Min operating distance	0.4 m	0.8 m
Max operating distance	4.2 m	4.2 m
Min modulation frequency	10 Mhz	10 Mhz
Max modulation frequency	320 Mhz	130 Mhz
Av modulation frequency	200 Mhz	80 Mhz
Fill Factor	≈100%	60%
Quantum effic. ($\lambda = 860$ nm)	44%	21%
Readout noise	$3e^-$ (210 µV)	(320 µV)
Modulation contrast	87% at 200 MHz, 78% at 320 MHz	68% at 50 MHz
Chip power	650 mW	2100 mW
Wavelength	860 µm	860 µm

5.6 Texture Mapping

Texture mapping refers to the task of mapping texture and color information acquired by the RGB camera to the computed depth information. It can be seen as a method to wrap a color image onto a 3D geometry. It is an important step for acquiring realistic 3D models of an object or a scene.

A naive way to add color to a 3D point cloud might be to overlap the color and depth images so that a pixel (x, y) in the color image maps to the pixel (x, y) in the depth image. However, in commercial RGB-D systems, the color camera and the depth sensor are generally separated by a few centimeters (distance referred to as the baseline), so their fields of view are slightly different. Thus, a simple overlap will result in color transitions not lining up with actual object contours. A registration, based on the geometric configuration of the whole RGB-D system, is thus built in commercial RGB-D sensors to realign depth and color images.

This registration can be performed in two directions: one can transform the color image from the viewpoint of the RGB camera into the viewpoint of the depth sensor, or the other way around. In the first direction, for each pixel in the depth image, the

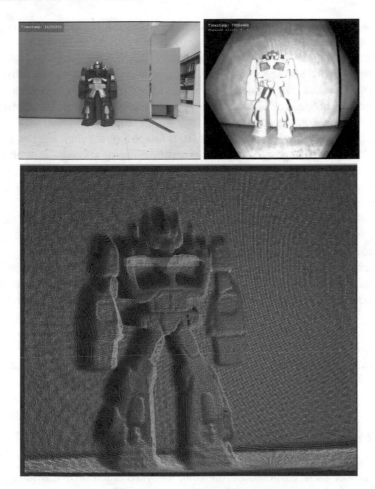

Fig. 5.18 Range acquisition using Microsoft's Kinect Azure RGB-D camera. Top-left: an image from the RGB camera used for texture mapping. Top-right: an image of the infrared camera used for the range measurement. Bottom-left: the range image displayed as a point cloud. Figure courtesy of NRC

depth value is used to compute the corresponding subpixel coordinates in the color image. A bilinear interpolation is then performed in the color image to compute the color value at subpixel precision. A hole in the depth image will result in a hole in the transformed color image.

To alleviate this limitation, the registration can be performed in the opposite direction, thus transforming the depth image from the viewpoint of the depth sensor into the viewpoint of the RGB camera. It warps a triangular mesh from the geometry of the depth sensor into the geometry of the RGB camera. A triangular mesh is used to avoid generating holes in the transformed depth image. A Z-buffer ensures that occlusions are handled correctly.

While commercial RGB-D sensors can model the 3D geometry of an object or a scene with interesting geometric detail, the fidelity of the recovered texture with respect to the 3D models is still less satisfactory [32]. Texture mapping lags behind 3D reconstruction. Misalignment between color and geometry can be attributable to numerous factors. First, texture information is usually of low-quality due to an RGB camera's limited resolution and vulnerability to motion and illumination conditions [28]. Some commercial systems such as Intel RealSense D400 series include a designated image signal processor for RGB image adjustments, scaling, and processing to improve image quality prior to texture mapping. Second, it is difficult to ensure precise synchronization between depth and RGB streams and perfect intrinsic and extrinsic camera calibration. Third, depth data are noisy and result in geometric inaccuracies in the reconstructed 3D model.

For these reasons, computer vision researchers usually avoid the use of the built-in color and depth registration provided in commercial range sensors and develop advanced methods for texture mapping. These methods usually rely on multiple views of the scene. The premise is that various images of the scene obtained by changing the viewpoint of the camera are ideally photometrically consistent, and thus, combining them produces a high-quality texture map. The methods can be categorized [32] into blending-based approaches which use different weighted average strategies to blend multiple color images into a texture map [12], projection-based approaches which associate to each vertex of the 3D mesh derived from the point cloud, an optimal color image [33], and warping-based approaches that warp different images locally to fit the 3D mesh [3].

5.7 Range Uncertainty and Lateral Resolution

This section contains advanced material and may be omitted on first reading. In this section, we first examine the uncertainty associated with 3D points measured by structured-light, active stereo, and time-of-flight RGB-D cameras. Some errors are systematic in nature, while others are random. In the remainder of this section, random errors are discussed. Since both structured-light and active stereo systems are based on triangulation, they share similar equations that describe their measurement uncertainties. Time-of-flight systems are based on time measurement and the equations that describe their measurement uncertainties are significantly different from those of triangulation-based systems. In Sect. 5.7.1, we present the range uncertainty for triangulation-based RGB-D cameras, followed in Sect. 5.7.2 by a presentation of the uncertainty associated with ToF-based RGB-D cameras. In Sects. 5.7.3 and 5.7.4, we discuss the lateral resolution and point spacing of RGB-D cameras. Finally, the tradeoffs between range uncertainty and lateral resolution are presented in Sect. 5.7.5.

5.7.1 Triangulation

The transformation of Eq. 5.9 from pixel coordinates to 3D points is non-linear, hence we introduce a first-order approximation using Taylor's expansion. When $s_x = s_y$, the solution in the neighborhood of $\hat{D}(x, y)$ can be approximated by

$$\mathbf{Q}^{\Delta}_{(x,y)}(\hat{D}(x, y) + \Delta D(x, y)) \approx \mathbf{Q}^{\Delta}_{(x,y)}(\hat{D}(x, y)) + \frac{d}{d\hat{D}(x, y)}\mathbf{Q}^{\Delta}_{(x,y)}(\hat{D}(x, y))\Delta D(x, y)$$

(5.17)

where

$$\frac{d}{d\hat{D}(x, y)}\mathbf{Q}^{\Delta}_{(x,y)}(\hat{D}(x, y)) = \frac{b}{\hat{D}(x, y)^2}\begin{bmatrix} o_x - x \\ o_y - y \\ -d/s_x \end{bmatrix}.$$

(5.18)

Since a first-order approximation is used, the covariance matrix associated with a 3D point can be computed explicitly [20, 21] as

$$\Sigma_{\Delta} = \begin{bmatrix} s_x^2(o_x - x)^2 & s_x^2(o_x - x)(o_y - y) & ds_x(x - o_x) \\ s_x^2(o_x - x)(o_y - y) & s_x^2(o_y - y)^2 & ds_x(y - o_y) \\ ds_x(x - o_x) & ds_x(y - o_y) & d^2 \end{bmatrix}\left(\frac{\sigma_{Z^{\Delta}}\sigma_D}{d}\right)^2 \quad (5.19)$$

where

$$\sigma_{Z^{\Delta}} = \frac{bd}{\hat{D}(x, y)^2 s_x} = \frac{s_x Z_W^2}{bd}$$

(5.20)

and σ_D depends on the type of triangulation system. We refer the reader to Chap. 3 for more details. Note that $\sigma_{Z^{\Delta}}$ increases with the square of the range Z_W. This is compatible with the results from the empirical studies by [11, 39] performed on Microsoft's Kinect I, which uses structured-light. The desire to reduce the physical size of electronic devices leads to a reduction of the baseline of triangulation-based RGB-D cameras. As seen in Eq. 5.20, this reduction induces an increase in range uncertainty.

5.7.2 Time-of-Flight

The transformation of Eq. 5.16 from a normalized image coordinates to 3D points is linear, hence the covariance matrix associated to a 3D point can be computed when $s_x = s_y$ as

$$\Sigma_{ToF} = \begin{bmatrix} s_x^2(o_x - x)^2 & s_x^2(o_x - x)(o_y - y) & ds_x(x - o_x) \\ s_x^2(o_x - x)(o_y - y) & s_x^2(o_y - y)^2 & ds_x(y - o_y) \\ ds_x(x - o_x) & ds_x(y - o_y) & d^2 \end{bmatrix}\left(\frac{\sigma_{Z^{ToF}}\sigma_{\delta\phi}}{d}\right)^2$$

(5.21)

where

$$\sigma_{Z^{ToF}} = \frac{c}{4\pi f_{cw}}. \tag{5.22}$$

Note that the value of $\sigma_{Z^{ToF}}$ is independent of the value of Z_W. This behavior was observed in the empirical studies of the performance of Microsoft's Kinect II by [11, 39]. Using a derivative similar to the one used in Chap. 3,

$$\sigma_{\delta\Phi} = \sqrt{\frac{2}{N}} \frac{\sigma}{B_{f_{cw}}} \tag{5.23}$$

where σ is the sensor's intrinsic uncertainty, N is the number of samples, and $B_{f_{cw}}$ is the amplitude of the sine wave for the continuous-wave modulation frequency f_{cw}. A formal presentation of the impact of readout error, fill factor, quantum efficiency, and other parameters on σ can be found in [77]. The case where $N = 4$ is presented in [83] for two different implementations of continuous-wave ToF. The amplitude of the sine wave is defined as

$$B_{f_{cw}} = m_{f_{cw}} B^{max} \tag{5.24}$$

where $m_{f_{cw}}$ is the modulation contrast at f_{cw} which varies from 0 to 1 and B^{max} is the maximum amplitude of the sine wave [77]. Typically, the value of $m_{f_{cw}}$ decreases as the value of f_{cw} increases. Some values of the modulation contrast for two ToF sensors arc given in Table 5.3.

5.7.3 Lateral Resolution

Intuitively, the lateral resolution is the capability of a 3D imaging system to discriminate two adjacent structures on the surface of a sample. A formal definition can be found in [109]. The lateral resolution is limited by two factors: the structural and the spatial resolution [109]. As an example, the lateral resolution of a digital camera, when working out-of-focus, is not limited by the camera pixel count (spatial resolution), but by the optical resolution (structural resolution) of the camera lens. Even when imaging in-focus, the digital camera's lateral resolution can be limited by the structural resolution rather than the spatial resolution. A method to evaluate the lateral resolution of a digital camera can be found in [51]. The extension of the lateral resolution evaluation from 2D camera to 3D camera has been investigated [37, 44, 59]. This extension is challenging since the range uncertainty also affects the capability of a 3D imaging system to discriminate two adjacent structures on the surface of a sample. A method to test the fidelity of depth-variation in range images was patented by one of the large RGB-D camera manufacturers [45].

A fundamental limitation of the structural resolution of RGB-D cameras, with respect to industrial 3D imaging systems, is the use of wavelengths within the near-infrared region of the spectrum. This choice is induced by the desire to not interfere with the human activities in the scene. In order to achieved high-structural resolution, industrial 3D imaging system typically uses blue or violet lasers (see Chap. 3). The spatial resolution of RGB-D cameras is significantly influenced by the measurement strategies used and is not necessarily related to the number of 3D points output by the RGB-D camera. The remainder of this subsection discusses the concept of point spacing which is then used to introduce the spatial resolution of each family of RGB-D cameras.

5.7.4   Point Spacing

The point spacing is often used by some 3D imaging manufacturers to describe the lateral resolution of 3D imaging systems. This value can be computed for structured-light, active stereo, and ToF RGB-D cameras. Point spacing varies with the range and it depends on the magnification of the optical system and on the size of a pixel. Point spacing is illustrated in Fig. 5.19. The concept of point spacing can be generalized to feature spacing when the distance between the center of two neighbor pixels is replaced by the distance between two features present on the detector image. Explicitly, the horizontal feature spacing S_x is defined as

$$S_x(Z, f_s) = \frac{Z}{d} f_s s_x \qquad (5.25)$$

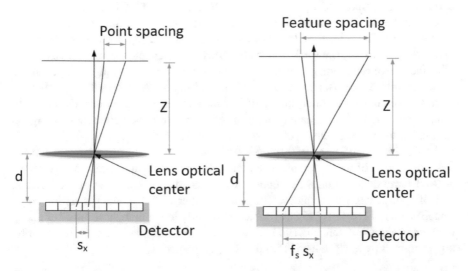

Fig. 5.19 Left: illustration of the point spacing. Right: illustration of the feature spacing. The distance between the optical center and the object plane is denoted Z, d is the distance between the optical center and the detector. The horizontal distance between the center of two neighboring pixels is s_x and f_s is the distance between two neighboring features given in pixel units. Figure courtesy of NRC

and the vertical feature spacing S_y is defined as

$$S_y(Z, f_s) = \frac{Z}{d} f_s s_y \qquad (5.26)$$

where Z/d is the magnification for the optical system at the distance Z from the optical center and d is the distance between the optical center and the detector. The horizontal and vertical pixel sizes are s_x and s_y, respectively, and f_s is the distance in pixels between two features. The point spacing is computed from Eqs. 5.25 and 5.26 by setting $f_s = 1$.

Typically, an RGB-D camera will output a range image that has the same resolution as the measurement camera. However, the spatial resolution of an RGB-D camera is dictated by the measurement strategies. Some RGB-D cameras measure significantly fewer 3D points than the number of outputs of the RGB-D camera. As is shown in the remainder of this subsection, for some systems, feature spacing is a better approximation of the spatial resolution than point spacing.

5.7.4.1 Time-Multiplexed Codification

For structured-light systems based on time-multiplexed encoding, the spatial resolution is limited by the number of rows of the camera and by the number of code transitions in the Gray code used by the projection system. The number of Gray code transitions is usually smaller than the number of columns of the measurement camera. The number of 3D points measured by this type of RGB-D camera is equal to the number of code transitions multiplied by the number of rows of the measurement camera. These measured 3D points can be arranged in a regular grid which is called the native range image. It is also possible to build an intensity image associated with the native range image since each 3D point of the native range image can be projected into the measurement camera image. Figure 5.20 shows the reduction of lateral resolution between an image of the measurement camera and the intensity image associated with the native range image. Typically, the native range image is resampled to fit the resolution of the measurement camera.

For the Intel RealSense SR300 presented in Sect. 5.4.1.3, the measurement camera has a resolution of 640×480 pixels and the projector uses nine Gray code patterns. A 9-bit Gray code contains 511 code transitions and for each row of the camera, 511 3D points can be computed. The total number of 3D points per native range image is thus 511×480 (245,280), which is slightly lower than the number of pixels of the measurement camera. The horizontal and vertical spatial resolutions can be approximated by $S_x(Z, 640/511)$ and $S_y(Z, 1)$, respectively.

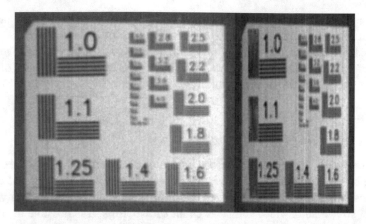

Fig. 5.20 Left: crop of an image of the measurement camera showing a line-pair resolution chart. Right: crop of the intensity channel of the native range image produced by a time-multiplexed codification. Notice the reduction of lateral resolution along the horizontal axis. The measurement camera has a resolution of 1498 × 800 and the Gray code has 1023 code transitions. Figure courtesy of NRC

5.7.4.2 Spatial Codification

Typically, for RGB-D cameras based on spatial encoding, the projected image contains approximately 30,000 feature points [119]. The position of each of these projector features can be computed in the measurement camera image and these correspondences can be used to compute 30,000 3D points. An RGB-D camera that uses a 640 × 480 measurement camera can typically output 307,200 3D points per range image which is about nine times the number of feature points. In this case, the horizontal and vertical spatial resolutions can be approximated by $S_x(Z, 3)$ and $S_y(Z, 3)$, respectively. Therefore, the spatial resolution of an RGB-D camera based on spatial codification is expected to be significantly lower than that of a time-multiplexed codification when the measurement camera of both RGB-D cameras have the same resolution.

5.7.4.3 Active Stereo

Some RGB-D camera manufacturers describe active stereo as a spatial codification structured-light system with an extra measurement camera. When the ambient lighting is moderated, it is expected that the depth of a pixel that views a projector feature will be accurate. One of the assumptions of active stereo is that the depth of a pixel that is not viewed by a projector feature will be estimated more accurately by a stereo matching algorithm than by interpolation. The horizontal and vertical spatial resolutions are expected to be in the range of $S_x(Z, 1)$ to $S_x(Z, 3)$ and $S_y(Z, 1)$ to $S_y(Z, 3)$, respectively, when the number of pixels of a measurement camera is nine times the number of projector features. When the projector features are not visible because of the ambient light, the active RGB-D camera is expected to perform as a passive stereo matching system. A comparative evaluation of a passive stereo algorithm can be found in [95]. The lateral resolution of a special family of stereo matching algorithms is presented in [59].

5.7.4.4 Time-of-Flight

For a phase-based system such as those presented in Sect. 5.5, the spatial resolution is given by the resolution of the measurement camera. The horizontal and vertical spatial resolutions can be approximated by $S_x(Z, 1)$ and $S_y(Z, 1)$, respectively. Given the pixel size, field of view, and pixel count of two ToFs, it is possible to compute the relative improvement of spatial resolution between two different ToF sensors (see the questions section at the end of this chapter). Table 5.3 contains such values for the Kinect II and Kinect Azure RGB-D cameras. Note that an improvement in spatial resolution will induce an improvement in lateral resolution only if the structural resolution is not the limiting factor. Even when one range measurement is obtained per pixel, an RGB-D camera's embedded post-processing steps can result in a significant amount of spatial filtering on the range data. This filtering affects the lateral resolution.

5.7.5 Lateral Resolution Versus Range Uncertainty

The depth value of each range image pixel is required in order to warp the texture image onto the range image. When the range information used for the warping is accurate, it is possible to have RGB-D cameras that have a lower lateral resolution in the depth channel (D) than in the color channels (RGB). Applying aggressive spatial filtering to the depth channel induces a reduction of the range uncertainty and a reduction of lateral resolution of the depth channel. However, this filtering may allow an increase in lateral resolution of the color channels. A modeling of the deviations of the texture image (RGB channels) and range image (D channel) of RGB-D camera is presented in [102]. The interpolation and filtering processes of the Intel RealSense SR300 are described in detail in [119]. Since the color channels of an RGB-D camera have potentially a higher resolution than the depth channel, it is possible to use a depth map up-sampling algorithm. The latter computes a high-resolution depth map that is plausible given the low-resolution depth map and the high-resolution RGB channels. More details can be found in [49, 50, 79, 117]. The evaluation of the lateral resolution of 3D imaging systems is a complex subject that is further discussed in [37, 41, 43, 44, 59, 67, 68].

5.8 System Characterization and Calibration

In this section, different studies that evaluate the performance of RGB-D cameras are discussed. We discourage the reader from comparing numerical values taken from different studies, as the experimental protocol may vary. We will first review metrological characterization approaches and then we present application-based characterization approaches. This is followed by a discussion on the different methods to improve the calibration of RGB-D cameras. We conclude the section with some final remarks related to system performance and RGB-D characterization.

5.8.1 Metrological Approaches

A comparative study between D415, SR300, Kinect II, and PrimeSense Carmine 1.09 is presented in [13]. The errors are measured using a calibrated sphere at a very close range. Between 5 and 10 m, errors are measured using the VDI/VDE 2634 Part 2 guideline [110]. Moreover, systematic depth errors are extracted using a planar surface at different distances. An in-depth comparative study that evaluates the RealSense D400, the Kinect II, and the Orbec Astral can be found in [35]. An empirical evaluation of ten RGB-D cameras is presented in [47]. The cameras tested are the Asus Xtion Pro Live, the Occipital Structure IO, the Orbbec Pro, the Kinect II, the RealSense D435, the RealSense ZR300, the RealSense R200, the RealSense F200, the RealSense SR300, and the Ensenso N35. Investigations of hand-held scanning systems, including RGB-D cameras, are presented in [42, 57, 58]. A metrological evaluation of Microsoft Kinect and Asus Xtion sensors is presented in [38]. An evaluation of the performance of the Intel RealSense SR300 is presented in [14]. An analysis of Intel RealSense D435 is presented in [4]. The proposed methodology uses a planar target with various orientations and distances to the RGB-D camera. Finally, a significant body of literature is available on the evaluation of the Kinect I and II [19, 26, 27, 30, 39, 69, 75, 94, 100].

5.8.2 Application-Based Approaches

Since the introduction of RGB-D cameras, a significant body of literature related to the quantitative evaluation of RGB-D cameras applied to many scientific fields has been produced. In this section, we provide a brief overview of some quantitative and qualitative evaluations related to two scientific disciplines.

5.8.2.1 Agriculture

In the context of agricultural applications, a comparative study of Microsoft's Kinect II, the Orbec Astra, the Intel RealSense SR300, and the Intel RealSense D435 is performed for close-range outdoor agricultural phenotyping [112]. Their experiments show that an active stereo camera outperforms other RGB-D cameras for outdoor agricultural applications. Many studies have examined the use of RGB-D cameras for characterizing crops such as sugar beets, maize, cotton, grapevine, and sweet onions [52, 53, 70, 80, 80, 113]. A review of the different sensors, including RGB-D cameras, used for plant phenotyping is presented in [85]. Another comparative study by Kuan et al. [61] examines the performance of Intel RealSense R200, Kinect II, and Xtion Pro Live in outdoor environments. In this study, the Intel RealSense R200, which is an active stereo sensor that predates the RealSense D435, had a larger operational range than the Kinect II. However, in terms of quality, the Kinect II outperformed the R200.

5.8.2.2 Biomedical Applications

Motion is a valuable descriptor of the functional and health status of a human subject. Consumer-grade RGB-D sensors are being exploited in various healthcare setups to analyze human shape and motion patterns. This tendency emanates from the need to base clinical decision making and outcome assessment on objective and quantitative measurements in a user-friendly and cost-effective manner [84].

RGB-D cameras are deployed in smart homes to monitor daily-life activities in elderly and/or disabled patients [76]. In rehabilitation, interactive remote physical therapy systems rely intensively on Microsoft's Kinect I and II to track body joints and compute kinematic measurements [15, 64, 72, 93]. Although sufficient accuracy has been reported for clinical use [8], reduced performance has been noted in cases of occlusions, either by an object or by other body parts [118] and in non-standing postures, such as sitting or lying down [116]. These applications generally require monitoring of the full body and address global motion patterns of large amplitude and low frequency.

At a smaller scale, RGB-D sensors are exploited for continuous and contactless monitoring of cardiac and respiratory vital signs in palliative and intensive care units [87, 92, 99] and for sleep monitoring in familiar environments [65]. However, difficulties related to large occlusions due to blankets and difficulties in distinguishing between front and back sleeping postures have been reported [84]. Limitations to the use of the Kinect have also been reported in the assessment of tremors in patients with Parkinson's disease [34] suggesting limited performance in the case of fine and local motion patterns.

5.8.3 Improving the Calibration of RGB-D Cameras

RGB-D cameras have to be calibrated by the manufacturer before being shipped to consumers. The calibration procedures used in factories for RGB-D cameras can be significantly different from the ones used for industrial scanners. The low cost and large volume of production for RGB-D cameras may require fast and automatic procedures. The in-factory calibration procedures for the Intel RealSense SR300 are described in [119]. The notable aspect of the method is that it does not require the extraction of fiducial markers.

Applications that focus on recreational human activities, such as motion tracking for video game interactions, only require a coarse calibration. For these applications, the factory calibration may be adequate. More demanding applications may require a recalibration of RGB-D cameras. Many methods have been proposed for recalibrating or improving the calibration of RGB-D cameras [6, 11, 17, 22, 23, 23, 54–56, 78, 103, 108, 111, 111, 120, 125]. While most methods use a parametric model, a non-parametric method is presented in [25]. Methods designed for the calibration of RGB-D cameras that are based on ToF are described in [63, 82, 115]. A review and quantitative comparison of methods for the Kinect sensor are presented in [114].

Some methods are specialized to recover the external parameters of an RGB-D cameras. Typically, recovering the pose of the RGB-D camera with respect to a world reference frame is of interest when combining multiple RGB-D cameras. Many methods have been proposed to calibrate multiple RGB-D cameras [2, 16, 31, 62, 74]. Some RGB-D cameras have trigger signals that can be used to synchronize multiple RGB-D cameras. These signals are used to avoid a simultaneous projection by one RGB-D camera and range measurement by another.

The calibration of a sensor requires a certain amount of training that operators of RGB-D cameras sometimes lack. In this situation, it may be useful to use fully automatic calibration methods that calibrate the system while in normal operating mode. These methods are known as auto-calibration or may sometimes be referred to as unsupervised calibration. Many methods have been proposed for the auto-calibration of RGB-D cameras [7, 24, 46, 71, 122]. Finally, some methods allowing the calibration of RGB-D cameras in the context of Simultaneous Localization and Mapping (SLAM) are presented in [86, 106, 123].

5.8.4 Final Remarks Related to System Performance and Characterization

A significant amount of post-processing is performed by RGB-D cameras. This processing may be optimized for specific applications and some of it can be disabled or enabled by interfacing with software developer kits. The user may not be fully aware that he/she had triggered a change in the behavior of the device. Different RGB-D cameras that use the same measurement principle may have been designed

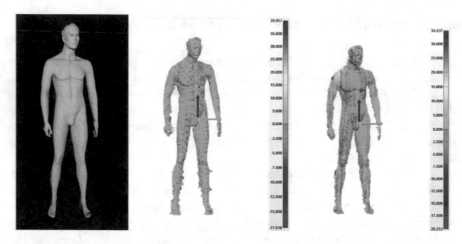

Fig. 5.21 Left: a rendering of the range image of a mannequin scanned by the system using temporal coding. Center: a color-coded difference between the range image acquired using temporal coding and active stereo. The matching algorithm is the semi-global matching method presented in Sect. 5.3.1.2. Right: a similar color-coded difference using an offline high-end, commercially available stereo matcher. Figure courtesy of NRC

for applications with different requirements. Thus, an RGB-D camera that uses a given implementation may not be a representative of all the RGB-D cameras that use that measurement principle.

Figure 5.21 shows the results obtained using a temporal coding structured-light system functioning in the near-infrared. The system is also equipped with a second camera that allows the conversion of the system into an active stereo system. The baseline of the active stereo system is twice the one of the temporal encoding configuration. This allows the quantitative evaluation of the tradeoffs between active stereo and temporal encoding using the same hardware. This setup also allows a quantitative evaluation of different stereo matching algorithms.

5.9   Research Challenges

Some research challenges are related to the development of new and improved hardware, while others are related to the development of mass-adopted applications. While the use of RGB-D cameras as input device for video games was initially envisioned as a mass market application, the number of video games that use the 3D imaging capabilities of RGB-D cameras is relatively small. In recent years, the increase in performance of computing platforms, combined with the rapid progression in the field of machine learning, has allowed significant advancement of passive vision technologies, such as structure-from-motion, that rely on regular cameras, rather than active sensors. The main challenge is the development of applications that can simultaneously reach a large user base and exploit the capabilities RGB-D cameras to perform tasks that are not possible with a regular camera. Without this large user base, it may be difficult to establish a viable business case supporting the development of new active 3D imaging systems for the consumer market.

Some research challenges related to all types of RGB-D camera hardware are the reduction of cost, size, and power consumption of the devices. The power output of the laser used in RGB-D cameras is typically fixed so that the devices are safe under all conditions during the normal use, including when using typical magnifying optics. Such regulatory and social-acceptance constraints leave little opportunity to increase the range of RGB-D cameras based on structured-light or ToF. Increasing the sensitivity of the near-infrared sensor integrated into the RGB-D cameras and reducing the ambient light generated by the projection system, thereby increasing the contrast, would allow designers to simultaneously increase the range and reduce the measurement uncertainty. Note that while only the modulated portion of the illuminated signal is used for the measurement, both the ambient and modulated illuminations have to be taken into account when computing the maximum permissible exposure.

Currently, there is a trend for manufacturers of RGB-D cameras to discontinue designs based on spatial encoding and these are being replaced by active stereo and ToF designs. Significant research and development activities are expected to occur on the topic of active stereo in the next few years. This technology allows RGB-D cameras to operate in outdoor environments and is, at the moment, cheaper than ToF to manufacture [119]. The expected growth of the ToF market related to the automobile sector, combined with the recent integration of ToF into high-end smartphones, creates new opportunities. Indeed, large industrial players are investing significant resources in the development of low-cost ToF chips that could also be used within RGB-D cameras.

5.10 Concluding Remarks

As factory workers, technicians, and engineers are exposed to 3D imaging technologies in their personal life, it can be expected that 3D systems, coupled with augmented reality systems, will enter the production floor of tomorrow's factories. Currently, several new manufacturing processes require the use of 3D imaging systems. RGB-D cameras can be used to build the first proof-of-concept of a manufacturing process even when it does not have the required accuracy. Note that for some industrial and commercial applications, the accuracy provided by consumer-grade RGB-D cameras may already be sufficient. The increase in price between an RGB-D camera and a low-end industrial 3D imaging systems is significant. This difference is in part related to the quality of the devices and in part related to the reduced volume of production. Manufacturers of industrial 3D imaging systems that use components contained in RGB-D cameras should see a significant reduction of production cost. It would not be surprising to see affordable low-end industrial 3D imaging systems produced in large volumes in the near future.

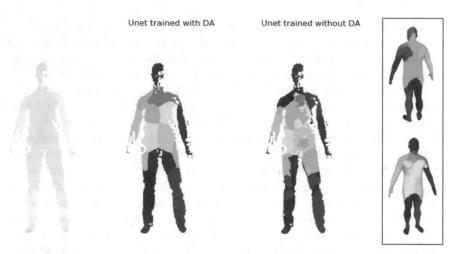

Fig. 5.22 From left to right: actual range image acquired with a temporal encoding structured-light system, where the depth is coded using Gray levels; results of a deep learning approach to human body parts segmentation trained with and without domain-specific data augmentation (DA) strategy that closely simulates the actual acquisition including the system parameters and typical artifacts present in the range images [96, 97]; a reference segmentation provided to qualitatively assess the results of the segmentation. Figure courtesy of NRC

The impact of RGB-D cameras on academic research activities is clear. Such cameras democratize the access to 3D data to hobbyists, students, and researchers and this leads to the creation of a significant body of literature presenting technologies that use range images as input. As a final remark, we would like to stress the importance of understanding the artifacts induced by the physical measurement process of RGB-D cameras, when using their output as input to other systems. As an example, Fig. 5.22 shows the results of a deep learning approach to human body parts segmentation from range images acquired using a structured-light system. A first convolutional neural network (UNet) was blindly trained using ideally generated synthetic range images [96]. The generalization performance on actual range images from the system was unsatisfactory (Fig. 5.22, second from the right). A second CNN (UNet) was trained using the same training images but introducing a domain-specific data augmentation (DA) strategy that emulates the actual range acquisition system with its sensor-specific artifacts, such as light occlusions, noise, and missing data. In this case, the generalization performance is much improved on actual data (Fig. 5.22, second from left) showing the importance of understanding and modeling the artifacts specific to a particular range sensor [96, 97].

5.11   Further Reading

Due to space constraints, many topics related to RGB-D cameras could not be included in this chapter. Readers not familiar with the related material contained in Chaps. 2–4 are invited to read these chapters. No description of the low-level hardware components of RGB-D cameras was included in this chapter. A good starting point for someone interested in the implementation details of RGB-D camera technologies can be found in [88, 121]. The exploitation of the range images produced by RGB-D cameras is described in [89, 98]. The metrological characterization of RGB-D cameras is presented in [35]. Finally, the fusion of multiple range images into a single 3D model is discussed in [124].

5.12   Questions

1. Name and explain the different types of RGB-D cameras.
2. Which type of RGB-D camera would you use in an outdoor environment?
3. For each type of RGB-D camera, what is the impact of having multiple sensors acquiring the same scene simultaneously?
4. Using the data from Table 5.3, what is the improvement in the spatial resolution between the Kinect II and Kinect Azure?
5. Some third parties sell kits that add lenses to the front of the projector, infrared camera, and RGB camera of the Kinect I. These kits are designed to reduce the operational range of the sensor. What is the impact of such kits on the recovery of scene geometry?
6. An engineer was asked to increase the modulation frequency of a ToF system by 20%. What is the impact on the range uncertainty, assuming that the modulation contrast is not changed?
7. An industrial designer informed you that the size of a triangulation-based RGB-D camera must be reduced by 50% while preserving the same range uncertainty. What modification could be made to achieve this?
8. How could a temperature variation within the RGB-D camera influence the recovery of scene geometry?

5.13   Exercises

1. Examine the Software Development Kit (SDK) of two different RGB-D cameras and identify all the parameters that could influence the quality of the resulting range images.
2. Using a commercially available DOE laser projector generating a random dot pattern and two monochromatic cameras, build an active stereo scanner using the

general design proposed in Fig. 5.4. Use the semi-global method presented in [48] to perform the stereo matching. Please refer to the discussion on laser safety at the end of Sect. 5.1.3.

3. Implement a Gray code structured-light system using the galvanometer-based projection system described in Sect. 5.4.1.1. Again, please refer to the discussion on laser safety at the end of Sect. 5.1.3.

4. Modify the system developed in the previous exercise to support the large-gap Gray Code (see Chap. 3).

5. Modify the system developed in the previous exercise to support phase shift patterns (see Chap. 3).

6. Add an RGB camera for performing texture mapping to the system developed in exercises 2 and 3.

Acknowledgements The authors would like to acknowledge the numerous contributions of their colleagues at the National Research Council Canada.

References

1. ANSI Z136 Part 1-6, American National Standard for safe use of lasers (2007)
2. Aalerud, A., Dybedal, J., Hovland, G.: Automatic calibration of an industrial RGB-D camera network using retroreflective fiducial markers. Sensors **19**(7), 1561 (2019)
3. Aganj, E., Monasse, P., Keriven, R.: Multi-view texturing of imprecise mesh. In: Lecture Notes in Computer Science, vol. 5995 LNCS, pp. 468–476 (2010)
4. Ahn, M.S., Chae, H., Noh, D., Nam, H., Hong, D.: Analysis and noise modeling of the Intel RealSense D435 for mobile robots. In: 16th International Conference on Ubiquitous Robots (UR), pp. 707–711 (2019)
5. Bamji, C.S., Mehta, S., Thompson, B., Elkhatib, T., Wurster, S., Akkaya, O., Payne, A., Godbaz, J., Fenton, M., Rajasekaran, V., Prather, L., Nagaraja, S., Mogallapu, V., Snow, D., McCauley, R., Mukadam, M., Agi, I., McCarthy, S., Xu, Z., Perry, T., Qian, W., Chan, V., Adepu, P., Ali, G., Ahmed, M., Mukherjee, A., Nayak, S., Gampell, D., Acharya, S., Kordus, L., O'Connor, P.: IMpixel 65nm BSI 320MHz demodulated TOF Image sensor with $3\mu m$ global shutter pixels and analog binning. In: 2018 IEEE International Solid - State Circuits Conference - (ISSCC), pp. 94–96 (2018)
6. Basso, F., Menegatti, E., Pretto, A.: Robust intrinsic and extrinsic calibration of RGB-D cameras. IEEE Trans. Robot. **34**(5), 1315–1332 (2018)
7. Basso, F., Pretto, A., Menegatti, E.: Unsupervised intrinsic and extrinsic calibration of a camera-depth sensor couple. In: IEEE International Conference on Robotics and Automation (ICRA), pp. 6244–6249 (2014)
8. Bonnechère, B., Jansen, B., Salvia, P., Bouzahouene, H., Sholukha, V., Cornelis, J., Rooze, M., Van Sint Jan, S.: Determination of the precision and accuracy of morphological measurements using the Kinect™ sensor: Comparison with standard stereophotogrammetry (2014)
9. British Standards Institution: BS EN 62471:2008, British Standards photobiological safety of lamps and lamp systems (2008)
10. Bronstein, A., Zabatani, A., Bronstein, M., Kimmel, R., Sperling, E., Surazhsky, V.: Projector distortion compensation in structured light depth reconstruction (2017). United States Patent Application 9,824,461
11. Cabrera, E.V., Ortiz, L.E., Silva B. M. F., Clua, E.W.G., Gonçalves, L.M.G.: A versatile method for depth data error estimation in RGB-D sensors. Sensors **18**(9) (2018)

12. Callieri, M., Cignoni, P., Corsini, M., Scopigno, R.: Masked photo blending: mapping dense photographic data set on high-resolution sampled 3D models. Comput. Graph. (Pergamon) **32**(4), 464–473 (2008)
13. Carfagni, M., Furferi, R., Governi, L., Santarelli, C., Servi, M., Uccheddu, F., Volpe, Y.: Metrological and critical characterization of the Intel D415 stereo depth camera. Sensors **19**(3), (2019)
14. Carfagni, M., Furferi, R., Governi, L., Servi, M., Uccheddu, F., Volpe, Y.: On the performance of the Intel SR300 depth camera: metrological and critical characterization. IEEE Sens. J. **17**(14), 4508–4519 (2017)
15. Chang, Y.J., Chen, S.F., Huang, J.D.: A Kinect-based system for physical rehabilitation: a pilot study for young adults with motor disabilities. Res. Dev. Disabil. **32**(6), 2566–2570 (2011)
16. Chen, C., Yang, B., Song, S., Tian, M., Li, J., Dai, W., Fang, L.: Calibrate multiple consumer RGB-D cameras for low-cost and efficient 3D indoor mapping. Remote Sens. **10**(2) (2018)
17. Chen, G., Cui, G., Jin, Z., Wu, F., Chen, X.: Accurate intrinsic and extrinsic calibration of RGB-D cameras with GP-based depth correction. IEEE Sens. J. **19**(7), 2685–2694 (2018)
18. Chugui, Y., Verkhoglyad, A., Poleshchuk, A., Korolkov, V., Sysoev, E., Zavyalov, P.: 3D optical measuring systems and laser technologies for scientific and industrial applications. Meas. Sci. Rev. **13**(6), 322–328 (2013)
19. Corti, A., Giancola, S., Mainetti, G., Sala, R.: A metrological characterization of the Kinect V2 time-of-flight camera. Robot. Auton. Syst. **75**, 584–594 (2016)
20. Cox, M.G., Siebert, B.R.L.: The use of a monte carlo method for evaluating uncertainty and expanded uncertainty. Metrologia **43**(4), S178 (2006)
21. Criminisi, A.: Accurate Visual Metrology from Single and Multiple Uncalibrated Images. Springer, New York Inc, New York (2001)
22. Darwish, W., Li, W., Tang, S., Wu, B., Chen, W.: A robust calibration method for consumer grade RGB-D sensors for precise indoor reconstruction. IEEE Access **7**, 8824–8833 (2019)
23. Darwish, W., Tang, S., Li, W., Chen, W.: A new calibration method for commercial RGB-D sensors. Sensors **17**(6) (2017)
24. Devaux, J.C., Hadj-Abdelkader, H., Colle, E.: Fully automatic extrinsic calibration of RGB-D system using two views of natural scene. In: 13th International Conference on Control Automation Robotics & Vision (ICARCV), pp. 894–900. IEEE (2014)
25. Di Cicco, M., Iocchi, L., Grisetti, G.: Non-parametric calibration for depth sensors. Robot Auton. Syst. **74**, 309–317 (2015)
26. Diaz, M., Tombari, F., Rodriguez-Gonzalvez, P., Gonzalez-Aguilera, D.: Analysis and evaluation between the first and the second generation of RGB-D sensors. IEEE Sens. J. **15**(11), 6507–6516 (2015)
27. Difilippo, N., Jouaneh, M.: Characterization of different Microsoft Kinect sensor models. IEEE Sens. J. **15**, 1–1 (2015)
28. Do, L., Ma, L., Bondarev, E., De With, P.H.: On multi-view texture mapping of indoor environments using Kinect depth sensors. In: VISAPP 2014 - Proceedings of the 9th International Conference on Computer Vision Theory and Applications, vol. 2, pp. 739–745 (2014)
29. Drouin, M.A.: Mise en correspondance active et passive pour la vision par ordinateur multivue. Université de Montréal (2007)
30. Fankhauser, P., Bloesch, M., Rodriguez, D., Kaestner, R., Hutter, M., Siegwart, R.: Kinect v2 for mobile robot navigation: Evaluation and modeling. In: 2015 International Conference on Advanced Robotics (ICAR), pp. 388–394 (2015)
31. Fernandez-Moral, E., González-Jiménez, J., Rives, P., Arévalo, V.: Extrinsic calibration of a set of range cameras in 5 seconds without pattern. In: 2014 IEEE/RSJ International Conference on Intelligent Robots and Systems, pp. 429–435 (2014)
32. Fu, Y., Yan, Q., Yang, L., Liao, J., Xiao, C.: Texture mapping for 3D reconstruction with RGB-D sensor. In: Proceedings of the IEEE Computer Society Conference on Computer Vision and Pattern Recognition, pp. 4645–4653 (2018)

33. Gal, R., Wexler, Y., Ofek, E., Hoppe, H., Cohen-Or, D.: Seamless montage for texturing models. Comput. Graph. Forum **29**(2), 479–486 (2010)
34. Galna, B., Barry, G., Jackson, D., Mhiripiri, D., Olivier, P., Rochester, L.: Accuracy of the Microsoft Kinect sensor for measuring movement in people with Parkinson's disease. Gait Post. **39**, 1062–1068 (2014)
35. Giancola, S., Valenti, M., Sala, R.: A Survey on 3D Cameras: Metrological Comparison of Time-of-Flight. Structured-Light and Active Stereoscopy Technologies. Springer (2018)
36. Giles, J.: Inside the race to hack the Kinect. New Sci. **208**(2789), 22–23 (2010)
37. Goesele, M., Fuchs, C., Seidel, H.P.: Accuracy of 3D range scanners by measurement of the slanted edge modulation transfer function. In: International Conference on 3D Digital Imaging and Modeling, p. 37 (2003)
38. Gonzalez-Jorge, H., Riveiro, B., Vazquez-Fernandez, E., Martínez-Sánchez, J., Arias, P.: Metrological evaluation of Microsoft Kinect and Asus Xtion sensors. Measurement **46**(6), 1800–1806 (2013)
39. Gonzalez-Jorge, H., Rodríguez-Gonzálvez, P., Martínez-Sánchez, J., González-Aguilera, D., Arias, P., Gesto, M., Díaz-Vilariño, L.: Metrological comparison between Kinect I and Kinect II sensors. Measurement **70**, 21–26 (2015)
40. Grunnet-Jepsen, A., Sweetser, J.N., Winer, P., Takagi, A., Woodfill, J.: Projectors for Intel RealSense Depth Cameras D4xx. Mouser Electronics (2018)
41. Guidi, G.: Metrological characterization of 3D imaging devices. In: Remondino, F., Shortis, M.R., Beyerer, J., León, F.P. (eds.) Videometrics, Range Imaging, and Applications XII; and Automated Visual Inspection, vol. 8791, pp. 163–172. International Society for Optics and Photonics, SPIE (2013)
42. Guidi, G., Gonizzi, S., Micoli, L.: 3D capturing performances of low-cost range sensors for mass-market applications. Int. Arch. Photogramm. Remote Sens. Spatial Inf. Sci. - ISPRS Arch. **41**, 33–40 (2016)
43. Guidi, G., Russo, M., Magrassi, G., Bordegoni, M.: Resolution characteritazion of 3D cameras. In: Three-dimensional Imaging Metrology, vol. 7239, p. 72390. International Society for Optics and Photonics (2009)
44. Guidi, G., Russo, M., Magrassi, G., Bordegoni, M.: Performance evaluation of triangulation based range sensors. Sensors **10**(8), 7192–7215 (2010)
45. Hall, M., Stewart, M.: Depth-spatial frequency-response assessment (2016). United States Patent Application US15/090,390
46. Halmetschlager-Funek, G., Prankl, J., Vincze, M.: Towards autonomous auto calibration of unregistered RGB-D setups: The benefit of plane priors. In: 2018 IEEE/RSJ International Conference on Intelligent Robots and Systems (IROS), pp. 5547–5554 (2018)
47. Halmetschlager-Funek, G., Suchi, M., Kampel, M., Vincze, M.: An empirical evaluation of ten depth cameras: bias, precision, lateral noise, different lighting conditions and materials, and multiple sensor setups in indoor environments. IEEE Robot. Autom. Mag. **26**(1), 67–77 (2019)
48. Hirschmüller, H.: Stereo processing by semiglobal matching and mutual information. IEEE Trans. Pattern Anal. Mach. Intell. **30**(2), 328–341 (2008)
49. Huhle, B., Schairer, T., Jenke, P., Straßer, W.: Fusion of range and color images for denoising and resolution enhancement with a non-local filter. Comput. Vis. Image Underst. **114**(12), 1336–1345 (2010). Special issue on Time-of-Flight Camera Based Computer Vision
50. Hui, T.W., Loy, C.C., Tang, X.: Depth map super-resolution by deep multi-scale guidance. In: European Conference on Computer Vision, pp. 353–369. Springer (2016)
51. International Organization for Standardization, Geneva, CH: Photography – Electronic still picture imaging – Resolution and spatial frequency responses (2014)
52. Jiang, Y., Li, C., Paterson, A.H.: High throughput phenotyping of cotton plant height using depth images under field conditions. Comput. Electron. Agric. **130**, 57–68 (2016)
53. Jiang, Y., Li, C., Paterson, A.H., Sun, S., Xu, R., Robertson, J.: Quantitative analysis of cotton canopy size in field conditions using a consumer-grade RGB-D camera. Front. Plant Sci. **8**, 2233 (2018)

54. Jin, B., Lei, H., Geng, W.: Accurate intrinsic calibration of depth camera with cuboids. In: European Conference on Computer Vision, pp. 788–803. Springer (2014)
55. Karan, B.: Accuracy improvements of consumer-grade 3D sensors for robotic applications. In: SISY 2013 - IEEE 11th International Symposium on Intelligent Systems and Informatics, Proceedings pp. 141–146 (2013)
56. Karan, B.: Calibration of Kinect-type RGB-D sensors for robotic applications. FME Trans. **43**(1), 47–54 (2015)
57. Kersten, T., Przybilla, H.J., Lindstaedt, M., Tschirschwitz, F., Misgaiski-Hass, M.: Comparative geometrical investigations of hand-held scanning systems. Int. Arch. Photogramm. Remote Sens. Spatial Inf. Sci. - ISPRS Arch. **41**, 507–514 (2016)
58. Kersten, T.P., Przybilla, H.J., Lindstaedt, M., Tschirschwitz, F., Misgaiski-Hass, M.: Comparative geometrical investigations of hand-held scanning systems. In: International Archives of the Photogrammetry, Remote Sensing & Spatial Information Sciences, vol. 41 (2016)
59. Klowsky, R., Kuijper, A., Goesele, M.: Modulation transfer function of patch-based stereo systems. In: 2012 IEEE Conference on Computer Vision and Pattern Recognition, pp. 1386–1393 (2012)
60. Konolige, K.: Projected texture stereo. In: IEEE International Conference on Robotics and Automation, pp. 148–155 (2010)
61. Kuan, Y.W., Ee, N.O., Wei, L.S.: Comparative study of Intel R200, Kinect v2, and Primesense RGB-D sensors performance outdoors. IEEE Sens. J. **19**(19), 8741–8750 (2019)
62. Kwon, Y.C., Jang, J.W., Choi, O.: Automatic sphere detection for extrinsic calibration of multiple RGBD cameras. In: 2018 18th International Conference on Control, Automation and Systems (ICCAS), pp. 1451–1454. IEEE (2018)
63. Lachat, E., Macher, H., Landes, T., Grussenmeyer, P.: Assessment and calibration of a RGB-D camera (Kinect v2 sensor) towards a potential use for close-range 3D modeling. Remote Sens. **7**, 13070–13097 (2015)
64. Lange, B., Chang, C.Y., Suma, E., Newman, B., Rizzo, A.S., Bolas, M.: Development and evaluation of low cost game-based balance rehabilitation tool using the Microsoft Kinect sensor. In: Proceedings of the Annual International Conference of the IEEE Engineering in Medicine and Biology Society, EMBS, pp. 1831–1834 (2011)
65. Lee, J., Hong, M., Ryu, S.: Sleep monitoring system using Kinect sensor. Int. J. Distrib. Sens. Netw. **2015**, 1–9 (2015)
66. Lim, J.: Optimized projection pattern supplementing stereo systems. In: 2009 IEEE International Conference on Robotics and Automation, pp. 2823–2829 (2009)
67. MacKinnon, D., Beraldin, J.A., Cournoyer, L., Carrier, B., Blais, F.: Proposed traceable structural resolution protocols for 3D imaging systems. In: Remondino, F., Shortis, M.R., El-Hakim, S.F. (eds.) Videometrics, Range Imaging, and Applications X, vol. 7447, pp. 38–46. International Society for Optics and Photonics, SPIE (2009)
68. MacKinnon, D.K., Beraldin, J.A., Cournoyer, L., Picard, M., Blais, F.: Lateral resolution challenges for triangulation-based three-dimensional imaging systems. Opt. Eng. **51**(2), 1–16–16 (2012)
69. Mallick, T., Das, P.P., Majumdar, A.K.: Characterizations of noise in Kinect depth images: a review. IEEE Sens. J. **14**(6), 1731–1740 (2014)
70. Milella, A., Marani, R., Petitti, A., Reina, G.: In-field high throughput grapevine phenotyping with a consumer-grade depth camera. Comput. Electron. Agric. **156**, 293–306 (2019)
71. Miller, S., Teichman, A., Thrun, S.: Unsupervised extrinsic calibration of depth sensors in dynamic scenes. In: 2013 IEEE/RSJ International Conference on Intelligent Robots and Systems, pp. 2695–2702 (2013)
72. Mishra, A.K., Skubic, M., Abbott, C.: Development and preliminary validation of an interactive remote physical therapy system. In: Proceedings of the Annual International Conference of the IEEE Engineering in Medicine and Biology Society, EMBS, pp. 190–193. IEEE (2015)
73. Molinier, T., Fofi, D., Salvi, J., Fougerolle, Y., Gorria, P.: Projector View Synthesis and Virtual Texturing. In: 2nd International Topical Meeting on Optical Sensing and Artificial Vision (2008)

74. Nakazawa, M., Mitsugami, I., Habe, H., Yamazoe, H., Yagi, Y.: Calibration of multiple Kinects with little overlap regions. IEEJ Trans. Electr. Electron. Eng. **10**, S108–S115 (2015)
75. Nguyen, C.V., Izadi, S., Lovell, D.: Modeling Kinect sensor noise for improved 3D reconstruction and tracking. In: Second International Conference on 3D Imaging, Modeling, Processing, Visualization Transmission, pp. 524–530 (2012)
76. Ni, Q., Hernando, A.B.G., de la Cruz, I.P.: The elderly's independent living in smart homes: A characterization of activities and sensing infrastructure survey to facilitate services development. Sensors (Switzerland) **15**(5), 11312–11362 (2015)
77. Nieuwenhove, D.V., Fotopoulou, K., López, C.E.: A 15 um CAPD Time-of-Flight pixel with 80% modulation contrast at 100 MHz (2015)
78. Paradiso, V., Crivellaro, A., Amgarou, K., de Lanaute, N., Fua, P., Liénard, E.: A versatile calibration procedure for portable coded aperture gamma cameras and RGB-D sensors. Nucl. Instrum. Methods Phys. Res. Sect. A: Accel. Spectrom. Detect. Assoc. Equip. **886**, 125–133 (2018)
79. Park, J., Kim, H., Yu-Wing Tai, Brown, M.S., Kweon, I.: High quality depth map upsampling for 3D-ToF cameras. In: 2011 International Conference on Computer Vision, pp. 1623–1630 (2011)
80. Paulus, S., Behmann, J., Mahlein, A.K., Plümer, L., Kuhlmann, H.: Low-cost 3D systems: suitable tools for plant phenotyping. Sensors **14**(2), 3001–3018 (2014)
81. Payne, A., Daniel, A., Mehta, A., Thompson, B., Bamji, C.S., Snow, D., Oshima, H., Prather, L., Fenton, M., Kordus, L., et al.: A 512× 424 CMOS 3D time-of-flight image sensor with multi-frequency photo-demodulation up to 130 MHz and 2Gs/s ADC. In: 2014 IEEE International Solid-State Circuits Conference Digest of Technical Papers (ISSCC), pp. 134–135 (2014)
82. Penne, R., Raposo, C., Mertens, L., Ribbens, B., Araújo, H.: Investigating new calibration methods without feature detection for ToF cameras. Image Vis. Comput. **43**, 50–62 (2015)
83. Perenzoni, M., Stoppa, D.: Figures of merit for indirect time-of-flight 3D cameras: definition and experimental evaluation. Remote Sens. **3**(11), 2461–2472 (2011)
84. Pöhlmann, S.T., Harkness, E.F., Taylor, C.J., Astley, S.M.: Evaluation of Kinect 3D sensor for healthcare imaging. J. Med. Biol. Eng. **36**(6), 857–870 (2016)
85. Qiu, R., Wei, S., Zhang, M., Li, H., Sun, H., Liu, G., Li, M.: Sensors for measuring plant phenotyping: a review. Int. J. Agric. Biol. Eng. **11**(2), 1–17 (2018)
86. Quenzel, J., Rosu, R.A., Houben, S., Behnke, S.: Online depth calibration for RGB-D cameras using visual SLAM. In: 2017 IEEE/RSJ International Conference on Intelligent Robots and Systems (IROS), pp. 2227–2234 (2017)
87. Rehouma, H., Noumeir, R., Bouachir, W., Jouvet, P., Essouri, S.: 3D imaging system for respiratory monitoring in pediatric intensive care environment. Comput. Med. Imaging Graph. **70**, 17–28 (2018)
88. Remondino, F., Stoppa, D. (eds.): TOF Range-Imaging Cameras. Springer, Berlin (2013)
89. Rosin, P., Lai, Y.K., Shao, L., Liu, Y. (eds.): RGB-D Image Analysis and Processing. Springer, Berlin (2019)
90. Salvi, J., Fernandez, S., Pribanic, T., Llado, X.: A state of the art in structured light patterns for surface profilometry. Pattern Recognit. **43**(8), 2666–2680 (2010)
91. Salvi, J., Pages, J., Batlle, J.: Pattern codification strategies in structured light systems. Pattern Recognit. **37**(4), 827–849 (2004)
92. Samir, M., Golkar, E., Rahni, A.A.A.: Comparison between the Kinect™V1 and Kinect™V2 for respiratory motion tracking. In: IEEE 2015 International Conference on Signal and Image Processing Applications, ICSIPA 2015 - Proceedings, pp. 150–155 (2016)
93. Saraee, E., Singh, S., Hendron, K., Zheng, M., Joshi, A., Ellis, T., Betke, M.: ExerciseCheck: remote monitoring and evaluation platform for home based physical therapy. ACM Int. Conf. Proc. Ser. Part **F1285**, 87–90 (2017)
94. Sarbolandi, H., Lefloch, D., Kolb, A.: Kinect range sensing: structured-light versus time-of-flight Kinect. Comput. Vis. Image Underst. **139**, 1–20 (2015)

95. Scharstein, D., Szeliski, R.: A taxonomy and evaluation of dense two-frame stereo correspondence algorithms. Int. J. Comput. Vis. **47**(1–3), 7–42 (2002)
96. Seoud, L., Boisvert, J., Drouin, M., Picard, M., Godin, G.: Training a CNN to robustly segment the human body parts in range image sequences. In: Optical Data Science II. SPIE (2019)
97. Seoud, L., Boisvert, J., Drouin, M.A., Picard, M., Godin, G.: Increasing the robustness of CNN-based human body segmentation in range images by modeling sensor-specific artifacts. In: Computer Vision – ECCV 2018 Workshops, pp. 729–743. Springer International Publishing (2019)
98. Shao, L., Han, J., Zhengyou, K.: Computer Vision and Machine Learning with RGB-D Sensors. Springer, Berlin (2014)
99. Shi, K., Will, C., Steigleder, T., Michler, F., Weigel, R., Ostgathe, C., Koelpin, A.: A contactless system for continuous vital sign monitoring in palliative and intensive care. 12th Annual IEEE International Systems Conference, SysCon 2018 - Proceedings, pp. 1–8 (2018)
100. Skalski, A., Machura, B.: Metrological analysis of Microsoft Kinect in the context of object localization. Metrol. Meas. Syst. **22**(4), 469–478 (2015)
101. Smith, W.J.: Modern Optical Engineering, 3rd edn. McGraw-Hill, New York City (2000)
102. Song, X., Zheng, J., Zhong, F., Qin, X.: Modeling deviations of RGB-D cameras for accurate depth map and color image registration. Multimed. Tools Appl. **77**(12), 14951–14977 (2018)
103. Staranowicz, A.N., Brown, G.R., Morbidi, F., Mariottini, G.L.: Practical and accurate calibration of RGB-D cameras using spheres. Comput. Vis. Image Underst. **137**, 102–114 (2015)
104. Surazhsky, V., Kimmel, R., Bronstein, A., Bronstein, M., Sperling, E., Zabatani, A.: Facilitating projection pre-sharping of digital images at computing devices (2017). United States Patent Application 9,792,673
105. Szeliski, R., Zabih, R., Scharstein, D., Veksler, O., Kolmogorov, V., Agarwala, A., Tappen, M., Rother, C.: A comparative study of energy minimization methods for Markov random fields with smoothness-based priors. IEEE Trans. Pattern Anal. Mach. Intell. **30**(6), 1068–1080 (2008)
106. Teichman, A., Miller, S., Thrun, S.: Unsupervised intrinsic calibration of depth sensors via SLAM. In: Robotics: Science and Systems, vol. 248, p. 3 (2013)
107. Trobina, M.: Error model of a coded-light range sensor. Technical Report BIWI-TR-164, ETH-Zentrum (1995)
108. Vasileiou, P.G., Psarakis, E.Z.: A new depth camera calibration algorithm. In: 2014 23rd International Conference on Robotics in Alpe-Adria-Danube Region (RAAD), pp. 1–8. IEEE (2014)
109. Verein Deutscher Ingenieure (VDI, Association of German Engineers): VDI 2617 Part 6.2, Accuracy of coordinate measuring machines – Characteristics and their testing – Guideline for the application of DIN EN ISO 10360 to coordinate measuring machines with optical distance sensors, Beuth Verlag GmbH (2005)
110. Verein Deutscher Ingenieure (VDI, Association of German Engineers): VDI 2634 Part 3 Optical 3-D measuring systems Optical system based on area scanning (2008)
111. Villena-Martínez, V., Fuster-Guilló, A., Azorín-López, J., Saval-Calvo, M., Mora-Pascual, J., Garcia-Rodriguez, J., Garcia-Garcia, A.: A quantitative comparison of calibration methods for RGB-D sensors using different technologies. Sensors **17**(2) (2017)
112. Vit, A., Shani, G.: Comparing RGB-D sensors for close range outdoor agricultural phenotyping. Sensors **18**(12) (2018)
113. Wang, W., Li, C.: Size estimation of sweet onions using consumer-grade RGB-depth sensor. J. Food Eng. **142**, 153–162 (2014)
114. Xiang, W., Conly, C., McMurrough, C.D., Athitsos, V.: A review and quantitative comparison of methods for Kinect calibration. In: Proceedings of the 2nd international Workshop on Sensor-based Activity Recognition and Interaction, p. 3. ACM (2015)
115. Xu, C., Li, C.: A flexible method for time-of-flight camera calibration using random forest. In: International Conference on Smart Multimedia, pp. 207–218. Springer (2018)
116. Xu, X., McGorry, R.W.: The validity of the first and second generation Microsoft Kinect for identifying joint center locations during static postures. Appl. Ergon. **49**, 47–54 (2015)

117. Yang, Q., Yang, R., Davis, J., Nister, D.: Spatial-depth super resolution for range images. In: 2007 IEEE Conference on Computer Vision and Pattern Recognition, pp. 1–8 (2007)
118. Yeung, L.F., Cheng, K.C., Fong, C.H., Lee, W.C., Tong, K.Y.: Evaluation of the Microsoft Kinect as a clinical assessment tool of body sway. Gait Post. **40**(4), 532–538 (2014)
119. Zabatani, A., Surazhsky, V., Sperling, E., Ben Moshe, S., Menashe, O., Silver, D.H., Karni, T., Bronstein, A.M., Bronstein, M.M., Kimmel, R.: Intel RealSense SR300 coded light depth camera. IEEE Trans. Pattern Anal. Mach. Intell. 1–1 (2019)
120. Zanuttigh, P., Marin, G., Dal Mutto, C., Dominio, F., Minto, L., Cortelazzo, G.M.: Calibration. In: Time-of-Flight and Structured Light Depth Cameras, pp. 117–159. Springer (2016)
121. Zanuttigh, P., Minto, L., Marin, G., Dominio, F., Cortelazzo, G.: Time-of-Flight and Structured Light Depth Cameras: Technology and Applications. Springer, Berlin (2016)
122. Zeisl, B., Pollefeys, M.: Structure-based auto-calibration of RGB-D sensors. In: 2016 IEEE International Conference on Robotics and Automation (ICRA), pp. 5076–5083 (2016)
123. Zhou, Q.Y., Koltun, V.: Simultaneous localization and calibration: Self-calibration of consumer depth cameras. In: Proceedings of the IEEE Conference on Computer Vision and Pattern Recognition, pp. 454–460 (2014)
124. Zollhöfer, M., Stotko, P., Görlitz, A., Theobalt, C., Nießner, M., Klein, R., Kolb, A.: State of the art on 3D reconstruction with RGB-D cameras. Comput. Graph. Forum **37**(2), 625–652 (2018)
125. Zuñiga-Noël, D., Ruiz-Sarmiento, J.R., Gonzalez-Jimenez, J.: Intrinsic calibration of depth cameras for mobile robots using a radial laser scanner. In: International Conference on Computer Analysis of Images and Patterns, pp. 659–671. Springer (2019)

Chapter 6
3D Data Representation, Storage and Processing

William A. P. Smith

Abstract In this chapter, we review methods for representing, storing and processing 3D data. We focus in particular on representations for raw 3D data, surface-based and solid-based models. We describe and compare various data structures available for representing triangular meshes and formats for mesh storage. We also provide details on three different subdivision schemes and explain how differential surface properties can be computed from different surface representations. In the context of data compression, we describe in detail the Quadric Error Metric algorithm for mesh simplification. Finally, we suggest areas for future work in this area and provide some concluding remarks.

6.1 Introduction

There is a wide range of 3D acquisition technologies and applications for 3D data. Perhaps not surprisingly, there are an equally wide number of systems for 3D data representation, compression, storage, search, manipulation and visualisation. 3D data representations serve as an intermediary between data acquisition and application, with constraints imposed from both sides.

In many cases, the method of acquisition dictates a specific native representation format. For example, classical stereo vision recovers disparity and hence depth values at each pixel and is therefore typically represented as a range image. On the other hand, the target application also imposes constraints on the method of representation. For example, certain operations are more efficient when a particular 3D representation is used. For this reason, it may be necessary to convert between representations, perhaps involving some level of approximation. In the case of graphics, representations may be different depending on whether the goal is physically accurate simulation of light transport [68] or real-time rendering for interactive applications [1].

W. A. P. Smith (✉)
Department of Computer Science, University of York, York YO10 5GH, UK
e-mail: william.smith@york.ac.uk

© Springer Nature Switzerland AG 2020
Y. Liu et al. (eds.), *3D Imaging, Analysis and Applications*,
https://doi.org/10.1007/978-3-030-44070-1_6

Examples of common 3D datasets range from the very small (molecules, microscopic tissue structures, 3D microstructures in materials science), to the human scale (3D human heart, 3D face, 3D body scans) to the large (3D modelling of buildings and landscapes) and beyond (3D modelling of astrophysical data). It is the scale, resolution and compression of this data that determines the volume of data stored. In turn, the challenges for storing, manipulating and visualising this data grow as the volume increases.

6.1.1 Overview

In this chapter, we provide an overview of how 3D data can be represented, stored and processed. We begin by providing a taxonomy of 3D data representations. We then delve in more detail into a selection of the most important 3D data representations. First, we focus on triangular meshes, describing the data structures available for efficiently processing such data. We take as an example the halfedge data structure and provide some implementation details. Second, we describe schemes for subdivision surfaces. Having considered methods for representing 3D data, we then discuss how local differential surface properties can be computed for the most common representation. Finally, we describe how 3D data can be compressed and simplified.

6.2 Representation of 3D Data

The representation of 3D data is the foundation of a number of important applications such as computer-aided geometric design, visualisation and graphics. In this section, we summarise various 3D representations which we classify as raw data (i.e. that is delivered by a 3D sensing device), surfaces (i.e. 2D manifolds embedded in 3D space) and solids (i.e. 3D objects with volume).

6.2.1 Raw Data

The raw output of a 3D sensor can take a number of forms, such as points, a depth map and polygons. Often, data represented in these raw forms requires further processing prior to analysis. Moreover, these representations may permit non-manifold or noisy surfaces to be represented which may hinder subsequent analysis.

6.2.1.1   Point Cloud

In its simplest form, 3D data exists as a set of unstructured three-dimensional coordinates called a *point cloud*, i.e. $P = \{\mathbf{v}_1, \ldots, \mathbf{v}_n\}$, where $\mathbf{v}_i \in \mathbb{R}^3$. Typically, a point cloud of n points is stored as an $n \times 3$ array of floating-point numbers or a linked list of n vertex records. Note that the ordering of the points is arbitrary so that any permutation of the point indices yields the same point cloud.

Point clouds arise most commonly in vision as the output of structure-from-motion (see [33] for general introduction or e.g. [78] for current state-of-the-art) or related techniques such as SLAM (simultaneous localisation and mapping) [82]. They also arise from laser range scanning devices, where the 3D positions of vertices lying along the intersection between a laser stripe and the surface are computed. Vertices may be augmented by additional information such as texture or, in the case of *oriented points*, a surface normal [41]. A visualisation of a point cloud is shown in Fig. 6.1a. A point cloud is unstructured. This means that there is no information about vertex connectivity, and hence no explicit notion of the underlying surface from which the points are sampled. This (usually unknown) sampling process results in a loss of information. It is not known how the captured points should be connected to approximate the surface and, depending on the sparsity of the sampling, parts of the surface may be missed or the genus changed by any possible triangulation. This makes further processing difficult. Local surface properties, such as the surface normal direction, can be estimated by assuming local planarity and fitting a plane to a given point and its k-nearest neighbours [36]. In other words, the k-nearest neighbours to a point are used as an approximation of the tangent plane at that point. This classical approach has subsequently been extended in many ways, see [6] for an up to date survey. Without requiring conversion to a surface-based representation, the direct rendering of vertex data (known as point-based rendering) has developed as a subfield within graphics which offers certain advantages over traditional polygon-based rendering [75].

Point clouds are ubiquitous and useful but lack structure. This is problematic when using them as input to machine learning systems such as deep neural networks. In particular, because they lack a regular grid structure, they cannot be used as input to a convolutional neural network without conversion to a different form with grid structure. Unfortunately, this conversion may introduce unwanted artefacts or involve making spurious assumptions. For this reason, there has been a lot of recent work on methods for supplying unstructured point cloud data to neural networks. Of particular note, PointNet [72] proposes an architecture for point cloud processing in which points are supplied and encoded in arbitrary order, respecting the permutation invariance of the representation. To extract global features from arbitrarily sized point clouds, pooling along point index dimension is performed.

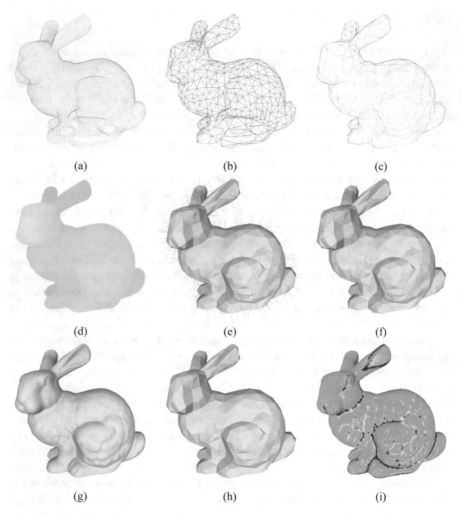

Fig. 6.1 Visualisation of different 3D representations: (**a**) point cloud, (**b**) wireframe, (**c**) wireframe with hidden surfaces removed, (**d**) depth map (brighter equals closer to the viewer), (**e**) vertex normals drawn in blue, (**f**) principal curvature directions drawn in red and blue, (**g**) smooth shaded, (**h**) flat shaded, (**i**) surface colour heat mapped to represent function value (in this case mean curvature)

6.2.1.2   Structured Point Cloud

A more constrained representation may be used when point cloud vertices adhere to an underlying structure, namely, a grid with arbitrary sampling. In this case, vertices are stored in an ordered $m \times n \times 3$ array and, for each point $i = 1, \ldots, m$, $j = 1, \ldots, n$, there is a corresponding 3D vertex $[x(i, j) \; y(i, j) \; z(i, j)]^T \in \mathbb{R}^3$. Moreover, the ordering of the points is such that adjacent vertices share adjacent

Fig. 6.2 Two of the possible
regular triangulations of a
3×3 grid. Note that the
single non-boundary vertex
has degree 6

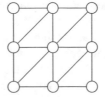 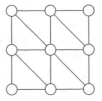

indices. There is an implicit mesh connectivity between neighbouring points, and non-boundary points are always degree 6. Conversion to a triangular mesh is straightforward, by constructing an edge between all pairs of adjacent vertices (and adding one of the two possible diagonals for each 2×2 neighbourhood). Two such triangulations are illustrated in Fig. 6.2.

Often, there is an additional binary 2D array of size $m \times n$ which indicates the presence or absence of 3D data (for example, parts of the surface being imaged may have poor reflectance). Instead of binary, a scalar "confidence" value can be stored providing an indication of measurement uncertainty at each point. Finally, a grayscale or colour texture image of the same dimensions may also be associated with the 3D data. In this case, the format provides an implicit correspondence between 2D pixels and 3D vertices, assuming that the 3D camera captures and stores such information. An example of a commonly used structured point cloud dataset is the 3D face images in the *Face Recognition Grand Challenge Version 2* data release [69].

6.2.1.3   Depth Maps and Range Images

A special case of a structured point cloud arises when the sampling of points in the x-y plane is viewer-centred, i.e. the 2D grid coordinates (i, j) are the result of a projection from 3D to 2D. Although often used interchangeably, we define a *range image* as a structured point cloud which arises from a perspective projection and a *depth map* as an orthogonal projection and regular sampling of 3D vertices over a 2D image plane. Both representations have the advantage that they can be represented by a 2D function $z(i, j)$ augmented by the projection parameters. Hence, these representations require less storage than those which allow variable spacing of points in the (x, y) plane and can effectively be stored (and compressed) as an image. In the case of a depth map, the only additional information required to reconstruct 3D vertex position is the fixed spacings, Δ_x and Δ_y (often $\Delta_x = \Delta_y = 1$, implying that the z values are in units of pixels). In the case of a range image, parameters related to the camera projection (e.g. focal length and centre of projection) must also be stored. Depth maps and range images can be visualised as greyscale images, whereby image intensity represents the distance to the surface (see Fig. 6.1d). Alternatively, they can be converted into a triangular mesh and rendered. Since the vertices are evenly distributed over the image plane, a regular triangulation can be used. Range images are the natural representations of binocular stereo [77] where, for each pixel, a disparity value is calculated which is related to depth. In addition, range images are often computed as an intermediate representation as part of the rendering pipeline. Here, they are used for z-buffering and to efficiently simulate many visual effects such as depth of field and atmospheric attenuation. Range images are the format supplied by depth cameras such as Microsoft Kinect [98] or Intel RealSense [42]. For this reason, they are in wide use in the now popular field of RGBD computer vision. The conversion from pixel coordinates (i, j) and depth value $z(i, j)$ in a range image to 3D point $P(i, j) \in \mathbb{R}^3$ in camera-centred coordinates is achieved via

$$P(i, j) = \begin{bmatrix} \frac{i-c_x}{f} z(i, j) \\ \frac{j-c_y}{f} z(i, j) \\ z(i, j) \end{bmatrix}, \tag{6.1}$$

where f is the focal length and (c_x, c_y) the principal point of the camera.

Depth maps and range images are stored in regular grids, just like conventional RGB images. This means that they can be supplied as input to convolutional neural networks or produced as the output from fully convolutional networks [52]. This has led to an explosion of interest in 3D deep learning using depth map-based representations. For example, a state-of-the-art method [50] estimates a range image from a single RGB image using supervised learning. The supervision labels are depth maps. These are estimated by a structure-from-motion and multiview stereo pipeline applied to unstructured image collections.

6.2.1.4 Normal Map

Photometric shape reconstruction methods often recover an intermediate representation comprising per-pixel estimates of the orientation of the underlying surface. In graphics, this is known as a *bump map*. This is either in the form of surface gradients, i.e. $p(x, y) = \partial_x z(x, y)$ and $q(x, y) = \partial_y z(x, y)$, or surface normals, i.e. $\mathbf{n}(x, y) = [-p(x, y) \ -q(x, y) \ 1]^T$. A normal map can be rendered by using a reflectance function to locally shade each pixel. Alternatively, a depth map can be estimated from surface normals via a process known as *surface integration* (see [73] for a recent survey and [31] for a state-of-the-art approach with publicly available source code). This is a difficult problem when the surface normal estimates are noisy or subject to bias. When augmented with (potentially lower resolution) depth estimates, the two sources of information can be combined to make a robust estimate of the surface using an efficient algorithm due to Nehab et al. [61]. This approach is particularly suitable where the depth map is subject to high-frequency noise (e.g. from errors in stereo correspondence) and the surface normals subject to low-frequency bias (e.g. when using photometric stereo with inaccurate light source directions). Normal maps are sometimes computed in rendering during the rasterisation process and referred to as normal buffers. This is useful in deferred shading [76] where the rendered image is computed in screen space in one pass after the rasterisation process. This is in contrast to conventional rasterisation where the image is rendered at the same time as rasterisation.

Often, normal maps are used to store high-frequency shape information to accompany geometry stored as a mesh. Here, the normal map no longer corresponds to a projection of the surface to 2D but uses an embedding of the 3D surface into a 2D texture space. The resolution of the normal map may be much higher than the number of vertices in the mesh, and the surface normals can be used during rendering to simulate having higher resolution geometry.

6.2.1.5 Polygon Soup

A polygon soup is in some senses analogous to point cloud data but comprises polygons rather than vertices. More precisely, it is a set of unstructured polygons [60], each of which connects vertices together but which is not themselves connected in a coherent structure such as a mesh. Such models may arise in an interactive modelling system where a user creates and places polygons into a scene without specifying how the polygons connect to each other. This sort of data may contain errors such as inconsistently oriented polygons; intersecting, overlapping or missing polygons; cracks (shared edges not represented as such); or T-junctions. This causes problems for many applications including rendering, collision detection, finite-element analysis and solid modelling operations. To create a closed surface, a surface fitting algorithm must be applied to the unstructured polygons. For example, Shen et al. [80] show how to fit an implicit surface to polygon soup data.

6.2.2 Surface Representations

The vast majority of geometric algorithms in computer vision and graphics operate on representations of 3D data based on surfaces. Of these representations, by far the most common is the triangular mesh. For this reason, we focus in more detail on this representation in Sect. 6.3. For many applications in *Computer-Aided Design* (CAD), it is necessary to be able to guarantee a certain class of surface smoothness. For example, this may relate to aerodynamic or aesthetic requirements. Smoothness can be categorised according to *differentiability class*. A surface belongs to class $\mathbb{C}^0$ if it is continuous (i.e. the surface or function value changes smoothly). The class $\mathbb{C}^1$ consists of all surfaces that are differentiable and whose derivative is continuous (i.e. the surface normal changes smoothly), while $\mathbb{C}^2$ surfaces have continuous second derivatives (i.e. the surface curvature changes smoothly). A representation which can provide such guarantees, as well as providing a convenient interface for interactive editing is subdivision surfaces. We focus in more detail on this representation in Sect. 6.4. Here, we give a brief overview of alternative surface representations and provide a comparison of the desirable features exhibited by each representation.

6.2.2.1 Triangular Mesh

The most common surface representation comprises 3D vertices, connected together to form triangular faces which in turn represent or approximate a 2D manifold embedded in 3D space. A number of categorisations are possible here. An important distinction is whether the mesh is closed (i.e. the surface completely encloses a volume) or open (i.e. the mesh contains "boundary" edges which are used by only one triangle). Meshes can represent surfaces with different genera. The *genus* of a surface is an integer representing the maximum number of cuttings along non-intersecting closed simple curves without rendering the resultant manifold disconnected. For example, a sphere has genus zero, whilst a torus has genus 1. An important property of a triangle is that it has a single surface normal. When a mesh is used to approximate a curved surface, the differential properties of the surface, such as normals and curvature, can only be approximately computed from the mesh faces. Mesh storage and representation is discussed in more detail in Sect. 6.3.

Often, meshes are augmented with *texture coordinates*, also known as UV coordinates [34]. These are most often 2D coordinates which describe a mapping from the surface to a 2D planar parameterisation. 1D, 3D (volumetric) and 4D (volumetric plus time) texture coordinates are also occasionally used. 2D texture coordinates range over the unit square, $(u, v) \in [0, 1] \times [0, 1]$ and associate with each triangle a corresponding triangle in texture space. For a triangle mesh containing N vertices and M triangles, the number of vertex coordinates lies between N and $3M$ (in the former case, vertices that are shared between triangles in the mesh are shared between the same triangles in the texture space; in the latter case no vertices are shared). RGB intensity (known as texture maps), surface normals (known as bump maps) or 3D displacements (known as displacement maps) are stored as images which are indexed by the texture coordinates. When rendering a polygonal mesh, texture within the interior of polygons can be looked up by interpolating the texture coordinates of the vertices of the polygon. Transforming an arbitrary mesh to a 2D parameterisation with minimal distortion is a difficult problem [79].

6.2.2.2 Quadrilateral Mesh

The polygons in a mesh need not be triangular. Meshes may contain polygons of arbitrary shape and number of vertices, though non-planar polygons will require additional processing for rendering (e.g. to interpolate surface normal direction over the polygon). One commonly used polygon mesh is based on quadrilateral polygons (sometimes known as a *quadmesh*). Quadmeshes can be easily converted to a triangular mesh by diagonally subdividing each quadrilateral. Quadrilateral meshes are preferred to triangular meshes in a number of circumstances. One example is when finite-element analysis is used to simulate surface deformation such as in automobile crash simulation or sheet-metal forming. In these cases, the solution accuracy is improved by using a quadmesh.

6.2.2.3   Subdivision Surface

Subdivision surfaces are used to represent a smooth surface using a low-resolution base mesh and a subdivision rule (or *refinement scheme*). When applied recursively, the subdivided surface tends towards the smooth surface. The *limit* subdivision surface is the surface produced when the refinement scheme is iteratively applied infinitely many times. The limit surface can be computed directly for most subdivision surfaces without the need to evaluate the iterative refinement. This allows a subdivision surface to be rendered without explicitly subdividing the original base mesh. We describe a number of subdivision schemes in Sect. 6.4.

6.2.2.4   3D Morphable Model

A space-efficient representation which can be used to approximate members of a class of surfaces (such as human faces [8] or automobiles [49]) is the *morphable model*. This is a compact statistical representation learnt from training samples. A mesh of N vertices may be written as a long vector: $\mathbf{s} = [x_1 \ y_1 \ z_1 \ \cdots \ x_N \ y_N \ z_N]^T$. From a sample of such meshes which are in dense correspondence (i.e. the ith vertex in each mesh corresponds to a point with the same meaning, such as the tip of the nose) a mean vector, $\bar{\mathbf{s}}$, and a set of orthonormal basis vectors, $\mathbf{e}_1, \ldots, \mathbf{e}_k \in \mathbb{R}^{3N}$, are derived using Principal Components Analysis (PCA). These vectors correspond to the most common modes of variation within the training data, and they are sorted by the variance captured by each mode, $\sigma_1 > \cdots > \sigma_k$. Hence, only the most important modes need to be retained to explain a large portion of the variance in the training data, i.e. klN. Any member of the class of objects can be approximated as a linear combination of the mean vector and the principal modes of variation:

$$\mathbf{s} = \mathbf{Pb} + \bar{\mathbf{s}}, \tag{6.2}$$

where $\mathbf{P} = [\mathbf{e}_1 | \ldots | \mathbf{e}_k] \in \mathbb{R}^{3N \times k}$ is the matrix formed by stacking the basis vectors and $\mathbf{b} \in \mathbb{R}^k$ is a vector of weights associated with each mode. The advantage of such a representation is that the high-dimensional mesh can be approximated by the low-dimensional parameter vector. Moreover, the parameter space is useful for recognition and classification, and the modes themselves often correspond to meaningful global descriptors. For example, in Fig. 6.3 we show a morphable model of human faces. The first mode appears to capture the difference between adult and child faces. A morphable model is limited to representing objects from within the same class as the training data. The ability of the model to generalise to unseen samples is characterised by the *generalisation error* which is a function of the diversity of the training samples. There is also an implicit assumption that the original high-dimensional data approximates a Gaussian distribution (hyperellipsoid) which can be accurately approximated by a small number of axes. Note that the mean shape and principal components are dependent on how the original shapes are rigidly aligned. Usually, this is done using generalised Procrustes analysis [29] but a recent nonlin-

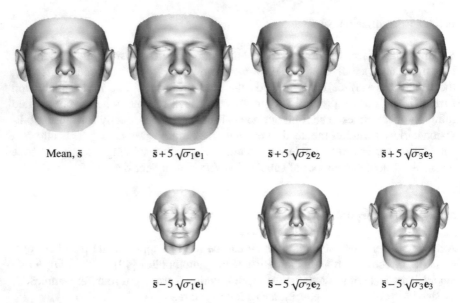

Mean, $\bar{\mathbf{s}}$ $\bar{\mathbf{s}}+5\sqrt{\sigma_1}\mathbf{e}_1$ $\bar{\mathbf{s}}+5\sqrt{\sigma_2}\mathbf{e}_2$ $\bar{\mathbf{s}}+5\sqrt{\sigma_3}\mathbf{e}_3$

$\bar{\mathbf{s}}-5\sqrt{\sigma_1}\mathbf{e}_1$ $\bar{\mathbf{s}}-5\sqrt{\sigma_2}\mathbf{e}_2$ $\bar{\mathbf{s}}-5\sqrt{\sigma_3}\mathbf{e}_3$

Fig. 6.3 A 3D morphable model of human faces [65]. The top left panel shows the mean face surface. The remainder shows the mean face deformed by ±5 standard deviations along the first three principal modes of variation

ear approach is able to build principal component shape models that are invariant to rigid body motion of the training shapes [35]. The parametric representation of a morphable model makes an ideal interface for the fixed size output of a deep neural network [4]. 3D morphable models are introduced and described in more detail in Chap. 10.

6.2.2.5 Implicit Surface

An implicit surface [9] (also known as a *level set* or an *isosurface*) is the set of all points $[x\ y\ z]^T$ which satisfy the function $f(x, y, z) = 0$. Typically, function values greater than zero indicate a point which is outside the object, while negative values indicate a point which is inside; this is known as a *signed distance function* (SDF). For example, the surface of a sphere of radius 5 can be represented by the set of points satisfying $x^2 + y^2 + z^2 - 25 = 0$. The surface normal to an implicit surface can be obtained simply by taking partial derivatives:

$$\mathbf{n}(x, y, z) = \left[\partial_x f(x, y, z)\ \partial_y f(x, y, z)\ \partial_z f(x, y, z)\right]^T. \tag{6.3}$$

Inside/outside tests can also be performed efficiently by simply evaluating the sign of the surface function at a given point. One of the most attractive properties of the implicit surface representation is that intersections can be computed analytically. By

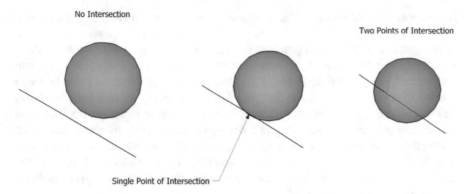

No Intersection

Two Points of Intersection

Single Point of Intersection

Fig. 6.4 The three possible cases for a line–sphere intersection

substituting a parametric ray equation into the implicit surface function and solving for the parameter, all intersections can be found exactly. For example, consider the ray described by

$$
\begin{bmatrix} x \\ y \\ z \end{bmatrix} = \begin{bmatrix} x_0 \\ y_0 \\ z_0 \end{bmatrix} + t \begin{bmatrix} a \\ b \\ c \end{bmatrix}. \tag{6.4}
$$

Substituting into the parametric surface for the radius 5 sphere given above yields

$$
t = \frac{-2(a+b+c) \pm \sqrt{(2a+2b+2c)^2 - 4(a^2+b^2+c^2)(x_0^2+y_0^2+z_0^2-25)}}{2(a^2+b^2+c^2)}. \tag{6.5}
$$

There are three possible cases for this intersection (see Fig. 6.4). Two real roots means that the ray intersects the sphere in two places. One real root means the ray touches the sphere tangentially. No real roots means the ray misses the surface. Higher order surfaces involve the solution of higher order intersection equations which may not be possible analytically.

In general, obtaining a function which exactly describes a general surface is difficult. However, for applications involving visualisation of physical effects such as fluid dynamics (where functional descriptions of the dynamics are readily available) an implicit surface is a natural representation. There are a number of commonly used ways to define an implicit surface. The example above is algebraic. The most common such form is a quadric which can be used to describe regular shapes such as spheres, ellipsoids and tori.

An alternative is to derive an algebraic representation from an intermediate representation [10] which is specified by a designer or fitted to data. The most common approach is to define a control structure from primitives such as points, line segments and planar patches. A field function is defined which is determined by the distance, r, from a point to a control structure. For example, $f(r) = \frac{1}{r^2}$. The value of this function is known as the *field strength*. The total field strength is the sum of the field strengths due to each control structure. Distances to line segments and planes are usually taken as the distance to the closest point on the structure. A single point yields a sphere whose radius is determined by the chosen contour value. Where there are more than one control point, the fields interact and the resulting isosurface bulges between points. Approaches along these lines are known variously as *metaballs*, *blobbies* and *soft objects*. Rendering isosurfaces for display is not straightforward. The most common approach is to converting to a polygonal model [11]. Alternatives include raytracing the surface [32] (which involves computing ray–surface intersections as described above) or using point sampling and point-based rendering. A particularly popular implicit surface representation for interpolation of missing parts of surfaces is the *Radial Basis Function* [14].

Very recently, implicit surfaces, specifically SDFs, have been rediscovered in the context of 3D shape modelling using deep neural networks. Initially, this was done by discretising SDFs over voxels [19, 87, 97]. However, the use of discrete voxels leads to very large memory requirements and networks with very large numbers of parameters, while the discretisation leads to low-quality shape representations. Very recently, continuous SDFs have been represented using the decision boundary of a deep network itself. Essentially, a shape represented by an SDF is encoded by a deep network that maps a point in $\mathbb{R}^3$ to a probability that the point is inside the object. Since deep neural networks are very effective at learning highly nonlinear decision boundaries, this provides an ideal representation for complex shape variations. This idea was proposed almost simultaneously as DeepSDF [64], Occupancy Networks [56], Deep Level Sets [58] and Learnt Implicit Fields [16].

6.2.2.6 Parametric Surface

A parametric surface [23] $\mathbf{x}(u, v) = [x(u, v), y(u, v), z(u, v)]^T$ is one which is defined by a parametric equation, $\mathbf{x} : \mathbb{R}^2 \mapsto \mathbb{R}^3$, with two parameters, u and v. For example, the radius 5 sphere example given above can be described in terms of spherical coordinate parameters:

$$\mathbf{x}(u, v) = \begin{bmatrix} 5 \sin u \cos v \\ 5 \sin u \sin v \\ 5 \cos u \end{bmatrix}. \tag{6.6}$$

A surface in such a form is easy to evaluate and, if the parametric equations are differentiable, it is straightforward to calculate differential properties of the surface. The problem is that it is very difficult to describe anything other than fairly simple shapes using an algebraic parametric description. For this reason, complex shapes are composed of piecewise parametric surfaces. These parametric patches are blended together to obtain the overall surface, and each patch is defined in terms of a set of control points over the unit square. To evaluate a parametric patch at a point, the tensor product of parametric curves defined by the control points is computed. This is achieved by combining control points with polynomial blending functions. Most commonly, these are order 3 (bicubic) functions for which $(3 + 1) \times (3 + 1) = 16$ coefficients are needed to define the function. These are usually defined in terms of a 4×4 grid of control points. The function can be written compactly in matrix form as

$$\mathbf{x}(u, v) = \begin{bmatrix} x(u, v) \\ y(u, v) \\ z(u, v) \end{bmatrix} = \begin{bmatrix} \mathbf{uMG}_x\mathbf{M}^T\mathbf{v}^T \\ \mathbf{uMG}_y\mathbf{M}^T\mathbf{v}^T \\ \mathbf{uMG}_z\mathbf{M}^T\mathbf{v}^T \end{bmatrix}, \tag{6.7}$$

where $\mathbf{u} = [u^3 \ u^2 \ u \ 1]$ and $\mathbf{v} = [v^3 \ v^2 \ v \ 1]$ and

$$\mathbf{G}_x = \begin{bmatrix} P_{1,1}^x & P_{1,2}^x & P_{1,3}^x & P_{1,4}^x \\ P_{2,1}^x & P_{2,2}^x & P_{2,3}^x & P_{2,4}^x \\ P_{3,1}^x & P_{3,2}^x & P_{3,3}^x & P_{3,4}^x \\ P_{4,1}^x & P_{4,2}^x & P_{4,3}^x & P_{4,4}^x \end{bmatrix}, \tag{6.8}$$

contains the x coordinates of the control points (i.e. $P_{i,j}^x$ is the x coordinate of the control point at position i, j in the control point grid), similarly for y and z. The matrix $\mathbf{M}$ describes a blending function for a parametric cubic curve. Two common examples include B-spline:

$$\mathbf{M}_{\text{B-Spline}} = \begin{bmatrix} \frac{-1}{6} & \frac{1}{2} & \frac{-1}{2} & \frac{1}{6} \\ \frac{1}{2} & -1 & \frac{1}{2} & 0 \\ \frac{-1}{2} & 0 & \frac{1}{2} & 0 \\ \frac{1}{6} & \frac{2}{3} & \frac{1}{6} & 0 \end{bmatrix}, \tag{6.9}$$

and Bézier:

$$\mathbf{M}_{\text{Bezier}} = \begin{bmatrix} -1 & 3 & -3 & 1 \\ 3 & -6 & 3 & 0 \\ -3 & 3 & 0 & 0 \\ 1 & 0 & 0 & 0 \end{bmatrix}. \tag{6.10}$$

Bézier patches have some useful properties. The patch will lie completely within the convex hull of its control points, and the Bézier surface will pass through the control points at the corner of the patch. It does not generally pass through the other control points. They are visually intuitive and popular in interactive editing applications for this reason. An example of a Bézier patch is shown in Fig. 6.5. To achieve $\mathbb{C}^0$ continuity between adjacent patches, the boundary control points (and hence boundary curve) must be aligned. $\mathbb{C}^1$ continuity is achieved by aligning the boundary curve and derivatives. This requires that four sets of three control points must be collinear.

An extremely useful generalisation of B-splines and Bézier surfaces is *Non-uniform Rational B-Splines* (NURBS) [70, 74]. The distribution of control points in a NURBS surface may be non-uniform. They are invariant to affine and perspec-

Fig. 6.5 A Bézier surface
patch. Control points are
shown in red, the control grid
in blue and the resulting
surface in black

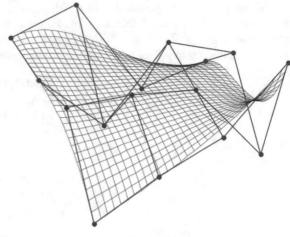

Fig. 6.6 An example
NURBS surface patch

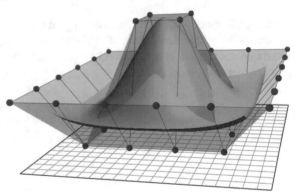

tive transformations which means that such transformations can be applied to the
control points to obtain the same surface as applying the transformation to the surface computed from the original control points. A NURBS surface is defined by
its *order*, a weighted set of *control points* and a *knot vector*. A point on a NURBS
surface is given by a weighted sum of a number of control points (usually only a
small subset) determined by a polynomial blending function. The parameter space
is divided up into intervals, and a control point only influences certain intervals.
This results in the desirable property of *local support* which means one part of the
surface can be adjusted without influencing others. The knot vector is a sequence of
parameter values which determine how and where a control point affects the NURBS
surface. The order of a NURBS surface determines the number of nearby control
points which influence a point on the surface. The NURBS surface is a unifying
representation which offers a single mathematical form for both standard analytical
shapes (e.g. conics) and free-form surfaces (Fig. 6.6).

Table 6.1 Comparison of surface representations

	Polygonal mesh	Subdivision surface	Morphable model	Implicit surface	Parametric surface
Accuracy	✗	✔	✗	✔	✔
Space-efficiency	✗	✔	✔	✔	✔
Display efficiency	✔	✔	✔	✗	✔
Intersection efficiency	✗	✗	✗	✔	✗
Intuitive specification	✗	✗	✔	✗	✔
Ease of editing	✗	✔	✔	✗	✗
Arbitrary topology	✔	✔	✗	✗	✗
Guaranteed continuity	✗	✔	✗	✔	✔

6.2.2.7 Comparison of Surface Representations

The best choice of surface representation is application dependent. Table 6.1 summarises some of the broad strengths and weaknesses of the surface representations discussed above. Generally speaking, polygonal meshes are the most widely used representation and the standard rendering pipeline, such as OpenGL, is optimised for their use. Subdivision surfaces are popular in animation and interactive editing applications. Parametric surfaces are widely used in CAD as are implicit surfaces which also find use in mathematical or scientific applications.

6.2.3 Solid-Based Representations

Solid-based representations are used where either the method of acquisition is volumetric in nature or where the application dictates a requirement for solid-based computations and manipulations. For example, consider the simple problem of wishing to compute the volume of a 3D object. If the object was stored, for example, as a closed surface represented using a mesh, there is no simple way in which this can be calculated. Using some of the solid-based representations described in this section, this is trivial. Common areas of application for solid-based representations include

1. **Medical imaging** [84]: Imaging modalities such as MRI and CT are volumetric in nature. Analysing and visualising such data necessitates volumetric representations.

2. **Engineering**: Components must be designed not only so that they fit together but so that their structural properties (determined by their 3D shape) meet specifications.
3. **Scientific visualisation** [62]: Volumetric data arises in fields ranging from oceanography to particle physics. In order for humans to interact with and draw inferences from such data, it must be possible to visualise it in a meaningful way.
4. **Finite-element analysis** [99]: A numerical technique for finding approximate solution of partial differential equations and integrals.
5. **Stereolithography** [3]: A process in which an ultraviolet laser is used to trace out cross sections through a 3D object, building up layers of resin until a complete object has been fabricated, commonly known as "3D printing".
6. **Interference fit** [48]: Designing object shapes so that two parts can be held together by friction alone.

Solids can either be represented volumetrically or by the surface which encloses them. In this section, we summarise the most common solid-based representations.

6.2.3.1 Voxels

Voxels are the 3D analogue of pixels (the name is a contraction of "volumetric pixel"). They are sometimes also referred to as a *spatial occupancy enumeration*. Each voxel corresponds to a small cubic volume within space. At each voxel, a boolean is stored which indicates the presence or absence of the volume at that point. Alternatively, it may be more appropriate to store a scalar which represents, for example, density at that point in the volume. The precision of the representation is determined by the size of the voxel. A voxel representation is very efficient for making volumetric calculations such as clearance checking. Data storage requirements are high, since the number of voxels grows cubically with the resolution along each dimension. Voxels are the natural representation for volumetric imaging modalities. This is where the sensing device measures surface properties at discrete spatial locations over a 3D volume. Common examples include Magnetic Resonance Imaging (MRI) and Computed Tomography (CT). In vision, volumetric representations are also appropriate for methods such as space carving [46] where image cues are used to determine whether a voxel lies within the volume of an object.

There are two common ways to visualise voxel data: direct volume rendering or conversion to polygonal surface for traditional mesh rendering. In direct volume rendering, voxels are projected to a 2D view plane and drawn from back to front using an appropriate colour and opacity for every voxel. Such visualisations allow multiple layered surfaces to be visualised simultaneously (often exploited in medical imaging where skin, soft tissue and bone can all be visualised in the same image). Conversion to a polygonal mesh requires extraction of an isosurface of equal surface value throughout the volume. The most commonly used approach for this purpose is the *marching cubes* algorithm of Lorensen and Cline [54]. The algorithm proceeds by examining cubes formed by eight neighbouring voxels. Each of the eight scalar

Fig. 6.7 The eight voxels produced by an octree voxel subdivision

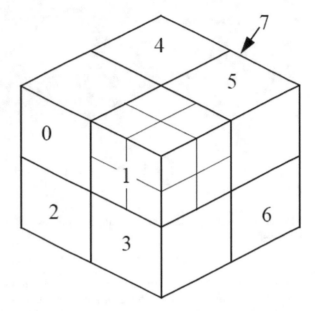

values is treated as a bit in an 8-bit integer. If a scalar value is higher than the iso-value (i.e. inside the surface), it is set to one; otherwise, it is set to zero. Hence, there are $2^8 = 256$ possible configurations. The 8-bit integer is used to access a lookup table which stores a polygon associated with each voxel configuration. The individual polygons are then fused to form a surface.

Like depth maps and range images, voxel representations have the advantage that they are stored in a regular grid structure (with three spatial dimensions rather than two in this case). This means that they can be used as input to or output from a convolutional neural network and, as for depth maps, there has been an explosion of interest in working with such data using deep learning. In fact, often surface-based representations are converted to volumetric representations solely for the purpose of enabling the use of deep learning. This has led to significant performance improvements [18] on tasks such as semantic voxel labelling, 3D object classification and CAD model retrieval.

A space-efficient representation for voxel data is the *octree*. This uses adaptive resolution depending on the complexity of the surface throughout the volume. The key idea is that voxels which are fully occupied or fully empty are not subdivided, while partially occupied voxels are. This continues until either all voxels are occupied or empty, or the smallest allowable voxel size is reached. Subdividing a voxel into smaller cubes results in eight smaller voxels (see Fig. 6.7). This representation can be stored in a tree structure in which nodes have eight children. Leaves are fully occupied or empty voxels; the root represents the complete volume in which the object lies. The finest resolution is determined by the depth of the tree. The example shown in Fig. 6.8 demonstrates how in regions of high curvature, subdivision can continue to obtain an arbitrarily high accuracy approximation to the underlying smooth volume. Deep

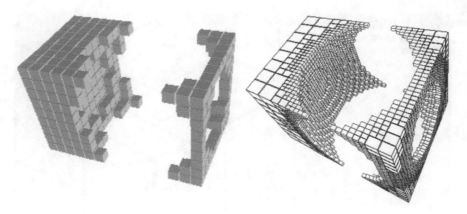

Fig. 6.8 A volume represented using equally sized voxels (left) and the octree adaptive representation (right)

learning architectures for volumetric data have been adapted to work with octrees [90]. A two-dimensional analogue of the octree representation in which pixels are recursively subdivided into four smaller pixels can be stored in a quadtree.

6.2.3.2 K-D Trees

K-d trees (short for *K-dimensional tree*) generalise the notion of space partitioning to arbitrary, axis-aligned planes. Whereas the octree uses a regular subdivision of space, a K-d tree is a data structure whose interior nodes represent a partition of space along a plane which is orthogonal to one of the axes. A K-d tree is stored in a binary tree where interior nodes represent a partition over an axis-aligned plane, and leaf nodes represent a volume in space. As well as a volumetric representation for shape, K-d trees are widely used for organising points to speed up multidimensional search [5], such as nearest neighbour.

For example, Fig. 6.9 shows a K-d tree constructed over a three-dimensional volume (initially comprising the white boxed region). The first subdivision is shown by the red plane. Each of the two subdivided regions is then split by the green planes, and finally the blue planes yield eight leaf volumes. The canonical method is of construction cycles through the axes of the space, subdividing along each in turn before returning to the first again. So in the example in Fig. 6.9, the next partitions would be parallel to the red plane. The position of the partitioning is chosen by the median point within the volume along the axis of partitioning. This strategy leads to balanced trees in which each leaf node is at the same depth ($\log n$ for a tree that partitions n points).

Practically, to build a K-d tree over a set of n points in k dimensions first, the points are pre-sorted along each dimension. Using an efficient sorting algorithm, this has complexity $O(kn \log n)$. By maintaining the order of these pre-sorted lists, the

Fig. 6.9   A 3D example of a
K-d tree

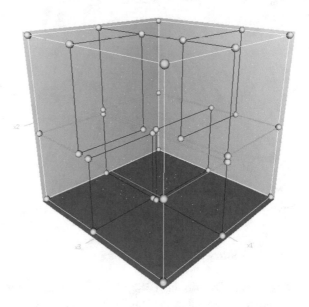

median at each partition can be computed in constant time, and constructing the tree
has complexity $O(n)$. Nearest neighbour search on a K-d tree is performed by binary
searching the tree using the input point position. The leaf node point becomes the
initial estimate of the nearest neighbour. This is updated as the algorithm unwinds
back up the tree, checking whether the point at each node is closer to the target and
also whether the other branch of the tree needs checking based on a simple rule. If
the K-d tree is balanced, this operation has complexity $O(\log n)$.

   K-d trees provide a way of reducing the complexity of nearest neighbour searches
or distance-based segmentation. For example, in the problem of range searching, the
aim is to find all vertices which lie within a certain Euclidean distance of a target
vertex (i.e. within a sphere centred on the target vertex with a radius given by the
distance threshold). This is an important problem for computing local features and
properties on surfaces. The brute force approach requires computation of the distance
between the target vertex and all others. With a K-d tree, the volume in which the
vertex lies can be found and only the distance to points within that volume need be
considered. The overhead of constructing the tree becomes worthwhile when many
such operations need to be performed. Note that for general range searching over a
surface, the use of a distance threshold will fail for complex, highly curved surfaces
(where Euclidean and geodesic distances vary greatly). In this case, it is necessary
to consider vertex connectivity to ensure only connected regions of the surface are
returned. This is discussed further in the next section.

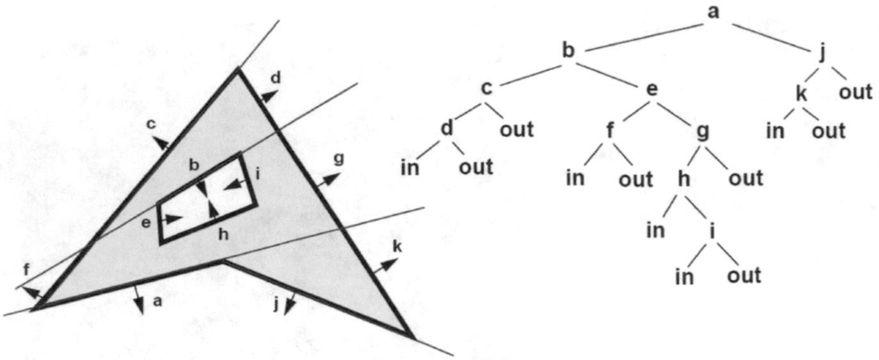

Fig. 6.10 A 2D example of a Binary Space Partitioning tree

6.2.3.3 Binary Space Partitioning

Binary Space Partitioning (BSP) further generalises the notion of space partitioning to arbitrary subdivisions, i.e. unlike the k-d tree, the cutting planes can be any orientation; thus, a k-d tree is an axis-aligned BSP tree. A volume (or in 2D, an area) is represented by a series of binary tests determining which side of a plane (or in 2D, a line) a point lies on. This representation leads to a binary tree structure with the leaf nodes indicating whether a point lies inside or outside the volume and branching at nodes representing the outcome of the binary test. This is a simple and elegant representation on which boolean operations and point classifications are easy to compute, though it potentially results in a high memory overhead. The representation was first proposed by Fuchs et al. [25] and is a popular representation in graphics calculating visible triangles from arbitrary viewpoints.

Each node stores the parameters of a plane and its outward-facing normal. Given a query point, at each node, an in/out test for the point is made and depending on the result of the test, the search recurses either left or right. When the search hits a leaf node, the final in/out classification can be returned. Algorithms for constructing BSP trees must make a choice of partitioning plane at each node and decide when to terminate the tree. These choices depend upon the intended application for the tree.

In Fig. 6.10 we provide an example of a BSP tree. In this case the tree operates in 2D, and hence the binary tests determine which side of each line a point lies and the resulting object is a 2D area. In this example, branching right signifies being outside the object, and left is inside. In/out classifications are stored at leaf nodes.

6.2.3.4 Constructive Solid Geometry

Constructive Solid Geometry (CSG) [47] is a representation of solid objects based on compositions of simple primitive solids. They are combined using boolean set operations. The primitives and operations can be stored efficiently in a binary tree

Fig. 6.11 An example of a
CSG object represented by a
binary tree of operations and
primitives

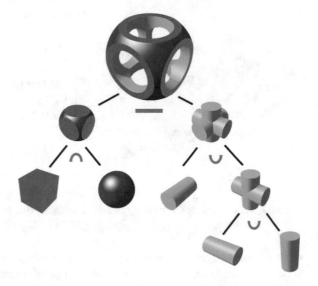

in which the leaves contain primitives, nodes contain operators and the represented object lies at the root. Figure 6.11 shows an example of a complex solid constructed from a small number of primitives and operations. The CSG representation is intuitive and relates well to CAD interfaces. However, representing arbitrary solids in this way can prove inefficient. In the context of 3D imaging, CSG can be useful for applications with "humans in the loop". For example, in content-based retrieval, a human must be able to construct a coarse 3D model with which to search. Another example is fitting a part-based model to 3D data (such as body parts to human motion data). In this case, the parts can be constructed by a human using CSG. Finally, for indexing 3D data, a very low-dimensional description of an object can be obtained by fitting a CSG model to the 3D data and comparing similarity by comparing CSG trees.

6.2.3.5   Boundary Representations

Boundary representations (known as *b-reps*) [86] describe solids by defining the boundary between solid and non-solid. They are widely used in computer-aided design. B-reps are composed of two parts. The first is the *topology*. This describes how the surface elements are connected and is specified in terms of faces, edges and vertices. See Fig. 6.12 for example. The second part is the *geometry* which specifies the shape of a face, edge or vertex in terms of surfaces, curves and points. A face is associated with a bounded portion of a surface and an edge with a bounded piece of a curve. The topology of a b-rep is stored in a data structure, most commonly the *winged-edge* which stores a face, edge and vertex table. Each edge stores pointers to its two vertices, the two faces adjacent to the edge and the four edges adjacent to both the edge and the adjacent faces. Each vertex and face stores a pointer to one

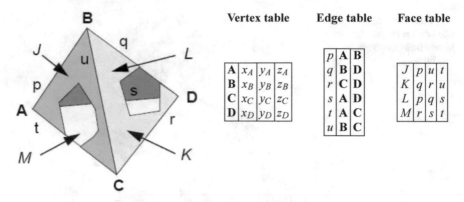

Fig. 6.12 An example of the topology of a solid described by a b-rep

of its adjacent edges. Adjacency relationship can therefore be computed in constant time. Compared to CSG representations, b-reps are more flexible and have a richer operation set.

6.2.3.6 Volumetric Mesh Representations

While triangle and quad meshes can be used to represent surfaces, it is also possible to represent volumes using mesh representations. The analogues of triangle and quad meshes for volumes are tetrahedral and hexahedral meshes (also called tet and hex meshes). A tetrahedron is a 3D shape formed of three triangles. A hexahedron is any 3D polyhedron with six faces, of which a cube is the canonical example. Figure 6.13 shows a hollow cylinder and cuboid represented as both hex and tet meshes.

6.2.4 Summary of Solid-Based Representations

The method of acquisition of 3D data determines in which of the raw representations the data is delivered. Although some operations are possible on such data (for example, point-based rendering of point clouds), most applications necessitate conversion to a higher level representation. This may require a degree of approximation (for example, integrating a depth map from surface normal data).

The choice between surface-based and solid-based representations is dictated by the nature of the data and the intended application. On the other hand, certain representations are amenable to creation and editing by hand, for example, by an animator or CAD designer. The requirements here may include ease and intuition of editing operations and guarantees about the nature of the resulting surface, such as smoothness. Other factors which may influence the choice of representation include

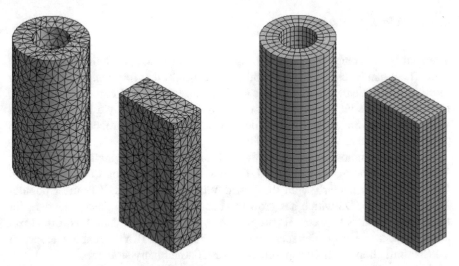

Fig. 6.13 A hollow cylinder and cuboid represented by tetrahedral (left) and hexahedral (right) meshes

storage and processing efficiency, representational power (e.g. some representations can only describe surfaces which are manifolds or continuous) and the efficiency with which the representation can be rendered for visualisation.

6.3 Polygon Meshes

Polygonal meshes are of such importance and are used so ubiquitously throughout computer graphics and vision that we provide a more in-depth discussion of the file formats and data structures available for their storage and representation. We focus particularly on triangular meshes, though the representations extend naturally to quad or arbitrary polygon meshes.

Formally, a triangular mesh of N vertices is defined as a pair: $M^N = (K^N, \mathbf{S})$. The topology, or connectivity, of the mesh is given by the *simplicial complex* K^N. A simplicial complex is a set of *simplices*, which in turn are generalisations of the notion of a triangle to arbitrary dimensions. A k-simplex is a polytope in k dimensions. So, a 0-simplex is a point, a 1-simplex is a line segment, a 2-simplex is a triangle and a 3-simplex is a tetrahedron. A triangle mesh can be represented using a 2-complex, meaning a simplicial complex whose highest dimension simplex is a 2-simplex. Concretely, the connectivity of a triangle mesh uses a 2-complex whose elements can be vertices $\{i\}$, edges $\{i, j\}$ or triangles $\{i, j, k\}$, with the indices $i, j, k \in [1 \ldots N]$. The actual shape of the mesh is given by the vector $\mathbf{S} \subset \mathbb{R}^{3N}$, where the ith vertex is given by $\mathbf{v}_i = [S_{3i-2} \ S_{3i-1} \ S_{3i}]^T$. There is some redundancy in this representation (for example, edges can be inferred from triangles) and so not all representations store all of this information.

6.3.1 Mesh Storage

There are a wide range of open and proprietary file formats for the storage of mesh data. These can be categorised into binary and ASCII text formats. The former are more space-efficient, while the latter are human readable and editable. In general, these file formats all comprise a list of 3D vertices followed by a list of polygons which index into the vertex list. The files may also store vertex or face attributes such as surface normals and texture coordinates.

The most commonly used text-based formats are OBJ (originally developed by Wavefront Technologies) and VRML (Virtual Reality Modelling Language) which was designed particularly with the World Wide Web in mind. The most popular binary format is 3DS which has grown to become a *de facto* industry standard for transferring models between 3D programmes. As well as 3D data, this format can also include scene properties such as lighting. Finally, the PLY format (developed at the Stanford Graphics Lab) supports both ASCII and binary storage.

As the most frequently used format for model archiving, we briefly describe the OBJ format. This is composed of up to four parts, two of which are required. The following snippet provides an example OBJ file:

```
# Vertex (x,y,z) coordinates
v 0.123 0.456 0.789
v ...
...

# Texture coordinates (u,v) coordinates
vt 0.500 0.600
vt ...
...

# Normals in (nx,ny,nz) form
vn 0.707 0.000 0.707
vn ...
...

# Face Definitions
f 1 2 3
f 3/1 4/2 5/3
f 6/4/1 3/5/3 7/6/5
f ...
...
```

Comments can appear anywhere within the file and are indicated by the line beginning with a hash symbol. The file must begin with a list of 3D vertex positions. Each is entered on a separate line, starting with "v". There are then two optional parts:

2D texture coordinates (line begins with "vt") and 3D vertex normals (line begins with "vn"). Texture coordinates are 2D coordinates in the range [0, 1], which index into a texture map (which is typically square). Texture coordinates are scaled by the dimensions of the texture map and colour values interpolated from the pixels surrounding the scaled texture coordinate position. The length of the texture coordinate and surface normal lists should be between N (one per vertex) and $3M$ (one per vertex per triangle with none shared between triangles). The final required part comprises face definitions. Each face definition can take four possible forms:

Vertex: A valid vertex index starts from 1 and indexes into the previously defined vertex list. Faces may have more than three vertices.

```
f v1 v2 v3 v4 ...
```

Vertex/texture coordinate: A vertex index may be followed by a texture coordinate index, separated by a slash.

```
f v1/vt1 v2/vt2 v3/vt3 ...
```

Vertex/texture coordinate/normal: A vertex index may be followed by both a texture coordinate and surface normal index, each separated by a slash.

```
f v1/vt1/vn1 v2/vt2/vn2 v3/vt3/vn3 ...
```

Vertex/normal: A vertex index may be followed by only a surface normal index, separated by a double slash.

```
f v1//vn1 v2//vn2 v3//vn3 ...
```

An OBJ file may be augmented by a companion MTL (Material Template Library) file which describes surface shading and material properties for the purposes of rendering.

6.3.2   Mesh Data Structures

To apply any processing to a mesh, such as rendering, manipulation or editing, we must be able to retrieve elements of the mesh and discover adjacency relationships. The most common such queries include finding the faces/edges which are incident on a given vertex, finding the faces which border an edge, finding the edges which border a face, finding the faces which are adjacent to a face and so on. Mesh data structures can be classified according to how efficiently these queries can be answered. This is often traded off against a storage overhead and representational power.

There are a large number of data structures available for the purpose of representing meshes. Some of the most common are summarised below.

Face list: A list of faces, each of which stores vertex positions. This representation is storage optimal if no two triangles share a vertex. However, where vertices are shared, there is a redundancy in storing the same vertex position multiple times. Connectivity between faces is not stored and must be inferred. Adjacency queries or transformations are inefficient and awkward.

Vertex-face list: A commonly used representation which is space-efficient. It comprises a list of shared vertices and a list of faces, each of which stores pointers into the shared vertex list for each of its vertices. Since this is the representation used in most 3D file formats, such as OBJ, it is straightforward to load archival data into this structure.

Vertex–vertex list: A list of vertices, each containing a list to the vertices to which it is adjacent. Face and edge information is implicit, and hence rendering is inefficient since it is necessary to traverse the structure to build lists of polygons. They are, however, extremely simple and are efficient when modelling complex changes in geometry [81].

Edge list: An edge list can be built from a vertex/face list in $O(M)$ time for a mesh of M faces. An edge list is useful for a number of geometric computer graphics algorithms such as computing stencil shadows.

Winged-edge: The best known boundary representation (b-rep). Each edge stores pointers to the two vertices at their ends, the two faces bordering them, and pointers to four of the edges connected to the end points. This structure allows edge-vertex and edge-face queries to be answered in constant time, though other adjacency queries can require more processing.

Halfedge: Also known as the FE-structure [96] or as a doubly connected edge list (DCEL) [20], although note that the originally proposed DCEL [59] described a different data structure. The halfedge is a b-rep structure which makes explicit the notion that an edge is shared by two faces by splitting an edge into two entities. It is restricted to representing manifold surfaces. Further implementation details are given below.

Adjacency Matrix: A symmetric matrix of size $N \times N$ which contains 1 if there is an edge between the corresponding vertices. It is highly space inefficient for meshes but allows some operations to be performed by applying linear algebra to the adjacency matrix. This forms the basis of algebraic graph theory [7].

We provide a summary of the time and space complexity of a representative sample of mesh data structures in Table 6.2. Note that different structures which support operations with the same asymptotic complexity may not be equally efficient in practice. For example, finding all vertices of a face using a winged-edge structure requires traversal from the face list to the edge list to the vertex list, whereas the vertex-face list structure can traverse directly from faces to vertices. Also, note that where we specify constant time, we refer to constant time per piece of information. So, for example, using a halfedge all of the edges incident on a vertex can be computed in a time which is linear in the number of edges incident on the vertex.

The halfedge structure allows all adjacency queries to be computed in constant time, whilst requiring only a modest overhead in storage requirements. For this

Table 6.2 Space and time complexity of mesh data structures for a mesh of M faces and N vertices

	Vertex-face list	Vertex–vertex list	Winged-edge	Halfedge
No. of pointers to store a cube	24	24	192	144
All vertices of a face	$O(1)$	$O(1)$	$O(1)$	$O(1)$
All vertices adjacent to a vertex	$O(M)$	$O(1)$	$O(1)$	$O(1)$
Both faces adjacent to an edge	$O(M)$	$O(N)$	$O(1)$	$O(1)$

reason, it is a good choice as a general-purpose data structure for mesh processing. On the other hand, a vertex-face list efficiently supports many of the most common operations and is much simpler to implement. For this reason, it is the most widely used representation. Finally, because an adjacency matrix is amenable to analysis using linear algebra, it is used widely in theoretical derivations. For this reason, we discuss these three representations in more detail in the following sections.

6.3.2.1   Vertex-Face List

A vertex-face list stores a triangle mesh of N vertices and M faces as a vertex table of size $3 \times N$ and a face table of size $3 \times M$. Since vertex coordinates are usually real numbers, the vertex table requires floating-point storage, whereas integer vertex indices in the face table require only integer storage. Note that the vertex indices in the face table are essentially pointers and could be implemented as such in some programming languages. The vertex-face list is ideal for operations involving enumerating all triangles, for example, rendering the mesh. This simply involves iterating over the face table. Similarly, applying a transformation to all vertices of a mesh simply requires iterating over the vertex table and applying the transformation to each vertex. The problem with this representation is that it does not store vertex–vertex adjacency (i.e. edges) explicitly. So, testing whether two vertices are adjacent or finding all vertices adjacent to a given vertex requires iterating over all triangles in the mesh (Fig. 6.14).

6.3.2.2   Halfedge Structure

The halfedge data structure comprises vertices, faces and "halfedges". Each edge in the mesh is represented by two halfedges. Conceptually, a halfedge is obtained

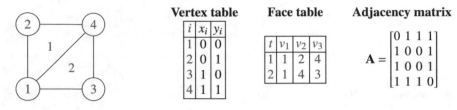

Vertex table

i	x_i	y_i
1	0	0
2	0	1
3	1	0
4	1	1

Face table

t	v_1	v_2	v_3
1	1	2	4
2	1	4	3

Adjacency matrix

$$A = \begin{bmatrix} 0 & 1 & 1 & 1 \\ 1 & 0 & 0 & 1 \\ 1 & 0 & 0 & 1 \\ 1 & 1 & 1 & 0 \end{bmatrix}$$

Fig. 6.14 A 2D mesh with four vertices (left) can be represented by the vertex table and one of the face tables or adjacency matrixes. Vertex indices are labelled blue, triangle indices red

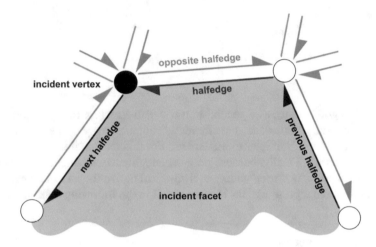

Fig. 6.15 Halfedge structure

by dividing an edge down its length. Figure 6.15 shows a small section of a mesh represented using the halfedge structure. Halfedges store pointers to

1. the next halfedge in the facet (and so they form a circularly linked list around the face);
2. its companion "opposite" halfedge;
3. the vertex at the end of the halfedge;
4. the face that the halfedge borders.

Note that halfedges can be linked in clockwise or counterclockwise direction about a face, but this must be consistent over the mesh.

Concretely, in C a minimal halfedge structure would be implemented as follows:

```
struct halfedge
{
    halfedge* next;
    halfedge* opposite;
    vertex* incidentvertex;
    face* incidentfacet;
};
```

In the halfedge data structure, a vertex stores 3D position (as well as any other per-vertex information) and a pointer to one of the halfedges which uses the vertex as a starting point:

```
struct vertex
{
    float x;
    float y;
    float z;
    // Additional per–vertex data here
    halfedge* outgoingedge;
}
```

Finally, a facet stores any per-facet information (for example, face normals) and a pointer to one of the halfedges bordering the face:

```
struct face
{
    // Additional per–facet data here
    halfedge* borderedge;
}
```

With the halfedge structure to hand, traversals are achieved by simply following the appropriate pointers. In the simplest case, the vertices adjacent to an edge can be found as follows:

```
vertex* vert1 = edge->incidentvertex;
vertex* vert2 = edge->opposite->incidentvertex;
```

Similarly for adjacent faces. Traversing the perimeter of a face is simply a case of following a circularly linked list:

```
halfedge* edge = face->borderedge;

do {
    // Process edge
    edge = edge->next;
} while (edge != face->borderedge)
```

Another useful operation is iterating over all the edges adjacent to a vertex (this is important for range searching and also for vertex deletion resulting from an edge collapse where pointers to this vertex must be changed to point to the vertex at the other end of the deleted edge). This is implemented as follows:

```
halfedge* edge = vert->outgoingedge;

do {
    // Process edge
```

```
        edge = edge->opposite->next;
    } while (edge != vert->outgoingedge)
```

Many other traversal operations can be implemented in a similar manner. In the context of range searching, edge lengths need to be considered (i.e. the Euclidean distance between adjacent vertices). Dijkstra's shortest path algorithm can be applied in this context for range searching using approximate geodesic distances or for exact geodesic distances the fast marching method can be used [43] or, even more efficiently, a recent heat flow method can be used [17]. Exercise 7 asks you to implement Dijkstra's shortest path algorithm on a halfedge structure.

6.3.2.3 Adjacency Matrix

The connectivity of a mesh comprising N vertices can be stored using an $N \times N$ adjacency matrix $\mathbf{A}$. Combined with a vertex table storing the vertex positions, this provides a complete representation for the mesh (see Fig. 6.14). If $\mathbf{A}_{ij} = 1$, it means that there is a mesh edge between vertex i and j. Since mesh edges are always undirected, $\mathbf{A}_{ij} = \mathbf{A}_{ji}$ for any i and j and so $\mathbf{A}$ is symmetric. Usually, an adjacency matrix for a mesh is sparse and so can be stored with better than $O(M^2)$ space complexity.

To test whether two vertices are adjacent, one simply needs to check a single entry in the matrix, taking $O(1)$ time. To find all vertices adjacent to vertex i, one simply needs to iterate over the ith row of $\mathbf{A}$ in $O(N)$ time. The analysis of adjacency matrices is an entire research area in itself. To give a flavour of the sort of analysis possible, the matrix powers of $\mathbf{A}$ are related to walks and distances. The nth power,

$$\mathbf{A}^n = \underbrace{\mathbf{A}\mathbf{A}\ldots\mathbf{A}}_{n \text{ times}}, \tag{6.11}$$

gives the number of walks of length n between any two vertices. Specifically, element (i, j) of $\mathbf{A}^n$ is the number of walks of length n between vertex i and j. Moreover, the smallest $n \in \mathbb{N}_0$ that makes element (i, j) of $\mathbf{A}^n$ positive is the distance (number of edges) between i and j. The number of triangles in a mesh is given by trace$(\mathbf{A}^3)/6$. However, there is no natural representation for triangles within an adjacency matrix so evaluating all triangles (for example for rendering) is not straightforward and inefficient.

6.4 Subdivision Surfaces

Subdivision surfaces are based on iterative refinement of a base mesh according to a refinement scheme. Each iteration of the subdivision results in a mesh which is smoother than the previous. Refinement schemes are divided into two classes:

approximating and *interpolating*. Interpolating schemes retain the positions of the original base mesh as part of the subdivided surfaces. Approximating schemes on the other hand is free to adjust the positions of these vertices. Approximating schemes generally leads to smoother surfaces but allow less precise control for designers who wish to specify the exact position of control vertices.

Subdivision surfaces exhibit a number of desirable features. The base mesh provides an easily editable representation. Often a coarse base mesh is built by combining basic shapes to obtain a desired topology. Alternatively, an object may be scanned or created using NURBS surfaces. A designer may adjust vertex positions at any level of subdivision, using a visualisation of the limit surface to guide vertex placement. This allows gross or finescale refinements to be made to the surface which are then reflected at lower levels of subdivision. Another important feature, for both aesthetic and engineering reasons, is the guarantees that subdivision surfaces can provide about surface continuity. Finally, they can be efficiently displayed, even allowing interactive editing.

In the context of 3D imaging, subdivision surfaces provide an ideal representation for storing and interacting with 3D data due to their space efficiency and ease of editing. However, a prerequisite step is to fit a subdivision surface to 3D data. This is a difficult problem on which much research has focussed. Popular approaches include that of Litke et al. [51] which is based on quasi-interpolation and that of Takeuchi et al. [89] which uses surface simplification to construct a control mesh. Subdivision surfaces can also be used to up-sample low-resolution sensed data by using measured vertices as control points and a subdivision scheme to interpolate a smooth surface.

One of the key developments in subdivision surfaces was to show that the limit surface could be efficiently evaluated directly without having to apply the iterative subdivision process. Stam [85] showed that a subdivision surface and all its derivatives can be evaluated in terms of a set of eigenbasis functions which depend only on the subdivision scheme.

We describe the two most popular approximating schemes due to Doo and Sabin [21] and Catmull and Clark [15] which can operate on quadrilateral meshes. We also describe the approximating scheme proposed by Loop [53] which operates on triangular meshes. Popular interpolating schemes include butterfly scheme, refined by Zorin et al. [100] and the method of Kobbelt [44].

6.4.1   Doo–Sabin Scheme

Commencing with a mesh of N vertices, $\mathcal{M}^N = (K^N, \mathbf{S})$, an iteration of the Doo–Sabin subdivision scheme proceeds as follows:

1. Every vertex $\mathbf{v}_i$, where $\{i\} \in K^N$, yields a new vertex, $\mathbf{v}_{i,f}$, for every face $f = \{i, j, k, \ldots\} \in K^N$ which has $\mathbf{v}_i$ as a vertex. This is known as the *image of* $\mathbf{v}_i$ *in* f.

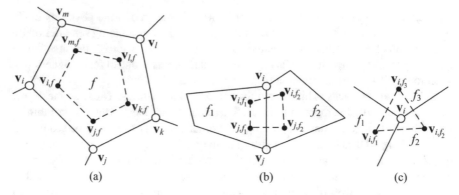

Fig. 6.16 Creation of (**a**) F-face, (**b**) E-face and (**c**) V-face in the Doo–Sabin subdivision scheme

2. The position of $\mathbf{v}_{i,f}$ can be computed using a number of different rules. A simple scheme sets $\mathbf{v}_{i,f}$ to the midpoint of the centroid of f and the vertex position $\mathbf{v}_i$, i.e.

$$\mathbf{v}_{i,f} = \frac{\mathbf{c}_f + \mathbf{v}_i}{2}, \tag{6.12}$$

where

$$\mathbf{c}_f = \frac{1}{\|f\|} \sum_{j \in f} \mathbf{v}_j. \tag{6.13}$$

3. Image vertices are connected to form three kinds of new face, the first of which is an F-face. An F-face is a smaller version of an original face, $f = \{i, j, k, \dots\} \in K^N$, formed by connecting the image vertices of the vertices of f, i.e. $\mathbf{v}_{i,f}, \mathbf{v}_{j,f}, \mathbf{v}_{k,f}, \dots$. If f is an n-sided face then so is the resulting F-face. This process is shown in Fig. 6.16a.
4. The second type of new face is an E-face. For every edge $\{i, j\} \in K^N$ shared by two vertices f_1 and f_2, a new rectangular face is formed from the four image vertices created from the endpoints of the edge, i.e. $\mathbf{v}_{i,f_1}$, $\mathbf{v}_{i,f_2}$, $\mathbf{v}_{j,f_1}$ and $\mathbf{v}_{j,f_2}$. This process is shown in Fig. 6.16b.
5. The final type of new face is a V-face. For every vertex $\{i\} \in K^N$, a new face is created by connecting the image vertices of $\mathbf{v}_i$ in all faces to which $\mathbf{v}_i$ is adjacent. If $\mathbf{v}_i$ has degree n then the new V-face is n-sided. This process is shown in Fig. 6.16c.

To summarise, the subdivided mesh will comprise a quadrilateral for each edge in the original mesh, an n-sided polygon for each n-sided polygon in the original mesh and an n-sided polygon for each degree-n vertex in the original mesh. After one round of subdivision, all vertices have degree four. Hence, subsequent divisions will create quadrilateral V-faces. Non-quadrilateral faces after one subdivision become *extraordinary points* in the limit surface. The limit surface is C^1 continuous, except at extraordinary points. An example of applying the Doo–Sabin scheme to a quadrilateral mesh is shown in Fig. 6.17.

Fig. 6.17 Two iterations of the Doo–Sabin subdivision scheme applied to a T-shaped quadrilateral base mesh. Extraordinary points are shown in blue

6.4.2   Catmull–Clark Scheme

Commencing with a mesh of N vertices, $\mathcal{M}^N = (K^N, \mathbf{S})$, an iteration of the Catmull–Clark subdivision scheme proceeds as follows:

1. For each face $f = \{i, j, \dots\} \in K^N$, add a new vertex to the mesh (known as a *face point*) with a position given by the centroid of the vertices of the face:

$$\mathbf{v}_f = \frac{1}{\|f\|} \sum_{i \in f} \mathbf{v}_i. \qquad (6.14)$$

2. For each edge $e = \{i, j\} \in K^N$ with adjacent faces f_1 and f_2, add a new vertex to the mesh (known as an *edge point*) with a position given by the average of the edge end points and adjacent face points:

$$\mathbf{v}_e = \frac{1}{4}\left(\mathbf{v}_i + \mathbf{v}_j + \mathbf{v}_{f_1} + \mathbf{v}_{f_2}\right). \qquad (6.15)$$

   The original edge is replaced by two new edges connected to the edge point.
3. Add edges from every edge point $\mathbf{v}_e$ to their adjacent face points, $\mathbf{v}_{f_1}$ and $\mathbf{v}_{f_2}$.
4. For each original point $\mathbf{v}_i$, where $\{i\} \in K^N$, compute a new position:

$$\mathbf{v}_i^{new} = \frac{\hat{\mathbf{v}}_f + 2\hat{\mathbf{v}}_e + (F - 3)\mathbf{v}_i}{F}, \qquad (6.16)$$

where $\hat{\mathbf{v}}_f$ is the average of the F-face points adjacent to the original point and $\hat{\mathbf{v}}_e$ is the average of the edge points adjacent to the original point.

The subdivided mesh is composed of quadrilaterals. In general, these will not be planar surfaces. The number of vertices with a degree other than four remains constant over iterations of the subdivision process. These are known as *extraordinary points*. The limit surface can be shown to be $\mathbb{C}^2$ continuous everywhere except at

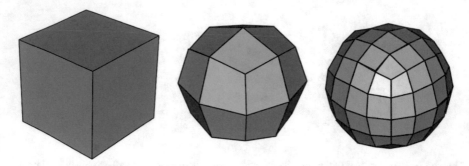

Fig. 6.18 Two iterations of the Catmull–Clark subdivision scheme applied to a cube base mesh

extraordinary vertices, where it is $\mathbb{C}^1$ continuous. An example of two iterations of the Catmull–Clark scheme is shown in Fig. 6.18.

6.4.3 Loop Scheme

Unlike the previous two subdivision schemes, Loop's method operates only on triangular meshes. Commencing with a triangular mesh of N vertices, $\mathcal{M}^N = (K^N, \mathbf{S})$, an iteration of Loop's scheme proceeds as follows:

1. For every edge $e = \{i, j\} \in K^N$ a new vertex $\mathbf{v}_e$ is created as a linear combination of the four vertices comprising the two faces, $f_1 = \{i, j, k_1\}$ and $f_2 = \{i, j, k_2\}$, which are adjacent to the edge as shown in Fig. 6.19a. They are combined using the following weights:

$$\mathbf{v}_e = \frac{1}{8}\mathbf{v}_{k_1} + \frac{1}{8}\mathbf{v}_{k_2} + \frac{3}{8}\mathbf{v}_i + \frac{3}{8}\mathbf{v}_j. \tag{6.17}$$

2. The position of each original point is adjusted according to its existing position and those of its adjacent vertices, as shown in Fig. 6.19b. For each original point $\mathbf{v}_i$, where $\{i\} \in K^N$, the new position is given by

$$\mathbf{v}_i^{\text{new}} = \alpha \left(\sum_{j \in \text{Adj}(i)} \frac{1}{d_i} \mathbf{v}_j \right) + (1 - n\alpha)\mathbf{v}_i, \tag{6.18}$$

where $\text{Adj}(i) = \{j | \{i, j\} \in K^N\}$ is the set of vertices adjacent to $\mathbf{v}_i$. The constant α is determined by the degree $d_i = \|\text{Adj}(i)\|$, and there are many variations available. The simplest choice is

$$\alpha = \begin{cases} \frac{3}{16} & \text{if } d_i = 3, \\ \frac{3}{8n} & \text{if } d_i > 3. \end{cases} \tag{6.19}$$

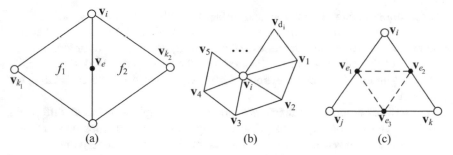

Fig. 6.19 Loop subdivision scheme: (**a**) creation of an edge vertex; (**b**) calculating new position for original points; (**c**) triangulation of new edge points

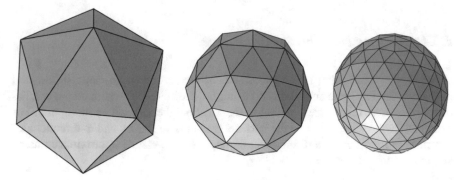

Fig. 6.20 Two iterations of the Loop subdivision scheme applied to an icosahedron base mesh

3. The subdivided surface is given by connecting the new edge vertices and the updated original vertices as shown in Fig. 6.19c.

After one subdivision, all vertices have degree six except those which were in the original mesh and had a degree other than six. These are the extraordinary vertices. The limit surface is C^2 continuous except at the extraordinary vertices (Fig. 6.20).

6.5 Local Differential Properties

Many useful 3D data processing operations require the computation of local differential properties of a surface. These range from the construction of local features such as spin images [39] to the computation of geodesic paths over a manifold [43]. However, most surface representations are discrete and contain only an approximate sampling of the underlying surface. The nature of the representation determines the manner in which these properties are computed.

First-order properties of the surface (normal vector and tangent plane) are most commonly used for shading (since surface reflectance is a function of orientation).

Interpolation shading uses interpolated surface normals to allow a polygonal approximation of a smooth surface to appear smooth when rendered (see Fig. 6.1g). Second-order properties (principal curvatures and directions) are often used for local characterisation of the surface topology, for example, the shape index [45]. Occasionally, even third-order properties (directional derivatives of the principal curvatures) can be useful.

For surfaces described in functional form (such as implicit surfaces), differential properties can be computed analytically using differential calculus. On the other hand, discrete representations require the assumption that the underlying surface is smooth and differential properties can only be approximated. Such operators should converge asymptotically to the true result as the sampling density increases.

6.5.1   Surface Normals

For uniformly sampled representations such as voxels and depth maps, differential properties can easily be approximated using finite differences which consider adjacent pixels or voxels, corresponding to the local neighbourhood about a point. For example, in the simplest case the surface gradients in the x- and y-directions of a surface represented as a discrete depth map, $z(x, y)$, can be approximated using single-forward differences:

$$\partial_x z(x, y) \approx \frac{z(x + 1, y) - z(x, y)}{\delta_x}, \quad \partial_y z(x, y) \approx \frac{z(x, y + 1) - z(x, y)}{\delta_y}, \quad (6.20)$$

where δ_x and δ_y are the spacings on the pixel array. The surface normal vector is then given by

$$\mathbf{n}(x, y) = \frac{[-\partial_x z(x, y) \; -\partial_y z(x, y) \; 1]^T}{\|[-\partial_x z(x, y) \; -\partial_y z(x, y) \; 1]^T\|}. \quad (6.21)$$

Note that computing gradients using only forward, backward or central differences results in high sensitivity to noise. A more stable estimate can be obtained by first smoothing the depth map prior to computing finite differences. If smoothing is done via convolution then, by associativity of the convolution operation, the smoothing and finite difference kernels can be pre-convolved giving a single kernel that provides a smoothed finite difference approximation. For example, using a 3×3 kernel, central finite differences and smoothing with a Gaussian filter with standard deviation 0.6, the following approximation is obtained [83]:

$$\partial_x z(x, y) \approx z * \frac{1}{12} \begin{bmatrix} -1 & 0 & 1 \\ -4 & 0 & 4 \\ -1 & 0 & 1 \end{bmatrix}, \quad (6.22)$$

similarly for the y gradient.

Fig. 6.21 Computation of
vertex normal by averaging
adjacent face normals

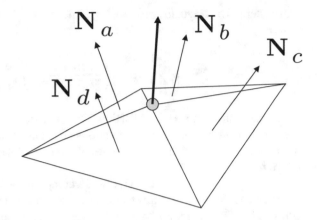

In the case of an arbitrary triangular mesh, such a simple approach is not possible. If the surface is truly piecewise planar, then it is enough to associate a *face normal* with each triangular facet. For a face composed of vertices $\mathbf{v}_1$, $\mathbf{v}_2$ and $\mathbf{v}_3$, the face normal is given by

$$\mathbf{n}_f = \frac{(\mathbf{v}_2 - \mathbf{v}_1) \times (\mathbf{v}_3 - \mathbf{v}_1)}{\|(\mathbf{v}_2 - \mathbf{v}_1) \times (\mathbf{v}_3 - \mathbf{v}_1)\|}. \tag{6.23}$$

For the normal to be directed to the outside of the object, the vertices must be ordered in an anticlockwise sense when viewed from the outside.

More commonly, the underlying surface is assumed smooth and the surface normal is approximated at each vertex. There are a number of alternative approaches to computing vertex normals [38] which are based on weighted averages of the adjacent facet normals (see Fig. 6.21).

Consider a vertex whose incident edges in anticlockwise order are given by the sequence $\langle \mathbf{e}_1, \ldots, \mathbf{e}_n \rangle$. The first edge is repeated at the end of the sequence so $\mathbf{e}_1 = \mathbf{e}_n$. The most well-known method which is very efficient to compute uses triangle areas as weights. The area weighted normal to a facet defined by edges $\mathbf{e}_i$ and $\mathbf{e}_{i+1}$ is given simply by $\mathbf{e}_i \times \mathbf{e}_{i+1}$. Hence, the area weighted vertex normal is

$$\mathbf{n}_v^{\text{Area}} = \sum_{i=1}^{n-1} \mathbf{e}_i \times \mathbf{e}_{i+1}. \tag{6.24}$$

Note that this result requires normalisation back to unit length. The efficiency of this approach lies in the fact that the cross-product computation factors in the area weight for free. In particular, no trigonometric calculations are required. The downside to this approach is that a triangle with large area but small angle between the edges incident on the vertex contributes disproportionately to the result. This can lead to highly inaccurate normals under certain circumstances, and the result depends heavily on the mesh triangulation (see [55] for an example).

An alternative, originally proposed by Thürmer and Wüthrich [93], uses the angle between pairs of edges incident on a vertex as the weight:

$$\mathbf{n}_v^{\text{Angle}} = \sum_{i=1}^{n-1} \arccos\left(\frac{\mathbf{e}_i \cdot \mathbf{e}_{i+1}}{\|\mathbf{e}_i\| \cdot \|\mathbf{e}_{i+1}\|}\right) \frac{\mathbf{e}_i \times \mathbf{e}_{i+1}}{\|\mathbf{e}_i \times \mathbf{e}_{i+1}\|}. \tag{6.25}$$

Again, the result requires normalisation. This approach is relatively simple and accurate but requires trigonometric calculations so is unsuitable for applications involving real-time computation of vertex normals (for example, interactive rendering of a deforming surface).

A method proposed by Max [55] offers a compromise. It does not require trigonometric calculations but is more stable in the special cases where area weighting performs badly. The weight is comprised of the sine of the angle between edge vectors and the edge length reciprocal:

$$\mathbf{n}_v^{\text{Max}} = \sum_{i=1}^{n-1} \frac{\sin\alpha_i}{\|\mathbf{e}_i\|\|\mathbf{e}_{i+1}\|} \frac{\mathbf{e}_i \times \mathbf{e}_{i+1}}{\|\mathbf{e}_i \times \mathbf{e}_{i+1}\|}, \tag{6.26}$$

where

$$\sin\alpha_i = \frac{\|\mathbf{e}_i \times \mathbf{e}_{i+1}\|}{\|\mathbf{e}_i\|\|\mathbf{e}_{i+1}\|}, \tag{6.27}$$

which simplifies to

$$\mathbf{n}_v^{\text{Max}} = \sum_{i=1}^{n-1} \frac{\mathbf{e}_i \times \mathbf{e}_{i+1}}{\|\mathbf{e}_i\|^2 \|\mathbf{e}_{i+1}\|^2}. \tag{6.28}$$

Again, the result requires normalisation. The derivation follows from an assumption of a locally spherical surface. For meshes representing surfaces which are exactly locally spherical, the result is exact.

6.5.2 Differential Coordinates and the Mesh Laplacian

When a surface is represented using a mesh, a transformation can be made to differential coordinates (δ-coordinates) which provides an alternate route to the computation of differential surface properties as well as a useful representation for other operations (including mesh compression). This is most easily accomplished when the mesh is stored in an adjacency matrix. A vertex $\mathbf{v}_i$, $\{i\} \in K^N$ which is a member of the mesh $\mathcal{M}^N = (K^N, \mathbf{S})$ may be represented in terms of δ-coordinates. This representation describes the difference between the absolute position of the vertex and the centre of mass of its adjacent vertices:

$$\delta_i = [\delta_i^x \; \delta_i^y \; \delta_i^z]^T = \mathbf{v}_i - \frac{1}{\|\mathrm{Adj}(i)\|} \sum_{j \in \mathrm{Adj}(i)} \mathbf{v}_j. \tag{6.29}$$

$d_i = \|\mathrm{Adj}(i)\|$ is the degree of the vertex i. This transformation can be represented in matrix form. Given the mesh adjacency matrix $\mathbf{A}$, where

$$A_{ij} = \begin{cases} 1 \text{ if } \{i, j\} \in K^N \\ 0 \text{ otherwise,} \end{cases} \tag{6.30}$$

and the diagonal degree matrix, $\mathbf{D}$, where $D_{ii} = d_i$, the *graph Laplacian matrix* (sometimes called the *topological Laplacian*) is defined by $\mathbf{L} = \mathbf{D} - \mathbf{A}$, i.e.

$$L_{ij} = \begin{cases} d_i & \text{if } i = j \\ -1 & \text{if } \{i, j\} \in K^N \\ 0 & \text{otherwise,} \end{cases} \tag{6.31}$$

The Laplacian relates absolute and differential coordinates as follows. If the long vector $\mathbf{x} \in \mathbb{R}^N$ contains the x coordinates of the vertices, then $\mathbf{L}\mathbf{x} = \mathbf{D}\delta^x$, where $\delta^x \in \mathbb{R}^N$ is a long vector of the x components of the differential coordinates of the vertices, and similarly for the y- and z-coordinates. Note that spectral analysis of the Laplacian can be used to perform signal processing operations on an irregularly triangulated mesh [91].

From differential geometry, it is known that an infinitesimal curvilinear integral about a point on a smooth surface is related to the mean curvature $H(\mathbf{v}_i)$ at $\mathbf{v}_i$ and the surface normal $\mathbf{n}_i$:

$$\lim_{|\gamma| \to 0} \frac{1}{|\gamma|} \int_{\mathbf{v} \in \gamma} (\mathbf{v}_i - \mathbf{v}) dl(\mathbf{v}) = -H(\mathbf{v}_i)\mathbf{n}_i, \tag{6.32}$$

where γ is a closed simple surface curve $l(\mathbf{v})$ around $\mathbf{v}_i$. By rewriting the differential coordinate vector, it can be seen that a discrete approximation to this integral can be made

$$\frac{1}{\|\mathrm{Adj}(i)\|} \sum_{j \in \mathrm{Adj}(i)} (\mathbf{v}_i - \mathbf{v}_j) \approx -H(\mathbf{v}_i)\mathbf{n}_i. \tag{6.33}$$

Hence, the direction of the differential coordinate vector approximates the surface normal, and the magnitude is proportional to the mean curvature [91]. This provides an alternative means to surface normal calculation for a mesh which is motivated by differential geometry. A final alternative proposed by Meyer et al. [57] is based on *cotangent weights*:

$$\delta_i^{\mathrm{cot}} = \frac{1}{|\Omega_i|} \sum_{j \in \mathrm{Adj}(i)} \frac{1}{2}(\cot \alpha_{ij} + \cot \beta_{ij})(\mathbf{v}_i - \mathbf{v}_j), \tag{6.34}$$

Fig. 6.22 The angles used in
the cotangent weights
scheme for surface normal
computation

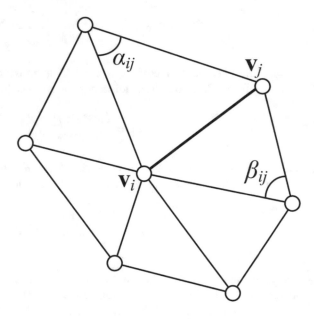

where $|\Omega_i|$ is the size of the Voronoi cell of i, and α_{ij} and β_{ij} denote the two angles
opposite to the edge $\{i, j\}$ (see Fig. 6.22).

6.6 Compression and Levels of Detail

Broadly speaking, the storage requirements for 3D data can be reduced in two ways:
storing a 3D representation in less space (compression) or deriving a lower resolution representation which approximates the original data. We have already seen
some representations which lead to space-efficient storage of 3D data. For example,
subdivision surfaces require only the storage of a low-resolution base mesh and subdivision rule while the octree representation uses adaptive resolution depending on
the complexity of the volume. Compression of 3D data in general [2, 66] is a more
challenging problem than is solved by the relatively mature technologies available
for compression of audio, image and video data. Techniques for 3D data compression
can be categorised into three classes of approach:

Mesh-based methods: Involve traversal of a polygonal mesh and encoding of the
mesh structure in a manner which can be compressed. An example of such an
approach is *topological surgery* [92]. This method proceeds by quantizing vertex
positions within the desired accuracy. A vertex spanning tree is then used to predict
the position of each vertex from 2, 3 or 4 of its ancestors in the tree. Finally, the
correction vectors required to recover the original positions are entropy encoded.
Another popular approach is based on a spectral analysis of the mesh Laplacian

[40]. An eigendecomposition of the Laplacian matrix (see Sect. 6.5.2) yields an orthonormal set of basis vectors onto which the geometry signals (vectors of x-, y- and z-components) can be projected. By discarding high-frequency components of the decomposition (i.e. those eigenvectors with small eigenvalues), the mesh can be compressed such that only high-frequency detail is lost.

Progressive and hierarchical methods: We have already seen subdivision surfaces which fall into this category. Another important approach is the *compressed progressive mesh* [37]. In the original progressive mesh, a mesh is encoded as a form of reverse simplification. The opposite of an edge collapse operation is a vertex split, in which a vertex is divided into two and additional edges and faces are added to the mesh. A progressive mesh represents a high-resolution mesh as a series of vertex split operations starting from a base mesh. Although this allows progressive transmission of increasingly detailed mesh data, there is a storage overhead which means space requirements increase. Pajarola and Rossignac [63] showed how this representation can be compressed.

Image-based methods: A 3D surface may be represented in image space. This can either be native to the representation (in the case of a range image or bump map) or via a process known as surface parameterisation or surface flattening [79]. Once represented as an image, any existing image compression algorithm may be applied to the data. However, it is important to note that the objectives of lossy image compression may not yield correspondingly high-quality results in the surface domain since the redundancies in the two data sources may not be the same. One example of an image-based approach is *geometry images* [30]. Geometry is captured as a 2D array of quantized points. To transform a mesh to this representation, an arbitrary mesh is cut along a network of edge paths, and the resulting single chart is parameterised onto a square. Face connectivity is implicit in the representation, and bump maps or texture can be stored in the same parameterisation. Compressing the resulting data using an image wavelet encoder allows dramatic reductions in storage requirements without severely affecting the resulting geometry.

As suggested above, an alternative to using compression to store a high-resolution mesh in less space is to derive a lower resolution mesh which approximates the original. This is known as mesh simplification and is described in the following section.

6.6.1   Mesh Simplification

Mesh simplification or decimation is the process of iteratively removing vertices, edges and faces from a mesh to reduce its complexity and storage requirements. As well as reducing storage requirements by removing redundant structures, simplified meshes can also be processed or rendered more efficiently. Most mesh simplification algorithms proceed using iterative edge collapse.

Fig. 6.23 An edge collapse operation

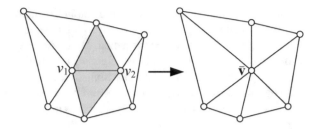

6.6.1.1   Edge Collapse

A pair contraction $(\mathbf{v}_1, \mathbf{v}_2) \to \bar{\mathbf{v}}$, transforms a pair of vertices $\mathbf{v}_1$ and $\mathbf{v}_2$ to a new position $\bar{\mathbf{v}}$, connects all their incident edges to $\mathbf{v}_1$ and deletes the vertex $\mathbf{v}_2$. Any edges or faces which became degenerate after the contraction are removed. An example is shown in Fig. 6.23.

Starting with the original high-resolution mesh $\mathcal{M}^N = (K^N, \mathbf{S})$, a sequence of pair contractions is applied until the simplification goals are satisfied (for example, the target number of vertices is reached). Each contraction corresponds to a local incremental modification of the complex K^N and shape vectors $\mathbf{S}$. The algorithm generates a sequence of meshes $\mathcal{M}^N, \mathcal{M}^{N-1}, \mathcal{M}^{N-2}, \ldots$ with decreasing resolution.

In general, only *edge* pairs are considered valid for contraction, i.e. where $\{i, j\} \in K^N$. When an edge is contracted: $(\mathbf{v}_i, \mathbf{v}_j) \to \bar{\mathbf{v}}_{ij}$, the simplicial complex, K^N, describing the mesh topology is modified. Degenerate faces (those that no longer have three distinct vertices), and duplicate edges are removed as well as the collapsed edge and redundant vertex j:

$$K^{N-1} = K^N \setminus \left\{ \{j\}, \{i, j\}, \{j, k\}, \{i, j, k\} : \{i, j, k\} \in K^N \right\}. \tag{6.35}$$

The shape vector of each individual mesh is also modified as the result of an edge collapse. The vertex $\mathbf{v}_j$ is deleted, and $\mathbf{v}_i$ is moved to $\bar{\mathbf{v}}_{ij}$.

6.6.1.2   Quadric Error Metric

Edge collapse algorithms operate by selecting the next edge for collapse as the one whose deletion will result in the least increase in error. The choice of error measure determines the nature of the simplification. For example, it may seek to preserve volume or surface orientation. The most successful and widely used error measure is based on the *Quadric Error Metric* (QEM), as proposed by Garland and Heckbert [26] in their QSlim algorithm.

Each vertex is a solution of a set of triangles (planes), which meet at that vertex. Hence, we can define the error of the vertex with respect to this set as the sum of squared distances to each triangle. Given a triangular plane $\mathbf{p}$ defined by the equation $ax + by + cz + d = 0$, where $\mathbf{n} = [a, b, c]$ is the plane normal and d is a scalar constant. A fundamental quadric is defined as

$$Q = (\mathbf{nn}^T, d\mathbf{n}, d^2) = (\mathbf{A}, \mathbf{b}, c), \tag{6.36}$$

where $\mathbf{A}$ is a 3×3 matrix, $\mathbf{b}$ is a 3-vector and c is a scalar. The quadric Q assigns a value $Q(\mathbf{v})$ to every point in space $\mathbf{v}$ by the second-order equation

$$Q(\mathbf{v}) = \mathbf{v}^T \mathbf{A} \mathbf{v} + 2\mathbf{b}^T \mathbf{v} + c. \tag{6.37}$$

Note that the level surface $Q(\mathbf{v}) = \epsilon$, which is a set of all points whose error with respect to Q is ϵ, is a quadratic surface. Also the value of this quadratic $Q(\mathbf{v})$ is precisely the squared distance of $\mathbf{v}$ to a given plane. The addition of quadrics can be naturally defined component-wise: $Q_1(\mathbf{v}) + Q_2(\mathbf{v}) = (Q_1 + Q_2)(\mathbf{v})$ where $(Q_1 + Q_2) = (\mathbf{A}_1 + \mathbf{A}_2, \mathbf{b}_1 + \mathbf{b}_2, c_1 + c_2)$. Thus, given a set of fundamental quadrics, determined by a set of planes, the quadric error at each vertex $\mathbf{v}_i$ is completely determined by

$$E_{Q_i}(\mathbf{v}_i) = \sum_p Q_p(\mathbf{v}_i) = Q_i(\mathbf{v}_i), \tag{6.38}$$

where $Q_i = \sum_p Q_p$ is the sum of the fundamental quadrics of all the planes incident on a vertex $\mathbf{v}_i$. Using this additive rule, for an edge collapse $(\mathbf{v}_i, \mathbf{v}_j) \rightarrow \bar{\mathbf{v}}_{ij}$, we can associate a quadric Q_{i+j} which approximates the error at $\bar{\mathbf{v}}_{ij}$, where $Q_{i+j} = Q_i + Q_j$. This simple additive rule is one of the reasons for the efficiency of this approach.

When considering the contraction of an edge $(\mathbf{v}_i, \mathbf{v}_j)$, we need to determine the target position $\bar{\mathbf{v}}_{ij}$. We select the optimum position $(\bar{\mathbf{v}})$ as the one that minimises Eq. 6.37. Since Eq. 6.37 is a quadratic, finding its minimum is a linear problem. Taking partial derivatives of Eq. 6.37

$$\nabla Q(\bar{\mathbf{v}}) = 2\mathbf{A}\bar{\mathbf{v}} + 2\mathbf{b}. \tag{6.39}$$

Solving for $\nabla Q(\bar{\mathbf{v}}) = 0$, we find the optimum position to be

$$\bar{\mathbf{v}} = -\mathbf{A}^{-1}\mathbf{b}. \tag{6.40}$$

Finally, after removal of t vertices the next edge to be collapsed is chosen as the one with minimal quadric error:

$$\{i^*, j^*\} = \underset{\{i,j\} \in K^{N-t}}{\arg \min} \; Q_{i+j}(\bar{\mathbf{v}}_{ij}). \tag{6.41}$$

Note that the algorithm is implemented efficiently by placing edges onto a priority queue. Priority is determined by the QEM for each edge. After each edge collapse, the QEM scores of edges sharing vertices with either end of the collapsed edge are updated (using the simple additive rule given above). Since an edge collapse is constant time complexity, the whole simplification is $O(n \log n)$, where the $\log n$ term corresponds to removing an edge from the queue. There are some additional technical considerations such as the preservation of an object boundary which are described in detail in the thesis of Garland [27].

6.6.2 QEM Simplification Summary

The QEM simplification algorithm is summarised as follows:

1. Compute quadrics for all triangles in the mesh (Eq. 6.36).
2. Compute errors associated with all edges $\{i, j\}$: $Q_{i+j}(\bar{v}_{ij})$ and place edge errors on a priority queue.
3. Delete edge with minimal error from priority queue, contract edge in mesh structure (removing redundant vertices and faces) and update QEM scores for adjacent edges.
4. If simplification goals not met, return to step 3.

6.6.3 Surface Simplification Results

In Fig. 6.24, we show results of applying the QEM simplification algorithm to a mesh containing 172,974 vertices. The original mesh is shown on the left. The middle image shows the surface after edges have been collapsed until the number of vertices has been reduced by 80% (to 34,595 vertices). Notice that there is almost no visual degradation of the rendering despite the large decrease in resolution. On the right, the original mesh has been simplified until the number of vertices has been reduced by 90% (17,296 vertices remain).

6.7 Current and Future Challenges

Although the representation, storage and processing of 3D data have been considered for many decades, there are still some major challenges to be faced. On the one hand, the size of 3D datasets is continuing to grow as sensing technology improves (e.g. the resolution of medical imaging devices) and we begin to process large sequences of dynamic data (acquired through 4D capture) or databases of meshes. Large databases arise in applications such as 3D face recognition where fine surface detail is required to distinguish faces, yet many millions of subjects may be enrolled in the database. Not only must the database be stored efficiently but it must be possible to perform

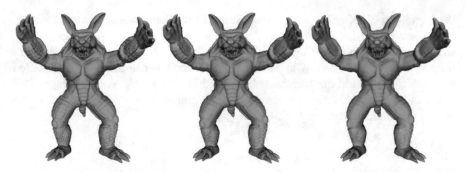

Fig. 6.24 Simplification results using the Quadric Error Metric. From left to right: original mesh (172,974 vertices), simplified by 80% (34,595 vertices) and simplified by 90% (17,296 vertices)

queries in real time to be of use in real-world applications. The progressive mesh representations described above allow progressive transmission of 3D data, but this must be extended to dynamic data. Moreover, the transformation of a mesh into a progressive mesh is expensive and may not be viable for huge datasets. The growing trend to outsource storage and processing of data to "the cloud" necessitates 3D representations which can be stored, interacted with and edited in a distributed manner.

However, on the other hand, there is a growing wish to be able to access such data in a resource-limited environment, for example, over bandwidth-limited network connections or on mobile devices with limited computational power. The advances in rendering technology exhibited in computer-generated movie sequences will begin to find its way into consumer products such as games consoles and mobile devices. These platforms are highly resource-limited in terms of both processing power and storage. Hence, the efficiency of the data structures used to store and process 3D data will be of critical importance in determining performance.

Statistical representations of 3D surfaces (such as the 3D morphable model [8], see Chap. 10) have proven extremely useful in vision applications where their compactness and robustness allow them to constrain vision problems in an efficient way. However, their application is limited because of *model dominance*, whereby low-frequency, global modes of variation dominate appearance. Extensions to such statistical representations which can capture high-frequency local detail whilst retaining the compact storage requirements are a significant future challenge. A related challenge is how such models can be learnt from a sparse sample of a very high-dimensional space, i.e. how can the generalisation capabilities of such a model be improved?

Finally, as machine learning (specifically deep learning) begins to move into the 3D domain, fundamental questions about the representation and processing of geometric data reappear. Convolutional neural networks have been extended to be applicable to meshes and graph structures [13]. Rapid advances have been made in the processing of 3D volumetric data using CNNs, including learning representations that can be used to generate new shapes [22]. However, we are only really at the beginning of this exciting line of development. There is a disconnect between artist- or renderer-friendly representations used in computer graphics and the grid structured data favoured by machine learning. Bridging this gap so that representations of a comparable quality to hand-crafted 3D models can be learnt or extracted from noisy real-world measurements in 2D and 3D is a truly grand challenge. This is a multifaceted challenge but one important component will be advanced in the representation and processing of 3D data.

6.8　Concluding Remarks

Representations of 3D data provide the interface between acquisition and sensing of 3D data and ultimately processing the data in a way which enables the development of useful applications. Anyone involved in 3D imaging and processing must be aware of the native representations used by sensing devices and the various advantages and limitations of higher level surface and volume-based representations. In many cases, data in a raw representation must be preprocessed before conversion to the desired higher level format, for example, through surface fitting, smoothing or resampling. Subsequently, in choosing the most suitable representation for a particular application, it must be established what operations need to be performed on the data and what requirements exist in terms of computational and storage efficiency. Whether involved with the low-level design of 3D sensors or interpreting and processing high-level 3D data, understanding these issues is important. Finally, as sensors and applications continue to develop the need for new representations and methods for compression and visualisation mean, this remains an active research area.

6.9　Further Reading

An introductory level text covering mathematics related to geometry processing is by Vince [94]. 3D representations in general are covered in some detail in the computer graphics textbooks of Watt [95] and Foley et al. [24]. Focussing in more detail on specific representations is a number of textbooks. With relation to meshes, geometry processing algorithms including error removal, mesh creation, smoothing, conversion and morphing are covered in detail in the textbook of Botsch et al. [12]. NURBS are described in detail in the textbook of Piegl and Tiller [70], subdivision surfaces are covered by Peters and Reif [67], implicit curves and surfaces are examined by Gomes et al. [28] and the textbook of Suetens [88] deals with volumetric representations in the context of medical imaging. A popular textbook describing techniques for visualisation is by Post et al. [71].

6.10   Questions and Exercises

6.10.1   Questions

1. Compare and contrast K-d point cloud structuring and octree structuring. When might one method be preferable over the other?
2. For each of the following methods and devices for 3D acquisition, explain what is the most suitable raw data representation. Justify your answer. You may need to research how each method operates.

   - time-of-flight camera,
   - multiview stereo,
   - shape-from-shading,
   - structured light and
   - MRI scanner (consider structural, functional and diffusion tensor modalities).

3. For a 3D imaging application of your choice, list the operations which would need to be applied to the data and use this to guide selection of an appropriate 3D representation. Explain any difficulties which may arise in converting to this representation from the raw data acquired in your chosen application.
4. What considerations are relevant when selecting a data structure for 3D meshes?
5. Describe an application in which lossy compression of 3D data is acceptable and an application in which only lossless compression is acceptable.
6. Explain three situations in which 3D data needs to be visualised. Each situation should employ a different visualisation of the data.

6.10.2   Exercises

1. Derive an algorithm for extracting a list of edges from a triangular mesh stored in a vertex-face list. The complexity should be linear in the number of triangles.
2. Using a data structure of your choice, show how to compute a vertex normal for a triangular mesh. You should choose one of the methods described in Sect. 6.5.1 to compute the normals.
3. In Sect. 6.3.2.2, code is given for traversing the edges incident on a vertex in a halfedge structure. Provide similar code for traversing the faces incident on a vertex.
4. Describe how to implement the *edge collapse* operation in a halfedge structure. The collapsed edge and one of the vertices must be removed from the structure, edges incident on the deleted vertex must be altered so that they are incident on the retained vertex and finally any degenerate faces must be removed.
5. A sphere can be represented as a subdivision surface using the following rule. The base mesh is a polyhedron, in this case use an icosahedron. The subdivision rule divides each triangle into four smaller triangles by adding vertices halfway along

each edge. The new vertices are translated such that their distance from the sphere centre is equal to the radius of the sphere. Derive a rule for computing the number of edges, faces and vertices in the representation as a function of the number of iterative subdivisions. Now, using a triangle mesh data structure of your choice, derive a similar rule for computing the number of pointers required to store the representation at each level of iteration.

6. Using a mesh representation of your choice, show how to evaluate the quadric error metric at a vertex.

7. A mesh can be considered as a weighted graph where edge weights correspond to Euclidean distance between the end nodes. Describe how to implement Dijkstra's shortest path algorithm in order to achieve fast range of searching over a mesh graph stored in a halfedge structure. Given a distance threshold over which to range search, what is the stopping criteria for this algorithm?

References

1. Akenine-Moller, T., Haines, E., Hoffman, N.: Real-time rendering. AK Peters/CRC Press (2018)
2. Alliez, P., Gotsman, C.: Recent advances in compression of 3d meshes. In: Dodgson, N., Floater, M., Sabin, M. (eds.) Advances in Multiresolution for Geometric Modelling, pp. 3–26. Springer, Berlin (2005)
3. Asberg, B., Blanco, G., Bose, P., Garcia-Lopez, J., Overmars, M., Toussaint, G., Wilfong, G., Zhu, B.: Feasibility of design in stereolithography. Algorithmica 19(1–2), 61–83 (1997)
4. Bas, A., Huber, P., Smith, W.A., Awais, M., Kittler, J.: 3d morphable models as spatial transformer networks. In: Proceedings of the IEEE International Conference on Computer Vision, pp. 904–912 (2017)
5. Bentley, J.L.: Multidimensional binary search trees used for associative searching. Commun. ACM 18(9), 509–517 (1975)
6. Berger, M., Tagliasacchi, A., Seversky, L.M., Alliez, P., Guennebaud, G., Levine, J.A., Sharf, A., Silva, C.T.: A survey of surface reconstruction from point clouds. In: Computer Graphics Forum, vol. 36, pp. 301–329. Wiley Online Library, Hoboken (2017)
7. Biggs, N.: Algebraic Graph Theory. Cambridge University Press, Cambridge (1993)
8. Blanz, V., Vetter, T.: A morphable model for the synthesis of 3D faces. In: Proceedings of the SIGGRAPH, pp. 187–194 (1999)
9. Bloomenthal, J., Bajaj, C., Blinn, J., Cani-Gascuel, M.P., Rockwood, A., Wyvill, B., Wyvill, G. (eds.): Introduction to Implicit Surfaces. Morgan Kaufmann, Burlington (1997)
10. Bloomenthal, J., Wyvill, B.: Interactive techniques for implicit modelling. In: Proceedings of the Symposium on Interactive 3D Computer Graphics (1990)
11. Bloomenthal, J.: Polygonization of implicit surfaces. Comput. Aided Geom. D. 5(4), 341–355 (1988)
12. Botsch, M., Kobbelt, L., Pauly, M., Alliez, P., Levy, B.: Polygon mesh processing. A K Peters/CRC Press, Natick (2011)
13. Bronstein, M.M., Bruna, J., LeCun, Y., Szlam, A., Vandergheynst, P.: Geometric deep learning: going beyond euclidean data. IEEE Signal Process. Mag. 34(4), 18–42 (2017)
14. Carr, J.C., Beatson, R.K., Cherrie, J.B., Mitchell, T.J., Fright, W.R., McCallum, B.C., Evans, T.R.: Reconstruction and representation of 3d objects with radial basis functions. In: Proceedings of the SIGGRAPH, pp. 67–76 (2001)

15. Catmull, E., Clark, J.: Recursively generated b-spline surfaces on arbitrary topological meshes. Comput. Aided Des. **10**(6), 350–355 (1978)
16. Chen, Z., Zhang, H.: Learning implicit fields for generative shape modeling. In: Proceedings of the IEEE Conference on Computer Vision and Pattern Recognition, pp. 5939–5948 (2019)
17. Crane, K., Weischedel, C., Wardetzky, M.: Geodesics in heat: a new approach to computing distance based on heat flow. ACM Trans. Graph. (TOG) **32**(5), 152 (2013)
18. Dai, A., Chang, A.X., Savva, M., Halber, M., Funkhouser, T.A., Nießner, M.: Scannet: Richly-annotated 3d reconstructions of indoor scenes. In: CVPR, vol. 2, p. 10 (2017)
19. Dai, A., Ruizhongtai Qi, C., Nießner, M.: Shape completion using 3d-encoder-predictor cnns and shape synthesis. In: Proceedings of the IEEE Conference on Computer Vision and Pattern Recognition, pp. 5868–5877 (2017)
20. de Berg, M., van Kreveld, M., Overmars, M., Schwarzkopf, O.: Computational Geometry: Algorithms and Applications. Springer, Berlin (1997)
21. Doo, D., Sabin, M.: Behavior of recursive division surfaces near extraordinary points. Comput. Aided Des. **10**(6), 356–360 (1978)
22. Dosovitskiy, A., Tobias Springenberg, J., Brox, T.: Learning to generate chairs with convolutional neural networks. In: Proceedings of the IEEE Conference on Computer Vision and Pattern Recognition, pp. 1538–1546 (2015)
23. Farin, G.: Curves and Surfaces for CAGD: A Practical Guide. Morgan Kaufmann, Burlington (2002)
24. Foley, J.D., van Dam, A., Feiner, S.K., Hughes, J.F.: Computer Graphics. Addison Wesley, Boston (1995)
25. Fuchs, H., Kedem, Z.M., Naylor, B.F.: On visible surface generation by a priori tree structures. ACM Comput. Graph. **14**, 124–133 (1980)
26. Garland, M., Heckbert, P.S.: Surface simplification using quadric error metrics. In: Proceedings of the SIGGRAPH, pp. 209–216 (1997)
27. Garland, M.: Quadric-based polygonal surface simplification. Ph.D. thesis, Computer Science Department, Carnegie Mellon University (1999)
28. Gomes, A.J.P., Voiculescu, I., Jorge, J., Wyvill, B., Galbraith, C.: Implicit Curves and Surfaces: Mathematics Data Structures and Algorithms. Springer, Berlin (2009)
29. Gower, J.C.: Generalized procrustes analysis. Psychometrika **40**(1), 33–51 (1975)
30. Gu, X., Gortler, S., Hoppe, H.: Geometry images. ACM Trans. Graphic. (Proc. SIGGRAPH) **21**, 3 (2002)
31. Harker, M., O'leary, P.: Regularized reconstruction of a surface from its measured gradient field. J. Math. Imaging Vis. **51**(1), 46–70 (2015)
32. Hart, J.C.: Ray tracing implicit surfaces. In: SIGGRAPH Course Notes (1993)
33. Hartley, R., Zisserman, A.: Multiple View Geometry in Computer Vision. Cambridge University Press, Cambridge (2000)
34. Heckbert, P.S.: Survey of texture mapping. IEEE Comput. Graph. Appl. **6**(11), 56–67 (1986)
35. Heeren, B., Zhang, C., Rumpf, M., Smith, W.: Principal geodesic analysis in the space of discrete shells. In: Computer Graphics Forum: vol. 37, pp. 173–184. Wiley Online Library, Hoboken (2018)
36. Hoppe, H., DeRose, T., Duchamp, T., McDonald, J., Stuetzle, W.: Surface reconstruction from unorganized points. In: Proceedings of the ACM SIGGRAPH, pp. 71–78 (1992)
37. Hoppe, H.: Efficient implementation of progressive meshes. Comput. Graph. **22**(1), 27–36 (1998)
38. Jin, S., Lewis, R.R., West, D.: A comparison of algorithms for vertex normal computations. Vis. Comput. **21**(1–2), 71–82 (2005)
39. Johnson, A.: Spin-images: a representation for 3-d surface matching. Ph.D. thesis, Robotics Institute, Carnegie Mellon University (1997)
40. Karni, Z., Gotsman, C.: Spectral compression of mesh geometry. In: Proceedings of the SIGGRAPH, pp. 279–286 (2000)
41. Kazhdan, M.: Reconstruction of solid models from oriented point sets. In: Proceedings of the Eurographics Symposium on Geometry Processing (2005)

42. Keselman, L., Woodfill, J.I., Grunnet-Jepsen, A., Bhowmik, A.: Intel realsense stereoscopic depth cameras. arXiv:1705.05548 (2017)
43. Kimmel, R., Sethian, J.A.: Computing geodesic paths on manifolds. Proc. Natl. Acad. Sci. **95**(15), 8431–8435 (1998)
44. Kobbelt, L.: Interpolatory subdivision on open quadrilateral nets with arbitrary topology. Comput. Graph. Forum **15**(3), 409–420 (1996)
45. Koenderink, J.J., van Doorn, A.J.: Surface shape and curvature scales. Image Vis. Comput. **10**(8), 557–565 (1992)
46. Kutulakos, K.N., Seitz, S.M.: A theory of shape by space carving. Int. J. Comput. Vis. **38**(3), 199–218 (2000)
47. Laidlaw, D.H., Trumbore, W.B., Hughes, J.F.: Constructive solid geometry for polyhedral objects. In: Proceedings of the SIGGRAPH, pp. 161–170 (1986)
48. Lebeck, A.O.: Principles and Design of Mechanical Face Seals. Wiley-Interscience, Hoboken (1991)
49. Leotta, M.J., Mundy, J.L.: Predicting high resolution image edges with a generic, adaptive, 3-d vehicle model. In: Proceedings of the CVPR, pp. 1311–1318 (2009)
50. Li, Z., Snavely, N.: Megadepth: Learning single-view depth prediction from internet photos. In: Computer Vision and Pattern Recognition (CVPR) (2018)
51. Litke, N., Levin, A., Schröder, P.: Fitting subdivision surfaces. In: Proceedings of the Conference on Visualization (2001)
52. Long, J., Shelhamer, E., Darrell, T.: Fully convolutional networks for semantic segmentation. In: Proceedings of the IEEE Conference on Computer Vision and Pattern Recognition, pp. 3431–3440 (2015)
53. Loop, C.: Smooth subdivision surfaces based on triangles. Master's thesis, University of Utah (1987)
54. Lorensen, W.E., Cline, H.E.: Arching cubes: a high resolution 3d surface construction algorithm. Comput. Graph. **21**(4) (1987)
55. Max, N.: Weights for computing vertex normals from facet normals. J. Graph. Tools **4**(2), 1–6 (1999)
56. Mescheder, L., Oechsle, M., Niemeyer, M., Nowozin, S., Geiger, A.: Occupancy networks: learning 3d reconstruction in function space. In: Proceedings of the IEEE Conference on Computer Vision and Pattern Recognition, pp. 4460–4470 (2019)
57. Meyer, M., Desbrun, M., Schröder, P., Barr, A.H.: Discrete differential-geometry operators for triangulated 2-manifolds. Vis. Math. **3**(7), 35–57 (2002)
58. Michalkiewicz, M., Pontes, J.K., Jack, D., Baktashmotlagh, M., Eriksson, A.: Implicit surface representations as layers in neural networks. In: Proceedings of the IEEE International Conference on Computer Vision, pp. 4743–4752 (2019)
59. Muller, D.E., Preparata, F.P.: Finding the intersection of two convex polyhedra. Theor. Comput. Sci. **7**, 217–236 (1978)
60. Murali, T.M., Funkhouser, T.A.: Consistent solid and boundary representations from arbitrary polygonal data. In: Proceedings of the Symposium on Interactive 3D Graphics (1997)
61. Nehab, D., Rusinkiewicz, S., Davis, J.E., Ramamoorthi, R.: Efficiently combining positions and normals for precise 3D geometry. ACM Trans. Graphic. (Proc. SIGGRAPH) **24**(3), 536–543 (2005)
62. Nielson, G.M., Hagen, H., Müller, H.: Scientific Visualization: Overviews, Methodologies, and Techniques. IEEE Computer Society Press, Washington, DC (1997)
63. Pajarola, R., Rossignac, J.: Compressed progressive meshes. IEEE Trans. Vis. Comp. Graph. **6**(1), 79–93 (2000)
64. Park, J.J., Florence, P., Straub, J., Newcombe, R., Lovegrove, S.: Deepsdf: learning continuous signed distance functions for shape representation. In: The IEEE Conference on Computer Vision and Pattern Recognition (CVPR) (2019)
65. Paysan, P., Knothe, R., Amberg, B., Romdhani, S., Vetter, T.: A 3D face model for pose and illumination invariant face recognition. In: Proceedings of the IEEE International Conference on Advanced Video and Signal based Surveillance (2009)

66. Peng, J., Kim, C.S., Kuo, C.C.J.: Technologies for 3d mesh compression: a survey. J. Vis. Commun. Image Represent. **16**(6), 688–733 (2005)
67. Peters, J., Reif, U.: Subdivision Surfaces. Springer, Berlin (2008)
68. Pharr, M., Jakob, W., Humphreys, G.: Physically based rendering: from theory to implementation. Morgan Kaufmann, Burlington (2016)
69. Phillips, P.J., Flynn, P.J., Scruggs, T., Bowyer, K.W., Chang, J., Hoffman, K., Marques, J., Jaesik, M., Worek, W.: Overview of the face recognition grand challenge. In: Proceedings of the CVPR, pp. 947–954 (2005)
70. Piegl, L., Tiller, W.: The NURBS Book. Springer, Berlin (1996)
71. Post, F.H., Nielson, G.M., Bonneau, G.P. (eds.): Data Visualization: The State of the Art. Springer, Berlin (2002)
72. Qi, C.R., Su, H., Mo, K., Guibas, L.J.: Pointnet: deep learning on point sets for 3d classification and segmentation. In: Proceedings of the IEEE Conference on Computer Vision and Pattern Recognition, pp. 652–660 (2017)
73. Quéau, Y., Durou, J.D., Aujol, J.F.: Normal integration: a survey. J. Math. Imaging Vis. **60**(4), 576–593 (2018)
74. Rogers, D.F.: An Introduction to NURBS with Historical Perspective. Morgan Kaufmann, Burlington (2001)
75. Rusinkiewicz, S., Levoy, M.: Qsplat: a multiresolution point rendering system for large meshes. In: Proceedings of the SIGGRAPH, pp. 343–352 (2000)
76. Saito, T., Takahashi, T.: Comprehensible rendering of 3-d shapes. In: ACM SIGGRAPH Computer Graphics, vol. 24, pp. 197–206. ACM, New York (1990)
77. Scharstein, D., Szeliski, R.: A taxonomy and evaluation of dense two-frame stereo correspondence algorithms. Int. J. Comput. Vis. **47**(1–3), 7–42 (2002)
78. Schönberger, J.L., Frahm, J.M.: Structure-from-motion revisited. In: Conference on Computer Vision and Pattern Recognition (CVPR) (2016)
79. Sheffer, A., Praun, E., Rose, K.: Mesh parameterization methods and their applications. Found. Trends Comput. Graph. Vis. **2**(2), 105–171 (2006)
80. Shen, C., O'Brien, J.F., Shewchuk, J.R.: Interpolating and approximating implicit surfaces from polygon soup. In: Proceedings of the SIGGRAPH, pp. 896–904 (2004)
81. Smith, C.: On vertex-vertex systems and their use in geometric and biological modelling. Ph.D. thesis, University of Calgary (2006)
82. Smith, R.C., Cheeseman, P.: On the representation and estimation of spatial uncertainty. Int. J. Robot. Res. **5**(4), 56–68 (1986)
83. Smith, W., Fang, F.: Height from photometric ratio with model-based light source selection. Comput. Vis. Image Understand. **145**, 128–138 (2016)
84. Smith, N.B., Webb, A.: Introduction to Medical Imaging: Physics Engineering and Clinical Applications. Cambridge University Press, Cambridge (2010)
85. Stam, J.: Exact evaluation of Catmull–Clark subdivision surfaces at arbitrary parameter values. In: Proceedings of the SIGGRAPH, pp. 395–404 (1998)
86. Stroud, I.: Boundary Representation Modelling Techniques. Springer, Berlin (2006)
87. Stutz, D., Geiger, A.: Learning 3d shape completion from laser scan data with weak supervision. In: Proceedings of the IEEE Conference on Computer Vision and Pattern Recognition, pp. 1955–1964 (2018)
88. Suetens, P.: Fundamentals of Medical Imaging. Cambridge University Press, Cambridge (2009)
89. Takeuchi, S., Kanai, T., Suzuki, H., Shimada, K., Kimura, F.: Subdivision surface fitting with qem-based mesh simplification and reconstruction of approximated b-spline surfaces. In: Proceedings of the Pacific Conference on Computer Graphics and Applications, pp. 202–212 (2000)
90. Tatarchenko, M., Dosovitskiy, A., Brox, T.: Octree generating networks: efficient convolutional architectures for high-resolution 3d outputs. In: Proceedings of the IEEE International Conference on Computer Vision, pp. 2088–2096 (2017)

91. Taubin, G.: A signal processing approach to fair surface design. In: Proceedings of the SIG-GRAPH, pp. 351–358 (1995)
92. Taubin, G., Rossignac, J.: Geometric compression through topological surgery. ACM Trans. Graphic. **17**(2), 84–115 (1998)
93. Thürmer, G., Wüthrich, C.A.: Computing vertex normals from polygonal facets. J. Graph. Tools **3**(1), 43–46 (1998)
94. Vince, J.A.: Mathematics for Computer Graphics. Springer, Berlin (2010)
95. Watt, A.: 3D Computer Graphics. Addison Wesley, Boston (1999)
96. Weiler, K.: Edge-based data structures for solid modeling in a curved surface environment. IEEE Comput. Graph. Appl. **5**(1), 21–40 (1985)
97. Zeng, A., Song, S., Nießner, M., Fisher, M., Xiao, J., Funkhouser, T.: 3dmatch: learning local geometric descriptors from rgb-d reconstructions. In: Proceedings of the IEEE Conference on Computer Vision and Pattern Recognition, pp. 1802–1811 (2017)
98. Zhang, Z.: Microsoft kinect sensor and its effect. IEEE Multimedia **19**(2), 4–10 (2012)
99. Zienkiewicz, O.C., Taylor, R.L., Zhu, J.Z.: The Finite Element Method: Its Basis and Fundamentals. Butterworth-Heinemann, Oxford (2005)
100. Zorin, D., Schröder, P., Sweldens, W.: Interpolating subdivision for meshes with arbitrary topology. In: Proceedings of the SIGGRAPH, pp. 189–192 (1996)

Part II
3D Shape Analysis and Inference

In the following chapter, we discuss local shape descriptors, both classical descriptors that are hand-crafted and those that are learned. Such descriptors allow us to find corresponding surface points on pairs of 3D images in a reasonable computational time. Chapter 8 then discusses 3D shape registration, which is the process of bringing one 3D shape into alignment with another similar 3D shape. The initial discussion centers on the well-known *Iterative Closest Points* algorithm of Besl and McKay and its variants. Advanced non-rigid registration approaches are covered. In Chap. 9, we discuss the 3D shape matching processes that allow us to build applications in both 3D shape retrieval (e.g. in shape search engines) and 3D object recognition. Although that chapter is largely application-based, we kept it within this book part, as it contains some basic concepts in 3D shape matching. Chapter 10 discussed 3D Morphable Models, both how they are trained and how they are fitted to data. The human face, ears and head are used as exemplars. Finally, in Chap. 11, we discuss deep learning on 3D datasets.

Chapter 7
3D Local Descriptors—from Handcrafted to Learned

Riccardo Spezialetti, Samuele Salti, Luigi Di Stefano, and Federico Tombari

Abstract Surface matching is a fundamental task in 3D computer vision, typically tackled by describing and matching local features computed from the 3D surface. As a result, description of local features lays the foundations for a variety of applications processing 3D data, such as 3D object recognition, 3D registration and reconstruction, and SLAM. A variety of algorithms for 3D feature description exists in the scientific literature. The majority of them are based on different, handcrafted ways to encode and exploit the geometric properties of a given surface. Recently, the success of deep neural networks for processing images has fueled also a data-driven approach to learn descriptive features from 3D data. This chapter provides a comprehensive review of the main proposals in the field.

7.1 Introduction

Nowadays, surface matching is solved by establishing point-to-point correspondences obtained by matching *local 3D descriptors* [13, 43, 72]. Local 3D descriptors are also referred to as *local features* and the paradigm, illustrated in Fig. 7.1, is referred to as *feature-based matching*. Examples of 3D computer vision tasks that leverage local 3D descriptors are as follows:

- **3D Object Detection:** Identification within a scene of an object from a library of models and estimation of its 6D pose.

R. Spezialetti (✉) · S. Salti · L. Di Stefano
University of Bologna, Bologna, Italy
e-mail: riccardo.spezialetti@unibo.it

S. Salti
e-mail: samuele.salti@unibo.it

L. Di Stefano
e-mail: luigi.distefano@unibo.it

F. Tombari
TU Munich and Google, Munich, Germany
e-mail: tombari@in.tum.de

© Springer Nature Switzerland AG 2020   319
Y. Liu et al. (eds.), *3D Imaging, Analysis and Applications*,
https://doi.org/10.1007/978-3-030-44070-1_7

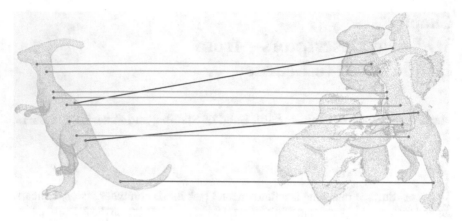

Fig. 7.1 Feature-based matching paradigm. Green lines correspond to good correspondences, while red lines correspond to mismatches

- **3D Object Reconstruction:** Recreate the shape and appearance of objects by registering a set of partial views.
- **3D Object Retrieval:** Retrieving three-dimensional models in large databases given a similar object as a query or given a textual description of the object.
- **SLAM (Simultaneous Localization and Mapping):** Building the map of an unknown environment while simultaneously localizing the sensor therein.

Descriptors or features are a compact but rich representation of the underlying 3D data designed to be either *invariant* or *robust* to a large set of nuisances, like rotation, point density variations, sensor noise, viewpoint changes, occlusions, and clutter.

Depending on the area involved, we can classify descriptors as either *global* or *local*. *Global* methods encode the entire 3D model in the descriptor [1, 39, 49] and are usually applied after a segmentation step to limit the influence of clutter. *Local* descriptors, instead, encode a small part of the surface, small with respect to the overall scene or object being matched (i.e., a neighborhood around a keypoint). The main advantage of using local descriptors versus global ones is higher robustness to partial occlusions of the surface and to the presence of clutter. For this reason, the latter are currently the dominant approach. In this chapter, we will focus uniquely on local descriptors, illustrating the main proposals in the literature and the way they have evolved from mostly handcrafted proposals to those based on deep learning.

According to [19], two key aspects for a 3D local descriptor are *descriptiveness* and *robustness*: descriptiveness refers to the capacity to capture predominant traits of the surface; and robustness is the ability to be not sensitive (i.e., to obtain a similar descriptor) in the presence of disturbances that can affect the data. Choosing the descriptor offering the right descriptiveness/robustness trade-off for a specific 3D computer vision application is a crucial step and still an open issue: usually, a few prominent alternatives are tested and the best performing one is used.

A typical *feature matching pipeline* consists of the following:

- **Feature detection:** The goal is to identify points of a surface particularly prominent with respect to a given saliency function computed on a local neighborhood of each point. These points are called *keypoints*.
- **Feature description:** As discussed, a descriptor is a compact representation of geometric properties of a point. Descriptors usually are designed to encode essential characteristics of points and to be invariant to nuisances like variations of point density and viewpoint. To speed up the overall feature matching process, typically just the keypoints of an object are described.
- **Feature matching:** The last phase of the pipeline yields correspondences between two or more surfaces by finding the most similar descriptors among the sets of descriptors computed at the keypoints of the surfaces. Several metrics can be used to compare descriptors, the most popular being the Euclidean distance in the descriptors space.

7.2   Background

Before we go into this chapter, let us provide some background definitions for a better understanding of the related works. We will start talking about the data structures most commonly used to represent 3D data (point clouds and meshes are described in more detail in Chap. 6), and then we will introduce the basic concepts related to the computation of local features, and finally conclude with some definitions about the most widespread noise sources that can be observed in 3D data.

- **Point cloud**: A point cloud is a set of points, which describes the shape of 3D object, characterized by their position in a coordinate system expressed with euclidean coordinates. In addition to the single coordinates, it is also possible to store information about the color of the points, as an RGB triplet, and their intensity (alpha channel). Cloud points are unorganized data structures, i.e., simple data collections, whose closeness in the data structure does not imply closeness in the observed space. The main limitation of this data structure is the high cost of searching for neighbors for a point in the 3D coordinate space.
- **Polygon mesh**: A polygon mesh is a collection of vertices, edges, and faces that defines the shape of 3D object. The faces usually consist of triangles, quadrilaterals, or other simple convex polygons. Unlike cloud points, meshes are organized data structures.
- **Feature point**: A feature point, denoted by **p**, is a point belonging to a 3D shape $\mathcal{M}$, for which the descriptor is being computed. Typically, feature points coincide with keypoints.
- **Support**: A support of a feature point **p** is the set of neighboring points lying within a spherical ball of radius $r > 0$ centered at **p**, denoted by $B_r(p) = \{s \in \mathcal{M} : \|p - s\|_2 < r\}$. Alternatively, the support can be made up of a fixed number of neighbors. Usually to the search for nearby points, a space-partitioning data

structure for organizing points in a k-dimensional space like k-trees [3] is utilized. The support of the feature point is used to compute the associated descriptor.

- **Local reference frame**: A Local Reference Frame (LRF) is a local system of Cartesian coordinates at each point, with respect to which the local geometric structure around that point is encoded. An LRF $\mathcal{L}(p)$ at point $\mathbf{p} \in \mathcal{M}$ is an orthogonal set of unit vectors:

$$\mathcal{L}(p) = \{\hat{\mathbf{x}}(p), \hat{\mathbf{y}}(p), \hat{\mathbf{z}}(p)\} \tag{7.1}$$

Invariance with respect to the object's pose is a fundamental trait of every 3D descriptor: state-of-the-art proposals achieve invariance using either a *Reference Axis* or a *Local Reference Frame (LRF)*, which co-variate with the object pose. Before descriptor computation, the support of the feature point is translated and oriented according to the Local Reference Frame or Reference Axis, effectively removing the pose change and making subsequent computations on geometric entities of the support pose-invariant. As is clear from this description and proven experimentally in [42], the repeatability of the reference system is key for the performance of the descriptor.

- **Clutter and cluttered scene**: The concept of clutter is related to object detection. In this context, we want to recognize a certain number of well-known objects within a scene. A clutter object is a distracting object that is not part of the set of known objects but can be present in the scene. Similarly, a scene containing a clutter object is defined as a cluttered scene.
- **Missing part**: Once scanned, objects may present missing parts due to the sensor's limited field of view or the shadow generated by the presence of other objects in the scene.

7.3 Related Works

This section reviews the main proposals for local 3D descriptors. In Fig. 7.2, we show a temporal evolution of the main proposals for 3D descriptors. A large body of work has been dedicated to define new and more effective solutions to the surface matching problem based on local 3D descriptors in the last 20 years: *Point Signature* [10], *Spin Images* [28], *3D Shape Context* [16], *Local Surface Patch*[9], *Point Feature Histograms*[48], *Scale-Dependent Local Shape Descriptor* [38], *Heat Kernel Signature* [58], *Fast Point Feature Histograms* [47], *Intrinsic Shape Signature* [73], *MeshHog* [71], *3D Surf* [32], *SHOT* [51], *Unique Shape Context* [60], *Rops* [20], *Trisi* [21], *Toldi* [68], *3D Match* [72], *CGF* [29], *PPFNet* [14], and *PPF-FoldNet* [13].

Local 3D descriptors can be further categorized into two main categories: those encoding handcrafted traits of the support and those obtained as output of a (deep) learning algorithm. In the latter case, typically a deep neural network is trained purposely to infer the 3D descriptor given a portion or the entire surface as input.

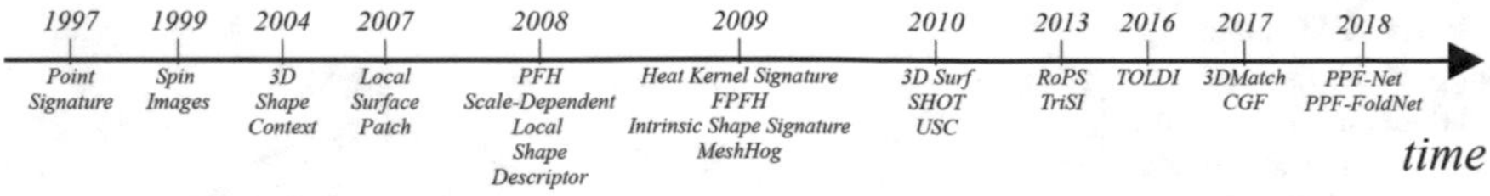

1997	1999	2004	2007	2008	2009	2010	2013	2016	2017	2018
Point Signature	Spin Images	3D Shape Context	Local Surface Patch	PFH Scale-Dependent Local Shape Descriptor	Heat Kernel Signature FPFH Intrinsic Shape Signature MeshHog	3D Surf SHOT USC	RoPS TriSI	TOLDI	3DMatch CGF	PPF-Net PPF-FoldNet

time

Fig. 7.2 Temporal evolution of 3D feature descriptors

Fig. 7.3 Bins of 3D shape context. The grid is divided into several bins along the radial, azimuth, and elevation dimensions

7.3.1   Handcrafted Local 3D Descriptors

A local 3D descriptor creates a compact representation of a 3D surface by collecting geometric or topological measurements into histograms. According to [19], hand-crafted local 3D descriptors can be grouped in *spatial distribution histogram* and *geometric attribute histogram*. Spatial distribution histogram counts the number of points falling in each histogram bin taking into account the spatial distribution of the points on the surface. Conversely, geometric attribute histogram generates histograms exploiting geometric properties of the surface like normals or curvatures.

In the following, we give an overview of methods belonging to both categories.

7.3.1.1   3D Shape Context

3D shape context (3DSC) directly extends the 2D shape context descriptor [2] to three dimensions. It was introduced by Frome et al. [16] in 2004.

The descriptor captures the local shape of a point cloud at a feature point **p** using the distribution of points in a spherical grid support. The normal **n** at **p** serves as a reference axis to align the north pole of the grid. Within the support region, a set of bins is constructed by equally dividing the azimuth and elevation dimensions, while the radial dimension is logarithmically spaced, as shown in Fig. 7.3. Due to this binning scheme, the descriptor is more robust to distortions in shape with distance from the feature point.

Each point p_i in the support is mapped to its corresponding bin using spherical coordinates, and the bin corresponding to them accumulates a weighted sum of local point density. The local point density for p_i is estimated as the number of

Fig. 7.4 USC unambiguous support. The spatial subdivision of 3DSC is aligned according to a Local Reference Frame to obtain a unique descriptor for each feature point

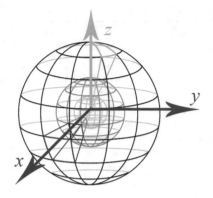

the points in a sphere of radius δ around p_i. Relying only on a reference axis and not on a full 3D reference frame, the descriptor is invariant up to a rotation along the north pole. Therefore, multiple descriptors for a single feature point have to be described and matched across different views of a surface, which significantly slows down the performance of the overall pipeline. The size of the final descriptor is $d_a \times d_e \times d_r$, where d_a, d_e, and d_r are, respectively, the numbers of bins along the azimuth, elevation, and radial axes, and the number of descriptors to be computed for a feature point is equal to d_a.

7.3.1.2 Unique Shape Context

Unique Shape Context (USC) improves 3DSC by leveraging a definition of repeatable and unambiguous Local Reference Frame as pointed out in Fig. 7.4. It was presented by Tombari et al. at the *ACM workshop on 3D object retrieval* in 2010.

One of the main drawbacks of 3DSC is the computation of multiple descriptors at a given feature point. Indeed, to take into account the degree of freedom on azimuth direction, a vector on the tangent plane at the normal **n** at the feature point **p** is randomly chosen and the grid support is then rotated about its north pole in to d_a positions. Each rotation defines a unique Local Reference Frame used to orientate the sphere grid and to compute the associated descriptor. As a consequence, d_a descriptors are estimated and stored for each feature point.

Differently from 3DSC, in USC the authors first estimate a Local Reference Frame using the same approach presented in Sect. 7.4.1.1 and proposed in [60], and then construct the descriptor likewise 3DSC.

Thanks to the adopted unique and repeatable Local Reference Frame, USC improves efficiency in terms of both performance and memory footprint with respect to 3DSC. The size of the final descriptor is the same as 3DSC.

7.3.1.3   Rotational Projection Statistics

Rotational Projection Statistics (RoPS) is a local 3D descriptor designed to operate on meshes. It was published by Guo et al. [20] in 2013. The first contribution of RoPS is the definition of a novel Local Reference Frame which relies on the eigenvalue decomposition of the covariance matrix. Differently from pre-existing approaches, the covariance matrix for a given feature point $\mathbf{p}$ is estimated by aggregating covariance matrices computed for every single triangle within the support. Every single matrix is weighted differently to mitigate the effect of mesh resolution variations and enhance the robustness of clutter and occlusion. The obtained $\hat{\mathbf{x}}$ and $\hat{\mathbf{z}}$ axes are disambiguated in order to achieve a unique and repeatable canonical orientation. The third axis, $\hat{\mathbf{y}}$, is derived as $\hat{\mathbf{z}} \times \hat{\mathbf{x}}$.

As for the histogram computation, the whole process is illustrated in Fig. 7.4 in [20]. Given the $\hat{\mathbf{x}}$-axis, the points within the support are rotated around it by a given angle, and projected onto three planes xy, yz, and xz. For each projection, a distribution matrix $\mathcal{D}$ is built by partitioning the plane into $L \times L$ bins and counting up the number of points falling into each bin. The number of bins represents the matrix dimension and is a parameter of the method. The distribution matrix $\mathcal{D}$ contains information about the local surface from a particular viewpoint. Hence, *five* statistics, including the central moments [12, 25] and Shannon entropy [54] are extracted from each distribution matrix. Different rotations along the same axis are taking into account to capture information from various viewpoints. The abovementioned process is repeated again for the $\hat{\mathbf{y}}$- and $\hat{\mathbf{z}}$-axes. The final descriptor is obtained by concatenating the statistics of all rotations. The size is $3 \times 3 \times 5 \times d_{rot}$, where d_{rot} is the number of rotations around each axis.

7.3.1.4   Point Feature Histogram

Point Feature Histogram (PFH) is designed to capture the surface variations based on the relationships between points in the local neighborhood and directions of the estimated normals. Hence, the performance is closely related to the quality of the surface normal estimations at each point. It was introduced by Rusu et al. [48] in 2008.

As shown in Fig. 7.5, for every pair of points $\mathbf{p}_i$ and $\mathbf{p}_j$, in the neighborhood of $\mathbf{p}$, a Darboux frame is built by choosing one point as source $\mathbf{p}_s$, and the other as target $\mathbf{p}_t$:

$$\mathbf{u} = \mathbf{n}_s, \mathbf{v} = \mathbf{u} \times \frac{\mathbf{p}_t - \mathbf{p}_s}{\|\mathbf{p}_t - \mathbf{p}_s\|}, \mathbf{w} = \mathbf{u} \times \mathbf{v} \qquad (7.2)$$

Next, using the frame defined above, three angular features, expressing the relationship between normals $\mathbf{n}_t$ and $\mathbf{n}_s$, and between normals and the difference vector between $\mathbf{p}_t$ and $\mathbf{p}_s$ are computed for each pair of points:

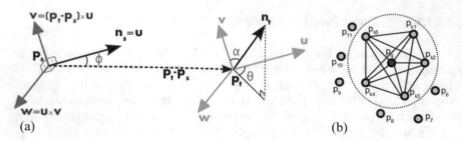

Fig. 7.5 PFH overview. (**a**) The u, v, and w vectors of a Darboux frame computed for a pair of points. Given two points $\mathbf{p}_i$ and $\mathbf{p}_j$ together with their normal $\mathbf{n}_i$ and $\mathbf{n}_j$, one is chosen as source point, $\mathbf{p}_s$, and the other as target point $\mathbf{p}_t$. (**b**) PFH computation for a feature point $\mathbf{p}$ shown in red. All the points enclosed in the support region are interconnected in a dense mesh. The histogram is built taking into account the angular features between all pairs of points, leading to $\mathbf{O}(k^2)$ computational complexity for a point with k neighbor points. Images from [41]

$$\alpha = \langle \mathbf{v}, \mathbf{n}_t \rangle, \phi = \langle \mathbf{u}, \mathbf{p}_t - \mathbf{p}_s \rangle / d, \theta = arctan(\langle \mathbf{w}, \mathbf{n}_t \rangle, \langle \mathbf{u}, \mathbf{n}_t \rangle), d = ||\mathbf{p}_t - \mathbf{p}_s|| \tag{7.3}$$

Also, the length of the difference vector d can be used as feature, although it is usually not considered as the distance between neighboring points increases with the distance from the viewpoint with standard 3D sensors. The PFH descriptor is obtained by binning each feature range with b bins and counting the occurrences for each bin. The final dimension is b^4, or b^3 if distance d is ignored.

7.3.1.5 Fast Point Feature Histogram

The computation of features for each pair of points makes PFH computationally expensive and not suitable for real-time application. Therefore, Rusu et al. introduced *Fast Point Feature Histogram* (FPFH) [47] in 2009. FPFH is a simplified variant of PFH and operates in two steps. First, a Simplified Point Feature Histogram (SPFH) is constructed using three angular features α, ϕ, and θ, for each point within support of and its own neighbors. The computed features are then binned into three separate histograms and concatenated to form the SPFH descriptor for each point. Secondly, the FPFH descriptor for $\mathbf{p}$ is obtained by summing up the SPFH descriptors belonging to each point within the support. The sum is weighted by the distance between the query point and a neighbor in the support region as shown in Fig. 7.6. The FPFH descriptor can reduce the computational complexity from $O(nk^2)$ to $O(nk)$, where k is the number of neighboring points.

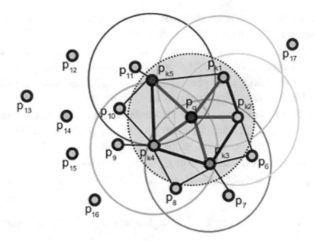

Fig. 7.6 FPFH overview. For a given feature point p_q, the algorithm first estimates its SPFH values by creating pairs between itself and its neighbors (illustrated using red lines). Then the SPFH values of p_q are weighted using the SPFH values of its p_k neighbors, thus creating the FPFH for p_q. The extra FPFH connections, resulting due to the additional weighting scheme, are shown with black lines. The connections marked with thicker lines will contribute to the FPFH twice. Image from [40]

7.3.2 Learned Local 3D Descriptors

The success of deep neural networks for processing images has motivated a data-driven approach to learning features from point clouds. Adaptation of deep learning to point cloud data is, however, far from straightforward. Indeed, the most effective deep neural networks deployed to process images, i.e., convolutional neural networks, are fed with input data arranged into a regular grid structure, but point clouds are inherently unstructured: a point cloud is a set of point coordinates without any obvious orderings between points.

3D deep learning approaches can be classified as follows:

- **View-based methods**: A 3D object is represented as a collection of 2D views. Standard 2D CNNs operate on every single view, and the learned features are merged together by a view pooling technique [57]. Moreover, these methods are suitable for application where the input data is a range image [64].
- **Voxel-based methods**: Early works were based on 3D voxels, regular 3D grids of occupancy, or density of points obtained from point clouds [11, 36, 56, 65, 72]. Although this representation is straightforward to obtain from point clouds, memory occupancy issues force the algorithm to operate with very small resolutions, which in turn introduces artifacts and makes it difficult to learn fine details of geometric structures. To address this limitation, some proposals rely on space partitions methods like k-d trees or octrees [31, 59]. References [44] combine view-based and voxel approaches to address 3D shape classification.

- **Point-based methods**: These methods operate directly on unordered point sets. The first pioneering work in this direction was PointNet [43], where a symmetric function is applied to 3D coordinates to achieve invariance to permutation. However, PointNet is not able to capture local information around points. Hence, the same authors introduced an improved multi-scale architecture, named PointNet++ [45], to exploit geometric features in a local point set.
- **Geometric Deep Learning**: These methods attempt to generalize deep learning model to non-Euclidean domains such as graphs and manifold [8]. The first formulation of neural networks on graphs was proposed in [52]. More recently, it has been extended to operate on non-rigid shape analysis [5, 6]. Finally, [63] proposes a graph convolution network (GCN) directly on point sets by means of *edge convolution*.

Chapter 11 will provide a more thorough overview of deep learning methods on 3D data.

When dealing with feature learning, two loss functions are usually taken into account to preserve in the feature space the proximity of neighboring patches in the Euclidean space: the contrastive loss [22] and the triplet loss [24], which consider pairs and triplets of patches, respectively. Usually, triplet loss is more favorable than contrastive loss because it takes an *anchor* example and tries to bring *positive* examples closer while also pushing away negative example. However, triplet loss performance heavily depends on the selection of the anchor, negative, and positive examples. Within this context, we can think of the anchor and the positive as the same 3D point captured from two different point of views, while the negative is from a viewpoint far from both. For more details as well as a graphic example of the difference between contrastive and triplet loss, we refer the reader to Fig. 7.4 in [14].

7.3.2.1   3DMatch

One of the first methods that learns a 3D local feature descriptor by means of deep learning algorithms is *3DMatch* [72], introduced by Zeng et al. in 2017.

Early work [36, 44] in this field-constructed voxel grid in the form of a binary-occupancy grid to represent sparse unstructured 3D data. 3DMatch extends this idea to more informative encoding based on the Truncated Signed Distance Function (TSDF) [37, 62].

In 3DMatch, a standard Siamese 3D ConvNet is trained with a contrastive loss function [22] that minimizes the l_2 distance between descriptors generated from matching points, and maximizes l_2 distance between non-corresponding points. The architecture of the network is inspired by AlexNet [33]. An overview of the method is depicted in Fig. 7.2 in [72]. The train set consists of RGB-D images of indoor scenes collected from existing popular datasets [23, 34, 55, 62, 66]. During the train stage, a local region is extracted around a randomly sampled interest point and voxelized with a grid of size $0.01 \, \text{m}^3$. Every voxel in the $30 \times 30 \times 30$ grid thus obtained stores a TDF value that indicates the distance between the center of that voxel to the nearest

3D surface. Since TSDF can be computed from meshes, point clouds, or depth maps, any one of these 3D data structures can be used as input to the network. The size of the final descriptor is 512.

7.3.2.2 PPFNet: Point Pair Feature NETwork

Point Pair Feature NETwork aims to learn a local descriptor by working directly on point coordinates augmented with handcrafted features. It was originally proposed by Deng et al. [14] in 2018.

PPFNet combines the permutation-invariant characteristics of PointNet [43] together with the high descriptive capacity of Point Pair Features (PPFs) [15]. The network is fed by geometries containing information about the local neighborhood of a 3D point such as raw point coordinates, normals, and PPFs. As depicted in Fig. 7.2 in [14], PPFNet architecture consists of three parts: a first cluster of mini-PointNets, a concatenation block, and a final group of MLPs.

The cluster of mini-PointNets processes N local patches uniformly sampled from a point cloud and extracts local features. Weights and gradients are shared within the cluster. With the aid of a max-pooling layer acting on local features, a global context information is created and then concatenated to every local feature. Max pool operation encapsulates the distinct local information capturing the global context of the whole point cloud. Finally, a group of MLPs merges the global and local features and creates the learned local descriptor.

PPFNet extends contrastive loss to N-patches by introducing a novel N-tuple loss, and it operates on a set of partial scans belonging to the same environment where the ground truth transformation $\mathbf{T}$ between scans is known. The distance between learned features of corresponding patches is minimized acting on two distance matrices: a correspondence matrix $\mathbf{M} \in \mathbb{R}^{N \times N}$, built on the points of the aligned scans, $\mathbf{M} = (m_{ij})$ with

$$m_{ij} = \mathbb{1}(\|\mathbf{x}_i - \mathbf{T}\mathbf{y}_j\|_2 < \tau) \tag{7.4}$$

and $\mathbb{1}$ is the indicator function; and a feature–space distance matrix $\mathbf{D} \in \mathbb{R}^{N \times N}$, $\mathbf{D} = (d_{ij})$ with

$$d_{ij} = \|f(\mathbf{x}_i) - f(\mathbf{y}_j)\|_2. \tag{7.5}$$

By defining the operator $\sum^*(\cdot)$ as the sum of all the elements in a matrix, the N-tuple loss can be formulated as

$$L = \sum{}^* \left(\frac{\mathbf{M} \circ \mathbf{D}}{\|\mathbf{M}\|_2^2} + \alpha \frac{max(\theta - (1 - \mathbf{M}) \circ \mathbf{D}, 0)}{N^2 - \|\mathbf{M}\|_2^2} \right) \tag{7.6}$$

where $\circ$ is the Hadamard product (element-wise multiplication), α is a hyper-parameter balancing the weight between matching and non-matching pairs, and θ is the lower bound on the expected distance between non-correspondent pairs.

PPFNet is trained using real data scenes from 3DMatch benchmark [72]. The dataset is described in Sect. 7.5. To explain how training data are sampled for PPFNet, however, it is important to anticipate that each of the 62 different real-world scenes in the dataset contains a variable number of *fragments*, i.e.,partial views, whose registration reconstructs the full scene.

Rather than randomly detecting keypoints in each fragment, mini-batches in PPFNet are created by randomly extracting the fragments and each point in a fragment acts as a keypoint. To reduce the amount of training data, each fragment is down-sampled to 2048 sample points. A radius search of 30 cm around each keypoint is performed to extract a local patch. Then, to increase robustness against point density variations each patch is down-sampled to 1024 points. If a patch contains less than 1024 points, points are randomly repeated. Due to memory limitations, each batch contains two fragment pairs with 8192 local patches. Number of combinations for the network at per batch is 2×2048^2.

7.4 Methods

Within this section, we provide a detailed presentation of some of the most popular methods for 3D local features description. The algorithms presented have been chosen on the basis of their heterogeneity, in order to provide a complete overview to the reader. We present two handcrafted methods, **SHOT** [51] and **Spin Images** [28], and two methods based on deep learning techniques, **CGF** [29] and **PPF-FoldNet** [13].

7.4.1 SHOT: Unique Signatures of Histograms for Local Surface Description

The *SHOT* descriptor [51] can be used both for surface description, as originally presented in [60], and for combined shape and texture description [61], if RGB information are available.

The approach is based on the observation that local 3D descriptors can be categorized into *signatures* and *histograms* (Fig. 7.7):

- **Signatures**: These descriptors use one or more geometric attributes computed separately at each point within the support to describe the surface. The computed measurements are encoded according to the local coordinates defined by an invariant local reference frame. Signatures are highly descriptive but small errors in the definition of the local reference frame or small perturbations in the encoded trait can substantially modify the final descriptor;
- **Histograms**: These descriptors use histograms to capture different characteristics of the surface. A specific domain of quantization (e.g., point coordinates, curva-

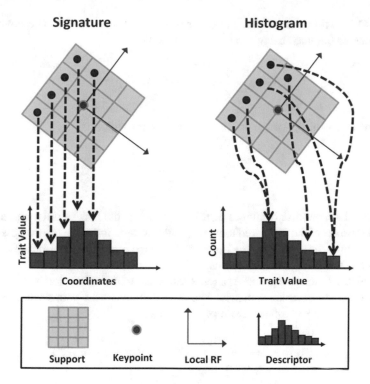

Fig. 7.7 Signatures and histograms. For the sake of clarity, the figure reports an example in a 2D domain

tures, normal angles) is discretized, and topological entities (e.g., vertices, mesh triangle areas) are accumulated into each spatial bin. If the descriptor domain is based on coordinates, the definition of a local reference frame is again required to obtain a pose-invariant descriptor. Histogram-like descriptor loses descriptive power due to the quantization error but offers greater robustness to noise.

Based on this taxonomy, SHOT was proposed to combine the advantages of signature-based methods with those of histogram-based methods, hence, the name Signature of Histograms of OrienTations (SHOT). This design choice makes SHOT representation operate at a good trade-off point between descriptiveness and robustness to noise.

7.4.1.1 Local Reference Frame

According to [67], the local reference frame proposed in SHOT belongs to *covariance analysis* methods. The computation of $\hat{\mathbf{x}}$-, $\hat{\mathbf{y}}$-, and $\hat{\mathbf{z}}$-axes rely on the Singular Value Decomposition (SVD) or Eigenvalue Decomposition (EVD) of a covariance matrix of the points, p_i, lying within a spherical support of radius R centered at the feature point **p**. We define k as the total number of points in the support. The covariance matrix can be obtained using the following equation:

$$C(\mathbf{p}) = \frac{1}{k} \sum_{i=0}^{k} (\mathbf{p}_i - \hat{\mathbf{p}})(\mathbf{p}_i - \hat{\mathbf{p}})^T \tag{7.7}$$

where $\hat{\mathbf{p}}$ is the centroid of the points lying within the support:

$$\hat{\mathbf{p}} = \frac{1}{k} \sum_{i=0}^{k} \mathbf{p}_i \tag{7.8}$$

One of the main disadvantages of this approach is the lack of uniqueness of the signs of the axes of the estimated local reference system. Indeed, as clearly discussed in [7], although the eigenvectors of Eq. 7.7 define the principal directions of the data, their sign is not defined unambiguously.

The SHOT descriptor proposes a local reference frame estimation that employs a slightly modified covariance matrix. The contributions of the points within support are weighted by their distance from **p**:

$$C_{\mathbf{w}}(\mathbf{p}) = \frac{1}{\sum_{i:d_i \leq R} (R-d_i)} \sum_{i:d_i \leq R} (R - d_i)(\mathbf{p}_i - \mathbf{p})(\mathbf{p}_i - \mathbf{p})^T \tag{7.9}$$

with $d_i = \|\mathbf{p}_i - \mathbf{p}\|_2$. By using a weighted covariance matrix, the repeatability in cluttered scenes in object recognition scenario is improved. Furthermore, to reduce computational complexity the centroid $\hat{\mathbf{p}}$ in (7.7) is replaced by the feature point **p**. Then, similar to [7], sign ambiguity is addressed by reorienting the sign of each eigenvector of $C_{\mathbf{w}}(\mathbf{p})$ so that its sign is coherent with the majority of the vectors it is representing. This procedure is applied to both $\hat{\mathbf{x}}$ and $\hat{\mathbf{z}}$. So, if we refer to the eigenvector corresponding to the largest eigenvalue as the $\mathbf{x}^+$ axis and we denote as $\mathbf{x}^-$ the opposite vector, the sign ambiguity is removed according to

$$S_x^+ \doteq \left\{ i : d_i \leq R \wedge (\mathbf{p}_i - \mathbf{p}) \cdot \mathbf{x}^+ \geq 0 \right\} \tag{7.10}$$

$$S_x^- \doteq \left\{ i : d_i \leq R \wedge (\mathbf{p}_i - \mathbf{p}) \cdot \mathbf{x}^- > 0 \right\} \tag{7.11}$$

$$\mathbf{x} = \begin{cases} \mathbf{x}^+, & |S_x^+| \geq |S_x^-| \\ \mathbf{x}^-, & \text{otherwise} \end{cases} \tag{7.12}$$

This results in the $\hat{\mathbf{x}}$ axis pointing in the direction of greater sample density. The same procedure is used to disambiguate the $\hat{\mathbf{z}}$-axis, while the third unit vector is computed via the cross-product $\hat{\mathbf{y}} = \hat{\mathbf{z}} \times \hat{\mathbf{x}}$.

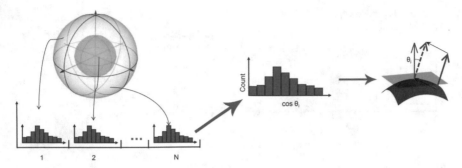

Fig. 7.8 The hybrid structure of shot. On the left side, the spherical support that acts as a signature, while on the right side the local histograms accumulate bin counters according to $cos\theta_i$

7.4.1.2   Histogram Computation

SHOT descriptor encodes the histograms of the surface normals at different spatial locations. This choice stems from the related field of 2D descriptors. According to the authors, there are two major reasons behind **SIFT** effectiveness [35], the most successful proposal among 2D descriptors. Firstly, SIFT computes a set of local histograms on specific subsets of pixels defined by a regular grid superimposed on the patch. Secondly, the elements of these local histograms are based on first-order derivatives describing the signal of interest, i.e., intensity gradients. Following these considerations, SHOT computes a set of local histograms over the 3D volumes defined by a 3D spherical grid superimposed on the support. As for the signature structure, the spherical grid is partitioned uniformly along the radial, azimuth, and elevation axes. The grid is aligned with the axes given by the estimated local reference frame. Each local histogram counts the number of points falling into each bin according to the cosine of the angle, θ_i, between the normal at each point $\mathbf{n}_i$ and the local $\hat{\mathbf{z}}_k$-axis. The hybrid structure of SHOT is sketched in Fig. 7.8.

The choice of cosine is mainly motivated by two aspects. The first is computational efficiency, as it can be computed as $cos\theta_i = \hat{\mathbf{z}}_k \cdot \mathbf{n}_i$. The second one is related to the descriptiveness of the algorithm. With an equally spaced binning on $cos\theta_i$, small differences in orthogonal directions to the normal, i.e., presumably the most informative ones, cause points to be accumulated in different bins leading to different histograms. Moreover, in the presence of quasi-planar regions (i.e., not very descriptive ones), this choice limits histogram differences due to noise by concentrating counts in a smaller number of bins.

Since the SHOT descriptor is generated by appending all the local histograms, the cardinality of the descriptor is related to the number of partitions. The authors indicate that 32 is a proper number of volumes, resulting from 8 azimuth divisions, 2 elevation divisions, and 2 radial divisions, while the number of bins for the internal histograms is 11, leading to total descriptor length of 352.

The use of histograms could render the description very sensitive to boundary effects. Furthermore, due to the spatial subdivision of the support, boundary effects

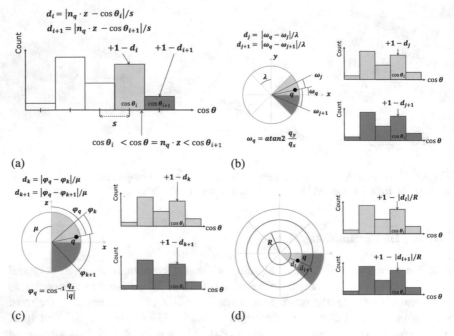

Fig. 7.9 SHOT quadrilinear interpolation. **a** Interpolation on normal cosines. **b** Interpolation on azimuth. **c** Interpolation on elevation. **d** Interpolation on distance

may also occur due to perturbations of the local reference frame. A commonly adopted solution is to perform linear interpolation between the point being accumulated into a specific local histogram bin and its neighbors, i.e., the neighboring bin in the local histogram and the bins having the same index in the local histograms corresponding to the neighboring subdivisions of the grid. In SHOT, this results in a quadrilinear interpolation, where each bin is incremented by a weight of $1 - d$ for each dimension. As for the local histogram, d is the distance of the current entry from the central value of the bin. As for elevation and azimuth, d is the angular distance of the entry from the central value of the volume. Along the radial dimension, d is the Euclidean distance of the entry from the central value of the volume. Along each dimension, d is normalized by the distance between two neighbor bins or volumes. Figure 7.9 illustrates a graphic description of the quadrilinear interpolation process. Finally, the whole descriptor is normalized to have Euclidean norm equal to 1, to increase robustness to point density variations.

7.4.2   Spin Images

The *Spin Images* is a surface representation technique that was initially introduced in [28]. The name gives an intuitive description about how the algorithm works. The term *image* means that a point is described using a 2D array, while *spin* mimics the process of constructing the image that can be thought as a 2D plane spinning around the normal at the keypoint and collecting counts of points of the support in the entries of the array. The spin image generation process is visualized in Fig. 7.8 in [27].

7.4.2.1   Oriented Basis

Differently from descriptors based on a local reference frame, spin images achieve rotation invariance using a reference axis. The surface normal at each point can be used to compute a 2D-oriented basis as shown in Fig. 7.2 in [27]. We define an oriented point O on the surface of an object using the 3D position of the point $\mathbf{p}$ and the surface normal $\mathbf{n}$ at the point. An oriented point allows us to define a partial system of cylindrical coordinates centered at the point. Only two coordinates are used: α is the radial coordinate defined as the perpendicular distance to the line through the surface normal, and β represents the elevation coordinate defined as the signed perpendicular distance to the tangent plane defined by $\mathbf{n}$ at $\mathbf{p}$. The polar angle coordinate is omitted because it cannot be defined robustly and unambiguously using just surface position and normal.

7.4.2.2   Histogram Computation

Using an oriented point basis, we can define a function called *spin-map* $S_o : R^3 \rightarrow R^2$ that projects a 3D point x to the 2D cylindrical coordinates of a particular basis $(\mathbf{p}, \mathbf{n})$ corresponding to the oriented point O:

$$S_o(x) \rightarrow (\alpha, \beta) = (\sqrt{\|(x - p)\|^2 - (n \cdot (x - p))^2}, n \cdot (x - p)) \qquad (7.13)$$

In order to create a spin image for an oriented point p, the space α-β is then discretized into a 2D array. Then, for each point x_i in the support region, the coordinates α and β are computed as in (7.13) and the bin indexed by (α, β) is incremented. Given a fixed *bin size (b)*, the size of the resultant spin image (i_{max}, j_{max}) can be calculated as

$$i_{max} = \frac{2\beta_{max}}{b} + 1 \qquad j_{max} = \frac{\alpha_{max}}{b} + 1 \qquad (7.14)$$

where α_{max} and β_{max} are the maximum α and $|\beta|$ values for all the oriented points within support region. The elevation coordinate β can be both positive and negative;

this is the reason why the size of the spin image in the β direction is twice β_{max}. Finally, the mapping between cylindrical coordinates α, β and the spin image is computed as

$$i = \lfloor \frac{2\beta_{max} - \beta}{b} \rfloor \quad j = \lfloor \frac{\alpha}{b} \rfloor \quad (7.15)$$

The discretization of the α-β domain makes the result of the spin image very sensitive to noise. Therefore, the contribution of the point is bi-linearly interpolated to the four surrounding bins in the 2D array. The creation of a 2D array representation of a spin image can be seen in Fig. 7.4 from [27].

The bilinear weights used to increment the bins in the spin image can be obtained as

$$a = \alpha - ib \quad b = \beta - jb \quad (7.16)$$

Spin images that are created using three different oriented points can be seen in Fig. 7.3 in [27]. Dark pixels correspond to bins with a high number of points.

7.4.2.3 Parameters

The generation of a spin image is regulated by three parameters: *bin size*, *image width*, and *support angle*.

The *bin size* is the width of each of the bins in the spin image. It is an important parameter because it defines the size in memory of the descriptor. As illustrated in Fig. 7.3 in [28], the size in memory of a spin image relates also to the descriptiveness of the spin image: having small-sized bins creates descriptive histograms. A common practice is to set the bin size approximately equal to the mesh or cloud resolution, i.e.,the median distance between vertices/points in the mesh/cloud.

The *image width* defines the number of rows and columns in a square spin image. The product between bin size and image width constitutes a new parameter called *support distance* (D_s). As shown in Fig. 7.4 in [28], this parameter acts on the amount of local versus global information embedded in the descriptor.

The *support angle* (A_s) allows to filter the points that contribute to the calculation of the spin image and make the spin image less sensitive to the effect of self-occlusion and clutter. We can define A_s as the maximum angle between the normal at the point for which we are computing the spin image and the normal of points that are allowed to contribute to the spin image. Suppose $\mathbf{p}$ is the oriented point for which we are computing the spin image and p_i is one of its oriented points within the support, the contribution of p_i will be accumulated in the histogram of $\mathbf{p}$ if

$$acos(n_p \cdot n_{p_i}) < A_s \quad (7.17)$$

The most appropriate value for this z parameter represents the right trade-off between shape descriptiveness and matching robustness. Decreasing support angle decreases the descriptiveness, while increasing it increases the sensitivity to occlusion and clutter. Typically, the support angle is kept small in object recognition and kept large in surface registration.

7.4.3 CGF: Compact Geometric Features

Compact Geometric Features (CGF) learns a mapping $f : \mathbb{R}^N \rightarrow \mathbb{R}^n$ from high-dimensional handcrafted representations to a very low-dimensional feature space. It was introduced by Khoury et al. [29] in 2017.

The authors try to overcome the point cloud representation problems by using a handcrafted approach to represent the raw local geometry around points. The neural networks perform a dimensionality reduction in order to compute compact embedding. Thanks to its low dimensionality, CGF enables faster nearest neighbor queries during the matching stage.

The network is trained using the triplet embedding loss [24]. In this regard, CGF is coupled with an effective negative sampling strategy which produces a highly discriminative embedding, described in Sect. 7.4.3.3.

7.4.3.1 Point Cloud Parametrization

Before CGF, the standard way to adapt point clouds to deep learning algorithms was to discretize the input into a uniform voxel grid. However, such representation is not efficient due to the high number of empty cells [26].

CGF captures the local geometry around each point into a handcrafted feature called spherical histogram. Inspired by 3DSC [16], a spherical histogram encodes the distribution of points in a local neighborhood with a nonuniform binned radial grid. A simplified view is shown in Fig. 7.2 from [29].

Given a feature point $\mathbf{p}$ a sphere $\mathbf{S}$ of radius r is centered at $\mathbf{p}$. To obtain rotational invariance, the local neighborhood is aligned to axes of a local reference frame computed as in Sect. 7.4.1.1. Considering the $\hat{\mathbf{z}}$-axis of the estimated LRF and the normal $\mathbf{n}$ at point $\mathbf{p}$, if the dot product $\langle \mathbf{n}, \hat{\mathbf{z}} \rangle < 0$, the signs of all three vectors in the local reference frame are flipped.

The volume bounded by $\mathbf{S}$ is divided into bins along the radial, elevation, and azimuth directions. The azimuth direction is split into $A = 12$ bins, each of extent $2\pi/A$. The elevation direction is subdivided into $E = 11$ bins, each of extent π/E. The radial direction, which has total span r, is logarithmically subdivided into 17 bins using the following thresholds:

$$r_i = \exp\left(\ln r_{\min} + \frac{i}{R} \ln\left(\frac{r}{r_{\min}}\right)\right). \tag{7.18}$$

Subdividing the radial direction in this fashion makes the histogram more robust to changes in shape near the center $\mathbf{p}$. The resulting spherical histogram has a size of 2,244 bins.

The value inside each bin reflects the point density of the local neighborhood around $\mathbf{p}$. Let $\mathcal{N} \subset \mathcal{P}$ be the set of neighboring points that lie inside the sphere $\mathbf{S}$. Each point $\mathbf{q} \in N$ is converted from euclidean to spherical coordinates, and the corresponding bin that contains $\mathbf{q}$ is incremented. The final histogram is normalized by dividing each bin by $|\mathcal{N}|$.

7.4.3.2   Network Architecture

CGF deep network maps supports from the high-dimensional space of spherical histograms to a very low-dimensional Euclidean space. The architecture is a fully connected network with five hidden layers. Each hidden layer contains 512 nodes and is followed by a ReLU non-linearity. Weights are initialized from a normal distribution with mean 0 and standard deviation 0.1. The mini-batch size is 512, and Adam [30] is used as optimizer. The dimension of the learned embedding which is then used as descriptor is 32.

As far as the loss function is concerned, a standard triplet loss [24] tries to keep similar features together while pushing dissimilar features apart. Starting from a mini-batch of triplets of input histograms $\mathcal{T} = \{(\mathbf{x}_i^a, \mathbf{x}_i^p, \mathbf{x}_i^n)\}_i$. Vector $\mathbf{x}_i^a$ is referred to as the anchor of triplet i, vector $\mathbf{x}_i^p$ is a positive example, and vector $\mathbf{x}_i^n$ is a negative example. Given such a set of triplets, triplet loss is written as

$$\mathcal{L}(\boldsymbol{\theta}) = \frac{1}{|\mathcal{T}|} \sum_{i=1}^{|\mathcal{T}|} \left[\|f(\mathbf{x}_i^a; \boldsymbol{\theta}) - f(\mathbf{x}_i^p; \boldsymbol{\theta})\|^2 \quad - \|f(\mathbf{x}_i^a; \boldsymbol{\theta}) - f(\mathbf{x}_i^n; \boldsymbol{\theta})\|^2 + 1 \right]_+$$

(7.19)

where $\boldsymbol{\theta}$ are the learned parameters and $[\cdot]_+$ denotes $\max(\cdot, 0)$.

7.4.3.3   Training Data

Triplet loss is often used to learn discriminative features. During training, a triplet of input histograms, $\mathcal{T} = \{(\mathbf{x}_i^a, \mathbf{x}_i^p, \mathbf{x}_i^n)\}_i$ is fed into the model as a single sample. The idea behind this is that distance between the learned embedding of anchor and positive should be smaller than that between anchor and negative embedding. In order to achieve this, it is essential to samples' negatives accurately. A common choice is to draw as negative, random points that are pretty far from the anchor.

Khoury et al. use a smarter strategy. Given a set of point clouds $\{\mathcal{P}_i\}_i$ that describe overlapping scans of a 3D object or scene, let $\{\mathcal{T}_i\}_i$ be a set of rigid transformations that align the point clouds $\{\mathcal{P}_i\}_i$ in a common coordinate frame. Consider the set $\mathcal{O}$ of overlapping pairs of point clouds from $\{\mathcal{P}_i\}_i$. Each point $\mathbf{p} \in \mathcal{P}_i$ in each pair

$(\mathcal{P}_i, \mathcal{P}_j) \in \mathcal{O}$ generates 40 triplets. These 40 triplets use as anchor point $\mathbf{p} \in \mathcal{P}_i$, while positives are grabbed from the local neighborhood of $\mathbf{p}$ in $\mathbf{T}_j \mathcal{P}_j$. With that in mind, we can denote as $\mathcal{N}^j_{\mathbf{p},\tau}$ in $\mathcal{P}_j$ the set of neighbors points that are at distance at most τ from $\mathbf{p}$. In addition, consider $\mathcal{N}^j_{\mathbf{p},2\tau}$, the set of points in $\mathcal{P}_j$ that are at distance at most 2τ from $\mathbf{p}$. While the points in $\mathcal{N}^j_{\mathbf{p},\tau}$ are good correspondences for $\mathbf{p}$ in $\mathcal{P}_j$, the set $\mathcal{N}^j_{\mathbf{p},2\tau} \setminus \mathcal{N}^j_{\mathbf{p},\tau}$ contains difficult negative examples for $\mathbf{p}$. This is visualized in Fig. 7.3 in [29]. They have similar local geometries of $\mathbf{p}$ but are far enough from it. Hence, 15 triplets are constructed by sampling negatives from $\mathcal{N}_{\mathbf{p},2\tau}$ and 25 are constructed by randomly sampling negatives from other scans.

7.4.4 PPF-FoldNet

PPF-FoldNet [13] is an extension of another descriptor, and it has been presented by Deng et al. [14] in 2018. The main limitations of learned 3D descriptors are the big amount of labeled data required, sensitivity to rotations, and the use of handcrafted input preparation. PPF-FoldNet improved upon these limitations by proposing an unsupervised rotation-invariant local descriptor. *FoldingNet* [69] introduced the idea of deforming a 2D grid to decode a 3D surface as a point set, given a latent codeword encoding the 3D surface, and offered an interesting paradigm for unsupervised learning with point clouds. Similarly, PPF-FoldNet uses folding operation to reconstruct the point pair feature [4, 15] of a support.

7.4.4.1 Point Cloud Parametrization

The local patch of a feature point $\mathbf{p}$ is represented by a collection of pair features, computed between $\mathbf{p}$ and the neighboring points:

$$\mathbf{F}_\Omega = \{ \mathbf{f}(\mathbf{p}, \mathbf{p}_1) \cdots \mathbf{f}(\mathbf{p}, \mathbf{p}_i) \cdots \mathbf{f}(\mathbf{p}, \mathbf{p}_N) \} \in \mathbb{R}^{4 \times N-1} \tag{7.20}$$

As far as Point Pair Features (PPFs) are concerned, for two points $\mathbf{x}_1$ and $\mathbf{x}_2$ the features are defined as

$$\boldsymbol{\psi}_{12} = (\|\mathbf{d}\|_2, \angle(\mathbf{n}_1, \mathbf{d}), \angle(\mathbf{n}_2, \mathbf{d}), \angle(\mathbf{n}_1, \mathbf{n}_2)) \tag{7.21}$$

where $\mathbf{d}$ denotes the difference vector between points, $\mathbf{n}_1$ and $\mathbf{n}_2$ are the surface normals at $\mathbf{x}_1$ and $\mathbf{x}_2$, $\|\cdot\|$ is the Euclidean distance, and $\angle$ is the angle operator computed in a numerically robust manner as in [4]:

$$\angle(\mathbf{v}_1, \mathbf{v}_2) = \operatorname{atan2}\big(\|\mathbf{v}_1 \times \mathbf{v}_2\|, \, \mathbf{v}_1 \cdot \mathbf{v}_2\big) \tag{7.22}$$

$\angle(\mathbf{v}_1, \mathbf{v}_2)$ is guaranteed to lie in the range $[0, \pi)$.

The main motivation behind the use of PPFs is their invariance to rotations. Rotation invariance is an essential trait for every local descriptor, and the PPFs are invariants under Euclidean isometry as distances and angles are preserved between every pair of points. A visualization of some local patches and their correspondent PPF signatures is shown in Fig. 7.2 in [13].

7.4.4.2   Network Architecture

PPF-FoldNet leverages on an encoder–decoder architecture, shown in Fig. 7.1 in [13], to reconstruct a set of PPFs computed on a local patch around a given feature point $\mathbf{p}$. The encoder is composed of a three-layer, point-wise Multi-Layer Perceptron (MLP) followed by a max-pooling layer that aggregates individual point features into a global one similar to [43, 69]. After the concatenation with skip links, a two-layer MLP compresses these features to the encoded codeword.

The decoder takes inspiration from FoldingNet [69], and try to deform a low-dimensional grid structure using the information encoded in the codeword learned by the encoder. Differently from [69], the decoder uses a deeper architecture, and each *folding* operation relies on a five-layer MLP. This choice is mainly due to higher dimensional of the reconstructed set, 4D versus 3D. The loss involved is the *Chamfer* distance between PPFs:

$$d(\mathbf{F}, \hat{\mathbf{F}}) = \max\left\{\frac{1}{|\mathbf{F}|}\sum_{\mathbf{f}\in\mathbf{F}}\min_{\hat{\mathbf{f}}\in\hat{\mathbf{F}}}\|\mathbf{f} - \hat{\mathbf{f}}\|_2, \ \frac{1}{|\hat{\mathbf{F}}|}\sum_{\hat{\mathbf{f}}\in\hat{\mathbf{F}}}\min_{\mathbf{f}\in\mathbf{F}}\|\mathbf{f} - \hat{\mathbf{f}}\|_2\right\} \qquad (7.23)$$

where F is computed as in (7.20) and the $\hat{\ }$ operator refers to the reconstructed set. The learned latent-dimensional vector is called *codeword* and used as local descriptor of the underlying geometry around which the patch is extracted. The weights of the network are initialized using Xavier initialization [17]. The loss is minimized by ADAM optimizer [30]. Batch size is 32, while the size of the final descriptor is 512.

7.4.4.3   Training Data

Thanks to the unsupervised approach, the network is trained by randomly sampling points from the fragments of the 3DMatch dataset. For each keypoint, the PPFs are computed using its neighboring points in a 30 cm vicinity. Since the number of points in a local patch is not fixed, each local patch is down-sampled to an arbitrary number of points, thereby facilitating the train by organizing the data into regular batches, and increasing the robustness to noises and different point densities.

7.5   Dataset and Evaluation

Within this section, we will validate some of the proposed algorithms in Sects. 7.3 and 7.4 using the popular 3D Match Benchmark Dataset [72]. This dataset is a collection of different real-world scenes retrieved from a pool of previously published ones such as Analysis-by-Synthesis [62], 7-Scenes [55], SUN3D [66], RGB-D Scenes v.2 [34], and Halber and Funkhouser [23]. The dataset includes indoor scenes like living rooms, offices, bedrooms, tabletops, and restrooms. Each scene is equipped by one or more RGB-D video sequences captured by real sensors, like Microsoft Kinect and Intel RealSense, together with camera intrinsic parameters. In order to be robust to noise point clouds for the fragments belonging to a single scene are generated by fusing 50 consecutive depth frames. The overall number of scenes in the dataset is 62, split into 54 for train and validation and 8 for benchmarking.

As for the selected descriptors, we have chosen FPFH [47], Spin Image [28], SHOT [51], USC [60], 3DMatch [72], CGF [29], PPFNet [14], and PPF-FoldNet [13]. The main reason behind the choice of handcrafted descriptors is to compare features based on point density, such as Spin Images and USC, and algorithms that operate on geometric properties such as FPFH and SHOT. On the other hand, for the learned ones we rely on the most recent proposals.

To test the rotation invariance of 3D feature descriptors, in [13] a rotated version of the 3D Match Benchmark Dataset is proposed. The fragments in the test split are rotated around randomly sampled axis with a randomly chosen angle. We refer to it as *Rotated 3D Match Benchmark*.

A good way to check the performance of a given descriptor is to use it within a registration pipeline. Given a set of K fragments available for each scene in the dataset, the aim is to find the rigid transformation matrix, $\mathbf{G}$, that aligns every pair of overlapping fragments. Each scene in the dataset comes with a list of overlapping fragments and the rigid transformations $\mathbf{T}_{ij} \in SE(3)$ between them. In order to check the performance of a given 3D local feature descriptor, the following steps are performed. For all the fragment pairs (V_i, V_j) with overlap at least 30 %, a list of correspondences between all the keypoints detected in V_i and all the keypoints detected in V_j is formed by finding all the pairs that lie mutually close in the feature space by applying nearest neighbor search [13]. The set containing all the correspondences is called $\mathbf{C}_{i,j}$. Then, given a pair of matched keypoints (k_i, k_j), $k_i \in V_i, k_j \in V_j$, the set of correct correspondences, $\mathbf{C}_{gnd_{i,j}}$, can be identified based on the available ground truth transformations by checking whether the matched keypoints lay within a certain distance τ_1 in the canonical reference frame:

$$\mathbf{C}_{gnd_{i,j}} = \{(k_i, k_j) : \|k_i - \mathbf{T}_{ij}k_j\| \leq \tau_1\} \tag{7.24}$$

We can define the inlier ratio for $\mathbf{C}_{i,j}$ as the percentage of true matches in $\mathbf{C}_{i,j}$, $r_{in} = |\mathbf{C}_{gnd_{i,j}}|/|\mathbf{C}_{i,j}|$. Instead of using the estimated correspondences within a RANSAC pipeline and check the resulting rigid transformation, a fragment pair is considered correctly aligned if $r_{in} > \tau_2$.

Given a set of fragment pairs $\mathbf{S} = \{(\mathbf{P}, \mathbf{Q})\}$ that are used in the evaluation, the quality of a given feature descriptor is measured by the recall R of fragment pairs matched in $\mathbf{S}$:

$$R = \frac{1}{|\mathbf{S}|} \sum_{i=1}^{|\mathbf{S}|} \mathbb{1}\left(r_{in}\left(\mathbf{S}_i = (\mathbf{P}_i, \mathbf{Q}_i)\right) > \tau_2\right) \qquad (7.25)$$

On both 3D Match Benchmark and Rotated 3D Match Benchmark, τ_1 and τ_2 are set to 10 cm and 5%, respectively. For each fragment, descriptors are computed in 5000 randomly sampled feature points, provided by [72]. The radius support used to compute a descriptor is 18 cm and for normal estimation it is 9 cm. For the handcrafted descriptors, we used the public implementation in **PCL** [50], while for the learned descriptors since the implementations are not public, the results were taken from [13].

7.6 Results

The experimental results on the standard 3D Match Benchmark are shown in Table 7.1. From the results, it is clear how the descriptors based on geometric attribute histograms tend to outperform those based on spatial distribution histograms. Indeed, SHOT, PPF-FoldNet build up their representations leveraging properties of the surface like normals. Except for SHOT and USC, PPFNet and PPF-FoldNet managed to match a higher number of fragment pairs compared to the other methods. This is a clear demonstration of how learning the descriptor using a stable and rich representation rather than using handcrafted techniques allows achieving higher performances.

Results on the rotated benchmark are illustrated in Table 7.2. They show how a robust local reference frame is an essential aspect of any descriptor. Comparing the results from Tables 7.1 and 7.2, FPFH, Spin Images, SHOT, USC, and CGF demonstrate robustness to rotations. Their performance remains stable despite the introduction of random rotations in the data. The significant drop in performance achieved by 3DMatch and PPFNet also demonstrates how these descriptors hardly learn to pose invariance directly from data. The best performance is obtained by PPF-FoldNet and SHOT: this proves how the use of rotation-invariant features, such as Point Pair Features, or a stable local reference frame, can lead to a robust and descriptive representation.

7.7 Open Challenges

Within this chapter, we have outlined how over the past few years there has been an intensive research activity in learning features for 3D data. Nevertheless, many challenges are still open. Although the use of deep learning algorithms has boosted the performance of local 3D descriptors, learning a rotation-invariant descriptor directly

Table 7.1 Results on the 3DMatch benchmark. Test data comes from SUN3D [66], except for *Red Kitchen* which is taken from 7-Scenes [55]

	FPFH [47]	Spin Image [28]	SHOT [51]	USC [60]	3DMatch [72]	CGF [29]	PPFNet [14]	PPF-FoldNet [13]
Kitchen	0.4802	0.5079	0.7470	0.7016	0.5830	0.6030	0.8972	0.7866
Home 1	0.7115	0.6987	0.8141	0.7756	0.7240	0.7110	0.5577	0.7628
Home 2	0.5769	0.6010	0.7548	0.6683	0.6150	0.5670	0.5913	0.6154
Hotel 1	0.6770	0.5973	0.7920	0.7788	0.5490	0.5710	0.5796	0.6814
Hotel 2	0.5673	0.5769	0.7692	0.6635	0.4810	0.5380	0.5796	0.7115
Hotel 3	0.7407	0.7222	0.8704	0.8148	0.6110	0.8330	0.6111	0.9444
Study	0.4486	0.4247	0.6918	0.5856	0.5170	0.3770	0.5342	0.6199
MIT Lab	0.3896	0.3506	0.5974	0.4675	0.5070	0.4550	0.6364	0.6234
Average	0.5740	0.5599	0.7546	0.6820	0.5730	0.5820	0.6231	0.7182

Table 7.2 Results on the rotated 3DMatch benchmark. Test data comes from SUN3D [66], except for *Red Kitchen* which is taken from 7-Scenes [55]

	FPFH [47]	Spin Image [28]	SHOT [51]	USC [60]	3DMatch [72]	CGF [29]	PPFNet [14]	PPF-FoldNet [13]
Kitchen	0.4921	0.5375	0.7470	0.7095	0.0240	0.6050	0.002	0.7885
Home 1	0.6987	0.7308	0.8141	0.8269	0.0380	0.7120	0.0000	0.7821
Home 2	0.5913	0.6250	0.7404	0.6490	0.0530	0.5720	0.0144	0.6442
Hotel 1	0.6903	0.6416	0.8053	0.7788	0.0180	0.5720	0.0044	0.6770
Hotel 2	0.5673	0.5673	0.7788	0.7115	0.0670	0.5380	0.0000	0.6923
Hotel 3	0.7407	0.7963	0.8519	0.8519	0.0190	0.8330	0.0000	0.963
Study	0.4555	0.4589	0.6952	0.6404	0.0270	0.3870	0.0000	0.6267
MIT Lab	0.4286	0.4675	0.6364	0.5714	0.0390	0.4550	0.0000	0.6753
Average	0.5831	0.6031	0.7586	0.7174	0.0360	0.5850	0.0026	0.7311

from 3D data such as point clouds remains an open problem. Indeed, most state-of-the-art methods achieve rotation invariance by relying on handcrafted features that are by design invariant to rotation. Moreover, many deep learning approaches still use handcrafted methods to operate on 3D data.

Additional open problems that 3D local descriptors will need to face in forthcoming years are the robustness to geometric transformation and noise. This is particularly relevant with learned-based approaches which suffer from the well-known domain shift problem when tested under unseen working conditions and data domains. Scalability toward large datasets (e.g., large scenes, many objects) and in general computational efficiency is also an important issue, especially considering the higher and higher relevance that mobile applications (such as, e.g., robotics, autonomous driving, augmented reality) are assuming in the context of 3D data processing.

7.8   Further Reading

We have presented an overview of methods proposed over the last two decades to describe the local properties of a 3D surface and successfully matched it under rigid transformations and in the presence of noise, clutter, and occlusions.

Interestingly, the successful research avenue aiming at adapting neural network architectures such as CNNs and auto-encoders to process 3D data—and in particular point clouds—has blurred the line between the standard distinction between global and local 3D descriptors, since such architectures could be employed indifferently under both fashions and for most 3D processing tasks. To name a few methods, we refer the reader to the recent point cloud-based auto-encoders proposed in Atlas-Net [18] and FoldingNet [69], or recent multi-resolution 3D descriptors for point clouds such as PointNet++ [45] and fully convolutional point networks [46]. All these methods have been, or could be, used for both global and local description tasks.

Although this chapter focuses on local features for 3D data, it is interesting to analyze how also in the field of images there has been a parallel line of research. One of the most remarkable works is represented by Lift [70]. For a more detailed discussion of learned 2D features, we refer the reader to the survey of Schonberger et al. [53].

7.9   Questions and Exercises

1. Based on the contents of Sect. 7.3, highlight the main differences between 3DSC and USC descriptors.
2. Explain the main differences between handcrafted and learned descriptors by highlighting the main advantages and disadvantages of the two approaches.

3. Explain the main problems related to the use of deep learning algorithms on point clouds and how the current state-of-the-art solutions try to overcome them.
4. In this chapter, local descriptors were mentioned. Why are they often preferred to global descriptors? In which applications are local descriptors most suitable?
5. In the 3DMatch descriptor, in order to create an organized structure for a point cloud, the local support of a feature point is voxelized. Explain the main disadvantage of this approach.
6. Considering a descriptor of your choice, handcrafted or learned, briefly explain how it works and what the advantages are compared to other state-of-the-art solutions.
7. What are the two main loss functions used to learn a local feature descriptor for point clouds?
8. What are the main sources of noise that make the calculation of a local reference frame not repeatable?
9. Considering a descriptor of your choice and using the dataset explained in Sect. 7.5, implement a feature matching pipeline as described in the Introduction.
10. Implement the estimation for the SHOT local reference frame described in Sect. 7.4.1.1.

7.10 Hands-On 3D Descriptors

As a supplement to this chapter, we provide some code snippets that show how to calculate some of the 3D descriptors presented in this chapter. The following examples use the open-source implementations available in the Point Cloud Library (PCL) [50]. In particular, the descriptors currently available are SHOT, FPFH, Spin Images, and USC.

In the following snippets 7.1 and 7.2, we provide the code to compute two of the descriptors seen in this chapter, SHOT and USC, respectively. As an exercise, we leave to the reader the extension of the presented snippets to the other aforementioned descriptors available in PCL.

```
#include <pcl/io/pcd_io.h>
#include <pcl/features/normal_3d.h>
#include <pcl/features/shot.h>

using namespace pcl;
using namespace std;

typedef PointXYZ PointT;
typedef Normal NormalT;
typedef SHOT352 ShotT;

int main(int argc, char** argv)
{
    /*Create point cloud for coordinates*/
```

```
15    PointCloud<PointT>::Ptr cloud(new PointCloud<
      PointT>);
16    /*Create point cloud for normals*/
17    PointCloud<NormalT>::Ptr normals(new PointCloud<
      NormalT>);
18    /*Create point cloud for descriptors */
19    PointCloud<ShotT>::Ptr descriptors(new PointCloud<
      ShotT>());
20
21    /*Read a point cloud from the disk, exit in case
      of failure*/
22    if (io::loadPCDFile<PointT>(argv[1], *cloud) != 0)
23        return -1;
24
25    /*Estimate the normals*/
26    const int number_of_neighbours_for_normals = 17;
27
28    NormalEstimation<PointT, NormalT>
      estimator_normals;
29
30    estimator_normals.setInputCloud(cloud);
31    estimator_normals.setKSearch(
      number_of_neighbours_for_normals);
32
33    estimator_normals.compute(*normals);
34
35    /*Estimate shot descriptor*/
36    SHOTEstimation<PointT, NormalT, ShotT> shot;
37    shot.setInputCloud(cloud);
38    shot.setInputNormals(normals);
39
40    const double radius_shot = 0.18;
41    shot.setRadiusSearch(radius_shot);
42
43    /*Set the radius to compute the Local Reference
      Frame*/
44    shot.setLRFRadius(radius_shot);
45
46    shot.compute(*descriptors);
47
48    /*Print descriptors*/
49    for(ShotT shot : (*descriptors))
50    {
51        for (int i = 0; i < shot.descriptorSize(); i
      ++)
52            cout << shot.descriptor[i] << endl;
53    }
54 }
```

Listing 7.1 Compute SHOT descriptor

```
1 #include <pcl/io/pcd_io.h>
2 #include <pcl/features/usc.h>
3
```

```
 4  using namespace pcl;
 5  using namespace std;
 6
 7  typedef PointXYZ PointT;
 8  typedef Normal NormalT;
 9  typedef UniqueShapeContext1960 UscT;
10  typedef ReferenceFrame FrameT;
11
12  int main(int argc, char** argv)
13  {
14      /*Create point cloud for coordinates*/
15      PointCloud<PointT>::Ptr cloud(new PointCloud<
        PointT>);
16      /*Create point cloud for descriptors */
17      PointCloud<UscT>::Ptr descriptors(new PointCloud<
        UscT>());
18
19      /*Read a point cloud from the disk, exit in case
        of failure*/
20      if (io::loadPCDFile<PointT>(argv[1], *cloud) != 0)
21          return -1;
22
23       /*Estimate USC descriptor*/
24      UniqueShapeContext<PointT, UscT, FrameT> usc;
25      usc.setInputCloud(cloud);
26
27      const double radius_usc = 0.18;
28      usc.setRadiusSearch(radius_usc);
29
30      /*Set the radius to compute the Local Reference
        Frame*/
31      usc.setLocalRadius(radius_usc);
32
33      /*The minimal radius value for the search sphere*/
34      const double radius_minimal = radius_usc / 10.0;
35      usc.setMinimalRadius(radius_minimal);
36
37      /*Radius used to compute the local point density
        for the neighbors*/
38      const double radius_density = radius_usc / 5.0;
39      usc.setPointDensityRadius(radius_density);
40
41      usc.compute(*descriptors);
42
43      /*Print descriptors*/
44      for(UscT usc : (*descriptors))
45      {
46          for (int i = 0; i < usc.descriptorSize(); i++)
47              cout << usc.descriptor[i] << endl;
48      }
49  }
```

Listing 7.2 Compute USC descriptor

References

1. Aldoma, A., Tombari, F., Rusu, R.B., Vincze, M.: OUR-CVFH–oriented, unique and repeatable clustered viewpoint feature histogram for object recognition and 6 DOF pose estimation. In: Joint DAGM (German Association for Pattern Recognition) and OAGM Symposium, pp. 113–122. Springer (2012)
2. Belongie, S., Malik, J., Puzicha, J.: Shape context: A new descriptor for shape matching and object recognition. In: Advances in Neural Information Processing Systems, pp. 831–837 (2001)
3. Bentley, J.L.: Multidimensional binary search trees used for associative searching. Commun. ACM **18**(9), 509–517 (1975)
4. Birdal, T., Ilic, S.: Point pair features based object detection and pose estimation revisited. In: 2015 International Conference on 3D Vision (3DV), pp. 527–535. IEEE (2015)
5. Boscaini, D., Masci, J., Melzi, S., Bronstein, M.M., Castellani, U., Vandergheynst, P.: Learning class-specific descriptors for deformable shapes using localized spectral convolutional networks. Comput. Graph. Forum **34**(5), 13–23 (2015)
6. Boscaini, D., Masci, J., Rodolà, E., Bronstein, M.: Learning shape correspondence with anisotropic convolutional neural networks. In: Advances in Neural Information Processing Systems, pp. 3189–3197 (2016)
7. Bro, R., Acar, E., Kolda, T.G.: Resolving the sign ambiguity in the singular value decomposition. J. Chemom.: A J. Chemom. Soc. **22**(2), 135–140 (2008)
8. Bronstein, M.M., Bruna, J., LeCun, Y., Szlam, A., Vandergheynst, P.: Geometric deep learning: going beyond Euclidean data. IEEE Signal Process. Mag. **34**(4), 18–42 (2017)
9. Chen, H., Bhanu, B.: 3D free-form object recognition in range images using local surface patches. Pattern Recognit. Lett. **28**(10), 1252–1262 (2007)
10. Chua, C.S., Jarvis, R.: Point signatures: a new representation for 3D object recognition. Int. J. Comput. Vis. **25**(1), 63–85 (1997)
11. Dai, A., Chang, A.X., Savva, M., Halber, M., Funkhouser, T., Nießner, M.: ScanNet: Richly-annotated 3D reconstructions of indoor scenes. In: Proceedings of IEEE Conference on Computer Vision and Pattern Recognition (CVPR), vol. 1, p. 1 (2017)
12. Demi, M., Paterni, M., Benassi, A.: The first absolute central moment in low-level image processing. Comput. Vis. Image Underst. **80**(1), 57–87 (2000)
13. Deng, H., Birdal, T., Ilic, S.: PPF-FoldNet: Unsupervised learning of rotation invariant 3D local descriptors. **2** (2018). arXiv:1808.10322
14. Deng, H., Birdal, T., Ilic, S.: PPFNet: Global context aware local features for robust 3D point matching. Comput. Vis. Pattern Recognit. (CVPR). IEEE **1** (2018)
15. Drost, B., Ulrich, M., Navab, N., Ilic, S.: Model globally, match locally: Efficient and robust 3D object recognition. In: 2010 IEEE Computer Society Conference on Computer Vision and Pattern Recognition, pp. 998–1005. IEEE (2010)
16. Frome, A., Huber, D., Kolluri, R., Bülow, T., Malik, J.: Recognizing objects in range data using regional point descriptors. In: European Conference on Computer Vision, pp. 224–237. Springer (2004)
17. Glorot, X., Bengio, Y.: Understanding the difficulty of training deep feedforward neural networks. In: Proceedings of the Thirteenth International Conference on Artificial Intelligence and Statistics, pp. 249–256 (2010)
18. Groueix, T., Fisher, M., Kim, V.G., Russell, B.C., Aubry, M.: A papier-mâché approach to learning 3D surface generation. In: Proceedings of the IEEE Conference on Computer Vision and Pattern Recognition, pp. 216–224 (2018)
19. Guo, Y., Bennamoun, M., Sohel, F., Lu, M., Wan, J., Kwok, N.M.: A comprehensive performance evaluation of 3D local feature descriptors. Int. J. Comput. Vis. **116**(1), 66–89 (2016)
20. Guo, Y., Sohel, F., Bennamoun, M., Lu, M., Wan, J.: Rotational projection statistics for 3D local surface description and object recognition. Int. J. Comput. Vis. **105**(1), 63–86 (2013)
21. Guo, Y., Sohel, F.A., Bennamoun, M., Lu, M., Wan, J.: TriSI: a distinctive local surface descriptor for 3D modeling and object recognition. In: GRAPP/IVAPP, pp. 86–93 (2013)

22. Hadsell, R., Chopra, S., LeCun, Y.: Dimensionality reduction by learning an invariant mapping. In: null, pp. 1735–1742. IEEE (2006)
23. Halber, M., Funkhouser, T.: Structured global registration of RGB-D scans in indoor environments. **2**(3), 9 (2016). arXiv:1607.08539
24. Hoffer, E., Ailon, N.: Deep metric learning using triplet network. In: International Workshop on Similarity-Based Pattern Recognition, pp. 84–92. Springer (2015)
25. Hu, M.K.: Visual pattern recognition by moment invariants. IRE Trans. Inf. Theory **8**(2), 179–187 (1962)
26. Itoh, T., Koyamada, K.: Automatic isosurface propagation using an extrema graph and sorted boundary cell lists. IEEE Trans. Vis. Comput. Graph. **1**(4), 319–327 (1995)
27. Johnson, A., Hebert, M.: Surface matching for object recognition in complex 3-d scenes. Image Visi. Comput. (1998)
28. Johnson, A., Hebert, M.: Using spin images for efficient object recognition in cluttered 3D scenes. IEEE Trans. Pattern Anal. Mach. Intell. **21**(5), 433–449 (1999)
29. Khoury, M., Zhou, Q.Y., Koltun, V.: Learning compact geometric features. In: 2017 IEEE International Conference on Computer Vision (ICCV), pp. 153–161. IEEE (2017)
30. Kinga, D., Adam, J.B.: A method for stochastic optimization. In: International Conference on Learning Representations (ICLR), vol. 5 (2015)
31. Klokov, R., Lempitsky, V.: Escape from cells: Deep kd-networks for the recognition of 3D point cloud models. In: 2017 IEEE International Conference on Computer Vision (ICCV), pp. 863–872. IEEE (2017)
32. Knopp, J., Prasad, M., Willems, G., Timofte, R., Van Gool, L.: Hough transform and 3D SURF for robust three dimensional classification. In: European Conference on Computer Vision, pp. 589–602. Springer (2010)
33. Krizhevsky, A., Sutskever, I., Hinton, G.E.: ImageNet classification with deep convolutional neural networks. In: Advances in Neural Information Processing Systems, pp. 1097–1105 (2012)
34. Lai, K., Bo, L., Fox, D.: Unsupervised feature learning for 3D scene labeling. In: 2014 IEEE International Conference on Robotics and Automation (ICRA), pp. 3050–3057. IEEE (2014)
35. Lowe, D.G.: Distinctive image features from scale-invariant keypoints. Int. J. Comput. Vis. **60**(2), 91–110 (2004)
36. Maturana, D., Scherer, S.: VoxNet: A 3D convolutional neural network for real-time object recognition. In: 2015 IEEE/RSJ International Conference on Intelligent Robots and Systems (IROS), pp. 922–928. IEEE (2015)
37. Newcombe, R.A., Izadi, S., Hilliges, O., Molyneaux, D., Kim, D., Davison, A.J., Kohi, P., Shotton, J., Hodges, S., Fitzgibbon, A.: KinectFusion: Real-time dense surface mapping and tracking. In: 2011 IEEE International Symposium on Mixed and Augmented Reality, pp. 127–136. IEEE (2011)
38. Novatnack, J., Nishino, K.: Scale-dependent/invariant local 3D shape descriptors for fully automatic registration of multiple sets of range images. In: European Conference on Computer Vision, pp. 440–453. Springer (2008)
39. Osada, R., Funkhouser, T., Chazelle, B., Dobkin, D.: Shape distributions. ACM Trans. Graph. (TOG) **21**(4), 807–832 (2002)
40. PCL, the point cloud library: Fast point feature histograms (FPFH) descriptors (2013). http://pointclouds.org/documentation/tutorials/fpfh_estimation.php. Aaccessed 16 Mar 2020
41. PCL, the point cloud library: Point feature histograms (PFH) descriptors (2013). http://pointclouds.org/documentation/tutorials/pfh_estimation.php. Accessed 16 Mar 2020
42. Petrelli, A., Di Stefano, L.: On the repeatability of the local reference frame for partial shape matching. In: 2011 IEEE International Conference on Computer Vision (ICCV), pp. 2244–2251. IEEE (2011)
43. Qi, C.R., Su, H., Mo, K., Guibas, L.J.: PointNet: Deep learning on point sets for 3D classification and segmentation. Proc. Comput. Vis. Pattern Recognit. (CVPR), IEEE **1**(2), 4 (2017)
44. Qi, C.R., Su, H., Nießner, M., Dai, A., Yan, M., Guibas, L.J.: Volumetric and multi-view cnns for object classification on 3D data. In: Proceedings of the IEEE Conference on Computer Vision and Pattern Recognition, pp. 5648–5656 (2016)

45. Qi, C.R., Yi, L., Su, H., Guibas, L.J.: PointNet++: Deep hierarchical feature learning on point sets in a metric space. In: Advances in Neural Information Processing Systems, pp. 5099–5108 (2017)
46. Rethage, D., Wald, J., Sturm, J., Navab, N., Tombari, F.: Fully-convolutional point networks for large-scale point clouds. In: European Conference on Computer Vision, pp. 625–640. Springer (2018)
47. Rusu, R.B., Blodow, N., Beetz, M.: Fast point feature histograms (FPFH) for 3D registration. In: 2009 IEEE International Conference on Robotics and Automation, pp. 3212–3217. IEEE (2009)
48. Rusu, R.B., Blodow, N., Marton, Z.C., Beetz, M.: Aligning point cloud views using persistent feature histograms. In: IEEE/RSJ International Conference on Intelligent Robots and Systems, IROS 2008, pp. 3384–3391. IEEE (2008)
49. Rusu, R.B., Bradski, G., Thibaux, R., Hsu, J.: Fast 3D recognition and pose using the viewpoint feature histogram. In: 2010 IEEE/RSJ International Conference on Intelligent Robots and Systems, pp. 2155–2162. IEEE (2010)
50. Rusu, R.B., Cousins, S.: 3D is here: Point Cloud Library (PCL). In: International Conference on Robotics and Automation. Shanghai, China (2011)
51. Salti, S., Tombari, F., Di Stefano, L.: SHOT: unique signatures of histograms for surface and texture description. Comput. Vis. Image Underst. **125**, 251–264 (2014)
52. Scarselli, F., Gori, M., Tsoi, A.C., Hagenbuchner, M., Monfardini, G.: The graph neural network model. IEEE Trans. Neural Netw. **20**(1), 61–80 (2009)
53. Schonberger, J.L., Hardmeier, H., Sattler, T., Pollefeys, M.: Comparative evaluation of hand-crafted and learned local features. In: Proceedings of the IEEE Conference on Computer Vision and Pattern Recognition, pp. 1482–1491 (2017)
54. Shannon, C.: A mathematical theory of communication, bell system technical journal, vol. 27(1948) (1948)
55. Shotton, J., Glocker, B., Zach, C., Izadi, S., Criminisi, A., Fitzgibbon, A.: Scene coordinate regression forests for camera relocalization in RGB-D images. In: Proceedings of the IEEE Conference on Computer Vision and Pattern Recognition, pp. 2930–2937 (2013)
56. Song, S., Yu, F., Zeng, A., Chang, A.X., Savva, M., Funkhouser, T.: Semantic scene completion from a single depth image. In: 2017 IEEE Conference on Computer Vision and Pattern Recognition (CVPR), pp. 190–198. IEEE (2017)
57. Su, H., Maji, S., Kalogerakis, E., Learned-Miller, E.: Multi-view convolutional neural networks for 3D shape recognition. In: Proceedings of the IEEE International Conference on Computer Vision, pp. 945–953 (2015)
58. Sun, J., Ovsjanikov, M., Guibas, L.: A concise and provably informative multi-scale signature based on heat diffusion. Comput. Graph. Forum **28**(5), 1383–1392 (2009)
59. Tatarchenko, M., Dosovitskiy, A., Brox, T.: Octree generating networks: Efficient convolutional architectures for high-resolution 3D outputs. In: Proceedings of the IEEE International Conf. on Computer Vision (ICCV), vol. 2, p. 8 (2017)
60. Tombari, F., Salti, S., Di Stefano, L.: Unique signatures of histograms for local surface description. In: European Conference on Computer Vision, pp. 356–369. Springer (2010)
61. Tombari, F., Salti, S., Di Stefano, L.: A combined texture-shape descriptor for enhanced 3D feature matching. In: 2011 18th IEEE International Conference on Image Processing, pp. 809–812. IEEE (2011)
62. Valentin, J., Dai, A., Nießner, M., Kohli, P., Torr, P., Izadi, S., Keskin, C.: Learning to navigate the energy landscape. In: 2016 Fourth International Conference on 3D Vision (3DV), pp. 323–332. IEEE (2016)
63. Wang, Y., Sun, Y., Liu, Z., Sarma, S.E., Bronstein, M.M., Solomon, J.M.: Dynamic graph CNN for learning on point clouds (2018). arXiv:1801.07829
64. Wei, L., Huang, Q., Ceylan, D., Vouga, E., Li, H.: Dense human body correspondences using convolutional networks. In: Proceedings of the IEEE Conference on Computer Vision and Pattern Recognition, pp. 1544–1553 (2016)

65. Wu, Z., Song, S., Khosla, A., Yu, F., Zhang, L., Tang, X., Xiao, J.: 3D ShapeNets: A deep representation for volumetric shapes. In: Proceedings of the IEEE Conference on Computer Vision and Pattern Recognition, pp. 1912–1920 (2015)
66. Xiao, J., Owens, A., Torralba, A.: Sun3D: A database of big spaces reconstructed using sfm and object labels. In: Proceedings of the IEEE International Conference on Computer Vision, pp. 1625–1632 (2013)
67. Yang, J., Xiao, Y., Cao, Z.: Toward the repeatability and robustness of the local reference frame for 3D shape matching: an evaluation. IEEE Trans. Image Process. 27(8), 3766–3781 (2018)
68. Yang, J., Zhang, Q., Xiao, Y., Cao, Z.: TOLDI: An effective and robust approach for 3D local shape description. Pattern Recognit. 65, 175–187 (2017)
69. Yang, Y., Feng, C., Shen, Y., Tian, D.: FoldingNet: Point cloud auto-encoder via deep grid deformation. In: Proceedings of IEEE Conference on Computer Vision and Pattern Recognition (CVPR), vol. 3 (2018)
70. Yi, K.M., Trulls, E., Lepetit, V., Fua, P.: Lift: Learned invariant feature transform. In: European Conference on Computer Vision, pp. 467–483. Springer (2016)
71. Zaharescu, A., Boyer, E., Horaud, R.: Keypoints and local descriptors of scalar functions on 2D manifolds. Int. J. Comput. Vis. 100(1), 78–98 (2012)
72. Zeng, A., Song, S., Nießner, M., Fisher, M., Xiao, J., Funkhouser, T.: 3Dmatch: Learning local geometric descriptors from RGB-D reconstructions. In: 2017 IEEE Conference on Computer Vision and Pattern Recognition (CVPR), pp. 199–208. IEEE (2017)
73. Zhong, Y.: Intrinsic shape signatures: A shape descriptor for 3D object recognition. In: 2009 IEEE 12th International Conference on Computer Vision Workshops, ICCV Workshops, pp. 689–696. IEEE (2009)

Chapter 8
3D Shape Registration

Umberto Castellani and Adrien Bartoli

Abstract Registration is the problem of bringing together two or more 3D shapes, either of the same object or of two different but similar objects. This chapter first introduces the classical Iterative Closest Point (ICP) algorithm which represents the gold standard registration method. Current limitations of ICP are addressed, and the most popular variants of ICP are described to improve the basic implementation in several ways. Challenging registration scenarios are analyzed, and a taxonomy of recent and promising alternative registration techniques is introduced. Four case studies are then described with an increasing level of difficulty. The first case study describes a simple but effective technique to detect outliers. The second case study uses the Levenberg–Marquardt (LM) optimization procedure to solve standard pairwise registration. The third case study focuses on the challenging problem of deformable object registration. The fourth case study introduces an ICP method for preoperative data registration in laparoscopy. Finally, open issues and directions for future work are discussed, and conclusions are drawn.

8.1 Introduction

Registration is a critical issue for various problems in computer vision and computer graphics. The overall aim is to find the best alignment between two objects or between several instances of the same object, in order to bring the shape data into the same reference system. The main high-level problems that use registration techniques are as follows:

1. **Model reconstruction**. The goal in model reconstruction is to create a complete object model from partial 3D views obtained by a 3D scanner. Indeed, it is rare that

U. Castellani (✉)
University of Verona, Verona, Italy
e-mail: Umberto.Castellani@univr.it

A. Bartoli
Université d'Auvergne, Clermont-Ferrand, France
e-mail: Adrien.Bartoli@gmail.com

© Springer Nature Switzerland AG 2020   353
Y. Liu et al. (eds.), *3D Imaging, Analysis and Applications*,
https://doi.org/10.1007/978-3-030-44070-1_8

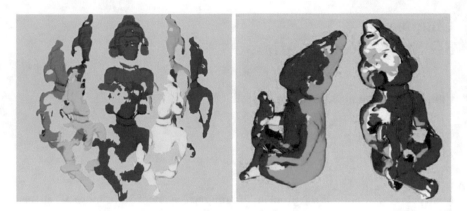

Fig. 8.1 Example of model reconstruction. Partial 3D views of the object of interest are acquired (left). After registration, all the 3D views are transformed to the common reference system and merged (right)

a single 3D view grabs the whole object structure, mainly due to self-occlusions. Registration allows one to obtain the alignment between the partial overlapping 3D views in order to build a complete object model, also called a mosaic (see Fig. 8.1). In this context, registration is first applied between pairs of views [11, 126]. The whole model is then reconstructed using multiple-view registration refinement [72, 126]. Typically, model reconstruction is employed in *cultural heritage* [10] to obtain 3D models of archeological findings. It has also been applied in applications such as *reverse engineering* and *rapid prototyping* [150] and for vision in hostile environments [29, 30].

2. **Model fitting**. The goal in model fitting is to compute the transformation between a partial 3D view and a known CAD model of the actual object. Model fitting is used in robotics for object grasping [41, 109] and model-based object tracking [123]. Model fitting is typically used with rigid objects but has recently been extended to deformable objects [31].

3. **Object recognition**. The goal in object recognition is to find, among a database of 3D models, which one best matches an input partial 3D view. This problem is more challenging than model fitting since a decision has to be made regarding which model, if any, is the sought one. Solving the recognition problem this way is called *recognition-by-fitting* [147]. Several works have been done for 3D face recognition [18, 20, 133] and for 3D object retrieval [56, 143]. Registration becomes more challenging in a cluttered environment [8, 76, 95].

4. **Multimodal registration**. The goal in multimodal registration is to align several views of the same object taken by different types of acquisition systems. After registration, the information from different modalities can be merged for comparison purposes or for creating a multimodal object model. This problem is typical in medical imaging where it is CT scans or MRI and PET scans [89, 134]. 3D medical image registration is discussed further in Chap. 11.

This chapter gives a general formulation of the registration problem. This formulation leads to computational solutions that can be used to solve the four above-mentioned tasks. It encompasses most of the existing registration algorithms. For a detailed description of registration techniques and experimental comparisons, we refer the reader to recent surveys [77, 96, 124, 126, 128, 141, 142]. It is worth mentioning that most of the existing computational solutions are based on the seminal Iterative Closest Point (ICP) [11] algorithm that we will describe shortly.

8.1.1   Chapter Outline

This chapter is organized as follows. We first present the two-view registration problem and the current algorithmic solutions. We then describe some advanced registration techniques. We give a comprehensive derivation of algorithms for registration by proposing four case studies. We give an overview of open challenges with future directions and conclusion. Further suggestions, additional reading, and exercises are finally proposed.

8.2   Registration of Two Views

We first give a mathematical formulation of the two-view registration problems and then derive the basic ICP algorithm and discuss its main variants.

8.2.1   Problem Statement

Given a pair of views $\mathbb{D}$ and $\mathbb{M}$ representing two scans (partial 3D views) of the same object, registration is the problem of finding the parameters $\mathbf{a}$ of the transformation function $T(\mathbf{a}, D)$ which best aligns D to M. Typically, $set\,D$ and $\mathbb{M}$ are either simple point clouds or triangulated meshes [26]. The moving view $\mathbb{D}$ is called *data-view*, while the fixed view $\mathbb{M}$ is called *model-view*. The registration problem is solved by estimating the parameters $\mathbf{a}^*$ of the transformation T that satisfy

$$\mathbf{a}^* = \arg\min_{\mathbf{a}} E(T(\mathbf{a}, \mathbb{D}), \mathbb{M}), \tag{8.1}$$

where E is called the *error function* and measures the registration error. Figure 8.2 illustrates the two-view registration process. The data-view and the model-view show different portions of *Bunny*. The transformation function $T(\mathbf{a}, \mathbb{D})$ is applied, and the registered views are shown.

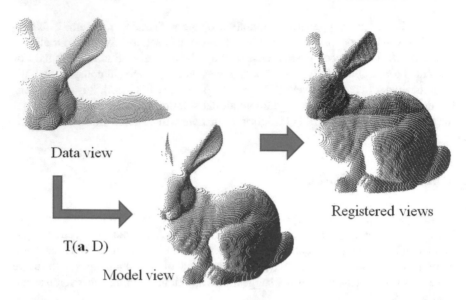

Fig. 8.2 Pairwise registration. The data-view and the model-view (left) are registered. The transformation function $T(\mathbf{a}, \mathbb{D})$ allows one to move the data-view to the model-view coordinate frame (right)

Most of the registration methods are based on the paradigm defined directly above and differ in the following aspects:

- **The transformation function**. The transformation function T usually implements a rigid transformation of the 3D space. It uses a translation vector $\mathbf{t}$ and a rotation matrix R whose values are encoded or parametrized in the parameter vector $\mathbf{a}$. The transformation function may also handle deformations; this requires a more complex formulation.
- **The error function**. The error function E measures the registration error or dissimilarity between $\mathbb{D}$ and $\mathbb{M}$ after alignment. When the transformation function T is rigid, E is a measure of *congruence* between the two views. In general, E takes the form of an L_2 approximation of the Hausdorff distance which further involves the so-called *point-to-point* distance [11] or the *point-to-plane* distance [36].
- **The optimization method**. This is the method or algorithm used to find the minimizer $\mathbf{a}$ in problem (8.1). The gold standard is the ICP algorithm [11] which was specifically designed for the problem at hand. General-purpose optimization methods such as Levenberg–Marquardt [54] have also been used for this problem.

8.2.2   The Iterative Closest Points (ICP) Algorithm

In the classical ICP algorithm [11], the overall aim is to estimate a rigid transformation with parameters $\mathbf{a}^* = (\mathsf{R}, \mathbf{t})$. Both views are treated as point clouds
$\mathbb{D} = \{\mathbf{d}_1, \ldots, \mathbf{d}_{N_d}\}$ and $\mathbb{M} = \{\mathbf{m}_1, \ldots, \mathbf{m}_{N_m}\}$. The error function is chosen as

$$E_{ICP}(\mathbf{a}, \mathbb{D}, \mathbb{M}) = \sum_{i=1}^{N_d} \|(\mathsf{R}\mathbf{d}_i + \mathbf{t}) - \mathbf{m}_j\|^2, \tag{8.2}$$

where we define $E_{ICP}(\mathbf{a}, \mathbb{D}, \mathbb{M}) = E(T(\mathbf{a}, \mathbb{D}), \mathbb{M})$ and where $(\mathbf{d}_i, \mathbf{m}_j)$ are corresponding points [126].[1] Fixing $\mathbf{d}_i \in \mathbb{D}$ the corresponding point $\mathbf{m}_j \in \mathbb{M}$ is computed
such that

$$j = \underset{k \in \{1, \ldots, N_m\}}{\arg\min} \|(\mathsf{R}\mathbf{d}_i + \mathbf{t}) - \mathbf{m}_k\|^2. \tag{8.3}$$

More specifically, the value

$$e_i^2 = \|(\mathsf{R}\mathbf{d}_i + \mathbf{t}) - \mathbf{m}_j\|^2 \tag{8.4}$$

is the square of the *residual*. Figure 8.3 illustrates the step of correspondence computation. For each data point (in red), the closest model point (in blue) is computed
using the Euclidean distance. The list of correspondences is thus obtained. Note
that, given point correspondences, computation of R and $\mathbf{t}$ to minimize E_{ICP} in
Eq. 8.2 can be solved in closed form [126]. Several approaches are possible for the
closed-form, least squares estimation of this 3D rigid body transformation. These
include approaches based on Singular Value Decomposition (SVD), unit quaternion,
dual quaternion, and orthonormal matrices. Although the study of Eggert et al. [49]
found little difference in the accuracy and robustness of all these approaches, perhaps the most well known of these is the SVD approach by Arun et al. [5]. Here, the
cross-covariance matrix is formed for the N_d correspondences, $(\mathbf{d}_i, \mathbf{m}_j)$, as

$$\mathsf{C} = \frac{1}{N_d} \sum_{i=1}^{N_d} (\mathbf{d}_i - \bar{\mathbf{d}})(\mathbf{m}_j - \bar{\mathbf{m}})^T, \tag{8.5}$$

where the means $\bar{\mathbf{d}}, \bar{\mathbf{m}}$ are formed over the N_d correspondences. Performing the SVD
of C gives us

$$\mathsf{U}\mathsf{S}\mathsf{V}^T = \mathsf{C}, \tag{8.6}$$

where U and V are two orthogonal matrices and S is a diagonal matrix of singular
values. The rotation matrix R can be calculated from the orthogonal matrices as

---

[1] Note that the pair $(\mathbf{d}_i, \mathbf{m}_j)$ is initially a putative correspondence, which becomes a true correspondence when convergence to a global minimum is attained.

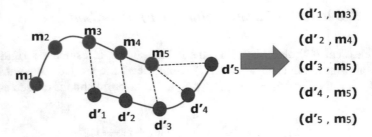

Fig. 8.3 Correspondence estimation in ICP. For each transformed data point $\mathbf{d}'_i = \mathsf{R}\mathbf{d}_i + \mathbf{t}$, the closest model point $\mathbf{m}_j$ is estimated (left). The list of corresponding points is then defined (right)

$$R = VU^T .$$ (8.7)

This solution may fail to give a correct rotation matrix and give a reflection instead when the data is severely corrupted [149]. Thus, it can be modified to always return a correct rotation matrix [149]:

$$R = VSU^T ,$$ (8.8)

where

$$S = \begin{cases} I & \text{if } \det(U)\det(V) = 1 \\ Diag(1, 1, \cdots, 1, -1) & \text{if } \det(U)\det(V) = -1. \end{cases}$$

Once the rotation matrix has been estimated, the translation vector $\mathbf{t}$ can be estimated as

$$\mathbf{t} = \bar{\mathbf{m}} - \mathsf{R}\bar{\mathbf{d}} .$$ (8.9)

The ICP algorithm is iterative because it iteratively improves the putative correspondences. If true correspondences were known, clearly the process could operate in one shot (one pass). ICP has two main steps in its inner loop: *(i)* closest point computation and *(ii)* rigid transformation estimation. In more detail, the algorithm operates as follows:

1. For each data point $\mathbf{d}_i \in \mathbb{D}$, compute the closest point $\mathbf{m}_j \in \mathbb{M}$ according to Eq. 8.3.
2. With the correspondences $(\mathbf{d}_i, \mathbf{m}_j)$ from step 1, estimate the new transformation parameters $\mathbf{a} = (\mathsf{R}, \mathbf{t})$.
3. Apply the new transformation parameters $\mathbf{a}$ from step 2 to the point cloud $\mathbb{D}$.
4. If the change in $E_{ICP}(\mathbf{a}, \mathbb{D}, \mathbb{M})$ between two successive iterations is lower than a threshold then terminate, else go to step 1.

It was proven [11] that this algorithm is guaranteed to converge monotonically to a local minimum of Eq. (8.2). Note that, as for any local iterative method, a strategy for initializing $\mathbf{a}$ must be used. An overview of the most popular initialization strategies is given in Sect. 8.2.3.1.

8.2.3   ICP Extensions

Although ICP has been successfully applied to many registration problems, there are several critical issues that need to be taken care of. In particular, ICP performs well when the following assumptions are met:

1. *The two views must be close to each other.* If not, ICP will probably get stuck in a local minimum. This issue is typically solved by pre-alignment of the two 3D views, also called *coarse* registration.
2. *The two views must fully overlap or the data-view $\mathbb{D}$ must be a subset of the model-view $\mathbb{M}$.* The problem arises from the fact that ICP always assigns a closest point to every data point. If a data point has no corresponding model point, this will create a spurious correspondence, an *outlier* with respect to the sought transformation, that will bias the solution or prevent the algorithm from finding the correct transformation parameters.

Two other important issues are the *speed* of computation and the *accuracy* of the ICP algorithm. Typically, methods focused on speed improvement for the closest point computation step which is the bottleneck of the algorithm. Other interesting approaches address instead of the speed of convergence by proposing new distance formulations for problem (8.1). Methods focusing on accuracy exploit additional information in order to measure the *similarity* between corresponding points not only in terms of proximity. In the following, we describe some registration techniques which improve the basic ICP method in several ways. Figure 8.4 illustrates the proposed taxonomy of ICP extensions so as to easily understand the organization of previous work in this field.

8.2.3.1   Techniques for Pre-alignment

The aim of pre-alignment techniques is to estimate a coarse transformation which will allow the two views to get closer. This helps the data-view to be transformed within basin of attraction of the correct local minimum. In practice, instead of searching *dense* point-to-point correspondences, pre-alignment techniques estimate the best matching between *features* extracted from the views. Roughly speaking, the features can be *global* or *local*. The former is a compact representation that effectively and concisely describes the entire view. The latter instead is a collection of local and discriminative descriptors computed on sub-parts of the views.

Global Approaches
Global approaches typically estimate and match the principal coordinate system of each view. The simplest approach is to compute the main translational alignment by shifting the centroids of the two point clouds to the origin of the coordinate system (i.e., zero-mean). In order to estimate also the orientation of the principal axes, Principal Component Analysis (PCA) to the 3D points can be performed. The problems with PCA as a pre-alignment method are (i) a 180° ambiguity in the

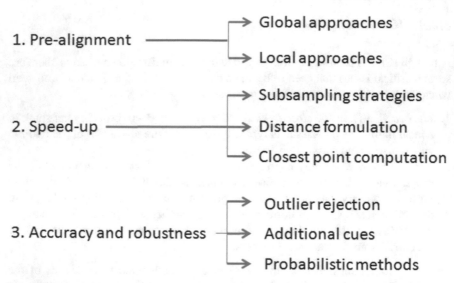

Fig. 8.4 A taxonomy of some ICP extensions

direction of the principal axes, (ii) principal axes may switch for shapes that have
eigenvalues similar in value, particularly if the object is able to deform slightly,
and (iii) a vulnerability to outliers in the raw shape data (as discussed). Even if
we enforce a right-handed frame using the sign of cross-product of basis vectors,
there still exists an overall 180° ambiguity, unless higher order moments are used.
Moments of higher orders are also useful to improve accuracy [21]. Of course, these
approaches perform well when the two views fully overlap. Otherwise, the non-
overlapping parts change the estimation of the principal axes and thus affect the
pre-alignment. Some improvements have been made by extracting and matching
the *skeletons* of the views [32, 99] but this is feasible for articulated objects only.
Recently, a method for registration between views in arbitrary pose was proposed as
the so-called *GO*-ICP method [157]. The key idea consists of solving the optimization
problem using a branch and bound algorithm to guarantee the estimation of a global
solution independently of the initialization.

Local Approaches
Local approaches define a *descriptor* (or signature) for each 3D point which encodes
local shape variation in the point neighborhood [27, 76, 78, 104, 140]. See also [63,
64, 145] for a comprehensive survey on local geometric descriptors. Point correspondences are then obtained as the best matches in regard to the point signatures.
Various methods to compute signatures were proposed. In the seminal work [76],
the *spin images* were introduced. In a spin image, the neighbors of some selected 3D
point (e.g., a 3D interest point [145]) are binned in a 2D cylindrical-polar coordinate
system. This consists of a distance from the selected point within that point's tangent
plane and a signed height above/below the tangent plane. Thus, the spin image is
a 2D histogram of 3D shape, where one dimension of information is sacrificed for

pose invariance. In [80], curvilinear features on the object are estimated from a small amount of points of interest. Gaussian and mean curvatures are used to this aim. Similarly, in [156], bitangent curve pairs were used as landmarks on the surface. In [104], a geometric scale-space analysis of 3D models was proposed from which a scale-dependent local shape descriptor was derived. Similarly in [27], registration involves few feature points by extending the approach for salient point detection to the 3D domain. A *generative model* is then estimated as a point descriptor by using hidden Markov models. In [78], the proposed descriptor encodes not only local information around the point, but also inter-point relationships. The method is inspired by the so-called *Shape Context* [9] which was improved using the *Bag-of-Words* paradigm [42]. Note that from the analysis of inter-point relationships, it is also possible to estimate the overlapping region between two views. It is worth noting that in general the estimation of the overlap area is not trivial. An interesting approach was proposed in [131] by combining local geometric features with advanced graph matching techniques. The method consists of representing all putative point matches as a graph, and then selecting as many *consistent* matches among them as possible. To this aim, a global discrete optimization problem is proposed based on the so-called *maximum strict sub-kernel algorithm* [130].

8.2.3.2 Techniques for Improving Speed

The speed of the algorithm is crucial for many applications. Unfortunately, when the number of points is very high, the basic ICP algorithm becomes very slow. In order to address this issue, several strategies were proposed. Many of these strategies are implemented by the Kinect fusion toolkit [101] for real-time modeling using dynamic RGBD sensors.

Subsampling
Subsampling can be applied to either the data-view only or to both the data-view and the model-view. *Random* and *uniform* strategies are common approaches [126]. *Normal space* sampling is a more sophisticated approach based on choosing points such that the distribution of normals among the selected points is as spread as possible. This increases the influence of smaller details which are crucial to better disambiguate the rigid transformation due to translational sliding. Another effective practice is based on a *hierarchical* subsampling where the *range* map is re-organized in a pyramidal fashion to obtain a coarse to fine representation of the source data. This approach is employed for online modeling as in [101] where the coarse levels with few points are used to estimate the rough motion, and vice-versa the detailed levels that involve more points are employed for refining the alignment.

Closest Point Computation
As mentioned above, closest point computation is the bottleneck of the registration process due to the quadratic complexity ($O(n^2)$) in finding the correspondence of each point. Early strategies were based on the organization of the model points in a *k-d* tree [136] structure in order to reduce the closest point complexity to $O(n \log n)$.

Closest point caching [136] also accelerates the speed of ICP (the data point correspondence search is only among a subset of model points which were the closest at
the previous iteration). Indeed, in [105] *k-d* tree and caching are combined in order
to further improve the speed of ICP. Other more effective approaches are based on
the so-called *reverse calibration* paradigm [13]. The idea is to project the source
data point onto the destination model-view which is encoded as a *range* image [124].
In particular, the projection from the 3D domain into the range image is performed
by using the calibration parameters of the 3D scanner. In this fashion, the correspondence is computed in one shot. The reverse calibration approach is especially
effective for real-time modeling purposes [30, 101, 125]. For instance, in [125] the
authors proposed the first real-time 3D model reconstruction system where the full
modeling pipeline is carried out during the acquisition using a real-time sensor. In
[30], online registration is performed to build a 3D mosaic of the scene in order
to improve the navigation in underwater environments. This online modeling using
reverse calibration alignment has been consolidated more recently with the large
availability of dynamic RGBD sensors [101]. Note that the one-shot computation
can be carried out also on generic point cloud (not necessarily coming from a range
image) by precomputing the so-called *distance transform* of the model-view [54].
Figure 8.5 illustrates the distance transform. In practice, the distance to closest model
points is pre-computed for all grid points of the discretized volume. The case for distance transform computed for the model is particularly compelling when one wishes
to align many instances of data scan to the same model scan. A more recent class of
methods is based on the GPU implementation of data representation to improve the
computation of corresponding points [47, 48]. A probabilistic approach is proposed
using Gaussian Mixture Models (GMMs) where a decoupling technique is introduced for parallel estimation of parameters. Also, in [101], a parallel computation
of local contributions of distance estimation is employed on a GPU to improve the
speed of real-time modeling.

Distance Formulation
Another crucial factor affecting the speed of ICP is the point-to-point or point-to-
plane distance used in problem (8.1). Figure 8.6 shows a schema of the two kinds
of distances: point-to-point computes the euclidean distance between the data point
and model point (left), and point-to-plane distance computes the projection of the
data point onto the surface of the model-view which is encoded in terms of piecewise
planar patches (for instance, a triangular mesh). In spite of an increased complexity
of the distance for point-to-plane formulation, the number of ICP iterations required
to converge is reduced [110, 115]. Whether this results in a reduced registration time
depends on the tradeoff between the increased per-iteration time and the reduced
number of iterations. Note that usually the point-to-plane distance is employed for
real-time modeling pipelines [101, 124] where pairwise registration is carried out
for subsequent views acquired very close in time with a very small motion among
them.

Recently, a new "distance formulation" has been proposed [112] where the model
surface is implicitly represented as the zero isosurface of a fitted Radial Basis Func-

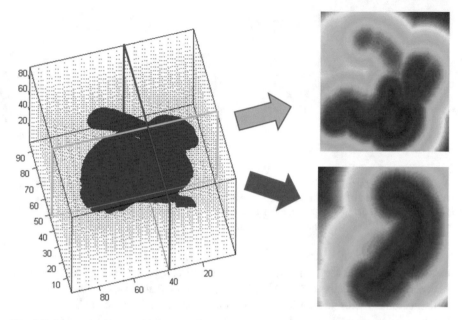

Fig. 8.5 Using the distance transform. The model-view is enclosed in a volumetric grid (left). For each point of the grid, the closest model point is computed. Two planes are highlighted on the XY- and YZ-axes, respectively, and the distance transform values of each grid point are visualized for both planes (right)

tion (RBF), $s(\mathbf{x}) = 0$, for any 3D point $\mathbf{x}$, where the function s represents *distance to surface*. For any point on the data scan (or on a pre-computed 3D grid), the distance and direction (gradient) to the zero isosurface can be computed directly from the RBF. The advantage of this RBF distance formulation is that it interpolates over holes that may exist in the model scan. Particularly for lower resolution scans, the interpolation is more accurate than the piecewise linear point-to-plane method. Both RBF model fitting and RBF model evaluation are $O(n \log n)$.

8.2.3.3 Techniques for Improving Accuracy

The accuracy of the alignment is the most critical aspect of the registration since even a small misalignment between two views can affect the whole 3D model reconstruction procedure. The simplest strategy that can be used is outlier rejection. Other methods improve the accuracy by using additional information such as color and texture or local geometric properties. Finally, an effective class of methods devoted to the improvement of accuracy are probabilistic methods.

Outlier Rejection
Closest point computation may yield spurious correspondences due to errors or to the presence of non-overlapping parts between the views. Typically, outlier rejection

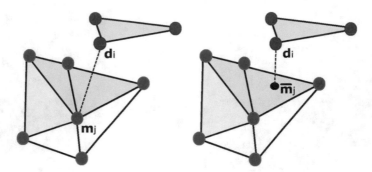

Fig. 8.6 Distance formulation. Point-to-point distance: the 3D vertex d_i is associated to the $3D$ point m_j which is a vertex of the source $3D$ mesh (left). Point-to-plane distance: the 3D vertex d_i is associated to the $3D$ point m_j which lies inside the plane defined by a triangle of the source $3D$ mesh (right)

techniques threshold the residuals. The threshold can be fixed manually, or as a percentage of worst pairs (e.g., 10% [117, 126]). Other techniques perform statistics on the residual vector and set the threshold as 2.5σ or apply the so-called *X84* rule [29, 66]. An evaluation of the use of the *X84* rule for automatic outlier rejection is presented in Sect. 8.5. More recently, statistical analysis has been introduced into the general registration problem (Eq. 8.1) by proposing a new error function named *Fractional Root Mean Squared Distance* [113]. In [17], an implicit approach to reject the outliers is introduced exploiting a sparse formulation of the closest point computation with L_1-norm distance.

Additional Information
The basic ICP algorithm computes the correspondences by taking into account only the *proximity* of points. However, corresponding points should be similar with respect to other aspects. Several studies have attempted to exploit additional information available from the acquisition process or from the analysis of the surface properties. In practice, the distance formulation is modified to integrate such additional information like local surface properties [59], intensity derived from the sensor [59, 154], or color [118]. In [74], the authors proposed to use color and texture information. In [135], the so-called *ICP using Invariant Feature* (ICPIF) was introduced where several geometric features are employed, namely, *curvatures*, *moments invariants*, and *spherical harmonics invariants*. In [25], additional information was integrated into the point descriptors using the spin image with color. More recently, with the availability of low-cost RGBD sensors [165], several methods have been proposed that exploit the matching computation on both the 2D and 3D domains (i.e., a 2D image is used as additional information) [67]. For instance, [162] uses camera pose optimization with 2D features to improve the accuracy of registration.

Probabilistic Method
In order to improve the robustness of the registration, several probabilistic versions of the standard ICP have been proposed [61, 119, 120]. In [119, 120], the idea

of multiple weighted matches justified by a probabilistic version of the matching problem is introduced. A new matching model is proposed based on Gaussian weight (SoftAssign [120]) and mutual information [119], leading to a smaller number of local minima and thus presenting the most convincing improvements. In [61], the authors introduced a probabilistic approach based on the Expectation Maximization (EM) paradigm, namely, EM-ICP. Hidden variables are used to model the point matching. Specifically, in the case of Gaussian noise, the proposed method corresponds to ICP with multiple matches weighted by normalized Gaussian weights. In practice, the variance of the Gaussian is interpreted as a scale parameter. At high scales, EM-ICP gets many matches while it behaves like standard ICP at lower scales. In [47], a hierarchical approach was introduced representing the partial views at multiple scales. In this fashion, the most appropriate level of geometric details is adaptively found to improve the point matching.

8.3 Advanced Techniques

Although registration is one of the most studied problems in computer vision, several cases are still open and new issues have emerged in recent years. In this section, we focus on some scenarios where registration becomes more challenging: registration of *more than two views*, registration in *cluttered scenes*, and registration of *deformable objects*. We also describe some emerging techniques based on machine learning to solve the registration problem. Figure 8.7 illustrates the proposed taxonomy for advanced registration techniques.

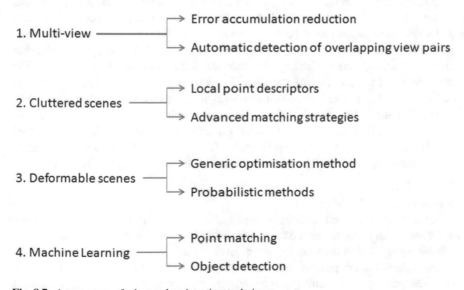

Fig. 8.7 A taxonomy of advanced registration techniques

8.3.1 Registration of More Than Two Views

Once registration has been performed pairwise, all the views need to be transformed into a global reference system by applying a *multiple-view* registration technique. Note that in this context the assumption that the data-view is a subset of the model-view is no longer true. There are two main issues: *(i)* error accumulation and *(ii)* the automation of the process.

Reducing Error Accumulation
When the ordering of the sequence of views $N_1, ..., N_p$ is available, the registration can be performed pairwise between consecutive views (i.e., between views N_i and N_{i+1}). In general, even if all the pairs are apparently well registered, some misalignment typically appears when the full model is reconstructed due to the accumulation and propagation of the registration error. The general idea of multiple-view registration techniques is to solve *simultaneously* for the global registration by exploiting the interdependencies between all views at the same time. This introduces additional constraints which reduce the global error. A comparative study of similar multiple-view registration schemes was performed [43]. In [117], a method is presented that first aligns the scans pairwise with each other and then uses the pairwise alignments as constraints in a multiview step. The aim is to evenly distribute the pairwise registration error, but the method itself is still based on pairwise alignments. In [29], a method that distributes registration errors evenly across all views was proposed. It operates in the space of estimated pairwise registration matrices; however, ordering of the views is required. More recently, [144] proposed a new approach based on the well-known generalized Procrustes analysis, seamlessly embedding the mathematical theory in an ICP framework. A variant of the method, where the correspondences are non-uniformly weighted using a curvature-based similarity measure, was also presented. In [161], a method that handles loop closures was proposed to perform a globally consistent reconstruction. Locally fused models are introduced for overlapping parts of the scene and used to initialize a global graph-based optimization that distributes residual error. The key idea consists in the detection of *points of interest* characterized by the areas with the highest density of information. This approach is particularly effective for large-scale scenarios where the reconstruction is obtained with a SLAM-like framework [51]. In [53], error accumulation is avoided by extending the LM-ICP algorithm [54] to work on multiple views. The idea consists of defining an effective optimization function that considers all the views simultaneously in the registration error, whose solution is obtained using standard numerical methods.

Automating Registration
Especially when the full model is composed of a large number of scans, the view order might not be available and therefore should be manually specified. Many methods were proposed to improve the automation of multiple-view registration. In [72], a global optimization process searches a graph constructed from the pairwise view matches for a connected sub-graph containing only correct matches, using a global

consistency measure to eliminate incorrect but locally consistent matches. Other approaches use both *global* and *local* pre-alignment techniques to select the overlapping views by computing a coarse alignment between all the pairs. In [90], the pre-alignment is performed by extracting global features from each view, namely, extended Gaussian images. Conversely, in [78], the pre-alignment is computed by comparing the signatures of feature points. Then, the best view sequence is estimated by solving a standard Travelling Salesman Problem (TSP). In [37], a robust strategy was introduced to detect wrong alignment between view pairs. A global optimization method is introduced based on the line processes algorithm. In [65], the authors introduced a *shape-growing* method where a seed shape is sequentially updated by registering it with the input partial views. In [53], a view matching method was proposed that combines salient point descriptors with a RANSAC-based robust correspondence computation. In this fashion, both the ordering of views and the pairwise pre-alignment are obtained leading to a fully automatic registration pipeline. Results regarding this aspect for example 3D scans are presented in Sect. 8.4.

8.3.2 Registration in Cluttered Scenes

Thanks to the recent availability of large-scale scanners, it is possible to acquire scenes composed of several objects. In this context, registration is necessary to localize each object present in the scene and estimate its pose. We call this scenario a *cluttered* case where the overlap between the registering views is very small since the object of interest to be localized may be made of a small subset of the entire view. This makes the registration problem more challenging. Figure 8.8 shows two examples of highly cluttered scenes: an entire square[2] and a scene composed of several mechanical objects.

Roughly speaking, two main strategies were proposed to address this problem: *(i)* the use of point signatures to improve point-to-point matching and *(ii)* the design of more effective matching methods.

Point Signatures
This approach is similar to local approaches for pre-alignment. However, in clutter scenarios, the problem becomes more challenging since, differently from the standard pre-alignment case, the neighborhood of one point of an object can cover part of other objects. Therefore, the descriptor may become useless, and the size of local neighborhood becomes crucial to get the best tradeoff between reliability of descriptor and robustness to clutter. A large number of methods for keypoint detection were proposed to reduce the considered points only to very few salient areas [145]. Then, using a local 3D Reference Frame (RF) is important to encode pose invariant 3D descriptors. For instance, in [146] the so-called *SHOT* descriptor was proposed to form a rotation invariant and robust to noise RF from which a descriptor is obtained combining geometric information with color. In [95], a descriptor

---

[2]Piazza Brà, Verona, Italy. Image courtesy of Gexcel: http://www.gexcel.it.

Fig. 8.8 Example of large scan acquisition (left) and scene with multiple mechanical objects (right)

that uses two reference points to define a local coordinate system is proposed. In particular, a three-dimensional tensor is built by sampling the space and storing the amount of surface intersecting each sample. In [8], a method that exploits surface scale properties is introduced. The geometric scale variability is encoded in the form of the intrinsic geometric scale of each computed feature by leading to a highly discriminative hierarchical descriptor.

Matching Methods

Since the number of corresponding points is very few within cluttered scenes, standard methods for outlier rejection are not useful but more complex matching algorithm can be exploited. In [95], descriptors are stored using a hash table that can be efficiently looked up at the matching phase by geometric hashing algorithm. In [8], matching is performed in hierarchical fashion by using the hierarchy induced from the definition of point descriptor. In [46], a method is proposed that creates a global model description using an oriented point pair feature and matches it by using a fast voting scheme. A fast voting scheme, similar to the generalized Hough transform, is used to optimize the model pose in a locally reduced search space. This space is parametrized in terms of points on the model and rotation around the surface normals.

In [155], a new voting scheme called *Intrinsic* Hough transform was introduced to exploit the sparsity of the voting space by sampling only at the areas where the matching probability is non-zero. In [2], a method is proposed to extract all coplanar 4-point sets from a 3D point set that are approximately congruent, under rigid transformation, to a given set of coplanar 4-points. This approach is further expanded in the so-called *Super*4PCS method [93] where an effective data structure is exploited to improve the core *instance problem*, i.e., finding all point pairs that are within a distance range $(r - \epsilon, r + \epsilon)$. In this fashion, a very fast registration can be obtained from arbitrary pose, with very few overlap. In [163], a method called *fast global* registration was introduced. A well-defined energy formulation is designed to encode the registration constraints, and a line process technique is exploited to efficiently solve for the optimal solution. This method is suitable for large scenes with clutter. Moreover, it can easily work with multiple views.

8.3.3 Deformable Registration

While rigidity in the aligning transformation is a largely applicable constraint, it is too restrictive in some cases. Imagine indeed that the object that has to be registered is not rigid but deformable. For instance, a typical deformable object is the human body and its parts such as the face or the hands. For the full body, it is very important to align the articulated parts (i.e., arms, legs, and so on), while for the face the deformations are caused mainly by the facial expressions. Another class of object is composed of planar shapes such as a piece of paper or a blanket that deform over time. Also, in the medical domain, there are mainly non-rigid scenarios caused by the deformation of the internal parts of the human body. Deformable registration has two main issues: the computation of stable correspondences and the use of an appropriate deformation model. Note that the need for registration of articulated or deformable objects has recently increased due to the availability of real-time range scanners [33, 34, 85, 97]. Roughly speaking, we can emphasize two classes of deformable registration methods: *(i)* methods based on general optimization techniques, and *(ii)* probabilistic methods.

Methods Based on General Optimization Techniques
The general formulation of deformable registration is more involved than the rigid case and it is more difficult to solve in closed form. Advanced optimization techniques are used instead. The advantage of using general optimization techniques consists of jointly computing the estimation of correspondences and the deformable parameters [33, 34, 38, 85, 138]. Moreover, other unknowns can be used to model further information like the overlapping area, the reliability of correspondences, the smoothness constraint, and so on [85]. Examples of transformation models which have been introduced for surface deformations are *(i)* affine transforms applied to nodes uniformly sampled from the range images [85], *(ii)* rigid transforms on patches automatically extracted from the surface [33], *(iii)* as rigid as possible constraint [138], *(iv)* Thin-Plate Splines (TPS) [38, 124], or *(v)* Linear Blend Skinning (LBS) model [34]. The error function can be optimized by the Levenberg–Marquardt Algorithm [85], GraphCuts [33], or Expectation–Maximization (EM) [34, 38, 100]. In [71], deformable registration is solved by alternating between correspondence and deformation optimization. Assuming approximately isometric deformations, robust correspondences are generated using a pruning mechanism based on geodesic consistency. Deformable alignment to account for errors in the point clouds obtained by scanning a rigid object is proposed in [22, 23]. Also, in this case, the authors use TPS to represent the deformable warp between a pair of views that they estimate through hierarchical ICP [124]. Note that using real-time RGBD sensors is possible to implement real-time modeling and reconstruction systems also for non-rigid objects

[73, 102]. For instance in [102], the so-called *Dynamic Fusion* method has been introduced for dense dynamic scene reconstruction. The idea is to estimate a dense volumetric motion field for each frame in order to provide increasingly denoised measurements and a complete representation of the observed scene as more measurements are acquired and integrated. This approach has been further extended in [73] where a sparse RGB feature matching strategy was introduced to improve the robustness of tracking.

A new class of methods are properly defined for human shapes and are based on the fitting of a template model (e.g., a morphable model) to the acquired shape [88]. In this scenario, the challenge consists of estimating both the shape and pose parameters within the same optimization procedure. For instance, in [14], the Skinned Multi-Person Linear (SMPL) model is registered to a monocular RGBD sequence for full-body reconstruction. This approach was further expanded for full-body dynamic shape and motion capture [15] where a new mesh registration method was proposed that uses both 3D geometry and texture information to register all scans in a sequence to a common reference topology. Another class of important method for non-rigid shapes is based on spectral shape analysis [84]. In particular, a new approach consists of moving the computation of matching from the physical to the spectral space exploiting the so-called *functional map* framework [106]. From the basic framework, several variants have been proposed to work on partial shapes [87, 122], to reduce the number of estimated parameters [103], and to exploit locality on the spectral domain [94]. It is worth noting that these methods provide the matching between points or shape parts but they cannot deform the pair of shapes to allow a full alignment between them. For this aim, a recent method called functional automatic registration for 3D human bodies (FARM) was proposed in [91] where the spectral approach based on the functional map is combined with the SMPL template model to obtain the registration of the full body in very challenging scenarios such as partiality, noise, and topological variation.

Probabilistic Methods

Using probabilistic methods, the uncertainty on the correct surface transformation can be addressed by adopting maximum likelihood estimation [4, 45, 70, 75, 100, 151]. Probabilistic approaches are based on modeling each of the point sets by a kernel density function [148]. The dissimilarity among such densities is computed by introducing appropriate distance functions. Registration is carried out without explicitly establishing correspondences. Indeed, the algorithm registers two meshes by optimizing a joint probabilistic model over all point-to-point correspondences between them [4]. In [75], the authors propose a correlation-based approach [148] to point set registration by representing the point sets as Gaussian mixture models. A closed-form solution for the L_2 norm distance between two Gaussian mixtures makes fast computation possible. In [151], registration is carried out simultaneously for several 3D range datasets. The method proposes an information-theoretic approach based on the Jensen–Shannon divergence measure. In [100], deformable registration is treated as a maximum likelihood estimation problem by introducing the coherent point drift paradigm. Smoothness constraints are introduced based on the assumption that points close to one another tend to move coherently over the velocity field. The proposed energy function is minimized with the EM algorithm. Similar approach has been proposed in [45] to track the full-hand motion. A stereo setup is employed to estimate the 3D surface. To improve the estimation of the hand pose, 2D motion (i.e., optical flow) is combined with 3D information. A well-defined hand model is employed to deal with articulated structures and deformations. Also, in this case, the standard ICP algorithm has been extended to its probabilistic version according to the EM-ICP approach. This approach has been further extended in [70] where the so-called expectation *conditional* maximization paradigm is introduced. A formal demonstration is proposed to show that it is convenient to replace the standard M-step by three conditional maximization steps, or CM steps, while preserving the convergence properties of EM. Experiments are reported for both the hand and body tracking. In [28], a statistical method has been proposed to model the local geometry properties variation as a local stochastic process encoded in a Hidden Markov Model (HMM). The idea is to learn local geometric configurations as hidden states and encoding the surface properties in terms of transitions among such states. In [166], the so-called *Stitched Puppet* model was proposed to encode the body parts of the human shapes in a generative model. The human body is represented by a graphical model whose nodes are associated to body parts that can independently translate and rotate in 3D.

8.3.4 Machine Learning Techniques

Recently, advanced machine learning techniques have been exploited to improve registration algorithms [3, 60, 98, 111, 139]. The general idea is to use data-driven approaches that learn the relevant registration criteria from examples. The most promising methods have been proposed for *(i)* improving the matching phase and *(ii)* detecting an object which is a general instance of one or more classes. Most of the recently proposed methods are based on deep learning architectures [82].

Improving the Matching
In these approaches, the emphasis is on the effectiveness of the correspondence computation. In [139], a new formulation for deformable registration (3D faces) is proposed. The distance function from corresponding points is defined as a weighted sum of contributions coming from different surface attributes (i.e., proximity, color/texture, normals). Instead of manually or heuristically choosing the weights, a machine learning technique is proposed to estimate them. A support vector machine framework is employed in a supervised manner, based on a dataset of pairs of correct and incorrect correspondences. In [3], the authors propose a novel unsupervised technique that allows one to obtain a fine surface registration in a single step, without the need of an initial motion estimation. The main idea of their approach is to cast the selection of correspondences between points on the surfaces in a *game theoretic* framework. In this fashion, a natural selection process allows one to select points

that satisfy a mutual rigidity constraint to thrive, eliminating all the other correspondences.

With the explosion of the deep learning technology [82], several methods have been proposed to extend this very effective approach to 3D registration. In [158], a neural network is trained on 3D shapes working on local volumetric patches. The need of a large number of training data is satisfied using the available dataset of already registered scans. This approach was further improved in [44], encoding simple geometric relationships such as normals and point pair features to better represent the local context of a given point. Furthermore, to explore the relationship across different views, a new descriptor was proposed in [160] where training is carried out by collecting information from multiple views. In [50] rather than using labeled data, the authors proposed an unsupervised method based on deep auto-encoders [68]. Deep learning methods are also effective for non-rigid objects like the human body [16, 86]. In [16], a geometric convolutional neural network was designed to effectively learn class-specific shape descriptors. In [86], a new neural network was proposed to directly estimating the shape correspondences within the functional map framework. Finally, interesting deep learning approaches have been successfully employed in the medical domain where different sources of information need to be integrated using a multimodal registration procedure [137].

Object Detection

A new class of methods is emerging from employing machine learning techniques for detecting specific classes of objects on large scenes [60, 98, 111]. In this context, the registration is important to be able to devise a *detection-by-localization* approach [147] where the pose of the object is also estimated. Several works have been done for the 2D domain, but its extension to 3D scenes is not trivial. In [111], the authors proposed to detect cars in cluttered scenes composed of millions of scanned points. The method is based on integrating *spin images* with *extended Gaussian images* in order to combine effectively local and global descriptors. Furthermore, the method is able to detect object classes and not only specific instances. In [98], the Associative Markov Network (AMN) has been extended to integrate the context of local features by exploiting directional information through a new non-isotropic model. In [60], different objects are simultaneously detected by hierarchical segmentation of point clouds. Indeed, clusters of points are classified using standard learning by example classifiers.

Deep learning methods have shown their benefit also for the object detection task. The so-called *3DMatch* method [158] enables 3D model alignment from cluttered RGBD scenes using a deep neural network to learn 3D matching. In [81], the object is localized using a regression procedure which, from the depth image, provides the 6D-pose parameters. Note that these deep-learning-based approaches naturally extend to multiple and different objects, leading to a complete 3D semantic segmentation. For instance, in [121] a new neural network architecture was proposed for the extraction of semantic components of a point cloud.

8.4   Registration at Work

In this section, we show some practical examples of registration algorithms at work on two views and then on more than two views.

8.4.1   Two-View Registration

As mentioned in Sect. 8.2, given a pair of partial views of the same object, the pairwise registration task consists in estimating the rigid transformation that brings the moving *data-view* to the reference *model-view*. In this example, we take a pair of scans from an RGBD sequence of a real scene that is acquired by a real-time sensor (i.e., kinect [101]). The scene contains a table and some objects of the real life. The data is online available from the *rgbd-scene-v2* dataset[3] and represents a very useful benchmark for the evaluation of real-time modeling techniques like *kinect fusion* [101].

Figure 8.9 shows the pair of evaluated scans. The RGB image (Fig. 8.9, left) shows a can, a box, a bowl, and a mug. The depth map (Fig. 8.9, center) highlights the relative positions among the involved objects (i.e., the bowl is the closest to the observer, the box is the farthest, and the other objects are in between). The colored point cloud (Fig. 8.9, right) gives the full 3D representation of the scene. As happens usually for a real scene acquired with real-time RGBD sensors, the scans are very noisy with the presence of many holes and outliers.

Figure 8.10 shows the 2D registration performance. Figure 8.10 shows the partial views before the registration. The second view is acquired after around 1 s from the first one. This means that the sensor motion is sufficiently large to introduce new details of the overall scene, and the two views are already heavily misaligned. For this experiment, we employed the standard ICP algorithm for pairwise registration after a manual pre-alignment. We use the ICP implementation from meshlab[4] and the enclosed aligning toolkit for the pre-registration. Finally, Fig. 8.10 shows the registered views. The two views are correctly aligned, and new details of the acquired scene can be correctly captured especially on the can and the bowl.

8.4.2   Multiple-View Registration

In this section, we evaluate a fully automatic 3D registration pipeline of multiple views. Given a sequence of unordered partial views of the same object, the registration task consists in finding the rigid transformation that brings each view to the global reference system. In this fashion, the views become aligned and a com-

---

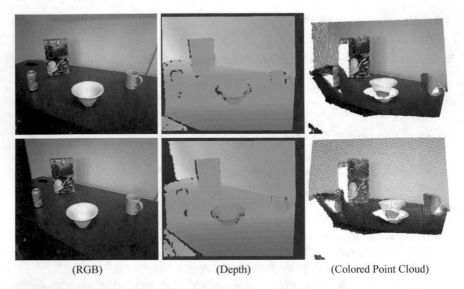

| (RGB) | (Depth) | (Colored Point Cloud) |

Fig. 8.9 Pair of RGBD scans: RGB image (left), depth map (center), and colored point cloud (right)

Fig. 8.10 2D Registration: starting views (left) and registered views (right)

plete model can be reconstructed. We adopt a local feature-based approach which is composed of the following main steps[5]:

1. **Keypoint detection**. Keypoint detection aims at detecting few and salient feature points from the shape. We employ the salient point detection method proposed in [27]. Inspired by the research on saliency measure on 2D images, the source mesh is decomposed into multiscale representations, and a saliency measure is defined by combining the results gathered at each scale. Finally, maximal points on the salient map are detected as feature points.

---

[5]Code and data for this automatic 3D registration pipeline is implemented on the Automatic 3D Registration toolkit available at http://profs.sci.univr.it/~castella/art.html.

2. **Keypoint description**. Keypoint description aims at attaching a descriptor to each keypoint that must be (i) distinctive of the point, (ii) invariant to rigid transformations, and (iii) resilient to as much nuisances as possible (noise, clutter, partial views, sampling rate, and so on). We use spin images [76], a well-known surface representation that has been successfully used in shape matching and object recognition.
3. **View matching**. Since the ordering of the views is unknown, a view matching step is required to estimate the set of view pairs to be registered. To this aim, the overlap between each view pair is computed using a voting scheme among the keypoint descriptors. The output of this stage is encoded in an adjacency matrix between the views.
4. **Pairwise registration**. The pairwise registration is obtained in two phases: (i) robust pre-alignment for which only feature points are involved, and (ii) ICP registration refinement where a more accurate alignment is estimated with ICP on the pre-aligned views using only the overlapping parts.
5. **Global registration**. A global alignment is produced by combining the pairwise rigid transformations found in the previous step. The idea (as in [92, 132]) is to estimate a global alignment of the views with the least accumulation error among the solutions based on chaining pairwise registrations.

A more detailed description of the steps involved in the proposed pipeline is available in [53]. Figure 8.11 shows a subset of partial views of Bunny (i.e., 6 over 24 views). The overlap between views is reliable for only a few view pairs (e.g., views 1 and 5). Conversely, for most of the view pairs, the overlap is not sufficient to guarantee a correct alignment. According to our pipeline, we detect the keypoints and their signatures for each view. Figure 8.12 (top) and (middle) shows some feature points on the Bunny ear from two overlapping views. It is worth to note that the extracted keypoints are coherent on the two observed views. Figure 8.12 (on the right side) shows the spin images of selected keypoints (red dots). As expected, corresponding points generate very similar signatures (Fig. 8.12 (top) and (middle) on the right side). When instead we consider a pair of non-corresponding points, their signatures appear very different (Fig. 8.12 (bottom) where a point around the eye is observed).

To compute the view matching, we follow the approach of [24] for 2D image mosaicing. In this phase, we consider only a constant number of descriptors in each view (we used 100, where a typical view contains thousands of keypoints). Then, each keypoint descriptor is matched to its l nearest neighbors in feature space (we use $l = 6$). This can be done efficiently by using a k-d tree to find approximate nearest neighbors. A 2D histogram is then built that records in each bin the number of matches between the corresponding views: we call it the keypoint co-occurrence matrix H. Finally, every view is matched to the $m(= 8)$ views that have the greatest values in H. Figure 8.13 (left) shows the keypoint co-occurrence matrix for our 24 views.

Once the set of overlapping views is available, we proceed with a robust pairwise registration procedure. At the first stage, a point-to point matching is computed

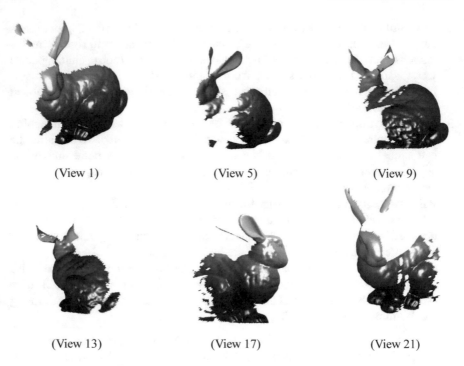

(View 1)   (View 5)   (View 9)

(View 13)   (View 17)   (View 21)

Fig. 8.11 Bunny. The full model is observed from partial views gradually sampled around the object (front to back views 1, 5, 9, and back to front views 13, 17, 21). Only 6 over 24 available views are shown (i.e., one every four views)

between keypoints using a nearest neighbor strategy among feature descriptor. Then, a geometric constraint is introduced using RANSAC on the absolute orientation. This leads to a robust pre-aligned between the views that are further refined using ICP. Figure 8.14 shows two overlapping views before (left) and after (right) registration. The overlapping points are colored in green. Note that for partially overlapping views, the inliers correspond to the area of overlap; hence, we can assign a weight $W(i, j)$ in the range [0, 1] to the pair (view i, view j), corresponding to the fraction of the overlapping points over the total number of points. The $n \times n$ matrix W is called the weighted adjacency matrix. For our experiment, the adjacency matrix is shown in Fig. 8.13 (right).

Finally, a weighted graph is constructed, whose vertices are the views and whose (weighted) adjacency matrix is W. Given a reference view chosen arbitrarily, which sets the global reference frame, for each view i, the transformation that aligns it with the reference view r is computed by chaining transformations along the shortest weighted path from i to r. This is equivalent to computing the (weighted) Minimum Spanning Tree (MST) with the root in r. In our experiment, the reference view is $r = 1$. Figure 8.15 shows the viewgraph (top) and the extracted path (bottom). In this fashion, the correct order for chaining the transformations is recovered, and all the

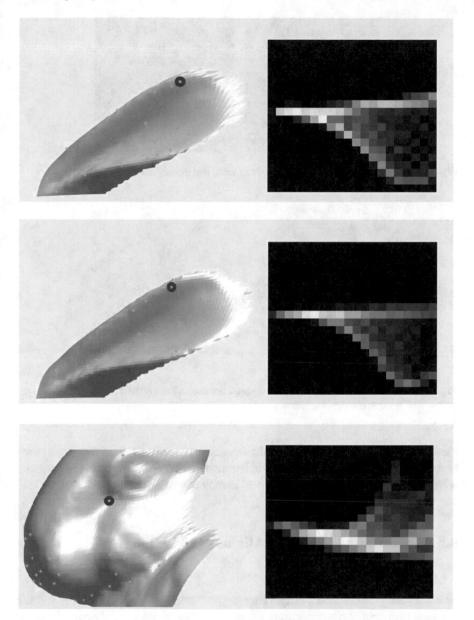

Fig. 8.12 Keypoint and signature. Keypoints are extracted from a small subpart of Bunny (i.e., the ear from two different views—top and middle—and the eye—bottom. For red points, the spin image signature is shown on the right

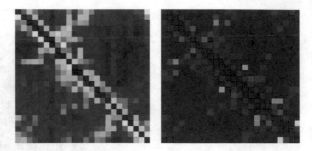

Fig. 8.13 The keypoint co-occurrence matrix H (left) and the adjacency matrix W (right)

Fig. 8.14 Pairwise registration. Two partial views are shown before (left) and after (right) registration. The overlap is colored in green

views can be represented on the global reference system. Figure 8.16 shows the views before (left) and after (right) the multiview registration. All the views are correctly aligned, and a full model of the observed Bunny can be reconstructed.

8.5 Case Study 1: Pairwise Alignment with Outlier Rejection

In this section, we describe a simple but effective strategy to make the ICP algorithm resistant to wrong correspondences. Especially when views are only partially overlapped, many points of the data-view do not have a correspondence in the model-view. We call those points *single points*. However, the basic ICP enforces single points to be associated to closest points in the model-view, therefore generating outliers. A robust outlier rejection procedure is introduced based on the so-called *X84* rule [29, 66]. The idea is to perform a robust statistical analysis of the residual errors e_i after closest point computation. The underlying hypothesis was pointed out in [159] and consists of considering the residuals of two fully overlapping sets as an approxima-

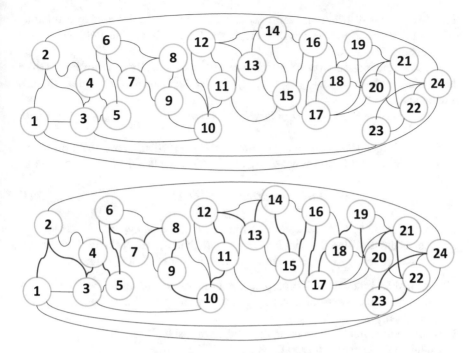

Fig. 8.15 The viewgraph is obtained from the adjacency matrix W (top). From the graph, the sequence of chaining transformations is computed using the minimum spanning tree algorithm (bottom). The root is node 1

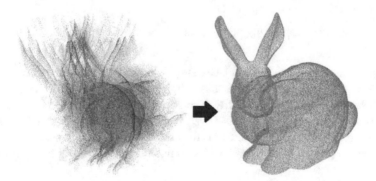

Fig. 8.16 Multiview registration. All 24 views before the registration (left) and after registration to the global reference system (right)

tion of a Gaussian distribution. Non-overlapping points can be detected by estimating a Gaussian distribution from residual errors and by defining a threshold on the tails of the estimated Gaussian.

The *X84* rule is a tool to estimate robustly and automatically this threshold. Given the residual errors $\mathbb{E} = \{e_i\}$, $i = 1 \ldots N_d$, the *Median Absolute Deviation* (MAD) is defined as

$$MAD = med(|e_i - location|), \tag{8.10}$$

where *med* is the *median* operator and *location* is the median of residual errors (i.e., $med(\mathbb{E})$). The X84 rule prescribes to reject values that violate the following relation:

$$|e_i - location| < k \cdot MAD. \tag{8.11}$$

Under the hypothesis of Gaussian distribution, a value of $k = 5.2$ is adequate in practice, as the resulting threshold contains more than 99.9% of the distribution.

Now we are ready to define the new procedure for robust outlier rejection:

1. For all data point $\mathbf{d}_i \in D$, compute the error e_i according to Eq. 8.4 (i.e., by estimating the closest point and by generating the pair of corresponding points $\mathbf{c}_i = (\mathbf{d}_i, \mathbf{m}_j)$).
2. Estimate *location* by computing the median of residuals $med(\mathbb{E})$.
3. Compute MAD according to Eq. 8.10.
4. For each residual error e_i $(i = 1, \ldots, N_d)$:

   a. If e_i satisfies Eq. 8.11 then keep $\mathbf{c}_i$ in the list of correspondences,
   b. If not, reject the correspondence.

5. A new list of corresponding points $\hat{\mathbf{c}}_i$ is obtained from which outliers have been filtered out.

In practice, this procedure replaces step 1 in the ICP algorithm described in Sect. 8.2.2. The X84 rejection rule has a breakdown point of 50%: any majority of the data can overrule any minority. The computational cost of X84 is dominated by the cost of the median, which is $O(n)$, where n is the size of the data point set. The most costly procedure inside ICP is the establishment of point correspondences, which costs $O(n \log n)$. Therefore, X84 does not increase the asymptotic complexity of ICP.

In Fig. 8.17, an example of registration between two views with a strong occluded part is shown. The non-overlapping area is wide: the ears and the whole face of *Bunny* are only visible in the data-view, while the bottom part of the body is observed in the model-view only. The number of data point is $N_d = 10000$, the number of model point $N_m = 29150$, and the number of points of the overlap is $\#(\mathbb{D} \cap \mathbb{M}) = 4000$. In this experiment, the two views are synthetically sampled from the whole 3D model. A view mask of 600×500 points is used in order to obtain highly dense views. Moreover, in this fashion we know the ground truth transformation, and no noise affects the views. Figure 8.18 shows the distribution of residual errors after X84-ICP registration. Note that most of the residuals are concentrated around zero.

Table 8.1 X-84 performance evaluations. Rotation and translation errors are reported

Method	Rot-error (rad.)	Transl-error (mm)	# Overlap. points	# Iterations	Time (s)
Besl [11]	0.22345	1.2636	10000	20	370
Picky [164]	0.10918	0.9985	9534	28	76
X84-ICP	0.06351	0.4177	4582	21	383
Ground truth	–	–	4000	–	–

It is confirmed that the behavior of the early part of the distribution is similar to a Gaussian [159]. The X84 rule is employed, and the threshold is automatically estimated on the tail of the Gaussian. The second peak of the distribution corresponds to residuals generated by the non-overlapping points.[6] In Fig. 8.18 (right), points of the data-view are colored differently between inliers and outliers. Note that non-overlapping parts are correctly registered.

Table 8.1 summarizes the performance of X84-ICP in comparison with Besl, i.e., the standard ICP [11], and Picky [164] which implements a combination of ICP variations described in Sect. 8.2.3. A hierarchical sampling strategy is introduced to improve the speed, and a thresholding approach on the residual distribution is employed. More specifically, a threshold is defined as $TH = \mu + 2.5\sigma$, where $\mu = $ mean($\{e_i\}$) and $\sigma = $ std($\{e_i\}$). The ground truth transformation is shown as well. Note that the basic ICP is strongly affected by outliers and is not able to correctly align the two views. The Picky ICP improves the accuracy, but it is not able to correctly

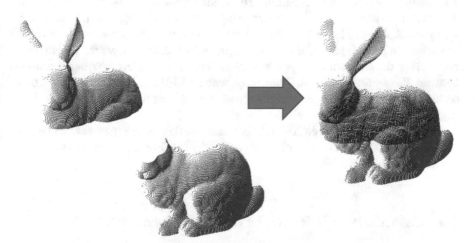

Fig. 8.17 Registration with robust outliers rejection. Two views at starting pose (left) and after registration (right). Note that the overlap area is quite restricted

---

[6]In order to visualize the peak, the second part of the histogram has been quantized with wider intervals.

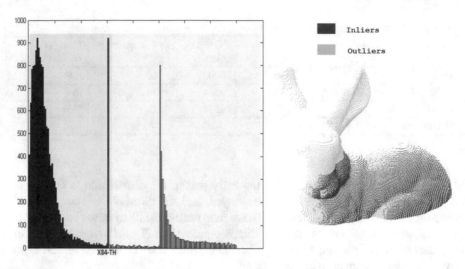

Fig. 8.18 Automatic residuals thresholding. From the distribution of residuals, the threshold is estimated according to the X84 rule. Points under the threshold are inliers (red), while outliers are over the threshold (blue). Outliers are points in non-overlapping areas

estimate the overlapping parts and it does not reach convergence. Conversely, by employing the X84 rule, wrong correspondences are well detected and a correct registration is obtained. In order to see the improvement in using robust methods, we evaluate the X84-ICP on a more challenging scenario composed of a pair of very noisy images with low resolution. The scene represents a tubular structure in an underwater environment that is acquired using acoustic devices [29, 30]. The starting views are depicted in Fig. 8.19 (left). In the red view, we clearly see a large amount of outliers in the left part of the scene. Figure 8.19 (center) shows the registration result using the standard ICP approach. Note that the blue view is wrongly moved between the two red structures. Conversely, when X84-ICP is used, the red structure on the left is recognized as outliers and the views are correctly aligned, see Fig. 8.19 (right).

We highlight that although X84-ICP performs well in these experiments, in more general cases if the number of outliers is greater than 50% of the residual distribution the X84 rule is likely to fail.

8.6 Case Study 2: ICP with Levenberg–Marquardt

In this section, we describe a registration method called Levenberg–Marquardt ICP (LM-ICP), which addresses several of the issues of ICP by modeling the registration as a general optimization problem. LM-ICP [54] was proposed in order to minimize the alignment error by employing a nonlinear optimization procedure. The advantage

Fig. 8.19 Registration with very noisy images from underwater scenarios composed of tubular structures. Starting views (left), registration using standard ICP, and registration using the robust X84-ICP

of the LM-ICP is the versatility in the definition of the optimization function in order to take into account several aspects of the registration, such as the outlier rejection and the speed.

8.6.1 The LM-ICP Method

The general problem formulation is defined as for the ICP algorithm. The error function $E(\mathbf{a}) = E_{ICP}(\mathbf{a}, \mathbb{D}, \mathbb{M})$ is nonlinear least squares and can thus be written as the sum of N_d squared residual vectors:

$$E(\mathbf{a}) = \sum_{i=1}^{N_d}(e_i(\mathbf{a}))^2, \qquad e_i(\mathbf{a}) = \|\mathsf{R}\mathbf{d}_i + \mathbf{t} - \mathbf{m}_j\|. \qquad (8.12)$$

Defining the residual vector as

$$\mathbf{e}(\mathbf{a}) = (e_1(\mathbf{a})\, e_2(\mathbf{a}) \,\cdots\, e_{N_d}(\mathbf{a}))^{\mathsf{T}}, \qquad (8.13)$$

we rewrite the error function as $E(\mathbf{a}) = \|\mathbf{e}(\mathbf{a})\|^2$.

The Levenberg–Marquardt algorithm combines the methods of gradient descent and Gauss–Newton. The goal at each iteration is to choose an update to the current estimate $\mathbf{a}_k$, say $\mathbf{x}$, so that setting $\mathbf{a}_{k+1} = \mathbf{a}_k + \mathbf{x}$ reduces the registration error.

We first derive the Gauss–Newton update. Expanding $E(\mathbf{a} + \mathbf{x})$ to second order yields

$$E(\mathbf{a} + \mathbf{x}) = E(\mathbf{a}) + (\nabla E(\mathbf{a}) \cdot \mathbf{x}) + \frac{1}{2!}((\nabla^2 E(\mathbf{a}) \cdot \mathbf{x}) \cdot \mathbf{x}) + h.o.t. \qquad (8.14)$$

This is rewritten in terms of $\mathbf{e}$ as

$$E(\mathbf{a}) = \mathbf{e}^\mathsf{T}\mathbf{e}$$
$$\nabla E(\mathbf{a}) = 2(\nabla\mathbf{e})^\mathsf{T}\mathbf{e}$$
$$\nabla^2 E(\mathbf{a}) = 2(\nabla^2\mathbf{e})\mathbf{e} + 2(\nabla\mathbf{e})^\mathsf{T}\nabla\mathbf{e}.$$

We now define the $N_d \times p$ *Jacobian* matrix $\mathbf{J} = \nabla\mathbf{e}$, with block (i, j) as $\mathbf{J}_{i,j} = \frac{\partial E_i}{\partial \mathbf{a}_j}$ (p is the number of elements in $\mathbf{a}$). Introducing the Gauss–Newton approximation (i.e., neglecting $(\nabla^2\mathbf{e})\mathbf{e}$), we get

$$E(\mathbf{a} + \mathbf{x}) \approx \mathbf{e}^\mathsf{T}\mathbf{e} + \mathbf{x}^\mathsf{T}\mathbf{J}^\mathsf{T}\mathbf{e} + \mathbf{x}^\mathsf{T}\mathbf{J}^\mathsf{T}\mathbf{J}\mathbf{x}. \tag{8.15}$$

Differentiating with respect to $\mathbf{x}$ and nullifying yields

$$\nabla_\mathbf{x} E(\mathbf{a} + \mathbf{x}) = \mathbf{J}^\mathsf{T}\mathbf{e} + \mathbf{J}^\mathsf{T}\mathbf{J}\mathbf{x} = 0, \tag{8.16}$$

and gives the Gauss–Newton update:

$$\mathbf{x}_{GN} = -(\mathbf{J}^\mathsf{T}\mathbf{J})^{-1}\mathbf{J}^\mathsf{T}\mathbf{e}. \tag{8.17}$$

Gauss–Newton is usually fast for mildly nonlinear problems (it has superlinear convergence speed), but there is no guarantee of convergence in the general case (an update may increase the error).

We now derive the gradient descent update. Since we deal with a least squares problem, the gradient descent update is simply given by

$$\mathbf{x}_{GD} = -\lambda^{-1}\mathbf{J}^\mathsf{T}\mathbf{e}, \tag{8.18}$$

where λ is the inverse step length. Gradient descent has the nice property that, unless a local minimum has been reached, one can always decrease the error by making the step length small enough. On the other hand, gradient descent is known to be slow and rather inefficient.

The Levenberg–Marquardt algorithm combines both Gauss–Newton and gradient descent updates in a relatively simple way:

$$\mathbf{x}_{LM} = -(\mathbf{J}^\mathsf{T}\mathbf{J} + \lambda\mathbf{I})^{-1}\mathbf{J}^\mathsf{T}\mathbf{e}. \tag{8.19}$$

A large value of λ yields a small, safe, gradient descent step while a small value of λ favor large and more accurate steps of Gauss–Newton that make convergence to a local minimum faster. The art of a Levenberg–Marquardt algorithm implementation is in tuning λ after each iteration to ensure rapid progress even where Gauss–Newton fails. The now-standard implementation is to multiply λ by 10 if the error increases and to divide it by 10 if the error decreases (with an upper bound at 10^8 and a lower bound at 10^{-4}, for instance). In order to make the method robust to outliers, one may attenuate the influence of points with a large error by replacing the square error function by an M-estimator ϵ and an Iterative Reweighted Least Squares (IRLS)-like reweighting procedure. For instance, the following robust functions can be used:

$$\text{Lorenzian: } \epsilon(r) = \log\left(1 + \frac{r^2}{\sigma}\right) \quad \text{or} \quad \text{Huber: } \epsilon(r) = \begin{cases} r^2 & r < \sigma \\ 2\sigma|r| - \sigma^2 & \text{otherwise.} \end{cases}$$

8.6.2   Computing the Derivatives

An important issue in how Levenberg–Marquardt is applied to ICP is the one of computing the derivatives of the error function. The simplest approach is based on using finite differencing, assuming that the error function is smooth. However, this leads to a cost of p extra function evaluations per inner loop. In [54], a more effective solution was proposed based on the *distance transform* which also drastically improves the computational efficiency. The distance transform is defined as

$$D_\epsilon(\mathbf{x}) = \min_j \epsilon^2(\|\mathbf{m}_j - \mathbf{x}\|), \tag{8.20}$$

where $\mathbf{x} \in \mathbb{X}$ and $\mathbb{X}$ is a discrete grid representing the volume which encloses the model-view $\mathbb{M}$. Indeed, each data point d_i can be easily associated to grid points by obtaining the residual error $e_i = X(d_i)$ in one shot.[7] In other words, LM-ICP merges the two main steps of ICP, namely, closest point computation and transformation estimation, in a single step. Note further that when the mapping $\|\mathbf{x}\| \to \epsilon^2(\|\mathbf{x}\|)$ is monotonic, we obtain that $D_\epsilon(\mathbf{x}) = \epsilon^2(\|D(\mathbf{x})\|)$, so existing algorithms to compute D may be used to compute D_ϵ, without requiring knowledge of the form of ϵ.

By combining Eq. (8.12) with Eq. (8.20), the new formulation of the registration problem becomes

$$E(\mathbf{a}) = \sum_{i=1}^{N_d} D_\epsilon(T(\mathbf{a}, \mathbf{d}_i)). \tag{8.21}$$

This formulation makes it much easier to compute the derivatives of E. In fact, since the distance transform is computed in a discrete form, it is possible to compute finite differences derivatives. More specifically, $\nabla_\mathbf{x} D_\epsilon = [\frac{\partial D_\epsilon}{\partial x}, \frac{\partial D_\epsilon}{\partial y}, \frac{\partial D_\epsilon}{\partial z}]$ is computed by defining $\frac{\partial D_\epsilon(x,y,z)}{\partial x} = \frac{D_\epsilon(x+1,y,z) - D_\epsilon(x-1,y,z)}{2}$, $\frac{\partial D_\epsilon(x,y,z)}{\partial y} = \frac{D_\epsilon(x,y+1,z) - D_\epsilon(x,y-1,z)}{2}$, and $\frac{\partial D_\epsilon(x,y,z)}{\partial z} = \frac{D_\epsilon(x,y,z+1) - D_\epsilon(x,y,z-1)}{2}$. In practice, $\nabla_\mathbf{x} D_\epsilon$ remains constant through the minimization, and we get

---

[7]Note that the volume is discretized into integer values; therefore, the data point d_i should be rounded to recover $X(d_i)$.

$$\nabla_{\mathbf{a}} E(\mathbf{a}) = \sum_{i=1}^{N_d} \nabla_{\mathbf{x}} D_\epsilon(T(\mathbf{a}, \mathbf{d}_i)) \nabla_{\mathbf{a}}^{\mathsf{T}} T(\mathbf{a}, \mathbf{d}_i). \tag{8.22}$$

Note that the computation of $\nabla_{\mathbf{a}}^{\mathsf{T}} T(\mathbf{a}, \mathbf{d}_i)$ depends on the rigid transformation parametrization being used. In [54], the author proposed model rotations by unitary quaternions for which the derivatives can be easily computed analytically. Finally, in order to compute the derivatives using matrix operators, the *Jacobian* matrix is defined as $\mathbf{J}_{i,j} = (\nabla_{\mathbf{x}} D_\epsilon(T(\mathbf{a}, \mathbf{d}_i)) \cdot \nabla_{a_j}^{\mathsf{T}} T(\mathbf{a}, \mathbf{d}_i))$, where $\nabla_{a_j} T(\mathbf{a}, \mathbf{d}_i) = [\frac{\partial T_x(\mathbf{a}, \mathbf{d}_i)}{\partial a_j}, \frac{\partial T_y(\mathbf{a}, \mathbf{d}_i)}{\partial a_j}, \frac{\partial T_z(\mathbf{a}, \mathbf{d}_i)}{\partial a_j}]$.

8.6.3 The Case of Quaternions

Let the quaternion be defined by $\mathbf{q} = [s, \mathbf{v}]$ where s and $\mathbf{v}$ are the scalar and vectorial components, respectively [153]. Let $\mathbf{d}$ be the point on which the rotation must be applied. To this aim such a point must be represented in quaternion space, leading to $\mathbf{r} = [0, \mathbf{d}]$. Therefore, the rotated point is obtained by

$$\mathbf{r}' = \mathbf{q}\mathbf{r}\mathbf{q}^{-1}.$$

By multiplying in quaternion space,[8] we obtain

$$\mathbf{r}' = [0, s^2\mathbf{d} + (\mathbf{d} \cdot \mathbf{v}) \cdot \mathbf{v} + 2s(\mathbf{v} \times \mathbf{d}) + \mathbf{v} \times (\mathbf{v} \times \mathbf{d})].$$

We represent this rotated point as

$$\mathbf{r}' = [0, T_x, T_y, T_z],$$

where

$$\begin{aligned} T_x &= s^2 d_x + (d_x v_x + d_y v_y + d_z v_z) v_x + 2s(v_y d_z - v_z d_y) + v_y(v_x d_y - v_y d_x) - v_z(v_z d_x - v_x d_z) = \\ &= s^2 d_x + v_x^2 d_x + v_x v_y d_y + v_x v_z d_z + 2s v_y d_z - 2s v_z d_y + v_x v_y d_y - v_y^2 d_x - v_z^2 d_x + v_x v_z d_z = \\ &= (s^2 + v_x^2 - v_y^2 - v_z^2) d_x + 2(v_x v_y - s v_z) d_y + 2(v_x v_z + s v_y) d_z \end{aligned}$$

$$\begin{aligned} T_y &= s^2 d_y + (d_x v_x + d_y v_y + d_z v_z) v_y + 2s(v_z d_x - v_x d_z) + v_z(v_y d_z - v_z d_y) - v_x(v_x d_y - v_y d_x) = \\ &= s^2 d_y + v_x v_y d_x + v_y^2 d_y + v_y v_z d_z + 2s v_z d_x - 2s v_x d_z + v_y v_z d_z - v_z^2 d_y - v_x^2 d_y + v_x v_y d_x = \\ &= 2(v_x v_y + s v_z) d_x + (s^2 - v_x^2 + v_y^2 - v_z^2) d_y + 2(v_y v_z - s v_x) d_z \end{aligned}$$

---

[8] A multiplication between two quaternions $\mathbf{q}$ and $\mathbf{q}'$ is defined as $[ss' - \mathbf{v} \cdot \mathbf{v}', \mathbf{v} \times \mathbf{v}' + s\mathbf{v}' + s'\mathbf{v}]$.

$$T_z = s^2 d_z + (d_x v_x + d_y v_y + d_z v_z)v_z + 2s(v_x d_y - v_y d_x) + v_x(v_z d_x - v_x d_z) - v_y(v_y d_z - v_z d_y) =$$
$$= s^2 d_z + v_x v_z d_x + v_y v_z d_y + v_z^2 d_z + 2s v_x d_y - 2s v_y d_x + v_x v_z d_x - v_x^2 d_z - v_y^2 d_z + v_y v_z d_y =$$
$$= 2(v_x v_z - s v_y)d_x + 2(v_y v_z + s v_x)d_y + (s^2 - v_x^2 - v_y^2 + v_z^2)d_z.$$

Now we introduce the translation component $[t_x, t_y, t_z]$ and normalize the quaternion by obtaining

$$T_x = \frac{(s^2 + v_x^2 - v_y^2 - v_z^2)d_x}{s^2 + v_x^2 + v_y^2 + v_z^2} + \frac{2(v_x v_y - s v_z)d_y}{s^2 + v_x^2 + v_y^2 + v_z^2} + \frac{2(v_x v_z + s v_y)d_z}{s^2 + v_x^2 + v_y^2 + v_z^2} + t_x$$

$$T_y = \frac{2(v_x v_y + s v_z)d_x}{s^2 + v_x^2 + v_y^2 + v_z^2} + \frac{(s^2 - v_x^2 + v_y^2 - v_z^2)d_y}{s^2 + v_x^2 + v_y^2 + v_z^2} + \frac{2(v_y v_z - s v_x)d_z}{s^2 + v_x^2 + v_y^2 + v_z^2} + t_y$$

$$T_z = \frac{2(v_x v_z - s v_y)d_x}{s^2 + v_x^2 + v_y^2 + v_z^2} + \frac{2(v_y v_z + s v_x)d_y}{s^2 + v_x^2 + v_y^2 + v_z^2} + \frac{(s^2 - v_x^2 - v_y^2 + v_z^2)d_z}{s^2 + v_x^2 + v_y^2 + v_z^2} + t_z.$$

According to this model for rotation and translation, the vector of unknowns is $\mathbf{a} = [s, v_x, v_y, v_z, t_x, t_y, t_z]$ (i.e., $\mathbf{a} \in \mathbb{R}^7$). Therefore, the Jacobian part $\nabla_{\mathbf{a}}^{\mathsf{T}} T(\mathbf{a}, \mathbf{d})$ is a 3×7 matrix:

$$\nabla_{\mathbf{a}}^{\mathsf{T}} T(\mathbf{a}, \mathbf{d}) = \begin{pmatrix} \frac{\partial T_x}{\partial s} & \frac{\partial T_x}{\partial v_x} & \frac{\partial T_x}{\partial v_y} & \frac{\partial T_x}{\partial v_z} & \frac{\partial T_x}{\partial t_x} & \frac{\partial T_x}{\partial t_y} & \frac{\partial T_x}{\partial t_z} \\ \frac{\partial T_y}{\partial s} & \frac{\partial T_y}{\partial v_x} & \frac{\partial T_y}{\partial v_y} & \frac{\partial T_y}{\partial v_z} & \frac{\partial T_y}{\partial t_x} & \frac{\partial T_y}{\partial t_y} & \frac{\partial T_y}{\partial t_z} \\ \frac{\partial T_z}{\partial s} & \frac{\partial T_z}{\partial v_x} & \frac{\partial T_z}{\partial v_y} & \frac{\partial T_z}{\partial v_z} & \frac{\partial T_z}{\partial t_x} & \frac{\partial T_z}{\partial t_y} & \frac{\partial T_z}{\partial t_z} \end{pmatrix}, \tag{8.23}$$

where T_x, T_y, and T_z have been defined above. For instance, we can compute the derivative component $\frac{\partial T_x}{\partial v_x}$ as

$$\frac{\partial T_x}{\partial v_x} = \frac{2v_x d_x}{s^2 + v_x^2 + v_y^2 + v_z^2} - \frac{2v_x(s^2 + v_x^2 - v_y^2 - v_z^2)d_x}{(s^2 + v_x^2 + v_y^2 + v_z^2)^2} +$$
$$+ \frac{2v_x d_y}{s^2 + v_x^2 + v_y^2 + v_z^2} - \frac{4v_x(v_x v_y - s v_z)d_y}{(s^2 + v_x^2 + v_y^2 + v_z^2)^2} +$$
$$+ \frac{2v_z d_z}{s^2 + v_x^2 + v_y^2 + v_z^2} - \frac{4v_x(v_x v_z + s v_y)d_z}{(s^2 + v_x^2 + v_y^2 + v_z^2)^2}.$$

Similarly, all the other components of the Jacobian can easily be computed.

8.6.4   Summary of the LM-ICP Algorithm

The algorithm for LM-ICP can be summarized as

1. Set $\lambda \leftarrow \lambda_0 = 10$,

2. compute distance transform $D_\epsilon(\mathbf{x})$,
3. set $\mathbf{a}_k \leftarrow \mathbf{a}_0$,
4. compute $\mathbf{e}_k = \mathbf{e}(\mathbf{a}_k)$,
5. compute J,
6. repeat

    a. compute update $\mathbf{a}_{k+1} = \mathbf{a}_k - (\mathbf{J}^T\mathbf{J} + \lambda\mathbf{I})^{-1}\mathbf{J}^T\mathbf{e}_k$ [9]
    b. compute $\Delta E = E(\mathbf{a}_{k+1}) - E(\mathbf{a}_k)$
    c. If $\Delta E > 0$ then $\lambda = 10\lambda$, go to a, else $\lambda = \frac{1}{10}\lambda$, go to 4.

7. If $\|\mathbf{e}_k\| > \nu$ go to 3, else terminate.

Note that ν is a constant which defines the convergence of the algorithm. As already highlighted, the algorithm above is the standard LM algorithm. The crucial components are *(i)* the choice of unknowns $\mathbf{a}$, *(ii)* the computation of error vector $\mathbf{e}$, and *(iii)* the computation of the Jacobian matrix J. In particular, the distance transform $D_\epsilon(\mathbf{x})$ enables an improvement in the computational efficiency of the error computation and makes the computation of the Jacobian feasible. The starting value $\mathbf{a}_0$ can be estimated by employing some of the techniques described in Sect. 8.2.3.1.

8.6.5 Results and Discussion

Figure 8.20 shows an example of LM-ICP alignment between two views. In this experiment, the emphasis is on the speed of the algorithm, since the accuracy is guaranteed by the fact that the two views are well overlapped. The LM-ICP takes less than 1 s for an LM iteration. A total of 20 iterations has been run to reach convergence. Both the data-view and the model-view have about 40,000 points. Using the basic ICP algorithm, the same number of iterations are required but each iteration takes more than 30 s. This confirms that a drastic improvement in speed is observed with LM-ICP, in comparison with basic ICP. Note that a crucial parameter is the grid size. It trades off computational efficiency with memory space. Moreover, it requires that the data scan is always inside the volume by requiring large memory space for storage when only a small overlap is observed between the views. Further experiments can be found in [54]. More details on experimental setup can be found on the LM-ICP website.[10] In practice, LM-ICP also enlarges the basin of convergence and estimates a more accurate solution (the minimum is reached with 50% fewer iterations on average, see [54] for more details).

    Finally, it is worth noting that LM-ICP can be easily extended to apply many other variants of the ICP. Multiview registration could also be solved in the LM-ICP framework.

---

[9] While we have chosen the identity as the damping matrix, some authors rather choose the diagonal part of the Gauss–Newton Hessian approximation.

[10] http://research.microsoft.com/en-us/um/people/awf/lmicp.

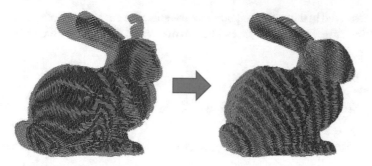

Fig. 8.20   LM-ICP. The starting pose (left) and merged views after registration (right)

8.7   Case Study 3: Deformable ICP with Levenberg–Marquardt

In this section, we describe an advanced registration technique: *Deformable-*
Levenberg Marquardt Iterative Closest Point (DLM-ICP) [31] . DLM-ICP extends
the LM-ICP approach, introduced in Sect. 8.6, to deformable objects. We focus on
continuous smooth surfaces such as the page of a book being turned in front of a
range sensor. To this aim, a *template* model is warped toward the input scans in order
to capture surface deformations. In this case, several instances of almost the entire
time-varying object are observed rather than different points of view of an object, and
the aim of registration is to align the views over time using a registration-by-fitting
approach.

The template model introduces a prior on the acquired shape by providing a joint
registration and reconstruction of the object with hole-filling and noise removal.
The proposed method exploits only geometric information without the extraction of
feature points. According to [54], described in Sect. 8.6, registration is modeled as
an optimization problem defined by an error function whose global minimum is the
sought after solution, estimated by the Levenberg–Marquardt algorithm. The error
function introduces the constraint that data points must be close to model points (i.e.,
the template). As for [54], it explicitly embeds a min operator, thus avoiding the
traditional two steps in ICP-like algorithms, through the use of a distance transform.
Furthermore, thanks to the flexibility of LM, many other terms are introduced to
model different expected behaviors of the deformation, namely, *surface*, and *temporal
smoothness* as well as *inextensibility* of the surface. Finally, a boundary constraint is
introduced to prevent the computed surface from sliding arbitrarily.

We highlight that, with this method, the unknowns are the template model, represented by a planar mesh that is deformed to fit each point cloud. More specifically,
we directly estimate the position of the model points without imposing any prior
about the kind of transformation function that has been applied. In particular, each
unknown (i.e., each vertex of the template) influences a very small portion of the
error function. Indeed, another interesting property of DLM-ICP is that the Jacobian

matrix, involved in the normal equations to be solved at each iteration, is highly sparse for all the terms. This makes the estimation of dense deformation fields tractable and fast.

8.7.1 Surface Representation

The sequence of 3D point clouds D_i, with $N_d = l_i$ points each, is represented by

$$D_i = \begin{pmatrix} d_{i,1}^x & d_{i,1}^y & d_{i,1}^z \\ \vdots & \vdots & \vdots \\ d_{i,l_i}^x & d_{i,l_i}^y & d_{i,l_i}^z \end{pmatrix}.$$

The unknown model, $a = M$, has a grid structure and is thus represented by three $R \times C$ matrices, giving the grid's deformation. Each matrix is reshaped in a single vector of size $N_m = RC$, giving M_i as

$$M_i = \begin{pmatrix} m_{i,1}^x & m_{i,1}^y & m_{i,1}^z \\ \vdots & \vdots & \vdots \\ m_{i,N_m}^x & m_{i,N_m}^y & m_{i,N_m}^z \end{pmatrix}.$$

In practice, the number of data points is much larger than the number of model points (i.e., $l_i \mathbf{g} N_m$). Upon convergence, the algorithm determines, for each model point, if there is a corresponding point in the current point cloud. Points may be missing because of occlusions or corrupted sensor output. This approach has the advantage that it naturally gives the reconstructed surface by interpolating the mesh points. Point cloud registration is obtained by composing the deformation fields. Note that, in contrast to Sect. 8.6, the registration is from model points to data points.

8.7.2 Cost Function

The cost function combines two *data* and three *penalty* terms:

$$E(M) = E_g(M) + \lambda_b E_b(M) + \lambda_s E_s(M) + \lambda_t E_t(M) + \lambda_x E_x(M), \qquad (8.24)$$

where $\lambda_b, \lambda_s, \lambda_x$, and λ_t are weights. Note that we drop the frame index i for purposes of clarity, and denote M_i as M and M_{i-1} as $\tilde{M}$.

The data terms are used to attract the estimated surface to the actual point cloud. The first term E_g is for global attraction, while the second one E_b deals with the boundary. In particular, the boundary term aims at preserving the method against possible sliding of the model along the observed surface. Moreover, these terms must account for possible erroneous points by using robust statistics. The penalty terms are E_s, E_t, and E_x. The first two account for *spatial smoothness* and *temporal smoothness* E_s, respectively. The third one penalizes the *surface stress* and is related to the non-extensibility of the surface, and therefore to material properties of the surface.

This cost function is minimized in an ICP-like manner, as described in the previous section. All five terms are explained below in detail.

Data Term: Global Surface Attraction
This term globally attracts the model to the data points in a closest point manner [126]. Denoting $\mathbb{B}_M$ as the set of boundary points in the model, $\mathbb{M}$, where

$$\mathbb{M} = \{(m_i^x \ m_i^y \ m_i^z)^T\}, \ i = 1 \ldots N_m \tag{8.25}$$

and $\mathbb{B}_D$ as the set of boundary points in the data, $\mathbb{D}$, where

$$\mathbb{D} = \{(d_i^x \ d_i^y \ d_i^z)^T\}, \ i = 1 \ldots l_i \tag{8.26}$$

we get the following data term, integrating the model to data points matching step:

$$\sum_{\mathbf{m} \in \mathbb{M} \setminus \mathbb{B}_M} \min_{\mathbf{d} \in \mathbb{D} \setminus \mathbb{B}_D} \| \mathbf{d} - \mathbf{m} \|^2, \tag{8.27}$$

where $\mathbf{d}$ and $\mathbf{m}$ are 3-vectors representing a data point and a model point, respectively. As we mentioned before, the unknowns are not the rigid transformation parameters (i.e., the classical rotation–translation) but correspond to the whole *deformable motion field* in $\mathbb{M}$.

An *outlier rejection* strategy is introduced by defining a robust function ϵ. Here, the $X84$ rule is employed [29]. Therefore, Eq. 8.27 is modified so as to get the following robustified data term:

$$E_g(\mathbb{M}) = \sum_{\mathbf{m} \in \mathbb{M} \setminus \mathbb{B}_M} \epsilon \left(\min_{\mathbf{d} \in \mathbb{D} \setminus \mathbb{B}_D} \| \mathbf{d} - \mathbf{m} \|^2 \right). \tag{8.28}$$

Data Term: Boundary Attraction
This term attracts boundary model points to boundary data points. It is defined in a similar manner to the global attraction term (Eq. 8.28) except that the sum and min operators are over the boundary points:

$$E_b(\mathbb{M}) = \sum_{\mathbf{m} \in \mathbb{B}_M} \epsilon \left(\min_{\mathbf{d} \in \mathbb{B}_D} \| \mathbf{d} - \mathbf{m} \|^2 \right). \tag{8.29}$$

Note that the boundaries can be computed by combining edge detection techniques with morphological operators.[11] More precisely, from the range image, we detect the portion of the image which is covered by the object we want to track (i.e., a piece of paper), and we impose the condition that boundaries of the model and the observed surface must coincide.

Penalty Term: Spatial Smoothness

This term discourages surface discontinuities by penalizing its second derivatives, as an approximation to its curvature. According to the definition of the geometry image [62], the model $\mathbb{M}$ is a displacement field parameterized[12] by (u, v) with $u = [1 \ldots R]$ and $v = [1 \ldots C]$, i.e., $\mathbf{M}(u, v) = (M^x(u, v) \; M^y(u, v) \; M^z(u, v))^\mathsf{T}$. The spatial smoothness term can thus be taken as the surface bending energy:

$$E_s(\mathbb{M}) = \int \int \left\| \frac{\partial \mathbb{M}^2}{\partial^2 u} \right\|^2 + 2 \left\| \frac{\partial \mathbb{M}^2}{\partial u \partial v} \right\|^2 + \left\| \frac{\partial \mathbb{M}^2}{\partial^2 v} \right\|^2 \; du \, dv.$$

Using a finite difference approximation for the first and second derivatives [116], the bending energy can be expressed in discrete form as a quadratic function of $\mathbb{M}$. More specifically, the derivative $\frac{\partial M^x}{\partial u}$ at a point (u, v) is discretely approximated as $\frac{\partial M^x(u,v)}{\partial u} = M^x(u + 1, v) - M^x(u - 1, v)$. This can be conveniently represented by a constant $N_m \times N_m$ matrix $\mathbf{C}_u$ such that $\nabla_u \mathbb{M}^x = \mathbf{C}_u \cdot \text{vect}(M^x)$, where $\text{vect}(M^x)$ is the vectorization operator which rearranges matrix $\mathbf{M}^x$ to a vector. A similar matrix $\mathbf{C}_v$ can be computed with respect to v. Indeed, the second derivatives are computed using Hessian operator matrices, namely, $\mathbf{C}_{uu}, \mathbf{C}_{uv}, \mathbf{C}_{vv}$. The surface bending energy can be expressed in discrete form by defining

$$E_s^x = \text{vect}(M^x)^\mathsf{T}(C_{uu}^\mathsf{T} C_{uu} + 2 C_{uv}^\mathsf{T} C_{uv} + C_{vv}^\mathsf{T} C_{vv}) \text{vect}(M^x),$$

and by computing

$$E_s(\mathbb{M}) = E_s^x(M^x) + E_s^y(M^y) + E_s^z(M^z),$$

which can be further expressed in matrix form as follows:

$$E_s(\mathbb{M}) = \text{vect}(\mathbb{M})^\mathsf{T} \mathcal{K} \text{vect}(\mathbb{M}), \tag{8.30}$$

where $\mathcal{K}$ is a $3N_m \times 3N_m$, highly sparse matrix.

Penalty Term: Temporal Smoothness

This term defines a dependency between the current and the previous point clouds, $\mathbb{M}$ and $\tilde{\mathbb{M}}$:

---

[11]The object boundaries can be estimated according to the kind of sensor being used. For instance, boundaries on range scans can be estimated on the range image. In stereo sensors, they can be estimated on one of the two optical views.

[12]Recall that the model points lie on a grid.

$$E_t(\mathbf{M}) = \| \mathbf{M} - \tilde{\mathbf{M}} \|^2 . \tag{8.31}$$

This makes the surface deformation smooth over time and can be used within a sequential processing approach. Obviously, it is not used in the first frame of the sequence.

Penalty Term: Non-extensibility
This term discourages surface stretching. It encourages mesh vertices to preserve their distance with their local neighborhood [129]:

$$E_X(\mathbf{M}) = \sum_{\mathbf{m}\in\mathbb{M}} \sum_{\mathbf{k}\in\mathcal{N}(\mathbf{m})} \left(\| \mathbf{m} - \mathbf{k} \|^2 - L_{m,k}^2 \right)^2 , \tag{8.32}$$

where $L_{m,k}$ are constants, which are computed at the first frame after robust initialization, and $\mathcal{N}(\mathbf{m})$ is the 8-neighborhood of the mesh vertex $\mathbf{m}$.

8.7.3 Minimization Procedure

The DLM-ICP cost function (8.24) is a sum of squared residuals, nonlinearly depending on the unknowns in $\mathbf{M}$. Therefore, as in Sect. 8.6, the Levenberg–Marquardt algorithm can be used. In order to provide partial derivatives of the residuals through a Jacobian matrix, all five terms in the cost function are separately differentiated and stacked as

$$J^{\mathsf{T}} = \left(J_d^{\mathsf{T}} \; J_b^{\mathsf{T}} \; J_s^{\mathsf{T}} \; J_t^{\mathsf{T}} \; J_x^{\mathsf{T}} \right) , \tag{8.33}$$

where $J_d^{N_m \times 3N_m}$, $J_b^{N_B \times 3N_m}$, $J_s^{3N_m \times 3N_m}$, $J_t^{N_m \times 3N_m}$, and $J_x^{\xi \times 3N_m}$ are related to the global attraction, boundary attraction, spatial smoothness, temporal smoothness, and non-extensibility terms, respectively, and $\xi = \mathbf{t}size(\mathcal{N}(\mathcal{M}))$. In particular, the Jacobians of global and boundary attraction terms are estimated by finite differences through distance transform, as described in Sect. 8.6.

Note that, in this case, since the Hessian matrix[13] $H = J^{\mathsf{T}}J + \lambda I$ must be inverted at each LM iteration, the problem is not tractable if the number of model points is too high (if the deformation field is too dense). One advantage of the proposed approach is that the Jacobian matrix J is very sparse. Thus, it uses the sparsity to speed up each iteration using the technique in [114]. In particular, a sparse Cholesky factorization package can be used, as in the Matlab "mldivide" function.

---

[13] We use "Hessian matrix" for the damped Gauss–Newton approximation to the true Hessian matrix.

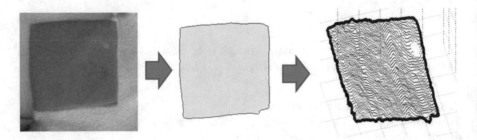

Fig. 8.21 Data acquisition: intensity image of the blanket (left), image boundary (center), and the 3D point cloud (right)

8.7.4 Summary of the Algorithm

The DLM-ICP algorithm can be summarized as follows:

1. Choose the model size $R \times C$ (for instance, 10×10)
2. Initialize the template model M_0
3. For each data frame $\mathbb{D}_i$

   a. Extract data boundary $\mathbb{B}_D$
   b. Set $M_i = M_{i-1}$ to initialize the LM algorithm
   c. Apply LM-ICP to estimate M_i by minimizing the error function
   d. Go to 3.

Step 3.c is described in Sect. 8.6.4. Here, the unknown is $a = M_i$, the error function $E(M_i)$ is defined by Eq. (8.24), and the Jacobian J is defined by Eq. (8.33).

8.7.5 Experiments

In the following experiment, the sensor is a real-time passive-stereo system.[14] The sensor acquires images at 25 FPS (frames-per-second) and provides both intensity (i.e., 2D) and 3D information. The deformation of a portion of a blanket is modeled. Figure 8.21 shows a picture of the blanket. Intensity information is used to segment the boundary; more precisely, only the portion delimited by the dark square is considered. Figure 8.21 also shows the image boundary extracted by combining a binary image segmentation method with 2D morphological operators and depicts the 3D data (i.e., the selected point cloud and 3D boundary).

The sequence is made of 100 point clouds. A model of size $R = 15$ and $C = 20$ is used. Model initialization M_0 is carried out by lying the model grid on a plane which is fitted to the extracted point cloud. Model initialization is employed in the first frame only. Then, each iteration uses the output of the previous one as an initial condition.

---

[14]Data courtesy of eVS (http://www.evsys.net).

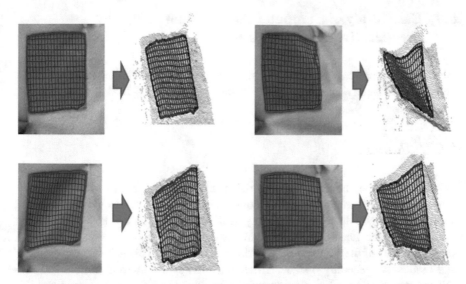

Fig. 8.22 Blanket sequence: 4 selected frames. For each frame, the 2D intensity and the 3D data are visualized. The grid models are shown in 3D space, as well as their projection in the 2D image

Note that a higher value of λ_b is necessary (i.e., $\lambda_b = 1.5$) for a correct convergence of the algorithm to the optimal solution. The other terms are set almost equally to 1. The distance transform parameters are important: the size of the voxels trades off speed and accuracy. In this experiment, the volume is divided into $36 \times 36 \times 18$ voxels. Figure 8.22 shows a selection of the output sequence. For each frame, we visualize *(i)* the intensity image with the extracted 2D boundary and the 2D projection of the estimated model and *(ii)* the point cloud, after the region-of-interest selection, evidencing both the 3D boundary and the grid. The blanket is handled from the bottom-left and upper-right corners, respectively. On the early frames, the blanket is gradually bent toward the square center; then, it is strongly stretched, moving the corners far from each other. Finally, in the late frames, random deformations are generated, especially around the corners. Results are satisfying since the fitting is correct for the whole sequence, in spite of the presence of strong occlusions and deformations. The mesh grids are well superimposed on data points maintaining a smooth shape. Nevertheless, the projection of the grids to the 2D images confirm the accuracy of the registration. More details on performance evaluation are available in [31].

8.8 Case Study 4: Computer-Aided Laparoscopy by Preoperative Data Registration

We describe a use case of 3D registration in laparoscopy. The technique involves 3D–3D deformable registration solved by customizing DLM-ICP.

8.8.1 Context

In laparoscopy, the surgeon uses keyholes in the patient's abdominal wall. The laparoscope is the observation device and consists of a camera connected to a thin rod containing an optic fiber. The surgeon typically uses between 2–4 keyholes of about 1 cm in diameter. Laparoscopy has many advantages over open surgery. However, some elements of the anatomy may be difficult to locate. This is because the organs and tissues are generally opaque. Structures such as the internal tumors and vessels are therefore invisible. Registration techniques can be used to circumvent this limitation of visualization by enabling intraoperative augmented reality. The most promising approach is to use preoperative data such as a Magnetic Resonance (MR) or Computed Tomography (CT) scan. These modalities are generally not available during surgery. They show the tumors and vessels well and can be used to create a 3D model of the target organ's outer surface and internal structures before surgery. The challenge is then to register this preoperative 3D model to the intraoperative 2D images given by the laparoscope. This is tremendously difficult because of the organ's deformation (due, for instance, to insufflation of the abdominal cavity) and because the vast majority of laparoscopes are monocular. Registration in laparoscopy is still an open problem but promising preliminary approaches have been proposed. We discuss the image-based approach, which uses the image contents to solve registration without requiring the use of fiducials. An example taken from [39] is shown in Fig. 8.23. This example represents the result of using a computer-aided laparoscopy system in a real surgery.

8.8.2 Problem Statement

Augmented reality laparoscopy follows three steps: preoperative 3D model reconstruction, intraoperative registration, and visualization. A complete pipeline is shown in Fig. 8.24. We here focus on the registration step but the visualization step is also highly challenging and researched, see, for instance, [6, 7, 12, 55, 107, 152]. The preoperative 3D model reconstruction consists in segmenting the preoperative 3D volume and interpolating the voxels to create a surface represented by a mesh. This may be extremely challenging to solve automatically but semi-automatic methods

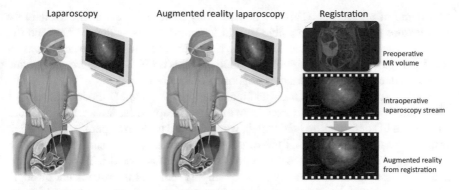

Fig. 8.23 Laparoscopy and the problem of registration in augmented reality laparoscopy. (left) The principle of laparoscopy, here with an example of a myomectomy procedure where the uterus contains two inner and thus invisible tumors. (middle) The principle of augmented reality laparoscopy, where the tumors are shown using virtual transparency. (right) The registration problem to be solved

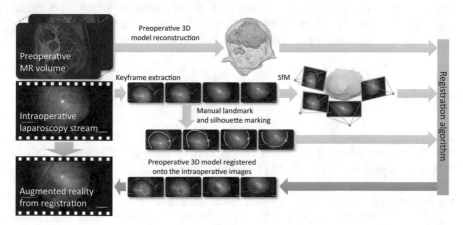

Fig. 8.24 Principle of an ICP-based solution to the problem of registration in augmented reality laparoscopy. The original problem is transformed into a special type of 3D surface-to-surface registration problem, which is solved using a particular instance of deformable ICP [39]

already exist which are very effective and available in software packages such as MITK (the Medical Imaging Interaction Toolkit [15]).

It is fundamental to understand that augmented reality laparoscopy involves two types of registration problem. The first and most complex type occurs at the start of surgery, when the preoperative 3D model has not been related at all to the 2D images yet. It implies that the preoperative 3D model is purely geometric, in other words untextured, as the preoperative data do not contain color, at least not color as we see it in laparoscopy. The second type of registration problem occurs in a later stage of surgery, after the preoperative 3D model has been texture mapped, thanks to the

---

[15] www.mitk.org.

first round of registration. This is a considerably easier problem as the availability of a texture map makes it possible to find keypoint correspondences between the preoperative 3D model and the 2D images, as, for instance, in [40]. We here focus on the first type of registration problem, which requires an ICP-like approach to draw correspondences and solve for deformation simultaneously.

The registration problem takes as inputs the preoperative 3D model and a set of intraoperative 2D images, extracted from the laparoscopy video stream and produces as output a 3D deformation field which, when applied to the preoperative 3D model, brings it to the state in which the organ was observed during surgery. We make the strong assumption that the organ does not deform across the 2D images. This is a valid assumption at the early steps of surgery, before the organ is cut through. This assumption means that the intraoperative state of the organ's outer part can be recovered by existing techniques such as Structure from Motion (SfM). The case of non-rigidly-related 2D images can be handled in two ways. First, the images can be dealt with individually, as was attempted for liver laparoscopic augmented reality [1, 79]. Second, advanced techniques extending SfM to deformable structures could be used, namely, Non-Rigid Structure from Motion (NRSfM) [19, 108, 127], but their applicability to laparoscopy data has not yet been demonstrated.

8.8.3 Registration

The registration has two main steps. The first step is to compute an intraoperative 3D reconstruction of the organ's outer surface from the 2D images. This is solved automatically by using SfM [39] or Simultaneous Localization and Mapping (SLAM) [57]. This produces a point cloud representing the organ's outer surface and the laparoscope's intrinsic and extrinsic parameters for each 2D image. The second step is to compute the registration for the organ's outer surface, which boils down to a 3D surface-to-surface registration. This can be solved by an existing technique such as DLM-ICP, the deformable ICP presented in the previous section. There is, however, a key difference between DLM-ICP and the case at hand: an organ has a spherical rather than a disk topology and therefore does not have boundaries, as opposed to a piece of paper or cloth. This means that the boundary term E_b from the cost (8.24) of DLM-ICP cannot be used. This second step is thus the most difficult: without the boundary term and as many organs tend to have smooth parts and the intraoperative 3D reconstruction tends to be partial, the 3D registration may easily drift to a false solution as the two surfaces can slide onto one another without changing the registration cost much. An equivalent of the boundary for spherical objects is the silhouette, which may be introduced as a new term in the cost, given that the organ's silhouette has been manually marked in some of the 2D images. The silhouette is, however, much weaker than the boundary term as it helps registration but does not prevent surface sliding. In practice, this effect is mitigated by using a few manually defined anatomical landmarks, depending on the organ at hand. For the uterus, for instance, these may be chosen as the junction points between the Fallopian tubes and the uterus' body. The general cost function is thus similar to, but not exactly like, the cost (8.24) of DLM-ICP. It combines three data terms and two penalty terms:

$$E(M) = \lambda_{dg} E_{dg}(M) + \lambda_{ds} E_{ds}(M) + \lambda_{dl} E_{dl}(M) + \lambda_{ps} E_{ps}(M) + \lambda_{px} E_{px}(M),$$

where $\lambda_{dg}, \lambda_{ds}, \lambda_{dl}, \lambda_{ps}, \lambda_{px} \in [0, 1]$ are weights.

Recall that the data terms attract the transformed preoperative 3D model to the intraoperative point cloud. The first data term E_{dg} is the global attraction term E_g of DLM-ICP. The second data term E_{ds} measures the distance on the organ's predicted silhouette. The third data term E_{dl} encapsulates the anatomical landmarks. The penalty terms convey prior knowledge on the organ's admissible deformations. The two penalty terms E_{ps} and E_{px} are, respectively, the spatial smoothness and surface stress terms E_s and E_x of DLM-ICP.

Once the organ's outer surface registration has been computed, a final step is to interpolate the surface deformation field to the desired 3D deformation field. This is desired because the registration found from the organ's outer surface is meant to bring the organ's inner structures, which do not belong to the organ's surface, from the preoperative 3D model to the intraoperative 2D images. This interpolation may be solved by means of a simple 3D spline interpolant estimated using the surface mesh's vertices as control points.

8.8.4   Validation

The accuracy of registration is obviously tremendously important in computer-aided laparoscopy, especially in the predicted position of tumors. It is, however, highly challenging to obtain data with ground truth, as by definition this information is not available during surgery. Quantitative validation is thus usually obtained from phantom or ex-vivo models. The above-described system was validated using synthetic tumors introduced in ex-vivo pig kidneys [35]. In this study, 33 tumors were resected by a control group, using standard laparoscopy, and 29 were resected by an AR group, using the computer-aided laparoscopy system. The resected tumors were analyzed a posteriori to see if the margins were negative (the tumor is entirely removed) or positive (the tumors were only partly removed). In the control group, 42.4% of the tumors were either completely missed or had positive margins. In the AR group, only 13.8% of the tumors had positive margins and none was completely missed. This shows that the registration system is sufficiently accurate to significantly improve the surgeon's performance at tumors localization and resection.

8.9 Challenges and Future Directions

Although the recent methods have brought important advances in 3D registration, especially in the challenging scenarios reported in Sects. 8.3–8.8, there are still many open issues to be addressed that make this research field still exciting and promising. New challenges arise from the rapid technological advances of new 3D acquisition systems. Even if recent deep learning methods have successfully exploited the possibility to recover 3D information using only 2D image, there are still convincing reasons to rely on RGBD sensors. Depth data naturally provides global positioning, and not just local 3D pose information or 2D bounding box information in the image space. Further, RGBD information helps one to solve the real-time reconstruction of entire scenes. At the device level, the new generation of depth sensors is now easily available on mobile phones and is more affordable for generic consumers.[16] Moreover, very often depth sensors are integrated on more complex systems for new emerging applications such as automotive, robotic surgery, or forensic tasks. This leads to an explosion of the available data (i.e., big data) that poses new problems for their manipulation. For instance, the integration between depth information acquired from such different acquisition sources yields new issues in dealing with very heterogeneous data characterized by different resolutions, levels of noise, scales, and so on. Moreover, depth sensors can be accompanied by other devices for the acquisition of other kind of information such as infrared data, GPS, Digital Elevation Model (DTM), or MRI scans (for the medical domain). Therefore, new advanced methods need to be studied for the fusion between information of different nature exploiting multimodal registration techniques.

New problems are emerging for the registration of very large-scale scenarios. Indeed, nowadays it is possible to reconstruct not only a scene composed of several buildings but an entire city. For this task, it is important to improve the methods for the matching at the view level by effectively combining features from both the 2D and 3D domains. In particular, it is important to well organize the previously stored information by introducing new indexing methods to combine shape retrieval strategy with registration techniques. Moreover, especially when the large-scale reconstruction is required for entertainment (i.e., video games or movies), a drastic reduction of the memory demand can be obtained by integrating the registration methods for the generation of procedural models (i.e., inverse procedural model).

In the context of deformable registration, the new issues regard the possibility to relax the prior information on the subject to be registered. Rather than working with a well-delimited class such as the human body or the human face, it is interesting to focus on subject with a more generic shape. For instance, an emerging and promising trend consists of modeling animals such as quadruped or birds. This is challenging due to the natural uncooperative behavior of the animals during the acquisition.

Finally, the advances on 3D registration are very important for several emerging applications. For instance, in the context of real-time interactive tasks, there is heavy expectation from new devices for modern Augmented Reality (AR), such

---

[16]See https://www.apple.com/iphone/ https://azure.microsoft.com/en-us/campaigns/kinect/.

as Hololens[17] or magic leap[18] to mention just a few, that already integrate several sensors to improve the device pose estimation. Also, Virtual Reality (VR) frameworks require very accurate and reliable 3D tracking systems for human parts like the head and the hands to reduce the typical disadvantages of immersive devices such as sickness, or to improve the gestural interaction. Another promising application regards self-driving cars where many of the open issues mentioned above like 3D data integration, 3D mapping, and object localization are crucial. In particular, it is very important to address methods for the matching between offline data with real-time information. Registration problems are very critical also in robotics applications for effective human–robot interaction where tracking and localization should be integrated with recognition systems. Also, in this case, real-time performance is very important.

8.10   Conclusion

Registration of 3D data is a well-studied problem but still new issues need to be solved. The ICP algorithm is the current standard method since it works well in general and it is easy to implement. Although the basic version is quite limited, several extensions and strong variants have been introduced that allow it to cope with many scenarios. For instance, the techniques described in Sects. 8.2.3 and 8.4 are sufficient to obtain an automatic full model reconstruction of a single object observed from a few dozen of viewpoints. However, in more challenging situations like in the presence of cluttered or deformable objects, the problem becomes more difficult. The point matching strategy needs to be improved as well as the transformation function needs to be properly designed. Therefore, more advanced techniques need to be employed like those described in Sect. 8.3. In order to give some examples of registration algorithms, four case studies were reported. Case study 1 shows in practice how a robust outliers rejection strategy can improve the accuracy of registration and estimate the overlapping area. Case study 2 exploits general Levenberg–Marquardt optimization to improve the basic ICP algorithm. In particular, the advantage of using the distance transform is clearly demonstrated. Case study 3 addresses a more challenging problem, namely, deformable registration from real-time acquisition. Also, in this case, the Levenberg–Marquardt approach enables the modeling of the expected behavior of surface deformations. In particular, effective data and penalty terms can be encoded easily in the general error function. Finally, case study 4 shows the benefits of deformable ICP for 3D registration in laparoscopy.

---

[17]https://www.microsoft.com/en-us/hololens.
[18]https://www.magicleap.com/.

New challenging scenarios can be addressed as described in Sect. 8.9 by exploiting recent machine learning and computer vision techniques already successfully employed for the 2D domain as well as new advances inspired from recent computer animation techniques.

8.11 Further Reading

In order to get a more comprehensive overview of 3D registration methods, the reader can refer to milestone surveys [77, 96, 126, 128]. In [126], Ruzinkiewicz et al. have analyzed some variants of ICP techniques, focusing on methods and suggestions to improve the computation speed. An extensive review of registration methods based on the definition of surface shape descriptors can be found in [96]. In [128], Salvi et al. proposed an extensive experimental comparison among different 3D pairwise registration methods. They evaluated the accuracy of the results for both coarse and fine registrations. More recently, Kaick et al. [77] proposed a survey on shape correspondence estimation by extensively reporting and discussing interesting methods for deforming scenarios. In [165], the most recent and promising registration methods for 3D reconstruction are exhaustively reported. In particular, this survey shows how algorithms are properly designed to best exploit the benefits of using RGBD data. In [69], different methods for 6D object pose estimation from dynamic range sensors are extensively evaluated on several publicly available benchmarks. The performance of several approaches such as point-pair-based features or learning-based methods are discussed and interesting open problems are raised. In [83], the authors reported several methods for data-driven modeling and synthesis of new scenes. To this aim advanced machine learning techniques are evaluated for the integration of real examples encoded by point clouds or meshes to the process of automatic generation of new plausible objects.

The reader interested in getting in-depth details on the theoretical evaluation of registration convergence should refer to work of Pottmann et al. [58, 115]. Convergence is discussed also by Ezra et al. [52] who provided lower and upper bounds on the number of ICP iterations.

Finally, to practice the registration, the reader can evaluate the following public available tools:

- Meshlab[19]
- Point Cloud Library (PLC)[20]
- Functional Automatic Registration for 3D Human Bodies (FARM).[21]

---

[19]http://www.meshlab.net/.

[20]http://pointclouds.org/.

[21]http://profs.scienze.univr.it/~marin/farm/.

8.12 Questions

Q.1 Give four examples of problem where 3D shape registration is an essential
      component. In each case explain why registration is required for their automated
      solution.
Q.2 Briefly outline the steps of the classical Iterative Closest Points (ICP) algorithm.
Q.3 What is usually the most computationally intensive step in a typical ICP appli-
      cation and what steps can be taken to reduce this?
Q.4 What is the common failure mode of ICP and what steps can be taken to attempt
      to avoid this?
Q.5 What steps can be taken to improve the final accuracy of an ICP-based regis-
      tration?
Q.6 Explain why registration in clutter is challenging and describe one solution that
      has been proposed.
Q.7 Explain why registration of deformable objects is challenging and describe one
      solution that has been proposed.
Q.8 Explain the effect of outliers in registration and describe one strategy that has
      been proposed for their detection.
Q.9 What advantages does LM-ICP have over classical ICP?
Q.10 Describe how DLM-ICP can be employed for computer-aided laparoscopy.

8.13 Exercises

1. Given two partial views very close to each other and an implementation of ICP,[22]
   try to register the views by gradually moving away from the data-view from the
   model-view until ICP diverges. Apply the perturbation to both the translational
   and rotational components. Repeat the exercise, decreasing the overlap area by
   removing points in the model-view.
2. Implement a pairwise pre-alignment technique based on PCA. Try to check the
   effectiveness of the pre-alignment by varying the shape of the two views.
3. Implement an outlier rejection technique to robustify ICP registration. Compare
   the robustness (i) fixed threshold, (ii) threshold estimated as 2.5σ of the residuals'
   distribution from their mean, and (iii) threshold estimated with the X84 technique.
4. Compute the Jacobian matrix of LM-ICP by encoding rotation with quaternions.[23]
5. Modify LM-ICP in order to work with multiple views, given a sequence of 10
   views which surround an object such that N_{10} is highly overlapping N_1. The
   global reference system is fixed on the first view. Estimate the global registration
   by including pairwise registration between subsequent views and by view N_{10} to
   view N_1. *Suggestion:* the number of unknowns is $9p$, where p is the dimension
   of the transformation vector (i.e., $p = 7$ for quaternions). The number of rows of

---

[22] A Matlab implementation can be found here http://www.csse.uwa.edu.au/ajmal/code.html.

[23] A Matlab implementation is available here: http://www.robots.ox.ac.uk/~awf/lmicp.

the Jacobian matrix is given by all residual vectors of each pairwise registration. Here, the key aspect is that view N_{10} should be simultaneously aligned pairwise with both view N_9 and view N_1.

References

1. Adagolodjo, Y., Trivisonne, R., Haouchine, N., Cotin, S., Courtecuisse, H.: Silhouette-based pose estimation for deformable organs application to surgical augmented reality. In: International Conference on Intelligent Robots and Systems (2017)
2. Aiger, D., Mitra, N.J., Cohen-Or, D.: 4-points congruent sets for robust surface registration. ACM Trans. Graph. **27**(3) (2008)
3. Albarelli, A., Torsello, A., Rodola, E.: A game-theoretic approach to fine surface registration without initial motion estimation. In: International Conference on Computer Vision and Pattern Recognition (2010)
4. Anguelov, D., Srinivasan, P., Pang, H.C., Koller D., Thrun, S., Davis, J.: The correlated correspondence algorithm for unsupervised registration of nonrigid surfaces. In: Neural Information Processing Systems Conference (2004)
5. Arun, K.S., Huang, T., Blostein, S.: Least-squares fitting of two 3-d point sets. IEEE Trans. Pattern Anal. Mach. Intell. **9**, 698–700 (1987)
6. Avery, B., Sandor, C., Thomas, B.H.: Improving spatial perception for augmented reality x-ray vision. In: IEEE Conference on Virtual Reality (2009)
7. Bajura, M., Fuchs, H., Ohbuchi, R.: Merging virtual objects with the real world: Seeing ultrasound imagery within the patient. In: International Conference on Computer Graphics and Interactive Techniques (1992)
8. Bariya, P., Nishino, K.: Scale-hierarchical 3d object recognition in cluttered scenes. In: International Conference on Computer Vision and Pattern Recognition (2010)
9. Belongie, S., Malik, J., Puzicha, J.: Shape matching and object recognition using shape contexts. IEEE Trans. Pattern Anal. Mach. Intell. **24**(4), 509–522 (2002)
10. Bernardini, F., Rushmeier, H.: The 3D model acquisition pipeline. Comput. Graph. Forum **21**(2), 149–172 (2002)
11. Besl, P., McKay, H.: A method for registration of 3-D shapes. IEEE Trans. Pattern Anal. Mach. Intell. **14**(2), 239–256 (1992)
12. Bichlmeier, C., Sielhorst, T., Heining, S., Navab, N.: Improving depth perception in medical AR: a virtual vision panel to the inside of the patient. In: Bildverarbeitung für die Medizin (2007)
13. Blais, G., Levine, M.: Registering multiview range data to create 3d computer objects. IEEE Trans. Pattern Anal. Mach. Intell. **17**(8) (1995)
14. Bogo, F., Black, M.J., Loper, M., Romero, J.: Detailed full-body reconstructions of moving people from monocular RGB-D sequences. In: International Conference on Computer Vision (2015)
15. Bogo, F., Romero, J., Pons-Moll, G., Black, M.J.: Dynamic FAUST: registering human bodies in motion. In: International Conference on Computer Vision and Pattern Recognition (2017)
16. Boscaini, D., Masci, J., Melzi, S., Bronstein, M., Castellani, U., Vandergheynst, P.: Learning class-specific descriptors for deformable shapes using localized spectral convolutional networks. Comput. Graph. Forum **34**(5) (2015)
17. Bouaziz, S., Tagliasacchi, A., Pauly, M.: Sparse iterative closest points. Comput. Graph. Forum **32**(5) (2013)
18. Bowyer, K.W., Chang, K., Flynn, P.: A survey of approaches and challenges in 3d and multimodal 3d + 2d face recognition. Comput. Vis. Image Underst. **101**(1) (2006)

19. Bregler, C., Hertzmann, A., Biermann, H.: Recovering non-rigid 3D shape from image streams. In: International Conference on Computer Vision and Pattern Recognition (2000)
20. Bronstein, A.M., Bronstein, M.M., Kimmel, R.: Three-dimensional face recognition. Int. J. Comput. Vis. **64**(1), 5–30 (2005)
21. Bronstein, A.M., Bronstein, M.M., Kimmel, R.: Numerical Geometry of Non-rigid Shapes. Springer, Berlin (2008)
22. Brown, B., Rusinkiewicz, S.: Non-rigid range-scan alignment using thin-plate splines. In: Symposium on 3D Data Processing, Visualization, and Transmission (2004)
23. Brown, B., Rusinkiewicz, S.: Global non-rigid alignment of 3-D scans. ACM Trans. Graph. (Proc. SIGGRAPH) **26**(3) (2007)
24. Brown, M., Lowe, D.: Recognising panoramas. In: ICCV (2003)
25. Brusco, N., Andreetto, M., Giorgi, A., Cortelazzo, G.: 3d registration by textured spin-images. In: 3DIM '05: Proceedings of the Fifth International Conference on 3-D Digital Imaging and Modeling, pp. 262–269 (2005)
26. Campbell, R., Flynn, P.: A survey of free-form object representation and recognition techniques. Comput. Vis. Image Underst. **81**(2), 166–210 (2001)
27. Castellani, U., Cristani, M., Fantoni, S., Murino, V.: Sparse points matching by combining 3D mesh saliency with statistical descriptors. In: Computer Graphics Forum, vol. 27, pp. 643–652. Blackwell Publishing (2008)
28. Castellani, U., Cristani, M., Murino, V.: Statistical 3d shape analysis by local generative descriptors. IEEE Trans. Pattern Anal. Mach. Intell. **33**(12) (2011)
29. Castellani, U., Fusiello, A., Murino, V.: Registration of multiple acoustic range views for underwater scene reconstruction. Comput. Vis. Image Underst. **87**(3), 78–89 (2002)
30. Castellani, U., Fusiello, A., Murino, V., Papaleo, L., Puppo, E., Pittore, M.: A complete system for on-line modelling of acoustic images. Image Commun. J. **20**(9–10), 832–852 (2005)
31. Castellani, U., Gay-Bellile, V., Bartoli, A.: Robust deformation capture from temporal range data for surface rendering. Comput. Animat. Virtual Worlds **19**(5), 591–603 (2008)
32. Chang, M., Leymarie, F., Kimia, B.: 3d shape registration using regularized medial scaffolds. In: International Symposium on 3D Data Processing, Visualization and Transmission (2004)
33. Chang, W., Zwicker, M.: Automatic registration for articulated shapes. Comput. Graph. Forum (Proc. SGP 2008) **27**(5), 1459–1468 (2008)
34. Chang, W., Zwicker, M.: Range scan registration using reduced deformable models. Comput. Graph. Forum **28**(2), 447–456 (2009)
35. Chauvet, P., Collins, T., Debize, C., Novais-Gameiro, L., Pereira, B., Bartoli, A., Canis, M., Bourdel, N.: Augmented reality in a tumor resection model. Surg. Endosc. **32**(3), 1192–1201 (2018)
36. Chen, Y., Medioni, G.: Object modelling by registration of multiple range images. Image Vis. Comput. **10**(3), 145–155 (1992)
37. Choi, S., Zhou, Q.Y., Koltun, V.: Robust reconstruction of indoor scenes. In: International Conference on Computer Vision and Pattern Recognition (2015)
38. Chui, H., Rangarajan, A.: A new point matching algorithm for non-rigid registration. Comput. Vis. Image Underst. **89**(2–3), 114–141 (2003)
39. Collins, T., Pizarro, D., Bartoli, A., Bourdel, N., Canis, M.: Computer-aided laparoscopic myomectomy by augmenting the uterus with pre-operative MRI data. In: International Symposium on Mixed and Augmented Reality (2014)
40. Collins, T., Pizarro, D., Bartoli, A., Canis, M., Bourdel, N.: Realtime wide-baseline registration of the uterus in monocular laparoscopic videos. In: International Workshop on Medical Imaging and Augmented Reality at MICCAI (2013)
41. Corey, G., Matei, C., Jaime, P., Hao, D., K., A.P.: Data-driven grasping with partial sensor data. In: IROS'09: Proceedings of the 2009 IEEE/RSJ international conference on Intelligent robots and systems, pp. 1278–1283 (2009)
42. Cruska, G., Dance, C.R., Fan, L., Willamowski, J., Bray, C.: Visual categorization with bags of keypoints. In: ECCV Workshop on Statistical Learning in Computer Vision, pp. 1–22 (2004)

43. Cunnington, S., Stoddart, A.: N-view point set registration: a comparison. In: British Machine Vision Conference (1999)
44. Deng, H., Birdal, T., Ilic, S.: PPFNet: Global context aware local features for robust 3d point matching. In: International Conference on Computer Vision and Pattern Recognition (2018)
45. Dewaele, G., Devernay, F., Horaud, R.: Hand motion from 3d point trajectories and a smooth surface model. In: European Conference on Computer Vision (2004)
46. Drost, B., Ulrich, M., Navab, N., Ilic, S.: Model globally, match locally: Efficient and robust 3d object recognition. In: International Conference on Computer Vision and Pattern Recognition (2010)
47. Eckart, B., Kim, K., Kautz, J.: HGMR: Hierarchical gaussian mixtures for adaptive 3d registration. In: European Conference on Computer Vision (2018)
48. Eckart, B., Kim, K., Troccoli, A., Kelly, A., Kautz, J.: MLMD: maximum likelihood mixture decoupling for fast and accurate point cloud registration. In: Proceedings of the International Conference on 3D Vision (2015)
49. Eggert, D., Lorusso, A., Fisher, R.: Estimating 3-d rigid body transformations: a comparison of four major algorithms. Mach. Vis. Appl. **9**, 272–290 (1997)
50. Elbaz, G., Avraham, T., Fischer, A.: 3d point cloud registration for localization using a deep neural network auto-encoder. In: International Conference on Computer Vision and Pattern Recognition (2017)
51. Endres, F., Hess, J., Sturm, J., Cremers, D., Burgard, W.: 3D mapping with an RGB-D camera. IEEE Trans. Robot. **30**(1), (2014)
52. Ezra, E., Sharir, M., Efrat, A.: On the performance of the ICP algorithm. Comput. Geom. **41**(1–2), 77–93 (2008)
53. Fantoni, S., Castellani, U., Fusiello, A.: Accurate and automatic alignment of range surfaces. In: Proceedings of the 2nd Joint 3DIM/3DPVT Conference: 3D Imaging, Modeling, Processing, Visualization and Transmission (3DIMPVT) (2012)
54. Fitzgibbon, A.: Robust registration of 2D and 3D point sets. Image Vis. Comput. **21**(13–14), 1145–1153 (2003)
55. Fuchs, H., Livingston, M., Raskar, R., Colucci, D., Keller, K., State, A., Crawford, J., Rademacher, P., Drake, S., Meyer, A.: Augmented reality visualization for laparoscopic surgery. In: Medical Image Computing and Computer-Assisted Intervention (1998)
56. Funkhouser, T., Kazhdan, M., Min, P., Shilane, P.: Shape-based retrieval and analysis of 3d models. Commun. ACM **48**(6), 58–64 (2005)
57. Garcia-Grasa, O., Bernal, E., Casado, S., Gil, I., Montiel, J.M.M.: Visual SLAM for hand-held monocular endoscope. IEEE Trans. Med. Imaging **33**(1), 135–146 (2014)
58. Gelfand, N., Mitra, N.J., Guibas, L.J., Pottmann, H.: Robust global registration. In: Desbrun, M., Pottmann, H. (eds.), Eurographics Association, pp. 197–206 (2005). ISBN 3-905673-24-X
59. Godin, G., Laurendeau, D., Bergevin, R.: A method for the registration of attributed range images. In: 3-D Digital Imaging and Modeling (3DIM), pp. 179–186 (2001)
60. Golovinskiy, A., Kim, V., Funkhouser, T.: Shape-based recognition of 3d point clouds in urban environments. In: International Conference on Computer Vision (2009)
61. Granger, S., Pennec, X.: Multi-scale EM-ICP: a fast and robust approach for surface registration. In: European Conference on Computer Vision (2002)
62. Gu, X., Gortler, S.J., Hoppe, H.: Geometry images. ACM Trans. Graph. **21**(3), 355–361 (2002)
63. Guo, Y., Bennamoun, M., Sohel, F., Lu, M., Wan, J.: 3d object recognition in cluttered scenes with local surface features: a survey. IEEE Trans. Pattern Anal. Mach. Intell. **36**(11) (2014)
64. Guo, Y., Bennamoun, M., Sohel, F., Lu, M., Wan, J., Kwok, N.M.: A comprehensive performance evaluation of 3d local feature descriptors. Int. J. Comput. Vis. **116**(1) (2016)
65. Guo, Y., Sohel, F., Bennamoun, M., Wan, J., Lu, M.: An accurate and robust range image registration algorithm for 3d object modeling. IEEE Trans. Multimed. **16**(5) (2014)
66. Hampel, F., Rousseeuw, P., Ronchetti, E., Stahel, W.: Robust Statistics: The Approach Based on Influence Functions. Wiley (1986)

67. Handa, A., Whelan, T., McDonald, J., Davison, A.: A benchmark for RGB-D visual odometry, 3D reconstruction and SLAM. In: IEEE International Conference on Robotics and Automation, ICRA (2014)
68. Hinton, G.E., Salakhutdinov, R.R.: Reducing the dimensionality of data with neural networks. Science **313**(5786) (2006)
69. Hodaň, T., Michel, F., Brachmann, E., Kehl, W., Buch, A.G., Kraft, D., Drost, B., Vidal, J., Ihrke, S., Zabulis, X., Sahin, C., Manhardt, F., Tombari, F., Kim, T.K., Matas, J., Rother, C.: BOP: Benchmark for 6d object pose estimation. In: Ferrari, V., Hebert, M., Sminchisescu, C., Weiss, Y. (eds.) European Conference on Computer Vision (2018)
70. Horaud, R., Forbes, F., Yguel, M., Dewaele, G., Zhang, J.: Rigid and articulated point registration with expectation conditional maximization. IEEE Trans. Pattern Anal. Mach. Intell. **33**, 587–602 (2011)
71. Huang, Q., Adams, B., Wicke, M., Guibas, L.: Non-rigid registration under isometric deformations. Comput. Graph. Forum **27**(5), 1449–1457 (2008)
72. Huber, D., Hebert, M.: Fully automatic registration of multiple 3D data sets. Image Vis. Comput. **21**(7), 637–650 (2003)
73. Innmann, M., Zollhöfer, M., Nießner, M., Theobalt, C., Stamminger, M.: Volumedeform: Real-time volumetric non-rigid reconstruction. In: European Conference on Computer Vision (2016)
74. Jhonson, A., Kang, S.: Registration and integration of textured 3d data. Image Vis. Comput. **19**(2), 135–147 (1999)
75. Jian, B., Vemuri, B.C.: A robust algorithm for point set registration using mixture of gaussians. In: International Conference on Computer Vision and Pattern Recognition (2005)
76. Johnson, A., Hebert, M.: Using spin images for efficient object recognition in cluttered 3D scenes. IEEE Trans. Pattern Anal. Mach. Intell. **21**(5), 433–449 (1999)
77. van Kaick, O., Zhang, H., Hamarneh, G., Cohen-Or, D.: A survey on shape correspondence. In: EuroGraphics: State-of-the-Art Report (2010)
78. Khoualed, S., Castellani, U., Bartoli, A.: Semantic shape context for the registration of multiple partial 3–D views. In: British Machine Vision Conference (2009)
79. Koo, B., Özgür, E., Roy, B.L., Buc, E., Bartoli, A.: Deformable registration of a preoperative 3D liver volume to a laparoscopy image using contour and shading cues. In: Medical Image Computing and Computer-Assisted Intervention (2017)
80. Krsek, P., Pajdla, T., Hlaváč, V.: Differential invariants as the base of triangulated surface registration. Comput. Vis. Image Underst. **87**(1–3), 27–38 (2002)
81. Krull, A., Brachmann, E., Michel, F., Yang, M.Y., Gumhold, S., Rother, C.: Learning analysis-by-synthesis for 6d pose estimation in RGB-D images. In: International Conference on Computer Vision (2015)
82. LeCun, Y., Bengio, Y., Hinton, G.: Deep learning. Nature **521**(436) (2015)
83. Lescoat, T., Ovsjanikov, M., Memari, P., Thiery, J.M., Boubekeur, T.: A survey on data-driven dictionary-based methods for 3d modeling. Comput. Graph. Forum **37**(2) (2018)
84. Lévy, B.: Laplace-Beltrami eigenfunctions towards an algorithm that understands geometry. In: Proceedings of SMI, pp. 13–25. IEEE, Washington, DC (2006)
85. Li, H., Sumner, R.W., Pauly, M.: Global correspondence optimization for non-rigid registration of depth scans. Comput. Graph. Forum (Proc. SGP'08) **27**(5) (2008)
86. Litany, O., Remez, T., Rodolá, E., Bronstein, A.M., Bronstein, M.M.: Functional maps: structured prediction for dense shape correspondence. In: International Conference on Computer Vision (2017)
87. Litany, O., Rodolà, E., Bronstein, A.M., Bronstein, M.M., Cremers, D.: Non-Rigid Puzzles. Comput. Graph. Forum **35**(5), 135–143 (2016)
88. Loper, M., Mahmood, N., Romero, J., Pons-Moll, G., Black, M.J.: SMPL: A skinned multi-person linear model. ACM Trans. Graph. **34**(6) (2015)
89. Maintz, J., Viergever, M.A.: A survey of medical image registration. Med. Image Anal. **2**(1), 1–36 (1998)

90. Makadia, A., Patterson, A., Daniilidis, K.: Fully Automatic Registration of 3D Point Clouds. In: Proceedings of the 2006 IEEE Computer Society Conference on Computer Vision and Pattern Recognition-Volume 1, pp. 1297–1304. IEEE Computer Society Washington, DC, USA (2006)

91. Marin, R., Melzi, S., Rodolà, E., Castellani, U.: Farm: Functional automatic registration method for 3d human bodies. (2018). arXiv:1807.10517

92. Marzotto, R., Fusiello, A., Murino, V.: High resolution video mosaicing with global alignment. In: ICCV (2004)

93. Mellado, N., Aiger, D., Mitra, N.J.: Super 4PCS fast global pointcloud registration via smart indexing. Comput. Graph. Forum 33(5) (2014)

94. Melzi, S., Rodolà, E., Castellani, U., Bronstein, M.M.: Localized manifold harmonics for spectral shape analysis. Comput. Graph. Forum 37(6), 20–34 (2018)

95. Mian, A.S., Bennamoun, M., Owens, R.: Three-dimensional model-based object recognition and segmentation in cluttered scenes. IEEE Trans. Pattern Anal. Mach. Intell. 28(10), 1584–1601 (2006)

96. Mian, A.S., Bennamoun, M., Owens, R.A.: Automatic correspondence for 3d modeling: an extensive review. Int. J. Shape Model. 11(2), 253–291 (2005)

97. Mitra, N.J., Flory, S., Ovsjanikov, M., Gelfand, N., Guibas, L., Pottmann, H.: Dynamic geometry registration. In: Symposium on Geometry Processing, pp. 173–182 (2007)

98. Munoz, D., Vandapel, N., Hebert, M.: Directional associative markov network for 3-d point cloud classification. In: International Symposium on 3-D Data Processing, Visualization, and Transmission (3DPVT) (2008)

99. Murino, V., Ronchetti, L., Castellani, U., Fusiello, A.: Reconstruction of complex environments by robust pre-aligned ICP. In: 3DIM (2001)

100. Myronenko, A., Song, X., Carreira-Perpinan, M.: Non-rigid point set registration: Coherent point drift. In: Neural Information Processing Systems Conference (2006)

101. Newcombe, R., Davison, A., Izadi, S., Kohli, P., O., H., Shotton, J., Molyneaux, D., Hodges, S., Kim, D., Fitzgibbon, A.: Kinectfusion: real-time dense surface mapping and tracking. In: IEEE ISMA (2011)

102. Newcombe, R.A., Fox, D., Seitz, S.M.: Dynamicfusion: Reconstruction and tracking of nonrigid scenes in real-time. In: International Conference on Computer Vision and Pattern Recognition (2015)

103. Nogneng, D., Melzi, S., Rodolà, E., Castellani, U., Bronstein, M., Ovsjanikov, M.: Improved functional mappings via product preservation. Comput. Graph. Forum 37(2), 179–190 (2018)

104. Novatnack, J., Nishino, K.: Scale-Dependent/Invariant Local 3D Shape Descriptors for Fully Automatic Registration of Multiple Sets of Range Images. In: Proceedings of the 10th European Conference on Computer Vision: Part III, pp. 440–453. Springer, Berlin, Heidelberg (2008)

105. Nuchter, A., Lingemann, K., Hertzberg, J.: Cached k-d tree search for ICP algorithms. In: 3DIM '07: Proceedings of the Sixth International Conference on 3-D Digital Imaging and Modeling, pp. 419–426 (2007)

106. Ovsjanikov, M., Ben-Chen, M., Solomon, J., Butscher, A., Guibas, L.: Functional maps: a flexible representation of maps between shapes. ACM Trans. Graph. (TOG) 31(4) (2012)

107. Özgür, E., Lafont, A., Bartoli, A.: Visualizing in-organ tumors in augmented monocular laparoscopy. In: International Symposium on Mixed and Augmented Reality (2017)

108. Parashar, S., Pizarro, D., Bartoli, A.: Isometric non-rigid shape-from-motion with Riemannian geometry solved in linear time. IEEE Trans. Pattern Anal. Mach. Intell. 40(10), 2442–2454 (2018)

109. Park, K., Germann, M., Breitenstein, M.D., Pfister, H.: Fast and automatic object pose estimation for range images on the GPU. Mach. Vis. Appl. 21(5), 749–766 (2009)

110. Park, S., Subbarao, M.: An accurate and fast point-to-plane registration technique. Pattern Recognit. Lett. 24(16), 2967–2976 (2003)

111. Patterson IV, A., Mordohai, P., Daniilidis, K.: Object detection from large-scale 3d datasets using bottom-up and top-down descriptors. In: Proceedings of the European Conference on Computer Vision (2008)

112. Pears, N.E., Heseltine, T., Romero, M.: From 3d point clouds to pose normalised depth maps. Int. J. Comput. Vis. **89**(2), 152–176 (2010)
113. Phillips, J., Liu, R., Tomasi, C.: Outlier robust ICP for minimizing fractional RMSD. In: 3-D Digital Imaging and Modeling (3DIM), pp. 427–434 (2007)
114. Pissanetzky, S.: Sparse Matrix Technology. Academic, New York (1984)
115. Pottmann, H., Huang, Q., Yang, Y., Hu, S.: Geometry and convergence analysis of algorithms for registration of 3D shapes. Int. J. Comput. Vis. **67**(3), 277–296 (2006)
116. Prasad, M., Zisserman, A., Fitzgibbon, A.W.: Single view reconstruction of curved surfaces. In: International Conference on Computer Vision and Pattern Recognition (2006)
117. Pulli, K.: Multiview registration for large data sets. In: 3DIM: Proceedings of the Fifth International Conference on 3-D Digital Imaging and Modeling, pp. 160–168 (1999)
118. Pulli, K., Piiroinen, S., Duchamp, T., Stuetzle, W.: Projective surface matching of colored 3d scans. In: 3-D Digital Imaging and Modeling (3DIM), pp. 531–538 (2005)
119. Rangarajan, A., Chui, H., Duncan, J.: Rigid point feature registration using mutual information. Med. Image Anal. **3**, 425–440 (1999)
120. Rangarajan, A., Chui, H., Mjolsness, E., Pappu, S., Davachi, L., Goldman-Rakic, P., Duncan., J.: A robust point-matching algorithm for autoradiograph alignment. Med. Image Anal. **1**, 379–398 (1997)
121. Rethage, D., Wald, J., Sturm, J., Navab, N., Tombari, F.: Fully-convolutional point networks for large-scale point clouds. In: Ferrari, V., Hebert, M., Sminchisescu, C., Weiss, Y. (eds.) European Conference on Computer Vision (2018)
122. Rodolà, E., Cosmo, L., Bronstein, M.M., Torsello, A., Cremers, D.: Partial functional correspondence. Comput. Graph. Forum **36**(1), 222–236 (2017)
123. Ruiter, H.D., Benhabib, B.: On-line Modeling for Real-Time, Model-Based, 3D Pose Tracking. Springer, Berlin (2007)
124. Rusinkiewicz, S., Brown, B., Kazhdan, M.: 3d scan matching and registration. ICCV Short Course (2005)
125. Rusinkiewicz, S., Hall-Holt, O., Levoy, M.: Real-time 3-D model acquisition. ACM Trans. Graph. (Proc. SIGGRAPH) **21**(3), 438–446 (2002)
126. Rusinkiewicz, S., Levoy, M.: Efficient variants of the ICP algorithm. In: 2001. Proceedings Third International Conference on 3-D Digital Imaging and Modeling, pp. 145–152 (2001)
127. Russell, C., Yu, R., Agapito, L.: Video pop-up: Monocular 3D reconstruction of dynamic scenes. In: European Conference on Computer Vision (2014)
128. Salvi, J., Matabosch, C., Fofi, D., Forest, J.: A review of recent range image registration methods with accuracy evaluation. Image Vis. Comput. **25**(5), 578–596 (2007)
129. Salzmann, M., Ilic, S., Fua, P.: Physically valid shape parameterization for monocular 3-D deformable surface tracking. In: British Machine Vision Conference (2005)
130. Sara, R.: Finding the largest unambiguous component of stereo matching. In: Proceedings of European Conference on Computer Vision (ECCV), pp. 900–914 (2002)
131. Sara, R., Okatani, I., Sugimoto, A.: Globally convergent range image registration by graph kernel algorithm. In: 3-D Digital Imaging and Modeling (3DIM) (2005)
132. Sawhney, H.S., Hsu, S., Kumar, R.: Robust video mosaicing through topology inference and local to global alignment. In: ECCV (1998)
133. Scheenstra, A., Ruifrok, A., Veltkamp, R.C.: A survey of 3d face recognition methods. In: Audio- and Video-Based Biometric Person Authentication, pp. 891–899 (2005)
134. Shams, R., Sadeghi, P., Kennedy, R.A., Hartley, R.I.: A survey of high performance medical image registration on multi-core, GPU and distributed architectures. IEEE Signal Process. Mag. **27**(2), 50–60 (2010)
135. Sharp, G., Sang, L., Wehe, D.: ICP registration using invariant features. IEEE Trans. Pattern Anal. Mach. Intell. **24**(1), 90–102 (2002)
136. Simon, D.A.: Fast and accurate shape-based registration. Ph.D. thesis, Carnegie Mellon University, Pittsburgh, PA, USA (1996)

137. Simonovsky, M., Gutiérrez-Becker, B., Mateus, D., Navab, N., Komodakis, N.: A deep metric for multimodal registration. In: Ourselin, S., Joskowicz, L., Sabuncu, M.R., Unal, G., Wells, W. (eds.) Medical Image Computing and Computer-Assisted Intervention – MICCAI 2016 (2016)
138. Sorkine, O., Alexa, M.: As-rigid-as-possible surface modeling. Symp. Geom. Process. **4**, 109–116 (2007)
139. Steinke, F., Scholkopf, B., Blanz, V.: Learning dense 3d correspondence. In: Annual Conference on Neural Information Processing Systems (NIPS 2006) (2007)
140. Taati, B., Bondy, M., Jasiobedzki, P., Greenspan, M.: Automatic registration for model building using variable dimensional local shape descriptors. In: International Conference on 3-D Digital Imaging and Modeling (2007)
141. Tabia, H., Guo, Y., Laga, H., Fisher, R.B., Bennamoun., M.: 3D Shape Analysis: Fundamentals, Theory, and Applications. Wiley, New York (2019)
142. Tam, G.K., Cheng, Z.Q., Lai, Y.K., Langbein, F.C., Liu, Y., Marshall, D., Martin, R.R., Sun, X.F., Rosin, P.L.: Registration of 3d point clouds and meshes: a survey from rigid to nonrigid. IEEE Trans. Vis. Comput. Graph. **19**(7), 1199–1217 (2012)
143. Tangelder, J., Veltkamp, R.: A survey of content based 3d shape retrieval methods. Multimed. Tools Appl. **39**(3), 441–471 (2008)
144. Toldo, R., Beinat, A., Crosilla, F.: Global registration of multiple point clouds embedding the generalized procrustes analysis into an ICP framework. In: Symposium on 3D Data Processing, Visualization, and Transmission (2010)
145. Tombari, F., Salti, S., Stefano, L.D.: Performance evaluation of 3d keypoint detectors. Int. J. Comput. Vis. **102**(1–3) (2013)
146. Tombari, F., Salti, S., Stefano, L.D.: SHOT: Unique signatures of histograms for surface and texture description. Int. J. Comput. Vis. **125** (2014)
147. Trucco, M., Verri, A.: Introductory Techniques for 3-D Computer Vision. Prentice Hall, Upper Saddle River (1998)
148. Tsin, Y., Kanade, T.: A correlation-based approach to robust point set registration. In: European Conference on Computer Vision, pp. 558–569 (2004)
149. Umeyama, S.: Least-squares estimation of transformation parameters between two points patterns. IEEE Trans. Pattern Anal. Mach. Intell. **13**(4), 376–380 (1991)
150. Vinesh, R., Kiran, F.: Reverse Engineering, an Industrial Perspective. Springer, Berlin (2008)
151. Wang, F., Vemuri, B.C., Rangarajan, A.: Groupwise point pattern registration using a novel CDF-based Jensen-Shannon Divergence. In: International Conference on Computer Vision and Pattern Recognition (2006)
152. Wang, R., Geng, Z., Zang, Z., Pei, R.: Visualization techniques for augmented reality in endoscopic surgery. In: Medical Imaging and Augmented Reality Workshop at MICCAI (2016)
153. Watt, A.: 3D Computer Graphics. Addison-Wesley, Boston (2000)
154. Weik, S.: Registration of 3-d partial surface models using luminance and depth information. In: 3-D Digital Imaging and Modeling (3DIM), pp. 93–100 (1997)
155. Woodford, O.J., Pham, M.T., Maki, A., Perbet, F., Stenger, B.: Demisting the hough transform for 3d shape recognition and registration. Int. J. Comput. Vis. **106**(3), (2014)
156. Wyngaerd, J.V., Gool, L.V.: Automatic crude patch registration: Toward automatic 3d model building. Comput. Vis. Image Underst. **87**(1–3), 8–26 (2002)
157. Yang, J., Li, H., Campbell, D., Jia, Y.: Go-ICP: a globally optimal solution to 3d ICP point-set registration. IEEE Trans. Pattern Anal. Mach. Intell. **38**(11) (2016)
158. Zeng, A., Song, S., Nießner, M., Fisher, M., Xiao, J., Funkhouser, T.: 3dmatch: Learning local geometric descriptors from rgb-d reconstructions. In: International Conference on Computer Vision and Pattern Recognition (2017)
159. Zhang, Z.: Iterative point matching of free-form curves and surfaces. Int. J. Comput. Vis. **13**, 119–152
160. Zhou, L., Zhu, S., Luo, Z., Shen, T., Zhang, R., Zhen, M., Fang, T., Quan, L.: Learning and matching multi-view descriptors for registration of point clouds. In: European Conference on Computer Vision (2018)

161. Zhou, Q.Y., Koltun, V.: Dense scene reconstruction with points of interest. ACM Trans. Graph. **32**(4) (2013)
162. Zhou, Q.Y., Koltun, V.: Color map optimization for 3d reconstruction with consumer depth cameras. ACM Trans. Graph. **33**(4) (2014)
163. Zhou, Q.Y., Park, J., Koltun, V.: Fast global registration. In: European Conference on Computer Vision (2016)
164. Zinsser, T., Schnidt, H., Niermann, J.: A refined ICP algorithm for robust 3D correspondences estimation. In: International Conference on Image Processing, pp. 695–698 (2003)
165. Zollhöfer, M., Stotko, P., Görlitz, A., Theobalt, C., Nießner, M., Klein, R., Kolb, A.: State of the Art on 3D Reconstruction with RGB-D Cameras. Comput. Graph. Forum **37**(2) (2018)
166. Zuffi, S., Black, M.J.: The stitched puppet: A graphical model of 3D human shape and pose. In: International Conference on Computer Vision and Pattern Recognition (2015)

Chapter 9
3D Shape Matching for Retrieval and Recognition

Benjamin Bustos and Ivan Sipiran

Abstract Nowadays, multimedia information such as images and videos are present in many aspects of our lives. Three-dimensional information is also becoming important in different applications, for instance, entertainment, medicine, security, art, just to name a few. It is therefore necessary to study how to properly process 3D information taking advantage of the properties that it provides. This chapter gives an overview of 3D shape matching and its applications in shape retrieval and recognition. In order to present the subject, we opted for describing in detail four approaches with good balance among maturity and novelty, namely, the PANORAMA descriptor, spin images, functional maps, and Heat Kernel Signatures for retrieval. We also aim at stressing the importance of this field in areas such as computer vision and computer graphics, as well as the importance of addressing the main challenges on this research field.

9.1 Introduction

The ability to store and manipulate large amounts of information have enabled the emergence of a number of applications. Generally, the information is given as text because it is easy to produce and understand by a computer. However, there are situations where information cannot be suitably represented by text, such as a tourists photo album.

Thus, the use and availability of multimedia information have increased considerably, on one hand to support new applications and on the other hand due to the proliferation and accessibility of inexpensive capture devices such as digital cameras. A number of applications have benefited from this availability of images, videos, and three-dimensional models, such as security, entertainment, and engineering pro-

B. Bustos (✉)
Department of Computer Science, University of Chile, Santiago, Chile
e-mail: bcbustos@dcc.uchile.cl

I. Sipiran
Department of Engineering, Pontifical Catholic University of Peru, Lima, Peru
e-mail: isipiran@pucp.edu.pe

© Springer Nature Switzerland AG 2020
Y. Liu et al. (eds.), *3D Imaging, Analysis and Applications*,
https://doi.org/10.1007/978-3-030-44070-1_9

413

cesses. Unlike text, multimedia information is difficult to be compared directly, and therefore we require techniques to manipulate it effectively.

Our goal in this chapter is to address the problem of comparing two 3D objects based on their shapes. Shape matching refers to the process of finding a correspondence between two shapes based on some similarity criterion. The criterion which has received most attention by the research community is the visual similarity, that is to say, two shapes should be matched if they share visually common features. In this chapter, we are interested in two processes involving 3D shapes matching, namely, recognition and retrieval.

Although these processes are related, they are slightly different. On the one hand, shape recognition consists of identifying a given 3D object within a set of possible alternatives. The outcome of this process is generally the class to which the object belongs or the recognized object as stored by the recognition system. The latter is useful when the queried object represents a partial or occluded portion such as a range scan. On the other hand, shape retrieval consists of defining a measure in order to quantify the similarity between shapes. A typical outcome of this process is an ordered list of objects according to their associated measure.

In recent years, we have witnessed increasing interest in computer graphics and computer vision communities for 3D shape retrieval and recognition. As a result, a number of techniques and approaches have been proposed for shape representation, object and feature description, feature selection, and matching algorithms. It is also important to note the number of applications that have emerged, such as

- Geometric 3D comparison for shoe industry [79].
- 3D hippocampi retrieval [59].
- Classification of pollen in 3D volume data sets [93].
- 3D retrieval for museums [46].
- Human ear recognition in 3D [27].
- 3D object classification for craniofacial research [1].
- 3D protein retrieval and classification [86, 87, 125].
- CAD/CAM [126].
- Archeology [53].
- 3D video sequences [52].

Therefore, it should be noted the importance of evaluating and comparing new approaches that may appear. Due to the large amount of research carried out and the large dissemination of 3D information obtained through increasingly better capture devices, several benchmarks have been presented such as the Princeton Shape Benchmark [99], the Konstanz 3D database [19], the TOSCA dataset [13], and the Shape Retrieval Contest (SHREC) datasets. More recently, with the adoption of deep learning techniques in 3D research community, large-scale datasets have been built such as ShapeNet [23] and ModelNet [122].

9.1.1   *Retrieval and Recognition Evaluation*

An important factor is also the methodology of evaluation for shape retrieval and recognition techniques. In this sense, the evaluation relies on the solid background of mature fields such as pattern recognition and information retrieval. In the case of shape retrieval, the common evaluation methods are Precision-Recall curves, cumulated gain-based measurements, nearest neighbor, first-tier, and second-tier [3]. For shape recognition, the ROC curves and error rates have commonly been used [34]. In order to maintain this chapter self-contained, we briefly describe the evaluation measures commonly used in the literature.

In retrieval, the evaluation measures mostly consider the ranked lists retrieved when queried objects are presented. The main measures are presented as follows:

- **Precision**: the extent to which the retrieved objects are relevant to a query. Formally, it is the ratio of correctly retrieved objects with respect to the total number of retrieved objects.
- **Recall**: the extent to which the relevant objects are correctly retrieved. Formally, it is the ratio of correctly retrieved objects with respect to the total number of relevant objects for the query.
- **R-Precision**: precision when the number of retrieved objects equals the number of relevant objects.
- **Cumulated gain-based measurements**: the idea is to use the ranked position of relevant objects. First, we need to convert the retrieved list into a binary list G with 1s in position where relevant objects appear. Second, the discounted cumulated gain vector DCG is defined as follows:

$$DCG[i] = \begin{cases} G[1] & \text{if } i = 1 \\ DCG[i - 1] + G[i]/\log_2 i & \text{otherwise} \end{cases} \tag{9.1}$$

where the log function penalizes the ranking of a relevant object.
- **Nearest neighbor, first-tier, and second-tier**: these evaluation measures check the ratio of relevant objects in the top K objects of the ranked list. Specifically, $K = 1$ for nearest neighbor, $K = |R| - 1$ for first-tier and $K = 2 \times (|R| - 1)$ for second-tier, where $|R|$ is the number of relevant objects to a query.

In recognition, the common measures are related to error rates after recognition. Some interesting terms are defined as follows:

- **True positive (TP)**: ratio of similar shapes identified as similar.
- **False positive (FP)**: ratio of dissimilar shapes identified as similar.
- **False negative (FN)**: ratio of similar shapes identified as dissimilar.

Using the aforementioned terms, the measures commonly used in recognition are as follows:

- **Equal error rate (EER)**: the value of false positive at which it equals the false negative rate. Similarly, a typical measure is the value of false positive at some percentage of false negatives.
- **ROC curves**: is a graphical plot representing the trade-off between the true positives and the false positives.

9.1.2 Chapter Outline

The organization of this chapter is as follows. Section 9.2 provides a brief overview of the proposed approaches and main ideas to date. Section 9.3 presents in detail some techniques for shape retrieval and recognition. The organization of this section is as follows:

- Section 9.3.1 describes a view-based technique in 3D shape retrieval known as PANORAMA descriptor.
- Section 9.3.2 presents spin images, an effective descriptor for 3D shape recognition.
- Section 9.3.3 presents the functional maps method to discover correspondences between objects with isometric transformations.
- Finally, Sect. 9.3.4 addresses two approaches for large-scale retrieval: Bag-of-Features with Heat Kernel Signatures and the Signature Quadratic Form Distance.

Section 9.4 is devoted to pose the main challenges in these fields and convenient directions for further research. Section 9.5 presents our concluding remarks. Section 9.6 suggests further readings and finally, in Sect. 9.7.2 we propose problems and exercises related to the presented material.

9.2 Literature Review

To support similarity search between two multimedia objects, we must define a model that allows us to find a relation between them. It cannot be done directly because we are interested in analyzing similar objects, rather than analyzing identical copies. A lot of work has been done to assess the relation between 3D objects when the required model is global. By global, we mean that given a 3D object, an algorithm encodes the information of the complete object and compares the result as analogy of visual similarity. The most widely used model consists in obtaining an abstract representation of an object such as feature vectors or graphs, and the similarity is calculated based upon these representations. For example, distance metrics are commonly used to calculate similarity among feature vectors. Another similarity model which has gained much interest involves local features specially in non-rigid and partial shape retrieval and recognition. The problem of defining a similarity model is very challenging. For example, a visual model allows us to represent a shape by its aspect. However, this model cannot be used to discriminate two shapes semantically similar but with different aspects. In this section, we cover a non-exhaustive set of methods and frameworks to deal with the shape matching problem. We divide our description into shape retrieval techniques, recognition techniques, and shape correspondence techniques.

9.2.1   Shape Retrieval

Bustos et al. [19] described a methodology that consists in representing 3D objects as real vectors of a certain dimension obtained through a transformation function. Then, these vectors can be organized in a multidimensional index, where the similarity corresponds to the proximity in the space where vectors are defined. The Minkowski distance family is usually used to measure the proximity of feature vectors. The authors presented experimental results comparing several transformation functions where the Depth-Buffer Descriptor proposed by Vranic [117] showed the best results. Iyer et al. [54] and Tangelder et al. [113] also discussed techniques for 3D object retrieval, identifying future trends and important issues to be addressed. Also, the Princeton Shape Benchmark [99] provides a reference collection and experimental tests for several descriptors. Other surveys and reports were written by Funkhouser et al. [41], Del Bimbo et al. [9], and Bustos et al. [18, 20]. In 3D shape recognition, Campbell and Flynn [21] presented a comprehensive study about representation and recognition of free-form shapes.

According to the information extracted from shapes, existing approaches use histograms, image-based representation, and local features. Histogram-based methods summarize certain shape properties such as distribution between points on the surface [80], angles information [85], distribution of face normals [58], and so forth. These properties are used to build histograms which represent shapes and matching is done with common histogram measures. Differently, transform-based methods apply some transform to the shapes to convert them in a numerical representation of the underlying object. Some examples of transforms applied are Fourier Transform [35], Radon Transform [33], and Wavelet Transform [63].

As well, image-based methods intend to represent a 3D object as a set of projected images, so the matching becomes an image matching problem. For instance, Vranic [117] proposed to take the frequency spectrum of depth images, Chen [25] considered silhouettes taken from directions according to the vertices of a dodecahedron, and Chaouch and Verroust-Blondet [24] converted a set of depth images in character strings with the matching being performed with variations of the well-known edit distance. More recently, helped by the fast adoption of deep learning techniques in computer vision and shape analysis, the attention has been put in the use of data-driven approaches to take advantage of image-based representations. The common approach is to render synthetic views from a 3D object and perform several tasks such as feature learning or metric learning. For example, Tabia and Laga [112] proposed to project image features computed with a neural network in a common target space, where images or sketches can also be represented. In the same spirit, He et al. [50] described a method to learn centroids of shape collections and apply a triplet-center loss function to determine the class of a given object, which is subsequently used for retrieval. The input is a set of rendered views from the input object. On the other hand, Chen and Fang [29] built a metric network that evaluates the cross-modality features between 3D shapes and sketches. Similarly, Liu et al. [75] used a cross-domain distance learning on 3D objects represented as a set of rendered views to teach a neural network to generalize between objects in different datasets. Also, Feng et al. [38] proposed a group-fusion technique that combines different projections from an object to learnt to discriminate 3D objects.

In classic shape retrieval, the image-based methods are sensitive to the object pose. This problem is partially addressed by data-driven approaches because we can get a good representation using different projections of the object, while a neural network learns to extract the important information for certain task. However, it is clear that partial and non-rigid matching could not be addressed with these methods. One natural choice to deal with these problems is the use of local features. Gal and Cohen-Or [42] proposed to represent a 3D object as a set of salient geometric features, which determine the complete object. Their scheme entirely relies on curvature information over the shape's surface and the matching is done by indexing the salient features using geometric hashing [120] with a vote scheme to determine similar objects.

One of the most widely used approaches for managing local descriptor is Bag-of-Features. This approach begins by clustering all the local descriptor from an entire collection and calculating the centroids for each cluster. Then, each shape is represented as a histogram with a number of bins equal to the number of clusters. Each descriptor adds one into the bin corresponding to the closest centroid. Toldo et al. [114] proposed to segment a given mesh and build a descriptor for each segment. Subsequently, a Bag-of-Features approach combines all the descriptors in the mesh. Similarly, Bronstein et al. [15] proposed a soft version of the Bag-of-Features approach applied on dense descriptors based on the heat kernel signature originally introduced by Sun et al. [110] which is related to the Laplace–Beltrami operator. The authors also presented a spatially sensitive bag-of-features technique which gave good results in shape retrieval. In the same direction, Litman et al. [74] applied the sparse coding approach to learn a dictionary of basis descriptors and sparse vectors over 3D local descriptors to retrieve similar non-rigid objects.

Obviously, the use of local features highlights a new problem: the amount of information used in the matching. With these approaches, a shape is represented with a set of descriptors and the problem of matching becomes non-trivial. In addition, the matching step is more expensive than computing a distance between points, as used in global matching. To this respect, future research directions could be motivated for this kind of matching.

9.2.2   Shape Recognition

As noted, most presented techniques make extensive use of local features because these can mitigate the effect of occlusion in cluttered scenes. Nevertheless, image-based proposals have also been considered. Lee and Drew [65] extracted contours from 2D projections around a 3D object, and subsequently scale-space curvature image was obtained for each projection. These images were used to identify the class of an object and determine the object in the selected class. As well, Cyr and Kimia [32] extracted 2D views which were grouped in view sets called aspects. These aspects were represented by a prototype view for accelerating the recognition process given views from new objects.

Although it is possible to apply any approach from shape retrieval proposals for object recognition, one that has received most attention is the matching by local features. In their seminal work, Chua and Jarvis [30] presented the point signature, a 1D descriptor for points over a surface. The descriptor is based on distance profiles among the surface and a circular curve generated as intersection of the tangent plane and a arbitrary-sized sphere centered in the analyzed point. In the matching, correspondences were found and a voting scheme allowed to determine the objects in a scene. Following the idea of representing the surrounding geometry in a point, Johnson and Hebert [56] proposed their well-known and well-studied spin images. Given an object, the authors constructed 2D descriptors for points over the surface. As the name suggests, a spin image was obtained by spinning a plane around the analyzed point's normal and accumulating the points lying in the plane. The matching was performed by finding correspondences using the spin images between an object and a scene and subsequently a geometric verification with a modified version of the iterative closest point algorithm [7] was performed. A variation of this technique was the spherical spin images presented by Ruiz-Correa et al. [94].

Simple information has also been considered. For instance, Hetzel et al. [51] used pixels depth, normals and curvature information in order to combine them in multidimensional histograms. Thus, the matching step was performed using χ^2-divergence and a posteriori Bayesian classifier. Alternatively, Sun et al. [111] proposed their point fingerprint which consisted of geodesic contours projected on a point's tangent plane. Frome et al. [40] introduced the 3D shape contexts and the harmonic shape contexts. The idea behind the shape context approach is accumulating the surrounding points using concentric spheres around the analyzed point. The authors proposed to use locality sensitive hashing for matching. Likewise, Li and Guskov [68] used spin images and normal-based signatures to describe selected points over range scans. A combination of pyramid matching and support vector machines (SVM) was applied for object recognition giving good results on CAD models and faces.

Chen and Bhanu [28] proposed an approach to recognize highly similar 3D objects in range images. As the authors claimed, several techniques have been proposed to recognize objects in dissimilar classes; however, the task of recognizing objects with high similarity is challenging. Given an object, the authors extracted local surface patches on interest points found using curvature information. Due to the high dimensionality of the descriptors, these were embedded in a low dimensional space using FastMap [37]. Then, the low dimensional descriptors were organized in a kd-tree where efficient nearest neighbor algorithms can be applied. Using the kd-tree, it is possible to find correspondences between two objects. A SVM classifier ranks the correspondences according to geometric constraints returning the most promising correspondences which were verified with the iterative closest point algorithm. The object with the least mean square error is selected.

9.2.3 Shape Correspondences

The problem of discovering the correspondences between objects with non-rigid transformations has received most attention in the scientific community. The problem is challenging because this kind of transformation cannot be easily parameterized with a single transformation, but with a set of local transformations whose search can be combinatorial. Probably, this difficulty has attracted the attention of researchers in different fields, and the result is a large number of methods that try to solve the problem effectively and efficiently. A survey with pioneering methods in shape correspondences was compiled in [57].

Bronstein et al. [16] formulated the problem as an embedding transformation of the geodesic space to the euclidean space. They used a generalization of the multidimensional scaling method to find the minimum-distortion embedding. Likewise, Lipman and Funkhouser [72] proposed a Mobius voting approach to count transformation votes on triplets of points defined in a conformal flattening embedding. Similarly, Kim et al. [60] defined a blended intrinsic method where the correspondences were extracted from the confidence and consistency of conformal maps.

In general, the matching problem is formulated as an optimization where the variable is an indicator function of matching. Rodola et al. [90] proposed a game-theoretic strategy to solve a quadratic optimization problem of dense correspondences. Interestingly, Rodola et al. [92] introduced the use of sparsity-inducing regularizers to control the density and stability of the found correspondences. On the other hand, Sipiran et al. [104] used hierarchical key-components [105] to split the optimization of a matching problem which is efficiently solved over tree representations.

A common shared characteristic of aforementioned methods is that correspondences are represented as pairs of points between analyzed shapes. Note that this representation is combinatorial and prevents the use of more complex operations on the correspondence map itself. To overcome this problem. Ovsjanikov et al. [81] proposed a new framework to represent and compute shape correspondences. Their method is based on the observation that a map that transfers functions from one shape to another is equivalent to the correspondence map itself. As result, the correspondences can be succinctly represented as a matrix of coefficients (functional map) that has interesting algebraic properties and can be computed efficiently. Nevertheless, a general assumption of a functional map is that analyzed shapes are near-isometric; therefore, this method cannot be applied to non-isometric similar shapes. To deal with this drawback, Kovnatsky et al. [61] and Eynard et al. [36] formulated the problem as a joint diagonalization of the corresponding Laplacians, whose solution was called the coupled quasi-harmonic bases. On the other hand, another drawback of the original formulation of functional maps is the uncertain behavior under partial data and corrupted shapes. In this direction, Litany et al. [73] and Rodola et al. [89] have made important contributions to compute an effective functional map between shapes with missing geometry.

9.3   3D Shape Matching Techniques

The objective of this section is to present both mature and updated material concerning 3D shape matching. We provide detailed descriptions of four approaches: the PANORAMA descriptor, spin images, functional maps for shape matching, and large-scale shape retrieval.

The aforementioned methods address different aspects of shape matching. First, PANORAMA descriptor is a technique suitable for global matching. Second, spin images method is a pioneer in 3D object recognition. Third, functional maps are a solid framework to establish correspondences between 3D models. And finally, Heat Kernel Signatures is an effective surface descriptor to deal with matching under isometric transformations and retrieval.

An important issue to be considered before describing the approaches is shape representation. Although there are many ways to represent a 3D object, boundary representation has mostly been used where objects are represented by a limit surface that distinguishes inside from outside of the object. Moreover, the surface can be approximated in a piece-wise manner, reducing the amount of information needed to represent it at the expense of losing details. The most common way is depicting the surface by a set of points (vertices) and polygons (faces), and in fact, it is preferable to take triangular faces for efficiency and effectiveness in computations involving them. Surprisingly, this representation allows to conceive almost any object with the desired level of detail.

All the techniques presented in this section use triangular meshes for representing shapes.

9.3.1   PANORAMA

PANORAMA [83] is a 3D shape descriptor that extracts features from a set of so-called "panoramic views" from the 3D model. The acronym PANORAMA stands for *PANoramic Object Representation for Accurate Model Attributing*.

9.3.1.1 Process for Computing the PANORAMA Descriptor

For computing the PANORAMA descriptor, there is a three-stage process that consists of

  i. Pose normalization of the 3D model.
 ii. Extraction of the so-called *Panoramic Views*.
iii. Generation of the set of features.

Pose Normalization

For obtaining scale, rotation, and translation invariance, the first step for computing PANORAMA is to normalize the pose of the 3D model. This is accomplished by combining two techniques [117]: Continuous Principal Component Analysis (CPCA) and Normals Principal Component Analysis (NPCA). The main idea behind both methods is to perform a Principal Component Analysis over the 3D model for obtaining its Principal Components. The main difference between the two techniques is the data they used for computing the Principal Components. In the case of CPCA, it uses the surface of the 3D model, considering it as a continuous function. In the case of NPCA, it uses the distribution orientation of the normals of the 3D model. Finally, the 3D model is rotated to align its coordinate axes with the computed Principal Components, thus obtaining a normalized pose.

PANORAMA uses different combinations of these two techniques for its pose normalization process. First, for obtaining translation invariance it uses the CPCA method. Second, for obtaining rotation invariance it uses both CPCA and NCPA, obtaining two different sets of Principal Components. The feature extraction process uses both sets to generate descriptors, which are at the end aggregated for computing a final single descriptor. Finally, for obtaining scale invariance it normalizes the features to the unit L_1 norm.

Panoramic Views

The PANORAMA descriptor is based on the so-called *Panoramic Views*, which are projections of the 3D model to the lateral surface of a cylinder. Let R and H be, respectively, the radius and height of the cylinder. The cylinder is oriented according to one of the axis of the 3D model (after pose normalization), and it is centered at the 3D model's origin. The method defines that $H = 2R$ and that $R = 3 \cdot d_{mean}$, where d_{mean} is "the mean distance of the model's surface from its centroid" [83]. The value of d_{mean} can be computed during the pose normalization. According to the authors of PANORAMA, the empirical value for R ($3 \cdot d_{mean}$) allows most of 3D models to lie completely within the cylinder, and it works better than computing a bounding cylinder for each 3D model.

Next, the method parametrizes the lateral surface of the cylinder. Let B be the rate of sampling (the authors recommend setting $B = 64$). Let $s(\phi, y)$ be a set of points on the surface of the cylinder, with $\phi \in [0, 2\pi]$ and $y \in [0, H]$. Coordinate ϕ is sampled $2B$ times, and coordinate y is sampled B times, thus obtaining $2B^2$ points that discretize the cylinder surface.

Finally, the method computes a value for each point in $s(\phi, y)$. From the axis that crosses the center of the cylinder, at a height coplanar to y, the method casts rays from the center to the surface of the cylinder. These rays capture two features from the 3D model's surface: (i) the maximum distance from the origin to the furthest point of intersection with the model's surface (a value in $[0, R]$) and (ii) the absolute value of the cosine of the angle between the ray and the normal vector of the corresponding triangle in the model's surface to the power of n (according to the authors, the best empirical values for n are in the range of $[4, 6]$).

Therefore, each point of the discretized cylinder allows the method to obtain a pair of values $(s_1(\phi, y), s_2(\phi, y))$, the first corresponding to information of the distance from the surface of the 3D model to the cylinder, and the second corresponding to information of the angle between the cast ray and its corresponding normal on the 3D model. The same process is repeated by aligning a cylinder with all coordinate axes, thus obtaining three sets of points $(s_1(\phi, y), s_2(\phi, y))$ (one for each cylinder).

Feature Computation

During the Panoramic Views step, the method computed six sets of descriptors (three cylinders and two different values per cylinder), which corresponds to a projection of the 3D model to the surface of a cylinder. For each of these projections, the method computes the 2D Discrete Fourier Transform (DFT). Because of symmetry properties of the Fourier Transform, the total number of non-redundant Fourier coefficients is $(B + 1) \cdot \left(\frac{B}{2} + 1\right)$ per projection. The method stores the absolute values of the real and imaginary parts of these coefficients and normalizes the coefficients to the unit L_1 norm. The number of computer features can be reduced by considering only those coefficients located outside an ellipse centered at the Fourier image. The size of the ellipse is chosen so that only about 65% of the high-energy coefficients per projection are taken into account for the descriptor computation. Finally, the resulting coefficients for each projection are aggregated to form a single DFT descriptor.

Similarly, for each cylindrical projection, the method computes the 2D Discrete Wavelet Transform (DWT) for all levels using both the Haar and Coiflet basis functions. The total number of levels is $\log_2(B)$. So, the method computes two sets of features, Haar and Coiflet. These coefficients are normalized to the unit L_1 norm. Next, the method computes for each sub-band in every level of the DWT a set of statistics that includes the mean, the standard deviation, and the skewness of the coefficients, obtaining a total of $18 \cdot \log(B) + 1$ features per cylindrical projection $(3 \cdot \log(B) + 1$ sub-bands times three different statistic values times two different basis functions). The features from all cylindrical projections are aggregated to form a single DWT-based descriptor.

Final Descriptor and Similarity Measure

Each Panoramic View produced different descriptors for the 3D model, but the authors of PANORAMA argue that not all projections are equally discriminative. Indeed, they propose weighting each projection by a factor w_t, which varies depending on the axis used to orient the cylinder. Let the t-cylindrical projection be the one oriented using the tth principal component. The authors determined experimentally the next fixed values for the weights: $w_x = 0.51$, $w_y = 0.31$, and $w_z = 0.18$.

For computing the distance between two 3D models x and y described using PANORAMA, one computes for each projection the distance between the corresponding set of descriptors using the function:

$$dist(x, y) = L_1(x_{DFT}, y_{DFT}) + D_{Canberra}(x_{DWT}, y_{DWT}), \qquad (9.2)$$

where L_1 denotes the Manhattan distance and $D_{Canberra}$ denotes the Canberra distance. Finally, the distance between the 3D models is the minimum value of $dist(x, y)$ among all three-cylinder projections.

9.3.1.2 Complexity Analysis

Let S be a 3D object with n vertices. The complexities for each stage of the method are as follows:

- Pose normalization: $O(n)$ (according to Vranic [117]).
- Computation of Panoramic Views: $O(B^2)$, with B be the rate of sampling of the cylinder.
- Features Computation: $O\left(B^2 \log B\right)$ (dominated by the computation of 2D DFT and 2D DWT).

Thus, the total complexity of this method is $\max\left(O(n), O\left(B^2 \log B\right)\right)$.

9.3.2 Spin Images for Object Recognition

In this section, we describe a 3D object recognition technique with support to occlusion and cluttered scenes. Originally, this work was proposed by Johnson and Hebert [55, 56] for recognizing objects in complex scenes obtained through a structured light range camera in order to be used in robotic systems. This has been recognized as pioneering work in the use of 3D shape matching for computer vision tasks and its relative success has allowed the increasing interest in these kinds of techniques to support high-level vision tasks. Although there exist more recent methods to perform matching with local descriptors, we believe Spin Images deserve our attention as pioneering work that gives good results in object recognition. Broadly speaking, this technique works as follows:

- Given a set of models, we calculate a spin image for each vertex and store them in a huge collection of spin images.
- Given a scene, possibly cluttered and with occlusions, random vertices are selected for which spin images are computed. Thus, we compare these spin images with those previously stored and select possible correspondences.

- Finally, we need to use geometric consistency and a variation of the iterative closest point algorithm to perform correspondences validation and matching.

In order to calculate the spin images for a 3D shape, this technique requires a uniform mesh. By uniform, we mean that distances between adjacent vertices remain close to the median of all distances. In fact, mesh resolution is defined as the median of all edge lengths from the shape. Johnson [55] proposed an efficient algorithm to control the mesh resolution which is based on mesh simplification schemes [43]. In addition, vertices have to be oriented, so each vertex must have an associated normal pointing out toward outside of the shape. We assume that a shape is uniform and each vertex is properly oriented.

To build a spin image of a vertex, we need to build a local basis defined on this vertex, so accumulating the surrounding vertices around the analyzed vertex using the local basis allows us to create a pose invariant local description. In addition, we can control how local this description is; hence, the spin images can be used with large support for alignment and registration tasks and with small support for cluttered recognition.

We denote an oriented point p as a pair $O = (p, \mathbf{n})$ which maintains coordinate information along with the associated normal vector $\mathbf{n}$. The local basis is formed by the following elements:

- The point p.
- The normal $\mathbf{n}$ and the line L through p parallel to $\mathbf{n}$.
- The tangent plane P through p oriented perpendicularly to $\mathbf{n}$.

We can represent any point q in this basis, as shown in Fig. 9.1, through two cylindrical coordinates: α, the perpendicular distance from q to the line L; and β, the signed perpendicular distance from q to the plane P. We define the spin map S_O as a function that projects 3D points q to the local 2D coordinates defined with the previous elements

$$S_O : \mathbb{R}^3 \rightarrow \mathbb{R}^2$$

$$S_O(q) \rightarrow (\alpha, \beta) = (\sqrt{\|q - p\|^2 - (\mathbf{n} \cdot (q - p))^2}, \mathbf{n} \cdot (q - p)) \qquad (9.3)$$

The process of spin image formation uses the function previously defined accumulating points in the (α, β) image coordinate. This can be seen as spinning a matrix around a point's normal and storing the occurrences of surrounding points in the respective coordinates in the matrix. Finally, the spin image looks like an occurrence histogram in the cylindrical coordinate system defined by the local basis.

In order to create a spin image, three useful parameters have to be defined as follows:

- Bin size (bin), spatial extent for the bins in the image.

Fig. 9.1 Local basis for
point p

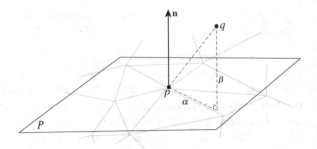

- Image width (W), number of bins in both image directions. Usually, spin images are square.
- Support angle (A_s), the maximum angle between normals for contributing points.

Let $A = (p_A, \mathbf{n_A})$ be an oriented point for which we want to build its spin image. For each oriented point $B = (p_B, \mathbf{n_B})$ on the shape, we use the local basis and the spin map function to obtain the coordinate (α, β). Then, the bin corresponding to that coordinate is given by

$$i = \left\lfloor \frac{\frac{W*bin}{2} - \beta}{bin} \right\rfloor$$

$$j = \left\lfloor \frac{\alpha}{bin} \right\rfloor \tag{9.4}$$

Instead of directly accumulating the occurrence in the respective bin, the authors suggested to use bilinear interpolation and thus accumulate the occurrence in neighboring positions. Therefore, the bilinear weights are calculated as follows:

$$a = \frac{\alpha}{bin} - j$$

$$b = \frac{\frac{W*bin}{2} - \beta}{bin} - i \tag{9.5}$$

With this weights, the image is updated as follows:

$$I(i, j) = I(i, j) + (1 - a)(1 - b)$$

$$I(i, j + 1) = I(i, j + 1) + (1 - a)b$$

$$I(i + 1, j) = I(i + 1, j) + a(1 - b)$$

$$I(i + 1, j + 1) = I(i + 1, j + 1) + ab \tag{9.6}$$

In addition, there is a constraint that the contributing points must hold with respect to the angle between normals. Only points which hold this condition are used in the spin image generation process.

$$acos(\mathbf{n_A}, \mathbf{n_B}) < A_s \tag{9.7}$$

where A_s is the support angle. When A_s is small, a better support to occlusion is provided, as points on the mesh with considerably different directions can be due to occlusion.

In practice, the bin size must be configured to the mesh resolution in order to preserve a good relation between sampling and descriptiveness. Also, in the original experiments carried out by Johnson [55], the image width was 15 and the support angle depends on how much we want to support occlusion; however, a common value in experiments can be 60°. Figure 9.2 shows spin images generated with different values for each parameter.

Once a spin image is calculated for each vertex within a model, these will be stored for matching process. Nevertheless, we need to compare spin images in order to determine possible correspondences. Given two spin images P and Q with N bins each, the cross-correlation can be used to measure their similarity

$$R(P, Q) = \frac{N \sum p_i q_i - \sum p_i \sum q_i}{\sqrt{(N \sum p_i^2 - (\sum p_i)^2)(N \sum q_i^2 - (\sum q_i)^2)}} \tag{9.8}$$

It is easy to note that R is in the range $[-1, 1]$ with high values when the spin images are similar and low values when they are not similar. However, there is a problem when we compare two spin images with this measure. Due to occlusions and cluttered scenes, a spin image often contains more information than others, so for limiting this effect, it is necessary to take only those pixels where data exists. Since the cross-correlation depends on the number of pixels to compute it, the amount of overlap will have effect on the comparison. Obviously, the confidence in the comparison is better when more pixels are used. In addition, the confidence can be measured by its variance, so combining the cross-correlation R and its variance we get a new similarity measure C previously changing the distribution of correlation coefficients by means of the hyperbolic arctangent function which has better statistical properties. As well, the variance is defined in terms of the new distribution.

$$C(P, Q) = (atanh(R(P, Q)))^2 - \lambda \left(\frac{1}{N - 3}\right) \tag{9.9}$$

where N is the number of overlapping pixels (whose values are different from zero), λ is a constant, and R is calculated using the N overlapping pixels. Note that some pixels in the spin images could not contain votes and thus have a value of zero, so it is important to consider only pixels with votes. This measure has a high value

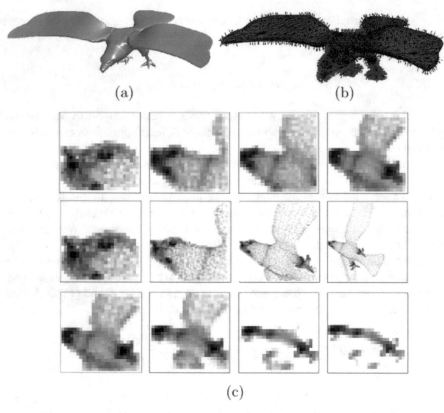

Fig. 9.2 Spin image generation process. **a** Input mesh, **b** mesh with normals, **c** Spin images. At top, the parameters were $W = 25$, $A_s = \pi$, and $bin = \{1, 2, 3, 4\}$ times the mesh resolution. At middle, the parameters were $W = \{25, 50, 100, 200\}$, $A_s = \pi$, and $bin = 1$ times the mesh resolution. At bottom, the parameters were $W = 25$, $bin = 4$ times the mesh resolution, and $A_s = \{\pi, \pi/2, \pi/3, \pi/4\}$. The resolution of the spin images is dependant of W

when the spin images are highly correlated and a large number of pixels overlap. In experiments, λ was configured to 3.

9.3.2.1 Matching

Given a scene, a random set of points is selected for matching. For each point, a set of correspondences is established using spin images from the scene and those calculated from models. Given a point from the scene, we calculate its spin image as previously described, thus this is compared with all the spin images in the huge collection using Eq. 9.9. From the comparison with the stored spin images, a histogram is built quantizing the similarity measure. This histogram maintains the information about occurrences of similarity measures when comparison is being performed and it can be seen as a distribution of similarities between the input spin image and the stored ones. As we are interested in high similarity values, these can be found as outliers in the histogram.

In practice, outliers are found by automatically evaluating the histogram. A standard way to localize outliers is to determine the fourth spread of the histogram defined as the difference between the median of the largest $N/2$ measurements and the median of the smallest $N/2$ measurements. Let f_s be the fourth spread, extreme outliers are $3f_s$ units above the median of the largest $N/2$ measurements. Note that with this method, the number of outliers can be greater than or equal to zero, so many correspondences per point can be found.

Once we have the set of correspondences for each point on the scene, we need to organize them in order to recognize the correct model object in the scene. As a large amount of correspondences have been detected, it is necessary to filter them out. Firstly, correspondences with similarity measure less than the half of the maximum similarity are discarded. Secondly, by using geometric consistency, it is possible to eliminate bad correspondences. Given two correspondences $C_1 = (s_1, m_1)$ and $C_2 = (s_2, m_2)$, the geometric consistency is defined as follows:

$$d_{gc}(C_1, C_2) = 2 \frac{\|S_{m_2}(m_1) - S_{s_2}(s_1)\|}{\|S_{m_2}(m_1) + S_{s_2}(s_1)\|}$$

$$D_{gc}(C_1, C_2) = max(d_{gc}(C_1, C_2), d_{gc}(C_2, C_1)) \qquad (9.10)$$

where $S_O(p)$ denotes the spin map function of point p using the local basis of point O, as defined in Eq. 9.3.

This geometric consistency measures the consistency in position and normals. D_{gc} is small when C_1 and C_2 are geometrically consistent. By using geometric consistency, correspondences which are not geometrically consistent with at least a quarter of the complete list of correspondences are eliminated. The final set of correspondences has a high probability of being correct, but it is still necessary to group and verify them.

Now, we group correspondences in order to calculate a good transformation and hence do the matching. A grouping measure is used which prioritizes correspondences that are far apart. The grouping measure is defined as

$$w_{gc}(C_1, C_2) = \frac{d_{gc}(C_1, C_2)}{1 - \exp(-(\|S_{m_2}(m_1)\| + \|S_{s_2}(s_1)\|)/2)}$$

$$W_{gc}(C_1, C_2) = max(w_{gc}(C_1, C_2), w_{gc}(C_2, C_1)) \qquad (9.11)$$

The same measure can also be defined between a correspondence C and a group of correspondences $\{C_1, C_2, \ldots, C_n\}$ as follows:

$$W_{gc}(C, \{C_1, C_2, \ldots, C_n\}) = max_i(W_{gc}(C, C_i)) \qquad (9.12)$$

Therefore, given a set of possible correspondences $L = \{C_1, C_2, \ldots, C_n\}$, the following algorithm has to be used for generating groups:

- For each correspondence $C_i \in L$, initialize a group $G_i = \{C_i\}$

  - Find a correspondence $C_j \in L - G_i$, such that $W_{gc}(C_j, G_i)$ is minimum. If $W_{gc}(C_j, G_i) < T_{gc}$ then update $G_i = G_i \cup \{C_j\}$. T_{gc} is set between zero and one. If T_{gc} is small, only geometrically consistent correspondences remain. A commonly used value is 0.25.
  - Continue until no more correspondences can be added.

As a result, we have n groups, which are used as starting point for final matching. For each group of correspondences $\{(m_i, s_i)\}$, a rigid transformation T is calculated by minimizing the following error using least-squares method:

$$E_T = \min_T \sum \|s_i - T(m_i)\|^2 \qquad (9.13)$$

where $T(m_i) = R(m_i) + t$, R and t are the rotation matrix and the translation vector, representing the rotation and position of the viewpoint s_i in the coordinate system of m_i.

As a last step, each transformation needs to be verified in order to be validated as a matching. The model points in the correspondences are transformed using T. For each point in the scene and the correspondences set, we extend correspondences for neighboring points in both points of a correspondence under a distance constraint. A threshold distance equal to twice the mesh resolution is used. If the final set of correspondences is greater than a quarter or a third of the number of vertices of the model, the transformation is considered valid and the matching is accepted. Finally, with the final correspondences set, the transformation is refined by using an iterative closest point algorithm.

9.3.2.2 Evaluation

Unfortunately, in the original work by Johnson [55], the models used in experiments were obtained using a scanner and they are not available to date. Johnson and Hebert [56] presented results trying to measure the robustness of their method against clutter and occlusion. They built 100 scenes involving four shapes, using a range scanner. The experiments were based on querying an object in a scene and determining if the object was present or not. In addition, the levels of occlusion and clutter were also determined.

The four shapes were used in each scene, so the number of runs was 400. Interestingly, there were no errors at levels of occlusion under 70% and the rate of recognition was above 90% at 80% of occlusion. In addition, the recognition rate was greater than 80% at levels of clutter under 60%.

Spin images have also been evaluated in the Robust Feature Detection and Description Benchmark [14] (SHREC 2010 track). In this track, the goal was to evaluate

Table 9.1 Robustness results for Spin Images. Each value indicates the normalized Euclidean distance between descriptors as defined in Eq. 9.14 (Taken from Bronstein et al. [14]. 2010 Eurographics)

Transform.	Strength				
	1	≤2	≤3	≤4	≤5
Isometry	0.12	0.10	0.10	0.10	0.10
Topology	0.11	0.11	0.11	0.11	0.11
Holes	0.12	0.12	0.12	0.12	0.12
Micro holes	0.15	0.15	0.16	0.16	0.16
Scale	0.18	0.15	0.15	0.15	0.15
Local scale	0.12	0.13	0.14	0.15	0.17
Sampling	0.13	0.13	0.13	0.13	0.15
Noise	0.13	0.15	0.17	0.19	0.20
Shot noise	0.11	0.13	0.16	0.17	0.18
Average	0.13	0.13	0.14	0.14	0.15

the robustness of the descriptors against mesh transformations such as isometry, topology, holes, micro holes, scale, local scale, sampling, noise, and shot noise. The dataset consisted of three shapes taken from the TOSCA dataset [13]. Subsequently, several transformations, in different levels, were applied to each shape. The resulting dataset contained 138 shapes. In addition, a set of correspondences was available in order to measure the distance between descriptors in corresponding points.

The evaluation was performed using the normalized euclidean distance between the descriptors of corresponding points of two shapes X and Y,

$$Q(X, Y) = \frac{1}{|F(X)|} \sum_{k=1}^{|F(X)|} \frac{\|f(y_k) - g(x_j)\|_2}{\|f(y_k)\|_2 + \|g(x_j)\|_2}, \qquad (9.14)$$

where (x_j, y_k) are corresponding points, $f(\cdot)$ and $g(\cdot)$ are the descriptors in a point, and $F(X)$ is the set of vertices to be considered. Here, we present the results obtained using $F(X) = X$.

The best results were obtained for isometry and topology transformation with 0.10 and 0.11 average distance, respectively. This is because spin images were extracted locally, and these transformations do not modify the local structure of the mesh. On the other hand, the noise and shot noise transformations got higher distances (up to 0.20 and 0.18, respectively). It is clear that higher levels of noise modify considerably the distribution of points on the surface, so spin images are not constructed robustly. See Tables 9.1 and 9.2 for the complete results. Table 9.2 shows the performance for dense heat kernel signatures calculated on 3D meshes. Clearly, regarding robustness, spin images show some drawbacks. However, an important aspect of this approach is its support to occlusion. In that sense, its application in recognition has been proved.

Table 9.2 Robustness results for Dense Heat Kernel Signatures. Each value indicates the normalized Euclidean distance between descriptors as defined in Eq. 9.14 (Taken from Bronstein et al. [14]. 2009 Eurographics)

Transform.	Strength				
	1	≤ 2	≤ 3	≤ 4	≤ 5
Isometry	0.01	0.01	0.01	0.01	0.01
Topology	0.02	0.02	0.02	0.02	0.02
Holes	0.02	0.02	0.02	0.03	0.03
Micro holes	0.01	0.01	0.01	0.01	0.02
Scale	0.25	0.15	0.13	0.14	0.16
Local scale	0.02	0.03	0.05	0.07	0.10
Sampling	0.02	0.02	0.02	0.02	0.02
Noise	0.03	0.06	0.09	0.12	0.15
Shot noise	0.01	0.01	0.02	0.02	0.02
Average	0.04	0.04	0.04	0.05	0.06

More recently, Guo et al. [47] presented a thorough evaluation of 3D local description methods with respect to five criteria: descriptiveness, compactness, robustness, scalability, and efficiency. The methods evaluated were Spin Images [55], 3D shape context [40], Unique shape context [115], Rotational projection statistic [48], Tri-spin image [49], Local surface patch [26], Thrift [39], Point feature histogram [97], Fast point feature histogram [96], and Signature of histogram of orientations [116]. The experiments showed the effectiveness of the evaluated methods under several scenarios such as retrieval and recognition. The evaluation also showed that every descriptor has its own strengths and weaknesses depending on the kind of data and the application.

9.3.2.3 Complexity Analysis

Let S be a 3D object with n vertices. In addition, let W be the number of rows and columns of a resulting spin image (we assume square spin images for the analysis). The complexity of each stage is given as follows:

- Computation of spin images for each vertex: $O(n^2)$. Given a vertex, each vertex on the mesh is mapped onto its spin image.
- Find the initial set of correspondences: $O(nPW^2)$, where P is the number of spin images in the collection. For each vertex on the query object, the cross-correlation is calculated with respect to each spin image in the collection.
- Filter the correspondences: $O(n^2)$.
- Group the correspondences: $O(n^2)$. For each correspondence, a group is computed by applying the W_{gc} measure.
- Find the transformation using least-square method: $O(n)$.
- Validation: $O(n)$.

The total complexity is dominated by the process of finding the initial set of correspondences. This is because $P \gg n$, so the complexity of this method is $O(nPW^2)$.

9.3.3   Functional Maps

Let M and N be 3D shapes and let $T : M \to N$ be a map that computes the correspondence in N for each point in M. The matching problem is the computation of the map T with shapes M and N as inputs. If the input shapes are discrete representations of 3D surfaces (triangular meshes, for example), the map T is commonly represented as a set of corresponding points $\{(m, n)\} \in M \times N$ such that $T(m) = n$. In practice, a more realistic criterion to search a good map is to minimize the distortion d of the map; therefore, the matching problem can be stated as

$$T^* = \arg\min_T \sum_m d(T(m), n) \tag{9.15}$$

where (m, n) is a corresponding point.

Note that the map T can be used to transfer information from shape M to shape N. For example, let us define a function $f : M \to \mathbb{R}$, on the surface of M, then we could use T to transfer the function from M to N. Let $g : N \to \mathbb{R}$ be the function that results from transferring f, we thus have

$$g = f \circ T^{-1} \tag{9.16}$$

If $(m, n) \in T$, then it holds that $g(n) = f(T^{-1}(n)) = f(m)$. We denote as $T_F : \mathcal{F}(M, \mathbb{R}) \to \mathcal{F}(N, \mathbb{R})$ the *functional map* that transfers real-valued functions defined on M to real-valued functions defined on N, where $T_F(f) = f \circ T^{-1}$. A nice property of T_F is the linearity over the corresponding function spaces. That is, given a bijective map $T : M \to N$, the following holds:

$$T_F(\alpha_1 f_1 + \alpha_2 f_2) = (\alpha_1 f_1 + \alpha_2 f_2) \circ T^{-1} = \alpha_1 f_1 \circ T^{-1} + \alpha_2 f_2 \circ T^{-1}$$
$$= \alpha_1 T_F(f_1) + \alpha_2 T_F(f_2) \tag{9.17}$$

In addition, if M is equipped with a basis $\{\phi_i^M\}$ such that any function $f : M \to \mathbb{R}$ can be represented as a linear combination of basis functions $f = \sum_i a_i \phi_i^M$ (see Fig. 9.3), then

$$T_F(f) = T_F\left(\sum_i a_i \phi_i^M\right) = \sum_i a_i T_F(\phi_i^M). \tag{9.18}$$

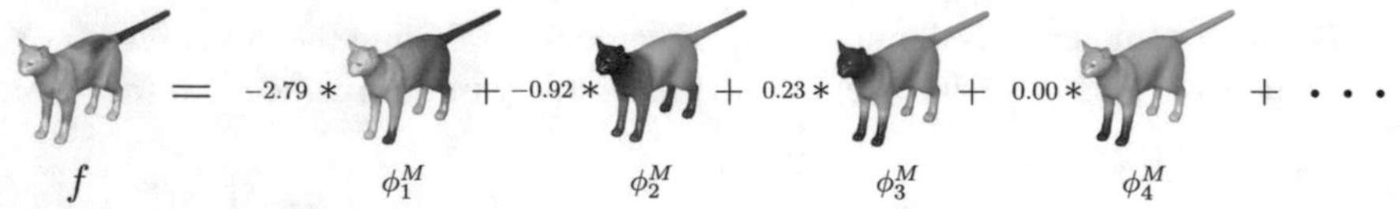

Fig. 9.3 Mean curvature (function defined on the surface of an object) represented as a linear combination of basis functions. The plot shows the eigenfunctions of the Laplace–Beltrami operator and the corresponding coefficients obtained in the decomposition. Shape was taken from the TOSCA dataset [13]

Furthermore, if N is also equipped with a basis $\{\phi_j^N\}$, then

$$T_F(\phi_i^M) = \sum_j c_{ji}\phi_j^N \tag{9.19}$$

It follows that

$$T_F(f) = \sum_i a_i \sum_j c_{ji}\phi_j^N = \sum_j \left(\sum_i a_i c_{ji}\right)\phi_j^N \tag{9.20}$$

Note that if f and g are represented as a vector of coefficients $\mathbf{a} = \{a_0, a_1, \ldots, a_i, \ldots\}$ and $\mathbf{b} = \{b_0, b_1, \ldots, b_j, \ldots\}$, respectively, coefficients $\mathbf{b}$ can be computed as $b_j = \sum_i a_i c_{ji}$, and therefore the functional map T_F can be represented as a matrix C such that $T_F(\mathbf{a}) = C\mathbf{a}$. In practice, the summations are truncated to the number k of basis elements used to represent the functions, and therefore $C \in \mathbb{R}^{k \times k}$.

9.3.3.1 Choice of Basis

The effective computation of a functional map depends on the basis we choose to find the matrix C. In general, the set of basis functions must be compact and stable. The basis must be compact because we are interested in representing functions approximately well with a few elements in the basis. On the other hand, the basis must be stable because the space of functions spanned from all the linear combinations of basis functions must be robust to small deformations in the surface.

In particular in shape matching, we would like to deal with isometric deformations, so a good choice is to take the first k eigenvalues and eigenvectors of the Laplace–Beltrami operator of the shape.

9.3.3.2 Inference of Functional Maps

The ideas around the functional map formulation translate the original shape matching problem to the effective computation of the matrix C from functions defined over the surfaces to match. Given two functions $f : M \to \mathbb{R}$ and $g : N \to \mathbb{R}$ represented as vector of coefficients $\mathbf{a}$ and $\mathbf{b}$, respectively, the correspondence between f and g can be written as

$$\mathbf{Ca} = \mathbf{b} \tag{9.21}$$

Moreover, we can generalize to any number of functions which can be stacked in a matrix notation, and we obtain the general equation $CA = B$. To effectively compute C, we can solve the above equation in a least-square sense

$$E_1(C) = \|CA - B\|_2^2 \tag{9.22}$$

A natural additional constraint is to allow the functional map to commute with linear operators over the space of functions, such as the Laplace–Beltrami operator. Let Λ^M and Λ^N be the functional representation of the Laplace–Beltrami operator of M and N, respectively, it is expected that $\Lambda^N C = C\Lambda^M$. In the least-square sense, we have

$$E_2(C) = \|\Lambda^N C - C\Lambda^M\|_2^2 \tag{9.23}$$

Finally, the functional map is the solution to the following optimization problem:

$$C^* = \arg\min_C E_1(C) + E_2(C) = \|CA - B\|_2^2 + \rho\|\Lambda^N C - C\Lambda^M\|_2^2 \tag{9.24}$$

where the solution can be found using a least-square minimization.

9.3.3.3 Conversion to Correspondences

The functional map C encodes the map between two shapes M and N. However, we need to compute the correspondences from the functional map. Let us suppose we want to get the correspondence of a point $x \in M$. The first step is to build an indicator function (or a highly peaked Gaussian around x). The second step is to use the functional map C to compute the destination function $g(\cdot)$ on N and finally select the point $y \in N$ such that $g(y)$ is maximum (Fig. 9.4). Nevertheless, if we apply this method for each point in M, the computation of the complete set of correspondences will take a quadratic complexity.

A more efficient method can be devised if we carefully observe the heat kernel defined on a point $x \in M$ in a given time t

$$k_t^M(x, \cdot) = \sum_i^\infty e^{-t\lambda_i} \phi_i^M(x)\phi_i^M(\cdot) \tag{9.25}$$

where λ_i and ϕ_i are the ith eigenvalue and eigenvector of the Laplace–Beltrami operator of M. The delta function δ_x in a point $x \in M$, which is a good indicator function to compute the correspondence, can be defined using the heat kernel as

Fig. 9.4 Left: Gaussian function defined on the geodesic distances to a source point. Right: Gaussian function transferred to the target shape. Note that we used the functional map between the shapes to transfer the function. Shapes were taken from the TOSCA dataset [13]

$\delta_x = \lim_{t \to 0^+} k_t^M(x, \cdot)$. Therefore, the delta function can be represented as the linear combination

$$\delta_x = \phi_0^M(x)\phi_0^M + \phi_1^M(x)\phi_1^M + \phi_2^M(x)\phi_2^M + \cdots \qquad (9.26)$$

It means that the functional representation of δ_x is the vector $\mathbf{x}$ with coefficients $(\phi_0^M(x), \phi_1^M(x), \phi_2^M(x), \ldots)$, and moreover we can compute the destination delta function on N by computing $C\mathbf{x}^T$, which in turn must have a functional representation in the shape N. Observe that we can compute all the destination delta functions for points in M by computing $C\Phi^M$, where matrix Φ^M contains the eigenfunctions of M in each row. Accordingly, if the matrix Φ^N contains the eigenfunctions of N in each row, the correspondence for point in M is the nearest neighbor of $C\Phi^M$ in Φ^N. Using a data structure to perform proximity queries, the correspondence search can be linear logarithmic in complexity.

The previous analysis also elucidates a way to refine the functional map C. Once we compute the functional map with Eq. 9.24, we would expect that the functional map C is a good transformation of Φ^M to Φ^N. We can use this observation to refine the functional map to fit such transformation. It is convenient to see that C works as a rotation matrix of Φ^M, and therefore we can use a ICP-like algorithm to iteratively refine the matrix C. The algorithm start with $C_0 = C$ and it iteratively finds the nearest neighbors between $C_i\Phi^M$ and Φ^N and subsequently it computes C_{i+1} as the rotation matrix that minimizes the distances between corresponding coefficients in the functional representations. Figure 9.5 shows an example of matching between two shapes using the algorithm described in this section.

Fig. 9.5 Left: Source shape with a color function on the surface. Center: Target shape with the color function transferred by using the functional map computed using the described method. Right: Correspondences extracted from the functional map using the ICP-like algorithm. Shapes were taken from the TOSCA dataset [13]

9.3.3.4   Implementation

Given two triangular meshes M and N with m and n vertices, respectively, we compute a vertex-wise descriptor. Although any vertex descriptor would be useful, we follow the choice of the original method to use the Wave Kernel Signature. The result of the description is a matrix $W_{m \times d}^M$ and a matrix $W_{n \times d}^N$ with rows representing a point descriptor of dimension d. In practice, we can use more than one descriptor for the inference of the functional map by concatenating the descriptors for each vertex. For the optimization, we need the functional representation of the descriptor, that is, the coefficients of the linear combination of basis functions to produce the input descriptor. Note that the functional decomposition $f = \sum_{i=0}^{k} a_i \phi_i$ can be expressed in matrix notation as follows:

$$
(\phi_0 \, \phi_1 \, \phi_2 \, \ldots \, \phi_{k-1}) \begin{pmatrix} a_0 \\ a_1 \\ a_2 \\ \vdots \\ a_{k-1} \end{pmatrix} = f \tag{9.27}
$$

where ϕ_i and f are functions defined over a triangular mesh; therefore, they are column vectors with the number of vertices as dimension. This matrix notation can be easily generalized to vector-valued functions

$$
\Phi A = F \tag{9.28}
$$

where Φ is the matrix of basis functions (as columns), A is the matrix of coefficients and F is the matrix of descriptors. Note that we have now a linear system and we want to find A. We can take advantage of the linear independence of the basis functions to solve the linear system above as follows:

$$A = \Phi^+ F \tag{9.29}$$

where Φ^+ is the pseudo-inverse of matrix Φ. In this way, we can compute matrices A and B in Eq. 9.24

For the second term of the optimization, we need to compute the Laplace–Beltrami operator for the given shapes. Let Δ_M and Δ_N be the matrix representation of the operators. The functional representation of operators is diagonal matrices composed of the eigenvalues of the Laplace–Beltrami operator. If we only consider k basis functions, the problem to optimize is

$$\|C_{k\times k} A_{k\times d} - B_{k\times d}\|_2^2 + \rho \|\Lambda_{k\times k}^N C_{k\times k} - C_{k\times k} \Lambda_{k\times k}^M\|_2^2 \tag{9.30}$$

where A and B are the d-dimensional descriptors in functional representation (as computed in Eq. 9.29), Λ^N and Λ^M are diagonal matrices with the eigenvalues of the Laplace–Beltrami operators. As we are interested in solving the above problem as a least-square problem, we need to slightly modify the first term. Note that the following formulation is equivalent:

$$\|(A^T)_{d\times k} (C^T)_{k\times k} - (B^T)_{d\times k}\|_2^2 + \rho \|(C^T)_{k\times k} \Lambda_{k\times k}^N - \Lambda_{k\times k}^M (C^T)_{k\times k}\|_2^2 \tag{9.31}$$

To numerically solve the optimization problem with least-squares, we need to represent it as a linear system $Ax = B$, where the constraints go in the matrices A and B and the solution we search is x. Therefore, the first step is to represent the matrix C^T as a column vector by concatenating its columns. Let us denote this column vector as $\mathbf{c}$. The matrices of constraint have two parts because of the terms involved in the optimization. First, we build the matrix $\mathbf{A}$ which is organized as follows:

$$\begin{pmatrix} A^T & \mathbf{0} & \mathbf{0} & \dots \\ \mathbf{0} & A^T & \mathbf{0} & \dots \\ \mathbf{0} & \mathbf{0} & A^T & \dots \\ \vdots & \vdots & \vdots & \vdots \end{pmatrix} \tag{9.32}$$

The matrix A^T is replicated as many times as columns in the matrix C^T. The bold zero denotes a zero matrix with the same size of A^T. Taking into account the dimensions we used in Eq. 9.31, matrix $\mathbf{A}$ has $d \times k$ rows and k^2 columns. Accordingly, we rearrange the matrix B^T in a column vector in the same way we did with matrix C^T. Let us denote as $\mathbf{b}$ the column vector representation of B^T, and therefore the first term of the optimization problem can be stated as

$$\mathbf{Ac} = \mathbf{b} \tag{9.33}$$

The second step is to rearrange the operator commutativity constraint accordingly. Recall that the functional representation of the Laplace–Beltrami operator is a diagonal matrix with the eigenvalues of the operator as elements. Without loss of generality, we use the notation of eigenvalues $\{\lambda_i^M\}$ and $\{\lambda_j^N\}$ to introduce the commutativity constraints in the linear system. After rearranging the matrix C^T as a column vector, the resulting linear constraints can be represented by a diagonal matrix $\mathbf{L}$ of dimension $k^2 \times k^2$, where the ith element can be calculated as

$$l_i = \lambda_{(i \bmod k)}^M - \lambda_{(i/k)}^N \tag{9.34}$$

where the index i/k takes the integer division of the values. Therefore, the commutativity constraint can be written as

$$\mathbf{Lc} = \mathbf{0} \tag{9.35}$$

where $\mathbf{c}$ is the column vectorization of C^T and $\mathbf{0}$ is a column vector of zeros with the right dimension to accommodate the system.

Finally, the linear system of equation to solve is defined as

$$\begin{pmatrix} \frac{\mathbf{A}}{\|A\|_\infty} \\ \rho \frac{\mathbf{L}}{\|L\|_\infty} \end{pmatrix} \mathbf{c} = \begin{pmatrix} \frac{\mathbf{B}}{\|B\|_\infty} \\ \mathbf{0} \end{pmatrix} \tag{9.36}$$

The normalization by the L_∞ norm is to deal with the scale of the matrices and it also facilitates the setup of parameter ρ. The solution to this system is the vectorized version of C^T, and therefore we must take care of the right rearrangement of the solution matrix C.

9.3.3.5   Experiments

We use the cotangent scheme for the computation of the Laplace–Beltrami operator on the input shapes [77]. For the sake of completeness, we briefly explain how to compute the Laplace Beltrami operator of a shape.

Given a 3D mesh, we can calculate the discrete Laplace–Beltrami operator in each vertex with the cotangent scheme proposed by Meyer et al. [77]:

$$K(p_i) = \frac{1}{2A_i} \sum_{p_j \in N_1(p_i)} (\cot \alpha_{ij} + \cot \beta_{ij})(p_i - p_j) \tag{9.37}$$

where A_i is the Voronoi region area around p_i, α_{ij} and β_{ij} are the angles opposite to the arc $\overline{p_i p_j}$ and $N_1(p_i)$ is the set of p_i's adjacent vertices. See Fig. 9.6 for details.

The computation of A_i, the Voronoi region around a vertex p_i, must be performed as follows. We accumulate a region for each adjacent face T to p_i, if T is non-obtuse

Fig. 9.6 Neighborhood
configuration around p_i. The
dashed lines enclose the
Voronoi region used in
computing the
Laplace–Beltrami operator

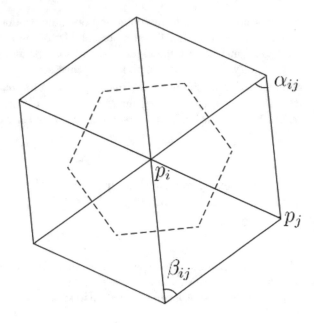

we add the Voronoi region for that face by using Eq. 9.38. If T is obtuse, we add
$area(T)/2$ if the angle of T in p_i is obtuse, or $area(T)/4$ otherwise.

$$A_T = \frac{1}{8} \sum_{j \in N_1(i)} (\cot \alpha_{ij} + \cot \beta_{ij}) \| p_i - p_j \|^2 \tag{9.38}$$

To numerically compute the Laplace–Beltrami operator, a matrix can be calculated
in the following way:

$$L_{ij} = \begin{cases} -\frac{\cot \alpha_{ij} + \cot \beta_{ij}}{2A_i} & \text{if } p_i \text{ is adjacent to } p_j \\ \sum_k \frac{\cot \alpha_{ik} + \cot \beta_{kj}}{2A_i} & \text{if } p_i = p_j \\ 0 & \text{otherwise,} \end{cases} \tag{9.39}$$

where p_k are the vertices adjacent to p_i.

We are interested in the eigenvalues and eigenvectors of this matrix. Thus, the
problem to be solved is

$$L\phi = \lambda\phi \tag{9.40}$$

However, it is clear to note that L might not be symmetric. This is to say, $L_{ij} \neq L_{ji}$ when $A_i \neq A_j$, which is very likely. Nevertheless, it can be represented as a
generalized eigenvalue problem where $L = S^{-1}M$. Then, we have

$$M\phi = \lambda S\phi \tag{9.41}$$

with

$$
M_{ij} = \begin{cases} -\dfrac{\cot \alpha_{ij} + \cot \beta_{ij}}{2} & \text{if } p_i \text{ is adjacent to } p_j \\ \sum_k \dfrac{\cot \alpha_{ik} + \cot \beta_{kj}}{2} & \text{if } p_i = p_j \\ 0 & \text{otherwise} \end{cases} \tag{9.42}
$$

and

$$
S_{ij} = \begin{cases} A_i & \text{if } i = j \\ 0 & \text{otherwise} \end{cases} \tag{9.43}
$$

The solution to this problem ensures that the eigenvalues and eigenvectors are real. In addition, two eigenvectors ϕ_i and ϕ_j corresponding to different eigenvalues λ_i and λ_j are orthogonal with respect to the S dot-product:

$$
\phi_i \cdot \phi_j = \phi_i^T S \phi_j = 0, \ i \neq j \tag{9.44}
$$

The shape spectrum is the set of eigenvalues $\{\lambda_0, \lambda_1, \lambda_2, ..., \lambda_{n-1}\}$. If the shape is closed, $\lambda_0 = 0$.

For our experiments, we compute the $k = 100$ first eigenvalues and eigenvectors of the Laplace–Beltrami. The eigenvectors are used as basis functions of input shapes. For the computation of the functional maps, we use the Wave Kernel Signature as point descriptor [2]. We also use a complementary descriptor for segments to introduce invariance to symmetric flips. We first segment each input shape using the consensus method proposed in [91] and describe each segment with the sum of the WKS descriptors of points in the segment. Subsequently, candidate pairs of matched segment are used to build functional constraints using the Heat Kernel Map. Figure 9.7 shows the result of computing the functional map and the subsequent correspondences in several objects with non-rigid transformations from the TOSCA dataset [13]. Figure 9.8 shows the application of functional maps in the transfer of regions between isometric shapes.

9.3.3.6 Complexity Analysis

Let M and N be two shapes with m and n vertices, respectively. Let k be the number of eigenfunctions used to compute the functional map. In addition, let d be the dimension of the local descriptors used for the optimization constraints. We split the complexity analysis into two parts: the computation of the functional map and the discovery of correspondences from the functional map. For the inference of the functional map, note that the final linear system of equations in Eq. 9.36 has $d \times k + k^2$ equations and k^2 unknowns. To simplify our analysis, we assume $d = O(k)$ and therefore the system has $O(k^2)$ equations and k^2 unknowns. Typical solvers are in the order of $O(n^3)$, where n is the number of unknowns. Therefore, the computation of the functional map is in the order of $O(k^5)$.

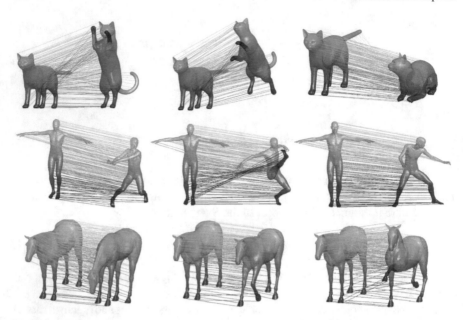

Fig. 9.7 Correspondences found after computing the functional map between pair of shapes. The color function has also been transferred from source shape to target shape. Shapes were taken from the TOSCA dataset [13]

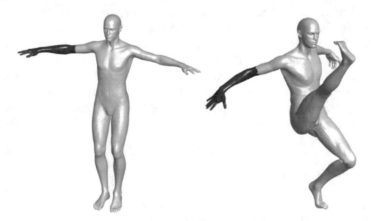

Fig. 9.8 Segmentation transfer between shapes with isometric transformation. Left: we select a region of the mesh using an editing software and export the segment indicator function. Right: the indicator function is transferred to the target shape using the functional maps computed between input shapes. Shapes were taken from the TOSCA dataset [13]

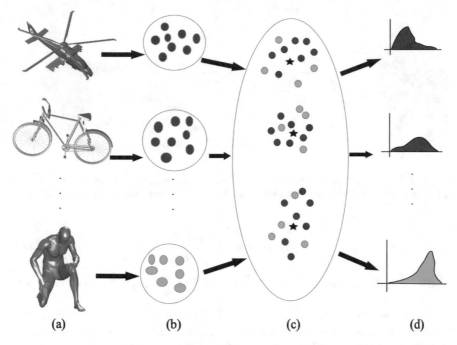

(a)   (b)   (c)   (d)

Fig. 9.9 Process to obtain a descriptor for a shape using the heat kernel signatures and bag-of-features. **a** Input shape, **b** local descriptors (heat kernel signatures) are extracted, **c** clustering of descriptor space (black stars are centroids of resulting clusters), and **d** Vector quantization, using local descriptors and clusters, results in shape descriptors

For the search of correspondences, for each point in $C\Phi^M$, we need to find the closest point in Φ^N. Using a spatial index to speed up the computation of nearest neighbor searches, this task takes $O(n \log n + m \log n)$.

9.3.4 Shape Retrieval with Heat Kernel Signatures

We observed in the previous approach the importance and applicability of the Laplace–Beltrami operator and its spectrum in shape description tasks. In this section, we describe the application of heat kernel signatures which are based on the intimate relation among the heat diffusion process and the Laplace–Beltrami operator. In addition, the presented technique utilizes a widely used approach for describing information entities based on their components and frequencies known as Bag-of-features [82]. Figure 9.9 summarizes the approach.

The heat diffusion process over a compact manifold S, possibly with boundary, is governed by the heat equation

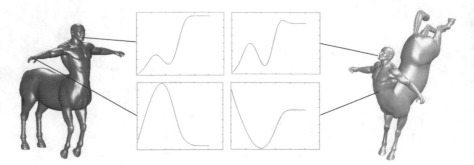

Fig. 9.10 Heat kernel signatures calculated on two isometric shapes. At top, signatures in corresponding points look very similar. At bottom, signatures in different points on the mesh differ

$$\Delta_S u(x, t) = -\frac{\partial u(x, t)}{\partial t} \tag{9.45}$$

where Δ_S is the Laplace–Beltrami operator of S and $u(., t)$ is the heat distribution over S in time t.

The fundamental solution of Eq. 9.45 is $K_t(x, y)$ called the heat kernel. This represents a solution with a point heat source in x and can be considered as the amount of heat transferred from x to y at time t supposing that the heat source is x. For compact manifolds, the heat kernel can be expressed using the eigenvalues and eigenvectors of the Laplace–Beltrami operator as follows:

$$K_t(x, y) = \sum_{i=0}^{\infty} \exp(-\lambda_i t)\mathbf{v_i}(x)\mathbf{v_i}(y) \tag{9.46}$$

where λ_i is the ith eigenvalue and $\mathbf{v_i}(\cdot)$ is the ith eigenvector's entry corresponding to a given point.

Sun et al. [110] formally proved that the heat kernel is isometric invariant, informative (enough, redundant information exists), multi-scale, and stable against perturbations on the surface. In addition, restricting the heat kernel to the temporal domain and fixing the spatial variables, we can obtain a representation for each point on the manifold:

$$K_t(x, x) = \sum_{i=0}^{\infty} \exp(-\lambda_i t)\mathbf{v_i}(x)^2 \tag{9.47}$$

Figure 9.10 shows heat kernel signatures for two isometric shapes. Given a shape S, we need to calculate the heat kernel signature for point on S. In practice, the heat kernel signature of a point $x \in S$ is a n-dimensional descriptor vector with each bin corresponding to some value of t:

$$p(x) = (p_1(x), \ldots, p_n(x)) \tag{9.48}$$

$$p_i(x) = c(x)K_{\alpha^{i-1}t_0}(x, x) \tag{9.49}$$

where $c(x)$ must be selected in order to have $\|p(x)\|_2 = 1$. Note that we need to restrict the number of eigenvalues and eigenvector to be considered in Eq. 9.47. As a result, we obtain a descriptor for each vertex on the mesh.

Once we compute the descriptors for each shape in the database, these must be grouped in a huge collection of local descriptors, which will be called the descriptor space. Next, it is necessary to quantize the n-dimensional descriptors space. The idea is to find a point set in the descriptor space in order to better cluster the whole descriptor set. Unsupervised techniques from machine learning field can be used such as k-means and its variants [34]. In order to make this section self-contained, we briefly describe k-means clustering on the descriptor space.

Let D be the huge set of n-dimensional descriptors and k be the number of clusters we want to find. The algorithm can be summarized as follows:

1. **Initial centroids selection:** Select k points in the n-dimensional space. This step can be performed in different ways, for instance, selecting random points in the n-dimensional space, selecting random descriptors from D, or using information about the distribution of descriptors in D, just to name a few. Let $M = (m_1, \ldots, m_k)$ be the set of selected centroids.
2. **Cluster assignment:** Assign each descriptor in D to the closest cluster C_i

$$C_i = \{d \in D : \|d - m_i\| \leq \|d - m_j\|, \forall j = 1 \ldots k\} \tag{9.50}$$

3. **Centroids update:** Compute the new centroids for each cluster

$$m_i = \frac{1}{|C_i|} \sum_{d \in C_i} d \tag{9.51}$$

4. **Stop criterion:** If centroids remain unchanged after update step, stop, and return M. Go to step 2, otherwise.

Using the set of centroids M and the heat kernel signatures previously calculated for a shape P, we need to compute a single descriptor for P, so it is necessary to combine the local descriptor in a shape descriptor. To tackle this issue, we calculate the feature distribution in a vertex $x \in P$ as $\theta(x) = (\theta_1(x), \ldots, \theta_k(x))^T$ where

$$\theta_i(x) = c(x) \exp\left(\frac{-\|p(x) - m_i\|_2}{2\sigma^2}\right) \tag{9.52}$$

where $c(x)$ is a constant selected such that $\|\theta(x)\|_2 = 1$, $p(x)$ is the heat kernel signature of x, m_i is the centroid of cluster C_i, and σ is constant. Each bin in $\theta(x)$ can be considered as the probability that x belongs to the cluster corresponding to such bin. This is a soft version of quantization because the classic bag-of-features approach considers placing a one in the bin corresponding to the closest cluster and zeros in the rest. Although the classic way can be performed here, the soft version has proved to be effective in experiments.

To obtain a shape descriptor, the feature distributions are simply added to obtain a shape descriptor of size k, the vocabulary size:

$$f(S) = \sum_{x \in S} \theta(x) \tag{9.53}$$

and the matching between two shapes S and T is performed by using the L_1 distance

$$d(S, T) = \| f(S) - f(T) \|_1 \tag{9.54}$$

Nevertheless, during the quantization process, the spatial information is lost. Obviously, this information could be useful in the matching process. Sipiran et al. [107] proposed representing the 3D shape by *feature signatures*, which can take into account the spatial information of the local descriptors. The problem is now finding an appropriate distance function for comparing two 3D shapes from their respective feature signatures.

9.3.4.1 Feature Signatures and the Signature Quadratic Form Distance

The Signature Quadratic Form Distance (SQFD) was proposed by Beecks et al. [4]. Originally, this distance measure was designed as a flexible measure for comparing multimedia objects. One interesting characteristic of this distance function is that an object can be represented by several feature vectors. Also, comparing two objects involves comparing two sets of feature vectors, and this is possible even if the sets have different cardinality.

Let P be a 3D shape. We represent this shape with a set of features $F = \{f_i\}$, $f_i \in FS$, where FS is a feature space of arbitrary dimensionality. Let $C_1, \ldots, C_n$ be the result of a clustering of F in n clusters, where C_i is the centroid of each obtained cluster. Finally, let w_i be a weight associated to each centroid C_i, which corresponds to the fraction of points on the cluster. We define the *feature signature* S^P of P as

$$S^P = \left\{ \left(C_i^P, w_i^P \right), 1 \le i \le n \right\} \tag{9.55}$$

The size of S^P depends on the clustering process, and this can be variable depending on each particular 3D object. Therefore, it is important to note that the feature signature of a shape a may have a different size than the feature signature of a shape b.

Let $S^P = \left\{ \left(C_i^P, w_i^P \right), 1 \le i \le n \right\}$ and $S^Q = \left\{ \left(C_i^Q, w_i^Q \right), 1 \le i \le m \right\}$ be the signatures of P and Q, respectively, and let $sim : FS \times FS \to \mathbb{R}$ be a positive semi-definite similarity function. For example, sim could be defined as $sim \left(C^i, C^j \right) =$

$e^{-\alpha d^2(C^i,C^j)}$, where d is the Euclidean distance and α is a positive real value. The SQFD is defined as

$$SQFD\left(S^P, S^Q\right) = \sqrt{\left(w^P| - w^Q\right) \cdot A_{sim} \cdot \left(w^P| - w^Q\right)^T} \qquad (9.56)$$

In Eq. 9.3.4.1, the notation $\left(w^P| - w^Q\right)$ corresponds to the concatenation of the weights from P and the negative value from the weights from Q in an $(n+m)$-dimensional vector. Also, the matrix $A_{sim} \in \mathbb{R}^{(n+m) \times (n+m)}$ is the similarity matrix between the centroids of S^P and S^Q, such that

$$a_{i,j} = \begin{cases} sim\left(C_i^P, C_j^P\right) & \text{if } i \le n \text{ and } j \le n; \\ sim\left(C_{i-n}^Q, C_j^P\right) & \text{if } i > n \text{ and } j \le n; \\ sim\left(C_i^P, C_{j-n}^Q\right) & \text{if } i \le n \text{ and } j > n; \\ sim\left(C_{i-n}^Q, C_{j-n}^Q\right) & \text{if } i > n \text{ and } j > n. \end{cases} \qquad (9.57)$$

9.3.4.2   3D Shape Matching Using Feature Signatures

The general algorithm for 3D shape matching based on features signatures can be described in the next steps:

- Compute Heat Kernel Signatures for surface points on the 3D shape.
- Apply a clustering process over the computed Heat Kernel Signatures. Then, compute the feature signature for each 3D shape. Sipiran et al. [107] recommend using the clustering algorithm proposed by Leow and Li [66], which is based on k-means but uses adaptive binning for determining the number k of clusters. This allows us to obtain feature signatures of different lengths depending on the distribution of the local descriptors on the 3D shape.
- Use the SQFD as distance function for implementing the shape matching by using similarity searches.

There are several ways to compute the feature signatures. For example, Sipiran et al. [107] proposed the next three different methods:

i. *SQFD-ALL.* In this method, one computes the Heat Kernel Signature for each vertex of the 3D shape. Next, one produces the clustering using all the computed features. Finally, using the result from the clustering process one computes the feature signature. From the three methods, SQFD-ALL is the most computationally expensive one.

ii. *SQFD-IP.* In this method, one computes the Heat Kernel Signature over selected vertices from the 3D shape. Thus, the first step is to compute interest points from the 3D shape, for example, using the Harris 3D interest point detector [103]. The idea behind this method is that not all points from the 3D shape are discriminative, thus the shape description may benefit from ignoring non-relevant points. An additional advantage of this method is that the clustering process is done over a smaller set of points, thus reducing the time spent on computing the feature signatures.

iii. *SQFD-Cluster.* This method takes into account that the interest points detected by Harris 3D tend to form clusters. Thus, one can filter isolated interest points that may have been detected not because of salient geometry, but because of noise in the data. The clusters are computed on the geodesic space of the triangle mesh. Once the method detects these clusters, it computes the Heat Kernel Signatures for each interest point belonging to the cluster. Finally, the feature signature corresponds to the centroids of each geodesic cluster, and its associated weight is proportional to the number of interest points located on the cluster.

Experimentally, Sipiran et al. [107] showed that the SQFD-Cluster method is able to obtain the best effectiveness among the three proposed methods.

Finally, it is worth noting that the SQFD is a metric distance function. Thus, one could implement index structures for efficiently performing the matching process. This can greatly accelerate the matching process while maintaining its effectiveness.

9.3.4.3 Complexity Analysis

Let S be a 3D object with n vertices. The complexities for each stage of the method are:

- Compute the Laplacian Matrix: $O(n^2)$.
- Compute the eigenvalues and eigenvectors: $O(n^3)$.
- Compute the HKS: $O(nm)$, where m is the dimension of each HKS.
- Clustering step and computation of the feature signature: $O(IKN)$, where I is the number of iterations of the clustering process, K is the number of clusters, and N is the number of local descriptors.

The total complexity of this method is $O(n^3)$.

9.4 Main Challenges for Future Research

If we observe the literature on shape retrieval and recognition as briefly reviewed in Sect. 9.2, we can observe that this is a relatively young field, and therefore presents a number of areas which require further work and progress. This section is devoted to present the trends in future researches and the challenges which concern to the community.

- **Query specification.** The research is commonly focused on testing the effectiveness and efficiency of the presented proposals; however, an important factor is left out, users. As a result, little work has been done in query specification. It is generally assumed that we have a query object in the representation allowed by applications. Nevertheless, we often are interested in retrieving objects similar to the query, so a natural question arises: *If we have an object (the query) visually similar to our needs, why do we proceed to search?* A more interesting approach is to provide the query as images, video, sketches, or text. However, this proposal involves to advice methods which support such kind of information and try to find a correspondence between the query and the shapes. For example, in content-based image retrieval, the research has turned into using sketches as a more natural way of querying an image. This trend has raised new challenges and research interests, which are also expected in shape retrieval and recognition community.

- **Efficiency and large-scale retrieval.** Although a relative level of effectiveness has recently been achieved both in shape retrieval and recognition, important issues related to the efficiency require attention, but even if approaches such as local features and the Laplace–Beltrami operator have begun to be extensively used. In addition, most techniques present results over publicly available datasets of no more than 2000 objects and even results about efficiency are not provided. Moreover, Laplace–Beltrami based approaches rely on extensive computations of eigenvalues and eigenvectors of huge matrices, so it is often necessary to simplify the meshes before processing at the expense of losing the level of detail. In this sense, efficient variants and alternatives are expected to be studied.

- **Object representation.** As can be noted from previous sections of this chapter, many approaches rely on boundary representation for 3D shapes. Perhaps this follows from the fact that this representation is preferred to others because its simplicity and suitability for rendering tasks. In addition, triangle meshes are widely available for processing and the vast majority of 3D objects on the Internet are found in this way. Nevertheless, some potential applications use different representations such as parametric surfaces in CAD and volumetric information in medicine. Each representation has intrinsic advantages which should be considered in order to exploit the information as it is.

- **Partial matching.** A lot of work has been done for 3D objects when the required matching model is global, visual similarity. By global, we mean that given a 3D object, and algorithm retrieves those objects in the database that look visually similar and the whole shape structure is used for comparison. However, many presented methods do not allow partial matching due to the restricted global model that they assume. So given a part of a shape as query, an interesting issue is trying to retrieve those objects in the database that contain visually similar parts to the query. Difficulties can arise due to the need to represent a model in a compact way, for instance, with local information which extent is unknown a priori. In addition, the matching becomes an expensive task because of the exponential amount of possible memberships of the query. Moreover, an even harder problem is to quantify the similarity and partiality due to the similarity strongly depends on the partiality level allowed while searching.

- **Domain applications.** With the increasing interest of the computer vision community for 3D shape retrieval and recognition, a current trend is to research the support that these can give to high-level vision tasks. What is more, computer vision aims at recognizing and understanding the real composition of a viewed scene through a camera, where a scene is part of a three-dimensional world. In the future, we could consider the combination of shape retrieval and recognition with 3D reconstructions of scenes from images as an attempt to break the semantic gap between a three-dimensional scene and the image which represents it. In the same way, the field of medicine could take advantage in building 3D image analysis automated systems such as magnetic resonance images (MRI) and computed tomographies. It is easy to obtain three-dimensional representations from this kind of information and further processing can be beneficial. Another interesting application is modeling support. Surely, the killer applications of computer graphics are videogames, 3D films, and special effects which need a large amount of work in modeling. These applications could benefit from shape retrieval and recognition tasks to reduce the time spent modeling.

- **Automatic 3D objects annotation.** In order to increase the effectiveness, we could require more information about semantic to complement the geometric information extracted from the shape. Information about composition is a good choice, so it is necessary to maintain textual information which represents rich semantic information to be used in retrieval tasks. Nevertheless, attaching tags to shapes by humans is an expensive task taking into account the amount of objects in a database. Thus, by using shape retrieval and recognition, we can assign textual tags based on visual similarity or functionality. Besides this approach can be used to add semantic information, it can be used to improve the visual search effectiveness.
- **3D Retrieval from Range Scans.** Another interesting problem is the 3D shape retrieval from range scans [108], where the query object is a range image (a point-cloud obtained from one view of an object using a 3D scanner or simulated) and the problem is to find matches within a collection of 3D objects. This problem is challenging because the range image only contains partial information from the original object, and the amount of this partial information depends on the "point of view" from where the range image was taken.
- **Cross-modal 3D Shape Matching.** A current open problem in this research area is cross-modal 3D shape matching, where additionally to geometry the user can use other modalities for performing the matching process. For example, Biasotti et al. [100] propose combining geometry and texture information for class identification in archeological artifacts. One SHREC track (standard benchmarks for evaluating and comparing 3D shape matching and retrieval algorithms) was devoted to the retrieval problem in textured 3D models [22].

9.5 Concluding Remarks

This chapter introduces the shape matching process from the point of view of representative approaches in the field, potential applications, and the main challenges that need to be addressed. A noteworthy issue is the form of the information embodied in the 3D shapes to be matched. There are many available datasets, so this aspect should not be a limitation to start. The wide variety of data allows us to choose between different characteristics such as level of detail, shapes classes, and so forth. In addition to the standard datasets, many shape recognition applications consider customized acquired data in order to test their proposals in domain-oriented information; however, it is important to use datasets accepted for the community to have consistent results and valuable comparison.

Just as the amount of available information has considerably grown in recent times, there is also an increasing interest of researchers for proposing new approaches for shape matching and studying the potential applications in several knowledge fields. We have witnessed the achieved benefits of fields such as medicine, engineering, art, entertainment, and security, by the development of shape retrieval and recognition techniques. What is more, it is evident the interest in computer vision applications based on shape matching. It is not so difficult to realize the great potential that has the three-dimensional information which can be used as complement for images and video processing in order to improve the effectiveness in high-level vision tasks. We believe that the 3D information will be used commonly in the future and processes such as retrieval and recognition will be the base for cutting-edge applications.

Likewise, it is beneficial to have a huge catalog of techniques because we can select a convenient technique depending on the application context. In addition, we often can combine them to improve the performance in general. In this chapter, we selected four techniques which were explained in detail in Sect. 9.3. The PANORAMA descriptor is an effective view-based representation for 3D shapes that have proven to be convenient for global shape retrieval. One of the main characteristics of this descriptor is its concise representation which can be exploited to build fast and effective 3D shape retrieval systems.

The other three presented techniques assume a non-global similarity model by exploiting local descriptors which can be used to do the matching. Both the functional map and shape google approaches make extensive use of a mathematical tool which has proven to be powerful for shape analysis, namely, the Laplace–Beltrami operator. This operator has desirable properties which makes it a valuable tool for shape matching, in addition to the good effectiveness achieved in shape retrieval. Nevertheless, a weak point of this tool is its high computational cost which making it an interesting challenge to be tackled in the future.

The spin image approach has proven to be effective in 3D shape recognition. Its versatility for describing shapes in different aspects has made it a standard technique for recognition tasks and new approaches often compare their results against results using spin images. Nevertheless, its dependency on uniform meshes and normals computation is restrictive and not suitable because shapes usually do not meet these requirements. A small difference in calculating normals can produce different spin images damaging the effectiveness.

As can be noted, there is a lot of work to be done, proposing new approaches in order to improve the effectiveness and primarily the efficiency, and studying new paradigms some of which we mention in Sect. 9.4. We are convinced that the future of this research field is promising and the growth in scientific and technological productivity will remain thanks to the enormous efforts that research communities in different fields are doing.

9.6 Further Reading

As expected, the increasing interest of research communities in shape retrieval and recognition areas has allowed a rapid advance, both in theory (new approaches) and applications. Obviously, due to space limitations, all the materials could not be addressed in this chapter, so this section is devoted to present additional material for interested readers.

A good starting point to introduce to the subject of shape retrieval and recognition are the surveys [19, 21, 54, 113]. Early evaluations of algorithms were also presented in the reports [9, 18, 20, 41]. For recent experimentation with state-of-the-art techniques, we recommend to review the reports of SHREC contest. For instance, some SHREC tracks are robust feature detection and description benchmark [12, 14], non-rigid 3D shape retrieval [69, 70], 3D hand gesture recognition [109], large-scale retrieval [98], point-cloud retrieval [71], retrieval for cultural heritage [8], and protein shape retrieval [64]. These reports represent a good reference for review recent approaches and their evaluation.

For readers interested in the Laplace–Beltrami operator and its applications in shape retrieval and recognition, we recommend the papers by Belkin et al. [5, 6], Bobenko [10], Chuang et al. [31], Ghaderpanah et al. [44], Levy [67], Rustamov [95], Wu et al. [121], and Xu [123, 124]. These papers have highly mathematical content, so it is recommended for more advanced level of research.

On the other hand, in addition to applications listed in Sect. 9.1, in the papers by Perakis et al. [88], Zhou et al. [127], and Giorgi et al. [45], we can find applications to face recognition, and in the work by Wessel et al. [119], the authors presented a benchmark for retrieval of architectural data. There are also proposals of application of shape matching in cultural heritage problems [84, 101, 102, 106].

Furthermore, more recent contributions on 3D shape matching and retrieval are using neural networks to learn the correspondence function between geometric information. Even more, we are witnessing the arise of an active research topic around all these new methods, which has been called geometric deep learning [17]. Pioneering works in this direction were applied to find point correspondences between two 3D shapes [76, 118]. The main challenge in the application of neural networks in 3D shape matching is the robust definition of convolutional operations on the 3D domain. Some proposals include anisotropic convolutional neural networks [11], mixture models [78] and deep functional maps [73].

9.7 Questions and Exercises

This section presents some questions and exercises related to the material presented in previous sections. We strongly recommend you to undertake these exercises to reinforce the knowledge you have learnt from this chapter.

9.7.1 Questions

Question 9.1 Explain the difference between shape retrieval and shape recognition and give an example application of each.

Question 9.2 Why is the matching of shapes that can deform (such as bending deformation) more difficult in general than matching of rigid shapes?

Question 9.3 Why is the matching using partial views of an object (for example, when using single viewpoint 3D scans) more difficult in general than when the complete object surface is available in the query shape?

Question 9.4 What properties of shape descriptor are desirable when addressing partial matching problems and non-rigid matching problems?

Question 9.5 Describe the "bag-of-features" approach to shape retrieval.

Question 9.6 Find interesting properties of the similarity matrix A_{sim} defined for the SQFD.

9.7.2 Exercises

9.1 Demonstrate that Laplacian commutativity constraint, in the functional map computation, is equivalent to the matrix whose diagonal elements are defined in Eq. 9.34.

9.2 In the functional map method, the number of coefficients of matrix C (and therefore the number of unknowns in the problem) is related to the number of eigenfunctions used in the input shapes. Note that fewer eigenfunctions will make a more succinct representation for the functional map. However, it could be interesting to see what is the effect of the number of eigenfunctions in the effectiveness of the matching. Experiment and compare the correspondences between two shapes when $k = 10, 20, 50, 100, 500, 1000$. Note also that more eigenfunctions require more computation. What is a good trade-off in your experiments?

9.3 Consider a neighborhood where four points are coplanar and three of them form an equilateral triangle. The fourth point lies in the barycenter of the triangle.

Let a be the length of a triangle's side. Compare the triangle area with the following quantities:

- Voronoi region of p by using only Eq. 9.38.
- Voronoi region of p taking into account the obtuse triangles as described in Sect. 9.3.3.

Argue why it is necessary to be aware of obtuse triangles while calculating the Voronoi region area.

9.4 Prove that the Laplace–Beltrami operator is not invariant to scale changes. Additionally, suppose a uniform mesh which has edges with the same length denoted by a. Conjecture what happens with the operator when a tends to zero.

9.5 Explain why the quantity $K_t(x, y)$ is a good choice for the spatial factor in shape google technique?

9.6 The direction of the normal in the spin images defines a horizontal line in the middle of the spin image. A little variation in this normal modifies the image, rotating the pixels around the central point in the first column of the image. Propose a method to tackle with little variation of the normals.

9.7 The spin image in a point p depends on the direction of its normal. Let suppose an object A with normals computed in each vertex and an object B, equal to A, with opposite normals. Propose a variation to spin image computation in order to generate the same descriptor for corresponding points in A and B.

9.8 Implement the spin images construction modifying the accumulation method. Instead of using bilinear interpolation, use a Gaussian weight centered in the corresponding pixel. Is this method more robust against noise and normal variations?

9.9 Implement the SQFD distance, using the *sim* function defined in Sect. 9.3.4.1. Which properties of matrix A_{sim} can be used for an efficient implementation of this distance function?

References

1. Atmosukarto, I., Wilamowska, K., Heike, C., Shapiro, L.G.: 3D object classification using salient point patterns with application to craniofacial research. Pattern Recognit. **43**(4), 1502–1517 (2010)
2. Aubry, M., Schlickewei, U., Cremers, D.: The wave kernel signature: a quantum mechanical approach to shape analysis. In: 2011 IEEE International Conference on Computer Vision Workshops (ICCV Workshops), pp. 1626–1633 (2011)
3. Baeza-Yates, R.A., Ribeiro-Neto, B.A.: Modern Information Retrieval. ACM Press/Addison-Wesley, Boston (1999)

4. Beecks, C., Uysal, M.S., Seidl, T.: Signature quadratic form distance. In: Proceedings of the ACM International Conference on Image and Video Retrieval, CIVR'10, pp. 438–445. ACM, New York (2010). https://doi.org/10.1145/1816041.1816105

5. Belkin, M., Sun, J., Wang, Y.: Discrete Laplace operator on meshed surfaces. In: Teillaud, M., Welzl, E. (eds.) Proceedings of the Symposium on Computational Geometry, pp. 278–287. ACM (2008)

6. Belkin, M., Sun, J., Wang, Y.: Constructing Laplace operator from point clouds in Rd. In: Mathieu, C. (ed.) Proceedings of the ACM-SIAM Symposium on Discrete Algorithms., pp. 1031–1040. SIAM (2009)

7. Besl, P.J., McKay, N.D.: A Method for Registration of 3D Shapes. IEEE Trans. Pattern Anal. Mach. Intell. **14**(2), 239–256 (1992)

8. Biasotti, S., Thompson, E.M., Aono, M., Hamza, A.B., Bustos, B., Dong, S., Du, B., Fehri, A., Li, H., Limberger, F.A., Masoumi, M., Rezaei, M., Sipiran, I., Sun, L., Tatsuma, A., Forero, S.V., Wilson, R.C., Wu, Y., Zhang, J., Zhao, T., Fornasa, F., Giachetti, A.: Retrieval of surfaces with similar relief patterns. In: Pratikakis, I., Dupont, F., Ovsjanikov, M. (eds.) Eurographics Workshop on 3D Object Retrieval. The Eurographics Association (2017)

9. Bimbo, A.D., Pala, P.: Content-based retrieval of 3D models. ACM Trans. Multimedia Comput. Commun. Appl. **2**(1), 20–43 (2006)

10. Bobenko, A.I.: Delaunay triangulations of polyhedral surfaces, a discrete Laplace-Beltrami operator and applications. In: Teillaud, M., Welzl, E. (eds.) Proceedings of the Symposium on Computational Geometry, p. 38. ACM (2008)

11. Boscaini, D., Masci, J., Rodoià, E., Bronstein, M.: Learning shape correspondence with anisotropic convolutional neural networks. In: Proceedings of the 30th International Conference on Neural Information Processing Systems, NIPS'16, pp. 3197–3205. Curran Associates Inc., USA. http://dl.acm.org/citation.cfm?id=3157382.3157455 (2016)

12. Boyer, E., Bronstein, A.M., Bronstein, M.M., Bustos, B., Darom, T., Horaud, R., Hotz, I., Keller, Y., Keustermans, J., Kovnatsky, A., Litmany, R., Reininghaus, J., Sipiran, I., Smeets, D., Suetens, P., Vandermeulen, D., Zaharescu, A., Zobel, V.: SHREC '11: robust feature detection and description benchmark. In: Laga et al. [62], pp. 71–78. http://diglib.eg.org/EG/DL/WS/3DOR/3DOR11/071-078.pdf

13. Bronstein, A., Bronstein, M., Kimmel, R.: Numerical Geometry of Non-Rigid Shapes. Springer Publishing Company, Incorporated (2008)

14. Bronstein, A.M., Bronstein, M.M., Bustos, B., Castellani, U., Crisani, M., Falcidieno, B., Guibas, L.J., Kokkinos, I., Murino, V., Sipiran, I., Ovsjanikov, M., Patanè, G., Spagnuolo, M., Sun, J.: SHREC 2010: robust feature detection and description benchmark. In: Proceedings of the Workshop on 3D Object Retrieval (3DOR'10). Eurographics Association (2010)

15. Bronstein, A.M., Bronstein, M.M., Guibas, L.J., Ovsjanikov, M.: Shape google: geometric words and expressions for invariant shape retrieval. ACM Trans. Graph. **30**(1), 1:1–1:20 (2011)

16. Bronstein, A.M., Bronstein, M.M., Kimmel, R.: Generalized multidimensional scaling: a framework for isometry-invariant partial surface matching. Proc. Natl. Acad. Sci. **103**(5), 1168–1172 (2006)

17. Bronstein, M.M., Bruna, J., LeCun, Y., Szlam, A., Vandergheynst, P.: Geometric deep learning: going beyond Euclidean data. IEEE Signal Process. Mag. **34**(4), 18–42 (2017). https://doi.org/10.1109/MSP.2017.2693418

18. Bustos, B., Keim, D., Saupe, D., Schreck, T.: Content-based 3D object retrieval. IEEE Comput. Graph. Appl. **27**(4), 22–27 (2007)

19. Bustos, B., Keim, D.A., Saupe, D., Schreck, T., Vranic, D.V.: Feature-based similarity search in 3D object databases. ACM Comput. Surv. **37**(4), 345–387 (2005)

20. Bustos, B., Keim, D.A., Saupe, D., Schreck, T., Vranic, D.V.: An experimental effectiveness comparison of methods for 3D similarity search. Int. J. Digital Libr. **6**(1), 39–54 (2006)

21. Campbell, R.J., Flynn, P.J.: A survey of free-form object representation and recognition techniques. Comput. Vis. Image Underst. **81**(2), 166–210 (2001)

22. Cerri, A., Biasotti, S., Abdelrahman, M., Angulo, J., Berger, K., Chevallier, L., El-Melegy, M.T., Farag, A.A., Lefebvre, F., Giachetti, A., Guermoud, H., Liu, Y.J., Velasco-Forero, S., Vigouroux, J.R., Xu, C.X., Zhang, J.B.: SHREC'13 track: retrieval on textured 3D models. In: Proceedings of the 6th Eurographics Workshop on 3D Object Retrieval, pp. 73–80. Eurographics Association (2013)
23. Chang, A.X., Funkhouser, T.A., Guibas, L.J., Hanrahan, P., Huang, Q., Li, Z., Savarese, S., Savva, M., Song, S., Su, H., Xiao, J., Yi, L., Yu, F.: ShapeNet: an information-rich 3d model repository. arXiv:1512.03012 (2015)
24. Chaouch, M., Verroust-Blondet, A.: 3D Model retrieval based on depth line descriptor. In: Proceedings of the IEEE International Conference Multimedia and Expo, pp. 599–602. IEEE (2007)
25. Chen, D.Y., Tian, X.P., Shen, Y.T., Ouhyoung, M.: On visual similarity based 3D model retrieval. Comput. Graph. Forum **22**(3), 223–232 (2003)
26. Chen, H., Bhanu, B.: 3d free-form object recognition in range images using local surface patches. Pattern Recognit. Lett. **28**(10), 1252–1262. http://www.sciencedirect.com/science/article/pii/S0167865507000621 (2007). https://doi.org/10.1016/j.patrec.2007.02.009
27. Chen, H., Bhanu, B.: Human ear recognition in 3D. IEEE Trans. Pattern Anal. Mach. Intell. **29**(4), 718–737 (2007)
28. Chen, H., Bhanu, B.: Efficient recognition of highly similar 3D objects in range images. IEEE Trans. Pattern Anal. Mach. Intell. **31**(1), 172–179 (2009)
29. Chen, J., Fang, Y.: Deep Cross-modality adaptation via semantics preserving adversarial learning for sketch-based 3D shape retrieval. In: Proceedings of the European Conference on Computer Vision, pp. 624–640 (2018)
30. Chua, C.S., Jarvis, R.: Point signatures: a new representation for 3D object recognition. Int. J. Comput. Vis. **25**(1), 63–85 (1997)
31. Chuang, M., Luo, L., Brown, B.J., Rusinkiewicz, S., Kazhdan, M.M.: Estimating the Laplace-Beltrami operator by restricting 3D functions. Comput. Graph. Forum **28**(5), 1475–1484 (2009)
32. Cyr, C.M., Kimia, B.B.: A similarity-based aspect-graph approach to 3D object recognition. Int. J. Comput. Vis. **57**(1), 5–22 (2004)
33. Daras, P., Zarpalas, D., Tzovaras, D., Strintzis, M.G.: Shape matching using the 3d radon transform. In: Proceedings of the International Symposium on 3D Data Processing, Visualization and Transmission, pp. 953–960. IEEE Computer Society (2004)
34. Duda, R.O., Hart, P.E., Stork, D.G.: Pattern Classification, 2nd edn. Wiley-Interscience, New York (2000)
35. Dutagaci, H., Sankur, B., Yemez, Y.: Transform-based methods for indexing and retrieval of 3D objects. In: Proceedings of the International Conference on 3D Digital Imaging and Modeling, pp. 188–195. IEEE Computer Society (2005)
36. Eynard, D., Kovnatsky, A., Bronstein, M.M., Glashoff, K., Bronstein, A.M.: Multimodal manifold analysis by simultaneous diagonalization of laplacians. IEEE Trans. Pattern Anal. Mach. Intell. **37**(12), 2505–2517 (2015)
37. Faloutsos, C., Lin, K.: FastMap: a fast algorithm for indexing, data-mining and visualization of traditional and multimedia datasets. In: Proceedings of the ACM International Conference on Management of Data(SIGMOD), pp. 163–174 (1995)
38. Feng, Y., Zhang, Z., Zhao, X., Ji, R., Gao, Y.: GVCNN: Group-view convolutional neural networks for 3D shape recognition. In: Proceedings of the Computer Vision and Pattern Recognition, pp. 264–272 (2018)
39. Flint, A., Dick, A., van den Hengel, A.: Thrift: local 3d structure recognition. In: 9th Biennial Conference of the Australian Pattern Recognition Society on Digital Image Computing Techniques and Applications (DICTA 2007), pp. 182–188 (2007). https://doi.org/10.1109/DICTA.2007.4426794
40. Frome, A., Huber, D., Kolluri, R., Bülow, T., Malik, J.: Recognizing objects in range data using regional point descriptors. In: Pajdla, T., Matas, J. (eds.) Proceedings of the European Conference on Computer Vision (ECCV), Lecture Notes in Computer Science, vol. 3023, pp. 224–237. Springer, Berlin (2004)

41. Funkhouser, T.A., Kazhdan, M.M., Min, P., Shilane, P.: Shape-based retrieval and analysis of 3D models. Commun. ACM **48**(6), 58–64 (2005)
42. Gal, R., Cohen-Or, D.: Salient geometric features for partial shape matching and similarity. ACM Trans. Graph. **25**(1), 130–150 (2006)
43. Garland, M., Heckbert, P.S.: Surface simplification using quadric error metrics. In: Proceedings of the International Conference and Exhibition on Computer Graphics and Interactive Techniques (SIGGRAPH), pp. 209–216 (1997)
44. Ghaderpanah, M., Abbas, A., Hamza, A.B.: Entropic hashing of 3D objects using Laplace-Beltrami operator. In: Proceedings of the International Conference Image Processing (ICIP), pp. 3104–3107. IEEE (2008)
45. Giorgi, D., Attene, M., Patanè, G., Marini, S., Pizzi, C., Biasotti, S., Spagnuolo, M., Falcidieno, B., Corvi, M., Usai, L., Roncarolo, L., Garibotto, G.: A critical assessment of 2D and 3D face recognition algorithms. In: Tubaro, S., Dugelay, J.L. (eds.) Proceedings of the International Conference on Advanced Video and Signal Based Surveillance (AVSS), pp. 79–84. IEEE Computer Society (2009)
46. Goodall, S., Lewis, P.H., Martinez, K., Sinclair, P.A.S., Giorgini, F., Addis, M., Boniface, M.J., Lahanier, C., Stevenson, J.: SCULPTEUR: Multimedia retrieval for museums. In: Proceedings of the ACM International Conference on Image and Video Retrieval (CIVR), Lecture Notes in Computer Science, vol. 3115, pp. 638–646. Springer, Berlin (2004)
47. Guo, Y., Bennamoun, M., Sohel, F., Lu, M., Wan, J., Kwok, N.M.: A comprehensive performance evaluation of 3d local feature descriptors. Int. J. Comput. Vis. **116**(1), 66–89 (2016). https://doi.org/10.1007/s11263-015-0824-y
48. Guo, Y., Sohel, F., Bennamoun, M., Lu, M., Wan, J.: Rotational projection statistics for 3d local surface description and object recognition. Int. J. Comput. Vis. **105**(1), 63–86 (2013). https://doi.org/10.1007/s11263-013-0627-y
49. Guo, Y., Sohel, F., Bennamoun, M., Lu, M., Wan., J.: TriSI a distinctive local surface descriptor for 3d modeling and object recognition. In: Proceedings of the International Conference on Computer Graphics Theory and Applications and International Conference on Information Visualization Theory and Applications - Volume 1: GRAPP, (VISIGRAPP 2013), pp. 86–93. INSTICC, SciTePress (2013). https://doi.org/10.5220/0004277600860093
50. He, X., Zhou, Y., Zhou, Z., Bai, S., Bai, X.: Triplet-center loss for multi-view 3d object retrieval. In: Proceedings of the Computer Vision and Pattern Recognition (2018)
51. Hetzel, G., Leibe, B., Levi, P., Schiele, B.: 3D Object Recognition from Range Images using Local Feature Histograms. In: Proceedings of the IEEE Conference on Computer Vision and Pattern Recognition (CVPR), pp. 394–399. IEEE Computer Society (2001)
52. Huang, P., Hilton, A., Starck, J.: Shape similarity for 3D video sequences of people. Int. J. of Comput. Vis. **89**(2–3), 362–381 (2010)
53. Huang, Q.X., Flöry, S., Gelfand, N., Hofer, M., Pottmann, H.: Reassembling fractured objects by geometric matching. ACM Trans. Graph. **25**(3), 569 (2006)
54. Iyer, N., Jayanti, S., Lou, K., Kalyanaraman, Y., Ramani, K.: Three-dimensional shape searching: state-of-the-art review and future trends. Comput.-Aided Des. **37**(5), 509–530 (2005)
55. Johnson, A.: Spin-images: A representation for 3D surface matching. Ph.D. Thesis, Robotics Institute, Carnegie Mellon University, Pittsburgh, PA (1997)
56. Johnson, A.E., Hebert, M.: Using spin images for efficient object recognition in cluttered 3D scenes. IEEE Trans. Pattern Anal. Mach. Intell. **21**(5), 433–449 (1999)
57. van Kaick, O., Zhang, H., Hamarneh, G., Cohen-Or, D.: A survey on shape correspondence. Comput. Graph. Forum **30**(6), 1681–1707 (2011)
58. Kang, S.B., Ikeuchi, K.: The Complex EGI: a new representation for 3D pose determination. IEEE Trans. Pattern Anal. Mach. Intell. **15**(1), 707–721 (1993)
59. Keim, D.A.: Efficient geometry-based similarity search of 3D spatial databases. In: Delis, A., Faloutsos, C., Ghandeharizadeh, S. (eds.) Proceedings of the ACM International Conference on Management of Data (SIGMOD), pp. 419–430. ACM Press (1999)
60. Kim, V.G., Lipman, Y., Funkhouser, T.: Blended intrinsic maps. ACM Trans. Graph. **30**(4), 79:1–79:12 (2011)

61. Kovnatsky, A., Bronstein, M.M., Bronstein, A.M., Glashoff, K., Kimmel, R.: Coupled quasi-harmonic bases. Comput. Graph. Forum **32**(2pt4), 439–448 (2013)
62. Laga, H., Schreck, T., Ferreira, A., Godil, A., Pratikakis, I., Veltkamp, R. (eds.): Eurographics Workshop on 3D Object Retrieval. Eurographics Association, Llandudno (2011)
63. Laga, H., Takahashi, H., Nakajima, M.: Spherical wavelet descriptors for content-based 3D model retrieval. In: Proceedings of the Shape Modeling International, p. 15. IEEE Computer Society (2006)
64. Langenfeld, F., Axenopoulos, A., Chatzitofis, A., Craciun, D., Daras, P., Du, B., Giachetti, A., Lai, Y.k., Li, H., Li, Y., Masoumi, M., Peng, Y., Rosin, P.L., Sirugue, J., Sun, L., Thermos, S., Toews, M., Wei, Y., Wu, Y., Zhai, Y., Zhao, T., Zheng, Y., Montes, M.: Protein shape retrieval. In: Telea, A., Theoharis, T., Veltkamp, R. (eds.) Eurographics Workshop on 3D Object Retrieval. The Eurographics Association (2018)
65. Lee, T.K., Drew, M.S.: 3D object recognition by eigen-scale-space of contours. In: Sgallari, F., Murli, A., Paragios, N. (eds.) Proceedings of the International Conference on Scale Space and Variational Methods in Computer Vision, Lecture Notes in Computer Science, vol. 4485, pp. 883–894. Springer (2007)
66. Leow, W.K., Li, R.: The analysis and applications of adaptive-binning color histograms. Comput. Vision Image Understanding **94**(1), 67–91. http://www.sciencedirect.com/science/article/pii/S1077314203001929 (2004). https://doi.org/10.1016/j.cviu.2003.10.010
67. Lévy, B.: Laplace-Beltrami eigenfunctions towards an algorithm that understands geometry. In: Proceedings of the Shape Modeling International, p. 13. IEEE Computer Society (2006)
68. Li, X., Guskov, I.: 3D object recognition from range images using pyramid matching. In: Proceedings of the International Conference on Computer Vision (ICCV), pp. 1–6. IEEE (2007)
69. Lian, Z., Godil, A., Bustos, B., Daoudi, M., Hermans, J., Kawamura, S., Kurita, Y., Lavoué, G., Nguyen, H.V., Ohbuchi, R., Ohkita, Y., Ohishi, Y., Porikli, F., Reuter, M., Sipiran, I., Smeets, D., Suetens, P., Tabia, H., Vandermeulen, D.: SHREC '11 Track: shape retrieval on non-rigid 3D watertight meshes. In: Laga et al. [62], pp. 79–88. http://diglib.eg.org/EG/DL/WS/3DOR/3DOR11/079-088.pdf
70. Lian, Z., Godil, A., Fabry, T., Furuya, T., Hermans, J., Ohbuchi, R., Shu, C., Smeets, D., Suetens, P., Vandermeulen, D., Wuhrer, S.: SHREC'10 Track: Non-rigid 3D shape retrieval. In: Daoudi, M., Schreck, T. (eds.) Proceedings of the 3th Eurographics Workshop on 3D Object Retrieval, pp. 101–108. Eurographics Association, Norrköping, Sweden. http://diglib.eg.org/EG/DL/WS/3DOR/3DOR10/101-108.pdf (2010)
71. Limberger, F.A., Wilson, R.C., Aono, M., Audebert, N., Boulch, A., Bustos, B., Giachetti, A., Godil, A., Saux, B.L., Li, B., Lu, Y., Nguyen, H.D., Nguyen, V.T., Pham, V.K., Sipiran, I., Tatsuma, A., Tran, M.T., Velasco-Forero, S.: Point-cloud shape retrieval of non-rigid toys. In: Pratikakis, I., Dupont, F., Ovsjanikov, M. (eds.) Eurographics Workshop on 3D Object Retrieval. The Eurographics Association (2017)
72. Lipman, Y., Funkhouser, T.: MÖbius voting for surface correspondence. ACM Trans. Graph. **28**(3), 72:1–72:12 (2009)
73. Litany, O., Remez, T., Rodolà, E., Bronstein, A.M., Bronstein, M.M.: Deep functional maps: structured prediction for dense shape correspondence. In: 2017 IEEE International Conference on Computer Vision (ICCV), pp. 5660–5668 (2017)
74. Litman, R., Bronstein, A., Bronstein, M., Castellani, U.: Supervised learning of bag-of-features shape descriptors using sparse coding. In: Proceedings of the Symposium on Geometry Processing, SGP '14, pp. 127–136. Eurographics Association, Aire-la-Ville, Switzerland (2014)
75. Liu, A., Xiang, S., Li, W., Nie, W., Su, Y.: Cross-domain 3D model retrieval via visual domain adaptation. In: International Joint Conference on Artificial Intelligence, pp. 828–834 (2018)
76. Masci, J., Boscaini, D., Bronstein, M.M., Vandergheynst, P.: Geodesic convolutional neural networks on riemannian manifolds. In: 2015 IEEE International Conference on Computer Vision Workshop (ICCVW), pp. 832–840 (2015). https://doi.org/10.1109/ICCVW.2015.112

77. Meyer, M., Desbrun, M., Schroder, P., Barr, A.H.: Discrete differential-geometry operators for triangulated 2-manifolds. Vis. Math. **III**, 35–57 (2003)
78. Monti, F., Boscaini, D., Masci, J., Rodolà, E., Svoboda, J., Bronstein, M.M.: Geometric deep learning on graphs and manifolds using mixture model cnns. In: 2017 IEEE Conference on Computer Vision and Pattern Recognition (CVPR), pp. 5425–5434 (2016)
79. Novotni, M., Klein, R.: A geometric approach to 3D object comparison. In: Proceedings of the Shape Modeling International, pp. 167–175. IEEE Computer Society (2001)
80. Osada, R., Funkhouser, T.A., Chazelle, B., Dobkin, D.P.: Shape distributions. ACM Trans. Graph. **21**(4), 807–832 (2002)
81. Ovsjanikov, M., Ben-Chen, M., Solomon, J., Butscher, A., Guibas, L.: Functional maps: a flexible representation of maps between shapes. ACM Trans. Graph. **31**(4), 30:1–30:11 (2012)
82. Ovsjanikov, M., Bronstein, A.M., Guibas, L.J., Bronstein, M.M.: Shape google: a computer vision approach to invariant shape retrieval. In: Proceedings of the Workshop on Non-Rigid Shape Analysis and Deformable Image Alignment (NORDIA) (2009)
83. Papadakis, P., Pratikakis, I., Theoharis, T., Perantonis, S.: PANORAMA: a 3D shape descriptor base on panoramic views for unsupervised 3D object retrieval. Int. J. Comput. Vis. **89**(2–3), 177–192 (2010)
84. Papaioannou, G., Schreck, T., Andreadis, A., Mavridis, P., Gregor, R., Sipiran, I., Vardis, K.: From reassembly to object completion: a complete systems pipeline. JOCCH **10**(2), 8:1–8:22 (2017)
85. Paquet, E., Rioux, M.: Nefertiti: a query by content software for three-dimensional models databases management. In: Proceedings of the International Conference on 3D Digital Imaging and Modeling, pp. 345–352. IEEE Computer Society (1997)
86. Paquet, E., Viktor, H.: Exploring protein architecture using 3D shape-based signatures. In: Proceedings of the International Conference on Engineering in Medicine and Biology, pp. 1204–1208 (2007)
87. Paquet, E., Viktor, H.L.: Capri/MR: exploring protein databases from a structural and physic-ochemical point of view. Proc. VLDB **1**(2), 1504–1507 (2008)
88. Perakis, P., Theoharis, T., Passalis, G., Kakadiaris, I.A.: Automatic 3D facial region retrieval from multi-pose facial datasets. In: Spagnuolo, M., Pratikakis, I., Veltkamp, R.C., Theoharis, T. (eds.) Proceedings of the Workshop on 3D Object Retrieval (3DOR), pp. 37–44. Eurographics Association (2009)
89. Rodolí, E., Cosmo, L., Bronstein, M.M., Torsello, A., Cremers, D.: Partial functional correspondence. Comput. Graph. Forum **36**(1), 222–236 (2017)
90. Rodolà, E., Bronstein, A.M., Albarelli, A., Bergamasco, F., Torsello, A.: A game-theoretic approach to deformable shape matching. In: 2012 IEEE Conference on Computer Vision and Pattern Recognition, pp. 182–189 (2012)
91. Rodolà, E., Bulò, S.R., Cremers, D.: Robust region detection via consensus segmentation of deformable shapes. Comput. Graph. Forum **33**(5), 97–106 (2014)
92. Rodolà, E., Torsello, A., Harada, T., Kuniyoshi, Y., Cremers, D.: Elastic net constraints for shape matching. In: 2013 IEEE International Conference on Computer Vision, pp. 1169–1176 (2013)
93. Ronneberger, O., Burkhardt, H., Schultz, E.: General-purpose object recognition in 3D volume data sets using gray-scale invariants - classification of airborne pollen-grains recorded with a confocal laser scanning microscope. In: Conference on Pattern Recognition, vol. 2 (2002)
94. Ruiz-Correa, S., Shapiro, L.G., Melia, M.: A New Signature-Based Method for Efficient 3D Object Recognition. In: Proceedings of the IEEE Conference on Computer Vision and Pattern Recognition (CVPR), vol. 1 (2001)
95. Rustamov, R.M.: Laplace-Beltrami eigenfunctions for deformation invariant shape representation. In: Belyaev, A.G., Garland, M. (eds.) Proceedings of the Symposium on Geometry Processing, ACM International Conference Proceeding Series, vol. 257, pp. 225–233. Eurographics Association (2007)
96. Rusu, R.B., Blodow, N., Beetz, M.: Fast point feature histograms (FPFH) for 3d registration. In: 2009 IEEE International Conference on Robotics and Automation, pp. 3212–3217 (2009). https://doi.org/10.1109/ROBOT.2009.5152473

97. Rusu, R.B., Blodow, N., Marton, Z.C., Beetz, M.: Aligning point cloud views using persistent feature histograms. In: 2008 IEEE/RSJ International Conference on Intelligent Robots and Systems, pp. 3384–3391 (2008). https://doi.org/10.1109/IROS.2008.4650967
98. Savva, M., Yu, F., Su, H., Kanezaki, A., Furuya, T., Ohbuchi, R., Zhou, Z., Yu, R., Bai, S., Bai, X., Aono, M., Tatsuma, A., Thermos, S., Axenopoulos, A., Papadopoulos, G.T., Daras, P., Deng, X., Lian, Z., Li, B., Johan, H., Lu, Y., Mk, S.: Large-scale 3D shape retrieval from ShapeNet core55. In: Pratikakis, I., Dupont, F., Ovsjanikov, M. (eds.) Eurographics Workshop on 3D Object Retrieval. The Eurographics Association (2017)
99. Shilane, P., Min, P., Kazhdan, M.M., Funkhouser, T.A.: The Princeton Shape Benchmark. In: Proceedings of the Shape Modeling International, pp. 167–178. IEEE Computer Society (2004)
100. Silvia, B., Cerri, A., Falcidieno, B., Spagnuolo, M.: Similarity assessment for the analysis of 3D artefacts. In: Proceedings of the Eurographics Workshop on Graphics and Cultural Heritage, pp. 155–164. Eurographics Association (2014)
101. Sipiran, I.: Analysis of partial axial symmetry on 3d surfaces and its application in the restoration of cultural heritage objects. In: 2017 IEEE International Conference on Computer Vision Workshops (ICCVW), pp. 2925–2933 (2017)
102. Sipiran, I.: Completion of cultural heritage objects with rotational symmetry. In: Proceedings of the 11th Eurographics Workshop on 3D Object Retrieval, 3DOR '18, pp. 87–93. Eurographics Association (2018)
103. Sipiran, I., Bustos, B.: Harris 3D: a robust extension of the Harris operator for interest point detection on 3d meshes. The Visual Computer **27**, 963–976 (2011). http://dx.doi.org/10.1007/s00371-011-0610-y
104. Sipiran, I., Bustos, B.: A fully hierarchical approach for finding correspondences in non-rigid shapes. In: 2013 IEEE International Conference on Computer Vision, pp. 817–824 (2013)
105. Sipiran, I., Bustos, B.: Key-components: detection of salient regions on 3d meshes. Vis. Comput. **29**(12), 1319–1332 (2013)
106. Sipiran, I., Gregor, R., Schreck, T.: Approximate symmetry detection in partial 3d meshes. Comput. Graph. Forum **33**(7), 131–140 (2014)
107. Sipiran, I., Lokoc, J., Bustos, B., Skopal, T.: Scalable 3d shape retrieval using local features and the signature quadratic form distance. Vis. Comput. **33**(12), 1571–1585 (2017). https://doi.org/10.1007/s00371-016-1301-5
108. Sipiran, I., Meruane, R., Bustos, B., Schreck, T., Li, B., Lu, Y., Johan, H.: A benchmark of simulated range images for partial shape retrieval. Vis. Comput. **30**(11), 1293–1308 (2014). https://doi.org/10.1007/s00371-014-0937-2
109. Smedt, Q.D., Wannous, H., Vandeborre, J.P., Guerry, J., Saux, B.L., Filliat, D.: 3D hand gesture recognition using a depth and skeletal dataset. In: Pratikakis, I., Dupont, F., Ovsjanikov, M. (eds.) Eurographics Workshop on 3D Object Retrieval. The Eurographics Association (2017)
110. Sun, J., Ovsjanikov, M., Guibas, L.J.: A concise and provably informative multi-scale signature based on heat diffusion. Comput. Graph. Forum **28**(5) (2009)
111. Sun, Y., Paik, J.K., Koschan, A., Page, D.L., Abidi, M.A.: Point fingerprint: a new 3D object representation scheme. IEEE Trans. Syst. Man Cybern. **33**(4), 712–717 (2003)
112. Tabia, H., Laga, H.: Learning shape retrieval from different modalities. Neurocomputing **253**, 24–33 (2017)
113. Tangelder, J.W.H., Veltkamp, R.C.: A survey of content based 3D shape retrieval methods. Multimedia Tools Appl. **39**(3), 441–471 (2008)
114. Toldo, R., Castellani, U., Fusiello, A.: Visual vocabulary signature for 3D object retrieval and partial matching. In: Spagnuolo, M., Pratikakis, I., Veltkamp, R.C., Theoharis, T. (eds.) Proceedings of the Workshop on 3D Object Retrieval(3DOR), pp. 21–28. Eurographics Association (2009)
115. Tombari, F., Salti, S., Di Stefano, L.: Unique shape context for 3d data description. In: Proceedings of the ACM Workshop on 3D Object Retrieval, 3DOR '10, pp. 57–62. ACM, New York, USA (2010). https://doi.org/10.1145/1877808.1877821

116. Tombari, F., Salti, S., Di Stefano, L.: Unique signatures of histograms for local surface description. In: Daniilidis, K., Maragos, P., Paragios, N. (eds.) Computer Vision - ECCV 2010, pp. 356–369. Springer, Berlin (2010)

117. Vranic, D.: 3D Model retrieval. Ph.D. Thesis, University of Leipzig (2004)

118. Wei, L., Huang, Q., Ceylan, D., Vouga, E., Li, H.: Dense human body correspondences using convolutional networks. In: The IEEE Conference on Computer Vision and Pattern Recognition (CVPR) (2016)

119. Wessel, R., Blümel, I., Klein, R.: A 3D shape benchmark for retrieval and automatic classification of architectural data. In: Spagnuolo, M., Pratikakis, I., Veltkamp, R.C., Theoharis, T. (eds.) Proceedings of the Workshop on 3D Object Retrieval (3DOR), pp. 53–56. Eurographics Association (2009)

120. Wolfson, H.J., Rigoutsos, I.: Geometric hashing: an overview. Comput. Sci. Eng. **4**, 10–21 (1997)

121. Wu, H.Y., Wang, L., Luo, T., Zha, H.: 3D shape consistent correspondence by using Laplace-Beltrami spectral embeddings. In: Spencer, S.N., Nakajima, M., Wu, E., Miyata, K., Thalmann, D., Huang, Z. (eds.) Proceedings of the ACM International Conference on Virtual-Reality Continuum and its Applications in Industry, pp. 307–309. ACM (2009)

122. Wu, Z., Song, S., Khosla, A., Yu, F., Zhang, L., Tang, X., Xiao, J.: 3D ShapeNets: a deep representation for volumetric shapes. In: 2015 IEEE Conference on Computer Vision and Pattern Recognition (CVPR), pp. 1912–1920 (2015)

123. Xu, G.: Convergent discrete Laplace-Beltrami operators over triangular surfaces. In: Proceedings of the Geometric Modeling and Processing, pp. 195–204. IEEE Computer Society (2004)

124. Xu, G.: Discrete Laplace-Beltrami operators and their convergence. Comput. Aided Geom. Des. **21**, 767–784 (2004)

125. Yeh, J.S., Chen, D.Y., Chen, B.Y., Ouhyoung, M.: A web-based three-dimensional protein retrieval system by matching visual similarity. Bioinformatics **21**(13), 3056–3057 (2005)

126. You, C.F., Tsai, Y.L.: 3D solid model retrieval for engineering reuse based on local feature correspondence. Int. J. Adv. Manuf. Technol. **46**(5–8), 649–661 (2009)

127. Zhou, X., Seibert, H., Busch, C., Funk, W.: A 3D face recognition algorithm using histogram-based features. In: Perantonis, S.J., Sapidis, N., Spagnuolo, M., Thalmann, D. (eds.) Proceedings of the Workshop on 3D Object Retrieval (3DOR), pp. 65–71. Eurographics Association (2008)

Chapter 10
3D Morphable Models: The Face, Ear and Head

Hang Dai, Nick Pears, Patrik Huber, and William A. P. Smith

Abstract With prior knowledge and experience, people can easily observe rich shape and texture variation for a certain type of object, such as human faces, cats or chairs, in both 2D and 3D images. This ability helps us recognise the same person, distinguish different kinds of creatures and sketch unseen samples of the same object class. The process of capturing prior knowledge relating to the normal variations in an object class is mathematically interpreted as statistical modelling. The outcome of such a modelling process is a morphable model, a compact description of an object class that captures the model's training set shape variance, and thus can act as a useful prior in many Computer Vision applications. Here, we are particularly concerned with 3D shape, and so we refer to the concept of a 3D Morphable Model (3DMM). However, in many applications, it is very important to capture and model the associated texture, where that texture is registered (i.e. aligned) with shape data. Typically, a 3DMM is a vector-space representation of objects that captures the variation of shape and texture. Any convex combination of vectors of a set of object class examples generates a real and valid example in this vector space. Morphable models have many applications in creative media, medical image analysis and biometrics, by providing a useful encoding and prior statistical distribution of both shape and texture. In this chapter, we introduce 3DMMs, provide historical context and recent literature and describe both classical and modern 3DMM construction pipelines that exploit deep learning. We also review the publicly available models that such pipelines generate.

H. Dai · N. Pears · P. Huber (✉) · W. A. P. Smith
Department of Computer Science, University of York,
Deramore Lane, York YO10 5GH, UK
e-mail: patrik.huber@york.ac.uk

N. Pears
e-mail: nick.pears@york.ac.uk

W. A. P. Smith
e-mail: william.smith@york.ac.uk

© Springer Nature Switzerland AG 2020
Y. Liu et al. (eds.), *3D Imaging, Analysis and Applications*,
https://doi.org/10.1007/978-3-030-44070-1_10

463

Finally, we illustrate the power of 3DMMs via case studies and examples. Throughout the chapter, our exemplar models will be 3DMMs of the human face and head, as these are widely employed in Computer Vision and Graphics literature.

10.1 Introduction

Statistical 3D shape modelling aims to encode 3D shapes in some object class, e.g. human faces, cars and chairs. Typically this employs a *fixed* and relatively *small* number of variables called model parameters. When the model parameters for one shape example interact through the mathematical structure of the 3D shape model that shape is reconstructed to some approximation. The model parameters are also sometimes called latent variables, as they are not directly observable in the raw data, but must be inferred in some form of model fitting process. As we smoothly vary the model parameters, within reasonable ranges, we expect to be able to view smoothly varying and plausible 3D shape reconstructions, hence the name *3D Morphable Model* (3DMM). This means that the structure of the model allows surface points or patches of the shape to change simultaneously, with a single shape parameter change, and so the model's capture of surface point/patch correspondences across the whole 3DMM training dataset is implied. Figure 10.1 illustrates instances generated from the Universal Head Model (UHM) [119].

A *fixed* number of model parameters, required to encode the many different shapes in the training dataset, implies that there is a form of normalisation of representation (cf. the variable number of raw 3D surface points). Also, the relatively *small* number of parameters implies that there is data compression (i.e. dimension reduction) that exploits the correlations and/or more complex relationships between different parts of the modelled object class. In other words, due to the regularity of shapes in an object class, their encodings occupy a manifold or *shape space* of relatively low dimension. As long as the model parameters stay within this space, it will generate a plausible face shape. Of course, some shapes are more common than others and

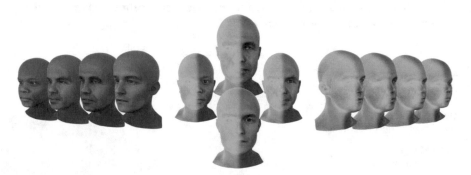

Fig. 10.1 3D heads synthesised by the Universal Head Model (UHM). Figure courtesy of [119]

therefore the model parameters are thought to occupy some distribution, which may be modelled in various ways, such as using a Gaussian or mixture of Gaussians.

There are many possible encodings that can represent the same raw datasets. Two that are commonly employed include the linear encoding of Principal Component Analysis (PCA) and the non-linear encodings of autoencoder neural nets. Modelling attempts to distill the essence of a shape into a compact description. Here, Occam's razor comes to mind, which invokes the law of parsimony; we wish to encode with a small number of parameters, yet when data is reconstructed with such models, we desire high representational accuracy. These two attributes can be in conflict with each other and often an application-based compromise is required.

A 3DMM provides a useful prior distribution over the model parameters, and knowing the range of shape variation expected for an object class, which is expressed through this prior, often makes analysis problems in Computer Vision much more tractable. Indeed this is the essence of *analysis-by-synthesis* approaches, where, if we model all the components that generate an image, such as 3D shape, surface reflectance, scene lighting and the projective imaging processes, and if we estimate these model components accurately by model fitting, then we can synthesise an image that is very similar to the actual image and thereby understand it. Furthermore, 3DMMs allow us to understand imaged 3D shapes in the context of the distribution of possible shapes for that object class, for example, determining if a particular example shape is an outlier for that class. 3DMMs also facilitate reconstruction of missing data from 2D and 3D images, since the model parameters that accurately reconstruct observable raw data are also able to estimate both the unobservable data and the variation around that estimate.

Throughout the chapter, our exemplar models will be 3DMMs of the human face, ear and head. These are of particular interest in both Computer Vision and Computer Graphics literature and are widely employed in practical applications. Full body models have also been widely studied, with the Skinned Multi-Person Linear Model (SMPL) being a recent example [105], which employs the FAUST full body dataset [19]. However, we do not attempt to cover the full body literature in this chapter.

We note that shape deformation fields that capture facial expressions are an important component of facial modelling. The prevalent approach is that of simple linear *blendshapes* [101], with a set of 3D facial expressions being made available by Cao et al. [36] in the *FaceWarehouse* project. However, in this chapter, we primarily focus on a tutorial approach to constructing and fitting statistical models that capture the variability of human faces and heads due to the different identities in the training dataset.

10.1.1   Model Training Data

In Computer Vision and Graphics, there are various ways of representing raw 3D object data (see Chap. 6 for an overview of 3D data representations). Here, we will be primarily concerned with constructing 3DMMs from *3D point clouds*, i.e. the set

Fig. 10.2 3D head capture, using the 3dMD system. *Left:* A subject being captured. *Right:* The resulting captured 3D image, shown as a textured mesh, and with the underlying 3D data

of 3D points that sample an imaged object's surface. We are also interested in the associated *3D mesh*, where neighbouring points are connected into a triangulation that approximates the surface of the object in a piecewise linear fashion. Such a mesh is useful for capturing surface neighbourhood information between points, and for rendering a colour-texture surface onto the 3D object. Our notion of a raw 3D image is where we have a set of unlabelled 3D points connected into a mesh triangulation, along with a bitmap image and a set of texture coordinates that indicate the correspondence (or registration) between the 3D mesh and the 2D image. Such a 3D image will have been created either by a passive or active 3D vision system (see Chaps. 2–5 for an overview of possible ways of capturing 3D data). Recently, efforts have been made to build or augment 3DMMs from standard 2D image datasets. This has mainly been due to the recent progress in model-based 3D shape inference from 2D images that has been made using deep convolutional networks [134] and, later in the chapter, we discuss this work.

Returning to 3D data capture, Fig. 10.2 shows a subject being captured using a 3dMD head capture system.[1] It consists of five active 3D camera units, where each of the units uses a combination of structured IR projection, IR cameras and standard cameras for the colour-texture capture. 3D surface points are triangulated, as in passive stereo, but only at the illuminated spots in the projected pattern. The 3dMD system software is able to stitch together the five separate 3D images into a single 3D image, additionally handling the texture-to-shape registration. Although this is presented in their propriety TSB format, it can easily be converted into open formats such as OBJ, that contains 3D point cloud coordinates, their mesh connectivity, and texture coordinates that index into an associated five-view composite bitmap. The right portion of Fig. 10.2 shows the resulting captured 3D image of the subject, firstly as a mesh with the texture rendered over it, and secondly the underlying 3D data. As 3D images, both of these can be rotated on the screen and examined with a 3D viewer, such as the freely available MeshLab application.[2] Typically, the human head images captured with this system have between 100K and 200K vertices.

---

[1] http://www.3dmd.com.

[2] https://www.meshlab.net.

Commercial 3D capture systems are now much faster and higher resolution than when such devices first came on the market. However, it must be remembered that all of the raw 3D image data provided by such devices both have a varying number of points per 3D image and each of those points is unlabelled. Thus, the ith point in the 3D point cloud has no semantic meaning across the dataset, and if we arbitrarily select some index number, the ith 3D point, this could be on the tip of the nose of one person and the middle of the cheek for another. So 3D image data in its raw form has limited utility; it could be used with a point-and-click user interface to measure Euclidean or geodesic distances between landmarks, as in a 'software callipers' application. However, this is very laborious if we want to know large population measurement statistics, and if we want to understand how different parts of the modelled object structure vary together (co-vary). The first key to solving this problem is to consider reparameterisation of the 3D mesh, such that the parameterisation is normalised across the dataset associated with the object class of interest, the second is alignment and the third is model construction by finding a parametrisation that encodes the main shape variations across the dataset. Each of these stages is first presented in outline and then in detail, later in the chapter.

10.1.2   The Analysis-by-synthesis Application

To illustrate the power of 3DMMs, and thus provide application context early in this chapter, we briefly overview the classical work of Blanz and Vetter [17] from the late 1990s, and that model's use in a typical analysis-by-synthesis setting. The term analysis-by-synthesis refers to the fact that, if the modelling of some system is theoretically well-founded, then it should be able to generate any reasonable data output instance of that system. The output is then 'understood', in some sense, by the parameterisation of the system output in terms of the model.

Blanz and Vetter built a 3DMM from 3D face scans [17] and employed it in 2D face recognition [18], in an analysis-by-synthesis framework. Two hundred scans were used to build the model (young adults, 100 males and 100 females). Dense correspondences were computed using optical flow with an energy term dependent on both shape and texture. Such morphable models incorporate a prior multi-dimensional distribution over the model's parameters, and this defines the expected variation of the object class shape. As such, a 3DMM defines a highly useful 'prior' (prior distribution of model parameters) and the model parameters can be varied over a reasonable range (e.g. equating to $\pm 3\sigma$ over any parameter), thus covering the variation in the training dataset. This makes them suitable for incorporation into a typical *analysis-by-synthesis* approach, depicted in Fig. 10.3. (In addition to shape and texture, an expression component can be incorporated into the morphable model. Often this is just linear, i.e. a weighted sum of expression modes that is added to the shape part of the morphable model.)

The idea is to model all of the physical ingredients that generate a (standard 2D) image, namely, 3D shape and surface reflectance (via a 3DMM), lighting, and object

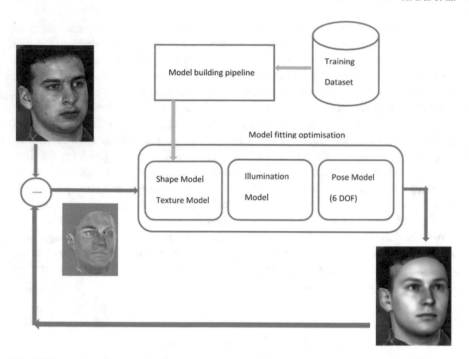

Fig. 10.3 *Analysis-by-synthesis.* The forward process of a system is modelled to produce an image of a person's face, here with a statistical 3D shape and texture model, illumination and pose (camera) model. A non-linear optimisation is then run that tries to minimise the difference between the synthesised image and the image that the system aims to model. Hence, the system is able to analyse an input image, by synthesising images, where the model parameters are known

pose (position and orientation), and gradually adjust all such parameters of the model until the difference between a synthesised 2D image and an actual 2D input image is minimised. Typically this is a challenging non-linear optimisation problem that is computationally expensive and has many local minima, and so a good initialisation is very important. The parameters associated with the 3DMM can then be used in a face recognition application, whereas the parameters associated with the specific image capture, lighting and pose, can be discarded as irrelevant. In a sense, the useful information relating to identity has been disentangled from the factors that can often confound face recognition, namely, lighting and pose variations.

More recently, Garrido et al. [70] have advanced this approach by considering 3D shape on *coarse*, *medium* and *fine* scales. In this work, it is recognised that modelling constructs such as Principal Component Analysis (PCA) capture shape variations that exist in a relatively low-dimensional linear subspace and these are low spatial frequency shape variations. To counter this, they employ medium-scale corrective shapes, via the use of manifold harmonics. However, these are still too low-frequency to capture details such as wrinkles, which are dealt with in a third level of their hierarchy: fine-scale modelling. Fine-scale shape variations are encoded in the gradient domain and are based on deformation gradients.

Many alternative approaches to analysis-by-synthesis with 3DMMs exist, and we provide a more detailed overview of historical and recent works in Sect. 10.16.1.

10.1.3   Chapter Structure

The rest of this chapter has the following structure:

- Section 10.2 presents a historical perspective that highlights some key shape modelling developments that pre-date modern 3DMMs. For the purposes of that discussion, we define this to be the 1999 3DMM face modelling work of Blanz and Vetter [17].
- In Sect. 10.3, we outline the key ingredients and processes in a classical 3DMM construction pipeline. Each of these ingredients is then presented in detail in the subsequent sections, i.e. Sects. 10.4–10.8.
- In Sect. 10.9, we present the various 3DMM construction pipelines presented in the literature, and we focus on their commonalities and differences.
- Sections 10.10–10.12 present 3DMMs of the human face, the human head (including the full cranium) and a 3DMM of the human ear.
- Section 10.13 discusses how to leverage the fact that human faces and heads have strong bilateral reflective symmetry, which could be used as a morphing constraint.
- Section 10.14 discusses evaluation criteria for morphable models.
- Section 10.15 details some recent approaches that employ deep learning for 3DMM construction.
- Section 10.16 presents a selection of 3DMM applications.
- Sections 10.17–10.21 present research challenges, conclusions, further reading, questions and exercises, respectively.

10.2   Historical Perspective

Early work in shape analysis was performed on 2D images. In 1942, Thompson et al. [135] sketched transformation grids to show how one shape had to be deformed to match another in terms of their corresponding landmarks. Kendall [93] derived statistical developments concerning the shape space for Procrustes-registered data in 1984. Bookstein's work on Thin Plate Splines (TPS) [24] was central to the development of the related field of statistical shape analysis [59], which provides the theoretical underpinnings of statistical shape modelling. Later Bookstein employed a combination of Procrustes analysis and TPS in order to analyse shapes in terms of their landmark positions [25]. Meanwhile, relevant work was produced in Computer Vision. For example, rigid transformation estimation between a pair of 3D shapes was solved by several Computer Vision researchers, with approaches based on Singular Value Decomposition (SVD) that lead to least-squares solutions being particularly popular [8].

In terms of 2D image modelling, Sirovich and Kirby described a low-dimensional procedure for the characterisation of 115 aligned 2D facial images using Principal Component Analysis and called the resulting eigenvectors *Eigenpictures* [95, 129]. Later in 1991, Turk and Pentland employed this modelling technique in a face recognition application and termed the eigenvectors *Eigenfaces* [141].

Also, in the 1990s, two groups of researchers, Besl and McKay [15] and Chen and Medioni [39], independently proposed the Iterative Closest Points (ICP) algorithm for rigid 2D and 3D shape alignment and registration. ICP cycles through three main steps: (i) finding surface correspondences as closest points; (ii) computing the rigid transformation estimation between them and (iii) applying the transformation to one of the surfaces to make it closer to the other. Later several research groups investigated non-rigid registration approaches where, for example, local affine deformations are permitted [5, 7].

In other work in the 1990s, Cootes et al. developed shape models applied to 2D images, termed Point Distribution Models (PDMs) [44]. The work is done with reference to 2D shapes, where corresponding points are manually marked on the boundaries of a set of training examples. The points are aligned to minimise the variance in distance between corresponding points. This is done by encapsulating a Procrustes-based alignment in an iterative procedure, where the mean is normalised to a default scale and pose at each iteration. After such alignment, a standard principal component analysis (PCA) captures how the shapes deviate from the mean shape. Cootes et al. presented Active Shape Models (ASM) in [45], where pose, scale and shape parameters are determined in order to fit the model to an image. This work was inspired by the earlier work on active contour models [91]. The same research team also went on to include texture in their models, giving birth to Active Appearance Models (AAMs) [42]. They further developed a set of shape modelling approaches where the best correspondences are those that define the most compact shape model given some quality of fit between the model and the data [55, 100]. In terms of 3D models, in 1996, Cootes et al. [43] proposed to build statistical 3D models from a set of uncalibrated 2D images. In that work, 2D landmark points from two views (images) of the same object are used to recover 3D shape, and then build a statistical 3D model of the variation of those points from multiple object instances.

10.3   Outline of a Classical 3DMM Construction Process

An outline of a classical 3DMM modelling pipeline is shown in Fig. 10.4. The following subsections give a brief overview of the processes in this pipeline.

Fig. 10.4 Classical 3DMM modelling pipeline, from 3D face data to the final statistical model

10.3.1 Normalised Mesh Parameterisation

In order to learn a meaningful statistical model of shape, all items in the model's training dataset must be reparameterised into a standard form. Thus we normalise the 3D meshes, such that each has the same number of points, N, and points with the same index, i, have the same label. This means that points on different object instances with the same index have the same meaning, at least to some approximation demanded by the application. (We recognise that such labels are easy to define for well-localised common structures on the object and very difficult for others. In the case of the human face, the eye and mouth corners are well-defined and well-localised anatomical structures, but points in the middle of the cheek and forehead are not.) A typical approach is to take a template mesh which, ideally, is close to the average size and shape of the object members in the dataset. We then apply transformations to this template, which is often termed the source mesh, such that it is in some sense optimally aligned to the data mesh, also termed the target mesh. Such transformations consist of rigid motion translations and rotations, scalings and other affine transformations such as stretching and shearing, and non-linear deformation. The latter is the most challenging due to the large space of possible non-linear, non-rigid deformations. The process of non-rigidly deforming a template mesh to match a data mesh is termed *non-rigid registration* or *morphing* and is discussed in detail later in the chapter. The point to note at present is that once the template has been morphed to each data item in the dataset in turn, then we can use the deformed templates in place of the data, and the whole dataset then has the same number of points, with the same semantic meaning and joined into a consistent triangulation. In other words, the template parameterisation has been transferred to all the dataset samples and this provides a good foundation for statistical modelling. One might say that an approximate *groupwise* correspondence has been achieved. The word *approximate* is used as the optimisations are conducted in a *pairwise* fashion between template and each data item, rather than jointly over the whole group, which is more challenging and addressed in various literature [55]. Note that template-based correspondence methods need very high quality shape registration for good performance [152, 153]. Figure 10.5 shows an example of the template morphing approach, where the *FaceWarehouse template* has been morphed to a 3D image in the *Headspace* dataset [51].

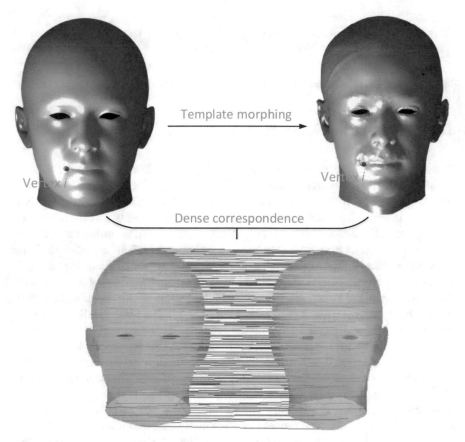

Fig. 10.5 Template morphing for dense correspondence: the dense correspondence is illustrated by the parallel connecting lines

10.3.2 Mesh Alignment

Typically the items in an object dataset will not be in a consistent pose and they will be in different positions and orientations relative to some coordinate system. Since the shape template (usually) moves towards the scan to align with it, the deformed templates will also be in inconsistent poses. Therefore, an alignment stage is often employed after the morphing stage, in a classical 3DMM construction pipeline, and this is an essential precursor to standard statistical modelling, which is based upon Principal Component Analysis (PCA). The process usually employed is termed Generalised Procrustes Alignment (GPA), which seeks to minimise the least-squares error between each shape and the mean shape. However, since computation of the mean shape itself depends on the alignment, the process is iterative, where a new mean shape is computed after each improved alignment until the mean shape converges. Before we build a statistical model, we can optionally scale-normalise the fitted templates by rescaling each of them. Scale can be computed as the mean (or RMS) distance to the centroid for each deformed template and an average scale can be computed, to which we can normalise. Scale normalisation gives a better shape alignment after GPA, and we can often observe this as tighter clusters of corresponding vertices. However, we will lose the correlation between shape and scale, unless scale is reintroduced in the modelling stage as an additional variable.

10.3.3 Statistical Modelling

The standard method to perform statistical modelling is to assume that the dataset objects lie on a linear manifold in shape space and employ PCA. (Here, we assume a basic understanding of PCA). The validity of this assumption is dataset dependent. In performing PCA, we encode the shape relative to the mean of the dataset, we capture the largest correlations between the variations of different parts of the object across the dataset, and we employ significantly fewer shape parameters relative to the the number of parameters associated with the raw data. In this sense, the modelling process performs a high degree of data compression. For example, the *FaceWarehouse* template of the human head has $N = 11,510$ 3D vertices, which requires $3N = 34,530$ parameters to express each morphed template across the dataset. After PCA, we can accurately express any shape with around 100 shape parameters. A refinement of PCA is to use Weighted PCA (WPCA) to ensure that the extraction of shape deformation is independent of varying resolution over the mesh. This can be achieved by constructing a sparse symmetric weighting matrix as a function of the average mesh face areas around and between vertices [51]. The choice between PCA and WPCA is application dependent.

In order to perform PCA (or WPCA) and encode shape variation, we consider each morphed template as a point in a high dimensional space of size $3N$, which is termed the shape space. Thus a $N \times 3$ matrix representing N 3D points is reshaped to a $3N$ vector. If there are M shape examples, we have a $M \times 3N$ matrix representing the full dataset. Often, we find that $M < 3N$, unless we have a particularly large dataset relative to 3D mesh size. In this case, we can extract at most $M - 1$ shape parameters. A particular shape instance $\mathbf{x}$ can be expressed in terms of the PCA model parameters $(\mathbf{x_m}, \mathbf{V})$ as follows:

$$\mathbf{x} = \mathbf{x_m} + \mathbf{Vb}, \tag{10.1}$$

where $\mathbf{x_m}$ is the mean shape, $\mathbf{V}$ are the eigenvectors representing shape variations (correlated surface point displacements) and $\mathbf{b}$ are the shape parameters that encode and represent the shape instance. Note that a 3DMM usually also has a texture model with the same structure as the shape model, but constructed from per vertex RGB colour values rather than X, Y, Z vertex position values. Such a texture model is usually independent from the shape model, i.e. correlations between shape and

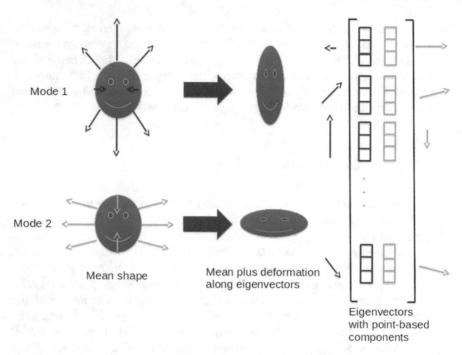

Fig. 10.6 Toy example for a PCA face model. It shows the mean face and the first two modes of variation, indicated with coloured arrows, and the resulting deformation applied to the mean. The right side shows the structure of the corresponding PCA basis matrix, where each column represents an eigenvector

texture are not captured. A notable exception to this is the Copula Eigenfaces work of Egger et al. [60].

Figure 10.6 illustrates a toy example of a PCA decomposition encoding face variation relative to the mean face, where we show eight surface points varying over the first two modes of shape variation. These shape variations are captured by the eigenvectors, or principal components, which are 3N column vectors that are unit vectors. Such eigenvectors are composed of the individual 3D point movement directions of the eight points on the shape surface, as illustrated. The size of these movements is exaggerated in the figure for the purposes of illustration. Note that by varying a single shape parameter, b_i, within the parameter vector, **b**, the whole face shape changes to a different and yet valid face shape, as long as we don't move too far away from the mean, as we slide along an eigenvector. The *principal components* are named as such since they capture the shape changes that have the most variance in the training set. Contrast the variation of a shape parameter with changing a single parameter of the raw representation which would just move a point on the surface and create a noisy spike. Any face should be able to be well described as the mean, plus a linear combination of the eigenvectors of the model, as described by Eq. 10.1 (of course a reasonable number of eigenvectors is likely to be far greater than the two illustrated).

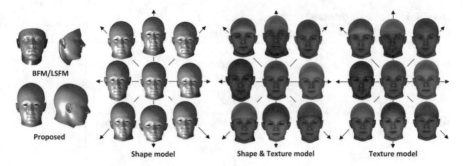

Fig. 10.7 The Liverpool-York Head Model (LYHM). *1st block:* shape compared to the Basel Face Model (BFM) [115] and Large-Scale Face Model (LSFM) [27]; *2nd-4th blocks:* the central head is the mean and the first four principal modes of variation are shown

Figure 10.7 shows a real example of a 3DMM, in this case the Liverpool-York Head Model (LYHM) [51], and the figure illustrates that the full cranium is modelled, where earlier models have only modelled the facial area. Both shape and texture are modelled and the means and first four modes of variations are illustrated.

10.4   3D Face and Head Datasets

The form of a 3D face/head dataset is application dependent. Most face databases are face recognition oriented. Only the Bosphorus dataset contains facial occlusions. FRGC v.2 [118] used to be the largest 3D face database. In 2016, MeIn3D replaced FRGC v.2 as the largest. The BU-3DFE [151] database has various emotional expressions. Every subject displays four intensity levels in each of six emotions. Table 10.1 lists the 3D face databases used in research. Not all of them are publicly available.

The Face Recognition Grand Challenge (FRGC) has been organised for several reasons. There were three main directions to be pursued: Face recognition on (1) high resolution still images, (2) multiple still images both on the enrollment and challenge side and on (3) 3D face shape. Such databases were a challenge for teams in industry and academia. Since this dataset contains various expressions, it is very challenging to localise facial landmarks in FRGC and other datasets, such as the University of York 3D face dataset. Additionally, the mesh quality and resolution are relatively low compared to those captured by the latest techniques.

The MeIn3D [27] database includes over 10,000 3D facial scans. It was collected in the Science Museum in London by the ibug group from Imperial College London. Booth et al. [27] used this dataset to construct a large-scale 3D morphable model of face. They aimed at 3D face reconstruction and surgical planning. However, this dataset is face-only and proprietary (not public). The 3D mesh in this dataset composes of about 60,000 vertices joined into 120,000 triangulated faces associated with a high-resolution texture image. Metadata, including gender, age and ethnicity, is

Table 10.1 List of 3D face/head databases

Database	Subjects	Total	Expression	Pose	Occlusions
FRGC v.2 [118]	466	4007	Anger, happiness, sadness, surprise, disgust, puffy	N/A	N/A
BU-3DFE [151]	100	2500	Anger, happiness, sadness, surprise, disgust, fear	N/A	N/A
ND2006 [65]	888	13450	Happiness, sadness, surprise, disgust, other	N/A	N/A
Univ. of York [85]	350	5250	Happiness, anger, eyes closed, eye-brows raised	N/A	N/A
CASIA [155]	123	1845	Smile, laugh, anger, surprise, closed eyes	N/A	N/A
GavabDB [110]	61	549	Smile, frontal accentuated laugh, frontal random gesture	Left, right, up, down	N/A
3DRMA [16]	120	720	N/A	Slight left/right and up/down	N/A
Bosphorus [124]	105	4652	34 expressions (action units and six emotions)	13 yaw, pitch and cross rotations	4 occlusions
MeIn3D [27]	9663	12000	N/A	N/A	N/A
FaceBase [126]	3500	3500	N/A	N/A	N/A
Headspace [51]	1519	1519	N/A	N/A	N/A

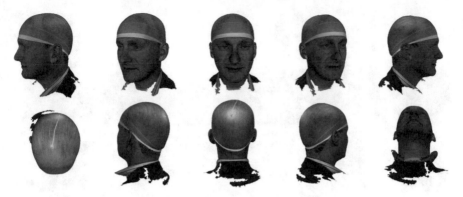

Fig. 10.8 Example 01242 from the Headspace dataset [51]. Subjects wear tight fitting latex caps to reduce the effect of hairstyle on captured cranial shape

provided to build specific demographic models and to analyse the shape variation for certain demographic groups.

The FaceBase [126] dataset collects 3D face meshes along with DNA information. This dataset includes 35 age groups from 3 to 40 years old. It aims at collecting 50 males and 50 females in each age group. They released their measurements of craniofacial shape. This dataset has the potential to explore the relation between craniofacial shape and gene information.

We note that the *MeIn3D* and *FaceBase* dataset for craniofacial researchers contain a large amount of 3D face scans, but the full cranium is not included. The only other full head (including full cranium) dataset that we are aware of is that of the *Size China* project; however, currently there is no 3DMM developed from Size China data and it is expensive for researchers to get access to the data. To date (2020), the Headspace dataset [51] is the only full head dataset both publicly available and free for researchers (Fig. 10.8).

10.5   Facial Landmarking

As mentioned earlier, template morphing methods are often employed to establish dense correspondences. Such methods need an automatic initialisation to bring them within the convergence basin of the global minimum of alignment and morphing. Automatic initialisation is to align the input 3D data to the template, which demands 3D facial landmarks to act as sparse correspondences. Figure 10.9 shows a more detailed process flow, where, in the *Initialisation* stage, the pose of the input data is normalised using facial landmarks to be approximately that of the template.

Landmark detection on 3D face scans can broadly be done in two main ways: (1) detection directly on the 3D mesh [46], (2) detection on the associated registered 2D image and projecting these 2D landmarks onto the 3D mesh [51]. The majority of the

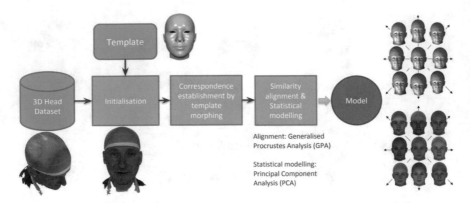

Fig. 10.9 Detailed 3DMM modelling pipeline. In the first step, 3D scans need to be roughly aligned, and the template mesh placed reasonably close to the scan. This can be done by manually annotating scans, or, more conveniently, by automatically detecting facial landmarks. Given this initial alignment, one can proceed with correspondence establishment and finally statistical modelling

research in facial landmark detection is done on 2D images, partly because it is much easier to obtain larger training datasets of 2D images, but also because the areas of applications are larger. Facial landmarking algorithms can loosely be grouped into three major classes: holistic methods, Constrained Local Model (CLM) methods and regression-based methods [146]. These classes of methods may use pixel values or extracted features on the face or in local facial patches around the landmarks. As automatic facial landmark detection is usually quite an important building block both for building and using morphable models, in the following, we briefly discuss the broad approaches.

Holistic Methods: Cootes et al. [42] introduced the Active Appearance Model (AAM) which aims at fitting the facial images with a small number of coefficients using a statistical model. An AAM consists of a 2D global facial shape model and a holistic facial appearance model, which can be learned by PCA. The appearance model can be learned from a set of holistic pixel values or extracted features, such as SIFT [92] and HOG [54]. In order to locate the landmarks, the learned appearance and shape models are fit to the test images for searching the best match. As a classic approach of facial landmark detection and pose estimation, many improvements over the original AAM have been proposed [83, 139].

Constrained Local Models: The CLM [11, 12, 47] strategies locate facial landmarks based wholly on the global facial shape models as well as the independent local appearance of each landmark. The AAM approach learns the appearance model for the whole face, while CLM models a set of local pixel values or extracted features [9]. The local features make it easier to deal with illumination variations and occlusion.

The popular Zhu and Ramanan [159] face detector and landmarker follows the CLM approach. They use a tree-structured part model of the face, which both detects faces and locates facial landmarks. One of the major advantages of their approach is that it can handle extreme head poses, even at relatively low image resolutions. A mixture-of-trees model encodes topological changes due to viewpoint and uses extracted features (HOG features) rather raw pixel values. The authors employ 13 viewpoints (spanning 180 degrees in azimuth) and 5 expressions that are limited to frontal viewpoints, yielding a total of 18 mixtures that use a shared pool of parts.

Regression Methods: The regression-based strategies use machine learning methods to learn the mapping from 2D images to the landmarks [34, 58, 67, 158]. The main difference from the previous two classes of methods is that regression methods normally do not construct any explicit global face shape constraints. The regression-based techniques can be categorised into direct regression methods [145] and cascaded regression methods [58]. The former strategies predict the landmark positions in one iteration with no initialisation, while the latter methods perform cascaded prediction and they normally require landmark ground-truth for learning. More recently, there have been deep learning-based methods that try to estimate 3D landmark positions from 2D images [34, 58].

10.6 Correspondence Establishment

Correspondence establishment is a very challenging problem, encompassing non-linear shape representation and non-rigid shape deformation. The main approach to dense correspondence is shape registration. As shown in Table 10.2, many methods exist to register a mesh using different transformations. Three main types are common: rigid transformation, rigid deformation followed with non-rigid deformation and non-rigid deformation.

Rigid transformation follows the assumption that the objects can be registered by a Euclidean transformation consisting of rotation and translation [14, 69, 81]. This transformation, which has 6 Degrees of Freedom (DoF), is applied for all the points. When global scaling is also permitted, this is termed a similarity transformation.

Rigid transformation with non-rigid deformation allows surfaces to undergo a combination of global rigid transformations and local non-rigid deformation. Allen et al. [4] used a skeleton template for articulation. Pekelny et al. [116] employed prior information from bones to estimate the transformations. Chang and Zwicker [37] used a finite set of rigid transformations to estimate the global transformations. Local

Table 10.2 Registration methods

Transformation	Examples
Rigid transformation	All rigid cases
Rigid transformation with non-rigid deformation	[4, 37, 116]
Non-rigid deformation	[7, 29, 30, 89, 102, 111, 112]

deformations can be estimated by blending the transformations of the adjacent parts [37].

Non-rigid deformation methods include more generic and local deformations. There are two ways to perform deformation: displacement fields [73, 111] and local transformations [7, 102]. In the following five subsections, we describe the leading non-rigid registration methods in the literature.

10.6.1 Non-rigid ICP

Amberg et al. [7] proposed the optimal-step Non-Rigid Iterative Closest Point (NICP) framework, which extended Iterative Closest Point (ICP) to non-rigid deformations. Like ICP, there is an iteration loop that finds closest points between source and target shapes, which helps retain the convergence property of ICP. However, rather than the source moving rigidly, small changes in movement are permitted between neighbouring vertices with mesh connectivity. Following Allen et al. [5] they define per-vertex locally affine deformations. Since these are underconstrained, regularisation is necessary and this is achieved by minimising the weighted difference of affine transformations between neighbouring mesh vertices. The weighting is relative to other terms in the cost function (primarily the sum of squared differences between each vertex and their corresponding points on the target surface) and can be thought of as a mesh stiffness, which is gradually reduced through the iteration sequence. Regularised movement and deformation are termed an optimal step, which is achieved via a single linear solve within each iteration, for some level of mesh stiffness.

10.6.2 Global Correspondence Optimisation

In contrast to rigid ICP, Li et al. [102] showed that using proximity heuristics to determine correspondences is less reliable when large deformations are present. Instead of estimating approximated corresponding points alone, the algorithm simultaneously solves for correspondences, confidence weights and deformation field within a single non-linear least-squares optimisation, using the Levenberg–Marquardt algorithm. The global correspondence optimisation solves simultaneously for both the deformation parameters as well as the correspondence positions.

10.6.3 Coherent Point Drift

Myronenko and Song [111] consider the alignment of two point sets as a probability density estimation and they call their method Coherent Point Drift (CPD). There is no closed-form solution for this optimisation, so they employ an Expectation-Maximisation (EM) algorithm to optimise a Gaussian Mixture Model (GMM) fitting. Algorithms are provided to solve for three different shape deformation models: rigid (CPD-rigid), affine (CPD-affine) and generally non-rigid (CPD-non-rigid). The *'non-rigid'* motion model in [111] employs an $M \times M$ Gaussian kernel $\mathbf{G}$ for motion field smoothing, and the M-step requires solving for an $M \times 3$ matrix $\mathbf{W}$ that generates the template deformation (GMM motion field) as $\mathbf{GW}$. Such motion regularisation is related to motion coherence and inspired the algorithm's name. The approach of CPD is to transform the point registration problem into a probability density estimation problem. The template point set is represented as a Gaussian Mixture Model (GMM), where the means of the mixture components are situated at M template points, $\mathbf{y}_m$, in the template point set, $\mathbf{Y}$. The Gaussian distribution around these points is equal for all points, and isotropic with variance σ^2. The CPD algorithm adjusts the position of the mixture components and the variance parameter to maximise the posterior probability of the GMM model generating the N data points $\mathbf{x}_n$ in the data point set, $\mathbf{X}$.

In the *expectation step* (E-step) of the EM algorithm, the probabilities of correspondence between template and data, $\mathbf{P}$ are computed, initially using assumed parameters for the GMM, i.e. the initial template position and shape, and a suitable estimate of isotropic variance σ^2. A given entry $P_{m,n} = P(m|\mathbf{x_n})$ in $\mathbf{P}$ is a posterior probability computed using Bayes theorem as

$$P(m|\mathbf{x_n}) = \frac{\exp^{-\frac{1}{2}\left(\frac{\|x_n - y_m(\theta)\|^2}{\sigma^2}\right)}}{\sum_{k=1}^{M} \exp^{-\frac{1}{2}\left(\frac{\|x_n - y_k(\theta)\|^2}{\sigma^2}\right)} + \frac{(2\pi\sigma^2)^{\frac{3}{2}}\omega M}{(1-\omega)N}}, \tag{10.2}$$

where ω is the weighting of a uniform distribution added to the GMM to account for data noise. The symbol θ indicates that the template points are deformed according to the current estimate of the template deformation parameters.

The *maximisation step* (M-step) then optimises the GMM parameters, based on these expected correspondence probabilities, and this two-step process iterates until convergence.

Assuming an implementation for 3D point clouds, the *'rigid'* motion model is a 7-parameter similarity transform including a 6-DoF 3D rigid transform and a global scale parameter, whereas the affine motion model is the standard unconstrained 12-parameter formulation. For the affine case they optimise for

$$\mathbf{B} = f_B(\mathbf{X}, \mathbf{Y}, \mathbf{P}), \ \mathbf{t} = f_t(\mathbf{X}, \mathbf{Y}, \mathbf{P}), \ \sigma^2 = f_\sigma(\mathbf{X}, \mathbf{Y}, \mathbf{P}), \tag{10.3}$$

where $\mathbf{B}$ is an affine transformation matrix (excluding translation), $\mathbf{t}$ is a translation vector and σ^2 is a scalar representing variance. For the functional forms of f_B, f_t, f_σ, see [111].

The CPD method has been extended by various groups [76, 86, 140, 143]. Compared to Thin Plate Spline Robust Point Matching, TPS-RPM, [150], CPD offers superior accuracy and stability with respect to non-rigid deformations in the presence of outliers. A modified version of CPD imposed a *Local Linear Embedding* topological constraint to cope with highly articulated non-rigid deformations [71]. However, this extension is more sensitive to noise than CPD. Zhou et al. formulated a non-rigid registration method using Student's Mixture Model (SMM) to do probability density estimation [157]. The results are more robust and accurate on noisy data than CPD. Dai et al. [51] presented a hierarchical parts-based CPD morphing framework, called CPD-LB, that employed mesh morphing constraints based on the Laplace–Beltrami (LB) operator. The approach is able to mitigate under-fitting, over-fitting and tangential surface sliding.

Recent techniques have emphasised isometric deformation of shapes, such that certain intrinsic surface properties (geodesic distances, face areas and angles) are preserved. Jain et al. [89] sought a low-dimensional embedding method to preserve all pairwise geodesic distances. Bronstein et al. [29] used generalised multi-dimensional scaling to embed one mesh in another for partial mesh matching. Based on previous work, Bronstein et al. [30] used a different distance measurement known as diffusion distance and Gromov–Hausdorff distance to deal with topological noise. The result in Ovsjanikov et al. [112] demonstrated that a single correspondence was able to be established for all points by means of the heat kernel.

10.6.4 Laplace–Beltrami Mesh Manipulation

The Laplace–Beltrami (LB) operator is widely used in 3D mesh manipulation. The LB term regularises the mesh manipulation in two ways: (1) the manipulated points on the mesh template are forced to move towards their corresponding position on the raw 3D scan; (2) all other points in mesh template are moved as rigidly as possible regarding the manipulated points' movement, according to an optimised cost function.

Following Sorkine et al. [130], the idea for quantifying the rigid deformation energy is to sum up the deviations from rigidity. Thus, the energy function can be formed as

$$\mathbf{E}(\mathbf{S}') = \sum_{i=1}^{n} \mathbf{w}_i \sum_{j \in N(i)} \mathbf{w}_{ij} \| (\mathbf{p}'_i - \mathbf{p}'_j) - \mathbf{R}_i (\mathbf{p}_i - \mathbf{p}_j) \|, \qquad (10.4)$$

where $\mathbf{S}'$ is the deformed mesh associated with a mesh $\mathbf{S}$ and $\mathbf{R}$ is a rotation. The mesh consists of n vertices and m faces. Also $N(i)$ is the set of vertices connected to vertex i. The parameters $\mathbf{w}_i$, $\mathbf{w}_{ij}$ are fixed vertex and edge weights, respectively. Note that $\mathbf{E}(\mathbf{S}')$ relies on the geometries of $\mathbf{S}$, $\mathbf{S}'$, which have vertex positions $\mathbf{p}$, $\mathbf{p}'$, respectively. Specifically, since the reference mesh (our input shape) is fixed, the only variables in $\mathbf{E}(\mathbf{S}')$ are the deformed vertex positions $\mathbf{p}'_i$. The gradient of $\mathbf{E}(\mathbf{S}')$ is computed with respect to the positions $\mathbf{p}'$. The partial derivatives $\mathbf{p}'_i$ can be written as

$$\frac{d\mathbf{E}(\mathbf{S}')}{d\mathbf{p}'_i} = \sum_{j \in N(i)} 4\mathbf{w}_{ij} \left((\mathbf{p}'_i - \mathbf{p}'_j) - \frac{1}{2}(\mathbf{R}_i + \mathbf{R}_j)(\mathbf{p}_i - \mathbf{p}_j) \right). \qquad (10.5)$$

Setting the partial derivatives to zero, each $\mathbf{p}'_i$ represents the following linear system of equations:

$$\sum_{j \in N(i)} \mathbf{w}_{ij}(\mathbf{p}'_i - \mathbf{p}'_j) = \sum_{j \in N(i)} \frac{\mathbf{w}_{ij}}{2}(\mathbf{R}_i + \mathbf{R}_j)(\mathbf{p}_i - \mathbf{p}_j). \qquad (10.6)$$

The linear combination on the left-hand side is the discrete Laplace–Beltrami operator applied to $\mathbf{p}'$; hence, the system of equations can be written as

$$\mathbf{L}\mathbf{p}' = \mathbf{b}, \qquad (10.7)$$

where $\mathbf{b}$ is an n-vector whose i-th row contains the right-hand side expression from (10.6). We also need to incorporate the modelling constraints into this system. In the simplest form, those can be expressed by some fixed positions

$$\mathbf{p}'_j = \mathbf{c}_k, k \in \mathcal{F}, \qquad (10.8)$$

where $\mathcal{F}$ is the set of indices of the constrained vertices.

10.6.5   Parameterisation Methods

Parameterisation is another approach to shape correspondence. Parameterisation of shape allows points insertion, points sliding and points deletion to establish correspondence. Some methods [35] use geodesic distances between each landmark to insert corresponding points. Others tend to find the best parameterisation among all the subjects [55].

Contour Subdivision: Correspondences can be found by localisation of salient feature points ('landmarks') and then by dividing the length of the contour equally in terms of geodesic distances between each landmark. Landmarks are detected and labelled by virtue of their learned local properties and their relative configuration. Relative local properties can be enforced by a model fitting approach based on sample consensus, such as RANSAC [35].

Minimum Description Length: Davies et al. [55] posed the correspondence establishment as one of finding the best parameterisation for each shape in the training set. The algorithm selects the set of parameterisations by minimising the description length of the training set. This objective function captures both the model complexity itself and the data values required to express each of the training scans with the model.

10.6.6 Correspondence Establishment Summary

There exist lots of correspondence establishment methods including template morphing, isometric deformation and shape parameterisation. The most recent progress in 3DMM construction pipelines reveals that template morphing method is a better choice in this case than other methods [132]. The goal of template morphing is to align and morph a *source* point set (or mesh) to a *target* point set. By using some form of template shape as the source, non-rigid shape morphing is able to reparameterise a collection of raw 3D scans of some object class into a consistent form. This is feasible when the optimisation of a cost function forces the template to morph towards the shape of target mesh. The cost function can be defined as a distance error or a functional energy between the morphed template and the target mesh. In most recent progress, there is a trend of correspondence matching by deep learning [28, 128, 144]. Once trained, correspondence matching can be a real-time process. Lots of features in the face can be used for the optimisation of the cost function. However, this is not the case in the cranium, which makes it a more complicated problem than face-only template morphing.

With correct correspondences, a 3DMM is able to sensibly describe the shape variation within the object class [131]. The ground-truth of dense correspondence is required for the evaluation of correspondence accuracy. Because that ground-truth of dense correspondence is often unknown, manual landmarks can be used as the ground-truth in evaluation [131, 132]. Based on this evaluation metric, Ericsson et al. [64] used the mean absolute distance, which is calculated between the manual landmarks and points corresponding to the same landmarks in a mesh template, for benchmarking.

10.7 Procrustes Alignment

In some techniques in the literature, establishing correspondences and attaining alignment are tightly coupled, whereas in others they are more separate. In the previous section, we considered tightly coupled methods and in following section, we consider the standalone alignment procedure GPA [77, 79, 133], which operates on the assumption that correspondences are known. It is of course possible to realign, if there is good rationale to do so, using GPA after correspondences have been found using any method.

We now briefly recap the well-known Procrustes alignment procedure. The collection of scans in dense correspondence are subjected to Generalised Procrustes Analysis (GPA) to remove similarity transformation effects (rotation, translation, scale), leaving only shape information. Let X and Y be a pair of $(m \times n)$ matrices representing two objects with n corresponding points in m dimensional space. Full Procrustes alignment seeks an optimal similarity transformation with $(\mathbf{R}, \mathbf{t}, s)$ denoted as rotation, translation and scaling, respectively, such that

$$(\mathbf{R}, \mathbf{t}, s) = \arg\min_{\mathbf{R}, \mathbf{t}, s} ||s(\mathbf{R}\mathbf{X} + \mathbf{t}\mathbf{u}^\mathrm{T}) - \mathbf{Y}||_2^2, \tag{10.9}$$

where $\mathbf{u}$ is an n-dimensional column vector of unit values. If one is interested in *form models* (models that retain the original scaling of all of the inputs used in the training), the scaling is constant $(s = 1)$, otherwise, it is determined by ensuring X and Y have the same mean (or RMS) distance to the centroid. The translation component can be eliminated by centering all shapes on their centroids. The solution to the rotation can readily be found using Singular Value Decomposition (SVD).

Generalising the above to many sets of corresponding points, Generalised Procrustes Analysis (GPA) is a widely used alignment method in statistical modelling for aligning training datasets. It aims to align to the mean shape of the dataset, but the mean shape depends on alignment and so the GPA process is iterative, as follows:

1. Set the initial estimate of the mean shape to one example from the dataset (e.g. the first or the nearest to mean size);
2. Align all the remaining shapes to the estimated mean shape (updated in every loop);
3. If the estimated mean has changed significantly, go to Step 2.

The convergence of GPA alignment is detected by the stabilisation of the mean shape.

10.8   Statistical Modelling

Statistical modelling is the final step of 3DMM construction. It represents shape using a reduced set of parameters and models their multivariate distribution. The number of parameters is small relative to 3N where N is the number of 3D points in the mesh. PCA is one form of this that decorrelates the parameters that control shape variation. The standard method (PCA) and recent progress are discussed in the following sections.

10.8.1   Principal Component Analysis

Principal Component Analysis (PCA) generates a 3DMM as a linear basis of shapes. This allows for the generation of novel shape instances. Each deformed shape template is represented by p 3D points (x_i, y_i, z_i) and is reshaped to a $3p$ row vector. Each of these vectors is then stacked in a $k \times 3p$ data matrix, for a dataset with k items, and each column is made zero mean. Singular Value Decomposition is applied from which eigenvectors are given directly and eigenvalues can be computed from the singular values. This yields a linear model as

$$\mathbf{X}^* = \bar{\mathbf{X}} + \mathbf{PU} = \bar{\mathbf{X}} + \sum_{i=1}^{k-1} \mathbf{P}_i U_i, \tag{10.10}$$

where $\bar{\mathbf{X}}$ is the mean shape vector and $\mathbf{P}$ is a matrix whose columns $\mathbf{U} = [U_1, \ldots, U_k]$ are the eigenvectors of the covariance matrix. The vector $\mathbf{P}$ holds the shape parameters $\{P_i\}$, that weight the shape variation modes which, when added to the mean shape, model a shape instance $\mathbf{X}^*$.

The standard assumption in PCA model construction is a multimodal Gaussian distribution with the associated ellipses of constant probability having their axes along the eigenvectors (principal components). However, Koppen et al. [99] observe that various ethnic groups have quite different means in shape space and therefore proposes a Gaussian mixture 3DMM to better model the global shape variation.

10.8.2 Gaussian Process Morphable Model

Lüthi et al. [106] employed Gaussian processes (GPs) to statistically model shape variations. The modelling by a GP is represented by the leading components of its Karhunen–Loève expansion. A Gaussian Process Morphable Model (GPMM) can use manually defined arbitrary kernel functions to describe the deformation's covariance matrix. This enables a GPMM to aid the construction of a 3DMM, without the need for training data. The posterior models of GPMMs are regression models of the shape deformation field. Given partial observations, such posterior models are able to determine what is the potential complete shape. A posterior model is able to estimate other points' movements when some set of landmarks and their target positions are given.

Instead of modelling absolute vertex positions using PCA, GPMMs represent the shape variation as a vector field $\mathbf{u}$ from a template $\mathbf{X} \in \mathbb{R}^{p \times 3}$ towards a target shape $\mathbf{X}'$ represented as

$$\mathbf{X}' = \mathbf{X} + \mathbf{u}(\mathbf{X}) \tag{10.11}$$

for some deformation vector field $\mathbf{u} \in \mathbb{R}^{p \times 3}$. We model the deformation as a Gaussian process $\mathbf{u} \sim GP(\mu, \mathbf{k})$ where $\mu \in \mathbb{R}^{p \times 3}$ is a mean deformation and $\mathbf{k} \in \mathbb{R}^{3 \times 3}$ a covariance function or kernel. The core idea behind this approach is that a parametric, low-dimensional model can be obtained by representing the Gaussian process using the r leading basis functions $\psi_i \in \mathbb{R}^{p \times 3}$ of its Karhunen–Loève expansion:

$$\mathbf{u} = \mu + \sum_{i=1}^{r} \alpha_i \sqrt{\lambda_i} \psi_i, \alpha_i \in \mathcal{N}(0, 1). \tag{10.12}$$

One possible choice for the kernel function is to build it from training data. In that case, the resulting model is the same as if using PCA. However, this kernel function can be combined with various other kernel functions, some of which can be manually defined. Since GPMMs have much more freedom in defining the covariance function, much more shape variation is modelled when compared to standard PCA models. However, the shapes generated by such models may be quite far away from the space of the training shapes, which can also be a potential problem.

10.8.3   Statistical Modelling Using Autoencoders

Recently Ranjan et al. [121] introduced a Convolutional Mesh Autoencoder (CoMA) consisting of mesh downsampling and mesh upsampling layers with fast localised convolutional filters defined on the mesh surface. Bagautdinov et al. [10] proposed a method to model multi-scale face geometry that learns the facial geometry using UV parameterisation for mesh representation, which started with the observation that both global and local linear models can be viewed as specific instances of autoencoders. This approach featured a variational autoencoder with multiple layers of hidden variables that capture various level of geometrical details. Although PCA is a very well-known and widely used procedure that works well for linear shape spaces, either Gaussian processes or autoencoders can replace PCA in statistical modelling.

10.9   Existing 3DMM Construction Pipelines

A 3DMM construction pipeline is an automatic procedure that includes initialisation, dense correspondence establishment, alignment and statistical modelling methods. The input is a 3D face dataset, and the output is a 3D morphable model. The pipeline should be able to be demonstrated on a publicly available dataset. We compare the three recent works of 3DMM construction pipelines: the LSFM pipeline (2017) [27], the Basel Open Framework (2017) [73], and (later introduced in the chapter) the LYHM pipeline [51].

10.9.1   LSFM Pipeline

The LSFM pipeline uses a 2D facial landmarker to detect 2D facial landmarks and then project them onto 3D mesh. These 3D landmarks are then used to globally align all meshes to a face template mesh, using NICP. With such a large cohort of data, there will be some convergence from either landmarking error or NICP. They employed an error pruning process to avoid undesirable deformation results because of the failures of algorithm convergence. Then the registered data is processed by GPA for alignment and PCA for the shape variation modelling.

Table 10.3 Pipelines comparison

	Initialisation	Dense correspondence	Alignment	Modelling
LSFM	Automatic facial landmarks	NICP with error pruning	GPA	PCA
OF	Manual landmarks needed	GPMM registration	GPA	GP
LYHM	Automatic facial landmarks	CPD (CPD-LB variant)	GPA	PCA

10.9.2 Basel Open Framework

The Basel Open Framework (OF) [73] requires manual landmarks for the initialisation of registration. They employed GPMM registration to establish dense correspondence, where the model is obtained by modelling the possible deformation of a reference mesh, using a Gaussian process. This initial GPMM models not the actual shape variation but the possible deformation defined by a combination of handcrafted Gaussian kernels. The registration process is both multi-scale as well as the face being divided into five regions, each associated with their own smoothness parameters. The deformation of ears is the most regularised and the nose and eye regions are the least regularised. There usually exists much noise in the ear region of 3D mesh, and more regularisation makes the ear deformation more robust to noise or missing data in a scan. In order to capture the detail of local region, less regularisation enables more flexible deformation. Subsequently, the registered data is subjected to GPA to remove similarity effects. The shape variation is modelled by Gaussian process using the leading components of its Karhunen–Loève expansion.

A comparison of the three 3DMM construction pipelines can be seen in Table 10.3.

10.10   3D Face Models

Existing 3D statistical face models mainly consist of either morphable models, multilinear models or part-based models, as shown in Table 10.4. As discussed earlier, in the late 1990s, Blanz and Vetter built a 3DMM from 3D face scans [17] and employed it in 2D face recognition [18]. Despite significant passage of time since that publication, there are very few publicly available morphable models of the human face and even fewer that include the full cranium (such models are presented in the following section).

The Basel Face Model (BFM) 2009 is the most well-known and widely-used morphable face model, and was developed by Paysan et al. [115]. Like in their seminal paper, again 200 scans were used, but the method of determining corresponding points was improved. Instead of optical flow, a set of hand-labelled feature points is

Table 10.4 An overview of 3D face modelling techniques

Basis functions	Method
Global	Morphable model (PCA) [6, 17, 88]
Global	Multilinear model [22, 27, 142, 148]
Part-based	Part-based model [13, 57, 82]
Localised detail	Hierarchical pyramids [74]
Local	Local wavelet model [32]

marked on each of the 200 training scans. The corresponding points on a template mesh are known, which is then morphed onto the training scan using the optimal-step Non-Rigid ICP algorithm of Amberg et al. [7].

The BFM 2009 [115] was released as both a global model and a part-based model that is learned for four regions (eyes, nose, mouth and the rest of face). In the part-based version, the regions are fitted to the data independently and merged in a post-processing step. The part-based model was shown to lead to a higher data accuracy than the global model. This method and its follow-up work [13, 82] are implemented by:

- Manual face segmentation into several local regions;
- Morphable model construction for each segmented part;
- A post-processing step to stitch the segmented parts.

De Smet et al. [57] proposed a method to find the optimal segmentation automatically by clustering the vertices, which is based on features derived from their displacements. In order to address the potential discontinuities at the boundaries of the segments, they smoothly weight the segments to obtain regionalised basis functions for the training data.

A statistical model called the multilinear model is a higher order generalisation of PCA [22, 142, 148, 149] and is employed to statistically model varying facial expressions. By using a multilinear model, Vlasic et al. [142] modelled facial shape using a combination of identity and expression variation. Yang et al. [149] modelled the expression of a face in a different input image of the same subject and built a PCA shape space for each expression. Follow-up works [22, 148] used multilinear models for a better description of expressions in videos. When a sequence of 3D meshes is given, Bolkart et al. [22] fitted a multilinear model to parametrise a 4D sequence. In 2015, they demonstrated a direct construction of multilinear model from a set of Bosphorus and BU-3DFE raw meshes using a global optimisation of 3DMM parameters along with a groupwise registration over the 3D scans [23]. Models and code are provided online [21].

Another alternative to modelling faces with expression is to blend different shape models with expressions, which was introduced by Salazar et al. [123] to establish correspondence among faces with expression.

A hierarchical pyramids method was introduced by Golovinskiy et al. [74] to build a localised model. In order to model the geometric details in a high-resolution face mesh, this statistical model is able to describe the varying geometric facial detail. Brunton et al. [31, 32] described 3D facial shape variation at multiple scales using wavelet basis. The wavelet basis provided a way to combine small signals in local facial regions which are difficult for PCA to capture. The group makes several of their models, built using the BU-3DFE face database [151], available online [20].

In 2016, Huber et al. [88] published a multi-resolution 3DMM of the face, built from 169 subjects, called the *Surrey Face Model*, publicly available for research use, and with landmark annotation and metadata for texture remapping. They published and since further developed *eos* [87], an open-source 3D morphable face model library for Python and C++, available on GitHub. It supports various 3D morphable face models and includes pose estimation, and fast landmarks and edge-based fitting functionality.

In 2017, Booth et al. [26, 27] built a Large-Scale Facial Model (LSFM), using the NICP template morphing approach, as was used in the BFM, but with error pruning, followed by Generalised Procrustes Analysis (GPA) for alignment, and PCA for the model construction. This 3DMM employs the largest 3D face dataset to date and is constructed from 9663 distinct facial identities.

Lüthi et al. [106] model the shape variations with a Gaussian process, which they represent using the leading components of its Karhunen–Loève expansion. These Gaussian Process Morphable Models (GPMMs) unify a variety of non-rigid deformation models, with B-splines and PCA models as examples. In their follow-on work, they present a novel pipeline for morphable face model construction based on Gaussian processes [73]. GPMMs separate problem-specific requirements from the registration algorithm by incorporating domain-specific adaptions as a prior model. The resulting model, the Basel Face Model 2017, has been made available to researchers.

Tran et al. [137] proposed a framework to construct a non-linear 3DMM model from a large set of unconstrained face images, without collecting 3D face scans. Specifically, given a face image as input, a network encoder estimates the projection, shape and texture parameters. Two decoders serve as the non-linear 3DMM to map from the shape and texture parameters to the 3D shape and texture, respectively.

To conclude, we note that, over the last 20 years, research in 3DMM construction has mainly been focused on two main techniques: (1) dense correspondence establishment and (2) statistical modelling methods. Most of the methods need landmarks or other annotations in either the initialisation or the correction of correspondence establishment and are often not fully automatic processes. For statistical modelling, the most popular models overwhelmingly use PCA or GPs, which cannot model high-frequency details very well. Only very recently, researchers have started to more actively propose alternative ways to learn and represent face shape and texture (see Sect. 10.15), which preserve more fine-scale detail. Additionally, most models consist of only the face area, sometimes including the ear and neck regions of the head. In practice, when using models that contain ears, the ear region is often excluded in the fitting process as fitting ears has proven a difficult task. The next section (Sect. 10.11) introduces the most recent full head 3DMMs, while Sect. 10.12 provides an overview of 3D ear models.

10.11   3D Head Models

In 2017, Dai et al. [51, 52] published the Liverpool-York Head Model (LYHM), a public 3DMM of the full human head in both shape and texture. One of the authors' aims was to model human face and cranium variation in order to support clinical planning and surgical intervention evaluation tools for craniofacial surgeons. The authors used a 3dMDhead scanning system to capture 3D images of the human face and cranium, and 1212 scans have been used to build the global LYHM. They also built several demographic-specific models from subsets of the data related to age and gender.

Li et al. [103], also in 2017, proposed the FLAME model, which uses a linear shape space trained from 3800 scans of human heads. FLAME combines this linear shape space with an articulated jaw, neck and eyeballs, pose-dependent corrective blendshapes and additional global expression blendshapes. The pose and expression dependent articulations are learned from 4D face sequences. In total, the model is trained from over 33,000 scans. FLAME is low-dimensional, but the authors show it to be more expressive than existing PCA-based models. The authors make the model available for research purposes.

In 2019, Gerig et al. released an updated version of the BFM, the Basel Face Model 2019, as part of the Open Framework [73] resources. It covers the full head, with the back of the head being based on little data and heuristics, and is available in three different resolution levels.

In the same year, Ploumpis et al. [119] presented a technique to merge statistical models of the face and the full head and applied this to the LSFM face model and the LYHM head model, respectively, in order to combine the best properties of both models, namely, full coverage of the cranium with data-derived statistical variation, plus fine detail in the facial area. This work developed into what is now known as the Universal Head Model (UHM), shown in Fig. 10.1. This model has independent statistical representation of the ears, eyes with position, gaze direction and pupil dilation parameters, as well as a basic inner-mouth surface that includes tongue and teeth, although these inner-mouth parts do not capture independent statistical variation derived from 3D image data.

10.12   3D Ear Models

The shape of the ear has long been recognised as a means of biometric identification [1, 117]. There are many existing ear recognition systems, with a recent survey by Emersic et al. [63] and ear biometrics continues to be an active research area [62]. Morphable models provide powerful statistical priors on shape and so can be used in biometric ear analysis.

Zolfaghari et al. [161] describe a construction of a morphable model for external ear shapes based on a deformation framework using diffeomorphic metric mapping.

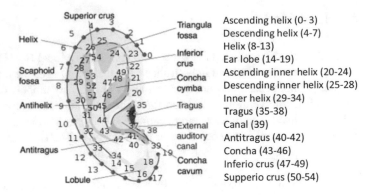

Fig. 10.10 55 landmarks on ears and their semantic annotations, as proposed by Zhou et al. [156]

To our knowledge, the morphable model is not publicly available. However, they released high-quality 3D meshes of the ear for 10 subjects [161]. This is insufficient to construct a high-quality 3D morphable model that is a good representation of the mean ear shape and the variance and covariances of size and shape, of a large population.

Recently, Zhou et al. [156] made a 2D ear image dataset available with 55 ground-truth landmarks over 600 images, partitioned into 500 training images and 100 test images. Figure 10.10 shows the 55 landmarks and their semantic annotations. It is possible to leverage this large annotated 2D ear dataset [156] to generate a large 3D ear dataset with a data augmentation process. Such a process was followed by Dai et al. [48] to create the first publicly available 3DMM of the human ear, the York Ear Model, illustrated in Fig. 10.11. The augmented 3D ear dataset was also released with this model, thus allowing researchers to construct 3DMMs using their own 3DMM construction pipelines, the performance of the models constructed could then be compared with the original model of Dai et al. [48].

10.13 3D Facial Symmetry and Asymmetry

Recent work in 3DMMs of the human head has employed symmetric morphing and explicit modelling of symmetric and asymmetric shape variation. Most biological objects, including human heads and bodies, possess approximate symmetries. Often this is principally extrinsic, bilateral symmetry (i.e. reflective symmetry about a vertical plane bisecting the object). Deviations from exact symmetry are an interesting and potentially important geometric property in terms of modelling and understanding 3D shape variation. The degree of asymmetry may convey information about an object. For example, there is evidence that facial asymmetry is used by humans to measure genetic health [90] and asymmetry in man-made objects may indicate imperfections in the manufacturing process. For such reasons, statistical shape mod-

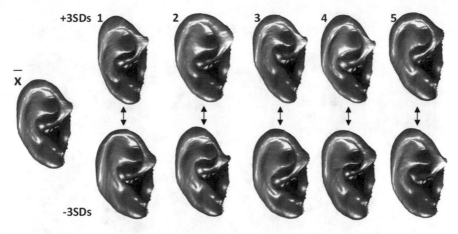

Fig. 10.11 The publicly available 3DMM of the human ear from Dai et al. [48], showing the mean ear on the left and the first five principal components of shape variation

els may separate symmetric from asymmetric shape variability in order to reveal interesting and potentially subtle aspects of shape variation over population datasets.

There is a large body of work on detecting symmetries in images [114], 2D shapes, 3D meshes and point clouds. These symmetries could be exact or approximate [109], extrinsic [120] or intrinsic [113], partial [114, 127], hierarchical or full [113]. Once detected, this enables symmetry-aware mesh processing [75] to take place in which symmetries help regularise and denoise a range of processing tasks.

The geometric morphometrics community [94, 96, 98, 107] has built models of deviations from symmetry, though this has largely been in 2D. Savriama et al. [125] present a decomposition of asymmetric shape into a symmetric shape and asymmetry variation. There are many works on how to measure facial asymmetry variation. There is much literature from both the Computer Vision perspective [38, 104, 108, 160] and the Biology perspective [41, 84, 96].

The ICP-based approach to computing the symmetry plane of bilateral objects in point sets [56, 147, 154] employed a rigid-body transformation-based approach to estimate the symmetry plane. The major advantage of this approach is to benefit from the ICP algorithm relying on a known closed-form solutions for the absolute orientation problem [8, 66].

Recent work by Dai et al. [50] has presented a method to constrain CPD-based template morphing such that all deformations are symmetric. This has been shown to be a useful form of shape deformation regularisation, giving high-quality correspondences. Further work by the same group has decomposed the modelled shape variations of a 3DMM into large symmetric variations and small asymmetric variations [53]. This can be employed to reveal interesting and subtle aspects of shape variation over population datasets. Figure 10.12 shows the first five principal components of symmetric head shape variation for 1212 subjects in the Headspace dataset. Note that ±5 standard deviations are employed to emphasise the shape variation.

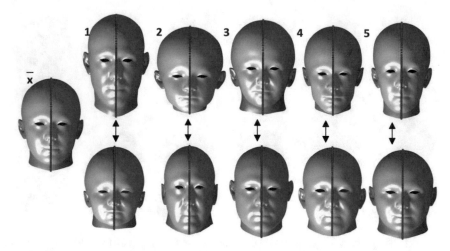

Fig. 10.12 Visualisation of five principal components (mean ± 5 SDs) of symmetry variation

10.14   3DMM Evaluation Criteria

For quantitative evaluation of 3DMM construction pipelines, three performance metrics are commonly used: compactness, generalisation and specificity (see e.g. [131]). The following subsections give a brief introduction to each of them.

10.14.1   Compactness

The compactness of the statistical shape model describes the number of parameters required to express some fraction of the variance in the training set used to construct that model. A more compact model uses fewer parameters to express a given fraction of variance or expresses a bigger fraction of variance for a given number of shape parameters. So compactness measures the efficiency of a model to capture the shape variability. Compactness can be defined as

$$C(m) = \frac{\sum_{i=1}^{m} \alpha_i}{\sum_{i=1}^{N} \alpha_i}, \tag{10.13}$$

where α_i is the i-th eigenvalue, m is the number of shape parameters and N is the total number of shape parameters in the model.

10.14.2   Generalisation

Generalisation measures the capability of the model to represent unseen examples of the class of objects. It can be measured using the *leave-one-out* strategy, where one example is omitted from the training set and used for reconstruction testing. The accuracy of describing the unseen example is calculated by the mean vertex to vertex Euclidean distance error. With an increasing number of model parameters, the generalisation error is expected to decrease. For the same number of model coefficients, the lower mean Euclidean distance error, the better the model.

10.14.3   Specificity

Specificity measures the ability to generate shape instances of the class that are similar to those in the training set. In order to assess specificity, a set of shape instances should be randomly sampled from the shape space. Then the Euclidean distance error to the closest training shape is calculated for each shape instance and the average is taken for all the shape instances. The mean Euclidean distance error is expected to increase with increasing number of parameters, as the increasing number of PCA coefficients gives more flexibility to shape reconstruction. It also increases the likelihood of the reconstructed shape instances being away from the real data. For specificity measurement, the lower Euclidean distance error, the closer the model is to the training data, so the specificity is better.

10.14.4   A Comparison of 3DMM Construction Pipelines

Recently Dai et al. [49] employed a variety of 3DMM construction pipelines to build a 3DMM of the human head using the 1212 subjects from the Headspace dataset. These include their own method [49], which employs an adaptive template and CPD-based morphing, the NICP-based morphing method of the Large-Scale Face Model [26] and the Open Framework pipeline [73]. Compactness results are shown in Fig. 10.13 for the three pipelines, and generalisation and specificity results are shown in Fig. 10.14. Each of these is a function of the number of model parameters employed.

   As can be seen from Fig. 10.13a, when less than 33 components are used, the LSFM pipeline model is more compact than the Adaptive Template (AT) method and the Open Framework (OF). Between the 33 and 79 components, the model constructed by OF is more compact than the other two. When more than 79 components used, the AT method has better compactness than LSFM [27] and OF [73]. With the first 56 and the first 146 components used, the 3DMM constructed by the AT method retains 95 and 98% of the shape variation in the training set.

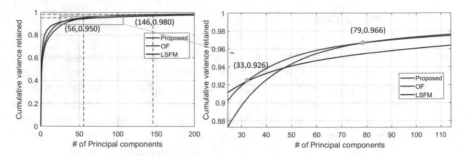

Fig. 10.13 Compactness in terms of number of model components. Higher is better. 'Proposed' is the Adaptive Template method of Dai et al. [49]

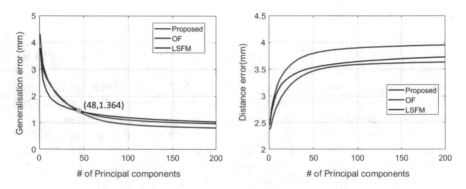

Fig. 10.14 Generalisation (left) versus number of model components, lower is better; Specificity (right), lower is better. 'Proposed' is the Adaptive Template method of Dai et al. [49]

The generalisation of the model demonstrates the ability in generating unseen examples. With fewer than 48 model parameters, LSFM is better than the AT method in terms of generalisation error. With more than 48 components, the AT method has the lowest generalisation error, which in this case implies that AT method has the best performance in describing unseen examples.

In [49], Dai et al. discuss how to select the number of model parameters employed in a 3DMM and this can be informed by plots of compactness, generalisation and specificity as a function of number of model parameters. Generally, these are soft curves, where the number selected is an application-dependent trade-off of performance metrics. Figure 10.15 clearly indicates that there are diminishing gains to be made, as the number of components increases, as the performance metric curves flatten, and a reasonable order-of-magnitude selection for the number of components may be 100.

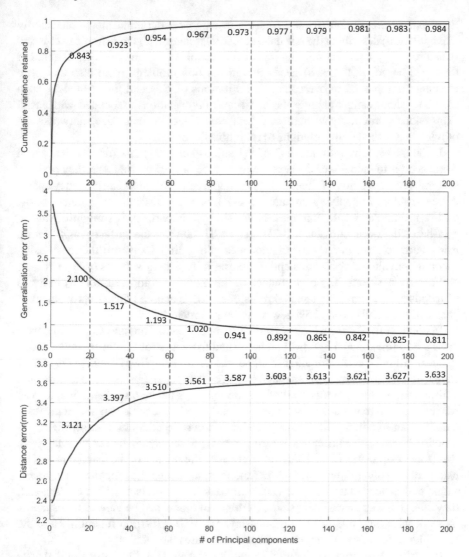

Fig. 10.15 Critical analysis of the model built from the Adaptive Template method, in terms of the number of model components

10.15 3DMM Construction Using Deep Learning

In applications that process, analyse and model 2D images, Convolutional Neural Networks (CNNs) have been immensely successful over the last decade. This is attributed to many desirable properties such as multi-scale, non-linear, hierarchical representation learning and translation invariance due to pooling. However, progress on their application to 3D meshes has been *relatively* limited. This is due to the non-

Euclidean nature of geometry and the different sample patterns and mesh connectivity (triangulation) describing the raw dataset (cf. 2D images with their simple grid-based structure). Any deep learning approach that employs 3D meshes directly (rather than grid-based depth maps) needs to address this problem. Note also that deep learning is employed to overcome the limitations of classical linear models, such as PCA, which cannot capture the non-linear deformations associated with facial expressions, particularly when these are extreme. Encoding using deep networks can provide better modelling solutions to such non-linear spaces.

In Sect. 10.8.3, we introduced *CoMA* (Ranjan et al. [121]), a Convolutional Mesh Autoencoder to model faces, where the input face is a 3D mesh. Here, they perform spectral decomposition of face meshes and apply convolutions in frequency space. A key problem in applying an autoencoder modelling structure to meshes is how to downsample and upsample meshes which, by comparison, is straightforward in grid-based data structures, such as 2D images. The authors use surface simplification using quadric error metrics for the downsampling, they transform the mesh using spectral convolution operations and upsample it by adding vertices back in at their barycentric positions. The performance of the model is compared to PCA in terms of reconstruction error for facial expressions, with a claimed 50% improvement of performance, whilst using 75% fewer model parameters.

In contrast to *CoMA*, which is learned from 3D data, Tran and Liu [137] developed a non-linear facial 3DMM that is learned from a set of 2D 'in-the-wild' facial images, without the need for 3D scans. The architecture employs an encoder to extract shape, texture and camera parameters, two decoders generate shape and texture, and a differentiable renderer fuses all of the models to generate a synthetic image. The renderer is differentiable and so an end-to-end training scheme can simultaneously learn the set of parameters for the encoder and two decoders by minimising a loss function based on the difference between real input and synthetic output images. In their follow-up works [136, 138], they improved the fidelity of the learned model by using, among other things, proxy loss functions, to reduce the influence of regularisation that is needed to make the task learnable. In comparison with a PCA model, they note that a standard linear shape (or texture) model can be viewed as a shallow network with only one fully connected layer and no activation function. Here the layer bias is the mean of the linear shape (or texture) model.

Recently, Generative Adversarial Networks (GANs, Goodfellow et al. [78]) have been explored in the context of face modelling. GANs employ a dual network structure, a generator network and a discriminator network, in a zero-sum game. They are very popular in modelling data distributions and hence are being used in 3DMM related applications. The *MeshGAN* system [40] is a Generative Adversarial Network that operates directly on 3D meshes to generate 3D faces and build non-linear 3DMMs of faces. Here Deep Generative Graph Convolutional Networks (DGCNs) are trained using spectral mesh convolutions that individually model identity and expression. Identity is trained on around 12000 subjects, using the same MeIn3D (3dMD acquisition) dataset as the LSFM, while expression is trained using around 14000 expression from the 4DFAB dataset. The authors demonstrate that the GAN-based architecture is able to generate higher frequency and hence more subtle details than autoencoders and can model the distribution of faces better. In [72], Gecer et al. propose *GANFIT*, which utilises a GAN to learn a 3DMM texture model from in-the-wild images and can reconstruct high-quality texture and geometry from a single image.

10.16 Applications of 3DMMs

Here we demonstrate the utility and power of 3DMMs by describing some of their applications.

10.16.1 Fitting a 3D Model to 2D Images

One of the most popular methods of fitting a 3D model to a 2D image is the *analysis-by-synthesis* approach, which we described in Sect. 10.1.2. 3DMMs are in particular useful for the task of reconstructing 3D from a single, monocular 2D input image, as that problem is ill-constrained. Prior information, in the form of a statistical model that contains knowledge about faces and their variability, makes that problem more feasible to solve.

The overall approach is to find the model parameters that, along with pose, imaging and lighting parameters, generate a synthetic image as similar as possible to the input, and this in an iterative optimisation. To be successful, good initialisations are required as the algorithm may get stuck in a local minimum. In practice it is much easier to achieve a successful result if landmarks are extracted from the 2D image and matched to corresponding landmarks on the 3D model, thus enabling a good estimate of the camera projection matrix.

Knothe [97], in their Ph.D. thesis, describe a complete model building and fitting pipeline in much detail, making it an ideal work for readers wanting to become more familiar with classical non-linear fitting methods, to reconstruct 3D face model parameters from 2D images. Additionally, they present a *global-to-local* approach to overcome some of the limitations of PCA being a holistic method. Their fitting method extends the seminal work of Romdhani et al. [122] who proposed a *Multi-Features Fitting* algorithm, advocating to use various image features such as edges, instead of only pixel intensities, to obtain a smoother overall cost function and to avoid local minima. Aldrian and Smith [3] equally published a seminal work, proposing to decompose the geometric and photometric part of the model fitting to state the problem as a multilinear system which can be solved accurately and efficiently.

Garrido et al. [70], whose work is briefly highlighted in Sect. 10.1.2, highlight shortcomings of PCA-based modelling, and propose a 3-stage fitting consisting of a coarse, medium and fine-scale process, with the modelling process being constrained to the PCA face space only in the first stage.

More recently, researchers have started to use deep learning and CNNs to replace traditional non-linear optimisation algorithms in 3DMM fitting. Among the most well-known, Terawi et al. [134] developed the *MoFA* system, a model-based deep convolutional face autoencoder for unsupervised monocular reconstruction. This approach blends together the powerful analysis capabilities of deep CNNs, with the same kind of model-based image synthesis approach that was used in Blanz and Vetter's facial analysis-by-synthesis [17]. The authors term this *'an expert-designed generative model that serves as a decoder'*. Here both face intrinsics are modelled, which includes 3D shape, reflectance and expression, and imaging extrinsics, which includes 6DoF pose and illumination. The whole pipeline is end-to-end differentiable with the extrinsic/intrinsic model parameters being explicit and with clear semantic meaning. Thus the CNN-based autoencoder is trained to extract model parameters that can be clearly interpreted, by design, in terms of their role in image synthesis.

The MoFA approach is very similar, at least in the image synthesis stage, to the generative part of early analysis-by-synthesis approaches [17]. The problem with both these approaches is that their optimisations are highly non-convex and can easily get stuck in local minima. This is mitigated by the use of landmark-based alignment. However, extracting the model parameters via a deep CNN encoding gives much faster inference, once the network is trained, because the parameters are directly inferred from the network rather than being iteratively optimised. Note that the MoFA 3D shape models are essentially the same linear models employed in PCA-based schemes.

10.16.2 Shape Reconstruction with Missing Data

The task of reconstruction of an unseen example with missing parts can validate the correspondence quality, model fitting and generalisation ability of a 3DMM [2]. In the first row of Fig. 10.16, Dai et al. [51] fix the shape of the cranium and reconstruct the full head from that shape, while permitting the shape of the face to vary. Here, they found that most variation occurs over the chin region. The second row of Fig. 10.16 is the reconstruction from the face only, and they note that the principal variation in reconstructed cranium is from high/short to low/long. This offers a way to augment existing face models with a cranium. Reconstruction from one side of the sagittal symmetry plane demonstrates asymmetrical variation of the head.

10.16.3 Age Regression

Model regression can validate the model's generalisation ability on some property (e.g. age, gender). Dai et al. [51] use a linear regression between the shape and texture parameters against age. After this learning process, shape parameters can be revisited when given the age value. Then the shape for the specific age can be reconstructed by

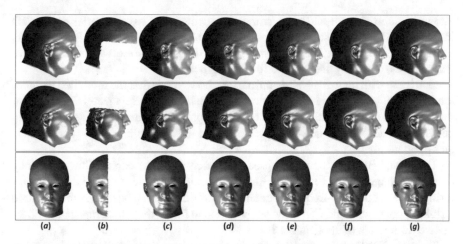

Fig. 10.16 The flexibility of reconstruction from incomplete data, using the method of Dai et al. [51]: (**a**) example; (**b**) crop (incomplete data); (**c**)–(**g**) are the flexibility modes, and (**e**) is the mean reconstruction

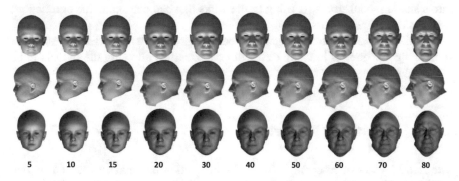

Fig. 10.17 Age regression from 5 years to 80 years, learned on the LYHM-male submodel

adding the shape variation to the mean shape. Figure 10.17 demonstrates a sequence of 3D images generated from age regression of the LYHM-male submodel (a model learned only on male scans of the Headspace dataset), ranging from 5 to 80 years. Note that the cranium develops before the face in children, and the shape of the cranium is not changing in adults.

10.17 Research Challenges

There are many open research challenges in the training and fitting of 3DMMs. First, there are many more 2D image datasets than 3D image datasets, and 2D datasets are usually significantly larger. This is due to 2D images being more easily captured, allowing much cheaper and more convenient cameras. If we can better exploit 2D images for 3DMM construction, as is starting to happen with the GAN networks already mentioned, then 3DMMs can exploit the large 2D datasets and online *in-the-wild* images, currently unexploited for this purpose.

One issue with network-based approaches, however, is that the modelled parameters are not always easily interpretable. Interpretable parameters generally allow for models to be deployed in a broader range of applications and so bridging the gap between uninterpretable network encodings and interpretable parametric models is an important goal.

Traditional 3DMM training approaches, such as PCA, capture low-frequency detail. Although this is now being addressed, more work needs to be done in capturing more subtle high-frequency details and, for the human head, this may include wrinkles, pores and hair. Can these be modelled in forms that are compact and informative for a range of applications?

Training 3DMMs from partial data is another important challenge, in order to exploit both 2D and 3D data that is occluded or self-occluded. This may lead to new parts-based methods. Here various component-based models may be integrated into a single model structure, using frameworks that can determine the correlations between the different parts.

Ultimately, we hope for very general, but interpretable models that can answer a broad range of queries in many different contexts, thus allowing the models to be deployed in a very broad range of applications.

10.18 Concluding Remarks

The last 20 years of research in 3DMM construction has mainly focused on two main techniques: (1) dense correspondence establishment and (2) statistical modelling methods. For dense correspondence establishment, one established method is template morphing, which aims to find the best combination of global and local transformation. This is formulated as the optimisation of a cost function that forces the template to morph towards the shape of the target mesh. The cost function can be defined as distance error or functional energy between morphed template and target mesh. The most recent progress has been in correspondence matching by deep learning.

In terms of statistical modelling methods, the standard method is PCA, which finds the directions in the vector space that have maximum variance, whilst being mutually orthogonal. Multilinear models use multiple PCA models to separate factors like identity and expressions. A Gaussian process can model shape variation by just defining different Gaussian kernels. With all these methods, high-frequency signals are lost in the statistical modelling. Recently, there is a trend in statistical modelling to use autoencoders. The input meshes either need re-meshing before the learning process when processing 3D meshes directly, or need to be transferred into a functional space, e.g. UV map representation. At the end of the decoder, there is a back-transformation required from the functional space to 3D spatial coordinates. The most recent work in 3DMMs has employed GANs both to reconstruct shape and texture from single 2D images and to improve statistical modelling of the underlying distributions.

After working through this chapter, you should be able to

- Explain what a 3DMM is, and why it is useful.
- Appreciate the various pipelines, and processes within pipelines, that are required to construct 3DMMs from large datasets that contain 3D images of some object class.
- Understand how deep learning is being used to build non-linear morphable models.
- Understand how to evaluate 3DMMs in terms of a set of performance metrics.
- Employ 3DMMs as a useful prior on shape in Computer Vision and Machine Learning applications.

10.19   Further Reading

A very recent survey work is that of Egger et al. [61], who take stock of the last 20 years of 3D morphable model history, since their inception. They provide a thorough review of the state-of-the-art literature and current challenges. To our knowledge, there is currently only little other work that surveys the 3DMM literature. Ferrari et al. [68] presented an introductory tutorial on *Statistical 3D Face Reconstruction with 3D Morphable Models* at the 2018 3D Vision Conference, with a particular focus on a dictionary-learning based approach for model building and fitting. Brunton et al. [33] present a review of statistical shape spaces for 3D data. In addition to the global PCA approach presented in this chapter, they cover *wavelet PCA*, where wavelet transforms project sampled data onto basis functions that are localised in space and frequency before PCA is applied. The Graphics and Vision Research Group of the University of Basel provide an online course on *Statistical Shape Modelling* [80] that is based on the work of Lüthi et al. [106], who model shape variations with a Gaussian process, which results in a more general framework than PCA for modelling shape deformations. In terms of modelling texture (appearance), this chapter has considered 3D shape and texture as independent models. The Copula Eigenfaces work of Egger et al. [60] enables a combined analysis of facial appearance and shape data.

   In terms of applications of 3D morphable face models to 2D images, Zollhöfer et al. [162] provide a recent and comprehensive overview and comparison of state-of-the-art methods for monocular 3D face reconstruction, where 3D morphable models are often an essential part.

10.20 Questions

1. Explain the difference between a raw 3D image and a version of that same 3D image generated by a 3DMM. Discuss both the underlying representations and visual appearance of the two entities.
2. Why are landmarks points often needed in 3DMM construction pipelines that use template morphing?
3. Explain how correspondence within a whole set of items is achieved by morphing a template N times to the N items (e.g. 3D face scans) in a dataset. Discuss the validity of the notion of *groupwise* correspondence using this mechanism.
4. If Euclidean rigid alignment is built into the morphing process, when morphing a template to a dataset, why is a Generalised Procrustes Analysis step applied after morphing, which is also an alignment process?
5. Explain how PCA is used to provide a mechanism to construct a 3DMM. What are PCA's limitations in this respect? Suggest an alternative approach to model construction that does not have this limitation.
6. Why is weighted PCA sometimes used in place of PCA for 3DMM construction?
7. Researchers are now increasingly using deep learning to build 3DMMs. Discuss the benefits you think that deep learning techniques bring to the 3DMM construction pipelines.

10.21 Exercises

1. To get started with 3DMMs without access to a 3D dataset, we suggest building a synthetic dataset of triangles in the plane, with random positions, shapes, sizes and rotations. Given the dataset is synthetic, the point correspondences are known. Use GPA and PCA to build a statistical model. Then use the model to generate an animation of the principal modes of shape variation.
2. Download the Basel Face Model (BFM) 2009 [115] and generate animations of the principal modes of both shape and texture variation.
3. Download a publicly available 3D face dataset. Use the mean BFM shape as a template and morph this to an example in the dataset. This requires selecting a shape morphing algorithm such as non-rigid ICP [7] or CPD [111], both of which take some time to tune for some given dataset. After completing the morph, fit the BFM model and observe the result compared to the raw data. Try this several times using varying numbers of principal components in the model and comment on your observations.
4. Implement a full pipeline that morphs the BFM 3D face template onto each example in your 3D face dataset and build a 3DMM using GPA and PCA applied to the warped templates. Again, animate the principal modes of shape variation.

References

1. Abaza, A., Ross, A., Hebert, C., Harrison, M.A.F., Nixon, M.S.: A survey on ear biometrics. ACM Comput. Surv. (CSUR) **45**(2), 22 (2013)
2. Albrecht, T., Knothe, R., Vetter, T.: Modeling the remaining flexibility of partially fixed statistical shape models. In: 2nd MICCAI Workshop on Mathematical Foundations of Computational Anatomy, pp. 160–169 (2008)
3. Aldrian, O., Smith, W.A.P.: Inverse rendering of faces with a 3d morphable model. IEEE Trans. Pattern Anal. Mach. Intell. **35**(5), 1080–1093 (2013). https://doi.org/10.1109/TPAMI. 2012.206
4. Allen, B., Curless, B., Popović, Z.: Articulated body deformation from range scan data. ACM Trans. Graph. (TOG) **21**, 612–619 (2002)
5. Allen, B., Curless, B., Popovic, Z.: The space of human body shapes: reconstruction and parameterization from range scans. ACM Trans. Graph. **22**(3), 587–594 (2003). https://doi. org/10.1145/882262.882311
6. Amberg, B., Knothe, R., Vetter, T.: Expression invariant 3d face recognition with a morphable model. In: 8th IEEE International Conference on Automatic Face and Gesture Recognition. FG, pp. 1–6 (2008)
7. Amberg, B., Romdhani, S., Vetter, T.: Optimal step nonrigid ICP algorithms for surface registration. In: IEEE Conference on Computer Vision and Pattern Recognition, pp. 1–7 (2007)
8. Arun, K.S., Huang, T.S., Blostein, S.D.: Least-squares fitting of two 3-d point sets. IEEE Trans. Pattern Anal. Mach. Intell. **PAMI-9**(5), 698–700 (1987)
9. Asthana, A., Zafeiriou, S., Cheng, S., Pantic, M.: Robust discriminative response map fitting with constrained local models. In: Proceedings of the IEEE Conference on Computer Vision and Pattern Recognition, pp. 3444–3451 (2013)
10. Bagautdinov, T.M., Wu, C., Saragih, J.M., Fua, P., Sheikh, Y.: Modeling facial geometry using compositional VAEs. In: IEEE Conference on Computer Vision and Pattern Recognition, CVPR, pp. 3877–3886 (2018). https://doi.org/10.1109/CVPR.2018.00408
11. Baltrusaitis, T., Robinson, P., Morency, L.P.: 3d constrained local model for rigid and non-rigid facial tracking. In: IEEE Conference on Computer Vision and Pattern Recognition (CVPR), pp. 2610–2617 (2012)
12. Baltrusaitis, T., Robinson, P., Morency, L.P.: Constrained local neural fields for robust facial landmark detection in the wild. In: Proceedings of the IEEE International Conference on Computer Vision Workshops, pp. 354–361 (2013)
13. Basso, C., Verri, A., Herder, J.: Fitting 3d morphable models using implicit representations. J. Virtual Real. Broadcast. **4**(18), 1–10 (2007)
14. Bergevin, R., Laurendeau, D., Poussart, D.: Estimating the 3d rigid transformation between two range views of a complex object. In: Proceedings of 11th IAPR International Conference on Pattern Recognition. Vol. I. Conference A: Computer Vision and Applications, pp. 478–482. IEEE (1992)
15. Besl, P.J., McKay, N.D.: Method for registration of 3-d shapes. In: Sensor Fusion IV: Control Paradigms and Data Structures, vol. 1611, pp. 586–607. International Society for Optics and Photonics (1992)
16. Beumier, C., Acheroy, M.: Face verification from 3d and grey level clues. Pattern Recogn. Lett. **22**(12), 1321–1329 (2001)
17. Blanz, V., Vetter, T.: A morphable model for the synthesis of 3d faces. In: Proceedings of the 26th Annual Conference on Computer Graphics and Interactive Techniques, pp. 187–194 (1999)
18. Blanz, V., Vetter, T.: Face recognition based on fitting a 3d morphable model. IEEE Trans. Pattern Anal. Mach. Intell. **25**(9), 1063–1074 (2003)
19. Bogo, F., Romero, J., Loper, M., Black, M.J.: Faust: Dataset and evaluation for 3d mesh registration. In: 2014 IEEE Conference on Computer Vision and Pattern Recognition, pp. 3794–3801 (2014)

20. Bolkart, T., Brunton, A., Salazar, A., Wuhrer, S.: Statistical 3d shape models of human faces. http://facepage.gforge.inria.fr/. Accessed 4 Mar 2020
21. Bolkart, T., Wuhrer, S.: A groupwise multilinear correspondence optimization for 3d faces. http://multilinear-mdl.gforge.inria.fr. Accessed 23 Aug 2019
22. Bolkart, T., Wuhrer, S.: Statistical analysis of 3d faces in motion. In: 2013 International Conference on 3D Vision-3DV, pp. 103–110. IEEE (2013)
23. Bolkart, T., Wuhrer, S.: A groupwise multilinear correspondence optimization for 3d faces. In: Proceedings of the IEEE International Conference on Computer Vision, pp. 3604–3612 (2015)
24. Bookstein, F.L.: Principal warps: thin-plate splines and the decomposition of deformations. IEEE Trans. Pattern Anal. Mach. Intell. **11**(6), 567–585 (1989)
25. Bookstein, F.L.: Landmark methods for forms without landmarks: morphometrics of group differences in outline shape. Med. Image Anal. **1**(3), 225–243 (1997)
26. Booth, J., Roussos, A., Ponniah, A., Dunaway, D., Zafeiriou, S.: Large scale 3d morphable models. Int. J. Comput. Vis. **126**(2–4), 233–254 (2018)
27. Booth, J., Roussos, A., Zafeiriou, S., Ponniah, A., Dunaway, D.: A 3d morphable model learnt from 10,000 faces. In: Proceedings of CVPR, pp. 5543–5552 (2016)
28. Boscaini, D., Masci, J., Rodolà, E., Bronstein, M.: Learning shape correspondence with anisotropic convolutional neural networks. In: Advances in Neural Information Processing Systems, pp. 3189–3197 (2016)
29. Bronstein, A.M., Bronstein, M.M., Kimmel, R.: Generalized multidimensional scaling: a framework for isometry-invariant partial surface matching. Proc. Natl. Acad. Sci. **103**(5), 1168–1172 (2006)
30. Bronstein, A.M., Bronstein, M.M., Kimmel, R., Mahmoudi, M., Sapiro, G.: A Gromov-Hausdorff framework with diffusion geometry for topologically-robust non-rigid shape matching. Int. J. Comput. Vis. **89**(2–3), 266–286 (2010)
31. Brunton, A., Bolkart, T., Wuhrer, S.: Multilinear wavelets: a statistical shape space for human faces. In: Fleet, D.J., Pajdla, T., Schiele, B., Tuytelaars, T. (eds.) Computer Vision - ECCV, Proceedings, Part I. Lecture Notes in Computer Science, vol. 8689, pp. 297–312. Springer, Berlin (2014). https://doi.org/10.1007/978-3-319-10590-1_20
32. Brunton, A., Lang, J., Dubois, E., Shu, C.: Wavelet model-based stereo for fast, robust face reconstruction. In: 2011 Canadian Conference on Computer and Robot Vision (CRV), pp. 347–354 (2011)
33. Brunton, A., Salazar, A., Bolkart, T., Wuhrer, S.: Statistical shape spaces for 3D data: a review. In: C.H. Chen (ed.) Handbook of Pattern Recognition and Computer Vision, 5th edn, pp. 217–238. World Scientific, Singapore (2016). https://doi.org/10.1142/9789814656535_0012
34. Bulat, A., Tzimiropoulos, G.: How far are we from solving the 2d and 3d face alignment problem? (and a dataset of 230,000 3d facial landmarks). In: International Conference on Computer Vision (2017)
35. Cantzler, H.: Random sample consensus (ransac). Action and Behaviour, Division of Informatics, University of Edinburgh, Institute for Perception (1981)
36. Cao, C., Weng, Y., Zhou, S., Tong, Y., Zhou, K.: Facewarehouse: a 3d facial expression database for visual computing. IEEE Trans. Vis. Comput. Graph. **20**(3), 413–425 (2014)
37. Chang, W., Zwicker, M.: Automatic registration for articulated shapes. Comput. Graph. Forum **27**, 1459–1468 (2008)
38. Chen, J., Yang, C., Deng, Y., Zhang, G., Su, G.: Exploring facial asymmetry using optical flow. IEEE Signal Process. Lett. **21**(7), 792–795 (2014)
39. Chen, Y., Medioni, G.: Object modelling by registration of multiple range images. Image Vis. Comput. **10**(3), 145–155 (1992)
40. Cheng, S., Bronstein, M.M., Zhou, Y., Kotsia, I., Pantic, M., Zafeiriou, S.: Meshgan: nonlinear 3d morphable models of faces (2019). arXiv:abs/1903.10384
41. Claes, P., Walters, M., Vandermeulen, D., Clement, J.G.: Spatially-dense 3d facial asymmetry assessment in both typical and disordered growth. J. Anat. **219**(4), 444–455 (2011)

42. Cootes, T.F., Edwards, G.J., Taylor, C.J.: Active appearance models. IEEE Trans. Pattern Anal. Mach. Intell. **23**(6), 681–685 (2001). https://doi.org/10.1109/34.927467
43. Cootes, T.F., Mauro, E.C.D., Taylor, C.J., Lanitis, A.: Flexible 3D models from uncalibrated cameras. Image Vis. Comput. **14**(8), 581–587 (1996). https://doi.org/10.1016/0262-8856(96)01099-2
44. Cootes, T.F., Taylor, C.J.: Combining point distribution models with shape models based on finite element analysis. Image Vis. Comput. **13**(5), 403–409 (1995)
45. Cootes, T.F., Taylor, C.J., Cooper, D.H., Graham, J.: Active shape models-their training and application. Comput. Vis. Image Underst. **61**(1), 38–59 (1995)
46. Creusot, C., Pears, N., Austin, J.: A machine-learning approach to keypoint detection and landmarking on 3d meshes. Int. J. Comput. Vis. **102**(1–3), 146–179 (2013)
47. Cristinacce, D., Cootes, T.F.: Feature detection and tracking with constrained local models. In: Bmvc, vol. 1, p. 3. Citeseer (2006)
48. Dai, H., Pears, N., Smith, W.: A data-augmented 3d morphable model of the ear. In: Proceedings of IEEE International Conference on Automatic Face Gesture Recognition, pp. 404–408 (2018)
49. Dai, H., Pears, N., Smith, W.: Non-rigid 3d shape registration using an adaptive template. In: Proceedings of PeopleCap Workshop, European Conference on Computer Vision (2018)
50. Dai, H., Pears, N., Smith, W., Duncan, C.: Symmetric shape morphing for 3d face and head modelling. In: Proceedings of IEEE International Conference on Automatic Face Gesture Recognition, pp. 91–97 (2018)
51. Dai, H., Pears, N.E., Smith, W.A.P., Duncan, C.: A 3d morphable model of craniofacial shape and texture variation. In: IEEE International Conference on Computer Vision, ICCV, pp. 3104–3112 (2017). https://doi.org/10.1109/ICCV.2017.335
52. Dai, H., Pears, N.E., Smith, W.A.P., Duncan, C.: Statistical modeling of craniofacial shape and texture. Int. J. Comput. Vis. **128**(2), 547–571 (2020). https://doi.org/10.1007/s11263-019-01260-7
53. Dai, H., Smith, W.A.P., Pears, N., Duncan, C.: Symmetry-factored statistical modelling of craniofacial shape. In: The IEEE International Conference on Computer Vision (ICCV) (2017)
54. Dalal, N., Triggs, B.: Histograms of oriented gradients for human detection. In: IEEE Computer Society Conference on Computer Vision and Pattern Recognition. CVPR, vol. 1, pp. 886–893 (2005)
55. Davies, R.H., Twining, C.J., Cootes, T.F., Waterton, J.C., Taylor, C.J.: A minimum description length approach to statistical shape modeling. IEEE Trans. Med. Imaging **21**(5), 525–537 (2002)
56. De Momi, E., Chapuis, J., Pappas, I., Ferrigno, G., Hallermann, W., Schramm, A., Caversaccio, M.: Automatic extraction of the mid-facial plane for cranio-maxillofacial surgery planning. Int. J. Oral Maxillofac. Surg. **35**(7), 636–642 (2006)
57. De Smet, M., Van Gool, L.: Optimal regions for linear model-based 3d face reconstruction. In: Asian Conference on Computer Vision, pp. 276–289 (2010)
58. Deng, J., Zhou, Y., Cheng, S., Zaferiou, S.: Cascade multi-view hourglass model for robust 3d face alignment. In: 13th IEEE International Conference on Automatic Face and Gesture Recognition (FG), pp. 399–403 (2018)
59. Dryden, I.L., Mardia, K.V., et al.: Statistical Shape Analysis (1998)
60. Egger, B., Kaufmann, D., Schönborn, S., Roth, V., Vetter, T.: Copula eigenfaces. In: Proceedings of the 11th Joint Conference on Computer Vision, Imaging and Computer Graphics Theory and Applications: Volume 1: GRAPP, pp. 50–58 (2016)
61. Egger, B., Smith, W.A.P., Tewari, A., Wuhrer, S., Zollhöfer, M., Beeler, T., Bernard, F., Bolkart, T., Kortylewski, A., Romdhani, S., Theobalt, C., Blanz, V., Vetter, T.: 3d morphable face models - past, present and future. ACM Trans. Graph. (2020)
62. Emersic, Z., Stepec, D., Struc, V., Peer, P., George, A., Ahmad, A., Omar, E., Boult, T.E., Safdaii, R., Zhou, Y., et al.: The unconstrained ear recognition challenge. In: IEEE International Joint Conference on Biometrics (IJCB), pp. 715–724 (2017)

63. Emersic, Z., Struc, V., Peer, P.: Ear recognition: more than a survey. Neurocomputing **255**, 26–39 (2017)
64. Ericsson, A., Karlsson, J.: Measures for benchmarking of automatic correspondence algorithms. J. Math. Imaging Vis. **28**(3), 225–241 (2007)
65. Faltemier, T.C., Bowyer, K.W., Flynn, P.J.: Using a multi-instance enrollment representation to improve 3d face recognition. In: 1st IEEE International Conference on Biometrics: Theory, Applications, and Systems. BTAS, pp. 1–6 (2007)
66. Faugeras, O.D., Hebert, M.: The representation, recognition, and locating of 3-d objects. Int. J. Robot. Res. **5**(3), 27–52 (1986)
67. Feng, Z., Kittler, J., Christmas, W.J., Huber, P., Wu, X.: Dynamic attention-controlled cascaded shape regression exploiting training data augmentation and fuzzy-set sample weighting. In: IEEE Conference on Computer Vision and Pattern Recognition, CVPR, pp. 3681–3690 (2017). https://doi.org/10.1109/CVPR.2017.392
68. Ferrari, C., Berretti, S., Bimbo, A.D.: Statistical 3d face reconstruction with 3d morphable models. https://www.micc.unifi.it/3dmm-tutorial/program/. Accessed 20 Jan 2020
69. Fitzpatrick, J.M., West, J.B., Maurer, C.R.: Predicting error in rigid-body point-based registration. IEEE Trans. Med. Imaging **17**(5), 694–702 (1998)
70. Garrido, P., Zollhöfer, M., Casas, D., Valgaerts, L., Varanasi, K., Pérez, P., Theobalt, C.: Reconstruction of personalized 3d face rigs from monocular video. ACM Trans. Graph. **35**(3), 28:1–28:15 (2016)
71. Ge, S., Fan, G., Ding, M.: Non-rigid point set registration with global-local topology preservation. In: IEEE Conference on Computer Vision and Pattern Recognition Workshops (CVPRW), pp. 245–251 (2014)
72. Gecer, B., Ploumpis, S., Kotsia, I., Zafeiriou, S.: GANFIT: generative adversarial network fitting for high fidelity 3d face reconstruction. In: IEEE Conference on Computer Vision and Pattern Recognition, CVPR, pp. 1155–1164 (2019). https://doi.org/10.1109/CVPR.2019.00125
73. Gerig, T., Morel-Forster, A., Blumer, C., Egger, B., Lüthi, M., Schönborn, S., Vetter, T.: Morphable face models - an open framework. In: 13th IEEE International Conference on Automatic Face and Gesture Recognition, FG, pp. 75–82 (2018). https://doi.org/10.1109/FG.2018.00021
74. Golovinskiy, A., Matusik, W., Pfister, H., Rusinkiewicz, S., Funkhouser, T.: A statistical model for synthesis of detailed facial geometry. ACM Trans. Graph. (TOG) **25**, 1025–1034 (2006)
75. Golovinskiy, A., Podolak, J., Funkhouser, T.: Symmetry-aware mesh processing. Mathematics of Surfaces XIII, pp. 170–188 (2009)
76. Golyanik, V., Taetz, B., Reis, G., Stricker, D.: Extended coherent point drift algorithm with correspondence priors and optimal subsampling. In: IEEE Winter Conference on Applications of Computer Vision (WACV), pp. 1–9 (2016)
77. Goodall, C.: Procrustes methods in the statistical analysis of shape. J. R. Stat. Society. Ser. B (Methodol.), 285–339 (1991)
78. Goodfellow, I.J., Pouget-Abadie, J., Mirza, M., Xu, B., Warde-Farley, D., Ozair, S., Courville, A.C., Bengio, Y.: Generative adversarial nets. In: Ghahramani, Z., Welling, M., Cortes, C., Lawrence, N.D., Weinberger, K.Q. (eds.) Advances in Neural Information Processing Systems 27: Annual Conference on Neural Information Processing Systems, pp. 2672–2680 (2014)
79. Gower, J.C.: Generalized procrustes analysis. Psychometrika **40**(1), 33–51 (1975)
80. Graphics and Vision Research Group, University of Basel: Statistical shape modelling. http://gravis.dmi.unibas.ch/PMM/lectures/ssm/. Accessed 4 Mar 2020
81. Guo, X.: Three dimensional moment invariants under rigid transformation. In: International Conference on Computer Analysis of Images and Patterns, pp. 518–522. Springer (1993)
82. ter Haar, F.B., Veltkamp, R.C.: 3d face model fitting for recognition. In: European Conference on Computer Vision, pp. 652–664 (2008)
83. Haase, D., Rodner, E., Denzler, J.: Instance-weighted transfer learning of active appearance models. In: Proceedings of CVPR, pp. 1426–1433 (2014)

84. Hennessy, R.J., McLearie, S., Kinsella, A., Waddington, J.L.: Facial shape and asymmetry by three-dimensional laser surface scanning covary with cognition in a sexually dimorphic manner. The Journal of neuropsychiatry and clinical neurosciences **18**(1), 73–80 (2006)
85. Heseltine, T., Pears, N., Austin, J.: Three-dimensional face recognition using combinations of surface feature map subspace components. Image Vis. Comput. **26**(3), 382–396 (2008)
86. Hu, Y., Rijkhorst, E.J., Manber, R., Hawkes, D., Barratt, D.: Deformable vessel-based registration using landmark-guided coherent point drift. In: International Workshop on Medical Imaging and Virtual Reality, pp. 60–69. Springer (2010)
87. Huber, P.: A lightweight 3D morphable face model fitting library in modern C++14. https://github.com/patrikhuber/eos. Accessed 4 Mar 2020
88. Huber., P., Hu., G., Tena., R., Mortazavian., P., Koppen., W.P., Christmas., W.J., Rätsch., M., Kittler., J.: A multiresolution 3d morphable face model and fitting framework. In: Proceedings of the 11th Joint Conference on Computer Vision, Imaging and Computer Graphics Theory and Applications - Volume 4: VISAPP, (VISIGRAPP), pp. 79–86 (2016)
89. Jain, V., Zhang, H.: Robust 3d shape correspondence in the spectral domain. In: IEEE International Conference on Shape Modeling and Applications (SMI), pp. 19–19 (2006)
90. Jones, B.C., Little, A.C., Penton-Voak, I.S., Tiddeman, B., Burt, D.M., Perrett, D.: Facial symmetry and judgements of apparent health: support for a "good genes" explanation of the attractiveness-symmetry relationship. Evol. Hum. Behav. **22**(6), 417–429 (2001)
91. Kass, M., Witkin, A., Terzopoulos, D.: Snakes: active contour models. Int. J. Comput. Vis. **1**(4), 321–331 (1988)
92. Ke, Y., Sukthankar, R.: Pca-sift: a more distinctive representation for local image descriptors. In: Proceedings of the IEEE Computer Society Conference on Computer Vision and Pattern Recognition. CVPR, vol. 2, pp. II–II (2004)
93. Kendall, D.G.: Shape manifolds, procrustean metrics, and complex projective spaces. Bull. Lond. Math. Soc. **16**(2), 81–121 (1984)
94. Kent, J.T., Mardia, K.V.: Shape, procrustes tangent projections and bilateral symmetry. Biometrika, 469–485 (2001)
95. Kirby, M., Sirovich, L.: Application of the Karhunen-Loeve procedure for the characterization of human faces. IEEE Trans. Pattern Anal. Mach. Intell. **12**(1), 103–108 (1990)
96. Klingenberg, C.P., Barluenga, M., Meyer, A.: Shape analysis of symmetric structures: quantifying variation among individuals and asymmetry. Evolution **56**(10), 1909–1920 (2002)
97. Knothe, R.: A global-to-local model for the representation of human faces. Ph.D. thesis, University of Basel, Basel, Switzerland (2009). https://doi.org/10.5451/unibas-004988894
98. Kolamunnage-Dona, R.R., Kent, J.T.: Decomposing departures from bilateral symmetry. In: Barber, S., Baxter, P., Mardia, K.V., Walls, R.E. (eds.) Quantitative Biology, Shape Analysis, and Wavelets, pp. 75–78. Leeds University Press, Leeds (2005)
99. Koppen, P., Feng, Z.H., Kittler, J., Awais, M., Christmas, W., Wu, X.J., Yin, H.F.: Gaussian mixture 3D morphable face model. Pattern Recogn. **74**, 617–628 (2018)
100. Kotcheff, A.C., Taylor, C.J.: Automatic construction of eigenshape models by direct optimization. Med. Image Anal. **2**(4), 303–314 (1998)
101. Lewis, J.P., Anjyo, K., Rhee, T., Zhang, M., Pighin, F.H., Deng, Z.: Practice and theory of blendshape facial models. In: Lefebvre, S., Spagnuolo, M. (eds.) Eurographics - State of the Art Reports, pp. 199–218 (2014). https://doi.org/10.2312/egst.20141042
102. Li, H., Sumner, R.W., Pauly, M.: Global correspondence optimization for non-rigid registration of depth scans. Eurographics Symp. Geom. Process. **27**(5), 1421–1430 (2008)
103. Li, T., Bolkart, T., Black, M.J., Li, H., Romero, J.: Learning a model of facial shape and expression from 4d scans. ACM Trans. Graph. **36**(6), 194:1–194:17 (2017). https://doi.org/10.1145/3130800.3130813
104. Liu, Y., Palmer, J.: A quantified study of facial asymmetry in 3d faces. In: IEEE International Workshop on Analysis and Modeling of Faces and Gestures (AMFG), Proceedings, pp. 222–229. IEEE Computer Society (2003). https://doi.org/10.1109/AMFG.2003.1240847
105. Loper, M., Mahmood, N., Romero, J., Pons-Moll, G., Black, M.J.: SMPL: A skinned multi-person linear model. ACM Trans. Graph. (Proc. SIGGRAPH Asia) **34**(6), 248:1–248:16 (2015)

106. Lüthi, M., Gerig, T., Jud, C., Vetter, T.: Gaussian process morphable models. IEEE Trans. Pattern Anal. Mach. Intell. (2017)
107. Mardia, K.V., Bookstein, F.L., Moreton, I.J.: Statistical assessment of bilateral symmetry of shapes. Biometrika, 285–300 (2000)
108. Milner, D., Raz, S., Hel-Or, H., Keren, D., Nevo, E.: A new measure of symmetry and its application to classification of bifurcating structures. Pattern Recogn. **40**(8), 2237–2250 (2007)
109. Mitra, N.J., Guibas, L.J., Pauly, M.: Partial and approximate symmetry detection for 3d geometry. ACM Trans. Graph. (TOG) **25**, 560–568 (2006)
110. Moreno, A.B., Sánchez, A.: GavabDB: a 3d face database. In: Proceedings of 2nd COST275 Workshop on Biometrics on the Internet, Vigo (Spain), pp. 75–80 (2004)
111. Myronenko, A., Song, X.B.: Point set registration: coherent point drift. IEEE Trans. Pattern Anal. Mach. Intell. **32**(12), 2262–2275 (2010). https://doi.org/10.1109/TPAMI.2010.46
112. Ovsjanikov, M., Mérigot, Q., Mémoli, F., Guibas, L.: One point isometric matching with the heat kernel. Comput. Graph. Forum **29**, 1555–1564 (2010)
113. Ovsjanikov, M., Sun, J., Guibas, L.: Global intrinsic symmetries of shapes. In: Computer graphics forum, vol. 27, pp. 1341–1348. Wiley Online Library (2008)
114. Patraucean, V., Grompone von Gioi, R., Ovsjanikov, M.: Detection of mirror-symmetric image patches. In: Proceedings of CVPR Workshops, pp. 211–216 (2013)
115. Paysan, P., Knothe, R., Amberg, B., Romdhani, S., Vetter, T.: A 3d face model for pose and illumination invariant face recognition. In: Tubaro, S., Dugelay, J. (eds.) Sixth IEEE International Conference on Advanced Video and Signal Based Surveillance, AVSS, Genova, Italy, pp. 296–301 (2009). https://doi.org/10.1109/AVSS.2009.58
116. Pekelny, Y., Gotsman, C.: Articulated object reconstruction and markerless motion capture from depth video. Comput. Graph. Forum **27**, 399–408 (2008)
117. Pflug, A., Busch, C.: Ear biometrics: a survey of detection, feature extraction and recognition methods. IET Biom. **1**(2), 114–129 (2012)
118. Phillips, P.J., Flynn, P.J., Scruggs, T., Bowyer, K.W., Chang, J., Hoffman, K., Marques, J., Min, J., Worek, W.: Overview of the face recognition grand challenge. In: 2005 IEEE Computer Society Conference on Computer Vision and Pattern Recognition (CVPR'05), vol. 1, pp. 947–954. IEEE (2005)
119. Ploumpis, S., Wang, H., Pears, N., Smith, W.A.P., Zafeiriou, S.: Combining 3d morphable models: a large scale face-and-head model. In: The IEEE Conference on Computer Vision and Pattern Recognition (CVPR) (2019)
120. Podolak, J., Shilane, P., Golovinskiy, A., Rusinkiewicz, S., Funkhouser, T.: A planar-reflective symmetry transform for 3d shapes. ACM Trans. Graph. (TOG) **25**(3), 549–559 (2006)
121. Ranjan, A., Bolkart, T., Sanyal, S., Black, M.J.: Generating 3d faces using convolutional mesh autoencoders. In: Ferrari, V., Hebert, M., Sminchisescu, C., Weiss, Y. (eds.) Computer Vision - ECCV, Proceedings, Part III. Lecture Notes in Computer Science, vol. 11207, pp. 725–741. Springer (2018). https://doi.org/10.1007/978-3-030-01219-9_43
122. Romdhani, S., Vetter, T.: Estimating 3d shape and texture using pixel intensity, edges, specular highlights, texture constraints and a prior. In: IEEE Computer Society Conference on Computer Vision and Pattern Recognition (CVPR), pp. 986–993 (2005). https://doi.org/10.1109/CVPR.2005.145
123. Salazar, A., Wuhrer, S., Shu, C., Prieto, F.: Fully automatic expression-invariant face correspondence. Mach. Vis. Appl. **25**(4), 859–879 (2014)
124. Savran, A., Alyüz, N., Dibeklioğlu, H., Çeliktutan, O., Gökberk, B., Sankur, B., Akarun, L.: Bosphorus database for 3d face analysis. In: European Workshop on Biometrics and Identity Management, pp. 47–56. Springer (2008)
125. Savriama, Y., Klingenberg, C.P.: Beyond bilateral symmetry: geometric morphometric methods for any type of symmetry. BMC Evol. Biol. **11**(1), 280 (2011)
126. Sharif, M., Ayub, K., Sattar, D., Raza, M., Mohsin, S.: Enhanced and fast face recognition by hashing algorithm. J. Appl. Res. Technol. **10**(4), 607–617 (2012)
127. Shehu, A., Brunton, A., Wuhrer, S., Wand, M.: Characterization of partial intrinsic symmetries. In: European Conference on Computer Vision, pp. 267–282. Springer (2014)

128. Simo-Serra, E., Trulls, E., Ferraz, L., Kokkinos, I., Fua, P., Moreno-Noguer, F.: Discriminative learning of deep convolutional feature point descriptors. In: Proceedings of the IEEE International Conference on Computer Vision, pp. 118–126 (2015)

129. Sirovich, L., Kirby, M.: Low-dimensional procedure for the characterization of human faces. J. Opt. Soc. Am. A **4**(3), 519–524 (1987)

130. Sorkine, O., Alexa, M.: As-rigid-as-possible surface modeling. In: Proceedings of the Fifth Eurographics Symposium on Geometry Processing, pp. 109–116 (2007)

131. Styner, M.A., Rajamani, K.T., Nolte, L.P., Zsemlye, G., Székely, G., Taylor, C.J., Davies, R.H.: Evaluation of 3d correspondence methods for model building. In: Information Processing in Medical Imaging, pp. 63–75 (2003)

132. Tam, G.K., Cheng, Z.Q., Lai, Y.K., Langbein, F.C., Liu, Y., Marshall, D., Martin, R.R., Sun, X.F., Rosin, P.L.: Registration of 3d point clouds and meshes: a survey from rigid to nonrigid. IEEE Trans. Vis. Comput. Graph. **19**(7), 1199–1217 (2013)

133. Ten Berge, J.M.: Orthogonal procrustes rotation for two or more matrices. Psychometrika **42**(2), 267–276 (1977)

134. Tewari, A., Zollhöfer, M., Kim, H., Garrido, P., Bernard, F., Perez, P., Theobalt, C.: Mofa: Model-based deep convolutional face autoencoder for unsupervised monocular reconstruction. In: The IEEE International Conference on Computer Vision (ICCV) (2017)

135. Thompson, D.W.: On Growth and Form. Cambridge University Press, Cambridge (1942)

136. Tran, L., Liu, F., Liu, X.: Towards high-fidelity nonlinear 3d face morphable model. In: IEEE Conference on Computer Vision and Pattern Recognition, CVPR, pp. 1126–1135 (2019). https://doi.org/10.1109/CVPR.2019.00122

137. Tran, L., Liu, X.: Nonlinear 3d face morphable model. In: IEEE Conference on Computer Vision and Pattern Recognition, CVPR, pp. 7346–7355 (2018). https://doi.org/10.1109/CVPR.2018.00767

138. Tran, L., Liu, X.: On learning 3d face morphable model from in-the-wild images. IEEE Trans. Pattern Anal. Mach. Intell. (2019). https://doi.org/10.1109/TPAMI.2019.2927975

139. Tresadern, P.A., Sauer, P., Cootes, T.F.: Additive update predictors in active appearance models. In: Proceedings of BMVC, vol. 2, p. 4 (2010)

140. Trimech, I.H., Maalej, A., Amara, N.E.B.: 3d facial expression recognition using nonrigid cpd registration method. In: International Conference on Information and Digital Technologies (IDT), pp. 478–481. IEEE (2017)

141. Turk, M., Pentland, A.: Eigenfaces for recognition. J. Cogn. Neurosci. **3**(1), 71–86 (1991)

142. Vlasic, D., Brand, M., Pfister, H., Popović, J.: Face transfer with multilinear models. ACM Trans. Graph. (TOG) **24**, 426–433 (2005)

143. Wang, P., Wang, P., Qu, Z., Gao, Y., Shen, Z.: A refined coherent point drift (cpd) algorithm for point set registration. Sci. China Inf. Sci. **54**(12), 2639–2646 (2011)

144. Wei, L., Huang, Q., Ceylan, D., Vouga, E., Li, H.: Dense human body correspondences using convolutional networks. In: Proceedings of the IEEE Conference on Computer Vision and Pattern Recognition, pp. 1544–1553 (2016)

145. Wu, Y., Hassner, T., Kim, K., Medioni, G., Natarajan, P.: Facial landmark detection with tweaked convolutional neural networks. IEEE Trans. Pattern Anal. Mach. Intell. (2017)

146. Wu, Y., Ji, Q.: Facial landmark detection: a literature survey. Int. J. Comput. Vis. 1–28 (2017)

147. Wu, Y., Pan, G., Wu, Z.: Face authentication based on multiple profiles extracted from range data. In: International Conference on Audio-and Video-Based Biometric Person Authentication, pp. 515–522 (2003)

148. Yang, F., Bourdev, L., Shechtman, E., Wang, J., Metaxas, D.: Facial expression editing in video using a temporally-smooth factorization. In: IEEE Conference on Computer Vision and Pattern Recognition (CVPR), pp. 861–868 (2012)

149. Yang, F., Wang, J., Shechtman, E., Bourdev, L., Metaxas, D.: Expression flow for 3d-aware face component transfer. ACM Trans. Graph. (TOG) **30**, 60 (2011)

150. Yang, J.: The thin plate spline robust point matching (TPS-RPM) algorithm: a revisit. Pattern Recogn. Lett. **32**(7), 910–918 (2011)

151. Yin, L., Wei, X., Sun, Y., Wang, J., Rosato, M.J.: A 3d facial expression database for facial behavior research. In: 7th International Conference on Automatic Face and Gesture Recognition (FGR06), pp. 211–216. IEEE (2006)
152. Yu, R., Russell, C., Campbell, N., Agapito, L.: Direct, dense, and deformable: template-based non-rigid 3d reconstruction from RGB video. In: IEEE International Conference on Computer Vision (ICCV) (2015)
153. Zhang, K., Cheng, Y., Leow, W.K.: Dense correspondence of skull models by automatic detection of anatomical landmarks. In: Computer Analysis of Images and Patterns, pp. 229–236 (2013)
154. Zhang, L., Razdan, A., Farin, G., Femiani, J., Bae, M., Lockwood, C.: 3d face authentication and recognition based on bilateral symmetry analysis. Vis. Comput. $22(1)$, 43–55 (2006)
155. Zhong, C., Sun, Z., Tan, T.: Robust 3d face recognition using learned visual codebook. In: 2007 IEEE Conference on Computer Vision and Pattern Recognition, pp. 1–6. IEEE (2007)
156. Zhou, Y., Zaferiou, S.: Deformable models of ears in-the-wild for alignment and recognition. In: 2017 12th IEEE International Conference on Automatic Face and Gesture Recognition (FG), pp. 626–633 (2017)
157. Zhou, Z., Zheng, J., Dai, Y., Zhou, Z., Chen, S.: Robust non-rigid point set registration using student's-t mixture model. PloS One $9(3)$, e91, 381 (2014)
158. Zhu, X., Lei, Z., Liu, X., Shi, H., Li, S.Z.: Face alignment across large poses: a 3d solution. In: Proceedings of the IEEE Conference on Computer Vision and Pattern Recognition, pp. 146–155 (2016)
159. Zhu, X., Ramanan, D.: Face detection, pose estimation, and landmark localization in the wild. In: Proceedings of CVPR, pp. 2879–2886 (2012)
160. Zhurov, A.I., Richmond, S., Kau, C.H., Toma, A.: Averaging facial images. Three-dimensional Imaging for Orthodontics and Maxillofacial Surgery, pp. 126–44. Wiley-Blackwell, London (2010)
161. Zolfaghari, R., Epain, N., Jin, C.T., Glaunès, J., Tew, A.: Generating a morphable model of ears. In: IEEE International Conference on Acoustics, Speech and Signal Processing (ICASSP), pp. 1771–1775 (2016)
162. Zollhöfer, M., Thies, J., Garrido, P., Bradley, D., Beeler, T., Pérez, P., Stamminger, M., Nießner, M., Theobalt, C.: State of the art on monocular 3d face reconstruction, tracking, and applications. Comput. Graph. Forum $37(2)$, 523–550 (2018). https://doi.org/10.1111/cgf.13382

Chapter 11
Deep Learning on 3D Data

Charles Ruizhongtai Qi

Abstract Emerging 3D related applications such as autonomous vehicles, AI-assisted design, and augmented reality have highlighted the demands for more robust and powerful 3D analyzing algorithms. Inspired by the success of deep learning on understanding images, audio, and texts, and backed by growing amounts of available 3D data and annotated 3D datasets, a new field that studies deep learning on 3D data has arisen recently. However, unlike images or audio that have a dominant representation as arrays, 3D has many popular representations. Among them, the two most common representations are point clouds (from raw sensor input) and meshes (widely used in shape modeling) that are both not defined on a regular grid. Due to their irregular format, current convolutional deep neural networks cannot be directly used. To analyze those 3D data, two major branches of methods exist. One family of methods first converts such irregular data to regular structures such as 3D volumetric grids (through quantization) or multi-view images (through rendering or projection) and then applies existing convolutional architectures on them. On the other hand, a new family of methods study how to design deep neural networks that *directly* consume irregular data such as point clouds (sets) and meshes (graphs). Those architectures are designed to respect the special properties of the input 3D representations such as the permutation invariance of the points in a set, or the intrinsic surface structure in a mesh. In this chapter we present representative deep learning models from both of those families, to analyze 3D data in representations of regular structures (multi-view images and volumetric grids) and irregular structures (point clouds and meshes). While we mainly focus on introducing the backbone networks that are general for deep 3D representation learning, we also show their successful applications ranging from semantic object classification, object part segmentation, scene parsing, to finding shape correspondences. At the end of the chapter we provide more pointers for further reading and discuss future directions.

C. Ruizhongtai Qi (✉)
Stanford University, Stanford, CA, USA
e-mail: charlesq34@gmail.com

© Springer Nature Switzerland AG 2020
Y. Liu et al. (eds.), *3D Imaging, Analysis and Applications*,
https://doi.org/10.1007/978-3-030-44070-1_11

513

11.1 Introduction

Deep learning is part of a broader family of machine learning methods, while machine learning itself belongs to the even broader field of artificial intelligence. Compared to designing handcrafted features, deep learning allows computational models with multiple processing layers to *learn representations* of data with multiple levels of abstraction [54]. Artificial neural networks are the most popular realizations of deep learning models. In recent years, the growing computing power provided by GPUs (graphics processing units) and the availability of large-scale training datasets have fueled the fast development of deep learning models and algorithms. This has led to breakthroughs in many areas of computer science, from speech recognition [2, 66, 101] to image understanding [37, 52, 79, 88], to machine translation [108]. Methods based on deep learning have even achieved super-human performance on many problems that were previously considered very hard for machines. One example is a computer Go program called AlphaGo [87] that beat multiple top human players, where deep learning plays a key role in its system. Nowadays, deep learning models have already been widely used in daily products, such as Siri and Face ID on iPhones, Google Image Search and Google Translate, and the Autopilot system in Tesla cars for semi-autonomous driving.

While deep learning has great success in processing data such as image, videos, audio, and texts, only until very recently researchers started to explore how to learn deep representations from 3D data such as point clouds and meshes, leading to a rising field named *3D deep learning*. The task space of 3D deep learning is vast but can be roughly divided into three categories: 3D analysis, 3D synthesis, and 3D assisted image understanding [91]. In 3D geometry analysis, some typical tasks include semantic classification of objects [65, 76, 92, 110] (given a 3D object, classify it into one of a few predefined categories such as chairs and tables), semantic parsing of objects or scenes [3, 19, 77] (segmenting an object or a scene into different semantic regions such as chair leg, chair back for a chair object, or floor, wall, table for a scan of an indoor room), and finding correspondences among different shapes [9] (such as human bodies). In 3D synthesis, a deep learning model generates 3D data either from conditioned input or an embedding vector. For example, one interesting problem is shape completion from partial scans, where given a partial scan we want to use a deep learning model to complete the scan based on its learned object shape priors [20]. Another example is automated shape modeling, where a model generates a mesh or parametric model of an object from unstructured input such as images and point clouds [100]. The third large category of tasks, 3D assisted image understanding, does not directly consume 3D data but uses 3D as a faithful surrogate to assist image understanding tasks [56, 86] that is hard to achieve without 3D data. For example, for the problem of intrinsic decomposition, we can generate synthetic data from existing 3D models to train our network.

Among those tasks this chapter focuses on 3D analysis tasks. Furthermore, we will focus on the "backbone" network architectures instead of discussing specific problems. These backbone architectures are the keys to deep 3D representation learning

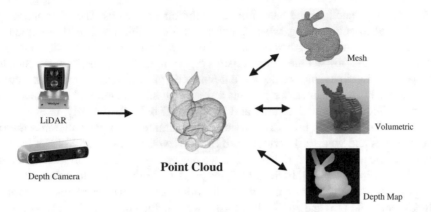

Fig. 11.1   3D representations. Among them, point clouds and meshes are in an irregular structure while depth maps (or projected views) and volumetric grids are in a regular structure that can be directly consumed by convolutional neural networks. Figure is from [74]

and are, therefore, the foundation for any applications built on top of 3D data. We will see that even just discussing about backbone architectures, we have a large space to explore and many challenges to solve.

One of the major challenges to develop deep learning models for 3D data is its representation issue. Unlike images that have a dominant representation as 2D pixel arrays, 3D has many popular representations, as shown in Fig. 11.1. In choosing or designing a deep learning model we need to first determine which 3D representation to use. The diversity of representations exists for a reason though: just as computational algorithms depend on data structures (lists, trees, graphs, etc.), different applications of 3D data have their own preferences for 3D representations. Among them, a point cloud is a set of points in space sampled from object surfaces, usually collected by 3D sensors such as LiDARs (Light Detection and Ranging) or depth cameras. A polygon mesh is a collection of triangles or quads and is heavily used in computer graphics because it is friendly to 3D modeling and rendering algorithms. Volumetric representation quantifies the space into small voxels (3D cubes) and is common in simulation and reconstruction (such as in medical imaging), because it is easier to aggregate signals in regular grids than other formats. Last but not least, we also represent 3D as multiple projected views, often used for visualization, as humans are more used to perceiving 2D than 3D. There are also more parametric representations such as those defined with cylinders, cubes, and NURBS, which are convenient to deform and simple to encode.

Among the above mentioned 3D representations the two most common ones are point clouds (from sensor data) and meshes (from geometric modeling). However, neither of them are defined on regular grids. Due to their irregularity, deep convolutional neural networks cannot be directly applied here. To analyze them, two branches of methods exist. One is to first convert such irregular data to a regular grid structure, such as volumetric grids (through voxelization) or images (through rendering or projection) and then apply convolutional networks. The other approach is more end-to-end learning, where point clouds or meshes are directly inputted to the networks without any conversion. This however, requires new types of deep neural networks that respect the characteristics of the input 3D representations, such as the permutation invariance of points in a point set, or the intrinsic surface structure of a mesh. In this chapter, we present a few relatively mature and representative deep architectures for both regular and irregular 3D data. Particularly, in Sect. 11.3 we show deep learning models on regularly structured 3D representations (multi-view images and volumetric grids), with Multi-view CNN [92] and VoxNet [65] as two example architectures. In Sect. 11.4, we present deep learning models on point clouds with PointNet [76]. In Sect. 11.5, we briefly introduce deep learning methods on processing meshes by explaining motivations behind two representative works SyncSpecCNN [115] and ACNN [9]. Lastly we conclude the chapter, discuss future research directions in Sect. 11.6 and point readers to more resources for further reading in Sect. 11.7. In the end of the chapter, there are questions and exercises that provide an opportunity to check the reader's understanding of this chapter.

After reading this chapter, the readers should understand the challenges of deep learning on 3D data, be able to describe and implement a deep learning model for multi-view images, be able to describe and implement volumetric CNNs, be able to describe and implement deep learning models for processing point clouds, know about the two common types of deep networks on meshes, and be aware of future research directions in 3D deep learning.

11.2 Background

Recent advances in deep learning are supported by high-performance computing hardware (GPU) and new software frameworks (Caffe [46], TensorFlow [1], PyTorch [71], etc.), but more importantly they are fueled by large-scale datasets (e.g., ImageNet [23]). Similarly, 3D deep learning rises because *3D data* and *3D datasets* become available.

The growth in 3D data is due to two forces. The first driving force is the progress in 3D sensing technology. As the costs of sensors decrease quickly, we now have access to very affordable depth cameras such as Kinect, Tango, Structure Sensor, Intel RealSense or even depth cameras in phones (e.g., iPhone X). Extremely accurate 3D sensors such as LiDARs are also more widespread thanks to the needs of the autonomous vehicle industry. A large number of 3D sensors directly result in much quicker growth of raw 3D data. The second force is the availability and popularity of free 3D modeling tools such as Blender and SketchUp, as well as 3D model sharing platforms such as the Trimble 3D Warehouse, leading to a fast growing number of 3D models that are publicly accessible.

However, while 3D data quickly grows from both sensing and modeling, they are not yet ready to be used by deep learning algorithms, because most models still require annotated data for training. Fortunately, we also observe a few recent efforts in organizing, cleaning, and annotating 3D data (e.g., ShapeNet [14]). The works in this chapter are only possible with these public 3D datasets.

In Scct. 11.2.1, we introduce the datasets we used in this chapter and discuss their characteristics. Then in Sect. 11.2.2, we survey previous work and also discuss recent advances in the field.

11.2.1 Datasets

We used various datasets for a variety of 3D analysis problems to test the performance of the presented deep architectures and algorithms. The datasets involved are diverse, ranging from single objects to multi-objects in scenes, from synthetic shapes to real scans.

- ModelNet40 [110]: A 3D dataset of CAD models from 40 categories (mostly man-made objects such as chairs, bathtubs, cars, etc.). All models are aligned in upright poses. In default, 10 of the 40 categories have aligned poses in azimuth angles. There is also a recent update in the dataset, providing fully aligned models for all categories. We use the official split with 9,843 shapes for training and 2,468 for testing to evaluate deep models in 3D shape classification, with random shape rotations in the azimuth direction (along the up-down axis).
- ShapeNetPart [114]: This is a dataset built on top of the ShapeNet [14] dataset (a large-scale, richly annotated 3D shape repository), containing 16,881 shapes from 16 of the ShapeNet classes, annotated with 50 parts in total. We use the official train/test split following [14]. We test deep models for object part segmentation on this dataset, which is a much finer grained task than whole shape classification in ModelNet40.
- S3DIS [3]: The Stanford 3D Indoor Spaces (S3DIS) dataset contains 3D scans from Matterport scanners in 6 building areas including 271 rooms. Each point in the scan is annotated as one of the 13 semantic categories (chair, table, floor, wall, etc., plus clutter). The dataset also provides annotations for depth and normal maps, as well as instance segmentations. We use this dataset for the evaluation of semantic segmentation (semantic scene parsing).

Besides the datasets mentioned above (those used in experiments in this chapter), there are many more other efforts in building 3D datasets. Examples include the SHREC15 [58] dataset with nonrigid objects, ScanNet [19] and Matterport3D [13] of large-scale indoor scans, as well as datasets with LiDAR scans such as KITTI [29] and Semantic3D [36]. There are also ongoing efforts to build large 3D/RGB-D video datasets and simulation platforms [85] for 3D understanding and interactions. We foresee that datasets will keep playing an important role in future 3D deep learning research.

11.2.2 Related Work

As 3D is prevalent in computer vision, graphics, and robotics, there have been tremendous works on topics of point clouds, 3D data learning, and 3D scene understanding. In this section, we briefly review previous works related to the topic, and introduce some concurrent and more recent efforts since the draft of this chapter. We first review prior attempts in designing and learning features for point clouds, then discuss 3D deep learning on point clouds and meshes.

11.2.2.1 3D Descriptors

Most existing features for point clouds and meshes are handcrafted toward specific tasks. These features or 3D descriptors often encode certain statistical properties of local points or surfaces and are designed to be invariant to certain transformations, which are typically classified as intrinsic (WKS [4], HKS [10, 94], etc.) or extrinsic (PFH [81], FPFH [82], D2 [69], inner-distance [60], Spin Image [47], LFD [15], etc.). They can also be categorized as local features and global features, or be classified based on the input format they take (e.g., 3D points, points with features, or depth maps). For a specific task, it is not trivial to find the optimal feature combination (feature selection), even with a deep neural network [28].

In this chapter we present deep learning approaches for 3D representation learning, which can be easily adapted to different tasks, such as classification, segmentation, shape retrieval, and finding correspondences.

11.2.2.2 Deep Learning on Point Clouds

Vinyals et al. [103] is one of the first researchers that studied deep learning on point sets. They designed a read-process-write network with attention mechanism to consume unordered input sets and showed that their network has the ability to sort numbers. However, since their work focuses on generic sets and natural language processing (NLP) applications, there lacks the role of geometry in the sets. Concurrent to the PointNet [76] we will introduce in this chapter, there are also works from Ravanbakhshet et al. [78] and Zaheer et al. [116], in which they designed deep networks that achieve invariance to set element ordering. However, their works emphasize a wide range of applications for point set learning, rather than focusing on 3D understanding. Compared with these prior work, the architecture we present in Sect. 11.4 exploits the geometry properties in 3D point sets (geometric transformations and distance spaces for sampling and local context). We also provide theoretical analysis and intuitive visualization of what has been learned by the deep network.

Real 3D point clouds from sensors or geometric estimation (e.g., structure from motion) are usually noisy and have nonuniform sampling densities. This affects effective point feature extraction and causes difficulty for learning. One of the key issues is to select a proper scale for point feature design. Previously several approaches have been developed regarding this [6, 22, 33, 67, 72, 107] either in the geometry processing community or photogrammetry and remote sensing community. In none of the above deep learning works, the problem of nonuniform sampling density has been explicitly considered. In a recent work [77], a new architecture called Point-Net++ was proposed which learns to extract point features and balance multiple feature scales in an end-to-end fashion. The PointNet++ has a hierarchical structure that applies shared subnetworks (based on the PointNet [76] architecture) at local regions of point clouds (similar to shared convolution kernels in a CNN) such that it is translation invariant. The hierarchical architecture shows stronger generalizability to large-scale 3D scene parsing than [76]. The nonuniform density problem has also been addressed more thoroughly in [39].

Recently there have been many more efforts in designing novel deep neural networks for point clouds [16, 32, 39, 44, 51, 55, 57, 80, 93, 97, 98, 104–106, 111, 113, 117]. For example, dynamic graph CNNs [105] extends PointNet++ by allowing neighborhood search in latent feature spaces. VoxelNet [117] combines PointNet with 3D CNNs. It computes local voxel features using a PointNet-like network, and then applies 3D CNNs on voxels for object proposals and classification. O-CNN [106], OctNet [80] and Kd-network [51] have introduced indexing trees to 3D deep learning, to avoid computations at empty spaces. ShapeContextNet [111] extends the traditional Shape Context [5] descriptor to a trainable setting with deep neural networks. SPLATNet [93] achieves efficient 3D convolution by sparse bilateral convolutions on a lattice structure. Tangent convolution network [97] exploits the fact that point clouds from 3D sensors are living on a 2D manifold in 3D space, and achieved point cloud learning by 2D convolutions on local tangent planes. KPConv networks [98] designed a point-based convolution kernel for point cloud learning. SparseConvNet [32] and MinkowskiCNN [16] have shown that one can train very deep networks with well-implemented sparse 3D convolutions, for point cloud processing. With diverse applications and representations of 3D data, we envision more research on deep networks for point clouds in the near future.

11.2.2.3   Deep Learning on Graphs

Recently there has been a strong interest to study how to generalize CNNs to graphs, and these new types of CNNs are called "graph CNNs" Graph CNNs take a graph with vertex functions as input. Conventional image CNNs can be viewed as graph CNNs on 2D regular grids of pixels, with RGB color as vertex values. There have been some previous works studying graph CNN on more general graphs instead of 2D regular grids [12, 21, 24, 38], and [8, 9, 64] have a special focus on near-isometric 3D shape graphs like human bodies. To generalize image CNNs, these works usually try to tackle the following three challenges: defining translation structures on graphs to allow parameter sharing, designing compactly supported filters on graphs, and aggregating multi-scale information. Their constructions of deep neural networks usually fall into two types: spatial construction and spectral construction. In Sect. 11.5 we will see two concrete examples from both of those types.

11.3   Deep Learning on Regularly Structured 3D Data

To deal with irregular 3D data such as point clouds or meshes, one popular approach is to first convert irregular data to a regularly structured form. The two most popular conversions are rendering/projection (to single-view or multi-view images) and voxelization (to volumetric grids). With regular structures, we can adopt the successful convolutional neural networks to learn deep representations of 3D data.

In multi-view images, a polygon mesh is rendered into 2D images from multiple viewpoints before any representation learning. This conversion leads to two benefits. First, rendering circumvents artifacts in the original geometric representations that are usually unfriendly to traditional geometric algorithms. Some examples of the artifacts include close but disconnected shape parts (which breaks the topology), empty interior structure, and non-manifold geometry. Second, as rendering produces images, so we can leverage both maturely designed convolutional neural network (CNN) architectures, as well as their pretrained weights from large-scale natural image datasets. Besides these two benefits, from a more intuitive perspective, the process of analyzing multi-view images to understand 3D is similar to the process humans perceive a 3D object—we understand the full shape of an object by observing it from multiple angles.

Another popular way to convert irregular 3D data to a regular form is to "voxelize" a 3D point cloud or a mesh to a volumetric grid. In its simplest form, the voxelization process produces an occupancy grid where each voxel (a 3D cube in space) is associated with a binary value, where one indicates the presence of a point or the voxel being crossed by a face in the mesh, while zero indicates an empty space without any point or mesh face crossing it. After this quantization step, the original irregular data is converted to a 3D array, which can be consumed by a 3D convolutional neural network (3D CNN). A 3D CNN (also referred to as a volumetric CNN) is very similar to an image CNN, except it uses 3D convolutions instead of 2D ones. Compared with multi-view images, 3D volumetric inputs preserve original 3D geometry (in a quantized version) and are able to capture interior structures of objects. In certain applications of 3D data such as analysis of CT scans, 3D CNNs are the de facto approach since the input is naturally in volumetric forms.

In the following part of this section, we first introduce a deep neural network that consumes multi-view images called Multi-view CNN (MVCNN) in Sect. 11.3.1. Then in Sect. 11.3.2, we go into details of volumetric CNNs/3D CNNs and describe a simple but effective volumetric CNN called VoxNet. Lastly in Sect. 11.3.3, we compare MVCNN and volumetric CNNs on the 3D object classification task, where we also discuss the gap between their performance. In the same section, we further provide more experiments to understand the gap, as well as introduce two new and more powerful volumetric CNNs trying to fill the gap.

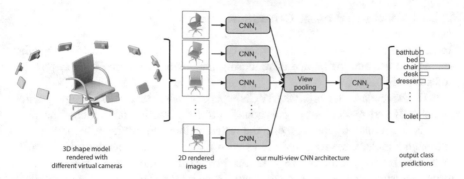

Fig. 11.2 Multi-view CNN for 3D shape recognition. At test time a 3D shape is rendered from 12 different views and is passed through CNN_1 to extract view based features. These are then pooled across views and passed through CNN_2 to obtain a compact shape descriptor. Figure is from [92]

11.3.1 Multi-view CNN

The work from Su et al. [92] proposed a simple but effective way to learn 3D shape descriptors for classification and retrieval with a multi-view representation of the 3D data. Because of the input data format and the use of CNNs to consume multi-view images, the proposed network is called Multi-view CNN (MVCNN). The system pipeline and the network architecture is shown in Fig. 11.2. In the MVCNN shape recognition pipeline, we first generate multiple views of a 3D shape by a rendering engine. Then MVCNN learns an aggregated representation combining features from multiple views, as a compact descriptor for the 3D shape. The learning process is supervised by a 3D shape classification task. The detailed process is explained in the following two subsections.

Note that compared with the proposed approach in MVCNN, there are several more naive approaches. For example, a simple way to use multiple views of a 3D shape for its classification is to generate 2D image descriptors from each view independently and then classify the shape based on these independent image descriptors, for example, with a voting scheme. Alternatively, if the input 3D shapes are aligned, we can render the 3D shape from a fixed set of viewpoints, extract 2D descriptors from each of the views and then concatenate the 2D descriptors in the same order as that of the views. We can use the concatenated vector as the shape descriptor and train a model to classify the shape based on it. However, aligning 3D shapes to a canonical orientation is hard by itself (or requires extra annotations). On the other hand, this approach cannot adapt to the varying number of views in case of partial 3D input. Compared to these two approaches, MVCNN is able to *learn* to aggregate views and is able to take the varying number of views. Details of the MVCNN pipeline is described below.

11.3.1.1   Multi-view Image Generation

To generate a multi-view representation of a 3D shape, we have to consider what renderer to use and the choice of rendering parameters including camera position and scene lighting.

As to the renderer, the original MVCNN paper chooses to use the Phong reflection model [73] and renders mesh polygons with a perspective projection. The pixel color is determined by interpolating the reflected intensity of the polygon vertices. Although simple, these rendered views with Phong reflection are very informative to summarize the geometry of the shape. For textured meshes, we can also use a more sophisticated renderer such as a ray traced renderer to respect more details in color and material properties. One can even generate beyond the common gray or RGB images, such as depth images, normal maps, etc., to capture more geometric properties of the shapes. For simplicity, in the following discussion and experiments we assume the shapes are rendered into gray images.

In the rendering scene the 3D shape is scaled into the same size and fits into a viewing volume at the center of the scene. In rendering engines with required scene lighting, we can uniformly place several point light sources around the 3D shape [75]. As long as renderings of all 3D shapes share the same lighting setup, the learned global 3D descriptors will be comparable. In another case, if we also want to test the deep network on views from natural images or under unknown lighting conditions, using a fixed lighting setup will cause issues as the model would overfit to the rendering process thus will not generalize to new images with different lighting. One way to resolve the issue is to randomly change the scene lighting parameters such as the number, energy, and color spectrum of the light sources, a process known as domain randomization [99].

Another key factor of generating multi-view representation is to choose the camera poses (viewpoints) for rendering. There are two common camera setups depending on our prior knowledge of the input 3D shape. In the first camera setup, we assume that the input shapes are upright oriented along a consistent axis (e.g., the z-axis). Most man-made CAD models in shape repositories such as the 3D Warehouse and datasets like ModelNet40 and ShapeNet satisfy this assumption. Based on this assumption, we render K views by placing K virtual cameras evenly spread around the 3D shape. Empirically, MVCNN takes $K = 12$ views such that every view is 30° from each other, and they are elevated 30° from the ground plane pointing to the center of the object (see Fig. 11.2). The center of the object is the weighted average of the mesh face vertices where the weight is the face area. For more complicated shapes (like mechanical components), we can also place another set of cameras elevated $-30°$ to capture its bottom geometry. In the second camera setup, we do not assume an upright orientation of the object, i.e., we have no prior knowledge of the shape's orientation. In this case we have to place more cameras than those in the first case in order not to miss representative views of the object. As in [92], we can place 20 virtual cameras at the 20 vertices of an icosahedron enclosing the shape, with all of them pointing to the center of the shape. Then we generate 4 rendered views from each camera using 0, 90, 180, 270° rotations along the optical axis (in-tilt rotations), yielding a total of 80 views.

As noted in [92], using different shading coefficients or illumination models did not have much effect on the learned 3D descriptors due to the invariance of the learned filters to illumination changes, as also observed in image-based CNNs. Also the currently proposed camera setups are already able to achieve successful results—adding more or different viewpoints is trivial but leads to marginal performance improvement. Finally, by using the simple Phong reflection model, rendering each mesh from all the viewpoints takes no more than ten milliseconds on modern graphics hardware [92].

11.3.1.2   Multi-view CNN Architecture

Given multi-view images of an object, a simple baseline method to classify the shape is to extract features from each individual image and then aggregate their features (similar to light-field descriptor) for a further linear classifier. Or one can predict classification scores (with a linear classifier, a SVM) separately for each image and then "bagging" the results by taking the average of scores from all images. While these two baselines work well, the information from multi-view images is not fully exploited. Multi-view CNN further exploits the input by learning to aggregate views. The architecture (as illustrated in Fig. 11.2) mainly has three parts: the image feature extraction (with CNN_1), view pooling, and 3D descriptor learning (with CNN_2).

As in Fig. 11.2, first, each image in the multi-view representation is processed by the first part of the network (CNN_1) separately. The same CNN_1 is shared across all views. Then image descriptors extracted by CNN_1 are aggregated through a view-pooling layer, which is simply an element-wise maximum operation. An alternative view-pooling is an element-wise mean operation, but its empirical results are not as effective. Then the pooled image descriptor is fed to another CNN_2 for further processing to form a final 3D shape descriptor. The 3D shape descriptor can readily be used for many different tasks, such as for shape classification (with a linear softmax classifier), or shape retrieval. As the entire architecture is a directed acyclic graph, the entire model can be trained end-to-end using stochastic gradient descent with back-propagation. The supervision signal is from an annotated dataset (ModelNet [110]) with shape category labels.

In implementation, it is possible to select different architectures for the subnetworks CNN_1 and CNN_2. However, in order to leverage the mature architecture design, it is recommended to split existing image CNN architectures to form CNN_1 and CNN_2, in which case we can also take advantage of the model's pretrained weights from much larger image datasets such as ImageNet [23]. For example, in the original work of MVCNN [92], the authors adopted VGG [88] architecture using its conv1 to conv5 layers to construct CNN_1 and the rest of the layers to construct CNN_2, with the fc7 output (after ReLU nonlinearity) as the final 3D shape descriptor. The VGG network is pretrained on ImageNet images from 1k categories and then

Fig. 11.3 VoxNet architectures. Conv(f, d, s) indicates f filters of size d and at strides s, Pool(m) indicates pooling with area m, and Full(n) indicates fully connected layer with n outputs. Inputs, example feature maps, and predicted outputs are shown. The point cloud on the left is from LiDAR and the one on the right is from a RGB-D scan. Cross sections are used for visualization purposes. Figure is from [65]

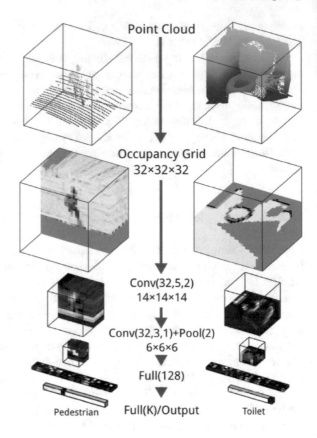

fine-tuned on all 2D views of the 3D shapes in the training set, with a classification task.

In Sect. 11.3.3, we will present a quantitative evaluation of the MVCNN architecture on a shape classification benchmark and compare it with the volumetric CNNs introduced in the next section.

11.3.2 Volumetric CNN

In this section, we present a simple, effective, and representative volumetric CNN/3D CNN architecture for object classification. The architecture called *VoxNet* [65] takes a volumetric occupancy grid, extracts hierarchical features from the 3D grid input, and finally gets a global descriptor of the 3D input for shape classification. In the following text, we first discuss how to prepare volumetric data from point clouds or polygon meshes, and then show the specific architecture design of VoxNet.

11.3.2.1 Voxelization

Voxelization is a discretization process that converts geometric data in a continuous domain (such as point clouds and meshes) into a discrete grid (a volumetric array). Depending on the input source, there are multiple ways to voxelize the irregular 3D data into volumetric data.

Given a point cloud, the simplest way of voxelization is to compute a binary occupancy grid based on whether there is any point in a voxel, which is called a hit grid in [65]. If we also know the pose of the sensor (such as a LiDAR or a depth camera) that acquires the point cloud, we may also encode the voxel as free (observed as empty), occupied, and unknown (occluded) through 3D ray tracing. There is also a more advanced way to compute an occupancy grid in a probabilistic way or compute a density grid with continuous values in each voxel (more details can be found in [65]).

We can also voxelize a polygon mesh (typically with triangles) into a volumetric occupancy grid. The first step is to subdivide the faces in the mesh until the longest edge of a face is small enough (e.g., half the length of a voxel size), and then set the voxels beneath the face vertices to one to create a "filled" voxelization (assuming space inside the object is occupied), or set voxels with vertices in them as occupied to create a "hollow" voxelization (assuming space inside the object is empty). Although the binary grid is simple and effective in many cases, we can encode more geometric information with a continuous value grid to enrich each voxel's information. The most popular encoding is a distance field and its variants, such as a truncated signed distance field (TSDF). In TSDF volumetric representation, each voxel stores a truncated distance from the voxel center to its nearest mesh surface, with a positive number if the voxel is outside or a negative number if the voxel is inside the surface. If there is no orientation in the faces, we can also build an unsigned distance field (DF) [20].

Without special notice, in the following sections, we assume we have a binary occupancy grid as input to all the volumetric CNNs.

11.3.2.2 VoxNet Architecture

The basic building blocks for a volumetric CNN include the input layer (preprocessing layer), 3D convolutional layers, pooling layers (average pooling or max pooling), fully connected layers, and up-convolution layers (omitted as up-convolutions are just strided convolutions). More detailed definitions are as follows:

The input layer takes a fixed size grid of $I \times J \times K$ voxels. Due to the computation and space complexity the resolution of the input grid is usually not high. For example, in [65], $I = J = K = 32$. The occupancy value is shifted by 0.5 and scaled by 2 so that they are in the range of $(-1, 1)$ (for binary occupancy grid the values are either -1 or 1). While for simplicity we only consider scalar valued inputs, we can easily add more feature channels for each voxel such as the LiDAR intensity values or the RGB color from an optical camera.

Fig. 11.4 Left: volumetric CNN (single orientation input). Right: multi-orientation volumetric CNN (MO-VCNN), which takes in various orientations of the 3D input, extracts features from shared CNN_1 and then pass pooled feature through another network CNN_2 to make a prediction

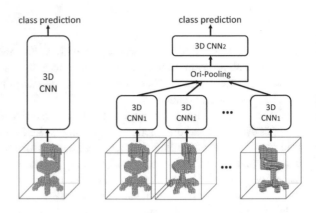

A 3D convolutional layer takes four-dimensional input volumes (height H, width W, length L, channel C), among them the first three dimensions are spatial and the last dimension contains the feature vectors for the voxels. In a batch mode (usually in GPU processing), the input becomes five-dimensional, with a batch size dimension B as the first dimension ($B \times H \times W \times L \times C$). A 3D convolution kernel (or filter) is in the size of $h \times w \times l \times C$, where h, w, l define the kernel size. Usually we use a square kernel with the same sizes on each side ($d \times d \times d \times C$). If we define F kernel functions for a given convolution layer, the total number of parameters (without counting the bias term) is $F \times d \times d \times d \times C$. The 3D convolution kernel will convolve with local volumetric regions by shifting its position in *3D space*, with stride and padding choices similar to those defined for 2D convolutions. In the VoxNet architecture, we use square kernels noted as $\text{Conv}(f, d, s)$ where f is the number of kernels, d is its spatial dimension, and s is the stride size in shifting. The output of the convolution is passed through a leaky rectified nonlinearity layer (leaky ReLU) [62].

A 3D max-pooling layer $\text{Pool}(m)$ downsamples the input volume by a factor of m along the three spatial dimensions. It replaces each $m \times m \times m$ nonoverlapping block of voxels with their maximum. There are also more parameter choices such as uneven spatial dimensions and strides, similar to 2D pooling layers.

A fully connected layer takes vector inputs and maps the vector to an output vector with a weight matrix multiplication, followed by a nonlinearity layer such as ReLU. In VoxNet, we use $\text{Full}(n)$ to denote a fully connected layer with n outputs. In the last layer, the number of output matches the number of object categories and a softmax nonlinearity is used to provide a probabilistic score.

Based on the definitions of layers above, the VoxNet architecture is simply a composition of those layers with $\text{Conv}(32, 5, 2) \rightarrow \text{Conv}(32, 3, 1) \rightarrow \text{Pool}(2) \rightarrow \text{Full}(128) \rightarrow \text{Full}(K)$ (Fig. 11.3) with K as the number of classes. The network is simple, and therefore, fast and portable, with just 921,736 parameters most of which are from the first fully connected layer (around 96% of the total parameters).

11.3.2.3   Tips to Improve Volumetric CNN Performance

There are several strategies to improve the performance of volumetric CNNs through data augmentation in training (to reduce overfitting), voting from multiple inputs, as well as learning to aggregate multi-orientation inputs and learning to align inputs.

Data Augmentation

Similar to learning on large image datasets, we can augment the training data with random rotation, shifting, and scaling, which helps reduce model overfitting in training. For example, we can create n copies of each input instance by rotating them with $360/n°$ along the upright axis. We can also shift the input in the three spatial dimensions with a random small distance or scale the input by a random factor in the range of $[1 - \delta, 1 + \delta]$ where δ is a small number, for example, 0.1.

Voting and Learning to Vote

At testing time, we can pool the activations of the output layer over all n rotated versions of the input by taking the average of their classification scores. We can even take a similar approach to Multi-view CNN, to learn to aggregate features from observations from different orientations of the object, which can be called multi-orientation pooling (Fig. 11.4).

Learning to Align

An alternative approach of learning to vote is learning to align objects in different orientations to a "canonical" orientation before it is processed by the volumetric CNN. This can be achieved through a 3D spatial transformer network [75], which is a subnetwork (a volumetric CNN by itself but with fewer parameters) that takes volumetric grid input and output a transformation matrix (e.g., a rotation matrix) that is applied on the input. Then a following volumetric CNN consumes the rotated version of the input. The transformer network is jointly optimized with the following network and is shown to be able to learn to canonicalize object poses. With available annotations on object poses, we can even explicitly supervise the transformer network to regress to the ground truth pose, a relative pose to a predefined canonical pose (e.g., a chair with its back facing the front).

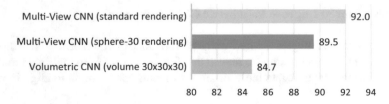

Fig. 11.5 Classification accuracy. Yellow and blue bars: performance drop of multi-view CNN due to the discretization of CAD models in rendering. Blue and green bars: volumetric CNN is significantly worse than multi-view CNN, even though their inputs have similar amounts of information. This indicates that the network of the volumetric CNN is weaker than that of the multi-view CNN

Fig. 11.6 3D shape representations

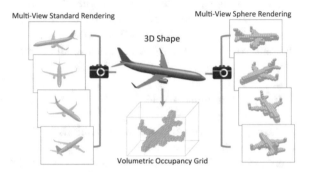

11.3.3   3D Volumetric CNN Versus Multi-view CNN

In the above two sections, we present two types of deep architecture on 3D shapes, volumetric and multi-view. In this section we make a shoulder to shoulder comparison of their performance, explain their performance gap, and briefly present two new volumetric deep networks with very different design intuitions to fill the gap.

The volumetric representation encodes a 3D shape as a 3D tensor of binary or real values. The multi-view representation encodes a 3D shape as a collection of renderings from multiple viewpoints. Stored as tensors, both representations can easily be used to train convolutional neural networks, i.e., volumetric CNNs and multi-view CNNs.

Intuitively, a volumetric representation should encode as much information, if not more, than its multi-view counterpart. However, experiments indicate that multi-view CNNs produce superior performance in object classification. Figure 11.5 reports the classification accuracy[1] on the ModelNet40 test set by two representative

---

[1]Average instance accuracy: the ratio between total number of correctly classified shapes and total number of tested shapes.

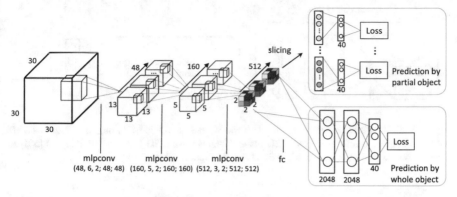

slicing

Fig. 11.7 Auxiliary training by subvolume supervision (Sect. 11.3.4.2). The main innovation is that we add auxiliary tasks to predict class labels that focus on part of an object, intended to drive the CNN to more heavily exploit local discriminative features. An mlpconv layer is a composition of three conv layers interleaved by ReLU layers. The five numbers under mlpconv are the number of channels, kernel size and stride of the first conv layer, and the number of channels of the second and third conv layers, respectively. The kernel size and stride of the second and third conv layers are 1. For example, mlpconv(48, 6, 2; 48; 48) is a composition of conv(48, 6, 2), ReLU, conv(48, 1, 1), ReLU, conv(48, 1, 1), and ReLU layers. Note that we add dropout layers with rate = 0.5 after fully connected layers

volumetric/multi-view architectures.[2] A volumetric CNN based on voxel occupancy (green) is 7.3% worse than a multi-view CNN (yellow).

It is interesting to ask why there is this performance gap. The gap seems to be caused by two factors: input resolution and network architecture differences. The multi-view CNN down-samples each rendered view to 227×227 pixels (Multi-view Standard Rendering in Fig. 11.6); to maintain a similar computational cost, the volumetric CNN uses a $30 \times 30 \times 30$ occupancy grid (Volumetric Occupancy Grid in Fig. 11.6).[3] As shown in Fig. 11.6, the input to the multi-view CNN captures more detail.

However, the difference in input resolution is not the primary reason for this performance gap, as evidenced by further experiments. If we compare the two networks by providing them with data containing a similar level of detail. To this end, we feed the multi-view CNN with renderings of the $30 \times 30 \times 30$ occupancy grid using *sphere rendering*,[4] i.e., for each occupied voxel, a ball is placed at its center, with radius equal to the edge length of a voxel. (Multi-View Sphere Rendering in Fig. 11.6.) We train the multi-view CNN from scratch using these sphere renderings. The accuracy of this multi-view CNN is reported in blue.

---

[2]We train models by replicating the architecture of [110] for volumetric CNNs and [92] for multi-view CNNs. All networks were trained in an end-to-end fashion. All methods were trained/tested on the same split for a fair comparison.

[3]Note that $30 \times 30 \times 30 \approx 227 \times 227(\times 0.5)$.

[4]It is computationally prohibitive to match the volumetric CNN resolution to multi-view CNN, which would be $227 \times 227 \times 227$.

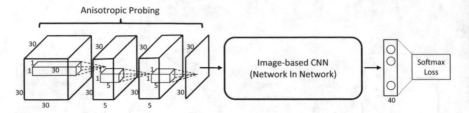

Fig. 11.8 CNN with anisotropic probing kernels. We use an elongated kernel to convolve the 3D cube and aggregate information to a 2D plane. Then we use a 2D NIN (NIN-CIFAR10 [59]) to classify the 2D projection of the original 3D shape. Figure is from [75]

Additionally, low-frequency information in 3D seems to be quite discriminative for object classification—it is possible to achieve 89.5% accuracy (blue) at a resolution of only $30 \times 30 \times 30$. This discovery motivates the architectures of a multi-resolution version of MVCNN.

11.3.4 Two New Volumetric Convolutional Neural Networks

11.3.4.1 Overview

We introduce two network variations that significantly improve the VoxNet architectures introduced in Sect. 11.3.2 on 3D volumetric data. These architecture designs are originally from [75]. The first network is designed to mitigate overfitting by introducing auxiliary training tasks, which are themselves challenging. These auxiliary tasks encourage the network to predict object class labels from partial subvolumes. Therefore, no additional annotation efforts are needed. The second network is designed to mimic multi-view CNNs, as they are strong in 3D shape classification. Instead of using rendering routines from computer graphics, the network projects a 3D shape to 2D by convolving its 3D volume with an anisotropic probing kernel. This kernel is capable of encoding long-range interactions between points. An image CNN is then appended to classify the 2D projection. Note that the training of the projection module and the image classification module is end-to-end. This emulation of multi-view CNNs achieves similar performance to them, using only standard layers in the CNN.

In order to mitigate overfitting from too many parameters, we adopt the mlpconv layer from [59] as the basic building block in both network variations (after each $d \times d \times d$ convolution layer, there are a few extra $1 \times 1 \times 1$ convolution layers following it, to further process the features maps).

11.3.4.2 Network 1: Auxiliary Training by Subvolume Supervision

Since current 3D datasets such as ModelNet40 are still limited in scale, we often observe significant overfitting when we train volumetric CNNs. When a volumetric CNN overfits to the training data, it has no incentive to continue learning. Reference [75] thus introduced auxiliary tasks that are closely correlated with the main task but are difficult to overfit, so that learning continues even if the main task is overfitted.

These auxiliary training tasks also predict the same object labels, but the predictions are made solely on a local subvolume of the input. Without complete knowledge of the object, the auxiliary tasks are more challenging, and can thus better exploit the discriminative power of local regions. This design is different from the classic multi-task learning setting of heterogeneous auxiliary tasks, which inevitably requires collecting additional annotations (e.g., conducting both object classification and detection [30]).

This design is implemented through an architecture shown in Fig. 11.7. The first three layers are mlpconv (multi-layer perceptron convolution) layers, a 3D extension of the 2D mlpconv proposed by [59]. The input and output of the mlpconv layers are both 4D tensors. Compared with the standard combination of linear convolutional layers and max-pooling layers, mlpconv has a three-layer structure and is thus a universal function approximator if enough neurons are provided in its intermediate layers. Therefore, mlpconv is a powerful filter for feature extraction of local patches, enhancing approximation of more abstract representations. In addition, mlpconv has been validated to be more discriminative with fewer parameters than ordinary convolution with pooling [59].

At the fourth layer, the network branches into two. The lower branch takes the whole object as input for traditional classification. The upper branch is a novel branch for auxiliary tasks. It slices the $512 \times 2 \times 2 \times 2$ 4D tensor (2 grids along x, y, z axes, and 512 channels) into $2 \times 2 \times 2 = 8$ vectors of dimension 512. We set up a classification task for each vector. A fully connected layer and a softmax layer are then appended independently to each vector to construct classification losses. A simple calculation shows that the receptive field of each task is $22 \times 22 \times 22$, covering roughly 2/3 of the entire volume.

11.3.4.3 Network 2: Anisotropic Probing

The success of multi-view CNNs is intriguing. Multi-view CNNs first project 3D objects to 2D and then make use of well-developed 2D image CNNs for classification. Inspired by its success, [75] designed a neural network that is also composed of the two stages. However, while multi-view CNNs use external rendering pipelines from computer graphics, the proposed network achieves the 3D-to-2D projection using differentiable layers,[5] in a manner similar to 'X-ray scanning'.

---

[5] A rising field related to this differentiable way of projection is called differentiable rendering [61] or neural rendering [49].

Key to this network is the use of an elongated anisotropic kernel which helps capture the global structure of the 3D volume. As illustrated in Fig. 11.8, the neural network has two modules: an anisotropic probing module and a network in network (NIN) module. The anisotropic probing module contains three convolutional layers of elongated kernels, each followed by a nonlinear ReLU layer. Note that both the input and output of each layer are 3D tensors.

In contrast to traditional isotropic kernels, an anisotropic probing module has the advantage of aggregating long-range interactions in the early feature learning stage with fewer parameters. As a comparison, with traditional neural networks constructed from isotropic kernels, introducing long-range interactions at an early stage can only be achieved through large kernels, which inevitably introduce many more parameters. After anisotropic probing, we use an adapted NIN network [59] to address the classification problem.

The anisotropic probing network is capable of capturing internal structures of objects through its X-ray like projection mechanism. This is an ability not offered by standard rendering. Combined with multi-orientation pooling (introduced below), it is possible for this probing mechanism to capture any 3D structure, due to its relationship with the Radon transform.

In addition, this architecture is scalable to higher resolutions, since all its layers can be viewed as 2D. While 3D convolution involves computation at locations of cubic resolution, we maintain quadratic computational cost.

11.3.5 Experimental Results

We show evaluation of volumetric CNNs and multi-view CNNs on the ModelNet40 dataset [110]. For convenience in the following discussions, we define *3D resolution* to be the discretization resolution of a 3D shape. That is, a $30 \times 30 \times 30$ volume has 3D resolution 30. The sphere rendering from this volume also has a 3D resolution 30, though it may have a higher 2D image resolution.

By default, we report classification accuracy on all models in the test set (average instance accuracy). For comparisons with other previous work we also report average class accuracy.

11.3.5.1 Classification Results

We compare the newly introduced methods with several strong baselines (previous state of the art) for shape classification on the ModelNet40 dataset. In the following, we discuss the results within volumetric CNN methods and within multi-view CNN methods.

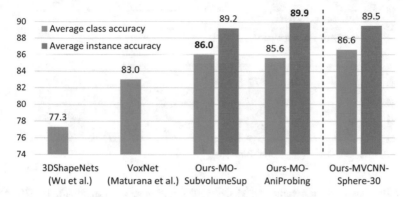

Fig. 11.9 Classification accuracy on ModelNet40 (resolution: 30). The newly introduced volumetric CNNs [75] have matched the performance of multi-view CNN at 3D resolution 30 (re-implementation of Su-MVCNN [92], rightmost group). Figure is from [75]

Volumetric CNNs

Figure 11.9 summarizes the performance of volumetric CNNs. MO-SubvolumeSup is the subvolume supervision network in Sect. 11.3.4.2 and MO-AniProbing is the anisotropic probing network in Sect. 11.3.4.3. Input data is augmented with random azimuth and elevation rotations. For clarity, we use MO- to denote that both networks are trained with an additional multi-orientation pooling step (20 orientations). For reference to multi-view CNN performance at the same 3D resolution, we also include MVCNN-Sphere-30, the result of the multi-view CNN with sphere rendering at 3D resolution 30.

As can be seen, both of these two new volumetric CNNs significantly outperform previous volumetric CNNs. Moreover, they both match the performance of multi-view CNN under the same 3D resolution. That is, *the gap between volumetric CNNs and multi-view CNNs is closed* under 3D resolution 30 on the ModelNet40 dataset, an issue that motivates us.

Multi-view CNNs

Figure 11.10 summarizes the performance of multi-view CNNs. MVCNN-MultiRes is the result of training an SVM over the concatenation of fc7 features from MVCNN-Sphere-30, 60, and MVCNN. HoGPyramid-LFD is the result by training an SVM over a concatenation of HoG features at three 2D resolutions (227×227, 114×114, and 57×57). Here LFD (lightfield descriptor) simply refers to extracting features from renderings. MVCNN-MultiRes achieves state-of-the-art accuracy.

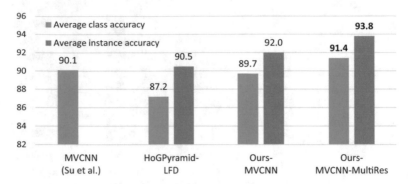

Fig. 11.10 Classification accuracy on ModelNet40 (multi-view representation). The 3D multi-resolution version is the strongest. It is worth noting that the simple baseline HoGPyramid-LFD performs quite well. Figure is from [75]

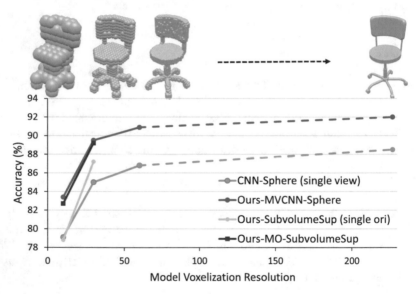

Fig. 11.11 Top: sphere rendering at 3D resolution 10, 30, 60, and standard rendering. Bottom: performance of image-based CNN and volumetric CNN with increasing 3D resolution. The two rightmost points are trained/tested from standard rendering. Figure is from [75]

11.3.5.2 Effect of 3D Resolution over Performance

Section 11.3.5.1 shows that the new volumetric CNN and multi-view CNN perform comparably at 3D resolution 30. Here we study the effect of 3D resolution for both types of networks.

Figure 11.11 shows the performance of volumetric CNN and multi-view CNN at different 3D resolutions (defined at the beginning of Sect. 11.3.5). Due to computational cost, we only test volumetric CNNs at 3D resolutions 10 and 30. The

Table 11.1 Comparison of volumetric CNN architectures. Numbers reported are classification accuracy on ModelNet40. Results from E2E-[110] (end-to-end learning version). All experiments are using the same set of azimuth and elevation augmented data

Network	Single-orientation	Multi-orientation
E2E-[110]	83.0	87.8
VoxNet [65]	83.8	85.9
3D-NIN	86.1	88.5
SubvolumeSup	**87.2**	89.2
AniProbing	84.4	**89.9**

observations are: first, the performance of volumetric CNNs and multi-view CNNs is on par at tested 3D resolutions; second, the performance of multi-view CNNs increases as the 3D resolution goes up. To further improve the performance of volumetric CNNs, this experiment suggests that it is worth exploring how to scale up volumetric CNNs to take input with higher 3D resolutions.

Comparison of Volumetric CNN Architectures

The architectures in comparison include VoxNet [65], E2E-[110] (the end-to-end learning variation of [110] implemented in Caffe [46]), 3D-NIN (a 3D variation of Network in Network [59] designed for 3D as in Fig. 11.7 without the "Prediction by partial object" branch), SubvolumeSup (Sect. 11.3.4.2) and AniProbing (Sect. 11.3.4.3).

From Table 11.1, first, the two volumetric CNNs we propose, SubvolumeSup and AniProbing networks, both show superior performance, indicating the effectiveness of the new architecture design; second, multi-orientation pooling increases performance for all network variations. This is especially significant for the anisotropic probing network, since each orientation usually only carries partial information of the object.

Comparison of Multi-view Methods

We compare different methods that are based on multi-view representations in Table 11.2. Methods in the second group are trained on the full ModelNet40 train set. Methods in the first group, SPH, LFD, FV, and Su-MVCNN, are trained on a subset of ModelNet40 containing 3,183 training samples. They are provided for reference. Also, note that the MVCNNs in the second group are re-implementations of MVCNN [92] in Caffe with AlexNet instead of VGG. We observe that MVCNNs are superior to methods by SVMs on handcrafted features.

Table 11.2 Comparison of multi-view based methods. Numbers reported are classification accuracy (class average and instance average) on ModelNet40. Note here the MVCNN is a replicated version of [92] trained on a larger training set

Method	#Views	Accuracy (class)	Accuracy (instance)
SPH (reported by [110])	–	68.2	–
LFD (reported by [110])	–	75.5	–
FV (reported by [92])	12	84.8	–
Su-MVCNN [92]	80	90.1	–
PyramidHoG-LFD	20	87.2	90.5
MVCNN	20	89.7	92.0
MVCNN-MultiRes	20	**91.4**	**93.8**

11.3.6 Further Discussion

In the text above we have introduced two types of deep neural networks to analyze 3D data: multi-view CNNs and volumetric CNNs (3D CNNs) and specifically described one multi-view CNN architecture: MVCNN from [92] and three volumetric CNNs: VoxNet from [65] and two stronger performing models from [75].

While we focused mainly on the semantic classification task, these two types of deep networks can be extended to many other applications such as shape part segmentation [48] and semantic scene segmentation [18] by aggregating multi-view image segmentation results, and 3D object detection [89] or 3D scan completion [20, 90] with volumetric CNNs.

These two types of networks have their own pros and cons as well. Multi-view CNNs are often good at capture fine-grained geometric structures (such as keys in a keyboard or thin bars on a chair back) thanks to the high-resolution image input and are very discriminative due to the well engineered and pretrained CNNs available—that's why MVCNNs are the leading methods in shape retrieval challenges such as the SHREC'16 [84]. However, multi-view CNNs have more strict requirements on the input format than volumetric CNNs. When the 3D input is not in the form of meshes or high density point clouds, or when the input is partial scans, it is not obvious how to render or project the input into multi-view images. For 3D input at the scene level, how to balance the quality, quantity, and efficiency of view-rendering is also a challenge. On the other hand, volumetric CNNs are more flexible with the input types (meshes, point clouds; partial or complete; single objects or scenes), as essentially it is just a quantization step. However, the main challenge with volumetric CNNs is on computation cost with high-resolution input as we discussed in the experiment subsection above. The network architecture is also coupled with the input resolution, i.e., adjusting the input resolution changes the physical receptive field sizes of the network layers. Recently there are a couple of new projects [16, 32] that proposed to use sparse 3D convolutions to achieve high efficiency while keeping high spatial resolution, which got promising results especially on the large-scale semantic scene parsing task [19].

A shared concern with both types of these networks (multi-view and volumetric CNNs) is that they all require a preprocessing step of the raw 3D point clouds or meshes before representation learning. These preprocessing steps on one hand could cause loss of 3D information and on the other hand lead to more hyper-parameter choices (e.g., viewpoints, rendering parameters or voxelization resolution) that are not obvious to determine in many scenarios. In the next two sections (Sects. 11.4 and 11.5) we introduce two new types of deep neural networks that directly consumes point cloud or mesh data without converting them to regular structures.

11.4   Deep Learning on Point Clouds

In this section, we explore deep learning architectures capable of reasoning about point clouds, a popular and important type of 3D geometric data. Typical convolutional deep networks require regular input data formats, like those of image grids or 3D voxels, in order to perform weight sharing and other kernel optimizations. Since point clouds are not in a regular format, most researchers typically transform such data to regular 3D voxel grids or collections of images (e.g., views) before feeding them to a deep net architecture as we discussed in Sect. 11.3. This data representation transformation, however, renders the resulting data unnecessarily voluminous—while also introducing quantization artifacts that can obscure natural invariances of the data.

For this reason, in this chapter, we focus on directly processing point clouds without converting them to other formats—and mainly introduce one representative deep network named *PointNet* [76]. The PointNet architecture directly takes point clouds as input and outputs either class labels for the entire input or per-point segment/part labels for each point of the input (Fig. 11.12).

Although point clouds are simple in representation, we still face two challenges in the deep architecture design. First, the model needs to respect the fact that a point cloud is just a set of points, and therefore, invariant to permutations of its members. Second, invariances to rigid transformations also need to be considered. To address the challenges, PointNet is constructed as a symmetric function composed of neural networks, which guarantees its invariance to input point orders. Furthermore, the input format is easy to apply rigid or affine transformations to, as each point transforms independently. Thus we can add a data-dependent spatial transformer network that attempts to canonicalize the data before the PointNet processes them, so as to further improve the results.

We provide both theoretical analysis and an experimental evaluation of the approach. We show that PointNet can approximate any set function that is continuous. More interestingly, it turns out that the network learns to summarize an input point cloud by a sparse set of key points, which roughly corresponds to the skele-

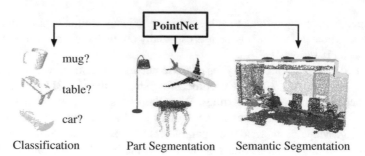

Fig. 11.12 Applications of PointNet. We propose a novel deep net architecture that consumes raw point clouds (sets of points) without voxelization or rendering. It is a unified architecture that learns both global and local point features, providing a simple, efficient, and effective approach for a number of 3D recognition tasks. Figure is from [76]

ton of objects according to visualization. The theoretical analysis and visualizations provide an understanding of why PointNet is highly robust to small perturbation of input points as well as to corruption through point insertion (outliers) or deletion (missing data).

We show the experimental results of PointNet on a number of benchmark datasets ranging from shape classification, part segmentation to scene segmentation, and compare it with deep learning methods with multi-view and volumetric representations. Under a unified architecture, the PointNet is much faster in speed, but it also exhibits strong performance on par or even better than the prior art.

In the rest of the section, Sect. 11.4.1 describes the problem formulation for deep learning on point clouds. Section 11.4.2 introduces the properties of point sets for which we refer to in the PointNet architecture design. Section 11.4.3 presents the detailed architecture of PointNet while Sect. 11.4.4 provides some theoretical analysis of the network. Lastly in Sect. 11.4.5 we show the experimental results of PointNet on shape recognition and semantic parsing benchmarks, and provide visualizations, as well as analysis experiments.

11.4.1 Problem Statement

We introduce a deep learning framework that directly consumes unordered point sets as inputs. A point cloud is represented as a set of 3D points $\{P_i | i = 1, \ldots, n\}$, where each point P_i is a vector of its (x, y, z) coordinate plus extra feature channels such as color, normal, etc. For simplicity and clarity, unless otherwise noted, we only use the (x, y, z) coordinate as point's channels.

For the object classification task, the input point cloud is either directly sampled from a shape or pre-segmented from a scene point cloud. The deep network outputs k scores for all the k candidate classes. For semantic segmentation, the input can be a single object for part region segmentation, or a subvolume from a 3D scene for object region segmentation. The model will output $n \times m$ scores for each of the n points and each of the m semantic subcategories.

11.4.2 Properties of Point Sets in $\mathbb{R}^N$

In theory a fully connected neural network with one hidden layer is able to approximate any continuous function, however, injecting more structure in the network architecture can greatly reduce the number of necessary parameters and improve approximation accuracy. A well-known example is the design of convolutional neural networks for images. To find out a proper architecture structure, we need to first understand the properties of the data.

The input is a subset of points from an Euclidean space. It has three main properties:

- Unordered. Unlike pixel arrays in images or voxel arrays in volumetric grids, a point cloud is a set of points without a specific order. In other words, a network that consumes n 3D points needs to be invariant to $n!$ permutations of the input.
- Interaction among points. The points are from a space with a distance metric. This means that points are not isolated, and neighboring points form a meaningful subset. Therefore, the model needs to be able to capture local structures from nearby points, and the combinatorial interactions among local structures.
- Invariance under transformations. As a geometric object, the learned representation of the point set should be invariant to certain transformations. For example, rotating and translating points all together should not modify the global point cloud category nor the segmentation of the points.

11.4.3 PointNet Architecture

The full PointNet architecture is illustrated in Fig. 11.13, where the classification network and the segmentation network share a great portion of the common structure. Please read the caption of Fig. 11.13 for the pipeline.

The network has three key modules: the max-pooling layer as a symmetric function to aggregate information from all the points, a local and global information combination structure, and two joint alignment networks that align both input points and point features. We will discuss the reason behind these design choices in separate paragraphs below.

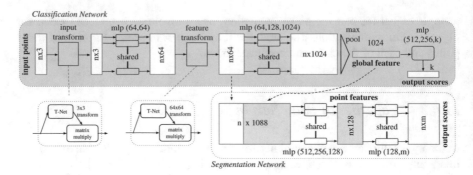

Fig. 11.13 PointNet architecture. The classification network takes *n* points as input, applies input and feature transformations, and then aggregates point features by max pooling. The output is classification scores for *k* classes. The segmentation network is an extension of the classification net. It concatenates global and local features and outputs per-point scores. "mlp" stands for multi-layer perceptron, numbers in bracket are layer sizes. Batchnorm is used for all layers with ReLU. Dropout layers are used for the last mlp in the classification net. Figure is from [76]

Symmetry Function for Unordered Input

In order to make a model invariant to input permutation, three strategies exist: (1) sort input into a canonical order; (2) treat the input as a sequence to train a RNN (recurrent neural network), but augment the training data by all kinds of permutations; (3) use a simple symmetric function to aggregate the information from each point. Here, a symmetric function takes *n* vectors as input and outputs a new vector that is invariant to the input order. For example, + and * operators are symmetric binary functions.

While sorting sounds like a simple solution, in high-dimensional space there, in fact, does not exist an ordering that is stable with respect to point perturbations in the general sense. This can be easily shown by contradiction. If such an ordering strategy exists, it defines a bijection map between a high-dimensional space and a $1D$ real line. It is not hard to see, to require an ordering to be stable with respect to point perturbations is equivalent to requiring that this map preserves spatial proximity as the dimension reduces, a task that cannot be achieved in the general case. Therefore, sorting does not fully resolve the ordering issue, and it is hard for a network to learn a consistent mapping from input to output as the ordering issue persists. As shown in experiments (Fig. 11.16), we find that a fully connected network applied on a sorted point set performs poorly, though slightly better than the one directly processing an unsorted input.

The idea to use an RNN considers the point set as a sequential signal and hopes that by training the RNN with randomly permuted sequences, the RNN will become invariant to order. However, in "OrderMatters" [103] the authors have shown that order does matter and cannot be totally omitted. While an RNN has relatively good robustness to input ordering for sequences with small lengths (dozens), it's hard to scale up to thousands of input elements, which is the common size for point sets. Empirically, we have also shown that a model based on RNNs does not perform as well as the proposed method (Fig. 11.16).

A more general idea is to approximate a general function defined on a point set by applying a symmetric function on transformed elements in the set

$$f(\{x_1, \ldots, x_n\}) \approx g(h(x_1), \ldots, h(x_n)), \tag{11.1}$$

where $f : 2^{\mathbb{R}^N} \to \mathbb{R}, h : \mathbb{R}^N \to \mathbb{R}^K, g : \mathbb{R}^K \times \cdots \times \mathbb{R}^K \to \mathbb{R}$ as a *symmetric function*. With this function composition, since g is symmetric and as h is shared across input elements $\{x_i\}$, the whole function f is guaranteed to be symmetric.

Empirically, the basic module is very simple: we approximate h by a multi-layer perceptron (MLP) network and g as a composition of (element-wise) max pooling (MAX $: \mathbb{R}^K \times \cdots \times \mathbb{R}^K \to \mathbb{R}^K$) and another multi-layer perceptron network $\gamma :$ $\mathbb{R}^K \to \mathbb{R}$, therefore, $g = \gamma \circ$ MAX.

The output dimension (K) of the function h is a key parameter as it specifies the latent space size for point aggregation. Empirically we take $K = 1024$. We also learn a number of f's, for example k of them as scores for k categories in the point cloud classification task. See Fig. 11.13 for detailed parameters of h and see visualizations (Fig. 11.20) in Sect. 11.4.5.3 for an intuitive explanation of what has been learned in the function h.

While the key module seems simple, it has interesting properties (see Sect. 11.4.5.3) and can achieve strong performance (see Sect. 11.4.5.1) in several different applications. Due to the simplicity of the module, we are also able to provide theoretical analysis as in Sect. 11.4.4.

Local and Global Information Aggregation

The output from the above max-pooling operator gives us a global signature of the input set. We can easily train a SVM or a multi-layer perceptron classifier (with γ and a linear layer) on this global feature for classification. However, point segmentation requires a combination of local and global knowledge (as a global descriptor cannot tell classes of individual points while a local descriptor has limited context). We can achieve this in a simple yet highly effective manner.

The solution can be seen in Fig. 11.13 (*Segmentation Network*). After computing the global point cloud feature after max pooling (1024-dim), we feed it back to per-point embeddings (64-dim) by concatenating the global feature with each of the points embeddings. Then we extract new per-point features based on the combined point descriptors—this time the per-point feature is aware of both the local and global information.

With this modification the network is able to predict per-point quantities that rely on both local geometry and global semantics. For example we can accurately predict per-point normals (see appendix in [76]), validating that the network is able to summarize information from the point's local neighborhood. In Sect. 11.4.5, we also show that the model can achieve superior performance on shape part segmentation and scene segmentation compared with prior work.

Joint Alignment Network

The semantic labeling of a point cloud has to be invariant if the point cloud undergoes certain geometric transformations, such as rigid transformation. We, therefore, expect that the learned representation of a point set is invariant to these transformations.

A natural solution is to align all input set to a canonical space before feature extraction. Jaderberg et al. [45] introduced the idea of the spatial transformer to align 2D images through sampling and interpolation, achieved by a specifically tailored layer implemented on GPU.

The input form of point clouds allows us to achieve this goal in a much simpler way compared with [45]. We do not need to invent any new layers and no alias is introduced as in the image case. We predict an affine transformation matrix by a mini-network (T-net in Fig. 11.13) and directly apply this transformation to the coordinates of input points. The mini-network itself resembles the form of (11.1), composed of point embedding functions, max pooling, and fully connected layers. It takes a point cloud input and outputs a 3×3 transformation matrix (or a 64×64 matrix in the feature transformation case described below). More details about the T-net are described in the appendix in [76].

By training the T-net along with the rest of the network, the T-net learns to geometrically transform point clouds such that they are more aligned (typically to a few canonical poses within each category) so that the classification task afterward becomes easier.

This idea can be further extended to the alignment of feature space as well. We can insert another alignment network on point features and predict a feature transformation matrix to align features from different input point clouds. However, the transformation matrix in the feature space has a much higher dimension than the spatial transform matrix, which greatly increases the difficulty of optimization. We, therefore, add a regularization term to the softmax training loss. We constrain the feature transformation matrix to be close to an orthogonal matrix

$$L_{reg} = \|I - AA^T\|_F^2, \tag{11.2}$$

where A is the feature alignment matrix predicted by a mini-network. An orthogonal transformation will not lose information in the input, thus it is desired. We find that by adding the regularization term, the optimization becomes more stable and the model achieves better performance.

11.4.4 Theoretical Analysis

Universal Approximation

We first show the universal approximation ability of PointNet to continuous set functions. By the continuity of set functions, intuitively, a small perturbation to the input point set should not greatly change the function values, such as classification or segmentation scores.

Formally, let $\mathcal{X} = \{S : S \subseteq [0, 1] \text{ and } |S| = n\}$, $f : \mathcal{X} \to \mathbb{R}$ is a continuous set function on $\mathcal{X}$ w.r.t to Hausdorff distance $d_H(\cdot, \cdot)$, i.e., $\forall \epsilon > 0, \exists \delta > 0$, for any $S, S' \in \mathcal{X}$, if $d_H(S, S') < \delta$, then $|f(S) - f(S')| < \epsilon$. The theorem says that f can be arbitrarily approximated by the network given enough neurons at the max-pooling layer, i.e., K in (11.1) is sufficiently large.

Theorem 11.1 *Suppose $f : \mathcal{X} \to \mathbb{R}$ is a continuous set function w.r.t Hausdorff distance $d_H(\cdot, \cdot)$. $\forall \epsilon > 0$, $\exists$ a continuous function h and a symmetric function $g(x_1, \ldots, x_n) = \gamma \circ MAX$, such that for any $S \in \mathcal{X}$,*

$$\left| f(S) - \gamma \left(\underset{x_i \in S}{MAX} \{h(x_i)\} \right) \right| < \epsilon$$

where $x_1, \ldots, x_n$ is the full list of elements in S ordered arbitrarily, γ is a continuous function, and MAX is a vector max operator that takes n vectors as input and returns a new vector of the element-wise maximum.

The proof of this theorem can be found in the appendix of [76]. The key idea is that in the worst case the network can learn to convert a point cloud into a volumetric representation, by partitioning the space into equal-sized voxels. In practice, however, the network learns a much smarter strategy to probe the space, as we shall see in point function visualizations.

Bottleneck Dimension and Stability

Theoretically and experimentally we find that the expressiveness of the network is strongly affected by the dimension of the max-pooling layer, i.e., K in (11.1). Here we provide an analysis, which also reveals properties related to the stability of the model.

We define $\mathbf{u} = \underset{x_i \in S}{MAX}\{h(x_i)\}$ to be the subnetwork of f which maps a point set in $[0, 1]^m$ to a K-dimensional vector. The following theorem tells us that small corruptions or extra noise points in the input set are not likely to change the output of the network

Theorem 11.2 *Suppose $\mathbf{u} : \mathcal{X} \to \mathbb{R}^K$ such that $\mathbf{u} = \underset{x_i \in S}{MAX}\{h(x_i)\}$ and $f = \gamma \circ \mathbf{u}$. Then,*

(a) $\forall S, \exists \, \mathcal{C}_S, \mathcal{N}_S \subseteq \mathcal{X}, \; f(T) = f(S) \; if \, \mathcal{C}_S \subseteq T \subseteq \mathcal{N}_S;$
(b) $|\mathcal{C}_S| \leq K$

We explain the implications of the theorem. (a) says that $f(S)$ is unchanged up to the input corruption if all points in $\mathcal{C}_S$ are preserved; it is also unchanged with extra noise points up to $\mathcal{N}_S$. (b) says that $\mathcal{C}_S$ only contains a bounded number of points, determined by K in (11.1). In other words, $f(S)$ is in fact totally determined by a finite subset $\mathcal{C}_S \subseteq S$ of less or equal to K elements. We, therefore, call $\mathcal{C}_S$ the *critical point set* of S and K the *bottleneck dimension* of f. Section 11.4.5.3 describes more details on how to compute $\mathcal{N}_S$ and $\mathcal{C}_S$ empirically and also provides some visualizations of a few sample critical sets.

Combined with the continuity of h, this explains the robustness of the model with respect to point perturbation, corruption, and extra noise points. The robustness is gained in analogy to the sparsity principle in machine learning models. *Intuitively, the network learns to summarize a shape by a sparse set of key points.* In the following section we see that the key points form the skeleton of an object.

11.4.5 Experimental Results

Experiments are divided into four parts. First, we show that PointNet can be applied to multiple 3D recognition tasks (Sect. 11.4.5.1). Second, we provide experiments to validate the network design (Sect. 11.4.5.2). At last, we visualize what the network learns (Sect. 11.4.5.3) and analyze time and space complexity (Sect. 11.4.5.4).

11.4.5.1 Applications

In this section we show how PointNet can be trained to perform 3D object classification, object part segmentation and semantic scene segmentation. Even though the network takes input with an unstructured, unordered data representation (point sets), PointNet is able to achieve comparable or even better performance compared with strong prior methods on benchmarks for several tasks.

3D Object Classification

The network learns a global point cloud feature that can be used for object classification. We evaluate the model on the ModelNet40 [110] shape classification benchmark. There are 12,311 CAD models from 40 man-made object categories, split into 9,843 for training and 2,468 for testing. While previous methods focus on volumetric and multi-view image representations, PointNet was the first deep architecture to directly work on raw point cloud data.

Table 11.3 Classification results on ModelNet40

	Input	#Views	Accuracy avg. class	Accuracy overall
SPH [50]	Mesh	–	68.2	–
3DShapeNets [110]	Volume	1	77.3	84.7
VoxNet [65]	Volume	12	83.0	85.9
Subvolume [75]	Volume	20	86.0	**89.2**
LFD [110]	Image	10	75.5	–
MVCNN [92]	Image	80	**90.1**	–
Baseline	Point	–	72.6	77.4
PointNet	Point	1	86.2	**89.2**

We uniformly sample 1024 points on mesh faces according to face areas[6] and scale the point cloud of each shape into a unit sphere. During training, we augment the point cloud on-the-fly by randomly rotating the object along the up-axis and jitter the position of each point by a Gaussian noise with zero mean and 0.02 standard deviation.

In Table 11.3, we compare the PointNet model with previous works, as well as a baseline using MLP on traditional features extracted from point cloud (point density, D2, shape contour, etc.). The PointNet model achieved the best performance among methods based on 3D input (volumetric and point cloud). With only fully connected layers and max pooling, the network gains a strong lead in inference speed and can be easily parallelized in GPU implementation. There is still a small gap between the PointNet method and multi-view based method (MVCNN [92]), which we think is due to the loss of fine geometry details that can be captured by rendered images.

3D Object Part Segmentation

Part segmentation is a challenging fine-grained 3D recognition task. Given a 3D scan or a mesh model, the task is to assign a part category label (e.g., chair leg, cup handle) to each point or face.

We evaluate on the ShapeNet part data set from [114], which contains 16,881 shapes from 16 categories, annotated with 50 parts in total. Most object categories are labeled with two to five parts. Ground truth annotations are labeled on sampled points on the shapes.

The part segmentation is formulated as a per-point classification problem. The evaluation metric is mIoU on points. For each shape S of category C, to calculate the shape's mIoU: For each part type in category C, compute IoU between ground

---

[6]To sample one point, we first randomly select a face. A face f_i is selected with probability $p_i = \text{area}(f_i)/\sum_{j=1}^{N} \text{area}(f_j)$. Then we randomly sample a point from the face.

Table 11.4 Segmentation results on ShapeNet part dataset. Metric is mIoU (%) on points. We compare PointNet with two traditional methods [109, 114] and a 3D fully convolutional network baseline. PointNet method achieved the best mIoU compared with the baselines

	Mean	Aero	Bag	Cap	Car	Chair	Ear	Guitar	Knife
#Shapes		2690	76	55	898	3758	69	787	392
Wu [109]	–	63.2	–	–	–	73.5	–	–	–
Yi [114]	81.4	81.0	78.4	77.7	**75.7**	87.6	61.9	**92.0**	85.4
3D CNN	79.4	75.1	72.8	73.3	70.0	87.2	63.5	88.4	79.6
PointNet	**83.7**	**83.4**	**78.7**	**82.5**	74.9	**89.6**	**73.0**	91.5	**85.9**
	Lamp	Laptop	Motor	Mug	Pistol	Rocket	Skate	Table
#Shapes	1547	451	202	184	283	66	152	5271
Wu [109]	74.4	–	–	–	–	–	-	74.8
Yi [114]	**82.5**	**95.7**	**70.6**	91.9	**85.9**	53.1	69.8	75.3
3D CNN	74.4	93.9	58.7	91.8	76.4	51.2	65.3	77.1
PointNet	80.8	95.3	65.2	**93.0**	81.2	**57.9**	**72.8**	**80.6**

truth and predicted part labeling (among points). If the union of ground truth and prediction points is empty, then count part IoU as 1. Then we average IoUs for all part types in category C to get mIoU for that shape. To calculate mIoU for the category, we take an average of mIoUs for all shapes in that category.

We compare the segmentation version PointNet (a modified version [76] of Fig. 11.13, *Segmentation Network*) with two traditional methods [109, 114] that both take advantage of pointwise geometry features and correspondences between shapes, as well as a 3D CNN baseline [76].

In Table 11.4, we report per-category and mean IoU(%) scores. We observe a 2.3% mean IoU improvement and the network beats the baseline methods in most categories.

We also perform experiments on simulated Kinect scans to test the robustness of these methods. For every CAD model in the ShapeNet part data set, we use Blensor Kinect Simulator [35] to generate incomplete point clouds from six random viewpoints. We train PointNet on the complete shapes and partial scans with the same network architecture and training setting. Results show that the network lost only 5.3% mean IoU. In Fig. 11.14, we present qualitative results on both complete and partial data. One can see that though partial data is fairly challenging, the predictions from PointNet are still reasonable.

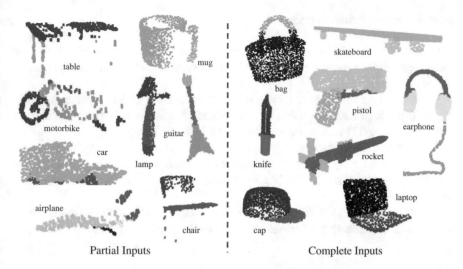

Fig. 11.14 Qualitative results for part segmentation. We visualize the CAD part segmentation results across all 16 object categories. We show both results for partial simulated Kinect scans (left block) and complete ShapeNet CAD models (right block). Figure is from [76]

Fig. 11.15 Qualitative results for semantic segmentation. Top row is an input point cloud with color. Bottom row is output semantic segmentation result (on points) displayed in the same camera viewpoint as input

Semantic Segmentation in Scenes

The segmentation PointNet on part segmentation can be easily extended to semantic scene segmentation, where point labels become semantic object classes instead of object part labels.

We show the experimental results on the Stanford 3D Indoor Spaces (S3DIS) dataset [3], which contains 3D scans from Matterport scanners in 6 areas (building floors) including 271 rooms annotated with 13 semantic categories.

To prepare training data, we first split points by room, and then split each room into blocks with 1 m by 1 m areas. We train the segmentation version of PointNet to predict a per-point class in each block. More details of the experimental setup can be found in [76].

Figure 11.15 shows the segmentation results from PointNet. We see the network is able to output smooth predictions and is robust to missing points and occlusions.

11.4.5.2   Architecture Design Analysis

In this section we validate the design choices of PointNet by control experiments. We also show the effects of the network's hyperparameters.

Comparison with Alternative Order-Invariant Methods

As mentioned in Sect. 11.4.3, there are at least three options for consuming unordered set inputs. We use the ModelNet40 shape classification problem as a test bed for comparisons of those options, the following two control experiment will also use this task.

The baselines (illustrated in Fig. 11.16) we compared with include multi-layer perceptron on unsorted (with permutation augmentation) and sorted (with lex-sort based on XYZ coordinates) points as $n \times 3$ arrays, an RNN model that considers input points as a sequence, and PointNet models (vanilla versions without input and feature transformations) based on symmetry functions. The symmetry operation that we experimented with include max pooling, average pooling and an attention-based weighted sum. The attention method is similar to that in [103], where a scalar score is predicted from each point feature, then the score is normalized across points by computing a softmax. The weighted sum is then computed on the normalized scores and the point features. As shown in Fig. 11.16, max-pooling operation achieved the best performance by a large margin, which validates the PointNet's design choice.

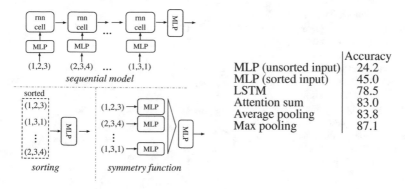

	Accuracy
MLP (unsorted input)	24.2
MLP (sorted input)	45.0
LSTM	78.5
Attention sum	83.0
Average pooling	83.8
Max pooling	87.1

Fig. 11.16 Three approaches to achieve order invariance. Multi-layer perceptron (MLP) applied on points consists of 5 hidden layers with neuron sizes 64, 64, 64, 128, 1024, all points share a single copy of MLP. The MLP close to the output consists of two layers with sizes 512, 256. Figure is from [76]

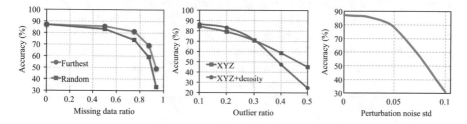

Fig. 11.17 PointNet robustness test. The metric is overall classification accuracy on ModelNet40 test set. Left: delete points. Furthest means the original 1024 points are sampled with furthest sampling. Middle: insertion. Outliers uniformly scattered in the unit sphere. Right: perturbation. Add Gaussian noise to each point independently. Figure is from [76]

Robustness Test

We show that PointNet, while simple and effective, is robust to various kinds of input corruptions. We use the same architecture as in Fig. 11.16's max-pooling network. Input points are normalized into a unit sphere. Results are in Fig. 11.17.

As to missing points, when there are 50% points missing, the accuracy only drops by 2.4 and 3.8% with respect to furthest and random input sampling. The network is also robust to outlier points, if it has seen those during training. We evaluate two models: one trained on points with (x, y, z) coordinates; the other on (x, y, z) plus point density. The network has more than 80% accuracy even when 20% of the points are outliers. Figure 11.17 (right) shows the network is robust to point perturbations.

We further compare PointNet and VoxNet [65] on robustness to missing data in the input point clouds. Both networks are trained with the same train-test split, using 1024 points per shape as input. For VoxNet we voxelize the point cloud to $32 \times 32 \times 32$ occupancy grids and augment the training data by random rotation around the up-axis and jittering.

Fig. 11.18 PointNet versus VoxNet [65] on incomplete input data. Metric is overall classification accuracy on ModelNet40 test set. Note that VoxNet is using 12 viewpoints averaging while PointNet is using only one view of the point cloud. Evidently PointNet presents much stronger robustness to missing points. Figure is from [76]

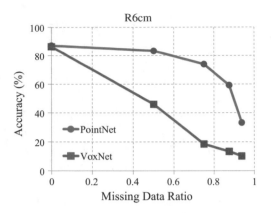

At test time, input points are randomly dropped out by a certain ratio. As VoxNet is sensitive to rotations, its prediction uses average scores from 12 viewpoints of a point cloud. As shown in Fig. 11.18, we see that the PointNet is much more robust to missing points. VoxNet's accuracy dramatically drops when half of the input points are missing, from 86.3 to 46.0% with a 40.3% difference, which is more than *10x* worse than PointNet (only 3.8% drop in accuracy). This can be explained by the theoretical analysis and explanation of PointNet—it learns to use a collection of *critical points* to summarize the shape, thus it is very robust to missing data.

11.4.5.3 Visualizing PointNet

Critical Point and Upper-Bound Shape Visualization

In Fig. 11.19, we visualize some results of the *critical point sets* C_S and the *upper-bound shapes* $\mathcal{N}_S$ (as discussed in Theorem 11.2) for some sample shapes S. The point sets between the two shapes will give exactly the same global shape feature $f(S)$.

We can see clearly from Fig. 11.19 that the *critical point sets* C_S, contributed to the max pooled feature, summarizes the skeleton of the shape. The *upper-bound shapes* $\mathcal{N}_S$ illustrates the largest possible point cloud that gives the same global shape feature $f(S)$ as the input point cloud S. C_S and $\mathcal{N}_S$ reflect the robustness of PointNet, meaning that losing some non-critical points does not change the global shape signature $f(S)$ at all.

The C_S is computed by comparing point embedding values, i.e., $h(x_i)$ with the max-pooled embedding for each embedding dimension and each point: if a point's embedding is smaller than the max-pooled embedding in all dimensions, then this point does not contribute to the pooled descriptor and thus is not a critical point; otherwise it is a critical point. The $\mathcal{N}_S$ is constructed (approximately) by forwarding a uniformly and densely sampled set of points in $[-1, 1]^3$ through the network and

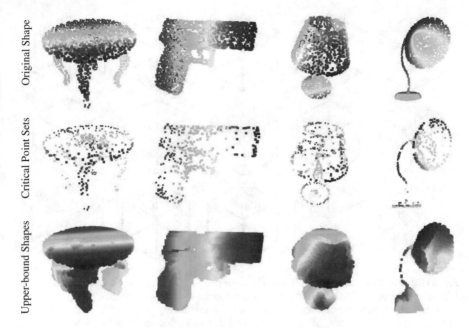

Fig. 11.19 Critical points and upper-bound shape. While critical points jointly determine the global shape feature for a given shape, any point cloud that falls between the critical points set and the upper-bound shape gives exactly the same feature. We color-code all figures to show the depth information. Figure is from [76]

select points p whose point function values $(h_1(p), h_2(p), \ldots, h_K(p))$ are no larger than the global shape descriptor.

Point Function Visualization

The classification PointNet computes a K-dimensional ($K = 1024$ in this visualization) point embedding for each point and aggregates all the per-point embeddings via a max-pooling layer into a single K-dim vector, which forms a global shape descriptor.

To gain more insights on what the point functions $h_1, \ldots, h_K$ have learned, we visualize the points x_i's that give high point function value $h(x_i)$ in Fig. 11.20. This visualization clearly shows that different point functions learn to detect points in different regions with various shapes scattered in the whole space.

In another perspective, the point function h_i can be viewed as a **space encoding function** for input space $\mathbb{R}^N$. To understand this view, we can take voxelization as an example. Voxelization is a predefined, static way to encode space. For example, in a $10 \times 10 \times 10$ binary occupancy grid of the $\mathbb{R}^3$ space, there are 1000 encoding functions corresponding to the 1000 voxels, which are all one-hot functions mapping from $\mathbb{R}^3$ to $\{0, 1\}$ with 0 noting an empty voxel and 1 noting an occupied one—the

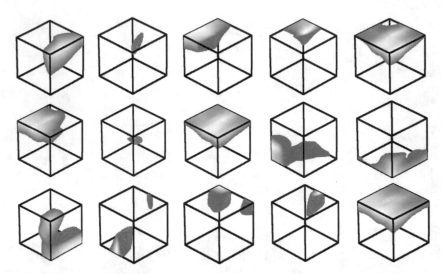

Fig. 11.20 Point function visualization. For each per-point function h, we calculate the values $h(p)$ for all the points p in a cube of diameter two located at the origin, which spatially covers the unit sphere to which our input shapes are normalized when training our PointNet. In this figure, we visualize all the points p that give $h(p) > 0.5$ with function values color-coded by the brightness of the voxel. We randomly pick 15 point functions and visualize the activation regions for them

ith function is activated only if there is a point in the ith voxel. In comparison, in PointNet, we are able to learn a set of smooth space encoding functions adaptive to data and task, which could encode the space in a more efficient and effective way than the simple voxelization.

11.4.5.4   Time and Space Complexity Analysis

Table 11.5 summarizes space (number of parameters in the network) and time (floating-point operations/sample) complexity of the classification PointNet. We also compare PointNet to a representative set of volumetric and multi-view based architectures in previous works.

While MVCNN [92] and Subvolume (3D CNN) [75] achieve high performance, PointNet is orders more efficient in computational cost (measured in FLOPS: *141x* and *8x* more efficient, respectively). Besides, PointNet is much more space efficient than MVCNN in terms of the number of parameters in the network (*17x* less parameters). Moreover, PointNet is much more scalable—its space and time complexity is $O(N)$-*linear* in the number of input points. However, since convolution dominates computing time, multi-view method's time complexity grows *quadratically* on image resolution and volumetric convolution-based method grows *cubically* with the volume size.

Table 11.5 Time and space complexity of deep architectures for 3D data classification. PointNet (vanilla) is the classification PointNet without input and feature transformations. FLOPS stands for floating-point operations per second. The "M" stands for million. Subvolume and MVCNN used pooling on input data from multiple rotations or views, without which they have much inferior performance

	Number of parameters	FLOPS
PointNet (vanilla) [76]	0.8M	148M
PointNet [76]	3.5M	440M
Subvolume [75]	16.6M	3633M
MVCNN [92]	60.0M	62057M

Empirically, PointNet is able to process more than one million points per second for point cloud classification (around 1 K objects/second) or semantic segmentation (around 2 rooms/second) with a 1080X GPU on TensorFlow, showing great potential for portable devices and real-time applications.

11.5 Deep Learning on Meshes

A polygon mesh is a collection of vertices, edges and faces that define the shape of a 3D object in computer graphics or solid modeling. Each vertex may be associated with extra data than its coordinates such as its local geometry property (such as normal and curvature) or other physical properties (such as surface tension and temperature). In the context of data structures, a polygon mesh is a *graph* thus the deep neural networks processing it are often called *graph CNNs* or *geometric deep learning* models, which are generalizations of convolutional neural networks defined on a Euclidean or grid-like structure to a non-Euclidean domain [11]. The architectures studied under geometric deep learning are not restricted to analyzing 3D objects or scenes, they can be used in much broader data types such as social networks (with users as vertices), sensor networks (with distributed interconnected sensors as vertices), or even gene expression data and brain structure data that are often modeled as graphs [11].

The methods of graph CNNs mainly fall into one of the following two categories. The first category of methods is based on the Convolution Theorem, to define convolution in the *spectral* domain [12, 21, 38, 115]. The main motivation behind this formulation is because there is no obvious definition of translation in the spatial domain. This branch of methods is tightly related to the field of spectral analysis on graphs. An alternative family of methods considers the convolution operation as a template matching process in the *spatial* domain [8, 9, 64, 68], and focuses on defining spatial operators on a local graph. However, as noted in [11], there is often not a clear cut between spectral and spatial methods. Aside from these two families of methods, there are also methods that convolve the graphs in an embedding

Fig. 11.21 Illustration of the
difference between extrinsic
and intrinsic deep learning
methods on geometric data.
Left: extrinsic methods.
Right: intrinsic methods.
Figure is from [9]

space mapped (such as a parameterization space in 2D) from the original mesh and
resort to traditional CNNs for feature learning [63]. However, in those cases the
parameterization is often not unique and introduces distortion to the data.

In the following text, we briefly introduce the design ideas and application results
behind two representative works of deep learning on meshes, one based on the spatial
domain (ACNN [9]) and the other on the spectral domain (SyncSpecCNN [115]).

11.5.1 Spatial Domain Graph CNN

While graph CNNs are also called CNNs, they have significant differences with image
CNNs and volumetric CNNs defined on Euclidean space/regular grid structures.
Figure 11.21 gives a clear illustration of their difference. On the left of the figure,
we see that volumetric CNNs define the convolution kernels, as well as translations
in the 3D Euclidean space. Such an operation is not invariant to deformations. For
example as seen in the figure the filter activated from a straight cylinder would not
respond if the tube is bent. In comparison, on the right we see an intrinsic convolution
operation, where the receptive field is defined on the surface itself, thus invariant to
deformations. For deformable objects such as human bodies, the ability to respect
deformation invariance is critical to achieve good performance in tasks like finding
correspondences.

In the work of the ACNN (anisotropic convolutional neural network) [9], a set
of oriented anisotropic diffusion kernels are constructed which operate on the local
intrinsic polar representation of the data. With several cascades of the filters using
both linear and nonlinear layers, a deep neural network is trained to learn intrinsic
dense correspondences between deformable human bodies. Figure 11.22 shows the
remarkable results achieved by the method.

11.5.2 Spectral Domain Graph CNN

In spectral methods of graph CNNs, a 3D shape S is modeled as a graph $\mathcal{G} = (\mathcal{V}, \mathcal{E})$
with vertices $\mathcal{V}$ as points in $\mathbb{R}^3$ and $|\mathcal{V}| = n$, and edges $\mathcal{E}$ as the set of edges in the
graph. The adjacency matrix associated with $\mathcal{G}$ is denoted as $W \in \mathbb{R}^{n \times n}$. One way

Fig. 11.22 Examples of correspondence on the FAUST humans dataset [7] obtained by ACNN. Shown is the texture transferred from the leftmost reference shape to different subjects in different poses by means of predicted correspondence. The correspondence is nearly perfect (only very few minor artifacts are noticeable). Figure is from [9]

to compute the Laplacian of the graph is $L = I - D^{-1/2}WD^{-1/2}$ where I is the identify matrix, and D is the degree matrix where $D_{i,i} = \sum_j W_{i,j}$. The eigenvalue decomposition gives a set of eigenvectors $u_l, l = 0, \ldots, n - 1$ as a set of orthogonal bases of the graph along with their corresponding eigenvalues $\lambda_l, l = 0, \ldots, n - 1$. As in Fourier analysis, this spectral decomposition also introduces the concept of frequency. For each basis u_l, the eigenvalue λ_l in the decomposition defines its frequency, depicting its smoothness. The convolution theorem of Fourier analysis can be extended to the Laplacian spectrum: the convolution between a kernel and a function on the shape graph is equivalent to the pointwise multiplication of their spectral representations [12].

In the work of SyncSpecCNN [115], the graph CNN is defined based on the spectral convolution theorem. It also combines processing in the spectral and spatial domains, where weight sharing among convolution kernels at different scales is by performing the convolutions in the spectral domain (as pointwise multiplications by the kernel duals), while the nonlinearity step (such operations are not easily dualized) happens in the spatial domain. The general process is illustrated in Fig. 11.23a.

One challenge of this spectral based method is on how to effectively share weights across shapes. Since different shapes give rise to different nearest neighbor graphs on their point clouds, the eigenbases we get for the graph Laplacians are not directly comparable. To address the issue in SyncSpecCNN, the authors proposed to synchronize all these Laplacians by applying a functional map [70] (a linear map between function spaces) in the spectral domain to align them to a common canonical space. The aligning functional maps succeed in encoding all the dual information on a common set of basis functions where global learning takes place. An initial version of the aligning maps is computed directly from the geometry and then is further refined during training, in the style of a data-dependent spatial transformer network. The newly proposed spectral convolution scheme is illustrated in Fig. 11.23b. With the ability to sync eigenbases across geometrically very different shapes, the Sync-SpecCNN is able to generalize to fine-grained tasks on man-made objects, which

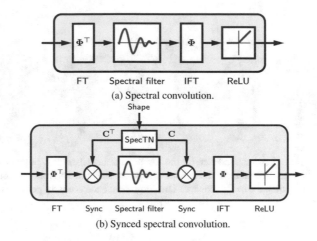

(a) Spectral convolution.

(b) Synced spectral convolution.

Fig. 11.23 Comparisons of spectral convolution and synced spectral convolution. Figure adapted from [40]

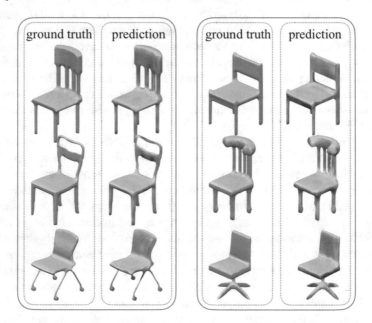

Fig. 11.24 Normal prediction task. The colors shown on the 3D shape are RGB-coded normals, namely putting XYZ components of normal directions into RGB channels. The SyncSpecCNN predicts reasonable normal directions even on very thin structures. Figure is from [115]

was previously hard for spectral graph CNN methods. Figure 11.24 demonstrates its successful normal predictions.

11.6   Conclusion and Outlook

This chapter has presented a rich family of methods on deep 3D representation learning. Starting from deep learning models on regularly structured 3D data, we showed how we can represent 3D shapes as multi-view images and how we can leverage existing CNNs to build a deep network to learn to aggregate information from those views to produce a powerful 3D descriptor. We presented a simple yet effective architecture for processing volumetric input. We discussed the reasons behind the performance gap between volumetric CNNs and multi-view CNNs, while also introducing two new volumetric architectures to fill the gap. Then in the next two sections, we presented deep learning models on irregular data: point clouds and meshes. A permutation invariant network PointNet is described in detail with both theoretical analysis and rich experimental and visualization results. Finally, we introduced two main families of deep networks for processing meshes.

Due to the high reproducibility of deep learning-based methods, now there is a trend in the general deep learning community to open source model architectures and experiment scripts. In fact, most methods presented in this paper have open sourced code and datasets from the original authors.[7] We believe such code releases encourage more reproducible research and to accelerates the development cycles of future work. We encourage readers interested in the details of the methods to inspect such code and run their experiments.

Future Work

3D deep learning is still a young field, there are many more interesting future directions for research. One such direction is to develop architectures that further respect rotation invariance or even achieve rotation equivariance (a rotated point cloud leads to "rotated" features). We have seen naive ways to address the issue through pooling (MVCNN and multi-orientation pooling in volumetric CNNs) or data augmentation, or input spatial transformer networks. However, they are not designed to guarantee any invariance or equivariance in rotations. Some very recent works try to address the problem with spherical CNNs [17, 25], but they are restricted to single objects and are not applicable to 3D scenes. In future work, it is worth exploring more generic architectures equivariant to rotations, for example as 3D variants of Capsule Networks [83].

Another timely research direction is joint learning of geometry and color data. In this chapter we focused on the geometry data alone, but real applications usually get access to both point clouds and 2D images. These two data sources are often complementary as point clouds describe accurate 3D geometry (but low in resolution)

---

[7]MVCNN: https://github.com/suhangpro/mvcnn.
VoxNet: https://github.com/dimatura/voxnet.
PointNet: http://github.com/charlesq34/pointnet.
SyncSpecCNN: https://github.com/ericyi/SyncSpecCNN.

and images capture high-resolution color textures (but lack 3D). We have already touched on some combined use cases of the two modalities. For example in PointNet semantic segmentation, the best results are achieved when we append RGB color as extra feature channels for each point. However, this is still an early attempt in this direction. More recently there are more efforts in joining 2D and 3D features for semantic segmentation [93, 97], as well as in 3D object detection [53, 112]. It is still interesting to study different design choices: whether we should aggregate both 2D and 3D features on 2D, on 3D or in another latent space, in which we need more research.

Last but not least, besides *analyzing* 3D data such as volumetric grids and point clouds, it is very fascinating to study how we can *generate* or *synthesize* high quality 3D geometry, for 3D reconstruction, shape completion or AI-assisted design/modeling. In image generation, a generative model only needs to decide pixel values since all pixel locations are already fixed. In comparison, to generate a point cloud, a model has to decide positions for points, which could be a much more challenging problem. Fan et al. [27] is one of the early works in this direction, where they reconstruct 3D geometry (with point clouds) from a single image. Another work called Octree generation network [96] manages to generate high-resolution 3D with Octree structures. Despite those early works, how to generate 3D point clouds with richer features such as position confidence and color, and how to deal with ambiguity in the generated space are still very open problems.

Broad Applications of Deep Learning on 3D Data

3D data is prevalent and how to process it is a fundamental problem. So its applications are also very diverse and are beyond the ones we mentioned in this chapter.

For example, AI-assisted design is a rising field where designers work with machine learning algorithms to accelerate the work cycle and improve overall design quality. In a project called ComplementMe [95], an algorithm can provide interactive design assistance to a 3D shape designer. The system provides suggestions to the designer in real time, on possible shape parts to use, as well as where to place them so that they are compatible with existing parts. In this system, PointNet is used to learn a latent representation for shape parts. Deep architectures on point clouds can also complement other deep networks in learning more robust 3D shape descriptors, for building large-scale 3D shape search engines. In AtlasNet [34], 3D deep learning models help model 3D meshes from simple raw point clouds or images as input.

Another promising field to apply 3D deep learning is robotics. In many robotics tasks such as grasping and manipulation, it is critical to get robust semantic understanding and accurate localization of 3D geometry. Point clouds are the prevalent sensor data in those tasks. A light-weight 3D deep learning architecture would provide a new machinery to directly process point clouds and understand their semantics and geometry. 3D deep learning models can also be used for learning intuitive physics, where we infer physical rules or properties by observing objects move. Direct learning in point clouds can potentially simplify the problem compared to learning in images.

The presented networks and future 3D deep learning models also have a potential impact on more general science. One interesting problem is to infer functions from structures in molecules, which can be formulated as a learning problem on point clouds. For example, given 3D arrangement of atoms in enzymes, machines can be trained to classify enzymes, which can potentially accelerate scientific discoveries and save labor costs. Another direction is to process and understand medical images, especially when the signals are sparse and represented as point clouds, in which successful algorithms could save lives.

We believe this chapter just marks the beginning of the exciting and fast growing field of 3D deep learning. We expect to see more exciting research in the future.

11.7 Further Reading

Lots of related resources on 3D deep learning are still in the forms of articles, courses, and conference tutorials. For a more broad overview of the topics mentioned in this chapter, we refer the reader to the 3D deep learning tutorial from CVPR 2017 [40], which covers more applications and example architectures. We also refer readers to two relevant University courses with notes available online: *Machine Learning for 3D Data* from Stanford University [42] and a similar course with more focus on deep learning methods from University of California San Diego [43]. While focusing on multi-view, volumetric, and point cloud representations, we put less content on deep learning models for meshes because it falls in another large research topic—deep learning on graphs. For readers with more interests in graph/geometric deep learning, we refer them to a very thorough review paper from Bronstein et al. [11]. Details of the ShapeNet dataset and the motivation and vision behind this effort can be found in [14]. For a detailed literature explaining how deep learning works, we recommend the reader to the *Deep Learning* textbook [31] and the Stanford course [41] while the latter has a particular focus on the convolutional neural networks.

11.8 Questions

1. Give three examples of applications of deep learning on 3D data.
2. Explain the challenges of applying convolutional neural networks on point clouds and meshes. What are some common ways to convert them such that we can use CNNs?
3. What are the pro and cons of multi-view CNNs?
4. What are the pro and cons of volumetric CNNs?
5. What are the possible reasons that a volumetric CNN lags behind in 3D object classification performance compared with a multi-view CNN?

6. What qualities do we look for in a deep learning model consuming raw point clouds?
7. What are the advantages of a PointNet model? Are there any limitations?
8. What are the two common ways to achieve deep learning on meshes?
9. What is the difference between extrinsic convolutions on regular grids and intrinsic convolutions on surfaces?
10. List three future research directions for deep learning on 3D data.

11.9 Exercises

1. Draw a t-SNE [102] visualization from 3D descriptors extracted by a trained MVCNN on a collection of 3D shapes (e.g., from ModelNet40 [110]). Do you observe that shapes from the same category are embedded close to each other? Can you also find some confusing cases from the visualization?
2. Given a trained MVCNN, test how the number of input images affects results. Assuming we know the alignment of objects, does a certain viewpoint (e.g., the front view of the aligned objects) matter more than the back view?
3. Given a CAD model, voxelize it to binary occupancy grids in different resolutions (using the hollow model), e.g., to $10 \times 10 \times 10$, $30 \times 30 \times 30$ and $60 \times 60 \times 60$. Observe how occupancy rate (the ratio between the number of the occupied voxels and that of all the voxels) decreases as we increase resolution.
4. Implement a sphere rendering engine that renders 2D views from point clouds. See if you can tell the category of an object from its low resolution sphere rendering. How many points do you need approximately to tell the correct categories?
5. Experiment with a VoxNet that takes truncated signed distance field (TSDF) or truncated distance field (TDF) grids as input. Do the TSDF or TDF features lead to a stronger classification performance compared with binary occupancy feature (e.g., on the ModelNet40 benchmark)?
6. Download a trained PointNet model and the ModelNet40 dataset, and then visualize the top-10 critical points from the PointNet on several shapes. Do they have patterns or consistency among shapes from the same category?
7. Implement a point cloud autoencoder using a PointNet architecture for the encoder and a fully connected layer for the decoder. Refer to [26] on how to define an optimization loss to compare two point clouds.
8. In 3D deep learning, there is often a need to code in GPU to achieve fast parallel layers for geometric processing. Sharpen your GPU coding skills by trying to implement the farthest point sampling in CUDA.
9. In [117], the authors proposed a 3D deep learning model with mixed representations. It first learns voxel features from local point clouds in each voxel and then uses 3D CNNs for voxel feature learning. Implement the VoxelNet structure for ModelNet40 object classification, and try to experiment with the hyperparameters such as grid resolution, network depth, and widths. Compare results with a VoxNet that is based on 3D CNN only.

10. Download the KITTI object detection dataset and extract the point clouds within all the ground truth 3D object bounding boxes. Train a PointNet to classify the LiDAR point clouds into different semantic categories (pedestrian, cars, and cyclists).
11. Implement a spatial method for a graph convolution network and test it on object part segmentation on ShapeNet objects. Refer to [11] to find a spatial graph CNN model you like. Compare results with those of the method in [115].

References

1. Abadi, M., Barham, P., Chen, J., Chen, Z., Davis, A., Dean, J., Devin, M., Ghemawat, S., Irving, G., Isard, M., et al.: TensorFlow: a system for large-scale machine learning. In: OSDI, vol. 16, pp. 265–283 (2016)
2. Amodei, D., Ananthanarayanan, S., Anubhai, R., Bai, J., Battenberg, E., Case, C., Casper, J., Catanzaro, B., Cheng, Q., Chen, G., et al.: Deep speech 2: end-to-end speech recognition in English and Mandarin. In: International Conference on Machine Learning, pp. 173–182 (2016)
3. Armeni, I., Sener, O., Zamir, A.R., Jiang, H., Brilakis, I., Fischer, M., Savarese, S.: 3D semantic parsing of large-scale indoor spaces. In: Proceedings of the IEEE International Conference on Computer Vision and Pattern Recognition (2016)
4. Aubry, M., Schlickewei, U., Cremers, D.: The wave kernel signature: a quantum mechanical approach to shape analysis. In: 2011 IEEE International Conference on Computer Vision Workshops (ICCV Workshops), pp. 1626–1633. IEEE (2011)
5. Belongie, S., Malik, J., Puzicha, J.: Shape context: a new descriptor for shape matching and object recognition. In: Advances in Neural Information Processing Systems, pp. 831–837 (2001)
6. Belton, D., Lichti, D.D.: Classification and segmentation of terrestrial laser scanner point clouds using local variance information. IAPRS **Xxxvi**(5), 44–49 (2006)
7. Bogo, F., Romero, J., Loper, M., Black, M.J.: FAUST: dataset and evaluation for 3D mesh registration. In: Proceedings of the IEEE Conference on Computer Vision and Pattern Recognition, pp. 3794–3801 (2014)
8. Boscaini, D., Masci, J., Melzi, S., Bronstein, M.M., Castellani, U., Vandergheynst, P.: Learning class-specific descriptors for deformable shapes using localized spectral convolutional networks. Computer Graphics Forum, vol. 34, pp. 13–23. Wiley Online Library, Hoboken (2015)
9. Boscaini, D., Masci, J., Rodolà, E., Bronstein, M.: Learning shape correspondence with anisotropic convolutional neural networks. In: Advances in Neural Information Processing Systems, pp. 3189–3197 (2016)
10. Bronstein, M.M., Kokkinos, I.: Scale-invariant heat kernel signatures for non-rigid shape recognition. In: 2010 IEEE Conference on Computer Vision and Pattern Recognition (CVPR), pp. 1704–1711. IEEE (2010)
11. Bronstein, M.M., Bruna, J., LeCun, Y., Szlam, A., Vandergheynst, P.: Geometric deep learning: going beyond Euclidean data. IEEE Signal Process. Mag. **34**(4), 18–42 (2017)
12. Bruna, J., Zaremba, W., Szlam, A., LeCun, Y.: Spectral networks and locally connected networks on graphs (2013). arXiv:1312.6203
13. Chang, A., Dai, A., Funkhouser, T., Halber, M., Niessner, M., Savva, M., Song, S., Zeng, A., Zhang, Y.: Matterport3D: learning from RGB-D data in indoor environments. In: International Conference on 3D Vision (3DV) (2017)

14. Chang, A.X., Funkhouser, T., Guibas, L., Hanrahan, P., Huang, Q., Li, Z., Savarese, S., Savva, M., Song, S., Su, H., Xiao, J., Yi, L., Yu, F.: ShapeNet: an information-rich 3D model repository. Technical report, Stanford University — Princeton University — Toyota Technological Institute at Chicago (2015). arXiv:1512.03012 [cs.GR]

15. Chen, D.Y., Tian, X.P., Shen, Y.T., Ouhyoung, M.: On visual similarity based 3D model retrieval. Computer Graphics Forum, vol. 22, pp. 223–232. Wiley Online Library, Hoboken (2003)

16. Choy, C., Gwak, J., Savarese, S.: 4D spatio-temporal ConvNets: Minkowski convolutional neural networks. (2019). arXiv:1904.08755

17. Cohen, T.S., Geiger, M., Köhler, J., Welling, M.: Spherical CNNs (2018). arXiv:1801.10130

18. Dai, A., Nießner, M.: 3DMV: joint 3D-multi-view prediction for 3D semantic scene segmentation. In: Proceedings of the European Conference on Computer Vision (ECCV), pp. 452–468 (2018)

19. Dai, A., Chang, A.X., Savva, M., Halber, M., Funkhouser, T.A., Nießner, M.: ScanNet: richly-annotated 3D reconstructions of indoor scenes. In: CVPR, vol. 2, p. 10 (2017)

20. Dai, A., Ruizhongtai Qi, C., Nießner, M.: Shape completion using 3D-encoder-predictor CNNs and shape synthesis. In: Proceedings of the IEEE Conference on Computer Vision and Pattern Recognition, pp. 5868–5877 (2017)

21. Defferrard, M., Bresson, X., Vandergheynst, P.: Convolutional neural networks on graphs with fast localized spectral filtering. In: Advances in Neural Information Processing Systems, pp. 3844–3852 (2016)

22. Demantké, J., Mallet, C., David, N., Vallet, B.: Dimensionality based scale selection in 3D lidar point clouds. Int. Arch. Photogramm. Remote Sens. Spat. Inf. Sci. 38(Part 5), W12 (2011)

23. Deng, J., Dong, W., Socher, R., Li, L.J., Li, K., Fei-Fei, L.: ImageNet: a large-scale hierarchical image database. In: IEEE Conference on Computer Vision and Pattern Recognition, CVPR 2009, pp. 248–255. IEEE (2009)

24. Duvenaud, D.K., Maclaurin, D., Iparraguirre, J., Bombarell, R., Hirzel, T., Aspuru-Guzik, A., Adams, R.P.: Convolutional networks on graphs for learning molecular fingerprints. In: Advances in Neural Information Processing Systems, pp. 2224–2232 (2015)

25. Esteves, C., Allen-Blanchette, C., Makadia, A., Daniilidis, K.: Learning so (3) equivariant representations with spherical CNNs. In: ECCV 2018 (2018)

26. Fan, H., Su, H., Guibas, L.J.: A point set generation network for 3D object reconstruction from a single image. In: CVPR, vol. 2, p. 6 (2017)

27. Fan, H., Su, H., Guibas, L.J.: A point set generation network for 3D object reconstruction from a single image. In: The IEEE Conference on Computer Vision and Pattern Recognition (CVPR) (2017)

28. Fang, Y., Xie, J., Dai, G., Wang, M., Zhu, F., Xu, T., Wong, E.: 3D deep shape descriptor. In: Proceedings of the IEEE Conference on Computer Vision and Pattern Recognition, pp. 2319–2328 (2015)

29. Geiger, A., Lenz, P., Stiller, C., Urtasun, R.: Vision meets robotics: the KITTI dataset. Int. J. Robot. Res. 32(11), 1231–1237 (2013)

30. Girshick, R.: Fast R-CNN. In: Proceedings of the IEEE International Conference on Computer Vision, pp. 1440–1448 (2015)

31. Goodfellow, I., Bengio, Y., Courville, A.: Deep Learning. MIT Press, Cambridge (2016). http://www.deeplearningbook.org

32. Graham, B., Engelcke, M., van der Maaten, L.: 3D semantic segmentation with submanifold sparse convolutional networks. In: Proceedings of the IEEE Conference on Computer Vision and Pattern Recognition, pp. 9224–9232 (2018)

33. Gressin, A., Mallet, C., Demantké, J., David, N.: Towards 3D lidar point cloud registration improvement using optimal neighborhood knowledge. ISPRS J. Photogramm. Remote Sens. 79, 240–251 (2013)

34. Groueix, T., Fisher, M., Kim, V.G., Russell, B.C., Aubry, M.: AtlasNet: a Papier-Mâché approach to learning 3D surface generation (2018). arXiv:1802.05384

35. Gschwandtner, M., Kwitt, R., Uhl, A., Pree, W.: BlenSor: blender sensor simulation toolbox. Advances in Visual Computing, pp. 199–208. Springer, Berlin (2011). https://doi.org/10. 1007/978-3-642-24031-7_20

36. Hackel, T., Savinov, N., Ladicky, L., Wegner, J.D., Schindler, K., Pollefeys, M.: Semantic3D.net: a new large-scale point cloud classification benchmark. ISPRS Ann. Photogramm. Remote Sens. Spat. Inf. Sci. **IV-1-W1**, 91–98 (2017)

37. He, K., Zhang, X., Ren, S., Sun, J.: Deep residual learning for image recognition. In: Proceedings of the IEEE Conference on Computer Vision and Pattern Recognition, pp. 770–778 (2016)

38. Henaff, M., Bruna, J., LeCun, Y.: Deep convolutional networks on graph-structured data (2015). arXiv:1506.05163

39. Hermosilla, P., Ritschel, T., Vázquez, P.P., Vinacua, À., Ropinski, T.: Monte Carlo convolution for learning on non-uniformly sampled point clouds. In: SIGGRAPH Asia 2018 Technical Papers, p. 235. ACM (2018)

40. Homepage of 3D deep learning tutorial at CVPR 2017, Honolulu, United States. http://3ddl. stanford.edu. Accessed 25 Oct 2018

41. Homepage of CS231N: Convolutional neural networks for visual recognition at Stanford University. http://cs231n.stanford.edu. Accessed 25 Oct 2018

42. Homepage of CS468: Machine learning for 3D data at Stanford University. http://graphics. stanford.edu/courses/cs468-17-spring/. Accessed 25 Oct 2018

43. Homepage of CS468: Machine learning for 3D data at University of California San Diego. https://cse291-i.github.io. Accessed 25 Oct 2018

44. Hua, B.S., Tran, M.K., Yeung, S.K.: Pointwise convolutional neural networks. In: Proceedings of the IEEE Conference on Computer Vision and Pattern Recognition, pp. 984–993 (2018)

45. Jaderberg, M., Simonyan, K., Zisserman, A., et al.: Spatial transformer networks. In: NIPS 2015

46. Jia, Y., Shelhamer, E., Donahue, J., Karayev, S., Long, J., Girshick, R., Guadarrama, S., Darrell, T.: Caffe: convolutional architecture for fast feature embedding (2014). arXiv:1408.5093

47. Johnson, A.E., Hebert, M.: Using spin images for efficient object recognition in cluttered 3D scenes. IEEE Trans. Pattern Anal. Mach. Intell. **21**(5), 433–449 (1999)

48. Kalogerakis, E., Averkiou, M., Maji, S., Chaudhuri, S.: 3D shape segmentation with projective convolutional networks. In: Proceedings of the IEEE Conference on Computer Vision and Pattern Recognition, pp. 3779–3788 (2017)

49. Kato, H., Ushiku, Y., Harada, T.: Neural 3D mesh renderer. In: Proceedings of the IEEE Conference on Computer Vision and Pattern Recognition, pp. 3907–3916 (2018)

50. Kazhdan, M., Funkhouser, T., Rusinkiewicz, S.: Rotation invariant spherical harmonic representation of 3D shape descriptors. In: Symposium on Geometry Processing, vol. 6, pp. 156–164 (2003)

51. Klokov, R., Lempitsky, V.: Escape from cells: deep Kd-networks for the recognition of 3D point cloud models. In: 2017 IEEE International Conference on Computer Vision (ICCV), pp. 863–872. IEEE (2017)

52. Krizhevsky, A., Sutskever, I., Hinton, G.E.: ImageNet classification with deep convolutional neural networks. In: Advances in Neural Information Processing Systems, pp. 1097–1105 (2012)

53. Ku, J., Mozifian, M., Lee, J., Harakeh, A., Waslander, S.: Joint 3D proposal generation and object detection from view aggregation (2017). arXiv:1712.02294

54. LeCun, Y., Bengio, Y., Hinton, G.: Deep learning. Nature **521**(7553), 436–444 (2015)

55. Li, J., Chen, B.M., Hee Lee, G.: SO-Net: self-organizing network for point cloud analysis. In: Proceedings of the IEEE Conference on Computer Vision and Pattern Recognition, pp. 9397–9406 (2018)

56. Li, Y., Su, H., Qi, C.R., Fish, N., Cohen-Or, D., Guibas, L.J.: Joint embeddings of shapes and images via CNN image purification. TOG (2015)

57. Li, Y., Bu, R., Sun, M., Wu, W., Di, X., Chen, B.: PointCNN: convolution on X-transformed points. In: Advances in Neural Information Processing Systems, pp. 820–830 (2018)

58. Lian, Z., Zhang, J., Choi, S., ElNaghy, H., El-Sana, J., Furuya, T., Giachetti, A., Guler, R.A., Lai, L., Li, C., Li, H., Limberger, F.A., Martin, R., Nakanishi, R.U., Neto, A.P., Nonato, L.G., Ohbuchi, R., Pevzner, K., Pickup, D., Rosin, P., Sharf, A., Sun, L., Sun, X., Tari, S., Unal, G., Wilson, R.C.: Non-rigid 3D shape retrieval. In: Pratikakis, I., Spagnuolo, M., Theoharis, T., Gool, L.V., Veltkamp, R. (eds.) Eurographics Workshop on 3D Object Retrieval. The Eurographics Association (2015). https://doi.org/10.2312/3dor.20151064
59. Lin, M., Chen, Q., Yan, S.: Network in network (2013). arXiv:1312.4400
60. Ling, H., Jacobs, D.W.: Shape classification using the inner-distance. IEEE Trans. Pattern Anal. Mach. Intell. **29**(2), 286–299 (2007)
61. Loper, M.M., Black, M.J.: OpenDR: an approximate differentiable renderer. In: European Conference on Computer Vision, pp. 154–169. Springer (2014)
62. Maas, A.L., Hannun, A.Y., Ng, A.Y.: Rectifier nonlinearities improve neural network acoustic models. In: Proceedings of the ICML, vol. 30, p. 3 (2013)
63. Maron, H., Galun, M., Aigerman, N., Trope, M., Dym, N., Yumer, E., Kim, V.G., Lipman, Y.: Convolutional neural networks on surfaces via seamless toric covers. ACM Trans. Graph. **36**(4), 71 (2017)
64. Masci, J., Boscaini, D., Bronstein, M., Vandergheynst, P.: Geodesic convolutional neural networks on Riemannian manifolds. In: Proceedings of the IEEE International Conference on Computer Vision Workshops, pp. 37–45 (2015)
65. Maturana, D., Scherer, S.: VoxNet: a 3D convolutional neural network for real-time object recognition. In: IEEE/RSJ International Conference on Intelligent Robots and Systems (2015)
66. Mikolov, T., Deoras, A., Povey, D., Burget, L., Černocký, J.: Strategies for training large scale neural network language models. In: 2011 IEEE Workshop on Automatic Speech Recognition and Understanding (ASRU), pp. 196–201. IEEE (2011)
67. Mitra, N.J., Nguyen, A., Guibas, L.: Estimating surface normals in noisy point cloud data. Int. J. Comput. Geom. Appl. **14**(04–05), 261–276 (2004)
68. Monti, F., Boscaini, D., Masci, J., Rodola, E., Svoboda, J., Bronstein, M.M.: Geometric deep learning on graphs and manifolds using mixture model CNNs. In: Proceedings of the CVPR, vol. 1, p. 3 (2017)
69. Osada, R., Funkhouser, T., Chazelle, B., Dobkin, D.: Shape distributions. ACM Trans. Graph. (TOG) **21**(4), 807–832 (2002)
70. Ovsjanikov, M., Ben-Chen, M., Solomon, J., Butscher, A., Guibas, L.: Functional maps: a flexible representation of maps between shapes. ACM Trans. Graph. (TOG) **31**(4), 30 (2012)
71. Paszke, A., Gross, S., Chintala, S., Chanan, G., Yang, E., DeVito, Z., Lin, Z., Desmaison, A., Antiga, L., Lerer, A.: Automatic differentiation in PyTorch. In: NIPS-W (2017)
72. Pauly, M., Kobbelt, L.P., Gross, M.: Point-based multiscale surface representation. ACM Trans. Graph. (TOG) **25**(2), 177–193 (2006)
73. Phong, B.T.: Illumination for computer generated pictures. Commun. ACM **18**(6), 311–317 (1975)
74. Qi, R.: Deep learning on point clouds for 3D scene understanding. Ph.D. thesis, Stanford University (2018)
75. Qi, C.R., Su, H., Nießner, M., Dai, A., Yan, M., Guibas, L.: Volumetric and multi-view CNNs for object classification on 3D data. In: Proceedings of the IEEE Conference on Computer Vision and Pattern Recognition (CVPR) (2016)
76. Qi, C.R., Su, H., Mo, K., Guibas, L.J.: PointNet: deep learning on point sets for 3D classification and segmentation. In: Proceedings of the IEEE Conference on Computer Vision and Pattern Recognition (CVPR) (2017)
77. Qi, C.R., Yi, L., Su, H., Guibas, L.J.: PointNet++: deep hierarchical feature learning on point sets in a metric space. In: NIPS 2017 (2017)
78. Ravanbakhsh, S., Schneider, J., Poczos, B.: Deep learning with sets and point clouds (2016). arXiv:1611.04500
79. Ren, S., He, K., Girshick, R., Sun, J.: Faster R-CNN: towards real-time object detection with region proposal networks. In: Advances in Neural Information Processing Systems, pp. 91–99 (2015)

80. Riegler, G., Ulusoy, A.O., Geiger, A.: OctNet: learning deep 3D representations at high reso-
    lutions. In: Proceedings of the IEEE Conference on Computer Vision and Pattern Recognition,
    vol. 3 (2017)
81. Rusu, R.B., Blodow, N., Marton, Z.C., Beetz, M.: Aligning point cloud views using persistent
    feature histograms. In: 2008 IEEE/RSJ International Conference on Intelligent Robots and
    Systems, pp. 3384–3391. IEEE (2008)
82. Rusu, R.B., Blodow, N., Beetz, M.: Fast point feature histograms (FPFH) for 3D registration.
    In: IEEE International Conference on Robotics and Automation, ICRA'09, pp. 3212–3217.
    IEEE (2009)
83. Sabour, S., Frosst, N., Hinton, G.E.: Dynamic routing between capsules. In: Advances in
    Neural Information Processing Systems, pp. 3856–3866 (2017)
84. Savva, M., Yu, F., Su, H., Aono, M., Chen, B., Cohen-Or, D., Deng, W., Su, H., Bai, S., Bai, X.,
    et al.: SHREC16 track: largescale 3D shape retrieval from ShapeNet Core55. In: Proceedings
    of the Eurographics Workshop on 3D Object Retrieval, pp. 89–98 (2016)
85. Savva, M., Kadian, A., Maksymets, O., Zhao, Y., Wijmans, E., Jain, B., Straub, J., Liu, J.,
    Koltun, V., Malik, J., Parikh, D., Batra, D.: Habitat: a platform for embodied AI research
    (2019). arXiv:1904.01201
86. Shi, J., Dong, Y., Su, H., Stella, X.Y.: Learning non-Lambertian object intrinsics across
    ShapeNet categories. In: 2017 IEEE Conference on Computer Vision and Pattern Recog-
    nition (CVPR), pp. 5844–5853. IEEE (2017)
87. Silver, D., Huang, A., Maddison, C.J., Guez, A., Sifre, L., Van Den Driessche, G., Schrit-
    twieser, J., Antonoglou, I., Panneershelvam, V., Lanctot, M., et al.: Mastering the game of go
    with deep neural networks and tree search. Nature 529(7587), 484 (2016)
88. Simonyan, K., Zisserman, A.: Very deep convolutional networks for large-scale image recog-
    nition (2014). arXiv:1409.1556
89. Song, S., Xiao, J.: Deep sliding shapes for a modal 3D object detection in RGB-D images.
    In: Proceedings of the IEEE Conference on Computer Vision and Pattern Recognition, pp.
    808–816 (2016)
90. Song, S., Yu, F., Zeng, A., Chang, A.X., Savva, M., Funkhouser, T.: Semantic scene completion
    from a single depth image. In: Proceedings of the IEEE Conference on Computer Vision and
    Pattern Recognition, pp. 1746–1754 (2017)
91. Su, H.: Deep 3D representation learning. Ph.D. thesis, Stanford University (2018)
92. Su, H., Maji, S., Kalogerakis, E., Learned-Miller, E.G.: Multi-view convolutional neural
    networks for 3D shape recognition. In: Proceedings of the ICCV (2015)
93. Su, H., Jampani, V., Sun, D., Maji, S., Kalogerakis, E., Yang, M.H., Kautz, J.: SPLATNet:
    sparse lattice networks for point cloud processing. In: Proceedings of the IEEE Conference
    on Computer Vision and Pattern Recognition, pp. 2530–2539 (2018)
94. Sun, J., Ovsjanikov, M., Guibas, L.: A concise and provably informative multi-scale signature
    based on heat diffusion. Computer Graphics Forum, vol. 28, pp. 1383–1392. Wiley Online
    Library, Hoboken (2009)
95. Sung, M., Su, H., Kim, V.G., Chaudhuri, S., Guibas, L.: ComplementMe: weakly-supervised
    component suggestions for 3D modeling. ACM Trans. Graph. (TOG) 36(6), 226 (2017)
96. Tatarchenko, M., Dosovitskiy, A., Brox, T.: Octree generating networks: efficient convolu-
    tional architectures for high-resolution 3D outputs (2017). arXiv:1703.09438
97. Tatarchenko, M., Park, J., Koltun, V., Zhou, Q.Y.: Tangent convolutions for dense prediction
    in 3D. In: Proceedings of the IEEE Conference on Computer Vision and Pattern Recognition,
    pp. 3887–3896 (2018)
98. Thomas, H., Qi, C.R., Deschaud, J.E., Marcotegui, B., Goulette, F., Guibas, L.J.: KPConv:
    flexible and deformable convolution for point clouds (2019). arXiv:1904.08889
99. Tobin, J., Fong, R., Ray, A., Schneider, J., Zaremba, W., Abbeel, P.: Domain randomization
    for transferring deep neural networks from simulation to the real world. In: 2017 IEEE/RSJ
    International Conference on Intelligent Robots and Systems (IROS), pp. 23–30. IEEE (2017)
100. Tulsiani, S., Su, H., Guibas, L.J., Efros, A.A., Malik, J.: Learning shape abstractions by
     assembling volumetric primitives. In: Computer Vision and Pattern Recognition (CVPR)
     (2017)

101. Van Den Oord, A., Dieleman, S., Zen, H., Simonyan, K., Vinyals, O., Graves, A., Kalchbrenner, N., Senior, A.W., Kavukcuoglu, K.: WaveNet: a generative model for raw audio. In: SSW, p. 125 (2016)
102. van der Maaten, L., Hinton, G.: Visualizing data using t-SNE. J. Mach. Learn. Res. **9**(Nov), 2579–2605 (2008)
103. Vinyals, O., Bengio, S., Kudlur, M.: Order matters: sequence to sequence for sets (2015). arXiv:1511.06391
104. Wang, S., Suo, S., Ma, W.C., Pokrovsky, A., Urtasun, R.: Deep parametric continuous convolutional neural networks. In: Proceedings of the IEEE Conference on Computer Vision and Pattern Recognition, pp. 2589–2597 (2018)
105. Wang, Y., Sun, Y., Liu, Z., Sarma, S.E., Bronstein, M.M., Solomon, J.M.: Dynamic graph CNN for learning on point clouds (2018). arXiv:1801.07829
106. Wang, P.S., Liu, Y., Guo, Y.X., Sun, C.Y., Tong, X.: O-CNN: octree-based convolutional neural networks for 3D shape analysis. ACM Trans. Graph. (TOG) **36**(4), 72 (2017)
107. Weinmann, M., Jutzi, B., Hinz, S., Mallet, C.: Semantic point cloud interpretation based on optimal neighborhoods, relevant features and efficient classifiers. ISPRS J. Photogramm. Remote Sens. **105**, 286–304 (2015)
108. Wu, Y., Schuster, M., Chen, Z., Le, Q.V., Norouzi, M., Macherey, W., Krikun, M., Cao, Y., Gao, Q., Macherey, K., et al.: Google's neural machine translation system: bridging the gap between human and machine translation (2016). arXiv:1609.08144
109. Wu, Z., Shou, R., Wang, Y., Liu, X.: Interactive shape co-segmentation via label propagation. Comput. Graph. **38**, 248–254 (2014)
110. Wu, Z., Song, S., Khosla, A., Yu, F., Zhang, L., Tang, X., Xiao, J.: 3D ShapeNets: a deep representation for volumetric shapes. In: Proceedings of the IEEE Conference on Computer Vision and Pattern Recognition, pp. 1912–1920 (2015)
111. Xie, S., Liu, S., Chen, Z., Tu, Z.: Attentional ShapeContextNet for point cloud recognition. In: Proceedings of the IEEE Conference on Computer Vision and Pattern Recognition, pp. 4606–4615 (2018)
112. Xu, D., Anguelov, D., Jain, A.: PointFusion: deep sensor fusion for 3D bounding box estimation (2017). arXiv:1711.10871
113. Xu, Y., Fan, T., Xu, M., Zeng, L., Qiao, Y.: SpiderCNN: deep learning on point sets with parameterized convolutional filters. In: Proceedings of the European Conference on Computer Vision (ECCV), pp. 87–102 (2018)
114. Yi, L., Kim, V.G., Ceylan, D., Shen, I.C., Yan, M., Su, H., Lu, C., Huang, Q., Sheffer, A., Guibas, L.: A scalable active framework for region annotation in 3D shape collections. In: SIGGRAPH Asia (2016)
115. Yi, L., Su, H., Guo, X., Guibas, L.J.: SyncSpecCNN: synchronized spectral CNN for 3D shape segmentation. In: CVPR, pp. 6584–6592 (2017)
116. Zaheer, M., Kottur, S., Ravanbakhsh, S., Poczos, B., Salakhutdinov, R.R., Smola, A.J.: Deep sets. In: Advances in Neural Information Processing Systems, pp. 3391–3401 (2017)
117. Zhou, Y., Tuzel, O.: VoxelNet: end-to-end learning for point cloud based 3D object detection (2017). arXiv:1711.06396

Part III
3D Imaging Applications

In this third and final part of this book, we discuss three application areas of 3D imaging and analysis: 3D face recognition, 3D digitization of cultural heritage, and 3D phenotyping of plants.

Chapter 12
3D Face Recognition

Nick Pears and Ajmal Mian

Abstract Face recognition using 3D cameras captures and processes explicit 3D shape information and is more resistant to spoofing security attacks than 2D face recognition. However, typical compact-baseline, triangulation-based 3D capture systems are generally only suitable for close-range applications. The 3D shape may be used alone, or in combination with simultaneously captured, standard 2D color images in multimodal 2D/3D face recognition. Like its 2D counterpart, modern 3D face recognition often uses a feature extraction phase followed by a classification phase. Traditionally, such features have been handcrafted, but recent approaches use the representational learning power of deep neural networks. Other approaches use shape alignment methods, or analysis-by-synthesis, which exploits the prior shape distribution information captured by 3D morphable models. Additionally, 3D face models have been used for pose correction and calculation of the facial albedo map, which is independent of illumination. Finally, 3D face recognition has also achieved significant success toward expression invariance by modeling nonrigid surface deformations, removing facial expressions or by using parts-based face recognition. This chapter is not intended to be a comprehensive survey. Rather, it gives a tutorial introduction to 3D face recognition and a representative sample of both well-established and more recent state-of-the-art 3D face recognition techniques in terms of their implementation and expected performance on benchmark datasets.

N. Pears (✉)
Department of Computer Science, University of York,
Deramore Lane, York YO10 5GH, UK
e-mail: nick.pears@cs.york.ac.uk

A. Mian
School of Computer Science and Software Engineering,
University of Western Australia, 35 Stirling Highway, Crawley, WA 6009, Australia
e-mail: ajmal.mian@uwa.edu.au

Fig. 12.1 A 3D image
sample from the UoY 3D
face dataset, with three
different renderings [49]

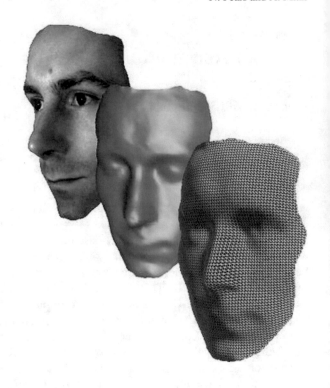

12.1 Introduction

Automatic measurement of the intrinsic characteristics of the human face is a socially-acceptable, computer-based biometric recognition method that can be implemented in a nonintrusive way [54]. This chapter will introduce the main concepts behind 3D face recognition algorithms, gives an overview of the literature, and elaborates upon some carefully-selected and representative techniques. Note that we do not intend to give a highly comprehensive literature review, due to the size of the field and the tutorial nature of this text.

A typical example of a 3D face image from the UoY dataset [49] is shown in Fig. 12.1. Note that 3D cameras often capture a standard 2D image that is registered to the captured 3D shape, and this can be texture-mapped onto the 3D mesh surface, as shown. Thus, one can consider that a 3D camera augments 2D images with explicit 3D shape information, rather than replacing them, i.e., such cameras often provide multimodal sensor data, which may be combined in the recognition process. However, this chapter mainly focuses on systems that make recognition decisions based on the 3D shape channel.

12.1.1   Chapter Outline

We provide a map for the contents of this chapter, as follows:

- Section 12.2 defines face recognition in terms of the identification and verification tasks and presents standard evaluation metrics and techniques.
- Section 12.3 presents the state-of-the-art in 2D face recognition to provide some context for 3D face recognition.
- Section 12.4 compares and contrasts 3D face recognition with 2D face recognition.
- Section 12.5 gives an overview of how facial surfaces are represented and visualized.
- Section 12.6 overviews the datasets that researchers have used to conduct comparative performance evaluations.
- Section 12.7 compares and contrasts two classes of approach to 3D face recognition, holistic, and local feature-based methods.
- Section 12.8 presents a typical processing pipeline for a 3D face recognition system and includes face detection, spike removal, hole filling, smoothing, pose correction, resampling, feature extraction, and classification.
- Section 12.9 outlines the Iterative Closest Points (ICP) algorithm for 3D face recognition in a tutorial format.
- Section 12.10 presents Principal Components Analysis (PCA) for 3D face recognition in a tutorial format.
- Section 12.11 outlines Linear Discriminant Analysis (LDA) for 3D face recognition in a tutorial format.
- Section 12.12 discusses how to extract fundamental local surface features such normals and curvature from 3D surfaces.
- Section 12.13 discusses a selection of five recent classical (i.e., non deep learning) approaches to 3D face recognition.
- Section 12.14 presents two recent deep learning approaches to 3D face recognition.

Sections 12.15–12.19 give research challenges, conclusions, further reading, questions and exercises, respectively.

12.2   Verification and Identification

All face recognition systems must perform matching operations. They do this by extracting some form of normalized descriptive representation of the live, captured face, known as the *probe* or *query*, and they compare that to the same normalized descriptive representations pre-extracted from one or more samples from the subject set stored on the system, known as the *gallery*. This *face recognition* task can be categorized as either *face verification* (also known as face authentication), where the system accepts or rejects a claimed identity, or *face identification*, where the system attempts to associate an identity label to an image. Before we can understand the state-of-the-art in face recognition, we need to explain the standard evaluation methodologies.

12.2.1 Evaluation of Face Verification

In a verification application, the face recognition system must supply a binary *accept* or *reject* decision, as a response to the subject's claimed identity, associated with one of a stored set of *gallery* scans. It does this by generating a match score between the probe and the gallery data of the subject's claimed identity. Often this is implemented as a distance metric between feature vectors. In the simplest cases, the Euclidean distance, cosine distance or Mahalanobis distance is used. The latter is only possible in the case of multiple images of the same person in the gallery, which forms a more effective *template* for that person. A low score on the distance metric indicates a close match and application of a suitable threshold generates the accept/reject decision. Verification systems are mainly used by authorized individuals, who want to gain their rightful access to a building or computer system. Consequently, they will usually be cooperative by adopting a neutral expression and frontal pose at a favorable distance from the camera. For cooperative scenarios, datasets such as FRGC v2 [82], discussed later, provide suitable training and validation datasets to perform verification tests.

In order to evaluate a verification system, a large number of verification tests need to be performed, where the subject's identity associated with the probe is known, so that it can be established whether the accept/reject decision was correct. Usually, this identity is extracted from the filename of a stored face capture within a dataset by means of a unique subject identifier.

A key point is that the accept/reject decision is threshold dependent and it is desirable to explore the system performance over a wide range of such thresholds. Given that a set of images is available, all with known identities, and there are at least two for each subject, we now describe a way of implementing this. Every image in the set is compared with every other, excluding itself, and a match score is formed. Two lists are then formed, one containing matches of the same subject identity and the other containing matches of different subjects. We then vary the threshold from zero, so that all decisions are *reject*, to the maximum score value, so that all decisions are *accept*. For each threshold value, we examine the two lists and count the number of *reject* decisions from the *same identity* (SI) list to form a *false rejection rate* (FRR) as a percentage of the SI list size and we count the number of *accept* decisions in the *different identity* (DI) list to form a *false acceptance rate* (FAR) as a percentage of the DI list size. Ideally, there is some threshold at which both FAR and FRR are zero, and this describes a perfect system performance. However, in sufficiently challenging datasets, both *false accepts* and *false rejects* exist. False accepts can be reduced by decreasing the threshold but this increases false rejects and vice-versa.

A *receiver operating characteristic* or ROC curve, as defined in biometric verification tests, is a plot of FRR against FAR for all thresholds, thus giving a visualization of the trade-off between these two performance metrics. Depending on the dataset size and the number of scans per person, the SI and DI list sizes can be very different, with DI usually much larger than SI. This has the implication that values on the FRR axis are noisier than on the FAR axis. In order to measure system performance using a FRR versus FAR ROC curve, we can use the concept of an *equal error rate* (EER), where $FRR = FAR$, and a lower value indicates a better performance for a given face verification system. However, given that a false accept is often a worse decision with a higher penalty than a false reject, alternative ways of expressing system performance are often used. For example, a ROC curve can also be plotted as *verification rate* against FAR, where verification rate is the percentage of subjects verified, in terms of the set of subjects making true claims of their identity. In other words, this is the *true positive* rate or *true accept rate* (TAR), where $TAR = 1 - FRR$. Using this curve, one can select a suitable low FAR and read off the verification rate from the ROC curve. Typically FAR values of 0.001 (0.1%) or 0.01 (1%) are used.

12.2.2   Evaluation of Face Identification

In face identification, the probe image is processed and matched to the full set of stored gallery captures, with known identifier labels, and a set of matching scores is generated. The match with the highest match score or, equivalently, the lowest distance metric, provides the identity of the probe. The percentage of correct identifications with respect to the total number of comparisons gives the identification rate. Note that identification requires a more time-consuming *one-to-many* match process, in contrast to verification's *one-to-one* match.

More generally, we can record the *rank*, r, of the match, which denotes that the match was the rth best across the full gallery. The percentage of correct top-match identifications already mentioned is thus more specifically termed the *rank-1* identification rate, and this is the most widely-used single performance figure for identification.

In some applications, such as semiautomatic face recognition, other $rank - r$ performance rates may be important. For example, suppose that it is of utmost importance to apprehend a dangerous criminal, whose processed image is stored in the gallery. Even if that person's gallery image is the 10th best match to some probe, then the police would be interested in the result. In this case, a human operator could receive an alarm to perform a manual inspection of the probe image and the top 10 gallery matches. Thus the system's *rank-10 identification rate* is important, which is defined as the rate at which subjects appear in the first 10 closest matches across the full gallery, given that the probe is known to be in the gallery (i.e., a closed-set evaluation is used). If in this scenario, the rank-10 identification rate was deemed to be too low, r could be increased, at the expense of an increased amount of manual checking.

More generally, it is possible to use a wide range of rank scores to capture a more comprehensive understanding of identification performance. Here, we record the rank of the correct match in a large number of tests, and we determine the percentage of identifications that are less than or equal to some value of r. Plotting the percentage of identifications against r allows us to compare systems at a range of possible rank operating points. Such a graph is known as a *Cumulative Match Curve* (CMC) and

r starts at 1 and is incremented until 100% recognition is attained for some large r associated with the weakest match.

The discussion so far has implicitly assumed a *closed-set* evaluation protocol, i.e., one where the identity of the probe exists in the gallery set. However, there are many real-world situations when this is not the case. Many applications have only a small number of subjects that need to be identified, whereas the probes are from a much wider population. For example, in a retail system, convicted shoplifters may be stored on a so-called *watch list*, but these are small minority of the subjects exposed to the recognition system. In this latter *open-set* case, the system most often will not be able to find a sufficiently close match to anyone in the gallery and a *null* response should be returned. Thus, if there were 100 subjects on the watch list gallery, the system has to provide one of 101 possible responses. The open-set face recognition problem has been addressed in recent literature by Scheirer et al. [89] and Günther et al. [43].

12.3   Context: A Brief Overview of 2D Face Recognition

Computer-based face recognition from 2D images has been studied extensively for more than half a century. Bledsoe's approach [11], dating from 1964, was semiautomatic and used a human operator to manually mark up facial features. Since that time, an extensive literature has demonstrated a very wide variety of approaches in 2D face recognition, with the latest and most successful approaches being based on Convolutional Neural Network (CNN) architectures. This has been a highly successful application area in the deep learning revolution, partly due to the wide availability of large volumes of online 2D facial images for training. For example, Google's FaceNet [90] was trained on 200M images of 8M identities while VGG-Face [77] used 2.6M images of 2,622 subjects for training. Indeed, deep CNNs have been so successful that automatic 2D face recognition systems can now match or even exceed human-level performance on a relatively recent leading benchmark dataset, *Labeled Faces in the Wild* (LFW) [52], which consists of 13,233 images of 5,749 people. In 2014, Facebook's DeepFace system [97] reported a verification accuracy of 97.35% at 1% FAR, closely approaching human-level performance, which was recorded at 97.5%. Interesting comparisons between different sets of humans (e.g., super recognizers, who are in the top 1–2% performers, and students) and different machine algorithms have been presented by Phillips et al. [83] and show similar performance between the best algorithms and the best humans (super recognizers), with other groups of humans performing at a lower level. Thus, deep learning solutions are impressive, but saturating relatively small datasets does not imply that automatic 2D face recognition is a solved problem, particularly considering the possibility of face identification on a planetary scale, potentially consisting of a gallery of several billion subjects. The MegaFace benchmark [57] proposed more challenging evaluations, where up to one million distractor images can be injected into the gallery of an existing benchmark dataset. This dataset consists of one million images of more than

690 K subjects. Their results show that by progressively adding up to one million distractors into some dataset gallery, the rank-1 identification performance of several leading approaches degrades. In the case of the FaceScrub celebrity benchmark [73], which comprises 108 K unconstrained face images of 530 subjects (about 200 images per person), systems with rank-1 recognition rates that are above 95% drop to somewhere in the region of 60 to 75% after the injection of the full 1 million distractors into the gallery.

12.4 3D Recognition Versus 2D Recognition

Compared to 2D, 3D face recognition research started much more recently and is thought to originate in the early 1990s, with the work of Gordon [41], which used depth and curvature features. More recently, with the increased availability of affordable 3D cameras, many 3D face recognition algorithms have been proposed and a number of competitions have been arranged for benchmarking their performance. Some commercial products have also appeared in the market and one can now purchase a range of *Commercial Off-The-Shelf* (COTS) 3D face recognition systems. In 2017, Apple released the *iPhone X*, the first smartphone to incorporate a 3D camera with 3D face authentication to unlock the device.

A 2D image is a function of the scene geometry, the scene reflectance, the illumination conditions, and the imaging geometry. The same scene appears completely different from different viewpoints or under different illuminations. For images of human faces, it is known that the variations due to pose and illumination changes are greater than the variations between images of different subjects under the same pose and illumination conditions [2]. As a result, 2D image-based face recognition algorithms have traditionally struggled to cope with such imaging variations. The recent revolution in deep learning, often thought to date from AlexNet [61] in 2012, has significantly mitigated these problems, although highly variable illumination, extreme poses, and extreme expressions still remain challenging.

On the other hand, a captured face surface[1] much more explicitly represents the geometry of the viewed scene, and the raw data that is being classified is often much less dependent on the facial pose and ambient illumination, particularly when using active 3D cameras that source their own scene illumination. Therefore, traditionally (i.e., at least pre-deep learning), 3D face capture and recognition algorithms have been more successful in dealing with the challenges of varying pose and illumination. Perhaps deep learning has weakened the argument for using 3D approaches over 2D. However, as stated earlier, 3D cameras often augment standard 2D image data, rather than replacing it, and there are some continuing advantages of 3D: (i) the face-background segmentation problem is significantly easier in 3D; in fact, it becomes trivial; (ii) 3D authentication systems are more resistant to spoofing security attacks. It is clearly more difficult and laborious for a spoofer to use a 3D printer to print a

---

[1]This may be referred to as a *3D scan* or a *3D image*, depending on the mode of shape capture.

true-to-scale 3D shape that is correctly colored than it is to supply a photograph.[2] (iii) Facial texture is not always stable for subjects, as it can change with variations in makeup and facial hair.

Despite the perceived advantages of 3D, we have to be careful not to over-emphasize some of them. First, we should observe that 3D imaging is not fully independent of the pose, because when imaging with a single 3D camera with its limited field of view, the part of the facial surface that is captured is clearly dependent on the pose. In other words, self-occlusion is a problem, and research issues concerning the fact that the surface view is *partial* come into play. Additionally, 3D cameras do have some sensitivity to strong and/or variable ambient lighting. In passive stereo, it is harder to do the image-to-image matching, required to find correspondences. Even in the active imaging case, it is more difficult to detect the projected light pattern, sometimes leading to missing parts in the 3D data. Camera designers often attempt to counter this by the use of optical filters, modulated projected light, and use of certain wavelengths, such as 940 nm, where those wavelengths from the sun are blocked by the Earth's atmosphere. Finally note that, as pose varies, the orientation of the imaged surface affects both the size and shape of the footprint of the projected light, and how much light is reflected back to the camera. This can reduce the signal-to-noise ratio of the visual sensing process, resulting in an increase in the amount of noise on the measured surface geometry. Thus, 3D imaging for face recognition can still provide benefits over 2D imaging, but usually at the cost of additional imaging and/or illumination hardware. 3D facial shape may be used both as an independent cue for face recognition, in multimodal 2D/3D recognition schemes [17, 70], or to assist (pose correct, segment) 2D image-based face recognition. Multimodal schemes are supported by COTS 3D cameras as most also capture color-texture in the form of a standard 2D image, along with the 3D shape, and the data from these two modalities (2D and 3D) is registered.

3D face recognition developments have also achieved significant success towards robust operation in the presence of facial expression variations. This is achieved either by building expression-invariant face surface representations [13], modeling nonrigid surface deformations [67], or avoiding expression deformations by only considering the more rigid upper parts of the face [70] or regions around the nose [16].

Whereas large volume 2D images can be obtained by crawling the web, large volume 3D data is significantly harder to obtain. Hence deep learning has had less impact on 3D face recognition, at least at the time of writing in early 2019. We do, however, present two recent works of deep learning [38, 58] applied to 3D recognition later in the chapter.

As well as being used directly in 3D face recognition systems, data from 3D cameras can also be used to assist 2D face recognition, by constructing generative 3D face models offline. The most common of these are known as 3D Morphable Models (3DMMs) [10], which can generate 3D face instances from a statistical

---

[2]Note that *liveness detection*, such as the detection of blinking, can be used to augment security [76] in both 2D and 3D modalities.

model. Such statistical models are often derived from Principal Component Analysis (PCA) applied to the aligned set of 3D training samples, to yield linear model, whereas nonlinear models may be extracted from deep autoencoder networks. The models are then used in an *analysis-by-synthesis* approach to recognize 2D images. Essentially, one builds parameterised models of illumination, facial surface reflectance, camera pose, and projection, as well as 3D shape. Then a model parameter optimisation attempts to synthesize an image that is highly similar to the actual 2D facial image. The resulting 3D face parameters are then used in the face recognition scheme, effectively as a global shape feature vector. Thus, using 3D shape models, trained offline with 3D data, an online 2D recognition system can be employed, obviating the need for a 3D scanner in the live system.

Of course, we would classify the *analysis-by-synthesis* approach as a 2D face recognition scheme as the probe input to the recognition system is 2D. It is important to note that 2D and 3D concepts are often mixed within the same system, however, the emphasis of this chapter is on recognition from 3D shape data only, where geometric features are extracted from the 3D face and matched against a dataset to determine the identity of an unknown subject or to verify his/her claimed identity. Even within these 3D facial shape recognition systems, there are many different approaches in the literature that can be categorized in different ways, and we discuss this later in the chapter.

12.5   3D Face Image Representation and Visualization

The fundamental measurement provided by most 3D cameras is a set of N 3D point coordinates, $\mathbf{p}_i = [x_i, y_i, z_i]^T$, $i = \{1 \ldots N\}$, described in some defined 3D camera frame. Since we are concerned with shape, encoded by relative depths of points and not absolute depths, knowledge of the exact definition of this frame is usually unimportant. If the set of points are unordered, it is termed a *point cloud* and there is no neighborhood or surface connectivity information explicit or implicit in the representation.

In contrast, a *range image* may be generated, which is a 2D arrangement of depth (Z coordinate) values of the scene corresponding to the pixels of the image plane of the 3D sensor. A range image only retains the Z coordinates of the sensed points and the corresponding (X, Y) coordinates can be obtained from the (calibrated) camera model parameters. It is possible to convert a point cloud representation to a centrally projected range image or orthogonally projected *depth map* (see Fig. 12.2), which is similar to a range image but resampled with orthogonal projection.

Since range only is retained in a range image, the inverse is also possible only if the camera model (i.e., projection model) is given, so that the correct (X, Y) coordinates can be computed for each range image pixel.

The software of many stereo-based 3D cameras augment 3D point data with surface connectivity information and thus provide the user with a *polygonal mesh*. For example, the OBJ format provides both mesh connectivity and texture coordinates

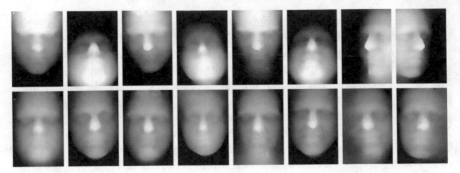

Fig. 12.2 Facial depth maps: the top row shows the captured pose when the subject has been asked to move their head 45° relative to the frontal. The rendering is the same as a range image, i.e., brighter pixels are closer to the 3D camera. The bottom row shows resampled depth maps after a pose normalization process has been applied to the captured point cloud. Figure adapted from [81]

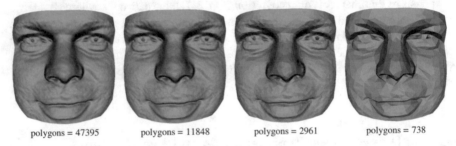

polygons = 47395   polygons = 11848   polygons = 2961   polygons = 738

Fig. 12.3 A 3D face mesh (rendered as flat shaded view in MeshLab [69]) is decimated three times using the *quadric error algorithm* [37]

which map each 3D point to a simultaneously captured and registered 2D image, so that the per-vertex color of each 3D point is known. This makes the object scan more suitable for the purposes of rendering and processing. Such mesh representations are common in computer graphics and are generated by constructing polygons from neighboring points such that each polygon is planar and simple (i.e. has nonintersecting edges). Both of these constraints are always satisfied with triangles, therefore, most meshes are made of triangles only. Delaunay triangulation is a common method used to generate triangular meshes from point clouds.

Range sensors sample a surface according to their relative orientation and the perspective view of the sensor. Therefore, surfaces that are closer and orthogonal to the sensor are sampled more densely compared to surfaces that are far or oblique to the sensor. For efficient memory utilization and rendering, points/vertices from the oversampled parts of the scene are removed using mesh decimation [46]. Mesh decimation works on the principle of collapsing edges that would minimally alter the surface geometry hence the decimated mesh contains only a fraction of points/polygons and yet retains the original 3D shape. Figure 12.3 shows a sample 3D face decimated three times using the *quadric error algorithm* [37].

Polygonal models are linear approximations of surfaces with flat polygons. A more accurate mathematical representation is given by *nonuniform rational B-splines* (NURBS). In addition to having greater accuracy, a NURBS representation is also more compact compared to the polygonal representation. NURBS represent surfaces continuously in two parametric directions with the help of control points and knots. Details of NURBS and B-splines can be found in [84].

A large number of visualization tools are available for rendering and manipulating 3D data. Most are built using the *Open Graphics Library* (OpenGL) and can render point clouds, meshes, filled polygons with constant shading or texture mappings. Likewise, file formats are numerous, however, they all follow the same convention, i.e. a header followed by the X, Y, Z coordinates of the point cloud and the list of polygons. The header usually contains information about the sensor, rendering parameters, the number of points and polygons, and so on. The polygon list contains index numbers of points that form a polygon. Examples of free visualization and manipulation tools are *MeshLab* [69] and *Blender* [99]. Proprietary software includes *Maya*, *Rhino* and *Poser*. Large online datasets of 3D faces are outlined in the following section.

12.6 3D Face Datasets

A range of 3D face datasets have been employed by the research community for 3D face recognition evaluations. Examples include:

- The Face Recognition Grand Challenge v2 3D dataset (FRGC v2) [82].
- The Bosphorus 3D face dataset (Bosphorus) [12].
- The Texas 3D face recognition dataset (Texas3DFRD) [100].
- The Notre Dame 3D face dataset (ND-2006) [30].
- The Binghamton University 3D facial expression dataset (BU-3DFE) [107].
- The Binghamton University 4D (3D + time) dynamic facial expression dataset (BU-4DFE, 3D video) [106].
- The Chinese Academy of Sciences Institute of Automation 3D dataset (CASIA) [53].
- The GavabDB 3D dataset.
- The 3D-TEC twins dataset [102].
- The University of Milano Bicocca 3D Face Database (UMB-DB) [20].
- The University of York (UoY) 3D face dataset [49].

Datasets are characterized by the number of 3D face images captured, the number of subjects imaged, the quality and resolution of the images, and the variations in facial pose, expression, and occlusion. Table 12.1 outlines this characterisation for the datasets mentioned above. Note that some of the datasets have particular qualities. For example, the BU-4DFE contains 3D video frames of facial expression enactment rather than still images, and the 214 3D-TEC subjects are 107 pairs of twins.

Table 12.1 A selection of 3D face datasets used for face recognition evaluation

Dataset	Subj.	Samp.	Size	Exp.	Pose	Occ.
FRGC v2	466	1–22	4950	Yes	No	No
Bosphorus	105	29–54	4666	Yes	Yes	Yes
Texas3DFR	118	1–89	1149	Yes	No	No
ND-2006	888	1–63	13450	Yes	Yes	No
BU-3DFE	100	25	2500	Yes	No	No
BU-4DFE	101	600	60600	Yes	No	No
CASAI	123	15	1845	Yes	No	No
GavabDB	61	9	549	Yes	Yes	No
3D-TEC	214	2	428	Yes	No	No
UMB-DB	143	≥ 6	1473	Yes	No	Yes
UoY	350	15	5250	Yes	Yes	No

Datasets comprising several thousand images gathered from several hundred subjects, allow researchers to observe relatively small differences in performance in a statistically significant way. Different datasets are more or less suitable for evaluating different types of face recognition scenario. For example, a frontal view, neutral expression dataset is suitable for *verification-of-cooperative-subject* evaluations, but a dataset with pose variations, expression variations and occlusion by head accessories (such as hat and spectacles) is necessary for evaluating a typical *identification-at-a-distance* scenario for non-cooperating subjects who may even be unaware that they are being imaged. This type of dataset is more challenging to collect as all common combinations of variations need to be covered, leading to a much larger number of captures per subject. Due to space limitations, we only describe the most influential of these, the FRGC v2 3D face dataset and the Bosphorus dataset. The reader is referred to the literature references for the details of other datasets.

12.6.1 FRGC V2 3D Face Dataset

For well over a decade, the *Face Recognition Grand Challenge* version 2 (FRGC v2) 3D face dataset [82] has been the most widely used dataset in benchmark face identification and verification evaluations, although for some evaluation protocols, it is now close to saturation (i.e., close to 100% performance). Many researchers used this dataset because it allowed them to compare the performance of their algorithm with many others. Indeed, it became almost expected within the research community that face recognition evaluations would include the use of this dataset, at least for the cooperating subject verification scenario.

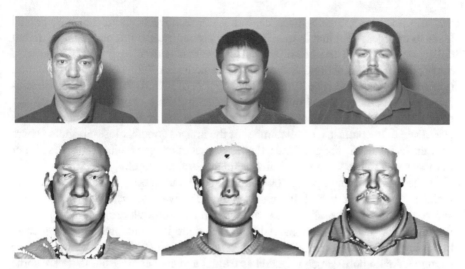

Fig. 12.4 Top row: 2D images reprinted from the FRGC v2 dataset [82]. Second row: a rendering of the corresponding 3D data, after conversion from ABS to OBJ format

The FRGC v2 dataset contains a 3D dataset of 4950 3D face images, where each capture contains two channels of information: a structured 3D point cloud[3] and registered color-texture image (i.e., a standard 2D image). An example of both of these channels of information, each of which has a 640 × 480 resolution, is shown in Fig. 12.4. Thus, in addition to 3D face recognition, 2D/3D multimodal recognition is supported. Results comparing 2D, 3D, and multimodal PCA-based recognition on this dataset are given in [17]. There is a direct correspondence between the 3D points in the 640 × 480 range data (abs format) and pixels in the 640 × 480 color-texture image (ppm format). The range data file is an ASCII text file, containing some header information, a 640 × 480 array of binary flags indicating where a valid range reading has been made, and the (X, Y, Z) tuples over a 640 × 480 array. Where a range flag reads invalid, each value in the tuple is set to −999999.0.

The range sensor employed collects the texture data just after the range data. This opens up the possibility of the subject moving their face slightly between these two captures and can lead to poor registration between the range and texture channels. Often the texture channel is used to mark up fiducial points on the face, such as eye corners, nose tip, and mouth corners, and these are then mapped onto the range data using the known, implicit registration to give 3D landmarks. In this case, and in other cases where channel registration is important, these 3D scans must be removed.

A key point in the proper evaluation of any supervised training system is that the differences between the training and testing 3D face scans must be compara-ble to what is expected when test data is gathered in a live operational recognition

---

[3] 3D points are structured in a rectangular array and since (x, y) values are included, strictly it is not a range image, which contains z-values only.

scenario. In dataset development, capturing consecutive scans of the same person leads to train/test data that is too similar for proper evaluation, hence the different collection periods of the FRGC v2 dataset, which is divided into three sections, *Spring-2003*, *Fall-2003* and *Spring-2004*, named after their periods of collection (University semesters). The Spring-2003 consists of 943 3D face images, with subjects in a cooperating, near-frontal pose and a neutral facial expression. The majority of the images in this subset are at a depth such that the neck and shoulder areas are also imaged. In contrast, a small number of the images contain close-up shots, where only the facial area is imaged. Thus, the resolution of imaged facial features is higher in these scans. Also, within this training subset, ambient lighting is controlled.

In the Fall-2003 and Spring-2004 datasets, ambient lighting is uncontrolled, and facial expressions are varied. Expressions include any of anger, happiness, sadness, surprise, disgust, and *puffy cheeks*, although many subjects are not scanned with the full set of these expressions. Additionally, there is less depth variation than in the Spring-2003 subset and all of the images are close-ups with little shoulder area captured. Again pose can be regarded as frontal and cooperative, but there are some mild pose variations. In these data subsets there are 4007 two-channel scans of 466 subjects (1–22 scans per subject).

To compare ROC curves the same training data and testing data partitions must be employed. The FRGC protocol defines a range of different experiments of increasing difficulty for the generation of ROC performance curves, where there is an increasing time gap between the collection of the gallery image and the probe. These evaluations are referred to as ROC I, ROC II, and ROC III. In the first within-semester evaluations are conducted, in the second they are within-year, and in the third they are between semesters. In this way, a significant passage of time is put between gallery data collection and the verification event, as would often be the case in real-world systems.

High performance 3D face recognition systems have reported rank-1 identification rates that typically range from around 96 to 98.5% [56, 70, 85] on the FRGC v2 3D face dataset. Verification rates that typically range from around 96.5% to 98.5% at 0.1% FAR have been reported for the full FRGC v2 dataset [56, 70, 72, 85]. This is a significant performance improvement on PCA-based baseline results [78]. It is reasonable to assume that in many verification scenarios the subject will be cooperating with a neutral expression. Verification rates for probes with neutral expressions range from around 98.5 to 99.9% [56, 70, 72] at 0.1% FAR. It appears that the ability of the dataset to challenge 3D recognition algorithms over neutral expressions is close to be saturated.

The development of the FRGC face dataset has made a huge contribution to the advancement of 3D face recognition algorithms. However, an interesting point to note is that pose invariance has been an often quoted advantage of 3D face recognition over 2D face recognition, and yet many recognition evaluations have been made on the FRGC dataset, which only contains the very mild pose variations associated with cooperative subjects. In noncooperative subject face recognition applications, other datasets are needed that contain scans from a wide range of different head poses including, for example, full profile views, thus challenging the recognition system in terms of its ability to represent and match partial surfaces. One example of such a dataset is the Bosphorus dataset, which we now briefly outline.

12.6.2   The Bosphorus Dataset

The Bosphorus dataset contains 4666 3D face images of 105 subjects, with 29–54 3D captures per subject [12, 88]. Thus, compared to FRGC v2, there are fewer subjects, but there are more images per subject so that a wider variety of natural, unconstrained viewing conditions, associated with noncooperative image capture, can be explored. There are three types of variation: expression, pose, and occlusion. The standard set of six expressions is included, which includes happiness, surprise, fear, anger, sadness, and disgust, but these are augmented with a set of more primitive expressions based on facial action units (FACS) to give 34 expressions in total. There are 14 different poses (with neutral expression) comprising eight yaw angles, four pitch angles, and two combined rotations of approximately 45° yaw and ±20° pitch. Finally there are up to four scans with occlusions, including *hand over eye*, *hand over mouth*, *spectacles* and *hair over face*.

The data is captured with an *Inspeck Mega Capturor II 3D* camera. Subjects sit at around 1.5 m from the camera and (X, Y, Z) resolution is 0.3 mm, 0.3 mm, 0.4 mm for each of these dimensions, respectively. The associated color-texture images are 1600×1200 pixels. Example captures from the Bosphorus dataset, which are stored as structured depth maps, are shown in Fig. 12.5. Registration with an associated 2D image is stored as two arrays of texture coordinates. More details of capture conditions can be found in [88].

Li et al. [64] present a registration-free 3D face recognition method that is evaluated on the Bosphorus dataset. Rank-1 recognition rates of 96.56%, 98.82%, 91.14%, and 99.21% are achieved on the entire database, and the expression, pose, and occlusion subsets, respectively. The system is also evaluated on FRGC v2 using the first-vs-all protocol and a 96.3% rank-1 identification rate is achieved.

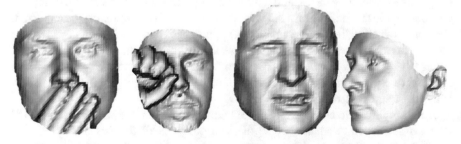

Fig. 12.5 Example 3D scans from the Bosphorus dataset with occlusions, expression variations, and pose variations [12, 88]. Figure adapted from [24]

12.7   Holistic Versus Local Feature-Based Methods for 3D Recognition

Two main categorisations of 3D face recognition systems are (i) classical versus deep learning approaches. In the former, local/global representations are handcrafted, whereas in the latter they are learnt; (ii) the use of *holistic* (global) face representations versus *local feature-based* face representations, which we now consider.

Holistic methods encode the full visible facial surface after its pose has been normalized to a canonical frontal pose, and the surface and its properties are resampled to produce a standard size feature vector. The feature vector could contain raw depth values and/or any combination of surface property, such as gradients and curvature. This approach has been employed, for example, using depth maps and the associated surface feature maps in nearest neighbor schemes within both *Principal Component Analysis* (PCA) and *Linear Discriminant Analysis* (LDA) derived subspaces [49]. Note that the counterpart of these methods for 2D images are often called *appearance-based* methods, since their low-dimensional representation is faithful to the original image. Often, such holistic methods are quite sensitive to pose, facial expressions, and occlusions. For example, a small change in the pose can alter the depth maps and normal maps of a 3D face. This error will propagate to the feature vector extraction stage, where a feature vector represents a 3D face scan, and subsequently affect matching. For global representation and features to be consistent between multiple 3D face scans of the same identity, the scans must be accurately normalized with respect to pose. Due to the difficulty of accurate localization of fiducial points, pose normalization is never perfect. Even the ICP-based pose normalization to a reference 3D face cannot perfectly normalize the pose with high repeatability because dissimilar surfaces may have several local minima rather than a single, distinctively low global minimum. Another source of error in pose normalization is a consequence of the nonrigid nature of the face. Facial expressions can change the curvatures of a face and displace fiducial points leading to errors in pose normalization.

In contrast, *local feature-based methods* refers to those techniques that only encode the facial surface around extracted *points of interest*, also known as *keypoints*. For example, these could be the local extrema of curvature on the facial surface or keypoints for which we have learnt their local properties. Keypoints should be repeatedly detectable at locations on a 3D face where descriptive features can be extracted. Structural matching (e.g., graph matching) approaches can then be employed where the relative spatial relations of features are key to the face matching process [71]. Alternatively, a *bag of features* approach could be employed, where spatial relations are completely discarded and the content of more complex *information rich* features is the key to the face matching process.

An example of a local feature-based 3D face recognition is that of Chua et al. [18] who extracted point signatures [19] of the rigid parts of the face for expression robust 3D face recognition. A point signature is a one-dimensional invariant signature describing the local surface around a point. The signature is extracted by centering a sphere with a fixed radius at that point. The intersection of the sphere with the object's surface gives a 3D curve whose orientation can be normalized using its normal and a reference direction. The 3D curve is projected perpendicularly to a plane, fitted to the curve, forming a 2D curve. This projection gives a signed distance profile called the point signature. The starting point of the signature is defined by a vector from the point to where the 3D curve gives the largest positive profile distance. Chua et al. [18] do not provide a detailed experimental analysis of the point signatures for 3D face recognition. Local features have also been combined with global features to achieve better performance. Xu et al. [104] combined local shape variations with global geometric features to perform 3D face recognition. Al-Osaimi et al. [3] combined local and global geometric cues for 3D face recognition. The local features represented local similarities between faces while the global features provided geometric consistency of the spatial organization of the local features.

In conclusion, an advantage of holistic methods is that they try to use all of the visible facial surfaces for discrimination. However, when 3D scans are noisy or low resolution or contaminated by occlusion, accurate and reliable pose normalization is difficult and local feature-based approaches may perform better. Our observation is that more recent approaches tend to use local feature-based approaches. Note that Soltanpour et al. [93] present a more comprehensive literature review on local feature methods for 3D face recognition, while Guo et al. [44] present a comprehensive performance evaluation of 3D local feature descriptors in a more general object recognition sense, with respect to their descriptiveness, compactness, and robustness.

12.8   Processing Stages in Classical 3D Face Recognition

We now present a typical set of processing stages in a classical 3D face recognition system. When developing a classical 3D face recognition system, one has to understand what information is provided from the camera or from the dataset, what format it is presented in, and what imperfections are likely to exist. The raw data obtained from even the best 3D cameras is imperfect as it may contain spikes, holes, and noise. Preprocessing stages are usually tailored to the form and quality of this raw data. Often, the face scans must be normalized with respect to pose (e.g., holistic approaches) and spatial sampling before extracting features for 3D face recognition. Although the 3D face processing pipeline shown in Fig. 12.6 is typical, many variations on this exist; in particular, there are some possible reorderings and not all of the preprocessing and pose normalization stages are always necessary. With this understanding, we discuss all of the stages of the pipeline in the following subsections.

12.8.1   Face Detection and Segmentation

Images acquired with a 3D sensor usually contain a larger area than just the face area and it is often desirable to segment and crop this extraneous data as early as

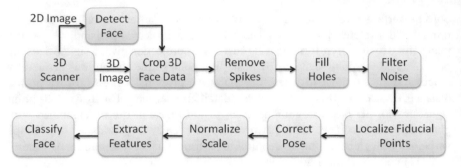

Fig. 12.6 Block diagram showing typical processing steps in a 3D face recognition system. There are several possible reorderings of this pipeline, depending on the input data quality and the performance priorities of the application

possible in the processing pipeline in order to speed up processing in the downstream sections of the pipeline. This face detection and cropping process, which yields 3D face segmentation, can be done on the basis of the camera's 3D range data, 2D texture image or a combination of both.

In the case of 2D images, face detection is a mature field (particularly for frontal poses) and popular approaches include skin detection, face templates, eigenfaces, neural networks, support vector machines, and hidden Markov models. A seminal approach for real-time face detection by Viola and Jones [103] is based on Haar wavelets and adaptive boosting (Adaboost) and is part of the *Open Computer Vision (OpenCV)* library.

However, some face recognition systems prefer not to rely on the existence of a 2D texture channel in the 3D camera data and crop the face on the basis of 3D information only. Also, use of 3D information is sometimes preferred for a more accurate localization of the face. If some pose assumptions are made, it is possible to apply some very basic techniques. For example, one could take the uppermost vertex (largest y value), assume that this is near to the top of the head and crop a sufficient distance downwards from this point to include the largest faces likely to be encountered. Note that this can fail if the uppermost vertex is on a hat, other head accessory, or some types of hairstyle. Alternatively, for cooperative subjects in frontal poses, one can make the assumption that the nose tip is the closest point to the camera and crop a spherical region around this point to segment the facial area. However, the chin, forehead or hair is occasionally closer. Thus, particularly in the presence of depth spikes, this kind of approach can fail and it may be better to move the cropping process further down the processing pipeline so that it is after a spike filtering stage.

If the system's computational power is such that it is acceptable to move cropping even further down the pipeline, more sophisticated cropping approaches can be applied, which could be based on facial feature localization and some of the techniques described earlier for 2D face detection. The nose is perhaps the most prominent feature that has been used alone [70], or in combination with the inner eye corners, for face region segmentation [21]. The latter approach uses the principal curvatures to detect the nose and eyes. The candidate triplet is then used by a PCA-based classifier for face detection.

12.8.2 Removal of Spikes

Spikes are caused mainly by specular regions. In the case of faces, the eyes, nose tip, and teeth are three main regions where spikes are likely to occur. The eye lens sometimes forms a real image in front of the face causing a positive spike. Similarly, the specular reflection from the eye forms an image of the laser behind the eye causing a negative spike. Shiny teeth seem to be bulging out in 3D scans and a small spike can sometimes form on top of the nose tip. Glossy facial makeup or oily skin can also cause spikes at other regions of the face. In medical applications such as craniofacial anthropometry, the face is powdered to make its surface Lambertian and the teeth are painted before scanning.

Spike detection works on the principle that surfaces, and faces, in particular, are generally smooth. One simple approach to filtering spikes is to examine a small neighborhood for each point in the mesh or range image and replace its depth (Z-coordinate value) by the median of this small neighborhood. This is a standard *median filter* which, although effective, can attenuate fine surface detail. Another approach is to threshold the absolute difference between the point's depth and the median of the depths of its neighbors. If the threshold is exceeded, the point's depth is replaced with the neighborhood median, or deleted to be filled later by a more sophisticated scheme. These approaches work well in high resolution data, but in sufficiently low resolution data, problems may occur when the facial surface is steep relative to the viewing angle, such as the sides of the nose in frontal views. In this case, we can detect spikes relative to the local surface orientation, but this requires that surface normals are computed, which are corrupted by the spikes. It is possible to adopt an iterative procedure where surface normals are computed and the spikes are removed in cycles, yielding a clean, uncorrupted set of surface normals even for relatively low resolution data [81].

12.8.3 Filling of Holes and Missing Data

In addition to the holes resulting from spike removal, the 3D data contains many other missing points due to occlusions, such as the nose occluding the cheek when, for example, the head pose is sufficiently rotated (in yaw angle) relative to the 3D camera. Obviously, such areas of the scene that are not visible to either the camera or the projected light cannot be acquired. Similarly, dark regions which do not reflect sufficient projected light are not sensed by the 3D camera. Both can cause large regions of missing data, which are often referred to as *missing parts*.

In the case of cooperative subject applications (e.g., a typical verification application) frontal face images are acquired and occlusion is not a major issue. However, dark regions such as the eyebrows and facial hair are usually not acquired. Moreover, for laser-based projection, power cannot be increased to acquire dark regions of the face due to eye-safety reasons.

Thus, the only option is to fill the missing regions using an interpolation technique such as nearest neighbor, linear or polynomial. For small holes, linear interpolation gives reasonable results however, bicubic interpolation has shown to give better results [70]. Alternatively, one can use implicit surface representations for interpolation, such as those provided by radial basis functions [81].

For larger size holes, symmetry or PCA-based approaches can be used, although these require a localized symmetry plane and a full 6-DOF rigid alignment, respectively, and hence would have to be moved further downstream in the processing pipeline. Alternatively, a model-based approach can be used to morph a model until it gives the best fit to the data points [109]. This approach learns the 3D face space offline and requires a significantly large training data in order to generalize to unseen faces. However, it may be very useful if the face being scanned was previously seen and obviously this is a common scenario in 3D face recognition.

For better generalization to unseen faces, an anthropometrically correct [32] *annotated face model* (AFM) [56] is used. The AFM is based on an average 3D face constructed using statistical data and the anthropometric landmarks are associated with its vertices. The AFM is then fitted to the raw data from the scanner using a deformable model framework. Blanz et al. [9] also used a morphable model to fit the 3D scan, filling up missing regions in addition to other preprocessing steps, in a unified framework.

12.8.4 *Removal of Noise*

For face scans acquired by laser scanners, noise can be attributed to optical components such as the lens and the mirror, or mechanical components which drive the mirror, or the CCD itself. Scanning and imaging conditions such as ambient light, laser intensity, surface orientation, texture, and distance from the scanner can also affect the noise levels in the scanner. Sun et al. [96] give a detailed analysis of noise in the Minolta Vivid scanner and noise in active sensors is discussed in another chapter of this book.

We have already mentioned the median filter as a mechanism for spike (impulsive noise) removal. More difficult is the removal of surface noise, which is less differentiated from the underlying object geometry, without removing fine surface detail or generally distorting the underlying shape, for example, from volumetric shrinkage. Clearly, there is a trade-off to be made and an optimal level of filtering is sought in order to give the best recognition performance. Removal of surface noise is particularly important as a preprocessing step in some methods of extraction of the differential properties of the surface, such as normals and curvatures.

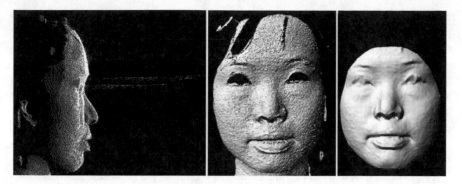

Fig. 12.7 From left to right. A 3D capture of a face with spikes in the point cloud. Shaded view with holes and noise. Final preprocessed 3D data after cropping, removal of spikes, hole filling, and noise removal. Figure courtesy of [70]

If the 3D data is in range image or depth map form, there are many methods available from the standard 2D image filtering domain, such as convolution with Gaussian filters. Many of these methods have been adapted so that they can be applied to 3D meshes. One example of this is *Bilateral Mesh Denoising* [35], which is based on shifting mesh vertices along their normal directions. Figure 12.7 shows a face scan with spikes, holes, and noise before and after preprocessing.

12.8.5   *Fiducial Point Localization and Pose Correction*

The pose of different subjects or the same subject can vary between 3D image captures, even when they are cooperative. Therefore, pose correction is a necessary preprocessing step for holistic approaches that require normalized resampling of the facial surface in order to generate a feature vector. (Such feature vectors are often subsequently mapped into a subspace—e.g., in PCA and LDA-based methods described later.) This may also be necessary for other algorithms that rely on features that are not inherently pose invariant. A common approach to pose correction uses fiducial points on the 3D face. Three points are necessary to normalize the pose to a canonical form. Automatic detection of such points is necessary for automatic online verification and identification processes.

The shape index, derived from principle curvatures, has been used to automatically detect the inside eye corners and the nose tip for facial pose correction [66]. Although a minimum of three fiducial points are sufficient to correct the pose, it has proved a challenging research problem to detect these points, where all three are identified correctly and localized with high repeatability. This problem is more difficult in the presence of varying facial expressions, which can change the local shape around a point. Worse still, as pose changes, one of the three fiducial points selected may become occluded. For example, the nose bridge occludes an inner eye corner as the head is turned from a frontal view toward a profile view. To counter this, some approaches have attempted to extract a large number of fiducial points so that three or more are always visible [25].

In addition to a shape scan, most 3D cameras capture a registered color-texture map of the face (i.e. a standard 2D image, where the color associated with each 3D point is known). Fiducial point detection can be performed on the basis of the 3D shape channel directly, or using the 2D images and then projecting the results onto the 3D shape using the known 2D-to-3D registration. This latter approach may be implemented by any of the many 2D facial image landmarkers that have recently become available [26].

Gupta et al. [45] detected 10 anthropometric fiducial points to calculate craniofacial proportions [32]. Three points were detected using the 3D face alone and the rest were detected based on 2D and 3D data. Mian et al. [70] performed pose correction based on a single point, i.e. the nose tip which is automatically detected. The 3D face was cropped using a sphere with a fixed radius centered at the nose tip and its pose was then corrected by iteratively applying PCA and resampling the face on a uniform grid. This process also filled the holes (due to self occlusions) that were exposed during pose correction. Pears et al. [81] performed pose correction by detecting the nose tip using pose invariant features based on the spherical sampling of a radial basis function (RBF) representation of the facial surface. Another sphere centered on the nose tip intersected the facial surface and the tangential curvature of this space curve was used in a correlation scheme to normalize facial pose. The interpolating properties of RBF representations gave all steps in this approach a good immunity to missing parts, although some steps in the method are computationally expensive. Creusot et al. [23, 25] presented a machine-learning approach to keypoint detection and landmarking on 3D meshes. This learnt which 3D surface features could best discriminate a set of 14 landmarks from their surrounding areas. The same authors demonstrate the use of graph matching techniques to label a set of fiducial surface points even under partial facial occlusion [22].

Another common pose correction approach is to register all 3D faces to a common reference face using the *Iterative Closest Points* (ICP) algorithm [7]. The reference is usually an average face model, in a canonical pose, calculated from training data. Sometimes only the rigid parts of the face are used in this face model, such as upper face area containing nose, eyes, and forehead. ICP can find the optimal registration only if the two surfaces are already approximately registered. Therefore, the query face is first coarsely aligned with the reference face, either by zero-meaning both scans or using fiducial points, before applying ICP to refine the registration [66]. In refining pose, ICP establishes correspondences between the closest points of the two surfaces and calculates the rigid transformation (rotation and translation) that minimizes the mean-squared distance between the corresponding points. These two steps are repeated until the change in mean-squared error falls below a threshold or the maximum number of iterations is reached. In the case of registering a probe face to an average face, the surfaces are dissimilar. Hence, there may be more than one comparable local minima and ICP may converge to a different minimum each time a query face is registered to the reference face. The success of ICP depends upon the initial coarse registration and the similarity between the two surfaces.

As a final note on pose correction, Blanz et al. [9] used a morphable model in a unified framework to simultaneously optimize pose, shape, texture, and illumination. The algorithm relies on manual identification of seven fiducial points and uses the Phong lighting model [4] to optimize shape, texture, and illumination (in addition to pose) which can be used for face recognition. This algorithm would be an expensive choice if only pose correction is the aim and it requires landmarks to work well.

12.8.6   Spatial Resampling

Unlike 2D images, 3D scans have an absolute scale, which means that the distance between any two fiducial points (landmarks), such as the inner corners of the eye, can be measured in absolute units (e.g., millimeters). Thus 3D imaging of the same face from near or far will only alter the spatial sampling rate and the measured distance between landmarks should vary very little, at least in scans of reasonable quality and resolution.

However, many face recognition algorithms require the face surface, or parts of the face surface, to be sampled in a uniform fashion, which requires some form of *spatial sampling normalization* or *spatial resampling* via an interpolation process. Basic interpolation processes usually involve some weighted average of neighbors, while more sophisticated schemes employ various forms of implicit or explicit surface fitting.

Assuming that we have normalized the pose of the face (or facial part), we can place a standard 2D resampling grid in the x, y plane (for example, it could be centered on the nose tip) and resample the facial surface depth orthogonally to generate a resampled depth map. In many face recognition schemes, a standard size feature vector needs to be created and the standard resampling grid of size $p \times q = m$ creates this. For example, in [70], all 3D faces were sampled on a uniform x, y grid of 161×161 where the planar distance between adjacent pixels was 1mm. Although the sampling rate was uniform in this case, subjects had a different number of points sampled on their faces, because of their different facial sizes. The resampling scheme employed cubic interpolation. In another approach, Pears et al. [81] used RBFs as implicit surface representations in order to resample 3D face scans.

An alternative way of resampling is to identify three noncollinear fiducial points on each scan and resample it such that the number of sample points between the fiducial points is constant. However, in doing this, we are discarding information contained within the absolute scale of the face, which often is useful for subject discrimination.

12.8.7 Feature Extraction on Facial Surfaces

Depth maps may not be the ideal representations for 3D face recognition because they are quite sensitive to pose. Although the pose of 3D faces can be normalized with better accuracy compared to 2D images, the normalization is never perfect. For this reason, it is usually preferable to extract features that are less sensitive to pose before applying holistic approaches. The choice of features extracted is crucial to the system performance and is often a trade-off between invariance properties and the richness of information required for discrimination. Example *features* include the raw depth values themselves, normals, curvatures, spin images [55], 3D adaptations of the *Scale Invariant Feature Transform* (SIFT) descriptor [65], and many others. A comprehensive performance evaluation of 3D local feature descriptors is given by Guo et al. [44].

12.8.8 Classifiers for 3D Face Matching

In the large array of published 3D face recognition work, all of the well-known classification schemes have been applied by various researchers. These include k-nearest neighbors (k-NN) in various subspaces, such as those derived from PCA and LDA, neural nets, Support Vector Machines (SVM), Adaboost, and many others. The choice (type, complexity) of classifier employed is related to the separation of subjects (classes) within their feature space. Good face recognition performance depends on choosing a classifier that fits the separation of the training data well without overfitting and hence generalizes well to unseen 3D face scans. Pattern classification is a huge subject in its own right and we can only detail a selection of the possible techniques in this chapter. We refer the reader to the many excellent texts on the subject, for example, [8, 28].

12.9 ICP-based 3D Face Recognition

In this section and the following sections on PCA and LDA, we present well-established holistic approaches to 3D face recognition, with a more tutorial style of presentation. These do not give state-of-the-art face recognition performance but are a good place to start when first implementing 3D face recognition systems, and can define a baseline performance level for some dataset. The aim is to give the reader a solid grounding before going on to more modern and more advanced techniques that have better performance. We will highlight the strengths and limitations of each technique and present clear implementation details.

One of the earliest algorithms employed for matching surfaces is the *iterative closest points* (ICP) algorithm [7], which aims to iteratively minimize the mean square error between two point sets. In brief, ICP has three basic operations is its iteration loop, as follows:

1. Find pairs of closest points between two point clouds (i.e., probe and gallery face scans).
2. Use these *putative* correspondences to determine a rigid 6-DOF Euclidean transformation that moves one point cloud closer to the other.
3. Apply the rigid transformation to the appropriate point cloud.

The procedure is repeated until the change in mean square error associated with the correspondences falls below some threshold, or the maximum number of iterations is reached. In the context of 3D face recognition, the remaining mean square error then can be used as a matching metric.

Due to its simplicity, ICP has been popular for rigid surface registration and 3D object recognition and many variants and extensions of ICP have been proposed in the literature [86].

Here, we will give a presentation in the context of 3D face recognition. Surface registration and matching are similar procedures except that, in the latter case, we are only interested in the final registration error between the two surfaces. A fuller and more formal outline of ICP is presented in the following subsection.

12.9.1   ICP Outline

Let $\mathbf{p}_j = [x_j \ y_j \ z_j]^T$ where $j = 1 \dots M$ be a zero-mean set of 3D points of a probe face scan and let $\mathbf{g}_i = [x_i \ y_i \ z_i]^T$ where $i = 1 \dots N$ be a zero-mean set of 3D points of a gallery face scan. Since both point clouds are zero mean, they have an implicit coarse translational alignment. An initial coarse orientation alignment *may* also be required to avoid convergence to a local minimum but, for now, we will assume that it is not required and we will discuss this issue later.

We can stack the points in $M \times 3$ and $N \times 3$ data matrices to give:

$$\mathsf{P} = \begin{bmatrix} \mathbf{p}_1^T \\ \vdots \\ \mathbf{p}_M^T \end{bmatrix}, \quad \mathsf{G} = \begin{bmatrix} \mathbf{g}_1^T \\ \vdots \\ \mathbf{g}_N^T \end{bmatrix}. \tag{12.1}$$

Let F be a function that, for each point in P, finds the nearest point in G:

$$(\mathbf{c}, \mathbf{d}) = F(\mathsf{P}, \mathsf{G}), \tag{12.2}$$

where $\mathbf{c}$ and $\mathbf{d}$ are vectors of size M each, such that $\mathbf{c}$ and $\mathbf{d}$ contain, respectively, the index number and distance of the jth point of P to its nearest point in G. This is called the *closest points* step where the pairs of closest points within the two-point clouds are assigned as *tentative correspondences*. (We use the word *putative* because they are not accurate correspondences until ICP has converged to the correct global minimum.) This is the most critical and computationally the most expensive step of the algorithm. It is critical because highly inaccurate tentative correspondences could, in the worst case, cause ICP convergence to a local minimum. Even if this is not the case, they will affect the accuracy of the final registration and hence the matching metric between the two-point clouds. Typically, the following filters are applied to minimize these effects:

1. Tentative correspondences whose distance is greater than a threshold are removed. The threshold is usually chosen as a multiple of the point cloud resolution which is initially set relatively high, depending on the quality of the initial registration. It is then gradually reduced through the iterations until it is equal to the resolution.
2. Tentative correspondences whose surface normals have a mutual angle above a threshold are removed. The threshold is chosen based on the accuracy of the normals and the quality of the initial registration. Also, it is possible to reduce this threshold through the iterations.
3. Tentative correspondences at the boundary points are avoided. This step is useful when the two-point clouds only partially overlap, as occurs with partial views of the probe face.
4. Sometimes additional information such as texture is also used to remove poor quality tentative correspondences.

To speed up the search for the nearest points within the gallery scan, the points in each gallery scan are arranged in a k-d tree and these structures are precomputed off-line. A further speed up can be achieved by storing the index of the nearest neighbor from the centers of a set of voxels in a voxelized space around the gallery scan [105]. Again this can be precomputed offline. (Note that the ICP technique based on Levenberg–Marquardt minimization [34], also uses a precomputed distance transform.)

Let $\mathbf{p}_k = [x_k \ y_k \ z_k]^T$ and $\mathbf{g}_k = [x_k \ y_k \ z_k]^T$ (where $k = 1, \ldots m$) be the remaining m corresponding pairs of points of the probe and gallery face, respectively. The next step is to find the rotation matrix R and translation vector $\mathbf{t}$ that minimizes the mean square error (MSE) between these tentative correspondences. The error to be minimized is given by

$$e = \frac{1}{m} \sum_{k=1}^{m} \|\mathsf{R}\mathbf{p}_k + \mathbf{t} - \mathbf{g}_k\|^2. \tag{12.3}$$

The unknowns (R and $\mathbf{t}$) in Eq. 12.3 can be calculated using a number of approaches including *quaternion* methods and *Singular Value Decomposition* (SVD). We will give details of the widely-used SVD approach [5]. The means of $\mathbf{p}_k$ and $\mathbf{g}_k$ are given by

$$\bar{\mathbf{p}} = \frac{1}{m} \sum_{k=1}^{m} \mathbf{p}_k \qquad (12.4)$$

$$\bar{\mathbf{g}} = \frac{1}{m} \sum_{k=1}^{m} \mathbf{g}_k \qquad (12.5)$$

and the cross-covariance matrix $\mathbf{C}$ is given by the mean of outer products

$$\mathbf{C} = \frac{1}{m} \sum_{k=1}^{m} (\mathbf{p}_k - \bar{\mathbf{p}})(\mathbf{g}_k - \bar{\mathbf{g}})^T. \qquad (12.6)$$

Equivalently, this can be expressed as

$$\mathbf{C} = \frac{1}{m} \mathbf{P}_m^T \mathbf{G}_m, \qquad (12.7)$$

where $\mathbf{P}_m, \mathbf{G}_m$ are the zero-centered data matrices in Eq. 12.1 trimmed to $m \times 3$ matrices of m tentative correspondences. Performing the SVD of $\mathbf{C}$ gives us

$$\mathbf{U}\mathbf{S}\mathbf{V}^T = \mathbf{C}, \qquad (12.8)$$

where $\mathbf{U}$ and $\mathbf{V}$ are two orthogonal matrices and $\mathbf{S}$ is a diagonal matrix of singular values. The rotation matrix $\mathbf{R}$ can be calculated from the orthogonal matrices as [5]

$$\mathbf{R} = \mathbf{V}\mathbf{U}^T. \qquad (12.9)$$

Note that if this is indeed a rotation matrix, then $\det(\mathbf{R}) = +1$. However, in principle, it is possible to obtain $\det(\mathbf{R}) = -1$, which corresponds to a reflection. This degeneracy is not what we want but, according to Arun et al. [5] and in our own experience, it usually does not occur. Once the rotation matrix has been computed, the translation vector $\mathbf{t}$ can be calculated as

$$\mathbf{t} = \bar{\mathbf{g}} - \mathbf{R}\bar{\mathbf{p}}. \qquad (12.10)$$

Then the original point cloud of the probe face is transformed as

$$\mathbf{P}'^T = \mathbf{R}\mathbf{P}^T + \mathbf{t}\mathbf{J}_{1,n}, \qquad (12.11)$$

where $\mathbf{J}_{1,n}$ is a $1 \times n$ matrix of ones.

Subsequently, tentative correspondences are established again between the transformed probe face and the gallery face (Eq. 12.2). This process is iterated until e approaches a minimum value, detected by its change over one iteration falling below some threshold. If the initial coarse alignment is within the convergence zone of the global minimum MSE, the final value of e is a good measure of the similarity between two face scans, where smaller values of e mean that the faces are more similar. In identification scenarios, the probe face is matched with every gallery face and the identity of the one with the minimum value of e is declared as the probe's identity. If two gallery identities have very similar low e values, sometimes the number of correspondences, m, in the final iteration can also be used to make a better judgment. Alternatively, a probe can be verified against a claimed gallery identity if the computed value of e falls below some appropriate threshold.

12.9.2   A Critical Discussion of ICP

The main advantage of the ICP algorithm is that it iteratively corrects registration errors as it matches two faces, provided that the initial alignment of the surfaces is within the zone of convergence of the global minimum. If the initial coarse registration is not good enough ICP can converge to a local minimum and hence the algorithm fails. Iterative realignment comes at a heavy computational cost, particularly in the establishment of the closest points. For this step, a basic search has complexity $O(MN)$, where M and N are the number of points in the probe and gallery scans, respectively. This is reduced to $O(M \log N)$ when using k-d tree structures for the closest points search in the gallery scans. It is important to remember that the average time per gallery scan match is also scaled by the average number of iterations per match which is often different for different ICP variants.

Another disadvantage of ICP is that it does not extract features from the face, thus ruling out the possibilities of training classifiers on multiple instances of a face, and ruling out indexing of features from gallery faces for faster matching or feature-level fusion. Thus, the probe must be matched to the complete gallery, thereby making the recognition time linear to the gallery size. This means that, in relation to scan resolution and gallery size, N_G, a single ICP-based probe to gallery match has overall complexity $O(N_G M \log N)$.

As a consequence of this, many variants of ICP try to reduce the face scan match time. Coarse to fine resolution schemes can be used and we can precompute as many aspects of the algorithm as possible on the whole gallery in an off-line batch process. Examples include extracting fiducial points for coarse registration, cropping to spherical volumes relative to the nose tip, building k-d trees, and placing the galley scans in voxel structures for fast lookup of the closest points.

The ICP algorithm can accurately match rigid surfaces. However, faces are not rigid and the facial surface can significantly deform due to expressions. Consequently, the performance of standard ICP degrades under facial expressions. For example, one study cropped the 3D face region manually and then applied standard ICP for neutral and non-neutral subsets of the FRGC dataset for a rank-1 recognition test. The neutral dataset gave an average result of 91% while the non-neutral subset was only 61.5% [16].

However, the second advantage of ICP is that it can operate in partial surface matching schemes. Thus, the problem of facial expressions can be significantly mitigated by applying ICP to the relatively rigid regions of the face [16, 70], which can be identified in the gallery scans in an offline batch process. The ability to do partial matching also allows ICP to handle pose variations by matching 2.5D scans to complete face models [66]. In the case of large pose variations, coarse prealignment using fiducial points (landmarks) may be necessary.

12.9.3   A Typical ICP-based 3D Face Recognition Implementation

We now outline typical steps involved in a standard ICP-based 3D face recognition application. This is intended as a guide on how to implement and start using this approach, but please note that there are many variants of this algorithm available in the literature and MATLAB has a built in function called `pcregistericp` that can be employed.

We assume that the probe and gallery faces are near-frontal in the pose. Some minor pose variations are allowable, such as is found in the FRGC v2 dataset and as might be seen in a typical cooperative verification application. Padia and Pears [74] show that, when registering a 3D face scan to an average face model, ICP converges to the correct global minimum for an initial misalignment between the scans of at least 30° in any of three orthogonal rotational axes. We preprocess each gallery scan, according to the steps below.

1. Determine the closest vertex to the camera. In most reasonable quality scans, this will be close to the nose tip. (Occasionally, the chin, lips or forehead can be closest to the camera and, in a first implementation, a quick visual check may be required so that the nose tip can be selected manually for these failure cases.)
2. Crop to a spherical region of radius 100 mm around this point. For smaller faces, this may include some neck and hair area.
3. Filter spikes and interpolate over any holes.
4. Compute the mean of the point cloud and perform a zero-mean operation (i.e., subtract the mean from each vertex).
5. Use an off-the-shelf algorithm to organize each gallery scan into a k-d tree. Many are publicly available on the web.

For each probe scan to be matched to the gallery, we follow the steps below.

1. Perform the processing steps 1–4 described for the gallery scans above. Given that both probe and gallery face scans are now zero-mean, this constitutes an initial coarse translational alignment.
2. Use a standard off-the-shelf algorithm to perform a closest-point search in the k-d tree of the gallery scan, for each point in the probe scan.
3. Delete tentative correspondences according to the filters given in the earlier 4-point list. (Use the distance and surface normal filters, at least.)

4. From the tentative correspondences, form the cross-covariance matrix using Eq. 12.7. (Note that the means used for this matrix are associated with the list of filtered tentative correspondences, not the full scans.)
5. Perform SVD on the cross-covariance matrix and hence extract the rotation matrix, $\mathbf{R}$, according to Eq. 12.9.
6. Compute the translation, $\mathbf{t}$ using Eq. 12.10.
7. Update the alignment of the probe scan with the gallery scan using Eq. 12.11.
8. Compute e and, unless on the first iteration, determine the change in e from the previous iteration. If this is below a threshold, or if the maximum number of iterations has been reached, finish. Otherwise go to step 2.

The smallest final value of e is used to determine the best match in the gallery for a rank-1 identification, although if e is not sufficiently low, it could be determined that the probe subject is not present in the gallery. Alternatively, the e value could be determined from a single gallery face scan match and thresholded in a verification test against a claimed gallery identity.

Once this basic implementation described above is operational, there are several immediate improvements that can be made. For those readers that want to improve the implementation, we suggest the following.

- The final number of correspondences may vary and this number may be included, along with e, in a cost function in order to make the verification or identification decision. (i.e., A slightly higher e value could be preferable if it is accompanied by a significantly higher number of correspondences.)
- Particularly for large datasets where a fast per-scan match is required, it is preferable to construct a voxel space around the gallery scans where, for the center of each voxel, the index of the nearest gallery surface point is stored. This means that for some probe point, we determine the voxel that it lies in and we just look up the corresponding gallery surface point [105].

When dealing with large pose variations of the probe, such as may be encountered in a noncooperating subject identification scenario, more sophisticated techniques than the above are required. The cropping of the probe based on the nose tip being the nearest point to the camera will often fail and, in profile views, the nose tip will often not be detected by many current methods. Worse still, the probe will often be outside of the global minimum convergence zone of the near-frontal gallery scan poses. To deal with these scenarios, techniques are needed to extract three fiducial points (landmarks) on the probe scans when they are in an arbitrary pose. Then, if a sufficiently wide range of these fiducial points is precomputed on the gallery scans, an initial coarse pose registration is possible. However, reliable landmarking of 3D face scans in arbitrary poses is not trivial. Creusot et al. [25] extract keypoints on 3D face scans and then label them from a set of fourteen possible labels.

12.9.4   ICP Variants and Other Surface Matching Approaches

Lu et al. [66] used *shape index* features along with some anchor points to perform an initial coarse registration of the faces which was later refined with ICP. They matched partial 2.5D scans to 3D face models in order to deal with large pose variations.

Chang et al. [16] proposed an *adaptive rigid multiregion selection* (ARMS) approach for ICP-based 3D face recognition. They automatically locate the inner eye corners, nose tip, and bridge of the nose based on mean and Gaussian curvatures. These landmarks are used to define an elliptical region around the nose of the gallery face. For a probe face, these landmarks are used to define multiple overlapping surface regions, which are individually matched to the gallery face using ICP and the results are combined. The results of Chang et al. show that using smaller regions around the nose can result in better recognition performance. A cross comparison of their ARMS approach with standard approaches on the FRGC v2 dataset gave a rank-1 performance of 97.1% on neutral faces and 86.1% on non-neutral faces, as compared to a PCA performance of 77.7% (neutral) and 61.3% (non-neutral), and a standard ICP performance of 91% (neutral) and 61.5% (non-neutral).

Mian et al. [70] used a variant of ICP for separately matching the *eyes-forehead* region and the nose. Their results show that the eyes-forehead region is more robust to facial expressions compared to the nose. Accurate automatic segmentation of the two regions was performed by first detecting the nose tip, aligning the face using PCA, and then detecting the points of inflection around the nose. In the ICP variant, correspondences were established along the z-dimension. Point clouds were projected to the xy-plane before establishing correspondences and reprojected to the xyz-space for alignment. Mian et al. [70] argued that correspondences should be forced between points that are far along the viewing direction as it gives useful information about the dissimilarity between faces.

Faltemier et al. [31] aligned the face using the nose tip and selected 28 subregions on the face that remain relatively consistent in the presence of expressions and matched each region independently using ICP. They used *Borda Count* and consensus voting to combine the scores. Matching expression insensitive regions of the face is a potentially useful approach to overcome the sensitivity of ICP to expressions. However, determining such regions is a problem worth exploring because these regions are likely to vary between individuals, as well as expressions. Another challenge in matching subregions is that it requires accurate segmentation of the subregions.

Finally, we note that, rather than minimizing a mean-squared error metric between the probe and gallery surfaces, other metrics are possible, although a significantly different approach to minimization must be adopted and the approach is no longer termed *ICP*. One such metric is termed the *Surface Interpenetration Measure* (SIM) [91] which measures the degree to which two aligned surfaces cross over each other. The SIM metric has recently been used with a *Simulated Annealing* approach to 3D face recognition [85]. A verification rate of 96.5% was achieved on the FRGC v2 dataset at 0.1% FAR and a rank-one accuracy of 98.4% was achieved in identification tests.

In the following two sections we discuss PCA and LDA-based 3D face recognition systems that operate on depth maps and surface feature maps (e.g., arrays of curvature values) rather than on point clouds.

12.10 PCA-based 3D Face Recognition

Once 3D face scans have been filtered, pose normalized, and resampled so that, for example, standard size depth maps are generated, the simplest way to implement a face recognition system is to compare the depth maps directly. In this sense we see a $p \times q$ depth map as an $m \times 1$ feature vector in an $m = pq$ dimensional space and we can implement a 1-nearest neighbor scheme, for example, based on either a Euclidean (L2 norm) metric or cosine distance metric. However, this is not generally recommended. Typical depth map sizes mean that m can be a large dimensional space with a large amount of redundancy, since we are only imaging faces and not other objects. Dimension reduction using *Principal Component Analysis* (PCA) can express the variation in the data in a smaller space, thus improving the speed of feature vector comparisons, and removing dimensions that express noise, thus improving recognition performance. Note that PCA is also known in various texts as the *Hotelling transform* or the *Karhunen–Lóeve transform*. The transform involves a zero-mean operation and rotation of the data such that the variables associated with each dimension become uncorrelated. It is then possible to form a reduced dimension subspace by discarding those dimensions that express little variance in the (rotated) data. This is equivalent to a projection into a subspace of the zero-mean dataset that decorrelates the data. It is based on the second-order statistical properties of the data and maps the general covariance matrix in the original basis to a diagonal matrix in the new rotated basis.

PCA-based 3D face recognition has become a baseline at least in near-frontal poses, such as is provided in the FRGC v2 dataset [82]. The method is the 3D analogy to where 2D facial images are decomposed into a linear combination of eigenvectors [92] and employed within a face recognition scenario [101]. Another important difference is that in 2D *eigenfaces*, the three most significant eigenvalues are usually affected by illumination variations and discarding them improves recognition performance [6]. Since depth maps do not contain any illumination component, all significant eigenvalues are used for 3D face recognition.

One of the earliest works on PCA-based 3D face recognition is of Achermann et al. [1]. Hesher et al. [50] explored the use of different numbers of eigenvectors and image sizes for PCA-based 3D face recognition. Heseltine et al. [48] generated a set of twelve feature maps based on the gradients and curvatures over the facial surface, and applied PCA-based face recognition to these maps. Pan et al. [75] constructed a circular depth map using the nose tip as center and axis of symmetry as the starting point. They applied a PCA-based approach to the depth map for face recognition. Chang et al. [15] performed PCA-based 3D face recognition on a larger dataset and later expanded their work to perform a comparative evaluation of PCA-based 3D face recognition with 2D eigenfaces and found similar recognition performance [17].

In order to implement and test PCA-based 3D face recognition, we need to partition our pose normalized 3D scans into a training set and a test set. The following subsections provide procedures for training and testing a PCA-based 3D face recognition system.

12.10.1 PCA System Training

1. For the set of n training images, $\mathbf{x}_i$, $i = 1 \ldots n$, where each training face is represented as an m-dimensional point (column vector) in depth map or surface feature space,

$$\mathbf{x} = [x_1, \ldots, x_m]^T, \tag{12.12}$$

   stack the n training face vectors together (as rows) to construct the $n \times m$ training data matrix

$$\mathbf{X} = \begin{bmatrix} \mathbf{x}_1^T \\ \vdots \\ \mathbf{x}_n^T \end{bmatrix}. \tag{12.13}$$

2. Perform a mean-centering operation by subtracting the mean of the training face vectors, $\bar{\mathbf{x}} = \frac{1}{n} \sum_{i=1}^{n} \mathbf{x}_i$, from each row of matrix $\mathbf{X}$ to form the zero-mean training data matrix

$$\mathbf{X}_0 = \mathbf{X} - \mathbf{J}_{n,1} \bar{\mathbf{x}}^T, \tag{12.14}$$

   where $\mathbf{J}_{n,1}$ is an $n \times 1$ matrix of ones.
3. Generate the $m \times m$ covariance matrix $\mathbf{C}$ of the training data as

$$\mathbf{C} = \frac{1}{n-1} \mathbf{X}_0^T \mathbf{X}_0. \tag{12.15}$$

   Note that dividing by $n - 1$ (rather than n) generates an unbiased covariance estimate from the training data (rather than a maximum likelihood estimate). As we tend to use large training sets (of the order of several hundred images), in practice there is no significant difference between these two covariance estimates.
4. Perform a standard eigendecomposition on the covariance matrix $\mathbf{C}$. Since the covariance matrix $\mathbf{C}$ is symmetric, its eigenvectors are orthogonal to each other, and can be chosen to have a unit length such that

$$\mathbf{V} \mathbf{D} \mathbf{V}^T = \mathbf{C}, \tag{12.16}$$

   where both $\mathbf{V}$ and $\mathbf{D}$ are $m \times m$ matrices. The columns of matrix $\mathbf{V}$ are the eigenvectors, $\mathbf{v}_i$, associated with the covariance matrix $\mathbf{C}$ and $\mathbf{D}$ is a diagonal matrix whose elements contain the corresponding eigenvalues, λ_i. Since the covariance C is a symmetric positive semidefinite matrix, these eigenvalues are real and non-negative. A key point is that these eigenvalues describe the variance along each of the eigenvectors. (Note that eigendecomposition can be achieved with a standard function call such as the MATLAB `eig` function.) Eigenvalues in D and their corresponding eigenvectors in V are in corresponding columns and we require them to be in descending order of eigenvalue. If this order is not automatically performed within the eigendecomposition function, column reordering should be implemented.

5. Select the number of subspace dimensions for projecting the 3D faces. This is the *dimensionality reduction* step and is usually done by analyzing the ratio of cumulative variance associated with the first k dimensions of the rotated image space to the total variance associated with the full set of m dimensions in that space. This *proportion of variance* ratio a_k is given by

$$a_k = \frac{\sum_{i=1}^{k} \lambda_i}{\sum_{i=1}^{m} \lambda_i} \qquad (12.17)$$

and takes a value between 0 and 1, which is often expressed as a percentage 0–100%. A common approach is to choose a minimum value of k such that a_k is greater than a certain percentage (90% or 95% are commonly used). Figure 12.8 shows a plot of a_k versus k for 455 3D faces taken from the FRGC v2 dataset [82]. From Fig. 12.8 one can conclude that the shape of human faces lies in a significantly lower dimensional subspace than the dimensionality of the original depth maps. Note that the somewhat arbitrary thresholding approach described here is likely to be suboptimal and recognition performance can be tuned later by searching for an optimal value of k in a set of face recognition experiments.

6. Project the training data set (the *gallery*) into the k-dimensional subspace

$$\tilde{X} = X_0 V_k. \qquad (12.18)$$

Here V_k is a $m \times k$ matrix containing the first k eigenvectors (columns, v_i) of V and $\tilde{X}$ is a $n \times k$ matrix of n training faces (stored as rows) in the k-dimensional subspace (k dimensions stored as columns).

12.10.2 PCA Training Using Singular Value Decomposition

Several variants of PCA-based 3D face recognition exist in the literature and one of the most important variants is to use *Singular Value Decomposition* (SVD) directly on the $n \times m$ zero-mean training data matrix, X_0, thus replacing Steps 3 and 4 in the previous subsection. The advantage of using SVD is that it can often provide superior numerical stability compared to eigendecomposition algorithms, additionally the

Fig. 12.8 Proportion of variance (%) of the first k eigenvalues to the total variance for 455 3D faces. The first 26 most significant eigenvalues retain 95% of the total variance and the first 100 eigenvalues retain 99% of the total variance [82]

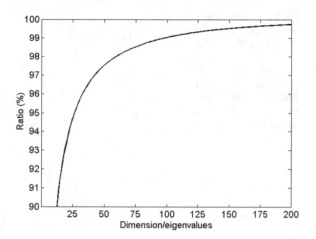

storage required for a data matrix is often much less than a covariance matrix (the number of training scans is much less than the dimension of the feature vector). The SVD is given as

$$USV^T = X_0, \tag{12.19}$$

where U and V are orthogonal matrices of dimension $n \times n$ and $m \times m$, respectively, and S is a $n \times m$ matrix of *singular values* along its diagonal. Note that, in contrast to the eigendecomposition approach, no covariance matrix is formed, yet the required matrix of eigenvectors, V, spanning the most expressive subspace of the training data is obtained. Furthermore, we can determine the eigenvalues from the corresponding singular values. By substituting for X_0 in Eq. 12.15, using its SVD in Eq. 12.19, and then comparing to the eigendecomposition of covariance in Eq. 12.16 we see that

$$D = \frac{1}{n-1}S^2. \tag{12.20}$$

The proof of this is given as one of the questions at the end of this chapter. Typically SVD library functions order the singular values from highest to lowest along the leading diagonal allowing a suitable number of eigenvectors to be selected for the subspace, as in Step 5 of the previous subsection.

12.10.3   PCA Testing

Once the above PCA training phase is completed, it is straightforward to implement a simple nearest neighbor face identification scheme, within the reduced k-dimensional space. We can also threshold a suitable distance metric to implement a face verification scheme.

Fig. 12.9 A two-class classification problem in which we wish to reduce the data dimension to one. The standard PCA result is given as the black axis passing through the pooled data mean, and the LDA result is given by the green axis

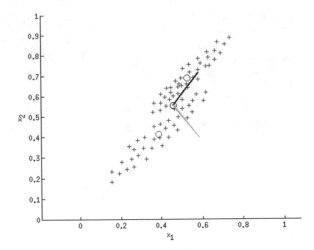

Each test or *probe* face, $\mathbf{x}_p$, must undergo the same transformations as the training faces, namely subtraction of the training data mean and projection into the subspace

$$\tilde{\mathbf{x}}_p^T = (\mathbf{x}_p - \bar{\mathbf{x}})^T \mathbf{V}_k. \qquad (12.21)$$

Euclidean distance and cosine distance are common metrics used to find the nearest neighbor in the gallery. Given some probe face, $\tilde{\mathbf{x}}_p$, and some gallery face, $\tilde{\mathbf{x}}_g$, both of which have been projected into the PCA-derived subspace, the Euclidean distance between them is given as

$$d_e(\tilde{\mathbf{x}}_p, \tilde{\mathbf{x}}_g) = ||\tilde{\mathbf{x}}_p - \tilde{\mathbf{x}}_g|| = \sqrt{(\tilde{\mathbf{x}}_p - \tilde{\mathbf{x}}_g)^T (\tilde{\mathbf{x}}_p - \tilde{\mathbf{x}}_g)} \qquad (12.22)$$

and the cosine distance is given as

$$d_c(\tilde{\mathbf{x}}_p, \tilde{\mathbf{x}}_g) = 1 - \frac{\tilde{\mathbf{x}}_p^T \tilde{\mathbf{x}}_g}{||\tilde{\mathbf{x}}_p|| \cdot ||\tilde{\mathbf{x}}_g||}. \qquad (12.23)$$

In both cases, a small value of the metric (preferably close to zero) indicates a good match. In testing of a PCA-based 3D face recognition system Heseltine et al. [48] found that, usually the Euclidean distance outperformed the cosine distance, but the difference between the two metrics depended on the surface feature type (depth, curvature or gradient) and in a minority of cases, the cosine distance gave a marginally better performance.

The distance metrics described above don't take any account of how the training data is spread along the different axes of the PCA-derived subspace. The *Mahalanobis distance* normalizes the spread along each axis, by dividing by its associated variance to give

$$d_m(\tilde{\mathbf{x}}_p, \tilde{\mathbf{x}}_g) = \sqrt{(\tilde{\mathbf{x}}_p - \tilde{\mathbf{x}}_g)^T \mathbf{D}^{-1}(\tilde{\mathbf{x}}_p - \tilde{\mathbf{x}}_g)}. \qquad (12.24)$$

This expresses the distance in units of standard deviation. Note that the inverse of $\mathbf{D}$ is fast to compute due to its diagonal structure. Equivalently, we can *whiten* the training and test data, by premultiplying all feature vectors by $\mathbf{D}^{-\frac{1}{2}}$, which maps the covariance of the training data to the identity matrix, and then Eq. 12.22 for the Euclidean distance metric can be used in this new space. Similarly, we can use the cosine distance metric in the whitened feature space. Heseltine et al. [48] found that using the information in $\mathbf{D}$ generally improved performance in their PCA-based 3D face recognition system. For many surface features, the cosine distance in the whitened space improved on the standard cosine distance so much that it became the best performing distance metric. This metric is also reported to be the preferred metric in the PCA-based work of Chang et al. [17].

Finally, 3D face recognition systems often display the match between the probe and the gallery. This can be done in terms of the original images, or alternatively the two $m \times 1$ 3D face vectors can be *reconstructed* from their k-dimensional subspace vectors as

$$\mathbf{x} = \mathbf{V}_k \tilde{\mathbf{x}} + \bar{\mathbf{x}}. \qquad (12.25)$$

We summarize a PCA face recognition testing phase as follows:

1. Project the test (probe) face into the PCA-derived subspace using Eq. 12.21
2. For every face in the training data set (gallery), compute a distance metric between the probe and gallery. Select the distance metric with the smallest value as the rank-1 identification match.
3. Optionally display the probe and gallery as reconstructions from the PCA space using Eq. 12.25.

For a verification system, we replace Step 2 with a check against the *claimed identity* gallery capture only, and if the distance metric is below some threshold, then the identity is verified. Performance metrics are then evaluated with reference to the true identities of probe and gallery, which are generally contained with the 3D face scan filenames. Obviously, for large-scale performance evaluations, Step 3 is omitted.

12.10.4 PCA Performance

PCA has been tested on 3D face datasets by many researchers. It is often used as a baseline to measure the performance of other systems (i.e., reported new systems are expected to be better than this.) As mentioned earlier, Chang et al. [16] report the PCA performance of rank-1 recognition on the FRGC dataset as 77.7% and 61.3% for neutral and non-neutral expressions, respectively. Problems with the PCA include (i) a vulnerability to expressions due to the holistic nature of the approach and (ii) the difficulty to get good pose normalization, which is a requirement of the preprocessing stages of the method. The most time-consuming part of online face processing is usually the pose normalization stage, particularly if automatic feature localization and cropping is used as a precursor to this. Once we have sampled the face scan into a standard size feature vector, its projection into 3D face space is a fast operation (linear in the dimension of the feature vector) and, in a nearest neighbor matching scheme, matching time is linear in the size of the gallery.

12.11 LDA-Based 3D Face Recognition

One reason that PCA-based approaches have been popular is that they can operate with only one training example per subject. This is because it does not take account of the per-subject (within-class) distribution of the training data. However, because of this reason, the projection axes computed by PCA may make class discrimination difficult. Indeed, in the worst case for some surface feature type, it could be that the very dimensions that are discarded by PCA are those that provide good discrimination between classes. With the advent of more sophisticated datasets with several (preferably many) 3D scans per subject, more sophisticated subspaces can be used, which attempt to find the linear combination of features that best separates each subject (class). This is the aim of *Linear Discriminant Analysis (LDA)*, while simultaneously performing dimension reduction. Thus, while PCA finds the most *expressive* linear combinations of surface feature map dimensions (in the simplest case, depth map pixels), LDA finds the most *discriminative* linear combinations.

Although 3D face recognition is an inherently multi-class classification problem in a high dimensional space, it is easier to initially look at LDA for a two-class problem in a two-dimensional space and compare it to PCA. Subsequently, we will look at the issues involved with high dimensional feature vectors and we will also generalize to multi-class problems.

12.11.1 Two-Class LDA

Suppose that we have the two-class, 2D problem shown in Fig. 12.9. Intuitively we want to project the data onto a direction for which there is the largest separation of the class means, relative to the within-class scatter in that same projection direction.

A scatter matrix is simply a scaled version of a covariance matrix, and for each set of training scans, $\mathbb{C}_c$, belonging to class $c \in \{1, 2\}$, they are formed as

$$S_c = X_{0c}^T X_{0c}, \tag{12.26}$$

where X_{0c} is a zero-mean data matrix, as described in Sect. 12.10.1 (although it is now class-specific), and n_c is the number of training scans in the set $\mathbb{C}_c$. We note that these scatter matrices are often expressed as a sum of outer products

$$S_c = \sum_{i=1}^{n_c} (\mathbf{x}_i - \bar{\mathbf{x}}_c)(\mathbf{x}_i - \bar{\mathbf{x}}_c)^T, \quad \mathbf{x}_i \in \mathbb{C}_c, \tag{12.27}$$

where $\bar{\mathbf{x}}_c$ is the mean of the feature vectors in class $\mathbb{C}_c$. Given that we have two classes, the *within-class scatter matrix* can be formed as

$$S_W = S_1 + S_2. \tag{12.28}$$

The *between-class scatter* is formed as the outer product of the difference between the two-class means

$$S_B = (\bar{\mathbf{x}}_1 - \bar{\mathbf{x}}_2)(\bar{\mathbf{x}}_1 - \bar{\mathbf{x}}_2)^T. \tag{12.29}$$

Fisher proposed to maximize the ratio of between class scatter to within class scatter relative to the projection direction [28], i.e., solve

$$J(\mathbf{w}) = \max_{\mathbf{w}} \frac{\mathbf{w}^T S_B \mathbf{w}}{\mathbf{w}^T S_W \mathbf{w}} \tag{12.30}$$

with respect to the 2×1 column vector $\mathbf{w}$. This is known as Fisher's criterion. A solution to this optimization can be found by differentiating Eq. 12.30 with respect to $\mathbf{w}$ and equating to zero. This gives

$$S_W^{-1} S_B \mathbf{w} - J\mathbf{w} = \mathbf{0}. \tag{12.31}$$

We recognize this as a generalized eigenvalue-eigenvector problem, where the eigenvector of $S_W^{-1} S_B$ associated with its largest eigenvalue (J) is our desired optimal direction, $\mathbf{w}^*$. (In fact, the other eigenvalue will be zero because the between class scatter matrix, being a simple outer product, can only have rank 1). Figure 12.9 shows the very different results of applying PCA to give the most expressive axis for the pooled data (both classes), and applying LDA which gives a near orthogonal axis, relative to that of PCA, for the best class separation in terms of Fisher's criterion. Once data is projected into the new space, one can use various classifiers and distance metrics, as described earlier.

12.11.2   *LDA with More Than Two Classes*

In order to extend the approach to a multiclass problem ($K > 2$ classes), we could train $\frac{K(K-1)}{2}$ pairwise binary classifiers and classify a test 3D face according to the class that gets most votes. This has the advantage of finding the projection that best separates each pair of distributions, but often results in a very large number of classifiers in 3D face recognition problems, due to the large number of classes (one per subject) often experienced. Alternatively, one can train K *one-versus-all* classifiers where the binary classifiers are of the form *subject X* and *not subject X*. Although this results in fewer classifiers, the computed projections are usually less discriminative.

Rather than applying multiple binary classifiers to a multi-class problem, we can generalize the binary LDA case to multiple classes. This requires the assumption that the number of classes is less than or equal to the dimension of the feature space (i.e., $K \leq m$ where m is the dimension of our depth map space or surface feature map space). For high dimensional feature vectors, such as encountered in 3D face recognition, we also require a very large body of training data to prevent the scatter matrices from being singular. In general, the required number of 3D face scans is not available, but we address this point in the following subsection.

The multi-class LDA procedure is as follows: Firstly, we form the means of each class (i.e., each subject in the 3D face dataset). Using these means, we can compute the scatter matrix for each class using Eq. 12.26 or 12.27. For the within-class scatter matrix, we simply sum the scatter matrices for each individual class

$$\mathbf{S}_W = \sum_{i=1}^{K} \mathbf{S}_i. \tag{12.32}$$

This is an $m \times m$ matrix, where m is the dimension of the feature vector. We form the mean of all training faces, which is the weighted mean of the class means

$$\bar{\mathbf{x}} = \frac{1}{n} \sum_{i=1}^{K} n_i \bar{\mathbf{x}}_i, \tag{12.33}$$

where n_i is the number of training face scans in each class and n is the total number of training scans. The between-class scatter matrix is then formed as

$$\mathbf{S}_B = \sum_{i=1}^{K} n_i (\bar{\mathbf{x}}_i - \bar{\mathbf{x}})(\bar{\mathbf{x}}_i - \bar{\mathbf{x}})^T. \tag{12.34}$$

This scatter matrix is also $m \times m$. Rather than finding a single m-dimensional vector to project onto, we now seek a reduced dimension subspace in which to project our data, so that a feature vector in the new subspace is given as

$$\tilde{\mathbf{x}} = \mathbf{W}^T \mathbf{x}. \tag{12.35}$$

We formulate Fisher's criterion as

$$J(\mathbf{W}) = \max_{\mathbf{W}} \frac{|\mathbf{W}^T \mathbf{S}_B \mathbf{W}|}{|\mathbf{W}^T \mathbf{S}_W \mathbf{W}|}, \tag{12.36}$$

where the vertical lines indicate that the determinant is to be computed. Given that the determinant is equivalent to the product of the eigenvalues, it is a measure of the square of the scattering volume. The projection matrix, $\mathbf{W}$, maps the original m-dimensional space to, at most, $K - 1$ dimensions and so its maximum size is $m \times (K - 1)$. This limit exists because $\mathbf{S_B}$ is the sum of K outer products and matrices formed from outer products are rank 1 or less. Additionally, only $K - 1$ of these are independent due to their dependence on the overall mean $\bar{\mathbf{x}}$ of the pooled training data. As with the two-class case, the optimal projection is found from the generalized eigenvalue-eigenvector problem

$$\mathbf{S}_W^{-1}\mathbf{S}_B\mathbf{W} - J\mathbf{W} = \mathbf{0}, \tag{12.37}$$

and the optimal projection $\mathbf{W}^*$ is the one whose columns are the eigenvectors corresponding to the largest eigenvalues. At most, there will be $K - 1$ nonzero eigenvalues. In practice we select the subset of eigenvectors with eigenvalues above some small threshold, as those close to zero provide little useful discrimination. Note that we can only form the solution in this way if $\mathbf{S}_W$ is non-singular and we discuss this issue in the following subsection.

12.11.3 LDA in High Dimensional 3D Face Spaces

When applying LDA to 3D face recognition, we have to address the problems associated with working in high dimensional spaces. In [49], for example, range maps of 60 pixels wide and 90 high are employed to give feature vectors of length $m = 5400$. Thus the scatter matrices, both $\mathbf{S}_W$ and $\mathbf{S_B}$ are extremely large (dimension $m \times m$) and worse still, due to the typically small number (10–100) of training images per class, they are singular (non invertible). This is referred to as LDA's *small sample size* problem. The more traditional approach to dealing with this is to initially apply PCA as a dimensional reduction stage, before LDA can proceed, as was done in Belhumeur et al.'s [6] seminal work in 2D face recognition and later in 3D face recognition work [40, 47, 49].

If the total number of pooled training vectors is n, then the rank of $\mathbf{S}_W$ is at most $k = n - K$. Thus, PCA can be applied to the data and the k eigenvectors with the largest eigenvalues are selected to give the $m \times k$ projection matrix $\mathbf{V}_k$. This is then reduced to $K - 1$ dimensions using the LDA-derived $k \times (K - 1)$ projection matrix, as described in the previous subsection.

Assuming that 3D faces can be represented as an m-dimensional vector, we can summarize this approach with the following training steps:

1. Determine the projection matrix of a PCA-derived subspace, of dimension $n - K$, as described in Sect. 12.10.
2. Project all of the 3D faces that constitute the training data into this subspace.

3. Form the within-class and between-class scatter matrices of the training data in this reduced dimension PCA-derived subspace, as described in Sect. 12.11.2.
4. Determine the smaller (maximum dimension $K - 1$) LDA-derived subspace of this PCA subspace by solving the generalized eigenvalue-eigenvector problem in the form of Eq. 12.37.
5. Project the training data from the PCA subspace into the LDA subspace.

Then, when we wish to classify a 3D face scan (a probe), it must be projected into the new space. Therefore, we combine the two projections by multiplying them together, and each probe feature vector is mapped directly into the smaller subspace (of maximum dimension $K - 1$) as

$$\tilde{\mathbf{x}}_p = \mathbf{W}^T \mathbf{V}_k^T (\mathbf{x}_p - \bar{\mathbf{x}}). \tag{12.38}$$

Although this approach can often give better results than PCA alone when there is enough training data within each class, a criticism of this two-stage approach is that the initial PCA stage could still discard dimensions that have useful discriminative information. Therefore, more recent approaches to applying LDA to high dimensional approaches have tried to avoid this and these techniques go under various names such as *direct LDA*. It is worth noting, however, that for some of these approaches there have been different viewpoints in the literature (e.g., in [108] and [36]) and we encourage the reader to investigate direct approaches after becoming comfortable with this more established two-stage approach.

12.11.4 LDA Performance

The work of Heseltine et al. [47] shows that LDA can give significantly better performance than PCA when multiple scans of the same subject are available in the training data, although this work predates the wide use of benchmark FRGC 3D face data. As with PCA, the most computationally expensive process is usually pose normalization. Again, projection into a subspace is a fast operation (linear in the dimension of the feature vector) and, in a nearest neighbor matching scheme, matching time is linear in the size of the gallery.

12.12 Normals and Curvature in 3D Face Recognition

When PCA, LDA, and other techniques are applied to 3D face recognition problems, surface features are often extracted. The simplest of these are related to the differential properties of the surface, namely the surface normals and the surface curvature. In *normal maps*, each pixel value is represented by the surface normal. Gokbert et al. [40] used the normal vectors in Cartesian form (n_x, n_y, n_z) and concatenated them to

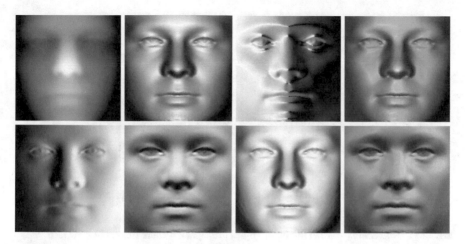

Fig. 12.10 Top row: a range image (Z values) and its normal maps of elevation ϕ and azimuth θ angles. The three (Z, ϕ, θ) values rendered as an RGB image. Bottom row: normal maps of x, y, and z normal components. The three (X, Y, Z) values rendered as an RGB image

perform PCA-based 3D face recognition. Note that this form has redundancy and a more compact way is to use the spherical coordinates, (θ, ϕ), which are the elevation and azimuth angles, respectively. Normals can be computed using the cross product on the mesh data and Max [68] provides an efficient way of doing this over the full mesh. Alternatively, we can fit a planar surface using orthogonal least-squares to the spherical neighborhood of a 3D point or range pixel. This is implemented via SVD and the eigenvector with the smallest eigenvalue is the surface normal. Figure 12.10 shows sample images of normal maps of a 3D face.

Surface normals can capture minor variations in the facial surface, however, being first order derivatives, they are more sensitive to noise compared to depth maps. Often, to overcome this problem, the 3D face is smoothed before computing the normals, or the normals are computed over a larger neighborhood. In either case, the ability of surface normals to capture subtle features is somewhat attenuated.

The surface normals of a shape can be represented by points on a unit sphere. This sphere is often called the Gaussian sphere. By associating weights to the normals based on the surface area with the same normal, an *extended Gaussian image* (EGI) is formed [51]. The EGI cannot differentiate between similar objects at different scales which is not a major problem in 3D face recognition. Another limitation, which can impact face recognition, is that the EGI of only convex objects is unique and many non-convex objects can have the same EGI. To work around this limitation, Lee and Milios [62] represent only the convex regions of the face by EGI and use a graph matching algorithm for face recognition.

Curvature-based measures, which are related to second-order derivatives of the raw depth measurements, have also been used to extract features from 3D face images and these measures are pose invariant. Several representations are prominent in this context, most of which are based on the principal curvatures of a point on a three-

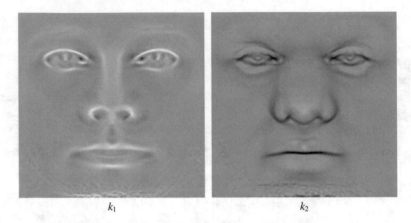

k_1 k_2

Fig. 12.11 Maximum (left) and minimum (right) principal curvature images of a 3D face

dimensional surface. To understand principal curvatures, imagine the normal on a surface and an infinite set of planes (a *pencil of planes*) each of which contains this normal. Each of these planes intersects the surface in a plane curve and the principal curvatures are defined as the maximum curvature, κ_1, and minimum curvature, κ_2, of this infinite set of plane curves. The directions that correspond to maximum and minimum curvatures are always perpendicular and are called the principal directions of the surface. Principal curvatures are in fact the eigenvalues of the *Weingarten matrix*, which is a 2×2 matrix containing the parameters of a quadratic local surface patch, fitted in a local plane that is aligned to the surface tangent plane. Figure 12.11 shows images of the maximum and minimum curvatures of a 3D face. Tanaka et al. [98] constructed a variant of the EGI by mapping the principal curvatures and their directions onto two unit spheres representing ridges and valleys, respectively. Similarity between faces was calculated by Fisher's spherical correlation [33] of their EGIs.

Gaussian curvature, K, is defined as the product of these principal curvatures, while *mean curvature*, H, is defined as the average, i.e.,

$$K = \kappa_1 \kappa_2, \quad H = \frac{\kappa_1 + \kappa_2}{2}. \tag{12.39}$$

Both of these are invariant to rigid transformations (and hence pose), but only Gaussian curvature is invariant to the surface bending that may occur during changes of facial expression. Lee and Shim [63] approximated 3×3 windows of the range image by quadratic patches and calculated the minimum, maximum, and Gaussian curvatures. Using thresholds, edge maps were extracted from these curvatures and a depth weighted Hausdorff distance was used to calculate the similarity between faces. Using depth values as weights, in fact, combines the range image with the curvatures giving it more discriminating power. The advantages of combining depth with curvature for face recognition have been known since the early 90's [41].

The *shape index* was proposed by Koenderink and van Doorn [60] as a surface shape descriptor. It is based on both principal curvatures and derived as

$$s = \frac{2}{\pi} \arctan \left(\frac{\kappa_2 + \kappa_1}{\kappa_2 - \kappa_1} \right) \quad (-1 \leq s \leq +1). \qquad (12.40)$$

It can be thought of a polar description of shape in the $\kappa_1 - \kappa_2$ plane, where different values distinguish between caps, cups, ridges, valleys, and saddle points. Since a ratio of curvatures is used in Eq. 12.40, the size of the curvature is factored out and hence the descriptor is scale invariant. Koenderink and van Doorn combine the principal curvatures in a different measure to measure the magnitude of the curvature, which they called *curvedness*, c, where $c = \sqrt{\frac{\kappa_1^2 + \kappa_2^2}{2}}$. Since principal curvatures are pose invariant, the shape index is also pose invariant. Lu et al. [66] used the shape index to find a rough estimate of registration which was then refined with a variant of the ICP algorithm [7]. In their earlier work, they also used the shape index map of the registered faces for recognition along with the texture and the Cartesian coordinates of the 3D face. This is an example where curvatures are combined with the point cloud, instead of the range image, for face recognition. Thus, we can conclude that curvatures offer viewpoint invariant and localized features that are useful for face alignment and matching. Moreover, face recognition performance generally improves when curvature-based features are combined with the range image or point cloud.

Samir et al. [87] represented a 3D face with continuous facial curves which were extracted using a depth function. We can think of these curves as the intersection of the 3D face with planes orthogonal to the camera and at different depths. Face recognition was performed by matching their corresponding facial curves using geodesic distance criteria [59]. Although, the facial curves of a face change with changes in the curvature of different identities, they are not completely invariant to pose [87]. Figure 12.12 shows a sample 3D face with facial curves.

12.12.1 Computing Curvature on a 3D Face Scan

Here we present a standard technique for computing curvatures on a 3D face scan. We assume that we start with a preprocessed mesh, which has spikes filtered and holes filled. Then, for each surface point, we implement the following procedure:

1. Find the neighbors within a local neighborhood, the neighbor set includes the point itself. The size of this neighborhood is a trade-off that depends on the scan resolution and the noise level. We can use connectivity information in the mesh or the structure in a range image to compute neighborhoods quickly. Otherwise, some form of data structuring of a point cloud is required to do a fast cuboidal region search, usually refined to a spherical region. Typically k-d trees and octrees are employed and standard implementations of these can be found online.

Fig. 12.12 Facial curves
mapped on the range image
of a face [87]. These are the
intersection of the 3D face
with planes orthogonal to the
camera, at different depths

2. Subtract the mean of the point cloud from all points in the set and then use eigendecomposition, via SVD, to fit a plane to this zero-mean point set. The eigenvector with the smallest eigenvalue is the estimated surface normal. The other two eigenvectors lie in the estimated tangent plane and can be used as a local basis.
3. Project all neighbors into this local basis. (This is the same procedure as was outlined for a full face scan in Sect. 12.10.1).
4. Recenter the data on the surface point.
5. Using least-squares fitting, fit a local quadratic surface patch, $z = \frac{A}{2}x^2 + Bxy + \frac{C}{2}y^2$, where $[x, y, z]^T$ are the neighboring points expressed in the recentered local basis and $[A, B, C]^T$ are the surface parameters to be found by least-squares.
6. Form the Weingarten matrix as

$$W = \begin{pmatrix} A & B \\ B & C \end{pmatrix}. \tag{12.41}$$

7. Determine the principal curvatures, κ_1, κ_2 as the eigenvalues of the Weingarten matrix.
8. Form the Gaussian curvature, mean curvature, and shape index, as required, using Eqs. 12.39 and 12.40

Of course, there are many variants of this approach. For example, in Step 2, it is faster to compute normals using cross products within Max's method [68] rather than using SVD, in which case we would use an arbitrary local basis to do the quadratic surface fit.

This section concludes the generic tutorial part of the chapter, we now go on to outline a selection of more specific advanced approaches.

12.13   A Selection of Classical Techniques in 3D Face Recognition

In this section, we present a selection of five classical (i.e., not deep learning) techniques in the field of 3D face recognition published in the 2010s decade. These are presented in chronological order and include: (i) Fusion of multiple region classifiers [94]; (ii) Iterative closest normal points [72]; (iii) Use of radial curve features [27]; (iv) A registration-free approach using keypoints [64] and (v) An approach that employs a Genetic Algorithm to select nasal patches [29]. We describe more recent deep learning approaches that use neural networks later, in Sect. 12.14.

12.13.1   Fusion of Multiple Region Classifiers

Spreeuwers [94] presented a method that uses registration to an intrinsic coordinate system and fusion of multiple region classifiers. The intrinsic coordinate system requires an origin and three angles to be defined. The former is defined by the tip of the nose and the latter uses two angles defined by the bilateral (sagittal) symmetry plane, and a third is either defined by the slope of the bridge of the nose or the line between the nasion and subnasale (both are used and the results are fused). These features are chosen for intrinsic registration, as they are relatively stable under facial expression. Standard depth images are generated from both registration methods.

A set of 30 overlapping regions are defined, as shown in Fig. 12.13, where the white area is the included part of the depth map. Ideally, independence of all regions is desired, but this would create smaller lower accuracy classification regions, and so a certain amount of overlap is accepted in the manual region specification. Regions are designed on the basis of their anticipated stability. For example, hair and spectacles often cause problems, as does the lower part of the face due to expression variation.

A PCA-LDA likelihood ratio classifier is employed for matching of individual regions to gallery subjects, and the scores from each individual region are fused into a single score, using simple majority voting, in order to make a match decision. Excellent rank-1 identification performance of 99% was reported for the *first versus all* test over the FRGC v2 dataset. A verification rate of 94.6% at 0.1% FAR was reported for the *all versus all* verification test. Later, the author introduced a set of optimisations to the method [95] to upgrade this performance figure significantly to 99.3%, with the identification rate increasing to 99.4%.

Fig. 12.13 Regions used in
the fusion of multiple region
classifiers. Figure courtesy
of [94]

12.13.2   *Iterative Closest Normal Points*

Given an algorithm that can find high quality 3D correspondences between facial 3D
images, Mohammadzade and Hatzinakos [72] show that Linear Discriminant Analysis (LDA) can provide excellent recognition results with good robustness to facial
expressions. In effect, LDA can find subject-specific expression-invariant regions of
the face.

There are several standard preprocessing steps in the approach, such as nose detection, denoising, and pose alignment. However, the key contribution in this approach
is to find good correspondences across the training dataset of faces. This takes inspiration from the ICP algorithm [7] and is called the Iterative Closest Normal Points
(ICNP) algorithm. One 3D image is randomly selected to be the template (source)
mesh, to be deformed to all other (target) meshes in the dataset. The aim of doing
this is to have correspondences across the whole dataset to allow PCA and LDA to
be applied. Correspondences are determined, as follows:

1. For every point in the source, find the closest point in the target.
2. The closest target point for some source point defines a search window on the
   target mesh, over which to search for the closest normal ([72] employs a 10 mm
   by 10 mm search window on a depth map).
3. The vectors that map source points to target points thus form a noisy 3D motion
   field, which can be filtered to give a smooth motion field. This is done by applying
   a 2D Wiener filter over the depth map, with the filter using a support region of
   20 mm by 20 mm. Note that motion vectors at the boundary of the face cannot be
   filtered with such a window, and so boundary motion is interpolated using nearest
   neighbors.

4. The displacement vectors of the motion field can then be added to their corresponding reference points in the template to find approximate correspondences, and clearly these may not lie on the target surface, so another nearest point search is required to establish correspondences.
5. Correspondences are used to update the alignment and SVD can be used, as with standard ICP.

The steps above are repeated until the magnitude of the rotation in the final rigid alignment step falls below some threshold.

The FRGC ROC III verification experiment was included in the evaluations, employing LDA (preceded by PCA for dimension reduction) for multiple captures of each subject in the gallery, thus minimizing the ratio of within-class variance to between class variance along the optimal projection direction. This was done for both point coordinates and surface normals and it was found that the use of normals significantly outperformed the use of point coordinates. At a FAR of 0.1% the method achieves a 99.9% verification rate for neutral expressions, when four or more scans are employed per gallery subject. For probes with expressions, the method achieves a 98.5% verification rate, but requires six or more scans per gallery subject to achieve this (with four gallery scans a 96.2% verification rate was achievable).

12.13.3   3D Face Recognition Using Radial Curves

Drira et al. [27] propose a 3D face recognition solution that is robust to expressions and occlusions using a local representation consisting of radial curves emanating from the detected nose tip. Curves are chosen as local features due to the efficiency of deformable curve matching—the curves being deformed being dependent on expression. The fact that the curves are radial permits a selection of them to represent regional shapes. (Other types of curves have been employed, such as isoradius contours, that orbit the nose tip at a set of predefined radii [80, 81].)

Radial curves are extracted by intersecting a pencil of planes, with the pencil axis parallel to the Z (depth) axis and intersecting the nose tip. A *quality filter* heuristic is used to filter occluded curves, which should have one continuous piece and should have a length greater than some threshold (70 mm). An elastic shape analysis framework is presented for analyzing the filtered radial curves. When both corresponding radial curves from a pair of 3D images pass the quality filter, they are matched using an elastic distance computation and an average distance is computed over all matching pairs. Evaluation of the FRGC v2 dataset gives a rank-1 recognition performance of 97%. Additionally, in the ROC III verification test for FRGC v2, 97% is achieved.

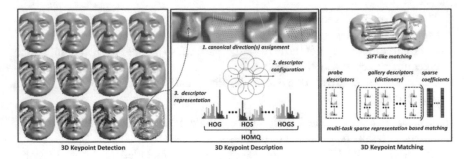

Fig. 12.14 Overview of a registration-free approach using matching of 3D keypoint descriptors. Figure courtesy of [64]

12.13.4 A Registration-free Approach Using Matching of 3D Keypoint Descriptors

Li et al. [64] present a registration-free approach based on keypoints and an overview of the approach is shown in Fig. 12.14. Three stages are employed: keypoint detection, keypoint description, and keypoint matching. Keypoint detection uses the standard approach of the two principal curvatures, although saliency of keypoints is incorporated using a scale-space approach, extracted using a set of Gaussian filters over the face mesh. Three keypoint descriptors are employed and evaluated, namely: (i) Histogram of Gradient (HOG), (ii) Histogram of Shape index (HOS), and (iii) Histogram of Gradient of Shape index (HOGS). Additionally, all three are combined into a single descriptor, which is named as a Histogram of Multiple surface differential Quantities (HOMQ). This descriptor is constructed in a similar spirit to SIFT-like descriptors, with a canonical direction for the descriptor being computed and eight local region descriptor histograms being concatenated onto the central local region. This is performed in a consistent rotational (spin) direction starting from that canonical direction, as illustrated in the quasi-daisy spatial configuration shown in Fig. 12.14 (center). To enable matching, a descriptor dictionary is constructed that concatenates all of the keypoint descriptors for all of the subjects in the gallery. The idea is then to express the descriptors of some probe as a reconstruction using a sparse selection of the dictionary descriptors. Images from the same person share a large set of keypoints with similar geometric characteristics and so, for any descriptor of the probe face, there is a high probability of selecting the descriptors of the matching gallery face. This approach is more robust to occlusions than the much simpler approach of just counting the number of matching descriptors.

The primary evaluation is performed on the Bosphorus dataset. This has an advantage over the FRGC dataset in the sense that it can test the system's robustness to occlusions. Rank-1 recognition rates of 96.56%, 98.82%, 91.14%, and 99.21% are achieved on the entire database, and the expression, pose, and occlusion subsets, respectively. The system is also evaluated on FRGC v2 using a first versus all protocol and a 96.3% rank-1 identification rate is achieved.

12.13.5   GA-based Nasal Patch Selection for Expression-Robustness

The nasal region is a relatively rigid part of the face and so has been targeted for expression-robust algorithms, with a recent approach by Emambakhsh and Evans [29]. The method generates an accurate 7-point landmarking of the nasal region. This is employed in an interpolation scheme to upscale the number of landmarks by around a factor of 10. (In Morphometrics, these interpolated surface points are termed *semi-landmarks*.) The augmented set of landmarks define sampling points within the nasal region which form the centers of small (7 mm radius) spherical cropping regions. These nasal patches are then candidate depth map parts over which to generate descriptive features. Features vectors are constructed as histograms of the normal vectors of the Gabor-filtered depth map, see [29] for full details. In training, there is a feature selection process, based on a Genetic Algorithm, that aims to select a set of nasal patches and Gabor filter scales that are robust against facial expressions. The Mahalanobis cosine distance is used to check the robustness of the match between neutral and non-neutral expressions.

Emambakhsh and Evans [29] present a complex set of processes in their paper. Its practical, multi-stage approach is highly heuristic and, in that sense, it is in sharp contrast to generic deep learning approaches that are trained end-to-end. Nevertheless, it gives good results on the FRGC v2.0 dataset. In the identification scenario, they achieved a Rank-1 Recognition Rate (R1RR) of 97.9%, with 98.45% and 98.5% for neutral and non-neutral probes, respectively. In verification, they achieved a 2.4% Equal Error Rate (EER) and a True Positive Rate (TPR) of 93.5% at a 0.1%FAR in the ROC III experiment.

12.14   Deep Learning Approaches to 3D Face Recognition

In recent years, deep learning has proved to provide state-of-the-art solutions to many problems in image classification, speech recognition, and natural language processing. Many researchers date the modern deep learning revolution back to 2012 when the AlexNet paper [61] on image classification was published. Essentially, application of this powerful technology involves the formulation of optimisation problems that have well-behaved differentials, thus enabling gradient descent to function well. In contrast to classical approaches that use human-designed (handcrafted) features, deep learning approaches learn the best hierarchical set of features that optimizes classification performance, and so is a form of representation learning. In many domains, given sufficient (possibly augmented) training data, deep learning outperforms classical systems with handcrafted features. This is because handcrafted features are almost always suboptimal for the classification task. Convolutional Neural Networks (CNNs) have proved to be particularly successful in 2D image classification tasks, and they are well-suited to the grid-like structure of the array of pixels

in such images. It is possible to represent 3D data in grid-like structures; in particular voxel representations or view-specific depth map representations, although there
are disadvantages with both of these approaches. For example, many voxels can be
empty, leading to inefficiency.

The size of 3D face datasets tends to be much smaller than 2D face datasets and
there are many more 2D face images than 3D that can be harvested from the web.
This has allowed deep Convolutional Neural Networks (CNNs) to be readily trained
for 2D face recognition, but often there is insufficient data for 3D network training. In
the following, we overview two deep learning approaches to 3D face recognition, the
first uses transfer learning from the 2D to the 3D domain and the second employs 3D
face data augmentation via model-based 3D face synthesis and 3D face interpolation.

12.14.1 Deep 3D Face Identification by Transfer Learning

As mentioned, large volume 2D face image data is much more readily available
to train deep networks for 2D face recognition. Recently, Kim et al. [58] adapted
the publicly available VGG 2D face recognition solution [77] to 3D using transfer
learning. A process of 3D data augmentation adds both pose variations and expression
variations to existing data. This requires fitting a 3D Morphable Model (3DMM) to
the data, and the Basel Face Model [79] is employed. Small random pose variations
are straightforward to add after the model has been fitted to the data. Expressions can
then be added using the FaceWarehouse [14] 3D facial expression database. Finally,
the model with expression is orthogonally projected back into a depth map. Missing
or occluded parts are simulated by placing eight 18 by 18 pixel patches at random
positions on each depth map, thus preventing overfitting to specific regions of the
face.

In the transfer learning process, the last fully connected layer (FC8) of the VGG
network is replaced with a new fully connected layer and a softmax layer with
the size of the number of subjects in the training data. The new layer is randomly
initialized and the learning rate of the new layer is an order of magnitude higher
than the transferred layers (0.01 vs. 0.001). The FRGC and CASIA datasets are
used for training and the system is tested on Bosphorus, BU3DFE, and 3D-TEC
datasets. State-of-the-art rank-1 identification accuracies are obtained for Bosphorus
and 3D-TEC (case I) with scores of 99.2% and 94.8%, respectively.

Our commentary on this work is that its strength is in the 3D data augmentation. However, one could argue that the optimal CNN features in 3D facial images
may be quite different from 2D, as 3D depth maps appear much smoother than 2D
facial images, i.e., the spatial frequencies are situated in lower frequency bands. Furthermore, recent discussion in the deep learning community suggests that unlearnt
random weights in CNNs can provide quite good performance as feature extractors,
as long as the classifying back end of the network is well trained. Therefore, using
networks trained on 2D images to perform 3D face recognition is likely to be sub-

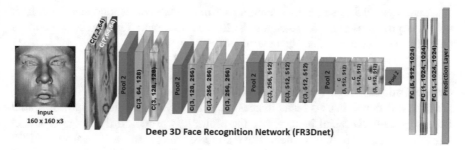

Fig. 12.15 The Fr3dNET deep 3D face recognition network. Figure courtesy of [38]

optimal as 3D data has its own peculiarities defined by the underlying shape and geometry.

12.14.2 Large-scale 3D Face Recognition, Trained from Scratch

Gilani and Mian [38] propose the first deep CNN model designed specifically for 3D face recognition. The publicly available Fr3dNET network, shown in Fig. 12.15 is trained from scratch on over 3 Million 3D facial images, with over 100 K distinct identities.

Due to the lack of availability of large-scale 3D images, data augmentation is a key enabling process to train a deep 3D face recognition network. Real 3D face images of 1785 individuals are used in the first stage. Pairs of individuals are selected that have a large shape difference, in terms of the bending energy required to deform one to the other. Just over 90.1 K pairings are used from the possible 499.5 K. New images are then generated that are in the span of the selected pair, which requires that the shapes are in correspondence and the approach of Gilani et al. [39] is employed. The advantage of this approach over sampling from a 3D Morphable Model, such as the Basel Face Model [79], is that more high frequency detail is retained.

In the second stage, commercial software[4] is employed that generates densely corresponded faces of 300 identities with varying facial shapes, each in four different expressions with three intensity levels. In this stage, faces are paired that are similar (i.e., small bending energy mapping), motivated by the fact that similar faces must be generated to enable a 3D face recognition system to be trained to a high real-world accuracy. Using linear spans of the pairings, 9950 new identities are generated.

Finally, pose variations are simulated in each 3D scan by deploying 15 synthetic cameras on a hemisphere in front of the 3D face, with self-occluded points being removed by applying a hidden point removal algorithm. The final result is over 3 million 3D images of over 100 K identities, as follows: 1785 identities, with a single

---

[4]Singular Inversions, Facegen Modeller, www.facegen.com.

expression and 15 poses, 90.1 K identities from dense correspondence modeling, with 2 expressions and 15 poses, and 8120 identities with 12 expressions and 15 poses from the synthetic face generation process.

Depth maps are created with the image centered on the detected nose tip, and surface normals are also computed as elevation and azimuth angles to give a 3-channel gridded input to a CNN. The CNN architecture is based on the VGG network [77], but it is noted that 3D facial images are generally of significantly lower spatial frequency than 2D facial images, and therefore, it is proposed that a larger kernel size (7×7) is used for CNN filters. The feature vectors of length 1024 from the FC7 layer are employed for face recognition using the cosine distance between probe and gallery faces.

The authors also propose a protocol for merging public 3D face datasets and they call this dataset *LS3DFace* for 3D recognition system testing. The dataset has 1853 identities with 31860 images, and samples data from 10 existing 3D face datasets, which are the first 10 in Table 12.1. The authors achieve an end-to-end rank-1 recognition rate of 98.74% on 27 K of these probes, significantly outperforming other face recognition techniques trained and tested using the same datasets.

12.15 Research Challenges

After more than two decades of extensive research in the area of 3D face recognition, new representations, new techniques, and new deep learning architectures that can be applied to this problem are continually being released in the literature. A number of challenges still remain to be surmounted.

Facial expressions remain a challenge as existing techniques often lose important information in the process of removing facial expressions or extracting expression-invariant features. Although small to medium pose variations can be handled by current 3D face recognition systems, large pose variations often cannot, due to significant self-occlusion. In systems that employ pose normalization, this will affect the accuracy of pose correction and, for any recognition system, it will result in large areas of missing data. For head yaw rotations, this may be mitigated by the fact that the symmetrical face contains redundant information for discrimination. Additional problems with capturing 3D data from a single viewpoint include noise at the edges of the scan and the inability to reliably define local regions (e.g., for local surface feature extraction), because these become eroded if they are positioned near the edges of the scan. Dark and specular regions of the face, such as the eyes, offer further challenges to the acquisition and subsequent preprocessing steps.

In addition to sensor technology improving, we expect to see improved 3D face datasets, with larger numbers of subjects and larger number of captures per subject, covering a very wide range of pose variation, expression variation, and occlusions caused by hair, hands, and common accessories (e.g., spectacles, hats, scarves, and phone). We expect to see publicly available datasets that start to combine pose variation, expression variation, and occlusion thus providing an even greater challenge to 3D face recognition algorithms.

Passive techniques are advancing rapidly, for example, some approaches may no longer explicitly reconstruct the facial surface but directly extract features from multiview stereo images. Of course, with a much increased input data size associated with high resolution images, an increase in computational power is required. 3D video cameras are also appearing in the market opening up yet another dimension for video-based 3D face recognition, known as 4D face recognition. Here dynamic facial expression change may be a useful biometric cue. Outdoor recognition is particularly challenging due to the highly variable interference of sunlight. Additionally, recognition at larger distances is particularly challenging and may require time-of-flight imaging mechanisms rather than those that rely on triangulation over a relatively small baseline.

12.16 Concluding Remarks

In this chapter, we presented the basic concepts behind 3D face recognition algorithms. In particular, we looked at the individual stages in a typical 3D face scan processing pipeline that takes raw face scans and is able to make verification or identification decisions. We presented a wide range of literature relating to all of these stages. We explained several well-established 3D face recognition techniques (ICP, PCA, and LDA) with a more tutorial approach and clear implementation steps in order to familiarize the reader with the most well-established techniques in 3D face recognition, presented in a tutorial style. We also presented a selection of five classical advanced methods published in the last decade that have shown promising recognition performance on benchmark datasets, and two recent approaches that employ deep learning.

12.17 Further Reading

The interested reader is encouraged to refer to the original publications of the methods described in this chapter, and their references, for more details concerning the algorithms discussed here.

There are several existing 3D face recognition surveys which give a good overview of the field, for example, a recent by Zhou and Xiao [110]. A survey of local feature methods for 3D face recognition is given by Soltanpour et al. [93] and a comprehensive performance evaluation of 3D local feature descriptors is given by Guo et al. [44]. No doubt further surveys on 3D and 3D/2D face recognition will be published periodically in the future.

In addition, the website www.face-rec.org [42] provides a range of information on all common face recognition modalities. Several of the chapters in this book are highly useful to the 3D face recognition researcher, particularly those that include detailed discussions on 3D image acquisition, surface representations, 3D features, shape registration, and shape matching. For good general texts on pattern recognition and machine learning, we recommend the texts of Duda et al. [28] and Bishop [8].

12.18 Questions

1. What advantages can 3D face recognition systems have over standard 2D face recognition systems?
2. How can a 3D sensor be used such that the 3D shape information that it generates aids 2D face recognition? Discuss this with respect to the probe images being 3D and the gallery 2D and vice-versa.
3. What are the main advantages and disadvantages of feature-based 3D face recognition approaches when compared to holistic approaches?
4. Outline the main processing stages of a classical (nonneural) 3D face recognition system and give a brief description of the primary function of each stage. Indicate the circumstances under which some of the stages may be omitted.
5. Briefly outline the main steps of the ICP algorithm and describe its advantages and limitations in the context of 3D face recognition.
6. Describe the steps of the Iterative Closest Normal Point (ICNP) algorithm [72] and contrast it with the ICP approach.
7. Provide a short proof of the relationship between eigenvalues and singular values given in Eq. 12.20.
8. Compare and contrast PCA and LDA in the context of 3D face recognition.
9. Why has deep learning been applied to 2D face recognition much earlier and more extensively than 3D face recognition?

12.19 Exercises

In order to do these exercises, you will need access to the FRGC v2 3D face dataset.

1. Build (or download) some utilities to load and display the 3D face scans stored in the ABS format files of the FRGC dataset.
2. Implement the cropping, spike removal, and hole filling preprocessing steps as described in Sect. 12.8. Apply them to a small selection of scans in the FRGC v2 data and check that they operate as expected.
3. Implement an ICP-based face verification system, as described in Sect. 12.9 and use the preprocessed scans as input.
4. Implement a PCA-based 3D face recognition system, as described in Sect. 12.10, using raw depth data only and compare your results with the ICP-based system.

5. Use a facial mask to only include the upper half of the 3D face scan in training and testing data. Rerun your experimentations for ICP and PCA and compare them with your previous results, particularly with a view to those scans that have non-neutral facial expressions.
6. Implement the Iterative Closest Normal Point (ICNP) algorithm [72] and test its verification performance on the FRGC dataset under the ROC III protocol [82].

References

1. Achermann, B., Jiang, X., Bunke, H.: Face recognition using range images. In: Proceedings of International Conference on Virtual Systems and MultiMedia VSMM '97 (Cat. No.97TB100182), pp. 129–136 (1997)
2. Adini, Y., Moses, Y., Ullman, S.: Face recognition: the problem of compensating for changes in illumination direction. IEEE Trans. Pattern Anal. Mach. Intell. 19(7), 721–732 (1997)
3. Al-Osaimi, F., Bennamoun, M., Mian, A.: Integration of local and global geometrical cues for 3D face recognition. Pattern Recognit. 41(3), 1030–1040 (2008)
4. Angel, E.: Interactive Computer Graphics: A Top-Down Approach Using OpenGL, 5th edn. Addison-Wesley Publishing Company, Reading (2008)
5. Arun, K.S., Huang, T.S., Blostein, S.D.: Least-squares fitting of two 3D point sets. IEEE Trans. Pattern Anal. Mach. Intell. 9(5), 698–700 (1987)
6. Belhumeur, P.N., Hespanha, J.P., Kriegman, D.J.: Eigenfaces vs. fisherfaces: recognition using class specific linear projection. IEEE Trans. Pattern Anal. Mach. Intell. 19(7), 711–720 (1997)
7. Besl, P.J., McKay, N.D.: A method for registration of 3D shapes. IEEE Trans. Pattern Anal. Mach. Intell. 14(2), 239–256 (1992)
8. Bishop, C.M.: Pattern Recognition and Machine Learning (Information Science and Statistics). Springer, Berlin (2006)
9. Blanz, V., Scherbaum, K., Seidel, H.: Fitting a morphable model to 3D scans of faces. In: Proceedings of 2007 IEEE 11th International Conference on Computer Vision, pp. 1–8 (2007)
10. Blanz, V., Vetter, T.: A morphable model for the synthesis of 3D faces. In: Proceedings of the 26th Annual Conference on Computer Graphics and Interactive Techniques, pp. 187–194. ACM Press/Addison-Wesley Publishing Co., USA (1999)
11. Bledsoe, W.W.: The model method in facial recognition, technical report pri 15. Technical Report, Panoramic Research, Inc. Palo Alto, California, USA (1964)
12. Bogazici University: The Bosphorus 3D face database. http://bosphorus.ee.boun.edu.tr/. Accessed 21 Jan 2020
13. Bronstein, A.M., Bronstein, M.M., Kimmel, R.: Three-dimensional face recognition. Int. J. Comput. Vis. 64(1), 5–30 (2005)
14. Cao, C., Weng, Y., Zhou, S., Tong, Y., Zhou, K.: Facewarehouse: a 3D facial expression database for visual computing. IEEE Trans. Vis. Comput. Graph. 20(3), 413–425 (2014)
15. Chang, J.K., Bowyer, K., Flynn, P.: Face recognition using 2D and 3D facial data. In: Proceedings of Multimodal User Authentication Workshop, pp. 25–32 (2004)
16. Chang, K.I., Bowyer, K.W., Flynn, P.J.: Multiple nose region matching for 3D face recognition under varying facial expression. IEEE Trans. Pattern Anal. Mach. Intell. 28(10), 1695–1700 (2006)
17. Chang, K.I., Bowyer, K.W., Flynn, P.J.: An evaluation of multimodal 2D+3D face biometrics. IEEE Trans. Pattern Anal. Mach. Intell. 27(4), 619–624 (2005)
18. Chua, C.-S., Han, F., Ho, Y.-K.: 3D human face recognition using point signature. In: Proceedings Fourth IEEE International Conference on Automatic Face and Gesture Recognition, pp. 233–238 (2000)

19. Chua, C.S., Jarvis, R.: Point signatures: a new representation for 3D object recognition. Int. J. Comput. Vis. **25**(1), 63–85 (1997)
20. Colombo, A., Cusano, C., Schettini, R.: UMB-DB: A database of partially occluded 3D faces. In: Proceedings of 2011 IEEE International Conference on Computer Vision Workshops (ICCV Workshops), pp. 2113–2119 (2011)
21. Colombo, A., Cusano, C., Schettini, R.: 3D face detection using curvature analysis. Pattern Recognit. **39**(3), 444–455 (2006)
22. Creusot, C., Pears, N.E., Austin, J.: 3D face landmark labelling. In: Proceedings of 1st ACM workshop on 3D object retrieval, pp. 27–32 (2010)
23. Creusot, C., Pears, N., Austin, J.: Automatic keypoint detection on 3D faces using a dictionary of local shapes. In: Proceedings of 2011 International Conference on 3D Imaging, Modeling, Processing, Visualization and Transmission, pp. 204–211 (2011)
24. Creusot, C.: Automatic landmarking for non-cooperative 3D face recognition. Ph.D. Thesis, Department of Computer Science, University of York, UK (2011)
25. Creusot, C., Pears, N., Austin, J.: A machine-learning approach to keypoint detection and landmarking on 3D meshes. Int. J. Comput. Vis. **102**(1), 146–179 (2013)
26. Deng, J., Roussos, A., Chrysos, G., Ververas, E., Kotsia, I., Shen, J., Zafeiriou, S.: The menpo benchmark for multi-pose 2D and 3D facial landmark localisation and tracking. Int. J. Comput. Vis. 1–26 (2018)
27. Drira, H., Ben Amor, B., Srivastava, A., Daoudi, M., Slama, R.: 3D face recognition under expressions, occlusions, and pose variations. IEEE Trans. Pattern Anal. Mach. Intell. **35**(9), 2270–2283 (2013)
28. Duda, R.O., Hart, P.E., Stork, D.G.: Pattern Classification, 2nd edn. Wiley-Interscience, New York (2001)
29. Emambakhsh, M., Evans, A.: Nasal patches and curves for expression-robust 3D face recognition. IEEE Trans. Pattern Anal. Mach. Intell. **39**(5), 995–1007 (2017)
30. Faltemier, T.C., Bowyer, K.W., Flynn, P.J.: Using a multi-instance enrollment representation to improve 3D face recognition. In: Proceedings of 2007 First IEEE International Conference on Biometrics: Theory, Applications, and Systems, pp. 1–6 (2007)
31. Faltemier, T.C., Bowyer, K.W., Flynn, P.J.: A region ensemble for 3D face recognition. IEEE Trans. Inf. Forensics Secur. **3**(1), 62–73 (2008)
32. Farkas, L.G.: Anthropometry of the Head and Face. Raven Press, New York (1994)
33. Fisher, N.I., Lee, A.J.: Correlation coefficients for random variables on a unit sphere or hypersphere. Biometrika **73**(1), 159–164 (1986)
34. Fitzgibbon, A.: Robust registration of 2D and 3D point sets. Image Vis. Comput. **21**, 1145–1153 (2002)
35. Fleishman, S., Drori, I., Cohen-Or, D.: Bilateral mesh denoising. ACM Trans. Graph. **22**(3), 950–953 (2003)
36. Gao, H., Davis, J.W.: Why direct lda is not equivalent to lda. Pattern Recognit. **39**(5), 1002–1006 (2006)
37. Garland, M., Heckbert, P.: Surface simplification using quadric error metrics. In: Proceedings of the ACM SIGGRAPH Conference on Computer Graphics (1997)
38. Gilani, S.Z., Mian, A.: Learning from millions of 3D scans for large-scale 3D face recognition. In: Proceedings of International Conference Computer Vision and Pattern Recognition (2018)
39. Gilani, S.Z., Mian, A., Shafait, F., Reid, I.: Dense 3D face correspondence. IEEE Trans. Pattern Anal. Mach. Intell. **40**(7), 1584–1598 (2018)
40. Gökberk, B., İrfanoğlu, M.O., Akarun, L.: 3D shape-based face representation and feature extraction for face recognition. Image Vis. Comput. **24**(8), 857–869 (2006)
41. Gordon, G.G.: Face recognition based on depth and curvature features. In: Proceedings 1992 IEEE Computer Society Conference on Computer Vision and Pattern Recognition, pp. 808–810 (1992)
42. Grgic, M., Delac, K.: Face recognition homepage. http://www.face-rec.org. Accessed 21 Jan 2020

43. Günther, M., Cruz, S., Rudd, E.M., Boult, T.E.: Toward open-set face recognition. In: Proceedings of IEEE Conference on Computer Vision and Pattern Recognition Workshops (CVPRw), pp. 573–582 (2017)
44. Guo, Y., Bennamoun, M., Sohel, F., Lu, M., Wan, J., Kwok, N.M.: A comprehensive performance evaluation of 3D local feature descriptors. Int. J. Comput. Vis. **116**(1), 66–89 (2016)
45. Gupta, S., Markey, M.K., Bovik, A.C.: Anthropometric 3D face recognition. Int. J. Comput. Vis. **90**(3), 331–349 (2010)
46. Heckbert, P., Garl, M.: Survey of polygonal surface simplification algorithms. In: SIGGRAPH, Course Notes: Multiresolution Surface Modeling (1997)
47. Heseltine, T., Pears, N.E., Austin, J.: Three-dimensional face recognition: a fishersurface approach. In: Proceedings of the International Conference Image Analysis and Recognition, pp. 684–691 (2004)
48. Heseltine, T., Pears, N.E., Austin, J.: Three-dimensional face recognition: an eigensurface approach. In: Proceedings of the IEEE International Conference Image Processing, Singapore, 2004 (ICIP'04), pp. 1421–1424 (2004)
49. Heseltine, T., Pears, N.E., Austin, J.: Three-dimensional face recognition using combinations of surface feature map subspace components. Image Vis. Comput. **26**(3), 382–396 (2008)
50. Hesher, C., Srivastava, A., Erlebacher, G.: A novel technique for face recognition using range imaging. In: Proceedings of Seventh International Symposium on Signal Processing and Its Applications, 2003. Proceedings., vol. 2, pp. 201–204(2003)
51. Horn, B.: Robot Vision, chapter 16. MIT Press, Cambridge (1986)
52. Huang, G., Mattar, M., Berg, T., Learned-Miller, E.: Labeled faces in the wild: a database for studying face recognition in unconstrained environments. Technical Report 07–49 (2007)
53. Institute of Automation, Chinese Academy of Sciences (CASIA): biometrics ideal test: CASIA-3D FaceV1. http://biometrics.idealtest.org. Accessed 21 Jan 2020
54. Jain, A.K., Ross, A., Prabhakar, S.: An introduction to biometric recognition. IEEE Trans. Circuits Syst. Video Technol. **14**(1), 4–20 (2004)
55. Johnson, A.E., Hebert, M.: Using spin images for efficient object recognition in cluttered 3D scenes. IEEE Trans. Pattern Anal. Mach. Intell. **21**(5), 433–449 (1999)
56. Kakadiaris, I.A., Passalis, G., Toderici, G., Murtuza, M.N., Lu, Y., Karampatziakis, N., Theoharis, T.: Three-dimensional face recognition in the presence of facial expressions: an annotated deformable model approach. IEEE Trans. Pattern Anal. Mach. Intell. **29**(4), 640–649 (2007)
57. Kemelmacher-Shlizerman, I., Seitz, S.M., Miller, D., Brossard, E.: The megaface benchmark: 1 million faces for recognition at scale. In: Proceedings of 2016 IEEE Conference on Computer Vision and Pattern Recognition (CVPR), pp. 4873–4882 (2016)
58. Kim, D., Hernandez, M., Choi, J., Medioni, G.: Deep 3D face identification. In: Proceedings of 2017 IEEE International Joint Conference on Biometrics (IJCB), pp. 133–142 (2017)
59. Klassen, E., Srivastava, A., Mio, M., Joshi, S.H.: Analysis of planar shapes using geodesic paths on shape spaces. IEEE Trans. Pattern Anal. Mach. Intell. **26**(3), 372–383 (2004)
60. Koenderink, J.J., van Doorn, A.J.: Surface shape and curvature scales. Image Vis. Comput. **10**(8), 557–565 (1992)
61. Krizhevsky, A., Sutskever, I., Hinton, G.: Imagenet classification with deep convolutional neural networks. Neural Inf. Process. Syst. **25** (2012)
62. Lee, J., Milios, E.: Matching range images of human faces. In: Proceedings of Third International Conference on Computer Vision, pp. 722–726. IEEE Computer Society (1990)
63. Lee, Y.-H., Shim, J.-C.: Curvature based human face recognition using depth weighted hausdorff distance. In: Proceedings of 2004 International Conference on Image Processing, 2004, vol. 3, pp. 1429–1432 (2004)
64. Li, H., Huang, D., Morvan, J.M., Wang, Y., Chen, L.: Towards 3D face recognition in the real: a registration-free approach using fine-grained matching of 3D keypoint descriptors. Int. J. Comput. Vis. **113**(2), 128–142 (2015)
65. Lo, T.W.R., Siebert, J.P.: Local feature extraction and matching on range images: 2.5D SIFT. Comput. Vis. Image Underst. **113**(12), 1235–1250 (2009)

66. Lu, X., Jain, A.K., Colbry, D.: Matching 2.5d face scans to 3D models. IEEE Trans. Pattern Anal. Mach. Intell. **28**(1), 31–43 (2006)
67. Lu, X., Jain, A.: Deformation modeling for robust 3D face matching. IEEE Trans. Pattern Anal. Mach. Intell. **30**(8), 1346–1357 (2008)
68. Max, N.: Weights for computing vertex normals from facet normals. J. Graph. Tools **4**(2), 1–6 (1999)
69. MeshLab: MeshLab. Open source system for processing and editing 3D triangular meshes. http://www.meshlab.net. Accessed 22 Jan 2020
70. Mian, A., Bennamoun, M., Owens, R.: An efficient multimodal 2D–3D hybrid approach to automatic face recognition. IEEE Trans. Pattern Anal. Mach. Intell. **29**(11), 1927–1943 (2007)
71. Mian, A., Bennamoun, M., Owens, R.: Keypoint detection and local feature matching for textured 3D face recognition. Int. J. Comput. Vis. **79**, 1–12 (2008)
72. Mohammadzade, H., Hatzinakos, D.: Iterative closest normal point for 3D face recognition. IEEE Trans. Pattern Anal. Mach. Intell. **35**(2), 381–397 (2013)
73. Ng, H., Winkler, S.: A data-driven approach to cleaning large face datasets. In: Proceedings of 2014 IEEE International Conference on Image Processing, pp. 343–347 (2014)
74. Padia, C., Pears, N.E.: A review and characterization of icp-based symmetry plane localisation in 3D face data. Technical Report 463, Department of Computer Science, University of York (2011)
75. Pan, G., Han, S., Wu, Z., Wang, Y.: 3D face recognition using mapped depth images. In: Proceedings of 2005 IEEE Computer Society Conference on Computer Vision and Pattern Recognition (CVPR'05) - Workshops, p. 175 (2005)
76. Pan, G., Wu, Z., Sun, L.: Recent Advances in Face Recognition (chap.: Liveness detection for face recognition), pp. 236–254. Intech Open, London (2008)
77. Parkhi, O.M., Vedaldi, A., Zisserman, A.: Deep face recognition. In: Proceedings of the British Machine Vision Conference 2015, pp. 41.1–41.12. BMVA Press (2015)
78. Passalis, G., Kakadiaris, I.A., Theoharis, T., Toderici, G., Murtuza, N.: Evaluation of the ur3d algorithm using the frgc v2 data set. In: Proceedings of the IEEE Workshop on Face Recognition Grand Challenge Experiments (2005)
79. Paysan, P., Knothe, R., Amberg, B., Romdhani, S., Vetter, T.: A 3D face model for pose and illumination invariant face recognition. In: Proceedings of 2009 Sixth IEEE International Conference on Advanced Video and Signal Based Surveillance, pp. 296–301 (2009)
80. Pears, N.E., Heseltine, T.: Isoradius contours: New representations and techniques for 3D face registration and matching. In: Proceedings of 3rd International Symposium on 3D Data Processing, Visualization, and Transmission, Chapel Hill, NC, USA, pp. 176–183 (2006)
81. Pears, N.E., Heseltine, T., Romero, M.: From 3D point clouds to pose normalised depth maps. Int. J. Comput. Vis. **89**(2), 152–176 (2010)
82. Phillips, P.J., Flynn, P., Scruggs, T., Bowyer, K., Chang, J.K., Hoffman, K., Marques, J., Min, J., Worek, W.: Overview of the face recognition grand challenge. In: Proceedings of IEEE Computer Society Conference on Computer Vision and Pattern Recognition, vol. 1, pp. 947–954 (2005)
83. Phillips, P.J., Yates, A., Hu, Y., Hahn, C., Noyes, E., Jackson, K., Cavazos, J., Jeckeln, G., Ranjan, R., Sankar, S., Chen, J.C., Castillo, C., Chellappa, R., White, D., O'Toole, A.: Face recognition accuracy of forensic examiners, superrecognizers, and face recognition algorithms. Proc. Natl. Acad. Sci. **115**, 201721,355 (2018)
84. Piegl, L., Tiller, W.: The NURBS Book. Monographs in Visual Communication, 2nd edn. Springer, Berlin (1997)
85. Queirolo, C.C., Silva, L., Bellon, O.R.P., Pamplona Segundo, M.: 3D face recognition using simulated annealing and the surface interpenetration measure. IEEE Trans. Pattern Anal. Mach. Intell. **32**(2), 206–219 (2010)
86. Rusinkiewicz, S., Levoy, M.: Efficient variants of the icp algorithm. In: Proceedings of Third International Conference on 3D Digital Imaging and Modeling, pp. 145–152 (2001)
87. Samir, C., Srivastava, A., Daoudi, M.: Three-dimensional face recognition using shapes of facial curves. IEEE Trans. Pattern Anal. Mach. Intell. **28**(11), 1858–1863 (2006)

88. Savran, A., Alyüz, N., Dibeklioğlu, H., Çeliktutan, O., Gökberk, B., Sankur, B., Akarun, L.: Bosphorus database for 3d face analysis. In: B. Schouten, N.C. Juul, A. Drygajlo, M. Tistarelli (eds.) Proceedings of European Workshop on Biometrics and Identity Management, pp. 47–56. Springer, Berlin (2008)
89. Scheirer, W.J., de Rezende Rocha, A., Sapkota, A., Boult, T.E.: Toward open set recognition. IEEE Trans. Pattern Anal. Mach. Intell. **35**(7), 1757–1772 (2013)
90. Schroff, F., Kalenichenko, D., Philbin, J.: Facenet: A unified embedding for face recognition and clustering. In: Proceedings of 2015 IEEE Conference on Computer Vision and Pattern Recognition (CVPR), pp. 815–823 (2015)
91. Silva, L., Bellon, O., Boyer, K.: Precision range image registration using a robust surface interpenetration measure and enhanced genetic algorithms. IEEE Trans. Pattern Anal. Mach. Intell. **27**, 762–776 (2005)
92. Sirovich, L., Kirby, M.: Low-dimensional procedure for the characterization of human faces. J. Opt. Soc. Amer. A, Opt. Image Sci. **4**, 519–524 (1987)
93. Soltanpour, S., Boufama, B., Wu, Q.J.: A survey of local feature methods for 3D face recognition. Pattern Recognit. **72**, 391–406 (2017)
94. Spreeuwers, L.: Fast and accurate 3D face recognition. Int. J. Comput. Vis. **93**(3), 389–414 (2011)
95. Spreeuwers, L.J.: Breaking the 99% barrier: optimisation of three-dimensional face recognition. IET Biometrics **4**, 169–178 (2015)
96. Sun, X., Rosin, P.L., Martin, R.R., Langbein, F.C.: Noise analysis and synthesis for 3D laser depth scanners. Graph. Models **71**(2), 34–48 (2009)
97. Taigman, Y., Yang, M., Ranzato, M., Wolf, L.: Deepface: Closing the gap to human-level performance in face verification. In: Proceedings of 2014 IEEE Conference on Computer Vision and Pattern Recognition, pp. 1701–1708 (2014)
98. Tanaka, H.T., Ikeda, M., Chiaki, H.: Curvature-based face surface recognition using spherical correlation. Principal directions for curved object recognition. In: Proceedings of Third IEEE International Conference on Automatic Face and Gesture Recognition, pp. 372–377 (1998)
99. The Blender Foundation: Open source 3D suite. https://www.blender.org/. Accessed 21 Jan 2020
100. The University of Texas at Austin: Texas 3D face recognition database. http://live.ece.utexas.edu/research/texas3dfr. Accessed 22 Jan 2020
101. Turk, M., Pentland, A.: Eigenfaces for recognition. J. Cognit. Neurosci. **3**(1), 71–86 (1991)
102. Vijayan, V., Bowyer, K.W., Flynn, P.J., Huang, D., Chen, L., Hansen, M., Ocegueda, O., Shah, S.K., Kakadiaris, I.A.: Twins 3D face recognition challenge. In: Proceedings of 2011 International Joint Conference on Biometrics (IJCB), pp. 1–7 (2011)
103. Viola, P., Jones, M.J.: Robust real-time face detection. Int. J. Comput. Vis. **57**(2), 137–154 (2004)
104. Xu, C., Wang, Y., Tan, T., Quan, L.: Automatic 3D face recognition combining global geometric features with local shape variation information. In: Proceedings of Sixth IEEE International Conference on Automatic Face and Gesture Recognition, 2004. Proceedings., pp. 308–313 (2004)
105. Yan, P., Bowyer, K.W.: A fast algorithm for icp-based 3D shape biometrics. In: Proceedings of Fourth IEEE Workshop on Automatic Identification Advanced Technologies (AutoID'05), pp. 213–218 (2005)
106. Yin, L., Chen, X., Sun, Y., Worm, T., Reale, M.: A high-resolution 3D dynamic facial expression database. In: Proceedings of 2008 8th IEEE International Conference on Automatic Face Gesture Recognition, pp. 1–6 (2008)
107. Yin, L., Wei, X., Sun, Y., Wang, J., Rosato, M.J.: A 3D facial expression database for facial behavior research. In: Proceedings of 7th International Conference on Automatic Face and Gesture Recognition (FGR06), pp. 211–216 (2006)
108. Yu, H., Yang, J.: A direct lda algorithm for high-dimensional data - with application to face recognition. Pattern Recognit. **34**, 2067–2070 (2001)

109. Zhang, L., Snavely, N., Curless, B., Seitz, S.M.: Spacetime faces: High-resolution capture for modeling and animation. In: Deng, Z., Neumann, U. (eds.) Data-Driven 3D Facial Animation, pp. 248–276. Springer, London (2008)
110. Zhou, S., Xiao, S.: 3D face recognition: a survey. Human-Centric Comput. Inf. Sci. **8**(1), (2018)

Chapter 13
3D Digitization of Cultural Heritage

Gabriele Guidi and Bernard D. Frischer

Abstract The chapter first analyzes the reasons for digitizing Cultural Heritage (CH), tracing the history of applying 3D technologies for the purpose of digitizing CH, and reviewing the current state of the art in the field. A detailed survey is offered for the digitization of different types of both tangible and intangible CH. The latter includes a section about the 3D digitization of damaged or no-longer existing CH monuments for the purpose of creating 3D hypotheses of restoration and reconstruction in virtual archaeology. A methodological section points out which 3D technologies are used in the field and how they can be best applied, taking into account digitization approaches appropriate to the different classes of CH object as well as the relative strengths and weaknesses of the various technologies. This is followed by a discussion of how CH can be modeled from raw data, and a section about the different 3D processing pipelines that can be implemented through active or passive 3D sensing techniques. Finally, a detailed section treats the creation of a 3D content repository for CH, taking into account both the relevant articulated metadata as well as the ways 3D data are stored and visualized for online access.

13.1 Introduction

Digitizing cultural heritage in order to generate 3D models of objects such as statues, buildings, cities, and even larger territories has become increasingly common during the past twenty years. Although coming from the technical domains of Optoelectronics, Computer Vision, Computer Graphics, Geomatics, and Virtual Reality, the technologies for 3D modeling in the real world have been adopted by several areas of the Humanities and Social Sciences including, e.g., Archaeology, Art History, Architectural History, Egyptology, and Paleontology. More recently, 3D digitization has

G. Guidi (✉)
Politecnico di Milano, 20156 Milan, Italy
e-mail: gabriele.guidi@polimi.it

B. D. Frischer
Indiana University, Bloomington, IN 47401, USA
e-mail: bernard.d.frischer@gmail.com

© Springer Nature Switzerland AG 2020
Y. Liu et al. (eds.), *3D Imaging, Analysis and Applications*,
https://doi.org/10.1007/978-3-030-44070-1_13

631

also become a topic of interest in the field of Archival Science, owing to its usefulness in documenting heritage artifacts. An early paper in this field [133] presciently foresaw that digitizing cultural heritage would have multiple purposes.

For this reason, in this introduction, we will give an updated summary of possible answers to the motivations behind the 3D digitization of cultural heritage, discussed in Sects. 13.1.1–13.1.8.

The rest of the chapter is divided into 7 sections (numbered 2 to 8). In Sect. 13.2, an overview of previous work about 3D digitization of cultural heritage is presented, subdividing the vast domain of cultural heritage by typology: tangible (13.2.1), intangible (13.2.2), and no-longer extant (13.2.3). Section 13.3 illustrates technologies and methods for 3D digitization of cultural heritage, with specific emphasis on 3D data capture (13.3.1), 3D modeling (13.3.2) as well as storage and visualization from accessible repositories (13.3.3). Section 13.4 is about how one of the methods described in Sect. 13.2 can be used in practice, showing an applicative example. Section 13.5 points out the open challenges in the field. Section 13.6 makes some concluding remarks, Sect. 13.7 provides a list of further readings, and Sect. 13.8 poses questions for a possible test on this topic. We begin with the fundamental question: why should we digitize cultural heritage?

13.1.1   Visualization and Interaction

Creating a 3D model of an existing heritage artifact, building, or site means "virtualizing" the monument in order to permit a user to visualize it and interact with it in different ways. From a simple 3D viewer showing a model on the screen of a computer to a virtual visit through a stereoscopic head-mounted display, the purpose is always to show the geometrical and visual qualities of the object through its digital simulacrum, supporting different levels of immersivity into the digital 3D world. The virtual model has a variety of potential uses—uses to which the original can rarely, if ever be put. For example, once we have a virtual model of a statue in a museum, we can recontextualize the work of art into a virtual model of the place where it was originally located (e.g., a sculpture now in a museum can be virtually, but for practical reasons hardly ever physically, restored to the chapel of a church for which it was originally created). A collection of virtual models of works of art that are logically connected but physically dispersed (e.g., the oeuvre of a sculptor scattered in many museums) can be brought together in a virtually created space resembling a museum gallery or exhibition hall that never actually existed. Moreover, visualization and interaction are the first functions required to make possible a number of other applications of a 3D model such as those described in the following subsections.

13.1.2 Remote Visit

When a cultural heritage asset is located in sites not easily reached for some reason, a digital model can be the best way to make possible the experience of a visit. Such reasons may range from (i) dangers to visitors (e.g., during wartime); (ii) temporary closure owing to restoration work; (iii) impact on a fragile object or environment of a massive public presence; (iv) inaccessibility of the location (e.g., on the top of a roof, at the bottom of the sea, or in the interior chamber of an Egyptian pyramid closed to the public); and (v) budgetary limitations making it impractical for a given person to visit a site. Even when these factors are not operative and the tourist is able to arrive at a cultural heritage site, preceding the visit with the use of a virtual model can quickly provide the background needed to improve comprehension of the site so that the experience of actually visiting it is enriched and perhaps speeded up, thereby increasing the museum's capacity to accommodate more visitors. In any case, the virtual model does not replace the original but complements it.

13.1.3 Study and Research

Documenting the surviving evidence of tangible heritage has traditionally been the starting point of any scholar in fields of the Humanities and Social Science such as Archaeology, Art History, or Architectural History. Since the nineteenth century, the typical tool for quick and effective documentation has been photography, a tool that is still effective for showing bi-dimensional objects such as paintings or aerial views of archaeological sites. But when a cultural object has more geometrical complexity such as, for example, a statue in the round, a photograph of it is generally inadequate to the task of full documentation. In addition, the metric representation of an object in a photograph can be done by including a scale in the image, but this form of scaling yields a rough approximation as compared to the submillimeter accuracy that can be obtained by a digital model generated with a 3D digitization technology. Depending on the field, this lack of accuracy may lead to a lack of information and to a resultant misinterpretation. Examining an artifact, building, or site through its 3D digital model makes it possible to navigate, section, see through, measure, and compare the heritage artifact in a way that would not be possible even with the actual physical object. This allows scholars from any part of the world to study in depth heritage assets located even very far from where they live, using all the tools available on their computers for an objective and quantitative analysis.

13.1.4   Digital Restoration and Reconstruction

Once a heritage artifact has its digital counterpart, different modifications or integrations of the 3D model can be implemented without touching the original object. Such restoration may be based on the reconstruction of missing elements according to formal rules or other clues deducible from the historical documentation [62]. Examples include the regeneration of the original colors of a sculpture inferred from pigment analysis on the surface of the original artifact [64, 152], or the virtual reconstruction of buildings [87] and cities [60], starting from a 3D scan of some of their surviving physical elements.

13.1.5   Heritage Monitoring for Conservation

The proper preservation of cultural heritage monuments requires continuous monitoring of its state of preservation. The evolution of the shape of a specific artifact, structure, or site, as documented through periodic 3D scanning, may reveal a process of degradation underway on a time scale not evident to the naked eye. This functional use of the model makes it possible, for example, to check the corrosion of stone elements in the open air caused by air pollution, the deformations of wood arising from different environmental changes such as humidity and temperature [80], the impact of restoration on an artwork [1], or the natural erosion of a cultural landscape [56].

13.1.6   Physical Replicas

Rapid prototyping through 3D printing and digital milling—widely used in industrial design—makes possible the use of the 3D model of a work of art to generate its physical replica [45]. Although this may be prone to give rise to ethical concerns [102], a prudent use of this process can be useful for several applications that do not require the extraordinary fidelity of the physical copy to the original piece. As examples might be cited, the creation of copies that temporarily replace museum pieces on loan elsewhere or providing copies near the original object in the gallery so that visitors can touch and handle them, thereby enhancing their museum experience. Such enhancement is particularly valuable for the blind.

13.1.7   3D Archives of Cultural Heritage

Handling the models that are created for any of the applications thus far mentioned raises the issue of the management of large repositories of 3D models of heritage artifacts, structures or sites, sometimes made accessible over the Internet. This involves a two-fold problem. On one hand, there is the technical infrastructure needed to store a large amount of data associated with the production of a model (e.g., raw laser scans or photogrammetric images). On the other hand, there is the production of metadata suitable for describing in an exhaustive way the content of the model and the technical process for transforming the original into its digital counterpart. The latter inherits all the insights and solutions developed in the library automation field as early as the 1980s for the digitization of other objects such as books, images, and multimedia contents.

13.1.8 Information Systems

The 3D model of a cultural heritage object has another realm of application: as a resource for a dedicated information system able to associate a specific piece of information with a specific geometrical position on the surface of the 3D model through a process commonly known as 3D annotation. This approach, similar to what is usually done on a geographical scale using Geographical Information Systems (GISs), can be applied at the different scales of an object [153], a building [119] or an entire archaeological site [42]. The number and kinds of pieces of information associable with a 3D model may vary from (i) conservation records useful for managing and planning possible restoration interventions [153]; (ii) stratigraphic information gathered during an archaeological excavation [71]; (iii) historical information about the artifact/building useful for touristic purposes; (iv) technical reports about possible scientific analyses made in a specific location of an artifact, like C14 or thermoluminescence dating, pigment analysis with X-Ray Fluorescence (XRF), DNA sequencing for biological materials, biochemical analyses, etc. The means of conveying knowledge through the 3D model can be done not only by linking a single large mesh with local annotations, possibly structured through a database, but also by properly segmenting the 3D model of the heritage object according to its different, hierarchically structured semantic components. This form of hierarchic 3D illustration originated in the field of Mechanical Engineering for representing complex systems such as an automobile, whose CAD model incorporates a huge information system from the single bolts of the engine to the assembly of the entire vehicle [142]. The same approach was then ported to the field of Architectural Design with the introduction of the "Building Information Model" (BIM), where a building is represented in 3D connecting single components typically collected from a library of components (e.g., wires, pipes, windows, stairs, doors, etc.) [91]. In both cases, the purpose is very practical: having a comprehensive list of components needed to build the vehicle or the house, making possible a precise estimate of production costs, management of the supplies, and, possibly, implementation of measures to reduce costs by sharing the same components between different cars or buildings. This way of structuring 3D models of components as information units has also been then extended to cultural heritage. The result is now known as Heritage Building

Information Model (HBIM), when specifically referred to heritage buildings [124] or more generally as semantically structured 3D models [38]. In this case, the purpose is not, obviously, to estimate the cost of reproducing a heritage asset, but to manage the conservation work in case of monuments requiring continuous maintenance to prevent their irreversible deterioration [3].

13.2 Previous Work on 3D Digitization of Heritage

The earliest work on 3D digitization of heritage objects was done in 1997 by the Institute for Information Technology at the National Research Council Canada, which developed and patented the first laser scanners based on triangulation [139]. They were applied to a number of different heritage objects [156]. But it was probably the Stanford Digital Michelangelo Project [108], begun in 1998, that first brought the new approach into prominence among professionals in the relevant fields of the Humanities and Engineering. The group headed by Marc Levoy scanned 20 sculptures by Michelangelo in Italy, including the worldwide famous 5m-tall statue of David. Thanks to significant coverage in the press, the Digital Michelangelo Project also made clear to the general public how much more informative the interactive 3D model could be as compared to the form of documentation hitherto used, namely, a still photograph. In the same years, thanks to research in the field of laser radar— where the radar techniques for measuring distances with electromagnetic waves are ported to the optical field—the first large-scale 3D laser scanners were marketed by Cyrax, a California company later purchased by Leica Geosystems. Initially conceived as a tool for surveying complex manufacturing plants, the first Cyrax 2400 was capable of measuring 800 points per second with 6mm uncertainty at a maximum distance of 50m [95]. It was soon experimentally deployed for the purpose of creating 3D surveys of cultural heritage sites [4].

From those early days, enormous progress has been made in terms of increased acquisition speed (currently done at more than one million points per second), resolution, addition of color superimposed over the geometric data, and reduction of measurement uncertainty. However, from the first applications it was clear that to exploit such extraordinary potential, substantial resources were needed in terms of time for the acquisition of the 3D data and, particularly, for the subsequent post-processing that leads to the final digital 3D model. Considering that such digital objects represent just the starting point for other possible applications in the Humanities and Social Sciences, such as, for example, creating virtual museums or producing physical reproductions of works of art, the research community concentrated its efforts in the intervening twenty years on making shorter, simpler and mostly automatic all the steps in the pipeline used to create 3D models of objects in the real world.

As a result, 3D digitization of cultural heritage has been pursued with different methodological approaches to (i) physical heritage assets like statues, paintings, buildings, etc., as they appear in their current form (Sect. 13.2.1); (ii) immaterial, or "intangible," heritage such as ritual gestures, dances, and other forms of performances that are defined by their temporal evolution in 3D space (Sect. 13.2.2); (iii) the reconstructed form of tangible heritage, sometimes starting from the digitization of the surviving remains (Sect. 13.2.3).

13.2.1   3D Digitization of Tangible Cultural Heritage

"Tangible cultural heritage" refers to physical artifacts produced, maintained, and transmitted intergenerationally in a society. It includes artistic creations, built heritage such as buildings and monuments, and other physical or tangible products of human creativity that are invested with cultural significance in a society. In this section, a review of 3D digitization works of tangible heritage, subdivided by category, is reported.

Sculpture and Other Museum Artifacts

This is a category of heritage objects that started being digitized by 3D scanning in the late 1990s. The earliest experiments were made with a triangulation laser scanner on a small stone sculpture by Giovanni Pisano representing "Madonna with Child" preserved in the Scrovegni Chapel in Padua (Italy) [17]; with a white light pattern projection device on the Michelangelo's "Pietà" in Florence [21]; and with a custom triangulation laser scanner mounted on a vertical rail supported by a 7.6 m tall gantry for the digitization of Michelangelo's "David" [108].

In addition to a number of logistical issues related to the use of advanced technologies in heritage venues, such early experiments made evident how the intrinsic error of 3D capturing devices [11], the response of the scanned material, and the propagation of such errors on the raw data during the following processing stage can produce a significant discrepancy between the real artifact and its final 3D representation [81]. This issue was addressed by integrating different 3D capturing technologies such as active range sensing and photogrammetry [18], leading to a high-accuracy digitization procedure used for the 3D modeling of the wooden statue of the "Magdalen" by Donatello in Florence (Italy) [79].

The difficulty in 3D scanning of non-cooperative optical materials was first raised by the Visual Information Technology group at NRC Canada, which noticed how the sponge-like structure of marble may lead to a reflection not only from the exterior surface, but also from internal layers of the material that might distort the light reflected back. As a result, the active laser device is deceived and renders an incorrect metric response [73]. Such error proved to be extremely large for phase-shift laser scanners, reaching 6 mm of systematic distance overestimation owing to the penetration of light into the material [20]. It was then verified with a systematic test on different types of marble that the error for laser triangulation devices is far smaller (40 micrometers), even if clearly detectable [85]. Bronze is another material widely used for sculpture that yielded a very poor optical response. For laser triangulation devices, the strong absorption of light owing to this dark material, especially evident in old and non-restored bronze statues, together with the potentially high specularity,

Fig. 13.1 Digital 3D model of the bronze "Davide" by Donatello (1440). It was the first 3D model of a heritage asset ever made with the laser radar technology, demonstrating how this approach eliminates the artifacts typically generated by a dark shiny surface

led in general to an increase in 3D data uncertainty with areas of absent data where there were reflections.

Such artifacts were found to be absent in the case of frequency-modulated laser radars, such as the one used for the digitization of the bronze "David" by Donatello in Florence (Italy) [88], as shown in Fig. 13.1.

In addition to the first test for establishing the proper active technologies and 3D processing methodologies for different types of statues, several applications of 3D digitization have been made in recent decades for specific conservation purposes. Some significant examples include virtual restorations based on 3D digitization of sculptural fragments. This was the case with the "Minerva d'Arezzo" preserved in Florence and disassembled into parts [58] after a possible incorrect reassembly during a previous restoration, or the reconstructive hypothesis of the sculpture of Epicurus made by Frischer et al. [65]. An instructive example of virtual restoration aimed at guiding the actual restoration is offered by the work done on the marble sculpture "Adam" by Tullio Lombardo, which on the evening of October 6, 2002 unexpectedly fell to the ground and smashed into hundreds of large and small pieces at the Metropolitan Museum in New York. Here the "3D puzzle" of the statue to be reconstructed was first solved using the 3D model in order to establish the sequence of steps needed to achieve a complete physical reconstruction [138].

A similar activity, involving not just a manual alignment of fragments, as in the cases just mentioned, but also an automatic identification of best matches was pursued to find joins of fragments of the "Forma Urbis Romae," a large map of Severan Rome (ca. AD 200) inscribed on marble blocks and subsequently removed from the wall on which it was displayed, despoiled, and broken into fragments to be melted down into lime in medieval times [103]. An analogous approach [161] was used to find matches in the fragments of wall paintings damaged by the eruption of the volcano on Santorini (Greece) in ca. 1500 BC [29]. A new instance of this method was recently tested on two sets of terracotta fragments, representing figurines of the Hu civilization [166]. The 3D scanning of sculptures as high-resolution documentation before restoring the physical artifact was then extended to statues of large and colossal size starting from the Great Buddha project. Here the digitization was completed on some monumental bronze sculptures of Buddha located in the municipalities of Asukain, Kamakura, and Nara, Japan, whose heights are 2.57 m, 13.35 m, and 14.98 m, respectively [93].

The idea of scanning sculpture was also extended to no-longer-existing objects, like the two colossal standing Buddha statues in Bamyan (Afghanistan), 35 m and 53 m high, originally carved into the living rock and blown up by the Taliban in 2001. Here a team based at the ETH Zurich reconstructed in 3D the two sculptures with image-based modeling by using historical images taken before their destruction [75].

A recent series of activities related to the digitization of material heritage, made possible by the latest advances in 3D capturing technologies, includes the systematic digitization of all the content belonging to a museum or cultural heritage site. The first museum which established a working relationship with a research group for the purpose of studying the opportunities presented by 3D digitization of artifacts was the Petrie Museum of Egyptian Archaeology at the University College London [113]. Here, starting in 2009, several experiments to test different active and passive methods for digitizing museum artifacts were performed [141]. The first museum to be systematically digitized was the Archaeological Museum of Milan within the framework of the 3DICONS European project (2012–2015). The aim was to add 3D models of Cultural Heritage objects to EUROPEANA, the portal dedicated to the European culture [131]. All the collections connected to European history were considered, including pieces from the Greek, Roman, Etruscan, late Egyptian, and Medieval periods. As a result, 427 objects and structures belonging to the museum were modeled in 3D. Of this total, 9% were models of buildings and large structures, 14% of small untextured museum artifacts, and 77% of small and medium texturized museum artifacts, like those shown in Fig. 13.2.

The decision was taken to 3D digitize buildings and large structures with phase-shift terrestrial laser scanning owing to its ability to give a metric 3D output independent of targets and other references that must be attached to the surface of the artifact. Small un-texturized museum artifacts were acquired with triangulation-based laser scanning owing to its ability to work well in the absence of any surface texturing. Small and medium texturized museum artifacts were then digitized with automatic photogrammetry (SFM/Image Matching).

Fig. 13.2 Examples of 3D models of different museum artifacts, produced in the framework of the 3DICONS project, digitized at the Archaeological Museum in Milan (Italy): **a** Etruscan pear wood head (seventh Century BC); **b** Greek amphora of decorated clay (sixth Century BC); **c** Roman stone sculpture representing the head of Zeus (first Century AD); **d** Roman marble basin sculpted with mythological creatures (second Century AD)

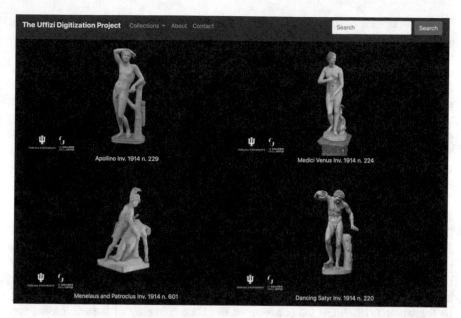

Fig. 13.3 Search page of the IU-Uffizi project, dedicated to the 3D digitization of the around 1000 Roman sculptures conserved at the "Uffizi Galleries" and all the connected sites (Pitti palace, Loggia dei Lanzi, Boboli garden) in Florence, Italy

This approach was chosen because of its efficiency in terms of processing time from the acquisition phase to the final 3D model. This turned out to be from 5 to 10 times faster than 3D digitization utilizing active sensors [78]. In the same period, the Smithsonian Institution started its 3D digitization program aiming at a systematic digitization of its collections in partnership with Autodesk Inc., which developed a customized online viewer [128]. However, until the present time, only one hundred models of his vast collection of over 150 million objects have been created, representing more the attempt to establish a workflow rather than to undertake a serious program of comprehensive digitization.

A more advanced approach for massive 3D digitization was proposed by the Fraunhofer Institute with the project CultLab3D. This is an automatic system made for quickly digitizing small museum artifacts utilizing a conveyor belt that moves the object along different stages of the digitization process [145]. Although limited to small artifacts, the system allows capture of the artifacts' geometries, textures as well as optical properties such as reflection and absorption. While on the conveyor belt, the artifact passes through two nested aluminum scanning arcs, each holding nine high-resolution cameras and nine ring lights. Each arc can describe a full hemisphere moving around the artifact. From the related images the 3D texturized model can be quickly generated with submillimeter accuracy using photogrammetry [151].

The latest example of systematic digitization is represented in Fig. 13.3 by the collaboration between Indiana University (Bloomington, IN, USA) and the Uffizi

Galleries (Florence, Italy). In May 2016, the two institutions signed an agreement to digitize, over a five-year period, all the collections of Greek and Roman sculpture belonging to the gallery, consisting of ca. 1,000 altars, basins, busts, herms, statues, statue groups, and fragments [125]. The project presented several practical difficulties arising, for example, from lighting conditions that are sometimes less than ideal, the location of some objects very close to walls, which makes it difficult to photograph the back sides, and the possibility of working in the gallery only at times when it is closed to the public [82]. Despite these difficulties, which are undoubtedly typical of what comparable projects will encounter at other museums, the project is proceeding on schedule and made its website, as shown in Fig. 13.3, publicly available in August 2018 with publication of the first 300 models (www.digitalsculpture.org/florence).

Paintings

The first experiment of 3D digitization was made on a painting by the French artist Jean-Baptiste-Camille Corot (1796–1875). In the first half of 1996, a large exhibition of 163 of his finest paintings was held at the Grand Palais, Paris. The show traveled to the National Gallery of Canada, Ottawa, where it was open from June 21 to September 22, 1996, and to The Metropolitan Museum of Art, New York from October 22, 1996 to January 19, 1997. On the occasion of the Canadian stop of the exhibition, the Centre de Recherche et de Restauration des Musées de France (CRRMF) asked the National Research Council (NRC) of Canada for permission to utilize their active 3D technologies based on laser triangulation. The goal was to use them as instruments in an experiment to evaluate their effectiveness for analyzing paintings [157]. The NRC used its High-Resolution Color Laser Scanner, based on three collimated lasers (respectively, red, green and blue), which had been specially developed for digitizing museum objects in color. It was used in a configuration giving 50 micrometers of resolution on the painting plane (xy) with uncertainty of less than 10 micrometers along the z-axis. From the experiment it emerged that, although the exterior surface of the painting was nearly flat owing to a layer of varnish, the 3D image captured by the range sensor derived from the paint layer beneath the varnish rather than directly from the varnish surface itself. This resulted in a detailed high-resolution recording of the 3D structure of the paint layer, including brush stroke details as well as crack patterns, paint losses, and other characteristics due to aging [72].

A second experiment of 3D scanning of paintings was made in 2002 during the monitoring of the painting "The Adoration of the Magi" (Fig. 13.4) by Leonardo da Vinci, displayed at the Uffizi Gallery in Florence, Italy. Over the centuries, the painting—made on a wooden support consisting of poplar planks—suffered periods of poor conservation leading to a significant bending of the wooden support with consequent deterioration of the painted layers. In addition, this Da Vinci masterpiece was only partially varnished (its upper left corner was unfinished), and for this reason it was very fragile and not suited to major restoration interventions. The 3D monitoring aimed therefore at establishing the deviation of the painting from its theoretical flat shape, the level of craquelure at the center of the painted surface and possible lack of material in the support. The digitization work was made with an active device based on the projection of white light patterns, with a lateral resolu-

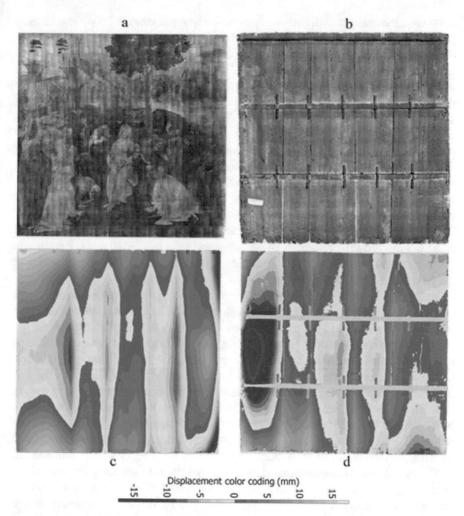

Fig. 13.4 Three-dimensional digitization of the painting on wood "Adoration of the Magi" by Leonardo da Vinci for monitoring purposes: **a** 3D model of the front side, with colors; **b** 3D model of the rear side, without colors; **c** deviation map from a fitting plane of the front side; **d** deviation map of the rear. From such analysis a quantitative evaluation, for example, of the deep depression on the rear side (−23 mm, pink spot in **d**), was possible [77]

tion on the painting plane of 270 μm over the whole painted surface, 90 μm for the central high-resolution area, and 350 μm for the rear side. As a result it was possible to measure deviations from planarity of 23 mm in the rear side of the painting as well as wrinkles in the painted layer of the central area as small as 50 μm with an uncertainty along z of 18 μm [77].

This analytical approach had its climactic early application in 2004, when a team from the NRC Canada traveled to Paris with a portable version of the high-resolution color laser scanner already used in the Corot experiment. The objective was to undertake 3D scanning of the worldwide famous Mona Lisa by Leonardo Da Vinci. When configured to render maximum resolution, this device was capable of sampling the surface of the painting with a resolution of $60\,\mu m$ and an uncertainty along z of $10\,\mu m$. The presence of three collimated RGB lasers allowed the scientists to precisely capture the color of the painting as well as the 3D geometry of its front and rear sides. By exploiting the presence of three different wavelengths associated with the three base colors, a variable penetration inside the painted layer was possible, making it possible to interpret some of Leonardo's painting techniques such as "sfumato." Finally, the ultra-high resolution of the device was able to document the 3D pattern of brush strokes and cracks in a way never before possible [25].

In 2013, a custom system for documenting painting was presented that was based on a high-resolution structured-light measurement head with no IR and UV emission. It was mounted on an industrial robot arm that could be automatically positioned over the painting surface [98].

In 2014, a team from TU-Delft developed a fringe encoded stereo vision system specifically designed for 3D capture of painting [165]. The metrological performance was similar to the NRC color laser scanner of 1996 ($50\,\mu m$ of resolution on the painting plane and $9\,\mu m$ of uncertainty along z), but without the complication of three collimated lasers. It also was able to observe the Technical Guidelines for Digitizing Cultural Heritage in the reproduction of the colors [94]. The system was used to document and physically reproduce a self-portrait by Rembrandt and the "Flowers in a Blue Vase" by Van Gogh. An unprecedented level of fidelity of the artist's brush strokes was achieved in the reproduction of the painting by a 3D print of the model. The digitization of paintings with strong 3D materiality was further explored in 2015 with the digitization of "Alchemy" by Jackson Pollock [32]. Completed in 1947, the work is a recognized masterpiece of the twentieth century and one of the first examples of so-called "action painting," performed by placing the canvas on the ground, and pouring/dripping/squeezing paint onto its surface. Digitization of the painting was performed with a commercial fringe projection device. A resolution of $200\,\mu m$ on the painting plane was used, with two areas acquired at higher resolution ($100\,\mu m$). The high-resolution 3D model allowed the conservators to investigate the relationship between the shape of the painting and the painting process which was, according to the artist, an essential part of the artwork.

Although 3D digitization of paintings at an instant in time, such as those mentioned above and several others available in the literature [2, 5], have provided useful documentation for conservators, an even more interesting form of digitization is the one repeated over time, since it can reveal deformations of the work of art. The fiber-based nature of wood, widely used as painting support or canvas frame, gives peculiar deformations arising from either such environmental conditions as humidity and temperature or from conservation issues. In 2004, a first test of this nature was made using multiple photogrammetric campaigns on the "Retable," an English panel painting of the thirteenth century on display in Westminster Abbey, London (UK)

[140]. Between 2005 and 2007, several subsequent acquisitions were performed on the "Pala Trivulzio," a painting on canvas by Andrea Mantegna in the collection of the Castello Sforzesco in Milan (Italy). The campaign started in March 2005, before the beginning of a major restoration, then in May 2006 at the end of the replacement of the frame, which resulted in flattening the whole canvas and eliminating macroscopic waves in its shape. It continued in July 2006 and in March 2007 for purposes of monitoring [10]. In all these examples, the comparison was made using the same equipment at different moments in time. More recently, an experiment of comparison between 3D digitization of the same painting at different times with completely different devices and processes was proposed, introducing a modified alignment algorithm for identifying the long-term deformation resulting from aging/environmental factors as well as the modification introduced by some restoration interventions [1].

Summarizing the technologies mentioned in the literature for the 3D digitization of paintings, we have reported use of active sensors based on laser triangulation [10, 25, 157], on white light fringe projection (the large majority) [1, 2, 5, 10, 32, 77], on active stereoscopy [165], and on standard (i.e., passive) photogrammetry [140].

Built Heritage

The survey of architecture has a long history. A well-established method based on the measurement of few salient points of a building with theodolites or traditional photogrammetry and the subsequent rendering of the surveyed building into 2D sections, plans, and elevations has been the standard approach for representing built structures, including those of cultural interest. The weight of this traditional approach undoubtedly contributed to the slow rate at which 3D digitization of buildings was introduced as compared to that of other types of cultural assets such as sculptures, where, as we have seen, the earliest experiments date to the mid-90s.

Initially, 3D digitization was introduced to capture the shape of specific buildings composed of a complex system of pipes and tubes as, for example, power plants. These were always difficult for the traditional approach to survey because of the intrinsic difficulty of surveying the many rounded surfaces with no salient points. However, soon the digital scanning method was ported to ancient and ruined heritage monuments, typically no longer composed of their original regular and symmetric shapes because of deterioration over time. So, the first works in this field date to early 2000 with the presentation of the technology and the related methodologies [27, 109], which were applied to a survey of ancient castles [33, 155].

After the first experiments, some general criteria were defined by those organizations involved in the documentation of cultural heritage such as the "International Council on Monuments and Sites" (ICOMOS) and its technical extension "Comité International de la Photogrammétrie Architecturale" (CIPA). Some of the criteria they emphasized included the importance of data integration, the advisability of capturing different components of a built heritage by means of the most suitable technologies for each component [19], and striving for redundancy in estimating the quality of the obtained 3D measurements [132].

The first experiment in integrating different sensors to solve the problems of 3D resolution dates to 2002. The first tests were done on the survey of a Roman villa

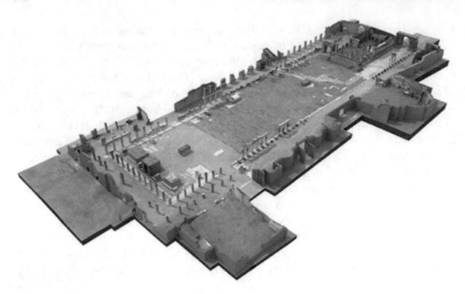

Fig. 13.5 Digital model of the Pompei forum, originated by the integration of aerial photogrammetry, TOF 3D laser scanning and terrestrial photogrammetry, covering a resolution ranging from 0.25 to 250 mm

beneath the Baptistry of the Florence Cathedral (Italy), and the 3D digitization of the Pomposa Abbey (Italy). The first case illustrated the advantages of integrating the high-resolution survey of a mosaic made with a triangulation device with the lower resolution 3D capture of the architectural structure taken with a TOF laser scanner through a common reference system measured by means of photogrammetry [89]. In the second case, a richly carved stone window captured with a triangulation-based laser scanner was merged with the low-resolution model of the entire abbey generated with traditional (non SFM/IM based) photogrammetry [54]. The concept was further developed in the survey of the forum of Pompeii (Fig. 13.5), where many different technologies were integrated to cover resolutions spanning three orders of magnitude from 0.25 to 250 mm [84].

Sensor integration is commonly applied also to solve a typical problem in surveying buildings with terrestrial technologies, such as the proper digitization of the top of each building. Although attempts to digitize with laser scanners raised above the building with hydraulic platforms have been successfully made, as has 3D scanning with Aerial Laser Scanners (ALS) [106], the problem has been solved in a much cheaper way with the introduction of photogrammetry using cameras mounted on drones. Their data is then integrated with that captured by terrestrial devices [120].

Unmanned Aerial Vehicles (UAVs) have also become frequently used in archaeology for capturing entire areas [127], including, for example, documenting the different layers of an ongoing excavation [41, 105].

Underwater Heritage

Cultural heritage evidence can be found in several environments including the bottom of water bodies such as lakes, seas, or oceans. Those environments, in addition to preserving sites, structures, buildings, and artifacts made of inorganic materials, can also include wooden vessels, human remains, or even food, thanks to the absence of oxygen. This led UNESCO to draw a specific convention in 2001 for the protection of what is conventionally referred to as "Underwater Cultural Heritage" (UCH), defined as "traces of human existence having a cultural, historical or archaeological character which have been partially or totally under water, periodically or continuously, for at least 100 years" [160].

UCH represents a great (and in large part still unexplored) cultural resource that is accessible only to the very limited public involved in scuba diving or with access to special equipment such as submersible vehicles. In this context, 3D digitization represents a valuable approach to document UCH assets for different purposes, including the presentation of such remains to the general public with the help of multimedia presentations or virtual reality applications [31].

The methods for underwater 3D data acquisition range from ultrasound to optical technologies, with significant differences in terms of resolution, sensor-to-surface distance, and acquisition speed [118].

Because acoustic waves can easily propagate in water, ultrasound is historically the most suitable method and has been used for decades in sonar. The working principle, also known as Bathymetry, is based on the measurement of sensor-to-surface distance through the measurement of the time needed by a burst of ultrasound energy to go from a probe to a surface and back to the receiver, similar to what happens when laser light measures distances with the approach known as Time of Flight (TOF). A proper scanning approach involves the measurement of the latitude and longitude dimensions with a GPS installed on a ship moving according to a precise scanning trajectory and equipped with an ultrasound unit pointed toward the sea bottom. This makes it possible to generate 3D maps of the bottom of the sea, including possible remains of archaeological interest [116].

Optical methods may use active devices such as an Aerial Laser Scanner (ALS). In general, a standard ALS does not provide information from the sea bottom because the wavelength of near-infrared light is reflected by the sea surface and does not penetrate the water. Using shorter wavelength lights (blue-green), a moderate penetration can be obtained, allowing the mapping of archaeological structures on the sea bottom in shallow waters [51].

However, the most commonly used approach for underwater 3D digitization at high resolution is photogrammetry, which has been applied for several decades in archaeology [12].

In underwater photogrammetry, the presence of multiple media with different refraction indexes such as air, glass, and water tend to complicate the actual optical configuration of the photogrammetric problem. For this reason, in traditional underwater photogrammetry, a specific camera calibration was required [69]. One of the reasons for the great success of SFM/IM photogrammetry in this context is its use

Fig. 13.6 Underwater photogrammetry of a Roman amphorae cargo, sunk not far from Toulon (France) and laying on the bottom of the sea at 300 meters of depth: **a** Remotely Operated Vehicle (ROV) run by COMEX (France), while capturing the image dataset with the ORUS3D system; **b** resulting 3D model published on the web (https://skfb.ly/6LnQz). Courtesy of the ROV3D project, Laboratoire des Sciences de l'Information et des Systèmes (LSIS), Marseille, France

of self-calibration of cameras that compensates for refraction issues, recalibrating the camera in its operating environment, thereby simplifying the photogrammetric process [149].

In the literature, this method has been used with handheld cameras controlled by a scuba diver [117] for 3D digitization of archaeological sites [30], shipwrecks [43], amphorae, and other cargo of ships [47]. As an alternative, a vehicle holding a camera and traveling around the object of interest can be used, for example, in the early archaeological survey of a shipwreck in Turkey, made in the 1960s by the archaeologist George F. Bass using the Asharan, a custom-built submersible equipped with stereophotogrammetric gear [13].

More recently, Remotely Operated Vehicles (ROVs) like that shown in Fig. 13.6 have been used [53], in a fashion comparable to the way drones are used in the air, or even Autonomously Operated Vehicles (AOVs), aquatic versions of a robot [96]. A vehicle without a human presence is particularly useful when the 3D survey has to be done under conditions not suitable for a scuba diver such as those requiring long periods of time, entry into dangerous conditions or into deep waters [9, 52].

Sensor fusion is sometimes utilized to take advantage of each of the aforementioned technologies [70], such as in the study of a World War II battle site combining Multibeam Bathymetry and SFM Photogrammetry [97].

13.2.2   3D Digitization of Intangible Cultural Heritage

As specified in the UNESCO Convention of 2003 about this topic [159], "intangible cultural heritage" means the practices, representations, expressions, knowledge, skills—as well as the instruments, objects, artifacts and cultural spaces associated therewith—that communities, groups and, in some cases, individuals recognize as part of their cultural heritage. According to this definition, examples of such forms of heritage include

- Oral traditions and expressions, including language as a vehicle of the intangible cultural heritage
- Performing arts
- Social practices, rituals, and festive events
- Knowledge and practices concerning nature and the universe
- Traditional craftsmanship

The approach for digitally documenting an example of intangible heritage generally privileges description through pictures, audio, and video recordings along with metadata organized according to proper ontologies [115]. In addition, recent studies emphasize how tangible and intangible heritage are strictly interconnected and should be jointly considered [34]. Studies about the optimal way of visualizing such forms of heritage [57] have also made clear how many forms of intangible heritage include 3D content or elements. Examples include the performing arts and rituals involving movement of a human body in 3D space. Such movement generates a 4D entity (3D + time) that can be conveniently captured with motion capture techniques used in the gaming, animation, and movie industries as well as in the biomechanical analysis of human postures and movements for sport or rehabilitation.

The most commonly used approach is based on dedicated studios equipped with multiple synchronized cameras and dedicated illuminators aiming at the active volume through which the actor moves. The actor might wear a special suit equipped with refractive targets for full body captures or spherical refractive targets attached directly on the moving part of the body that is involved in this type of digitization. Triangulation among homologous points identified by the targets on frames corresponding to the same time instant generates the 3D information required, as is the case in standard photogrammetry. A set of 3D points representing the position in space of the targets for each time frame is, therefore, generated and used both for visual analysis or for extracting geometrical data of interest. Several commercial systems on the market perform this kind of motion capture, such as Vicon (www.vicon.com) or Optitrack (www.optitrack.com). Although the precision of the system is submillimetric, the limitation is represented by the 3D capture of only the targets' positions, and not of the geometry of the entire moving scene.

A low-cost version of such a visual method is possible with RGBD devices developed for video gaming, such as the Microsoft Kinect, ASUS Xion, Structure Sensor, or the Intel Realsense, which can provide streams of 3D data in real time from the investigated volume. In this way, the motion capture of a skeleton extracted by the raw 3D data can be provided [150]. An alternative approach is represented by miniaturized Inertial Measurement Units (IMUs). A magneto-inertial measurement unit typically embeds a triaxial gyroscope, a triaxial accelerometer, and a triaxial magnetic sensor in the same assembly. By combining the information provided by each sensor within a sensor fusion framework, it is possible to determine the unit orientation with respect to a common global coordinate system. Recent advances in the construction of microelectromechanical system devices have made possible the manufacturing of small and light devices that makes it possible to apply them to the moving body under investigation [36].

Among the few applications in the cultural heritage field worth mentioning are the digitization and visualization of several Kung Fu moves for the exhibition "300 Years of Hakka Kung Fu" (Fig. 13.7), held in 2017 at the Hong Kong Heritage Museum (China) [37, 101]; the 4D capturing of the classical dances of India made by School of Art Design at the Nanyang Technological University in Singapore [46]; and the European project i-Treasures, dedicated to the study of an integrated system for capturing intangible heritage [48].

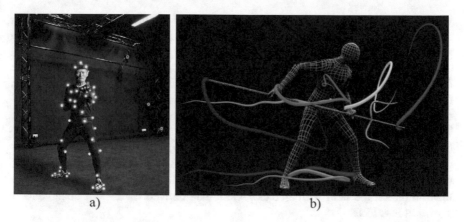

Fig. 13.7 Digitization of intangible heritage: **a** Kung Fu master in motion capture studio at City University of Hong Kong; **b** graphic representation of movements with colored trajectories of a few nodes of the moving 3D model. (Both images by courtesy of Sarah Kenderdine, EPFL, Lausanne, Switzerland)

13.2.3   3D Reconstruction of Damaged or No-Longer Extant Monuments

In addition to the reality-based digital modeling of heritage assets described in the previous sections, the 3D modeling of buildings, monuments, or entire cities that do not physically exist anymore in their original status has defined from the 1990s a new field of studies known as "Virtual Archeology" [126, 137], or more broadly "Virtual Heritage" [143].

A Virtual Archaeology 3D model can be created by purely philological considerations, using as source the existing archaeological literature on the monument to be reconstructed. In this case, the geometrical deductions about shape and size of the building and its components are entirely based on preexisting written documents, possibly containing older surveys of the area, often made with survey technologies much less accurate than those used in more recent times. This approach, although useful for illustrative purposes, may involve a considerable uncertainty in the resulting reconstruction model [135].

By using a 3D digitization of the existing elements, it is possible to improve the accuracy of the final reconstruction model by integrating the literature with trusted data collected from the existing remains. Examples of this might include a building's footprint or the height of remains still standing, both generally very valuable pieces of evidence in making a 3D reconstruction model.

This approach makes it possible to improve the accuracy of the initial data, for example, published plans or sections. They can be normalized by taking into account the new, trustworthy measured data, providing thereby a new starting point for drafting the plan, sections and elevations of the structure [144]. Similarly, when the older graphic documentation is not scientific but artistic, finding securely measurable surviving common elements in the older pictorial representation and in the monument today can improve the reliability of the resulting 3D model [55]. Furthermore, a precise three-dimensional representation of a building's remains can provide useful clues for estimating its height, a parameter not infrequently more difficult to estimate from ancient documents than is the footprint provided by the foundations. Moreover, the current height of a surviving architectural detail as well as its relationship to surrounding features in the environment can provide clues helpful to the reconstruction. The 3D measurement of any surviving decorative elements (such as a statue) can also help determine the size of niches and other architectural components, influencing the general shape of the reconstructed monument [87]. An example of such a complete reconstruction based on the integration of actual geometrical information currently measurable on the field with archaeological data derived by ancient documents is shown in Fig. 13.8.

However, the early 3D reconstructions [40, 59, 66] made clear that the many degrees of freedom of an archaeological 3D reconstruction can produce several different outcomes, and, therefore, they have to be governed by agreed-upon principles that make scientifically traceable each 3D modeling choice. This led to the introduction of the "London Charter," offering recommendations for the use of computer-based visualization methods in relation to intellectual integrity, reliability, documentation, sustainability, and access [15, 44]. Such guidelines, proposed in 2006 and refined in 2009, were further enriched in 2013 by the "International Principles on Virtual Archaeology" (also known as the Seville Principles) [16], endorsed by ICOMOS in 2017 [92]. This framework gives a set of rules upon which to structure a solid digital reconstruction of a site or building that no longer exists.

Apart from the technical issues of creating a 3D reconstruction of damaged or destroyed monuments, it is important to recognize that such creations are visualizations and as such conform to the general use cases defined by Ware in [162]:

1. Facilitating the cognition of large amounts of data
2. Promoting the perception of unanticipated emergent properties
3. Highlighting problems in the quality of the data
4. Clarifying the relationship of large- and small-scale features
5. Formulating research hypotheses

The first use relates to the use of cultural heritage reconstruction models in education in schools or public outreach by cultural heritage institutions. Generally, beginning students and the general public have a hard time imagining how a building reduced to its foundations originally looked and functioned, or how a statue reduced to a fragmentary torso once appeared in terms of its geometry and polychromy. A 3D reconstruction is a highly effective way to present an integration of the surviving evidence complemented by the various hypotheses of restoration. In this case, it ideally synthesizes and illustrates the collective views of experts who have studied the relevant issues underlying a hypothesis of restoration.

Fig. 13.8 Example of digital reconstruction of an archaeological site [87]: **a** 3D model of the current state of the templar group G at the archaeological site My Son (Vietnam); **b** virtual reconstruction of its hypothetical ancient structure based on the state model and on archaeological information about the area

The second through fifth use cases relate more readily to research. A digitally restored statue can be recontextualized into the digital reconstruction of its original house or religious sanctuary, which itself can be embedded into a reconstruction model of the entire settlement and set under a digitally recreated, dynamic, and historically correct daytime and nighttime sky. This series of digital creations can, to be sure, serve the purpose of the first use case (education and public outreach), but it can also allow experts to make discoveries or have insights that would have otherwise been impossible or impractical. For example, the recreated scene just described might reveal that there is an alignment between the sun and the statue at sunrise on a significant religious holiday. An example of such an alignment is the statue of Osirantinous in the Antoneion at Hadrian's Villa [61]. This might be considered an unanticipated emergent property of the dataset constituted by the statue and the foundations of the sanctuary as supplemented by various hypotheses of restoration. Regarding Ware's third use case, it does not infrequently happen that when a 3D reconstruction is made of a building that has already been the subject of a printed monograph by a building historian, it is discovered that some element or other of the building has been neglected, e.g., there is a room without an entrance, a floor that cannot be reached by a staircase, etc. [67]. In effect, creating a detailed 3D reconstruction is a rigorous exercise that forces the creative team to make a complete inventory of what is securely known, probably known, possibly known, and not known at all. In short, it highlights the problems of the quality of the underlying archaeological data.

Most interesting of all is Ware's fifth use case, where the 3D visualization helps the expert formulate, test, and refine research hypotheses, whether new or old. In the case of the study of history by Humanists and Social Scientists, one great limitation has always been the impossibility of turning back the clock to make observations of past environments and the activities taking place in them. With an interactive 3D reconstruction, this limitation is mitigated, if not eliminated: now, for the first time, it is possible for practitioners of historical disciplines to make observations, recreate experiences, and run experiments in an environment that either no longer exists or exists in a highly damaged form. This is the use of the 3D model as a cognitive tool, a characteristic cultural heritage models share with a wide range of scientific models in fields such as Astronomy, Biology, Chemistry, Engineering, and Physics. It has been recognized by philosophers of science that such tools not only illustrate previously accumulated knowledge but—because they are dynamic and, in the case of cultural heritage models, often involve hypotheses of restoration— can also generate new knowledge [163]. This use case has been recently termed "simpiricism," a portmanteau word combining "simulation" and "empiricism" [63].

13.3   Capture, Modeling, and Storage of Digitized Cultural Heritage

13.3.1   Capturing 3D Data from Cultural Heritage Assets

Digitization Approaches Versus Type of Cultural Heritage Object

Referring to tangible heritage, a first distinction among the 3D capturing techniques can be made according to the size of the object to be digitized, that can range from (a) small museum artifacts; (b) large museum artifacts like life-size or colossal statues; (c) buildings; (d) urban areas or archaeological sites; and (e) territories. This has a direct impact on some functional parameters that directly define the most suitable 3D technology needed. The most evident parameters include the possibility of working indoors or outdoors, the maximum spatial resolution, and the measurement uncertainty.

It is, therefore, important to consider what needs to be captured. In addition to the most strict 3D features associated with the object's shape, its accurate visual representation can be crucial, so that we should distinguish between (a) internal shape; (b) external shape; (c) color texture; and (d) material reflectance. These features also influence the physical principle behind the 3D technology to be chosen.

In addition, the methods we are considering involve no physical contact between the 3D sensor and the heritage asset to be digitized. Therefore, every 3D technology uses a radiating form of energy which, interacting with the surface to be measured, is somehow altered by the interaction and is then collected by a sensor that produces its measurement according to the amount of alteration arising from the interaction. In most cases the radiated energy is light, and the response of the 3D sensing method is affected by the nature of the material in terms of (a) reflectance (i.e., how shiny is the material?); (b) transmittance (i.e., how transparent is the material?); and (c) absorbance (i.e., how dark is the material?). In addition, if the light used for gathering the 3D information is not generated by the 3D sensor itself, as happens in active 3D devices, but is a natural or non-coded artificial light typically used in passive 3D methods, the presence of recognizable visual features on the surface to be digitized is also something that heavily influences the choice of 3D technology.

In addition to all the constraints to 3D digitization in terms of logistics, budget, timing, and cost/benefit ratio, the single most important element driving technological decision-making is the final purpose of the 3D model motivating the campaign of digitization in the first place. Between the two extremes of, on one hand, a metric model rendering a highly accurate virtual replica of the heritage object/scenario and, on the other hand, a rough non-metric 3D model for an approximate visual representation of the object (e.g., on a website aimed at the general public), there are several mid-points on the spectrum of design choices available to any 3D digitization project. Of course, the more accurate the model, the more analytical options are open to its end-user in making geometric measurements and visual evaluations. However, accuracy can come at a steep price in terms of 3D acquisition and processing time.

Digitization Approaches Versus Type of Technology

The available tools can be divided into classes depending on their operating principle. As mentioned above, in any case a form of radiating energy is always used for gathering geometrical and visual information, so a first distinction can be made between penetrating and non-penetrating radiations.

In the penetrating category, methods based on the same x-ray devices used in medicine, or, at higher energy, in the mechanical industry, and in airport security, make it possible to capture the inaccessible surfaces of heritage objects [35]. The typical opto-geometrical configuration in this case involves a source of radiation on one side of the object, and a sensing device on the opposite side.

Objects like Egyptian mummies may have amulets or materials used for the mummification process under the exterior bandages that can be conveniently imaged with penetrating radiations. Besides, the analysis of bones and teeth may reveal age, sex, health state, and death reason of the deceased person (Fig. 13.9), resulting in an informative complement for its historical interpretation [164].

X-Ray Computer Tomography (CT) is also useful for reverse engineering heritage objects in order to determine how they were assembled. In the research done on a Japanese wooden statue of the XIII century preserved at "La Venaria Reale" (Turin, Italy), the internal structure of its joints was identified with a portable CT system for restoration purposes, as was the presence of nails and screws used in previous restoration work to reattach the pieces with damaged joints [122]. This analysis becomes even more important when complex metallic mechanisms have to be analyzed without physically dismounting them on account of their fragility [68, 129].

Because it is not based on light, as is photogrammetry and active 3D sensing, X-ray 3D imaging does not suffer from the typical limitations of the interactions of light and materials that can compromise 3D digitization. This problem is typically encountered in artworks made of translucid or transparent materials such as glass, gemstones, amber, or ivory [107].

Although x-rays are the most common, different types of radiation such as accelerated neutrons can be involved in creating tomographic images that render a 3D volumetric representation of the investigated heritage object [121]. Recent developments based on the use of alternative radiation frequencies have made it possible to extend the approach from objects to larger structures, such as the attempt to 3D scan the interiors of the Egyptian pyramids using cosmic rays [123].

For *non-penetrating* 3D, the electromagnetic energy covers the visible and the infrared spectrum. The latter may also allow a little penetration under the illuminated surface depending on the actual wavelength used, ranging from fractions of a millimeter for Near InfraRed (NIR), to several millimeters for the Far Infrared (FIR) used in so-called TeraHertz imaging. However, in most 3D applications in the field of cultural heritage, penetrations inside the material are not important or useful, and this is the reason why light sources for 3D never go beyond NIR.

Within non-penetrating devices a further distinction has to be made between active and passive 3D methods.

Fig. 13.9 Different volume renderings of a Computer Tomography of a mummy conserved at the Archaeological Museum of Milan, Italy, making evident different structures: **a** exterior bandage; **b** skin around the head; **c** skull and bones, showing an impacted canine tooth

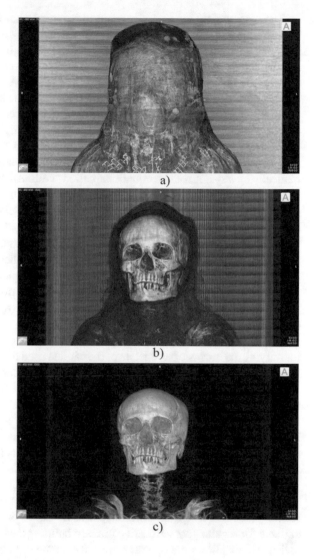

a)

b)

c)

In a *passive 3D method*, light is used only to illuminate the details of the scene. These details must be plainly visible elements contrasting with the background and richly present on all the points of the surface of interest. All 3D passive devices (e.g., theodolites) or methods (e.g., photogrammetry) use this feature, since the measurement process requires, first of all, that the same points be recognized in different views of a scene from various positions, and this is possible only if the measured object is provided with a contrast texture, or—when the object is uniformly colored with no salient points—if the operator has added reference targets over the surface of interest at a number of points sufficient for the task of estimating its 3D shape.

The most widely used passive method is digital photogrammetry, that estimates the 3D coordinates of a recognizable point in space by using at least two photos of it taken from different positions. The position of the imaged point on each photo implicitly defines a ray going from the point in the 3D space to its projection over the camera sensor plane. The presence of at least two rays originated by two different camera positions allows us to find an intersection in the space that identifies the 3D coordinates of the imaged point, starting from the 2D coordinates of its projections on two photographs. This condition is called "collinearity," referring to the alignment on the same line of the 3D point in space, the projection center of the camera, and the projected point on the photograph. The collinearity condition is represented mathematically by a system of two equations, called "collinearity equations," providing the projection coordinates on the sensor of a point, given its 3D coordinates, the camera position and orientation (extrinsic parameters), and a set of parameters representing how the projection is affected by the camera (intrinsic parameters). The intrinsic parameters include the focal length of the objective used for taking the image and a set of parameters taking into account the physical phenomena occurring in a real camera that tend to make different and actual photographic images from a theoretical perspective projection. Such parameters define the various lens distortions and the misalignment of the sensor to the lens optical axis due to the mechanical tolerances of the camera.

Therefore the photogrammetric process involves three phases: (i) calibration, for identifying the intrinsic parameters of the camera used for taking the image; (ii) resection, for establishing the extrinsic parameters of the camera; and (iii) intersection, for calculating the 3D coordinates of an imaged point starting from its projections on two or more images taken from different positions.

A crucial activity for making the method work is identifying correspondences among projections of the same points in different images. In general, the more reliable correspondences are found, the better are the results for the redundancy of information that makes more robust the identification of intrinsic and extrinsic parameters. In its early days, such identification was based on a significant manual process of a specialized operator who had to find out corresponding features on different images framing the same area from different points of view. For this reason, the method was suitable for regular geometries like modern buildings, where the knowledge of a few salient points allows the operator to easily remodel their shape in 3D, but not particularly attractive for 3D digitizing the complex shapes of cultural heritage assets, where the object's contours are often geometrically complex and/or blurred by aging or ruptures. However, Digital Photogrammetry has been extraordinarily improved in the last twenty years thanks to the automation of feature recognition provided by Computer Vision algorithms such as "Scale-Invariant Feature Transform" (SIFT) [111] or "Speeded Up Robust Feature" (SURF) [14]. Such algorithms are at the basis of the automation of the photogrammetric process. When the identification of correspondences among different images is made by a computer rather than a human operator, the considerable time needed for manually selecting the corresponding features is reduced of several orders of magnitude and is performed automatically by unattended computers. In this way, the number of correspondences can grow easily from a few tens to many thousands, making the calibration and resection processes, usually indicated as "Structure From Motion" (SFM) more reliable. The following triangulation among corresponding elements of images is obtained by means of the "Image Matching" (IM) process. Starting from picture elements of an oriented image, it looks systematically for the most likelihood correspondence in another oriented image (stereo matching), or group of images (multi-view matching), calculating the 3D coordinates of the point corresponding to the intersection of the two or more rays associated with such picture elements. Each picture elements represent a regular subdivision of the original image made of square sub-images whose side ranges from a few pixels to one single pixel. The output of that process is a dense cloud of points, made of a 3D point for every matching sub-image [112]. Therefore, if each sub-image is just one pixel, the maximum number of 3D points contained in the cloud associated to each matching, can be as large as the number of overlapping pixels among the two or more images involved. Considering that the number of images of a project may range from a few tens to thousands, and each image is made by several millions of pixels, the SFM/IM process can easily generate several millions of 3D points.

Although a manual intervention is always needed for scaling the 3D data according to one or more reference points to be set on the 3D digitized scene and measured with a different device, this highly automated version of the photogrammetric process makes it possible to greatly improve 3D productivity with respect to the traditional approach.

This is particularly valuable for 3D digitizing cultural heritage for the characteristics of the majority of aged materials typical of heritage artifacts and sites, which makes automatic feature extraction easy to be implemented. SFM/IM works well with all the materials that have a nearly Lambertian (diffusive) reflection, no transparency or translucency, and an irregular texture such as stone, bricks, and wood. It might be problematic when light reflection is diffusive, but no texture nor micro-irregularities are present at all, like, for example, in some white plaster copies of sculptures. It might also give poor results when a recognizable texture is associated with a high surface specularity like in ceramic vases or rough metal artifacts. Finally, it becomes very faulty when the material is transparent or specular and with little or no texture like, for example, glasses and polished metallic surfaces.

In an *active 3D method*, a coded light is projected onto the surface to be measured in such a way as to represent a reference visible from a sensing device such as a camera or a photodetector [26]. In this way, 3D measurement can also be done on completely textureless surfaces. If the projected light intensity is not too high, then environmental light may interfere with the coded light, making the device not usable, for example, outdoors. In this domain a further distinction is made between

- Devices based on triangulation, where the optical sensor is made by a light source and a camera set at a known distance, able to measure only small volumes but with a very small uncertainty (below 0.2 mm);
- Devices based on the direct measurement of distance, such as Time-Of-Flight (TOF) and Phase-Shift (PS) laser scanners, where the sensor-to-surface distance

is evaluated by the time needed by light to go from the sensor to the surface and back. These devices can be used at distances from few meters to few kilometers, and are, therefore, suitable for digitizing buildings, large artifacts, archaeological sites, or entire territories. In this case a much larger measurement uncertainty occurs, ranging from few millimeters to a few decimeters. The same principle is used in Laser Radars (LR), where the method for evaluating the distance is based on frequency-modulated light and where the measurement uncertainty can be reduced 20 times with respect to TOF laser scanners. Interferometry also works on the same principle, even if the method in this case is suitable for 3D digitization of very small samples (e.g., coins) with measurement uncertainty in the order of few micrometers;

- Devices based on laser-driven selective focusing of the imaged scene such as confocal microscopy, suitable for ultra-small samples or for the matter structure.

In any case, 3D active devices are the only ones capable of metrically acquiring the geometry of a surface automatically, with no need to resize the final 3D results. The result they produce is a "range image" representing the 3D view of the device from the point of acquisition.

The range image, or structured 3D point cloud, is a matrix of 3D coordinates similar to a color image where the color pixels are substituted by 3D coordinates. Often the gray level or the color associated with the surface reflectivity in the 3D recorded point is also provided as complementary information. 3D devices based on a rectangular sensor, or on a 360-degree scanning, typically generate a structured 3D point cloud that has the advantage to contain the implicit information about the normals associated with each point, pointing from the surface to the sensor measuring it. Such a piece of information is crucial for the following post-processing phases of the 3D data.

As an alternative, the 3D data can be represented as an unstructured cloud of 3D points made by a list of xyz coordinates generated by saving the 3D data in neutral interchange file formats based on text, like, for example, pts.

We have to point out that while a photogrammetric process provides a dense cloud of points of the 3D digitized object all defined in the same coordinate system, an active device gives a set of 3D images of the object taken from various points of view, each one represented in the internal coordinate system of the device. Such a non-negligible difference involves an entirely different procedure in the following processing, as explained in the next section.

13.3.2   Modeling Cultural Heritage from Raw Data

After 3D data acquisition, a post-processing phase is crucial for transforming a set of 3D points originated by a dense sampling of the heritage object's surface, into a reality-based 3D model.

Point Cloud Provided by 3D Active Devices

When the scene is imaged from different points of view with an active 3D device, each one provides a range image, whose 3D coordinates are represented in a local reference system centered on the 3D device. Since all these coordinate systems are unrelated it is necessary to align all 3D data into the same coordinate system for obtaining a single 3D point cloud representing the object surface. Such process can be achieved in three different ways:

1. Measuring some reference targets on the scene with a different 3D device providing their coordinates in a common reference. This approach is used more frequently with laser scanners based on direct measurement of distance (TOF, PS, LR), thanks to their large region of interest [146];
2. Using as references natural 3D features recognizable in more range images and finding the best possible match between them through the "Iterative Closest Point" (ICP) algorithm. This is the most used approach with triangulation-based devices, but it is often used also with the other active devices when no reference targets are available [22];
3. Using a complementary equipment like GPS+IMU, CMMs, Laser Trackers, or Motion Capture cameras, to measure the range device position and orientation of each acquired range image in a global reference system. The 3 coordinates and 3 rotations (6 degrees of freedom) of the 3D device can be used to calculate the transformation matrix of each range image from the local coordinate system of the 3D device to the global one. This allows us to provide on-the-fly the 3D data gathered from different positions in a single global reference. For this reason, this approach is at the heart of most mobile mapping device gathering 3D data from aerial vehicles, cars, robots, or handheld 3D devices [86].

Once the set of 3D data is available in the same reference system, a meshing process is able to transform them into a 3D polygonal model whose precision, accuracy, and resolution are determined by the quality of the initial raw data. This can afterward be edited and textured with an additional process [136].

Point Cloud Provided by a Photogrammetric Process

In the modern automatic photogrammetry techniques, the modeling process is far more straightforward, since the measuring phase provides directly 3D data all oriented within the same reference system.

The subsequent modeling phase consists in generating the polygonal from the point cloud originated by the photogrammetric process, representing a dense sampling of the exterior surface of the cultural heritage object.

Point Cloud Generated by Sensor Fusion

Integrating different devices for capturing cultural heritage sites or objects may give both a set of point clouds suitable for being pre-meshed, as for a single active device, or an unstructured point cloud as with photogrammetry, depending on the specific use of such integration. This approach has been proved to be useful for two specific purposes: (a) improving the global accuracy of the final result and (b) adapting the space resolution of the 3D capturing phase to the local richness of features of any specific 3D object.

Creating a 3D Model from Raw 3D Data This step of the process can vary depending on the technology providing 3D data and on the consequent structuring of such data. Before to see in detail how the process of transforming a set of raw 3D data into a 3D model works, it is appropriate to specify what is intended as a digital 3D model.

In general, a computer-based 3D model is defined as a digital representation of an object, made by a collection of geometric primitives connected to each other. Depending on the type and dimension of the primitives forming the 3D model, the way it is generated, its digital representation into the computer memory, and even its visual aspect can be very different.

A critical difference between modeling primitives is their dimensionality (i.e., 1D, 2D, or 3D). We can make a distinction among

- Mono-dimensional primitives: segments or curves connecting two points in the 3D space;
- Bi-dimensional primitives: planar or curved surface patches whose edges are represented by 1D primitives. They can be planar polygons like triangles, quadrangles (quads), or polygons with more than four sides (n-gons). As an alternative, they can be made of curved surface patches represented by polynomial expressions like the "Non-Uniform Rational B-Splines" (NURBS) or by surfaces obtained by iteratively subdividing a polygonal model according to a specific subdivision algorithm (Subdivision surfaces).
- Three-dimensional primitives: volumetric components like tetrahedrons, hexahedrons, cylinders, etc., aiming at representing the entire volume enclosed in the primitive and not only the surface surrounding it.

According to the modeling primitive used, the resulting model will result in a different category.

When 1D primitives connect 3D points of the object surface, the resulting 3D object is called a wireframe model. This type of representation describes the object shape with coarse approximation. It was used at the beginning of the computer graphics era when hardware resources were insufficient to render in real time a 3D model represented in a more sophisticated way. Nowadays, the structuring of a 3D model solely as a wireframe is obsolete. However, the associate visual rendering is still used for more complex forms of models, for 3D editing purposes, since the wireframe may help in making evident the inner model structure.

When 2D primitives connect lines or curves built upon 3D points of the objects, trying to approximate at best the object shape, the resulting 3D object is called a surface model. It can have different aspects depending on the actual 2D primitive employed.

We talk about mesh models when planar polygons, generally triangular or quadrangular (quad) connect 3D points belonging to the object surface. Such points, called nodes or vertices, can be either defined by an operator through a Computer-Aided

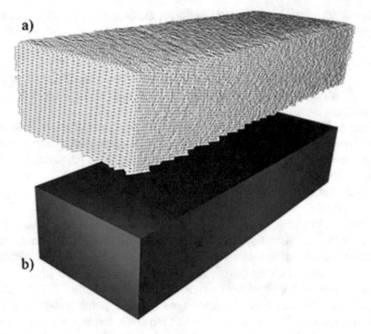

Fig. 13.10 Different surface models of the same parallelepiped made of: **a** triangular polygons built over the 3D point cloud originated by its 3D scanning; **b** manually edited quads

Design (CAD) tool or measured by a 3D sensor. In the first case, a minimal number of salient points can be used for representing a shape, while in the second one the 3D model is originated by a high-resolution sampling of the same form, and the generation of a mesh model made by many more polygons for representing the same geometrical information.

Figure 13.10 exemplifies the concept showing a 3D polygonal model of a parallelepiped test object in our lab, measuring 100 mm × 60 mm × 270 mm, made with a CAD program using the exact values of its size along x, y, and z (Fig. 13.10b). Since this object is made of rectified iron and painted matte white to avoid reflections, it was also 3D scanned, and the resulting mesh is shown in Fig. 13.10a. The lower model exhibits the ideal representation of the geometry of that object, while the upper one shows its possible physical imperfections as well as the measurement uncertainty of the 3D digitization process.

When a model is made by the connection of 3D primitives, it is called solid model and it is intended as a volumetric description of the modeled object, including its physical materiality. This type of models is generated as the combination of actions typical of an industrial process for physically manufacturing the object, and for this reason, they are mainly used in the mechanical engineering field since they work for both a visual representation of the object and the physical simulation of its static and dynamic behavior.

In digital 3D modeling of cultural heritage, the large majority of the models are surface models.

If generated by plans or blueprints, a surface model can be hand-drawn with a CAD modeler allowing NURBS design (e.g., Rhinoceros by MacNeel, Alias Studio, Maya, 3D Studio Max by Autodesk or the open-source package Blender), or polygon design (e.g., Modo by Foundry, Maya and 3D Studio Max by Autodesk or the open-source package Blender).

If generated by acquired point clouds, a dense polygonal mesh is instead the most suitable 3D modeling approach, considering that the measured points can shape a polygonal mesh representing the closest estimate of the object surface, within the tolerance of the 3D acquisition device measurement error.

The available approaches for generating a mesh out of 3D scanned data changes also depend on the nature and organization of the raw 3D data.

As seen in Sect. 13.3.1, we may have 3D sensors providing structured clouds of 3D points where the meshing can be easily made on each 3D image using as complementary information the relative position of each point to his neighbors. This allows a direct transformation from cloud to mesh on the single 3D image, where for each point on the sensor plane (xy), only one z value is available. This is also called range map or 2.5D point cloud. On such range maps, each point can be connected with the neighbors, that is known due to the data structure, through a regular triangular mesh. Each pre-meshed range map can be adequately segmented using the normals (i.e., the normals of each polygon forming the mesh) as feedback for determining break-lines over the mesh. This is generally made setting a threshold for the maximum angular difference of normals associated with adjacent polygons. Therefore, for a set of structured 3D data, the alignment phase ends up with a set of aligned 3D point clouds that can also be represented as a set of mesh patches of the whole object surface. The final mesh, in this case, can be obtained by merging different patches and smoothing the data over the overlapping areas. This can be done with a technique called zippering, consisting of eroding the regions at the intersection of the views and re-triangulating the eroded areas for building the final model [158], or making a smoothing on the overlapped region based on Venn diagrams [154].

If the raw 3D data that are not structured due to the way they are stored after being collected by the sensor, or because they are generated by a photogrammetric process, the triangulation is operated directly on the final dense 3D cloud. Such triangulation is far more complex than the straightforward triangulation of a 2.5D range map, and may involve two different strategies (Fig. 13.11) based on

- 3D data approximation, initially proposed in the Computer Graphics domain;
- 3D data interpolation, developed in the Geometric Processing domain.

The 3D data approximation approach aims at calculating a polygonal surface fitting the 3D captured data but not passing from the actual measured points. The methods belonging to this category can filter out possible noise and artifacts overlapped on the real 3D information but, at the same time, tend to smooth possible fine details. Such approximation may be convenient, for example, with data provided by 3D scanning

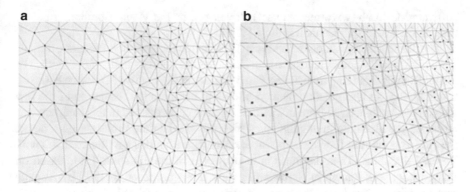

Fig. 13.11 Meshing of a point cloud, represented by yellow dots, with different meshing approaches: **a** data interpolation. Here all the points of the 3D cloud are also nodes of the mesh; **b** data approximation. The mesh fits the 3D points leaving part of them invisible below the surface, some visible because above the surface, and none of them corresponding to mesh nodes

archaeological sites with noisy TOF laser scanners or with poor photogrammetric photo set.

The oldest algorithm belonging to this category, called "Marching Cubes," is derived from the medical imaging domain where devices like Computer Tomography (CT) or Magnetic Resonance (MR) provide volumetric 3D data. This means that a volume is subdivided into regular small cells shaped as rectangular boxes (voxels), each associated with a measured density. Such data are mainly shown as a sequence of adjacent images. But if a 3D shape, for example of a bone, has to be extracted as a 3D entity from the entire dataset, all the cells containing a range of densities associated with a bone, will be identified. The corresponding iso-surface, generated in the form of a triangular mesh, will provide the 3D model of the bone [110]. The 3D scanned data are technically very different from CT or MR scans, since only the surface of an object is described and not his inner densities, and the surface sampling can be nonuniform. However, by defining a volume corresponding to the geometrical extent of the digitized object along the three dimensions and subdividing it with a proper granularity, it is possible to differentiate cells filled with a 3D point from those empty and apply the same concept for extracting a triangular mesh in correspondence of the filled cells [76]. Another very popular algorithm in this area is the Poisson surface reconstruction [99], which identifies an approximating function as a solution of a Poisson equation, using as inputs the coordinates of the 3D points, and the corresponding normals as samples of the gradients. This method was implemented, for example, in the proprietary software Agisoft Photoscan to generate a mesh from photogrammetric data. Although it provides a regular mesh without empty zones even in the presence of nonuniform input data, it is characterized by a significant smoothing of 3D details. For this reason, in 2013, it was improved with a version able to reduce smoothing called "screened Poisson surface reconstruction" [100]. An implementation of this algorithm is available for example on the open-source 3D processing software MeshLab (www.meshlab.net), developed by the Visual Computing Lab of the National Research Council in Italy [136].

The 3D data interpolation methods can be valuable for generating accurate meshes from high-quality point clouds using each measured point as node of the mesh. For example, after digitizing a small decorated artifact with an active 3D device based on triangulation, an interpolation method allows to maintain the resolution of the raw data on the mesh derived from it. The first algorithm introduced in this category was based on the Delaunay triangulation, where the 3D data are projected on a plane, the closest points are found, and possible redundant triangles are filtered in 2D with Voronoi diagrams. Then the mesh is re-projected in the 3D space [39]. Based on this concept well-known implementations are those proposed in 1999 by Amenta and Bern [6], refined with the name "power crust" in 2001 [8]. Another idea was implementing the "mesh growing" concept, as, for example, in the ball pivoting algorithm. Here, starting with a seed triangle, a ball touching three points of the 3D cloud is imagined, revolving around the edge while keeping in contact with the edge's endpoints until it touches another point, forming another triangle [23]. The co-cone algorithm is built on the same idea. In this case the mesh is originated by the union of co-cones (double cones with an opening angle of $\pi/8$ with respect to the estimated normal) placed at each point [7]. An efficient interpolation algorithm has also been recently proposed by Boltcheva and Lévy [28].

3D Editing

This phase of the 3D content generation mainly consists in (a) cleaning of the unavoidable topological errors in the mesh; (b) elimination of possible holes in the mesh that may arise during the automatic process; (c) smoothing of details determined just by artifacts and not corresponding to actual geometric details; and (d) possible rearrangement of the polygonal structure for optimizing the model size while minimizing the lack of geometrical information.

Topological issues are particularly vicious because, especially when large meshes are involved, they might be not evident at first, but they can produce issues in the following processing phases. This includes wrong model texturing, visual impairments in model rendering, unpredictable outcome of mesh simplification, or slower 3D interaction due to the presence of unexpected polygons inside the external mesh shell.

There are several types of topological errors that can occur on a mesh, representing a situation impossible on a real surface. Most of the times, these are originated by computational errors in the generation of the mesh, mostly due to noisy datasets or to the presence of outliers in the point cloud.

We should recall that the building blocks of a mesh are vertexes (or nodes) connected by triangular faces, each one characterized by a normal. And the digital description of the model consists in a list of nodes, represented by their x, y, and z coordinates in space, and a list of triangles, describing the connections between nodes addressed through their index. With this in mind, a comprehensive list of possible topological errors is presented in Fig. 13.12, where the following cases are shown:

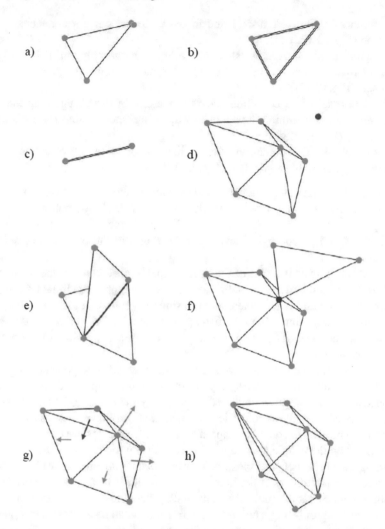

Fig. 13.12 Possible topology errors in a 3D mesh: **a** duplicate vertex; **b** duplicate face; **c** zero area face; **d** unreferenced vertex; **e** non-manifold edge; **f** non-manifold vertex; **g** flipped normal; **h** crossing faces

- Duplicate vertex—The same vertex is present twice in the list of mesh nodes (Fig. 13.12a)
- Duplicate face—The same face is repeated twice in the list of polygons despite the nodes are the same (Fig. 13.12b)
- Zero area face—A triangle is generated between one vertex and two separate instances of the same node, originating a degenerate triangle with zero area (Fig. 13.12c)

- Unreferenced vertex—A node listed in the node list but not connected to any polygon (Fig. 13.12d)
- Non-manifold edge—An edge shared by more than two polygons (Fig. 13.12e)
- Non-manifold vertex—A node shared by polygons not connected each other except for itself (Fig. 13.12f)
- Flipped normal—This condition occurs when one of the polygons in the mesh has a normal orientation in the opposite way with respect to those of its neighbor polygon(s) (Fig. 13.12g)
- Crossing faces—This condition occurs when one or more polygons intersect the rest of the mesh sharing no edges (Fig. 13.12h).

Such errors can be identified and corrected by some of the most diffused commercial programs for mesh editing like Polyworks Modeler from Innovmetric (Canada) or Geomagic Wrap from 3D Systems (USA). However, the most comprehensive set of tools for spotting topological errors can be found in the open-source software MeshLab.

Closing mesh holes is a part of the process that is needed when the focus of 3D modeling is cultural heritage visualization. The mesh represents in fact the support over which the texture is projected, and missing polygons in a mesh involve also a missing part in the texture, that is visually rather humble. This action is also needed if the model has to be 3D printed, because 3D printing is possible only on closed (aka watertight) meshes.

On the other hand, if the model is aiming at the most accurate geometric representation of a cultural heritage object, any alteration of the shape produced by closing the mesh with non-measured nodes extrapolated by the existing data while closing holes, may result in a false geometric document that, for this reason, is avoided.

Whenever needed, the practical approaches for closing holes in a mesh (Fig. 13.13) can be based on the simple closure with a plane fitting the nodes of the hole border smoothing the borders of such closure. This approach works in case of flat or quasi-flat surfaces. Alternatively, if the hole lies in the middle of a surface characterized by a significant curvature, the nodes surrounding the hole can be taken into account with their normal for fitting a polynomial surface that can be afterward sampled and meshed at the same spatial resolution of the surrounding mesh.

In the software packages that allow mesh editing, these two approaches are indicated as "flat filling" (Fig. 13.13b) and smooth filling (Fig. 13.13c), respectively.

Another process that might be used is the smoothing filtering that can be applied to the whole model or selectively if specific bad 3D digitization condition occurs in a specific area of the mesh. These can be due to a material not optically cooperating with the 3D digitization process (e.g., very dark or shiny surfaces acquired with a triangulation laser scanner) or errors made by the 3D digitization operator (e.g., insufficient image overlap in a photogrammetric process).

When the operator is aware that the details shown on the mesh are not actually present on the object but are just artifacts of the process, filtering—even if it is still a "falsification" of the original data—can improve the quality of the final result, as shown in Fig. 13.14.

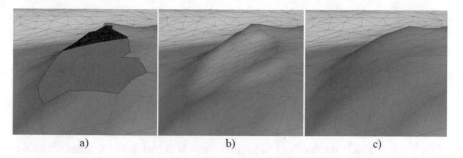

Fig. 13.13 Hole closure in the mesh representing a small terracotta sculpture: **a** mesh with the hole; **b** closure with flat filling; **c** closure with smooth filling

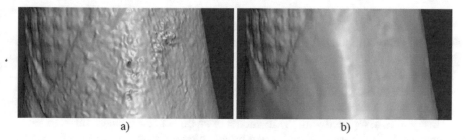

Fig. 13.14 Mesh smoothing: **a** mesh artifacts originated by an insufficient image overlap in a photogrammetric 3D digitization process; **b** smooth filtering of the surface

This rationalization of the mesh is useful also for the following simplification stage that might be based on different criteria: arbitrary determination of the total number of polygons in the final mesh or maximum deviation between the original and simplified mesh. The first approach can be useful, for example, if the mesh has to be used in an application with strong limitations in handling large numbers of polygons (e.g., a virtual museum app implemented on a smartphone). Otherwise the second criterion generally allows to maintain a better coherence between the simplified mesh and the original one, especially if the maximum deviation between the two is set smaller than the intrinsic measurement uncertainty of the 3D method for digitizing the heritage asset.

13.3.3   Creating a 3D Repository for Cultural Heritage

Today, the wide range of digital 3D objects considered for digitization and the technological and methodological improvements have generated a considerable increase in the production of digital 3D cultural heritage models, propelling the scientific community to start moving from keeping unstructured repositories of 3D models to devising structured databases. The design of a digital library containing 3D models of cultural heritage objects comprises two critical macro-components:

1. The semantic description of the digitized object through appropriately descriptive attributes useful for searching the object in a database. Such attributes are data describing other data (i.e., the actual 3D digital content), and for this reason are called "metadata".
2. The 3D content generation consisting of (i) the actual 3D digitization of the object by means of a technology appropriate to its size and details; (ii) storage of the 3D digitized object in a repository of considerable size owing to the large amount of data usually associated with 3D content; (iii) online access to the resource; and (iv) the availability of a suitable 3D viewer for visualizing the digitized heritage asset.

Description of CH Object for Online Access

The two macro-components just cited are equally important. Generally, the first step is defining a general structure for the attributes describing the heritage objects to be digitized. This step comes first because such structuring may influence the way the raw data are collected during the digitization process and stored in a directory tree coherent with the metadata structure [83].

Everything associated with the metadata of an object or a concept through terms interconnected with each other for use by a computer is part of the much broader areas of Artificial Intelligence (AI) and the Semantic Web. Both have been greatly developed in the last three decades [74]. In this context, the way metadata is inter-related with each other is called the "ontology". This is a term generally inspired by philosophy, where an ontology is a theory about the nature of existence, but in our context "ontology" is a terminus technicus relating to a collection of statements that define the relations between concepts in a language readable by a computer as well as the logical rules making it possible for a computer to apply them correctly [24]. Such "reasoning" is allowed by the "Resource Description Framework" (RDF) which facilitates representing structured information about any resource in the form of simple triple statements (subject, predicate, object). The assumption underlying RDF is that resources can be described by means of semantically meaningful connections between them.

Metadata and ontologies can be focused on specific disciplinary areas like healthcare, legislation, or biomedical research. The organization of information through this approach started in the field of library automation, where in the 1980s a large-scale digitization of library card catalogues was started in order to make it possible to perform book searches with computers. This led to the creation of large databases often arranged according to proprietary criteria and suitable for a search on a local computer with a specific software package. The explosion of the Internet encouraged organizations and operators to find a way to make such databases searchable independently of proprietary rules by adding a layer of "intelligence" to metadata, making web searches more effective than they otherwise would have been.

The first structured attempt to give a semantic connotation to bibliographic descriptions came at a workshop organized in 1995 by the Online Computer Library

Table 13.1 Dublin core metadata elements

Dublin core element	Use
Title	A name given to the resource
Subject	The topic of the resource
Description	An account of the resource
Creator	An entity primarily responsible for making the resource
Publisher	An entity responsible for making the resource available
Contributor	An entity responsible for making contributions to the resource
Date	A point or period of time associated with an event in the lifecycle of the resource
Type	The nature or genre of the resource
Format	The file format, physical medium, or dimensions of the resource
Identifier	An unambiguous reference to the resource within a given context
Source	A related resource from which the described resource is derived
Language	A language of the resource
Relation	A related resource
Coverage	The spatial or temporal topic of the resource, the spatial applicability of the resource, or the jurisdiction under which the resource is relevant
Rights	Information about rights held in and over the resource

Center (OCLC) at their headquarters located at Dublin (Ohio), USA. Here more than fifty people discussed how a core set of semantics for Web-based resources could be useful for easier search and retrieval using the World Wide Web. The results of that discussion became the "Dublin Core Metadata Schema," a name that refers to the location of the workshop. Originally developed to describe web resources, "Dublin Core" (DC) has been used to describe a variety of physical and digital resources. It is based on a "core" of 15 metadata elements (Table 13.1).

From 1996 the "International Council of Museums" (ICOM), through its "International Committee for Documentation" (CIDOC), extended the reasoning from web resources to generic cultural objects, developing its "Conceptual Reference Model" (CIDOC-CRM), an ontology for documenting cultural heritage and museum objects. In order to better describe, for example, the history of a manufactured item or a historical event, a set of refinements to the DC were added to make the schema able to describe spatiotemporal events, with the introduction of actors, temporal entities, and places where an action took place. Similarly, the active or passive involvement of actors in a historical event was mapped through hierarchical metadata.

This was done with the conviction, demonstrated by practical applications, that the explicit modeling of events leads to models of cultural contents that can better be integrated [50].

The CIDOC-CRM was progressively refined until 2006, when it became an ISO standard (ISO 21127).

In 2005, the effort to offer an improved level of interoperability among cultural heritage data coming from different institutions was further pursued with the creation of Europeana. It was conceived as an online resource for making Europe's cultural heritage accessible to all. To make this vast effort technically feasible, Europeana was designed to give access to different kinds of digital contents hosted by the heritage institutions in Europe rather than to collect the contents in a large central repository. Therefore, the digital objects that the user can find through Europeana remain with the cultural institution that created them, which is responsible for its preservation and accessibility. Europeana collects only the metadata describing each object, including a small picture of it (thumbnail). In functional terms, any user can search a resource on Europeana through an online search engine running on its local database of metadata provided by the various participating institutions. Once the user finds what he is looking for, he can click a link to the actual content, and he is automatically connected to a landing page arranged by the owner organization that owns and maintains the original resource.

A specific data model was proposed, the "Europeana Data Model" (EDM), for structuring the data that Europeana ingests, manages, and publishes, taking into account the development status of the Semantic Web at that time [49]. EDM was also an attempt to transcend the respective perspectives of the sectors represented in Europeana, namely, museums, archives, audiovisual collections, libraries, and research institutions.

However, it was only with the EU-funded project CARARE that the issue of describing 3D models of cultural heritage for publication on Europeana was considered. CARARE was a "Best Practice Network" active from 2010 to 2013. It was designed to involve and support Europe's network of heritage agencies and organizations, archaeological museums and research institutions and specialist digital archives in i) making available through Europeana their digital content for archaeological and architectural heritage; ii) aggregating content and delivering services; and iii) enabling access to 3D and Virtual Reality content through Europeana. One of the significant outcomes of the project was the development of a metadata schema with specialized fields specifically designed for describing 3D content. The schema was based on various semantic web pillars such as the Dublin Core and the CIDOC-CRM, but also on some more specialized standards including

- EDM, for maintaining compatibility with the Europeana Data Model
- MIDAS Heritage, for information about the historical environment
- POLIS DTD, conceived as an interoperability framework for cultural heritage
- LIDO (Lightweight Information Describing Objects), resulting from an international effort in the museum sector

In recent years, the CARARE schema has been enriched thanks to the 3DICONS project, another EU-financed initiative specifically aimed at populating Europeana with 3D models of cultural heritage (http://3dicons-project.eu). Through 3DICONS, more than 3,000 models were produced and stored in local repositories in sixteen European countries, and the related metadata was ingested into Europeana. The critical issues raised by this experience led to progressive refinements climaxing in CARARE 3.0, a draft of which was circulating while this chapter is being written.

Apart from the many specific standards that cannot be analyzed in depth here because of space limitations, any metadata schema associated with 3D digital content derived by a cultural heritage object will contain at least the following typologies of data:

- Descriptive metadata. They include the name and identifier (e.g., inventory number) of the heritage asset. They also describe features like material, author (if known), history, and significant dates of the described object, as well as its typology (archaeological monument, historic building, industrial monument, archaeological landscape area, shipwreck, artifact, ecofact, etc).
- Technical metadata. They include technical information that applies to any 3D object, including the sensor used for the 3D digitization, the process for creating the 3D model from the raw data, the 3D model size in terms of polygons and texture size, the file type and information about the software and hardware on which the digital object can be rendered or executed.
- Administrative metadata. They include provenance information about who is responsible for the digital preservation of the digital object as well as rights and permission information that specifies, for example, what access to the digital object is permissible.

Production and Online Access to CH Digital Object

The techniques used for 3D digitization of large sets of heritage objects are the same as those described in Sect. 13.3.1, except for the fact that large-scale digitization requires an optimized serialization of activities to make sustainable the production of a large number of 3D models per operator and per time unit.

Previous experiences of this type to be reviewed here include i) the EU-financed project 3DICONS (http://3dicons-project.eu), where the Politecnico di Milano provided more than 500 3D models under the leadership of one of the coauthors of this chapter; and ii) The "Uffizi-Indiana University" project (www.digitalsculpture.org/florence), led by the other coauthor of this chapter. In the latter project, currently still underway, the Virtual World Heritage Lab at Indiana University is digitizing the ca. 1,000 ancient sculptures housed in the various collections of the Uffizi Galleries in Florence (Italy).

As already mentioned in Sect. 13.2.1, the 3DICONS experience has shown that, in case of the large-scale production of 3D models, the photogrammetric approach is by far more suitable than 3D capture with active range sensors [78]. On average, each operator in the 3DICONS project was able to produce six models per month. The same approach with some further optimization was applied in the Uffizi-Indiana University project. As a result, productivity was increased to sixteen models per operator per month. The optimization of the process consisted in (i) the systematization of image capture according to predefined settings suitable for gathering the level of detail needed by the application (and not more); (ii) use of a monopod and a remote control of the camera when dealing with large artifacts; (iii) the use of fixed focal length lenses to improve 3D data quality; (iv) capturing geometry normalized according to a fixed base schema with local variations determined by the specific peculiarity of each piece; (v) use of a quick single laser scan to speed up the scaling phase of photogrammetric modeling; (vi) use of wide-angle lenses and illumination devices for capturing surfaces of the artifacts positioned close to walls or to other occluding elements; and (vii) systematic storing of the raw images and intermediate processing in a way coherent with the object metadata [114].

Once the 3D models are available, the next technical issue concerns the design of the repository. Fixed rules are difficult to prescribe owing to the great variability of the size of the 3D models to be accessed from the database, the kind of cultural heritage objects included, and the level of detail chosen for their data capture. The previously mentioned experiences suggest some key best practices.

The two main requirements for a 3D repository are that it offers enough space for accommodating all the 3D models expected to be included in the collection and that it offers a Uniform Resource Locator (URL) for each model which is added to its identifying metadata record. For example, in the 3DICONS project all the digital objects were allocated on a Network Attached Storage (NAS) made of four physical hard disks connected as a Redundant Array of Independent Disks (RAID). The data protection was provided with internal redundancy with RAID 5, a RAID schema with parity blocks cyclically distributed over the array, which is used to recover the data in case of failure of one of the four disks of the array.

For the Uffizi-Indiana University project, the space for the 3D models was allocated on a series of hard disks of the Virtual World Heritage Laboratory. A tape unit provided by the Scholarly Data Archive of Indiana University (https://kb.iu.edu/d/aiyi) provided for backup.

In general, the prediction of the actual space needed for an application like this is very dependent on the digitized material and on the level of detail required by end-users who will consult the 3D material. Usually, for the simple textured 3D model (i.e., excluding all the images/measurements taken on the field to generate the final three-dimensional representation of a museum artifact), a reasonable upper limit is 500 MB per model. This results in a rough estimation of 2,000 models per TB. Obviously, such an estimate may change dramatically in cases of models representing large architectural structures not subdivided into elementary components or of territorial models derived, for example, from aerial laser scanning or drone photogrammetry.

The space required might be very different if the storage area is used for all the material associated with the production of the model as well as for the model itself. The latter is sometimes generated in a high-resolution master version with one or more low-resolution variants for online delivery, depending on the purpose of the repository. For example, this was the approach followed in the 3DICONS project because of the need to respect the strict copyright laws of Italy. In Italy, a low-resolution digital representation of a museum object can be freely distributed, but a special authorization from the museum which owns the object is required if the representation is above a certain resolution. Owing to the need for dual-model generation (at low and high resolution) and the decision to preserve both the raw data and the final high- and low-resolution models, the space needed in the 3DICONS project was on average 3 GB per item, leading to an average of ca. 300 models per TB. Thus, the total space required for the 550 models of architectural structures and museum objects, including the raw 3D data collected on the field for the generation of the 3D models, was ca. 1.7 terabytes (TB).

Regarding web visualization of 3D content, both Open Source and commercial solutions have become available in recent years. User interaction with a model can be achieved in two different modes:

1. The 3D model is stored remotely in a standard format such as *obj*, *ply* or *3Dpdf* which can be read by a 3D viewer installed on the local computer of the end-user;
2. The 3D model is stored remotely on a dedicated portal in a format that is not necessarily standard or known to the end-user, but the portal itself provides a 3D viewer for accessing the material.

The way the model is visualized can also follow three different modalities, according to the rendering type chosen:

a. Local rendering. The 3D content is first entirely downloaded by the end-user before it can be visualized. Once the model is fully downloaded, in a time period depending on its size and on bandwidth, the rendering is produced on the local computer of the end-user, with a frame rate of the rendered scene depending on the processing capability of the local computer. This approach is used either if the 3D model is first downloaded in a standard format and shown with a local 3D viewer (mode 1), or if after downloading, the 3D viewing function is provided by the portal itself through a WebGL application (mode 2).
b. Remote rendering. The 3D model is preserved and rendered remotely while the end-user accesses it [148]. Instead of downloading the 3D content locally, only a stream of frames originated by the rendering is sent to the local end-user, resulting in much higher protection of the copyrighted 3D material. This rendering approach always involves the use of mode 2.
c. Local rendering of 3D model chunks remotely preserved. This approach offers two advantages: (i) good data protection because the entire model is not transmitted but only pieces of it at different resolutions depending on the virtual navigation chosen by the user and (ii) low latency time since the rendering is done locally on only a small part of the entire model.

For example, most of the 3D models accessible on Europeana from the 3DICONS project are stored as 3Dpdf files, downloadable through the link provided by a Europeana search from the content provider. To access the 3D content the end-user must have the original Acrobat Reader from Adobe, the only one able to read 3D contents in pdf files. Hence, here we see exemplified implementation of interaction mode 1 with rendering type 1.

Nowadays, the most commonly used platform for sharing a 3D model online is Sketchfab (https://sketchfab.com), a commercial web service conceived as a general-purpose platform for accessing 3D content through the web, offering for 3D models a service similar to what YouTube offers for videos. It is widely used in the cultural heritage community [90]. It exemplifies the case of interaction in mode 2 with rendering of type 1.

In connection with the Stanford Digital Michelangelo Project, in the early 2000s, a set of tools was developed that included Scanview, software for visualizing the project's 3D content using interaction mode 2 and rendering type 2 [104]. In the early 2010s, the concepts behind this tool were further developed to exploit WebGL (a standard that did not exist when Scanview was first conceived) by the Digital Sculpture Project of the Virtual World Heritage Laboratory (http://www.digitalsculpture. org).

A system that is sometimes used today to visualize cultural heritage content is the "3D Heritage Online Presenter" (3DHOP), a framework for the creation of advanced web-based visual presentations of high-resolution 3D content such as those needed in the cultural heritage field. By using multi-resolution encoding, it is able to efficiently stream high-resolution 3D models such as those originated by 3D digitization employed in cultural heritage applications [134]. In this case, the interaction uses mode 2 with rendering type 3.

13.4   Experimental Application

13.4.1   3D Digitization of a Little Clay Sculpture with Photogrammetry

The test object is a 48 cm tall low-cost reproduction of one of the soldiers in the so-called Terracotta Army, namely, a collection of terracotta sculptures depicting the armies of Qin Shi Huang, the first Emperor of China.

For this example, the commercial tool Agisoft Metashape—one of the most widely available SFM/IM tools used today—was employed. Among its various features, it has the possibility to print coded targets to be used on the scene for scaling purposes. Therefore, after having printed several sheets with 6 targets per page and having cut three pairs of targets per page, four of these pairs were used for preparing the set where the object was photographed, as shown in Fig. 13.15.

The table where the object was located, surrounded by illuminators, was first prepared with coded targets taped over it. The targets' relative distances were measured with a metallic tape meter for having a scaling reference, as shown in the following figure.

Two long distances between the centers of the coded targets were taken for controlling the model scale:

- d(100, 107) = 492 mm
- d(98, 101) = 509.5 mm

Fig. 13.15 Field preparation before starting the photogrammetric 3D digitization. Two long distances between coded targets are taken with a tape meter for controlling the model scale (d(100, 107) = 492 mm and d(98, 101) = 509.5 mm), while the shorter distances d(97, 98), d(99, 100), d(101, 102), and d(107, 108), all equal to 95 mm, are used for checking the scaling result

The shorter distances [d(97, 98), d(99, 100), d(101, 102), d(107, 108)], all equal to 95 mm, were used for checking the scaling result at the end of the process.

The sequence of images was taken at a distance suitable for capturing all the details of the surface whose minimal size was estimated in 0.5 mm with a caliper, before starting the photogrammetric campaign. According to the Shannon–Nyquist sampling theorem [147], the minimal 3D sampling spacing that allows to reconstruct such detail is half its size, therefore 0.25 mm emerged to be the minimal 3D resolution of the point cloud originated by this process, allowing to "see" such detail. In order to correlate such value to the image resolution we have to consider that Agisoft Metashape will be set in the following processing in a modality that generates one 3D sample for every 4 pixels, therefore we have to aim at an image resolution equal to 0.25/4 = 0.0625 mm.

This value, also called in the photogrammetric literature as "Ground Sampling Distance" (GSD) based on its original meaning in aerial photogrammetry, is determined by the camera-surface distance (d), the size of the pixel over the photographic sensor (px), and the focal length of the lens used for taking the images (f). To find the relationship between those parameters, it is sufficient to consider the diagram in Fig. 13.16.

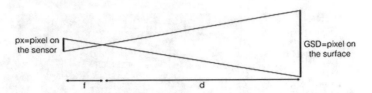

Fig. 13.16 Geometrical relationship between the active cell of a photographic sensor and the GSD, i.e., the spacing among adjacent pixels once projected over the imaged surface

Here a portion of the surface to be imaged, lying at a distance d by the projection center of the camera, is projected over the sensor inside the photo-camera, lying at a distance f from the projection center of the camera. The portion of the object's surface indicated as GSD is the one corresponding to the active pixels px over the sensor. The two triangles sharing one vertex in the projection center are similar, therefore the base/height ratio will be equal, which means

$$px/f = \frac{GSD}{d}.$$

If we want to know, what is the maximum distance at which to operate the camera in order to guarantee the desired resolution, we need also to know some technical details about the camera to be used. In our case, a Sony Alpha 6300 equipped with a macro 30 mm lens was used. This gives us two useful parameters of the problem: $f = 30$ mm and the pixel size px. The latter value requires some additional technical information, viz., the size of the sensor in terms of both geometrical extension and number of pixels. As easily found in the technical specifications of the camera, it is equipped with an APS-C sensor whose size is 23.5 mm × 15.6 mm, providing 24 Mega Pixels organized as a 6000 × 4000 matrix. For this reason, the pixel size over the sensor can be found either as 23.5 mm/6000 or 15.6 mm/4000 since the matrix geometry tends to be dimensioned to ensure a square pixel. In both cases we get $px = 0.0039$ mm.

Hence, if our digitization problem required an assigned GSD, the minimal camera-object distance will be given by

$$d = \frac{GSD}{px} f.$$

That with the number of the problem gives $d = (0.0625/0.0039) * 30$ mm $= 481$ mm. So, keeping the camera at least at 48.1 cm from the object will ensure the needed 3D resolution at the end of the photogrammetric process.

Of course, such reasoning is exact for a planar surface while for a round object like the one in this example it gives a value depending on the point of the object where the camera distance is evaluated, giving anyway an order of magnitude and an upper limitation for the camera-object distance.

Such precise estimation of resolution does not take into account the presence of measurement uncertainty and 3D artifacts in the captured point cloud which can hide details even if the 3D resolution is appropriate.

In addition, these considerations about 3D resolution have to be evaluated in relation to the final purpose of the model. If the purpose is an accurate geometrical documentation, the proper resolution is crucial. Contrariwise, if the goal is to create a 3D object for purposes of visualization, the information contained in the texture can be enough, and the geometrical resolution can be strongly reduced.

The second step in the preparatory phase is determining the camera positioning that requires a set of views from different locations in order to capture all the surface features of the object, maintaining an overlap level of at least two thirds from one shot to the next, so that in the fully overlapped zone the same feature can be seen in at least 3 subsequent images. We should first consider that for a camera equipped with a sensor whose size is $w_s * h_s$, shooting at a distance d with a lens having focal length f, the framed area has width w_f and height h_f, given by

$$w_f = \frac{d}{f}w_s, \quad h_f = \frac{d}{f}h_s.$$

For the settings evaluated before the camera-target distance is 481 mm, the focal length is $f = 30$ mm and the APS-C sensor has width $w_s = 23.5$ mm and height $h_s = 15.6$ mm. Hence, $w_f = (481/30) * 23.5$ mm $= 377$ mm and $h_f = (481/30) * 15.6$ mm $= 250$ mm, corresponding to an angular view of 43° horizontally and 29° vertically.

In these conditions, assuming we take portrait-oriented images in order to ensure better capture of the geometry of a specific object, the 2/3 overlap rule will give a lateral displacement s between adjacent images given by 1/3 of the horizontal frame size, given in this case by h_f since we are using the portrait orientation. In the case of a lateral displacement (i.e., with the camera kept orthogonal to the imaged surface) we would have $s = 250$ mm$/3 = 83$ mm. However, we have to take into account that in this case the framing covers the entire sculpture, and there is a circular movement of the shooting position around the object. The actual sculpture has a rectangular base of 16 cm by 14 cm and is 48 cm tall. So, if we assume, for the sake of simplicity, that we can approximate this sculpture with a cylinder whose diameter is 15 cm, photographed from a distance of 48 cm (see Fig. 13.17), we can evaluate the angular portion of the object "seen" by the camera considering the two right triangles having the optical axis of the camera as the hypotenuse.

Each one has one side tangent to the cylinder and the smallest angle given approximately by arctan $(7.5/48) = 8.9°$. So, the other non-right angle will be 90°-8.9°=81.1°. By doubling these values, we will obtain the angular coverage of the object from the camera (17.8°), and therefore the angular portion of the object seen from that point of view (162.2°).

By applying the 1/3 rule to this convergent shooting, we can see that the minimum number of images will be one every 162.2°/3=54°, that means about 6.6 images around the object. A higher number of images results in a better overlap that generates

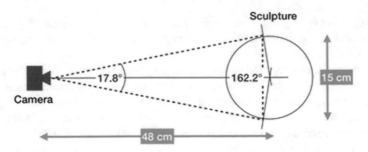

Fig. 13.17 Angular coverage of each image given the camera-target relative position

more redundancy and improved results. Therefore, the images actually taken in this case numbered about 12 (nearly double of the minimum) at three different vertical positions, in order to cover all the surfaces of the object, with the addition of a few close-ups for some details like the legs or the arms.

Regarding the camera setting, the A mode was used (i.e., automatic with aperture priority), in order to maintain a fixed aperture throughout the whole image set. This allows a better estimation of the radial distortion parameters, strongly influenced by aperture variations. The actual aperture was set to F8, which at the chosen operating distance and with the selected lens and camera gives a depth of field of 8.5 cm, sufficient for the depth of sculpture chosen. The total number of images taken ended up being 57. A sample of the photo set is shown in Fig. 13.18.

The photogrammetric process could be therefore started with the image alignment step that includes the automatic estimation of thousands of corresponding features on the selected images, called in the vocabulary of the specific software used in this example, "tie points." This massive identification of corresponding features originates a redundant system of collinearity equations made by thousands of equations (two for every feature).

The best approximate solution of such a system is found with the bundle adjustment technique that gives as output the 3D coordinates of each tie point, the extrinsic parameters of the cameras (i.e., the positions and angular orientations of the images in the project), and the intrinsic parameters of the camera (i.e., the calibration parameters, the same for each image). It should be noted that the system of coordinates used at this stage is relative and arbitrary, determined by the first image used as a starting point for the process. The oriented images for this example are shown in Fig. 13.19.

Good feedback for the quality of the alignment process is provided by reprojecting the tie points over the images and checking the deviation from the coordinates of the corresponding features initially identified over the images. Such quantity, called reprojection error, should be generally below one pixel. The Metashape software allows us to estimate this error and also to select the tie points with a reprojection error above a predefined threshold. Once the tie points producing a larger reprojection error are deleted, the bundle adjustment can be reiterated until the result gives a

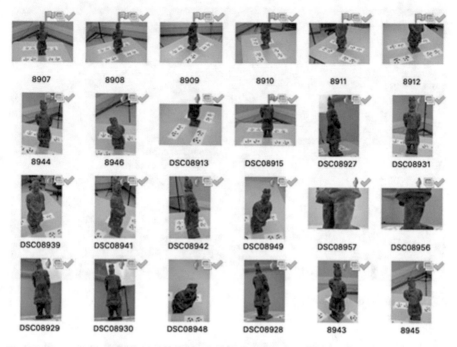

Fig. 13.18 A sample of the images taken for the photogrammetric 3D digitization of the sculpture

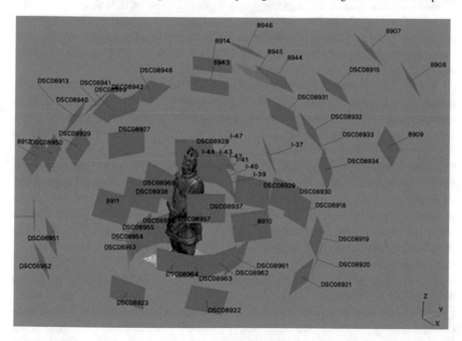

Fig. 13.19 Image distribution in space

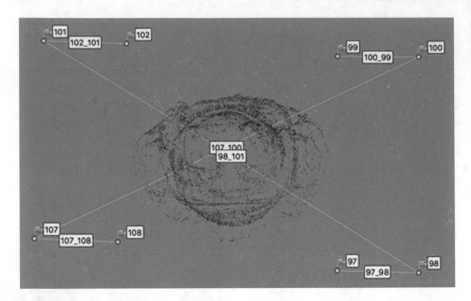

Fig. 13.20 Image distribution in space

satisfactory outcome. In the case of this example after one step of refinement, about 25,000 tie points were used, providing a reprojection error of 0.38 pixel.

After the images' orientation, the project can be scaled using the reference points measured at the beginning. The software used allows us to automatically identify the coded targets on the scene. The user can then select pairs of identified targets, defining one or more scale bars and assigning a size to it.

In Fig. 13.20 the targets photographed in Fig. 13.15 are shown in the photogrammetric environment. Two scaling bars represented by the two diagonal distances between (107, 100) and (98, 101) have been used for scaling the project, while the short distances between (97, 98), (99, 100), (101, 102), (107, 108) for checking the scaling result, as shown in Fig. 13.21.

These numbers provide a good feedback about the metrological quality of the result, resulting 0.092 mm on the control scale bars and better than 0.3 mm on the checking scalebars. Once the images in the set are oriented in space and the camera parameters are known, it is possible to perform the image matching phase, that for every image of the set, systematically generates a 3D point for each pixel or group of pixels recognized in other images of the same set. Given the size of each image, this process can easily generate millions of 3D points.

The software used in this example makes it possible to set the size of the matching entity with a parameter indicated (rather misleadingly) as "quality." A "super-high" quality means matching pixel-by-pixel, a "high" quality matching 2×2 pixel windows, a quality "medium" matching 4×4 pixel windows and so forth, halving the linear image resolution at each step. So, starting from the same oriented images, the number of 3D points originated at a certain quality level is reduced by four passing to

Scale Bars	▲ Distance (m)	Accuracy (m)	Error (m)
☐ ▤ 97_98	95.000000	0.001000	0.201431
☑ ▤ 98_101	509.500000	0.001000	0.104543
☐ ▤ 100_99	95.000000	0.001000	-0.459790
☐ ▤ 102_101	95.000000	0.001000	-0.083347
☑ ▤ 107_100	492.000000	**0.001000**	-0.077077
☐ ▤ 107_108	95.000000	0.001000	0.302530
Total Error			
Control scale bars			0.091842
Check scale bars			0.295995

Fig. 13.21 Scaling results. The distances between (98, 101) and (107, 100), measured in the field with a tape measure, were used for imposing two scaling factors with an average error of 92 micrometers. The other recorded distances, theoretically equal to 95 mm, provide an average error lower than 0.3 mm. Despite the caption of the table, all the values are expressed in mm

the lower level or multiplied by four passing to the higher level because the "quality" is actual "density" or "3D sampling frequency."

In this case, we chose a "medium" quality determining the 1:4 resolution ratio between the 3D cloud and the images, mentioned at the beginning of this section. The dense cloud created in this way turned out to have 4.3 million 3D points (Fig. 13.22b).

The following step consisted in creating the mesh from this high definition set of data. Theoretically, to maintain all the details contained in the dense cloud, a mesh should contain approximately a number of polygons twice the number of 3D points. However, since the software contains an intelligent simplification process that tends to dynamically adapt the size of the polygon to the size of the represented feature, it is possible to reduce the number of actual polygons in the final mesh. Depending on the details in the 3D shape, the number of polygons may range from 20% to 50% the number of 3D points in the dense cloud without a significant detail loss.

In addition, it has to be noted that the meshing algorithm implemented in this software package belongs to the "3D data approximation" category, mentioned in the subsection "Creating a 3D Model from Raw 3D Data" of Sect. 13.3.2. This always implies a certain level of smoothing passing from the dense cloud to the mesh. For this reason, certain applications of SFM/IM photogrammetry to cultural heritage, like for example 3D survey for monitoring purposes, tend to use the raw 3D point cloud rather than the meshed model in order to reduce to a minimum any loss of geometric details [130].

In this example, given the presence of large sections of the model with few details, we arbitrarily decided to generate a mesh with 1.5 million polygons, that after some editing with an external program was reduced to 1.2 million, owing to the cut of the plane in the bottom part. The latter is shown untextured in Fig. 13.22c.

The final stage of the modeling consists in texturing the 3D model with the images initially used for creating its geometry (Fig. 13.22d). To map a 2D space on a three-

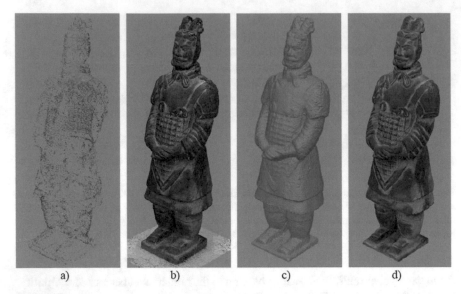

a)   b)   c)   d)

Fig. 13.22 Four processing steps in the photogrammetric 3D modeling of the sculpture used in this example: **a** 25,000 tie points identified on the surface of the object and in the close neighborhood; **b** dense cloud made of 4.2 million 3D points; **c** untextured edited mesh made of 1.2 million polygons; **d** same mesh textured using a 8k × 8k UV mapping space

dimensional surface, we use the well-known process called UV mapping, which is a standard process in computer graphics.

The process consists in defining a square area whose axes are denoted U and V and unwrapping the 3D model over such area, if necessary, breaking its geometry into parts. This creates a bi-univocal mapping between the 3D surface and the 2D area of the UV space whose extension goes conventionally from 0 to 1 on each axis (Fig. 13.23). When this ideal space has to be converted in a digital map, this is practically made with a square image whose side is, in general, a power of two, typically 4096 x 4096, 8192 x 8192, and so forth.

When this operation is completed, every surface of the model has a correspondence with the pixels of this square image that is used for projecting the images of the photogrammetric image set. The projection can be made with all the images of the dataset or with a limited subset, for example, avoiding the images very inclined with respect to the model surface, in order to avoid strong nonuniformity in the texture resolution.

In order to optimize the uniformity of texture resolution, it is also possible to include in the photogrammetric image set a few shots taken with the camera orthogonal to the artifact's surface, taken from the main views (front, right, left, etc.), selecting only those images and few integrative views in the texturing phase.

Once the UV parametrization is done, the same mapping space can be used not only by a texture, but potentially by other maps that can be used in computer graphics,

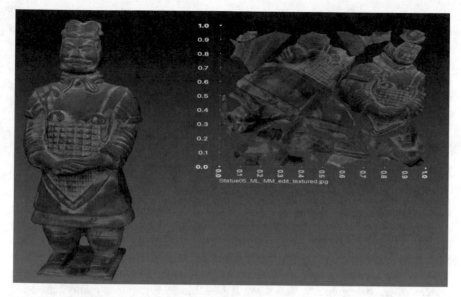

Fig. 13.23 UV parametrization for the model shown in Fig. 13.21

like displacement, normals, ambient occlusion, opacity, emission, or transparency, if the visualization environment used for interacting with the 3D model is able to accommodate them. For some purely visual applications, this may allow us to greatly reduce the model's polygon count, baking the visual information into a set of maps, as usually happens in 3D computer games, which require light 3D models to support real-time rendering of dynamic interactions.

13.4.2   Overview of the Software Tools Used

As made clear in the previous section, digitizing an ancient artifact in 3D with photogrammetry involves different tools that pertain to the different phases of the process. In our specific example, we have used the software packages specified below for the different phases of the process:

- Photogrammetry (feature extraction/camera calibration/image orientation): Metashape by Agisoft (www.agisoft.com). The choice of this commercial tool was motivated by the universally recognized stability of this tool for that part of the process, together with the possibility to intervene manually on the refinement of camera calibration parameters. Possible commercial alternatives to this program are RealityCapture by Capturing Reality (www.capturingreality.com), ReCap by Autodesk (www.autodesk.com/products/recap), Photomodeler by Photo-Modeler Technologies (www.photomodeler.com), 3DF Zephyr by 3DFlow (www.3dflow.

net), Pix4D by Pix4D SA (www.pix4d.com), and iWitnessPRO by DeChant Consulting Services DCS Inc. (www.iwitnessphoto.com).

- Photogrammetry (Image matching): Metashape
- Mesh topology check/correction: Meshlab
- Mesh holes correction: Meshmixer
- Mesh smoothing: Meshmixer
- Mesh texturing: Metashape

13.5   Open Challenges

Technically, the production of 3D models for cultural heritage can be considered a solved problem with respect to the geometrical component for many categories of scenarios that are optically cooperative, independently of their size. A significant difference does exist in terms of modeling time between steady active devices, which still need substantial manual effort for post-processing the data, and mobile active devices or photogrammetry, that make it possible to generate a reality-based 3D model with minimal human effort. With the same types of materials, the generation of the texture component can also be considered a solved problem for all applications where the quality of a photographic image is considered adequately accurate.

In particular, the experience with recent EU-financed projects such as 3DICONS, the project CultLab3D by Fraunhofer Institute, or the Indiana University-Uffizi 3D Digitization Project, whose goal is digitizing the entire collection of ancient sculptures in the Uffizi Galleries, demonstrated how today automatic photogrammetry based on SfM/IM is the preferred technology for massive digitization of CH, making it possible to produce a textured model 5 to 20 times faster than that required by steady active 3D devices [82].

However, if the 3D digitization involves scenarios with non-cooperative materials (e.g., those that are shiny or transparent), apart from penetrating radiations that may work in some cases, we still lack efficient technological solutions for obtaining a mesh model.

Regarding material reflectance, which is important for accurately rendering the visual aspect of a digitized heritage asset, the existing methods give good results only on specific categories of objects, typically those small enough to fit into complex structures for generating sequences of images with various illumination geometries. Here 3D technology needs to progress to extend reflectance estimation to a broader category of heritage objects while also reducing the time needed for making the estimate.

What is still lacking in the Humanities and Social Science side is a complete understanding of the metrological aspects related to 3D digitization. Any 3D capturing technology gives limited resolution, accuracy, and precision, and a full awareness of what is needed for a specific cultural heritage application has a direct impact on the whole 3D digitization pipeline, with direct consequences for feasibility and costs. Therefore, the nature, strengths, and limitations of the 3D capture technology chosen for any given project should be completely understood by end-users in the Humanities and Social Sciences when they must determine how best to handle the inevitable trade-off between costs and benefits in any proposed 3D digitization project.

3D digitization of cultural heritage is triggering new opportunities and challenges for sharing heritage goods. These changes are leading to an evolution of the economic, cultural, and social value of heritage, which requires more innovative policy and governance solutions than those generally adopted. This novel approach, also known as "participatory governance of cultural heritage," is becoming—especially in Europe—a growing interdisciplinary area. It is a direct consequence of the multiple possibilities of interconnections between artifacts, sites, historical events, and narratives, once in digital form. Historically speaking, the governance of cultural heritage has often been a top-down approach: from institutions (i.e., the "experts") to the public. By contrast, participatory governance of cultural heritage combines knowledge of the real interests and needs of the society with those of the cultural heritage assets (collections, staff competence, etc.). As a result, it recognizes many different "experts," involving the participation of local communities and shaping the perception of an identity related to a place and its cultural heritage.

13.6 Conclusion

After initial resistance by the cultural authorities to the introduction of the new technologies discussed herein, over the past twenty years, 3D digitization has gradually become a routine activity for recording and preserving heritage. Especially in the countries more endowed with tangible heritage such as Greece, Italy, France, or the UK and that are fortunate to belong to a governmental structure (the European Union) which typically offers strong financial backing to cultural activities of all kinds, 3D digitization is even required as a standard form of documentation for heritage sites and monuments.

More generally, globalization, digitization, and the pervasive adoption of ICTs are changing the way cultural heritage is produced, presented, accessed, and used. At the same time, cultural heritage is increasingly recognized as a competitive advantage in some areas of the world, leading to an evolution of the economic, cultural, and social value of heritage, which requires more innovative policy and governance solutions than those generally adopted.

The paradigm shift involved by those changes generates several challenges determined by the porting of cultural heritage to the digital era, for example, the strong need of an interdisciplinarity approach bridging the humanities and the highly technical disciplines, or a new threat in the form of the long-term conservation of digital objects, which are much more fragile than the pyramids or marble sculptures.

Such new scenarios also open up new opportunities and new areas of study and research that will require new professional figures up to the task of facing this aspect of the digital revolution. We hope that the training of such new professionals will benefit from this chapter.

13.7   Further Reading

This chapter touches several scientific areas, and of necessity it could not go into too much depth when discussing the topics treated above, some of them, indeed, are suitable for an entire book.

For this reason, several articles and books have been cited throughout the chapter, both to support the statements made but also to suggest links to external readings useful for deepening knowledge about specific topics.

Therefore, instead of suggesting other texts, we invite readers to search inside the text the specific subject of interest and to refer to the papers/books mentioned there, with particular emphasis on the review and state-of-the-art papers.

13.8   Questions

1. What are, in general, the possible purposes of 3D digitizing cultural heritage?
2. What makes a 3D model more effective than an image in documenting a heritage object?
3. What is meant by the acronym HBIM?
4. In the 3D digitization of sculpture and other museum artifacts, what is the most difficult material to scan: wood, marble, or bronze? And, why?
5. Assuming you wish to create the 3D model of a sculpture, what is the quicker method to obtain a texturized mesh: laser scanning or photogrammetry?
6. Does it make sense to digitize in 3D a painting? Can you cite any examples of this being done?
7. Why is it sometimes useful to integrate different 3D technologies?
8. In the case of underwater photogrammetry of an ancient relic in deep waters (i.e., $> 100\,\text{m}$) a ROV is generally used. What is that?
9. What type of technologies are used for digitizing intangible cultural heritage?
10. To what does the term "Virtual Heritage" refer?
11. What is the purpose of the criteria contained in the "London Charter" and in the "Seville Principles"?
12. Which are the five benefits of visualization such as 3D reconstructions of cultural heritage defined by Ware?
13. What is "simpiricism"?
14. Should the final purpose of a cultural heritage 3D model influence the cost of the related 3D digitization process? If so, why?

15. When is it appropriate to make 3D models of heritage assets by the use of penetrating radiation such as X-rays?
16. What is the difference between active and passive 3D digitization methods?
17. What does the collinearity condition mean in photogrammetry?
18. How could the photogrammetric process become automatic in SFM/IM?
19. Which category of 3D active devices can be used in cultural heritage digitization?
20. How can 3D range maps originated by a 3D active device be registered in the same coordinate system?
21. Considering the same heritage object, how is the genesis of a dense cloud originated by an active device different from one of a dense cloud originated by SFM/IM photogrammetry?
22. Are 3D scanned heritage assets generally modeled as surface or volume 3D models?
23. Meshing a 3D cloud can be done with two alternative approaches: data approximation or data interpolation. Which one is the most suitable for creating a detailed mesh whose nodes are exactly corresponding with the measured points?
24. How does the "marching cubes" algorithm operate to generate a mesh from the raw data?
25. What does it mean when a mesh has a non-manifold edge?
26. Would it be better to close a hole in the mesh of a sculpture in a quasi-planar region of the model by flat or smooth filling?
27. What do we mean when we speak about metadata for the 3D model of a cultural heritage object?
28. In discussing metadata, to what does the term "ontology" refer?
29. What is the "Dublin Core"?
30. What are the possible approaches to create an online visualization of a 3D model?
31. What are the open challenges in the 3D digitization of cultural heritage?

References

1. G., P., Pingi, P., Siotto, E., Bellucci, R., Guidi, G., Scopigno, R.: Deformation analysis of Leonardo da Vinci's "Adorazione dei magi" through temporal unrelated 3D digitization. J. Cult. Herit. **38**, 174–185 (2019)
2. Abate, D., Menna, F., Remondino, F., Gattari, M.: 3d painting documentation: evaluation of conservation conditions with 3d imaging and ranging techniques. Int. Arch. Photogramm. Remote Sens. Spat. Inf. Sci. - ISPRS Arch. **40**, 1–8 (2014)
3. Achille, C., Fassi, F., Fregonese, L.: 4 years history: From 2D to BIM for ch: The main spire on milan cathedral. In: Proceedings of 2012 18th International Conference on Virtual Systems and Multimedia, pp. 377–382 (2012)
4. Addison, A.: Emerging trends in virtual heritage. IEEE Multimedia **7**, 22–25 (2000)
5. Akca, D., Grun, A., Breuckmann, B., Lahanier, C.: High definition 3D-scanning of arts objects and paintings. In: Proceedings of Optical 3D Measurement Techniques VIII, pp. 50–58 (2007)
6. Amenta, N., Bern, M.: Surface reconstruction by Voronoi filtering. Discret. Comput. Geom. **22**, 481–504 (1999)

7. Amenta, N., Choi, S., Dey, T., Leekha, N.: A simple algorithm for homeomorphic surface reconstruction. In: Proceedings of the Sixteenth Annual Symposium on Computational Geometry - SCG '00, pp. 213–222. ACM Press, New York (2000)

8. Amenta, N., Choi, S., Kolluri, R.: The power crust. In: Proceedings of the Symposium on Solid Modeling and Applications, pp. 249–266 (2001)

9. Ballard, R., McCann, A., Yoerger, D., Whitcomb, L., Mindell, D., Oleson, J., Singh, H., Foley, B., Adams, J., Piechota, D., Giangrande, C.: The discovery of ancient history in the deep sea using advanced deep submergence technology. Deep. Res. Part I Oceanogr. Res. Pap. **47**, 1591–1620 (2000)

10. Barazzetti, L., Remondino, F., Scaioni, M., Brutto, M.L., Rizzi, A., Brumana, R.: Geometric and radiometric analysis of paintings. Int. Arch. Photogram., Remote Sens. Spatial Inf. Sci. **XXXVIII**, 62–67 (2010)

11. Baribeau, R., Rioux, M.: Influence of speckle on laser range finders. Appl. Opt. **30**, 2873–2878 (1991)

12. Bass, G.: Archaeology Under Water. Thames & Hudson, London (1966)

13. Bass, G., van Doorninck, F.: A fourth-century shipwreck at yassi ada. Am. J. Archaeol. **75**, 27–37 (1971)

14. Bay, H., Tuytelaars, T., Van Gool, L.: Surf: Speeded up robust features. In: Leonardis, A., Bischof, H., Pinz A., (eds.) Proceedings of 9th European Conference on Computer Vision, pp. 404–417. Springer, Berlin (2006)

15. Beacham, R., Nicolucci, F.: The London charter for the computer-based visualisation of cultural heritage. Technical report, King's College London (2009)

16. Bendicho, V.M.: International guidelines for virtual archaeology: The Seville principles. In: Corsi C., Slapsak, B., Vermeulen, F. (eds.) Good Practice in Archaeological Diagnostics: Non-invasive Survey of Complex Archaeological Sites, pp. 269–283. Springer International Publishing, Cham (2013)

17. Beraldin, J.A., Blais, F., Cournoyer, L., Rioux, M., Bernier, F., Harrison, N.: Portable digital 3D imaging system for remote sites. In: Proceedings of 1998 IEEE International Symposium on Circuits and Systems (Cat. No.98CH36187), pp. 488–493 (1998)

18. Beraldin, J.A., Guidi, G., Ciofi, S., Atzeni, C., et al.: Improvement of metric accuracy of digital 3D models through digital photogramme-try. a case study: Donatello's Maddalena. In: Proceedings of International Symposium on 3D data Processing Visualization and Transmission, pp. 3–6 (2002)

19. Beraldin, J.A.: Integration of laser scanning and close-range photogrammetry - the last decade and beyond. In: ISPRS Archives – Volume XXXV Part B5 (2004). http://www.isprs.org/proceedings/xxxv/congress/comm5/papers/188.pdf

20. Beraldin, J.A.: Modelling the Erechteion. Technical Report, National Research Council, Canada (2009). https://www.gim-international.com/content/article/modelling-the-erechteion

21. Bernardini, F., Rushmeier, H., Martin, I., Mittleman, J., Taubin, G.: Building a digital model of Michelangelo's florentine pieta. IEEE Comput. Graph. Appl. **22**, 59–67 (2002)

22. Bernardini, F., Rushmeier, H.: The 3D model acquisition pipeline. Comput. Graph. Forum. **21**, 149–172 (2002)

23. Bernardini, F., Mittleman, J., Rushmeier, H., Silva, C., Taubin, G.: The ball-pivoting algorithm for surface reconstruction. IEEE Trans. Vis. Comput. Graph. **5**, 349–359 (1999)

24. Berners-Lee, T., Hendler, J., Lassila, O.: The semantic web. Sci. Am. **284**, 34–43 (2001)

25. Blais, F., Taylor, J., Cournoyer, L., Picard, M., Borgeat, L., Godin, G., Beraldin, J.A., Rioux, M., Lahanier, C.: Ultra high-resolution 3D laser color imaging of paintings: the Monalisa by Leonardo da Vinci. In: Proceedings of 7th International Conference on Lasers in the Conservation of Artworks, pp. 1–8 (2008)

26. Blais, F.: Review of 20 years of range sensor development. J. Electron. Imaging **13**, 231–243 (2004)

27. Böhler, W., Marbs, A.: 3D scanning instruments. In: Bohler, W., (ed.) Proceedings of the CIPA WG 6 International Workshop on Scanning for Cultural Heritage Recording, pp. 9–12 (2002)

28. Boltcheva, D., Lévy, B.: Simple and scalable surface reconstruction. Technical report, LORIA - Université de Lorraine; INRIA Nancy (2016)
29. Brown, B., Toler-Franklin, C., Nehab, D., Burns, M., Dobkin, D., Vlachopoulos, A., Doumas, C., Rusinkiewicz, S., Weyrich, T.: A system for high-volume acquisition and matching of fresco fragments. ACM Trans. Graph. **27**(84), 1–9 (2008)
30. Bruno, F., Gallo, A., De Filippo, F., Muzzupappa, M., Davidde Petriaggi, B., Caputo, P.: 3D documentation and monitoring of the experimental cleaning operations in the underwater archaeological site of Baia (Italy). In: Proceedings of 2013 Digital Heritage International Congress (DigitalHeritage), pp. 105–112. IEEE (2013)
31. Bruno, F., Lagudi, A., Muzzupappa, M., Lupia, M., Cario, G., Barbieri, L., Passaro, S., Saggiomo, R.: Project visas: Virtual and augmented exploitation of submerged archaeological sites-overview and first results. Mar. Technol. Soc. J. **50**, 119–129 (2016)
32. Callieri, M., Pingi, P., Potenziani, M., Dellepiane, M., Pavoni, G., Lureau, A., Scopigno, R.: Alchemy in 3D: a digitization for a journey through matter. In: Proceedings of 2015 Digital Heritage, pp. 223–230. IEEE (2015)
33. Capra, A., Costantino, D., Rossi, G., Angelini, M., Leserri, M., Politecnico, D., Turismo, V.: Survey and 3d modelling of castel del monte. In: Proceedings of CIPA 2005 XX International Symposium, pp. 183–188 (2005)
34. Carboni, N., De Luca, L.: Towards a conceptual foundation for documenting tangible and intangible elements of a cultural object. Digit. Appl. Archaeol. Cult. Herit. **3**, 108–116 (2016)
35. Casali, F.: X-ray and neutron digital radiography and computed tomography for cultural heritage. In: Bradley, D., Creagh, D., (eds.) Physical Techniques in the Study of Art, Archaeology and Cultural Heritage, pp. 41–123. Elsevier (2006)
36. Cereatti, A., Della Croce, U., Sabatini, A.: Three-dimensional human kinematic estimation using magneto-inertial measurement units. In: Müller, B., Wolf, S., Brueggemann, G.P., Deng, Z., McIntosh, A., Miller, F., Selbie, W. (eds.) Hand-Book of Human Motion, pp. 1–24. Springer International Publishing, Cham (2017)
37. Chao, H., Shaw, J., Kenderdine, S.: 300 years of Bakka kung fu: digital vision of its legacy and future. Tech. report, International Guoshu Association, Hong Kong (2016)
38. De Luca, L., Veron, P., Florenzano, M.: Reverse engineering of architectural buildings based on a hybrid modeling approach. Comput. Graph. **30**, 160–176 (2006)
39. de Berg, M., Cheong, O., Kreveld, M.V., Overmars, M.: Delaunay triangulations. In: Computational Geometry, pp. 191–218. Springer, Berlin (2008)
40. Debevec, P.: The Parthenon. In: Proceedings of ACM SIGGRAPH 2004 Computer Animation Festival, p. 188. ACM, New York (2004)
41. Dellepiane, M., Dell'Unto, N., Callieri, M., Lindgren, S., Scopigno, R.: Archeological excavation monitoring using dense stereo matching techniques. J. Cult. Herit. **14**, 201–210 (2013)
42. Dell'Unto, N., Leander, A., Dellepiane, M., Callieri, M., Ferdani, D., Lindgren, S.: Digital reconstruction and visualization in archaeology: case-study drawn from the work of the Swedish Pompeii project. In: Proceedings of 2013 Digital Heritage International Congress (DigitalHeritage), pp. 621–628 (2013)
43. Demesticha, S., Skarlatos, D., Neophytou, A.: The 4th-century b.c. shipwreck at Mazotos, Cyprus: new techniques and methodologies in the 3D mapping of shipwreck excavations. J. F. Archaeol. **134**–150 (2014)
44. Denard, H.: A New Introduction to the London Charter. Ashgate Publishing Ltd (2012)
45. Denker, A.: Rebuilding Palmyra virtually: recreation of its former glory in digital space. Virtual Archaeol. Rev. **8**(17), 20–30 (2017)
46. Dhanapalan, B.: Capturing kathakali: Performance capture, digital aesthetics, and the classical dance of India. In: Proceedings of 2016 22nd International Conference on Virtual System and Multimedia (VSMM), pp. 1–7. IEEE, Kuala Lumpur (2016)
47. Diamanti, E., Vlachaki, F.: 3D recording of underwater antiquities in the South Euboean Gulf. ISPRS - Int. Arch. Photogramm. Remote Sens. Spat. Inf. Sci. **XL-5/W5**, 93–98 (2015)
48. Dimitropoulos, K., Tsalakanidou, F., Nikolopoulos, S., Kompatsiaris, I., Grammalidis, N., Manitsaris, S., Denby, B., Crevier-Buchman, L., Dupont, S., Charisis, V., Hadjile-ontiadis,

L., Pozzi, F., Cotescu, M., Ciftci, S., Katos, A., Manitsaris, A.: A multimodal approach for the safeguarding and transmission of intangible cultural heritage: the case of i-Treasures. IEEE Intell. Syst. **33**, 3–16 (2018)

49. Doerr, M., Gradmann, S., Hennicke, S., Isaac, A.: The European Data Model (EDM). In: Proceedings of World Library and Information Congress: 76th IFLA General Conference and Assembly, pp. 1–12. Gothenburg, Sweden (2010)

50. Doerr, M.: The CIDOC conceptual reference module: an ontological approach to semantic interoperability of metadata. AI Mag. **24**, 75–92 (2003)

51. Doneus, M., Miholjek, I., Mandlburger, G., Doneus, N., Verhoeven, G., Briese, C., Preges-bauer, M.: Airborne laser bathymetry for documentation of submerged archaeological sites in shallow water. ISPRS - Int. Arch. Photogramm. Remote Sens. Spat. Inf. Sci. **XL-5/W5**, 99–107 (2015)

52. Drap, P., Merad, D., Hijazi, B., Gaoua, L., Nawaf, M., Saccone, M., Chemisky, B., Seinturier, J., Sourisseau, J.C., Gambin, T., Castro, F.: Underwater photogrammetry and object modeling: a case study of Xlendi wreck in Malta. Sensors **15**, 30351–30384 (2015)

53. Drap, P., Seinturier, J., Hijazi, B., Merad, D., Boi, J.M., Chemisky, B., Seguin, E., Long, L.: The rov 3D project. J. Comput. Cult. Herit. **8**, 1–24 (2015)

54. El-Hakim, S., Beraldin, J., Picard, M., Godin, G.: Detailed 3D reconstruction of large-scale heritage sites with integrated techniques. IEEE Comput. Graph. Appl. **24**, 21–29 (2004)

55. El-Hakim, S., Lapointe, J.F., Whiting, E.: Digital reconstruction and 4D presentation through time. In: Proceedings of ACM SIGGRAPH 2008 Talks, pp. 44:1–44:1. ACM, New York (2008)

56. Fieber, K., Mills, J., Peppa, M.V., Haynes, I., Turner, S., Turner, A., Douglas, M., Bryan, P.: Cultural heritage through time: a case study at Hadrian's wall, United Kingdom. Int. Arch. Photogramm. Remote Sens. Spat. Inf. Sci. - ISPRS Arch. **42**, 297–302 (2017)

57. Foni, A., Papagiannakis, G., Magnenat-Thalmann, N.: A taxonomy of visualization strategies for cultural heritage applications. J. Comput. Cult. Herit. **3**, 1–21 (2010)

58. Fontana, R., Greco, M., Materazzi, M., Pampaloni, E., Pezzati, L., Rocchini, C., Scopigno, R.: Three-dimensional modelling of statues: the Minerva of Arezzo. J. Cult. Herit. **3**, 325–331 (2002)

59. Forte, M., Pescarin, S., Pietroni, E., Dell'Unto, N.: The Appia antica project. Archaeological landscapes through digital technologies. In: Forte, M. (ed.) Proceedings of the 2nd Italy United States Workshop, Rome, Italy, November, 2003; BAR International Series 1379. BAR Archaeopress, Oxford (2005)

60. Frischer, B., Abernathy, D., Guidi, G., Myers, J., Thibodeau, C., Salvemini, A., Müller, P., Hofstee, P., Minor, B.: Rome reborn. In: Proceedings of ACM SIGGRAPH, Article No. 34 (2008)

61. Frischer, B., Zotti, G., Mari, Z., Vittozzi, G.: Archaeoastronomical experiments supported by virtual simulation environments: celestial alignments in the Antinoeion at Hadrian's villa (Tivoli, Italy). Digit. Appl. Archaeol. Cult. Herit. **3**, 55–79 (2016)

62. Frischer, B.: 3D data capture, restoration and online publication of sculpture. In: Campana, S., Remondino, F. (eds.) 3D Modeling in Archaeology and Cultural Heritage, pp. 137–144. BAR Archeopress, Oxford (2014)

63. Frischer, B.: Edmund Buchner's solarium Augusti: New observations and simpirical studies. Atti della Pontif. Accad. Rom. di Archeol. **89**, 80–81 (2018)

64. Frischer, B.: Introduction with remarks on digital restoration of the Richmond Caligula and its methodological implications. Technical Report, University of Virginia (2013). http://www. digitalsculpture.org/papers/frischer/frischer_paper.htm

65. Frischer, B.: Reconstructing Epicurus' lost portrait statue. Technical Report, University of Virginia (2013). http://digitalsculpture.org/epicurus/index02.html

66. Frischer, B.: The digital roman forum project: remediating the traditions of roman topography. In: Forte, M. (ed.) Proceedings of Acts of the 2nd Italy-United States Workshop, Rome, Italy, November, 2003; BAR International Series 1379, pp. 9–21. BAR Archaeopress, Oxford (2005)

67. Frischer, B., Abernathy, D., Caroli Giuliani, F., Scott, R., Ziemssen, H.: A new digital model of the roman forum. J. Roman Archaeol. JRA Suppl. Ser. Numb. **61**, 163–182 (2006)
68. Fritsch, D., Wagner, J., Simon, S., Ceranski, B., Niklaus, M., Zhan, K., Schweizer, T., Wang, Z.: Gyrolog — towards VR preservations of gyro instruments for historical and didactical research. In: Proceedings of 2018 Pacific Neighborhood Consortium Annual Conference and Joint Meetings (PNC), p. 1–7 (2018)
69. Fryer, J., Fraser, C.: On the calibration of underwater cameras. Photogramm. Rec. **12**, 73–85 (2006)
70. Fusiello, A., Murino, V.: Augmented scene modeling and visualization by optical and acoustic sensor integration. IEEE Trans. Vis. Comput. Graph. **10**, 625–636 (2004)
71. Galeazzi, F., Callieri, M., Dellepiane, M., Charno, M., Richards, J., Scopigno, R.: Web-based visualization for 3D data in archaeology: the ads 3D viewer. J. Archaeol. Sci. Rep. **9**, 1–11 (2016)
72. Godin, G., Beraldin, J.A., Taylor, J., Cournoyer, L., Rioux, M., El-Hakim, S., Baribeau, R., Blais, F., Boulanger, P., Domey, J., Picard, M.: Active optical 3D imaging for heritage applications. IEEE Comput. Graph. Appl. **22**, 24–35 (2002)
73. Godin, G., Rioux, M., Beraldin, J., Levoy, M., Cournoyer, L., Blais, F.: An assessment of laser range measurement on marble surfaces. In: Proceedings of 5th Conference on Optical 3D Measurement Techniques, pp. 49–56 (2001)
74. Gray, P., Storrs, G., du Boulay, J.: Knowledge representations for database metadata. Artif. Intell. Rev. **2**, 3–29 (1988)
75. Gruen, A., Remondino, F., Zhang, L.: Image-based reconstruction of the great Buddha of Bamiyan, Afghanistan. In: Proceedings of SPIE, vol. 5013. Videometrics VII (2003)
76. Guennebaud, G., Gross, M.: Algebraic point set surfaces. ACM Trans. Graph. **26**, 23 (2007)
77. Guidi, G., Atzeni, C., Seracini, M., Lazzari, S.: Painting survey by 3D optical scanning: the case of "Adorazione dei Magi" by Leonardo da Vinci. Stud. Conserv. **49**, 1–12 (2004)
78. Guidi, G., Barsanti, S., Micoli, L., Russo, M.: Massive 3D digitization of museum contents. In: Toniolo, L., Boriani, M., Guidi, G., (eds.) Built Heritage: Monitoring Conservation Management, pp. 335–346. Springer, Berlin (2015)
79. Guidi, G., Beraldin, J.A., Atzeni, C.: High-accuracy 3D modeling of cultural heritage: the digitizing of Donatello's "Maddalena". IEEE Trans. Image Process. **13**, 370–380 (2004)
80. Guidi, G., Beraldin, J.A., Atzeni, C.: Wood artworks monitoring through high-resolution 3D cameras. In: Proceedings of SPIE Videometrics IX, pp. 1–7 (2007)
81. Guidi, G., Cioci, A., Atzeni, C., Beraldin, J.A.: Accuracy verification and enhancement in 3D modeling: Application to Donatello's maddalena. In: Proceedings of Fourth International Conference on 3D Digital Imaging and Modeling, pp. 334–341 (2003)
82. Guidi, G., Malik, U., Frischer, B., Barandoni, C., Paolucci, F.: The Indiana University-Uffizi project: Metrological challenges and workflow for massive 3D digitization of sculptures. In: Proceedings of 2017 23rd International Conference on Virtual System and Multimedia (VSMM), pp. 1–8. IEEE, Dublin, Ireland (2017)
83. Guidi, G., Micoli, L., Gonizzi, S., Navarro, P., Russo, M.: 3D digitizing a whole museum: a metadata centered workflow. p. 307–310. IEEE (2013)
84. Guidi, G., Remondino, F., Russo, M., Menna, F., Rizzi, A., Ercoli, S.: A multi-resolution methodology for the 3D modeling of large and complex archaeological areas. Int. J. Archit. Comput. **7**, 39–56 (2009)
85. Guidi, G., Remondino, F., Russo, M., Spinetti, A.: Range sensors on marble surfaces: quantitative evaluation of artifacts. In: Proceedings of SPIE on Videometrics, Range Imaging, and Applications X, pp. 744703 (2009)
86. Guidi, G., Remondino, F.: 3D modelling from real data. In: Modeling and Simulation in Engineering, pp. 69–102. IntechOpen Limited (2012)
87. Guidi, G., Russo, M., Angheleddu, D.: 3D survey and virtual reconstruction of archeological sites. Digit. Appl. Archaeol. Cult. Herit. **1**, 55–69 (2014)
88. Guidi, G., Spinetti, A., Carosso, L., Atzeni, C.: Digital three-dimensional modelling of Donatello's David by frequency-modulated laser radar. Stud. Conserv. **54**, 3–11 (2009)

89. Guidi, G., Tucci, G., Beraldin, J.A.A., Ciofi, S., Damato, V., Ostuni, D., Costanti-no, F., El Hakim, S.: Multiscale archaeological survey based on the integration of 3D scanning and photogrammetry. In: Proceedings of CIPA WG 6 International Workshop on Scanning for Cultural Heritage Recording, pp. 13–18 (2002)

90. Hagmann, D.: Reflections on the use of social networking sites as an interactive tool for data dissemination in digital archaeology. Interdiscip. Archaeol. - Nat. Sci. Archaeol. **IX**, 7–20 (2018)

91. Howard, R., Björk, B.C.: Building information modelling - experts' views on standardisation and industry deployment. Adv. Eng. Inform. **22**, 271–280 (2008)

92. ICOMOS: Draft resolutions of the general assembly. Technical report, 19th General Assembly of ICOMOS New Delhi, India (2017)

93. Ikeuchi, K., Oishi, T., Takamatsu, J., Sagawa, R., Nakazawa, A., Kurazume, R., Nishino, K., Kamakura, M., Okamoto, Y.: The great Buddha project: digitally archiving, restoring, and analyzing cultural heritage objects. Int. J. Comput. Vis. **75**, 189–208 (2007)

94. Initiative, F.F.A.D.G.: Technical guidelines for digitizing cultural heritage materials: Creation of raster image master files. Technical Report, Federal Agencies Digitization Guidelines Initiative (2017). http://www.digitizationguidelines.gov/

95. Jacobs, G.: New large-scale 3D laser scanning, modeling & visualization technology provides advanced capabilities for scene reconstruction and interpretation. In: Proceedings of SPIE - The International Society for Optical Engineering, pp. 92 – 101 (2000)

96. Johnson-Roberson, M., Bryson, M., Friedman, A., Pizarro, O., Troni, G., Ozog, P., Henderson, J.: High-resolution underwater robotic vision-based mapping and three-dimensional reconstruction for archaeology. J. F. Robot. **34**, 625–643 (2017)

97. Kan, H., Katagiri, C., Nakanishi, Y., Yoshizaki, S., Nagao, M., Ono, R.: Assessment and significance of a World War II battle site: recording the USS Emmons using a high-resolution DEM combining multibeam bathymetry and SFM photogrammetry. Int. J. Naut. Archaeol. **47**, 267–280 (2018)

98. Karaszewski, M., Adamczyk, M., Sitnik, R., Michoński, J., Załuski, W., Bunsch, E., Bolewicki, P.: Automated full-3D digitization system for documentation of paintings. In: Pezzati, L., Targowski, P., (eds.) Proceedings of SPIE Optical Metrology, p. 87900X (2003)

99. Kazhdan, M., Bolitho, M., Hoppe, H.: Poisson surface reconstruction. In: Proceedings of Eurographics Symposium on Geometry Processing, pp. 61–70 (2006)

100. Kazhdan, M., Hoppe, H.: Screened Poisson surface reconstruction. ACM Trans. Graph. **32**, 1–13 (2013)

101. Kenderdine, S., Shaw, J.: Archives in motion: motion as meaning. In: Grau, O., Coones, W., Rühse, V. (eds.) Museum and Archive on the Move: Changing Cultural Institutions in the Digital Era, pp. 211–233. De Gruyter, Berlin (2017)

102. Khunti, R.: The problem with printing Palmyra: exploring the ethics of using 3D printing technology to reconstruct heritage. Stud. Digit. Herit. **3**, 1–12 (2018)

103. Koller, D., Jennifer, T., Tina, N., Natasha, G., Marc, L.: Fragments of the City: stanford's digital forma urbis Romae project. J. Roman Archaeol. 61. In: Proceedings of the Third Williams Symposium on Classical Architecture, pp. 237–252. Rome, Italy, 20–23 May (2006)

104. Koller, D., Turitzin, M., Levoy, M., Tarini, M., Croccia, G., Cignoni, P., Scopigno, R.: Protected interactive 3D graphics via remote rendering. ACM Trans. Graph. **23**, 695–703 (2004)

105. Lai, L., Sordini, M., Campana, S., Usai, L., Condò, F.: 4D recording and analysis: the case study of nuraghe Oes (Giave, Sardinia). Digit. Appl. Archaeol. Cult. Herit. **2**, 233–239 (2015)

106. Lasaponara, R., Coluzzi, R., Masini, N.: Flights into the past: full-waveform airborne laser scanning data for archaeological investigation. J. Archaeol. Sci. **38**, 2061–2070 ((2011)

107. Laycock, S., Bell, G., Corps, N., Mortimore, D., Cox, G., May, S., Finkel, I.: Using a combination of micro-computed tomography, cad and 3D printing techniques to reconstruct incomplete 19th-century cantonese chess pieces. J. Comput. Cult. Herit. **7**, 1–6 (2015)

108. Levoy, M., Pulli, K., Curless, B., Rusinkiewicz, S., Koller, D., Pereira, L., Ginzton, M., Anderson, S., Davis, J., Ginsberg, J., Shade, J., Fulk, D., Pulli, K., Koller, D., Anderson, S.,

Shade, J., Curless, B., Pereira, L., Davis, J., Fulk, D.: The digital Michelangelo project: 3D scanning of large statues. In: Proceedings of SIGGRAPH, pp. 131–144 (2000)

109. Lichti, D., Gordon, S., Stewart, M.: Ground-based laser scanners: operation, systems and applications. Geomatica **56**, 21–33 (2002)

110. Lorensen, W., Cline, H.: Marching cubes: a high resolution 3D surface construction algorithm. In: Proceedings of the 14th Annual Conference on Computer Graphics and Interactive Techniques - SIGGRAPH '87, pp. 163–169. ACM Press, New York (1987)

111. Lowe, D.: Distinctive image features from scale-invariant keypoints. Int. J. Comput. Vis. **60**, 91–110 (2004)

112. Ma, Z., Liu, S.: A review of 3D reconstruction techniques in civil engineering and their applications. Adv. Eng. Inform. **37**, 163–174 (2018)

113. Macdonald, S., Nelson, T.: A space for innovation and experimentation: university museums as test beds for new digital technologies. In: A Handbook for Academic Museums: Beyond Exhibitions and Education, pp. 418–444 (2012)

114. Malik, U., Guidi, G.: Massive 3d digitization of sculptures: methodological approaches for improving efficiency. IOP Conf. Ser. Mater. Sci. Eng. **364**, 012,015 (2018)

115. Mallik, A., Chaudhury, S., Ghosh, H.: Nrityakosha: preserving the intangible heritage of Indian classical dance. J. Comput. Cult. Herit. **4**, (2011)

116. Mayer, L., Calder, B., Schmidt, J., Malzone, C.: Providing the third dimension: High-resolution multibeam sonar as a tool for archaeological investigations - an example from the D-Day beaches of Normandy. University of New Hampshire, Technical report (2003)

117. McCarthy, J., Benjamin, J.: Multi-image photogrammetry for underwater archaeological site recording: an accessible, diver-based approach. J. Marit. Archaeol. **9**, 95–114 (2014)

118. Menna, F., Agrafiotis, P., Georgopoulos, A.: State of the art and applications in archaeological underwater 3D recording and mapping. J. Cult. Herit. **33**, 231–248 (2018)

119. Messaoudi, T., Véron, P., Halin, G., De Luca, L.: An ontological model for the reality-based 3D annotation of heritage building conservation state. J. Cult. Herit. **29**, 100–112 (2018)

120. Meyer, D., Fraijo, E., Lo, E., Rissolo, D., Kuester, F.: Optimizing UAV systems for rapid survey and reconstruction of large scale cultural heritage sites. In: Proceedings of 2015 Digital Heritage, pp. 151–154. IEEE (2015)

121. Mongy, T.: Application of neutron tomography in culture heritage research. Appl. Radiat. Isot. **85**, 54–59 (2014)

122. Morigi, M., Casali, F., Bettuzzi, M., Brancaccio, R., D'Errico, V.: Application of X-ray computed tomography to cultural heritage diagnostics. Appl. Phys. A **100**, 653–661 (2010)

123. Morishima, K., Kuno, M., Nishio, A., Kitagawa, N., Manabe, Y., Moto, M., Takasaki, F., Fujii, H., Satoh, K., Kodama, H., Hayashi, K., Odaka, S., Procureur, S., Attié, D., Bouteille, S., Calvet, D., Filosa, C., Magnier, P., Mandjavidze, I., Riallot, M., Marini, B., Gable, P., Date, Y., Sugiura, M., Elshayeb, Y., Elnady, T., Ezzy, M., Guerriero, E., Steiger, V., Serikoff, N., Mouret, J.B., Charlès, B., Helal, H., Tayoubi, M.: Discovery of a big void in Khufu's pyramid by observation of cosmic-ray muons. Nature **552**, 386 (2017)

124. Murphy, M., McGovern, E., Pavia, S.: Historic building information modelling - adding intelligence to laser and image based surveys of European classical architecture. ISPRS J. Photogramm. Remote Sens. **76**, 89–102 (2013)

125. Newsroom, I.B.: IU and Uffizi gallery partner to digitize in 3D the museum's Greek and Roman sculpture collection. Technical Report, Indiana University (2016). http://archive.news.indiana.edu/releases/iu/2016/05/iu-uffizi-gallery-partnership-digitize-sculptures.shtml

126. Nicolucci, F.: Virtual archaeology: an introduction. In: Virtual archaeology: Proceedings of the VAST Euroconference, Arezzo 24–25 November 2000, pp. 3–6 (2002)

127. O'Driscoll, J.: Landscape applications of photogrammetry using unmanned aerial vehicles. J. Archaeol. Sci. Rep. **22**, 32–44 (2018)

128. Office, S.D.P.: Smithsonian x 3D. Technical Report, Smithsonian 3D Labs (2018). https://3d.si.edu

129. Pakzad, A., Iacoviello, F., Ramsey, A., Speller, R., Griffiths, J., Freeth, T., Gibson, A.: Improved X-ray computed tomography reconstruction of the largest fragment of the antikythera mechanism, an ancient greek astronomical calculator. PLoS One **13**, 1–11 (2018)

130. Pamart, A., Ponchio, F., Abergel, V., Alaoui M'Darhri, A., Corsini, M., Dellepiane, M., Morlet, F., Scopigno, R., De Luca, L.: A complete framework operating spatially-oriented RTI in a 3D/2D cultural heritage documentation and analysis tool. ISPRS - Int. Arch. Photogramm. Remote Sens. Spat. Inf. Sci. **XLII-2/W9**, 573–580 (2019)

131. Petras, V., Stiller, J.: A decade of evaluating Europeana - constructs, contexts, methods and criteria. In: Kamps, J., Tsakonas, G., Manolopoulos, Y., Iliadis, L., Karydis, I. (eds.) Research and Advanced Technology for Digital Libraries: Proceedings of 21st International Conference on Theory and Practice of Digital Libraries, TPDL, pp. 233–245 (2017)

132. Petros, P.: Cultural heritage documentation. In: Applications of 3D Measurement from Images, pp. 225–250. Whittle Publishing Co., United Kingdom (2007)

133. Pieraccini, M., Guidi, G., Atzeni, C.: 3D digitizing of cultural heritage. J. Cult. Herit. **2**, 63–70 (2001)

134. Potenziani, M., Callieri, M., Dellepiane, M., Corsini, M., Ponchio, F., Scopigno, R.: 3Dhop: 3D heritage online presenter. Comput. Graph. **52**, 129–141 (2015)

135. Potier, S., Maltret, J., Zoller, J.: Computer graphics: assistance for archaelogical hypotheses. Autom. Constr. **9**, 117–128 (2000)

136. Ranzuglia, G., Callieri, M., Dellepiane, M., Cignoni, P., Scopigno, R.: Meshlab as a complete tool for the integration of photos and color with high resolution 3D geometry data. In: CAA 2012 Conference Proceedings, pp. 406–416. Pallas Publications - Amsterdam University Press (AUP) (2013)

137. Reilly, P.: Towards a virtual archaeology. In: Proceedings of CAA90. Computer Applications and Quantitative Methods in Archaeology, pp. 132–139 (1991)

138. Riccardelli, C., Morris, M., Wheeler, G., Soultanian, J., Becker, L., Street, R.: The treatment of Tullio Lombardo's Adam: A new approach to the conservation of monumental marble sculpture. Metrop. Museum J. **49**, 48–116 (2014)

139. Rioux, M.: Digital 3D imaging: theory and applications. In: SPIE Proceedings, Videometrics III, vol. 2350, pp. 2314–2350 (1994)

140. Robson, S., Bucklow, S., Woodhouse, N., Papadakia, H.: Periodic photogrammetric monitoring and surface reconstruction of a historical wood panel painting for restoration purposes. In: International Archives of Photogrammetry and Remote Sensing, pp. 395–400 (2004)

141. Robson, S., MacDonald, S., Were, G., Hess, M.: 3D recording and museums. In: Warwick, C., Terras, M., Hyhan, J. (eds.) Digital Humanities in Practice, pp. 91–115. Facet Publishing, London (2012)

142. Roller, D.: An approach to computer-aided parametric design. Comput. Des. **23**, 385–391 (1991)

143. Roussou, M.: Virtual heritage: from the research lab to the broad public. In: Virtual Archaeology: Proceedings of the VAST Euroconference, Arezzo 24–25 November 2000, pp. 93–100 (2002)

144. Russo, M., Guidi, G.: Diachronic 3D reconstruction for lost cultural heritage. In: Remondino, F., (ed.) Proceedings of 4th International Workshop 3D-ARCH, ISPRS, Trento, Italy, pp. 1–6 (2011)

145. Santos, P., Ritz, M., Tausch, R., Schmedt, H., Rodriguez, R., Fuhrmann, C., Domajnko, M., Knuth, M., Fellner, D.: Cultlab3D - fast and economic 3D mass-digitization. In: Pescarin, S., Cano, P., Grande, A., (eds.) Proceedings of International Congress on Digital Heritage - EXPO. IEEE (2015)

146. Shan, J., Toth, C.: Topographic Laser Ranging and Scanning: Principles and Processing. CRC Press (2008)

147. Shannon, C.: A mathematical theory of communication. Bell Syst. Tech. J. (1948)

148. Shi, S., Hsu, C.H.: A survey of interactive remote rendering systems. ACM Comput. Surv. **47**, 57:1–57:29 (2015)

149. Shortis, M.: Calibration techniques for accurate measurements by underwater camera systems. Sensors **15**, 30810–30826 (2015)

150. Shuai, L., Li, C., Guo, X., Prabhakaran, B., Chai, J.: Motion capture with ellipsoidal skeleton using multiple depth cameras. IEEE Trans. Vis. Comput. Graph. **23**, 1085–1098 (2017)

151. Singh, G.: Cultlab3D - digitizing cultural heritage. IEEE Comput. Graph. Appl. **34**, 4–5 (2014)
152. Siotto, E., Dellepiane, M., Callieri, M., Scopigno, R., Gratziu, C., Moscato, A., Burgio, L., Legnaioli, S., Lorenzetti, G., Palleschi, V.: A multidisciplinary approach for the study and the virtual reconstruction of the ancient polychromy of roman sarcophagi. J. Cult. Herit. **16**(3), 307–314 (2015)
153. Soler, F., Melero, F., Luzón, M.: A complete 3D information system for cultural heritage documentation. J. Cult. Herit. **23**, 49–57 (2017)
154. Soucy, M., Laurendeau, D.: A general surface approach to the integration of a set of range views. IEEE Trans. Pattern Anal. Mach. Intell. **17**, 344–358 (1995)
155. Sternberg, H., Kersten, T., Jahn, I., Kinzel, R.: Terrestrial 3D laser scanning – data acquisition and object modeling for industrial as-built documentation and architectural applications. In: The International Archives of Photogrammetry, Remote Sensing and Spatial Information Sciences, vol. XXXV, pp. 942–947 (2004)
156. Taylor, J., Beraldin, J.A., Godin, G., Cournoyer, L., Baribeau, R., Blais, F., Rioux, M., Domey, J.: NRC 3D imaging technology for museum and heritage applications. J. Vis. Comput. Animat. **14**, 121–138 (2003)
157. Taylor, J., Beraldin, J., Godin, G.: 3D imaging collaboration between the national research council of Canada and European museums and cultural organizations. In: Proceedings of the Electronic Imaging and the Visual Arts (EVA 2001), pp. 1–11. NRC, Montreal, Quebec, CA (2001)
158. Turk, G., Levoy, M.: Zippered polygon meshes from range images. In: Proceedings of the 21st Annual Conference on Computer Graphics and Interactive Techniques, pp. 311–318. ACM, New York (1994)
159. UNESCO: 2003 Convention for the safeguarding of the intangible cultural heritage. Technical report, UNESCO (2003)
160. UNESCO: Convention on the protection of the underwater cultural heritage. Technical report, UNESCO (2001)
161. Velios, A., John, H.: Digital reconstruction of fragmented archaeological objects. Stud Conserv **52**(1), 19–36 (2007). https://doi.org/10.1179/sic.2007.52.1.19
162. Ware, C.: Information Visualization. Perception for Design, 3rd edn. Elsevier, Amsterdam (2013)
163. Winsberg, E.: Computer simulations in science. In: Stanford Encyclopedia of Philosophy Archive, Summer 2018 Edition, Stanford University (2018). https://plato.stanford.edu/archives/sum2018/entries/simulations--science/
164. Ynnerman, A., Rydell, T., Antoine, D., Hughes, D., Persson, A., Ljung, P.: Interactive visualization of 3D scanned mummies at public venues. Commun. ACM **59**, 72–81 (2016)
165. Zaman, T., Jonker, P., Lenscigne, B., Dik, J.: Simultaneous capture of the color and topography of paintings using fringe encoded stereo vision. Herit. Sci. **2**, Article 23 (2014)
166. Zhang, Y., Li, K., Chen, X., Zhang, S., Geng, G.: A multi feature fusion method for reassembly of 3D cultural heritage artifacts. J. Cult. Herit. **33**, 191–200 (2018)

Chapter 14
3D Phenotyping of Plants

Ayan Chaudhury and John L. Barron

Abstract In recent years, there has been significant progress in computer vision based plant phenotyping technologies. Due to their non-invasive and non-contact properties, imaging techniques are becoming state of the art in automated plant phenotyping analysis. There are several aspects of phenotyping, including plant growth, organ classification and tracking, disease detection, etc. This chapter presents a broad overview of computer vision based 3D plant phenotyping techniques. Some case studies of state-of-the-art techniques are described in detail. In the first case study, automated robotic systems for 3D plant phenotyping are discussed. The second study focuses on general registration techniques of point cloud and alignment of multiple view challenging plant point cloud data. Next, recently successful plant organ segmentation techniques are reviewed. Finally, some open challenges of vision-based plant phenotyping are discussed, followed by conclusion and some hands on exercises.

14.1 Introduction

Due to the increase in the world population in recent years, the demand of food/crop is increasing very fast. Automated analysis for crop production systems is of extreme demand in order to fulfil the task of mass production as well as efficient monitoring of crops. Computer vision based techniques can be very efficient because of the non-invasive and non-contact nature of image-based analysis. Also, imaging systems can be more accurate than other approaches. In recent years, there has been

A. Chaudhury (✉)
School of EECS, KTH Royal Institute of Technology, Stockholm, Sweden
e-mail: ayanc@kth.se

A. Chaudhury · J. L. Barron
Department of Computer Science, University of Western Ontario, London, Canada
e-mail: barron@csd.uwo.ca

© Springer Nature Switzerland AG 2020
Y. Liu et al. (eds.), *3D Imaging, Analysis and Applications*,
https://doi.org/10.1007/978-3-030-44070-1_14

tremendous progress in image-based analysis of plant phenotyping (measuring biologically significant properties of plants) technologies. 3D imaging based approaches are becoming state of the art in quantifying biological properties of plants. The advantage of 3D over 2D are numerous. For example, in order to analyze the growth of a plant, representing that plant as a 3D mesh model is a very effective methodology. From the 3D mesh, it is possible to compute the 3D volume (the convex hull) and 3D surface area of the plant, in addition to analyzing other desirable properties. As we will see later in this chapter, 3D laser scanners are widely used to perform 3D plant phenotyping. Also consider the area of a leaf. If the leaf is curved, its 3D area will be significantly different from the area computed from its 2D image.

Additionally, apart from the 3D based analysis of plants, data collection is also an important aspect of an automated phenotyping system and cannot be ignored. However, building a high throughput real-time system is a challenging task. Several challenges include the following factors: communication among the hardware devices, reliable data transfer and analysis, fault tolerance, etc. Ideally, the system should be simple enough for a naive user to operate and obtain the phenotyping result as a ready-made product. An ideal system should also be able to be general enough to handle several varieties of plants and analyze their phenotypes accurately. With the advancements of recent robotic technologies and high precision mechanical devices, fully automated real-time systems are becoming possible. These systems are shown to be reliable enough to capture and analyze the data throughout the lifetime of a plant. Automation is also important to study the effect of several environmental factors (e.g. lighting, temperature, humidity, etc.) on a plant. Designing controlled chamber can fulfil the needs of restricted environmental factors. For example, if we need to study the effect of light on a specific plant under certain temperature, then we need to place the plant in a chamber where the temperature is controlled and the lighting can be turned on/off at desired time of the day. This is an example of an embedded system that can be programmatically controlled as needed. This is an integral part of a 3D plant phenotyping system.

Recently, laser scanning systems have gained popularity to capture 3D data on the surface of a plant. Laser scanning is an excellent way to perform non-invasive 3D analysis of plant phenotyping. Kinect laser scanners are now available at cheap cost and are being widely used in various fields including plant phenotyping, 3D modelling and remote sensing applications. Depending on the need of the application, the resolution of the scanner can be controlled. For example, dense spacing of points is needed in order to model a very detailed surface, whereas sparse scans might be sufficient for applications that do not need much local details to be modelled. The 3D model of the plant can be obtained by aligning multiple overlapping views of the scans taken from different directions around the plant. Then the merged point cloud data can be used to analyze different aspects of phenotyping.

Phenotyping refers to measuring (or quantifying) various biologically interesting properties of plants. There are several aspects of phenotyping. State-of-the-art techniques in computer vision are adopted for different application areas. For example, consider tracking a particular organ over time. To make the system fully automated, first we need to set up a robotic system that will be able to place the laser scanner at a suitable position, scan the plant and extract the point cloud data. Having the raw point cloud data, computer vision algorithms need to be designed to perform shape matching of point clouds in order to identify the organ of interest. As the plant grows, the robot should dynamically change its position to perform the scanning. There are many challenges involved in this type of phenotyping. As the plant grows bigger, the leaves occlude each other and the organ of interest might become partially or fully occluded by some other organs. In these cases, a single scan might not be sufficient to recognize the organ and the robot needs to be moved at suitable positions around the occlusion and take multiple scans of the occluded object. This is just an example of a challenging 3D phenotyping problem. Other types of phenotyping include the growth analysis of living plants. In that case, multi-view points cloud data needs to be aligned into a single point cloud, which can be triangulated to obtain a 3D mesh model of the plant. This is a challenging task since aligning multiple views of a complex plant structure is a difficult problem. Also, efficient triangulation is very important to retain the detailed structure of the plant. From the 3D mesh model, several properties like volume and surface area can be computed. Segmentation of plant organs has also gained attention for phenotyping tasks. Estimation of leaf area, stem diameter, etc. requires proper segmentation of the organs. Different types of shape primitives are often used to extract the required structure. For example, tubular shape fitting is a common technique to extract the round-shaped stem of a plant.

3D plant phenotyping is highly inspired from computer vision algorithms. Through-out this chapter, we will see some applications of 3D plant phenotyping. Although there are several components of phenotyping, we will discuss certain key areas, which are the most popular, as well as challenging. Initially we will discuss about automated systems for 3D plant phenotyping. Then registration of multi-view point cloud data are described. Next, some popular techniques of plant organ segmentation are studied. We also discuss in brief about related phenotyping problems to give an overview of the recent focus of the phenotyping research community.

The organization of the chapter is as follows. In the next section, related literature is summarized. Then we discuss the key techniques in 3D plant phenotyping, followed by the current challenges and concluding remarks. We end the chapter with some hands-on exercises related to plant phenotyping techniques.

14.2   Related Work

A large body of work has been reported on computer vision based plant pheno-typing in the last decade. In recent literature, several aspects of plant phenotyping are discussed. Tremendous progress in automated plant phenotyping and imaging technologies have created a mini-renaissance [1]. Software products are becoming available for building high throughout phenotyping systems [2, 3]. Automated data collection systems [4, 5] are becoming prevalent over tedious manual techniques [6]. However, most of the automated systems have some limitations on the type, size or geometrical properties of the plants that can be processed. The ultimate goal of computer vision-based automation techniques is to generalize these type of systems [7–9]. Recently, a fully automated robotic system has been proposed [10]. The system works in a fully automated way throughout the lifetime of a plant and analyzes the growth pattern from the reconstructed 3D point cloud data. The system is general and can be customized to perform different types of automated tasks related to 3D plant phenotyping. We discuss the related literature on different aspects of plant phenotyping in the next subsections.

14.2.1 Organ Tracking

Detection and tracking of plant organ is a well-studied problem. Jimenez et al. [11] proposed a fruit harvesting system that can detect fruits of a plant from their colour and morphological properties. It was one of the first methods where laser scanners were used in plant phenotyping analysis. These types of systems are of extreme demand in agricultural applications. Chattopadhyay et al. [12] presented 3D reconstruction of apple trees for dormant pruning (cutting off certain primary branches to improve the yield and crop quality of the plant) applications in an automated manner. These techniques can be very helpful in the pruning process as a part of intelligent agricultural robotic application. Paulus et al. [13, 14] performed organ segmentation of wheat, grapevine and barley plants using a surface feature-based histogram analysis of 3D point cloud data. Klodt et al. [15] performed segmentation to monitor the growth of grapevines. Similar type of work on plant organ segmentation was proposed in [16] via unsupervised clustering technique. Paproki et al. [17] measured plant growth in the vegetative stage. They generated 3D point cloud from 2D images. Golbach et al. [18] setup a multiple camera system and the 3D model of the plant was reconstructed using a shape-from-silhouette method. Then the geometric properties (e.g. area, length) of the leaves and stems are computed by segmenting these organs. The final results are validated by comparing with the ground truth data obtained by destructing the plant by hand. Dellen et al. [19] built up a system to analyze leaf growth of tobacco plants by tracking the leaves over time from time-lapsed video. In each video frame, leaves are detected by assuming a circular leaf shape model. A graph-based method is employed to track leaves through the temporal sequence of video frames.

14.2.2 Plant Health Monitoring

Another type of plant phenotyping that has gained attention is determining the condition of a plant from specific patterns of its leaves. Usually, the texture properties of the leaves are exploited to perform the analyses, and then the leaves are tracked over time. A challenging task to perform this type of analysis is to segment the leaves in different imaging conditions [20]. Active contour model was used in [21] to detect

lesions in *Zea Mayes*. This crop is widely used and lesion detection can be very helpful in disease detection at the early stages. Xu et al. [22] detected nitrogen-deficient
tomatoes from the texture of the leaves. Tracking the leaves of rosette plants can be
very useful for growth rate measurement. Similar type of work was presented in [23].

14.2.3   3D Reconstruction

3D reconstruction from multiple views is a quintessential part of many 3D phenotyping applications. This is a very challenging problem. The complex geometrical
structure of the plants makes the problem extremely difficult to handle. Pound et
al. [24, 25] reconstructed the 3D model of a plant using level set based technique.
Santos et al. [26] performed a structure from motion technique to reconstruct the 3D
point cloud model of the plant surface, and then a spectral clustering technique is
used to segment the leaves. Similar type of approach was used for visual odometry
applications in [27]. Kumar et al. [28] used a mirror-based system to obtain multiple
views of the plant. A visual hull algorithm is used to perform the reconstruction.
The setup alleviates the need for camera calibration due to the use of the mirrors.
Recently, Gibbs et al. [29] proposed to improve the image acquisition that results in
improving the overall 3D reconstruction. Instead of using a fixed camera position
for all types of plants, they proposed to change the camera position dynamically,
depending on the geometry of the plant. This type of approach can be embedded
in the intelligent robotic systems. Simek et al. [30] modelled spatial smoothness of
the branches of plant by Gaussian Process. Their method is designed to estimate the
thin structures of a plant from monocular images. Brophy et al. [31] presented an
approach to align multiple views of a plant into a single point cloud. The approach
exploits recently successful Gaussian Mixture Model registration and mutual nearest
neighbour techniques. However, the method needs a good initial guess, which can
be rectified by automatic feature matching of junction points [32].

14.2.4   Rhythmic Pattern Detection

Rhythmic pattern of plant growth is a well-known phenomenon [33]. There have
been attempts to capture the circadian rhythm of plant movements using imaging
techniques [34]. Plant leaves are known to be affected by various lighting conditions.
Dornbusch et al. [35] captured the effect of rhythmic leaf movements by lighting via
laser scanning system. Tracking and growth analysis of seedling was studied in [36].
Corn seedling growth was studied by Barron and Liptay [37–39]. They demonstrated
that the growth is well correlated with room temperature.

14.2.5 Structural Analysis

Structural analysis of plants is also studied in the literature [40]. Augustin et al. [41] extracted geometric features of Arabidopsis plant for phenotypic analysis. Li et al. [42] performed a 4D analysis to track budding and bifurcation events of plants from point cloud data.

14.3 Key Techniques

In this section, we will focus on some specific aspects of 3D plant phenotyping and explain the state-of-the-art techniques. Before we explain the key techniques, we briefly discuss some terminologies that will be used throughout this section. The flow of the section is as follows. First, we give an overview of some key terms. Then we discuss different types of automated systems for 3D plant phenotyping. These systems aim at collecting data without (or minimal) manual intervention. We focus on 3D model building of plants, and that is why we discuss about aligning multiple datasets to obtain a 3D point cloud model of a plant. Although the problem is basically the general point cloud registration and alignment problem, we will discuss certain variations of the standard algorithms related to plant structures. Finally, some segmentation algorithms are discussed.

14.3.1 Terminologies

14.3.1.1 Point Cloud

A point cloud is simply a set of data points. Point clouds are typically generated by range scanners, which record the point coordinates at the surface of an object. The density of points depends on the scanner settings. In the general case, high density of points encodes fine geometry of the object, and requires high computation time to process the data. On the contrary, low density of points encodes less local geometry and mostly keep the global shape of the object, and usually requires less computational time to process. 3D point clouds are usually stored as raw coordinate values (x, y, z). However, the fourth attribute can be the colour or intensity information, depending on the type of scanner used. Among different file formats for storing the point cloud, the most commonly used extensions are: *.xyz*, *.pcd*, *.asc*, *.pts*, and *.csv* formats.

14.3.1.2   3D Mesh

A 3D mesh or a polygonal mesh is a data structure that connects the points in the cloud by means of a set of vertices (which are the points themselves), a set of edges, and polygonal elements (e.g. triangles for triangular mesh). Polygon meshes are also referred as *surface* meshes which represent both the surface and the volumetric structure of the object. The process of making a triangular mesh is also called the *triangulation*. The efficient rendering of the triangles can produce a realistic representation of a synthetic object, which is a center of attention in the computer graphics research community. Among different types of triangulation technique, most commonly used are the Delaunay and Alpha shape triangulation algorithms. Let us consider a set of points $P = \{p_1, \ldots, p_n\} \subset \mathbb{R}^d$. Let's call these as *sites*. A *Voronoi diagram* is a decomposition of $\mathbb{R}^d$ into convex polyhedra. Each region or *Voronoi cell* $\mathcal{V}(p_i)$ for p_i is defined to be the set of points x that are closer to p_i than to any other site. Mathematically,

$$\mathcal{V}(p_i) = \{x \in \mathbb{R}^d \mid ||p_i - x|| \leq ||p_j - x|| \, \forall j \neq i\},$$

where $||.||$ denotes the Euclidean distance. The *Delaunay triangulation* of P is defined as the dual of the Voronoi diagram.

The α-*complex* of P is defined as the Delaunay triangulation of P having an empty circumscribing sphere with a squared radius equal to or smaller than α. The *Alpha shape* is the domain covered by alpha complex. If $\alpha = 0$, the α-shape is the point set P, and for $0 \leq \alpha \leq \infty$, the boundary $\partial \mathcal{P}_\alpha$ of the α-shape is a subset of the Delaunay triangulation of P.

14.3.1.3   Registration of Point Cloud

In the general sense, registration of two point clouds refers to aligning one point cloud to the other. One of the point cloud is called the *model* point set, which remains "fixed" in space. The other point cloud, referred as the *data*, is the "moving" point set. We seek to find the transformation parameters (typically the rotation, translation and scaling) of the *data* point cloud, that best aligns it to the *model* point cloud. By *best*, we mean the alignment that has the minimal error with respect to the ground truth. There are usually two cases in this regard: *rigid* and *non-rigid*. Rigid point cloud registration problems are usually easier to handle, since estimation of the transformation parameters is relatively less complicated. On the other hand, non-rigid point cloud registration problems are hard in nature, and typically a single set of transformation parameters are not sufficient to align the data to the model point cloud. Among various types of challenges associated with non-rigid point cloud registration, the following are the most prevalent ones: occlusion, deformation and minimal overlap between the two point clouds.

Fig. 14.1 A typical green house system [2]. Plants are placed on conveyor belts and images are taken automatically as the belt moves around (licensed under the Creative Commons Attribution 4.0 International License)

14.3.1.4   Viewing Software

There are a variety of software available to visualize the point clouds and meshes. The following software are widely used in the computer vision and graphics community: Meshlab,[1] CloudCompare,[2] Point Cloud Library[3] (also offers lots of functionalities for point cloud processing), etc.

14.3.2   Automated Systems for 3D Phenotyping

The goal of a high throughput plant phenotyping system is to monitor a mass crop production system and analyze several phenotypic parameters related to growth, yield and stress tolerance in different environmental conditions. An automated green house system looks like the one in Fig. 14.1. The plants are placed on conveyor belts and the image acquisition devices capture images in different time frames.

In many applications, the phenotyping demands high precision results. In order to obtain high precision quality, robots can be used to perform the task in more efficient manner. Subramanian et al. [5] developed a high throughput robotic system in order to quantify seedling development. A 3-axis gantry robot system is used to move the robot in the vertical X-Z plane. The movement of each axis is controlled by linear servo motors. Two cameras are attached to the robot, one of them is of high resolution and the other one is of low resolution. Perpendicular to the optical axis of the cameras, a series of petri dish containing plant seedlings are attached to a sample fixture.

---

[1] http://www.meshlab.net/.

[2] https://www.danielgm.net/cc/.

[3] http://pointclouds.org/.

The robot periodically moves along the gantries and captures images of each petri dish. A probabilistic localization is performed to locate the seedling. Focusing is also performed automatically. As the seedlings grow over time, the system dynamically analyzes the images with high accuracy. This type of automated system is very useful in studying growth of mini-seedlings (a young plant grown from seed).

However, the system described above is not designed to monitor a whole plant throughout its lifetime. Also, the robot system does not have enough degrees of freedom (DOF) to move anywhere around a plant to perform real-time 3D data capture. Recently, a machine vision system has been proposed in order to perform real-time 3D system [10]. The system is fully automated, including the growth chamber, robot operation, data collection and analysis. A naive user can obtain phenotyping results with a few mouse clicks.

The system comprises of an adjustable pedestal and a 2-axis overhead gantry which carries a 7-DOF robotic arm. A near-infrared laser scanner is attached at the end of the arm, which can measure dense depth map of the surface of an object. The arm provides high level of flexibility for controlling the position and orientation of the scanner attached at the end. The plant is placed on a pedestal, which can be moved vertically to adjust the room for different plant sizes. The whole setup is housed in a programmable chamber, which is fully controllable in terms of lighting, temperature, humidity, etc. Different components of the system are integrated together as a single system. The setup is shown in Fig. 14.2.

During an experiment, the chamber is programmed according to the requirements. The plant is placed on the pedestal, and other parameters such as number of scans, resolution, timings, etc., are provided by the user. Initially the robot remains at the home position. When the scan starts, the robot moves to the scan position and takes an initial scan. This initial scan is performed to compute the bounding box comprising the whole plant. The bounding box calculation is needed to dynamically change the robot position as the plant grows over time. When the bounding box is determined, actual scanning is performed. The laser scanner records point cloud data in xyz format on the surface of the plant. If the scanner field of view is not able to enclose the whole plant due to size constraint, multiple overlapping partial scans are taken. After the first scan, the robot moves to the next scanning position and performs a similar scanning routine. When the scan sets are complete, the robot goes back to the home position until the next set of scan is scheduled. Captured data are transferred to the server automatically and processing gets started immediately (aligning multiple views are discussed in the next subsection).

The system is designed for general use of phenotyping applications, and can be customized according to the need. The robot arm can be exploited for tracking specific organs by exploiting the high degree of flexibility of the arm. To handle the case of occlusion of the organs, the robot arm can be programmed to move to specific coordinates in order to obtain full view of the occluded organ. In recent years, automated data collection through robotic system is performed in outdoor environment for agricultural applications [43, 44].

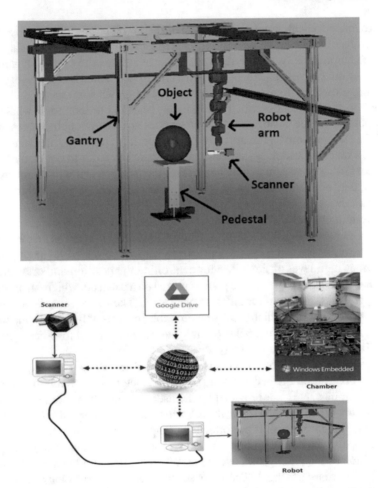

Fig. 14.2 Complete autonomous robotic system for 3D plant phenotyping applications. Top: Schematic diagram of the gantry robot system. Bottom: High-level view of the system

14.3.3 Multiple-View Alignment

Although registration of 3D point cloud data has been studied extensively in the literature, registration of plant structures is a challenging task. The self recursive and thin structure makes the problem of pairwise registration extremely complicated and non-rigid. Although different types of approaches exist for solving the pairwise registration and multiple view alignment problem, recently probabilistic methods have been successful in many applications. We first discuss the background of general registration problem and then end by discussing the adaptation of the technique for registration of plant structures.

Recently, Gaussian Mixture Models (GMM) have been very successful in the registration of non-rigid point sets. Let us consider two overlapping views (point clouds) of a plant. One point cloud is called the *model* point set, and the other is called the *data* point set. The target is to transform the data point set to the model point set in order to obtain the merged point cloud. Mathematically, let's say the model point set is denoted as $\mathcal{M} = (x_1, x_2, ..., x_M)^T$, and the observed data point set is denoted as $\mathcal{S} = (y_1, y_2, ..., y_N)^T$. The model point set undergoes a non-rigid transformation $\mathcal{T}$, and our goal is to estimate $\mathcal{T}$ so that the two point sets become aligned. Then the GMM probability density function can be written as,

$$p(y_n) = \sum_{i=1}^{M+1} P(z_n = i) p(y_n | z_n = i), \qquad (14.1)$$

where z_n are latent variables that assign an observed data point y_n to a GMM centroid. Usually all the GMM components are modelled as having equal covariances σ^2, and the outlier distribution is considered as uniform, i.e. $1/a$, where a is usually set as the number of points in the model point set. The unknown parameter $\omega \in [0, 1]$ is the percentage of the outliers. The membership probabilities π_{mn} are assumed to be equal for all GMM components. Denoting the set of unknown parameters $\theta = \{\mathcal{T}, \sigma^2, \omega\}$, the mixture model can be written as

$$p(y_n | \theta) = \omega \frac{1}{a} + (1 - \omega) \sum_{i=1}^{M} \frac{\pi_{mn}}{(2\pi\sigma^2)^{D/2}} exp[-\frac{||y_n - \mathcal{T}(x_m)||^2}{2\sigma^2}]. \qquad (14.2)$$

The goal is to find the transformation $\mathcal{T}$. Sometimes a prior is used to estimate the transformation parameters. A common form of prior [45] is

$$P(\mathcal{T}) \propto exp[-\frac{\lambda}{2}\phi(\mathcal{T})],$$

where $\phi(\mathcal{T})$ is the smoothness factor, and λ is a positive real number. The parameters θ are estimated using the Bayes' rule. The optimal parameters can be obtained as

$$\theta^* = \arg\max_{\theta} P(\theta | \mathcal{S}) = \arg\max_{\theta} P(\mathcal{S} | \theta) P(\mathcal{T}),$$

which is equivalent to minimizing the negative log-likelihood:

$$\mathcal{L}(\theta | \mathcal{S}) = -\sum_{n=1}^{N} \ln P(y_n | \theta) - \ln P(\mathcal{T}). \qquad (14.3)$$

Jian and Vemuri [46] followed this approach and represented the point set by Gaussian mixtures. They proposed an approach to minimize the discrepancy between two Gaussian mixtures by minimizing the L_2 distance between two mixtures.

The Coherent Point Drift (CPD) registration method was proposed by Myronenko et al. [47, 48]. Their method is based on GMM, where the centroids are moved together. Given two point clouds, $\mathcal{M} = (x_1, x_2, ..., x_M)^T$ and $\mathcal{S} = (y_1, y_2, ..., y_N)^T$, in general for a point x, the GMM probability density function will be $p(x) = \sum_{i=1}^{M+1} P(i)p(x|i)$, where:

$$p(x|i) = \frac{1}{(2\pi\sigma^2)^{D/2}} exp[-\frac{||x - y_i||^2}{2\sigma^2}]. \qquad (14.4)$$

They minimize the following negative log-likelihood function to obtain the optimal alignment:

$$E(\theta, \sigma^2) = -\sum_{j=1}^{N} log \sum_{i=1}^{M+1} P(i)p(x_j|i). \qquad (14.5)$$

There are many ways to estimate the parameters, such as gradient descent, Expectation Maximization (EM) algorithm and variational inference. EM is a standard and widely used technique to optimize the cost function. Basically the E-step (or the *Expectation*) computes the posterior probability, and the M-step (or the *Maximization*) computes the new parameter values from the likelihood function. The aim is to find the parameters θ and σ^2.

Let us denote the initial and updated probability distributions as P^{old} and P^{new}, respectively. The E-step basically computes the "old" parameter values, and then computes the posterior probability distributions $P^{old}(i|x_j)$. In the M-step, the new parameter values are computed by minimizing the log-likelihood function:

$$\mathcal{E} = -\sum_{j=1}^{N} \sum_{i=1}^{M+1} P^{old}(i|x_j)log(P^{new}(i)p^{new}(x_j|i)), \qquad (14.6)$$

which can be rewritten as

$$\mathcal{E}(\theta, \sigma^2) = \frac{1}{2\sigma^2} \sum_{j=1}^{N} \sum_{i=1}^{M+1} P^{old}(i|x_j)||x_j - \mathcal{T}(y_i, \theta)||^2 + \frac{N_p D}{2}log\sigma^2, \qquad (14.7)$$

where

$$N_p = \sum_{j=0}^{N} \sum_{i=0}^{M} P^{old}(i|x_j) \leq N. \qquad (14.8)$$

Now the current parameter values θ^{old} is used to find the posterior probabilities:

$$P^{old}(i|x_j) = \frac{exp(-\frac{1}{2\sigma^{old 2}}||x_j - \mathcal{T}(y_i, \theta^{old})||^2)}{\sum_{k=1}^{M} exp(-\frac{1}{2\sigma^{old 2}}||x_j - \mathcal{T}(y_k, \theta^{old})||^2) + (2\pi\sigma^2)^{D/2}\frac{\omega}{1-\omega}\frac{M}{N}}. \qquad (14.9)$$

Although pairwise registration works reasonably well, aligning multiple views is problematic. The reason is that, the errors from pairwise registrations accumulate during multiple alignment and as a result, the merging does not yield good results. To handle this problem, Brophy et al. [31] proposed a solution based on the Mutual Nearest Neighbour (MNN) [49] algorithm. The algorithm is based on CPD which can align many views with minimal error. More specifically, it is a drift-free algorithm for merging non-rigid scans, where *drift* is the build-up of alignment error caused by sequential pairwise registration. Although CPD alone is effective in registering pairs with a fair amount of overlap, when registering multiple scans, especially scans that have not been pre-aligned; this method achieves a much better fit both visually and quantitatively than CPD by itself, utilizing sequential pairwise registration.

First, the scans are aligned sequentially, and then a global method is used to refine the result. The global method involves registering each scan X_i to an "average" shape, which we construct using the centroids of the *mutual nearest neighbors* (MNN) [49] of each point. For X_i, we use scans X_j where $j \neq i$ to obtain the average shape Y_{cent} from the centroids, and X_i is then registered to this average shape. This is repeated for every scan until the result converges.

For a point x, the density function is written as

$$p(x|i) = \frac{1}{(2\pi\sigma^2)^{D/2}} \exp[-\frac{||x - \hat{y}_i||^2}{2\sigma^2}], \qquad (14.10)$$

where $\hat{y}_i \in Y_{cent}$ are the points in the target scan Y_{cent}, which is constructed from all scans other than itself.

For a pair of scans X and Y, a point $x_i \in X$ and $y_j \in Y$ is called MNN if $x_i = x_{i_n}$ and $y_{j_n} = y_j$, where

$$x_{i_n} = \min(|x_p - y_j|), \forall x_p \in X, \qquad (14.11)$$

and

$$y_{j_n} = \min(|y_q - x_i|), \forall y_q \in Y. \qquad (14.12)$$

For each point x_j in scan X_i, the set of points $\{x_k | x_k \in X_l \land MNN(x_k, x_j)\}$ are found, where $l \neq i$, i.e. all scans other than X_i. For each of these sets of points x_k, the centroid is computed as

$$x_{cent} = \sum_{k=1}^{n-1} \frac{x_k}{n-1}. \qquad (14.13)$$

X_{cent}, the set of centroids calculated for each x_j, is registered to scan X_i.

Fig. 14.3 12 scans of the Arabidopsis plant, prior to registration, but with rotation and translation pre-applied. Different colours indicate different scans [31]

14.3.3.1 Approximate Alignment

In general, to reconstruct a 3D model of a plant, a set of scans are captured around the plant at specific increments. After acquiring them, the idea is to solve for the rigid transformation $T_0 = (R_0, t_0)$ (where R is a rotation matrix and $\mathbf{t}$ is a translation vector) between the first scan (X_0) and the second scan (X_1) using the rigid version of CPD. After we solve for T_0 only once, for each scan X_i, the transformation is applied i times

The new set of transformed scans $\hat{X}$ should now be roughly aligned in the coordinate system of the last scan. This method is used to obtain a rigid registration. The initial registration is important when the pair of scans to be registered has minimal overlap. The result of approximately aligned scans on some real plant data is shown in Fig. 14.3.

14.3.3.2 Global Non-rigid Registration via MNN

Once the initial registration is complete, CPD is used in conjunction with MNN to recover the non-rigid deformation field that the plant undergoes between the capture of each scan. At this point, the scans should be approximately aligned to one another. The centroid/average scan is constructed and the scan is registered to it.

14.3.3.3 Global Registration

Algorithm 14.1 is used to merge all scans, where $MNN(\cdot)$ computes the mutual nearest neighbour for each point in scans X_i and X_j and the centroids function likewise takes the centroids computed for each point in each scan and combines them into one average scan using Eq. 14.13. For each point in scan X_i, the single nearest neighbour from all other scans is found and we use this set of distances to compute the L^2-norm.

Algorithm 14.1 MNN Registration

1: $\mathbf{X} = [X_1, \ldots, X_n]$, where each X_i is a range scan that has been approximately adjusted. A predefined tolerance tol_{max}.
2: $tol = \sum_{i=1}^{n} error\_L^2(X_i)/n$
3: **while** $tol < tol_{max}$ **do**
4:    **for** $i = 1$ to n **do**
5:       **for** $j = 1$ to n **do**
6:          **if** $j \neq i$ **then**
7:             $X_{i_{cent}} = MNN(\, X_j, X_i\,)$
8:          **end if**
9:       **end for**
10:      $X_{cent} = centroids(\, X_{1_{cent}}, \ldots, X_{N_{cent}}\,)$
11:      $X_i = register\_cpd(\, X_{cent}, X_i)$
12:   **end for**
13: **end while**

Figure 14.4 shows all 12 scans, merged into a single point cloud after subsampling each scan. Each colour in the point cloud represents a different scan.

A problem with GMM based registration is that the views need to have been approximately aligned before the registration. For large rotation angle differences, the algorithm fails drastically. In the literature, there has been significant work on feature matching of two point cloud datasets. For example, Fast Feature Point Histogram (FPFH) [50] is a popular technique for feature matching in point cloud. However, these type of descriptors exploit surface normal information to uniquely characterize an interest point. For thin structured plant data, accurately computing surface normal is an extremely difficult and error-prone task. Traditional descriptors fail to produce reasonable results for plant feature correspondence.

Bucksch et al. [51] presented a method to register two plant point clouds. Their method performs skeletonization of the input point cloud and then estimates the

Fig. 14.4 12 scans captured in 30° increments about the plant and then merged into a single point cloud using MNN. Shown from two viewpoints, are the front facing scans on the left and the above facing scans on the right. Different colours indicate different scans [31]

transformation parameters by minimizing point-to-line distances. The idea is to map a point p_0 from one point cloud to the line joining two nearest neighbour points p_1 and p_2 in the skeletonized second point cloud. That is, the mapping condition is the following:

$$||\mathbf{p_0'p_2} \times \mathbf{p_1p_2}|| = 0.$$

where $p_0' = Rp_0 + t$ is the transformed point, R is the rotation matrix and t is the translation vector. However, the algorithm needs the point clouds to be roughly aligned in order to obtain good registration results.

A remedy to the above problem can be obtained by exploiting the junction points as features, as proposed by Chaudhury et al. [32]. The advantage of using junctions as feature points is that, even if there is deformation and non-rigidity in the point cloud data, a junction point will not be affected by these factors. Initially, the neighbourhood of each 3D point is transformed into 2D by performing the appropriate 3D coordinate transformations. The method is two step. First, a statistical dip test of multi-modality is performed to detect non-linearity of the local structure. Then each branch is approximated by sequential RANSAC line fitting and an Euclidean clustering technique. The straight line parameters of each branch are extracted using Total Least Squares (TLS) estimation. Finally, the straight line equations are solved to determine if they intersect in the local neighbourhood. Such junction points are good candidates for subsequent correspondence algorithms. Using these detected junction points, the correspondence algorithm is formulated as an optimized sub-graph matching problem.

14.3.3.4 Coordinate Transformation

Using a kd-tree algorithm, the nearest neighbour points of a point within a certain radius can be obtained. Given such points in a local neighbourhood about some 3D point, the data is transformed so that the surface normal of the plane fitting the data is

Fig. 14.5 Planar vector
orientations

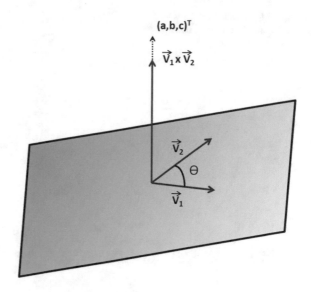

a line-of-sight vector $(0, 0, 1)$. More specifically, the center of mass (x_{cm}, y_{cm}, z_{cm})
of the neighbourhood 3D points is computed first. To reformulate as a 2D problem,
the following steps are performed: translate the origin to the center of mass by
$-(x_{cm}, y_{cm}, z_{cm})$, rotate about the x-axis onto the $x - z$ plane by some Euler angle
α, rotate about the y-axis onto the longitudinal axis $(0, 0, 1)$ by some Euler angle β
and finally transform the origin back to the previous location by (x_{cm}, y_{cm}, z_{cm}). The
detailed calculations are shown below.

A plane of the form $ax + by + cz + d = 0$ is fitted to the neighbourhood data and
the parameters are obtained. Consider 3 points on a planar surface: $P_1(x_1, y_1, z_1)$,
$P_2(x_2, y_2, z_2)$ and $P_3(x_3, y_3, z_3)$. Compute the vectors $\mathbf{V_1}$ and $\mathbf{V_2}$ (see Fig. 14.5) as

$$\mathbf{V_1} = \begin{bmatrix} x_2 - x_1 \\ y_2 - y_1 \\ z_2 - z_1 \end{bmatrix}, \mathbf{V_2} = \begin{bmatrix} x_3 - x_1 \\ y_3 - y_1 \\ z_3 - z_1 \end{bmatrix}$$

Then $\mathbf{V_1} \times \mathbf{V_2}$ is the normal to the surface $ax + by + cz + 1 = 0$. That is, $\mathbf{V_1} \times \mathbf{V_2}$ and $(a, b, c)^T$ are in the same direction.

We aim to nullify the effect of z-coordinates, which require the following steps.
First we translate the origin to the center of mass (CM) $(-x_m, -y_m, -z_m)$ so that
the origin coincides with the CM. We use 4D homogeneous coordinates to perform
all the matrix multiplications. In 3D heterogeneous coordinates, translation is specified as vector addition but in the equivalent 4D homogeneous coordinates it is now
specified by matrix multiplication, as are all the other operations, allowing matrix
concatenation of all matrices to be performed by one matrix. The 4D homogeneous
transformation matrix has the following form:

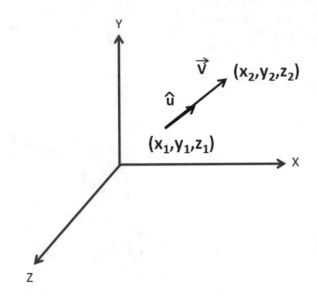

$$T(T_x, T_y, T_z) = \begin{pmatrix} 1 & 0 & 0 & T_x \\ 1 & 0 & 0 & T_y \\ 1 & 0 & 0 & T_z \\ 0 & 0 & 0 & 1 \end{pmatrix} \qquad (14.14)$$

Thus, $T(-x_m, -y_m, -z_m)$ does the translation to the center of mass (the new origin). Next we project the rotation axis onto the z-axis. This requires two steps: rotate by some unknown α angle about x-axis so that the vector $\hat{u}$ is in the xz-plane, and then rotate by some unknown β angle about the y-axis to bring vector $\hat{u}$ onto the z-axis. We show how to calculate α and β in the next 2 subsections. Finally we re-translate back the origin to the previous location by the inverse translation $T(x_m, y_m, z_m)$.

Let us consider rotation about the z-axis. In that case, **V** is the rotation axis with endpoints (x_1, y_1, z_1) and (x_2, y_2, z_2). We rotate about **V** (see Fig. 14.6), given by

$$\mathbf{V} = \begin{bmatrix} x_2 - x_1 \\ y_2 - y_1 \\ z_2 - z_1 \end{bmatrix} = \begin{bmatrix} x \\ y \\ z \end{bmatrix}$$

In this case, $\hat{u} = \frac{\mathbf{V}}{||\mathbf{V}||_2} = (a, b, c)$ is the unit vector in **V**'s direction. The direction cosines of **V** (the Euler angles) are given by

$$a = \frac{x}{||\mathbf{V}||_2}, \quad b = \frac{y}{||\mathbf{V}||_2} \text{ and } c = \frac{z}{||\mathbf{V}||_2}.$$

We use the following convention: $\hat{u}$ is the normal vector, and $\mathbf{u}$ is the unnormalized vector (of the projection of $\hat{u}$ onto $y - z$ plane).

14.3.3.5 Rotate $\hat{u}$ into the XZ-Plane

Let α be the rotation angle between the projection of $\mathbf{u}$ in the yz-plane and the positive z-axis and $\mathbf{u}'$ be the projection of $\hat{u}$ in the yz-plane (Fig. 14.7). That is, $\hat{u} = (a, b, c)^T \implies \mathbf{u}' = (0, b, c)^T$.

Then the angle α can be obtained simply from the equation,

$$\mathbf{u}' \cdot \hat{k} = ||\mathbf{u}'||_2 ||\hat{k}||_2 \cos \alpha.$$

Let $\hat{k} = (0, 0, 1)$ is the unit vector in the z-direction, i.e. $||\hat{k}||_2 = 1$. Then

$$||\mathbf{u}'||_2 = \sqrt{\mathbf{u}' \cdot \mathbf{u}'} = \sqrt{(0, b, c) \cdot (0, b, c)} = \sqrt{b^2 + c^2}$$
$$\implies \mathbf{u}' \cdot \hat{k} = (0, b, c) \cdot (0, 0, 1) = c.$$

Thus,

$$c = \sqrt{b^2 + c^2} \cdot 1 \cdot \cos \alpha \implies \cos \alpha = \frac{c}{\sqrt{b^2 + c^2}}.$$

The vector product can also be used to compute $\sin \alpha$. Note that $\mathbf{u}' \times \hat{k}$ is a vector in x's direction, i.e., $\hat{i}$. Then

$$\mathbf{u}' \times \hat{k} = \hat{i} ||\mathbf{u}'||_2 ||\hat{k}||_2 \sin \alpha = \hat{i} \sqrt{b^2 + c^2} \sin \alpha.$$

and

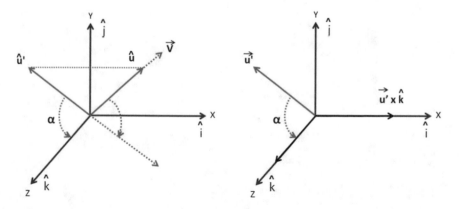

Fig. 14.7 Rotate $\hat{u}$ about the xz-plane. Left: first, project $\hat{u}$ onto the y z plane as $\hat{u}'$. Right: second, $\hat{u}'$ is rotated by α about the x axis onto the $\hat{k}$ axis

$$\mathbf{u}' \times \hat{k} = \begin{vmatrix} \hat{i} & \hat{j} & \hat{k} \\ 0 & b & c \\ 0 & 1 & 1 \end{vmatrix} = b\hat{i}.$$

Then $b\hat{i} = \hat{i}\sqrt{b^2 + c^2}\sin\alpha$, or $\sin\alpha = \frac{b}{\sqrt{b^2+c^2}}$.

Given $\sin\alpha$ and $\cos\alpha$, we can specify the 4D homogeneous rotation matrix for rotation about the x-axis as

$$R_X(\alpha) = \begin{pmatrix} 1 & 0 & 0 & 0 \\ 0 & \frac{c}{\sqrt{b^2+c^2}} & \frac{-b}{\sqrt{b^2+c^2}} & 0 \\ 0 & \frac{b}{\sqrt{b^2+c^2}} & \frac{c}{\sqrt{b^2+c^2}} & 0 \\ 0 & 0 & 0 & 1 \end{pmatrix} \quad (14.15)$$

This matrix rotates $\hat{u}$ onto the xz-plane.

14.3.3.6 Align $\hat{u}_{xz}$ Along Z-Axis

As shown in Fig. 14.8, we need to compute $\sin\beta$ and $\cos\beta$ in this case.

Using the dot product we can write

$$\hat{u}_{xz} \cdot \hat{k} = \overbrace{||\hat{u}_{xz}||_2}^{=1} \overbrace{||\hat{k}||_2}^{=1} \cos\beta$$
$$= (a, 0, \sqrt{b^2 + c^2}) \cdot (0, 0, 1)^T = \sqrt{b^2 + c^2}$$
$$\implies \cos\beta = \sqrt{b^2 + c^2}.$$

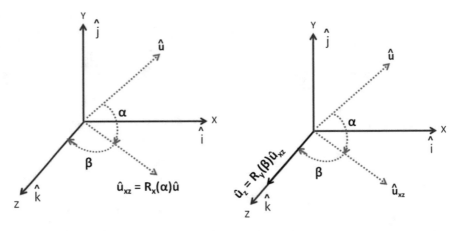

Fig. 14.8 Aligning $\hat{u}$ along the z-axis. Left: $\hat{u}$ is rotated by α about the x axis onto the $x - z$ plane as $\hat{u}_{xz}$. Right: $\hat{u}_{xz}$ is rotated by β about the y-axis onto the $\hat{k}$ axis as $\hat{u}_z$

Also, using the vector product, $\hat{k} \times \hat{u}_{xz}$ is a vector in the direction of the y-axis, thus resulting

$$\hat{u}_{xz} \times \hat{k} = \hat{j} \overbrace{||\hat{u}_{xz}||_2}^{=1} \overbrace{||\hat{k}||_2}^{=1} \sin \beta$$

and

$$\begin{vmatrix} \hat{i} & \hat{j} & \hat{k} \\ a & 0 & \sqrt{b^2 + c^2} \\ 0 & 0 & 1 \end{vmatrix} = -a\hat{j}.$$

Thus, $-a\hat{j} = \hat{j} \sin \beta$, or $\sin \beta = -a$. Then the 4D homogeneous rotation matrix about the y-axis can be specified as

$$R_Y(\beta) = \begin{pmatrix} \sqrt{b^2 + c^2} & 0 & -a & 0 \\ 0 & 1 & 0 & 0 \\ a & 0 & \sqrt{b^2 + c^2} & 0 \\ 0 & 0 & 0 & 1 \end{pmatrix} \tag{14.16}$$

which aligns $\hat{u}_{xz}$ with the z-axis. Thus we apply the transformations:

$$R_y(\beta) R_x(\alpha) T(-x_m, -y_m, -z_m) \tag{14.17}$$

to all 3D points. If we wish to undo this transformation we could use

$$T(x_m, y_m, z_m) R_x^T(\alpha) R_y^T(\beta), \tag{14.18}$$

where $R_x^T(\alpha) \equiv R_y^{-1}(\alpha)$ and $R_y^T(\beta) \equiv R_y^{-1}(\beta)$ because rotation matrices are unitary and orthogonal.

Next, a plane of the form $ax + by + cz + d = 0$ is fit to the neighbourhood data using Cramer's rule. The parameters $\mathbf{n} = (a, b, c)$ are the plane's surface normal. Since these transformations result in vertical surface normals we need only be concerned with the structure in the $x - y$ plane, i.e. the problem is now 2D.

14.3.3.7 Dip Test for Multi-modality

The detection of multi-modality in numeric data is a well-known problem in statistics. A probability density function having more than one mode is denoted as a multi-modal distribution. Hartigan et al. [52] proposed a dip test for unimodality by maximizing the difference between the empirical distribution function and the unimodal distribution function. In the case of a unimodal distribution, the value for the dip should asymptotically approach 0, while for the multi-modal case it should yield a positive floating point number. Zhao et al. [53] exploited this idea to detect bifurcations in the coronary artery. A similar idea is applicable in this case too. Points

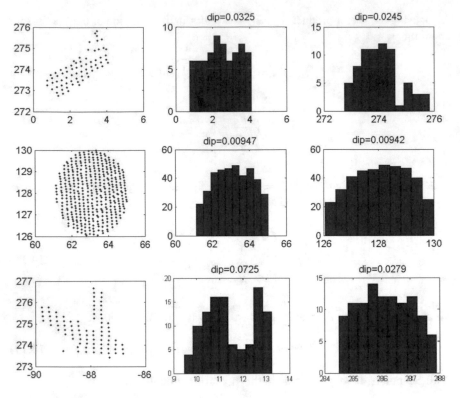

Fig. 14.9 Distribution of data: column 1 are the neighbourhood point clouds under consideration, column 2 are the histograms of the x coordinate distribution and column 3 are the histograms of the y coordinate distribution for a single stem (first row), a leaf (second row) and a stem with 2 branches (last row). The later is potentially a junction point

having non-linear local neighbourhood are potential candidates for a junction point. The idea is to perform the dip test for a local neighbourhood of a point. If it is a stem or a leaf, the data should be uniform and the distribution should only be unimodal. For a junction point likely due to a bifurcation, it should exhibit multi-modality. The dip value can thus be used as a measure of multi-modality (Fig. 14.9).

The dip test is performed along the x and y directions (note that as we have reduced the dimensionality from 3D to 2D the z-coordinates can be ignored) and obtain the maximum dip value. The neighbourhood is determined to be multi-modal if the dip value is over some threshold. However, the threshold value of the dip value is highly dependent on the data and should be tuned carefully (done visually for now).

The dip measurement is used for initial filtering of non-junction neighbourhood data. Note that non-linearity and high dip values in local neighbourhood do not guarantee that those points are junction points. For some leaf and stem data, sometimes the data shows high dip values. Instead of relying blindly on dip test results, further processing is needed in order to confirm the presence of junction in the neighbour-hood.

14.3.3.8   RANSAC Fitting and TLS Approximation

Consider the case of a maximum three branches at an intersection point (which is typically the case in real life): the branches may intersect at a single point (the red dot in Fig. 14.10c) or at two different points (the red dots in Fig. 14.10d).

Assuming the fact that the main stem will be thicker than the branches, the thick stem can be extracted simply by using RANSAC straight line fitting using a high distance threshold for inliers. Other branches can be estimated by sequential RANSAC fitting. However, there may be other points due to additional branches, a leaf or a

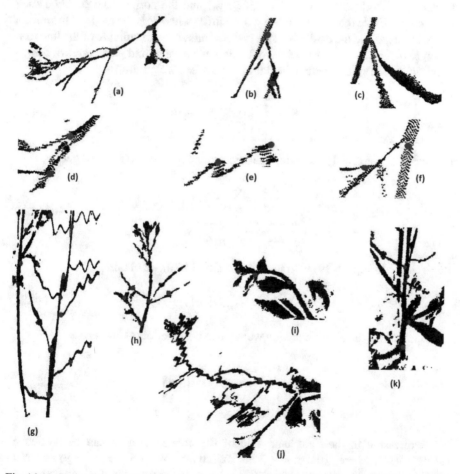

Fig. 14.10 Examples of detected junction points (red dots) on the real Arabidopsis plant data [32]

noise event (or some combination of the three). After removing the RANSAC fitted main stem, Euclidean clustering is performed on the rest of the data to choose
the biggest connected component(s) to extract the sub-branches. Two sets of points,
$X_i = \{p_i \in \mathcal{P}\}$ and $X_j = \{p_j \in \mathcal{P}\}$ form two different clusters, if the following condition holds

$$\mathbf{min}||p_i - p_j||_2 \geq \tau,$$

where τ is the distance threshold. The branches may be straight or curved, but by
using RANSAC we can estimate the principal direction of the branch [54]. A criterion
is imposed to estimate a broken branch shape (due to occlusion): two branches are
merged if they are spatially close to each other and have the roughly same direction.

After estimating the points for each branch, we need to know the straight line
parameters in order to estimate their intersection (if any). We use TLS to approximate
the straight line represented by a set of points in a branch and extract the parameters.
Consider a set of points $(x_1, y_1), \ldots, (x_n, y_n)$ and the normal line equation $ax +
by + c = 0$. [Note that a is $\cos(\theta)$ and b is $\sin(\theta)$ where θ is the angle of the normal
line with respect to the positive x axis and c is minus the magnitude of the line from
(x, y) to $(0,0)$.] To fit all the points to the line, we have to find parameters a, b and c
to minimize the sum of perpendicular distances, i.e. we minimize

$$E = \sum_{i=1}^{n}(ax_i + by_i + c)^2 \tag{14.19}$$

(as $\cos^2 \theta + \sin^2 \theta = 1$). Equating the first order derivative to zero we get

$$\frac{\partial E}{\partial c} = \sum -2(ax_i + by_i + c) = 0$$
$$\implies c = -\frac{a}{n} \sum x_i + -\frac{b}{n} \sum y_i = -a\bar{x} + -b\bar{y}. \tag{14.20}$$

Replacing c in Eq. (14.19) with its value in Eq. (14.20) we obtain

$$E = \sum \left[a(x_i - \bar{x}) + b(y_i - \bar{y})\right]^2. \tag{14.21}$$

To minimize the above equation we rewrite it in the following form:

$$E = \left\| \begin{bmatrix} x_1 - \bar{x} & y_1 - \bar{y} \\ \vdots & \vdots \\ x_n - \bar{x} & y_n - \bar{y} \end{bmatrix} \begin{bmatrix} a \\ b \end{bmatrix} \right\|^2. \tag{14.22}$$

The expression in the right-hand side of the above equation can be written as
$(UN)^T(UN)$, where U is an $n \times 2$ matrix having rows $(x_i - \bar{x}, y_i - \bar{y})$ and N is
$(a, b)^T$. Setting $\frac{dE}{dN} = 0$, we obtain $2(U^TU)N = 0$, the solution of which (subject to

$||N||^2 = 1$), is the eigenvector of $U^T U$ associated with the smallest eigenvalue. We extract the parameters a, b, $\bar{x}$ and $\bar{y}$ from the equation $a(x_i - \bar{x}) + b(y_i - \bar{y}) = 0$.

After approximating the straight lines, we solve the equations given below to determine if these lines intersect or not. Recall that two branches are approximated by two straight lines, and the presence of junction is confirmed if the lines intersect. For two straight line equations of the form $ax + by + c = 0$ and $dx + ey + f = 0$, the intersection point can be obtained as

$$x = \frac{-bf - ce}{ae - db} \quad \text{and} \quad y = \frac{cd - fa}{ae - db}. \tag{14.23}$$

If the straight lines are parallel, the discriminant $(ae - db)$ will be equal to zero. If the lines are non-parallel, we check if the intersection point is contained in the local neighbourhood or not. Note that the obtained intersection point is 2D, so we apply the reverse transformation to find the actual 3D point. Finally non-maximal suppression is performed based on the highest dip value to reduce the number of points.

14.3.3.9   Correspondence Matching

The detected junction points from the last phase are potential candidates for correspondences and can be used as features points for matching. For raw 3D point cloud data, local surface normals, neighbourhood information, etc., are typically used for encoding the local structure and points are matched based on the descriptor similarities. This idea typically fails for plant data because the thin structures do not allow for good local surface normal calculations and because of deformations, the local structure can change abruptly in adjacent images. An approach to solve the problem is to exploit sub-graph matching theory as discussed below.

First, the data is triangulated using Delaunay triangulation in 3D (note that we converted the problem temporarily to 2D just for detection of junction points). Using the vertex information from triangulation, we can construct a graph connecting all the points. To handle the cases of missing or occluded data, the points to the nearest triangle vertex can be connected so that all the points are included in a single graph. Then, for each junction point, Dijkstra's shortest path algorithm can compute geodesic distance to all other junction points. The same procedure is followed for the second point cloud as well. Then the pairwise distances will be used to be the criteria for graph matching.

Consider two graphs $G_1 = (V_1, E_1)$ and $G_2 = (V_2, E_2)$. Each junction point is considered to be a node of the graph. Each node stores the geodesic distances to all other nodes. In the end, this yields a set of edges. Compatibility of two nodes in G_1 and G_2 are defined as a closest distance match. For example, let us suppose two graphs G_1 and G_2 have n_1 and n_2 nodes. Each node V_{1_i} in G_1 stores all distances to all other nodes. We denote this is as the set of attributes of node V_{1_i}: $\mathcal{D}_{v_{1_i}} = \{d_{v_{1_i} v_{1_j}}\}, \forall j \subset n_1$. Similarly in G_2, the set of attributes of node V_{2_i} is defined as $\mathcal{D}_{v_{2_i}} = \{d_{v_{2_i} v_{2_k}}\}, \forall k \in n_2$.

The compatibility of two nodes, V_{1_i} and V_{2_i}, are formulated as the sum of the squares of the difference of nearest distances, multiplied by the number of matches. Suppose G_1 and G_2 contain 5 and 7 nodes, respectively. Let the attributes of a node V_{1_i} contain the following distances: $\{d_1, d_2, d_3, d_4\}$ (ignoring self distance). Similarly, V_{2_i} contains the distances $\{d'_1, d'_2, d'_3, d'_4, d'_5, d'_6\}$. We use a threshold ϵ (= 0.2) for the match of two distances. Suppose there are 3 distance matches given by $d_1 \sim d'_4$, $d_3 \sim d'_2$, $d_4 \sim d'_1$. Then the affinity of the two vertices is computed as

$$\mathcal{A}_{v_{1_i} v_{2_i}} = 3 * [(d_1 - d'_4)^2 + (d_3 - d'_2)^2 + (d_4 - d'_1)^2] \qquad (14.24)$$

The logic for using this kind of distance matching is that any outlier is likely to be eliminated by a lower number of matches. On the other hand, compatible points will only have the maximum number of distance matches.

Using the compatibility of two vertices, we can obtain the initial node correspondence by using the Hungarian algorithm [55]. The outliers are likely to get rejected by unmatched distance attributes. However, there still may be non-optimal matches of the vertices. Cour et al. [56] proposed a graph matching technique, which is shown to be robust and unambiguous. Given two graphs, $G_1 = (V_1, E_1, A_1)$ and $G_2 = (V_2, E_2, A_2)$, where each edge $e = V_i V_j \in E$ has an attribute A_{ij}. The objective is to find N pairs of correspondences (V_i, V_j) where $V_i \in V_1$ and $V_j \in V_2$. The affinity A_{ij} (Eq. 14.24) defines the quality of the match between nodes V_i and V'_i. Denoting the similarity function of pairwise affinity as $f(\cdot, \cdot)$, the matching score can be computed as:

$$\lambda(\mathcal{N}) = \sum_{ii', jj' \subset \mathcal{N}} f(\mathcal{A}_{ij}, \mathcal{A}'_{i'j'}) \qquad (14.25)$$

Representing $\mathcal{N}$ as a binary vector x so that $x(ii') = 1$ if $ii' \in \mathcal{N}$, the above equation can be written as

$$max_x \ \lambda(x) = x^T W x, \qquad (14.26)$$

where $W_{ii', jj'} = f(\mathcal{A}_{ij}, \mathcal{A}'_{i'j'})$. The optimal solution of the above equation is given by

$$x^* = argmax_x (x^T W x). \qquad (14.27)$$

The permutation matrix provides the correspondence among the vertices (or the junction points in this case). Finally the outliers (or wrong matches) can be pruned out using RANSAC.

14.3.4   Organ Segmentation

Classification of different plant organs from point cloud data is an important plant phenotyping. Segmenting leaves, stems, fruits and other plant parts can help in tracking specific organ over time. There are different approaches of organ segmentation in the literature. Paulus et al. [13] presented a surface feature-based histogram technique to segment stems and leaves of grapevines, and wheat ears. The method is based on Fast Point Feature Histogram (FPFH) [50]. The idea is to build histogram for each point in the cloud and classify the histograms using Support Vector Machine (SVM). For every point p in the cloud, the surface normal is computed by considering a local neighbourhood within radius r_H around the point. For each point p_n in the neighbourhood, three types of features are computed. Let us say n_p and n_{pn} are the estimated normals at p and p_n, respectively. A coordinate frame uvw is defined as follows:

$$u = n_p, v = (p_n - p) \times u, w = u \times v.$$

Then for each p and p_n, the following features are computed,

$$f_0 = v \cdot n_{pn},$$
$$f_1 = (u \cdot (p_n - p))/\|p_n - p\|,$$
$$f_2 = \arctan(w \cdot n_{pn}, u \cdot n_{pn}).$$

Then for every point, a histogram is built, where the index of the histogram bin is calculated by using the following formula: $\sum_{i=0}^{2}(\frac{f_i \cdot b}{f_{i(max)} - f_{i(min)}}) \cdot b^i$, where b is the division factor for the histogram size.

Next, the histogram for each point is represented as the normalized weighted sum of the histograms of the neighbouring points. For k neighbours around a point p having their histograms as $h_n(p_k)$, the weighted histogram of a point is expressed as

$$h_w(p) = \frac{1}{k} \sum_k wb(k) \cdot h_n(p_k) + (1 - wb(k)) \cdot h_n(p), \qquad (14.28)$$

$wb = 1 - (0.5 + \frac{d}{r_H} \cdot 0.5)$, d is the distance from the source to the target point. These histograms encode primitive shapes like plane, sphere, cone and cylinder, which will be able to classify plant organs like flat leaf surface, cylinder-shaped stems, etc. The histograms are classified using SVM.

Wahabzada et al. [16] developed an unsupervised clustering method as an extension of the histogram-based method discussed above. The idea is to compare the histograms by some efficient metric, and then perform clustering like k-means using Euclidean distance measure. However, Euclidean distance metric performs poorly in presence of noise. As other alternatives, two different types of distance measures are used for histogram comparison. The first one is the standard Kullback–Leibler (KL) divergence, which uses *Hellinger distance* for computing the distance between two histograms. This is basically a probabilistic analog of the Euclidean distance. For two histograms $\mathbf{x}$ and $\mathbf{y}$, the *Hellinger distance* is given by

$$d_H(\mathbf{x}, \mathbf{y}) = \sum_i (\sqrt{x_i} - \sqrt{y_i})^2. \qquad (14.29)$$

The other metric is to use the *Aitchison distance* given by

$$d_A(\mathbf{x}, \mathbf{y}) = \sqrt{\sum_i (ln\frac{x_i}{g(\mathbf{x})} - ln\frac{y_i}{g(\mathbf{y})})^2}, \tag{14.30}$$

where $g(\cdot)$ is the geometric mean. The k-means objective function is iteratively optimized by the standard EM algorithm.

In a different approach, Li et al. [42] formulated the organ segmentation task as an energy minimization problem. The goal of their work was to detect events (such as budding and bifurcation) from time lapse range scans. A key stage to detect these events is to segment the plant point cloud into leaves and stems. The problem is formulated as a two stage binary labelling problem. In the first stage of labelling, leaves and stems are classified, and in the second stage, individual leaves are classified separately. An organ hypothesis $\mathcal{H}^t$ is formulated as, $\mathcal{H}^t := L_l^t \cup S_s^t$ for frame F^t, where L and S are leaf and stem categories, L_l^t is the l-th leaf, S_s^t is the s-th stem. For any point, p^t in the point cloud $\mathcal{P}^t$ in the current frame F^t, the aim is to find a labelling that maps p^t into $\mathcal{H}^t$. The first stage finds a binary labeling f_B that maps $\mathcal{P}^t$ to $\{L^t, S^t\}$, and the second stage consists of two labellings f_L and f_S that decompose L^t and S^t into individual leaves L_l^t and S_s^t.

The energy function to find the labelling f_B is formulated as

$$E(f_B) = \sum_{p^t \in \mathcal{P}^t} D_{p^t}(f_B(p^t)) + \sum_{(p^t, q^t) \in N_{p^t}} V(f_B(p^t), f_B(q^t)) \tag{14.31}$$

where N_{p^t} is the neighbourhood around a point. The data term D_{p^t} penalizes the cost of classifying p^t as leaf or stem, and the smoothness term $V(f_B(p^t), f_B(q^t))$ ensures spatial coherence.

The data term is formulated based on the curvature values, considering the fact that leaves are generally flatter than stems. For the smoothness term, penalty of labelling is designed as high for neighbouring points to different organs, but less near organ borders. The term is defined as

$$V(f_B(p^t), f_B(q^t)) = \begin{cases} max(\frac{1}{C(p^t)}, \frac{1}{C(q^t)}), \text{ if } f(p^t) \neq f(q^t) \\ 0, \text{ if } f(p^t) = f(q^t) \end{cases} \tag{14.32}$$

where $C(p^t)$ is the curvature of p^t, obtained from the eigenvalues from principal component analysis of neighbourhood points.

Similar approach is followed for labelling in the second stage, with some modifications. To segment the individual leaves (which might be touching each other, thus forming a single connected component), adjacent frames are looked at simultaneously to confirm the hypothesis. Similar hypothesis is built for the data term, and short stems are trimmed out based on a threshold. The energy is minimized by the well-known α-expansion algorithm [57, 58].

A more recent work on segmentation can be found in the work of Jin et al. [59]. They performed segmentation of stem and leaf of Maize plants on 3D Light detection and ranging (LiDAR) data.

14.4   Main Challenges

There are several challenging problems associated with vision-based plant phenotyping. First of all, no efficient registration algorithm exists that can handle every dataset. In the presence of occlusion and non-rigidity, most of the existing algorithms fail to generate good results. Incorporation of prior knowledge about the plant structure in the registration process might be worth studying. Environmental factors such as wind make a plant to jitter constantly. This can make the pairwise registration problem extremely challenging. Occlusion is still an unsolved problem. Handling these cases are open research problems. Also, the optimal number of scans needed to capture the geometric details of a plant has not been studied.

In general, Delaunay or alpha shape triangulations are widely used to polygonize 3D point cloud data. However, in order to retain the thin structure, perfect tuning of the parameters is very crucial in these cases. However, if the application demands very tiny details to be visible in the polygonized mesh, more efficient triangulation algorithms will be more demanding.

Regarding 3D point cloud segmentation methods, although it has been studied widely in the literature, the problem is still challenging for different scenarios with complex background. Also, segmentation in the case of highly occluded point cloud structure is a challenging problem. In fact, the problem is more complicated in terms of generalizing the algorithm for the sheer variety of phenotypes presented by plants.

14.5   Conclusion

This chapter has summarized the basic concepts of some recently successful 3D plant phenotyping techniques. Emphasis has been put on an automated system for 3D phenotyping, pairwise registration and alignment of plant point cloud data and organ segmentation techniques. Vision-based plant phenotyping is becoming more demanding these days, dedicated conferences and workshops are getting organized frequently.[4,5] Challenging datasets are getting released also. Although we have not covered the recent deep learning techniques in plant phenotyping, interested readers are encouraged to read some recent work like [60] for 3D segmentation.

---

[4] https://www.plant-phenotyping.org/CVPPP2019.

[5] http://liris.univ-lyon2.fr/IAMPS2019/.

14.6 Further Reading

An interesting mathematical aspect of plant structures can be found in the book by Prusinkiewicz and Lindenmayer [61]. For an overview of recent plant phenotyping technologies, the readers are invited to read [1] and a more recent review [62]. Other reviews of imaging techniques can be found in [9, 63]. A detailed description of the setup, procedure and experiments of annotated datasets is available in [64]. The details of plant organ segmentation in energy minimization framework can be found in [42].

14.7 Exercises

1. Vascusynth[6] is a software for generating synthetic vascular (tree-like) structures. Generate some custom data using the software. Then perform CPD registration and report the average Root Mean Square (RMS) error from ground truth data. Source code of CPD is available both in Matlab[7] and Python.[8]
2. Add some Gaussian noise in the data above and perform CPD registration again. Increase the level of noise and report the threshold beyond which the registration algorithm fails (you can consider error up to say 5% as acceptable).
3. Add some deformation (e.g. applying random rotation to some random parts) to the data and repeat the registration task.
4. Extend the pairwise registration into a multi-view alignment problem. Align multiple views to obtain a single point cloud by exploiting the idea of pairwise registration in a sequential manner.
5. Obtain the ground truth junction points in the point cloud data in Vascusynth. Assume that the matching of junction points are available. Now apply large amount of rotation to one of the views and perform pairwise registration. The results might not be good at this stage. In order to improve the registration result, we will test if initial rough alignment of the junction points help or not. Using the ground truth matching of the junction points, retrieve the transformation parameters (rotation, translation and scaling), and apply reverse transformation to the data. Now perform the registration. Report the effect of pre-alignment on the registration error.
6. Select some random points in the 3D point cloud above. Extract small neighbourhoods (say 50 × 50) around these points. These neighbourhoods will also be 3D. Then apply the coordinate transformation as described in Sect. 14.3.3.4 to convert the data into 2D. Now compare the original 3D data of these neighbourhood structures and the transformed point cloud. If you are getting all the z-coordinate values of the transformed point cloud as almost the same, then the

---

[6]http://vascusynth.cs.sfu.ca/Welcome.html.

[7]https://sites.google.com/site/myronenko/research/cpd.

[8]https://github.com/siavashk/pycpd.

result is correct. Also, plot both 3D and 2D data and see if the transformation has preserved the original structure or not.

7. Perform Principal Component Analysis (PCA) of the above 3D neighbourhood structures. Look at the eigenvalues and eigenvectors. Can you tell anything about the local structure from these quantities?

8. Obtain the challenging vegetation dataset from ASL database.[9] Apply state-of-the-art point cloud feature matching algorithms and report their limitations on this type of data.

9. Perform CPD registration of the same dataset as above.

10. Triangulate the point cloud data using some standard algorithms like Delaunay triangulation[10] or alpha shape algorithm.[11] Adjust the parameters to get the best result. Do you think that these algorithms are efficient enough to triangulate the dataset?

11. Obtain the dataset of Li et al. [42].[12] Implement the segmentation method as described in detail in the paper.

References

1. Spalding, E.P., Miller, N.D.: Image analysis is driving a renaissance in growth measurement. Current Opinion Plant Biol. **16**(1), 100–104 (2013)
2. Hartmann, A., Czauderna, T., Hoffmann, R., Stein, N., Schreiber, F.: HTpheno: An image analysis pipeline for high-throughput plant phenotyping. BMC Bioinform. **12**, Article number: 148 (2011)
3. Klukas, C., Chen, D., Pape, J.M.: Integrated analysis platform: an open-source information system for high-throughput plant phenotyping. Plant Physiol. **165**(2), 506–518 (2014)
4. Scanalyzer-HTS, http://www.lemnatec.com/products/hardware-solutions/scanalyzer-hts/
5. Subramanian, R., Spalding, E., Ferrier, N.: A high throughput robot system for machine vision based plant phenotype studies. Mach. Vis. Appl. **24**(3), 619–636 (2013)
6. Paulus, S., Schumann, H., Kuhlmann, H., Leon, J.: High-precision laser scanning system for capturing 3D plant architecture and analysing growth of cereal plants. Biosyst. Eng. **121** (2014)
7. Fiorani, F., Schurr, U.: Future scenarios for plant phenotyping. Ann. Rev. Plant Biol. **64** (2013)
8. Furbank, R.T., Tester, M.: Phenomics - technologies to relieve the phenotyping bottleneck. Trends Plant Sci. **16**(12), 635–644 (2011)
9. Li, L., Zhang, Q., Huang, D.: A review of imaging techniques for plant phenotyping. Sensors **14**(11) (2014)
10. Chaudhury, A., Ward, C., Talasaz, A., Ivanov, A.G., Brophy, M., Grodzinski, B., Hüner, N.P.A., Patel, R.V., Barron, J.L.: Machine vision system for 3D plant phenotyping. In: IEEE/ACM Transactions on Computational Biology and Bioinformatics (2018)
11. Jiménez, A.R., Ruíz, R.C., Rovira, J.L.P.: A vision system based on a laser rangefinder applied to robotic fruit harvesting. Mach. Vis. Appl. **11**(6), 321–329 (2000)

---

[9]https://projects.asl.ethz.ch/datasets/doku.php?id=laserregistration:laserregistration.

[10]https://mathworks.com/help/matlab/ref/delaunaytriangulation.html.

[11]https://www.mathworks.com/matlabcentral/mlc-downloads/downloads/submissions/28851/versions/4/previews/alphavol.m/index.html.

[12]http://web.siat.ac.cn/~vcc/publications/2013/Planalyze/.

12. Chattopadhyay, S., Akbar, S.A., Elfiky, N.M., Medeiros, H., Kak, A.C.: Measuring and modeling apple trees using time-of-flight data for automation of dormant pruning applications. In: Proceedings of IEEE Winter Conference on Applications of Computer Vision (WACV) (2016)
13. Paulus, S., Dupuis, J., Mahlein, A.K., Kuhlmann, H.: Surface feature based classification of plant organs from 3D laser scanned point clouds for plant phenotyping. BMC Bioinform. **14**(238) (2013)
14. Paulus, S., Dupuisemail, J., Riedelemail, S., Kuhlmann, H.: Automated analysis of barley organs using 3D laser scanning: an approach for high throughput phenotyping. Sensors **14**(7), 12670–12686 (2014)
15. Klodt, M., Herzog, K., Töpfer, R., Cremers, D.: Field phenotyping of grapevine growth using dense stereo reconstruction. BMC Bioinform. **16**, 143 (2015)
16. Wahabzada, M., Paulus, S., Kersting, K., Mahlein, A.-K.: Automated interpretation of 3d laserscanned point clouds for plant organ segmentation. BMC Bioinform. **16**, 248 (2015)
17. Paproki, A., Sirault, X., Berry, S., Furbank, R., Fripp, J.: A novel mesh processing based technique for 3d plant analysis. BMC Plant Biol. **12**(1) (2012)
18. Golbach, F., Kootstra, G., Damjanovic, S., Otten, G., Zedde, R.: Validation of plant part measurements using a 3D reconstruction method suitable for high-throughput seedling phenotyping. Mach. Vis. Appl. (2015)
19. Dellen, B., Scharr, H., Torras, C.: Growth signatures of rosette plants from timelapse video. IEEE/ACM Trans. Comput. Biol. Bioinform. **12**(6), 1470–1478 (2015)
20. Scharr, H., Minervini, M., French, A.P., Klukas, C., Kramer, D.M., Liu, X., Luengo, I., Pape, J., Polder, G., Vukadinovic, D., Yin, X., Tsaftaris, S.A.: Leaf segmentation in plant phenotyping: a collation study. Mach. Vis. Appl. **27**(4), 585–606 (2016)
21. Kelly, D., Vatsa, A., Mayham, W., Kazic, T.: Extracting complex lesion phenotypes in zea mays. Mach. Vis. Appl. **27**(1), 145–156 (2016)
22. Xu, G., Zhang, F., Shah, S.G., Ye, Y., Mao, H.: Use of leaf color images to identify nitrogen and potassium deficient tomatoes. Pattern Recognit. Lett. **32**(11), 1584–1590 (2011)
23. Aksoy, E.E., Abramov, A., Wörgötter, F., Scharr, H., Fischbach, A., Dellen, B.: Modeling leaf growth of rosette plants using infrared stereo image sequences. Comput. Electron. Agricult. **110**, 78–90 (2015)
24. Pound, M.P., French, A.P., Fozard, J.A., Murchie, E.H., Pridmore, T.P.: A patch based approach to 3D plant shoot phenotyping. Mach. Vis. Appl. (2016)
25. Pound, M.P., French, A.P., Murchie, E.H., and Pridmore, T.P.: Surface reconstruction of plant shoots from multiple views. In: Proceedings of ECCV Workshops (2014)
26. Santos, T.T., Koenigkan, L.V., Barbedo, J.G.A., Rodrigues, G.C.: 3D plant modeling: localization, mapping and segmentation for plant phenotyping using a single hand-held camera. In: Proceedings of ECCV 2014 Workshops, Lecture Notes in Computer Science, vol. 8928
27. Santos, T.T., Rodrigues, G.C.: Flexible three-dimensional modeling of plants using low-resolution cameras and visual odometry. Mach. Vis. Appl. **27**(5), 695–707 (2016)
28. Kumar, P., Cai, J., Miklavcic, S.: High-throughput 3D modelling of plants for phenotypic analysis. In: Proceedings of of 27th Conference on Image and Vision Computing New Zealand (IVCNZ) (2012)
29. Gibbs, J.A., Pound, M., French, A.P., Wells, D.M., Murchie, E., Pridmore, T.: Plant phenotyping: an active vision cell for three-dimensional plant shoot reconstruction. Plant Physiol. **178**, 524–534 (2018)
30. Simek, K., Palanivelu, R., Barnard, K.: Branching gaussian processes with applications to spatiotemporal reconstruction of 3d trees. In: Proceedings of European Conference on Computer Vision (ECCV) (2016)
31. M. Brophy, A. Chaudhury, S. S. Beauchemin, and J. L. Barron, "A method for global non-rigid registration of multiple thin structures", Proceedings of Conference on Computer and Robot Vision (CRV), 2015
32. Chaudhury, A., Brophy, M., Barron, J.L.: Junction-based correspondence estimation of plant point cloud data using subgraph matching. IEEE Geosci. Remote Sens. Lett. **13**(8), 1119–1123 (2016)

33. Cox, M.C., Millenaar, F.F., van Berkel, Y.E.D.J., Peeters, A.J., Voesenek, L.A.: Plant movement. submergence-induced petiole elongation in Rumex palustris depends on hyponastic growth. Plant Physiol. **132**, 282–291 (2003)
34. Navarro, P.J., Ferníndez, C., Weiss, J., Egea-Cortines, M.: Development of a configurable growth chamber with a computer vision system to study circadian rhythm in plants. Sensors **12**(11), 15356 (2012)
35. Dornbusch, T., Lorrain, S., Kuznetsov, D., Fortier, A., Liechti, R., Xenarios, I., Fankhauser, C.: Measuring the diurnal pattern of leaf hyponasty and growth in Arabidopsis a novel phenotyping approach using laser scanning. Funct. Plant Biol. **39**(11), 860–869 (2012)
36. Benoit, L., Rousseau, D., Belin, E., Demilly, D., Chapeau-Blondeau, F.: Simulation of image acquisition in machine vision dedicated to seedling elongation to validate image processing root segmentation algorithms. Comput. Electron. Agricult. **104** (2014)
37. Barron, J.L., Liptay, A.: Optic flow to measure minute increments in plant growth. BioImaging (BI1994) **2**(1), 57–61 (1994)
38. Barron, J.L., Liptay, A.: Measuring 3d plant growth using optical flow. BioImaging (BI1997) **5**(2), 82–86 (1997)
39. Liptay, A., Barron, J.L., Jewett, T., Wesenbeeck, I.V.: Oscillations in corn seedling growth as measured by optical flow. J. Am. Soc. Hort. Sci. **120**(3) (1995)
40. Godin, C., Ferraro, P.: Quantifying the degree of self-nestedness of trees: application to the structural analysis of plants. IEEE/ACM Trans. Comput. Biol. Bioinform. **7**(4), 688–703 (2010)
41. Augustin, M., Haxhimusa, Y., Busch, W., Kropatsch, W.G.: A framework for the extraction of quantitative traits from 2D images of mature Arabidopsis thaliana. Mach. Vis. Appl. (2015)
42. Li, Y., Fan, X., Mitra, N.J., Chamovitz, D., Cohen-Or, D., Chen, B.: Analyzing growing plants from 4d point cloud data. In: ACM Transactions on Graphics (Proceedings of SIGGRAPH Asia 2013), vol. 32 (2013)
43. Medeiros, F., Kim, D., Sun, J., Seshadri, H., Akbar, S.A., Elfiky, N.M., Park, J.: Modeling dormant fruit trees for agricultural automation. J. Field Robot. **34**(7), 1203–1224 (2016)
44. Sa, I., Lehnert, C., English, A., McCool, C., Dayoub, F., Upcroft, B., Perez, T.: Peduncle detection of sweet pepper for autonomous crop harvesting-combined color and 3D information. IEEE Robot. Autom. Lett. **2**(2) (2017)
45. Yuille, A.L., Grzywacz, N.M.: A computational theory for the perception of coherent visual motion. Nature **333**(6168) (1988)
46. Jian, B., Vemuri, B.C.: Robust point set registration using gaussian mixture models. IEEE Trans. Pattern Anal. Mach. Intell. **33**(8) (2011)
47. Myronenko, A., Song, X., Carreira-Perpinan, M.A.: Non-rigid point set registration: coherent point drift. In: Advances in Neural Information Processing Systems (NIPS) (2006)
48. Myronenko, A., Song, X.: Point set registration: coherent point drift. IEEE Trans. Pattern Anal. Mach. Intell. **32**(12) (2010)
49. Toldo, R., Beinat, A., Crosilla, F.: Global registration of multiple point clouds embedding the generalized procrustes analysis into an ICP framework. In: Proceedings of 3DPVT 2010 (2010)
50. Rusu, R.B., Blodow, N., Beetz, M.: Fast point feature histograms (FPFH) for 3D registration (2009)
51. Bucksch, A., Khoshelham, K.: Localized registration of point clouds of botanic trees. IEEE Geosci. Remote Sens. Lett. **10**(3) (2013)
52. Hartigan, J.A., Hartigan, P.M.: The dip test of unimodality. Ann. Stat. **13**(1), 70–84 (1985)
53. Zhao, F., Bhotika, R.: Coronary artery tree tracking with robust junction detection in 3D CT angiography. In: Proceedings of the 8th IEEE International Symposium on Biomedical Imaging (ISBI), pp. 2066–2071 (2011)
54. Uhercik, M., Kybic, J., Liebgott, H., Cachard, C.: Model fitting using RANSAC for surgical tool localization in 3D ultrasound images. IEEE Trans. Biomed. Eng. **57**(8), 1907–1916 (2010)
55. Kuhn, H.: The Hungarian method for the assignment problem. Naval Res. Logist. Quart. **2**(1–2), 83–97 (1955)
56. Cour, T., Srinivasan, P., Shi, J.: Balanced graph matching. In: Proceedings of Advances in Neural Information Processing Systems (NIPS), pp. 313–320 (2007)

57. Boykov, Y., Kolmogorov, V.: An experimental comparison of min-cut/max-flow algorithms for energy minimization in vision. IEEE Trans. Pattern Anal. Mach. Intell. **26**(9), 1124–1137 (2004)
58. Boykov, Y., Veksler, O., Zabih, R.: Fast approximate energy minimization via graph cuts. IEEE Trans. Pattern Anal. Mach. Intell. **23**(11), 1222–1239 (2001)
59. Jin, Y., Su, Y., Wu, F., Pang, S., Gao, S., Hu, T., Liu, J., Guo, Q.: Stem-leaf segmentation and phenotypic trait extraction of individual maize using terrestrial LiDAR data. IEEE Trans. Geosci. Remote Sens. **57**(3), 1336–1346 (2018)
60. Jin, S., Su, Y., Gao, S., Wu, F., Hu, T., Liu, J., Li, W., Wang, D., Chen, S., Jiang, Y., Pang, S., Guo, Q.: Deep learning: individual maize segmentation from terrestrial lidar data using faster R-CNN and regional growth algorithms. Frontiers Plant Sci. (2018)
61. Prusinkiewicz, P., Lindenmayer, A.: The Algorithmic Beauty of Plants. Springer, Berlin (1990)
62. Gibbs, J.A., Pound, M., French, A.P., Wells, D.M., Murchie, E., Pridmore, T.: Approaches to three-dimensional reconstruction of plant shoot topology and geometry. Funct. Plant Biol. **44**(1), 62–75 (2017)
63. Dhondt, S., Wuyts, N., Inzé, D.: Cell to whole-plant phenotyping: the best is yet to come. Trends Plant Sci. **18**(8), 428–439 (2013)
64. Minervini, M., Fischbach, A., Scharr, H., Tsaftaris, S.A.: Finely-grained annotated datasets for image-based plant phenotyping. Pattern Recognit. Lett. **81**, 80–89 (2016)

Index

© Springer Nature Switzerland AG 2020
Y. Liu et al. (eds.), *3D Imaging, Analysis and Applications*,
https://doi.org/10.1007/978-3-030-44070-1

Printed in the United States
by Baker & Taylor Publisher Services